*The Editors*

DONALD H. REIMAN is Adjunct Professor of English at the University of Delaware and Editor of *Shelley and his Circle* at the Carl H. Pforzheimer Collection, New York Public Library. In addition to contributing articles and reviews to scholarly journals, Professor Reiman has written, edited, co-edited, or compiled some two hundred volumes of literary and textual criticism, biographical and textual sources materials, and critically edited texts of the English Romantics. Prominent among these are editions of manuscripts of the Shelleys, Byron, and their circles at the Pforzheimer Collection; the Bodleian Library, Oxford; and the Houghton Library, Harvard University. He is a director and officer of the Keats-Shelley Association of America, founder of the Wordsworth-Coleridge Association, a founding director of the Society for Textual Scholarship and the Byron Society of America, and a co-founder of the Romantic Circles Web site.

NEIL FRAISTAT is Professor of English at the University of Maryland and a founder and General Editor of the *Romantic Circles* Web site. He has published widely in journals on Romantic Period literature and on textual scholarship and in such books as *The Poem and the Book, Poems in Their Place*, and *The "Prometheus Unbound" Notebooks*. He is co-editor with Susan S. Lanser of Helen Maria Williams's *Letters Written in France*; with Elizabeth B. Loizeaux of *Reimagining Textuality: Textual Studies in the Late Age of Print*; and with Donald H. Reiman of *The Complete Poetry of Percy Bysshe Shelley*. He is also a recipient of the Society for Textual Scholarship's Fredson Bowers Memorial Prize, the Keats-Shelley Association's Prize, and the Keats-Shelley Association's Distinguished Scholar Award.

# W. W. NORTON & COMPANY, INC.
### *Also Publishes*

A NORTON CRITICAL EDITION

# SHELLEY'S POETRY
# AND PROSE

AUTHORITATIVE TEXTS
CRITICISM

SECOND EDITION

*Selected and Edited by*

## DONALD H. REIMAN

UNIVERSITY OF DELAWARE

*and*

## NEIL FRAISTAT

UNIVERSITY OF MARYLAND, COLLEGE PARK

*First Edition co-edited by*
SHARON B. POWERS

W · W · NORTON & COMPANY · *New York* · *London*

The text of this book is composed in Fairfield Medium
with the display set in Bernhard Modern.
Composition by PennSet, Inc.
Manufacturing by the Courier Companies, Inc.
Book design by Antonina Krass.

Library of Congress Cataloging-in-Publication Data

Shelley, Percy Bysshe, 1792–1822.
   [Selections 2001]
   Shelley's poetry and prose : authoritative texts, criticism / selected and edited
   by Donald H. Reiman and Neil Fraistat.—2nd ed.
      p. cm.
   Includes bibliographical references and index.

ISBN 0-393-97752-8 (pbk.)

   1. Shelley, Percy Bysshe, 1792–1822—Criticism and interpretation. I. Reiman,
   Donald H. II. Fraistat, Neil, 1952– III. Title.
   PR5403 .R4 2001
   821'.7—dc21                                                              2001030903

W. W. Norton & Company, Inc., 500 Fifth Avenue, New York, N.Y. 10110
www.wwnorton.com

W. W. Norton & Company Ltd., Castle House, 75/76 Wells Street,
London W1T 3QT

5 6 7 8 9 0

# Contents

# The Prose

# Criticism

# Preface to the Second Edition

The years since 1977, when the first edition of the Norton Critical Edition of *Shelley's Poetry and Prose* (*SPP*) appeared, have witnessed a renaissance in Shelley scholarship and criticism greater than any since the years 1870–92. A typical year of the past two decades has seen the publication of two or three significant critical or contextual books that treat aspects of Shelley's life, thought, or writings, and from two- to three-dozen substantive essays in collective volumes, periodicals, and recently on the internet. Many of these publications feature new perspectives from both the practitioners and the opponents of such critical stances as psychoanalytic and deconstructive analysis, the New Historicism, globalism, ecology, and gender studies. More important—at least for those of us who function as textual scholars as well as critics—has been the wealth of transcription, publication, and analysis of Shelley's manuscripts and other primary textual authorities for his writings, such as are found in *Shelley and his Circle* (*SC*), *The Bodleian Shelley Manuscripts* (*BSM*), and the Shelley series in *The Manuscripts of the Younger Romantics* (*MYR: Shelley*), which provide new evidence that bears upon disputed issues in Shelley's life, thought, and art.

Thus, even though *SPP* has established itself as a popular choice for teaching Shelley to advanced undergraduate and graduate classes in English Romanticism and although local corrections were made in the reprintings of the edition in 1980 and 1982, we recognize that, as the original Preface to the first edition stipulated: "Like all works of scholarship . . . the Norton Critical Edition of Shelley exists to be used, tested, and corrected." Limitations of space have prevented us from adding to the substantial selection of Shelley's works offered in the first edition, but the order of these poems has been rearranged on the basis of redating or other reconsiderations; each text has been reedited from the ground up; all headnotes have been either replaced or updated; and many footnotes have been replaced, revised, or added for the first time. The Chronology of Shelley's life and Selected Bibliography have similarly been updated to reflect the current state of Shelley scholarship.

All the critical selections in this edition are new to *SPP*. The first edition, prepared when Shelley's poetic reputation was still suspect in large areas of the academy in both Britain and North America, featured carefully argued complete essays or sections of books that presented a sympathetic understanding of the poet's thought and art, including many examples of close reading of individual poems. Now, when Shelley's reputation as an artist and thinker is probably higher than it has ever been, we include a brief historical overview that draws upon some of the debates about his merits as a person and a poet that raged from the High Victorian period through the ascendency of the New Critics—roughly from 1860 to 1960. This sketch is followed by more substantial discussions by recent academic scholar-critics to illustrate a variety of the approaches and interests that have contributed to the current understanding and appreciation of the poet in his larger contexts—linguistic, historical, social, biographical, and artistic.

Having in 1992 begun our collaboration on a comprehensive scholarly edition of *The Complete Poetry of Percy Bysshe Shelley* (CPPBS), we decided, after Sharon Barbara Powers's untimely death in May 1994, also to edit jointly this new edition of SPP. Students, teachers, critics, and scholars should be aware, however, that CPPBS and SPP have different functions, audiences, and textual principles that may lead, at times, to local differences in punctuation and wording. Both editions, nonetheless, aspire to be *"authoritative"*—that is, to identify and base their texts upon those documents and printings that most nearly record or suggest the intentions of the author, Percy Bysshe Shelley, rather than modern handbooks of publishing style. Although within the limited parameters of the Norton Critical Editions we cannot communicate (or even cite) all of our research or present the full range of evidence that underlies these texts and annotations, the present edition makes use of much that we have learned from dozens of publications and years of research on the primary authorities for Shelley's texts and attempts to present his texts in the words, orthography, and style of punctuation found in the documents that Shelley himself either wrote or saw through the press.

Neither our factual introductions to the major poems, the informational notes at the bottom of the pages, nor the extended critical selections by others are designed to force teachers or students into specific readings of Shelley's poems and essays. Instead, they afford readers a range of contexts and opinions meant to provide them with information useful to their understanding of the literary conventions that Shelley employed, as well as the biographical and historical events that influenced him when he wrote and published his works, and enough varying views on the meaning and value of his writings to free both students and teachers from dogmatic judgments.

We do not normally gloss the common meanings of words found in standard collegiate dictionaries, but point out the special significance of certain words to Shelley, as well as the connotations and denotations of other words current in his own lifetime that have now become less common or even obsolete. The notes also name and characterize briefly some sources of the historical, scientific, and philosophical knowledge available to the poet through his life experiences, education, and omnivorous reading, thus aiding modern readers to understand what Shelley strove to communicate to his British contemporaries. After using these aids and applying their own knowledge, teachers, students—all readers of poetry—should be able to derive for themselves the present-day significance and value of Shelley's writings.

*Newark, Delaware*                                     DONALD H. REIMAN
*College Park, Maryland*                                  NEIL FRAISTAT

# Preface to the First Edition

This edition includes all of Shelley's greatest poetry and other poems frequently taught or discussed (including *Queen Mab, Alastor,* and all the book-length poems Shelley wrote in Italy except *Swellfoot the Tyrant*), as well as three of his most important prose works. The critical selections include what we believe to be among the best and most helpful scholarly and critical studies that elucidate Shelley's art and thought and his most difficult poems. These selections are all recent because it is in the nature of scholarship that the best new work absorbs and builds upon the true elements of earlier scholarship and in the nature of criticism that the most sensitive current voices raise and attempt to answer the literary and philosophical questions that concern present readers.

We have reedited the texts of Shelley's writings from the primary authorities according to the principles stated in the Textual Introduction, and we have annotated the works with the aim of making the meaning of the words and allusions in the text immediately comprehensible without sending the reader to a reference library. Beyond glossing individual words and allusions, we provide brief accounts of the circumstances under which each poem was written and published. We also comment succinctly on the structural divisions of those poems that teaching experience and the history of Shelley criticism have shown us to require such elucidation. Finally, for some poems that lend themselves to interpretation at more than one level, we have mentioned the directions taken by allegorical or symbolic interpretations that seem to us consonant with Shelley's thought and artistic methods. Detailed interpretation of the poems remains the task and the privilege of students and teachers.

The texts of Shelley's poetry and prose presented here are closer to the primary authorities (and, we believe, to Shelley's intention) than those found in any previous edition. Our annotation—though not embodying all that has been known and thought about Shelley—is far more detailed and precise than that in earlier editions and contains considerable information not available otherwise in Shelley studies. Like all works of scholarship, however, the Norton Critical Edition of Shelley exists to be used, tested, and corrected.

*New York, New York*                DONALD H. REIMAN
*Montclair, New Jersey*              SHARON B. POWERS

# Acknowledgments

The texts of Shelley's writings in this edition, while based on the First Edition of *Shelley's Poetry and Prose* (1977), have been checked and revised extensively after consulting a wealth of new information on the primary sources of his texts that has been gathered and published by numerous scholars all over the world, from documents and editions in a large number of libraries and private collections. Among the many scholars whose publications (listed in the Bibliography), counsels, or specialized information have been especially helpful to us either in reediting or in revising the annotation of these works, we should single out a few for special mention: B. C. Barker-Benfield, the late Kenneth Neill Cameron, Nora Crook, Stuart Curran, Kelvin Everest, Doucet Devin Fischer, Arthur Freeman, Jerrold E. Hogle, William Keach, the late G(eoffrey) M. Matthews, Michael J. Neth, Michael O'Neill, M. Byron Raizis, Charles E. Robinson, Jack Stillinger, Tatsuo Tokoo, the late Earl R. Wasserman, and Timothy Webb.

Users of *Shelley's Poetry and Prose* who called attention to specific errors or omissions in the first printing that have been rectified, either in the second and third states of the First Edition or in this edition, include James Bieri, James A. Butler, P. H. Butter, David Clark, Hélène Dworzan, David V. Erdman, John E. Grant, Robert A. Hartley, Parks C. Hunter, Sally Laura Hyman, E. B. Murray, Evan Radcliffe, Mary A. Quinn, Susan Shaw Sailer, Susan J. Wolfson, the late Robert Yampolsky, and Curt R. Zimansky.

Libraries, collections, and other institutions to which we are indebted for invaluable assistance and cooperation include The Carl H. Pforzheimer Collection of Shelley and His Circle at the New York Public Library; the Bodleian Library, Oxford; The Library of Congress; the University of Maryland; the University of Delaware; The Carl and Lily Pforzheimer Foundation, Inc.; and the National Endowment for the Humanities, an independent Federal Agency.

Most of all, we wish to recognize those colleagues who played a direct part in various stages of our labors in preparing the manuscript, vetting and styling it, proofreading it, and bringing it to production: at the University of Maryland, Dr. Melissa J. Sites and David Brookshire; at the University of Delaware, Dr. Shiela Pardee; and at W. W. Norton, Carol Bemis, Kate Lovelady, Brian Baker, and Ben Reynolds.

For permission to publish the critical selections in the back of the book, as edited and/or revised for this edition, we thank the authors, original publishers, or other copyright holders as specified in the bibliographical note to each.

# Textual Introduction

The texts of Shelley's poems in this edition have been reedited after a comparison of the primary authorities—extant holograph manuscripts, transcripts, first editions, and selected later editions (especially those of Mary Shelley) that may have incorporated authorial emendations.[1] The resulting texts were then compared with one another and with responsible critical editions, including the collected editions of H. Buxton Forman, C. D. Locock, Thomas Hutchinson (corrected by G. M. Matthews), and Roger Ingpen and Walter E. Peck, and the first volume of the Longman edition by G. M. Matthews and Kelvin Everest (1989), as well as selective editions and textual studies by Irving Massey, G. M. Matthews, Judith Chernaik, Lawrence John Zillman, and Timothy Webb.[2] During these steps we examined peculiarities of punctuation and orthography that seemed persistent (though not universal) in Shelley's holographs and in the texts printed under his direct supervision; in some instances, we regularized our texts to these apparently preferred forms, though we allowed to stand his archaic, anomalous, and unconventional usages in those places where we could not find enough evidence to determine with high probability his preferences or intentions.

*Spelling:* Where it can be established that Shelley employed two distinct forms of a word with a demonstrable difference in pronunciation, such as "sat" (rhymed with "hat") and "sate" (rhymed with "hate"), or a possible differentiation in meaning or function, such as "desert" (which seems usually reserved for the adjectival meaning) as opposed to "desart" (often a noun), these distinctions have been maintained. Shelley's original or preferred spellings—as nearly as they could be determined—have been followed, except in the case of certain repeatedly misspelled words ("thier" for "their," "recieve" for "receive"), such contemporary but obsolescent forms as "it's" for the possessive case of *it*, and certain abbreviations such as the ampersand ("&") and "w^ch" (for "which"); these, though often found in both Shelley's manuscripts and his printed books of certain periods, are not much in evidence in his late manuscripts or editions, and we have, therefore, normalized these words to their conventional and unabbreviated forms.

---

1. On criteria for determining the relative authority of various kinds of textual evidence, see Donald H. Reiman's review of vol. I of *The Complete Works of Percy Bysshe Shelley,* ed. Neville Rogers (*JEGP* 73 [April 1974]: 250–60), as reprinted in Reiman, *Romantic Texts and Contexts,* pp. 41–54.
2. For an overview of the history of Shelley's texts, giving the contributions of the various editors, see our *Complete Poetry of Percy Bysshe Shelley* (CPPBS), I, xxii–xxix.

Students may find themselves less confused by Shelley's other archaic spellings (e.g., "antient" for "ancient," "controul" for "control," "gulph" for "gulf") than by the changed pronunciation in modern American English of words such as "again" (which Shelley rhymed with "pain"), words ending in "-ing" (which were shortened so that "pursuing" rhymed with "ruin"), and the noun "wind" (which Shelley often rhymed with "kind" and "find").

*Punctuation:* The punctuation found in Shelley's surviving holograph manuscripts has been supplemented but has not ordinarily been altered, unless the change originated in a printed text of similar authority. The function of Shelley's commas, semicolons, and dashes differs from that of standard modern usage. But just as twentieth-century poets such as E. E. Cummings and T. S. Eliot often break their poetry into short lines that identify the patterned grouping of phrases and clauses, so Shelley and the poets of his day habitually punctuated their poetry to show the reader how the words were to be grouped when voiced aloud. These usages were recognized by the rhetoric and elocution manuals of the day; William Scott wrote, for example, in his *Elements of Elocution* (2nd ed., Edinburgh, 1808):

> The comma generally admits of a very short pause; in some situations, none: the semicolon requires a pause somewhat longer than the comma; the colon a still longer pause; and the period a longer still. The pause at the end of a paragraph, or where a dash is added to the period, should be greater than at the end of an ordinary sentence.—It has been said, that the pauses at the comma, semicolon, colon, and period, should be in the proportion of the numbers 1, 2, 3, 4; which may, in general, be pretty near the truth. (p. 57)

In "Mont Blanc," Shelley inserts commas between the subject and the verb in lines 115 and 118 (as William Scott does in the last sentence quoted above) to show where he wants the break in phrasing. This practice was recognized by the leading grammarian Lindley Murray, who wrote:

> The Comma usually separates those parts of a sentence, which, though very closely connected in sense and construction, require a pause between them. . . . A simple sentence, . . . when it is a long one, and the nominative case is accompanied with inseparable adjuncts, may admit of a pause immediately before the verb: as, "The good taste of the present age, has not allowed us to neglect the cultivation of the English language." "To be totally indifferent to praise or censure, is a real defect in character." (*English Grammar*, 2nd ed., improved [York, London, & Edinburgh, 1809], I, 376)

Shelley's draft manuscripts usually omit quotation marks and often omit commas at the ends of poetic lines (and sometimes full stops at the ends of stanzas) simply because the natural pause at the end of the line (or stanza) obviated the need for any punctuation at that early stage of composition, when the manuscript was meant merely as a guide to the poet. In his fair copies destined for the press (or for friends to whom some personal poems were addressed) Shelley is much more careful in punctuating, but even in these he often depended on the natural pause at the end of the line to serve instead of an optional comma, and there he sometimes employed a comma to indicate a pause where modern usage would require a colon or semicolon. While this practice is, again, analogous to that of T. S. Eliot and other twentieth-century poets and could easily be accepted by readers, Shelley's printers generally supplemented his punctuation, and, by not deleting their added pointing from volumes for which he read proofs, Shelley seems to have accepted, if not quite endorsed, the more heavily punctuated style of his day. We must remember, however, that contemporary pointing was primarily rhetorical rather than grammatical and that it was not as heavy as many subsequent editors have tried to impose on Shelley's poems.

In treating those texts for which the primary authority is either a rough draft manuscript or a safekeeping copy—e.g., the Esdaile Notebook or the two Harvard Shelley notebooks (see *MYR: Shelley*, I and V)—we have attempted to approximate the spirit of the punctuation in Shelley's press-copy manuscripts and in *The Cenci* and *Adonais*, printed under his direct supervision by Italian printers who would have been less likely than their English colleagues to "correct" Shelley's style. (In this edition of *SPP*, for example, we return in many instances to the orthography and punctuation of the first printing of *The Cenci* in preference to those of the second, London edition.) By the same rationale, we have slightly reduced the punctuation of some poems—particularly those for which the primary authority is the *Prometheus Unbound* volume—that seem to have been overpunctuated without Shelley's acquiescence.

*Capitalization:* Though the significance of Shelley's practice of capitalization is not yet fully understood in all details, he probably followed to an extent the practice of his time in capitalizing common nouns to indicate rhetorical emphasis. In "A Plain and Compendious Grammar of the English Tongue" prefixed to *The Complete Letter-Writer* (London: J. Brambles, A. Meggitt, and J. Waters, 1804), the anonymous author writes, under the heading "Of Capitals, or great Letters" (rule 2): "It is become customary to begin any substantive in a sentence with a capital, if it bears some considerable stress of the author's sense upon it, to make it the more remarkable." This rule is reinforced by rule 6, which states: "Sometimes capitals are used in whole words and sentences, when something extraordinary great is expressed" (p. 27). Shelley uses this latter mode of emphasis in "Hymn to Intellectual Beauty," lines 13, 71, and 83. For Shelley, who was hypersensitive to the aural effects of his poetry when read aloud, adding subtle emphasis by selectively capitalizing initial letters (rather than, say, italicizing whole words) may have been one way to articulate the rhythms of his verse as well as his meaning.

In any case, wherever Shelley's own usage (as nearly as that can be determined from the surviving evidence) parallels either the rules or practice of a number of his contemporaries or his older literary models, it seems best to follow him rather than to impose on his work the usage of either a typesetter or a later editor. In almost every instance where such persons have attempted to revise the capitalization of one of Shelley's manuscripts or first editions, they have merely replaced his preferences with others equally erratic and personal.

# Abbreviations

| | |
|---|---|
| *BSM* | *The Bodleian Shelley Manuscripts*, gen. ed. Donald H. Reiman, 23 vols. (New York & London: Garland Publishing, 1986–2001). |
| *CPPBS* | *The Complete Poetry of Percy Bysshe Shelley*, vol. I, ed. Donald H. Reiman and Neil Fraistat (Baltimore, MD: Johns Hopkins University Press, 2000). |
| *ELH* | *English Literary History* |
| *JEGP* | *Journal of English and Germanic Philology* |
| *KSJ* | *Keats-Shelley Journal* |
| *KSR* | *Keats-Shelley Review* |
| *Letters* | *The Letters of Percy Bysshe Shelley*, ed. Frederick L. Jones, 2 vols. (Oxford: Clarendon Press, 1964). |
| *MYR: Shelley* | *The Manuscripts of the Younger Romantics: Shelley*, gen. ed. Donald H. Reiman, 9 vols. (New York & London: Garland Publishing, 1985–1996). |
| *PMLA* | *Publications of the Modern Language Association* |
| *PQ* | *Philological Quarterly* |
| *RES* | *Review of English Studies* |
| *RR* | *The Romantics Reviewed: Contemporary Reviews of British Romantic Writers*, ed. Donald H. Reiman, 9 vols. (New York: Garland, 1972). |
| *SC* | *Shelley and his Circle, 1773–1822*, ed. Kenneth Neill Cameron and Donald H. Reiman, 10 vols. (Cambridge, MA: Harvard University Press, 1961–   ). |
| *SiR* | *Studies in Romanticism* |

SPP    *Shelley's Poetry and Prose: A Norton Critical Edition*, first edition, ed. Donald H. Reiman and Sharon B. Powers (New York: W. W. Norton, 1977); 2nd edition—the present text.

Works   *The Complete Works of Percy Bysshe Shelley*, ed. Roger Ingpen and Walter E. Peck, 10 vols. (Julian Edition) (London: Ernest Benn; New York: Charles Scribners' Sons, 1926–1930).

# THE POEMS

THE POEMS

# *From* THE ESDAILE NOTEBOOK

In 1813 Shelley planned to have Thomas Hookham publish two volumes of his poetry—*Queen Mab* and the volume of miscellaneous short poems that has become known as *The Esdaile Notebook*. Shelley, even in proposing the second volume, showed his mixed feelings about it: "My poems, will, I fear, little stand the criticism even of friendship. Some of the later ones have the merit of conveying a meaning in every word, and these are all faithful pictures of my feelings at the time of writing them. But they are, in a great measure, abrupt and obscure—all breathing hatred to government and religion, but I think not too openly for publication" (*Letters*, I, 348). Hookham ultimately declined to publish either volume, and Shelley gave the Notebook containing his early poems to his first wife, Harriet Westbrook Shelley.

The texts of these poems survive in a bound Notebook into which Shelley copied his poems for safekeeping while he submitted a more carefully punctuated manuscript (now lost) to potential publishers. When Shelley eloped with Mary Godwin, this Notebook remained with Harriet Shelley, who added to the poems that Shelley had copied a few more of his poems and fragments from other manuscripts in her possession, bringing the total number of pieces in the Notebook to fifty-eight. After Harriet's suicide in November or December 1816 (see *SC*, IV, 769–802), the Notebook was preserved for her surviving child, Eliza Ianthe, who in 1837 married Edward Jeffries Esdaile. In the 1880s the two sons of Ianthe Shelley Esdaile permitted Edward Dowden to publish biographically interesting excerpts from the poems in his two-volume *Life of Percy Bysshe Shelley* (1886). These fragments were collected in 1887 by T. J. Wise and H. Buxton Forman, who surreptitiously issued thirty copies of a thin volume entitled *Poems and Sonnets* with a false Philadelphia imprint. Most of the other poetry remained unpublished until Mrs. Lettice A. Worrall (née Esdaile), Shelley's great-granddaughter, sold the notebook at auction in London in July 1962, where it was purchased for The Carl H. Pforzheimer Library.

In 1964 Alfred A. Knopf published the first complete edition of the poems, *The Esdaile Notebook: A Volume of Early Poems by Percy Bysshe Shelley*, edited by Kenneth Neill Cameron. (Faber and Faber's English edition of Cameron's text corrected some errors.) Neville Rogers's edition, entitled *The Esdaile Poems* (1966), added little to the scholarship but provided the basis of the text of these poems in the first volume of his ill-fated Oxford edition of the *Poetical Works* (1972). Cameron, meanwhile, provided a diplomatic transcription of the poems in an Appendix to *SC*, IV (1970), and Reiman later edited a photofacsimile of the Notebook as volume I of *MYR: Shelley* (1985). The initial volume of G. M. Matthews and Kelvin Everest's *The Poems of Shelley* (1989) includes the Esdaile poems among other early poetry, arranged chronologically according to each poem's supposed date of initial composition. Volume II of our *Complete Poetry of Percy Bysshe Shelley* (CPPBS) includes *Queen Mab* and *The Esdaile Notebook* together, as Shelley originally planned to issue them, with the Esdaile poems in the order in which they appear in his Notebook. The four poems included in the present edition are also arranged in the order they are found in the Esdaile Notebook, where they are the seventh, twenty-sixth, forty-ninth, and fiftieth poems—the last two probably being the last two in the volume as Shelley finally tried to have it published.

This limited selection can only hint at the wide range of forms, subject-matter, and tone in the ambitious variety of apprentice poetry that Shelley assembled between 1811 and 1813 to represent his early ideas and feelings.

## To the Emperors of Russia and Austria who eyed the battle of Austerlitz from the heights whilst Buonaparte was active in the thickest of the fight[1]

Coward Chiefs! who while the fight
   Rages in the plain below
Hide the shame of your affright
   On yon distant mountain's brow,
Does one human feeling creep      5
Through your hearts' remorseless sleep.
On that silence cold and deep,
   Does one impulse flow
Such as fires the Patriot's breast,
Such as breaks the Hero's rest?[2]      10

No, cowards! ye are calm[3] and still,
   Keen frosts that blight the human bud,
Each opening petal blight and kill
   And bathe its tenderness in blood.
Ye hear the groans of those who die,      15
Ye heard the whistling death shots fly
And when the yells of Victory
   Float o'er the murdered good
Ye smile secure.—On yonder plain
The game if lost begins again.      20

Think ye the restless fiend[4] who haunts
   The tumult of yon gory field,
Whom neither shame nor danger daunts,
   Who dares not fear, who cannot yield,
Will not with Equalizing blow      25
Abase the high, exalt the low

1. Napoleon Bonaparte brilliantly defeated the combined armies of Russia and Austria at Austerlitz in Moravia on December 2, 1805, when Shelley was only thirteen. (For the classic fictional description of the battle, see Tolstoy's *War and Peace*, Part III, chaps. XIIff.) Shelley completed another poem in the same relatively sophisticated stanza form as this one in February 1812, and his attack on the emperors of Austria and Russia may date either from that year, when the British were gloating over Napoleon's retreat from Moscow, or possibly from early 1813, when England again allied itself with the two lesser emperors in its sixth anti-French coalition.
2. In lines 5–10 Shelley supplied no end punctuation except for a period at the end of the stanza. One editor inserted a question mark at the end of line 6 after *sleep*, instead of after *deep* in line 7.
3. Sometimes, when speaking of human emotions, Shelley uses *calm* in a negative sense to mean "unmoved" or "insensitive" (e.g., *Prometheus Unbound*, I.238, 259).
4. Napoleon as a "restless fiend" resembles Satan in Milton's *Paradise Lost*; cf. Shelley's remarks on *Paradise Lost* in the Preface to *Prometheus Unbound* and in *A Defence of Poetry*.

And in one mighty shock o'erthrow
   The slaves that sceptres wield
Till from the ruin of the storm
   Ariseth Freedom's awful form?         30

Hushed below the battle's jar
   Night rests silent on the Heath,
Silent save when vultures soar
   Above the wounded warrior's death.
How sleep ye now, unfeeling Kings!      35
Peace seldom folds her snowy wings
On poisoned memory's conscience-stings
   Which lurk bad hearts beneath:
Nor downy beds procure repose
Where crime and terror mingle throes.[5]    40

Yet may your terrors rest secure.
   Thou, Northern chief,[6] why startest thou?
Pale Austria,[7] calm those fears. Be sure
   The tyrant needs such slaves as you.
Think ye the world would bear his sway    45
Were dastards such as you away?
No! they would pluck his plumage gay
   Torn from a nation's woe[8]
And lay him in the oblivious gloom
Where Freedom now prepares your tomb.    50

# Sonnet[1]

## To a balloon, laden with <u>Knowledge</u>

Bright ball of flame that through the gloom of even
Silently takest thine etherial way
And with surpassing glory dimm'st each ray
Twinkling amid the dark blue Depths of Heaven:

5. *throes:* pangs, spasms.
6. Czar Alexander I (reigned 1801–25).
7. Francis Hapsburg reigned as Holy Roman Emperor Francis II from 1792 to 1806 (when Napoleon dissolved the Holy Roman Empire) and as Francis I, Emperor of Austria, from 1804 to 1835 (having assumed the title of emperor the same year that the Corsican crowned himself Emperor of France).
8. Lines 47–48 allude to Thomas Paine's retort in *The Rights of Man* to Edmund Burke's lament for Marie Antoinette in *Reflections on the Revolution in France*: "He pities the plumage [i.e., the Queen], but forgets the dying bird [France]."
1. In August 1812, Shelley, his wife Harriet, her sister Eliza Westbrook, and an Irish servant were in Devonshire distributing two broadsides (single-sheet publications): a poem entitled *The Devil's Walk* and the prose *Declaration of Rights*. Shelley disseminated some of these by sealing them in empty bottles that he set afloat in the sea, a gesture that he commemorated in another Esdaile sonnet entitled, "On launching some bottles filled with knowledge into the Bristol Channel." Though there is no outside evidence that he also launched one or more of these broadsides in "a balloon," the penalties for being caught distributing such seditious documents in person were severe enough (as we show in *CPPBS*, I, 283–85) to warrant the practicality of all such unorthodox methods.

Unlike the Fire thou bearest,[2] soon shalt thou                5
Fade like a meteor in surrounding gloom
Whilst that,[3] unquencheable is doomed to glow—
A watch light by the patriot's lonely tomb,
A ray of courage to the opprest and poor,
A spark, though gleaming on the hovel's hearth,              10
Which through the tyrant's gilded domes shall roar,
A beacon in the darkness of the Earth,
A Sun which o'er the renovated scene
Shall dart like Truth where Falshood yet has been.


# Zeinab and Kathema[1]

Upon the lonely beach Kathema lay;
    Against his folded arm his heart beat fast.
Through gathering tears the Sun's departing ray
    In coldness o'er his shuddering spirit past
And all unfelt the breeze of evening came               5
That fanned with quivering wing his wan cheek's feeble flame.

"Oh!" cried the mourner, "could this widowed soul
    But fly where yonder Sun now speeds to dawn."
He paused—a thousand thoughts began to roll;
    Like waves they swept in restless tumult on,          10
Like those fast waves that quick-succeeding beat
Without one lasting shape the beach beneath his feet.

And now the beamless, broad and yellow sphere
    Half sinking lingered on the crimson sea;
A shape of darksome distance does appear                15
    Within its semicircled radiancy.
All sense[2] was gone to his betrothed one—
His eye fell on the form that dimmed the setting sun,—

He thought on his betrothed . . . for his youth
    With her that was its charm to ripeness grew.         20
All that was dear in love, or fair in truth,
    With her was shared as childhood's moments flew,
And mingled with sweet memories of her
Was life's unveiling morn with all its bliss and care.

---

2. Shelley regularly uses fire as a symbol of spiritual energy—here as knowledge that can overcome evil error; when he was young, he held the Socratic view that much human evil results
from ignorance rather than malice.
3. Fire (line 5).
1. "Zeinab and Kathema," perhaps composed in June 1811, fuses incidents from popular Gothic
and orientalist romances with a violent attack on British imperialism abroad and social injustice at home. The name "Zeinab" comes from Robert Southey's *Thalaba the Destroyer*
(1801), where Zeinab is the widowed mother of the young Arab warrior Thalaba.
2. Emotional consciousness.

O wild and lovely Superstition's[3] spell, 25
  Love for the friend that life and freedom gave—
Youth's growing hopes that watch themselves so well,
  Passion, so prompt to blight, so strong to save,
And childhood's host of memories combine
Her life and love around his being to entwine. 30

And to their wishes with its joy-mixed pain
  Just as the veil of hope began to fall,
The Christian murderers over-ran the plain,
  Ravaging, burning and polluting all.
Zeinab was reft[4] to grace the robbers' land; 35
Each drop of kindred blood stained the invaders' brand.

Yes! they had come their holy book to bring
  Which God's own son's apostles had compiled
That charity and peace, and love might spring
  Within a world by God's blind ire defiled, 40
But rapine,[5] war and treachery rushed before
Their hosts, and murder dyed Kathema's bower in gore.

Therefore his soul was widowed, and alone
  He stood in the world's wide and drear expanse.
No human ear could shudder at his groan, 45
  No heart could thrill with his unspeaking glance;
One only hope yet lingering dared to burn,
Urging to high emprize[6] and deeds that danger spurn.

The glow has failed on Ocean's western line,
  Faded from every moveless cloud above. 50
The moon is up—she that was wont to shine
  And bless thy childish nights of guileless love,
Unhappy one, ere Christian rapine tore
All ties, and stain'd thy hopes in a dear mother's gore.

The form that in the setting Sun was seen 55
  Now in the moonlight slowly nears the shore,
The white sails gleaming o'er the billows green
  That sparkle into foam its prow before;
A wanderer of the deep it seems to be,
On high adventures bent, and feats of chivalry. 60

Then hope and wonder filled the mourner's mind.
  He gazed till vision even began to fail,
When to the pulses of the evening wind[7]
  A little boat approaching gave its sail,

3. Shelley intended this word for false or pagan religion to include Christianity.
4. Stolen.
5. Pillage, robbery.
6. An undertaking, especially one of adventure or chivalry.
7. In this early effort, young Shelley rhymed the noun "wind" three times with "mind" and once with "kind"—accepted contemporary poetic eye rhymes.

Rode o'er the slow raised surges near the strand,                    65
Ran up the beach and gave some stranger men to land.

"If thou wilt bear me to far England's shore
    Thine is this heap—the Christian's God!"
The chief with gloating rapture viewed the ore
    And his pleased avarice gave the willing nod.        70
They reach the ship, the fresh'ning breezes rise
And smooth and fast they speed beneath the moonlight skies.

What heart e'er felt more ardent longings now?
    What eye than his e'er beamed with riper hope
As curbed impatience on his open brow                    75
    There painted fancy's unsuspected scope,
As all that's fair the foreign land appeared
By ever present love, wonder and hope endeared?

Meanwhile through calm and storm, through night and day,
    Unvarying in her aim the vessel went                 80
As if some inward spirit ruled her way
    And her tense sails were conscious of intent
Till Albion's⁸ cliffs gleamed o'er her plunging bow
And Albion's river floods bright sparkled round her prow.

Then on the land in joy Kathema leaped                   85
    And kissed the soil in which his hopes were sown;
These even now in thought his heart has reaped.
    Elate of body and soul he journeyed on
And the strange things of a strange land past by
Like motes⁹ and shadows prest upon his charmed eye.      90

Yet Albion's changeful skies and chilling wind
    The change from Cashmire's vale might well denote.
There Heaven and Earth are ever bright and kind;
    Here, blights and storms and damp forever float
Whilst hearts are more ungenial than the zone—           95
Gross, spiritless, alive to no pangs but their own.

There flowers and fruits are ever fair and ripe;
    Autumn there mingles with the bloom of spring
And forms unpinched by frost or hunger's gripe¹
    A natural veil o'er natural spirits fling;            100
Here, woe on all but wealth has set its foot.
Famine, disease and crime even wealth's proud gates pollute.

Unquiet death and premature decay,
    Youth tottering on the crutches of old age,

8. England's.
9. Particles of dust; especially the innumerable minute specks seen in a sunbeam.
1. Grip, grasp.

And, ere the noon of manhood's riper day,    105
  Pangs that no art of medicine can assuage,
Madness and passion, ever mingling flames,—
And souls that well become such miserable frames—

These are the bribes which Art to man has given
  To yield his taintless nature to her sway.    110
So might dank night with meteors[2] tempt fair Heav'n
  To blot the sunbeam and forswear the day
Till gleams of baleful light alone might shew
The pestilential mists, the darkness and the woe.

Kathema little felt the sleet and wind,    115
  He little heeded the wide altered scene;
The flame that lived within his eager mind
  There kindled all the thoughts that once had been.
He stood alone in England's varied woe,
Safe, mid the flood of crime that round his steps did flow.    120

It was an evening when the bitterest breath
  Of dark December swept the mists along
That the lone wanderer came to a wild heath.
  Courage and hope had staid[3] his nature long;
Now cold, and unappeased hunger spent    125
His strength; sensation failed in total languishment.

When he awaked to life cold horror crept
  Even to his heart, for a damp deathy smell
Had slowly come around him while he slept.
  He started . . . lo! the fitful moonbeams fell    130
Upon a dead and naked female form
That from a gibbet[4] high swung to the sullen storm.

And wildly in the wind its dark hair swung,
  Low mingling with the clangor of the chain
Whilst ravenous birds of prey that on it clung    135
  In the dull ear of night poured their sad strain,
And ghastlily her shapeless visage shone
In the unsteady light, half mouldered through the bone.

Then madness seized Kathema, and his mind
  A prophecy of horror filled. He scaled    140
The gibbet which swung slowly in the wind
  High o'er the heath.—Scarcely his strength avail'd
To grasp the chain, when by the moonlight's gleam
His palsied gaze was fixed on Zeinab's altered frame.

2. Any luminous optical phenomenon in the earth's atmosphere.
3. Sustained.
4. An upright post with a projecting arm from which the bodies of criminals were hung in
chains or irons after execution. See the note to "The Sensitive-Plant," III.69.

Yes! in those orbs once bright with life and love     145
    Now full-fed worms bask in unnatural light;
That neck on which his eyes were wont to rove
    In rapture, changed by putrefaction's blight,
Now rusts the ponderous links that creak beneath
Its weight, and turns to life the frightful sport of death.     150


Then in the moonlight played Kathema's smile
    Calmly.—In peace his spirit seemed to be.
He paused, even like a man at ease awhile,
    Then spoke—"My love! I will be like to thee,
A mouldering carcase or a spirit blest,     155
With thee corruption's prey, or Heaven's happy guest."


He twined the chain around his neck, then leaped
    Forward, in haste to meet the life to come.
An iron-souled son of Europe might have wept
    To witness such a noble being's doom     160
As on the death scene Heaven indignant frowned
And Night in horror drew her veil the dead around.


For they had torn his Zeinab from her home—
    Her innocent habits were all rudely shriven[5]—
And dragged to live in love's untimely tomb     165
    To prostitution, crime and woe was driven.
The human race seemed leagued against her weal
And indignation cased her naked heart in steel.


Therefore against them she waged ruthless war
    With their own arms of bold and bloody crime,—     170
Even like a mild and sweetly-beaming star
    Whose rays were wont to grace the matin prime[6]
Changed to a comet, horrible and bright,
Which wild careers[7] awhile then sinks in dark-red night.


    175
Thus, like its God, unjust and pityless,
    Crimes first are made and then avenged by man,
For where's the tender heart, whose hope can bless
    Or man's, or God's, unprofitable plan—
A universe of horror and decay,
Gibbets, disease, and wars and hearts as hard as they.     180

---

5. Confessed, absolved; here used ironically. The penance for Zeinab's "innocent habits" was "prostitution, crime and woe."
6. Public morning prayers in the Church of England include matins, lauds, and prime: *matin prime* would be morning prayers generally.
7. Moves at full speed.

# The Retrospect.[1]

## Cwm Elan, 1812

To trace Duration's lone career,
To check the chariot of the year[2]
Whose burning wheels forever sweep
The boundaries of oblivion's deep. . . .
To snatch from Time, the monster's, jaw     5
The children which she just had borne
And, ere entombed within her maw,[3]
To drag them to the light of morn
And mark each feature with an eye
Of cold and fearless scrutiny. . . .     10
It asks a soul not formed to feel,
An eye of glass, a hand of steel,
Thoughts that have passed and thoughts that are
With truth and feeling to compare;
A scene which wildered[4] fancy viewed     15
In the soul's coldest solitude,
With that same scene when peaceful love
Flings rapture's colour o'er the grove
When mountain, meadow, wood and stream
With unalloying glory gleam     20
And to the spirit's ear and eye
Are unison and harmony.

The moonlight was my dearer day:—
Then would I wander far away
And lingering on the wild brook's shore     25
To hear its unremitting roar,
Would lose in the ideal flow
All sense of overwhelming woe;
Or at the noiseless noon of night,
Would climb some heathy[5] mountain's height     30
And listen to the mystic sound
That stole in fitful gasps around.
I joyed to see the streaks of day
Above the purple peaks decay
And watch the latest line of light     35
Just mingling with the shades of night;

1. In July and August 1811, Shelley visited Cwm Elan (the Welsh estate of his cousin Thomas Grove) just before he returned to London to elope with Harriet Westbrook. In June 1812 he returned to Cwm Elan—this time with Harriet as his wife. The poem may owe its name and the theme of its opening lines to Southey's "The Retrospect" (1794), but Wordsworth's "Tintern Abbey" (1798) exerted the strongest influence on Shelley's poem.
2. The image of the chariot of Being appears repeatedly in Shelley's poetry; see the notes to *Queen Mab*, I.134 and IX.154.
3. Kronos (Saturn) devoured his children; through confusion of his name with Chronos, he was also identified with Time.
4. Lost, straying.
5. Covered with heather or other low herbage.

For day with me, was time of woe
When even tears refused to flow;
Then would I stretch my languid frame
Beneath the wild-woods' gloomiest shade          40
And try to quench the ceaseless flame
That on my withered vitals preyed;
Would close mine[6] eyes and dream I were
On some remote and friendless plain
And long to leave existence there          45
If with it I might leave the pain
That with a finger cold and lean
Wrote madness on my withering mien.


It was not unrequited love
That bade my wildered spirit rove;          50
'T was not the pride, disdaining life,
That with this mortal world at strife
Would yield to the soul's inward sense,
Then groan in human impotence,
And weep, because it is not given          55
To taste on Earth the peace of Heaven.
'T was not, that in the narrow sphere
Where Nature fixed my wayward fate
There was no friend or kindred dear
Formed to become that spirit's mate,          60
Which, searching on tired pinion,[7] found
Barren and cold repulse around. . . .
Ah no! yet each one sorrow gave
New graces to the narrow grave:


For broken vows had early quelled          65
The stainless spirit's vestal[8] flame.
Yes! whilst the faithful bosom swelled,
Then the envenomed arrow came
And apathy's unaltering eye
Beamed coldness on the misery;          70
And early I had learned to scorn
The chains of clay that bound a soul
Panting to seize the wings of morn,[9]
And where its vital fires were born
To soar, and spurn the cold control          75
Which the vile slaves of earthly night
Would twine around its struggling flight.
O, many were the friends whom fame

6. In poetry of this period, the forms "mine" and "thine" replace "my" or "thy" when followed
by a vowel.
7. Wing.
8. Chaste or virgin.
9. Cf. Psalms 139:9: "If I take the wings of the morning . . ."

Had linked with the unmeaning name[1]
Whose magic marked among mankind                    80
The casket of my unknown mind,
Which hidden from the vulgar glare
Imbibed[2] no fleeting radiance there.
My darksome spirit sought. It found
A friendless solitude around.—                    85
For who, that might undaunted stand
The saviour of a sinking land,
Would crawl, its ruthless tyrant's slave,
And fatten upon freedom's grave,[3]
Though doomed with her to perish, where                    90
The captive clasps abhorred despair.[4]

*They* could not share the bosom's feeling,
Which, passion's every throb revealing,
Dared force on the world's notice cold
Thoughts of unprofitable mould,                    95
Who bask in Custom's fickle ray,—
Fit sunshine of such wintry day!
*They* could not in a twilight walk
Weave an impassioned web of talk
Till mysteries the spirit press                    100
In wild yet tender awfulness,[5]
Then feel within our narrow sphere
How little yet how great we are!
But they might shine in courtly glare,
Attract the rabble's cheapest stare,                    105
And might command where'er they move
A thing that bears the name of love;
They might be learned, witty, gay,
Foremost in fashion's gilt array,
On Fame's emblazoned pages shine,                    110
Be princes' friends, but never mine!

Ye jagged peaks that frown sublime,
Mocking the blunted scythe of Time,
Whence I would watch its lustre pale
Steal from the moon o'er yonder vale!                    115

Thou rock, whose bosom black and vast
Bared to the stream's unceasing flow,
Ever its giant shade doth cast
On the tumultuous surge below!

1. Gossip or public notice (*fame*) linked him with those in his social class as *friends,* but he considered his *name* as a Shelley, heir to a baronetcy, *unmeaning* compared to his inner feelings and aspirations that they did not share (lines 92–111 below).
2. Absorbed or received.
3. I.e., continue to enjoy the material benefits and prerogatives of the aristocracy.
4. I.e., even if he were doomed to die in prison, *clasp*ing despair.
5. Impressive solemnity; dreadfulness.

Woods, to whose depth retires to die                          120
The wounded echo's melody,
And whither this lone spirit bent
The footstep of a wild intent—

Meadows! Whose green and spangled breast
These fevered limbs have often pressed           125
Until the watchful fiend despair
Slept in the soothing coolness there!
Have not your varied beauties seen
The sunken eye, the withering mien,
Sad traces of the unuttered pain                     130
That froze my heart and burned my brain?

How changed since nature's summer form
Had last the power my grief to charm
Since last ye soothed my spirit's sadness—
Strange chaos of a mingled madness!            135
Changed!—not the loathsome worm that fed
In the dark mansions of the dead,
Now soaring through the fields of air
And gathering purest nectar there,
A butterfly whose million hues                       140
The dazzled eye of wonder views,
Long lingering on a work so strange,
Has undergone so bright a change!

How do I feel my happiness?
I cannot tell, but they may guess                    145
Whose every gloomy feeling gone,
Friendship and passion feel alone;
Who see mortality's dull clouds
Before affection's murmur fly,
Whilst the mild glances of her eye               150
Pierce the thin veil of flesh that shrouds
The spirit's radiant sanctuary.[6]

O thou![7] whose virtues latest known,
First in this heart yet claim'st a throne;
Whose downy sceptre still shall share            155
The gentle sway with virtue there;
Thou fair in form and pure in mind,
Whose ardent friendship rivets fast
The flowery band our fates that bind,
Which incorruptible shall last                         160
When duty's hard and cold control
Had thawed around the burning soul;
The gloomiest retrospects that bind

6. Shelley here represents the inner sanctum of his soul as being pierced by the looks of first
love as the hymen is broken during first intercourse.
7. Harriet Westbrook Shelley.

With crowns of thorn the bleeding mind,
The prospects of most doubtful hue   165
That rise on Fancy's shuddering view,
Are gilt by the reviving ray
Which thou hast flung upon my day.

## QUEEN MAB

Shelley conceived *Queen Mab*, his first major poem, in December 1811, and he composed it primarily between April 1812 and mid-February 1813. On February 19, 1813, Shelley wrote to his publisher friend Thomas Hookham that it was "finished & transcribed," though the notes were then still in progress. By May 21, 1813, *Queen Mab* was in press, but it may not have been produced until the end of December, when the first known reading of the printed volume is recorded by William Godwin in a journal entry for December 26. Shelley was by that time convinced that the poem was too radical to be published. Instead he distributed about 70 of the 250 copies printed to individuals he believed would be sympathetic, cutting out his name and address—which appeared as those of the printer—and, frequently, the dedicatory poem to Harriet Shelley. No manuscript of the original survives, though Shelley marked up two printed copies with cancellations and revisions for a different version that he never completed. One of these copies is at the Carl H. Pforzheimer Collection at the New York Public Library (SC 296; see SC, IV, 487–568) and the other is at the British Library (Ashley 4040).

 *Queen Mab* received some notice in 1817, when its moral quality figured in the decision of the Chancery Court to deprive Shelley of custody of his children by Harriet Shelley. In 1821, the poem was pirated both by William Clark of 201 Strand and—in a fake New York imprint—by William Benbow, R. C. Fair, and George Cannon, pretending to be "J. Baldwin." Clark was prosecuted by the Society for the Suppression of Vice; his edition was turned over for sale to Richard Carlile, the most courageous of all the radical booksellers, who also discovered, advertised, and (probably) sold the 180 remaining copies of Shelley's original 1813 edition of the poem.

 Thereafter *Queen Mab* was reprinted frequently in various editions. It became the bible of the Chartist movement and later had great influence on British Marxists, including George Bernard Shaw. Shelley himself, however, when he heard of the 1821 reprinting, wrote from Italy in a public letter: "I regret this publication, not so much from literary vanity, as because I fear it is better fitted to injure than to serve the cause of freedom."

 Queen Mab, "the fairies' midwife," appears in a famous speech by Mercutio in Shakespeare's *Romeo and Juliet* (I.iv.53–94), in which her mischievous dreammaking is described in terms that Shelley was later to echo in "The Witch of Atlas," lines 617ff. During the eighteenth century Queen Mab was the title character (like Mother Goose) in numerous collections of children's stories. Shelley's choice of this innocent-sounding name for the intermediary between the divine and the human who teaches the soul of Ianthe the revolutionary lessons of the past, situation of the present, and hopes of the future is in keeping with his directions to his publisher to have the poem printed "on fine paper & so as to catch the aristocrats:

They will not read it, but their sons & daughters may" (Shelley to Hookham, March 1813; *Letters*, I, 361). For useful discussions of aspects of
the poem, see the essays in this volume by Alan Bewell (pp. 627–36;
colonialism and disease), Annette Wheeler Cafarelli (pp. 607–16; libertinism and feminism), and Neil Fraistat (pp. 645–53; cultural implications
of the piracies).

# Queen Mab;
# A Philosophical Poem

ECRASEZ L'INFAME![1]
*Correspondance de Voltaire.*

———

Avia Pieridum peragro loca, nullius ante
Trita solo; juvat integros accedere fonteis;
Atque haurire: juvatque novos decerpere flores.
.    .    .    .    .    .    .
Unde prius nulli velarint tempora musæ.
Primum quod magnis doceo de rebus; et arctis
Religionum animos nodis exsolvere pergo.[2]
*Lucret.* lib. iv.

———

Δὸς ποῦ στῶ, καὶ κόσμον κινήσω.[3]
*Archimedes.*

———

## To Harriet * * * * *[4]

Whose is the love that, gleaming through the world,
Wards off the poisonous arrow of its scorn?
Whose is the warm and partial praise,
Virtue's most sweet reward?

1. "Crush the demon!" In his later years at Ferney, near Geneva, Voltaire included the phrase
   in most of his letters. Shelley himself used the phrase at least twice in his letters, once in
   French (Dec. 20, 1810; *Letters*, I, 29) and again in English (Jan. 3, 1811; *Letters*, I, 35).
   According to Peter Gay, Voltaire, like Shelley, meant Christianity rather than "religion" by
   the term *l'infame*.
2. The Latin epigraph comes from the opening of Book IV of Lucretius' Epicurean poem *De
   rerum natura* (*Of the Nature of Things*). The lines may be translated "I blaze a trail through
   pathless tracks of the Pierian realm, where no foot has ever trod before. What joy it is to
   discover virgin springs and drink their waters, and what joy to gather new flowers . . . never
   before wreathed by the Muses around anyone's head! First, I teach of great matters, and
   [secondly] I free men's minds from the crippling bonds of superstition." The main subject
   of Book IV is the nature of sensation and erotic love. Shelley later wrote of Lucretius' poem:
   "The 4th book is perhaps the finest. The whole of that passage about love is full of irresistible
   energy of language as well as the profoundest truth" (*Letters*, I, 545).
3. "Give me somewhere to stand, and I will move the earth," attributed to the Syracusan Greek
   scientist Archimedes (287–212 B.C.), refers to his enthusiasm for the power of the lever, a
   trope frequently used by radicals of the day to link mechanical forces with revolutionary
   actions. Shelley reused the epigraph on the title page of *Laon and Cythna*.
4. Shelley first intended this tribute to his first wife, Harriet Westbrook Shelley, to stand as
   the dedicatory poem in the collection of shorter works now known as *The Esdaile Notebook*,
   but when he failed to find a publisher for that volume, he transferred it (slightly revised) to
   *Queen Mab*.

Beneath whose looks did my reviving soul 5
Riper in truth and virtuous daring grow?
    Whose eyes have I gazed fondly on,
    And loved mankind the more?

Harriet! on thine:—thou wert my purer mind;
Thou wert the inspiration of my song; 10
    Thine are these early wilding flowers,
    Though garlanded by me.

Then press unto thy breast this pledge of love,
And know, though time may change and years may roll,
    Each flowret gathered in my heart 15
    It consecrates to thine.

### I.[5]

        How wonderful is Death,
        Death and his brother Sleep!
    One, pale as yonder waning moon
        With lips of lurid blue;
    The other, rosy as the morn 5
        When throned on ocean's wave
        It blushes o'er the world:
    Yet both so passing wonderful!

        Hath then the gloomy Power
    Whose reign is in the tainted sepulchres 10
        Seized on her sinless soul?
        Must then that peerless form
    Which love and admiration cannot view
    Without a beating heart, those azure veins
    Which steal like streams along a field of snow, 15
        That lovely outline, which is fair
            As breathing marble, perish?
            Must putrefaction's breath
    Leave nothing of this heavenly sight
            But loathsomeness and ruin? 20
    Spare nothing but a gloomy theme,
    On which the lightest heart might moralize?
        Or is it only a sweet slumber
            Stealing o'er sensation,
        Which the breath of roseate morning 25
            Chaseth into darkness?
        Will Ianthe[6] wake again,

---

5. Shelley described his choice of verse form in a letter to Hogg: "The didactic is in blank heroic verse, & the descriptive in blank lyrical measure. If authority is of any weight in support of this singularity, Miltons Samson Agonistes, the Greek Choruses, & (you will laugh) Southeys Thalaba may be adduced" (Feb. 7, 1813; *Letters*, I, 352).
6. The character is modeled on Harriet Shelley (Ianthe's name was given to Shelley and Harriet's first child, a daughter born June 23, 1813).

And give that faithful bosom joy
Whose sleepless spirit waits to catch
Light, life and rapture from her smile?                    30

      Yes! she will wake again,
Although her glowing limbs are motionless,
     And silent those sweet lips,
     Once breathing eloquence,
That might have soothed a tyger's rage,                    35
Or thawed the cold heart of a conqueror.
     Her dewy eyes are closed,
And on their lids, whose texture fine
Scarce hides the dark blue orbs beneath,
     The baby Sleep is pillowed:                         40
     Her golden tresses shade
     The bosom's stainless pride,
Curling like tendrils of the parasite[7]
     Around a marble column.

     Hark! whence that rushing sound?                    45
     'Tis like the wondrous strain
That round a lonely ruin swells,
Which, wandering on the echoing shore,
     The enthusiast hears at evening:
'Tis softer than the west wind's sigh;                     50
'Tis wilder than the unmeasured notes
Of that strange lyre whose strings
The genii of the breezes sweep:[8]
     Those lines of rainbow light
Are like the moonbeams when they fall                      55
Through some cathedral window, but the teints[9]
     Are such as may not find
     Comparison on earth.

Behold the chariot of the Fairy Queen!
Celestial coursers paw the unyielding air;[1]              60
Their filmy pennons[2] at her word they furl,
And stop obedient to the reins of light:
     These the Queen of spells drew in,
     She spread a charm around the spot,
And leaning graceful from the etherial car,               65
     Long did she gaze, and silently,
       Upon the slumbering maid.

---

7. I.e., ivy.
8. The Aeolian harp or wind lyre, an instrument popular in Shelley's time, was designed to be placed in an open window or on a porch, where its strings would vibrate in the wind, producing musical sounds (like wind chimes). The image of the poet as an Aeolian harp moved by the winds of a spiritual force or being is prominent in Romantic poetry.
9. Hues or tints.
1. The air gives solid footing to the hooves of "celestial coursers," whose density is no greater than that of air.
2. I.e., wings ("pinions").

Oh! not the visioned poet in his dreams,
When silvery clouds float through the 'wildered brain,
When every sight of lovely, wild and grand                    70
   Astonishes, enraptures, elevates,
      When fancy at a glance combines
      The wondrous and the beautiful,—
So bright, so fair, so wild a shape
      Hath ever yet beheld,                    75
As that which reined the coursers of the air,
   And poured the magic of her gaze
      Upon the maiden's sleep.

      The broad and yellow moon
      Shone dimly through her form—                    80
That form of faultless symmetry;
The pearly and pellucid³ car
      Moved not the moonlight's line:
      'Twas not an earthly pageant:
Those who had looked upon the sight,                    85
      Passing all human glory,
      Saw not the yellow moon,
      Saw not the mortal scene,
      Heard not the night-wind's rush,
      Heard not an earthly sound,                    90
      Saw but the fairy pageant,
      Heard but the heavenly strains
      That filled the lonely dwelling.

The Fairy's frame was slight, yon fibrous cloud,
That catches but the palest tinge of even,                    95
And which the straining eye can hardly seize
When melting into eastern twilight's shadow,
Were scarce so thin, so slight; but the fair star
That gems the glittering coronet of morn,⁴
Sheds not a light so mild, so powerful,                    100
As that which, bursting from the Fairy's form,
Spread a purpureal⁵ halo round the scene,
   Yet with an undulating motion,
   Swayed to her outline gracefully.

      From her celestial car                    105
      The Fairy Queen descended,
      And thrice she waved her wand
Circled with wreaths of amaranth:⁶
      Her thin and misty form

---

3. Translucent or transparent.
4. The planet Venus as morning star.
5. Purple; a poetic usage also found in Wordsworth and Byron.
6. From the Greek meaning "unfading" or "incorruptible"; the name given to a mythical flower whose blossoms never die.

Moved with the moving air,                                    110
And the clear silver tones,
As thus she spoke, were such
As are unheard by all but gifted ear.


FAIRY.

Stars! your balmiest influence shed!
Elements! your wrath suspend!                                 115
Sleep, Ocean, in the rocky bounds
    That circle thy domain!
Let not a breath be seen to stir
Around yon grass-grown ruin's height,
    Let even the restless gossamer                            120
    Sleep on the moveless air!
Soul of Ianthe! thou,
Judged alone worthy of the envied boon,
That waits the good and the sincere; that waits
Those who have struggled, and with resolute will             125
Vanquished earth's pride and meanness, burst the chains,
The icy chains of custom, and have shone
The day-stars[7] of their age;—Soul of Ianthe!
    Awake! arise!

Sudden arose[8]                                              130
    Ianthe's Soul; it stood
All beautiful in naked purity,
The perfect semblance of its bodily frame,
Instinct[9] with inexpressible beauty and grace;
    Each stain of earthliness                                135
    Had passed away, it reassumed
    Its native dignity, and stood
        Immortal amid ruin.

Upon the couch the body lay
    Wrapt in the depth of slumber:                           140
Its features were fixed and meaningless.
    Yet animal life was there,
And every organ yet performed
Its natural functions: 'twas a sight
Of wonder to behold the body and soul.                       145
    The self-same lineaments, the same
    Marks of identity were there:

---

7. Stars so bright that they are visible during the day; Milton uses the phrase (*Lycidas*,
   line 168) to refer to the sun.
8. The sharp distinction found in lines 130–56 between a perishable body and an immortal,
   everlasting (*sempiternal*, 149) soul is strongly present in Shelley's early poetry through *Queen
   Mab* but appears to be more figurative in such later poems as *Adonais*.
9. Animated, impelled; the word appears in Milton's description of the Chariot of Paternal
   Deitie (*Paradise Lost*, VI.749ff.), which underlies this and several other descriptions of chariots in Shelley's poetry.

Yet, oh, how different! One aspires to Heaven,
Pants for its sempiternal heritage,
And ever changing, ever rising still,
    Wantons in endless being.          150
The other, for a time the unwilling sport
Of circumstance and passion, struggles on;
Fleets through its sad duration rapidly;
Then, like an useless and worn-out machine,          155
    Rots, perishes, and passes.

FAIRY.

  Spirit! who hast dived so deep;
  Spirit! who hast soared so high;
    Thou the fearless, thou the mild,
Accept the boon thy worth hath earned,          160
    Ascend the car with me.

SPIRIT.

Do I dream? is this new feeling
But a visioned ghost of slumber?
    If indeed I am a soul,
A free, a disembodied soul,          165
    Speak again to me.

FAIRY.

I am the Fairy MAB: to me 'tis given
The wonders of the human world to keep:
The secrets of the immeasurable past,
In the unfailing consciences of men,          170
Those stern, unflattering chroniclers, I find:
The future, from the causes which arise
In each event, I gather: not the sting
Which retributive memory implants
In the hard bosom of the selfish man;          175
Nor that extatic and exulting throb
Which virtue's votary feels when he sums up
The thoughts and actions of a well-spent day,
Are unforeseen, unregistered by me:
And it is yet permitted me, to rend          180
The veil of mortal frailty, that the spirit
Clothed in its changeless purity, may know
How soonest to accomplish the great end
For which it hath its being, and may taste
That peace, which in the end all life will share.          185
This is the meed of virtue; happy Soul,
    Ascend the car with me!

The chains of earth's immurement
   Fell from Ianthe's spirit;
They shrank and brake[1] like bandages of straw     190
   Beneath a wakened giant's strength.
     She knew her glorious change,
And felt in apprehension uncontrolled
   New raptures opening round:
Each day-dream of her mortal life,     195
Each frenzied vision of the slumbers
   That closed each well-spent day,
   Seemed now to meet reality.

The Fairy and the Soul proceeded;
   The silver clouds disparted;     200
And as the car of magic they ascended,
   Again the speechless music swelled,
   Again the coursers of the air
Unfurled their azure pennons, and the Queen
   Shaking the beamy reins     205
   Bade them pursue their way.

   The magic car moved on.
The night was fair, and countless stars
Studded heaven's dark blue vault,—
   Just o'er the eastern wave     210
Peeped the first faint smile of morn:—
   The magic car moved on—
   From the celestial hoofs
The atmosphere in flaming sparkles flew,
   And where the burning wheels     215
Eddied above the mountain's loftiest peak,
   Was traced a line of lightning.
Now it flew far above a rock,
   The utmost verge of earth,
The rival of the Andes,[2] whose dark brow     220
   Lowered o'er the silver sea.

Far, far below the chariot's path,
   Calm as a slumbering babe,
   Tremendous Ocean lay.
The mirror of its stillness shewed     225
   The pale and waning stars,
   The chariot's fiery track,
   And the grey light of morn
   Tinging those fleecy clouds
   That canopied the dawn.     230
   Seemed it, that the chariot's way
Lay through the midst of an immense concave,

1. Broke.
2. In Shelley's day natural historians believed that the Andes were the highest mountains in the world and that the mountains of Japan were among those that rivaled them in height.

Radiant with million constellations, tinged
   With shades of infinite colour,
   And semicircled with a belt                                                    235
   Flashing incessant meteors.

     The magic car moved on.
    As they approached their goal
 The coursers seemed to gather speed;
The sea no longer was distinguished; earth                        240
  Appeared a vast and shadowy sphere;
    The sun's unclouded orb
  Rolled through the black concave;[3]
    Its rays of rapid light
Parted around the chariot's swifter course,                        245
  And fell, like ocean's feathery spray
    Dashed from the boiling surge
    Before a vessel's prow.

     The magic car moved on.
    Earth's distant orb appeared                                       250
The smallest light that twinkles in the heaven;
    Whilst round the chariot's way
    Innumerable systems rolled,[4]
   And countless spheres diffused
    An ever-varying glory.                                              255
  It was a sight of wonder: some
 Were horned like the crescent moon;
  Some shed a mild and silver beam
 Like Hesperus[5] o'er the western sea;
 Some dash'd athwart with trains of flame,                        260
 Like worlds to death and ruin driven;
Some shone like suns, and as the chariot passed,
    Eclipsed all other light.

    Spirit of Nature! here!
 In this interminable wilderness                                       265
Of worlds, at whose immensity
  Even soaring fancy staggers,
  Here is thy fitting temple.
   Yet not the lightest leaf
That quivers to the passing breeze                                     270
  Is less instinct with thee:
  Yet not the meanest worm

3. "Beyond our atmosphere the sun would appear a rayless orb of fire in the midst of a black concave. The equal diffusion of its light on earth is owing to the refraction of the rays by the atmosphere, and their reflection from other bodies" (the beginning of Shelley's note).
4. "The plurality of worlds,—the indefinite immensity of the universe is a most awful subject of contemplation. He who rightly feels its mystery and grandeur, is in no danger of seduction from the falshoods of religious systems, or of deifying the principle of the universe. . . . Millions and millions of suns are ranged around us, all attended by innumerable worlds, yet calm, regular, and harmonious, all keeping the paths of immutable necessity" (from Shelley's note).
5. The planet Venus as the evening star; also called Vesper.

That lurks in graves and fattens on the dead
    Less shares thy eternal breath.
        Spirit of Nature! thou!                         275
    Imperishable as this scene,
        Here is thy fitting temple.


## II.

If solitude hath ever led thy steps
    To the wild ocean's echoing shore,
        And thou hast lingered there,
        Until the sun's broad orb
    Seemed resting on the burnished wave,           5
        Thou must have marked the lines
Of purple gold, that motionless
        Hung o'er the sinking sphere:
Thou must have marked the billowy clouds
    Edged with intolerable radiancy                   10
        Towering like rocks of jet
        Crowned with a diamond wreath.
        And yet there is a moment,
        When the sun's highest point
Peeps like a star o'er ocean's western edge,          15
When those far clouds of feathery gold,
    Shaded with deepest purple, gleam
    Like islands on a dark blue sea;
Then has thy fancy soared above the earth,
    And furled its wearied wing                       20
        Within the Fairy's fane.[6]


        Yet not the golden islands
        Gleaming in yon flood of light,
            Nor the feathery curtains
        Stretching o'er the sun's bright couch,       25
        Nor the burnished ocean waves
            Paving that gorgeous dome,
        So fair, so wonderful a sight
As Mab's etherial palace could afford.
Yet likest evening's vault, that faery Hall!          30
As Heaven, low resting on the wave, it spread
        Its floors of flashing light,
        Its vast and azure dome,
        Its fertile golden islands
        Floating on a silver sea;                     35
Whilst suns their mingling beamings darted
Through clouds of circumambient[7] darkness,
    And pearly battlements around
    Looked o'er the immense of Heaven.


6. Temple.
7. Surrounding.

The magic car no longer moved. 40
    The Fairy and the Spirit
    Entered the Hall of Spells:
       Those golden clouds
    That rolled in glittering billows
    Beneath the azure canopy 45
With the etherial footsteps trembled not:
    The light and crimson mists,
Floating to strains of thrilling melody
    Through that unearthly dwelling,
Yielded to every movement of the will. 50
Upon their passive swell the Spirit leaned,
And, for the varied bliss that pressed around,
    Used not the glorious privilege
    Of virtue and of wisdom.

     "Spirit!" the Fairy said, 55
And pointed to the gorgeous dome,
    "This is a wondrous sight
    And mocks all human grandeur;
But, were it virtue's only meed,[8] to dwell
In a celestial palace, all resigned 60
To pleasurable impulses, immured
Within the prison of itself, the will
Of changeless nature would be unfulfilled.
Learn to make others happy. Spirit, come!
This is thine high reward:—the past shall rise; 65
Thou shalt behold the present; I will teach
    The secrets of the future."

    The Fairy and the Spirit
Approached the overhanging battlement.—
    Below lay stretched the universe! 70
    There, far as the remotest line
    That bounds imagination's flight,
      Countless and unending orbs
    In mazy motion intermingled,
    Yet still fulfilled immutably 75
      Eternal nature's law.
      Above, below, around,
      The circling systems formed
    A wilderness of harmony;
    Each with undeviating aim, 80
In eloquent silence, through the depths of space
    Pursued its wondrous way.

    There was a little light
That twinkled in the misty distance:

8. Reward.

None but a spirit's eye                                    85
Might ken[9] that rolling orb;
None but a spirit's eye,
And in no other place
But that celestial dwelling, might behold
Each action of this earth's inhabitants.                   90
    But matter, space and time
In those aërial mansions cease to act;
And all-prevailing wisdom, when it reaps
The harvest of its excellence, o'erbounds
Those obstacles, of which an earthly soul                  95
    Fears to attempt the conquest.


    The Fairy pointed to the earth.
    The Spirit's intellectual eye
    Its kindred beings recognized.
The thronging thousands, to a passing view,               100
    Seemed like an anthill's citizens.
    How wonderful! that even
The passions, prejudices, interests,
That sway the meanest being, the weak touch
    That moves the finest nerve,                           105
    And in one human brain
Causes the faintest thought, becomes a link
    In the great chain of nature.


    "Behold," the Fairy cried,
"Palmyra's ruined palaces![1]—                             110
    Behold! where grandeur frowned;
    Behold! where pleasure smiled;
What now remains?—the memory
    Of senselessness and shame—
    What is immortal there?                                115
    Nothing—it stands to tell
    A melancholy tale, to give
    An awful warning: soon
Oblivion will steal silently
    The remnant of its fame.                               120
    Monarchs and conquerors there
Proud o'er prostrate millions trod—
The earthquakes of the human race;
Like them, forgotten when the ruin
    That marks their shock is past.                        125

9. Recognize.
1. Palmyra, in what is now Syria, was once a flourishing city. Under its princess Zenobia Sep-
tima (who became first the wife and then the heir of Odenatus, co-ruler of the Roman
Empire) Palmyra challenged Rome itself, but the city was totally destroyed in A.D. 273 after
Aurelian successfully besieged Zenobia there. Palmyra's ruins were invoked by authors, especially in Volney's *Ruins of Empire,* as an illustration of the ephemeral nature of human
glory; Shelley's friend Thomas Love Peacock published a poem entitled *Palmyra* on this
theme in 1806.

"Beside the eternal Nile,
The Pyramids have risen.
Nile shall pursue his changeless way:
    Those pyramids shall fall;
Yea! not a stone shall stand to tell                                    130
    The spot whereon they stood!
Their very site shall be forgotten,
    As is their builder's name!

    "Behold yon sterile spot;
Where now the wandering Arab's tent                                    135
    Flaps in the desart-blast.
There once old Salem's haughty fane[2]
Reared high to heaven its thousand golden domes,
    And in the blushing face of day
    Exposed its shameful glory.                                    140
Oh! many a widow, many an orphan cursed
The building of that fane; and many a father,
Worn out with toil and slavery, implored
The poor man's God to sweep it from the earth,
And spare his children the detested task                                    145
Of piling stone on stone, and poisoning
    The choicest days of life,
    To soothe a dotard's[3] vanity.
There an inhuman and uncultured race
Howled hideous praises to their Demon-God;                                    150
They rushed to war, tore from the mother's womb
The unborn child,—old age and infancy
Promiscuous[4] perished; their victorious arms
Left not a soul to breathe.[5] Oh! they were fiends:
But what was he[6] who taught them that the God                                    155
Of nature and benevolence had given
A special sanction to the trade of blood?
His name and theirs are fading, and the tales
Of this barbarian nation,[7] which imposture
Recites till terror credits, are pursuing                                    160
    Itself into forgetfulness.

    "Where Athens, Rome, and Sparta stood,
    There is a moral desert now:
    The mean and miserable huts,
    The yet more wretched palaces,                                    165
    Contrasted with those antient fanes,

2. The Temple at Jerusalem, sacked by the Emperor Vespasian and his son Titus in A.D. 70.
3. The dotard is King Solomon.
4. Indiscriminately.
5. Shelley's attack on the religion of the Jews grew out of similar attacks by moralistic skeptics
   throughout the eighteenth century, from Voltaire to Thomas Paine. Attacks on Judaism
   were more acceptable in England than attacks on Christianity, which was Shelley's ultimate
   target.
6. Moses
7. tales . . . nation: The Old Testament and perhaps the Apocrypha, sacred writings of the Jews.

Now crumbling to oblivion;
The long and lonely colonnades,
Through which the ghost of Freedom stalks,[8]
    Seem like a well-known tune,                    170
Which, in some dear scene we have loved to hear,
Remembered now in sadness.
But, oh! how much more changed,
How gloomier is the contrast
Of human nature there!                                          175
Where Socrates expired, a tyrant's slave,
A coward and a fool, spreads death around—
Then, shuddering, meets his own.
Where Cicero and Antoninus lived,[9]
A cowled and hypocritical monk                                  180
Prays, curses and deceives.


    "Spirit! ten thousand years
Have scarcely past away,
Since, in the waste where now the savage drinks
His enemy's blood, and aping Europe's sons,                     185
Wakes the unholy song of war,
Arose a stately city,[1]
Metropolis of the western continent:
There, now, the mossy column-stone,
Indented by time's unrelaxing grasp,                            190
Which once appeared to brave
All, save its country's ruin;
There the wide forest scene,
Rude in the uncultivated loveliness
Of gardens long run wild,                                       195
Seems, to the unwilling sojourner, whose steps
Chance in that desart has delayed,
Thus to have stood since earth was what it is.
Yet once it was the busiest haunt,
Whither, as to a common centre, flocked                         200
Strangers, and ships, and merchandize:
Once peace and freedom blest
The cultivated plain:
But wealth, that curse of man,
Blighted the bud of its prosperity:                             205
Virtue and wisdom, truth and liberty,
Fled, to return not, until man shall know
That they alone can give the bliss
Worthy a soul that claims
Its kindred with eternity.                                      210

---

8. The spirit of Freedom from the Greek and Roman republics haunts the monuments of their past glories.
9. Cicero, republican orator and Skeptic philosopher, and the good emperor Marcus Aurelius Antoninus, also a Stoic philosopher, are named as the virtuous spirits of ancient Rome.
1. Lines 182–210 probably refer to the ruins of Mayan cities in Central America.

"There's not one atom of yon earth
        But once was living man;
Nor the minutest drop of rain,
That hangeth in its thinnest cloud,
        But flowed in human veins:                    215
        And from the burning plains
        Where Libyan monsters yell,
        From the most gloomy glens
        Of Greenland's sunless clime,
        To where the golden fields                    220
        Of fertile England spread
        Their harvest to the day,
        Thou canst not find one spot
        Whereon no city stood.

        "How strange is human pride!                   225
I tell thee that those living things,
To whom the fragile blade of grass,
        That springeth in the morn
        And perisheth ere noon,
        Is an unbounded world;                        230
I tell thee that those viewless[2] beings,
Whose mansion is the smallest particle
Of the impassive[3] atmosphere,
        Think, feel and live like man;
That their affections and antipathies,                235
        Like his, produce the laws
        Ruling their moral state;
        And the minutest throb
        That through their frame diffuses
        The slightest, faintest motion,              240
        Is fixed and indispensable
        As the majestic laws
        That rule yon rolling orbs."[4]

        The Fairy paused. The Spirit,
In extacy of admiration, felt                          245
All knowledge of the past revived; the events
        Of old and wondrous times,
Which dim tradition interruptedly
Teaches the credulous vulgar, were unfolded
        In just perspective to the view;              250
        Yet dim from their infinitude.
        The Spirit seemed to stand
High on an isolated pinnacle;
The flood of ages combating below,

2. Invisible.
3. Insensate; unable to feel pain.
4. Shelley's conception that there are minute universes within atoms comparable to the universe
   people inhabit (lines 225–43) is given another form in his "Ode to Heaven."

The depth of the unbounded universe                    255
   Above, and all around
Nature's unchanging harmony.


### III.

"FAIRY!" the Spirit said,
And on the Queen of spells
Fixed her etherial eyes,
"I thank thee. Thou hast given
A boon which I will not resign, and taught          5
A lesson not to be unlearned. I know
The past, and thence I will essay to glean
A warning for the future, so that man
May profit by his errors, and derive
   Experience from his folly:                   10
For, when the power of imparting joy
Is equal to the will, the human soul
   Requires no other Heaven."[5]


MAB.

Turn thee, surpassing Spirit!
Much yet remains unscanned.                          15
Thou knowest how great is man,
Thou knowest his imbecility:[6]
Yet learn thou what he is;
Yet learn the lofty destiny
Which restless time prepares                         20
For every living soul.


Behold a gorgeous palace, that amid
Yon populous city, rears its thousand towers
And seems itself a city. Gloomy troops
Of sentinels, in stern and silent ranks,            25
Encompass it around: the dweller there
Cannot be free and happy; hearest thou not
The curses of the fatherless, the groans
Of those who have no friend? He passes on:
The King, the wearer of a gilded chain              30
That binds his soul to abjectness, the fool
Whom courtiers nickname monarch, whilst a slave
Even to the basest appetites—that man
Heeds not the shriek of penury; he smiles

5. The discrepancy between the will to do good and the power of doing so is a major theme
throughout Shelley's poetry; in *Queen Mab* he advocates increasing the human power for
doing good by increasing the sum of human knowledge, and he finds no absolute need for
Heaven or an afterlife.
6. Weakness, feebleness.

At the deep curses which the destitute                              35
Mutter in secret, and a sullen joy
Pervades his bloodless heart when thousands groan
But for those morsels which his wantonness
Wastes in unjoyous revelry, to save
All that they love from famine: when he hears                       40
The tale of horror, to some ready-made face
Of hypocritical assent he turns,
Smothering the glow of shame, that, spite of him,
Flushes his bloated cheek.
                          Now to the meal
Of silence, grandeur, and excess, he drags                          45
His palled[7] unwilling appetite. If gold,
Gleaming around, and numerous viands[8] culled
From every clime, could force the loathing sense
To overcome satiety,—if wealth
The spring it draws from poisons not,—or vice,                      50
Unfeeling, stubborn vice, converteth not
Its food to deadliest venom; then that king
Is happy; and the peasant who fulfils
His unforced task, when he returns at even,
And by the blazing faggot[9] meets again                            55
Her welcome for whom all his toil is sped,
Tastes not a sweeter meal.
                          Behold him now
Stretched on the gorgeous couch; his fevered brain
Reels dizzily awhile: but ah! too soon
The slumber of intemperance subsides,                               60
And conscience, that undying serpent, calls
Her venomous brood to their nocturnal task.
Listen! he speaks! oh! mark that frenzied eye—
Oh! mark that deadly visage.


                              KING.

                              No cessation!
Oh! must this last for ever? Awful death,                           65
I wish, yet fear to clasp thee!—Not one moment
Of dreamless sleep! O dear and blessed peace!
Why dost thou shroud thy vestal purity
In penury and dungeons? wherefore lurkest
With danger, death, and solitude; yet shunn'st                      70
The palace I have built thee? Sacred peace!
Oh visit me but once, but pitying shed
One drop of balm upon my withered soul.

---

7. Weakened, enfeebled.
8. Articles of food, victuals.
9. A bundle of twigs or small sticks tied together for use as fuel.

THE FAIRY.

Vain man! that palace is the virtuous heart,
And peace defileth not her snowy robes                              75
In such a shed as thine. Hark! yet he mutters;
His slumbers are but varied agonies,
They prey like scorpions on the springs of life.[1]
There needeth not the hell that bigots frame
To punish those who err: earth in itself                           80
Contains at once the evil and the cure;
And all-sufficing nature can chastise
Those who transgress her law,—she only knows
How justly to proportion to the fault
The punishment it merits.
                              Is it strange                        85
That this poor wretch should pride him in his woe?
Take pleasure in his abjectness, and hug
The scorpion that consumes him? Is it strange
That, placed on a conspicuous throne of thorns,
Grasping an iron sceptre, and immured                              90
Within a splendid prison, whose stern bounds
Shut him from all that's good or dear on earth,
His soul asserts not its humanity?
That man's mild nature rises not in war
Against a king's employ? No—'tis not strange.                      95
He, like the vulgar, thinks, feels, acts and lives
Just as his father did; the unconquered powers
Of precedent and custom interpose
Between a *king* and virtue. Stranger yet,
To those who know not nature, nor deduce                           100
The future from the present, it may seem,
That not one slave, who suffers from the crimes
Of this unnatural being; not one wretch,
Whose children famish, and whose nuptial bed
Is earth's unpitying bosom, rears an arm                           105
To dash him from his throne!
                              Those gilded flies[2]
That, basking in the sunshine of a court,
Fatten on its corruption!—what are they?
—The drones[3] of the community; they feed
On the mechanic's labour: the starved hind                         110

1. The sting of the scorpion, besides being potentially deadly, was believed to be a cause of syphilis.
2. The king's courtiers; the literary allusion is to the description of Sporus in Pope's *Epistle to Dr. Arbuthnot*, lines 305–33, especially lines 309–11.
3. The natural analogy is to a beehive community and the literary allusion to Bernard de Mandeville's *The Fable of the Bees* (1714). The comparison of aristocrats to drones and the lower classes to worker bees became commonplace in radical discourse of the late eighteenth and early nineteenth centuries and was subsequently used by Shelley in "Song to the Men of England" and *A Philosophical View of Reform*.

For them compels the stubborn glebe⁴ to yield
Its unshared harvests; and yon squalid form,
Leaner than fleshless misery, that wastes
A sunless life in the unwholesome mine,
Drags out in labour a protracted death,                         115
To glut their grandeur; many faint with toil,
That few may know the cares and woe of sloth.

Whence, thinkest thou, kings and parasites arose?
Whence that unnatural line of drones, who heap
Toil and unvanquishable penury                                  120
On those who build their palaces, and bring
Their daily bread?—From vice, black loathsome vice;
From rapine, madness, treachery, and wrong;
From all that genders⁵ misery, and makes
Of earth this thorny wilderness; from lust,                     125
Revenge, and murder. . . . And when reason's voice,
Loud as the voice of nature, shall have waked
The nations; and mankind perceive that vice
Is discord, war, and misery; that virtue
Is peace, and happiness and harmony;                            130
When man's maturer nature shall disdain
The playthings of its childhood;—kingly glare
Will lose its power to dazzle; its authority
Will silently pass by; the gorgeous throne
Shall stand unnoticed in the regal hall,                        135
Fast falling to decay; whilst falsehood's trade
Shall be as hateful and unprofitable
As that of truth is now.
                            Where is the fame
Which the vainglorious mighty of the earth
Seek to eternize? Oh! the faintest sound                        140
From time's light footfall, the minutest wave
That swells the flood of ages, whelms in nothing
The unsubstantial bubble. Aye! to-day
Stern is the tyrant's mandate, red the gaze
That flashes desolation, strong the arm                         145
That scatters multitudes. To-morrow comes!
That mandate is a thunder-peal that died
In ages past; that gaze, a transient flash
On which the midnight closed, and on that arm
The worm has made his meal.
                            The virtuous man,                   150
Who, great in his humility, as kings
Are little in their grandeur; he who leads
Invincibly a life of resolute good,

---

4. *hind . . . glebe:* The hired agricultural laborer plows the stubborn soil or clod of earth. The phrase "stubborn glebe" echoes Thomas Gray's *Elegy Written in a Country Churchyard,* line 26.
5. Creates, engenders.

And stands amid the silent dungeon-depths
More free and fearless than the trembling judge,              155
Who, clothed in venal power, vainly strove
To bind the impassive[6] spirit;—when he falls,
His mild eye beams benevolence no more:
Withered the hand outstretched but to relieve;
Sunk Reason's simple eloquence, that rolled                   160
But to appal the guilty. Yes! the grave
Hath quenched that eye, and death's relentless frost
Withered that arm: but the unfading fame
Which virtue hangs upon its votary's tomb;
The deathless memory of that man, whom kings                  165
Call to their mind and tremble; the remembrance
With which the happy spirit contemplates
Its well-spent pilgrimage on earth,
Shall never pass away.

Nature rejects the monarch, not the man;                      170
The subject, not the citizen: for kings
And subjects, mutual foes, for ever play
A losing game into each other's hands,
Whose stakes are vice and misery. The man
Of virtuous soul commands not, nor obeys.                     175
Power, like a desolating pestilence,
Pollutes whate'er it touches; and obedience,
Bane of all genius, virtue, freedom, truth,
Makes slaves of men, and, of the human frame,
A mechanized automaton.                When Nero,             180
High over flaming Rome, with savage joy
Lowered[7] like a fiend, drank with enraptured ear
The shrieks of agonizing death, beheld
The frightful desolation spread, and felt
A new-created sense within his soul                           185
Thrill to the sight, and vibrate to the sound;
Thinkest thou his grandeur had not overcome
The force of human kindness? and, when Rome,
With one stern blow, hurled not the tyrant down,
Crushed not the arm red with her dearest blood,              190
Had not submissive abjectness destroyed
Nature's suggestions?                Look on yonder earth:
The golden harvests spring; the unfailing sun
Sheds light and life; the fruits, the flowers, the trees,
Arise in due succession; all things speak                     195
Peace, harmony, and love. The universe,
In nature's silent eloquence, declares

6. Unyielding (cf. II.233).
7. Frowned.

That all fulfil the works of love and joy,—
All but the outcast man. He fabricates[8]
The sword which stabs his peace; he cherisheth          200
The snakes that gnaw his heart; he raiseth up
The tyrant, whose delight is in his woe,
Whose sport is in his agony. Yon sun,
Lights it the great alone? Yon silver beams,
Sleep they less sweetly on the cottage thatch,          205
Than on the dome of kings? Is mother earth
A step-dame to her numerous sons, who earn
Her unshared gifts with unremitting toil;
A mother only to those puling[9] babes
Who, nursed in ease and luxury, make men               210
The playthings of their babyhood, and mar,
In self-important childishness, that peace
Which men alone appreciate?

     Spirit of Nature! no.
The pure diffusion of thy essence throbs               215
  Alike in every human heart.
    Thou, aye, erectest there
  Thy throne of power unappealable:
  Thou art the judge beneath whose nod
Man's brief and frail authority                        220
    Is powerless as the wind
    That passeth idly by.
Thine the tribunal which surpasseth
  The shew of human justice,
    As God surpasses man.                   225

    Spirit of Nature! thou
Life of interminable multitudes;
  Soul of those mighty spheres
Whose changeless paths through Heaven's deep silence lie;
    Soul of that smallest being,            230
    The dwelling of whose life
    Is one faint April sun-gleam;—
    Man, like these passive things,
Thy will unconsciously fulfilleth:
  Like theirs, his age of endless peace,          235
    Which time is fast maturing,
    Will swiftly, surely come;
And the unbounded frame, which thou pervadest,
    Will be without a flaw
  Marring its perfect symmetry.                    240

8. Makes.
9. Whining or complaining.

## IV.

[THE FAIRY CONTINUES:]

How beautiful this night! the balmiest sigh,
Which vernal zephyrs breathe in evening's ear,
Were discord to the speaking quietude
That wraps this moveless scene. Heaven's ebon vault,[1]
Studded with stars unutterably bright,                                    5
Through which the moon's unclouded grandeur rolls,
Seems like a canopy which love had spread
To curtain her sleeping world. Yon gentle hills,
Robed in a garment of untrodden snow;
Yon darksome rocks, whence icicles depend,[2]                            10
So stainless, that their white and glittering spires
Tinge not the moon's pure beam; yon castled steep,
Whose banner hangeth o'er the time-worn tower
So idly, that rapt fancy deemeth it
A metaphor of peace;—all form a scene                                    15
Where musing solitude might love to lift
Her soul above this sphere of earthliness;
Where silence undisturbed might watch alone,
So cold, so bright, so still.
                              The orb of day,
In southern climes, o'er ocean's waveless field                          20
Sinks sweetly smiling: not the faintest breath
Steals o'er the unruffled deep; the clouds of eve
Reflect unmoved the lingering beam of day;
And vesper's[3] image on the western main
Is beautifully still. To-morrow comes:                                   25
Cloud upon cloud, in dark and deepening mass,
Roll o'er the blackened waters; the deep roar
Of distant thunder mutters awfully;
Tempest unfolds its pinion o'er the gloom
That shrouds the boiling surge; the pityless fiend,                      30
With all his winds and lightnings, tracks his prey;
The torn deep yawns,—the vessel finds a grave
Beneath its jagged gulph.
                              Ah! whence yon glare
That fires the arch of heaven?—that dark red smoke
Blotting the silver moon? The stars are quenched                        35
In darkness, and the pure and spangling snow
Gleams faintly through the gloom that gathers round!
Hark to that roar, whose swift and deaf'ning peals
In countless echoes through the mountains ring,
Startling pale midnight on her starry throne!                           40
Now swells the intermingling din; the jar

1. Black (ebony) arch.
2. Hang down.
3. The planet Venus as the evening star (see I.259).

Frequent and frightful of the bursting bomb;
The falling beam, the shriek, the groan, the shout,
The ceaseless clangor, and the rush of men
Inebriate with rage:—loud, and more loud        45
The discord grows; till pale death shuts the scene,
And o'er the conqueror and the conquered draws
His cold and bloody shroud.—Of all the men
Whom day's departing beam saw blooming there,
In proud and vigorous health; of all the hearts       50
That beat with anxious life at sun-set there;
How few survive, how few are beating now!
All is deep silence, like the fearful calm
That slumbers in the storm's portentous pause;
Save when the frantic wail of widowed love       55
Comes shuddering on the blast, or the faint moan
With which some soul bursts from the frame of clay
Wrapt round its struggling powers.
                       The grey morn
Dawns on the mournful scene; the sulphurous smoke
Before the icy wind slow rolls away,          60
And the bright beams of frosty morning dance
Along the spangling snow. There tracks of blood
Even to the forest's depth, and scattered arms,
And lifeless warriors, whose hard lineaments
Death's self could change not, mark the dreadful path    65
Of the outsallying[4] victors: far behind,
Black ashes note where their proud city stood.
Within yon forest is a gloomy glen—
Each tree which guards its darkness from the day,
Waves o'er a warrior's tomb.
                  I see thee shrink,     70
Surpassing Spirit!—wert thou human else?
I see a shade of doubt and horror fleet
Across thy stainless features: yet fear not;
This is no unconnected misery,
Nor stands uncaused, and irretrievable.        75
Man's evil nature, that apology
Which kings who rule, and cowards who crouch, set up
For their unnumbered crimes, sheds not the blood
Which desolates the discord-wasted land.
From kings, and priests, and statesmen, war arose,    80
Whose safety is man's deep unbettered[5] woe,
Whose grandeur his debasement. Let the axe
Strike at the root, the poison-tree[6] will fall;

---

4. A *sally* was a sudden charge out of a besieged place in an attack upon the besiegers.
5. Unrelieved.
6. This is a reference to the mythical upas tree of Java, which was thought to kill all life within miles of it and which contemporary radicals often used to represent the poisonous British social order. Its story was invented ca. 1783 and appears in Erasmus Darwin's *Loves of the Plants* (1789). For Shelley's further use of the upas tree in *Queen Mab*, see IV.260–65 (where it represents the tools of tyranny), V.44–52 (where it represents Commerce), and VI.207–08 (where it represents Religion).

And where its venomed exhalations spread
Ruin, and death, and woe, where millions lay          85
Quenching the serpent's famine, and their bones
Bleaching unburied in the putrid blast,
A garden shall arise, in loveliness
Surpassing fabled Eden.
                        Hath Nature's soul,
That formed this world so beautiful, that spread          90
Earth's lap with plenty, and life's smallest chord
Strung to unchanging unison, that gave
The happy birds their dwelling in the grove,
That yielded to the wanderers of the deep
The lovely silence of the unfathomed main,          95
And filled the meanest worm that crawls in dust
With spirit, thought, and love; on Man alone,
Partial in causeless malice, wantonly
Heaped ruin, vice, and slavery; his soul
Blasted with withering curses; placed afar          100
The meteor-happiness, that shuns his grasp,
But serving on the frightful gulph to glare,
Rent wide beneath his footsteps?
                        Nature!—no!
Kings, priests, and statesmen, blast the human flower
Even in its tender bud; their influence darts          105
Like subtle poison through the bloodless veins
Of desolate society. The child,
Ere he can lisp his mother's sacred name,
Swells with the unnatural pride of crime, and lifts
His baby-sword even in a hero's mood.          110
This infant-arm becomes the bloodiest scourge
Of devastated earth; whilst specious names,
Learnt in soft childhood's unsuspecting hour,
Serve as the sophisms[7] with which manhood dims
Bright reason's ray, and sanctifies the sword          115
Upraised to shed a brother's innocent blood.
Let priest-led slaves cease to proclaim that man
Inherits vice and misery, when force
And falshood hang even o'er the cradled babe,
Stifling with rudest grasp all natural good.          120

Ah! to the stranger-soul, when first it peeps
From its new tenement,[8] and looks abroad
For happiness and sympathy, how stern
And desolate a tract is this wide world!
How withered all the buds of natural good!          125
No shade, no shelter from the sweeping storms
Of pityless power! On its wretched frame,
Poisoned, perchance, by the disease and woe

---

7. False yet plausible arguments, especially those urging expediency.
8. *stranger-soul . . . tenement:* The image is that of a complete soul coming from another realm
to enter the "house" or "dwelling-place" of the human body.

Heaped on the wretched parent whence it sprung
By morals, law, and custom, the pure winds                      130
Of heaven, that renovate the insect tribes,[9]
May breathe not. The untainting light of day
May visit not its lodgings.[1] It is bound
Ere it has life: yea, all the chains are forged
Long ere its being: all liberty and love                        135
And peace is torn from its defencelessness;
Cursed from its birth, even from its cradle doomed
To abjectness and bondage!

Throughout this varied and eternal world
Soul is the only element; the block                             140
That for uncounted ages has remained
The moveless pillar of a mountain's weight
Is active, living spirit. Every grain
Is sentient both in unity and part,
And the minutest atom comprehends                              145
A world of loves and hatreds; these beget
Evil and good: hence truth and falshood spring;
Hence will and thought and action, all the germs
Of pain or pleasure, sympathy or hate,
That variegate the eternal universe.                            150
Soul is not more polluted than the beams
Of heaven's pure orb, ere round their rapid lines
The taint of earth-born atmospheres arise.[2]

Man is of soul and body, formed for deeds
Of high resolve, on fancy's boldest wing                       155
To soar unwearied, fearlessly to turn
The keenest pangs to peacefulness, and taste
The joys which mingled sense and spirit yield.
Or he is formed for abjectness and woe,
To grovel on the dunghill of his fears,                        160
To shrink at every sound, to quench the flame
Of natural love in sensualism, to know
That hour as blest when on his worthless days
The frozen hand of death shall set its seal,
Yet fear the cure, though hating the disease.                  165
The one is man that shall hereafter be;
The other, man as vice has made him now.

War is the statesman's game, the priest's delight,
The lawyer's jest, the hired assassin's trade,

9. *pure winds . . . insect tribes:* According to Pliny's *Natural History,* locusts.
1. Though the first edition reads "longings," the context would suggest that this was a typo-
graphical error that slipped through unnoticed.
2. Shelley's doctrine in lines 139–53 is that good and evil arise from the nature of soul, or
active, living spirit, which is *sentient* and exhibits *loves* and *hatreds* (attractions and repul-
sions), whence spring all moral qualities. The question of whether matter had sentient qualities was hotly debated in England throughout the seventeenth and eighteenth centuries.

And, to those royal murderers, whose mean thrones      170
Are bought by crimes of treachery and gore,
The bread they eat, the staff on which they lean.
Guards, garbed in blood-red livery, surround
Their palaces, participate[3] the crimes
That force defends, and from a nation's rage      175
Secure the crown, which all the curses reach
That famine, frenzy, woe and penury breathe.
These are the hired bravos who defend
The tyrant's throne—the bullies of his fear:[4]
These are the sinks and channels of worst vice,      180
The refuse of society, the dregs
Of all that is most vile: their cold hearts blend
Deceit with sternness, ignorance with pride,
All that is mean and villainous, with rage
Which hopelessness of good, and self-contempt,      185
Alone might kindle; they are decked in wealth,
Honour and power, then are sent abroad
To do their work. The pestilence that stalks
In gloomy triumph through some eastern land
Is less destroying. They cajole with gold,      190
And promises of fame, the thoughtless youth
Already crushed with servitude: he knows
His wretchedness too late, and cherishes
Repentance for his ruin, when his doom
Is sealed in gold and blood!      195
Those too the tyrant serve, who, skilled to snare
The feet of justice in the toils of law,
Stand, ready to oppress the weaker still;
And, right or wrong, will vindicate for gold,
Sneering at public virtue, which beneath      200
Their pityless tread lies torn and trampled, where
Honour sits smiling at the sale of truth.

Then grave and hoary-headed hypocrites,
Without a hope, a passion, or a love,
Who, through a life of luxury and lies,      205
Have crept by flattery to the seats of power,
Support the system whence their honours flow. . . .
They have three words:—well tyrants know their use,
Well pay them for the loan, with usury
Torn from a bleeding world!—God, Hell, and Heaven.      210
A vengeful, pityless, and almighty fiend,
Whose mercy is a nickname for the rage
Of tameless tygers hungering for blood.
Hell, a red gulph of everlasting fire,

---

3. Share, take part in.
4. Shelley, in a long note, quotes from Essay V of William Godwin's *Enquirer*: "A soldier is a man whose business it is to kill those who never offended him, and who are the innocent martyrs of other men's iniquities. Whatever may become of the abstract question of the justifiableness of war, it seems impossible that the soldier should not be a depraved and unnatural being."

Where poisonous and undying worms prolong                215
Eternal misery to those hapless slaves
Whose life has been a penance for its crimes.
And Heaven, a meed for those who dare belie
Their human nature, quake, believe, and cringe
Before the mockeries of earthly power.                   220

These tools the tyrant tempers to his work,
Wields in his wrath, and as he wills destroys,
Omnipotent in wickedness: the while
Youth springs, age moulders, manhood tamely does
His bidding, bribed by short-lived joys to lend          225
Force to the weakness of his trembling arm.

They rise, they fall; one generation comes
Yielding its harvest to destruction's scythe.
It fades, another blossoms: yet behold!
Red glows the tyrant's stamp-mark on its bloom,          230
Withering and cankering deep its passive prime.
He has invented lying words and modes,
Empty and vain as his own coreless heart;
Evasive meanings, nothings of much sound,
To lure the heedless victim to the toils                 235
Spread round the valley of its paradise.

Look to thyself, priest, conqueror, or prince!
Whether thy trade is falshood, and thy lusts
Deep wallow in the earnings of the poor,
With whom thy master⁵ was:—or thou delight'st            240
In numbering o'er the myriads of thy slain,
All misery weighing nothing in the scale
Against thy short-lived fame: or thou dost load
With cowardice and crime the groaning land,
A pomp-fed king. Look to thy wretched self!              245
Aye, art thou not the veriest slave that e'er
Crawled on the loathing earth? Are not thy days
Days of unsatisfying listlessness?
Dost thou not cry, ere night's long rack⁶ is o'er,
"When will the morning come?" Is not thy youth           250
A vain and feverish dream of sensualism?
Thy manhood blighted with unripe disease?
Are not thy views of unregretted death
Drear, comfortless, and horrible? Thy mind,
Is it not morbid as thy nerveless frame,                 255
Incapable of judgment, hope, or love?
And dost thou wish the errors to survive
That bar thee from all sympathies of good,
After the miserable interest

5. Jesus Christ.
6. The would-be sleeper's bed is here compared to the instrument of torture on which victims
were stretched.

Thou hold'st in their protraction? When the grave          260
Has swallowed up thy memory and thyself,
Dost thou desire the bane that poisons earth
To twine its roots around thy coffined clay,
Spring from thy bones, and blossom on thy tomb,
That of its fruit thy babes may eat and die?[7]          265

## V.

[THE FAIRY CONTINUES:]

Thus do the generations of the earth
Go to the grave, and issue from the womb,
Surviving still the imperishable change
That renovates the world; even as the leaves
Which the keen frost-wind of the waning year          5
Has scattered on the forest soil, and heaped
For many seasons there, though long they choke,
Loading with loathsome rottenness the land,
All germs of promise. Yet when the tall trees
From which they fell, shorn of their lovely shapes,          10
Lie level with the earth to moulder there,
They fertilize the land they long deformed,
Till from the breathing lawn a forest springs
Of youth, integrity, and loveliness,
Like that which gave it life, to spring and die.          15
Thus suicidal selfishness, that blights
The fairest feelings of the opening heart,
Is destined to decay, whilst from the soil
Shall spring all virtue, all delight, all love,
And judgment cease to wage unnatural war          20
With passion's unsubduable array.

Twin-sister of religion, selfishness!
Rival in crime and falshood, aping all
The wanton horrors of her bloody play;
Yet frozen, unimpassioned, spiritless,          25
Shunning the light, and owning not its name;
Compelled, by its deformity, to screen
With flimsy veil of justice and of right,
Its unattractive lineaments, that scare
All, save the brood of ignorance: at once          30
The cause and the effect of tyranny;
Unblushing, hardened, sensual, and vile;
Dead to all love but of its abjectness,
With heart impassive[8] by more noble powers

---

7. A reference to the deadly upas tree (see note to IV.83) conflated with Genesis 3:3: "But of the fruit of the tree which is in the midst of the garden, God hath said, Ye shall not eat of it, neither shall ye touch it, lest ye die."
8. Unmoved; Shelley uses the word with two different meanings at II.233 and III.157.

Than unshared pleasure, sordid gain, or fame;     35
Despising its own miserable being,
Which still it longs, yet fears to disenthrall.

Hence commerce springs, the venal interchange
Of all that human art or nature yield;
Which wealth should purchase not, but want demand,     40
And natural kindness hasten to supply
From the full fountain of its boundless love,
For ever stifled, drained, and tainted now.
Commerce! beneath whose poison-breathing shade
No solitary virtue dares to spring,[9]     45
But poverty and wealth with equal hand
Scatter their withering curses, and unfold
The doors of premature and violent death,
To pining famine and full-fed disease,
To all that shares the lot of human life,     50
Which poisoned, body and soul, scarce drags the chain,
That lengthens as it goes and clanks behind.

Commerce has set the mark of selfishness,
The signet of its all-enslaving power
Upon a shining ore, and called it gold:     55
Before whose image bow the vulgar great,
The vainly rich, the miserable proud,
The mob of peasants, nobles, priests, and kings,
And with blind feelings reverence the power
That grinds them to the dust of misery.[1]     60
But in the temple of their hireling hearts
Gold is a living god, and rules in scorn
All earthly things but virtue.

Since tyrants, by the sale of human life,
Heap luxuries to their sensualism, and fame     65
To their wide-wasting and insatiate pride,
Success has sanctioned to a credulous world
The ruin, the disgrace, the woe of war.
His hosts of blind and unresisting dupes
The despot numbers; from his cabinet     70
These puppets of his schemes he moves at will,
Even as the slaves by force or famine driven,
Beneath a vulgar master, to perform
A task of cold and brutal drudgery;—
Hardened to hope, insensible to fear,     75
Scarce living pullies of a dead machine,
Mere wheels of work and articles of trade,
That grace the proud and noisy pomp of wealth!

9. See note to III.83.
1. In a note Shelley quotes the first fourteen lines of Book II of Lucretius' *De rerum natura*,
ending: "O wretched minds of men! O blinded hearts!"

The harmony and happiness of man
Yields to the wealth of nations;[2] that which lifts          80
His nature to the heaven of its pride,
Is bartered for the poison of his soul;
The weight that drags to earth his towering hopes,
Blighting all prospect but of selfish gain,
Withering all passion but of slavish fear,          85
Extinguishing all free and generous love
Of enterprize and daring, even the pulse
That fancy kindles in the beating heart
To mingle with sensation, it destroys,—
Leaves nothing but the sordid lust of self,          90
The groveling hope of interest and gold,
Unqualified, unmingled, unredeemed
Even by hypocrisy.
                    And statesmen boast
Of wealth![3] The wordy eloquence, that lives
After the ruin of their hearts, can gild          95
The bitter poison of a nation's woe,
Can turn the worship of the servile mob
To their corrupt and glaring idol, fame,
From virtue, trampled by its iron tread,
Although its dazzling pedestal be raised          100
Amid the horrors of a limb-strewn field,[4]
With desolated dwellings smoking round.
The man of ease, who, by his warm fire-side,
To deeds of charitable intercourse
And bare fulfilment of the common laws          105
Of decency and prejudice, confines
The struggling nature of his human heart,
Is duped by their cold sophistry; he sheds
A passing tear perchance upon the wreck
Of earthly peace, when near his dwelling's door          110
The frightful waves are driven,—when his son
Is murdered by the tyrant, or religion
Drives his wife raving mad.[5] But the poor man,
Whose life is misery, and fear, and care;
Whom the morn wakens but to fruitless toil;          115
Who ever hears his famished offsprings scream,
Whom their pale mother's uncomplaining gaze
For ever meets, and the proud rich man's eye

2. Shelley alludes here to the title of Adam Smith's classic rationale for laissez-faire capitalism.
3. "There is no real wealth but the labour of man. Were the mountains of gold and the vallies of silver, the world would not be one grain of corn the richer; no one comfort would be added to the human race. . . .
   "I will not insult common sense by insisting on the doctrine of the natural equality of man. The question is not concerning its desirableness, but its practicability: so far as it is practicable, it is desirable. That state of human society which approaches nearer to an equal partition of its benefits and evils should . . . be preferred . . ." (from Shelley's note).
4. These lines are based upon the Hindu procession of the Juggernaut, for which see the note to VII.36.
5. "I am acquainted with a lady of considerable accomplishments, and the mother of a numerous family, whom the Christian religion has goaded to incurable insanity. A parallel case is, I believe, within the experience of every physician" (Shelley's note).

Flashing command, and the heart-breaking scene
Of thousands like himself;—he little heeds          120
The rhetoric of tyranny; his hate
Is quenchless as his wrongs; he laughs to scorn
The vain and bitter mockery of words,
Feeling the horror of the tyrant's deeds,
And unrestrained but by the arm of power,          125
That knows and dreads his enmity.

The iron rod of penury still compels
Her wretched slave to bow the knee to wealth,
And poison, with unprofitable toil,
A life too void of solace to confirm          130
The very chains that bind him to his doom.
Nature, impartial in munificence,
Has gifted man with all-subduing will.
Matter, with all its transitory shapes,
Lies subjected and plastic⁶ at his feet,          135
That, weak from bondage, tremble as they tread.
How many a rustic Milton has past by,
Stifling the speechless longings of his heart,
In unremitting drudgery and care!
How many a vulgar Cato has compelled          140
His energies, no longer tameless then,
To mould a pin, or fabricate a nail!
How many a Newton, to whose passive ken
Those mighty spheres that gem infinity
Were only specks of tinsel, fixed in heaven          145
To light the midnights of his native town!⁷

Yet every heart contains perfection's germ:
The wisest of the sages of the earth,
That ever from the stores of reason drew
Science and truth, and virtue's dreadless tone,          150
Were but a weak and inexperienced boy,
Proud, sensual, unimpassioned, unimbued
With pure desire and universal love,
Compared to that high being, of cloudless brain,
Untainted passion, elevated will,          155
Which death (who even would linger long in awe
Within his noble presence, and beneath
His changeless eyebeam) might alone subdue.
Him, every slave now dragging through the filth
Of some corrupted city his sad life,          160
Pining with famine, swoln with luxury,
Blunting the keenness of his spiritual sense

6. Susceptible of being molded or shaped; malleable.
7. John Milton, Marcus Porcius Cato Uticensis (line 140), a staunch defender of the Roman
Republic against Catiline and Julius Caesar, and Sir Isaac Newton (line 143) are representatives of noble achievements in writing, political life, and scientific inquiry, respectively.
This entire verse paragraph is heavily influenced by Thomas Gray's *Elegy Written in a Country Churchyard* (1750).

With narrow schemings and unworthy cares,
Or madly rushing through all violent crime,
To move the deep stagnation of his soul,—          165
Might imitate and equal.
                    But mean lust[8]
Has bound its chains so tight around the earth,
That all within it but the virtuous man
Is venal: gold or fame will surely reach
The price prefixed by selfishness, to all          170
But him of resolute and unchanging will;
Whom, nor the plaudits of a servile crowd,
Nor the vile joys of tainting luxury,
Can bribe to yield his elevated soul
To tyranny or falshood, though they wield          175
With blood-red hand the sceptre of the world.

All things are sold: the very light of heaven
Is venal;[9] earth's unsparing gifts of love,
The smallest and most despicable things
That lurk in the abysses of the deep,          180
All objects of our life, even life itself,
And the poor pittance which the laws allow
Of liberty, the fellowship of man,
Those duties which his heart of human love
Should urge him to perform instinctively,          185
Are bought and sold as in a public mart
Of undisguising selfishness, that sets
On each its price, the stamp-mark of her reign.
Even love is sold;[1] the solace of all woe
Is turned to deadliest agony, old age          190
Shivers in selfish beauty's loathing arms,
And youth's corrupted impulses prepare
A life of horror from the blighting bane
Of commerce; whilst the pestilence that springs
From unenjoying sensualism, has filled          195
All human life with hydra-headed[2] woes.

Falshood[3] demands but gold to pay the pangs
Of outraged conscience; for the slavish priest
Sets no great value on his hireling faith:
A little passing pomp, some servile souls,          200

8. In the broad sense of strong desire for *mean* (small, low, unexalted) things.
9. Lines 177–78 may refer to the tax on windows in houses, *light of heaven* being excluded from poor homes.
1. "Not even the intercourse of the sexes is exempt from the despotism of positive institution. . . . Love withers under constraint: its very essence is liberty. . . . A husband and wife ought to continue so long united as they love each other: any law which should bind them to cohabitation for one moment after the decay of their affection, would be a most intolerable tyranny . . ." (from Shelley's note).
2. The Hydra was a monster in Greek mythology that had many heads (various authorities number them from nine to one hundred); whenever one head was cut off, two grew unless that neck was immediately cauterized by fire.
3. Shelley uses the word "falsehood" (usually spelled by him without the silent "e") to mean organized Christian religion.

Whom cowardice itself might safely chain,
Or the spare mite of avarice could bribe
To deck the triumph of their languid zeal,
Can make him minister to tyranny.
More daring crime requires a loftier meed:              205
Without a shudder, the slave-soldier lends
His arm to murderous deeds, and steels his heart,
When the dread eloquence of dying men,
Low mingling on the lonely field of fame,
Assails that nature, whose applause he sells             210
For the gross blessings of a patriot mob,
For the vile gratitude of heartless kings,
And for a cold world's good word,—viler still!

There is a nobler glory, which survives
Until our being fades, and, solacing                     215
All human care, accompanies its change;
Deserts not virtue in the dungeon's gloom,
And, in the precincts of the palace, guides
Its footsteps through that labyrinth of crime;
Imbues his lineaments with dauntlessness,                220
Even when, from power's avenging hand, he takes
Its sweetest, last and noblest title—death;
—The consciousness of good, which neither gold,
Nor sordid fame, nor hope of heavenly bliss
Can purchase; but a life of resolute good,               225
Unalterable will, quenchless desire
Of universal happiness, the heart
That beats with it in unison, the brain,
Whose ever wakeful wisdom toils to change
Reason's rich stores for its eternal weal.               230

This commerce of sincerest virtue needs
No mediative signs of selfishness,
No jealous intercourse of wretched gain,
No balancings of prudence, cold and long;
In just and equal measure all is weighed,                235
One scale contains the sum of human weal,
And one, the good man's heart.
                            How vainly seek
The selfish for that happiness denied
To aught but virtue! Blind and hardened, they,
Who hope for peace amid the storms of care,              240
Who covet power they know not how to use,
And sigh for pleasure they refuse to give,—
Madly they frustrate still their own designs;
And, where they hope that quiet to enjoy
Which virtue pictures, bitterness of soul,               245
Pining regrets, and vain repentances,
Disease, disgust, and lassitude, pervade
Their valueless and miserable lives.

But hoary-headed selfishness has felt
Its death-blow, and is tottering to the grave:                    250
A brighter morn awaits the human day,
When every transfer of earth's natural gifts
Shall be a commerce of good words and works;
When poverty and wealth, the thirst of fame,
The fear of infamy, disease and woe,                             255
War with its million horrors, and fierce hell
Shall live but in the memory of time,
Who, like a penitent libertine, shall start,
Look back, and shudder at his younger years.


### VI.

All touch, all eye, all ear,
The Spirit felt the Fairy's burning speech.
O'er the thin texture of its frame,
The varying periods painted changing glows,
As on a summer even,                                             5
When soul-enfolding music floats around,
The stainless mirror of the lake
Re-images the eastern gloom,
Mingling convulsively its purple hues
With sunset's burnished gold.                                   10

Then thus the Spirit spoke:
"It is a wild and miserable world!
Thorny, and full of care,
Which every fiend can make his prey at will.
O Fairy! in the lapse of years,                                15
Is there no hope in store?
Will yon vast suns roll on
Interminably, still illuming
The night of so many wretched souls,
And see no hope for them?                                       20
Will not the universal Spirit e'er
Revivify this withered limb of Heaven?"

The Fairy calmly smiled
In comfort, and a kindling gleam of hope
Suffused the Spirit's lineaments.                               25
"Oh! rest thee tranquil; chase those fearful doubts,
Which ne'er could rack an everlasting soul,
That sees the chains which bind it to its doom.
Yes! crime and misery are in yonder earth,
Falshood, mistake, and lust;                                    30
But the eternal world
Contains at once the evil and the cure.
Some eminent in virtue shall start up,
Even in perversest time:
The truths of their pure lips, that never die,                  35

Shall bind the scorpion falshood with a wreath
    Of ever-living flame,
Until the monster sting itself to death.[4]

"How sweet a scene will earth become!
Of purest spirits, a pure dwelling-place,                              40
Symphonious with the planetary spheres;[5]
When man, with changeless Nature coalescing,
Will undertake regeneration's work,
When its ungenial poles no longer point
    To the red and baleful sun                       45
    That faintly twinkles there.[6]

"Spirit! on yonder earth,
  Falshood now triumphs; deadly power
Has fixed its seal upon the lip of truth!
  Madness and misery are there!                               50
The happiest is most wretched! Yet confide,
Until pure health-drops, from the cup of joy,
Fall like a dew of balm upon the world.
Now, to the scene I shew, in silence turn,
And read the blood-stained charter of all woe,                         55
Which nature soon, with recreating hand,
Will blot in mercy from the book of earth.
How bold the flight of passion's wandering wing,
How swift the step of reason's firmer tread,
How calm and sweet the victories of life,                              60
How terrorless the triumph of the grave!
How powerless were the mightiest monarch's arm,
Vain his loud threat, and impotent his frown!
How ludicrous the priest's dogmatic roar!
The weight of his exterminating curse,                                 65
How light! and his affected charity,
To suit the pressure of the changing times,
What palpable deceit!—but for thy aid,
Religion![7] but for thee, prolific fiend,

4. *scorpion . . . death:* Pliny and other natural historians of antiquity wrote that scorpions commit suicide if surrounded by fire; Shelley used the metaphor more than once for the self-destructive nature of evil. (See *The Cenci*, II.ii.70–71.)
5. An allusion to the music of the spheres, the harmonious sound that, according to classical and Renaissance authorities, the planets make in their travels through space.
6. "The north polar star, to which the axis of the earth . . . points" (from Shelley's note). Shelley goes on to suggest that the angle of the earth's axis is gradually diminishing and that someday, when "the equator coincides with the ecliptic" (the line marking the points closest to the sun), "the nights and days will then become equal on the earth during the year, and probably the seasons also." He quotes contemporary scientists in support of his idea, but his real motivation (like that of some of the scientists) was the mythical notion, reflected by Milton in *Paradise Lost*, X.668–87, that the discrepancy between the equator and the ecliptic—the variation in the seasons and in the length of days and nights—was a physical manifestation of the moral Fall of Man.
7. In lines 72–145, Shelley personifies *Religion* and addresses "him" on his life cycle. Shelley published lines 72–102, with some alterations, as a separate poem entitled "Superstition" in the *Alastor* volume. The process of abstraction described in these lines was already a radical commonplace, used, for instance, by Baron d'Holbach, Constantin Volney, and Blake (though Shelley did not know Blake's work). See, for instance, Blake's *The Marriage of Heaven and Hell* (Plate 11).

Who peoplest earth with demons, hell with men,                    70
And heaven with slaves!

"Thou taintest all thou lookest upon!—the stars,
Which on thy cradle beamed so brightly sweet,
Were gods to the distempered playfulness
Of thy untutored infancy: the trees,                              75
The grass, the clouds, the mountains, and the sea,
All living things that walk, swim, creep, or fly,
Were gods: the sun had homage, and the moon
Her worshipper. Then thou becamest, a boy,
More daring in thy frenzies: every shape,                         80
Monstrous or vast, or beautifully wild,
Which, from sensation's relics, fancy culls;
The spirits of the air, the shuddering ghost,
The genii of the elements, the powers
That give a shape to nature's varied works,                       85
Had life and place in the corrupt belief
Of thy blind heart: yet still thy youthful hands
Were pure of human blood. Then manhood gave
Its strength and ardour to thy frenzied brain;
Thine eager gaze scanned the stupendous scene,                    90
Whose wonders mocked the knowledge of thy pride:
Their everlasting and unchanging laws
Reproached thine ignorance. Awhile thou stoodst
Baffled and gloomy; then thou didst sum up
The elements of all that thou didst know;                         95
The changing seasons, winter's leafless reign,
The budding of the heaven-breathing trees,
The eternal orbs that beautify the night,
The sun-rise, and the setting of the moon,
Earthquakes and wars, and poisons and disease,                   100
And all their causes, to an abstract point
Converging, thou didst bend, and called it GOD!
The self-sufficing, the omnipotent,
The merciful, and the avenging God!
Who, prototype of human misrule, sits                            105
High in heaven's realm, upon a golden throne,
Even like an earthly king; and whose dread work,
Hell, gapes for ever for the unhappy slaves
Of fate, whom he created, in his sport,
To triumph in their torments when they fell!                     110
Earth heard the name; earth trembled, as the smoke
Of his revenge ascended up to heaven,
Blotting the constellations; and the cries
Of millions, butchered in sweet confidence
And unsuspecting peace, even when the bonds                       115
Of safety were confirmed by wordy oaths
Sworn in his dreadful name, rung through the land;
Whilst innocent babes writhed on thy stubborn spear,
And thou didst laugh to hear the mother's shriek

Of maniac gladness, as the sacred steel          120
Felt cold in her torn entrails!

"Religion! thou wert then in manhood's prime:
But age crept on: one God would not suffice
For senile puerility; thou framedst
A tale to suit thy dotage, and to glut          125
Thy misery-thirsting soul, that the mad fiend
Thy wickedness had pictured, might afford
A plea for sating the unnatural thirst
For murder, rapine, violence, and crime,
That still consumed thy being, even when          130
Thou heardst the step of fate;—that flames might light
Thy funeral scene, and the shrill horrent[8] shrieks
Of parents dying on the pile that burned
To light their children to thy paths, the roar
Of the encircling flames, the exulting cries          135
Of thine apostles, loud commingling there,
    Might sate thine hungry ear
    Even on the bed of death!

"But now contempt is mocking thy grey hairs;
Thou art descending to the darksome grave,          140
Unhonoured and unpitied, but by those
Whose pride is passing by like thine, and sheds,
Like thine, a glare that fades before the sun
Of truth, and shines but in the dreadful night
That long has lowered above the ruined world.          145

"Throughout these infinite orbs of mingling light,
Of which yon earth is one, is wide diffused
A spirit of activity and life,
That knows no term, cessation, or decay;
That fades not when the lamp of earthly life,          150
Extinguished in the dampness of the grave,
Awhile there slumbers, more than when the babe
In the dim newness of its being feels
The impulses of sublunary[9] things,
And all is wonder to unpractised sense:          155
But, active, stedfast, and eternal, still
Guides the fierce whirlwind, in the tempest roars,
Cheers in the day, breathes in the balmy groves,
Strengthens in health, and poisons in disease;
And in the storm of change, that ceaselessly          160
Rolls round the eternal universe, and shakes
Its undecaying battlement, presides,
Apportioning with irresistible law
The place each spring of its machine shall fill;

8. Shuddering, expressing horror.
9. Because, in classical and Renaissance thought, all things beneath the moon were subject to
change and decay, *sublunar(y)* came to mean "mortal," "mundane."

So that, when waves on waves tumultuous heap          165
Confusion to the clouds, and fiercely driven
Heaven's lightnings scorch the uprooted ocean-fords,
Whilst, to the eye of shipwrecked mariner,
Lone sitting on the bare and shuddering rock,
All seems unlinked contingency and chance:          170
No atom of this turbulence fulfils
A vague and unnecessitated task,
Or acts but as it must and ought to act.¹
Even the minutest molecule of light,
That in an April sunbeam's fleeting glow          175
Fulfils its destined, though invisible work,
The universal Spirit guides; nor less,
When merciless ambition, or mad zeal,
Has led two hosts of dupes to battle-field,
That, blind, they there may dig each other's graves,          180
And call the sad work glory, does it rule
All passions: not a thought, a will, an act,
No working of the tyrant's moody mind,
Nor one misgiving of the slaves who boast
Their servitude, to hide the shame they feel,          185
Nor the events enchaining every will,
That from the depths of unrecorded time
Have drawn all-influencing virtue, pass
Unrecognised, or unforeseen by thee,
Soul of the Universe! eternal spring          190
Of life and death, of happiness and woe,
Of all that chequers the phantasmal scene
That floats before our eyes in wavering light,
Which gleams but on the darkness of our prison,
    Whose chains and massy² walls          195
    We feel, but cannot see.

"Spirit of Nature! all-sufficing Power,
Necessity!³ thou mother of the world!
Unlike the God of human error, thou
Requirest no prayers or praises; the caprice          200
Of man's weak will belongs no more to thee
Than do the changeful passions of his breast
To thy unvarying harmony: the slave,

1. In a note to lines 171–73, Shelley quotes from Holbach's *Système de la nature*, illustrating the operation of Necessity in the realms of physical nature and social interaction.
2. Solid, weighty.
3. "He who asserts the doctrine of Necessity, means that, contemplating the events which compose the moral and material universe, he beholds only an immense and uninterrupted chain of causes and effects, no one of which could occupy any other place than it does occupy. . . . Motive is, to voluntary action in the human mind, what cause is to effect in the material universe. The word liberty, as applied to mind, is analogous to the word chance, as applied to matter: they spring from an ignorance of the certainty of the conjunction of antecedents and consequents. . . . The doctrine of Necessity tends to introduce a great change into the established notions of morality, and utterly to destroy religion. . . . We are taught, by the doctrine of Necessity, that there is neither good nor evil in the universe, otherwise than as the events to which we apply these epithets have relation to our own peculiar mode of being" (from Shelley's note).

Whose horrible lusts spread misery o'er the world,
And the good man, who lifts, with virtuous pride,      205
His being, in the sight of happiness,
That springs from his own works; the poison-tree,
Beneath whose shade all life is withered up,[4]
And the fair oak, whose leafy dome affords
A temple where the vows of happy love      210
Are registered, are equal in thy sight:
No love, no hate thou cherishest; revenge
And favoritism, and worst desire of fame
Thou knowst not: all that the wide world contains
Are but thy passive instruments, and thou      215
Regardst them all with an impartial eye,
Whose joy or pain thy nature cannot feel,
    Because thou hast not human sense,
    Because thou art not human mind.

    "Yes! when the sweeping storm of time      220
Has sung its death-dirge o'er the ruined fanes
And broken altars of the almighty fiend,[5]
Whose name usurps thy honors, and the blood
Through centuries clotted there, has floated down
The tainted flood of ages, shalt thou live      225
Unchangeable! A shrine is raised to thee,
    Which, nor the tempest-breath of time,
    Nor the interminable flood,
    Over earth's slight pageant rolling,
       Availeth to destroy,—      230
The sensitive extension of the world.
    That wonderous and eternal fane,
Where pain and pleasure, good and evil join,
To do the will of strong necessity,
    And life, in multitudinous shapes,      235
Still pressing forward where no term can be,
    Like hungry and unresting flame
Curls round the eternal columns of its strength."

## VII.

### SPIRIT.

I was an infant when my mother went
To see an atheist burned. She took me there:
The dark-robed priests were met around the pile;
The multitude was gazing silently;
And as the culprit passed with dauntless mien,      5
Tempered disdain in his unaltering eye,
Mixed with a quiet smile, shone calmly forth:
The thirsty fire crept round his manly limbs;

4. The upas tree. See note to III.83.
5. The ordinary conception of God.

His resolute eyes were scorched to blindness soon;
His death-pang rent my heart! the insensate[6] mob          10
Uttered a cry of triumph, and I wept.
"Weep not, child!" cried my mother, "for that man
Has said, 'There is no God.' "


FAIRY.

                    There is no God![7]
Nature confirms the faith his death-groan sealed:
Let heaven and earth, let man's revolving race,          15
His ceaseless generations tell their tale;
Let every part depending on the chain
That links it to the whole, point to the hand
That grasps its term! let every seed that falls
In silent eloquence unfold its store          20
Of argument: infinity within,
Infinity without, belie creation;
The exterminable spirit it contains
Is nature's only God; but human pride
Is skilful to invent most serious names          25
To hide its ignorance.
                    The name of God
Has fenced about all crime with holiness,
Himself the creature of his worshippers,
Whose names and attributes and passions change,
Seeva, Buddh, Foh, Jehovah, God, or Lord,[8]          30
Even with the human dupes who build his shrines,
Still serving o'er the war-polluted world
For desolation's watch-word; whether hosts
Stain his death-blushing chariot wheels, as on
Triumphantly they roll, whilst Brahmins raise          35
A sacred hymn to mingle with the groans;[9]
Or countless partners of his power divide
His tyranny to weakness; or the smoke
Of burning towns, the cries of female helplessness,

6. Unfeeling; devoid of moral feeling.
7. "This negation must be understood solely to affect a creative Deity. The hypothesis of a
   pervading Spirit coeternal with the universe remains unshaken. . . . God is an hypothesis,
   and, as such, stands in need of proof. . . . From the phenomena, which are the objects of
   our senses, we attempt to infer a cause, which we call God. . . . From this hypothesis we
   invent this general name, to conceal our ignorance of causes and essences" (from Shelley's
   note). Shelley took this note from the text of *The Necessity of Atheism*, the pamphlet for
   which he was expelled from Oxford in March 1811.
8. *Seeva*, or Shiva, is the Hindu name for God in his role as destroyer; *Buddh* is the Buddha;
   *Foh*, or Fohi, was the name used in England in Shelley's day for Fu Hsi, the legendary or
   quasi-historical "first king of China, who is said to have founded this empire soon after the
   deluge" (George Crabb, *Universal Historical Dictionary*, London, 1833); *Jehovah*, or "Yahweh," is the Hebrew god; *Lord* (the Hebrew *Adonai*) is the name used instead of "Yahweh"
   when the name is pronounced.
9. *hosts . . . groans:* The reference is to the massive car of Vishnu, a title of whom is Jagannāth
   (hence "Juggernaut"), under whose wheels devotees were said sometimes to have immolated
   themselves; in general, an overwhelming force. *Brahmins* are the highest caste Hindus.

Unarmed old age, and youth, and infancy,                40
Horribly massacred, ascend to heaven
In honor of his name; or, last and worst,
Earth groans beneath religion's iron age,[1]
And priests dare babble of a God of peace,
Even whilst their hands are red with guiltless blood,                45
Murdering the while, uprooting every germ
Of truth, exterminating, spoiling all,
Making the earth a slaughter-house!

        O Spirit! through the sense
By which thy inner nature was apprised                50
    Of outward shews, vague dreams have rolled,
    And varied reminiscences have waked
        Tablets that never fade;
All things have been imprinted there,
The stars, the sea, the earth, the sky,                55
Even the unshapeliest lineaments
    Of wild and fleeting visions
        Have left a record there
        To testify of earth.

These are my empire, for to me is given                60
The wonders of the human world to keep,
And fancy's thin creations to endow
With manner, being, and reality;
Therefore a wondrous phantom, from the dreams
Of human error's dense and purblind[2] faith,                65
I will evoke, to meet thy questioning.
        Ahasuerus,[3] rise!

    A strange and woe-worn wight[4]
    Arose beside the battlement,
        And stood unmoving there.                70
His inessential figure cast no shade
    Upon the golden floor;

1. There were four traditional ages in classical thought: the Golden Age, the Silver Age, the Bronze Age, and the Iron Age; Shelley implies that religion has descended to this last, ignoble phase.
2. Of impaired or defective vision.
3. The Wandering Jew of ancient legend. Shelley's note, quoting from a German source, reads in part: "When our Lord was wearied with the burthen of his ponderous cross, and wanted to rest before the door of Ahasuerus, the unfeeling wretch drove him away with brutality. The Savior of mankind staggered, sinking under the heavy load, but uttered no complaint. An angel of death appeared before Ahasuerus, and exclaimed indignantly, 'Barbarian! thou has denied rest to the Son of Man: be it denied thee also, until he comes to judge the world.' . . .
    "A black demon . . . goads him now from country to country: he is denied the consolation which death affords, and precluded from the rest of the peaceful grave."
    Shelley had an abiding interest in the figure of the Wandering Jew, who is the protagonist of his earliest completed book-length poem, *The Wandering Jew; or, The Victim of the Eternal Avenger*, and who appears in his last completed major poem, *Hellas*. (See CPPBS, I, 200–204.)
4. A human being; usually used to express either contempt or sympathy.

His port and mien bore mark of many years,
And chronicles of untold antientness
Were legible within his beamless eye:                         75
    Yet his cheek bore the mark of youth;
Freshness and vigor knit his manly frame;
The wisdom of old age was mingled there
    With youth's primæval dauntlessness;
        And inexpressible woe,                                80
Chastened by fearless resignation, gave
An awful grace to his all-speaking brow.


SPIRIT.

Is there a God?


AHASUERUS.

Is there a God!—aye, an almighty God,
And vengeful as almighty! Once his voice                      85
Was heard on earth: earth shuddered at the sound;
The fiery-visaged firmament expressed
Abhorrence, and the grave of nature yawned
To swallow all the dauntless and the good
That dared to hurl defiance at his throne,                    90
Girt as it was with power. None but slaves
Survived,—cold-blooded slaves, who did the work
Of tyrannous omnipotence; whose souls
No honest indignation ever urged
To elevated daring, to one deed                               95
Which gross and sensual self did not pollute.
These slaves built temples for the omnipotent fiend,
Gorgeous and vast: the costly altars smoked
With human blood, and hideous pæans[5] rung
Through all the long-drawn aisles. A murderer[6] heard        100
His voice in Egypt, one whose gifts and arts
Had raised him to his eminence in power,
Accomplice of omnipotence in crime,
And confidant of the all-knowing one.
        These were Jehovah's words.                           105


"From an eternity of idleness
I, God, awoke; in seven days' toil made earth
From nothing; rested, and created man:
I placed him in a paradise, and there
Planted the tree of evil, so that he                          110
Might eat and perish, and my soul procure
Wherewith to sate its malice, and to turn,
Even like a heartless conqueror of the earth,

5. Songs of praise or thanksgiving; shouts of joy.
6. Moses.

All misery to my fame. The race of men
Chosen to my honor, with impunity                                115
May sate the lusts I planted in their heart.
Here I command thee hence to lead them on,
Until, with hardened feet, their conquering troops
Wade on the promised soil through woman's blood,
And make my name be dreaded through the land.                    120
Yet ever-burning flame and ceaseless woe
Shall be the doom of their eternal souls,
With every soul on this ungrateful earth,
Virtuous or vicious, weak or strong,—even all
Shall perish, to fulfil the blind revenge                       125
(Which you, to men, call justice) of their God."

        The murderer's brow
Quivered with horror.
            "God omnipotent,
Is there no mercy? must our punishment
Be endless? will long ages roll away,                           130
And see no term? Oh! wherefore hast thou made
In mockery and wrath this evil earth?
Mercy becomes the powerful—be but just:
O God! repent and save."

            "One way remains:
I will beget a son, and he shall bear                           135
The sins of all the world;[7] he shall arise
In an unnoticed corner of the earth,
And there shall die upon a cross, and purge
The universal crime; so that the few
On whom my grace descends, those who are marked                 140
As vessels to the honor of their God,
May credit this strange sacrifice, and save
Their souls alive: millions shall live and die,
Who ne'er shall call upon their Saviour's name,
But, unredeemed, go to the gaping grave.                        145
Thousands shall deem it an old woman's tale,
Such as the nurses frighten babes withal:
These in a gulph of anguish and of flame
Shall curse their reprobation endlessly,
Yet tenfold pangs shall force them to avow,                     150
Even on their beds of torment, where they howl,
My honor, and the justice of their doom.

---

7. Shelley attacks Christianity and the Bible in a long note that reads, in part: "A Roman
governor of Judea, at the instances of a priest-led mob, crucified a man called Jesus eighteen
centuries ago. He was a man of pure life, who desired to rescue his countrymen from the
tyranny of their barbarous and degrading superstitions. The common fate of all who desire
to benefit mankind awaited him. . . . Jesus was sacrificed to the honour of that God with
whom he was afterwards confounded. It is of importance, therefore, to distinguish between
the pretended character of this being as the Son of God and the Saviour of the world, and
his real character as a man, who, for a vain attempt to reform the world, paid the forfeit of
his life to that overbearing tyranny which has since so long desolated the universe in his
name."

What then avail their virtuous deeds, their thoughts
Of purity, with radiant genius bright,
Or lit with human reason's earthly ray?                                    155
Many are called, but few will I elect.
Do thou my bidding, Moses!"

                                   Even the murderer's cheek
Was blanched with horror, and his quivering lips
Scarce faintly uttered—"O almighty one,
I tremble and obey!"                                                       160


O Spirit! centuries have set their seal
On this heart of many wounds, and loaded brain,
Since the Incarnate came: humbly he came,
Veiling his horrible Godhead in the shape
Of man, scorned by the world, his name unheard,                            165
Save by the rabble of his native town,
Even as a parish demagogue. He led
The crowd; he taught them justice, truth, and peace,
In semblance; but he lit within their souls
The quenchless flames of zeal, and blest the sword                         170
He brought on earth to satiate with the blood
Of truth and freedom his malignant soul.
At length his mortal frame was led to death.
I stood beside him: on the torturing cross
No pain assailed his unterrestrial sense;                                  175
And yet he groaned. Indignantly I summed
The massacres and miseries which his name
Had sanctioned in my country, and I cried,
"Go! go!" in mockery.
A smile of godlike malice reillumined                                      180
His fading lineaments.—"I go," he cried,
"But thou shalt wander o'er the unquiet earth
Eternally."——The dampness of the grave
Bathed my imperishable front. I fell,
And long lay tranced upon the charmed soil.                                185
When I awoke hell burned within my brain,
Which staggered on its seat; for all around
The mouldering relics of my kindred lay,
Even as the Almighty's ire arrested them,
And in their various attitudes of death                                    190
My murdered children's mute and eyeless sculls
Glared ghastily upon me.
                             But my soul,
From sight and sense of the polluting woe
Of tyranny, had long learned to prefer
Hell's freedom to the servitude of heaven.                                 195
Therefore I rose, and dauntlessly began
My lonely and unending pilgrimage,
Resolved to wage unweariable war
With my almighty tyrant, and to hurl

Defiance at his impotence to harm                                    200
Beyond the curse I bore. The very hand
That barred my passage to the peaceful grave
Has crushed the earth to misery, and given
Its empire to the chosen of his slaves.
These have I seen, even from the earliest dawn          205
Of weak, unstable and precarious power,
Then preaching peace, as now they practise war;
So, when they turned but from the massacre
Of unoffending infidels, to quench
Their thirst for ruin in the very blood                         210
That flowed in their own veins, and pityless zeal
Froze every human feeling, as the wife
Sheathed in her husband's heart the sacred steel,
Even whilst its hopes were dreaming of her love;
And friends to friends, brothers to brothers stood     215
Opposed in bloodiest battle-field, and war,
Scarce satiable by fate's last death-draught, waged,
Drunk from the winepress of the Almighty's wrath;[8]
Whilst the red cross, in mockery of peace,
Pointed to victory! When the fray was done,               220
No remnant of the exterminated faith
Survived to tell its ruin, but the flesh,
With putrid smoke poisoning the atmosphere,
That rotted on the half-extinguished pile.

Yes! I have seen God's worshippers unsheathe           225
The sword of his revenge, when grace descended,
Confirming all unnatural impulses,
To sanctify their desolating deeds;
And frantic priests waved the ill-omened cross
O'er the unhappy earth: then shone the sun               230
On showers of gore from the upflashing steel
Of safe assassination, and all crime
Made stingless by the spirits of the Lord,
And blood-red rainbows canopied the land.

Spirit! no year of my eventful being                            235
Has passed unstained by crime and misery,
Which flows from God's own faith. I've marked his slaves
With tongues whose lies are venomous, beguile
The insensate mob, and, whilst one hand was red
With murder, feign to stretch the other out              240
For brotherhood and peace; and that they now
Babble of love and mercy, whilst their deeds
Are marked with all the narrowness and crime

---

8. The account in this passage of the bloody internecine wars among Christian factions is
punctuated here by a reference to Revelation 14:19–20, where an Angel thrusts his sickle
into the earth "and gathered the vine of the earth, and cast *it* into the great winepress of
the wrath of God. And . . . blood came out of the winepress, even unto the horse bridles,
by the space of a thousand *and* six hundred furlongs."

That freedom's young arm dare not yet chastise,
Reason may claim our gratitude, who now                        245
Establishing the imperishable throne
Of truth, and stubborn virtue, maketh vain
The unprevailing malice of my foe,
Whose bootless rage heaps torments for the brave,
Adds impotent eternities to pain,                             250
Whilst keenest disappointment racks his breast
To see the smiles of peace around them play,
To frustrate or to sanctify their doom.

Thus have I stood,—through a wild waste of years
Struggling with whirlwinds of mad agony,                      255
Yet peaceful, and serene, and self-enshrined,
Mocking my powerless tyrant's horrible curse
With stubborn and unalterable will,
Even as a giant oak, which heaven's fierce flame
Had scathed in the wilderness, to stand                       260
A monument of fadeless ruin there;
Yet peacefully and movelessly it braves
The midnight conflict of the wintry storm,
  As in the sun-light's calm it spreads
  Its worn and withered arms on high                          265
To meet the quiet of a summer's noon.⁹
    The Fairy waved her wand:
    Ahasuerus fled
Fast as the shapes of mingled shade and mist,
That lurk in the glens of a twilight grove,                   270
    Flee from the morning beam:
  The matter of which dreams are made¹
Not more endowed with actual life
Than this phantasmal portraiture
Of wandering human thought.²                                  275

## VIII.

### THE FAIRY.

The present and the past thou hast beheld:
It was a desolate sight. Now, Spirit, learn
  The secrets of the future.—Time!
Unfold the brooding pinion of thy gloom,
Render thou up thy half-devoured babes,                        5
And from the cradles of eternity,

9. Ahasuerus' determined refusal to surrender to God, as depicted by Shelley, harks back to Milton's Satan in *Paradise Lost*, whom he often echoes, and anticipates the character of Prometheus in *Prometheus Unbound*.
1. An echo of Prospero in Shakespeare's *The Tempest* ("We are such stuff / As dreams are made on . . . ," IV.i.156–57). The final stanza of Canto VII, with the disappearance of the phantasmal Ahasuerus, recalls the ending of the masque staged in *The Tempest* (the occasion for Prospero's remarks), in which "These our actors, / . . . were all spirits and / Are melted into air" (IV.i.148–50).
2. That is, Ahasuerus only has reality as an aberrant human idea.

Where millions lie lulled to their portioned sleep
By the deep murmuring stream of passing things,
Tear thou that gloomy shroud.—Spirit, behold
    Thy glorious destiny!                                    10

    Joy to the Spirit came.
Through the wide rent in Time's eternal veil,
Hope was seen beaming through the mists of fear:
    Earth was no longer hell;
    Love, freedom, health, had given                  15
Their ripeness to the manhood of its prime,
    And all its pulses beat
Symphonious to the planetary spheres:
    Then dulcet music swelled
Concordant[3] with the life-strings of the soul;              20
It throbbed in sweet and languid beatings there,
Catching new life from transitory death,—
Like the vague sighings of a wind at even,
That wakes the wavelets of the slumbering sea
And dies on the creation of its breath,                       25
And sinks and rises, fails and swells by fits:
    Was the pure stream of feeling
    That sprung from these sweet notes,
And o'er the Spirit's human sympathies
With mild and gentle motion calmly flowed.                    30

    Joy to the Spirit came,—
  Such joy as when a lover sees
The chosen of his soul in happiness,
    And witnesses her peace
Whose woe to him were bitterer than death,                    35
    Sees her unfaded cheek
Glow mantling[4] in first luxury of health,
    Thrills with her lovely eyes,
Which like two stars amid the heaving main
    Sparkle through liquid bliss.                      40

Then in her triumph spoke the Fairy Queen:
"I will not call the ghost of ages gone
To unfold the frightful secrets of its lore;
    The present now is past,
And those events that desolate the earth                      45
Have faded from the memory of Time,
Who dares not give reality to that
Whose being I annul. To me is given
The wonders of the human world to keep,
Space, matter, time, and mind. Futurity                       50
Exposes now its treasure; let the sight

3. Harmonious; *dulcet:* sweet.
4. Suffused with color, blushing.

Renew and strengthen all thy failing hope.
O human Spirit! spur thee to the goal
Where virtue fixes universal peace,
And midst the ebb and flow of human things,          55
Shew somewhat stable, somewhat certain still,
A lighthouse o'er the wild of dreary waves.

"The habitable earth is full of bliss;
Those wastes of frozen billows that were hurled
By everlasting snow-storms round the poles,          60
Where matter dared not vegetate or live,
But ceaseless frost round the vast solitude
Bound its broad zone of stillness, are unloosed;
And fragrant zephyrs there from spicy isles
Ruffle the placid ocean-deep, that rolls             65
Its broad, bright surges to the sloping sand,
Whose roar is wakened into echoings sweet
To murmur through the heaven-breathing groves
And melodize with man's blest nature there.

"Those desarts of immeasurable sand,                 70
Whose age-collected fervors scarce allowed
A bird to live, a blade of grass to spring,
Where the shrill chirp of the green lizard's love
Broke on the sultry silentness alone,
Now teem with countless rills and shady woods,       75
Corn-fields and pastures and white cottages;
And where the startled wilderness beheld
A savage conqueror stained in kindred blood,
A tygress sating with the flesh of lambs
The unnatural famine of her toothless cubs,          80
Whilst shouts and howlings through the desart rang,
Sloping and smooth the daisy-spangled lawn,
Offering sweet incense to the sun-rise, smiles
To see a babe before his mother's door,
    Sharing his morning's meal                       85
  With the green and golden basilisk[5]
    That comes to lick his feet.

"Those trackless deeps, where many a weary sail
Has seen above the illimitable plain,
Morning on night, and night on morning rise,         90
Whilst still no land to greet the wanderer spread
Its shadowy mountains on the sun-bright sea,
Where the loud roarings of the tempest-waves
So long have mingled with the gusty wind
In melancholy loneliness, and swept                  95
The desert of those ocean solitudes,

5. A mythical reptile, also called a cockatrice, whose breath and glance were supposed to be fatal.

But vocal to the sea-bird's harrowing shriek,
The bellowing monster, and the rushing storm,
Now to the sweet and many mingling sounds
Of kindliest human impulses respond.                              100
Those lonely realms bright garden-isles begem,
With lightsome clouds and shining seas between,
And fertile vallies, resonant with bliss,
Whilst green woods overcanopy the wave,
Which like a toil-worn labourer leaps to shore,                   105
To meet the kisses of the flowrets there.

"All things are recreated, and the flame
Of consentaneous[6] love inspires all life:
The fertile bosom of the earth gives suck
To myriads, who still grow beneath her care,                     110
Rewarding her with their pure perfectness:
The balmy breathings of the wind inhale
Her virtues, and diffuse them all abroad:
Health floats amid the gentle atmosphere,
Glows in the fruits, and mantles[7] on the stream:               115
No storms deform the beaming brow of heaven,
Nor scatter in the freshness of its pride
The foliage of the ever verdant trees;
But fruits are ever ripe, flowers ever fair,
And autumn proudly bears her matron grace,                       120
Kindling a flush on the fair cheek of spring,
Whose virgin bloom beneath the ruddy fruit
Reflects its tint and blushes into love.

"The lion now forgets to thirst for blood:
There might you see him sporting in the sun                       125
Beside the dreadless kid; his claws are sheathed,
His teeth are harmless, custom's force has made
His nature as the nature of a lamb.[8]
Like passion's fruit, the nightshade's[9] tempting bane
Poisons no more the pleasure it bestows:                          130
All bitterness is past; the cup of joy
Unmingled mantles to the goblet's brim,
And courts the thirsty lips it fled before.

"But chief, ambiguous man, he that can know
More misery, and dream more joy than all;                        135
Whose keen sensations thrill within his breast
To mingle with a loftier instinct there,
Lending their power to pleasure and to pain,

6. Simultaneous, mutual.
7. Foams or bubbles (see also VIII.132).
8. Shelley's two chief precedents for this peaceable vision of the future are Isaiah 11 and Virgil's
   Fourth Eclogue (see Shelley's last note to *Hellas*).
9. A poisonous plant, either of the genus *Solanum*, including black nightshade (which has white
   flowers and black berries) and woody nightshade (purple flowers and red berries), or else of
   the genus *Atropa*, deadly nightshade (belladonna).

Yet raising, sharpening, and refining each;
Who stands amid the ever-varying world,                         140
The burthen or the glory of the earth;
He chief perceives the change, his being notes
The gradual renovation, and defines
Each movement of its progress on his mind.


"Man, where the gloom of the long polar night                   145
Lowers o'er the snow-clad rocks and frozen soil,
Where scarce the hardiest herb that braves the frost
Basks in the moonlight's ineffectual glow,
Shrank with the plants, and darkened with the night;
His chilled and narrow energies, his heart,                     150
Insensible to courage, truth, or love,
His stunted stature and imbecile frame,
Marked him for some abortion of the earth,
Fit compeer of the bears that roamed around,
Whose habits and enjoyments were his own:                       155
His life a feverish dream of stagnant woe,
Whose meagre wants, but scantily fulfilled,
Apprised him ever of the joyless length
Which his short being's wretchedness had reached;
His death a pang which famine, cold and toil,                   160
Long on the mind, whilst yet the vital spark
Clung to the body stubbornly, had brought:
All was inflicted here that earth's revenge
Could wreak on the infringers of her law;
One curse alone was spared—the name of God.                     165


"Nor where the tropics bound the realms of day
With a broad belt of mingling cloud and flame,
Where blue mists through the unmoving atmosphere
Scattered the seeds of pestilence, and fed
Unnatural vegetation, where the land                            170
Teemed with all earthquake, tempest and disease,
Was man a nobler being; slavery
Had crushed him to his country's bloodstained dust;
Or he was bartered for the fame of power,
Which all internal impulses destroying,                         175
Makes human will an article of trade;
Or he was changed with Christians for their gold,
And dragged to distant isles, where to the sound
Of the flesh-mangling scourge, he does the work
Of all-polluting luxury and wealth,                             180
Which doubly visits on the tyrants' heads
The long-protracted fulness of their woe;
Or he was led to legal butchery,
To turn to worms beneath that burning sun,
Where kings first leagued against the rights of men,            185
And priests first traded with the name of God.

"Even where the milder zone afforded man
A seeming shelter, yet contagion there,
Blighting his being with unnumbered ills,
Spread like a quenchless fire; nor truth till late                    190
Availed to arrest its progress, or create
That peace which first in bloodless victory waved
Her snowy standard o'er this favoured clime:
There man was long the train-bearer of slaves,
The mimic of surrounding misery,                    195
The jackal of ambition's lion-rage,
The bloodhound of religion's hungry zeal.

"Here now the human being stands adorning
This loveliest earth with taintless body and mind;
Blest from his birth with all bland impulses,                    200
Which gently in his noble bosom wake
All kindly passions and all pure desires.
Him, still from hope to hope the bliss pursuing
Which from the exhaustless lore of human weal
Draws on the virtuous mind, the thoughts that rise                    205
In time-destroying infiniteness, gift
With self-enshrined eternity, that mocks
The unprevailing hoariness of age,
And man, once fleeting o'er the transient scene
Swift as an unremembered vision, stands                    210
Immortal upon earth:[1] no longer now
He slays the lamb that looks him in the face,
And horribly devours his mangled flesh,
Which still avenging nature's broken law,
Kindled all putrid humours in his frame,                    215
All evil passions, and all vain belief,
Hatred, despair, and loathing in his mind,
The germs of misery, death, disease, and crime.[2]

1. "Time is our consciousness of the succession of ideas in our mind. Vivid sensation, of either pain or pleasure, makes the time seem long. . . . If, therefore, the human mind . . . should become conscious of an infinite number of ideas in a minute, that minute would be eternity. I do not hence infer that the actual space between the birth and death of a man will ever be prolonged; but that his sensibility is perfectible. . . . the life of a man of virtue and talent, who should die in his thirtieth year, is, with regard to his own feelings, longer than that of a miserable priest-ridden slave, who dreams out a century of dulness" (from Shelley's note; Shelley actually died in his thirtieth year).
2. In Shelley's day comparative anatomists studying humans and apes concluded that man was naturally an eater of fruits and nuts—a vegetarian. Shelley was a vegetarian on both medical and moral grounds and remained one most of his life. Shelley's note states: "I hold that the depravity of the physical and moral nature of man originated in his unnatural habits of life. . . . All vice arose from the ruin of healthful innocence. Tyranny, superstition, commerce, and inequality, were then first known, when reason vainly attempted to guide the wanderings of exacerbated passion. . . .
    "Comparative anatomy teaches us that man resembles frugivorous animals in everything, and carnivorous in nothing; he has neither claws wherewith to seize his prey, nor distinct and pointed teeth to tear the living fibre. . . .
    "The intestines are also identical with those of herbivorous animals. . . .
    "On a natural system of diet, we should require no spices from India; no wines from Portugal, Spain, France, or Madeira; none of those multitudinous articles of luxury, for which every corner of the globe is rifled, and which are the causes of so much individual rivalship, such calamitous and sanguinary national disputes. . . .
    "The advantage of a reform in diet is obviously greater than that of any other. It strikes at the root of the evil."

No longer now the winged habitants,
That in the woods their sweet lives sing away,          220
Flee from the form of man; but gather round,
And prune their sunny feathers on the hands
Which little children stretch in friendly sport
Towards these dreadless partners of their play.
All things are void of terror: man has lost          225
His terrible prerogative, and stands
An equal amidst equals: happiness
And science dawn though late upon the earth;
Peace cheers the mind, health renovates the frame;
Disease and pleasure cease to mingle here,          230
Reason and passion cease to combat there;
Whilst each unfettered o'er the earth extend
Their all-subduing energies, and wield
The sceptre of a vast dominion there;
Whilst every shape and mode of matter lends          235
Its force to the omnipotence of mind,
Which from its dark mine drags the gem of truth
To decorate its paradise of peace."

## IX.

[THE FAIRY CONTINUES:]

"O happy Earth! reality of Heaven!
To which those restless souls that ceaselessly
Throng through the human universe, aspire;
Thou consummation of all mortal hope!
Thou glorious prize of blindly-working will!          5
Whose rays, diffused throughout all space and time,
Verge to one point and blend for ever there:
Of purest spirits thou pure dwelling-place!
Where care and sorrow, impotence and crime,
Languor, disease, and ignorance dare not come:          10
O happy Earth, reality of Heaven!

"Genius has seen thee in her passionate dreams,
And dim forebodings of thy loveliness
Haunting the human heart, have there entwined
Those rooted hopes of some sweet place of bliss          15
Where friends and lovers meet to part no more.
Thou art the end of all desire and will,
The product of all action; and the souls
That by the paths of an aspiring change
Have reached thy haven of perpetual peace,          20
There rest from the eternity of toil
That framed the fabric of thy perfectness.

"Even Time, the conqueror, fled thee in his fear;
That hoary giant, who, in lonely pride,

So long had ruled the world, that nations fell                              25
Beneath his silent footstep. Pyramids,
That for millenniums had withstood the tide
Of human things, his storm-breath drove in sand
Across that desart where their stones survived
The name of him whose pride had heaped them there.          30
Yon monarch, in his solitary pomp,
Was but the mushroom of a summer day,
That his light-winged footstep pressed to dust:
Time was the king of earth: all things gave way
Before him, but the fixed and virtuous will,                        35
The sacred sympathies of soul and sense,
That mocked his fury and prepared his fall.

"Yet slow and gradual dawned the morn of love;
Long lay the clouds of darkness o'er the scene,
Till from its native heaven they rolled away:                       40
First, crime triumphant o'er all hope careered
Unblushing, undisguising, bold and strong;
Whilst falshood, tricked in virtue's attributes,
Long sanctified all deeds of vice and woe,
Till done by her own venomous sting to death,                  45
She left the moral world without a law,
No longer fettering passion's fearless wing,
Nor searing reason with the brand of God.
Then steadily the happy ferment worked;
Reason was free; and wild though passion went              50
Through tangled glens and wood-embosomed meads,[3]
Gathering a garland of the strangest flowers,
Yet like the bee returning to her queen,
She bound the sweetest on her sister's brow,
Who meek and sober kissed the sportive child,                55
No longer trembling at the broken rod.

"Mild was the slow necessity of death:
The tranquil spirit failed beneath its grasp
Without a groan, almost without a fear,
Calm as a voyager to some distant land,                             60
And full of wonder, full of hope as he.
The deadly germs of languor and disease
Died in the human frame, and purity
Blest with all gifts her earthly worshippers.
How vigorous then the athletic form of age!                     65
How clear its open and unwrinkled brow!
Where neither avarice, cunning, pride, or care,
Had stamped the seal of grey deformity
On all the mingling lineaments of time.
How lovely the intrepid front of youth!                            70
Which meek-eyed courage decked with freshest grace;

3. Meadows enclosed by woods.

Courage of soul, that dreaded not a name,
And elevated will, that journeyed on
Through life's phantasmal scene in fearlessness,
With virtue, love, and pleasure, hand in hand.                    75

"Then, that sweet bondage which is freedom's self,
And rivets with sensation's softest tie
The kindred sympathies of human souls,
Needed no fetters of tyrannic law:
Those delicate and timid impulses                                 80
In nature's primal modesty arose,
And with undoubting confidence disclosed
The growing longings of its dawning love,
Unchecked by dull and selfish chastity,
That virtue of the cheaply virtuous,                              85
Who pride themselves in senselessness[4] and frost.
No longer prostitution's venomed bane
Poisoned the springs of happiness and life;
Woman and man, in confidence and love,
Equal and free and pure together trod                             90
The mountain-paths of virtue, which no more
Were stained with blood from many a pilgrim's feet.

"Then, where, through distant ages, long in pride
The palace of the monarch-slave had mocked
Famine's faint groan, and penury's silent tear,                   95
A heap of crumbling ruins stood, and threw
Year after year their stones upon the field,
Wakening a lonely echo; and the leaves
Of the old thorn, that on the topmost tower
Usurped the royal ensign's grandeur, shook                        100
In the stern storm that swayed the topmost tower
And whispered strange tales in the whirlwind's ear.

"Low through the lone cathedral's roofless aisles
The melancholy winds a death-dirge sung:
It were a sight of awfulness to see                               105
The works of faith and slavery, so vast,
So sumptuous, yet so perishing withal![5]
Even as the corpse that rests beneath its wall.
A thousand mourners deck the pomp of death
To-day, the breathing marble glows above                          110
To decorate its memory, and tongues
Are busy of its life: to-morrow, worms
In silence and in darkness seize their prey.

4. An absence of sensuous feelings.
5. Nonetheless, in spite of everything. Lines 107–08 form an accidentally rhymed couplet; in
   revising the poem as *Queen of the Universe*, Shelley eliminated this imperfection by moving
   *withal* between *yet* and *so*.

"Within the massy prison's mouldering courts,
Fearless and free the ruddy children played,                    115
Weaving gay chaplets[6] for their innocent brows
With the green ivy and the red wall-flower,
That mock the dungeon's unavailing gloom;
The ponderous chains, and gratings of strong iron,
There rusted amid heaps of broken stone                    120
That mingled slowly with their native earth:
There the broad beam of day, which feebly once
Lighted the cheek of lean captivity
With a pale and sickly glare, then freely shone
On the pure smiles of infant playfulness:                    125
No more the shuddering voice of hoarse despair
Pealed through the echoing vaults, but soothing notes
Of ivy-fingered winds and gladsome birds
And merriment were resonant around.

"These ruins soon left not a wreck[7] behind:                    130
Their elements, wide scattered o'er the globe,
To happier shapes were moulded, and became
Ministrant to all blissful impulses:
Thus human things were perfected, and earth,
Even as a child beneath its mother's love,                    135
Was strengthened in all excellence, and grew
Fairer and nobler with each passing year.

"Now Time his dusky pennons o'er the scene
Closes in stedfast darkness, and the past
Fades from our charmed sight. My task is done:                    140
Thy lore is learned. Earth's wonders are thine own,
With all the fear and all the hope they bring.
My spells are past: the present now recurs.
Ah me! a pathless wilderness remains
Yet unsubdued by man's reclaiming hand.                    145

"Yet, human Spirit, bravely hold thy course,
Let virtue teach thee firmly to pursue
The gradual paths of an aspiring change:
For birth and life and death, and that strange state
Before the naked soul has found its home,                    150
All tend to perfect happiness, and urge
The restless wheels of being on their way,
Whose flashing spokes, instinct with infinite life,
Bicker[8] and burn to gain their destined goal:
For birth but wakes the spirit to the sense                    155
Of outward shews, whose unexperienced shape

6. Garlands or wreaths worn on the head.
7. The *Oxford English Dictionary* gives this use (with one from Wordsworth's *Evening Walk*) as an example of the mistaken use of "wreck" for "wrack" (sb.¹5.b), meaning vestige or trace left after a destructive process.
8. Flash, gleam, quiver (see *Paradise Lost*, VI.766, in the description of the Chariot of Paternal Deitie alluded to in the note to I.134).

New modes of passion to its frame may lend;
Life is its state of action, and the store
Of all events is aggregated there
That variegate the eternal universe;                          160
Death is a gate of dreariness and gloom,
That leads to azure isles and beaming skies
And happy regions of eternal hope.
Therefore, O Spirit! fearlessly bear on:
Though storms may break the primrose on its stalk,            165
Though frosts may blight the freshness of its bloom,
Yet spring's awakening breath will woo the earth
To feed with kindliest dews its favorite flower,
That blooms in mossy banks and darksome glens,
Lighting the green wood with its sunny smile.                 170

"Fear not then, Spirit, death's disrobing hand,
So welcome when the tyrant is awake,
So welcome when the bigot's hell-torch burns;
'Tis but the voyage of a darksome hour,
The transient gulph-dream of a startling sleep.              175
Death is no foe to virtue: earth has seen
Love's brightest roses on the scaffold bloom,
Mingling with freedom's fadeless laurels there,
And presaging the truth of visioned bliss.
Are there not hopes within thee, which this scene            180
Of linked and gradual being has confirmed?
Whose stingings bade thy heart look further still,
When to the moonlight walk by Henry[9] led,
Sweetly and sadly thou didst talk of death?
And wilt thou rudely tear them from thy breast,             185
Listening supinely to a bigot's creed,
Or tamely crouching to the tyrant's rod,
Whose iron thongs are red with human gore?
Never: but bravely bearing on, thy will
Is destined an eternal war to wage                          190
With tyranny and falshood, and uproot
The germs of misery from the human heart.
Thine is the hand whose piety would soothe
The thorny pillow of unhappy crime,
Whose impotence an easy pardon gains,                       195
Watching its wanderings as a friend's disease:
Thine is the brow whose mildness would defy
Its fiercest rage, and brave its sternest will,
When fenced by power and master of the world.
Thou art sincere and good; of resolute mind,               200
Free from heart-withering custom's cold control,
Of passion lofty, pure and unsubdued.
Earth's pride and meanness could not vanquish thee,
And therefore art thou worthy of the boon

9. Ianthe's lover.

Which thou hast now received: virtue shall keep            205
Thy footsteps in the path that thou hast trod,
And many days of beaming hope shall bless
Thy spotless life of sweet and sacred love.
Go, happy one, and give that bosom joy
   Whose sleepless spirit waits to catch               210
   Light, life and rapture from thy smile."

   The Fairy waves her wand of charm.
Speechless with bliss the Spirit mounts the car,
   That rolled beside the battlement,
Bending her beamy eyes in thankfulness.                    215
   Again the enchanted steeds were yoked,
   Again the burning wheels inflame
The steep descent of heaven's untrodden way.
   Fast and far the chariot flew:
   The vast and fiery globes that rolled              220
   Around the Fairy's palace-gate
Lessened by slow degrees, and soon appeared
Such tiny twinklers as the planet orbs
That there attendant on the solar power
With borrowed light pursued their narrower way.            225

     Earth floated then below:
   The chariot paused a moment there;
   The Spirit then descended:
The restless coursers pawed the ungenial soil,
Snuffed the gross air, and then, their errand done,        230
Unfurled their pinions to the winds of heaven.

   The Body and the Soul united then,
A gentle start convulsed Ianthe's frame:
Her veiny eyelids quietly unclosed;
Moveless awhile the dark blue orbs remained:               235
She looked around in wonder and beheld
Henry, who kneeled in silence by her couch,
Watching her sleep with looks of speechless love,
   And the bright beaming stars
   That through the casement shone.                    240

# ALASTOR

Shelley wrote *Alastor* in the fall and early winter of 1815 while he and
Mary Godwin were living quietly in a cottage at Bishopsgate, one of the
eastern entrances to the Great Park of Windsor, in the Thames Valley
west of London. He arranged for the printer Samuel Hamilton to produce
250 copies of a volume comprised of *Alastor* and eleven shorter poems,
the copyright for which he offered to the publisher John Murray in early
January 1816 (*Letters*, I, 438–39). After Murray refused Shelley's offer,
the volume was published jointly in February 1816 by Baldwin, Cradock

and Joy (an important London bookselling-publishing firm of the period) and Carpenter & Son.

The *Alastor* volume was no best seller, but by the time of Shelley's death in 1822 all copies had been sold, and Mary Shelley, who had difficulty obtaining a copy for her own use, reprinted *Alastor* with Shelley's *Posthumous Poems* (1824). Although no manuscript of the original poem survives, Leigh Hunt's presentation copy of the *Alastor* volume at the University of California at Santa Barbara Library contains an emendation in Shelley's hand for line 291, as noted by Mary A. Quinn (*KSJ* XXXV [1986]: 17–20). There is also a copy of the volume containing Shelley's corrections for one of the poems published with it (see *SC*, IV, 592–94). Beyond the emendation in Hunt's presentation copy, the only significant textual authorities are the first edition (upon which our text is based) and Mary Shelley's reprint in *Posthumous Poems*.

Still the most influential reading of the poem to date is by Earl R. Wasserman, who views *Alastor* as exploring the interrelations between the universal human need for love and social ties and the idealist's solitary search for ultimate truths and ideal love. Wasserman suggests that the poem contains two chief characters, neither of whom is named: (1) the Narrator, who invokes the elements of nature and tells of his own early search for knowledge of the Ultimate (lines 1–49), and (2) the idealistic "Poet," whose story the Narrator tells in the main body of the poem and whose fate he regrets in the closing 49 lines. The numerous echoes of Wordsworth's poems are concentrated in the opening and closing addresses by the Narrator, leading Wasserman to consider the Narrator not Shelley's personal voice, but a Wordsworthian poet who compromises with mortal limitations and who, therefore, contrasts with the absolutism of the visionary young Poet. Important subsequent readings of *Alastor* include essays by William Keach, "Reflexive Imagery in Shelley," *KSJ* XXIV (1975): 49–69, and by Tilottama Rajan, "The Web of Human Things: Narrative and Identity in *Alastor*," in *New Romanticisms: Theory and Critical Practice*, ed. David L. Clark and Donald C. Goellnicht (Toronto: University of Toronto Press, 1994), pp. 27–51. Neil Fraistat reads *Alastor* within the context of the other poems with which it was first published in "Poetic Quests and Questionings in Shelley's *Alastor* Collection," *KSJ* XXXIII (1984): 161–81. For a useful discussion of the issues raised by the poem, see the essay by Michael Ferber reprinted in this volume, pp. 654–63.

# Alastor; or, The Spirit of Solitude

## Preface.

The poem entitled "ALASTOR," may be considered as allegorical of one of the most interesting situations of the human mind. It represents a youth of uncorrupted feelings and adventurous genius led forth by an imagination inflamed and purified through familiarity with all that is excellent and majestic, to the contemplation of the universe. He drinks deep of the fountains of knowledge, and is still insatiate. The magnificence and beauty of the external world sinks profoundly into the frame of his conceptions, and affords to their modifications a variety not to be exhausted. So long as it is possible for his desires to point towards objects thus infinite and unmeasured, he is joyous, and tranquil, and self-possessed. But the period arrives when these objects cease to suffice. His mind is at length suddenly awakened and thirsts for intercourse with an intelligence similar to itself. He images to himself the Being whom he loves. Conversant with speculations of the sublimest and most perfect natures, the vision in which he embodies his own imaginations unites all of wonderful, or wise, or beautiful, which the poet, the philosopher, or the lover could depicture. The intellectual faculties, the imagination, the functions of sense, have their respective requisitions on the sympathy of corresponding powers in other human beings. The Poet is represented as uniting these requisitions, and attaching them to a single image. He seeks in vain for a prototype of his conception. Blasted by his disappointment, he descends to an untimely grave.

The picture is not barren of instruction to actual men. The Poet's self-centred seclusion was avenged by the furies of an irresistible passion pursuing him to speedy ruin. But that Power which strikes the luminaries of the world with sudden darkness and extinction, by awakening them to too exquisite a perception of its influences, dooms to a slow and poisonous decay those meaner spirits that dare to abjure its dominion. Their destiny is more abject and inglorious as their deliquency is more contemptible and pernicious. They who, deluded by no generous error, instigated by no sacred thirst of doubtful knowledge, duped by no illustrious superstition, loving nothing on this earth, and cherishing no hopes beyond, yet keep aloof from sympathies with their kind, rejoicing neither in human joy nor mourning with human grief; these, and such as they, have their apportioned curse. They languish, because none feel with them their common nature. They are morally dead. They are neither friends, nor lovers, nor fathers, nor citizens of the world, nor benefactors of their country. Among those who attempt to exist without human sympathy, the pure and tenderhearted perish through the intensity and passion of their search after its communities, when the vacancy of their spirit suddenly makes itself felt. All else, selfish, blind, and torpid, are those unforeseeing multitudes who constitute, together with their own, the lasting misery and loneliness of the world. Those who love not their fellow-beings, live unfruitful lives, and prepare for their old age a miserable grave.

> "The good die first,
> And those whose hearts are dry as summer dust,
> Burn to the socket!"[1]

*December* 14, 1815.

---

1. Slightly misquoted from Wordsworth's *The Excursion*, I.500–502.

## Alastor; or, The Spirit of Solitude

*Nondum amabam, et amare amabam, quærebam quid amarem, amans amare.*
*—Confess. St. August.*[2]

Earth, ocean, air, beloved brotherhood!
If our great Mother has imbued my soul
With aught of natural piety[3] to feel
Your love, and recompense the boon with mine;[4]
If dewy morn, and odorous noon, and even,                          5
With sunset and its gorgeous ministers,[5]
And solemn midnight's tingling silentness;
If autumn's hollow sighs in the sere wood,
And winter robing with pure snow and crowns
Of starry ice the grey grass and bare boughs;                     10
If spring's voluptuous pantings when she breathes
Her first sweet kisses, have been dear to me;
If no bright bird, insect, or gentle beast
I consciously have injured, but still loved
And cherished these my kindred; then forgive                      15
This boast, beloved brethren, and withdraw
No portion of your wonted favour now!

Mother of this unfathomable world!
Favour my solemn song, for I have loved
Thee ever, and thee only; I have watched                          20
Thy shadow, and the darkness of thy steps,
And my heart ever gazes on the depth
Of thy deep mysteries. I have made my bed
In charnels and on coffins, where black death
Keeps record of the trophies won from thee,                       25
Hoping to still these obstinate questionings[6]
Of[7] thee and thine, by forcing some lone ghost,
Thy messenger, to render up the tale
Of what we are. In lone and silent hours,
When night makes a weird sound of its own stillness,              30
Like an inspired and desperate alchymist
Staking his very life on some dark hope,

2. This epigraph from St. Augustine's *Confessions*, III.i, has been translated: "Not yet did I love, yet I was in love with loving; . . . I sought what I might love, loving to love." Shelley had earlier used this quotation in the Advertisement to the "Poems to Mary" in 1810 in *The Esdaile Notebook* and had written it in a notebook that Claire Claremont used for her journal in 1814.
3. From Wordsworth's "My Heart Leaps Up": "And I could wish my days to be / Bound each to each by natural piety."
4. I.e., "repay your gift [of love] with my love."
5. Colors accompanying the sunset.
6. From Wordsworth, *Ode: Intimations of Immortality*, lines 142–43: "those obstinate questionings / Of sense and outward things."
7. I.e., about, concerning.

Have I mixed awful talk and asking looks
With my most innocent love, until strange tears
Uniting with those breathless kisses, made                    35
Such magic as compels the charmed night
To render up thy charge: . . . and, though ne'er yet
Thou hast unveil'd thy inmost sanctuary,[8]
Enough from incommunicable dream,
And twilight phantasms, and deep noonday thought,             40
Has shone within me, that serenely now
And moveless, as a long-forgotten lyre
Suspended in the solitary dome
Of some mysterious and deserted fane,[9]
I wait thy breath, Great Parent, that my strain              45
May modulate with murmurs of the air,
And motions of the forests and the sea,
And voice of living beings, and woven hymns
Of night and day, and the deep heart of man.

There was a Poet whose untimely tomb                         50
No human hands with pious reverence reared,
But the charmed eddies of autumnal winds
Built o'er his mouldering bones a pyramid
Of mouldering leaves in the waste wilderness:—
A lovely youth,—no mourning maiden decked                    55
With weeping flowers, or votive cypress wreath,[1]
The lone couch of his everlasting sleep:—
Gentle, and brave, and generous,—no lorn[2] bard
Breathed o'er his dark fate one melodious sigh:
He lived, he died, he sung, in solitude.                     60
Strangers have wept to hear his passionate notes,
And virgins, as unknown he past, have pined
And wasted for fond love of his wild eyes.
The fire of those soft orbs has ceased to burn,
And Silence, too enamoured of that voice,                    65
Locks its mute music in her rugged cell.

By solemn vision, and bright silver dream,
His infancy was nurtured. Every sight
And sound from the vast earth and ambient[3] air,
Sent to his heart its choicest impulses.                     70
The fountains of divine philosophy[4]
Fled not his thirsting lips, and all of great,
Or good, or lovely, which the sacred past

---

8. Shelley in his youth actually hunted ghosts and tried to raise the Devil and spirits of the
   dead in churchyards and burial vaults.
9. A sanctuary or temple.
1. The cyprus tree was sacred to mourners (Ovid, *Metamorphoses*, Book X), who offered wreaths
   of cypress boughs to the gods on behalf of the dead.
2. Forsaken, abandoned.
3. Surrounding.
4. An echo of Milton's *Comus*, line 476: "How charming is divine Philosophy!"

In truth or fable consecrates, he felt
And knew. When early youth had past, he left                    75
His cold fireside and alienated home
To seek strange truths in undiscovered lands.
Many a wide waste and tangled wilderness
Has lured his fearless steps; and he has bought
With his sweet voice and eyes, from savage men,                 80
His rest and food. Nature's most secret steps
He like her shadow has pursued, where'er
The red volcano overcanopies
Its fields of snow and pinnacles of ice
With burning smoke, or where bitumen lakes⁵                     85
On black bare pointed islets ever beat
With sluggish surge, or where the secret caves
Rugged and dark, winding among the springs
Of fire and poison, inaccessible
To avarice or pride, their starry domes                         90
Of diamond and of gold expand above
Numberless and immeasurable halls,
Frequent with⁶ crystal column, and clear shrines
Of pearl, and thrones radiant with chrysolite.⁷
Nor had that scene of ampler majesty                            95
Than gems or gold, the varying roof of heaven
And the green earth lost in his heart its claims
To love and wonder; he would linger long
In lonesome vales, making the wild his home,
Until the doves and squirrels would partake                    100
From his innocuous hand his bloodless food,⁸
Lured by the gentle meaning of his looks,
And the wild antelope, that starts whene'er
The dry leaf rustles in the brake,⁹ suspend
Her timid steps to gaze upon a form                            105
More graceful than her own.

               His wandering step,
Obedient to high thoughts, has visited
The awful ruins of the days of old:
Athens, and Tyre, and Balbec, and the waste
Where stood Jerusalem, the fallen towers                       110
Of Babylon, the eternal pyramids,
Memphis and Thebes, and whatsoe'er of strange¹
Sculptured on alabaster obelisk,
Or jasper tomb, or mutilated sphynx,

5. Molten lava flows; the exact phrase appears in Southey's *Thalaba*, VI.15, but the significance possibly derives from Milton's *Paradise Lost*, X.562 and XII.41, where bituminous lakes are associated with Hell.
6. Crowded with (see *Paradise Lost*, I.797).
7. Olivine, a greenish semi-precious stone.
8. The Poet, like Shelley, is a vegetarian.
9. A thicket of bushes, brushwood, or briers.
1. The unusual or the mysterious (a noun).

Dark Æthiopia in her desert hills                             115
Conceals. Among the ruined temples there,
Stupendous columns, and wild images
Of more than man, where marble dæmons[2] watch
The Zodiac's brazen mystery, and dead men
Hang their mute thoughts on the mute walls around,           120
He lingered, poring on memorials
Of the world's youth, through the long burning day
Gazed on those speechless shapes, nor, when the moon
Filled the mysterious halls with floating shades
Suspended he that task, but ever gazed                       125
And gazed, till meaning on his vacant mind
Flashed like strong inspiration, and he saw
The thrilling secrets of the birth of time.[3]

 Meanwhile an Arab maiden brought his food,
Her daily portion, from her father's tent,                   130
And spread her matting for his couch, and stole
From duties and repose to tend his steps:—
Enamoured, yet not daring for deep awe
To speak her love:—and watched his nightly sleep,
Sleepless herself, to gaze upon his lips                     135
Parted in slumber, whence the regular breath
Of innocent dreams arose: then, when red morn
Made paler the pale moon, to her cold home
Wildered,[4] and wan, and panting, she returned.

 The Poet wandering on, through Arabie                       140
And Persia, and the wild Carmanian waste,
And o'er the aërial mountains which pour down
Indus and Oxus from their icy caves,
In joy and exultation held his way;[5]
Till in the vale of Cashmire, far within                     145
Its loneliest dell, where odorous plants entwine
Beneath the hollow rocks a natural bower,
Beside a sparkling rivulet he stretched
His languid limbs. A vision on his sleep
There came, a dream of hopes that never yet                  150
Had flushed his cheek. He dreamed a veiled maid

2. Intermediate spirits with ability to communicate between the gods and men (from Plato and Greek mythology).
3. The Poet's journey in lines 106–28 carries him to the sites of great civilizations of the past in search of knowledge; he moves backward in time from the Greeks to the Phoenicians (Tyre and Balbec or Heliopolis), the Jews, the Babylonians, the Egyptians (Memphis and Thebes), and finally to Ethiopia, which the French writer Volney in his *Ruins of Empire* (1791) described as the "cradle of the sciences." In the temple of Dendera in Upper Egypt, the gods were arranged within the pattern of the Zodiac.
4. Lost or perplexed.
5. The Poet journeys eastward through Arabia, Persia, the Desert of Karmin (southeast Iran), across the Hindu Kush Mountains (the Indian Caucasus of *Prometheus Unbound*) and the source of the rivers Indus and Oxus, to the fabled Vale of Kashmir in northwest India (see *Prometheus Unbound*, II.i).

Sate near him, talking in low solemn tones.
Her voice was like the voice of his own soul
Heard in the calm of thought; its music long,
Like woven sounds of streams and breezes, held          155
His inmost sense suspended in its web
Of many-coloured woof and shifting hues.
Knowledge and truth and virtue were her theme,
And lofty hopes of divine liberty,
Thoughts the most dear to him, and poesy,          160
Herself a poet. Soon the solemn mood
Of her pure mind kindled through all her frame
A permeating fire: wild numbers then
She raised, with voice stifled in tremulous sobs
Subdued by its own pathos: her fair hands          165
Were bare alone, sweeping from some strange harp
Strange symphony, and in their branching veins
The eloquent blood told an ineffable tale.
The beating of her heart was heard to fill
The pauses of her music, and her breath          170
Tumultuously accorded with those fits
Of intermitted song. Sudden she rose,
As if her heart impatiently endured
Its bursting burthen: at the sound he turned,
And saw by the warm light of their own life          175
Her glowing limbs beneath the sinuous veil
Of woven wind, her outspread arms now bare,
Her dark locks floating in the breath of night,
Her beamy bending eyes, her parted lips
Outstretched, and pale, and quivering eagerly.          180
His strong heart sunk and sickened with excess
Of love. He reared his shuddering limbs and quelled
His gasping breath, and spread his arms to meet
Her panting bosom: . . . she drew back a while,
Then, yielding to the irresistible joy,          185
With frantic gesture and short breathless cry
Folded his frame in her dissolving arms.
Now blackness veiled his dizzy eyes, and night
Involved[6] and swallowed up the vision; sleep,
Like a dark flood suspended in its course,          190
Rolled back its impulse on his vacant brain.

Roused by the shock he started from his trance—
The cold white light of morning, the blue moon
Low in the west, the clear and garish hills,
The distinct valley and the vacant woods,          195
Spread round him where he stood. Whither have fled
The hues of heaven that canopied his bower
Of yesternight? The sounds that soothed his sleep,

6. Wrapped up, obscured.

The mystery and the majesty of Earth,
The joy, the exultation? His wan eyes                    200
Gaze on the empty scene as vacantly
As ocean's moon looks on the moon in heaven.
The spirit of sweet human love has sent
A vision to the sleep of him who spurned
Her choicest gifts. He eagerly pursues                   205
Beyond the realms of dream that fleeting shade;
He overleaps the bounds. Alas! alas!
Were limbs, and breath, and being intertwined
Thus treacherously? Lost, lost, for ever lost,
In the wide pathless desart of dim sleep,                210
That beautiful shape! Does the dark gate of death
Conduct to thy mysterious paradise,
O Sleep? Does the bright arch of rainbow clouds,
And pendent mountains seen in the calm lake,
Lead only to a black and watery depth,                   215
While death's blue vault, with loathliest vapours hung,
Where every shade which the foul grave exhales
Hides its dead eye from the detested day,
Conduct, O Sleep, to thy delightful realms?
This doubt with sudden tide flowed on his heart,         220
The insatiate hope which it awakened, stung
His brain even like despair.


                              While day-light held
The sky, the Poet kept mute conference
With his still soul. At night the passion came,
Like the fierce fiend of a distempered dream,            225
And shook him from his rest, and led him forth
Into the darkness.—As an eagle grasped
In folds of the green serpent, feels her breast
Burn with the poison, and precipitates[7]
Through night and day, tempest, and calm, and cloud,     230
Frantic with dizzying anguish, her blind flight
O'er the wide aëry wilderness: thus driven
By the bright shadow of that lovely dream,
Beneath the cold glare of the desolate night,
Through tangled swamps and deep precipitous dells,       235
Startling with careless step the moon-light snake,
He fled. Red morning dawned upon his flight,
Shedding the mockery of its vital hues
Upon his cheek of death. He wandered on
Till vast Aornos seen from Petra's steep                 240
Hung o'er the low horizon like a cloud;
Through Balk, and where the desolated tombs
Of Parthian kings scatter to every wind

7. Hastens.

Their wasting dust, wildly he wandered on,[8]
Day after day, a weary waste of hours,                            245
Bearing within his life the brooding care
That ever fed on its decaying flame.
And now his limbs were lean; his scattered hair
Sered by the autumn of strange suffering
Sung dirges in the wind; his listless hand                        250
Hung like dead bone within its withered skin;
Life, and the lustre that consumed it, shone
As in a furnace burning secretly
From his dark eyes alone. The cottagers,
Who ministered with human charity                                 255
His human wants, beheld with wondering awe
Their fleeting visitant. The mountaineer,
Encountering on some dizzy precipice
That spectral form, deemed that the Spirit of wind
With lightning eyes, and eager breath, and feet                   260
Disturbing not the drifted snow, had paused
In its career: the infant would conceal
His troubled visage in his mother's robe
In terror at the glare of those wild eyes,
To remember their strange light in many a dream                   265
Of after-times; but youthful maidens, taught
By nature, would interpret half the woe
That wasted him, would call him with false names
Brother, and friend, would press his pallid hand
At parting, and watch, dim through tears, the path                270
Of his departure from their father's door.


    At length upon the lone Chorasmian shore
He paused, a wide and melancholy waste
Of putrid marshes. A strong impulse urged

---

8. The Poet flees from Kashmir to the northwest into what is now Afghanistan and then into
the central Asian areas that in classical times (the geographical terms of which Shelley
employs) were Persian provinces; some of these areas were later parts of the former Soviet
Union. *Aornos* (240) was a mountain fortress on the upper Indus River captured by Alexander
the Great; its name means "without birds." *Petra* (240), the Sogdian Rock, is part of the
Pamir Range in Tajikistan. *Balk* (242), the ancient Persian province of Bactria, was south
of the River Oxus (now Amu Darya). Though at some periods Bactria and Parthia (which
was to the southwest, in the heartland of modern Iran) were distinct provinces, after the
decline of the post-Alexandrian Seleucid empire, a strong independent Parthian kingdom
spread over the region; its kings were buried at the city of Nysa (modern Nisa) in Bactria
proper. The Chorasmia was the swampy region between the Caspian and the Aral Sea, but
here the latter body of water seems intended; in classical times the Oxus flowed into the
Aral Sea.
    If we understand the Poet to embark on the Aral Sea, his shallop (a small open boat) would
be carried by a supernatural impulse up the Oxus to its headwaters in the Hindu Kush
Mountains (see note to 144). In Shelley's day the scientist Buffon and others believed that
the Hindu Kush (Indian Caucasus) region was the cradle of the human race. Several of
Shelley's geographical terms (especially *Chorasmian*, 272, and *Caucasus*, 353, 377) are ambiguous. If the Poet embarked on the Caspian Sea and ended up in the western Caucasus
Mountains, between the Caspian and the Black Sea, his journey would end somewhere near
the traditional site of the Garden of Eden (see Luther L. Scales, Jr., *KSJ* 21–22 [1972–73]:
137–39). Thus Shelley may have used the ambiguous names to combine biblical legend with
contemporary science.

His steps to the sea-shore. A swan was there,                       275
Beside a sluggish stream among the reeds.
It rose as he approached, and with strong wings
Scaling the upward sky, bent its bright course
High over the immeasurable main.
His eyes pursued its flight.—"Thou hast a home,                     280
Beautiful bird; thou voyagest to thine home,
Where thy sweet mate will twine her downy neck
With thine, and welcome thy return with eyes
Bright in the lustre of their own fond joy.
And what am I that I should linger here,                             285
With voice far sweeter than thy dying notes,
Spirit more vast than thine, frame more attuned
To beauty, wasting these surpassing powers
In the deaf air, to the blind earth, and heaven
That echoes not my thoughts?" A gloomy smile                        290
Of desperate hope convulsed his curling lips.[9]
For sleep, he knew, kept most relentlessly
Its precious charge, and silent death exposed,
Faithless perhaps as sleep, a shadowy lure,
With doubtful smile mocking its own strange charms.                 295

   Startled by his own thoughts he looked around.
There was no fair fiend[1] near him, not a sight
Or sound of awe but in his own deep mind.
A little shallop floating near the shore
Caught the impatient wandering of his gaze.                         300
It had been long abandoned, for its sides
Gaped wide with many a rift, and its frail joints
Swayed with the undulations of the tide.
A restless impulse urged him to embark
And meet lone Death on the drear ocean's waste;                     305
For well he knew that mighty Shadow loves
The slimy caverns of the populous deep.

   The day was fair and sunny; sea and sky
Drank its inspiring radiance, and the wind
Swept strongly from the shore, blackening the waves.                310
Following his eager soul, the wanderer
Leaped in the boat, he spread his cloak aloft
On the bare mast, and took his lonely seat,
And felt the boat speed o'er the tranquil sea
Like a torn cloud before the hurricane.                             315

   As one that in a silver vision floats
Obedient to the sweep of odorous winds

---

9. Shelley corrected "wrinkled his quivering lips" to the reading given here in Leigh Hunt's presentation copy of the *Alastor* volume now at the University of California at Santa Barbara Library.
1. The Poet fears he has been tempted to suicide (lines 285–95) by a seductive "fiend" external to his mind.

Upon resplendent clouds, so rapidly
Along the dark and ruffled waters fled
The straining boat.—A whirlwind swept it on,                    320
With fierce gusts and precipitating force,
Through the white ridges of the chafed sea.
The waves arose. Higher and higher still
Their fierce necks writhed beneath the tempest's scourge
Like serpents struggling in a vulture's grasp.                  325
Calm and rejoicing in the fearful war
Of wave ruining[2] on wave, and blast on blast
Descending, and black flood on whirlpool driven
With dark obliterating course, he sate:
As if their genii were the ministers                            330
Appointed to conduct him to the light
Of those beloved eyes, the Poet sate
Holding the steady helm. Evening came on,
The beams of sunset hung their rainbow hues
High 'mid the shifting domes of sheeted spray                   335
That canopied his path o'er the waste deep;
Twilight, ascending slowly from the east,
Entwin'd in duskier wreaths her braided locks
O'er the fair front and radiant eyes of day;
Night followed, clad with stars. On every side                 340
More horribly the multitudinous streams
Of ocean's mountainous waste to mutual war
Rushed in dark tumult thundering, as to mock
The calm and spangled sky. The little boat
Still fled before the storm; still fled, like foam             345
Down the steep cataract of a wintry river;
Now pausing on the edge of the riven wave;
Now leaving far behind the bursting mass
That fell, convulsing ocean. Safely fled—
As if that frail and wasted human form,                        350
Had been an elemental god.
                              At midnight
The moon arose: and lo! the etherial[3] cliffs
Of Caucasus, whose icy summits shone
Among the stars like sunlight, and around
Whose cavern'd base the whirlpools and the waves               355
Bursting and eddying irresistibly
Rage and resound for ever.—Who shall save?—
The boat fled on,—the boiling torrent drove,—
The crags closed round with black and jagged arms,
The shattered mountain overhung the sea,                       360
And faster still, beyond all human speed,
Suspended on the sweep of the smooth wave,
The little boat was driven. A cavern there
Yawned, and amid its slant and winding depths

2. Bursting.
3. Rising high in the air.

Ingulphed the rushing sea. The boat fled on                    365
With unrelaxing speed.—"Vision and Love!"
The Poet cried aloud, "I have beheld
The path of thy departure. Sleep and death
Shall not divide us long!"

                          The boat pursued
The windings of the cavern. Day-light shone               370
At length upon that gloomy river's flow;
Now, where the fiercest war among the waves
Is calm, on the unfathomable stream
The boat moved slowly. Where the mountain, riven,
Exposed those black depths to the azure sky,            375
Ere yet the flood's enormous volume fell
Even to the base of Caucasus, with sound
That shook the everlasting rocks, the mass
Filled with one whirlpool all that ample chasm;
Stair above stair the eddying waters rose,               380
Circling immeasurably fast, and laved
With alternating dash the knarled roots
Of mighty trees, that stretched their giant arms
In darkness over it. I' the midst was left,
Reflecting, yet distorting every cloud,                  385
A pool of treacherous and tremendous calm.
Seized by the sway of the ascending stream,
With dizzy swiftness, round, and round, and round,
Ridge after ridge the straining boat arose,
Till on the verge of the extremest curve,                390
Where, through an opening of the rocky bank,
The waters overflow, and a smooth spot
Of glassy quiet mid those battling tides
Is left, the boat paused shuddering.—Shall it sink
Down the abyss? Shall the reverting stress               395
Of that resistless gulph embosom it?
Now shall it fall?—A wandering stream of wind,
Breathed from the west, has caught the expanded sail,
And, lo! with gentle motion, between banks
Of mossy slope, and on a placid stream,                  400
Beneath a woven grove it sails, and, hark!
The ghastly torrent mingles its far roar,
With the breeze murmuring in the musical woods.
Where the embowering trees recede, and leave
A little space of green expanse, the cove                405
Is closed by meeting banks, whose yellow flowers
For ever gaze on their own drooping eyes,[4]
Reflected in the crystal calm. The wave
Of the boat's motion marred their pensive task,
Which nought but vagrant bird, or wanton wind,           410
Or falling spear-grass, or their own decay

4. The narcissi recall the legend of the Greek youth who pined away for self-love.

Had e'er disturbed before. The Poet longed
To deck with their bright hues his withered hair,
But on his heart its solitude returned,
And he forbore. Not the strong impulse hid          415
In those flushed cheeks, bent eyes, and shadowy frame,
Had yet performed its ministry: it hung
Upon his life, as lightning in a cloud
Gleams, hovering ere it vanish, ere the floods
Of night close over it.
                           The noonday sun          420
Now shone upon the forest, one vast mass
Of mingling shade, whose brown magnificence
A narrow vale embosoms. There, huge caves,
Scooped in the dark base of their aëry rocks
Mocking[5] its moans, respond and roar for ever.          425
The meeting boughs and implicated[6] leaves
Wove twilight o'er the Poet's path, as led
By love, or dream, or god, or mightier Death,
He sought in Nature's dearest haunt, some bank,
Her cradle, and his sepulchre. More dark          430
And dark the shades accumulate. The oak,
Expanding its immense and knotty arms,
Embraces the light beech. The pyramids
Of the tall cedar overarching, frame
Most solemn domes within, and far below,          435
Like clouds suspended in an emerald sky,
The ash and the acacia floating hang
Tremulous and pale. Like restless serpents, clothed
In rainbow and in fire, the parasites,
Starred with ten thousand blossoms, flow around          440
The grey trunks, and, as gamesome infants' eyes,
With gentle meanings, and most innocent wiles,
Fold their beams round the hearts of those that love,
These twine their tendrils with the wedded boughs
Uniting their close union; the woven leaves          445
Make net-work of the dark blue light of day,
And the night's noontide clearness, mutable
As shapes in the weird clouds. Soft mossy lawns
Beneath these canopies extend their swells,
Fragrant with perfumed herbs, and eyed with blooms          450
Minute yet beautiful. One darkest glen
Sends from its woods of musk-rose, twined with jasmine,
A soul-dissolving odour, to invite
To some more lovely mystery. Through the dell,
Silence and Twilight here, twin-sisters, keep          455
Their noonday watch, and sail among the shades,
Like vaporous shapes half seen; beyond, a well,
Dark, gleaming, and of most translucent wave,

---

5. Imitating or mimicking; its: the *forest* (line 421).
6. Intertwined.

Images all the woven boughs above,
And each depending leaf, and every speck                    460
Of azure sky, darting between their chasms;
Nor aught else in the liquid mirror laves
Its portraiture, but some inconstant star
Between one foliaged lattice twinkling fair,
Or, painted bird, sleeping beneath the moon,                465
Or gorgeous insect floating motionless,
Unconscious of the day, ere yet his wings
Have spread their glories to the gaze of noon.

    Hither the Poet came. His eyes beheld
Their own wan light through the reflected lines             470
Of his thin hair, distinct in the dark depth
Of that still fountain; as the human heart,
Gazing in dreams over the gloomy grave,
Sees its own treacherous likeness there. He heard
The motion of the leaves, the grass that sprung            475
Startled and glanced and trembled even to feel
An unaccustomed presence, and the sound
Of the sweet brook that from the secret springs
Of that dark fountain rose. A Spirit seemed
To stand beside him—clothed in no bright robes            480
Of shadowy silver or enshrining light,
Borrowed from aught the visible world affords
Of grace, or majesty, or mystery;—
But, undulating woods, and silent well,
And leaping rivulet, and evening gloom                     485
Now deepening the dark shades, for speech assuming
Held commune with him, as if he and it
Were all that was,—only . . . when his regard
Was raised by intense pensiveness, . . . two eyes,
Two starry eyes, hung in the gloom of thought,             490
And seemed with their serene and azure smiles
To beckon him.

            Obedient to the light
That shone within his soul, he went, pursuing
The windings of the dell.—The rivulet
Wanton and wild, through many a green ravine               495
Beneath the forest flowed. Sometimes it fell
Among the moss with hollow harmony
Dark and profound. Now on the polished stones
It danced; like childhood laughing as it went:
Then, through the plain in tranquil wanderings crept,      500
Reflecting every herb and drooping bud
That overhung its quietness.—"O stream!
Whose source is inaccessibly profound,
Whither do thy mysterious waters tend?
Thou imagest my life. Thy darksome stillness,             505
Thy dazzling waves, thy loud and hollow gulphs,

Thy searchless[7] fountain, and invisible course
Have each their type in me: and the wide sky,
And measureless ocean may declare as soon
What oozy cavern or what wandering cloud                      510
Contains thy waters, as the universe
Tell where these living thoughts reside, when stretched
Upon thy flowers my bloodless limbs shall waste
I' the passing wind!"
                              Beside the grassy shore
Of the small stream he went; he did impress                   515
On the green moss his tremulous step, that caught
Strong shuddering from his burning limbs. As one
Roused by some joyous madness from the couch
Of fever, he did move; yet, not like him,
Forgetful of the grave, where, when the flame                 520
Of his frail exultation shall be spent,
He must descend. With rapid steps he went
Beneath the shade of trees, beside the flow
Of the wild babbling rivulet; and now
The forest's solemn canopies were changed                     525
For the uniform and lightsome[8] evening sky.
Grey rocks did peep from the spare moss, and stemmed
The struggling brook: tall spires of windlestrae[9]
Threw their thin shadows down the rugged slope,
And nought but knarled stumps[1] of antient pines             530
Branchless and blasted, clenched with grasping roots
The unwilling soil. A gradual change was here,
Yet ghastly. For, as fast years flow away,
The smooth brow gathers, and the hair grows thin
And white, and where irradiate dewy eyes                      535
Had shone, gleam stony orbs:—so from his steps
Bright flowers departed, and the beautiful shade
Of the green groves, with all their odorous winds
And musical motions. Calm, he still pursued
The stream, that with a larger volume now                     540
Rolled through the labyrinthine dell; and there
Fretted a path through its descending curves
With its wintry speed. On every side now rose
Rocks, which, in unimaginable forms,
Lifted their black and barren pinnacles                       545
In the light of evening, and its precipice[2]
Obscuring the ravine, disclosed above,

7. Undiscoverable.
8. Luminous, evidently from light reflected by the atmosphere after sunset.
9. Dry stalks left from flowering plants after blossoms have died.
1. We have conjecturally emended the first "roots" of lines 530–31 to "stumps." The first edition's reading of "knarled (gnarled) roots" that clench the soil with "grasping roots" has long been considered an error, and Shelley's correction of "roots" to "stumps" in his translation of Homer's "Hymm to Mercury" (MYR: Shelley V, 110 and 182 n) provides the evidence for our emendation.
2. Headlong descent—its refers to dell, line 541.

Mid toppling stones, black gulphs and yawning caves,
Whose windings gave ten thousand various tongues
To the loud stream. Lo! where the pass expands          550
Its stony jaws, the abrupt mountain breaks,
And seems, with its accumulated crags,
To overhang the world: for wide expand
Beneath the wan stars and descending moon
Islanded seas, blue mountains, mighty streams,          555
Dim tracts and vast, robed in the lustrous gloom
Of leaden-coloured even, and fiery hills
Mingling their flames with twilight, on the verge
Of the remote horizon. The near scene,
In naked and severe simplicity,                         560
Made contrast with the universe. A pine,[3]
Rock-rooted, stretched athwart the vacancy
Its swinging boughs, to each inconstant blast
Yielding one only response, at each pause
In most familiar cadence, with the howl                 565
The thunder and the hiss of homeless streams
Mingling its solemn song, whilst the broad river,
Foaming and hurrying o'er its rugged path,
Fell into that immeasurable void
Scattering its waters to the passing winds.             570

   Yet the grey precipice and solemn pine
And torrent, were not all;—one silent nook
Was there. Even on the edge of that vast mountain,
Upheld by knotty roots and fallen rocks,
It overlooked in its serenity                           575
The dark earth, and the bending vault of stars.
It was a tranquil spot, that seemed to smile
Even in the lap of horror. Ivy clasped
The fissured stones with its entwining arms,
And did embower with leaves for ever green,             580
And berries dark, the smooth and even space
Of its inviolated floor, and here
The children of the autumnal whirlwind bore,
In wanton sport, those bright leaves, whose decay,
Red, yellow, or etherially pale,                        585
Rivals the pride of summer. 'Tis the haunt
Of every gentle wind, whose breath can teach
The wilds to love tranquillity. One step,
One human step alone, has ever broken
The stillness of its solitude:—one voice                590
Alone inspired its echoes;—even that voice
Which hither came, floating among the winds,
And led the loveliest among human forms

---

3. In Shelley's poetry pine trees recur as emblems of human hopes and symbolize the persistence of life in the face of adversity.

To make their wild haunts the depository
Of all the grace and beauty that endued                          595
Its motions, render up its majesty,
Scatter its music on the unfeeling storm,
And to the damp leaves and blue cavern mould,
Nurses of rainbow flowers and branching moss,
Commit the colours of that varying cheek,                        600
That snowy breast, those dark and drooping eyes.

    The dim and horned moon[4] hung low, and poured
A sea of lustre on the horizon's verge
That overflowed its mountains. Yellow mist
Filled the unbounded atmosphere, and drank                       605
Wan moonlight even to fulness: not a star
Shone, not a sound was heard; the very winds,
Danger's grim playmates, on that precipice
Slept, clasped in his embrace.—O, storm of death!
Whose sightless[5] speed divides this sullen night:              610
And thou, colossal Skeleton, that, still
Guiding its irresistible career
In thy devastating omnipotence,
Art king of this frail world, from the red field
Of slaughter, from the reeking hospital,                         615
The patriot's sacred couch, the snowy bed
Of innocence, the scaffold and the throne,
A mighty voice invokes thee. Ruin calls
His brother Death. A rare and regal prey
He hath prepared, prowling around the world;                     620
Glutted with which thou mayst repose, and men
Go to their graves like flowers or creeping worms,
Nor ever more offer at thy dark shrine
The unheeded tribute of a broken heart.

    When on the threshold of the green recess              625
The wanderer's footsteps fell, he knew that death
Was on him. Yet a little, ere it fled,
Did he resign his high and holy soul
To images of the majestic past,
That paused within his passive being now,                        630
Like winds that bear sweet music, when they breathe
Through some dim latticed chamber. He did place
His pale lean hand upon the rugged trunk
Of the old pine. Upon an ivied stone
Reclined his languid head, his limbs did rest,                   635
Diffused and motionless, on the smooth brink
Of that obscurest chasm;—and thus he lay,

4. The moon is crescent-shaped with the points rising, as in Coleridge's *Dejection: An Ode*: "the new Moon / With the old Moon in her arms" (see also "The Triumph of Life," lines 79–85).
5. Some critics have glossed this word as "invisible," but "blind" or "unseeing" seems to be the more likely meaning; like the charioteers in *Hellas* (lines 711ff.) and "The Triumph of Life" (lines 86–106), Death is blind in not apprehending moral distinctions.

Surrendering to their final impulses
The hovering powers of life. Hope and despair,
The torturers, slept; no mortal pain or fear                    640
Marred his repose, the influxes of sense,
And his own being unalloyed by pain,
Yet feebler and more feeble, calmly fed
The stream of thought, till he lay breathing there
At peace, and faintly smiling:—his last sight                   645
Was the great moon, which o'er the western line
Of the wide world her mighty horn suspended,
With whose dun[6] beams inwoven darkness seemed
To mingle. Now upon the jagged hills
It rests, and still as the divided frame                        650
Of the vast meteor[7] sunk, the Poet's blood,
That ever beat in mystic sympathy
With nature's ebb and flow, grew feebler still:
And when two lessening points of light alone
Gleamed through the darkness,[8] the alternate gasp             655
Of his faint respiration scarce did stir
The stagnate night:—till the minutest ray
Was quenched, the pulse yet lingered in his heart.
It paused—it fluttered. But when heaven remained
Utterly black, the murky shades involved                        660
An image, silent, cold, and motionless,
As their own voiceless earth and vacant air.
Even as a vapour[9] fed with golden beams
That ministered[1] on sunlight, ere the west
Eclipses it, was now that wonderous frame—                      665
No sense, no motion, no divinity—
A fragile lute, on whose harmonious strings
The breath of heaven did wander—a bright stream
Once fed with many-voiced waves—a dream
Of youth, which night and time have quenched for ever,          670
Still, dark, and dry, and unremembered now.

   O, for Medea's[2] wondrous alchemy,
Which wheresoe'er it fell made the earth gleam
With bright flowers, and the wintry boughs exhale
From vernal blooms fresh fragrance! O, that God,                675
Profuse of poisons, would concede the chalice
Which but one living man[3] has drained, who now,

6. Brownish; as the moon sinks lower, its light is more refracted and turns from a whitish to a
   dark yellow or orange color.
7. The term originally meant any phenomenon (including weather) within the earth's atmosphere, whose outer limits were thought to be marked by the moon.
8. As the moon sets, its center sinks first below the horizon, eventually leaving the tips of the
   crescent as *two lessening points of light* (654).
9. Cloud.
1. Attended, as a servant.
2. Medea, the sorceress of Greek legend and tragedy, brewed a magic potion to rejuvenate
   Aeson (Jason's father): when she spilled some on the ground, flowers and grass sprang up.
   (For an influential depiction of this incident, see Ovid, *Metamorphoses*, VII.275ff.)
3. Ahasuerus, the Wandering Jew, doomed to eternal life, who appears also in *Queen Mab*
   (VII.66ff.) and *Hellas* (lines 137–85, 638–40, 738ff.), among other works by Shelley.

Vessel of deathless wrath, a slave that feels
No proud exemption in the blighting curse
He bears, over the world wanders for ever, 680
Lone as incarnate death! O, that the dream
Of dark magician[4] in his visioned cave,
Raking the cinders of a crucible
For life and power, even when his feeble hand
Shakes in its last decay, were the true law 685
Of this so lovely world! But thou art fled
Like some frail exhalation; which the dawn
Robes in its golden beams,—ah! thou hast fled!
The brave, the gentle, and the beautiful,
The child of grace and genius. Heartless things 690
Are done and said i' the world, and many worms
And beasts and men live on, and mighty Earth
From sea and mountain, city and wilderness,
In vesper low or joyous orison,
Lifts still its solemn voice:—but thou art fled— 695
Thou canst no longer know or love the shapes
Of this phantasmal scene, who have to thee
Been purest ministers, who are, alas!
Now thou art not. Upon those pallid lips
So sweet even in their silence, on those eyes 700
That image sleep in death, upon that form
Yet safe from the worm's outrage, let no tear
Be shed—not even in thought. Nor, when those hues
Are gone, and those divinest lineaments,
Worn by the senseless[5] wind, shall live alone 705
In the frail pauses of this simple strain,
Let not high verse, mourning the memory
Of that which is no more, or painting's woe
Or sculpture, speak in feeble imagery
Their own cold powers. Art and eloquence, 710
And all the shews o' the world are frail and vain
To weep a loss that turns their lights to shade.
It is a woe too "deep for tears,"[6] when all
Is reft at once, when some surpassing Spirit,
Whose light adorned the world around it, leaves 715
Those who remain behind, not sobs or groans,
The passionate tumult of a clinging hope;
But pale despair and cold tranquillity,
Nature's vast frame, the web of human things,
Birth and the grave, that are not as they were. 720

4. An alchemist searching for the elixir of life and the power to change base metals into gold within a cave in which he sees visions.
5. Lacking sensation, insensate.
6. Wordsworth, Ode: Intimations of Immortality, line 203.

# Stanzas.—April, 1814.[1]

Away! the moor is dark beneath the moon,
    Rapid clouds have drank the last pale beam of even:
Away! the gathering winds will call the darkness soon,
    And profoundest midnight shroud the serene lights of heaven.

Pause not! The time is past! Every voice cries, Away!                    5
    Tempt not with one last tear thy friend's ungentle mood:
Thy lover's eye, so glazed and cold, dares not entreat thy stay:
    Duty and dereliction[2] guide thee back to solitude.

Away, away! to thy sad and silent home;
    Pour bitter tears on its desolated hearth;                          10
Watch the dim shades as like ghosts they go and come,
    And complicate strange webs of melancholy mirth.[3]

The leaves of wasted autumn woods shall float around thine head:
    The blooms of dewy spring shall gleam beneath thy feet:
But thy soul or this world must fade[4] in the frost that binds
        the dead,                                                       15
    Ere midnight's frown and morning's smile, ere thou and
        peace may meet.

The cloud shadows of midnight possess their own repose,
    For the weary winds are silent, or the moon is in the deep:
Some respite to its turbulence unresting ocean knows;
    Whatever moves, or toils, or grieves, hath its appointed sleep.     20

Thou in the grave shalt rest—yet till the phantoms flee
    Which that house and heath and garden made dear to
        thee erewhile,[5]
Thy remembrance, and repentance, and deep musings are not free
    From the music of two voices and the light of one sweet smile.

# Mutability.[1]

We are as clouds that veil the midnight moon;
    How restlessly they speed, and gleam, and quiver,
Streaking the darkness radiantly!—yet soon
    Night closes round, and they are lost for ever:

1. Composed at Bracknell, a village west of London, in April 1814, this poem refers to Shelley's infatuation with Cornelia Boinville Turner, daughter of Shelley's friend Harriet Collins de Boinville and wife of Thomas Turner, a lawyer and protégé of William Godwin. It appeared as the third poem in the *Alastor* volume (1816).
2. The condition of being forsaken or abandoned.
3. Lines 9–12 signal the deterioration of Shelley's first marriage to Harriet Westbrook Shelley. *Complicate:* form in an intricate way.
4. If the soul is immortal, then the world will fade first.
5. A while before, formerly.
1. "Mutability," like "To Wordsworth," was published with *Alastor* (1816); no MSS survive for either poem and their actual dates of composition are unknown.

Or like forgotten lyres,[2] whose dissonant strings          5
    Give various response to each varying blast,
To whose frail frame no second motion brings
    One mood or modulation like the last.

We rest.—A dream has power to poison sleep;
    We rise.—One wandering thought pollutes the day;          10
We feel, conceive or reason, laugh or weep;
    Embrace fond woe, or cast our cares away:

It is the same!—For, be it joy or sorrow,
    The path of its departure still is free:
Man's yesterday may ne'er be like his morrow;          15
    Nought may endure but Mutability.

## To Wordsworth.[1]

Poet of Nature, thou hast wept to know
That things depart which never may return:
Childhood and youth, friendship and love's first glow,
Have fled like sweet dreams, leaving thee to mourn.
These common woes I feel. One loss is mine          5
Which thou too feel'st, yet I alone deplore.
Thou wert as a lone star, whose light did shine
On some frail bark in winter's midnight roar:
Thou hast like to a rock-built refuge stood
Above the blind and battling multitude:          10
In honoured poverty thy voice did weave
Songs consecrate to truth and liberty,—
Deserting these, thou leavest me to grieve,
Thus having been, that thou shouldst cease to be.

## HYMN TO INTELLECTUAL BEAUTY

Composed in the summer of 1816 during Shelley's stay with Byron on the
shores of Lake Geneva, the "Hymn" was drafted (with the fourth stanza
missing) into the notebook now designated Bodleian MS Shelley adds.
e.16, pp. 57–61 (BSM, XI). The following fall, Shelley sent a copy of the
poem to Leigh Hunt for publication in his weekly newspaper the Examiner.
After Hunt misplaced this copy (which remains lost), Shelley sent him
another, presumably reconstructed from his draft, and the poem appeared
in the Examiner for January 19, 1817. A clipping from the Examiner con-

---

2. Aeolian harps or wind lyres (see note to *Queen Mab*, I.52 and cf. *Alastor*, lines 41–49, 663–
    68).
1. This sonnet stands as Shelley's comment on the growing political and religious conservatism
    of both William Wordsworth (whom he knew only through his writings) and Wordsworth's
    friend Robert Southey (whom Shelley had known well during his stay at Keswick, Cumber-
    land, from November 1812 through January 1813). On September 14, 1814, Mary Shelley
    recorded in her journal: "Shelley . . . brings home Wordsworth's Excursion, of which we read
    a part, much disappointed. He is a slave."

taining two corrections of the "Hymn" in Shelley's hand is now located at Harvard University. These corrections (for lines 27 and 58), reproduced in photofacsimile in *MYR: Shelley*, V, 8–9, have been adopted in our text. A revised version of the "Hymn" that Shelley was unable to see through the press was printed, along with "Lines written among the Euganean Hills" and "Ozymandias," with *Rosalind and Helen* (1819).

A new wrinkle was introduced into the textual history of the "Hymn" in December 1976, when an old studded trunk that once belonged to Byron's friend Scrope Davies was discovered in the vaults of the Pall Mall branch of Barclay's Bank in London. Left more than 150 years earlier, when Davies hastily fled England to evade pressing gambling debts, the trunk included among its contents a notebook containing new versions of "Hymn" (in Mary Shelley's hand) and "Mont Blanc" (in Shelley's hand), as well as two previously unknown sonnets, "To Laughter" and "Upon the wandering winds" (both transcribed by Mary Shelley). Shelley left the notebook, perhaps unintentionally, with Byron in Geneva at the end of August 1816, shortly before returning to England. Presumably to restore the notebook to Shelley, Byron entrusted it to Davies, who returned to England only a few days after Shelley. For reasons that remain unknown, however, Davies retained the notebook. The Scrope Davies Notebook (*SDN*) is now located at the British Library. For the history of its discovery, see the essay by Judith Chernaik and Timothy Burnett in *RES* XXIX (Feb. 1978): 37–49. Our text is based on the corrected *Examiner* text, with selected substantive variants in *SDN* noted below. For the significance of some of these variants, see Michael O'Neill's essay in this volume (pp. 616–26). See the essay by Forest Pyle (pp. 663–69) for a detailed reading of the poem.

"Intellectual," as used in the title, means nonmaterial.

# Hymn to Intellectual Beauty

## 1.

The awful shadow of some unseen Power[1]
   Floats though unseen amongst us,—visiting
   This various world with as inconstant wing
As summer winds that creep from flower to flower.—
Like moonbeams that behind some piny mountain shower,          5
      It visits with inconstant glance
      Each human heart and countenance;
Like hues and harmonies of evening,—
      Like clouds in starlight widely spread,—
      Like memory of music fled,—                              10
      Like aught that for its grace may be
Dear, and yet dearer for its mystery.

---

1. This line in *SDN* reads "The Lovely shadow of some awful Power . . ."

2.

Spirit of BEAUTY, that dost[2] consecrate
    With thine own hues all thou dost shine upon
    Of human thought or form,—where art thou gone?        15
Why dost thou pass away and leave our state,
This dim vast vale of tears, vacant and desolate?
        Ask why the sunlight not forever
        Weaves rainbows o'er yon mountain river,
Why aught should fail and fade that once is shewn,        20
        Why fear and dream and death and birth
        Cast on the daylight of this earth
        Such gloom,—why man has such a scope
For love and hate,[3] despondency and hope?

3.

No voice from some sublimer world hath ever        25
    To sage or poet these responses given—
    Therefore the name of God and ghosts and Heaven,[4]
Remain the records of their[5] vain endeavour,
Frail spells—whose uttered charm might not avail to sever,
        From all we hear[6] and all we see,        30
        Doubt, chance, and mutability.
Thy light alone—like mist o'er mountains driven,
        Or music by the night wind sent
        Through strings of some still instrument,[7]
        Or moonlight on a midnight stream,        35
Gives grace and truth to life's unquiet dream.

4.

Love, Hope, and Self-esteem, like clouds depart
    And come, for some uncertain moments lent.
    Man were immortal, and omnipotent,
Didst thou, unknown and awful as thou art,[8]        40
Keep with thy glorious train firm state within his heart.[9]
        Thou messenger of sympathies,
        That wax and wane in lovers' eyes—
Thou—that to human thought[1] art nourishment,

---

2. SDN reads "Shadow" for *Spirit*. Although the draft reads "that dost" and the second person familiar form is correct in this situation, "doth" remains uncorrected in the *Examiner* text and appears also in SDN.
3. SDN reads "joy."
4. Shelley corrected this line in the *Examiner* from the printed reading: "Therefore the names of Demon, Ghost, and Heaven . . ."
5. Sage and poet (line 26).
6. SDN reads "feel."
7. The Aeolian harp or wind lyre. SDN reads "mute" for *still.*
8. I.e., "Man would be . . . If thou didst . . ."
9. Shelley's hyperbole in lines 39–41 derives from his belief in the primary importance of psychological, rather than chronological, time. In his note to *Queen Mab*, VIII.203–07, he asserts the perfectibility of the human sensibility and, therefore, the possibility of virtual (not literal) immortality.
1. SDN reads "the poet[']s thought" for *to human thought*.

Like darkness to a dying flame![2]                               45
Depart not as thy shadow came,
Depart not—lest the grave should be,
Like life and fear, a dark reality.


5.

While yet a boy I sought for ghosts, and sped
  Through many a listening chamber, cave and ruin,          50
  And starlight wood, with fearful steps pursuing
Hopes of high talk with the departed dead.[3]
  I called on poisonous names with which our youth is fed;[4]
    I was not heard—I saw them not—
    When musing deeply on the lot                           55
Of life, at that sweet time when winds are wooing
    All vital things that wake to bring
    News of buds[5] and blossoming,—
    Sudden, thy shadow fell on me;
I shrieked, and clasped my hands in extacy!                 60


6.

I vowed that I would dedicate my powers
  To thee and thine—have I not kept the vow?
  With beating heart and streaming eyes, even now
I call the phantoms of a thousand hours
Each from his voiceless grave: they have in visioned bowers  65
    Of studious zeal or love's[6] delight
    Outwatched with me the envious night—
They know that never joy illumed my brow
    Unlinked with hope that thou wouldst free
    This world from its dark slavery,                       70
    That thou—O awful LOVELINESS,
Wouldst give whate'er these words cannot express.


7.

The day becomes more solemn and serene
  When noon is past—there is a harmony
  In autumn, and a lustre in its sky,                       75
Which through the summer is not heard or seen,
As if it could not be, as if it had not been!
    Thus let thy power,[7] which like the truth
    Of nature on my passive youth

2. The Spirit Shelley invokes is said to nourish human thought as darkness nourishes a dying
   flame; i.e., the Spirit does not really feed human thought at all but sets off and calls attention
   to it because of its opposite, antithetical nature. This contrast is also found in "Mont Blanc"
   and "The Triumph of Life."
3. SDN reads "Hopes of strange converse with the storied dead."
4. Religious terms such as God, ghosts, and Heaven (line 27). SDN reads: "that false name with
   which our youth is fed / He heard me not. . . ."
5. Shelley corrected the Examiner text to read buds instead of "birds"; SDN also reads "buds."
6. SDN reads "lore's."
7. SDN reads "shade."

Descended, to my onward life supply                         80
   Its calm—to one who worships thee,
   And every form containing thee,
   Whom, Spirit fair, thy spells did bind
To fear[8] himself, and love all human kind.


# MONT BLANC

Composition on "Mont Blanc" began at the end of July 1816, when the
Shelleys and Claire Clairmont toured the magnificent countryside of the
Chamonix Valley, at the foot of Europe's highest mountain. Shelley com-
pleted drafting the poem sometime before the end of August in a notebook
now designated Bodleian MS Shelley adds. e.16, pp. 1–4 (*BSM*, XI).
"Mont Blanc" was first published in 1817, at the end of the Shelleys'
*History of a Six Weeks' Tour* (*HSW*; 1817).
    A previously unknown version of "Mont Blanc" in Shelley's hand was
discovered in December 1976 within the Scrope Davies Notebook (*SDN*),
for the background to which see the headnote to "Hymn to Intellectual
Beauty." After having lost the fair copy of "Mont Blanc" that he had prepared in *SDN*, Shelley presumably returned to his draft to generate the
text for *HSW*. There are significant differences between these two versions
of "Mont Blanc," and rather than conflate them into a single eclectic text,
we base our text on *HSW*, with selected substantive variants in *SDN* noted
below. See the essay by Michael O'Neill in this volume (pp. 616–26) for
a discussion of these variants.
    The actual scene of the poem—the place where Shelley stood when he
was inspired to write it—is on a bridge over the Arve River in the Valley
of Chamonix in Savoy, now southeastern France, not far from Geneva,
Switzerland. Shelley sees only the rushing river; he hears the falling of the
streams melting off the glacier, Mer de Glace, above; but he images to
himself—and in the poem—the snows and lightning storms, unseen and
unheard, at the upper reaches of the mountain that feed the glacier and
start the chain of Necessity that first destroys life as the glacier moves
down the mountain and then supports life as the River Arve and, later,
the River Rhone carry water and life to peoples far away (lines 100–26).
    One of Shelley's most challenging poems, both formally and philosoph-
ically, "Mont Blanc" has received a wealth of modern critical attention,
much of which has focused on questions of epistemology and language,
especially in terms of the human mind's understanding of itself in relation
to Nature and to any ultimate source of Power. As is also generally recognized, the subtitle of the poem, "Lines Written in the Vale of Chamouni," indicates that Shelley was responding to issues in Coleridge's
earlier "Hymn before Sun-rise, in the Vale of Chamouni" (1802), a poem
that credits God for the sublime wonders of the landscape. Charles H.
Vivian's "The One 'Mont Blanc' " (*KSJ* IV [1955]: 55–65) laid the foundation for the modern understanding of the poem, which was developed
further in Earl Wasserman's seminal reading in *The Subtler Language* (Baltimore, MD: Johns Hopkins University Press, 1959, pp. 195–240). For a

---

8. Revere, have respect for.

more recent approach to the complex issues engaged by "Mont Blanc,"
see the essay by William Keach in this volume (pp. 669–75).

## Mont Blanc

### LINES WRITTEN IN THE VALE OF CHAMOUNI[1]

#### I.

The everlasting[2] universe of things
Flows through the mind, and rolls its rapid waves,
Now dark—now glittering—now reflecting gloom—
Now lending splendour, where from secret springs
The source of human thought its tribute brings                    5
Of waters,—with a sound but half[3] its own,
Such as a feeble brook will oft assume
In the wild woods, among the mountains lone,
Where waterfalls around it leap for ever,
Where woods and winds contend, and a vast river                  10
Over its rocks ceaselessly bursts and raves.

#### II.

Thus thou, Ravine of Arve—dark, deep Ravine—
Thou many-coloured, many-voiced vale,
Over whose pines, and crags, and caverns sail
Fast cloud shadows and sunbeams: awful[4] scene,                 15
Where Power in likeness of the Arve comes down
From the ice gulphs that gird his secret throne,
Bursting through these dark mountains like the flame
Of lightning through the tempest;—thou dost lie,
Thy giant brood of pines[5] around thee clinging,                20
Children of elder time, in whose devotion
The chainless[6] winds still come and ever came
To drink their odours, and their mighty swinging
To hear—an old and solemn harmony;
Thine earthly rainbows stretched across the sweep                25
Of the etherial waterfall, whose veil
Robes some unsculptured image;[7] the strange sleep
Which when the voices of the desart fail[8]
Wraps all in its own deep eternity;—

1. Instead of this subtitle, SDN reads "Scene — Pont Pellisier in the vale of Servox."
2. SDN reads "In day the eternal."
3. SDN reads "not all" for *but half.*
4. Inspiring awe, reverence.
5. Shelley uses the pine tree in several poems to symbolize the persistence of human values in the face of obstacles. (But see lines 109–11, in which that resistance is overcome.)
6. SDN reads "charmed."
7. The image that appears in the rocks behind the veil of the waterfall has not been sculptured by man.
8. This line is followed in SDN by the following two lines: "And its hues wane, doth blend them all & steep / Their periods in its own eternity. . . ."

Thy caverns echoing to the Arve's commotion,                    30
A loud, lone sound no other sound can tame;
Thou art pervaded with that ceaseless motion,
Thou art the path of that unresting sound—
Dizzy[9] Ravine! and when I gaze on thee
I seem as in a trance sublime[1] and strange                    35
To muse on my own separate phantasy,[2]
My own, my human mind, which passively
Now renders and receives fast influencings,
Holding an unremitting[3] interchange
With the clear universe of things around;                       40
One legion of wild thoughts, whose wandering wings
Now float above thy darkness, and now rest
Where that or thou art no unbidden guest,[4]
In the still cave of the witch Poesy,
Seeking among the shadows[5] that pass by                       45
Ghosts of all things that are, some shade of thee,
Some phantom, some faint image; till the breast
From which they fled recalls them,[6] thou art there!

## III.

Some say that gleams of a remoter world
Visit the soul in sleep,—that death is slumber,                 50
And that its shapes the busy thoughts outnumber
Of those who wake and live.—I look on high;
Has some unknown omnipotence unfurled
The veil of life and death? or do I lie
In dream, and does the mightier world of sleep                  55
Spread far around and inaccessibly
Its circles? For the very spirit fails,
Driven like a homeless cloud from steep to steep
That vanishes among the viewless gales!
Far, far above, piercing the infinite sky,                      60
Mont Blanc appears,—still, snowy, and serene—
Its subject mountains their unearthly forms
Pile around it, ice and rock; broad vales between
Of frozen floods, unfathomable deeps,
Blue as the overhanging heaven, that spread                     65
And wind among the accumulated steeps;
A desert[7] peopled by the storms alone,
Save when the eagle brings some hunter's bone,

9. SDN reads "Mighty."
1. SDN reads "vision deep" for *trance sublime.*
2. The phrase *my own separate phantasy* is in apposition to *My own, my human mind* (line 37) and *One legion of wild thoughts* (line 41). In SDN, *separate* is canceled and replaced with "various." And line 41 begins "A legion of swift thoughts."
3. SDN reads "unforeseeing."
4. This entire line is omitted in SDN.
5. In apposition to *Ghosts* (line 46).
6. *breast . . . fled:* The *Ghosts of all things that are* found in the imaginative mind must come from a source, here anthropomorphized as a *breast*; the poet explores the nature of this source in lines 49–57. *they . . . them* refers to *shadows . . . Ghosts* (lines 45–46).
7. SDN reads "Vast deserts."

And the wolf tracks[8] her there—how hideously
Its shapes[9] are heaped around! rude, bare, and high,                    70
Ghastly, and scarred, and riven.—Is this the scene
Where the old Earthquake-dæmon[1] taught her young
Ruin? Were these their toys? or did a sea
Of fire, envelope once this silent snow?
None can reply—all seems eternal now.                                    75
The wilderness has a mysterious tongue
Which teaches awful doubt,[2] or faith so mild,
So solemn,[3] so serene, that man may be
But for such faith[4] with nature reconciled;
Thou hast a voice, great Mountain, to repeal                             80
Large codes of fraud and woe; not understood
By all, but which the wise, and great, and good
Interpret, or make felt, or deeply feel.

### IV.

The fields, the lakes, the forests, and the streams,
Ocean, and all the living things that dwell                              85
Within the dædal[5] earth; lightning, and rain,
Earthquake, and fiery flood, and hurricane,
The torpor of the year when feeble dreams
Visit the hidden buds, or dreamless sleep
Holds every future leaf and flower;—the bound                           90
With which from that detested trance they leap;
The works and ways of man, their death and birth,
And that of him and all that his may be;
All things that move and breathe with toil and sound
Are born and die; revolve, subside and swell.                           95
Power dwells apart in its tranquillity
Remote, serene,[6] and inaccessible:
And *this*,[7] the naked countenance of earth,
On which I gaze, even these primæval mountains

8. Pursues, traces. SDN reads "watches her" for *tracks her there.*
9. SDN reads "rocks."
1. Daemons, in Greek mythology, are spirits intermediate between the gods and men, usually personifying natural forces.
2. Reverent open-mindedness.
3. SDN reads "simple."
4. *But for such faith* probably means "only through such faith"; in the manuscript draft this passage reads (canceled words in italics):

> Which teaches awful doubt,—or a *belief* faith so mild
> So solemn, so serene, that man *again* may be
> *To such high thoughts of With such a faith*
> In such wise faith with Nature reconciled!—

On the basis of this evidence both Wasserman and Chernaik concluded that *But* is used here not as a preposition meaning "except," but rather as an adverb meaning "only" or "merely." This reading is further bolstered by the variant in SDN "In such a faith" for *But for such faith.*
5. Intricately, cleverly fashioned; this favorite adjective of Shelley comes ultimately from Daedalus, the craftsman of Greek mythology who built the Cretan labyrinth and, later, wings to escape from it.
6. SDN reads "sublime"; the bald statement of the aloof nature of *Power* contrasts with the endless cyclical activities of mortal creatures described in lines 84–95.
7. I.e., the contrast drawn in lines 84–97, but especially the nature of *Power* stated in 96–97.

Teach the adverting mind. The glaciers creep
Like snakes that watch their prey, from their far fountains,
Slow rolling on; there, many a precipice,
Frost and the Sun in scorn of mortal[8] power
Have piled: dome, pyramid, and pinnacle,
A city of death, distinct with many a tower          105
And wall impregnable of beaming ice.
Yet not a city,[9] but a flood of ruin
Is there, that from the boundaries of the sky
Rolls its perpetual stream; vast pines are strewing
Its destined path, or in the mangled soil          110
Branchless and shattered stand: the rocks, drawn down
From yon remotest waste, have overthrown
The limits of the dead and living world,
Never to be reclaimed. The dwelling-place
Of insects, beasts, and birds, becomes its spoil;          115
Their food and their retreat for ever gone,
So much of life and joy is lost. The race
Of man, flies far in dread; his work and dwelling
Vanish, like smoke before the tempest's stream,
And their place is not known.[1] Below, vast caves          120
Shine in the rushing torrents' restless gleam,
Which from those secret chasms in tumult welling
Meet in the vale, and one majestic River,
The breath and blood of distant lands,[2] for ever
Rolls its loud waters to the ocean waves,          125
Breathes its swift vapours to the circling air.

## V.

Mont Blanc yet gleams on high:—the power is there,
The still and solemn power of many sights,
And many sounds, and much of life and death.
In the calm darkness of the moonless nights,          130
In the lone glare of day, the snows descend
Upon that Mountain; none beholds them there,
Nor when the flakes burn in the sinking sun,[3]
Or the star-beams dart through them:—Winds contend
Silently there, and heap the snow with breath          135
Rapid and strong,[4] but silently! Its home
The voiceless lightning in these solitudes
Keeps innocently, and like vapour broods
Over the snow. The secret strength of things

8. SDN reads "human."
9. SDN reads "A city's phantom . . but"; "phantom" replaces a canceled "spectre."
1. "As for man, his days are as grass. . . . For the wind passeth over it, and it is gone; and the place thereof shall know it no more" (Psalms 103:15–16).
2. The River Arve, which originates in the Valley of Chamonix at the foot of Mont Blanc, flows into Lake Geneva near the city of Geneva; nearby, the River Rhone flows out of Lake Geneva to begin its course through France to the Mediterranean Sea.
3. SDN reads "sunset wraps thier flakes in fire."
4. SDN reads "Blasting & swift."

Which governs thought, and to the infinite dome                    140
Of heaven is as a law, inhabits thee!⁵
And what were thou, and earth, and stars, and sea,
If to the human mind's imaginings
Silence and solitude were vacancy?


# *From* Laon and Cythna;
# or The Revolution of the Golden City¹

[Dedication] *To Mary——— ———*

### 1.

So now my summer task is ended, Mary,
    And I return to thee, mine own heart's home;
As to his Queen some victor Knight of Faëry,²
    Earning bright spoils for her inchanted dome;
    Nor thou disdain, that ere my fame become                      5
A star among the stars of mortal night,
    If it indeed may cleave its natal gloom,
Its doubtful promise thus I would unite
With thy beloved name, thou Child of love and light.

### 2.

The toil which stole from thee so many an hour                     10
    Is ended,—and the fruit is at thy feet!
No longer where the woods to frame a bower
    With interlaced branches mix and meet,
    Or where with sound like many voices sweet,
Water-falls leap among wild islands green,                         15
    Which framed for my lone boat a lone retreat
Of moss-grown trees and weeds, shall I be seen:
But beside thee, where still my heart has ever been.


5. *SDN* reads "is as a column, rests on thee."
1. *Laon and Cythna* (later revised and retitled *The Revolt of Islam*), Shelley's longest poem, is a symbolic romance-epic of twelve cantos in Spenserian stanzas. Uniting Shelley's philosophical, social, and personal concerns, it tells the story of two lovers (brother and sister in the original version) who inspire and lead a bloodless revolution against the sultan of Turkey. After a period of celebration, the revolution is overthrown by reactionary forces from the kingdoms of Europe, with Laon and Cythna themselves—martyrs to their idealistic cause—being guided to a Valhalla in the Temple of the Spirit. Shelley composed this "idealism of moral excellence"—his vision of how the leaders ought to have conducted the French Revolution—between March or April and September 1817 and wrote the Dedication "To Mary——— ———" (i.e., Mary Wollstonecraft Shelley) after the completion of this "summer task."
2. The poem owes much to Edmund Spenser's *The Faerie Queen* in diction, as well its stanza form.

### 3.

Thoughts of great deeds were mine, dear Friend, when first
   The clouds which wrap this world from youth did pass.    20
I do remember well the hour which burst
   My spirit's sleep: a fresh May-dawn it was,
   When I walked forth upon the glittering grass,
And wept, I knew not why; until there rose
   From the near school-room, voices, that, alas!    25
Were but one echo from a world of woes—
The harsh and grating strife of tyrants and of foes.

### 4.

And then I clasped my hands and looked around—
   —But none was near to mock my streaming eyes,
Which poured their warm drops on the sunny ground—    30
   So without shame, I spake:—"I will be wise,
   And just, and free, and mild, if in me lies
Such power, for I grow weary to behold
   The selfish and the strong still tyrannise
Without reproach or check." I then controuled    35
My tears, my heart grew calm, and I was meek and bold.

### 5.

And from that hour did I with earnest thought
   Heap knowledge from forbidden mines of lore,
Yet nothing that my tyrants knew or taught
   I cared to learn, but from that secret store    40
   Wrought linked armour for my soul, before
It might walk forth to war among mankind;
   Thus power and hope were strengthened more and more
Within me, till there came upon my mind
A sense of loneliness, a thirst with which I pined.[3]    45

### 6.

Alas, that love should be a blight and snare
   To those who seek all sympathies in one!—
Such once I sought in vain; then black despair,
   The shadow of a starless night, was thrown
   Over the world in which I moved alone:—    50
Yet never found I one not false to me,
   Hard hearts, and cold, like weights of icy stone
Which crushed and withered mine, that could not be
Aught but a lifeless clog,[4] until revived by thee.

3. Lines 21–45 give Shelley's most specific and detailed account of his conversion to revolutionary principles; the circumstances of the scene fit aristocratic Eton College, a leading
"public school" (endowed private preparatory school), where Shelley studied from 1804 to
1810.
4. A log, block of wood, or other dead weight that impedes movement.

### 7.

Thou Friend, whose presence on my wintry heart                                     55
    Fell, like bright Spring upon some herbless plain;
How beautiful and calm and free thou wert
    In thy young wisdom, when the mortal chain
Of Custom thou didst burst and rend in twain,[5]
And walked as free as light the clouds among,                                      60
    Which many an envious slave then breathed in vain
From his dim dungeon, and my spirit sprung
To meet thee from the woes which had begirt it long.

### 8.

No more alone through the world's wilderness,
    Although I trod the paths of high intent,                                       65
I journeyed now: no more companionless,
    Where solitude is like despair, I went.—
    There is the wisdom of a stern content
When Poverty can blight the just and good,
    When Infamy dares mock the innocent,                                            70
And cherished friends turn with the multitude
To trample: this was ours, and we unshaken stood!

### 9.

Now has descended a serener hour,
    And with inconstant fortune, friends return;
Though suffering leaves the knowledge and the power                                75
    Which says:—Let scorn be not repaid with scorn.
    And from thy side two gentle babes are born
To fill our home with smiles,[6] and thus are we
    Most fortunate beneath life's beaming morn;
And these delights, and thou, have been to me                                      80
The parents of the Song I consecrate to thee.

### 10.

Is it, that now my inexperienced fingers
    But strike the prelude of a loftier strain?
Or, must the lyre on which my spirit lingers
    Soon pause in silence, ne'er to sound again,[7]                                85
    Though it might shake the Anarch Custom's reign,
And charm the minds of men to Truth's own sway
    Holier than was Amphion's?[8] I would fain

5. Mary Godwin was sixteen years old when she declared her love to Shelley, who was then twenty-one and married to Harriet Westbrook Shelley.
6. William Shelley (born Jan. 24, 1816) and Clara Everina Shelley (born Sept. 2, 1817).
7. Shelley thought that he might be dying at this time.
8. In Greek myth Amphion, a son of Zeus, was so creative with his lyre that stones formed themselves into the walls of Thebes in response to his music. (His unholy acts were to avenge his human mother by conquering Thebes and putting to death her husband and that man's second wife.)

Reply in hope—but I am worn away,
And Death and Love are yet contending for their prey.                    90

### 11.

And what art thou? I know, but dare not speak:
    Time may interpret to his silent years.
Yet in the paleness of thy thoughtful cheek,
    And in the light thine ample forehead wears,
    And in thy sweetest smiles, and in thy tears,                    95
And in thy gentle speech, a prophecy
    Is whispered, to subdue my fondest fears:
And through thine eyes, even in thy soul I see
A lamp of vestal fire[9] burning internally.

### 12.

They say that thou wert lovely from thy birth,                    100
    Of glorious parents, thou aspiring Child.
I wonder not—for One then left this earth[1]
    Whose life was like a setting planet mild
    Which clothed thee in the radiance undefiled
Of its departing glory; still her fame                    105
    Shines on thee, through the tempests dark and wild
Which shake these latter days; and thou canst claim
The shelter, from thy Sire,[2] of an immortal name.

### 13.

One voice[3] came forth from many a mighty spirit,
    Which was the echo of three thousand years;                    110
And the tumultuous world stood mute to hear it,
    As some lone man who in a desart hears
    The music of his home:—unwonted fears
Fell on the pale oppressors of our race,
    And Faith, and Custom, and low-thoughted cares,                    115
Like thunder-stricken dragons, for a space
Left the torn human heart, their food and dwelling-place.

### 14.

Truth's deathless voice pauses among mankind!
    If there must be no response to my cry—
If men must rise and stamp with fury blind                    120
    On his pure name who loves them,—thou and I,

---

9. Sacred fire tended by virgins in the temple of Vesta, Roman goddess of the hearth and
household.
1. In 1797 Mary Wollstonecraft Godwin had died from complications connected with giving
birth to her second daughter, Mary Wollstonecraft Godwin (later Shelley).
2. William Godwin was then regarded by young liberals as England's greatest political theorist
and novelist of the decade following the French Revolution.
3. Godwin's *An Enquiry concerning Political Justice* (1793).

Sweet Friend! can look from our tranquillity
Like lamps into the world's tempestuous night,—
Two tranquil stars, while clouds are passing by
Which wrap them from the foundering[4] seaman's sight,      125
That burn from year to year with unextinguished light.

## *from* Canto IX[5]

### XX.

"We know not what will come—yet Laon, dearest,      3640
    Cythna shall be the prophetess of love,
Her lips shall rob thee of the grace thou wearest,
    To hide thy heart, and clothe the shapes which rove
    Within the homeless future's wintry grove;
For I now, sitting thus beside thee, seem      3645
    Even with thy breath and blood to live and move,
And violence and wrong are as a dream
Which rolls from stedfast truth an unreturning stream.

### XXI.

"The blasts of autumn drive the winged seeds
    Over the Earth,—next come the snows, and rain,      3650
And frosts, and storms, which dreary winter leads
    Out of his Scythian[6] cave, a savage train;
    Behold! Spring sweeps over the world again,
Shedding soft dews from her ætherial wings;
    Flowers on the mountains, fruits over the plain,      3655
And music on the waves and woods she flings,
And love on all that lives, and calm on lifeless things.

### XXII.

"O Spring, of hope, and love, and youth, and gladness
    Wind-winged emblem! brightest, best and fairest!
Whence comest thou, when, with dark Winter's sadness      3660
    The tears that fade in sunny smiles thou sharest?
    Sister of joy, thou art the child who wearest
Thy mother's dying smile, tender and sweet;
    Thy mother Autumn, for whose grave thou bearest
Fresh flowers, and beams like flowers, with gentle feet,      3665
Disturbing not the leaves which are her winding-sheet.

4. Stumbling, sinking because the ship is filled with water.
5. After escaping the armies sent by reactionary allies to restore the tyrant to power, Laon and
   his sister Cythna have told each other how, since being separated years earlier, each came
   to participate in the bloodless Revolution of the Golden City. In this speech, Cythna assures
   Laon that their struggle has not been in vain. Shelley later reused the imagery in "Ode to
   the West Wind."
6. Classical Scythia included two regions: Scythia intra Imaum (central Asia east of the Aral
   Sea) and Scythia extra Imaum (Tibet and Sinkiang province of western China).

### XXIII.

"Virtue, and Hope, and Love, like light and Heaven,
    Surround the world.—We are their chosen slaves.
Has not the whirlwind of our spirit driven
    Truth's deathless germs to thought's remotest caves?          3670
    Lo, Winter comes!—the grief of many graves,
The frost of death, the tempest of the sword,
    The flood of tyranny, whose sanguine waves
Stagnate like ice at Faith, the inchanter's word,
And bind all human hearts in its repose abhorred.               3675

### XXIV.

"The seeds are sleeping in the soil: meanwhile
    The tyrant peoples dungeons with his prey,
Pale victims on the guarded scaffold smile
    Because they cannot speak; and, day by day,
    The moon of wasting Science[7] wanes away                    3680
Among her stars, and in that darkness vast
    The sons of earth to their foul idols pray,
And grey Priests triumph, and like blight or blast
A shade of selfish care o'er human looks is cast.

### XXV.

"This is the winter of the world;—and here                      3685
    We die, even as the winds of Autumn fade,
Expiring in the frore[8] and foggy air.—
    Behold! Spring comes, though we must pass, who made
    The promise of its birth,—even as the shade
Which from our death, as from a mountain, flings                3690
    The future, a broad sunrise; thus arrayed
As with the plumes of overshadowing wings,
From its dark gulph of chains, Earth like an eagle springs.

### XXVI.

"O dearest love! we shall be dead and cold
    Before this morn may on the world arise;                     3695
Wouldst thou the glory of its dawn behold?
    Alas! gaze not on me, but turn thine eyes
    On thine own heart—it is a Paradise
Which everlasting Spring has made its own,
    And while drear Winter fills the naked skies,                3700
Sweet streams of sunny thought, and flowers fresh blown,
Are there, and weave their sounds and odours into one.

7. Knowledge and reasoned discourse.
8. Intensely cold, frosty.

### XXVII.

"In their own hearts the earnest of the hope
    Which made them great, the good will ever find;
And though some envious shade may interlope                    3705
    Between the effect and it, One comes behind,
    Who aye the future to the past will bind—
Necessity,[9] whose sightless strength forever
    Evil with evil, good with good must wind
In bands of union, which no power may sever:                   3710
They must bring forth their kind, and be divided never!

### XXVIII.

"The good and mighty of departed ages
    Are in their graves, the innocent and free,
Heroes, and Poets, and prevailing Sages,
    Who leave the vesture[1] of their majesty                  3715
    To adorn and clothe this naked world;—and we
Are like to them—such perish, but they leave
    All hope, or love, or truth, or liberty,
Whose forms their mighty spirits could conceive
To be a rule and law to ages that survive."[2]                3720

\*   \*   \*

# TO CONSTANTIA

Written at Marlow between mid-1817 and January 19, 1818, "To Constantia" celebrates Clara Mary Jane ("Claire") Clairmont, the stepsister of
Mary Shelley and a member for several years of the Shelley household,
one of whose nicknames was "Constantia" (a character in *Ormond*, by the
American novelist Charles Brockden Brown). Claire Clairmont, who had
a lovely singing voice, notes in her journal for January 19, 1818, that she
is copying the poem, probably for its appearance in the *Oxford University
and City Herald* on January 31, 1818—a publication that had been overlooked by editors of Shelley's poetry until Judith Chernaik discovered it
(*Times Literary Supplement*, Feb. 6, 1969, p. 140). For publication in the
*Herald*, Shelley gave the author's name as "Pleyel," the name not only of
a famous piano maker of the day but also—as Chernaik points out—of a
character in *Wieland*, Brown's best-known novel, who loves a woman
named Clara (*The Lyrics of Shelley* [1972], p. 197).
    Shelley's holograph fair copy (lacking line 44) appears in Harvard
MS.Eng.258.3, fols. 43v rev.–42v rev. (*MYR: Shelley*, V). His draft of the
poem appears in Bodleian MS Shelley e.4, fols. 36v rev.–34v rev. (*BSM*,
III), a transcription of which—with the stanza order confused—by Mary
Shelley is in Bodleian MS Shelley adds. d.7, pp. 38–40 (*BSM*, II). Mary
Shelley published a version of the poem based on her transcription in

9. See note to *Queen Mab*, VI.198.
1. Clothing, raiment.
2. Cf. the end of *A Defence of Poetry*: "Poets are the unacknowledged legislators of the world."

*Posthumous Poems*, under the title "To Constantia, Singing." Our text is
based on the version in the *Herald*, with some corrections in punctuation
and capitalization from Shelley's fair copy.

# To Constantia

Thy voice, slow rising like a Spirit, lingers
O'ershadowing me with soft and lulling wings;
The blood and life within thy snowy fingers
Teach witchcraft to the instrumental strings.
      My brain is wild, my breath comes quick,      5
      The blood is listening in my frame,
      And thronging shadows fast and thick
      Fall on my overflowing eyes,
      My heart is quivering like a flame;
As morning dew, that in the sunbeam dies,      10
I am dissolved in these consuming extacies.

I have no life, Constantia, but in thee;[1]
Whilst, like the world-surrounding air, thy song
Flows on, and fills all things with melody:
Now is thy voice a tempest, swift and strong,      15
      On which, as one in trance upborne,
      Secure o'er woods and waves I sweep
      Rejoicing, like a cloud of morn:
      Now 'tis the breath of summer's night[2]
      Which, where the starry waters sleep      20
Round western isles with incense blossoms bright,
Lingering, suspends my soul in its voluptuous flight.

A deep and breathless awe, like the swift change
Of dreams unseen, but felt in youthful slumbers;
Wild, sweet, yet incommunicably strange,      25
Thou breathest now, in fast ascending numbers:
      The cope of Heaven seems rent and cloven[3]
      By the inchantment of thy strain,
      And o'er my shoulders wings are woven
      To follow its sublime career,      30
      Beyond the mighty moons that wane
Upon the verge of Nature's utmost sphere,
Till the world's shadowy walls are past, and disappear.

---

1. In the Bodleian manuscript of Shelley's first draft this line reads "I am not body or soul or ought but thee."
2. A metaphor for the quality of her voice (not a reference to the season of the poem's composition, as has sometimes been assumed).
3. I.e., "The vault of Heaven seems torn and split." In traditional artistic representations of St. Cecilia, patron saint of music, the heavens are opened by the power of her singing while accompanied by the organ.

Cease, cease—for such wild lessons madmen learn:
Long thus to sink,—thus to be lost and die                    35
Perhaps is death indeed—Constantia turn!
Yes! in thine eyes a power like light doth lie,
    Even though the sounds, its voice, that were
    Between thy lips are laid to sleep—
    Within thy breath and on thy hair                    40
    Like odour it is lingering yet—
    And from thy touch like fire doth leap:
Even while I write my burning cheeks are wet—
Such things the heart can feel and learn, but not forget![4]

# OZYMANDIAS

Ozymandias was the Greek name for Ramses II (1304–1237 B.C.), the
pharaoh of Egypt with whom Moses contended during the Exodus. Shelley
wrote this sonnet—in December 1817 or January 1818—in a contest with
his friend Horace (Horatio) Smith. The chief textual authorities for Shelley's poem are a partial rough draft and a complete fair-copy holograph
(i.e., manuscript in the author's hand) in Bodleian MS Shelley e.4 (*BSM*,
III, 340–43); a first printing in Leigh Hunt's weekly newspaper the *Examiner* for January 11, 1818; and a revised printing in Shelley's *Rosalind
and Helen* volume (1819). Our substantive text derives from a comparison
of the two printings during Shelley's lifetime, but we return to the punctuation and orthography of Shelley's fair-copy manuscript.

Smith's competing sonnet, also initially titled "Ozymandias," appeared
in the *Examiner* for February 1 and was later reprinted with Smith's works
as "On a Stupendous Leg of Granite, Discovered Standing by Itself in the
Deserts of Egypt, with the Inscription Inserted Below." Though scholars
have long debated about which travel-book descriptions of Egypt Shelley
may have had in mind, discrepancies between the facts in his and Smith's
sonnets suggest that the poems were composed extemporaneously, probably after the two had discussed "a magnificent bust of Ramses, found
near a shattered colossus at the pharaoh's funerary temple in Thebes" that
the British Museum had acquired in 1817. (See Rick Gore, "Ramses the
Great," *National Geographic*, April 1991.)

## Ozymandias.

I met a traveller from an antique land,
Who said—"Two vast and trunkless legs of stone
Stand in the desert. . . . Near them, on the sand,
Half sunk a shattered visage lies, whose frown,
And wrinkled lip, and sneer of cold command,                    5
Tell that its sculptor well those passions read

---

4. The Bodleian draft reads "Alas, that the torn heart can bleed but not forget."

Which yet survive,[1] stamped on these lifeless things,[2]
The hand that mocked them, and the heart that fed;[3]
And on the pedestal, these words appear:
My name is Ozymandias, King of Kings,        10
Look on my Works, ye Mighty, and despair!
Nothing beside remains. Round the decay
Of that colossal Wreck, boundless and bare
The lone and level sands stretch far away."—

# Lines written among the Euganean Hills[1]

### October, 1818.

Many a green isle needs must be
In the deep wide sea of Misery,
Or the mariner, worn and wan,
Never thus could voyage on—
Day and night, and night and day,        5
Drifting on his dreary way,
With the solid darkness black
Closing round his vessel's track;
Whilst above the sunless sky,
Big with clouds, hangs heavily,        10
And behind the tempest fleet
Hurries on with lightning feet,
Riving[2] sail, and cord, and plank,
Till the ship has almost drank
Death from the o'er-brimming deep;        15
And sinks down, down, like that sleep
When the dreamer seems to be
Weltering[3] through eternity;
And the dim low line before
Of a dark and distant shore        20
Still recedes, as ever still
Longing with divided will,

1. Outlive.
2. The phrase *stamped . . . things* is parenthetical, identifying the medium through which survive the *passions* (line 6) of the two ancients—one who ordered and the other who produced the sculpture.
3. The sculptor's *hand . . . mocked* (both imitated and satirized) the *passions* that the pharaoh's *heart . . . fed.*

1. Shelley began writing this poem while living at Este, amid the Euganean Hills near Padua, probably between September 29 and October 11, 1818, soon after the death of the Shelleys' infant daughter Clara. In December 1818 or January 1819 he mailed it to his publisher Charles Ollier, who published it with *Rosalind and Helen* (May 1819). No draft has been authenticated, and only two short fragments of the press-copy manuscript survive: lines 56–81 at the Huntington Library (HM 331; in Mary Shelley's hand) and a holograph insert of lines 167–87 on Byron in the Tinker Collection at Yale University Library; facsimiles and critical discussion of these fragments appear in *MYR: Shelley*, III, 113–20, and VIII, 186–93, respectively. For a detailed reading of the poem, see Donald H. Reiman, "Structure, Symbol, and Theme in 'Lines written among the Euganean Hills,' " *PMLA* 77 (Sept. 1962): 404–13.
2. Tearing or pulling apart; rending.
3. Tossing and tumbling; floundering.

But no power to seek or shun,
He is ever drifted on
O'er the unreposing wave                                   25
To the haven of the grave.
What, if there no friends will greet;
What, if there no heart will meet
His with love's impatient beat;
Wander wheresoe'er he may,                                 30
Can he dream before that day
To find refuge from distress
In friendship's smile, in love's caress?
Then 'twill wreak⁴ him little woe
Whether such there be or no:                               35
Senseless⁵ is the breast, and cold,
Which relenting love would fold;
Bloodless are the veins and chill
Which the pulse of pain did fill;
Every little living nerve                                  40
That from bitter words did swerve
Round the tortured lips and brow,
Are like sapless leaflets now
Frozen upon December's bough.

On the beach of a northern sea                             45
Which tempests shake eternally,
As once the wretch⁶ there lay to sleep,
Lies a solitary heap,
One white skull and seven dry bones,⁷
On the margin of the stones,                               50
Where a few grey rushes⁸ stand,
Boundaries of the sea and land:
Nor is heard one voice of wail
But the sea-mews,⁹ as they sail
O'er the billows of the gale;                              55
Or the whirlwind up and down
Howling, like a slaughtered town,
When a King in glory rides
Through the pomp of fratricides:
Those unburied bones around                                60
There is many a mournful sound;
There is no lament for him

---

4. Cause harm or damage.
5. Incapable of perception or emotion.
6. A pitiable, unlucky being.
7. In his *PMLA* essay, Reiman suggests that the figures here symbolize the death of Shelley's past life in England: "The seven bones symbolize the seven years between his expulsion from Oxford (March 1811) and his final departure from England (March 1818)."
8. Plants having naked stalks growing in marshy ground; used here to signify something of little value.
9. Seagulls; Shelley alludes to Milton's *Paradise Lost*, where, after the Fall of Adam and Eve, the archangel Michael tells them how the Mount of Paradise will be washed away by the great flood and become "an Island salt and bare, / The haunt of Seals and Orcs and Sea-mews' clang" (XI.829–38).

Like a sunless vapour dim
Who once clothed with life and thought
What now moves nor murmurs not.                    65

Aye, many flowering islands lie
In the waters of wide Agony.
To such a one this morn was led
My bark by soft winds piloted—
'Mid the mountains Euganean[1]                      70
I stood listening to the pæan
With which the legioned rooks did hail
The sun's uprise majestical;
Gathering round with wings all hoar,
Through the dewy mist they soar                     75
Like grey shades, till th'eastern heaven
Bursts, and then, as clouds of even
Flecked with fire and azure lie
In the unfathomable sky,
So their plumes of purple grain,                    80
Starred with drops of golden rain,
Gleam above the sunlight woods,
As in silent multitudes
On the morning's fitful gale
Through the broken mist they sail,                  85
And the vapours cloven and gleaming
Follow down the dark steep streaming,
Till all is bright, and clear, and still,
Round the solitary hill.

Beneath is spread like a green sea                  90
The waveless plain of Lombardy,
Bounded by the vaporous air,
Islanded by cities fair;
Underneath day's azure eyes
Ocean's nursling Venice lies,                       95
A peopled labyrinth of walls,
Amphitrite's[2] destined halls
Which her hoary sire now paves
With his blue and beaming waves.—
Lo! the sun upsprings behind,                      100
Broad, red, radiant, half-reclined
On the level quivering line
Of the waters chrystalline;
And before that chasm of light,
As within a furnace bright,                        105
Column, tower, and dome, and spire,
Shine like obelisks of fire,

1. This line shows how Shelley pronounced Euganean (yoo-gä-ne'-un); *pæan:* song of
thanksgiving.
2. Amphitrite, in Greek myth, was the daughter of Oceanus (*sire,* line 98) and the wife of
Poseidon (Neptune), both gods of the sea.

Pointing with inconstant motion
From the altar of dark ocean
To the sapphire-tinted skies;                                    110
As the flames of sacrifice
From the marble shrines did rise,
As to pierce the dome of gold
Where Apollo spoke of old.[3]


Sun-girt City, thou hast been                                    115
Ocean's child, and then his queen;
Now is come a darker day,
And thou soon must be his prey,
If the power that raised thee here
Hallow so thy watery bier.                                       120
A less drear ruin then than now,
With thy conquest-branded brow[4]
Stooping to the slave of slaves
From thy throne, among the waves
Wilt thou be, when the sea-mew                                   125
Flies, as once before it flew,
O'er thine isles depopulate,
And all is in its antient state,
Save where many a palace gate
With green sea-flowers overgrown                                 130
Like a rock of ocean's own,
Topples o'er the abandoned sea
As the tides change sullenly.
The fisher on his watery way,
Wandering at the close of day,                                   135
Will spread his sail and seize his oar
Till he pass the gloomy shore,
Lest thy dead should, from their sleep
Bursting o'er the starlight deep,
Lead a rapid masque[5] of death                                 140
O'er the waters of his path.


Those who alone thy towers behold
Quivering through aerial gold,
As I now behold them here,
Would imagine not they were                                      145
Sepulchres, where human forms,
Like pollution-nourished worms,
To the corpse of greatness cling,
Murdered, and now mouldering:
But if Freedom should awake                                      150
In her omnipotence, and shake

3. *dome . . . old:* the oracle of Apollo at Delphi.
4. Venice is disfigured both by having in the past been a conqueror and recently by having
   been enslaved by Napoleonic France and Austria.
5. An elaborately staged dramatic performance.

From the Celtic Anarch's⁶ hold
All the keys of dungeons cold,
Where a hundred cities lie
Chained like thee, ingloriously,                      155
Thou and all thy sister band
Might adorn this sunny land,
Twining memories of old time
With new virtues more sublime;
If not, perish thou and they!—                        160
Clouds which stain truth's rising day
By her sun consumed away—
Earth can spare ye: while like flowers,
In the waste of years and hours,
From thy dust shall nations spring⁷                   165
With more kindly blossoming.

Perish—let there only be
Floating o'er thy hearthless sea,
As the garment of the sky
Clothes the world immortally,                         170
One remembrance, more sublime
Than the tattered pall⁸ of time,
Which scarce hides thy visage wan;—
That a tempest-cleaving Swan⁹
Of the songs of Albion,¹                              175
Driven from his ancestral streams
By the might of evil dreams,
Found a nest in thee; and Ocean
Welcomed him with such emotion
That its joy grew his, and sprung                     180
From his lips like music flung
O'er a mighty thunder-fit,
Chastening terror:—what though yet
Poesy's unfailing River,
Which through Albion winds forever                    185
Lashing with melodious wave
Many a sacred Poet's grave,
Mourn its latest nursling fled?
What though thou with all thy dead
Scarce can for this fame repay                        190
Aught thine own? oh, rather say
Though thy sins and slaveries foul

6. Austrian tyrant; in Shelley's day *Celtic* (pronounced "Keltic") referred in the Greek manner to northern, non-Mediterranean barbarian tribes, while *Anarch* had gained associations with Chaos from uses of the word in *Paradise Lost*, II.988, and Alexander Pope's *The Dunciad*, IV.655.
7. Lines 165 and 169 have been newly corrected on the basis of the Tinker-Yale holograph fragment, reproduced and discussed by Reiman in *MYR: Shelley*, VIII, 186–93, and Shelley's corrections in a copy of *Rosalind and Helen* (1819), in private hands.
8. Robe or cloak.
9. Lord Byron.
1. England.

Overcloud a sunlike soul?
As the ghost of Homer clings
Round Scamander's[2] wasting springs;        195
As divinest Shakespeare's might
Fills Avon[3] and the world with light
Like Omniscient power which he
Imaged 'mid mortality;
As the love from Petrarch's urn[4]      200
Yet amid yon hills doth burn,
A quenchless lamp by which the heart
Sees things unearthly;—so thou art,
Mighty Spirit—so shall be
The City that did refuge thee.      205

Lo, the sun floats up the sky
Like thought-winged Liberty,
Till the universal light
Seems to level plain and height;
From the sea a mist has spread,      210
And the beams of morn lie dead
On the towers of Venice now,
Like its glory long ago.
By the skirts of that grey cloud
Many-domed Padua proud      215
Stands, a peopled solitude,
'Mid the harvest-shining plain,
Where the peasant heaps his grain
In the garner[5] of his foe,
And the milk-white oxen slow      220
With the purple vintage strain,
Heaped upon the creaking wain,[6]
That the brutal Celt[7] may swill
Drunken sleep with savage will;
And the sickle to the sword      225
Lies unchanged, though many a lord,
Like a weed whose shade is poison,
Overgrows this region's foizon,[8]
Sheaves of whom are ripe to come
To destruction's harvest home:      230
Men must reap the things they sow,
Force from force must ever flow—
Or worse; but 'tis a bitter woe
That love or reason cannot change
The despot's rage, the slave's revenge.      235

2. Scamander was a river near Troy in Homer's *Iliad*.
3. The river near Shakespeare's birthplace, Stratford-on-Avon.
4. The last home and the tomb of the great Italian poet and humanist Francesco Petrarca ("Francis Petrarch," 1304–74) are shrines at the village of Arqua in the Euganean Hills.
5. Storehouse, granary.
6. A large open wagon for carrying heavy loads, especially of agricultural produce.
7. See note to line 152.
8. A plentiful crop or harvest.

Padua, thou within whose walls
Those mute guests at festivals,
Son and Mother, Death and Sin,[9]
Played at dice for Ezzelin,
Till Death cried, "I win, I win!"[1]                     240
And Sin cursed to lose the wager,
But Death promised, to assuage her,
That he would petition for
Her to be made Vice-Emperor,
When the destined years were o'er,                     245
Over all between the Po
And the eastern Alpine snow,
Under the mighty Austrian.
Sin smiled so as Sin only can,
And since that time, aye, long before,                     250
Both have ruled from shore to shore,—
That incestuous pair, who follow
Tyrants as the sun the swallow,
As Repentance follows Crime,
And as changes follow Time.                     255

In thine halls the lamp of learning,
Padua, now no more is burning;[2]
Like a meteor, whose wild way
Is lost over the grave of day,
It gleams betrayed and to betray:                     260
Once remotest nations came
To adore that sacred flame,
When it lit not many a hearth
On this cold and gloomy earth:
Now new fires from antique light                     265
Spring beneath the wide world's might;
But their spark lies dead in thee,
Trampled out by tyranny.
As the Norway woodman quells,
In the depth of piny dells,                     270
One light flame among the brakes,[3]
While the boundless forest shakes,
And its mighty trunks are torn
By the fire thus lowly born:
The spark beneath his feet is dead,                     275
He starts to see the flames it fed
Howling through the darkened sky

9. Cf. Milton's allegory of Sin and Death in *Paradise Lost*, Book II.
1. Cf. Coleridge's "Rime of the Ancient Mariner," lines 196–97, where Death and Life-in-Death cast dice for the soul of the Ancient Mariner. *Ezzelin:* Ezzelino da Romano (1194–1259), the first despot to overthrow republican medieval communes in Northern Italy, ruled Padua, Verona, and Vicenza with great cruelty from 1237 until he was hunted down and killed in 1259.
2. Padua's university was one of the oldest and most famous in medieval Europe.
3. Thickets, clumps of bushes.

With a myriad tongues victoriously,
And sinks down in fear: so thou,
O tyranny, beholdest now                               280
Light around thee, and thou hearest
The loud flames ascend, and fearest:
Grovel on the earth: aye, hide
In the dust thy purple pride!

Noon descends around me now:                           285
'Tis the noon of autumn's glow,
When a soft and purple mist
Like a vaporous amethyst,
Or an air-dissolved star
Mingling light and fragrance, far                      290
From the curved horizon's bound
To the point of heaven's profound,[4]
Fills the overflowing sky;
And the plains that silent lie
Underneath, the leaves unsodden                        295
Where the infant frost has trodden
With his morning-winged feet,
Whose bright print is gleaming yet;
And the red and golden vines,
Piercing with their trellised lines                    300
The rough, dark-skirted wilderness;
The dun and bladed grass no less,
Pointing from this hoary tower
In the windless air; the flower
Glimmering at my feet; the line                        305
Of the olive-sandalled Apennine
In the south dimly islanded;
And the Alps, whose snows are spread
High between the clouds and sun;
And of living things each one;                         310
And my spirit which so long
Darkened this swift stream of song,
Interpenetrated lie
By the glory of the sky:
Be it love, light, harmony,                            315
Odour, or the soul of all
Which from heaven like dew doth fall,
Or the mind which feeds this verse
Peopling the lone universe.

Noon descends, and after noon                          320
Autumn's evening meets me soon,
Leading the infantine moon,

4. A vast depth, or abyss.

And that one star,[5] which to her
Almost seems to minister
Half the crimson light she brings                    325
From the sunset's radiant springs:
And the soft dreams of the morn
(Which like winged winds had borne
To that silent isle, which lies
'Mid remembered agonies,                             330
The frail bark[6] of this lone being)
Pass, to other sufferers fleeing,
And its antient pilot, Pain,
Sits beside the helm again.

Other flowering isles must be                        335
In the sea of Life and agony:
Other spirits float and flee
O'er that gulph: even now, perhaps,
On some rock the wild wave wraps,
With folded wings they waiting sit                   340
For my bark, to pilot it
To some calm and blooming cove,
Where for me, and those I love,
May a windless bower be built,
Far from passion, pain, and guilt,                   345
In a dell 'mid lawny hills,
Which the wild sea-murmur fills,
And soft sunshine, and the sound
Of old forests echoing round,
And the light and smell divine                       350
Of all flowers that breathe and shine:
We may live so happy there,
That the spirits of the air,
Envying us, may even entice
To our healing paradise                              355
The polluting multitude;
But their rage would be subdued
By that clime divine and calm,
And the winds whose wings rain balm
On the uplifted soul, and leaves                     360
Under which the bright sea heaves;
While each breathless interval
In their whisperings musical
The inspired soul supplies
With its own deep melodies,                          365
And the love which heals all strife
Circling, like the breath of life,
All things in that sweet abode
With its own mild brotherhood:

5. Venus as the evening star (Vesper, Hesperus).
6. A small ship or rowing boat.

They, not it, would change;[7] and soon          370
Every sprite[8] beneath the moon
Would repent its envy vain,
And the earth grow young again.

## JULIAN AND MADDALO

Late in 1818, Shelley began a drama on the love and madness of the Italian epic poet Torquato Tasso. Abandoning that drama, he started to write—perhaps at Naples early in 1819—a dialogue between himself (Julian) and Byron (Maddalo), reflecting their conversations at Venice in August 1818. Finally, while writing *The Cenci* near Leghorn during the summer of 1819, he took the materials thus far composed, incorporated within the Maniac's speeches some emotional lines that reflect his own estrangement from Mary Shelley following the death of their son William at Rome, June 7, 1819, and shaped a philosophical dialogue in the conversational or "familiar" style that embodies a personal outcry in the objectified portrait of the madman. Shelley himself copied the poem on minute strips of paper torn from the standard letter-paper of the day and sent it to Leigh Hunt to have published anonymously. While affirming the impersonal nature of his portrait of the Maniac, he told Hunt that the poem had been "composed last year at Este," a remark probably also designed to screen the personal origin of the madman's outcries. *Julian and Maddalo* remained unpublished, however, during Shelley's lifetime and first appeared in Mary Shelley's edition of his *Posthumous Poems* (1824).

Our text is based on the manuscript that Shelley sent to Leigh Hunt for publication, now in the Pierpont Morgan Library (MA 974; reproduced and transcribed in *MYR: Shelley*, VIII). To that text we have added punctuation—some drawn from the text in *Posthumous Poems* that Mary Shelley based upon another fair copy, now lost. Shelley's first draft of the poem survives in Bodleian MS Shelley adds. e.11 (*BSM*, XV), and there is an intermediate fair copy of the first 107 lines in the hand of Mary Shelley in Bodleian MS Shelley adds. e.12 (pp. 177–71 *reverso*; *BSM*, XVIII, 215–08 *reverso*). Additional drafts possibly relating to the poem have been identified in one of the three Huntington Shelley notebooks (MS. HM 2176, fols. 3[r] and 13[r]; see *MYR: Shelley*, IV, xxxv–xxxviii, 14–15, 60–61).

In his letter to Hunt of August 15, 1819, Shelley included some sentences on poetic style that may have been intended for the Preface: "I have employed a certain familiar style of language to express the actual way in which people talk with each other whom education and a certain refinement of sentiment have placed above the use of vulgar idioms. I use the word *vulgar* in its most extensive sense; the vulgarity of rank and fashion is as gross in its way as that of Poverty, and its cant terms equally expressive of base conceptions, and therefore equally unfit for Poetry. Not that the familiar style is to be admitted in the treatment of a subject wholly

---

7. Literary analogues underlying lines 352–70 include Shakespeare's *The Tempest* and Dante's sonnet to Guido Cavalcanti, of which Shelley's translation (published with *Alastor*) begins: "Guido, I would that Lappo, thou, and I, / Led by some strong enchantment, might ascend / A magic ship. . . ." Shelley explored the theme again in the "l'envoy" at the end of *Epipsychidion*.
8. Spirit.

ideal, or in that part of any subject which relates to common life, where the passion exceeding a certain limit touches the boundaries of that which is ideal. Strong passion expresses itself in metaphor borrowed from objects alike remote or near, and casts over all the shadow of its own greatness" (Shelley, *Letters*, II, 108). The genesis and dating of the poem were first established in *SC*, VI, 850–65. For a discussion of its meaning see Kelvin Everest, "Shelley's Doubles: An Approach to 'Julian and Maddalo,' " in this volume (pp. 675–83).

For the poem's epigraph, Shelley translated ll. 28–30 of Virgil's *Tenth Eclogue*, which laments the unsuccessful wooing of "Lycoris" (actually Cytheris) by G. Cornelius Gallus, Virgil's patron and fellow poet. In Dryden's translation of Virgil's poem, "false Lycoris flies thy love and thee, / And, for thy rival [perhaps Mark Anthony], tempts the raging sea" (ll. 34–35). The words Shelley quotes are spoken by "Great Pan," who attempts to calm the "immod'rate grief" of Gallus.

# Julian and Maddalo;

## A *Conversation*

The meadows with fresh streams, the bees with thyme,
The goats with the green leaves of budding spring,
Are saturated not—nor Love with tears.
                                    VIRGIL's *Gallus*.

Count Maddalo is a Venetian nobleman of antient family and of great fortune, who, without mixing much in the society of his countrymen, resides chiefly at his magnificent palace in that city. He is a person of the most consummate genius, and capable, if he would direct his energies to such an end, of becoming the redeemer of his degraded country. But it is his weakness to be proud: he derives, from a comparison of his own extraordinary mind with the dwarfish intellects that surround him, an intense apprehension of the nothingness of human life. His passions and his powers are incomparably greater than those of other men; and, instead of the latter having been employed in curbing the former, they have mutually lent each other strength. His ambition preys upon itself, for want of objects which it can consider worthy of exertion. I say that Maddalo is proud, because I can find no other word to express the concentered and impatient feelings which consume him; but it is on his own hopes and affections only that he seems to trample, for in social life no human being can be more gentle, patient, and unassuming than Maddalo. He is cheerful, frank, and witty. His more serious conversation is a sort of intoxication; men are held by it as by a spell. He has travelled much; and there is an inexpressible charm in his relation of his adventures in different countries.

Julian is an Englishman of good family, passionately attached to those philosophical notions which assert the power of man over his own mind, and the immense improvements of which, by the extinction of certain moral superstitions, human society may be yet susceptible.

Without concealing the evil in the world, he is for ever speculating
how good may be made superior. He is a complete infidel, and a scoffer
at all things reputed holy; and Maddalo takes a wicked pleasure in
drawing out his taunts against religion. What Maddalo thinks on these
matters is not exactly known. Julian, in spite of his heterodox opinions,
is conjectured by his friends to possess some good qualities. How far
this is possible, the pious reader will determine. Julian is rather
serious.

Of the Maniac I can give no information. He seems by his own
account to have been disappointed in love. He was evidently a very
cultivated and amiable person when in his right senses. His story, told
at length, might be like many other stories of the same kind: the unconnected exclamations of his agony will perhaps be found a sufficient
comment for the text of every heart.

I rode one evening with Count Maddalo[1]
Upon the bank of land which breaks the flow
Of Adria towards Venice:[2]—a bare Strand
Of hillocks, heaped from ever-shifting sand,
Matted with thistles and amphibious weeds                      5
Such as from earth's embrace the salt ooze breeds
Is this;—an uninhabitable sea-side
Which the lone fisher, when his nets are dried,
Abandons; and no other object breaks
The waste, but one dwarf tree and some few stakes             10
Broken and unrepaired, and the tide makes
A narrow space of level sand thereon,—
Where 'twas our wont[3] to ride while day went down.
This ride was my delight.—I love all waste
And solitary places; where we taste                            15
The pleasure of believing what we see
Is boundless, as we wish our souls to be:
And such was this wide ocean, and this shore
More barren than its billows;—and yet more
Than all, with a remembered friend I love                      20
To ride as then I rode;—for the winds drove
The living spray along the sunny air
Into our faces; the blue heavens were bare,
Stripped to their depths by the awakening North;
And from the waves, sound like delight broke forth            25
Harmonizing with solitude, and sent
Into our hearts aërial merriment . . .
So, as we rode, we talked; and the swift thought,
Winging itself with laughter, lingered not,
But flew from brain to brain,—such glee was ours—             30
Charged with light memories of remembered hours,

1. At least some details of the scene in lines 1–140 are based on Shelley's conversation with
   Byron of August 23, 1818 (as described by Shelley in *Letters*, II, 36).
2. The *bank of land* is the Lido of Venice, then a barren offshore barrier island, though now a
   crowded beach resort; *Adria*: the Adriatic Sea.
3. Custom, habit.

None slow enough for sadness; till we came
Homeward, which always makes the spirit tame.
This day had been cheerful but cold, and now
The sun was sinking, and the wind also. 35
Our talk grew somewhat serious, as may be
Talk interrupted with such raillery
As mocks itself, because it cannot scorn
The thoughts it would extinguish:—'twas forlorn
Yet pleasing, such as once, so poets tell, 40
The devils held within the dales of Hell
Concerning God, freewill and destiny:[4]
Of all that earth has been or yet may be,
All that vain men imagine or believe,
Or hope can paint or suffering may atchieve, 45
We descanted,[5] and I (for ever still
Is it not wise to make the best of ill?)
Argued against despondency, but pride
Made my companion take the darker side.
The sense that he was greater than his kind 50
Had struck, methinks, his eagle spirit blind
By gazing on its own exceeding light.[6]
—Meanwhile the sun paused ere it should alight,[7]
Over the horizon of the mountains;—Oh,
How beautiful is sunset, when the glow 55
Of Heaven descends upon a land like thee,
Thou Paradise of exiles, Italy!
Thy mountains, seas and vineyards and the towers
Of cities they encircle!—it was ours
To stand on thee, beholding it; and then 60
Just where we had dismounted, the Count's men
Were waiting for us with the gondola.[8]—
As those who pause on some delightful way
Though bent on pleasant pilgrimage, we stood
Looking upon the evening and the flood 65
Which lay between the city and the shore
Paved with the image of the sky . . . the hoar
And aery Alps towards the North appeared
Through mist, an heaven-sustaining bulwark reared
Between the East and West; and half the sky 70
Was roofed with clouds of rich emblazonry
Dark purple at the zenith, which still grew

4. Lines 40–42 allude to *Paradise Lost*, II.555–61, where the fallen angels in Hell "reason'd high / Of Providence, Foreknowledge, Will, and Fate, . . . / And found no end, in wandring mazes lost."
5. Discussed at length, discoursed upon.
6. *eagle spirit . . . light:* According to tradition, the eagle not only possessed the keenest vision of all creatures but could renew its vision by flying directly toward the sun, which burned the scales from its eyes.
7. *light . . . alight:* Although *rime riche,* the exact repetition of a phonetic syllable of different meaning, is considered a virtue in French and Italian poetry, most English poets since the eighteenth century have avoided it; Shelley, however, employs it with some frequency in the poems he wrote in Italy.
8. Shelley, both here and at lines 139–40, rhymes *gondola* with "way," suggesting the contemporary British pronunciation of the word.

Down the steep West into a wondrous hue
Brighter than burning gold, even to the rent
Where the swift sun yet paused in his descent                    75
Among the many folded hills: they were
Those famous Euganean hills, which bear
As seen from Lido through the harbour piles
The likeness of a clump of peaked isles—
And then—as if the Earth and Sea had been                    80
Dissolved into one lake of fire, were seen
Those mountains towering as from waves of flame
Around the vaporous sun, from which there came
The inmost purple spirit of light, and made
Their very peaks transparent. "Ere it fade,"                    85
Said my Companion, "I will shew you soon
A better station"—so, o'er the lagune
We glided, and from that funereal bark[9]
I leaned, and saw the city, and could mark
How from their many isles in evening's gleam                    90
Its temples and its palaces did seem
Like fabrics of enchantment piled to Heaven.
I was about to speak, when—"We are even
Now at the point I meant," said Maddalo,
And bade the gondolieri cease to row.                    95
"Look, Julian, on the West, and listen well
If you hear not a deep and heavy bell."
I looked, and saw between us and the sun
A building on an island; such a one
As age to age might add, for uses vile,                    100
A windowless, deformed and dreary pile;
And on the top an open tower, where hung
A bell, which in the radiance swayed and swung;
We could just hear its hoarse and iron tongue:
The broad sun sunk behind it, and it tolled                    105
In strong and black relief.—"What we behold
Shall be the madhouse and its belfry tower,"
Said Maddalo, "and ever at this hour
Those who may cross the water, hear that bell
Which calls the maniacs each one from his cell                    110
To vespers."—"As much skill as need to pray
In thanks or hope for their dark lot have they
To their stern maker,"[1] I replied. "O ho!
You talk as in years past," said Maddalo.
"'Tis strange men change not. You were ever still                    115
Among Christ's flock a perilous infidel,
A wolf for the meek lambs—if you can't swim
Beware of Providence." I looked on him,
But the gay smile had faded in his eye.

9. "These gondolas are . . . finely carpeted & furnished with black & painted black" (Shelley
to Mary Shelley, Aug. 23, 1818). "It glides along the water looking blackly, / Just like a coffin
clapt in a canoe" (Byron, *Beppo*, lines 150–51).
1. The tone in lines 111–13 is ironic.

"And such,"—he cried, "is our mortality                                    120
And this must be the emblem and the sign
Of what should be eternal and divine!—
And like that black and dreary bell, the soul,
Hung in a heaven-illumined tower, must toll
Our thoughts and our desires to meet below                                 125
Round the rent heart and pray—as madmen do
For what? they know not,—till the night of death
As sunset, that strange vision, severeth
Our memory from itself, and us from all
We sought and yet were baffled!" I recall                                  130
The sense of what he said, although I mar
The force of his expressions. The broad star
Of day meanwhile had sunk behind the hill
And the black bell became invisible
And the red tower looked grey, and all between                             135
The churches, ships and palaces were seen
Huddled in gloom;—into the purple sea
The orange hues of heaven sunk silently.
We hardly spoke, and soon the gondola
Conveyed me to my lodging by the way.                                      140

    The following morn was rainy, cold and dim:
Ere Maddalo arose, I called on him,
And whilst I waited, with his child[2] I played;
A lovelier toy sweet Nature never made,
A serious, subtle, wild, yet gentle being,                                 145
Graceful without design and unforeseeing,
With eyes—oh speak not of her eyes!—which seem
Twin mirrors of Italian Heaven, yet gleam
With such deep meaning, as we never see
But in the human countenance: with me                                      150
She was a special favourite: I had nursed
Her fine and feeble limbs when she came first
To this bleak world; and she yet seemed to know
On second sight her antient playfellow,
Less changed than she was by six months or so;                             155
For after her first shyness was worn out
We sate there, rolling billiard balls about.
When the Count entered—salutations past[3]—
"The words you spoke last night might well have cast
A darkness on my spirit—if man be                                         160
The passive thing you say, I should not see
Much harm in the religions and old saws

---

2. Allegra Byron (or Biron) was the natural child of Byron and Mary Jane Clara ("Claire")
Clairmont, Mary Shelley's stepsister. Allegra had been raised by Claire under the Shelleys'
care from her birth (January 12, 1817) until they sent the child from Milan to Byron in
Venice on April 28, 1818. (Line 155 thus alludes to Shelley's *six months or so* of separation
from the child.)
3. In Shelley's draft this word replaced "o'er" to rhyme with *cast*.

(Though I may never own[4] such leaden laws)
Which break a teachless[5] nature to the yoke:
Mine is another faith"—thus much I spoke                    165
And noting he replied not, added: "See
This lovely child, blithe, innocent and free;
She spends a happy time with little care
While we to such sick thoughts subjected are
As came on you last night—it is our will                    170
That thus enchains us to permitted ill—
We might be otherwise—we might be all
We dream of happy, high, majestical.
Where is the love, beauty and truth we seek
But in our mind? and if we were not weak                    175
Should we be less in deed than in desire?"
"Ay, if we were not weak—and we aspire
How vainly to be strong!" said Maddalo:
"You talk Utopia." "It remains to know,"[6]
I then rejoined, "and those who try may find                180
How strong the chains are which our spirit bind;
Brittle perchance as straw . . . We are assured
Much may be conquered, much may be endured
Of what degrades and crushes us. We know
That we have power over ourselves to do                     185
And suffer—what, we know not till we try;
But something nobler than to live and die—
So taught those kings of old philosophy
Who reigned, before Religion made men blind;
And those who suffer with their suffering kind              190
Yet feel their faith, religion." "My dear friend,"
Said Maddalo, "my judgement will not bend
To your opinion, though I think you might
Make such a system refutation-tight
As far as words go. I knew one like you                     195
Who to this city came some months ago
With whom I argued in this sort, and he
Is now gone mad,—and so he answered me,—
Poor fellow! but if you would like to go,
We'll visit him, and his wild talk will show               200
How vain are such aspiring theories."
"I hope to prove the induction otherwise,
And that a want of that true theory, still,
Which seeks a 'soul of goodness'[7] in things ill
Or in himself or others has thus bowed                      205
His being—there are some by nature proud,
Who patient in all else demand but this:

4. Acknowledge.
5. Unteachable.
6. In the Pierpont Morgan manuscript the word is "see"; but *Posthumous Poems* and all subsequent texts give *know*, which completes the rhyme.
7. Shakespeare, *King Henry V*, IV.i.4.

To love and be beloved with gentleness;
And being scorned, what wonder if they die
Some living death? this is not destiny                              210
But man's own wilful ill." As thus I spoke[8]
Servants announced the gondola, and we
Through the fast-falling rain and high-wrought sea
Sailed to the island where the madhouse stands.
We disembarked. The clap of tortured hands,                        215
Fierce yells and howlings and lamentings keen,
And laughter where complaint had merrier been,
Moans, shrieks and curses and blaspheming prayers
Accosted us. We climbed the oozy stairs
Into an old courtyard. I heard on high,                             220
Then, fragments of most touching melody,
But looking up saw not the singer there—
Through the black bars in the tempestuous air
I saw, like weeds on a wrecked palace growing,
Long tangled locks flung wildly forth, and flowing,                225
Of those who on a sudden were beguiled
Into strange silence, and looked forth and smiled,
Hearing sweet sounds.—Then I: "Methinks there were
A cure of these with patience and kind care,
If music can thus move . . . but what is he                        230
Whom we seek here?" "Of his sad history
I know but this," said Maddalo: "he came
To Venice a dejected man, and fame
Said he was wealthy, or he had been so;
Some thought the loss of fortune wrought him woe;                  235
But he was ever talking in such sort
As you do—far more sadly—he seemed hurt,
Even as a man with his peculiar wrong,
To hear but of the oppression of the strong,
Or those absurd deceits (I think with you                          240
In some respects, you know) which carry through
The excellent impostors of this Earth
When they outface detection—he had worth,
Poor fellow! but a humourist[9] in his way"—
"Alas, what drove him mad?" "I cannot say;                         245
A Lady came with him from France, and when
She left him and returned, he wandered then
About yon lonely isles of desart sand
Till he grew wild—he had no cash or land
Remaining,—the police had brought him here—                       250
Some fancy took him and he would not bear

---

8. This came to be the only unrhymed line in the poem when Shelley elected to drop three
   and a half lines from his draft after line 210: "At least tho all the past c^d not have been /
   Other than as it was—yet things foreseen / Reason and Love may force beneath their yoke
   / Warned by a fate foregone—*as thus I spoke*" (*BSM*, XV, 89).
9. One exhibiting strong peculiarities in a particular direction, as if caused by the predominance
   of one of the four "humours" or vital fluids of classical and medieval physiology—blood,
   phlegm, choler (yellow bile), and melancholy (black bile).

Removal; so I fitted up for him
Those rooms beside the sea, to please his whim,
And sent him busts and books and urns for flowers,
Which had adorned his life in happier hours,                    255
And instruments of music—you may guess
A stranger could do little more or less
For one so gentle and unfortunate—
And those are his sweet strains which charm the weight
From madmen's chains, and make this Hell appear               260
A heaven of sacred silence, hushed to hear."—
"Nay, this was kind of you—he had no claim,
As the world says"—"None—but the very same
Which I on all mankind were I, as he,
Fallen to such deep reverse;—his melody                       265
Is interrupted now—we hear the din
Of madmen, shriek on shriek again begin;
Let us now visit him; after this strain
He ever communes with himself again,
And sees nor hears not any." Having said                      270
These words we called the keeper, and he led
To an apartment opening on the sea—
There the poor wretch was sitting mournfully
Near a piano, his pale fingers twined
One with the other, and the ooze and wind                     275
Rushed through an open casement, and did sway
His hair, and starred it with the brackish[1] spray;
His head was leaning on a music book,
And he was muttering, and his lean limbs shook;
His lips were pressed against a folded leaf                    280
In hue too beautiful for health, and grief
Smiled in their motions as they lay apart—
As one who wrought from his own fervid heart
The eloquence of passion, soon he raised
His sad meek face and eyes lustrous and glazed                285
And spoke—sometimes as one who wrote and thought
His words might move some heart that heeded not
If sent to distant lands; and then as one
Reproaching deeds never to be undone
With wondering self-compassion; then his speech               290
Was lost in grief, and then his words came each
Unmodulated, cold, expressionless;
But that from one jarred accent you might guess
It was despair made them so uniform:
And all the while the loud and gusty storm                    295
Hissed through the window, and we stood behind
Stealing his accents from the envious wind
Unseen. I yet remember what he said
Distinctly: such impression his words made.

1. Somewhat salty.

"Month after month," he cried, "to bear this load          300
And as a jade[2] urged by the whip and goad
To drag life on, which like a heavy chain
Lengthens behind with many a link of pain!—
And not to speak my grief—O not to dare
To give a human voice to my despair,                       305
But live and move, and wretched thing! smile on
As if I never went aside to groan
And wear this mask of falshood even to those
Who are most dear—not for my own repose—
Alas, no scorn or pain or hate could be                    310
So heavy as that falshood is to me—
But that I cannot bear more altered faces
Than needs must be, more changed and cold embraces,
More misery, disappointment and mistrust
To own me for their father . . . Would the dust            315
Were covered in upon my body now!
That the life ceased to toil within my brow!
And then these thoughts would at the least be fled;
Let us not fear such pain can vex the dead.

     "What Power delights to torture us? I know            320
That to myself I do not wholly owe
What now I suffer, though in part I may.
Alas, none strewed sweet flowers upon the way
Where wandering heedlessly, I met pale Pain
My shadow, which will leave me not again—                  325
If I have erred, there was no joy in error,
But pain and insult and unrest and terror;
I have not as some do, bought penitence
With pleasure, and a dark yet sweet offence,
For then,—if love and tenderness and truth                330
Had overlived hope's momentary youth,
My creed should have redeemed me from repenting;
But loathed scorn and outrage unrelenting
Met love excited by far other seeming
Until the end was gained . . . as one from dreaming        335
Of sweetest peace, I woke, and found my state
Such as it is.——
                    "O Thou, my spirit's mate
Who, for thou art compassionate and wise,
Wouldst pity me from thy most gentle eyes
If this sad writing thou shouldst ever see—                340
My secret groans must be unheard by thee,
Thou wouldst weep tears bitter as blood to know
Thy lost friend's incommunicable woe.

     "Ye few by whom my nature has been weighed
In friendship, let me not that name degrade                345

2. A cart horse, or a worn-out, inferior horse.

By placing on your hearts the secret load
Which crushes mine to dust. There is one road
To peace and that is truth, which follow ye!
Love sometimes leads astray to misery.
Yet think not though subdued—and I may well          350
Say that I am subdued—that the pale Hell
Within me would infect the untainted breast
Of sacred nature with its own unrest;
As some perverted beings think to find
In scorn or hate a medicine for the mind          355
Which scorn or hate hath wounded—O how vain!
The dagger heals not but may rend again . . . .
Believe that I am ever still the same
In creed as in resolve, and what may tame
My heart, must leave the understanding free          360
Or all would sink in this keen agony—
Nor dream that I will join the vulgar cry,
Or with my silence sanction tyranny,
Or seek a moment's shelter from my pain
In any madness which the world calls gain,          365
Ambition or revenge or thoughts as stern
As those which make me what I am, or turn
To avarice or misanthropy or lust . . . .
Heap on me soon, o grave, thy welcome dust!
Till then the dungeon may demand its prey,          370
And poverty and shame may meet and say—
Halting beside me on the public way—
'That love-devoted[3] youth is ours—let's sit
Beside him—he may live some six months yet.'
Or the red scaffold, as our country bends,          375
May ask some willing victim, or ye friends
May fall under some sorrow which this heart
Or hand may share or vanquish or avert;
I am prepared—in truth, with no proud joy—
To do or suffer aught,[4] as when a boy          380
I did devote to justice and to love
My nature, worthless now![5] . . .
                              "I must remove
A veil from my pent[6] mind. 'Tis torn aside!
O, pallid as death's dedicated bride,
Thou mockery which art sitting by my side,          385
Am I not wan like thee? at the grave's call
I haste, invited to thy wedding ball
To greet the ghastly paramour, for whom
Thou hast deserted me . . . and made the tomb
Thy bridal bed . . . But I beside your feet          390
Will lie and watch ye from my winding sheet—

3. Sacrificed to love.
4. *aught:* anything at all.
5. Cf. lines 380–82 with "Hymn to Intellectual Beauty" and the Dedication to *Laon and Cythna.*
6. Locked up, imprisoned.

Thus . . . wide awake, though dead . . . yet stay, o stay!
Go not so soon—I know not what I say—
Hear but my reasons . . . I am mad, I fear,
My fancy is o'erwrought . . . thou art not here . . .                    395
Pale art thou, 'tis most true . . . but thou art gone,
Thy work is finished . . . I am left alone!—
      x    x    x    x    x    x    x[7]
  "Nay, was it I who wooed thee to this breast
Which, like a serpent, thou envenomest
As in repayment of the warmth it lent?                    400
Didst thou not seek me for thine own content?
Did not thy love awaken mine? I thought
That thou wert she who said, 'You kiss me not
Ever, I fear you do not love me now'—
In truth I loved even to my overthrow                    405
Her, who would fain forget these words: but they
Cling to her mind, and cannot pass away.
      x    x    x    x    x    x    x
  "You say that I am proud—that when I speak
My lip is tortured with the wrongs which break
The spirit it expresses . . . Never one                    410
Humbled himself before, as I have done!
Even the instinctive worm on which we tread
Turns, though it wound not—then with prostrate head
Sinks in the dust and writhes like me—and dies?
No: wears a living death of agonies!                    415
As the slow shadows of the pointed grass
Mark the eternal periods, his pangs pass
Slow, ever-moving,—making moments be
As mine seem—each an immortality!
      x    x    x    x    x    x    x
  "That you had never seen me—never heard                    420
My voice, and more than all had ne'er endured
The deep pollution of my loathed embrace—
That your eyes ne'er had lied love in my face—
That, like some maniac monk, I had torn out
The nerves of manhood by their bleeding root                    425
With mine own quivering fingers, so that ne'er
Our hearts had for a moment mingled there
To disunite in horror—these were not
With thee like some suppressed and hideous thought
Which flits athwart our musings, but can find                    430
No rest within a pure and gentle mind . . .
Thou sealedst them with many a bare broad word
And cearedst[8] my memory o'er them,—for I heard
And can forget not . . . they were ministered
One after one, those curses. Mix them up                    435

7. Shelley's lines of x's (usually printed as asterisks) indicate silent pauses between the inter-
   mittent outcries of the Maniac; no poetic lines are omitted.
8. Wrapped in waxed cloth, embalmed; previous editors changed the word to "searedst."

Like self-destroying poisons in one cup,
And they will make one blessing which thou ne'er
Didst imprecate for, on me,—death.

    x    x    x    x    x    x    x

                                "It were
A cruel punishment for one most cruel,
If such can love, to make that love the fuel                    440
Of the mind's hell; hate, scorn, remorse, despair:
But *me*—whose heart a stranger's tear might wear
As water-drops the sandy fountain-stone,
Who loved and pitied all things, and could moan
For woes which others hear not, and could see              445
The absent with the glance of phantasy,
And with the poor and trampled sit and weep,
Following the captive to his dungeon deep;
*Me*—who am as a nerve o'er which do creep
The else unfelt oppressions of this earth                     450
And was to thee the flame upon thy hearth
When all beside was cold—that thou on me
Shouldst rain these plagues of blistering agony—
Such curses are from lips once eloquent
With love's too partial praise—let none relent              455
Who intend deeds too dreadful for a name
Henceforth, if an example for the same
They seek . . . for thou on me lookedst so, and so—
And didst speak thus . . . and thus . . . I live to shew
How much men bear and die not!

    x    x    x    x    x    x    x

                      "Thou wilt tell              460
With the grimace of hate how horrible
It was to meet my love when thine grew less;
Thou wilt admire how I could e'er address
Such features to love's work . . . this taunt, though true,
(For indeed nature nor in form nor hue                       465
Bestowed on me her choicest workmanship)
Shall not be thy defence . . . for since thy lip
Met mine first, years long past, since thine eye kindled
With soft fire under mine, I have not dwindled
Nor changed in mind or body, or in aught                    470
But as love changes what it loveth not
After long years and many trials.
                        "How vain
Are words! I thought never to speak again,
Not even in secret,—not to my own heart—
But from my lips the unwilling accents start                 475
And from my pen the words flow as I write,
Dazzling my eyes with scalding tears . . . my sight
Is dim to see that charactered in vain
On this unfeeling leaf which burns the brain
And eats into it . . . blotting all things fair              480
And wise and good which time had written there.

"Those who inflict must suffer, for they see
The work of their own hearts and this must be
Our chastisement or recompense—O child!
I would that thine were like to be more mild          485
For both our wretched sakes . . . for thine the most
Who feelest already all that thou hast lost
Without the power to wish it thine again;
And as slow years pass, a funereal train
Each with the ghost of some lost hope or friend          490
Following it like its shadow, wilt thou bend
No thought on my dead memory?
                    x     x     x     x     x     x     x
                                        "Alas, love,
Fear me not . . . against thee I would not move
A finger in despite. Do I not live
That thou mayst have less bitter cause to grieve?          495
I give thee tears for scorn and love for hate,
And that thy lot may be less desolate
Than his on whom thou tramplest, I refrain
From that sweet sleep⁹ which medicines all pain.
Then, when thou speakest of me, never say,          500
'He could forgive not.' Here I cast away
All human passions, all revenge, all pride;
I think, speak, act no ill; I do but hide
Under these words like embers, every spark
Of that which has consumed me—quick and dark          505
The grave is yawning . . . as its roof shall cover
My limbs with dust and worms under and over
So let Oblivion hide this grief . . . the air
Closes upon my accents, as despair
Upon my heart—let death upon despair!"          510

     He ceased, and overcome leant back awhile,
Then rising, with a melancholy smile
Went to a sofa, and lay down, and slept
A heavy sleep, and in his dreams he wept
And muttered some familiar name, and we          515
Wept without shame in his society.
I think I never was impressed so much;
The man who were not, must have lacked a touch
Of human nature . . . then we lingered not,
Although our argument was quite forgot,          520
But calling the attendants, went to dine
At Maddalo's; yet neither cheer nor wine
Could give us spirits, for we talked of him
And nothing else, till daylight made stars dim;
And we agreed his was some dreadful ill          525
Wrought on him boldly, yet unspeakable
By a dear friend; some deadly change in love

9. I.e., death.

Of one vowed deeply which he dreamed not of;
For whose sake he, it seemed, had fixed a blot
Of falshood on his mind which flourished not        530
But in the light of all-beholding truth;
And having stamped this canker[1] on his youth
She had abandoned him—and how much more
Might be his woe, we guessed not—he had store
Of friends and fortune once, as we could guess      535
From his nice[2] habits and his gentleness;
These were now lost . . . it were a grief indeed
If he had changed one unsustaining reed
For all that such a man might else adorn.
The colours of his mind seemed yet unworn;          540
For the wild language of his grief was high,
Such as in measure were called poetry;
And I remember one remark which then
Maddalo made. He said: "Most wretched men
Are cradled into poetry by wrong,                   545
They learn in suffering what they teach in song."

    If I had been an unconnected man[3]
I, from this moment, should have formed some plan
Never to leave sweet Venice,—for to me
It was delight to ride by the lone sea;             550
And then, the town is silent—one may write
Or read in gondolas by day or night,
Having the little brazen[4] lamp alight,
Unseen, uninterrupted; books are there,
Pictures, and casts from all those statues fair     555
Which were twin-born with poetry, and all
We seek in towns, with little to recall
Regrets for the green country. I might sit
In Maddalo's great palace, and his wit
And subtle talk would cheer the winter night        560
And make me know myself, and the firelight
Would flash upon our faces, till the day
Might dawn and make me wonder at my stay:
But I had friends in London too: the chief
Attraction here, was that I sought relief           565
From the deep tenderness that maniac wrought
Within me—'twas perhaps an idle thought,
But I imagined that if day by day
I watched him, and but seldom went away,
And studied all the beatings of his heart           570
With zeal, as men study some stubborn art
For their own good, and could by patience find
An entrance to the caverns of his mind,

---

1. A consuming, spreading sore or ulcer (cf. cancer).
2. Refined, cultured.
3. A man without family or other responsibilities.
4. Made of brass.

I might reclaim him from his dark estate:
In friendships I had been most fortunate[5]                   575
Yet never saw I one whom I would call
More willingly my friend; and this was all
Accomplished not; such dreams of baseless[6] good
Oft come and go in crowds and solitude
And leave no trace—but what I now designed          580
Made for long years impression on my mind.
The following morning, urged by my affairs,
I left bright Venice.
                    After many years
And many changes I returned; the name
Of Venice, and its aspect, was the same;               585
But Maddalo was travelling far away
Among the mountains of Armenia.[7]
His dog was dead. His child had now become
A woman; such as it has been my doom[8]
To meet with few, a wonder of this earth               590
Where there is little of transcendent worth,
Like one of Shakespeare's women: kindly she
And with a manner beyond courtesy
Received her father's friend; and when I asked
Of the lorn[9] maniac, she her memory tasked          595
And told as she had heard the mournful tale:
That the poor sufferer's health began to fail
Two years from my departure, but that then
"The Lady who had left him, came again.[1]
Her mien had been imperious, but she now             600
Looked meek—perhaps remorse had brought her low.
Her coming made him better, and they stayed
Together at my father's—for I played
As I remember with the lady's shawl—
I might be six years old—but after all                 605
She left him" . . . "Why, her heart must have been tough:
How did it end?" "And was not this enough?
They met—they parted"—"Child, is there no more?"
"Something within that interval which bore
The stamp of *why* they parted, *how* they met:        610
Yet if thine aged eyes disdain to wet
Those wrinkled cheeks with youth's remembered tears,
Ask me no more, but let the silent years
Be closed and ceared[2] over their memory

5. Shelley uses the same formulation in his dedication of *The Cenci* to Hunt.
6. Having no foundation; see Shakespeare, *The Tempest*, IV.i.151.
7. During 1817–18, Byron was studying the Armenian language in Venice.
8. Fate.
9. Abandoned, desolate.
1. Though the Pierpont Morgan manuscript gives the opening quotation marks at the beginning of line 597, the word *my* in line 598 identifies that line as Julian's self-reference in his indirect reporting of the substance of the response of Maddalo's daughter; his direct quotation of her words begins at 599.
2. Sealed up, embalmed (cf. line 433).

As yon mute marble where their corpses lie."                    615
I urged and questioned still, she told me how
All happened—but the cold world shall not know.


## STANZAS WRITTEN IN DEJECTION— DECEMBER 1818, NEAR NAPLES

The heading that Shelley gave the holograph fair copy of this poem was simply "Naples— December 1818." Though Mary Shelley produced a slightly
different text when she first published it in *Posthumous Poems* (1824), we
have followed Shelley's holograph safekeeping copy for the words of our
text, supplementing his sparse punctuation where appropriate.

This holograph—once part of the larger of the two Harvard Shelley
notebooks (Harvard MS.Eng.258.2)—was later removed and is now located in the Pierpont Morgan Library (MA 406; annotated facsimile in
*MYR: Shelley*, V, 73–75). The placement of the draft in Bodleian MS
Shelley adds. e.11 (*BSM*, XV) indicates that he gave the place and date to
reveal—not to obfuscate—the circumstances under which this very personal lament was composed. Mary Shelley certainly saw the poem while
it was still part of the Harvard Shelley Notebook, for it appears on the list
of contents in her hand at the back of the Notebook. Later—probably
after mid-1821—Shelley himself must have showed the poem to Edward
Williams, for one word in MA 406 is corrected in Williams's hand: he
wrote "cold" over "dead" in line 37, correcting the first rhyme in the final
stanza. Thus scholars were wrong to assume that Shelley removed these
leaves from the Harvard Notebook to send with others ("my saddest verses
raked up into one heap") to Charles Ollier on November 10, 1820, urging
him to publish them with *Julian and Maddalo*. For reasons adduced by
Reiman (*MYR: Shelley*, V, xxii–xxiii), the Pierpont Morgan MS was probably neither sent through the mail nor served as printer's copy when Mary
Shelley first published the poem.


## Stanzas written in Dejection— December 1818, Near Naples

The sun is warm, the sky is clear,
The waves are dancing fast and bright,
Blue isles and snowy mountains wear
The purple noon's transparent might,
The breath of the moist earth is light                    5
Around its unexpanded buds;
Like many a voice of one delight—
The winds, the birds, the Ocean-floods—
The City's voice itself is soft, like Solitude's.

I see the Deep's untrampled floor                    10
With green and purple seaweeds strown;
I see the waves upon the shore

Like light dissolved in star-showers, thrown . . .
I sit upon the sands alone:
The lightning of the noontide Ocean                         15
Is flashing round me, and a tone
Arises from its measured motion,
How sweet! did any heart now share in my emotion.

Alas, I have nor hope nor health
Nor peace within nor calm around,                           20
Nor that content surpassing wealth
The sage in meditation found
And walked with inward glory crowned,[1]
Nor fame nor power nor love nor leisure—
Others I see whom these surround—                           25
Smiling they live and call life pleasure:[2]
To me that cup has been dealt in another measure.

Yet now despair itself is mild,
Even as the winds and waters are;
I could lie down like a tired child                         30
And weep away the life of care
Which I have borne and yet must bear
Till Death like Sleep might steal on me
And I might feel in the warm air
My cheek grow cold, and hear the Sea                        35
Breathe o'er my dying brain its last monotony.

Some might lament that I were cold,
As I, when this sweet day is gone[3]
Which my lost heart, too soon grown old,
Insults with this untimely moan—                            40
They might lament—for I am one
Whom men love not, and yet regret:
Unlike this day, which, when the Sun
Shall on its cloudless glory set,
Will linger though enjoyed, like joy in Memory yet.[4]      45

1. *content . . . crowned:* though M. H. Abrams plausibly suggested that the allusion in lines 21–23 is to the Roman emperor and Stoic philosopher Marcus Aurelius (A.D. 121–180), whose *Meditations* Shelley admired, the poet could be referring to any wise person who had learned "to rule the empire of himself " (see page 327).
2. If lines 25–26 were indeed written on the date and at the place Shelley gives, the chief reference is surely to Byron and his circle at Venice.
3. I.e., Some might mourn (or *regret*, line 42) my death, as I shall lament the passing of this sweet day.
4. Lines 43–45: the stainless day, unlike the poet, will leave a joyful memory that will reproduce its original pleasure.

# The Two Spirits—An Allegory[1]

FIRST SPIRIT

O Thou who plumed with strong desire
Would float above the Earth—beware!
A shadow tracks thy flight of fire—
    Night is coming!
Bright are the regions of the air                5
And when winds and beams [       ]
It were delight to wander there—
    Night is coming!

SECOND SPIRIT

The deathless stars are bright above;
If I should cross the shade of night          10
Within my heart is the lamp of love
    And that is day—
And the moon will smile with gentle light
On my golden plumes where'er they move;
The meteors[2] will linger around my flight     15
    And make night day.

FIRST SPIRIT

But if the whirlwinds of darkness waken
Hail and Lightning and stormy rain—
See, the bounds of the air are shaken,
    Night is coming.                20
The red swift clouds of the hurricane
Yon declining sun have overtaken,
The clash of the hail sweeps o'er the plain—
    Night is coming.

1. At the time of Shelley's death this poetic dialogue between optimistic and pessimistic views of human destiny existed only in Shelley's original draft, Bodleian MS Shelley adds. e.12, pp. 13–17 (*BSM*, XVIII). Mary Shelley then transcribed it, with some errors (Bod. MS Shelley adds. d.7, pp. 62–65; *BSM*, II), and published it in Shelley's *Posthumous Poems* (1824)—later placing it among his poems of 1820. Judith Chernaik reedited it, along with most of Shelley's other major lyrical poems, in *The Lyrics of Shelley* (1972); she and Earl R. Wasserman (*Shelley: A Critical Reading*, pp. 42–44) are both convinced the poem is earlier. Chernaik suggests the poem may have been composed as early as 1818—a dating with which Charles E. Robinson (*Shelley and Byron*, pp. 263–64) and Nancy Goslee concur (*BSM*, XVIII, 280). We agree that the position in the Bodleian notebook suggests a date earlier than 1820 and date it tentatively between October 1818 and February 1819. Our text, based on the Bodleian draft, differs verbally from Chernaik's redaction in line 21, where we believe that *Posthumous Poems* correctly renders Shelley's draft of the line (Chernaik reads "And swift the clouds of the hurricane").
2. Probably shooting stars.

SECOND SPIRIT

I see the glare and I hear the sound—                                    25
I'll sail on the flood of the tempest dark
With the calm within and light around
          Which make night day;
And thou when the gloom is deep and stark,
Look from thy dull earth slumberbound—                                    30
My moonlike flight thou then mayst mark
          On high, far away.

———

Some say there is a precipice
Where one vast pine hangs frozen to ruin
O'er piles of snow and chasms of ice                                    35
          Mid Alpine mountains;
And that the languid storm pursuing
That winged shape forever flies
Round those hoar branches, aye renewing
          Its aery[3] fountains.                                    40

Some say when the nights are dry [and] clear
And the death dews sleep on the morass,[4]
Sweet whispers are heard by the traveller
          Which make night day—
And a shape like his early love doth pass                                    45
Upborne by her wild and glittering hair,
And when he awakes on the fragrant grass
          He finds night day.

# THE CENCI

Shelley began to compose this tragedy in May 1819, probably inspired by viewing the supposed Guido Reni portrait of Beatrice Cenci, then at the Palazzo Colonna in Rome. This portrait and a visit to the Palazzo Cenci stimulated Shelley to reread a manuscript of the Cenci family history that Mary Shelley had copied or translated in May 1818 from a manuscript owned by John Gisborne. (By 1964, the painting—no longer judged to be Guido's—was displayed at the Palazzo Corsini, across the Tiber from the Palazzo Cenci.) A photofacsimile of Mary Shelley's English version of the Cenci story—though perhaps not the same version that she had originally copied in 1818—appears in Bodleian MS Shelley adds. e.13 (*BSM*, X, 161ff). For additional evidence and complications concerning the transcript, see *SC*, VI, 896–98.

Shelley's composition of his drama at Rome was cut short by the illness and death of his son William Shelley (June 7, 1819), but he resumed work in late June and July after the Shelleys moved from Rome to the Villa

3. Ethereal.
4. Marsh or bog, here depicted as a breeding ground for disease.

Valsovano, near Livorno (Leghorn). By July 25, Shelley could write to Thomas Love Peacock, "I have written a tragedy" (*Letters*, II, 102; for the date of this letter, see *SC*, VI, 897n). On August 11, Shelley was copying his drama for the press; by August 20, Mary Shelley notes, she was copying it; and by September 21, 1819, the Leghorn printer Glauco Masi had produced 250 copies ready to ship to England.

Earlier, on September 10, Shelley had mailed a single printed copy of the text (without the Dedication and Preface) to Peacock, asking him to submit it anonymously to the Theatre Royal, Covent Garden, where Shelley hoped that Eliza O'Neill (1791–1872), the leading female tragedian of the day, would play Beatrice. But unknown to Shelley, O'Neill had just married and retired from the stage, and Covent Garden refused even to consider producing the play because of its emphasis on incest. This opinion was echoed by theatrical censors in Britain throughout the nineteenth century; *The Cenci* received its first staging in a private performance sponsored by the Shelley Society in 1886, but though George Bernard Shaw attempted to organize another performance for the centennial of Shelley's birth in 1892, *The Cenci* was not produced on the public stage in London until 1922, the centenary of his death. Prior to that date, the play had been produced professionally in Paris (1891); Coburg, Germany (1919); Moscow (1919–20); and Prague (1922). These and numerous subsequent productions in Europe and America have confirmed Shelley's confidence that *The Cenci* is "fitted for the stage" (see Stuart Curran, *Shelley's "Cenci"*). When Shelley, however, realized that the play would not be staged in London in 1820, he sent the Italian printing (dated 1819) to Charles Ollier, who published *The Cenci* early in 1820, the first reviews appearing in March and April. It alone of Shelley's works sold well enough to require an authorized second edition during his lifetime. For that 1820 London edition, Shelley sent Ollier a short list of verbal errors in the first edition, in Mary Shelley's hand, now bound into one of the Bodleian Library's copies of *The Cenci*, formerly owned by H. Buxton Forman (shelf mark Don.d.130). The only extant manuscript materials for the original edition are drafts for the Dedication and Preface, originally in Huntington notebook HM 2177 (see *MYR: Shelley*, IV, 28–37 and 400–47, respectively), of which the pages containing the Dedication were at some time removed and are in the Pforzheimer Collection, New York Public Library (*SC*, VI, 864–74).

The first editions of *The Cenci* and *Adonais*, both printed in Italy, are marred by minor inconsistencies—in the case of *The Cenci* due, in part, to different spelling practices of Shelley and Mary Shelley in their transcriptions of different parts of the copy-text. But both volumes provide valuable evidence of how Shelley wished his mature poetry to appear in print. Because Shelley himself saw the play through the press, guiding the Italian compositors, who would not have taken as many liberties with the forms of Shelley's words and punctuation as did the British printers of the second edition, our text is based on the first edition, as corrected from the errata list in the hand of Mary Shelley. We also correct palpable errors (for example, Æ instead of Œ at the beginning of "Œdipus"), the punctuation where the printed text fails to conform with Shelley's own practice in his polished fair-copy manuscripts, and anomalies that occur because of differences between the Italian and English type fonts (e.g., in the form of quotation marks).

See Jerrold E. Hogle's analysis of the play, pages 684–94.

# The Cenci
## A Tragedy, in Five Acts

*Dedication*[1]
To Leigh Hunt, Esq.

My DEAR FRIEND,

I inscribe with your name, from a distant country, and after an absence whose months have seemed years, this the latest of my literary efforts.

Those writings which I have hitherto published,[2] have been little else than visions which impersonate my own apprehensions of the beautiful and the just. I can also perceive in them the literary defects incidental to youth and impatience; they are dreams of what ought to be, or may be. The drama which I now present to you is a sad reality. I lay aside the presumptuous attitude of an instructor, and am content to paint, with such colours as my own heart furnishes, that which has been.

Had I known a person more highly endowed than yourself with all that it becomes a man to possess,[3] I had solicited for this work the ornament of his name. One more gentle, honourable, innocent and brave; one of more exalted toleration for all who do and think evil, and yet himself more free from evil; one who knows better how to receive, and how to confer a benefit though he must ever confer far more than he can receive; one of simpler, and, in the highest sense of the word, of purer life and manners I never knew: and I had already been fortunate in friendships when your name was added to the list.

In that patient and irreconcileable enmity with domestic and political tyranny and imposture which the tenor of your life has illustrated, and which, had I health and talents should illustrate mine, let us, comforting each other in our task, live and die.

All happiness attend you!

Your affectionate friend,
Percy B. Shelley.

*Rome, May* 29, 1819.

## Preface

A Manuscript was communicated to me during my travels in Italy which was copied from the archives of the Cenci Palace at Rome, and contains a detailed account of the horrors which ended in the extinction of one of the noblest and richest families of that city during the

---

1. Shelley drafted this Dedication to his closest friend at Villa Valsovano, near Livorno (Leghorn) in the period August 16–19, 1819; for Shelley's reasons for dating it May 29, 1819, see SC, VI, 865–74.
2. E.g., *Queen Mab, Alastor*, and *Laon and Cythna*.
3. I.e., all [the good qualities] that are becoming to a man.

Pontificate of Clement VIII,[4] in the year 1599. The story is, that an old man having spent his life in debauchery and wickedness, conceived at length an implacable hatred towards his children; which shewed itself towards one daughter under the form of an incestuous passion, aggravated by every circumstance of cruelty and violence. This daughter, after long and vain attempts to escape from what she considered a perpetual contamination both of body and mind, at length plotted with her mother-in-law[5] and brother to murder their common tyrant. The young maiden who was urged to this tremendous deed by an impulse which overpowered its horror, was evidently a most gentle and amiable being, a creature formed to adorn and be admired, and thus violently thwarted from her nature by the necessity of circumstance and opinion. The deed was quickly discovered and in spite of the most earnest prayers made to the Pope by the highest persons in Rome the criminals were put to death. The old man had during his life repeatedly bought his pardon from the Pope for capital crimes of the most enormous and unspeakable kind, at the price of a hundred thousand crowns; the death therefore of his victims can scarcely be accounted for by the love of justice. The Pope, among other motives for severity, probably felt that whoever killed the Count Cenci deprived his treasury of a certain and copious source of revenue.[6] Such a story, if told so as to present to the reader all the feelings of those who once acted it, their hopes and fears, their confidences and misgivings, their various interests, passions and opinions acting upon and with each other, yet all conspiring to one tremendous end, would be as a light to make apparent some of the most dark and secret caverns of the human heart.

On my arrival at Rome I found that the story of the Cenci was a subject not to be mentioned in Italian society without awakening a deep and breathless interest; and that the feelings of the company never failed to incline to a romantic pity for the wrongs, and a passionate exculpation of the horrible deed to which they urged her, who has been mingled two centuries with the common dust. All ranks of people knew the outlines of this history, and participated in the overwhelming interest which it seems to have the magic of exciting in the human heart. I had a copy of Guido's picture of Beatrice which is preserved in the Colonna Palace, and my servant instantly recognized it as the portrait of *La Cenci*.

This national and universal interest which the story produces and has produced for two centuries and among all ranks of people in a great City, where the imagination is kept for ever active and awake, first suggested to me the conception of its fitness for a dramatic pur-

---

4. Clement VIII (Ippolito Aldobrandino; 1536–1605), Pope from 1592 to 1605, was advised by Saint Philip Neri and was also a patron of Saint Francis de Sales; his pontificate actively supported the moral reforms in the Catholic Church known as the Counter-Reformation.
5. In Shelley's day *mother-in-law* could mean either stepmother or spouse's mother: in this case, stepmother.
6. "The Papal government formerly took the most extraordinary precautions against the publicity of facts which offer so tragical a demonstration of its own wickedness and weakness; so that the communication of the MS. had become, until very lately, a matter of some difficulty" (Shelley's note).

pose. In fact it is a tragedy which has already received, from its capacity of awakening and sustaining the sympathy of men, approbation and success. Nothing remained as I imagined, but to clothe it to the apprehensions of my countrymen in such language and action as would bring it home to their hearts. The deepest and the sublimest tragic compositions, *King Lear* and the two plays in which the tale of Œdipus is told, were stories which already existed in tradition, as matters of popular belief and interest, before Shakspeare and Sophocles made them familiar to the sympathy of all succeeding generations of mankind.

This story of the Cenci is indeed eminently fearful and monstrous: any thing like a dry exhibition of it on the stage would be insupportable. The person who would treat such a subject must increase the ideal, and diminish the actual horror of the events, so that the pleasure which arises from the poetry which exists in these tempestuous sufferings and crimes may mitigate the pain of the contemplation of the moral deformity from which they spring. There must also be nothing attempted to make the exhibition subservient to what is vulgarly termed a moral purpose. The highest moral purpose aimed at in the highest species of the drama, is the teaching the human heart, through its sympathies and antipathies, the knowledge of itself; in proportion to the possession of which knowledge, every human being is wise, just, sincere, tolerant and kind. If dogmas can do more, it is well: but a drama is no fit place for the enforcement of them. Undoubtedly, no person can be truly dishonoured by the act of another; and the fit return to make to the most enormous injuries is kindness and forbearance, and a resolution to convert the injurer from his dark passions by peace and love. Revenge, retaliation, atonement, are pernicious mistakes. If Beatrice had thought in this manner she would have been wiser and better; but she would never have been a tragic character: the few whom such an exhibition would have interested, could never have been sufficiently interested for a dramatic purpose, from the want of finding sympathy in their interest among the mass who surround them. It is in the restless and anatomizing casuistry[7] with which men seek the justification of Beatrice, yet feel that she has done what needs justification; it is in the superstitious horror with which they contemplate alike her wrongs and their revenge; that the dramatic character of what she did and suffered, consists.

I have endeavoured as nearly as possible to represent the characters as they probably were, and have sought to avoid the error of making them actuated by my own conceptions of right or wrong, false or true, thus under a thin veil converting names and actions of the sixteenth century into cold impersonations of my own mind. They are represented as Catholics, and as Catholics deeply tinged with religion. To a Protestant apprehension there will appear something unnatural in

---

7. The analytic reasoning of the casuist; casuistry is that part of ethics which resolves complex cases of conscience by applying the general rules of religion and morality to particular instances in which circumstances alter cases, or in which there seems to be a conflict of duties.

the earnest and perpetual sentiment of the relations between God and man which pervade the tragedy of the Cenci. It will especially be startled at the combination of an undoubting persuasion of the truth of the popular religion with a cool and determined perseverance in enormous guilt. But religion in Italy is not, as in Protestant countries, a cloak to be worn on particular days; or a passport which those who do not wish to be railed at carry with them to exhibit; or a gloomy passion for penetrating the impenetrable mysteries of our being, which terrifies its possessor at the darkness of the abyss to the brink of which it has conducted him. Religion coexists, as it were, in the mind of an Italian Catholic with a faith in that of which all men have the most certain knowledge. It is interwoven with the whole fabric of life. It is adoration, faith, submission, penitence, blind admiration; not a rule for moral conduct. It has no necessary connexion with any one virtue. The most atrocious villain may be rigidly devout, and without any shock to established faith, confess himself to be so.[8] Religion pervades intensely the whole frame of society, and is according to the temper of the mind which it inhabits, a passion, a persuasion, an excuse, a refuge; never a check. Cenci himself built a chapel in the court of his Palace, and dedicated it to St. Thomas the Apostle, and established masses for the peace of his soul. Thus in the first scene of the fourth act Lucretia's design in exposing herself to the consequences of an expostulation with Cenci after having administered the opiate, was to induce him by a feigned tale to confess himself before death; this being esteemed by Catholics as essential to salvation; and she only relinquishes her purpose when she perceives that her perseverance would expose Beatrice to new outrages.

I have avoided with great care in writing this play the introduction of what is commonly called mere poetry, and I imagine there will scarcely be found a detached simile or a single isolated description, unless Beatrice's description of the chasm appointed for her father's murder should be judged to be of that nature.[9]

In a dramatic composition the imagery and the passion should interpenetrate one another, the former being reserved simply for the full development and illustration of the latter. Imagination is as the im-

---

8. Here Shelley reinterprets his Italian source. According to Mary Shelley's text of "Relation of the death of the family of the Cenci," "Sodomy was the least and Atheism the greatest, of the vices of Francesco [Cenci] as is proved by the tenor of his life. For he was three times accused of Sodomy and paid the sum of 100,000 crowns to government in commutation of the punishment rightfully awarded to this crime. And concerning his religion it is sufficient to state that he never frequented any church & although he caused a small chapel dedicated to the Apostle St. Thomas to be built in the court of his palace his intention in so doing was to bury there all his children whom he cruelly hated" (BSM, X, 172–75).

9. "An idea in this speech was suggested by a most sublime passage in El Purgatorio de San Patricio of Calderon: the only plagiarism which I have intentionally committed in the whole piece" (Shelley's note). As Stuart Curran points out, most of Shelley's supposed verbal and situational "plagiarisms" from Shakespeare, John Webster, and other Jacobean dramatists appear in the Italian manuscript that was Shelley's chief source; Curran, therefore, reasons that by the time Shakespeare wrote Macbeth and Measure for Measure, the English could have known the story of the Cenci through comparable contemporary accounts of the murder and trial of 1599 transmitted from Rome, and some of the parallel phrasings from these plays and The Cenci might derive from their authors' use of related accounts of that murder trial.

mortal God which should assume flesh for the redemption of mortal passion. It is thus that the most remote and the most familiar imagery may alike be fit for dramatic purposes when employed in the illustration of strong feeling, which raises what is low, and levels to the apprehension that which is lofty, casting over all the shadow of its own greatness. In other respects I have written more carelessly; that is, without an over-fastidious and learned choice of words. In this respect I entirely agree with those modern critics who assert that in order to move men to true sympathy we must use the familiar language of men. And that our great ancestors the antient English poets are the writers, a study of whom might incite us to do that for our own age which they have done for theirs. But it must be the real language of men in general and not that of any particular class to whose society the writer happens to belong. So much for what I have attempted; I need not be assured that success is a very different matter; particularly for one whose attention has but newly been awakened to the study of dramatic literature.

I endeavoured whilst at Rome to observe such monuments of this story as might be accessible to a stranger. The portrait of Beatrice at the Colonna Palace is admirable as a work of art: it was taken by Guido during her confinement in prison. But it is most interesting as a just representation of one of the loveliest specimens of the workmanship of Nature. There is a fixed and pale composure upon the features: she seems sad and stricken down in spirit, yet the despair thus expressed is lightened by the patience of gentleness. Her head is bound with folds of white drapery from which the yellow strings of her golden hair escape, and fall about her neck. The moulding of her face is exquisitely delicate; the eye brows are distinct and arched: the lips have that permanent meaning of imagination and sensibility which suffering has not repressed and which it seems as if death scarcely could extinguish. Her forehead is large and clear; her eyes, which we are told were remarkable for their vivacity, are swollen with weeping and lustreless, but beautifully tender and serene. In the whole mien there is a simplicity and dignity which united with her exquisite loveliness and deep sorrow are inexpressibly pathetic. Beatrice Cenci appears to have been one of those rare persons in whom energy and gentleness dwell together without destroying one another: her nature was simple and profound. The crimes and miseries in which she was an actor and a sufferer are as the mask and the mantle in which circumstances clothed her for her impersonation on the scene of the world.

The Cenci Palace is of great extent; and though in part modernized, there yet remains a vast and gloomy pile of feudal architecture in the same state as during the dreadful scenes which are the subject of this tragedy. The Palace is situated in an obscure corner of Rome, near the quarter of the Jews, and from the upper windows you see the immense ruins of Mount Palatine[1] half hidden under their profuse

1. Monte Palatino was the Italian name of the Palatine, one of the fabled seven hills on which ancient Rome was built and, according to myth, the earliest, where Romulus and Remus were deposited by the Tiber River after having been abandoned as infants.

overgrowth of trees. There is a court in one part of the palace (perhaps that in which Cenci built the Chapel to St. Thomas), supported by granite columns and adorned with antique friezes of fine workmanship and built up, according to the antient Italian fashion, with balcony over balcony of open work. One of the gates of the palace formed of immense stones and leading through a passage, dark and lofty and opening into gloomy subterranean chambers, struck me particularly.

Of the Castle of Petrella, I could obtain no further information than that which is to be found in the manuscript.

### Dramatis Personæ

COUNT FRANCESCO CENCI.          SAVELLA, *the Pope's Legate.*
GIACOMO. ⎫                       OLIMPIO. ⎫
         ⎬ *his sons.*                   ⎬ *Assassins.*
BERNARDO. ⎭                      MARZIO. ⎭
CARDINAL CAMILLO.                ANDREA, *servant to Cenci.*
ORSINO, *a Prelate.*             Nobles—Judges—Guards—Servants.
LUCRETIA, *Wife of* CENCI, *and step-mother of his children.*
BEATRICE, *his daughter.*

The Scene lies principally in Rome, but changes during the Fourth
     Act to Petrella, a castle among the Apulia Apennines.

Time. During the Pontificate of Clement VIII.

### Act I

SCENE I.—*An apartment in the Cenci Palace. Enter* COUNT CENCI,
                    *and* CARDINAL CAMILLO.

*Camillo.* That matter of the murder is hushed up
If you consent to yield his Holiness
Your fief that lies beyond the Pincian gate.[2]—
It needed all my interest in the conclave
To bend him to this point: he said that you                    5
Bought perilous impunity with your gold;
That crimes like yours if once or twice compounded
Enriched the Church, and respited from hell
An erring soul which might repent and live:—
But that the glory and the interest                           10
Of the high throne he fills, little consist
With making it a daily mart of guilt
As manifold and hideous as the deeds
Which you scarce hide from men's revolted eyes.

---

2. The gate at the north end of the Via Veneto and now leading to the Borghese Gardens; *fief:* an estate.

*Cenci.* The third of my possessions—let it go!                    15
Aye, I once heard the nephew of the Pope[3]
Had sent his architect to view the ground,
Meaning to build a villa on my vines
The next time I compounded[4] with his uncle:
I little thought he should outwit me so!                           20
Henceforth no witness—not the lamp—shall see
That which the vassal threatened to divulge
Whose throat is choked with dust for his reward.
The deed he saw could not have rated higher
Than his most worthless life:—it angers me!                        25
Respited me from Hell!—So may the Devil
Respite their souls from Heaven. No doubt Pope Clement,
And his most charitable nephews, pray
That the apostle Peter and the saints
Will grant for their sake that I long enjoy                        30
Strength, wealth, and pride, and lust, and length of days
Wherein to act the deeds which are the stewards
Of their revenue.—But much yet remains
To which they shew no title.
     *Camillo.*               Oh, Count Cenci!
So much that thou migh'st honourably live                          35
And reconcile thyself with thine own heart
And with thy God, and with the offended world.
How hideously look deeds of lust and blood
Through those snow white and venerable hairs!—
Your children should be sitting round you now,                     40
But that you fear to read upon their looks
The shame and misery you have written there.
Where is your wife? Where is your gentle daughter?
Methinks her sweet looks, which make all things else
Beauteous and glad, might kill the fiend within you.               45
Why is she barred from all society
But her own strange and uncomplaining wrongs?[5]
Talk with me, Count,—you know I mean you well.
I stood beside your dark and fiery youth
Watching its bold and bad career, as men                           50
Watch meteors, but it vanished not—I marked
Your desperate and remorseless manhood; now
Do I behold you in dishonoured age
Charged with a thousand unrepented crimes.
Yet I have ever hoped you would amend,                             55
And in that hope have saved your life three times.
     *Cenci.* For which Aldobrandino[6] owes you now
My fief beyond the Pincian.—Cardinal,
One thing, I pray you, recollect henceforth,

---

3. The illegitimate children of Roman clergy were euphemistically called "nephews" and "nieces."
4. Accepted terms of settlement in lieu of prosecution.
5. The evils done to Beatrice.
6. I.e., the Pope (his family name).

And so we shall converse with less restraint.                    60
A man you knew spoke of my wife and daughter—
He was accustomed to frequent my house;
So the next day *his* wife and daughter came
And asked if I had seen him; and I smiled:
I think they never saw him any more.                    65
    *Camillo.* Thou execrable man, beware!—
    *Cenci.*                              Of thee?
Nay this is idle:—We should know each other.
As to my character for what men call crime
Seeing I please my senses as I list,[7]
And vindicate that right with force or guile,                    70
It is a public matter, and I care not
If I discuss it with you. I may speak
Alike to you and my own conscious heart—
For you give out that you have half reformed me,
Therefore strong vanity will keep you silent                    75
If fear should not; both will, I do not doubt.
All men delight in sensual luxury,
All men enjoy revenge; and most exult
Over the tortures they can never feel—
Flattering their secret peace with others' pain.                    80
But I delight in nothing else. I love
The sight of agony, and the sense of joy,
When this shall be another's, and that mine.
And I have no remorse and little fear,
Which are, I think, the checks of other men.                    85
This mood has grown upon me, until now
Any design my captious[8] fancy makes
The picture of its wish, and it forms none
But such as men like you would start to know,
Is as my natural food and rest debarred                    90
Until it be accomplished.
    *Camillo.*               Art thou not
Most miserable?
    *Cenci.*          Why, miserable?—
No.—I am what your theologians call
Hardened;—which they must be in impudence,
So to revile a man's peculiar taste.                    95
True, I was happier than I am, while yet
Manhood remained to act the thing I thought;
While lust was sweeter than revenge; and now
Invention palls:—Aye, we must all grow old—
And but that there remains a deed to act                    100
Whose horror might make sharp an appetite
Duller than mine—I'd do,—I know not what.
When I was young I thought of nothing else
But pleasure; and I fed on honey sweets:

7. Wish or choose.
8. Designed to entrap or entangle by subtlety.

Men, by St. Thomas! cannot live like bees          105
And I grew tired:—yet, till I killed a foe,
And heard his groans, and heard his children's groans,
Knew I not what delight was else on earth,
Which now delights me little. I the rather
Look on such pangs as terror ill conceals,          110
The dry fixed eye ball; the pale quivering lip,
Which tell me that the spirit weeps within
Tears bitterer than the bloody sweat of Christ.
I rarely kill the body which preserves,
Like a strong prison, the soul within my power,          115
Wherein I feed it with the breath of fear
For hourly pain.
    *Camillo.*    Hell's most abandoned fiend
Did never, in the drunkenness of guilt,
Speak to his heart as now you speak to me;
I thank my God that I believe you not.          120

                             *Enter* ANDREA.

    *Andrea.* My Lord, a gentleman from Salamanca[9]
Would speak with you.
    *Cenci.*        Bid him attend me in
The grand saloon.[1]             [*Exit* ANDREA.
    *Camillo.*       Farewell; and I will pray
Almighty God that thy false, impious words
Tempt not his spirit to abandon thee.    [*Exit* CAMILLO.
    *Cenci.* The third of my possessions! I must use          126
Close husbandry,[2] or gold, the old man's sword,
Falls from my withered hand. But yesterday
There came an order from the Pope to make
Fourfold provision for my cursed sons;          130
Whom I had sent from Rome to Salamanca,
Hoping some accident might cut them off;
And meaning if I could to starve them there.
I pray thee, God, send some quick death upon them!
Bernardo and my wife could not be worse          135
If dead and damned:—then, as to Beatrice—
               [*Looking around him suspiciously.*
I think they cannot hear me at that door;
What if they should? And yet I need not speak
Though the heart triumphs with itself in words.
O, thou most silent air, that shalt not hear          140
What now I think! Thou, pavement, which I tread
Towards her chamber,—let your echoes talk
Of my imperious step scorning surprise,
But not of my intent!—Andrea!
                       *Enter* ANDREA.

    *Andrea.*          My lord?

9. A university city in Old Castile, Spain—not far from northern Portugal.
1. A principal reception room in a palace or great house; salon.
2. Secret or careful thrift, economy.

*Cenci.* Bid Beatrice attend me in her chamber                145
This evening:—no, at midnight and alone.          [*Exeunt.*


SCENE II.—*A garden of the Cenci Palace.*
*Enter* BEATRICE *and* ORSINO, *as in conversation.*

*Beatrice.* Pervert not truth,
Orsino. You remember where we held
That conversation;—nay, we see the spot
Even from this cypress;—two long years are past
Since, on an April midnight, underneath                       5
The moon-light ruins of mount Palatine,
I did confess to you my secret mind.
  *Orsino.* You said you loved me then.
  *Beatrice.*                    You are a Priest,
Speak to me not of love.
  *Orsino.*           I may obtain
The dispensation of the Pope to marry.                        10
Because I am a Priest do you believe
Your image, as the hunter some struck deer,
Follows me not whether I wake or sleep?
  *Beatrice.* As I have said, speak to me not of love;
Had you a dispensation I have not;                            15
Nor will I leave this home of misery
Whilst my poor Bernard, and that gentle lady
To whom I owe life, and these virtuous thoughts,
Must suffer what I still have strength to share.
Alas, Orsino! All the love that once                         20
I felt for you, is turned to bitter pain.
Ours was a youthful contract, which you first
Broke, by assuming vows no Pope will loose.
And thus I love you still, but holily,
Even as a sister or a spirit might;                          25
And so I swear a cold fidelity.
And it is well perhaps we shall not marry.
You have a sly, equivocating vein
That suits me not.—Ah, wretched that I am!
Where shall I turn? Even now you look on me                   30
As you[3] were not my friend, and as if you
Discovered that I thought so, with false smiles
Making my true suspicion seem your wrong.
Ah! No, forgive me; sorrow makes me seem
Sterner than else my nature might have been;                 35
I have a weight of melancholy thoughts,
And they forebode,—but what can they forebode
Worse than I now endure?
  *Orsino.*
                    All will be well.

3. I.e., As if you.

Is the petition yet prepared? You know
My zeal for all you wish, sweet Beatrice;                                    40
Doubt not but I will use my utmost skill
So that the Pope attend to your complaint.
    *Beatrice.* Your zeal for all I wish;—Ah me, you are cold!
Your utmost skill . . . speak but one word . . . (*Aside.*) Alas!
Weak and deserted creature that I am,                                        45
Here I stand bickering with my only friend!        [*To* ORSINO.
This night my father gives a sumptuous feast,
Orsino; he has heard some happy news
From Salamanca, from my brothers there,
And with this outward shew of love he mocks                                  50
His inward hate. 'Tis bold hypocrisy
For he would gladlier celebrate their deaths,
Which I have heard him pray for on his knees:
Great God! that such a father should be mine!
But there is mighty preparation made,                                       55
And all our kin, the Cenci, will be there,
And all the chief nobility of Rome.
And he has bidden me and my pale Mother
Attire ourselves in festival array.
Poor lady! She expects some happy change                                     60
In his dark spirit from this act; I none.
At supper I will give you the petition:
Till when—farewell.
    *Orsino.*        Farewell. (*Exit* BEATRICE.) I know the Pope
Will ne'er absolve me from my priestly vow
But by absolving me from the revenue                                         65
Of many a wealthy see;[4] and, Beatrice,
I think to win thee at an easier rate.
Nor shall he read her eloquent petition:
He might bestow her on some poor relation
Of his sixth cousin, as he did her sister,                                   70
And I should be debarred from all access.
Then as to what she suffers from her father,
In all this there is much exaggeration:—
Old men are testy and will have their way;
A man may stab his enemy, or his vassal,                                     75
And live a free life as to wine or women,
And with a peevish temper may return
To a dull home, and rate[5] his wife and children;
Daughters and wives call this, foul tyranny.
I shall be well content if on my conscience                                  80
There rest no heavier sin than what they suffer
From the devices of my love—a net
From which she shall escape not. Yet I fear
Her subtle mind, her awe-inspiring gaze,

---

4. *revenue / Of many a wealthy see:* Orsino, a clergyman from an influential Roman family, has
   been given title to several bishoprics, from which he retains a portion of the revenues while
   subordinates perform the duties.
5. Scold, reprove angrily or vehemently.

Whose beams anatomize[6] me nerve by nerve                    85
And lay me bare, and make me blush to see
My hidden thoughts.—Ah, no! A friendless girl
Who clings to me, as to her only hope:—
I were a fool, not less than if a panther
Were panic-stricken by the Antelope's eye,                    90
If she escape me.                                      [*Exit.*


SCENE III.—*A magnificent Hall in the Cenci Palace. A Banquet.*
      *Enter* CENCI, LUCRETIA, BEATRICE, ORSINO, CAMILLO, NOBLES.

   *Cenci.* Welcome, my friends and Kinsmen; welcome ye,
Princes and Cardinals, pillars of the church,
Whose presence honours our festivity.
I have too long lived like an Anchorite,[7]
And in my absence from your merry meetings               5
An evil word is gone abroad of me;
But I do hope that you, my noble friends,
When you have shared the entertainment here,
And heard the pious cause for which 'tis given,
And we have pledged a health or two together,            10
Will think me flesh and blood as well as you;
Sinful indeed, for Adam made all so,
But tender-hearted, meek and pitiful.
   *First Guest.* In truth, my Lord, you seem too light of heart,
Too sprightly and companionable a man,                   15
To act the deeds that rumour pins on you.
(*To his Companion.*) I never saw such blithe and open cheer
In any eye!
   *Second Guest.* Some most desired event,
In which we all demand a common joy,
Has brought us hither; let us hear it, Count.            20
   *Cenci.* It is indeed a most desired event.
If, when a parent from a parent's heart
Lifts from this earth to the great father of all
A prayer, both when he lays him down to sleep,
And when he rises up from dreaming it;                   25
One supplication, one desire, one hope,
That he would grant a wish for his two sons
Even all that he demands in their regard—
And suddenly beyond his dearest hope,
It is accomplished, he should then rejoice,              30
And call his friends and kinsmen to a feast,
And task their love to grace his merriment,
Then honour me thus far—for I am he.
   *Beatrice* (*to* LUCRETIA). Great God! How horrible! Some
      dreadful ill
Must have befallen my brothers.

6. Analyze minutely.
7. One who has secluded himself from the world, usually for religious reasons.

*Lucretia.*                    Fear not, Child,                    35
He speaks too frankly.
    *Beatrice.*          Ah! My blood runs cold.
I fear that wicked laughter round his eye
Which wrinkles up the skin even to the hair.
    *Cenci.* Here are the letters brought from Salamanca;
Beatrice, read them to your mother. God!                    40
I thank thee! In one night didst thou perform,
By ways inscrutable, the thing I sought.
My disobedient and rebellious sons
Are dead!—Why, dead!—What means this change of cheer?
You hear me not, I tell you they are dead;                    45
And they will need no food or raiment more:
The tapers that did light them the dark way
Are their last cost. The Pope, I think, will not
Expect I should maintain them in their coffins.
Rejoice with me—my heart is wondrous glad.                    50
            [LUCRETIA *sinks, half fainting;* BEATRICE *supports her.*
    *Beatrice.* It is not true!—Dear lady, pray look up.
Had it been true, there is[8] a God in Heaven,
He would not live to boast of such a boon.
Unnatural man, thou knowest that it is false.
    *Cenci.* Aye, as the word of God, whom here I call                    55
To witness that I speak the sober truth;—
And whose most favouring Providence was shewn
Even in the manner of their deaths. For Rocco[9]
Was kneeling at the mass, with sixteen others,
When the Church fell and crushed him to a mummy,[1]                    60
The rest escaped unhurt. Cristofano[2]
Was stabbed in error by a jealous man,
Whilst she he loved was sleeping with his rival;
All in the self-same hour of the same night;
Which shews that Heaven has special care of me.                    65
I beg those friends who love me, that they mark
The day a feast upon their calendars.
It was the twenty-seventh of December:[3]
Aye, read the letters if you doubt my oath.
        *The assembly appears confused; several of the guests rise.*
    *First Guest.* Oh, horrible! I will depart.—
    *Second Guest.*                    And I.—
    *Third Guest.*                    No, stay!                    70
I do believe it is some jest; though faith!
'Tis mocking us somewhat too solemnly.
I think his son has married the Infanta,
Or found a mine of gold in El Dorado;[4]

8. I.e., because there is.
9. One of Count Cenci's sons.
1. A pulpy substance or mass.
2. Another of Cenci's sons.
3. The feast day of John the Evangelist, who wrote "God is love" (1 John 4:8).
4. A fictitious country or city abounding in gold, believed by the Spaniards and Sir Walter
   Ralegh to exist upon the Amazon; *Infanta:* the title given a daughter of the king of Spain.

'Tis but to season some such news; stay, stay!                    75
I see 'tis only raillery by his smile.
  *Cenci (filling a bowl of wine, and lifting it up).*
Oh, thou bright wine whose purple splendor leaps
And bubbles gaily in this golden bowl
Under the lamp light, as my spirits do,
To hear the death of my accursed sons!                             80
Could I believe thou wert their mingled blood,
Then would I taste thee like a sacrament,
And pledge with thee the mighty Devil in Hell,
Who, if a father's curses, as men say,
Climb with swift wings after their children's souls,               85
And drag them from the very throne of Heaven,
Now triumphs in my triumph!—But thou art
Superfluous; I have drunken deep of joy
And I will taste no other wine to-night.
Here, Andrea! Bear the bowl around.
  *A Guest (rising).*                Thou wretch!                   90
Will none among this noble company
Check the abandoned villain?
  *Camillo.*                For God's sake
Let me dismiss the guests! You are insane,
Some ill will come of this.
  *Second Guest.*          Seize, silence him!
  *First Guest.* I will!
  *Third Guest.*      And I!
  *Cenci (addressing those who rise with a threatening gesture).*
                      Who moves? Who speaks?
                      (*Turning to the Company.*)
                            'tis nothing,   95
Enjoy yourselves.—Beware! For my revenge
Is as the sealed commission of a king
That kills, and none dare name the murderer.
  [*The Banquet is broken up; several of the Guests are departing.*
  *Beatrice.* I do entreat you, go not, noble guests;
What although tyranny, and impious hate                            100
Stand sheltered by a father's hoary hair?
What, if 'tis he who clothed us in these limbs
Who tortures them, and triumphs? What, if we,
The desolate and the dead, were his own flesh,
His children and his wife, whom he is bound                        105
To love and shelter? Shall we therefore find
No refuge in this merciless wide world?
Oh, think what deep wrongs must have blotted out
First love, then reverence in a child's prone mind
Till it thus vanquish shame and fear! O, think!                    110
I have borne much, and kissed the sacred hand
Which crushed us to the earth, and thought its stroke
Was perhaps some paternal chastisement!
Have excused much, doubted; and when no doubt
Remained, have sought by patience, love and tears                  115

To soften him, and when this could not be
I have knelt down through the long sleepless nights
And lifted up to God, the father of all,
Passionate prayers: and when these were not heard
I have still borne,—until I meet you here,                    120
Princes and kinsmen, at this hideous feast
Given at my brothers' deaths. Two yet remain,
His wife remains and I, whom if ye save not,
Ye may soon share such merriment again
As fathers make over their children's graves.                 125
Oh! Prince Colonna,[5] thou art our near kinsman,
Cardinal, thou art the Pope's chamberlain,
Camillo, thou art chief justiciary,[6]
Take us away!
    *Cenci.* (*He has been conversing with* CAMILLO *during the first*
      *part of* BEATRICE's *speech; he hears the conclusion, and now*
      *advances.*)
               I hope my good friends here
Will think of their own daughters—or perhaps                  130
Of their own throats—before they lend an ear
To this wild girl.
    *Beatrice* (*not noticing the words of Cenci*). Dare no one look
      on me?
None answer? Can one tyrant overbear
The sense of many best and wisest men?
Or is it that I sue not in some form                          135
Of scrupulous law, that ye deny my suit?
Oh, God! That I were buried with my brothers!
And that the flowers of this departed spring
Were fading on my grave! And that my father
Were celebrating now one feast for all!                       140
    *Camillo.* A bitter wish for one so young and gentle;
Can we do nothing?—
    *Colonna.*              Nothing that I see.
Count Cenci were a dangerous enemy:
Yet I would second any one.
    *A Cardinal.*           And I.
    *Cenci.* Retire to your chamber, insolent girl!            145
*Beatrice.* Retire thou impious man! Aye hide thyself
Where never eye can look upon thee more!
Wouldst thou have honour and obedience
Who art a torturer? Father, never dream
Though thou mayst overbear this company,                      150
But ill must come of ill.—Frown not on me!
Haste, hide thyself, lest with avenging looks
My brothers' ghosts should hunt thee from thy seat!
Cover thy face from every living eye,

---

5. The Colonna family, rivals of the Orsinis for power in Rome, were at this period at the height
    of their power.
6. *justiciary:* one who administers justice.

And start if thou but hear a human step:                                      155
Seek out some dark and silent corner, there,
Bow thy white head before offended God,
And we will kneel around, and fervently
Pray that he pity both ourselves and thee.
   *Cenci.* My friends, I do lament this insane girl                    160
Has spoilt the mirth of our festivity.
Good night, farewell; I will not make you longer
Spectators of our dull domestic quarrels.
Another time.—        *[Exeunt all but* CENCI *and* BEATRICE.
        My brain is swimming round;
Give me a bowl of wine!        *[To* BEATRICE.
        Thou painted viper!                                       165
Beast that thou art! Fair and yet terrible!
I know a charm shall make thee meek and tame,
Now get thee from my sight!       *[Exit* BEATRICE.
        Here, Andrea,
Fill up this goblet with Greek wine. I said
I would not drink this evening; but I must;                                    170
For, strange to say, I feel my spirits fail
With thinking what I have decreed to do.—  *[Drinking the wine.*
Be thou the resolution of quick youth
Within my veins, and manhood's purpose stern,
And age's firm, cold, subtle villainy;                                        175
As if thou wert indeed my children's blood
Which I did thirst to drink! The charm works well;
It must be done; it shall be done, I swear!       *[Exit.*

END OF THE FIRST ACT.

*Act II*

SCENE I.—*An apartment in the Cenci Palace.*
*Enter* LUCRETIA *and* BERNARDO.

   *Lucretia.* Weep not, my gentle boy; he struck but me
Who have borne deeper wrongs. In truth, if he
Had killed me, he had done a kinder deed.
O, God Almighty, do thou look upon us,
We have no other friend but only thee!                                          5
Yet weep not; though I love you as my own
I am not your true mother.
   *Bernardo.*        O more, more,
Than ever mother was to any child,
That have you been to me! Had he not been
My father, do you think that I should weep?                                    10
   *Lucretia.* Alas! Poor boy, what else could'st thou have done?
                *Enter* BEATRICE.
   *Beatrice (in a hurried voice).* Did he pass this way? Have you
    seen him, brother?

Ah! No, that is his step upon the stairs;
'Tis nearer now; his hand is on the door;
Mother, if I to thee have ever been                                          15
A duteous child, now save me! Thou, great God,
Whose image upon earth a father is,
Dost thou indeed abandon me! He comes;
The door is opening now; I see his face;
He frowns on others, but he smiles on me,                                    20
Even as he did after the feast last night.
                                                           *Enter a Servant.*
Almighty God, how merciful thou art!
'Tis but Orsino's servant.—Well, what news?
    *Servant.* My master bids me say, the Holy Father
Has sent back your petition thus unopened.      [*Giving a paper.*
And he demands at what hour 'twere secure                                    26
To visit you again?
    *Lucretia.*          At the Ave Mary.[7]                  [*Exit Servant.*
So, daughter, our last hope has failed; Ah me!
How pale you look; you tremble, and you stand
Wrapped in some fixed and fearful meditation,                                30
As if one thought were over strong for you:
Your eyes have a chill glare; O, dearest child!
Are you gone mad? If not, pray speak to me.
    *Beatrice.* You see I am not mad; I speak to you.
    *Lucretia.* You talked of something that your father did                  35
After that dreadful feast? Could it be worse
Than when he smiled, and cried, "My sons are dead!"
And every one looked in his neighbour's face
To see if others were as white as he?
At the first word he spoke I felt the blood                                   40
Rush to my heart, and fell into a trance;
And when it past I sat all weak and wild;
Whilst you alone stood up, and with strong words
Checked his unnatural pride; and I could see
The devil was rebuked that lives in him.                                     45
Until this hour thus you have ever stood
Between us and your father's moody wrath
Like a protecting presence: your firm mind
Has been our only refuge and defence:
What can have thus subdued it? What can now                                  50
Have given you that cold melancholy look,
Succeeding to your unaccustomed fear?
    *Beatrice.* What is it that you say? I was just thinking
'Twere better not to struggle any more.
Men, like my father, have been dark and bloody,                             55
Yet never—O! Before worse comes of it
'Twere wise to die: it ends in that at last.

---

7. I.e., at the hour when the bell is rung for the recitation of the salutation to the Virgin (*Ave Maria*).

*Lucretia.* Oh, talk not so, dear child! Tell me at once
What did your father do or say to you?
He stayed not after that accursed feast          60
One moment in your chamber.—Speak to me.
    *Bernardo.* Oh, sister, sister, prithee, speak to us!
    *Beatrice* (*speaking very slowly with a forced calmness*).
It was one word, Mother, one little word;
One look, one smile. (*Wildly.*) Oh! He has trampled me
Under his feet, and made the blood stream down          65
My pallid cheeks. And he has given us all
Ditch water, and the fever-stricken flesh
Of buffaloes, and bade us eat or starve,
And we have eaten.—He has made me look
On my beloved Bernardo, when the rust          70
Of heavy chains has gangrened his sweet limbs,
And I have never yet despaired—but now!
What would I say?                                   [*Recovering herself.*
                  Ah! No, 'tis nothing new.
The sufferings we all share have made me wild:
He only struck and cursed me as he passed;          75
He said, he looked, he did;—nothing at all
Beyond his wont, yet it disordered me.
Alas! I am forgetful of my duty,
I should preserve my senses for your sake.
    *Lucretia.* Nay, Beatrice; have courage, my sweet girl.          80
If any one despairs it should be I
Who loved him once, and now must live with him
Till God in pity call for him or me.
For you may, like your sister, find some husband,
And smile, years hence, with children round your knees;          85
Whilst I, then dead, and all this hideous coil[8]
Shall be remembered only as a dream.
    *Beatrice.* Talk not to me, dear lady, of a husband.
Did you not nurse me when my mother died?
Did you not shield me and that dearest boy?          90
And had we any other friend but you
In infancy, with gentle words and looks,
To win our father not to murder us?
And shall I now desert you? May the ghost
Of my dead Mother plead against my soul          95
If I abandon her who filled the place
She left, with more, even, than a mother's love!
    *Bernardo.* And I am of my sister's mind. Indeed
I would not leave you in this wretchedness,
Even though the Pope should make me free to live          100
In some blithe place, like others of my age,
With sports, and delicate food, and the fresh air.

---

8. Turmoil, confusion; cf. "mortal coil" (*Hamlet*, III.i.67).

Oh, never think that I will leave you, Mother!
*Lucretia.* My dear, dear children!
                                        *Enter* CENCI, *suddenly.*
   *Cenci.*
                                    What, Beatrice here!
Come hither!          [*She shrinks back, and covers her face.*
          Nay, hide not your face, 'tis fair;                   105
Look up! Why, yesternight you dared to look
With disobedient insolence upon me,
Bending a stern and an inquiring brow
On what I meant; whilst I then sought to hide
That which I came to tell you—but in vain.                    110
   *Beatrice* (*wildly, staggering towards the door*).
Oh, that the earth would gape! Hide me, O God!
   *Cenci.* Then it was I whose inarticulate words
Fell from my lips, and who with tottering steps
Fled from your presence, as you now from mine.
Stay, I command you—from this day and hour                   115
Never again, I think, with fearless eye,
And brow superior, and unaltered cheek,
And that lip made for tenderness or scorn,
Shalt thou strike dumb the meanest of mankind;
Me least of all. Now get thee to thy chamber!                120
Thou too, loathed image of thy cursed mother,    [*To* BERNARDO.
Thy milky, meek face makes me sick with hate!
                      [*Exeunt* BEATRICE *and* BERNARDO.
(*Aside.*) So much has passed between us as must make
Me bold, her fearful.—'Tis an awful[9] thing
To touch such mischief as I now conceive:                    125
So men sit shivering on the dewy bank,
And try the chill stream with their feet; once in—
How the delighted spirit pants for joy!
   *Lucretia* (*advancing timidly towards him*).
Oh, husband! Pray forgive poor Beatrice,
She meant not any ill.
   *Cenci.*              Nor you perhaps?                      130
Nor that young imp, whom you have taught by rote
Parricide with his alphabet? Nor Giacomo?
Nor those two most unnatural sons, who stirred
Enmity up against me with the Pope?
Whom in one night merciful God cut off:                      135
Innocent lambs! They thought not any ill.
You were not here conspiring? You said nothing
Of how I might be dungeoned as a madman;
Or be condemned to death for some offence,
And you would be the witnesses?—This failing,               140
How just it were to hire assassins, or
Put sudden poison in my evening drink?
Or smother me when overcome by wine?

9. Awe-inspiring.

Seeing we had no other judge but God,
And he had sentenced me, and there were none          145
But you to be the executioners
Of his decree enregistered in heaven?
Oh, no! You said not this?
    *Lucretia.*          So help me God,
I never thought the things you charge me with!
    *Cenci.* If you dare speak that wicked lie again          150
I'll kill you. What! It was not by your counsel
That Beatrice disturbed the feast last night?
You did not hope to stir some enemies
Against me, and escape, and laugh to scorn
What every nerve of you now trembles at?          155
You judged that men were bolder than they are;
Few dare to stand between their grave and me.
    *Lucretia.* Look not so dreadfully! By my salvation
I knew not aught that Beatrice designed;
Nor do I think she designed any thing          160
Until she heard you talk of her dead brothers.
    *Cenci.* Blaspheming liar! You are damned for this!
But I will take you where you may persuade
The stones you tread on to deliver you:
For men shall there be none but those who dare          165
All things—not question that which I command.
On Wednesday next I shall set out: you know
That savage rock, the Castle of Petrella,
'Tis safely walled, and moated round about:
Its dungeons underground, and its thick towers          170
Never told tales; though they have heard and seen
What might make dumb things speak.—Why do you linger?
Make speediest preparation for the journey!     [*Exit* LUCRETIA.
The all-beholding sun yet shines; I hear
A busy stir of men about the streets;          175
I see the bright sky through the window panes:
It is a garish, broad, and peering day;
Loud, light, suspicious, full of eyes and ears,
And every little corner, nook and hole
Is penetrated with the insolent light.          180
Come darkness! Yet, what is the day to me?
And wherefore should I wish for night, who do
A deed which shall confound both night and day?
'Tis she shall grope through a bewildering mist
Of horror: if there be a sun in heaven          185
She shall not dare to look upon its beams;
Nor feel its warmth. Let her then wish for night;
The act I think shall soon extinguish all
For me: I bear a darker deadlier gloom
Than the earth's shade,[1] or interlunar air,          190
Or constellations quenched in murkiest cloud,

---

1. The shadow that the earth casts away from the sun; *interlunar:* pertaining to the dark period
between the old and new moon.

In which I walk secure and unbeheld
Towards my purpose.—Would that it were done!          [*Exit.*

SCENE II.—*A chamber in the Vatican. Enter* CAMILLO *and*
GIACOMO, *in conversation.*

*Camillo.* There is an obsolete and doubtful law
By which you might obtain a bare provision
Of food and clothing—
    *Giacomo.*          Nothing more? Alas!
Bare must be the provision which strict law
Awards, and aged, sullen avarice pays.          5
Why did my father not apprentice me
To some mechanic trade? I should have then
Been trained in no highborn necessities
Which I could meet not by my daily toil.
The eldest son of a rich nobleman          10
Is heir to all his incapacities;
He has wide wants, and narrow powers. If you,
Cardinal Camillo, were reduced at once
From thrice-driven beds of down,[2] and delicate food,
An hundred servants, and six palaces,          15
To that which nature doth indeed require?—
    *Camillo.* Nay, there is reason in your plea; 'twere hard.
    *Giacomo.* 'Tis hard for a firm man to bear: but I
Have a dear wife, a lady of high birth,
Whose dowry in ill hour I lent my father          20
Without a bond or witness to the deed:
And children, who inherit her fine senses,
The fairest creatures in this breathing world;
And she and they reproach me not. Cardinal,
Do you not think the Pope would interpose          25
And stretch authority beyond the law?
    *Camillo.* Though your peculiar case is hard, I know
The Pope will not divert the course of law.
After that impious feast the other night
I spoke with him, and urged him then to check          30
Your father's cruel hand; he frowned and said,
"Children are disobedient, and they sting
Their fathers' hearts to madness and despair
Requiting years of care with contumely.[3]
I pity the Count Cenci from my heart;          35
His outraged love perhaps awakened hate,
And thus he is exasperated to ill.
In the great war between the old and young
I, who have white hairs and a tottering body,
Will keep at least blameless neutrality."          40

2. Apparently down (the soft underfeathers of birds) that has been separated from larger, coarser feathers by beating the feathers until the lightest are blown away from the others (see V.ii.169–70).
3. Insulting or offensively contemptuous language or treatment.

                                          *Enter* ORSINO.
You, my good Lord Orsino, heard those words.
*Orsino.* What words?
*Giacomo.*                    Alas, repeat them not again!
There then is no redress for me, at least
None but that which I may atchieve⁴ myself,
Since I am driven to the brink.—But, say,                    45
My innocent sister and my only brother
Are dying underneath my father's eye.
The memorable torturers of this land,
Galeaz Visconti, Borgia, Ezzelin,⁵
Never inflicted on their meanest slave                    50
What these endure; shall they have no protection?
*Camillo.* Why, if they would petition to the Pope
I see not how he could refuse it—yet
He holds it of most dangerous example
In aught to weaken the paternal power,                    55
Being, as 'twere, the shadow of his own.
I pray you now excuse me. I have business
That will not bear delay.                    [*Exit* CAMILLO.
*Giacomo.*                    But you, Orsino,
Have the petition: wherefore not present it?
*Orsino.* I have presented it, and backed it with                    60
My earnest prayers, and urgent interest;
It was returned unanswered. I doubt not
But that the strange and execrable deeds
Alledged in it—in truth they might well baffle
Any belief—have turned the Pope's displeasure                    65
Upon the accusers from the criminal:
So I should guess from what Camillo said.
*Giacomo.* My friend, that palace-walking devil Gold
Has whispered silence to his Holiness:
And we are left, as scorpions ringed with fire,                    70
What should we do but strike ourselves to death?⁶
For he who is our murderous persecutor
Is shielded by a father's holy name,

---

4. According to an eighteenth-century dictionary the spelling "atchieve" is used "when speaking
   of some noble Enterprize," and the first edition of the *Encyclopædia Britannica* (1771; I,
   501) defines "atchievement" as a term in heraldry denoting "the arms of a person, or family,
   together with all the exterior ornaments of the shield . . . marshalled in order." Shelley used
   the word only four times in the poetry surveyed in F. S. Ellis's *Concordance*, but twice in
   this scene: here Giacomo uses it in Orsino's presence, and at line 151, the latter—the
   drama's dark counselor—plans to use the "atchieved" parricide to ensnare Beatrice. Shelley's
   spelling may be meant to suggest the view that murdering their monstrous father can bring
   both vengeance and atonement for the Cenci family's honor—ideas that Shelley's Preface
   cites as "pernicious mistakes."
5. Three noted Italian tyrants featured as villains in Sismondi's *History of the Italian Republics
   in the Middle Ages*. Gian Galeazzo Visconti (1351–1402), first Duke of Milan, imprisoned
   or killed his relatives and then conquered much of northern Italy; Cesare Borgia (1475–
   1507), the son of the Spanish Pope Alexander VI, tried to carve out a personal state in
   Romagna, the marches of Ancona, and Tuscany by cruelly suppressing the warring petty
   rulers of the region; Ezzelino (Eccelino) da Romano (1194–1259) led the Ghibelline faction
   in Lombardy as bloody ruler of Verona, Vicenza, and Padua. (See "Lines . . . Euganean
   Hills," lines 239–40 and note.)
6. According to bestiary tradition, when scorpions are surrounded by fire, they commit suicide
   by stinging themselves. (See *Queen Mab*, VI.36–38 and note.)

Or I would—                            [*Stops abruptly.*
   *Orsino.*   What? Fear not to speak your thought.
Words are but holy as the deeds they cover:                75
A priest who has forsworn the God he serves;
A judge who makes truth weep at his decree;
A friend who should weave counsel, as I now,
But as the mantle of some selfish guile;
A father who is all a tyrant seems,                       80
Were the prophaner for his sacred name.
   *Giacomo.* Ask me not what I think; the unwilling brain
Feigns often what it would not; and we trust
Imagination with such phantasies
As the tongue dares not fashion into words,              85
Which have no words, their horror makes them dim
To the mind's eye.—My heart denies itself
To think what you demand.
   *Orsino.*        But a friend's bosom
Is as the inmost cave of our own mind
Where we sit shut from the wide gaze of day,            90
And from the all-communicating air.
You look what I suspected—
   *Giacomo.*       Spare me now!
I am as one lost in a midnight wood,
Who dares not ask some harmless passenger
The path across the wilderness, lest he,                95
As my thoughts are, should be—a murderer.
I know you are my friend, and all I dare
Speak to my soul that will I trust with thee.
But now my heart is heavy and would take
Lone counsel from a night of sleepless care.           100
Pardon me, that I say farewell—farewell!
I would that to my own suspected self
I could address a word so full of peace.
   *Orsino.* Farewell!—Be your thoughts better or more bold.
                       [*Exit* GIACOMO.
I had disposed the Cardinal Camillo                     105
To feed his hope with cold encouragement:
It fortunately serves my close designs
That 'tis a trick of this same family
To analyse their own and other minds.
Such self-anatomy[7] shall teach the will               110
Dangerous secrets: for it tempts our powers,
Knowing what must be thought, and may be done,
Into the depth of darkest purposes:
So Cenci fell into the pit; even I,
Since Beatrice unveiled me to myself,                   115
And made me shrink from what I cannot shun,
Shew a poor figure to my own esteem,
To which I grow half reconciled. I'll do

7. Self-dissection or analysis.

As little mischief as I can; that thought
Shall fee⁸ the accuser conscience.
    (*After a pause.*)       Now what harm 120
If Cenci should be murdered?—Yet, if murdered,
Wherefore by me? And what if I could take
The profit, yet omit the sin and peril
In such an action? Of all earthly things
I fear a man whose blows outspeed his words; 125
And such is Cenci: and while Cenci lives
His daughter's dowry were a secret grave
If a priest wins her.—Oh, fair Beatrice!
Would that I loved thee not, or loving thee
Could but despise danger and gold and all 130
That frowns between my wish and its effect,
Or smiles beyond it! There is no escape . . .
Her bright form kneels beside me at the altar,
And follows me to the resort of men,
And fills my slumber with tumultuous dreams, 135
So when I wake my blood seems liquid fire;
And if I strike my damp and dizzy head
My hot palm scorches it: her very name,
But spoken by a stranger, makes my heart
Sicken and pant; and thus unprofitably 140
I clasp the phantom of unfelt delights
Till weak imagination half possesses
The self-created shadow. Yet much longer
Will I not nurse this life of feverous hours:
From the unravelled hopes of Giacomo 145
I must work out my own dear purposes.
I see, as from a tower, the end of all:
Her father dead; her brother bound to me
By a dark secret, surer than the grave;
Her mother scared and unexpostulating 150
From the dread manner of her wish atchieved:
And she!—Once more take courage, my faint heart;
What dares a friendless maiden matched with thee?
I have such foresight as assures success:
Some unbeheld divinity doth ever, 155
When dread events are near, stir up men's minds
To black suggestions; and he prospers best,
Not who becomes the instrument of ill,
But who can flatter the dark spirit, that makes
Its empire and its prey of other hearts 160
Till it become his slave . . . as I will do.     [*Exit.*

      END OF THE SECOND ACT.

---

8. Pay, or bribe.

## Act III

SCENE I.—*An apartment in the Cenci Palace.* LUCRETIA,
*to her enter* BEATRICE.

*Beatrice.* (*She enters staggering, and speaks wildly.*)
Reach me that handkerchief!—My brain is hurt;
My eyes are full of blood; just wipe them for me . . .
I see but indistinctly . . .
    *Lucretia.*        My sweet child,
You have no wound; 'tis only a cold dew
That starts from your dear brow . . . Alas! Alas!                    5
What has befallen?
    *Beatrice.*       How comes this hair undone?
Its wandering strings must be what blind me so,
And yet I tied it fast.—O, horrible!
The pavement sinks under my feet! The walls
Spin round! I see a woman weeping there,                    10
And standing calm and motionless, whilst I
Slide giddily as the world reels. . . . My God!
The beautiful blue heaven is flecked with blood!
The sunshine on the floor is black! The air
Is changed to vapours such as the dead breathe                    15
In charnel pits! Pah! I am choked! There creeps
A clinging, black, contaminating mist
About me . . . 'tis substantial, heavy, thick,
I cannot pluck it from me, for it glues
My fingers and my limbs to one another,                    20
And eats into my sinews, and dissolves
My flesh to a pollution, poisoning
The subtle, pure, and inmost spirit of life!
My God! I never knew what the mad felt
Before; for I am mad beyond all doubt!                    25
(*More wildly.*) No, I am dead! These putrefying limbs
Shut round and sepulchre the panting soul
Which would burst forth into the wandering air! (*A pause.*)
What hideous thought was that I had even now?
'Tis gone; and yet its burthen remains here                    30
O'er these dull eyes . . . upon this weary heart!
O, world! O, life! O, day! O, misery!
    *Lucretia.* What ails thee, my poor child? She answers not:
Her spirit apprehends the sense of pain,
But not its cause; suffering has dried away                    35
The source from which it sprung . . .
    *Beatrice* (*franticly*).       Like Parricide . . .
Misery has killed its father: yet its father
Never like mine . . . O, God! What thing am I?
    *Lucretia.* My dearest child, what has your father done?
    *Beatrice* (*doubtfully*). Who art thou, questioner? I have no
      father.                    40
(*Aside.*) She is the madhouse nurse who tends on me,

It is a piteous office.          [*To* LUCRETIA, *in a slow, subdued voice.*
                    Do you know
I thought I was that wretched Beatrice
Men speak of, whom her father sometimes hales[9]
From hall to hall by the entangled hair;                              45
At others, pens up naked in damp cells
Where scaly reptiles crawl, and starves her there,
Till she will eat strange flesh. This woful story
So did I overact in my sick dreams,
That I imagined . . . no, it cannot be!                               50
Horrible things have been in this wild world,
Prodigious mixtures, and confusions strange
Of good and ill; and worse have been conceived
Than ever there was found a heart to do.
But never fancy imaged such a deed                                    55
As . . .          [*Pauses, suddenly recollecting herself.*
          Who art thou? Swear to me, ere I die
With fearful expectation, that indeed
Thou art not what thou seemest . . . Mother!
     *Lucretia.*                    Oh!
My sweet child, know you . . .
     *Beatrice.*                Yet speak it not:
For then if this be truth, that other too                            60
Must be a truth, a firm enduring truth,
Linked with each lasting circumstance of life,
Never to change, never to pass away.
Why so it is. This is the Cenci palace;
Thou art Lucretia; I am Beatrice.                                     65
I have talked some wild words, but will no more.
Mother, come near me: from this point of time,
I am . . .          [*Her voice dies away faintly.*
     *Lucretia.* Alas! What has befallen thee, child?
What has thy father done?
     *Beatrice.*                What have I done?
Am I not innocent? Is it my crime                                     70
That one with white hair, and imperious brow,
Who tortured me from my forgotten years,
As parents only dare, should call himself
My father, yet should be!—Oh, what am I?
What name, what place, what memory shall be mine?                     75
What retrospects, outliving even despair?
     *Lucretia.* He is a violent tyrant, surely, child:
We know that death alone can make us free;
His death or ours. But what can he have done
Of deadlier outrage or worse injury?                                 80
Thou art unlike thyself; thine eyes shoot forth
A wandering and strange spirit. Speak to me,
Unlock those pallid hands whose fingers twine
With one another.

---

9. Drags, especially by force or violence.

*Beatrice.*          'Tis the restless life
Tortured within them. If I try to speak                          85
I shall go mad. Aye, something must be done;
What, yet I know not . . . something which shall make
The thing that I have suffered but a shadow
In the dread lightning which avenges it;
Brief, rapid, irreversible, destroying                          90
The consequence of what it cannot cure.
Some such thing is to be endured or done:
When I know what, I shall be still and calm,
And never any thing will move me more.
But now!—Oh blood, which art my father's blood,              95
Circling through these contaminated veins,
If thou, poured forth on the polluted earth,
Could wash away the crime, and punishment
By which I suffer . . . . no, that cannot be!
Many might doubt there were a God above                        100
Who sees and permits evil, and so die:
That faith no agony shall obscure in me.
     *Lucretia.* It must indeed have been some bitter wrong;
Yet what, I dare not guess. Oh, my lost child,
Hide not in proud impenetrable grief                           105
Thy sufferings from my fear.
     *Beatrice.*               I hide them not.
What are the words which you would have me speak?
I, who can feign no image in my mind
Of that which has transformed me. I, whose thought
Is like a ghost shrouded and folded up                         110
In its own formless horror. Of all words,
That minister to mortal intercourse,[1]
Which wouldst thou hear? For there is none to tell
My misery: if another ever knew
Aught like to it, she died as I will die,                      115
And left it, as I must, without a name.
Death! Death! Our law and our religion call thee
A punishment and a reward . . . Oh, which
Have I deserved?
     *Lucretia.*      The peace of innocence;
Till in your season you be called to heaven.                   120
Whate'er you may have suffered, you have done
No evil. Death must be the punishment
Of crime, or the reward of trampling down
The thorns which God has strewed upon the path
Which leads to immortality.
     *Beatrice.*                    Aye, death . . .         125
The punishment of crime. I pray thee, God,
Let me not be bewildered while I judge.
If I must live day after day, and keep
These limbs, the unworthy temple of thy spirit,

1. Conversation; social communication.

As a foul den from which what thou abhorrest                    130
May mock thee, unavenged . . . it shall not be!
Self-murder . . . no, that might be no escape,
For thy decree yawns like a Hell between
Our will and it:—O! In this mortal world
There is no vindication and no law                    135
Which can adjudge and execute the doom
Of that through which I suffer.

                                        *Enter* ORSINO.

(*She approaches him solemnly.*) Welcome, Friend!
I have to tell you that, since last we met,
I have endured a wrong so great and strange,
That neither life or death can give me rest.                    140
Ask me not what it is, for there are deeds
Which have no form, sufferings which have no tongue.
        *Orsino.* And what is he who has thus injured you?
        *Beatrice.* The man they call my father: a dread name.
        *Orsino.* It cannot be . . .
        *Beatrice.*                What it can be, or not,                    145
Forbear to think. It is, and it has been;
Advise me how it shall not be again.
I thought to die; but a religious awe
Restrains me, and the dread lest death itself
Might be no refuge from the consciousness                    150
Of what is yet unexpiated. Oh, speak!
        *Orsino.* Accuse him of the deed, and let the law
Avenge thee.
        *Beatrice.*  Oh, ice-hearted counsellor!
If I could find a word that might make known
The crime of my destroyer; and that done                    155
My tongue should like a knife tear out the secret
Which cankers² my heart's core; aye, lay all bare
So that my unpolluted fame should be
With vilest gossips a stale mouthed story;
A mock, a bye-word, an astonishment:—                    160
If this were done, which never shall be done,
Think of the offender's gold, his dreaded hate,
And the strange horror of the accuser's tale,
Baffling belief, and overpowering speech;
Scarce whispered, unimaginable, wrapt                    165
In hideous hints . . . Oh, most assured redress!
        *Orsino.* You will endure it then?
        *Beatrice.*                Endure?—Orsino,
It seems your counsel is small profit.
                    [*Turns from him, and speaks half to herself.*
                                        Aye,
All must be suddenly resolved and done.
What is this undistinguishable mist                    170
Of thoughts, which rise, like shadow after shadow,

---

2. Corrupts; consumes slowly and secretly.

Darkening each other?
   *Orsino.*            Should the offender live?
Triumph in his misdeed? and make, by use,
His crime, whate'er it is, dreadful no doubt,
Thine element; until thou mayest become           175
Utterly lost; subdued even to the hue
Of that which thou permittest?
   *Beatrice (to herself).*       Mighty death!
Thou double visaged shadow![3] Only judge!
Rightfullest arbiter!        [*She retires absorbed in thought.*
   *Lucretia.*      If the lightning
Of God has e'er descended to avenge . . .       180
   *Orsino.* Blaspheme not! His high Providence commits
Its glory on this earth, and their own wrongs
Into the hands of men; if they neglect
To punish crime . . .
   *Lucretia.*      But if one, like this wretch,
Should mock with gold, opinion, law and power?   185
If there be no appeal to that which makes
The guiltiest tremble? If because our wrongs,
For that they are, unnatural, strange and monstrous,
Exceed all measure of belief? Oh God!
If, for the very reasons which should make     190
Redress most swift and sure, our injurer triumphs?
And we the victims, bear worse punishment
Than that appointed for their torturer?
   *Orsino.*               Think not
But that there is redress where there is wrong,
So we be bold enough to seize it.
   *Lucretia.*           How?      195
If there were any way to make all sure,
I know not . . . but I think it might be good
To . . .
   *Orsino.* Why, his late outrage to Beatrice;
For it is such, as I but faintly guess,
As makes remorse dishonour, and leaves her     200
Only one duty, how she may avenge:
You, but one refuge from ills ill endured;
Me, but one counsel . . .
   *Lucretia.*        For we cannot hope
That aid, or retribution, or resource
Will arise thence, where every other one     205
Might find them with less need.    [BEATRICE *advances.*
   *Orsino.*           Then . . .
   *Beatrice.*              Peace, Orsino!
And, honoured Lady, while I speak, I pray,
That you put off, as garments overworn,

---

3. This image associates death with the myth of Janus, the Roman god of beginnings and
   endings, who is usually depicted with two faces, one to view the past and one the future.

Forbearance and respect, remorse and fear,
And all the fit restraints of daily life,                                      210
Which have been borne from childhood, but which now
Would be a mockery to my holier plea.
As I have said, I have endured a wrong,
Which, though it be expressionless, is such
As asks atonement; both for what is past,                                      215
And lest I be reserved, day after day,
To load with crimes an overburthened soul,
And be . . . what ye can dream not. I have prayed
To God, and I have talked with my own heart,
And have unravelled my entangled will,                                         220
And have at length determined what is right.
Art thou my friend, Orsino? False or true?
Pledge thy salvation ere I speak.
    *Orsino.*                 I swear
To dedicate my cunning, and my strength,
My silence, and whatever else is mine,                                         225
To thy commands.
    *Lucretia.*       You think we should devise
His death?
    *Beatrice.* And execute what is devised,
And suddenly. We must be brief and bold.
    *Orsino.* And yet most cautious.
    *Lucretia.*             For the jealous laws
Would punish us with death and infamy                                          230
For that which it became themselves to do.
    *Beatrice.* Be cautious as ye may, but prompt. Orsino,
What are the means?
    *Orsino.*          I know two dull, fierce outlaws,
Who think man's spirit as a worm's, and they
Would trample out, for any slight caprice,                                     235
The meanest or the noblest life. This mood
Is marketable here in Rome. They sell
What we now want.
    *Lucretia.*       To-morrow before dawn,
Cenci will take us to that lonely rock,
Petrella, in the Apulian Apennines.[4]                                         240
If he arrive there . . .
    *Beatrice.*         He must not arrive.
    *Orsino.* Will it be dark before you reach the tower?
    *Lucretia.* The sun will scarce be set.
    *Beatrice.*            But I remember
Two miles on this side of the fort, the road
Crosses a deep ravine; 'tis rough and narrow,                                  245
And winds with short turns down the precipice;
And in its depth there is a mighty rock,
Which has, from unimaginable years,

---

4. Mountains in Apulia, a region of southeast Italy.

Sustained itself with terror and with toil
Over a gulph, and with the agony                                      250
With which it clings seems slowly coming down;
Even as a wretched soul hour after hour,
Clings to the mass of life; yet clinging, leans;
And leaning, makes more dark the dread abyss
In which it fears to fall: beneath this crag                          255
Huge as despair, as if in weariness,
The melancholy mountain yawns . . . below,
You hear but see not an impetuous torrent
Raging among the caverns, and a bridge
Crosses the chasm; and high above there grow,                         260
With intersecting trunks, from crag to crag,
Cedars, and yews, and pines; whose tangled hair
Is matted in one solid roof of shade
By the dark ivy's twine. At noon day here
'Tis twilight, and at sunset blackest night.[5]                       265
    *Orsino.* Before you reach that bridge make some excuse
For spurring on your mules, or loitering
Until . . .
    *Beatrice.* What sound is that?
    *Lucretia.* Hark! No, it cannot be a servant's step;
It must be Cenci, unexpectedly                                        270
Returned . . . Make some excuse for being here.
    *Beatrice* (*to* ORSINO, *as she goes out*).
That step we hear approach must never pass
The bridge of which we spoke. [*Exeunt* LUCRETIA *and* BEATRICE.
    *Orsino.*              What shall I do?
Cenci must find me here, and I must bear
The imperious inquisition of his looks                                275
As to what brought me hither: let me mask
Mine own in some inane and vacant smile.
              *Enter* GIACOMO, *in a hurried manner.*
How! Have you ventured hither? know you then
That Cenci is from home?
    *Giacomo.*        I sought him here;
And now must wait till he returns.
    *Orsino.*          Great God!                        280
Weigh you the danger of this rashness?
    *Giacomo.*          Aye!
Does my destroyer know his danger? We
Are now no more, as once, parent and child,
But man to man; the oppressor to the oppressed;
The slanderer to the slandered; foe to foe:                          285
He has cast Nature off, which was his shield,
And Nature casts him off, who is her shame;
And I spurn both. Is it a father's throat

---

5. Lines 243–65 contain the description that, in the Preface, Shelley says he modeled on a passage near the end of the second act of *El Purgatorio de San Patricio* by the Spanish dramatist Pedro Calderón de la Barca (1600–81). Calderón's description depicts the entrance to Hell.

Which I will shake, and say, I ask not gold;
I ask not happy years; nor memories                                    290
Of tranquil childhood; nor home-sheltered love;
Though all these hast thou torn from me, and more;
But only my fair fame; only one hoard
Of peace, which I thought hidden from thy hate,
Under the penury heaped on me by thee,                                 295
Or I will . . . God can understand and pardon,
Why should I speak with man?
    *Orsino.*                  Be calm, dear friend.
    *Giacomo.* Well, I will calmly tell you what he did.
This old Francesco Cenci, as you know,
Borrowed the dowry of my wife from me,                                 300
And then denied the loan; and left me so
In poverty, the which I sought to mend
By holding a poor office in the state.
It had been promised to me, and already
I bought new clothing for my ragged babes,                            305
And my wife smiled; and my heart knew repose.
When Cenci's intercession, as I found,
Conferred this office on a wretch, whom thus
He paid for vilest service. I returned
With this ill news, and we sate sad together                          310
Solacing our despondency with tears
Of such affection and unbroken faith
As temper life's worst bitterness; when he,
As he is wont, came to upbraid and curse,
Mocking our poverty, and telling us                                   315
Such was God's scourge for disobedient sons.
And then, that I might strike him dumb with shame,
I spoke of my wife's dowry; but he coined
A brief yet specious tale, how I had wasted
The sum in secret riot; and he saw                                    320
My wife was touched, and he went smiling forth.
And when I knew the impression he had made,
And felt my wife insult with silent scorn
My ardent truth, and look averse and cold,
I went forth too: but soon returned again;                            325
Yet not so soon but that my wife had taught
My children her harsh thoughts, and they all cried,
"Give us clothes, father! Give us better food!
What you in one night squander were enough
For months!" I looked, and saw that home was hell.                    330
And to that hell will I return no more
Until mine enemy has rendered up
Atonement, or, as he gave life to me
I will, reversing nature's law . . .
    *Orsino.*                  Trust me,
The compensation which thou seekest here                              335
Will be denied.
    *Giacomo.*    Then . . . Are you not my friend?

Did you not hint at the alternative,
Upon the brink of which you see I stand,
The other day when we conversed together?
My wrongs were then less. That word parricide,                    340
Although I am resolved, haunts me like fear.
    *Orsino.* It must be fear itself, for the bare word
Is hollow mockery. Mark, how wisest God
Draws to one point the threads of a just doom,
So sanctifying it: what you devise                                345
Is, as it were, accomplished.
    *Giacomo.*                    Is he dead?
    *Orsino.* His grave is ready. Know that since we met
Cenci has done an outrage to his daughter.
    *Giacomo.* What outrage?
    *Orsino.*                    That she speaks not, but you may
Conceive such half conjectures as I do,                           350
From her fixed paleness, and the lofty grief
Of her stern brow bent on the idle air,
And her severe unmodulated voice,
Drowning both tenderness and dread; and last
From this; that whilst her step-mother and I,                     355
Bewildered in our horror, talked together
With obscure hints; both self-misunderstood
And darkly guessing, stumbling, in our talk,
Over the truth, and yet to its revenge,
She interrupted us, and with a look                               360
Which told before she spoke it, he must die . . .
    *Giacomo.* It is enough. My doubts are well appeased;
There is a higher reason for the act
Than mine; there is a holier judge than me,
A more unblamed avenger. Beatrice,                                365
Who in the gentleness of thy sweet youth
Hast never trodden on a worm, or bruised
A living flower, but thou hast pitied it
With needless tears! Fair sister, thou in whom
Men wondered how such loveliness and wisdom                       370
Did not destroy each other! Is there made
Ravage of thee? O, heart, I ask no more
Justification! Shall I wait, Orsino,
Till he return, and stab him at the door?
    *Orsino.* Not so; some accident might interpose              375
To rescue him from what is now most sure;
And you are unprovided where to fly,
How to excuse or to conceal. Nay, listen:
All is contrived; success is so assured
That . . .
                              *Enter* BEATRICE.

    *Beatrice.* 'Tis my brother's voice! You know me not?        380
    *Giacomo.* My sister, my lost sister!
    *Beatrice.*                    Lost indeed!
I see Orsino has talked with you, and

That you conjecture things too horrible
To speak, yet far less than the truth. Now, stay not,
He might return: yet kiss me; I shall know                    385
That then thou hast consented to his death.
Farewell, Farewell! Let piety to God,
Brotherly love, justice and clemency,
And all things that make tender hardest hearts
Make thine hard, brother. Answer not . . . farewell.         390

                    [*Exeunt severally.*

      SCENE II.—*A mean apartment in* GIACOMO's *house.*
            GIACOMO, *alone.*

*Giacomo.* 'Tis midnight, and Orsino comes not yet.
             [*Thunder, and the sound of a storm.*
What! can the everlasting elements
Feel with a worm like man? If so the shaft
Of mercy-winged lightning would not fall
On stones and trees. My wife and children sleep:             5
They are now living in unmeaning dreams:
But I must wake, still doubting if that deed
Be just which is most necessary. O,
Thou unreplenished lamp! whose narrow fire
Is shaken by the wind, and on whose edge                      10
Devouring darkness hovers! Thou small flame,
Which, as a dying pulse rises and falls,
Still flickerest up and down, how very soon,
Did I not feed thee, wouldst thou fail and be
As thou hadst never been! So wastes and sinks                15
Even now, perhaps, the life that kindled mine:
But that no power can fill with vital oil
That broken lamp of flesh. Ha! 'tis the blood
Which fed these veins that ebbs till all is cold:
It is the form that moulded mine that sinks                   20
Into the white and yellow spasms of death:
It is the soul by which mine was arrayed
In God's immortal likeness which now stands
Naked before Heaven's judgement seat!          [*A bell strikes.*
               One! Two!
The hours crawl on; and when my hairs are white,             25
My son will then perhaps be waiting thus,
Tortured between just hate and vain remorse;
Chiding the tardy messenger of news
Like those which I expect. I almost wish
He be not dead, although my wrongs are great;                30
Yet . . . 'tis Orsino's step . . .
                  *Enter* ORSINO.
          Speak!
*Orsino.*               I am come
To say he has escaped.
  *Giacomo.*          Escaped!

*Orsino.*                  And safe
Within Petrella. He past by the spot
Appointed for the deed an hour too soon.
    *Giacomo.* Are we the fools of such contingencies?      35
And do we waste in blind misgivings thus
The hours when we should act? Then wind and thunder,
Which seemed to howl his knell, is the loud laughter
With which Heaven mocks our weakness! I henceforth
Will ne'er repent of aught designed or done           40
But my repentance.
    *Orsino.*         See, the lamp is out.
    *Giacomo.* If no remorse is ours when the dim air
Has drank this innocent flame, why should we quail
When Cenci's life, that light by which ill spirits
See the worst deeds they prompt, shall sink for ever?    45
No, I am hardened.
    *Orsino.*          Why, what need of this?
Who feared the pale intrusion of remorse
In a just deed? Although our first plan failed
Doubt not but he will soon be laid to rest.
But light the lamp; let us not talk i' the dark.        50
    *Giacomo* (*lighting the lamp*). And yet once quenched I cannot
      thus relume[6]
My father's life: do you not think his ghost
Might plead that argument with God?
    *Orsino.*                  Once gone
You cannot now recall your sister's peace;
Your own extinguished years of youth and hope;      55
Nor your wife's bitter words; nor all the taunts
Which, from the prosperous, weak misfortune takes;
Nor your dead mother; nor . . .
    *Giacomo.*           O, speak no more!
I am resolved, although this very hand
Must quench the life that animated it.          60
    *Orsino.* There is no need of that. Listen: you know
Olimpio, the castellan[7] of Petrella
In old Colonna's time; him whom your father
Degraded from his post? And Marzio,
That desperate wretch, whom he deprived last year    65
Of a reward of blood, well earned and due?
    *Giacomo.* I knew Olimpio; and they say he hated
Old Cenci so, that in his silent rage
His lips grew white only to see him pass.
Of Marzio I know nothing.
    *Orsino.*             Marzio's hate     70
Matches Olimpio's. I have sent these men,
But in your name, and as at your request,
To talk with Beatrice and Lucretia.

6. Relight, rekindle.
7. The governor or constable of a castle.

*Giacomo.* Only to talk?

*Orsino.*                    The moments which even now

Pass onward to tomorrow's midnight hour                                    75

May memorize[8] their flight with death: ere then

They must have talked, and may perhaps have done,

And made an end . . .

    *Giacomo.*          Listen! What sound is that?

    *Orsino.* The housedog moans, and the beams crack: nought else.

    *Giacomo.* It is my wife complaining in her sleep:                         80

I doubt not she is saying bitter things

Of me; and all my children round her dreaming

That I deny them sustenance.

    *Orsino.*                    Whilst he

Who truly took it from them, and who fills

Their hungry rest with bitterness, now sleeps                              85

Lapped in bad pleasures, and triumphantly

Mocks thee in visions of successful hate

Too like the truth of day.

    *Giacomo.*          If e'er he wakes

Again, I will not trust to hireling hands . . .

    *Orsino.* Why, that were well. I must be gone; good night!              90

When next we meet . . . may all be done—

    *Giacomo.*                    And all

Forgotten—Oh, that I had never been!          [*Exeunt.*

END OF THE THIRD ACT.


## Act IV


SCENE I.—*An apartment in the Castle of Petrella. Enter* CENCI.

*Cenci.* She comes not; yet I left her even now

Vanquished and faint. She knows the penalty

Of her delay: yet what if threats are vain?

Am I now not within Petrella's moat?

Or fear I still the eyes and ears of Rome?                                  5

Might I not drag her by the golden hair?

Stamp on her? Keep her sleepless till her brain

Be overworn? Tame her with chains and famine?

Less would suffice. Yet so to leave undone

What I most seek! No, 'tis her stubborn will                               10

Which by its own consent shall stoop as low

As that which drags it down.

                               *Enter* LUCRETIA.

                Thou loathed wretch!

Hide thee from my abhorrence; Fly, begone!

Yet stay! Bid Beatrice come hither.

    *Lucretia.*                    Oh,

8. Memorialize.

Husband! I pray for thine own wretched sake                          15
Heed what thou dost. A man who walks like thee
Through crimes, and through the danger of his crimes,
Each hour may stumble o'er a sudden grave.
And thou art old; thy hairs are hoary grey;
As thou wouldst save thyself from death and hell,                    20
Pity thy daughter; give her to some friend
In marriage: so that she may tempt thee not
To hatred, or worse thoughts, if worse there be.
  *Cenci.* What! like her sister who has found a home
To mock my hate from with prosperity?                                25
Strange ruin shall destroy both her and thee
And all that yet remain. My death may be
Rapid—her destiny outspeeds it. Go,
Bid her come hither, and before my mood
Be changed, lest I should drag her by the hair.                      30
  *Lucretia.* She sent me to thee, husband. At thy presence
She fell, as thou dost know, into a trance;
And in that trance she heard a voice which said,
"Cenci must die! Let him confess himself!
Even now the accusing Angel waits to hear                            35
If God, to punish his enormous crimes,
Harden his dying heart!"
  *Cenci.*     Why—such things are . . .
No doubt divine revealings may be made.
'Tis plain I have been favoured from above,
For when I cursed my sons they died.—Aye . . . so . . .              40
As to the right or wrong that's talk . . . repentance . . .
Repentance is an easy moment's work
And more depends on God than me. Well . . . well . . .
I must give up the greater point, which was
To poison and corrupt her soul.
     [*A pause;* LUCRETIA *approaches anxiously,*
      *and then shrinks back as he speaks.*
        One, two;                       45
Aye . . . Rocco and Cristofano my curse
Strangled: and Giacomo, I think, will find
Life a worse Hell than that beyond the grave:
Beatrice shall, if there be skill in hate
Die in despair, blaspheming: to Bernardo,                            50
He is so innocent, I will bequeath
The memory of these deeds, and make his youth
The sepulchre of hope, where evil thoughts
Shall grow like weeds on a neglected tomb.
When all is done, out in the wide Campagna,[9]                       55
I will pile up my silver and my gold;
My costly robes, paintings and tapestries;

---

9. The Roman Campagna is the level valley of the Tiber River surrounding Rome; in Count
Cenci's (and in Shelley's) day it was almost deserted because of its unhealthy climate—
malaria was rife there—and because Italian warlords, such as the Orsini and Colonna families, had ravaged it.

My parchments and all records of my wealth,
And make a bonfire in my joy, and leave
Of my possessions nothing but my name;                          60
Which shall be an inheritance to strip
Its wearer bare as infamy. That done,
My soul, which is a scourge,[1] will I resign
Into the hands of him who wielded it;
Be it for its own punishment or theirs,                         65
He will not ask it of me till the lash[2]
Be broken in its last and deepest wound;
Until its hate be all inflicted. Yet,
Lest death outspeed my purpose, let me make
Short work and sure . . .                    [*Going.*
   *Lucretia* (*Stops him.*) Oh, stay! It was a feint:    70
She had no vision, and she heard no voice.
I said it but to awe thee.
   *Cenci.*                That is well.
Vile palterer[3] with the sacred truth of God,
Be thy soul choked with that blaspheming lie!
For Beatrice worse terrors are in store                          75
To bend her to my will.
   *Lucretia.*            Oh! to what will?
What cruel sufferings more than she has known
Canst thou inflict?
   *Cenci.*        Andrea! Go call my daughter,
And if she comes not tell her that I come.
What sufferings? I will drag her, step by step,                 80
Through infamies unheard of among men:
She shall stand shelterless in the broad noon
Of public scorn, for acts blazoned[4] abroad,
One among which shall be . . . What? Canst thou guess?
She shall become (for what she most abhors                      85
Shall have a fascination to entrap
Her loathing will), to her own conscious self
All she appears to others; and when dead,
As she shall die unshrived[5] and unforgiven,
A rebel to her father and her God,                              90
Her corpse shall be abandoned to the hounds;[6]
Her name shall be the terror of the earth;
Her spirit shall approach the throne of God
Plague-spotted with my curses. I will make
Body and soul a monstrous lump of ruin.                         95
                    *Enter* ANDREA.
   *Andrea.* The lady Beatrice . . .
   *Cenci.*                Speak, pale slave! What
Said she?

1. A person seen as an instrument of divine chastisement.
2. I.e., the *soul* of line 63.
3. An equivocator, or trifler with serious matters.
4. Conspicuously displayed, proclaimed.
5. Unconfessed.
6. "And the dogs shall eat Jezebel . . . and there shall be none to bury her" (2 Kings 9:10).

*Andrea.* My Lord, 'twas what she looked; she said:
"Go tell my father that I see the gulph
Of Hell between us two, which he may pass,
I will not."                                    [*Exit* ANDREA.
  *Cenci.*  Go thou quick, Lucretia,                    100
Tell her to come; yet let her understand
Her coming is consent: and say, moreover,
That if she come not I will curse her.          [*Exit* LUCRETIA.
       Ha!
With what but with a father's curse doth God
Panic-strike armed victory, and make pale                             105
Cities in their prosperity? The world's Father
Must grant a parent's prayer against his child
Be he who asks even what men call me.
Will not the deaths of her rebellious brothers
Awe her before I speak? For I on them                                 110
Did imprecate quick ruin, and it came.

        *Enter* LUCRETIA.

Well; what? Speak, wretch!
  *Lucretia.*      She said, "I cannot come;
Go tell my father that I see a torrent
Of his own blood raging between us."
  *Cenci (kneeling).*     God!
Hear me! If this most specious mass of flesh,                         115
Which thou hast made my daughter; this my blood,
This particle of my divided being;
Or rather, this my bane and my disease,
Whose sight infects and poisons me; this devil
Which sprung from me as from a hell, was meant                        120
To aught good use; if her bright loveliness
Was kindled to illumine this dark world;
If nursed by thy selectest dew of love
Such virtues blossom in her as should make
The peace of life, I pray thee for my sake,                           125
As thou the common God and Father art
Of her, and me, and all; reverse that doom!
Earth, in the name of God, let her food be
Poison, until she be encrusted round
With leprous stains! Heaven, rain upon her head                       130
The blistering drops of the Maremma's dew,[7]
Till she be speckled like a toad; parch up
Those love-enkindled lips, warp those fine limbs
To loathed lameness! All-beholding sun,
Strike in thine envy those life-darting eyes                          135
With thine own blinding beams!
  *Lucretia.*      Peace! Peace!
For thine own sake unsay those dreadful words.
When high God grants He punishes such prayers.

---

7. The Maremma, a coastal plain and tidewater swamp near Pisa, was noted for its unhealthy climate.

*Cenci (leaping up, and throwing his right hand towards Heaven).*
He does his will, I mine! This in addition,
That if she have a child . . .
   *Lucretia.*               Horrible thought!       140
   *Cenci.* That if she ever have a child; and thou,
Quick Nature! I adjure thee by thy God,
That thou be fruitful in her, and encrease
And multiply, fulfilling his command,
And my deep imprecation! May it be            145
A hideous likeness of herself, that as
From a distorting mirror, she may see
Her image mixed with what she most abhors,
Smiling upon her from her nursing breast.
And that the child may from its infancy       150
Grow, day by day, more wicked and deformed,
Turning her mother's love to misery:
And that both she and it may live until
It shall repay her care and pain with hate,
Or what may else be more unnatural.          155
So he may hunt her through the clamorous scoffs
Of the loud world to a dishonoured grave.
Shall I revoke this curse? Go, bid her come,
Before my words are chronicled in heaven.     [*Exit* LUCRETIA.
I do not feel as if I were a man,           160
But like a fiend appointed to chastise
The offences of some unremembered world.
My blood is running up and down my veins;
A fearful pleasure makes it prick and tingle:
I feel a giddy sickness of strange awe;       165
My heart is beating with an expectation
Of horrid joy.
                   *Enter* LUCRETIA.
          What? Speak!
   *Lucretia.*          She bids thee curse;
And if thy curses, as they cannot do,
Could kill her soul . . .
   *Cenci.*         She would not come. 'Tis well,
I can do both: first take what I demand,      170
And then extort concession. To thy chamber!
Fly ere I spurn[8] thee: and beware this night
That thou cross not my footsteps. It were safer
To come between the tiger and his prey.     [*Exit* LUCRETIA.
It must be late; mine eyes grow weary dim     175
With unaccustomed heaviness of sleep.
Conscience! Oh, thou most insolent of lies!
They say that sleep, that healing dew of heaven,
Steeps not in balm the foldings of the brain
Which thinks thee an impostor. I will go      180
First to belie thee with an hour of rest,

---

8. Kick.

Which will be deep and calm, I feel: and then . . .
O, multitudinous Hell, the fiends will shake
Thine arches with the laughter of their joy!
There shall be lamentation heard in Heaven                              185
As o'er an angel fallen; and upon Earth
All good shall droop and sicken, and ill things
Shall with a spirit of unnatural life
Stir and be quickened[9] . . . even as I am now.                  [*Exit.*


SCENE II.—*Before the Castle of Petrella. Enter* BEATRICE *and* LUCRETIA
                              *above on the ramparts.*

*Beatrice.* They come not yet.
*Lucretia.*                              'Tis scarce midnight.
*Beatrice.*                                        How slow
Behind the course of thought, even sick with speed,
Lags leaden-footed time!
*Lucretia.*                    The minutes pass . . .
If he should wake before the deed is done?
*Beatrice.* O, Mother! He must never wake again.                    5
What thou hast said persuades me that our act
Will but dislodge a spirit of deep hell
Out of a human form.
*Lucretia.*              'Tis true he spoke
Of death and judgement with strange confidence
For one so wicked; as a man believing                              10
In God, yet recking[1] not of good or ill.
And yet to die without confession! . . .
*Beatrice.*                                Oh!
Believe that heaven is merciful and just,
And will not add our dread necessity
To the amount of his offences.
                                *Enter* OLIMPIO *and* MARZIO, *below.*
*Lucretia.*                            See,                          15
They come.
*Beatrice.* All mortal things must hasten thus
To their dark end. Let us go down.
                         [*Exeunt* LUCRETIA *and* BEATRICE *from above.*
*Olimpio.* How feel you to this work?
*Marzio.*                                As one who thinks
A thousand crowns excellent market price
For an old murderer's life. Your cheeks are pale.                  20
*Olimpio.* It is the white reflexion of your own,
Which you call pale.
*Marzio.*              Is that their natural hue?
*Olimpio.* Or 'tis my hate and the deferred desire
To wreak[2] it, which extinguishes their blood.

---

9. Brought to life.
1. Heeding the consequences, caring.
2. Give vent or expression to.

*Marzio.* You are inclined then to this business?
*Olimpio.*                                        Aye.                    25
If one should bribe me with a thousand crowns
To kill a serpent which had stung my child,
I could not be more willing.
                    *Enter* BEATRICE *and* LUCRETIA, *below.*
                    Noble ladies!
*Beatrice.* Are ye resolved?
*Olimpio.*                    Is he asleep?
*Marzio.*                                        Is all
Quiet?
*Lucretia.* I mixed an opiate with his drink:            30
He sleeps so soundly . . .
*Beatrice.*                    That his death will be
But as a change of sin-chastising dreams,
A dark continuance of the Hell within him,
Which God extinguish! But ye are resolved?
Ye know it is a high and holy deed?                    35
*Olimpio.* We are resolved.
*Marzio.*                    As to the how this act
Be warranted, it rests with you.
*Beatrice.*                    Well, follow!
*Olimpio.* Hush! Hark! What noise is that?
*Marzio.*                                        Ha! some one comes!
*Beatrice.* Ye conscience-stricken cravens,[3] rock to rest
Your baby hearts. It is the iron gate,                    40
Which ye left open, swinging to the wind,
That enters whistling as in scorn. Come, follow!
And be your steps like mine, light, quick and bold.        [*Exeunt.*


                    SCENE III.—*An apartment in the Castle.*
                    *Enter* BEATRICE *and* LUCRETIA.

*Lucretia.* They are about it now.
*Beatrice.*                         Nay, it is done.
*Lucretia.* I have not heard him groan.
*Beatrice.*                             He will not groan.
*Lucretia.* What sound is that?
*Beatrice.*                     List! 'tis the tread of feet
About his bed.
*Lucretia.*     My God!
If he be now a cold stiff corpse . . .
*Beatrice.*                         O, fear not                    5
What may be done, but what is left undone:
The act seals all.
                    *Enter* OLIMPIO *and* MARZIO.
                    Is it accomplished?
*Marzio.*                    What?
*Olimpio.* Did you not call?

─────────────
3. Confessed or acknowledged cowards.

*Beatrice.*                When?
*Olimpio.*                 Now.
*Beatrice.*                        I ask if all is over?
  *Olimpio.* We dare not kill an old and sleeping man;
His thin grey hair, his stern and reverent brow,                        10
His veined hands crossed on his heaving breast,
And the calm innocent sleep in which he lay,
Quelled me. Indeed, indeed, I cannot do it.
  *Marzio.* But I was bolder; for I chid Olimpio,
And bade him bear his wrongs to his own grave                          15
And leave me the reward. And now my knife
Touched the loose wrinkled throat, when the old man
Stirred in his sleep, and said, "God! hear, O, hear,
A father's curse! What, art thou not our father?"
And then he laughed. I knew it was the ghost                           20
Of my dead father speaking through his lips,
And could not kill him.
  *Beatrice.*            Miserable slaves!
Where, if ye dare not kill a sleeping man,
Found ye the boldness to return to me
With such a deed undone? Base paltcrers!                               25
Cowards and traitors! Why, the very conscience
Which ye would sell for gold and for revenge
Is an equivocation:[4] it sleeps over
A thousand daily acts disgracing men;
And when a deed where mercy insults heaven . . .                       30
Why do I talk?
          [*Snatching a dagger from one of them and raising it.*
                Hadst thou a tongue to say,
"She murdered her own father," I must do it!
But never dream ye shall outlive him long!
  *Olimpio.* Stop, for God's sake!
  *Marzio.*                     I will go back and kill him.
  *Olimpio.* Give me the weapon, we must do thy will.                  35
  *Beatrice.* Take it! Depart! Return!
                    [*Exeunt* OLIMPIO *and* MARZIO.
                    How pale thou art!
We do but that which 'twere a deadly crime
To leave undone.
  *Lucretia.*      Would it were done!
  *Beatrice.*                     Even whilst
That doubt is passing through your mind, the world
Is conscious of a change. Darkness and hell                           40
Have swallowed up the vapour they sent forth
To blacken the sweet light of life. My breath
Comes, methinks, lighter, and the jellied blood
Runs freely through my veins. Hark!
                    *Enter* OLIMPIO *and* MARZIO.
                    He is . . .

_____
4. The expression of a falsehood in a form that is verbally true.

*Olimpio.*                           Dead!
*Marzio.* We strangled him that there might be no blood;          45
And then we threw his heavy corpse i' the garden
Under the balcony; 'twill seem it fell.
  *Beatrice (giving them a bag of coin).* Here take this gold, and
      hasten to your homes.
And, Marzio, because thou wast only awed
By that which made me tremble, wear thou this!          50
                    [*Clothes him in a rich mantle.*
It was the mantle which my grandfather
Wore in his high prosperity, and men
Envied his state: so may they envy thine.
Thou wert a weapon in the hand of God
To a just use. Live long and thrive! And, mark,          55
If thou hast crimes, repent: this deed is none.   [*A horn is sounded.*
  *Lucretia.* Hark, 'tis the castle horn; my God! it sounds
Like the last trump.[5]
  *Beatrice.*          Some tedious guest is coming.
  *Lucretia.* The drawbridge is let down; there is a tramp
Of horses in the court; fly, hide yourselves!          60
                    [*Exeunt* OLIMPIO *and* MARZIO.
  *Beatrice.* Let us retire to counterfeit deep rest;
I scarcely need to counterfeit it now:
The spirit which doth reign within these limbs
Seems strangely undisturbed. I could even sleep
Fearless and calm: all ill is surely past.          65
                    [*Exeunt.*

SCENE IV.—*Another apartment in the Castle. Enter on one side
the* LEGATE SAVELLA *introduced by a servant,
and on the other* LUCRETIA *and* BERNARDO.

  *Savella.* Lady, my duty to his Holiness
Be my excuse that thus unseasonably
I break upon your rest. I must speak with
Count Cenci; doth he sleep?
  *Lucretia (in a hurried and confused manner).* I think he sleeps;
Yet wake him not, I pray, spare me awhile,          5
He is a wicked and a wrathful man;
Should he be roused out of his sleep to-night,
Which is, I know, a hell of angry dreams,
It were not well; indeed it were not well.
Wait till day break. . . . (*Aside.*) O, I am deadly sick!          10
  *Savella.* I grieve thus to distress you, but the Count
Must answer charges of the gravest import,
And suddenly;[6] such my commission is.
  *Lucretia (with increased agitation).* I dare not rouse him: I
      know none who dare . . .

5. The end of the world, when Gabriel's trumpet will announce the Last Judgment.
6. Immediately.

'Twere perilous; . . . you might as safely waken          15
A serpent; or a corpse in which some fiend
Were laid to sleep.
    *Savella.*           Lady, my moments here
Are counted. I must rouse him from his sleep,
Since none else dare.
    *Lucretia* (*aside*).    O, terror! O, despair!
(*To* BERNARDO.) Bernardo, conduct you the Lord Legate to          20
Your father's chamber.        [*Exeunt* SAVELLA *and* BERNARDO.
                        *Enter* BEATRICE.

    *Beatrice.*          'Tis a messenger
Come to arrest the culprit who now stands
Before the throne of unappealable God.
Both Earth and Heaven, consenting arbiters,
Acquit our deed.
    *Lucretia.*     Oh, agony of fear!          25
Would that he yet might live! Even now I heard
The legate's followers whisper as they passed
They had a warrant for his instant death.
All was prepared by unforbidden means
Which we must pay so dearly, having done.          30
Even now they search the tower, and find the body;
Now they suspect the truth; now they consult
Before they come to tax us with the fact;
O, horrible, 'tis all discovered!
    *Beatrice.*           Mother,
What is done wisely, is done well. Be bold          35
As thou art just. 'Tis like a truant child
To fear that others know what thou hast done,
Even from thine own strong consciousness, and thus
Write on unsteady eyes and altered cheeks
All thou wouldst hide. Be faithful to thyself,          40
And fear no other witness but thy fear.
For if, as cannot be, some circumstance
Should rise in accusation, we can blind
Suspicion with such cheap[7] astonishment,
Or overbear[8] it with such guiltless pride,          45
As murderers cannot feign. The deed is done,
And what may follow now regards not me.
I am as universal as the light;
Free as the earth-surrounding air; as firm
As the world's centre. Consequence, to me,          50
Is as the wind which strikes the solid rock
But shakes it not.          [*A cry within and tumult.*
    *Voices.*       Murder! Murder! Murder!
              *Enter* BERNARDO *and* SAVELLA.
    *Savella* (*to his followers*). Go, search the castle round;
    sound the alarm;

7. Easily accomplished.
8. Overcome.

Look to the gates that none escape!
 *Beatrice.*      What now?
 *Bernardo.* I know not what to say . . . my father's dead.  55
 *Beatrice.* How; dead! he only sleeps; you mistake, brother.
His sleep is very calm, very like death;
'Tis wonderful how well a tyrant sleeps.
He is not dead?
 *Bernardo.*  Dead; murdered.
 *Lucretia (with extreme agitation).* Oh, no, no,
He is not murdered though he may be dead;  60
I have alone the keys of those apartments.
 *Savella.* Ha! Is it so?
 *Beatrice.*   My Lord, I pray excuse us;
We will retire; my mother is not well:
She seems quite overcome with this strange horror.
        *[Exeunt* LUCRETIA *and* BEATRICE.
 *Savella.* Can you suspect who may have murdered him?  65
 *Bernardo.* I know not what to think.
 *Savella.*    Can you name any
Who had an interest in his death?
 *Bernardo.*   Alas!
I can name none who had not, and those most
Who most lament that such a deed is done;
My mother, and my sister, and myself.  70
 *Savella.* 'Tis strange! There were clear marks of violence.
I found the old man's body in the moonlight
Hanging beneath the window of his chamber
Among the branches of a pine: he could not
Have fallen there, for all his limbs lay heaped  75
And effortless; 'tis true there was no blood . . .
Favour me, Sir; it much imports your house
That all should be made clear; to tell the ladies
That I request their presence.    *[Exit* BERNARDO.
      *Enter* GUARDS *bringing in* MARZIO.
 *Guard.*    We have one.
 *Officer.* My Lord, we found this ruffian and another  80
Lurking among the rocks; there is no doubt
But that they are the murderers of Count Cenci:
Each had a bag of coin; this fellow wore
A gold-inwoven robe, which shining bright
Under the dark rocks to the glimmering moon  85
Betrayed them to our notice: the other fell
Desperately fighting.
 *Savella.*   What does he confess?
 *Officer.* He keeps firm silence; but these lines found on him
May speak.
 *Savella.* Their language is at least sincere.   *[Reads.*
"To the Lady Beatrice.  90
That the atonement of what my nature
Sickens to conjecture may soon arrive,
I send thee, at thy brother's desire, those

Who will speak and do more than I dare
Write. . . .
                    Thy devoted servant, Orsino."                    95
                    *Enter* LUCRETIA, BEATRICE, *and* BERNARDO.
Knowest thou this writing, Lady?
    *Beatrice.*                    No.
    *Savella.*                         Nor thou?
    *Lucretia.* (*Her conduct throughout the scene is marked by extreme
        agitation.*) Where was it found? What is it? It should be
Orsino's hand! It speaks of that strange horror
Which never yet found utterance, but which made
Between that hapless child and her dead father          100
A gulph of obscure hatred.
    *Savella.*                    Is it so?
Is it true, Lady, that thy father did
Such outrages as to awaken in thee
Unfilial hate?
    *Beatrice.*    Not hate, 'twas more than hate:
This is most true, yet wherefore question me?          105
    *Savella.* There is a deed demanding question done;
Thou hast a secret which will answer not.
    *Beatrice.* What sayest? My Lord, your words are bold and rash.
    *Savella.* I do arrest all present in the name
Of the Pope's Holiness. You must to Rome.          110
    *Lucretia.* O, not to Rome! Indeed we are not guilty.
    *Beatrice.* Guilty! Who dares talk of guilt? My Lord,
I am more innocent of parricide
Than is a child born fatherless . . . Dear Mother,
Your gentleness and patience are no shield          115
For this keen judging world, this two-edged lie,
Which seems, but is not. What! will human laws,
Rather will ye who are their ministers,
Bar all access to retribution first,
And then, when heaven doth interpose to do          120
What ye neglect, arming familiar things
To the redress of an unwonted[9] crime,
Make ye the victims who demanded it
Culprits? 'Tis ye are culprits! That poor wretch
Who stands so pale, and trembling, and amazed,          125
If it be true he murdered Cenci, was
A sword in the right hand of justest God,
Wherefore should I have wielded it? Unless
The crimes which mortal tongue dare never name
God therefore scruples to avenge.
    *Savella.*                    You own          130
That you desired his death?
    *Beatrice.*                    It would have been
A crime no less than his, if for one moment
That fierce desire had faded in my heart.

9. Unusual.

'Tis true I did believe, and hope, and pray,
Aye, I even knew . . . for God is wise and just,                    135
That some strange sudden death hung over him.
'Tis true that this did happen, and most true
There was no other rest for me on earth,
No other hope in Heaven . . . now what of this?
    *Savella.* Strange thoughts beget strange deeds; and here are both:
I judge thee not.
    *Beatrice.*     And yet, if you arrest me,                    141
You are the judge and executioner
Of that which is the life of life: the breath
Of accusation kills an innocent name,
And leaves for lame acquittal the poor life                    145
Which is a mask without it.¹ 'Tis most false
That I am guilty of foul parricide;
Although I must rejoice, for justest cause,
That other hands have sent my father's soul
To ask the mercy he denied to me.                    150
Now leave us free: stain not a noble house
With vague surmises of rejected crime;
Add to our sufferings and your own neglect
No heavier sum: let them have been enough:
Leave us the wreck we have.
    *Savella.*     I dare not, Lady.                    155
I pray that you prepare yourselves for Rome:
There the Pope's further pleasure will be known.
    *Lucretia.* O, not to Rome! O, take us not to Rome!
    *Beatrice.* Why not to Rome, dear mother? There as here
Our innocence is as an armed heel                    160
To trample accusation. God is there
As here, and with his shadow ever clothes
The innocent, the injured and the weak;
And such are we. Cheer up, dear Lady, lean
On me; collect your wandering thoughts. My Lord,                    165
As soon as you have taken some refreshment,
And had all such examinations made
Upon the spot, as may be necessary
To the full understanding of this matter,
We shall be ready. Mother; will you come?                    170
    *Lucretia.* Ha! they will bind us to the rack, and wrest
Self-accusation from our agony!
Will Giacomo be there? Orsino? Marzio?
All present; all confronted; all demanding
Each from the other's countenance the thing                    175
Which is in every heart! O, misery!
             [*She faints, and is borne out.*
    *Savella.* She faints: an ill appearance this.
    *Beatrice.*          My Lord,

1. The sense of lines 141–46 is that a good reputation (*an innocent name*) is the *life of life*, which will be killed by the accusation of so serious a crime, leaving only *acquittal* to give insufficient substance to the life that would, without acquittal, be merely a *mask*.

She knows not yet the uses of the world.
She fears that power is as a beast which grasps
And loosens not: a snake whose look transmutes          180
All things to guilt which is its nutriment.
She cannot know how well the supine slaves
Of blind authority read the truth of things
When written on a brow of guilelessness:
She sees not yet triumphant Innocence          185
Stand at the judgement-seat of mortal man,
A judge and an accuser of the wrong
Which drags it there. Prepare yourself, my Lord;
Our suite[2] will join yours in the court below.          [*Exeunt.*

END OF THE FOURTH ACT.

## Act V

SCENE I.—*An apartment in* ORSINO's *Palace.*
*Enter* ORSINO *and* GIACOMO.

*Giacomo.* Do evil deeds thus quickly come to end?
O, that the vain remorse which must chastise
Crimes done, had but as loud a voice to warn
As its keen sting is mortal to avenge!
O, that the hour when present had cast off          5
The mantle of its mystery, and shewn
The ghastly form with which it now returns
When its scared game is roused, cheering the hounds
Of conscience to their prey! Alas! Alas!
It was a wicked thought, a piteous deed,          10
To kill an old and hoary-headed father.
    *Orsino.* It has turned out unluckily, in truth.
    *Giacomo.* To violate the sacred doors of sleep;
To cheat kind nature of the placid death
Which she prepares for overwearied age;          15
To drag from Heaven an unrepentant soul
Which might have quenched in reconciling prayers
A life of burning crimes . . .
    *Orsino.*                    You cannot say
I urged you to the deed.
    *Giacomo.*              O, had I never
Found in thy smooth and ready countenance          20
The mirror of my darkest thoughts; hadst thou
Never with hints and questions made me look
Upon the monster of my thought, until
It grew familiar to desire . . .
    *Orsino.*                    'Tis thus
Men cast the blame of their unprosperous acts          25
Upon the abettors of their own resolve;

2. Retinue; train of followers or servants.

Or any thing but their weak, guilty selves.
And yet, confess the truth, it is the peril
In which you stand that gives you this pale sickness
Of penitence; confess 'tis fear disguised                          30
From its own shame that takes the mantle now
Of thin remorse. What if we yet were safe?
   *Giacomo.* How can that be? Already Beatrice,
Lucretia and the murderer are in prison.
I doubt not officers are, whilst we speak,                          35
Sent to arrest us.
   *Orsino.*        I have all prepared
For instant flight. We can escape even now,
So we take fleet occasion by the hair.[3]
   *Giacomo.* Rather expire in tortures, as I may.
What! will you cast by self-accusing flight                         40
Assured conviction upon Beatrice?
She, who alone in this unnatural work,
Stands like God's angel ministered upon
By fiends; avenging such a nameless wrong
As turns black parricide to piety;                                  45
Whilst we for basest ends . . . I fear, Orsino,
While I consider all your words and looks,
Comparing them with your proposal now,
That you must be a villain. For what end
Could you engage in such a perilous crime,                         50
Training me on with hints, and signs, and smiles,
Even to this gulph? Thou art no liar? No,
Thou art a lie! Traitor and murderer!
Coward and slave! But, no, defend thyself;
                                                      [*Drawing.*
Let the sword speak what the indignant tongue                       55
Disdains to brand thee with.
   *Orsino.*               Put up your weapon.
Is it the desperation of your fear
Makes you thus rash and sudden with a friend,
Now ruined for your sake? If honest anger
Have moved you, know, that what I just proposed                    60
Was but to try you. As for me, I think,
Thankless affection led me to this point,
From which, if my firm temper could repent,
I cannot now recede. Even whilst we speak
The ministers of justice wait below:                                65
They grant me these brief moments. Now if you
Have any word of melancholy comfort
To speak to your pale wife, 'twere best to pass
Out at the postern,[4] and avoid them so.
   *Giacomo.* O, generous friend! How canst thou pardon me?      70
Would that my life could purchase thine!

---

3. Gain power or leverage over, while the time is right.
4. Back or side door.

*Orsino.*                                        That wish
Now comes a day too late. Haste; fare thee well!
Hear'st thou not steps along the corridor?          [*Exit* GIACOMO.
I'm sorry for it; but the guards are waiting
At his own gate, and such was my contrivance                    75
That I might rid me both of him and them.
I thought to act a solemn comedy
Upon the painted scene of this new world,
And to attain my own peculiar ends
By some such plot of mingled good and ill                       80
As others weave; but there arose a Power
Which graspt and snapped the threads of my device
And turned it to a net of ruin . . . Ha!          [*A shout is heard.*
Is that my name I hear proclaimed abroad?
But I will pass, wrapt in a vile disguise;                      85
Rags on my back, and a false innocence
Upon my face, through the misdeeming crowd
Which judges by what seems. 'Tis easy then
For a new name and for a country new,
And a new life, fashioned on old desires,                       90
To change the honours of abandoned Rome.
And these must be the masks of that within,
Which must remain unaltered . . . Oh, I fear
That what is past will never let me rest!
Why, when none else is conscious, but myself,                   95
Of my misdeeds, should my own heart's contempt
Trouble me? Have I not the power to fly
My own reproaches? Shall I be the slave
Of . . . what? A word? which those of this false world
Employ against each other, not themselves;                     100
As men wear daggers not for self-offence.
But if I am mistaken, where shall I
Find the disguise to hide me from myself,
As now I skulk from every other eye?              [*Exit.*


SCENE II.—*A Hall of Justice.* CAMILLO, JUDGES, *etc.,*
*are discovered seated;* MARZIO *is led in.*

*First Judge.* Accused, do you persist in your denial?
I ask you, are you innocent, or guilty?
I demand who were the participators
In your offence? Speak truth and the whole truth.
*Marzio.* My God! I did not kill him; I know nothing;           5
Olimpio sold the robe to me from which
You would infer my guilt.
*Second Judge.*            Away with him!
*First Judge.* Dare you, with lips yet white from the rack's kiss
Speak false? Is it so soft a questioner,
That you would bandy lover's talk with it                       10
Till it wind out your life and soul? Away!
*Marzio.* Spare me! O, spare! I will confess.

*First Judge.*                               Then speak.
*Marzio.* I strangled him in his sleep.
*First Judge.*                          Who urged you to it?
*Marzio.* His own son Giacomo, and the young prelate
Orsino sent me to Petrella; there                                    15
The ladies Beatrice and Lucretia
Tempted me with a thousand crowns, and I
And my companion forthwith murdered him.
Now let me die.
*First Judge.*   This sounds as bad as truth. Guards, there,
Lead forth the prisoners!
            *Enter* LUCRETIA, BEATRICE, *and* GIACOMO, *guarded.*
                    Look upon this man;                              20
When did you see him last?
*Beatrice.*                    We never saw him.
*Marzio.* You know me too well, Lady Beatrice.
*Beatrice.* I know thee! How? where? when?
*Marzio.*                            You know 'twas I
Whom you did urge with menaces and bribes
To kill your father. When the thing was done                        25
You clothed me in a robe of woven gold
And bade me thrive: how I have thriven, you see.
You, my Lord Giacomo, Lady Lucretia,
You know that what I speak is true.
            [BEATRICE *advances towards him; he covers his face,*
                                    *and shrinks back.*
                    O, dart
The terrible resentment of those eyes                               30
On the dead earth! Turn them away from me!
They wound: 'twas torture forced the truth. My Lords,
Having said this let me be led to death.
    *Beatrice.* Poor wretch, I pity thee: yet stay awhile.
    *Camillo.* Guards, lead him not away.
    *Beatrice.*                       Cardinal Camillo,                35
You have a good repute for gentleness
And wisdom: can it be that you sit here
To countenance a wicked farce like this?
When some obscure and trembling slave is dragged
From sufferings which might shake the sternest heart                40
And bade to answer, not as he believes,
But as those may suspect or do desire
Whose questions thence suggest their own reply:
And that in peril of such hideous torments
As merciful God spares even the damned. Speak now                   45
The thing you surely know, which is that you,
If your fine frame were stretched upon that wheel,
And you were told: "Confess that you did poison
Your little nephew; that fair blue-eyed child
Who was the loadstar⁵ of your life:"—and though                     50

---

5. I.e., "lodestar" or guiding star, on which one's attentions or hopes are fixed.

All see, since his most swift and piteous death,
That day and night, and heaven and earth, and time,
And all the things hoped for or done therein
Are changed to you, through your exceeding grief,
Yet you would say, "I confess any thing:"                         55
And beg from your tormentors, like that slave,
The refuge of dishonourable death.
I pray thee, Cardinal, that thou assert
My innocence.
    *Camillo* (*much moved*). What shall we think, my lords?
Shame on these tears! I thought the heart was frozen          60
Which is their fountain. I would pledge my soul
That she is guiltless.
    *Judge.*        Yet she must be tortured.
*Camillo.* I would as soon have tortured mine own nephew:
(If he now lived he would be just her age;
His hair, too, was her colour, and his eyes                       65
Like hers in shape, but blue and not so deep)
As that most perfect image of God's love
That ever came sorrowing upon the earth.
She is as pure as speechless infancy!
    *Judge.* Well, be her purity on your head, my Lord,       70
If you forbid the rack. His Holiness
Enjoined us to pursue this monstrous crime
By the severest forms of law; nay even
To stretch a point against the criminals.
The prisoners stand accused of parricide                         75
Upon such evidence as justifies
Torture.
    *Beatrice.* What evidence? This man's?
    *Judge.*            Even so.
    *Beatrice* (*to* MARZIO). Come near. And who art thou thus
    chosen forth
Out of the multitude of living men
To kill the innocent?
    *Marzio.*        I am Marzio,                          80
Thy father's vassal.
    *Beatrice.*      Fix thine eyes on mine;
Answer to what I ask.           [*Turning to the* JUDGES.
                  I prithee mark
His countenance: unlike bold calumny
Which sometimes dares not speak the thing it looks,
He dares not look the thing he speaks, but bends                 85
His gaze on the blind earth.
(*To* MARZIO.)          What! wilt thou say
That I did murder my own father?
    *Marzio.*           Oh!
Spare me! My brain swims round . . . I cannot speak . . .
It was that horrid torture forced the truth.
Take me away! Let her not look on me!                            90
I am a guilty miserable wretch;

I have said all I know; now, let me die!
   *Beatrice.* My Lords, if by my nature I had been
So stern, as to have planned the crime alledged,
Which your suspicions dictate to this slave,                    95
And the rack makes him utter, do you think
I should have left this two edged instrument
Of my misdeed; this man, this bloody knife
With my own name engraven on the heft,
Lying unsheathed amid' a world of foes,                    100
For my own death? That with such horrible need
For deepest silence, I should have neglected
So trivial a precaution, as the making
His tomb the keeper of a secret written
On a thief's memory? What is his poor life?                    105
What are a thousand lives? A parricide
Had trampled them like dust; and, see, he lives!
(*Turning to* MARZIO.) And thou . . .
   *Marzio.*                    Oh, spare me! Speak to me no more!
That stern yet piteous look, those solemn tones,
Wound worse than torture.
(*To the* JUDGES.)                    I have told it all;                    110
For pity's sake lead me away to death.
   *Camillo.* Guards, lead him nearer the Lady Beatrice,
He shrinks from her regard like autumn's leaf
From the keen breath of the serenest north.
   *Beatrice.* Oh, thou who tremblest on the giddy[6] verge                    115
Of life and death, pause ere thou answerest me;
So mayest thou answer God with less dismay:
What evil have we done thee? I, alas!
Have lived but on this earth a few sad years
And so my lot was ordered, that a father                    120
First turned the moments of awakening life
To drops, each poisoning youth's sweet hope; and then
Stabbed with one blow my everlasting soul;
And my untainted fame; and even that peace
Which sleeps within the core of the heart's heart;                    125
But the wound was not mortal; so my hate
Became the only worship I could lift
To our great father, who in pity and love,
Armed thee, as thou dost say, to cut him off;
And thus his wrong becomes my accusation; .                    130
And art thou the accuser? If thou hopest
Mercy in heaven, shew justice upon earth:
Worse than a bloody hand is a hard heart.
If thou hast done murders, made thy life's path
Over the trampled laws of God and man,                    135
Rush not before thy Judge, and say: "My maker,
I have done this and more; for there was one
Who was most pure and innocent on earth;

6. Apt to cause dizziness.

And because she endured what never any
Guilty or innocent endured before:                                    140
Because her wrongs could not be told, not thought;
Because thy hand at length did rescue her;
I with my words killed her and all her kin."
Think, I adjure you, what it is to slay
The reverence living in the minds of men                              145
Towards our ancient house, and stainless fame!
Think what it is to strangle infant pity,
Cradled in the belief of guileless looks,
Till it become a crime to suffer. Think
What 'tis to blot with infamy and blood                               150
All that which shews like innocence, and is,
Hear me, great God! I swear, most innocent,
So that the world lose all discrimination
Between the sly, fierce, wild regard of guilt,
And that which now compels thee to reply                              155
To what I ask: Am I, or am I not
A parricide?
   *Marzio.*   Thou art not!
   *Judge.*            What is this?
   *Marzio.* I here declare those whom I did accuse
Are innocent. 'Tis I alone am guilty.
   *Judge.* Drag him away to torments; let them be          160
Subtle and long drawn out, to tear the folds
Of the heart's inmost cell. Unbind him not
Till he confess.
   *Marzio.*      Torture me as ye will:
A keener pain has wrung a higher truth
From my last breath. She is most innocent!                            165
Bloodhounds, not men, glut yourselves well with me;
I will not give you that fine piece of nature
To rend and ruin.            [*Exit* MARZIO, *guarded.*
   *Camillo.*   What say ye now, my Lords?
   *Judge.* Let tortures strain the truth till it be white
As snow thrice sifted by the frozen wind.                             170
   *Camillo.* Yet stained with blood.
   *Judge* (*to* BEATRICE).        Know you this paper, Lady?
   *Beatrice.* Entrap me not with questions. Who stands here
As my accuser? Ha! wilt thou be he,
Who art my judge? Accuser, witness, judge,
What, all in one? Here is Orsino's name;                              175
Where is Orsino? Let his eye meet mine.
What means this scrawl? Alas! ye know not what,
And therefore on the chance that it may be
Some evil, will ye kill us?
                              *Enter an Officer.*
   *Officer.*          Marzio's dead.
   *Judge.* What did he say?
   *Officer.*            Nothing. As soon as we          180
Had bound him on the wheel, he smiled on us,

As one who baffles a deep[7] adversary;
And holding his breath, died.
   *Judge.*            There remains nothing
But to apply the question to those prisoners,
Who yet remain stubborn.
   *Camillo.*          I overrule          185
Further proceedings, and in the behalf
Of these most innocent and noble persons
Will use my interest with the Holy Father.
   *Judge.* Let the Pope's pleasure then be done. Meanwhile
Conduct these culprits each to separate cells;      190
And be the engines[8] ready: for this night
If the Pope's resolution be as grave,
Pious,[9] and just as once, I'll wring the truth
Out of those nerves and sinews, groan by groan.    [*Exeunt.*

SCENE III.—*The cell of a prison.* BEATRICE *is discovered asleep*
*on a couch. Enter* BERNARDO.

   *Bernardo.* How gently slumber rests upon her face,
Like the last thoughts of some day sweetly spent
Closing in night and dreams, and so prolonged.
After such torments as she bore last night,
How light and soft her breathing comes. Ay, me!      5
Methinks that I shall never sleep again.
But I must shake the heavenly dew of rest
From this sweet folded flower, thus . . . wake! awake!
What, sister, canst thou sleep?
   *Beatrice* (*awaking*).        I was just dreaming
That we were all in Paradise. Thou knowest      10
This cell seems like a kind of Paradise
After our father's presence.
   *Bernardo.*         Dear, dear sister,
Would that thy dream were not a dream! O, God!
How shall I tell?
   *Beatrice.*    What wouldst thou tell, sweet brother?
   *Bernardo.* Look not so calm and happy, or even whilst    15
I stand considering what I have to say
My heart will break.
   *Beatrice.*       See now, thou mak'st me weep:
How very friendless thou wouldst be, dear child,
If I were dead. Say what thou hast to say.
   *Bernardo.* They have confessed; they could endure no more    20
The tortures . . .
   *Beatrice.*    Ha! What was there to confess?
They must have told some weak and wicked lie

---

7. Profoundly cunning.
8. Machines of torture, especially the rack.
9. *Pope's resolution . . . Pious:* While Shelley was in Italy, Pope Pius VII (1740–1823) ruled
    Rome and the Papal States with a reactionary government employing spies, secret police and
    assassins, torture, slavery in the galleys, exile, and execution.

To flatter their tormentors. Have they said
That they were guilty? O, white innocence,
That thou shouldst wear the mask of guilt to hide                25
Thine awful and serenest countenance
From those who know thee not!
       *Enter* JUDGE *with* LUCRETIA *and* GIACOMO, *guarded.*
                Ignoble hearts!
For some brief spasms of pain, which are at least
As mortal as the limbs through which they pass,
Are centuries of high splendour laid in dust?                30
And that eternal honour which should live
Sunlike, above the reek of mortal fame,
Changed to a mockery and a bye-word? What!
Will you give up these bodies to be dragged
At horse's heels, so that our hair should sweep                35
The footsteps of the vain and senseless crowd,
Who, that they may make our calamity
Their worship and their spectacle, will leave
The churches and the theatres as void
As their own hearts? Shall the light multitude                40
Fling, at their choice, curses or faded pity,
Sad funeral flowers to deck a living corpse,
Upon us as we pass to pass away,
And leave . . . what memory of our having been?
Infamy, blood, terror, despair? O thou,                45
Who wert a mother to the parentless,
Kill not thy child! Let not her wrongs kill thee!
Brother, lie down with me upon the rack,
And let us each be silent as a corpse;
It soon will be as soft as any grave.                50
'Tis but the falsehood it can wring from fear
Makes the rack cruel.
    *Giacomo.*        They will tear the truth
Even from thee at last, those cruel pains:
For pity's sake say thou art guilty now.
    *Lucretia.* O, speak the truth! Let us all quickly die;                55
And after death, God is our judge, not they;
He will have mercy on us.
    *Bernardo.*        If indeed
It can be true, say so, dear sister mine;
And then the Pope will surely pardon you,
And all be well.
    *Judge.*      Confess, or I will warp                60
Your limbs with such keen tortures . . .
    *Beatrice.*             Tortures! Turn
The rack henceforth into a spinning-wheel!
Torture your dog, that he may tell when last
He lapped the blood his master shed . . . not me!
My pangs are of the mind, and of the heart,                65
And of the soul; aye, of the inmost soul,
Which weeps within tears as of burning gall

To see, in this ill world where none are true,
My kindred false to their deserted selves.
And with considering all the wretched life                    70
Which I have lived, and its now wretched end,
And the small justice shewn by Heaven and Earth
To me or mine; and what a tyrant thou art,
And what slaves these; and what a world we make,
The oppressor and the oppressed . . . . such pangs compel     75
My answer. What is it thou wouldst with me?
  *Judge.* Art thou not guilty of thy father's death?
  *Beatrice.* Or wilt thou rather tax high judging God
That he permitted such an act as that
Which I have suffered, and which he beheld;                   80
Made it unutterable, and took from it
All refuge, all revenge, all consequence,
But that which thou hast called my father's death?
Which is or is not what men call a crime,
Which either I have done, or have not done;                   85
Say what ye will. I shall deny no more.
If ye desire it thus, thus let it be,
And so an end of all. Now do your will;
No other pains shall force another word.
  *Judge.* She is convicted, but has not confessed.       90
Be it enough. Until their final sentence
Let none have converse with them. You, young Lord,
Linger not here!
  *Beatrice.*      O, tear him not away!
  *Judge.* Guards, do your duty.
  *Bernardo* (*embracing* BEATRICE). Oh! would ye divide
Body from soul?
  *Officer.*      That is the headsman's business.     95
      [*Exeunt all but* LUCRETIA, BEATRICE, *and* GIACOMO.
  *Giacomo.* Have I confessed? Is it all over now?
No hope! No refuge! O, weak, wicked tongue
Which hast destroyed me, would that thou hadst been
Cut out and thrown to dogs first! To have killed
My father first, and then betrayed my sister;                 100
Aye, thee! the one thing innocent and pure
In this black guilty world, to that which I
So well deserve! My wife! my little ones!
Destitute, helpless, and I . . . Father! God!
Canst thou forgive even the unforgiving,                      105
When their full hearts break thus, thus! . . .
         [*Covers his face and weeps.*
  *Lucretia.*           O my child!
To what a dreadful end are we all come!
Why did I yield? Why did I not sustain
Those torments? Oh, that I were all dissolved
Into these fast and unavailing tears,                         110
Which flow and feel not!
  *Beatrice.*        What 'twas weak to do,

'Tis weaker to lament, once being done;
Take cheer! The God who knew my wrong, and made
Our speedy act the angel of his wrath,
Seems, and but seems to have abandoned us.                115
Let us not think that we shall die for this.
Brother, sit near me; give me your firm hand,
You had a manly heart. Bear up! Bear up!
O, dearest Lady, put your gentle head
Upon my lap, and try to sleep awhile:                     120
Your eyes look pale, hollow and overworn,
With heaviness of watching and slow grief.
Come, I will sing you some low, sleepy tune,
Not cheerful, nor yet sad; some dull old thing,
Some outworn and unused monotony,                         125
Such as our country gossips sing and spin,
Till they almost forget they live: lie down!
So, that will do. Have I forgot the words?
Faith! They are sadder than I thought they were.

SONG

    False friend, wilt thou smile or weep     130
    When my life is laid asleep?
    Little cares for a smile or a tear,
    The clay-cold corpse upon the bier!
        Farewell! Heigho!
        What is this whispers low?             135
    There is a snake in thy smile, my dear;
    And bitter poison within thy tear.

    Sweet sleep, were death like to thee,
    Or if thou couldst mortal be,
    I would close these eyes of pain;                    140
    When to wake? Never again.
      O, World! Farewell!
      Listen to the passing bell!
    It says, thou and I must part,                       144
    With a light and a heavy heart.      *[The scene closes.*

SCENE IV.—*A Hall of the Prison. Enter* CAMILLO *and* BERNARDO.

*Camillo.* The Pope is stern; not to be moved or bent.
He looked as calm and keen as is the engine
Which tortures and which kills, exempt itself
From aught that it inflicts; a marble form,
A rite, a law, a custom: not a man.                       5
He frowned, as if to frown had been the trick
Of his machinery, on the advocates[1]
Presenting the defences, which he tore
And threw behind, muttering with hoarse, harsh voice:

1. Those who plead a case in court.

"Which among ye defended their old father                    10
Killed in his sleep?" Then to another: "Thou
Dost this in virtue of thy place; 'tis well."
He turned to me then, looking deprecation,
And said these three words, coldly: "They must die."
    *Bernardo.* And yet you left him not?
    *Camillo.*             I urged him still;           15
Pleading, as I could guess, the devilish wrong
Which prompted your unnatural parent's death.
And he replied: "Paolo Santa Croce
Murdered his mother yester evening,
And he is fled. Parricide grows so rife                      20
That soon, for some just cause no doubt, the young
Will strangle us all, dozing in our chairs.
Authority, and power, and hoary hair
Are grown crimes capital. You are my nephew,
You come to ask their pardon; stay a moment;                 25
Here is their sentence; never see me more
Till, to the letter, it be all fulfilled."
    *Bernardo.* O, God, not so! I did believe indeed
That all you said was but sad preparation
For happy news. O, there are words and looks                 30
To bend the sternest purpose! Once I knew them,
Now I forget them at my dearest need.
What think you if I seek him out, and bathe
His feet and robe with hot and bitter tears?
Importune him with prayers, vexing his brain                 35
With my perpetual cries, until in rage
He strike me with his pastoral cross, and trample
Upon my prostrate head, so that my blood
May stain the senseless dust on which he treads,
And remorse waken mercy? I will do it!                       40
O, wait till I return!                  [*Rushes out.*
    *Camillo.*        Alas! poor boy!
A wreck-devoted seaman thus might pray
To the deaf sea.
              *Enter* LUCRETIA, BEATRICE, *and* GIACOMO, *guarded.*
    *Beatrice.*      I hardly dare to fear
That thou bring'st other news than a just pardon.
    *Camillo.* May God in heaven be less inexorable           45
To the Pope's prayers, than he has been to mine.
Here is the sentence and the warrant.
    *Beatrice* (*wildly*).             Oh,
My God! Can it be possible I have
To die so suddenly? So young to go
Under the obscure, cold, rotting, wormy ground!             50
To be nailed down into a narrow place;
To see no more sweet sunshine; hear no more
Blithe voice of living thing; muse not again
Upon familiar thoughts, sad, yet thus lost—
How fearful! to be nothing! Or to be . . .                  55

What? O, where am I? Let me not go mad!
Sweet Heaven, forgive weak thoughts! If there should be
No God, no Heaven, no Earth in the void world;
The wide, grey, lampless, deep, unpeopled world!
If all things then should be . . . my father's spirit          60
His eye, his voice, his touch surrounding me;
The atmosphere and breath of my dead life!
If sometimes, as a shape more like himself,
Even the form which tortured me on earth,
Masked in grey hairs and wrinkles, he should come          65
And wind me in his hellish arms, and fix
His eyes on mine, and drag me down, down, down!
For was he not alone omnipotent
On Earth, and ever present? Even though dead,
Does not his spirit live in all that breathe,          70
And work for me and mine still the same ruin,
Scorn, pain, despair? Who ever yet returned
To teach the laws of death's untrodden realm?
Unjust perhaps as those which drive us now,
O, whither, whither?
    *Lucretia.*          Trust in God's sweet love,          75
The tender promises of Christ: ere night
Think we shall be in Paradise.
    *Beatrice.*          'Tis past!
Whatever comes my heart shall sink no more.
And yet, I know not why, your words strike chill:
How tedious, false and cold seem all things. I          80
Have met with much injustice in this world;
No difference has been made by God or man,
Or any power moulding my wretched lot,
'Twixt good or evil, as regarded me.
I am cut off from the only world I know,          85
From light, and life, and love, in youth's sweet prime.
You do well telling me to trust in God,
I hope I do trust in him. In whom else
Can any trust? And yet my heart is cold.
    [*During the latter speeches* GIACOMO *has retired conversing with*
                CAMILLO, *who now goes out;* GIACOMO *advances.*
    *Giacomo.* Know you not, Mother . . . Sister, know you not?          90
Bernardo even now is gone to implore
The Pope to grant our pardon.
    *Lucretia.*          Child, perhaps
It will be granted. We may all then live
To make these woes a tale for distant years:
O, what a thought! It gushes to my heart          95
Like the warm blood.
    *Beatrice.*          Yet both will soon be cold.
O, trample out that thought! Worse than despair,
Worse than the bitterness of death, is hope:
It is the only ill which can find place
Upon the giddy, sharp and narrow hour          100

Tottering beneath us. Plead with the swift frost
That it should spare the eldest flower of spring:
Plead with awakening Earthquake, o'er whose couch
Even now a city stands, strong, fair and free;
Now stench and blackness yawns, like death. O, plead          105
With famine, or wind-walking Pestilence,
Blind lightning, or the deaf sea, not with man!
Cruel, cold, formal man; righteous in words,
In deeds a Cain.[2] No, Mother, we must die:
Since such is the reward of innocent lives;          110
Such the alleviation of worst wrongs.
And whilst our murderers live, and hard, cold men,
Smiling and slow, walk through a world of tears
To death as to life's sleep; 'twere just the grave
Were some strange joy for us. Come, obscure Death,          115
And wind me in thine all-embracing arms!
Like a fond mother hide me in thy bosom,
And rock me to the sleep from which none wake.
Live ye, who live, subject to one another
As we were once, who now . . .

                              BERNARDO *rushes in.*
  *Bernardo.*                    Oh, horrible!          120
That tears, that looks, that hope poured forth in prayer,
Even till the heart is vacant and despairs,
Should all be vain! The ministers of death
Are waiting round the doors. I thought I saw
Blood on the face of one . . . what if 'twere fancy?          125
Soon the heart's blood of all I love on earth
Will sprinkle him, and he will wipe it off
As if 'twere only rain. O, life! O, world!
Cover me! let me be no more! To see
That perfect mirror of pure innocence          130
Wherein I gazed, and grew happy and good,
Shivered[3] to dust! To see thee, Beatrice,
Who made all lovely thou didst look upon . . .
Thee, light of life . . . dead, dark! while I say, sister,
To hear I have no sister; and thou, Mother,          135
Whose love was a bond to all our loves . . .
Dead! The sweet bond broken!

                    *Enter* CAMILLO *and* GUARDS.
                    They come! Let me
Kiss those warm lips before their crimson leaves
Are blighted . . . white . . . cold. Say farewell, before
Death chokes that gentle voice! O, let me hear          140
You speak!
  *Beatrice.* Farewell, my tender brother. Think
Of our sad fate with gentleness, as now:
And let mild, pitying thoughts lighten for thee

2. In Dante's *Inferno* the area of Hell where those who murdered relatives were punished was
   called Caina, after the first fratricide and murderer.
3. Shattered.

Thy sorrow's load. Err not in harsh despair,
But tears and patience. One thing more, my child,      145
For thine own sake be constant to the love
Thou bearest us; and to the faith that I,
Though wrapt in a strange cloud of crime and shame,
Lived ever holy and unstained. And though
Ill tongues shall wound me, and our common name      150
Be as a mark stamped on thine innocent brow
For men to point at as they pass, do thou
Forbear, and never think a thought unkind
Of those, who perhaps love thee in their graves.
So mayest thou die as I do; fear and pain      155
Being subdued. Farewell! Farewell! Farewell!
    *Bernardo.* I cannot say, farewell!
    *Camillo.*                 O, Lady Beatrice!
    *Beatrice.* Give yourself no unnecessary pain,
My dear Lord Cardinal. Here, Mother, tie
My girdle for me, and bind up this hair      160
In any simple knot; aye, that does well.
And yours I see is coming down. How often
Have we done this for one another; now
We shall not do it any more. My Lord,
We are quite ready. Well, 'tis very well.      165

THE END.

# PROMETHEUS UNBOUND

*Prometheus Unbound* was first published in August 1820, in a volume entitled *Prometheus Unbound: A Lyrical Drama in Four Acts, with Other Poems.* No poem but *Queen Mab* cost Shelley more pains to compose or occupied him for so long. It took him almost a year and a half to write the principal parts of the poem, beginning in late August or early September 1818 and ending in December 1819. But he appears to have been planning *Prometheus Unbound* as early as March 1818, and to have been revising it as late as May 26, 1820, when he mailed "two little papers of corrections & additions" for interpolations into the press transcript.

The standard account of the poem's composition, based partly on Mary Shelley's comments in her 1839 first edition of Shelley's complete poetry, is that Shelley began *Prometheus Unbound* at Este at the beginning of September 1818, completing Act I by early October. Then, after a hiatus, he wrote Acts II–III in Rome in early Spring 1819, apparently finishing the drama as a whole to his satisfaction before he undertook work on *The Cenci* in mid-May. Finally, in the oft-echoed words of Edward Dowden— "as a sublime after-thought"—he composed Act IV in Florence, in late Fall 1819.

However, as Neil Fraistat has demonstrated (*BSM*, IX, pp. lxii–lxxv), the manuscript evidence indicates that the composition of *Prometheus Unbound* was a more fluid, continuous, and revisionary process than has yet been widely recognized. Shelley probably did begin writing his lyrical drama at Este at the very beginning of September, but he worked inter-

mittently on the composition of Acts II and III in the fall and winter of
1818, until he caught fire in Rome during March and early April of 1819,
when he brought the poem to its tentative completion—and he continued
to work on the first three acts even after they were supposedly completed,
adding as many as 175 lines and canceling at least 10. Over one hundred
lines of Act II alone (among them the song at II.iii.54–98) were apparently
not written until the fall or winter of 1819, after Shelley had begun writing
Act IV—and they appear to derive *from* the stylistic experimentation of
Act IV, rather than vice versa. Although as late as September 6, 1819, in
a letter to his publisher Charles Ollier, Shelley is still describing *Prometheus Unbound* as complete, manuscript evidence suggests that he had
already begun drafting what was to become Act IV during the summer of
1819, months before that "sublime after-thought" was supposedly conceived.

Shelley's additions to the original three-act play broadened the scope of
his most ambitious work from a myth of the renovation of the human
psyche to a renewing of the whole cosmos. Given Shelley's ethics and his
theory of knowledge (epistemology), it seems likely that he believed that
when human beings viewed the universe correctly, it would appear to be
beneficent rather than hostile. *Queen Mab*, VIII–IX, provides a clearer,
more literal representation of such universal amelioration and can be used
to gloss and gauge the significance of the vision embodied in Act IV.

In its final form *Prometheus Unbound* exhibits Shelley's preferred sym-
metrical structure. Act I and Act IV each consists of a single scene that
has three clear-cut divisions (Act I, 1–305, 306–634, and 635–833; Act
IV, 1–184, 185–502, 503–78); these acts flank two acts divided into nine
scenes, of which the central one—Act II, scene v—depicts the journey
and transformation of Asia as she moves backward through time, reversing
the gyres of history to make "the world grow young again." Another obvious
structural parallel comprises the dialogues of mythological characters in
II.ii and III.ii. And whereas Acts I and III deal primarily with conditions
in the human world—with the psychology of tyranny (Act I) and of freedom (Act III)—the other two acts explore the metaphysical implications
of human bondage—how a slave psychology distorts the human view of
the universe.

Woven into these abstract structures is the action of the drama itself,
which Shelley drew—with modifications, as he explains in his Preface—
from Aeschylus' drama *Prometheus Bound* and what is known of its lost
sequel entitled *Prometheus Unbound*. In Act I of Shelley's version, Prometheus' curse of Jupiter is repeated to him, Prometheus repents it, he
resists the psychological torments sent by the tyrant, and he is comforted
by human hopes and ideals.

In Act II Panthea communicates to Asia two dreams she has had that
presage the release of Prometheus and the renewal of the world; Asia and
Panthea are called away and drawn down to the realm of Demogorgon.
Asia questions him on the nature of things. Demogorgon ascends the
chariot of the Hour in which Jupiter is destined to be overthrown and
directs the Oceanides to the car of the following Hour that will redeem
Prometheus.

In Act III Jupiter, having married and raped Thetis, awaits the offspring
of their union; this proves to be Demogorgon, who drags Jupiter down into
the abyss of chaos. Hercules releases Prometheus, and—after directing
the Spirit of the Hour of redemption to spread the good news around
the world and after hearing that spirit's report of the effects of the

proclamation—Prometheus and Asia retire to an oracular cave to cultivate the arts. The action itself having come to an end, Act IV is a hymn of rejoicing—first by a chorus of Spirits of the Hours and another chorus of Spirits of the Human Mind; then by the Spirit of the Earth (male) and the Spirit of the Moon (female). Finally, as Prometheus in his opening speech had described his situation in relation to past events, so Demogorgon, addressing the spirits of all creatures in the Universe, summarizes the present joy and tells how to recapture freedom, should it be lost again.

There have been several books and dozens of scholarly articles devoted solely or chiefly to explaining *Prometheus Unbound* or parts of it. For a summary and liberal sampling of interpretations up through the mid-1950s, students can consult Lawrence John Zillman's *Shelley's "Prometheus Unbound": A Variorum Edition* (University of Washington Press, 1959), and for supplementary references up through 1985, pages 648–51 of Stuart Curran's chapter "Shelley" in *The English Romantic Poets: A Review of Research and Criticism*, ed. Frank Jordan, Jr. (4th ed., Modern Language Association, 1985). Jerrold E. Hogle's chapter "Percy Bysshe Shelley" in Michael O'Neill's *Literature of the Romantic Period: A Bibliographical Guide* (Oxford University Press, 1998) provides more recent citations. In this volume, see the critical selections from G. M. Matthews (550–68) and Timothy Webb (694–711). Three other essays deserve special mention for their cogency and influence on subsequent criticism of *Prometheus Unbound*: Susan H. Brisman's " 'Unsaying His High Language': The Problem of Voice in *Prometheus Unbound*" (*SiR* 16 [1977]: 51–86), Stuart M. Sperry's "Necessity and the Role of the Hero in Shelley's *Prometheus Unbound*" (*PMLA* 96 [1981]: 242–54), and John Rieder's "The 'One' in *Prometheus Unbound*" (*Studies in English Literature* 25 [Autumn 1985]: 775–800.

Shelley ultimately drafted *Prometheus Unbound* in parts of five extant notebooks, three of which were not used until relatively late in the process of composition—not until after April 1819, when Shelley claimed that the first three acts were already completed. Of the 2,610 lines in the published poem, there is known draft for less than a third, the bulk of which is for Act IV (about 500 lines). The intermediate fair copy (Bodleian MSS Shelley e.1, e.2, and e.3) served as Shelley's safekeeping copy, and he recorded in it revisions made to the poem after the press transcript had already been sent to England. In some ways, however, the fair copy might more appropriately be termed a "fair draft": several passages in the poem are drafted directly in the MS; some lines and passages that we can infer were deleted in the press transcript are left uncanceled in the MS; and many details in such matters as punctuation, word choice, and stage directions that apparently were decided on in the press transcript are not recorded in the MS.

Mary Shelley transcribed for the press most or all of Acts I–III between September 5 and 12, 1819, and all of Act IV in mid-December 1819. As was his usual practice, Shelley appears to have corrected the press transcripts, making a series of small final revisions to prepare the poem for the press. He, however, was extremely dissatisfied with the state of the printed text of the poem, the only edition of *Prometheus Unbound* to appear during his lifetime, for which he had not been allowed to read proof. But the "formidable list" of errata he prepared has been lost or destroyed—as has been the press transcript itself, which best would have reflected his intentions for the printed text.

The textual difficulty of *Prometheus Unbound*, consequently, has been an anvil that has broken many hammers. Our text mediates between the three most important but nonetheless imperfect authorities—Shelley's intermediate fair copy, the first edition of 1820, and Mary Shelley's edition of 1839, which incorporates some (though *how many* remains the problem) authoritative corrections of the first edition. We have thus adopted the following principles: (1) Because the (now lost) manuscript copied by Shelley and/or Mary Shelley that served as press copy for the first edition certainly contained his final choices of words, which neither the compositors nor Shelley's friend Thomas Love Peacock (who corrected the proofs) would have felt free to alter, we have retained the verbal text of *1820*, unless either *1839* returns to the reading of the fair copy, or the fair-copy reading makes much better sense than *1820*. (2) Because the punctuation—especially in the lyric passages—is much heavier than that in either Shelley's surviving press-copy manuscripts or those poems that he personally saw through the press (but resembles the punctuation of Peacock's own poetry), we have made Shelley's fair copy the chief authority for punctuation, capitalization, and spelling; in numerous cases, where the fair copy was manifestly underpunctuated, we have added pointing either from *1820* or on analogy with punctuation in parallel lines and passages in the fair copy itself. (3) We have regularized spellings and, to a lesser extent, capitalization in those instances where the *Prometheus Unbound* fair copy and his other MSS and authorized printed texts show that Shelley maintained a reasonably consistent practice.

The punctuation, especially in the lyrics, is primarily rhetorical, not grammatical (see Textual Introduction, p. xviii). For example, Shelley's manuscript invariably contains a comma after internal rhyme words in lyric passages (e.g., "To stay steps proud, o'er the slow cloud" [I.236]); in other passages Shelley inserted commas, semicolons, and full stops, to indicate pauses at the beginnings and ends of phrases to be read as units, as well as suspension points ( . . . ) to mark sentences interrupted by another speaker or longer pauses. Thus, if the meaning is not immediately clear, try reading the passage aloud, with pauses whose length is governed by the heaviness of the punctuation.

The capitalization in the fair copy seems far less erratic to us now than it first appeared years ago. Since Peacock or the compositors at Marchant, the printer, obviously lowercased many capitals in Shelley's manuscript (of the type that appear in print in those volumes that he saw through the press), we have preferred Shelley's manuscript *except* that we have included capitals found in the first edition (and not in the MS) where they are congruent with the pattern of capitalization found in the fair copy—and hence may have been added to the lost press copy.

# Prometheus Unbound

## A Lyrical Drama in Four Acts

AUDISNE HÆC, AMPHIARAE, SUB TERRAM ABDITE?[1]

### Preface.[2]

The Greek tragic writers, in selecting as their subject any portion of their national history or mythology, employed in their treatment of it a certain arbitrary discretion. They by no means conceived themselves bound to adhere to the common interpretation or to imitate in story as in title their rivals and predecessors. Such a system would have amounted to a resignation of those claims to preference over their competitors which incited the composition. The Agamemnonian story was exhibited on the Athenian theatre with as many variations as dramas.

I have presumed to employ a similar licence.—The *Prometheus Unbound* of Æschylus, supposed the reconciliation of Jupiter with his victim as the price of the disclosure of the danger threatened to his empire by the consummation of his marriage with Thetis. Thetis, according to this view of the subject, was given in marriage to Peleus, and Prometheus by the permission of Jupiter delivered from his captivity by Hercules.—Had I framed my story on this model I should have done no more than have attempted to restore the lost drama of Æschylus; an ambition, which, if my preference to this mode of treating the subject had incited me to cherish, the recollection of the high comparison such an attempt would challenge, might well abate. But in truth I was averse from a catastrophe so feeble as that of reconciling the Champion with the Oppressor of mankind. The moral interest of the fable which is so powerfully sustained by the sufferings and endurance of Prometheus, would be annihilated if we could conceive of him as unsaying his high language, and quailing before his successful and perfidious adversary. The only imaginary being resembling in any degree Prometheus, is Satan; and Prometheus is, in my judgement, a

1. "Do you hear this, Amphiarus, hidden away under the earth?" Shelley found this line from Aeschylus' lost tragedy *Epigoni* in Cicero's *Tusculan Disputations* (II.xxv.60), where it is addressed to Zeno, the dead founder of Stoicism, by Cleanthes, who thereby voices his disgust at Dionysus' (and by extension, his contemporary world's) inability to endure physical suffering stoically. When Shelley copied this line into one of his notebooks, he entitled it "To the Ghost of Aeschylus," turning Aeschylus' own words against him, just as his *Prometheus Unbound* was intended to do. The epigraph appeared on the title page of the *Prometheus Unbound* volume, not on the title page of the lyrical drama itself.
2. MS evidence indicates that the Preface was composed in two distinct sections, written months apart. The first section, consisting of paragraphs 1–4, was written as fair copy sometime between April and early September 1819, to accompany the original three-act drama to the press. The second section, consisting of paragraphs 5–9, was written as fair copy sometime between mid-October and late December 1819, presumably in December, after Act IV was completed, in response to the notoriously harsh review of *Laon and Cythna* that appeared in the *Quarterly Review* for April 1819, which Shelley probably saw for the first time on October 15, 1819.

more poetical character than Satan because, in addition to courage and majesty and firm and patient opposition to omnipotent force, he is susceptible of being described as exempt from the taints of ambition, envy, revenge, and a desire for personal aggrandisement, which in the Hero of *Paradise Lost*, interfere with the interest. The character of Satan engenders in the mind a pernicious casuistry which leads us to weigh his faults with his wrongs and to excuse the former because the latter exceed all measure. In the minds of those who consider that magnificent fiction with a religious feeling, it engenders something worse. But Prometheus is, as it were, the type of the highest perfection of moral and intellectual nature, impelled by the purest and the truest motives to the best and noblest ends.

This Poem was chiefly written upon the mountainous ruins of the Baths of Caracalla, among the flowery glades, and thickets of odoriferous blossoming trees which are extended in ever winding labyrinths upon its immense platforms and dizzy arches suspended in the air. The bright blue sky of Rome, and the effect of the vigorous awakening of spring in that divinest climate, and the new life with which it drenches the spirits even to intoxication, were the inspiration of this drama.

The imagery which I have employed will be found in many instances to have been drawn from the operations of the human mind, or from those external actions by which they are expressed. This is unusual in modern Poetry; although Dante and Shakespeare are full of instances of the same kind: Dante indeed more than any other poet and with greater success. But the Greek poets, as writers to whom no resource of awakening the sympathy of their contemporaries was unknown, were in the habitual use of this power, and it is the study of their works (since a higher merit would probably be denied me) to which I am willing that my readers should impute this singularity.

One word is due in candour to the degree in which the study of contemporary writings may have tinged my composition, for such has been a topic of censure with regard to poems far more popular, and indeed more deservedly popular than mine. It is impossible that any one who inhabits the same age with such writers as those who stand in the foremost ranks of our own, can conscientiously assure himself, that his language and tone of thought may not have been modified by the study of the productions of those extraordinary intellects. It is true, that, not the spirit of their genius, but the forms in which it has manifested itself, are due, less to the peculiarities of their own minds, than to the peculiarity of the moral and intellectual condition of the minds among which they have been produced. Thus a number of writers possess the form, whilst they want the spirit of those whom, it is alleged, they imitate; because the former is the endowment of the age in which they live, and the latter must be the uncommunicated lightning of their own mind.

The peculiar style of intense and comprehensive imagery which distinguishes the modern literature of England, has not been, as a general power, the product of the imitation of any particular writer. The mass of capabilities remains at every period materially the same; the circumstances which awaken it to action perpetually change. If England were divided into forty republics, each equal in population and extent to Athens, there is no reason to suppose but that, under institutions not more perfect than those of Athens, each would produce philosophers and poets equal to those who (if we except Shakespeare) have never been surpassed. We owe the great writers of the golden age of our literature to that fervid awakening of the public mind which shook to dust the oldest and most oppressive form of the Christian Religion. We owe Milton to the progress and developement of the same spirit; the sacred Milton was, let it ever be remembered, a Republican and a bold enquirer into morals and religion. The great writers of our own age are, we have reason to suppose, the companions and forerunners of some unimagined change in our social condition or the opinions which cement it. The cloud of mind is discharging its collected lightning, and the equilibrium between institutions and opinions is now restoring, or is about to be restored.

As to imitation; Poetry is a mimetic art. It creates, but it creates by combination and representation. Poetical abstractions are beautiful and new, not because the portions of which they are composed had no previous existence in the mind of man or in nature, but because the whole produced by their combination has some intelligible and beautiful analogy with those sources of emotion and thought, and with the contemporary condition of them: one great poet is a masterpiece of nature, which another not only ought to study but must study. He might as wisely and as easily determine that his mind should no longer be the mirror of all that is lovely in the visible universe, as exclude from his contemplation the beautiful which exists in the writings of a great contemporary. The pretence of doing it would be a presumption in any but the greatest; the effect, even in him, would be strained, unnatural and ineffectual. A Poet, is the combined product of such internal powers as modify the nature of others, and of such external influences as excite and sustain these powers; he is not one, but both. Every man's mind is in this respect modified by all the objects of nature and art, by every word and every suggestion which he ever admitted to act upon his consciousness; it is the mirror upon which all forms are reflected, and in which they compose one form. Poets, not otherwise than philosophers, painters, sculptors and musicians, are in one sense the creators and in another the creations of their age. From this subjection the loftiest do not escape. There is a similarity between Homer and Hesiod, between Æschylus and Euripides, between Virgil and Horace, between Dante and Petrarch, between Shakespeare and Fletcher, between Dryden and Pope; each has a generic resemblance under which their specific distinctions are arranged. If this similarity be the result of imitation, I am willing to confess that I have imitated.

Let this opportunity be conceded to me of acknowledging that I have, what a Scotch philosopher characteristically terms, 'a passion for reforming the world:' what passion incited him to write and publish his book, he omits to explain.[3] For my part I had rather be damned with Plato and Lord Bacon, than go to Heaven with Paley and Malthus.[4] But it is a mistake to suppose that I dedicate my poetical compositions solely to the direct enforcement of reform, or that I consider them in any degree as containing a reasoned system on the theory of human life. Didactic poetry is my abhorrence; nothing can be equally well expressed in prose that is not tedious and supererogatory in verse. My purpose has hitherto been simply to familiarize the highly refined imagination of the more select classes of poetical readers with beautiful idealisms of moral excellence; aware that until the mind can love, and admire, and trust, and hope, and endure, reasoned principles of moral conduct are seeds cast upon the highway of life which the unconscious passenger tramples into dust, although they would bear the harvest of his happiness. Should I live to accomplish what I purpose, that is, produce a systematical history of what appear to me to be the genuine elements of human society, let not the advocates of injustice and superstition flatter themselves that I should take Æschylus rather than Plato as my model.

The having spoken of myself with unaffected freedom will need little apology with the candid; and let the uncandid consider that they injure me less than their own hearts and minds by misrepresentation. Whatever talents a person may possess to amuse and instruct others, be they ever so inconsiderable, he is yet bound to exert them: if his attempt be ineffectual, let the punishment of an unaccomplished purpose have been sufficient; let none trouble themselves to heap the dust of oblivion upon his efforts; the pile they raise will betray his grave which might otherwise have been unknown.

# Prometheus Unbound

## Act I

*Scene: A Ravine of Icy Rocks in the Indian Caucasus. Prometheus is discovered bound to the Precipice. Panthea and Ione are seated at his feet. Time, Night. During the Scene, Morning slowly breaks.*

PROMETHEUS
Monarch of Gods and Dæmons,[1] and all Spirits
But One, who throng those bright and rolling Worlds

3. Robert Forsyth, who uses this phrase as the title for Chapter XVI of *The Principles of Moral Science* (Edinburgh, 1805).
4. Shelley viewed both William Paley (1743–1805) and Robert Malthus (1766–1834) as pernicious theorists—in religion and political economy, respectively—whose works sought to perpetuate and justify an unjust social order. He had earlier coupled their names in a review of William Godwin's novel *Mandeville* in 1817, in which he claims that if Godwin "had devoted his high accomplishments to flatter the selfishness of the rich, or enforce those doctrines on which the powerful depend for power, they would no doubt have rewarded him with their countenance, and he might have been more fortunate in that sunshine than Mr. Malthus or Dr. Paley."
1. Supernatural beings of secondary rank who could communicate with both gods and men.

Which Thou and I alone of living things
Behold with sleepless eyes! regard this Earth
Made multitudinous with thy slaves, whom thou                    5
Requitest for knee-worship, prayer and praise,
And toil, and hecatombs[2] of broken hearts,
With fear and self-contempt and barren hope;
Whilst me, who am thy foe, eyeless[3] in hate,
Hast thou made reign and triumph, to thy scorn,                  10
O'er mine own misery and thy vain revenge.—
Three thousand years[4] of sleep-unsheltered hours
And moments—aye[5] divided by keen pangs
Till they seemed years, torture and solitude,
Scorn and despair,—these are mine empire:—                       15
More glorious far than that which thou surveyest
From thine unenvied throne, O Mighty God!
Almighty, had I deigned to share the shame
Of thine ill tyranny, and hung not here
Nailed to this wall of eagle-baffling mountain,                  20
Black, wintry, dead, unmeasured; without herb,
Insect, or beast, or shape or sound of life.
Ah me, alas, pain, pain ever, forever!

No change, no pause, no hope!—Yet I endure.
I ask the Earth, have not the mountains felt?                    25
I ask yon Heaven—the all-beholding Sun,
Has it not seen? The Sea, in storm or calm
Heaven's ever-changing Shadow, spread below—
Have its deaf waves not heard my agony?
Ah me, alas, pain, pain ever, forever!                           30

The crawling glaciers pierce me with the spears
Of their moon-freezing chrystals; the bright chains
Eat with their burning cold into my bones.
Heaven's winged hound,[6] polluting from thy lips
His beak in poison not his own, tears up                         35
My heart; and shapeless sights come wandering by,
The ghastly people of the realm of dream,
Mocking me: and the Earthquake-fiends are charged
To wrench the rivets from my quivering wounds
When the rocks split and close again behind;                     40
While from their loud abysses howling throng
The genii of the storm, urging the rage
Of whirlwind, and afflict me with keen hail.
And yet to me welcome is Day and Night,

---

2. Sacrifices of many victims presented as offerings.
3. Blind.
4. The time span that contemporary scientists believed separated the development of early
   civilizations (Egypt, etc.) from their own time.
5. Continually.
6. The eagle or vulture of Jupiter that daily tortured Prometheus.

Whether one breaks the hoar frost of the morn,                45
Or starry, dim, and slow, the other climbs
The leaden-coloured East; for then they lead
Their wingless, crawling Hours,[7] one among whom
—As some dark Priest hales[8] the reluctant victim—
Shall drag thee, cruel King, to kiss the blood              50
From these pale feet, which then might trample thee
If they disdained not such a prostrate slave.—
Disdain? Ah no! I pity thee.—What Ruin
Will hunt thee undefended through the wide Heaven!
How will thy soul, cloven to its depth with terror,         55
Gape like a Hell within! I speak in grief
Not exultation, for I hate no more
As then, ere misery made me wise.—The Curse
Once breathed on thee I would recall.[9] Ye Mountains,
Whose many-voiced Echoes, through the mist                  60
Of cataracts,[1] flung the thunder of that spell!
Ye icy Springs, stagnant with wrinkling frost,
Which vibrated to hear me, and then crept
Shuddering through India![2] Thou serenest Air,
Through which the Sun walks burning without beams!          65
And ye swift Whirlwinds, who on poised wings
Hung mute and moveless o'er yon hushed abyss,
As thunder louder than your own made rock
The orbed world! If then my words had power
—Though I am changed so that aught evil wish                70
Is dead within, although no memory be
Of what is hate—let them not lose it now!
What was that curse? for ye all heard me speak.

FIRST VOICE: *from the Mountains*
Thrice three hundred thousand years
    O'er the Earthquake's couch we stood;                   75
Oft as men convulsed with fears
    We trembled in our multitude.

SECOND VOICE: *from the Springs*
Thunderbolts had parched our water,
    We had been stained with bitter blood,
And had run mute 'mid shrieks of slaughter                  80
    Through a city and a solitude!

7. In classical art and myth the Horae, representations of the hours and seasons, are winged
   human figures.
8. Hauls or drags by force.
9. Remember; the word also foreshadows his *revoking* the curse.
1. Large waterfalls.
2. As the stage direction indicates, Shelley has relocated the scene of the play from the European Caucasus (between the Black and Caspian Seas) to the Hindu Kush, or Indian Caucasus, which some writers identified with the Himalayas. Shelley's reasons for the shift have
   been much speculated on, but he was certainly reflecting contemporary ideas that human
   life originated in central Asia; he was attempting to universalize the Greek myth to a general
   human myth.

THIRD VOICE: *from the Air*
I had clothed since Earth uprose
  Its wastes in colours not their own,
And oft had my serene repose
  Been cloven by many a rending groan.          85


FOURTH VOICE: *from the Whirlwinds*
We had soared beneath these mountains
  Unresting ages;—nor had thunder
Nor yon Volcano's flaming fountains
  Nor any power above or under
  Ever made us mute with wonder!          90


FIRST VOICE
But never bowed our snowy crest
As at the voice of thine unrest.


SECOND VOICE
Never such a sound before
To the Indian waves we bore.—
A pilot asleep on the howling sea          95
Leaped up from the deck in agony
And heard, and cried, "Ah, woe is me!"
And died as mad as the wild waves be.


THIRD VOICE
By such dread words from Earth to Heaven
My still realm was never riven;          100
When its wound was closed, there stood
Darkness o'er the Day, like blood.


FOURTH VOICE
And we shrank back—for dreams of ruin
To frozen caves our flight pursuing[3]
Made us keep silence—thus—and thus—          105
Though silence is as hell to us.


THE EARTH
The tongueless Caverns of the craggy hills
Cried "Misery!" then; the hollow Heaven replied,
"Misery!" And the Ocean's purple waves,
Climbing the land, howled to the lashing winds.          110
And the pale nations heard it,—"Misery!"

3. In Shelley's day, *ruin* and *pursuing* were an exact rhyme ("pursuin"). According to William Scott's *Elements of Elocution* (1808), apart from a few exceptions (which he lists), "G is silent before and after *n* in the same syllable, as gnat, gnarl, resign, . . . thinking, learning" (p. 11).

PROMETHEUS

I hear a sound of voices—not the voice
Which I gave forth.—Mother,[4] thy sons and thou
Scorn him, without whose all-enduring will
Beneath the fierce omnipotence of Jove                                    115
Both they and thou had vanished like thin mist
Unrolled on the morning wind!—Know ye not me,
The Titan, he who made his agony
The barrier to your else all-conquering foe?
O rock-embosomed lawns and snow-fed streams                               120
Now seen athwart frore[5] vapours deep below,
Through whose o'er-shadowing woods I wandered once
With Asia, drinking life from her loved eyes;
Why scorns the spirit which informs ye, now
To commune with me? me alone, who checked—                               125
As one who checks a fiend-drawn charioteer—
The falshood and the force of Him who reigns
Supreme, and with the groans of pining slaves
Fills your dim glens and liquid wildernesses?
Why answer ye not, still? brethren!

THE EARTH
                                        They dare not.                    130

PROMETHEUS

Who dares? for I would hear that curse again. . . .
Ha, what an awful whisper rises up!
'Tis scarce like sound, it tingles through the frame
As lightning tingles, hovering ere it strike.—
Speak, Spirit! from thine inorganic voice                                135
I only know that thou art moving near
And love. How cursed I him?

THE EARTH
                                        How canst thou hear
Who knowest not the language of the dead?

PROMETHEUS

Thou art a living spirit—speak as they.

THE EARTH

I dare not speak like life, lest Heaven's fell King                      140
Should hear, and link me to some wheel of pain
More torturing than the one whereon I roll.—
Subtle thou art and good, and though the Gods
Hear not this voice—yet thou art more than God
Being wise and kind—earnestly hearken now.—                             145

---

4. The Earth; in Hesiod's *Theogony*, Earth (Gaea or Tithea) was the mother and Sky (Uranus)
   the father of the Titans.
5. Frosty.

PROMETHEUS

Obscurely through my brain like shadows dim
Sweep awful[6] thoughts, rapid and thick.—I feel
Faint, like one mingled in entwining love,
Yet 'tis not pleasure.

THE EARTH

                    No, thou canst not hear:
Thou art immortal, and this tongue is known          150
Only to those who die . . .

PROMETHEUS

                    And what art thou,
O melancholy Voice?

THE EARTH

                    I am the Earth,
Thy mother, she within whose stony veins
To the last fibre of the loftiest tree
Whose thin leaves trembled in the frozen air          155
Joy ran, as blood within a living frame,
When thou didst from her bosom, like a cloud
Of glory, arise, a spirit of keen joy!
And at thy voice her pining sons uplifted
Their prostrate brows from the polluting dust          160
And our almighty Tyrant with fierce dread
Grew pale—until his thunder chained thee here.—
Then—see those million worlds which burn and roll
Around us: their inhabitants beheld
My sphered light wane in wide Heaven; the sea          165
Was lifted by strange tempest, and new fire
From earthquake-rifted mountains of bright snow
Shook its portentous hair beneath Heaven's frown;
Lightning and Inundation vexed the plains;
Blue thistles bloomed in cities; foodless toads          170
Within voluptuous chambers panting crawled;
When Plague had fallen on man and beast and worm,
And Famine,—and black blight on herb and tree,
And in the corn and vines and meadow-grass
Teemed ineradicable poisonous weeds          175
Draining their growth, for my wan breast was dry
With grief,—and the thin air, my breath, was stained
With the contagion of a mother's hate
Breathed on her child's destroyer—aye, I heard
Thy curse, the which if thou rememberest not          180
Yet my innumerable seas and streams,
Mountains and caves and winds, and yon wide Air
And the inarticulate people of the dead
Preserve, a treasured spell. We meditate

6. Awe-inspiring.

In secret joy and hope those dreadful words                                185
But dare not speak them.

PROMETHEUS
                         Venerable Mother!
All else who live and suffer take from thee
Some comfort; flowers and fruits and happy sounds
And love, though fleeting; these may not be mine.
But mine own words, I pray, deny me not.                                   190

THE EARTH
They shall be told.—Ere Babylon was dust,
The Magus Zoroaster,[7] my dead child,
Met his own image walking in the garden.
That apparition, sole of men, he saw.
For know there are two worlds of life and death:                           195
One that which thou beholdest, but the other
Is underneath the grave, where do inhabit
The shadows of all forms that think and live
Till death unite them, and they part no more;
Dreams and the light imaginings of men                                     200
And all that faith creates, or love desires,
Terrible, strange, sublime and beauteous shapes.
There thou art, and dost hang, a writhing shade
'Mid whirlwind-peopled mountains; all the Gods
Are there, and all the Powers of nameless worlds,                          205
Vast, sceptred Phantoms; heroes, men, and beasts;
And Demogorgon,[8] a tremendous Gloom;
And he, the Supreme Tyrant,[9] on his throne
Of burning Gold. Son, one of these shall utter
The curse which all remember. Call at will                                 210
Thine own ghost, or the ghost of Jupiter,
Hades or Typhon,[1] or what mightier Gods

---

7. Zoroaster (sixth or seventh century B.C.), a king of Bactria in what became part of Persia, founded a dualistic religion that worshiped fire and light in opposition to the evil principle of darkness. Priests of the religion were called Magi (singular: Magus). The exact source of Shelley's reference has not yet been discovered, but there had been a revival of interest in Zoroaster in France in the eighteenth century, and Peacock was much interested in the subject.
8. The name originated from a medieval error in transcribing the word "Demiourgos" (Demiurge) from Plato's myth of the creation in *Timaeus* (sections 28–40). In a note to the name in a poem written and published in 1817 while he and Shelley both lived at Marlow and conversed daily, Thomas Love Peacock alludes to Milton's mention of Demogorgon (*Paradise Lost*, II.965) and outlines the available information, from which we abstract: "Pronapides . . . makes Pan and the three sister Fates the offspring of Dæmogorgon. Boccaccio . . . gives some account of him. . . . He was the Genius of the Earth, and the Sovereign Power of the Terrestrial Dæmons. He dwelt originally with Eternity and Chaos, till, becoming weary of inaction, he organised the chaotic elements, and surrounded the earth with the heavens. In addition to Pan and the Fates, his children were Uranus, Titæa, Pytho, Eris, and Erebus" (*Rhododaphne* [London, 1818], pp. 179–80). Thus, in Peacock's account, Demogorgon is the father of the Sky, the Earth, and the Underworld, as well as the Fates. Some critics note that the name can be broken etymologically into "Demo" and "gorgon"—People-monster, symbol of a politically activated populace.
9. The shade or simulacrum of Jupiter.
1. *Hades* (Pluto), brother of Zeus (Jupiter) and king of the underworld; *Typhon*, a hundred-headed giant, warred with *Jupiter* and was finally imprisoned beneath volcanic Mt. Aetna.

From all-prolific Evil, since thy ruin
Have sprung, and trampled on my prostrate sons.—
Ask and they must reply—so the revenge                           215
Of the Supreme may sweep through vacant shades
As rainy wind through the abandoned gate
Of a fallen palace.

             PROMETHEUS
          Mother, let not aught
Of that which may be evil, pass again
My lips, or those of aught resembling me.—                        220
Phantasm of Jupiter, arise, appear![2]

          IONE
  My wings are folded o'er mine ears,
  My wings are crossed over mine eyes,
  Yet through their silver shade appears
  And through their lulling plumes arise                       225
    A Shape, a throng of sounds:
      May it be, no ill to thee[3]
    O thou of many wounds!
Near whom for our sweet sister's sake
Ever thus we watch and wake.                                      230

          PANTHEA
  The sound is of whirlwind underground,
  Earthquake and fire, and mountains cloven,—
  The Shape is awful like the sound,
  Clothed in dark purple, star-inwoven.
    A sceptre of pale gold                                   235
      To stay steps proud, o'er the slow cloud
    His veined hand doth hold.
Cruel he looks but calm and strong
Like one who does, not suffers wrong.

          PHANTASM OF JUPITER
Why have the secret powers of this strange world                  240
Driven me, a frail and empty phantom, hither
On direst storms? What unaccustomed sounds
Are hovering on my lips, unlike the voice
With which our pallid race hold ghastly talk
In darkness? And, proud Sufferer, who art thou?                   245

          PROMETHEUS
Tremendous Image! as thou art must be
He whom thou shadowest forth. I am his foe

2. Critics have suggested that Prometheus, when he cursed Jupiter, resembled the tyrant—that, in fact, Jupiter may be merely a distortion of Prometheus himself—and that it is therefore appropriate to have the Phantasm of Jupiter repeat the curse.
3. Shelley uses the comma in the middle of lines like these to emphasize the internal rhymes.

The Titan. Speak the words which I would hear,
Although no thought inform thine empty voice.

THE EARTH
Listen! and though your echoes must be mute,                    250
Grey mountains and old woods and haunted springs,
Prophetic caves and isle-surrounding streams
Rejoice to hear what yet ye cannot speak.

PHANTASM
A spirit seizes me, and speaks within:
It tears me as fire tears a thunder-cloud!                    255

PANTHEA
See how he lifts his mighty looks, the Heaven
Darkens above.

IONE
                He speaks! O shelter me—

PROMETHEUS
I see the curse on gestures proud and cold,
And looks of firm defiance, and calm hate,
And such despair as mocks itself with smiles,                    260
Written as on a scroll . . . yet speak—O speak!

PHANTASM
Fiend, I defy thee! with a calm, fixed mind,
   All that thou canst inflict I bid thee do;
Foul Tyrant both of Gods and Humankind,
   One only being shalt thou not subdue.                    265
      Rain then thy plagues upon me here,
      Ghastly disease and frenzying fear;
      And let alternate frost and fire
      Eat into me, and be thine ire
Lightning and cutting hail and legioned⁴ forms                    270
Of furies, driving by upon the wounding storms.

Aye, do thy worst. Thou art Omnipotent.
   O'er all things but thyself I gave thee power,
And my own will. Be thy swift mischiefs sent
   To blast mankind, from yon etherial tower.                    275
      Let thy malignant spirit move
      In darkness over those I love:
      On me and mine I imprecate⁵
      The utmost torture of thy hate
And thus devote to sleepless agony                    280
This undeclining head while thou must reign on high.

4. Arrayed in legions, as armies.
5. Invoke or call down evil or calamity.

But thou who art the God and Lord—O thou
　Who fillest with thy soul this world of woe,
To whom all things of Earth and Heaven do bow
　In fear and worship—all-prevailing foe!                              285
　　I curse thee! let a sufferer's curse
　　Clasp thee, his torturer, like remorse,
　　Till thine Infinity shall be
　　A robe of envenomed agony;
And thine Omnipotence a crown of pain                                 290
To cling like burning gold round thy dissolving brain.[6]

Heap on thy soul by virtue of this Curse
　Ill deeds, then be thou damned, beholding good,
Both infinite as is the Universe,
　And thou, and thy self-torturing solitude.                          295
　　An awful Image of calm power
　　Though now thou sittest, let the hour
　　Come, when thou must appear to be
　　That which thou art internally.
And after many a false and fruitless crime                            300
Scorn track thy lagging fall through boundless space and time.
                                        [*The Phantasm vanishes.*]

PROMETHEUS
Were these my words, O Parent?

THE EARTH
                                        They were thine.

PROMETHEUS
It doth repent me: words are quick and vain;
Grief for awhile is blind, and so was mine.
I wish no living thing to suffer pain.                                305

THE EARTH
Misery, O misery to me,
That Jove at length should vanquish thee.
Wail, howl aloud, Land and Sea,
The Earth's rent heart shall answer ye.
Howl, Spirits of the living and the dead,                             310
Your refuge, your defence lies fallen and vanquished.

FIRST ECHO
Lies fallen and vanquished?

SECOND ECHO
                                        Fallen and vanquished!

6. In lines 286–91 Shelley combines tortures from Greek myths (a poisoned shirt or tunic from
the centaur Nessus caused the death of Hercules) and the mocking of Jesus with a "gorgeous
robe" and a crown of thorns (Matthew 27:28–29; Mark 15:17; Luke 23:11).

IONE

Fear not—'tis but some passing spasm,
   The Titan is unvanquished still.                                      315
But see, where through the azure chasm
   Of yon forked and snowy hill,
Trampling the slant winds on high
   With golden-sandalled feet, that glow
Under plumes of purple dye                                                    320
Like rose-ensanguined[7] ivory,
   A Shape comes now,
Stretching on high from his right hand
   A serpent-cinctured[8] wand.


PANTHEA

'Tis Jove's world-wandering Herald, Mercury.                                  325


IONE

And who are those with hydra tresses[9]
   And iron wings that climb the wind,
Whom the frowning God represses
   Like vapours steaming up behind,
Clanging loud, an endless crowd—                                             330


PANTHEA

   These are Jove's tempest-walking hounds,[1]
   Whom he gluts with groans and blood,
When charioted on sulphurous cloud
   He bursts Heaven's bounds.


IONE

Are they now led, from the thin dead                                         335
On new pangs to be fed?


PANTHEA

The Titan looks as ever, firm, not proud.


FIRST FURY

Ha! I scent life!


SECOND FURY

   Let me but look into his eyes!


THIRD FURY

The hope of torturing him smells like a heap
Of corpses to a death-bird after battle!                                     340

---

7. Stained blood color.
8. Mercury carries a caduceus, a staff encircled by two snakes with their heads facing each
   other, a symbol of peace befitting the role of Hermes/Mercury as the messenger of the Gods:
   The caduceus is used today as a symbol of the physician.
9. Hair of snakes like a Gorgon's (see note to line 347).
1. I.e., the Furies.

**FIRST FURY**

Darest thou delay, O Herald! take cheer, Hounds
Of Hell—what if the Son of Maia[2] soon
Should make us food and sport? Who can please long
The Omnipotent?

**MERCURY**

       Back to your towers of iron
And gnash, beside the streams of fire, and wail[3]       345
Your foodless teeth! . . . Geryon, arise! and Gorgon,
Chimæra,[4] and thou Sphinx, subtlest of fiends,
Who ministered to Thebes Heaven's poisoned wine,
Unnatural love and more unnatural hate:[5]
These shall perform your task.

**FIRST FURY**

             O mercy! mercy!       350
We die with our desire—drive us not back!

**MERCURY**

Crouch then in silence.—
             Awful[6] Sufferer!
To thee unwilling, most unwillingly
I come, by the great Father's will driven down
To execute a doom of new revenge.       355
Alas! I pity thee, and hate myself
That I can do no more.—Aye from thy sight
Returning, for a season, Heaven seems Hell,
So thy worn form pursues me night and day,
Smiling reproach. Wise art thou, firm and good,       360
But vainly wouldst stand forth alone in strife
Against the Omnipotent, as yon clear lamps
That measure and divide the weary years
From which there is no refuge, long have taught
And long must teach.—Even now thy Torturer arms       365
With the strange might of unimagined pains

2. Mercury, whose father was Jupiter. Maia, the most luminous of the seven sisters in the constellation Pleiades, was the daughter of Atlas and Pleione.
3. We have repunctuated this line according to the argument of E. B. Murray, *KSJ* 24 (1975): 17–20.
4. *Geryon*, a monster with three heads and three bodies, lived with his man-eating flocks and his three-headed dog on an island beyond the Straits of Gibraltar, where he was destroyed by Hercules. The three *Gorgons* were mythical personages, with snakes for hair, who turned beholders into stone. The only mortal one, Medusa, was slain by Perseus and her head fixed on Athena's (Minerva's) shield. The *Chimera*, a fabled fire-breathing monster of Greek mythology with three heads (lion, goat, and dragon), the body of a lion and a goat, and a dragon's tail, was killed by Bellerophon.
5. The Sphinx, a monster with the body of a lion, wings, and the face and breasts of a woman, besieged Thebes by devouring those who could not answer her riddle. Oedipus solved the riddle (causing the Sphinx to kill herself), only to marry his mother (*unnatural love*), leading to the tragic events depicted in the Greek Theban plays, in which first the royal family and then all Thebes are destroyed by mutual hatreds.
6. Inspiring reverence.

The powers who scheme slow agonies in Hell,
And my commission is, to lead them here,
Or what more subtle, foul or savage fiends
People the abyss, and leave them to their task.                    370
Be it not so! . . . There is a secret known
To thee and to none else of living things
Which may transfer the sceptre of wide Heaven,
The fear of which perplexes the Supreme . . .
Clothe it in words, and bid it clasp his throne                    375
In intercession; bend thy soul in prayer
And like a suppliant in some gorgeous fane[7]
Let the will kneel within thy haughty heart;
For benefits and meek submission tame
The fiercest and the mightiest.

PROMETHEUS
                                Evil minds                          380
Change good to their own nature. I gave all
He has; and in return he chains me here
Years, ages, night and day: whether the Sun
Split my parched skin, or in the moony night
The chrystal-winged snow cling round my hair—                      385
Whilst my beloved race is trampled down
By his thought-executing ministers.
Such is the tyrant's recompense—'tis just:
He who is evil can receive no good;
And for a world bestowed, or a friend lost,                        390
He can feel hate, fear, shame—not gratitude:
He but requites me for his own misdeed.
Kindness to such is keen reproach, which breaks
With bitter stings the light sleep of Revenge.
Submission, thou dost know, I cannot try:                          395
For what submission but that fatal word,
The death-seal of mankind's captivity—
Like the Sicilian's hair-suspended sword[8]
Which trembles o'er his crown—would he accept,
Or could I yield?—which yet I will not yield.                      400
Let others flatter Crime where it sits throned
In brief Omnipotence; secure are they:
For Justice when triumphant will weep down
Pity not punishment on her own wrongs,
Too much avenged by those who err. I wait,                         405
Enduring thus the retributive hour
Which since we spake is even nearer now.—

7. Temple.
8. Dionysius the Elder, the ruler of Syracuse in Sicily, when pronounced by Damocles to be
   the happiest man on earth because of his wealth, persuaded the flatterer to take his place
   as sovereign. Amidst the splendor, Damocles perceived a sword hanging by one horsehair
   above his head and begged Dionysius to remove him from the terrifying situation.

But hark, the hell-hounds clamour. Fear delay!
Behold! Heaven lowers[9] under thy Father's frown.

MERCURY

O that we might be spared—I to inflict           410
And thou to suffer! Once more answer me:
Thou knowest not the period[1] of Jove's power?

PROMETHEUS

I know but this, that it must come.

MERCURY

                Alas!
Thou canst not count thy years to come of pain?

PROMETHEUS

They last while Jove must reign, nor more nor less    415
Do I desire or fear.

MERCURY

          Yet pause, and plunge
Into Eternity, where recorded time,
Even all that we imagine, age on age,
Seems but a point, and the reluctant mind
Flags wearily in its unending flight          420
Till it sink, dizzy, blind, lost, shelterless;
Perchance it has not numbered the slow years
Which thou must spend in torture, unreprieved.

PROMETHEUS

Perchance no thought can count them—yet they pass.

MERCURY

If thou might'st dwell among the Gods the while    425
Lapped in voluptuous joy?—

PROMETHEUS

           I would not quit
This bleak ravine, these unrepentant pains.

MERCURY

Alas! I wonder at, yet pity thee.

PROMETHEUS

Pity the self-despising slaves of Heaven,
Not me, within whose mind sits peace serene    430
As light in the sun, throned. . . . How vain is talk!
Call up the fiends.

9. Cowers.
1. The end or conclusion.

IONE

          O sister, look! White fire
Has cloven to the roots yon huge snow-loaded Cedar;
How fearfully God's thunder howls behind!

MERCURY

I must obey his words and thine—alas!                  435
Most heavily remorse hangs at my heart!

PANTHEA

See where the child of Heaven with winged feet
Runs down the slanted sunlight of the dawn.

IONE

Dear sister, close thy plumes over thine eyes
Lest thou behold and die—they come, they come       440
Blackening the birth of day with countless wings,
And hollow underneath, like death.

FIRST FURY

                    Prometheus!

SECOND FURY

Immortal Titan!

THIRD FURY

        Champion of Heaven's slaves!

PROMETHEUS

He whom some dreadful voice invokes is here,
Prometheus, the chained Titan.—Horrible forms,      445
What and who are ye? Never yet there came
Phantasms[2] so foul through monster-teeming Hell
From the all-miscreative brain of Jove;
Whilst I behold such execrable shapes,
Methinks I grow like what I contemplate             450
And laugh and stare in loathsome sympathy.

FIRST FURY

We are the ministers of pain and fear
And disappointment and mistrust and hate
And clinging[3] crime; and as lean dogs pursue

---

2. Spirits or incorporeal beings; apparitions.
3. Clasping.

Through wood and lake some struck and sobbing fawn,          455
We track all things that weep and bleed and live
When the great King betrays them to our will.[4]


PROMETHEUS

O many fearful natures in one name!
I know ye, and these lakes and echoes know
The darkness and the clangour of your wings.          460
But why more hideous than your loathed selves
Gather ye up in legions from the deep?


SECOND FURY

We knew not that—Sisters, rejoice, rejoice!


PROMETHEUS

Can aught exult in its deformity?


SECOND FURY

The beauty of delight makes lovers glad          465
Gazing on one another—so are we.
As from the rose which the pale priestess kneels
To gather for her festal crown of flowers
The aerial crimson falls, flushing her cheek—
So from our victim's destined agony          470
The shade which is our form invests us round,
Else we are shapeless as our Mother Night.[5]


PROMETHEUS

I laugh your power and his who sent you here
To lowest scorn.—Pour forth the cup of pain.


FIRST FURY

Thou thinkest we will rend thee bone from bone?          475
And nerve from nerve, working like fire within?


PROMETHEUS

Pain is my element as hate is thine;
Ye rend me now: I care not.


SECOND FURY

                              Dost imagine
We will but laugh into thy lidless eyes?


4. The comparison of human fears, hatreds, and evil thoughts with hunting dogs that pursue
a deer embodies both the myth of Actaeon (a hunter who was turned into a deer and devoured by his own hounds for seeing Diana naked) and an image deriving from it in Shakespeare's *Twelfth Night*: "That instant was I turn'd into a hart; / And my desires, like fell and
cruel hounds, / E'er since pursue me" (I.i.21–23).
5. The children of Night (according to Hesiod's *Theogony*) included Destruction, Death, Blame,
Grief, the Specters of Vengeance, Retribution, Deceit, Old Age, and Strife.

PROMETHEUS

I weigh not what ye do, but what ye suffer                    480
Being evil. Cruel was the Power which called
You, or aught else so wretched, into light.


THIRD FURY

Thou think'st we will live through thee, one by one,
Like animal life, and though we can obscure not
The soul which burns within, that we will dwell          485
Beside it, like a vain loud multitude
Vexing the self-content of wisest men—
That we will be dread thought beneath thy brain
And foul desire round thine astonished heart
And blood within thy labyrinthine veins                   490
Crawling like agony.


PROMETHEUS
                    Why, ye are thus now;
Yet am I king over myself, and rule
The torturing and conflicting throngs within
As Jove rules you when Hell grows mutinous.


CHORUS OF FURIES

From the ends of the Earth, from the ends of the Earth,          495
Where the night has its grave and the morning its birth,
            Come, Come, Come!
O ye who shake hills with the scream of your mirth
When cities sink howling in ruin, and ye
Who with wingless[6] footsteps trample the Sea,          500
And close upon Shipwreck and Famine's track
Sit chattering with joy on the foodless wrack;
            Come, Come, Come!
    Leave the bed, low, cold and red,
    Strewed beneath a nation dead;
    Leave the hatred—as in ashes                          505
      Fire is left for future burning,—
    It will burst in bloodier flashes
      When ye stir it, soon returning;
    Leave the self-contempt implanted                    510
    In young spirits sense-enchanted,
      Misery's yet unkindled fuel;
    Leave Hell's secrets half-unchanted
      To the maniac dreamer: cruel
    More than ye can be with hate,                       515
        Is he with fear.
        Come, Come, Come!
We are steaming up from Hell's wide gate
And we burthen the blasts of the atmosphere,

6. Heavy, evil.

But vainly we toil till ye come here.                          520

IONE

Sister, I hear the thunder of new wings.


PANTHEA

These solid mountains quiver with the sound
Even as the tremulous air:—their shadows make
The space within my plumes more black than night.


FIRST FURY

Your call was as a winged car                                  525
Driven on whirlwinds fast and far;
It rapt[7] us from red gulphs of war—


SECOND FURY

From wide cities, famine-wasted—


THIRD FURY

Groans half heard, and blood untasted—


FOURTH FURY

Kingly conclaves, stern and cold,                              530
Where blood with gold is bought and sold—


FIFTH FURY

From the furnace, white and hot,
In which—


A FURY

Speak not—whisper not!
I know all that ye would tell,
But to speak might break the spell                             535
Which must bend the Invincible,
    The stern of thought;
He yet defies the deepest power of Hell.


A FURY

Tear the veil!—


ANOTHER FURY

It is torn!


CHORUS

The pale stars of the morn
Shine on a misery dire to be borne.                            540
Dost thou faint, mighty Titan? We laugh thee to scorn.
Dost thou boast the clear knowledge thou waken'dst for man?
Then was kindled within him a thirst which outran

7. Carried from one place to another.

Those perishing waters: a thirst of fierce fever,
Hope, love, doubt, desire—which consume him forever.    545
  One[8] came forth, of gentle worth,
  Smiling on the sanguine earth;
  His words outlived him, like swift poison
    Withering up truth, peace and pity.
  Look! where round the wide horizon    550
    Many a million-peopled city
  Vomits smoke in the bright air.—
  Hark that outcry of despair!
  'Tis his mild and gentle ghost
    Wailing for the faith he kindled.    555
  Look again,—the flames almost
    To a glow-worm's lamp have dwindled:
  The survivors round the embers
    Gather in dread.
      Joy, Joy, Joy!    560
Past ages crowd on thee, but each one remembers,
And the future is dark, and the present is spread
Like a pillow of thorns for thy slumberless head.


      SEMICHORUS I
  Drops of bloody agony flow
  From his white and quivering brow.    565
  Grant a little respite now—
  See! a disenchanted Nation[9]
  Springs like day from desolation;
  To truth its state, is dedicate,
  And Freedom leads it forth, her mate;    570
  A legioned band of linked brothers
  Whom Love calls children—


      SEMICHORUS II
                    'Tis another's—
  See how kindred murder kin!
  'Tis the vintage-time for Death and Sin:
  Blood, like new wine, bubbles within    575
    Till Despair smothers
The struggling World—which slaves and tyrants win.
              [*All the* Furies *vanish, except one.*]


      IONE
Hark, sister! what a low yet dreadful groan
Quite unsuppressed is tearing up the heart
Of the good Titan—as storms tear the deep    580
And beasts hear the Sea moan in inland caves.
Darest thou observe how the fiends torture him?


8. Jesus Christ,
9. France, after it was freed of its enchantment by monarchy during the French Revolution,
   perverted the Revolution into bloody civil strife and then wars of conquest.

PANTHEA

Alas, I looked forth twice, but will no more.

IONE

What didst thou see?

PANTHEA
                    A woeful sight—a youth[1]
With patient looks nailed to a crucifix.                              585

IONE

What next?

PANTHEA
          The Heaven around, the Earth below
Was peopled with thick shapes of human death,
All horrible, and wrought by human hands,
And some appeared the work of human hearts,
For men were slowly killed by frowns and smiles:                     590
And other sights too foul to speak and live
Were wandering by. Let us not tempt worse fear
By looking forth—those groans are grief enough.

FURY

Behold, an emblem[2]—those who do endure
Deep wrongs for man, and scorn and chains, but heap                  595
Thousand-fold torment on themselves and him.

PROMETHEUS

Remit the anguish of that lighted stare—
Close those wan lips—let that thorn-wounded brow
Stream not with blood—it mingles with thy tears!
Fix, fix those tortured orbs in peace and death                      600
So thy sick throes shake not that crucifix,
So those pale fingers play not with thy gore.—
O horrible! Thy name I will not speak,
It hath become a curse. I see, I see
The wise, the mild, the lofty and the just,                          605
Whom thy slaves hate for being like to thee,
Some hunted by foul lies from their heart's home,
An early-chosen, late-lamented home,
As hooded ounces[3] cling to the driven hind,
Some linked to corpses in unwholesome cells:                         610
Some—hear I not the multitude laugh loud?—
Impaled in lingering fire: and mighty realms
Float by my feet like sea-uprooted isles

1. Jesus Christ.
2. A symbol; a fable or allegory such as might be expressed pictorially.
3. Cheetahs or hunting leopards; *hind*: a female deer in and after its third year.

Whose sons are kneaded down in common blood
By the red light of their own burning homes.—                    615

FURY

Blood thou canst see, and fire; and canst hear groans;
Worse things, unheard, unseen, remain behind.

PROMETHEUS

Worse?

FURY

    In each human heart terror survives
The ravin it has gorged: the loftiest fear
All that they would disdain to think were true:                  620
Hypocrisy and custom make their minds
The fanes of many a worship, now outworn.
They dare not devise good for man's estate
And yet they know not that they do not dare.
The good want power, but to weep barren tears.                   625
The powerful goodness want: worse need for them.
The wise want love, and those who love want wisdom;
And all best things are thus confused to ill.
Many are strong and rich,—and would be just,—
But live among their suffering fellow men                        630
As if none felt—they know not what they do.[4]

PROMETHEUS

Thy words are like a cloud of winged snakes
And yet, I pity those they torture not.

FURY

Thou pitiest them? I speak no more!              [*Vanishes.*]

PROMETHEUS

                          Ah woe!
Ah woe! Alas! pain, pain ever, forever!                          635
I close my tearless eyes, but see more clear
Thy works within my woe-illumed mind,
Thou subtle Tyrant! . . . Peace is in the grave—
The grave hides all things beautiful and good—
I am a God and cannot find it there—                             640
Nor would I seek it. For, though dread revenge,
This is defeat, Fierce King, not victory!
The sights with which thou torturest gird my soul
With new endurance, till the hour arrives
When they shall be no types of things which are.                 645

---

4. Lines 625–31 show the moment of Prometheus' ultimate temptation to despair, ending with
   the words of Christ on the cross (Luke 23:34).

PANTHEA
Alas! what sawest thou?

PROMETHEUS
                    There are two woes:
To speak and to behold; thou spare me one.
Names are there, Nature's sacred watchwords—they
Were borne aloft in bright emblazonry.
The nations thronged around, and cried aloud          650
As with one voice, "Truth, liberty and love!"
Suddenly fierce confusion fell from Heaven
Among them—there was strife, deceit and fear;
Tyrants rushed in, and did divide the spoil.
This was the shadow of the truth I saw.               655

THE EARTH
I felt thy torture, Son, with such mixed joy
As pain and Virtue give.—To cheer thy state
I bid ascend those subtle and fair spirits
Whose homes are the dim caves of human thought
And who inhabit, as birds wing the wind,              660
Its world-surrounding ether; they behold
Beyond that twilight realm, as in a glass,
The future—may they speak comfort to thee!

PANTHEA
Look, Sister, where a troop of spirits gather
Like flocks of clouds in spring's delightful weather,  665
Thronging in the blue air!

IONE
                    And see! more come
Like fountain-vapours when the winds are dumb,
That climb up the ravine in scattered lines.
And hark! is it the music of the pines?
Is it the lake? is it the waterfall?                  670

PANTHEA
'Tis something sadder, sweeter far than all.

CHORUS OF SPIRITS[5]
        From unremembered ages we
        Gentle guides and guardians be
        Of Heaven-oppressed mortality—
        And we breathe, and sicken not,               675
        The atmosphere of human thought:
        Be it dim and dank and grey
        Like a storm-extinguished day
        Travelled o'er by dying gleams;

5. Identified by Earth at lines 658–63.

Be it bright as all between                                    680
Cloudless skies and windless streams,
　Silent, liquid and serene—
As the birds within the wind,
　As the fish within the wave,
As the thoughts of man's own mind                              685
　Float through all above the grave,
We make there, our liquid lair,
Voyaging cloudlike and unpent[6]
Through the boundless element—
Thence we bear the prophecy                                    690
Which begins and ends in thee!

IONE

More yet come, one by one: the air around them
Looks radiant as the air around a star.

FIRST SPIRIT

On a battle-trumpet's blast
I fled hither, fast, fast, fast,                               695
Mid the darkness upward cast—
From the dust of creeds outworn,
From the tyrant's banner torn,
Gathering round me, onward borne,
There was mingled many a cry—                                  700
Freedom! Hope! Death! Victory!
Till they faded through the sky
And one sound—above, around,
One sound beneath, around, above,
Was moving; 'twas the soul of love;                            705
'Twas the hope, the prophecy,
Which begins and ends in thee.

SECOND SPIRIT

A rainbow's arch stood on the sea,
Which rocked beneath, immoveably;
And the triumphant Storm did flee,                            710
Like a conqueror swift and proud
Between, with many a captive cloud
A shapeless, dark and rapid crowd,
Each by lightning riven in half.—
I heard the thunder hoarsely laugh.—                          715
Mighty fleets were strewn like chaff
And spread beneath, a hell of death
O'er the white waters. I alit
On a great ship lightning-split
And speeded hither on the sigh                                 720
Of one who gave an enemy
His plank—then plunged aside to die.

6. Unconfined.

THIRD SPIRIT
I sate beside a sage's bed
And the lamp was burning red
Near the book where he had fed,                    725
When a Dream with plumes of flame
To his pillow hovering came,
And I knew it was the same
Which had kindled long ago
Pity, eloquence and woe;                            730
And the world awhile below
Wore the shade its lustre made.
It has borne me here as fleet
As Desire's lightning feet:
I must ride it back ere morrow,                     735
Or the sage will wake in sorrow.


FOURTH SPIRIT
On a Poet's lips I slept
Dreaming like a love-adept
In the sound his breathing kept;
Nor seeks nor finds he mortal blisses              740
But feeds on the aerial kisses
Of shapes that haunt thought's wildernesses.
He will watch from dawn to gloom
The lake-reflected sun illume
The yellow bees i' the ivy-bloom                   745
Nor heed nor see, what things they be;
But from these create he can
Forms more real than living man,
Nurslings of immortality!—
One of these awakened me                            750
And I sped to succour thee.


IONE
Behold'st thou not two shapes from the East and West
Come, as two doves to one beloved nest,
Twin nurslings of the all-sustaining air,
On swift still wings glide down the atmosphere?    755
And hark! their sweet, sad voices! 'tis despair
Mingled with love, and then dissolved in sound.—


PANTHEA
Canst thou speak, sister? all my words are drowned.


IONE
Their beauty gives me voice. See how they float
On their sustaining wings of skiey grain,          760
Orange and azure, deepening into gold:
Their soft smiles light the air like a star's fire.

CHORUS OF SPIRITS

Hast thou beheld the form of Love?


FIFTH SPIRIT
As over wide dominions
I sped, like some swift cloud that wings the wide air's wildernesses,
That planet-crested Shape swept by on lightning-braided pinions,[7]
   Scattering the liquid joy of life from his ambrosial[8] tresses:    766
His footsteps paved the world with light—but as I past 'twas fading
   And hollow Ruin yawned behind. Great Sages bound in madness
And headless patriots and pale youths who perished unupbraiding,
   Gleamed in the Night I wandered o'er—till thou, O King of sadness,
Turned by thy smile the worst I saw to recollected gladness.    771


SIXTH SPIRIT

Ah, sister! Desolation is a delicate thing:
It walks not on the Earth, it floats not on the air,
But treads with silent footstep, and fans with silent wing
The tender hopes which in their hearts the best and gentlest bear,
Who, soothed to false repose by the fanning plumes above    776
And the music-stirring motion of its soft and busy feet,
Dream visions of aerial joy, and call the monster, Love,
And wake, and find the shadow Pain—as he whom now we greet.


CHORUS
Though Ruin now Love's[9] shadow be,    780
Following him destroyingly
   On Death's white and winged steed,
Which the fleetest cannot flee—
   Trampling down both flower and weed,
Man and beast and foul and fair,    785
Like a tempest through the air;
Thou shalt quell this Horseman grim,
Woundless though in heart or limb.—


PROMETHEUS

Spirits! how know ye this shall be?


CHORUS
In the atmosphere we breathe—    790
As buds grow red when snow-storms flee
From spring gathering up beneath,
Whose mild winds shake, the elder brake[1]
And the wandering herdsmen know

---

7. Wings.
8. Divine or worthy of the gods.
9. It may be relevant to the thought here (and in lines 763 and 778) that in Hesiod's *Theogony*, Love is among the children of Night (along with those mentioned in the note to line 472 above). The Spirits here describe the effects of Love in the imperfect, unredeemed world.
1. Thicket.

That the white-thorn soon will blow—                          795
Wisdom, Justice, Love and Peace,
When they struggle to increase,
Are to us as soft winds be
To shepherd-boys—the prophecy
Which begins and ends in thee.                                800

IONE

Where are the Spirits fled?

PANTHEA

                          Only a sense
Remains of them, like the Omnipotence
Of music when the inspired voice and lute
Languish, ere yet the responses are mute
Which through the deep and labyrinthine soul,                 805
Like echoes through long caverns, wind and roll.

PROMETHEUS

How fair these air-born shapes! and yet I feel
Most vain all hope but love, and thou art far,
Asia! who when my being overflowed
Wert like a golden chalice to bright wine                     810
Which else had sunk into the thirsty dust.
All things are still—alas! how heavily
This quiet morning weighs upon my heart;
Though I should dream, I could even sleep with grief
If slumber were denied not . . . I would fain                 815
Be what it is my destiny to be,
The saviour and the strength of suffering man,
Or sink into the original gulph of things. . . .
There is no agony and no solace left;
Earth can console, Heaven can torment no more.                820

PANTHEA

Hast thou forgotten one who watches thee
The cold dark night, and never sleeps but when
The shadow of thy spirit falls on her?

PROMETHEUS

I said all hope was vain but love—thou lovest . . .

PANTHEA

Deeply in truth—but the Eastern star looks white,            825
And Asia waits in that far Indian vale,
The scene of her sad exile—rugged once
And desolate and frozen like this ravine;
But now invested with fair flowers and herbs

And haunted by sweet airs and sounds, which flow                    830
Among the woods and waters, from the ether[2]
Of her transforming presence—which would fade
If it were mingled not with thine.—Farewell!

END OF THE FIRST ACT.

## Act II

### SCENE I

*Morning. A lovely Vale in the Indian Caucasus.* Asia *alone.*

ASIA
From all the blasts of Heaven thou hast descended—
Yes, like a spirit, like a thought which makes
Unwonted[3] tears throng to the horny[4] eyes
And beatings haunt the desolated heart
Which should have learnt repose,—thou hast descended        5
Cradled in tempests; thou dost wake, O Spring!
O child of many winds! . . . As suddenly
Thou comest as the memory of a dream
Which now is sad because it hath been sweet;
Like genius, or like joy which riseth up                    10
As from the Earth, clothing with golden clouds
The desart of our life. . . .
This is the season, this the day, the hour;
At sunrise thou shouldst come, sweet sister mine . . .
Too long desired, too long delaying, come! . . .            15
How like death-worms the wingless moments crawl!
The point of one white star[5] is quivering still
Deep in the orange light of widening morn
Beyond the purple mountains; through a chasm
Of wind-divided mist the darker lake                        20
Reflects it—now it wanes—it gleams again
As the waves fade, and as the burning threads
Of woven cloud unravel in pale air. . . .
'Tis lost! and through yon peaks of cloudlike snow
The roseate sunlight quivers—hear I not                     25
The Æolian music of her[6] sea-green plumes
Winnowing[7] the crimson dawn?
                                          [Panthea *enters.*]
                I feel, I see
Those eyes which burn through smiles that fade in tears
Like stars half quenched in mists of silver dew.—

2. The air breathed by the gods.
3. Not usual.
4. Semi-opaque like horn.
5. I.e., Venus, the morning star.
6. I.e., Panthea (*sister*, line 14).
7. Beating or flapping in.

Beloved and most beautiful, who wearest                          30
The shadow of that soul by which I live,
How late thou art! the sphered sun had climbed
The sea, my heart was sick with hope, before
The printless air felt thy belated plumes.

PANTHEA

Pardon, great Sister! but my wings were faint                    35
With the delight of a remembered dream
As are the noontide plumes of summer winds
Satiate with sweet flowers. I was wont to sleep
Peacefully, and awake refreshed and calm
Before the sacred Titan's fall, and thy                          40
Unhappy love, had made through use and pity
Both love and woe familiar to my heart
As they had grown to thine . . . erewhile[8] I slept
Under the glaucous[9] caverns of old Ocean,
Within dim bowers of green and purple moss;                      45
Our young Ione's soft and milky arms
Locked then as now behind my dark moist hair
While my shut eyes and cheek were pressed within
The folded depth of her life-breathing bosom . . .
But not as now since I am made the wind                          50
Which fails beneath the music that I bear
Of thy most wordless converse; since dissolved
Into the sense with which love talks, my rest
Was troubled and yet sweet—my waking hours
Too full of care and pain.

ASIA
                              Lift up thine eyes                 55
And let me read thy dream.—

PANTHEA
                              As I have said,
With our sea-sister at his feet I slept.
The mountain mists, condensing at our voice
Under the moon, had spread their snowy flakes
From the keen ice shielding our linked sleep . . .              60
Then two dreams came.[1] One I remember not.
But in the other, his pale, wound-worn limbs
Fell from Prometheus, and the azure night
Grew radiant with the glory of that form
Which lives unchanged within, and his voice fell                65
Like music which makes giddy the dim brain
Faint with intoxication of keen joy:
"Sister of her whose footsteps pave the world

8. Formerly, or some time ago.
9. Of a dull or pale green color passing into grayish blue.
1. The communication of these two dreams of Panthea to Asia is the main action in this scene.

With loveliness—more fair than aught but her
Whose shadow thou art—lift thine eyes on me!"          70
I lifted them—the overpowering light
Of that immortal shape was shadowed o'er
By love; which, from his soft and flowing limbs
And passion-parted lips, and keen faint eyes
Steamed forth like vaporous fire; an atmosphere          75
Which wrapt me in its all-dissolving power
As the warm ether of the morning sun
Wraps ere it drinks some cloud of wandering dew.
I saw not—heard not—moved not—only felt
His presence flow and mingle through my blood          80
Till it became his life and his grew mine
And I was thus absorbed—until it past
And like the vapours when the sun sinks down,
Gathering again in drops upon the pines
And tremulous as they, in the deep night          85
My being was condensed, and as the rays
Of thought were slowly gathered, I could hear
His voice, whose accents lingered ere they died
Like footsteps of far melody. Thy name,
Among the many sounds alone I heard          90
Of what might be articulate; though still
I listened through the night when sound was none.
Ione wakened then, and said to me:
"Canst thou divine what troubles me tonight?
I always knew what I desired before          95
Nor ever found delight to wish in vain.
But now I cannot tell thee what I seek;
I know not—something sweet since it is sweet
Even to desire—it is thy sport, false sister!
Thou hast discovered some inchantment old          100
Whose spells have stolen my spirit as I slept
And mingled it with thine;—for when just now
We kissed, I felt within thy parted lips
The sweet air that sustained me, and the warmth
Of the life-blood for loss of which I faint          105
Quivered between our intertwining arms."
I answered not, for the Eastern star grew pale,
But fled to thee.

ASIA
          Thou speakest, but thy words
Are as the air. I feel them not. . . . oh, lift
Thine eyes that I may read his written soul!          110

PANTHEA
I lift them, though they droop beneath the load
Of that they would express—what canst thou see
But thine own fairest shadow imaged there?

ASIA

Thine eyes are like the deep blue, boundless Heaven
Contracted to two circles underneath                              115
Their long, fine lashes—dark, far, measureless,—
Orb within orb, and line through line inwoven.—


PANTHEA

Why lookest thou as if a spirit past?


ASIA

There is a change: beyond their inmost depth
I see a shade—a shape—'tis He, arrayed                           120
In the soft light of his own smiles which spread
Like radiance from the cloud-surrounded moon.
Prometheus, it is thou—depart not yet!
Say not those smiles that we shall meet again
Within that bright Pavilion which their beams                     125
Shall build o'er the waste world? The dream is told.
What shape[2] is that between us? Its rude hair
Roughens the wind that lifts it; its regard
Is wild and quick, yet 'tis a thing of air
For through its grey robe gleams the golden dew                   130
Whose stars the noon has quenched not.


DREAM
                                    Follow, follow!


PANTHEA

It is mine other dream.—


ASIA
                         It disappears.


PANTHEA

It passes now into my mind. Methought
As we sate here the flower-infolding buds
Burst on yon lightning-blasted almond tree,[3]                   135
When swift, from the white Scythian wilderness,
A wind swept forth wrinkling the Earth with frost . . .
I looked, and all the blossoms were blown down;
But on each leaf was stamped—as the blue bells
Of Hyacinth tell Apollo's written grief[4]—                      140
O *follow, follow!*

2. This is the second dream, which relates to the Spirits of the Hours that are to usher in the
   fall of Jupiter and the release of Prometheus, and to the course of necessity.
3. Earl R. Wasserman has pointed out that in Pliny's *Natural History* (a book Shelley knew
   well) the almond tree is mentioned as the first tree to bud in winter (January) and to bear
   fruit (March), and that the prophet Jeremiah puns on the Hebrew word for "almond," which
   also means "hasten" (Jeremiah 1:11–12).
4. After Hyacinthus, beloved of Apollo, was killed by the jealous Zephyrus, Apollo changed his
   blood into a flower and wrote his lament, "Ai" ("alas" or "woe!" in Greek) on the petals.

ASIA
As you speak, your words
Fill, pause by pause my own forgotten sleep
With shapes. . . . Methought among these lawns together
We wandered, underneath the young grey dawn,
And multitudes of dense white fleecy clouds                    145
Were wandering in thick flocks along the mountains
Shepherded by the slow, unwilling wind;
And the white dew on the new-bladed grass,
Just piercing the dark earth, hung silently—
And there was more which I remember not;                    150
But, on the shadows of the morning clouds
Athwart the purple mountain slope was written
*Follow, O follow!* as they vanished by,
And on each herb from which Heaven's dew had fallen
The like was stamped as with a withering fire;                    155
A wind arose among the pines—it shook
The clinging music from their boughs, and then
Low, sweet, faint sounds, like the farewell of ghosts,
Were heard—O *follow, follow, follow me!*
And then I said: "Panthea, look on me."                    160
But in the depth of those beloved eyes
Still I saw, *follow, follow!*

ECHO
Follow, follow!

PANTHEA
The crags, this clear spring morning, mock our voices,
As they were spirit-tongued.

ASIA
It is some being
Around the crags.—What fine clear sounds! O list!                    165

ECHOES *unseen*
Echoes we—listen!
We cannot stay
As dew-stars glisten
Then fade away—
Child of Ocean![5]                    170

ASIA
Hark! Spirits speak! The liquid responses
Of their aerial tongues yet sound.—

PANTHEA
I hear.

5. Asia, Panthea, and Ione are Oceanides, daughters of Oceanus, one of the earliest gods in
  all classical theogonies.

ECHOES
O follow, follow,
    As our voice recedeth
Through the caverns hollow                        175
    Where the forest spreadeth;
        [*More distant.*]
O follow, follow,
    Through the caverns hollow,
As the song floats, thou pursue
Where the wild-bee never flew,                     180
Through the noontide darkness deep,
By the odour breathing sleep
Of faint night-flowers, and the waves
At the fountain-lighted caves,
While our music, wild and sweet,                   185
Mocks thy gently-falling feet,
    Child of Ocean!


                ASIA
Shall we pursue the sound?—It grows more faint
And distant.


                PANTHEA
List!—the strain floats nearer now.


            ECHOES
In the world unknown                               190
    Sleeps a voice unspoken;[6]
By thy step alone
    Can its rest be broken,
        Child of Ocean!


                ASIA
How the notes sink upon the ebbing wind!           195


            ECHOES
O follow, follow!
    Through the caverns hollow,
As the song floats, thou pursue,
By the woodland noontide dew,
By the forests, lakes and fountains,               200
Through the many-folded mountains,
To the rents and gulphs and chasms
Where the Earth reposed from spasms
On the day when He and thou
Parted—to commingle now,                           205
    Child of Ocean!


6. Such descriptions in negatives (see *world unknown*, line 190) suggest that the echoes are leading Asia and Panthea from the realm of actuality into a world of potentiality. See Timothy Webb's essay in this volume (pp. 694–711) and D. J. Hughes's seminal essay, "Potentiality in *Prometheus Unbound*," *SiR* II (1963): 107–26.

ASIA

Come, sweet Panthea—link thy hand in mine
And follow, ere the voices fade away.


SCENE II

*A Forest, intermingled with Rocks and Caverns.* Asia *and* Panthea *pass
into it. Two young Fauns are sitting on a Rock, listening.*

SEMICHORUS I OF SPIRITS

The path through which that lovely twain[7]
   Have past, by cedar, pine and yew,[8]
   And each dark tree that ever grew
   Is curtained out from Heaven's wide blue;
Nor sun nor moon nor wind nor rain                         5
     Can pierce its interwoven bowers;
    Nor aught save where some cloud of dew,
Drifted along the earth-creeping breeze
Between the trunks of the hoar[9] trees,
    Hangs each a pearl in the pale flowers          10
   Of the green laurel,[1] blown anew;
And bends and then fades silently
One frail and fair anemone;[2]
Or when some star of many a one
That climbs and wanders through steep Night,               15
Has found the cleft through which alone
Beams fall from high those depths upon,
Ere it is borne away, away,
By the swift Heavens that cannot stay—
It scatters drops of golden light                          20
Like lines of rain that ne'er unite;
And the gloom divine is all around
And underneath is the mossy ground.


SEMICHORUS II

There the voluptuous nightingales
   Are awake through all the broad noonday.         25
When one with bliss or sadness fails—
    And through the windless ivy-boughs,
   Sick with sweet love, droops dying away
On its mate's music-panting bosom—
Another from the swinging blossom,                         30
    Watching to catch the languid close
   Of the last strain, then lifts on high
   The wings of the weak melody,

---

7. I.e., Asia and Panthea.
8. Though the yew tree is commonly associated with death, the *cedar* and *pine*—evergreens
with more hopeful symbolism—suggest that Shelley's description aims at a neutral portrayal
of *the gloom divine* (line 22) of the path leading down to Demogorgon's underworld.
9. Old and venerable.
1. Also called "bay," a symbol of success in poetry; *blown:* blooming.
2. Windflower; it belongs to the buttercup family.

Till some new strain of feeling bear
    The song, and all the woods are mute;                    35
When there is heard through the dim air
The rush of wings, and rising there
    Like many a lake-surrounded flute,
Sounds overflow the listener's brain
So sweet, that joy is almost pain.                           40

SEMICHORUS I

There those inchanted eddies play
    Of echoes, music-tongued, which draw,
    By Demogorgon's mighty law
    With melting rapture or sweet awe,
All spirits on that secret way,                              45
    As inland boats are driven to Ocean
Down streams made strong with mountain-thaw;
    And first there comes a gentle sound
    To those in talk or slumber bound,
And wakes the destined—soft emotion                         50
Attracts, impels them: those who saw
    Say from the breathing Earth behind
    There steams a plume-uplifting wind
Which drives them on their path, while they
    Believe their own swift wings and feet                   55
The sweet desires within obey:
And so they float upon their way
Until, still sweet but loud and strong,
The storm of sound is driven along,
    Sucked up and hurrying—as they fleet                     60
    Behind its gathering billows meet
And to the fatal mountain bear
Like clouds amid the yielding air.[3]

FIRST FAUN

Canst thou imagine where those spirits live
Which make such delicate music in the woods?                 65
We haunt within the least frequented caves
And closest coverts,[4] and we know these wilds,
Yet never meet them, though we hear them oft:
Where may they hide themselves?

SECOND FAUN

                                'Tis hard to tell—
I have heard those more skilled in spirits say,             70
The bubbles which the enchantment of the sun
Sucks from the pale faint water-flowers that pave
The oozy bottom of clear lakes and pools
Are the pavilions where such dwell and float

3. Lines 24–63 deal with sounds—following the closing out of light and the sense of sight in
the scene's opening lines.
4. Most secret shelters or thickets.

Under the green and golden atmosphere                    75
Which noontide kindles through the woven leaves,
And when these burst, and the thin fiery air,
The which they breathed within those lucent⁵ domes,
Ascends to flow like meteors through the night,
They ride on them, and rein their headlong speed,                    80
And bow their burning crests, and glide in fire
Under the waters of the Earth again.⁶

FIRST FAUN

If such live thus, have others other lives
Under pink blossoms or within the bells
Of meadow flowers, or folded violets deep,                    85
Or on their dying odours, when they die,
Or in the sunlight of the sphered dew?

SECOND FAUN

Aye, many more, which we may well divine.
But should we stay to speak, noontide would come,
And thwart Silenus find his goats undrawn⁷                    90
And grudge to sing those wise and lovely songs
Of fate and chance and God, and Chaos old,
And love, and the chained Titan's woful doom
And how he shall be loosed, and make the Earth
One brotherhood—delightful strains which cheer                    95
Our solitary twilights, and which charm
To silence the unenvying nightingales.

SCENE III

A *Pinnacle of Rock among Mountains.* Asia *and* Panthea.

PANTHEA

Hither the sound has borne us—to the realm
Of Demogorgon, and the mighty portal,
Like a Volcano's meteor-breathing chasm,
Whence the oracular vapour is hurled up
Which lonely men drink wandering in their youth                    5
And call truth, virtue, love, genius or joy—
That maddening wine of life, whose dregs they drain
To deep intoxication, and uplift
Like Mænads who cry loud, Evoe! Evoe!⁸
The voice which is contagion to the world.                    10

5. Shining or luminous.
6. Lines 70–82 portray the hydrogen cycle, as it was understood in Shelley's day, explaining
   the origin of the swamp gas that, when ignited, becomes the *ignis fatuus* or will-o'-the-wisp.
7. A demigod who became the nurse, preceptor, and attendant of Bacchus, Silenus is generally
   represented as a fat and jolly old man riding an ass, crowned with flowers, and always
   intoxicated; *undrawn:* not yet milked.
8. Maenads were fanatic female worshipers of Dionysus, Greek god of wine (Roman Bacchus);
   when in an intoxicated frenzy, they would surge through the wilderness, crying *"Evoe!"* and
   killing every living thing in their path. (See Euripides' late drama *The Bacchae.*)

ASIA

Fit throne for such a Power! Magnificent!
How glorious art thou, Earth! and if thou be
The shadow of some Spirit lovelier still,
Though evil stain its work and it should be
Like its creation, weak yet beautiful,                                    15
I could fall down and worship that and thee.[9]—
Even now my heart adoreth.—Wonderful!
Look Sister, ere the vapour dim thy brain;
Beneath is a wide plain of billowy mist,
As a lake, paving in the morning sky,                                     20
With azure waves which burst in silver light,
Some Indian vale . . . Behold it, rolling on
Under the curdling winds, and islanding
The peak whereon we stand—midway, around
Encinctured[1] by the dark and blooming forests,                          25
Dim twilight lawns and stream-illumined caves
And wind-inchanted shapes of wandering mist;
And far on high the keen sky-cleaving mountains
From icy spires of sunlike radiance fling
The dawn, as lifted Ocean's dazzling spray                                30
From some Atlantic islet scattered up
Spangles the wind with lamp-like water drops.
The vale is girdled with their walls—a howl
Of cataracts from their thaw-cloven ravines
Satiates the listening wind, continuous, vast,                            35
Awful as silence.—Hark! the rushing snow!
The sun-awakened avalanche! whose mass,
Thrice sifted by the storm, had gathered there
Flake after flake, in Heaven-defying minds
As thought by thought is piled, till some great truth                     40
Is loosened, and the nations echo round
Shaken to their roots: as do the mountains now.[2]


PANTHEA

Look, how the gusty sea of mist is breaking
In crimson foam, even at our feet!—it rises
As Ocean at the inchantment of the moon                                   45
Round foodless men wrecked on some oozy isle.


ASIA

The fragments of the cloud are scattered up—
The wind that lifts them disentwines my hair—

9. The central imagery in lines 12–16 echoes *Paradise Lost*, where Raphael implies to Adam
   that Earth may be "but the shadow of Heav'n, and things therein / Each to other like, more
   than on earth is thought" (V.574–76).
1. Belted, girdled.
2. This simile is one of the best examples of the reversal of imagery that Shelley mentions in
   the fourth paragraph of the Preface, for here an external natural event (the avalanche, lines
   36–38) is compared to a figure "drawn from the operations of the human mind"—in this
   case, the slow growth of new concepts in *Heaven-defying minds* until there is an intellectual
   revolution.

Its billows now sweep o'er mine eyes—my brain
Grows dizzy—I see thin shapes within the mist.          50


PANTHEA

A countenance with beckoning smiles—there burns
An azure fire within its golden locks—
Another and another—hark! they speak!


SONG OF SPIRITS
   To the Deep, to the Deep,
       Down, Down!          55
   Through the shade of Sleep,
   Through the cloudy strife
   Of Death and of Life;
   Through the veil and the bar
   Of things which seem and are,          60
Even to the steps of the remotest Throne,
       Down, Down!


   While the sound,[3] whirls around,
       Down, Down!
   As the fawn draws the hound,          65
   As the lightning the vapour,
   As a weak moth the taper;
   Death, Despair; Love, Sorrow;
   Time both; to-day, to-morrow;
As steel obeys the Spirit of the stone,[4]          70
       Down, Down!


   Through the grey, void Abysm,
       Down, Down!
   Where the air is no prism[5]
   And the moon and stars are not          75
   And the cavern-crags wear not
   The radiance of Heaven,
   Nor the gloom to Earth given;
Where there is One pervading, One alone,
       Down, Down!          80


   In the depth of the Deep,
       Down, Down!
   Like veil'd Lightning asleep,
   Like the spark nursed in embers,
   The last look Love remembers,          85
   Like a diamond which shines

3. Again, the comma is metrical (marking a pause after the internal rhyme) rather than grammatical.
4. The magnet draws the *steel*; the *fawn* attracts the *hound* (line 65); there is mutual attraction between *lightning* and *vapour*, *moth* and *taper* (candle), *Death* and *Despair*, etc.
5. I.e., out of the earth's atmosphere, which, acting as a prism, breaks the pure white sunlight of eternity into the variegated colors of mortal perception (cf. *Adonais*, lines 462–64).

On the dark wealth of mines,[6]
A spell is treasured but for thee alone—
        Down, Down!

We have bound thee, we guide thee                          90
        Down, Down!
With the bright form beside thee—
Resist not the weakness—
Such strength is in meekness—
That the Eternal, the Immortal,                            95
Must unloose through life's portal
The snake-like Doom coiled underneath his throne
        By that alone!


SCENE IV

*The Cave of* Demogorgon. Asia *and* Panthea.


PANTHEA
What veiled form sits on that ebon throne?


ASIA
The veil has fallen! . . .


PANTHEA
                I see a mighty Darkness
Filling the seat of power; and rays of gloom
Dart round, as light from the meridian Sun,
Ungazed upon and shapeless:—neither limb                    5
Nor form nor outline,[7] yet we feel it is
A living Spirit.


DEMOGORGON
        Ask what thou wouldst know.


ASIA
What canst thou tell?


DEMOGORGON
        All things thou dar'st demand.


ASIA
Who made the living world?


6. According to eighteenth-century scientists, the diamond was phosphorescent, first absorbing light and then glowing in the dark (see Robert A. Hartley, "Phosphorescence in Canto I of *The Revolt of Islam,*" *Notes and Queries,* n.s., 20 [August 1973]: 293–94).
7. Panthea's description of Demogorgon echoes Milton's description of Death in *Paradise Lost* (II.666–73), beginning, "The other shape, / If shape it might be call'd that shape had none / Distinguishable in member, joynt, or limb. . . ."

DEMOGORGON
      God.

ASIA
              Who made all
That it contains—thought, passion, reason, will,      10
Imagination?[8]

DEMOGORGON
God, Almighty God.

ASIA
Who made that sense which, when the winds of spring
In rarest visitation, or the voice
Of one beloved heard in youth alone,
Fills the faint eyes with falling tears, which dim      15
The radiant looks of unbewailing flowers
And leaves this peopled earth a solitude
When it returns no more?

DEMOGORGON
      Merciful God.

ASIA
And who made terror, madness, crime, remorse,
Which from the links of the great chain of things      20
To every thought within the mind of man
Sway and drag heavily—and each one reels
Under the load towards the pit of death;
Abandoned hope, and love that turns to hate;
And self-contempt, bitterer to drink than blood;      25
Pain whose unheeded and familiar speech
Is howling and keen shrieks, day after day;
And Hell, or the sharp fear of Hell?

DEMOGORGON
      He reigns.

ASIA
Utter his name—a world pining in pain
Asks but his name; curses shall drag him down.      30

DEMOGORGON
He reigns.

ASIA
I feel, I know it—who?

8. The metaphysical implication of Asia's statement is that all the universe is made up of mental activities, yet this—like Asia's other assertions—is neither confirmed nor denied by Demogorgon and should be seen as a useful myth rather than a declaration of Shelley's beliefs about reality.

DEMOGORGON
He reigns.


ASIA

Who reigns? There was the Heaven and Earth at first
And Light and Love;—then Saturn, from whose throne
Time fell, an envious shadow;[9] such the state
Of the earth's primal spirits beneath his sway                        35
As the calm joy of flowers and living leaves
Before the wind or sun has withered them
And semivital worms; but he refused
The birthright of their being, knowledge, power,
The skill which wields the elements, the thought                     40
Which pierces this dim Universe like light,
Self-empire and the majesty of love,
For thirst of which they fainted. Then Prometheus
Gave wisdom, which is strength, to Jupiter
And with this Law alone: "Let man be free,"                          45
Clothed him with the dominion of wide Heaven.
To know nor faith nor love nor law, to be
Omnipotent but friendless, is to reign;
And Jove now reigned; for on the race of man
First famine and then toil and then disease,                         50
Strife, wounds, and ghastly death unseen before,
Fell; and the unseasonable seasons drove,
With alternating shafts of frost and fire,
Their shelterless, pale tribes to mountain caves;
And in their desart[1] hearts fierce wants he sent                   55
And mad disquietudes, and shadows idle
Of unreal good, which levied mutual war,
So ruining the lair wherein they raged.
Prometheus saw, and waked the legioned[2] hopes
Which sleep within folded Elysian flowers,                           60
Nepenthe, Moly, Amaranth, fadeless blooms;[3]
That they might hide with thin and rainbow wings
The shape of Death; and Love he sent to bind
The disunited tendrils of that vine
Which bears the wine of life, the human heart;                       65
And he tamed fire, which like some beast of prey
Most terrible, but lovely, played beneath
The frown of man, and tortured to his will

9. Shelley plays on the Greek names for Saturn (Kronos), during whose reign was the mythical
   Golden Age, and Time (Chronos).
1. Forsaken or lonely.
2. Arrayed in legions, as armies.
3. *Elysian*: conducive to complete happiness (from "Elysium," the abode of virtuous Greeks
   after death); *Nepenthe*: a drug mentioned in the *Odyssey* (IV.220ff.) capable of banishing
   grief or trouble; *Moly*: a magical herb with a white flower and a black root, given to Odysseus
   by Hermes as a charm against the sorceries of Circe (*Odyssey*, X.302ff.); *Amaranth*: from the
   Greek adjective meaning "everlasting," "not fading," or "incorruptible" (cf. *Paradise Lost*,
   III.352–60).

Iron and gold, the slaves and signs of power,
And gems and poisons, and all subtlest forms                          70
Hidden beneath the mountains and the waves.
He gave man speech, and speech created thought,
Which is the measure of the Universe;
And Science struck the thrones of Earth and Heaven,
Which shook but fell not; and the harmonious mind                     75
Poured itself forth in all-prophetic song,
And music lifted up the listening spirit
Until it walked, exempt from mortal care,
Godlike, o'er the clear billows of sweet sound;
And human hands first mimicked[4] and then mocked                     80
With moulded limbs more lovely than its own
The human form, till marble grew divine,
And mothers, gazing, drank the love men see
Reflected in their race—behold, and perish.—[5]
He told the hidden power of herbs and springs,                        85
And Disease drank and slept—Death grew like sleep.—
He taught the implicated[6] orbits woven
Of the wide-wandering stars, and how the Sun
Changes his lair, and by what secret spell
The pale moon is transformed, when her broad eye                      90
Gazes not on the interlunar[7] sea;
He taught to rule, as life directs the limbs,
The tempest-winged chariots of the Ocean,[8]
And the Celt[9] knew the Indian. Cities then
Were built, and through their snow-like columns flowed                95
The warm winds, and the azure æther shone,
And the blue sea and shadowy hills were seen . . .
Such the alleviations of his state
Prometheus gave to man—for which he hangs
Withering in destined pain—but who rains down                        100
Evil, the immedicable plague, which while
Man looks on his creation like a God
And sees that it is glorious, drives him on,
The wreck of his own will, the scorn of Earth,
The outcast, the abandoned, the alone?—                              105
Not Jove: while yet his frown shook Heaven, aye when
His adversary from adamantine[1] chains
Cursed him, he trembled like a slave. Declare
Who is his master? Is he too a slave?

---

4. Copied or faithfully reproduced.
5. Swinburne suggested that lines 83–84 describe the positive prenatal influence on children whose mothers had viewed sculptures that achieved such idealized beauty that men fell desperately in love with them. He compares Virgil's phrase on the sorcery of love: "Ut vidi, ut perii" (*Eclogues*, VIII.41; "As I saw, how I was lost!").
6. Intertwined or entangled.
7. Dark; the time between the old and the new moon.
8. *tempest . . . Ocean:* a periphrasis for "sailboats."
9. From classical Greek times to Shelley's day the term "Celts" meant any of the barbarians to the north of the Graeco-Roman Mediterranean civilization.
1. Incapable of being broken.

DEMOGORGON

All spirits are enslaved which serve things evil.                    110
Thou knowest if Jupiter be such or no.


ASIA

Whom called'st thou God?


DEMOGORGON

                    I spoke but as ye speak—
For Jove is the supreme of living things.


ASIA

Who is the master of the slave?


DEMOGORGON

                    —If the Abysm
Could vomit forth its secrets:—but a voice                           115
Is wanting, the deep truth is imageless;
For what would it avail to bid thee gaze
On the revolving world? what to bid speak
Fate, Time, Occasion, Chance and Change?—To these
All things are subject but eternal Love.                             120


ASIA

So much I asked before, and my heart gave
The response thou hast given; and of such truths
Each to itself must be the oracle.—
One more demand . . . and do thou answer me
As my own soul would answer, did it know                             125
That which I ask.—Prometheus shall arise
Henceforth the Sun of this rejoicing world:
When shall the destined hour arrive?


DEMOGORGON

                    Behold!


ASIA

The rocks are cloven, and through the purple night
I see Cars drawn by rainbow-winged steeds                            130
Which trample the dim winds—in each there stands
A wild-eyed charioteer, urging their flight.
Some look behind, as fiends pursued them there
And yet I see no shapes but the keen stars:
Others with burning eyes lean forth, and drink                       135
With eager lips the wind of their own speed
As if the thing they loved fled on before
And now—even now they clasped it; their bright locks
Stream like a comet's flashing hair: they all
Sweep onward.—

DEMOGORGON

       These are the immortal Hours          140
Of whom thou didst demand.—One waits for thee.


ASIA

A Spirit with a dreadful countenance
Checks its dark chariot by the craggy gulph.
Unlike thy brethren—ghastly charioteer,
What art thou? whither wouldst thou bear me? Speak!    145


SPIRIT

I am the shadow of a destiny
More dread than is my aspect—ere yon planet
Has set, the Darkness which ascends with me
Shall wrap in lasting night Heaven's kingless throne.


ASIA

What meanest thou?


PANTHEA

         That terrible shadow[2] floats       150
Up from its throne, as may the lurid[3] smoke
Of earthquake-ruined cities o'er the sea.—
Lo! it ascends the Car . . . the coursers fly
Terrified; watch its path among the stars
Blackening the night!


ASIA

         Thus I am answered—strange!     155


PANTHEA

See, near the verge[4] another chariot stays:
An ivory shell inlaid with crimson fire
Which comes and goes within its sculptured rim
Of delicate strange tracery—the young Spirit
That guides it, has the dovelike eyes of hope.     160
How its soft smiles attract the soul!—as light
Lures winged insects through the lampless air.


SPIRIT

   My coursers are fed with the lightning,
     They drink of the whirlwind's stream
   And when the red morning is brightning     165
     They bathe in the fresh sunbeam;
       They have strength for their swiftness, I deem:
        Then ascend with me, Daughter of Ocean.
I desire—and their speed makes night kindle;

2. I.e., Demogorgon.
3. Shining with a red glow or glare amid darkness.
4. Outermost limits, horizon.

I fear—they outstrip the Typhoon;                                        170
Ere the cloud piled on Atlas[5] can dwindle
We encircle the earth and the moon;
We shall rest from long labours at noon:—
    Then ascend with me, Daughter of Ocean.


### SCENE V

*The Car pauses within a Cloud on the Top of a snowy Mountain.* Asia,
Panthea *and the* Spirit of the Hour.


#### SPIRIT

On the brink of the night and the morning
    My coursers are wont to respire,[6]
But the Earth has just whispered a warning
    That their flight must be swifter than fire:
They shall drink the hot speed of desire!                                  5


#### ASIA

Thou breathest on their nostrils—but my breath
Would give them swifter speed.


#### SPIRIT

                        Alas, it could not.


#### PANTHEA

O Spirit! pause and tell whence is the light
Which fills the cloud? the sun is yet unrisen.


#### SPIRIT

The sun will rise not until noon.—Apollo                                  10
Is held in Heaven by wonder—and the light
Which fills this vapour, as the aerial hue
Of fountain-gazing roses fills the water,
Flows from thy mighty sister.


#### PANTHEA

                        Yes, I feel . . .


#### ASIA

What is it with thee, sister? Thou art pale.                              15


#### PANTHEA

How thou art changed! I dare not look on thee;
I feel, but see thee not. I scarce endure
The radiance of thy beauty. Some good change

---

5. Atlas, a Titan and brother of Prometheus, refused hospitality to Perseus, who (by means of
   Medusa's head) changed Atlas into a mountain. (The real mountain was so high that the
   ancients believed the heavens rested on its top and that Atlas supported the world on his
   shoulders.)
6. I.e., usually rest or slow down.

Is working in the elements which suffer
Thy presence thus unveiled.—The Nereids[7] tell                    20
That on the day when the clear hyaline[8]
Was cloven at thy uprise, and thou didst stand
Within a veined shell, which floated on
Over the calm floor of the chrystal sea,
Among the Ægean isles, and by the shores                           25
Which bear thy name,[9] love, like the atmosphere
Of the sun's fire filling the living world,
Burst from thee, and illumined Earth and Heaven
And the deep ocean and the sunless caves,
And all that dwells within them; till grief cast                   30
Eclipse upon the soul from which it came:
Such art thou now, nor is it I alone,
Thy sister, thy companion, thine own chosen one,
But the whole world which seeks thy sympathy.
Hearest thou not sounds i' the air which speak the love            35
Of all articulate beings? Feelest thou not
The inanimate winds enamoured of thee?—List!

                                                    [*Music.*]


                ASIA
Thy words are sweeter than aught else but his
Whose echoes they are—yet all love is sweet,
Given or returned; common as light is love                         40
And its familiar voice wearies not ever.
Like the wide Heaven, the all-sustaining air,
It makes the reptile equal to the God . . .
They who inspire it most are fortunate
As I am now; but those who feel it most                            45
Are happier still, after long sufferings
As I shall soon become.


                PANTHEA
                List! Spirits speak.


                VOICE (*in the air, singing*)
            Life of Life! thy lips enkindle
                With their love the breath between them
            And thy smiles before they dwindle                     50
                Make the cold air fire; then screen them
            In those looks where whoso gazes
            Faints, entangled in their mazes.


7. Water nymphs who were daughters of Nereus (the Old Man of the Sea) and Doris (Hesiod's
   *Theogony*).
8. The glassy, transparent surface of the sea.
9. *shores . . . name:* In his syncretic way of treating myths, Shelley draws upon various traditions
   of Aphrodite/Venus mentioned by Cicero. One saw her as the daughter of Celus (Sky) and
   Light, another saw her rising from the froth of the sea and standing "within a veined shell,"
   and still another located her birth near Tyre and identified her with Astarte of the Phoenicians and Syrians. But by naming her Asia, Shelley frees his creation from the specific
   limitations associated with any specific myth of Aphrodite/Venus.

Child of Light! thy limbs are burning
   Through the vest which seems to hide them                              55
As the radiant lines of morning
   Through the clouds ere they divide them,
And this atmosphere divinest
Shrouds thee wheresoe'er thou shinest.


Fair are others;—none beholds thee                                              60
   But thy voice sounds low and tender
Like the fairest—for it folds thee
   From the sight, that liquid splendour,
And all feel, yet see thee never
As I feel now, lost forever!                                                    65


Lamp of Earth! where'er thou movest
   Its dim shapes are clad with brightness
And the souls of whom thou lovest
   Walk upon the winds with lightness
Till they fail, as I am failing,                                                70
. . . Dizzy, lost . . . yet unbewailing!


       ASIA
My soul is an enchanted Boat
Which, like a sleeping swan, doth float
Upon the silver waves of thy sweet singing,
   And thine doth like an Angel sit                                       75
   Beside the helm conducting it
Whilst all the winds with melody are ringing.
   It seems to float ever—forever—
   Upon that many winding River
   Between mountains, woods, abysses,                                     80
   A Paradise of wildernesses,
Till like one in slumber bound
Borne to the Ocean, I float down, around,
Into a Sea profound, of ever-spreading sound.


   Meanwhile thy Spirit lifts its pinions[1]                            85
   In Music's most serene dominions,
Catching the winds that fan that happy Heaven.
   And we sail on, away, afar,
   Without a course—without a star—
But by the instinct of sweet Music driven                                      90
   Till, through Elysian garden islets,
   By thee, most beautiful of pilots,
   Where never mortal pinnace[2] glided,
   The boat of my desire is guided—

1. Wings.
2. A small, light boat.

Realms where the air we breathe is Love                                95
Which in the winds and on the waves doth move,
Harmonizing this Earth with what we feel above.


We have past Age's icy caves,
    And Manhood's dark and tossing waves
And Youth's smooth ocean, smiling to betray;                           100
    Beyond the glassy gulphs we flee
    Of shadow-peopled Infancy,
Through Death and Birth, to a diviner day,[3]
    A Paradise of vaulted bowers
    Lit by downward-gazing flowers                                     105
    And watery paths that wind between
    Wildernesses calm and green,
Peopled by shapes too bright to see,
And rest, having beheld—somewhat like thee,
Which walk upon the sea, and chaunt melodiously!                       110

END OF THE SECOND ACT.


## Act III


### SCENE I

*Heaven.* Jupiter *on his Throne;* Thetis *and the other Deities assembled.*


JUPITER
Ye congregated Powers of Heaven who share
The glory and the strength of him ye serve,
Rejoice! henceforth I am omnipotent.
All else has been subdued to me—alone
The soul of man, like unextinguished fire,                             5
Yet burns towards Heaven with fierce reproach and doubt
And lamentation and reluctant prayer,
Hurling up insurrection, which might make
Our antique empire insecure, though built
On eldest faith, and Hell's coeval,[4] fear.                           10
And though my curses through the pendulous air
Like snow on herbless peaks, fall flake by flake[5]
And cling to it—though under my wrath's night
It climb the crags of life, step after step,
Which wound it, as ice wounds unsandalled feet,                        15
It yet remains supreme o'er misery,
Aspiring . . . unrepressed; yet soon to fall:
Even now have I begotten a strange wonder,

3. The reversal of time and mortal aging described here parallels a myth in Plato's *Statesman* (270e and 271b).
4. Equal in antiquity or contemporary in origin.
5. Jupiter's picture of his curses, falling "flake by flake," echoes Asia's simile of the avalanche of change loosed after building up "flake after flake, in Heaven-defying minds" (II.iii.39), and thus prepares for Jupiter's overthrow; *pendulous:* floating in space or undulating.

That fatal child,[6] the terror of the Earth,
Who waits but till the destined Hour arrive,                    20
Bearing from Demogorgon's vacant throne
The dreadful might of ever living limbs
Which clothed that awful spirit unbeheld—
To redescend and trample out the spark . . .
Pour forth Heaven's wine, Idæan Ganymede,[7]                    25
And let it fill the dædal[8] cups like fire
And from the flower-inwoven soil divine
Ye all triumphant harmonies arise
As dew from Earth under the twilight stars;
Drink! be the nectar circling through your veins               30
The soul of joy, ye everliving Gods,
Till exultation burst in one wide voice
Like music from Elysian winds.—
                                        And thou
Ascend beside me, veiled in the light
Of the desire which makes thee one with me,                     35
Thetis,[9] bright Image of Eternity!—
When thou didst cry, "Insufferable might!
God! spare me! I sustain not the quick flames,
The penetrating presence;[1] all my being,
Like him whom the Numidian seps did thaw                        40
Into a dew with poison,[2] is dissolved,
Sinking through its foundations"—even then
Two mighty spirits, mingling, made a third
Mightier than either—which unbodied now
Between us, floats, felt although unbeheld,                     45
Waiting the incarnation, which ascends—
Hear ye the thunder of the fiery wheels
Griding[3] the winds?—from Demogorgon's throne.—
Victory! Victory! Feel'st thou not, O World,
The Earthquake of his chariot thundering up                     50
Olympus?
[*The Car of the* Hour *arrives.* Demogorgon *descends
    and moves towards the Throne of* Jupiter.]

        Awful Shape, what art thou? Speak!

---

6. Jupiter describes at lines 37–48 more fully how he begot this child by raping Thetis. The
   present speech is an example of irony in the classical sense in which everything the speaker
   says is true, but in a way that he does not comprehend.
7. While tending his father's flocks on Mt. Ida, *Ganymede* was carried away by an eagle to
   satisfy Jupiter's lust; he replaced Hebe as cupbearer to the gods.
8. Displaying artistic cunning or fertile invention; variously adorned (from Daedalus, the mythical craftsman).
9. A sea nymph (nereid) who became the mother of Achilles by Peleus.
1. *sustain . . . presence:* Semele, daughter of Cadmus, was consumed by fire when—through a
   trick by Hera (Juno)—Zeus (Jupiter) was bound by an oath to lie with Semele in his own
   undisguised form. (The child of this union was Dionysus [Bacchus].)
2. *him . . . poison:* In Lucan's *Pharsalia* (IX.762–88) Sabellus dissolves when bitten by a seps,
   a legendary poisonous snake, while crossing the Numidian desert.
3. Clashing or grating against.

DEMOGORGON

Eternity—demand no direr name.
Descend, and follow me down the abyss;
I am thy child, as thou wert Saturn's child,
Mightier than thee;[4] and we must dwell together          55
Henceforth in darkness.—Lift thy lightnings not.
The tyranny of Heaven none may retain,
Or reassume, or hold succeeding thee . . .
Yet if thou wilt—as 'tis the destiny
Of trodden worms to writhe till they are dead—           60
Put forth thy might.

JUPITER
                    Detested prodigy!
Even thus beneath the deep Titanian prisons[5]
I trample thee! . . . Thou lingerest?
                              Mercy! mercy!
No pity—no release, no respite! . . . Oh,
That thou wouldst make mine enemy my judge.              65
Even where he hangs, seared by my long revenge
On Caucasus—he would not doom me thus.—
Gentle and just and dreadless, is he not
The monarch of the world?—what then art thou? . . .
No refuge! no appeal— . . .
                          Sink with me then—            70
We two will sink on the wide waves of ruin
Even as a vulture and a snake outspent
Drop, twisted in inextricable fight,
Into a shoreless sea.—Let Hell unlock
Its mounded Oceans of tempestuous fire,                  75
And whelm on them into the bottomless void
This desolated world and thee and me,
The conqueror and the conquered, and the wreck
Of that for which they combated.
                              Ai! Ai!
The elements obey me not . . . I sink . . .              80
Dizzily down—ever, forever, down—
And, like a cloud, mine enemy above . . .
Darkens my fall with victory!—Ai! Ai!


SCENE II

*The Mouth of a great River in the Island Atlantis.* Ocean *is discovered
reclining near the Shore;* Apollo *stands beside him.*

---

4. *I am thy child . . . than thee*: Hesiod's *Theogony*—at the very beginning of the literary
   transmission of the Greek myths—states the possibility that Zeus (Jupiter) will be overthrown
   by his second child by Metis (Wisdom), an "unruly son, the future king of gods and men"
   (lines 889–900).
5. The Titans, after their overthrow by Jupiter and the Olympian gods, were imprisoned in
   Tartarus, so far below the earth that it would take an anvil ten days to fall there from the
   earth (the same distance as from heaven to earth).

OCEAN

He fell, thou sayest, beneath his conqueror's frown?

APOLLO

Aye, when the strife was ended which made dim
The orb I rule, and shook the solid stars.[6]
The terrors of his eyes illumined Heaven
With sanguine[7] light, through the thick ragged skirts          5
Of the victorious Darkness, as he fell:
Like the last glare of day's red agony
Which from a rent among the fiery clouds
Burns far along the tempest-wrinkled Deep.

OCEAN

He sunk to the abyss? to the dark void?                          10

APOLLO

An eagle so, caught in some bursting cloud
On Caucasus, his thunder-baffled wings
Entangled in the whirlwind, and his eyes
Which gazed on the undazzling sun, now blinded
By the white lightning, while the ponderous hail               15
Beats on his struggling form which sinks at length
Prone, and the aerial ice clings over it.

OCEAN

Henceforth the fields of Heaven-reflecting sea
Which are my realm, will heave, unstain'd with blood
Beneath the uplifting winds—like plains of corn                20
Swayed by the summer air; my streams will flow
Round many-peopled continents and round
Fortunate isles; and from their glassy thrones
Blue Proteus and his humid Nymphs shall mark
The shadow of fair ships, as mortals see                       25
The floating bark of the light-laden moon
With that white star,[8] its sightless pilot's crest,
Borne down the rapid sunset's ebbing sea;
Tracking their path no more by blood and groans
And desolation, and the mingled voice                          30
Of slavery and command—but by the light
Of wave-reflected flowers, and floating odours,
And music soft, and mild, free, gentle voices,
That sweetest music,—such as spirits love.

APOLLO

And I shall gaze not on the deeds which make                   35
My mind obscure with sorrow, as Eclipse

6. The orb is the sun, and the solid stars are the fixed stars (those that classical and medieval
   cosmologists thought did not move).
7. Blood-red.
8. Venus, the morning star of line 39.

Darkens the sphere I guide—but list, I hear
The small, clear, silver lute of the young Spirit
That sits i' the Morning star.

OCEAN
                    Thou must away?
Thy steeds will pause at even—till when, farewell.                    40
The loud Deep calls me home even now, to feed it
With azure calm out of the emerald urns
Which stand forever full beside my throne. . . .
Behold the Nereids under the green sea,
Their wavering limbs borne on the windlike stream,                    45
Their white arms lifted o'er their streaming hair
With garlands pied[9] and starry sea-flower crowns,
Hastening to grace their mighty Sister's joy.
                              [*A sound of waves is heard.*]
It is the unpastured Sea hung'ring for Calm.
Peace, Monster—I come now! Farewell.

APOLLO
                         Farewell!—                    50

SCENE III

*Caucasus.* Prometheus, Hercules,[1] Ione, *the* Earth, Spirits. Asia *and*
Panthea *borne in the Car with the* Spirit of the Hour. Hercules *unbinds*
Prometheus, *who descends.*

HERCULES
Most glorious among Spirits, thus doth strength
To wisdom, courage, and long suffering love,
And thee, who art the form they animate,
Minister, like a slave.

PROMETHEUS
                    Thy gentle words
Are sweeter even than freedom long desired                    5
And long delayed.
                    Asia, thou light of life,
Shadow of beauty unbeheld, and ye
Fair sister nymphs, who made long years of pain
Sweet to remember through your love and care:
Henceforth we will not part. There is a Cave                    10
All overgrown with trailing odorous plants
Which curtain out the day with leaves and flowers
And paved with veined emerald, and a fountain
Leaps in the midst with an awakening sound;

---

9. With variegated colors.
1. In the Greek legend Herakles (Roman Hercules), the human hero who has been made
immortal, kills the eagle (or vulture) that tortures Prometheus and frees him after Prometheus had made his peace with Zeus (Jupiter). Shelley omits the killing of the bird because,
as III.ii had made clear, bloodshed was banished after Jupiter's fall.

From its curved roof the mountain's frozen tears                    15
Like snow or silver or long diamond spires
Hang downward, raining forth a doubtful light;
And there is heard the ever-moving air
Whispering without from tree to tree, and birds,
And bees; and all around are mossy seats                           20
And the rough walls are clothed with long soft grass;
A simple dwelling, which shall be our own,
Where we will sit and talk of time and change
As the world ebbs and flows, ourselves unchanged—
What can hide man from Mutability?—                                25
And if ye sigh, then I will smile, and thou
Ione, shall chant fragments of sea-music,
Until I weep, when ye shall smile away
The tears she brought, which yet were sweet to shed;
We will entangle buds and flowers, and beams                       30
Which twinkle on the fountain's brim, and make
Strange combinations out of common things
Like human babes in their brief innocence;
And we will search, with looks and words of love
For hidden thoughts each lovelier than the last,                   35
Our unexhausted spirits, and like lutes
Touched by the skill of the enamoured wind,
Weave harmonies divine, yet ever new,
From difference sweet where discord cannot be.
And hither come, sped on the charmed winds                         40
Which meet from all the points of Heaven, as bees
From every flower aerial Enna[2] feeds
At their known island-homes in Himera,
The echoes of the human world, which tell
Of the low voice of love, almost unheard,                          45
And dove-eyed pity's murmured pain, and music,
Itself the echo of the heart, and all
That tempers or improves man's life, now free.
And lovely apparitions dim at first
Then radiant—as the mind, arising bright                           50
From the embrace of beauty (whence the forms
Of which these are the phantoms) casts on them
The gathered rays which are reality—
Shall visit us, the progeny immortal
Of Painting, Sculpture and rapt Poesy                              55
And arts, though unimagined, yet to be.
The wandering voices and the shadows these
Of all that man becomes, the mediators
Of that best worship, love, by him and us
Given and returned, swift shapes and sounds which grow             60
More fair and soft as man grows wise and kind,
And veil by veil evil and error fall . . .

---

2. The famous meadow in Sicily from which Hades (Pluto) abducted Persephone (Proserpine)
was *aerial* because it was in the air of earth (rather than in the underworld); not far from it
in Sicily are two rivers and a town named *Himera*.

Such virtue has the cave and place around.
                    [*Turning to the* Spirit of the Hour.]
For thee, fair Spirit, one toil remains. Ione,
Give her that curved shell, which Proteus old[3]                     65
Made Asia's nuptial boon, breathing within it
A voice to be accomplished, and which thou
Didst hide in grass under the hollow rock.


          IONE
Thou most desired Hour, more loved and lovely
Than all thy sisters, this is the mystic shell;                     70
See the pale azure fading into silver
Lining it with a soft yet glowing light.
Looks it not like lulled music sleeping there?


          SPIRIT
It seems in truth the fairest shell of Ocean:
Its sound must be at once both sweet and strange.                   75


          PROMETHEUS
Go, borne over the cities of mankind
On whirlwind-footed coursers! once again
Outspeed the sun around the orbed world
And as thy chariot cleaves the kindling air,
Thou breathe into the many-folded Shell,                            80
Loosening its mighty music;—it shall be
As thunder mingled with clear echoes.—Then
Return and thou shalt dwell beside our cave.
                              [*Kissing the ground.*]
And thou, O Mother Earth!—


          THE EARTH
               I hear—I feel—
Thy lips are on me, and their touch runs down                       85
Even to the adamantine central gloom
Along these marble nerves—'tis life, 'tis joy,
And through my withered, old and icy frame
The warmth of an immortal youth shoots down

---

3. Proteus was a sea deity who not only could change himself into various forms, but could also predict future events. In Francis Bacon's explanation of classical myths, Proteus represents physical nature and natural law. Shelley's motivation in having Proteus give Asia the wedding gift of a conch shell to proclaim the fall of Jupiter and the beginning of a new Golden Age may be explained partly by a legend surrounding the three conch shells in the Shelley family's coat of arms (probably deriving from the magic bugle of Arthur's squire in Spenser's *Fairie Queene*, Book I, VIII), as told by Shelley's college friend and biographer, Thomas Jefferson Hogg: "Sir Guyon de Shelley, one of the most famous of the Paladins . . . carried about with him at all times three conchs fastened to the inside of his shield . . . When he blew the first shell, all giants, however huge, fled before him. When he put the second to his lips, all spells were broken, all enchantments dissolved; and when he made the third conch, the golden one, vocal, the law of God was immediately exalted, and the law of the Devil annulled and abrogated, wherever the potent sound reached" (Hogg, *Life of . . . Shelley*, ed. Edward Dowden [1906], p. 18). This story may be tongue-in-cheek, but it is probably based on something the young Shelley told Hogg about his hopes for the significance of the conch shells in his armorial shield.

Circling.—Henceforth the many children fair                    90
Folded in my sustaining arms—all plants,
And creeping forms, and insects rainbow-winged
And birds and beasts and fish and human shapes
Which drew disease and pain from my wan bosom,
Draining the poison of despair—shall take                      95
And interchange sweet nutriment; to me
Shall they become like sister-antelopes
By one fair dam, snowwhite and swift as wind
Nursed among lilies near a brimming stream;
The dewmists of my sunless sleep shall float                  100
Under the stars like balm; night-folded flowers
Shall suck unwithering hues in their repose;
And men and beasts in happy dreams shall gather
Strength for the coming day and all its joy:
And death shall be the last embrace of her                    105
Who takes the life she gave, even as a mother
Folding her child, says, "Leave me not again!"

ASIA

O mother! wherefore speak the name of death?
Cease they to love and move and breathe and speak
Who die?

THE EARTH

It would avail not to reply:                                  110
Thou art immortal and this tongue is known
But to the uncommunicating dead.—
Death is the veil which those who live call life:
They sleep—and it is lifted[4] . . . and meanwhile
In mild variety the seasons mild                              115
With rainbow-skirted showers, and odorous winds
And long blue meteors cleansing the dull night,
And the life-kindling shafts of the keen Sun's
All-piercing bow, and the dew-mingled rain
Of the calm moonbeams, a soft influence mild;                 120
Shall clothe the forests and the fields—aye, even
The crag-built desarts of the barren deep—
With ever-living leaves and fruits and flowers.
And Thou! . . . There is a Cavern[5] where my spirit
Was panted forth in anguish whilst thy pain                   125
Made my heart mad, and those who did inhale it
Became mad too, and built a Temple there
And spoke and were oracular, and lured
The erring nations round to mutual war
And faithless faith, such as Jove kept with thee;            130

4. *Death is the veil . . . lifted:* Cf. Shelley's sonnet: "Lift not the painted veil . . ." (p. 327). See also III.iv. 190–93, below.
5. This cavern is, apparently, the "mighty Portal" described by Panthea at II.iii.2–10, now redeemed from its former unhappy role. Lines 127–30 identify this location with such oracles as that at Delphi.

Which breath now rises as among tall weeds
A violet's exhalation, and it fills
With a serener light and crimson air
Intense yet soft the rocks and woods around;
It feeds the quick growth of the serpent vine     135
And the dark linked ivy tangling wild
And budding, blown, or odour-faded blooms
Which star the winds with points of coloured light
As they rain through them, and bright, golden globes
Of fruit, suspended in their own green heaven;     140
And, through their veined leaves and amber stems,
The flowers whose purple and translucid bowls
Stand ever mantling[6] with aerial dew,
The drink of spirits; and it circles round
Like the soft waving wings of noonday dreams,     145
Inspiring calm and happy thoughts, like mine
Now thou art thus restored . . . This Cave is thine.
Arise! Appear!
        [*A Spirit rises in the likeness of a winged child.*]
          This is my torch-bearer,
Who let his lamp out in old time, with gazing
On eyes from which he kindled it anew     150
With love which is as fire, sweet Daughter mine,
For such is that within thine own.—Run, Wayward!
And guide this company beyond the peak
Of Bacchic Nysa,[7] Mænad-haunted mountain,
And beyond Indus, and its tribute rivers,     155
Trampling the torrent streams and glassy lakes
With feet unwet, unwearied, undelaying;
And up the green ravine, across the vale,
Beside the windless and chrystalline pool
Where ever lies, on unerasing waves,     160
The image of a temple built above,
Distinct with column, arch and architrave[8]
And palm-like capital, and overwrought,
And populous most with living imagery—
Praxitelean shapes,[9] whose marble smiles     165
Fill the hushed air with everlasting love.
It is deserted now, but once it bore
Thy name, Prometheus; there the emulous youths
Bore to thine honour through the divine gloom
The lamp, which was thine emblem[1] . . . even as those     170

---

6. Foaming, bubbling.
7. In classical geography and legend there were no less than ten places named Nysa, all associated with Dionysus (Bacchus). One, a city in India, was the reputed birthplace of Dionysus and his capital during his legendary conquest of the East.
8. The main beam that rests on the tops of the capitals (column tops) in post and lintel architecture.
9. Statues by or exhibiting the perfection of the Greek sculptor Praxiteles (fourth century B.C.).
1. At Athens there was a cult that annually celebrated Prometheus' exploits as the fire bringer in the Lampadephoria, a race by torch-bearing youths (who thus *emulated* the feat of Prometheus). The lost third play of Aeschylus' Promethean trilogy was called *Prometheus the Fire Bringer*.

Who bear the untransmitted torch of hope
Into the grave across the night of life . . .
As thou hast borne it most triumphantly
To this far goal of Time . . . Depart, farewell.
Beside that Temple is the destined Cave . . .                    175


SCENE IV

*A Forest. In the Background a Cave.* Prometheus, Asia, Panthea, Ione,
*and the* Spirit of the Earth.


IONE

Sister, it is not Earthly . . . how it glides
Under the leaves! how on its head there burns
A light like a green star, whose emerald beams
Are twined with its fair hair! how, as it moves
The splendour drops in flakes upon the grass!                    5
Knowest thou it?


PANTHEA
          It is the delicate spirit
That guides the earth through Heaven. From afar
The populous constellations call that light
The loveliest of the planets, and sometimes
It floats along the spray of the salt sea                        10
Or makes its chariot of a foggy cloud
Or walks through fields or cities while men sleep
Or o'er the mountain tops, or down the rivers,
Or through the green waste wilderness, as now,
Wondering at all it sees. Before Jove reigned                    15
It loved our sister Asia, and it came
Each leisure hour to drink the liquid light
Out of her eyes, for which it said it thirsted
As one bit by a dipsas;[2] and with her
It made its childish confidence, and told her                    20
All it had known or seen, for it saw much,
Yet idly reasoned what it saw; and called her—
For whence it sprung it knew not nor do I—
"Mother, dear Mother."

SPIRIT OF THE EARTH [*running to* Asia]
          Mother, dearest Mother!
May I then talk with thee as I was wont?                         25
May I then hide mine eyes in thy soft arms
After thy looks have made them tired of joy?
May I then play beside thee the long noons
When work is none in the bright silent air?


2. A poisonous snake of classical legend (mentioned in Lucan's *Pharsalia*, IX.737–60, and
Milton's *Paradise Lost*, X.526), the bite of which caused an unquenchable thirst (cf.
dipsomaniac).

ASIA

I love thee, gentlest being, and henceforth 30
Can cherish thee unenvied.—Speak, I pray:
Thy simple talk once solaced . . . now delights.

SPIRIT OF THE EARTH

Mother, I am grown wiser, though a child
Cannot be wise like thee, within this day
And happier too, happier and wiser both. 35
Thou knowest that toads and snakes and loathly worms
And venomous and malicious beasts, and boughs
That bore ill berries in the woods, were ever
An hindrance to my walks o'er the green world,
And that, among the haunts of humankind 40
Hard-featured men, or with proud, angry looks
Or cold, staid gait, or false and hollow smiles
Or the dull sneer of self-loved ignorance
Or other such foul masks with which ill thoughts
Hide that fair being whom we spirits call man; 45
And women too, ugliest of all things evil,—
Though fair, even in a world where thou art fair
When good and kind, free and sincere like thee,—
When false or frowning made me sick at heart
To pass them, though they slept, and I unseen. 50
Well—my path lately lay through a great City
Into the woody hills surrounding it.
A sentinel was sleeping at the gate:
When there was heard a sound, so loud, it shook
The towers amid the moonlight, yet more sweet 55
Than any voice but thine, sweetest of all,
A long long sound, as it would never end:
And all the inhabitants leapt suddenly
Out of their rest, and gathered in the streets,
Looking in wonder up to Heaven, while yet 60
The music pealed along. I hid myself
Within a fountain in the public square
Where I lay like the reflex³ of the moon
Seen in a wave under green leaves—and soon
Those ugly human shapes and visages 65
Of which I spoke as having wrought me pain,
Past floating through the air, and fading still
Into the winds that scattered them;⁴ and those
From whom they past seemed mild and lovely forms
After some foul disguise had fallen—and all 70
Were somewhat changed—and after brief surprise
And greetings of delighted wonder, all

---

3. Reflection.
4. *Those ugly human shapes . . . scattered them:* This image of the masks of ugly human nature
floating away from the creatures that produced and wore them derives (with a reversal of
emphasis) from the passage on the *simulacra,* or "images," in Lucretius' *De rerum natura,*
IV.46ff. See also "The Triumph of Life," lines 480–516.

Went to their sleep again: and when the dawn
Came—wouldst thou think that toads and snakes and efts[5]
Could e'er be beautiful?—yet so they were            75
And that with little change of shape or hue:
All things had put their evil nature off.
I cannot tell my joy, when o'er a lake,
Upon a drooping bough with nightshade twined,
I saw two azure halcyons clinging downward          80
And thinning one bright bunch of amber berries
With quick long beaks, and in the deep there lay
Those lovely forms imaged as in a sky.[6]—
So with my thoughts full of these happy changes
We meet again, the happiest change of all.          85

ASIA

And never will we part, till thy chaste Sister
Who guides the frozen and inconstant moon
Will look on thy more warm and equal light
Till her heart thaw like flakes of April snow
And love thee.

SPIRIT OF THE EARTH
What, as Asia loves Prometheus?                     90

ASIA

Peace, Wanton[7]—thou art yet not old enough.
Think ye, by gazing on each other's eyes
To multiply your lovely selves, and fill
With sphered fires the interlunar[8] air?

SPIRIT OF THE EARTH
Nay, Mother, while my sister trims[9] her lamp      95
'Tis hard I should go darkling.

ASIA
                    —Listen! look!
            [*The* Spirit of the Hour *enters.*]

PROMETHEUS
We feel what thou hast heard and seen—yet speak.

SPIRIT OF THE HOUR
Soon as the sound had ceased whose thunder filled
The abysses of the sky, and the wide earth,

5. Small lizards or lizardlike animals; newts.
6. *I cannot tell my joy . . . as in a sky:* The double point of lines 78–83 is that the berries of
   the deadly nightshade are no longer poisonous (cf. *Queen Mab*, VIII.129 30) and that the
   halcyons, or kingfishers, have turned vegetarian.
7. A spoiled child (with overtones of lasciviousness).
8. Dark; the time between the old and the new moon.
9. Puts into proper order for lighting by cleaning, cutting the wick, or adding fresh fuel.

There was a change . . . the impalpable thin air                100
And the all-circling sunlight were transformed
As if the sense of love dissolved in them
Had folded itself round the sphered world.
My vision then grew clear and I could see
Into the mysteries of the Universe.[1]                          105
Dizzy as with delight I floated down,
Winnowing[2] the lightsome air with languid plumes,
My coursers sought their birthplace in the sun
Where they henceforth will live exempt from toil,
Pasturing flowers of vegetable fire—                            110
And where my moonlike car will stand within
A temple, gazed upon by Phidian forms,[3]
Of thee, and Asia and the Earth, and me
And you fair nymphs, looking the love we feel,
In memory of the tidings it has borne,                          115
Beneath a dome fretted with graven flowers,
Poised on twelve columns of resplendent stone
And open to the bright and liquid sky.
Yoked to it by an amphisbænic snake
The likeness of those winged steeds will mock                   120
The flight from which they find repose.[4]—Alas,
Whither has wandered now my partial[5] tongue
When all remains untold which ye would hear!—
As I have said, I floated to the Earth:
It was, as it is still, the pain of bliss                       125
To move, to breathe, to be; I wandering went
Among the haunts and dwellings of mankind
And first was disappointed not to see
Such mighty change as I had felt within
Expressed in outward things; but soon I looked,                 130
And behold! thrones were kingless, and men walked
One with the other even as spirits do,
None fawned, none trampled; hate, disdain or fear,
Self-love or self-contempt on human brows
No more inscribed, as o'er the gate of hell,                    135
"All hope abandon, ye who enter here";[6]
None frowned, none trembled, none with eager fear
Gazed on another's eye of cold command
Until the subject of a tyrant's will

---

1. In the general regeneration the earth's atmosphere ceases to act as a prism, thus no longer
   distorting sunlight into varied colors and a glare that hides realities.
2. Flapping or beating.
3. Statues by or approaching the quality of the great Athenian sculptor Phidias (fifth century
   B.C.).
4. The scene described in lines 111–21 is based on the Pantheon and the Sala della Biga in
   the Vatican Museum—both places Shelley visited in Rome. The *biga*, two-horse chariot, was
   the emblem of the moon (*my moonlike car*), as opposed to the four-horse chariot of the sun-
   god; in the museum the yoke of the two-horse chariot is a snake with a head on each end
   —the legendary *amphisbaena* (Reiman, *Romantic Texts and Contexts*, pp. 278–88).
5. Biased in favor of.
6. This line translates literally the last words of the inscription written above the gate leading
   into Dante's Inferno (III.9).

Became, worse fate, the abject[7] of his own                    140
Which spurred him, like an outspent horse, to death.
None wrought his lips in truth-entangling lines
Which smiled the lie his tongue disdained to speak;
None with firm sneer trod out in his own heart
The sparks of love and hope, till there remained          145
Those bitter ashes, a soul self-consumed,
And the wretch crept, a vampire among men,
Infecting all with his own hideous ill.
None talked that common, false, cold, hollow talk
Which makes the heart deny the *yes* it breathes           150
Yet question that unmeant hypocrisy
With such a self-mistrust as has no name.
And women too, frank, beautiful and kind
As the free Heaven which rains fresh light and dew
On the wide earth, past: gentle, radiant forms,           155
From custom's evil taint exempt and pure;
Speaking the wisdom once they could not think,
Looking emotions once they feared to feel
And changed to all which once they dared not be,
Yet being now, made Earth like Heaven—nor pride           160
Nor jealousy nor envy nor ill shame,
The bitterest of those drops of treasured gall,
Spoilt the sweet taste of the nepenthe,[8] love.

Thrones, altars, judgement-seats and prisons; wherein
And beside which, by wretched men were borne              165
Sceptres, tiaras, swords and chains, and tomes
Of reasoned wrong glozed[9] on by ignorance,
Were like those monstrous and barbaric shapes,
The ghosts of a no more remembered fame,
Which from their unworn obelisks look forth               170
In triumph o'er the palaces and tombs
Of those who were their conquerors, mouldering round.[1]
Those imaged to the pride of Kings and Priests
A dark yet mighty faith, a power as wide
As is the world it wasted, and are now                    175
But an astonishment; even so the tools
And emblems of its last captivity
Amid the dwellings of the peopled Earth,
Stand, not o'erthrown, but unregarded now.
And those foul shapes,[2] abhorred by God and man—        180
Which under many a name and many a form

7. Outcast or degraded person.
8. A magic drink that banished grief and pain.
9. Glossed; commented on or explained.
1. The Egyptian *obelisks*, brought to Rome by the conquering armies of the empire, had in the
   Renaissance been erected in the principal piazzas of the city, while the palaces of their
   conquerors (the ancient Romans) had fallen into decay. The *shapes* on the obelisks seemed
   *monstrous and barbaric* (line 168) because, when Shelley wrote, hieroglyphics could not be
   deciphered.
2. A generalized term for all gods of vengeance who inspired fear.

Strange, savage, ghastly, dark and execrable
Were Jupiter, the tyrant of the world;
And which the nations panic-stricken served
With blood, and hearts broken by long hope, and love          185
Dragged to his altars soiled and garlandless
And slain amid men's unreclaiming tears,
Flattering the thing they feared, which fear was hate—
Frown, mouldering fast, o'er their abandoned shrines.
The painted veil, by those who were, called life,              190
Which mimicked,[3] as with colours idly spread,
All men believed and hoped, is torn aside—
The loathsome mask has fallen, the man remains
Sceptreless, free, uncircumscribed—but man:
Equal, unclassed, tribeless and nationless,                    195
Exempt from awe, worship, degree,—the King
Over himself; just, gentle, wise—but man:
Passionless? no—yet free from guilt or pain
Which were, for his will made, or suffered them,
Nor yet exempt, though ruling them like slaves,                200
From chance and death and mutability,
The clogs[4] of that which else might oversoar
The loftiest star of unascended Heaven
Pinnacled dim in the intense inane.[5]

END OF THE THIRD ACT.

*Act IV*

*Scene: A Part of the Forest near the Cave of* Prometheus. Panthea *and*
Ione *are sleeping: they awaken gradually during the first Song.*

VOICE OF UNSEEN SPIRITS
  The pale Stars are gone,—
  For the Sun, their swift Shepherd,
  To their folds them compelling
  In the depths of the Dawn
Hastes, in meteor-eclipsing array, and they flee               5
  Beyond his blue dwelling,
  As fawns flee the leopard . . .
   But where are ye?

[*A Train of dark Forms and Shadows passes by confusedly, singing.*]
  Here, oh here!
  We bear the bier                                     10
Of the Father of many a cancelled year!
  Spectres we

---

3. Mocked (because the appearance is copied ineffectively).
4. Impediments or encumbrances.
5. The formless void of infinite space.

Of the dead Hours be,
We bear Time to his tomb in eternity.

Strew, oh strew                                    15
    Hair, not yew!
Wet the dusty pall with tears, not dew!
    Be the faded flowers
    Of Death's bare bowers
Spread on the corpse of the King of Hours!         20

Haste, oh haste!
    As shades are chased
Trembling, by Day, from Heaven's blue waste,
    We melt away
    Like dissolving spray                          25
From the children of a diviner day,
    With the lullaby
    Of winds that die
On the bosom of their own harmony!

                    IONE
What dark forms were they?                          30

                    PANTHEA
The past Hours weak and grey
With the spoil, which their toil
    Raked together
From the conquest but One could foil.

                    IONE
Have they past?

                    PANTHEA
            They have past;                         35
They outspeeded the blast;
While 'tis said, they are fled—

                    IONE
Whither, oh whither?

                    PANTHEA
To the dark, to the past, to the dead.

                    VOICE OF UNSEEN SPIRITS
Bright clouds float in Heaven,                      40
Dew-stars gleam on Earth,
Waves assemble on Ocean,
They are gathered and driven
By the Storm of delight, by the panic of glee!

They shake with emotion—                                    45
They dance in their mirth—
   But where are ye?


The pine boughs are singing
Old songs with new gladness,
The billows and fountains                                   50
Fresh music are flinging
Like the notes of a spirit from land and from sea;
  The storms mock the mountains
  With the thunder of gladness.
   But where are ye?                        55


IONE

What charioteers are these?


PANTHEA

          Where are their chariots?


SEMICHORUS OF HOURS I

The voice of the Spirits of Air and of Earth
Has drawn back the figured curtain of sleep
Which covered our being and darkened our birth
In the deep—


A VOICE

  In the deep?


SEMICHORUS II

        Oh, below the deep.           60


SEMICHORUS I

An hundred ages we had been kept
Cradled in visions of hate and care
And each one who waked as his brother slept
Found the truth—


SEMICHORUS II

      Worse than his visions were!


SEMICHORUS I

We have heard the lute of Hope in sleep,                    65
We have known the voice of Love in dreams,
We have felt the wand of Power, and leap—


SEMICHORUS II

As the billows leap in the morning beams!

CHORUS

Weave the dance on the floor of the breeze,
  Pierce with song Heaven's silent light,                          70
Enchant the Day that too swiftly flees,
  To check its flight, ere the cave of Night.

Once the hungry Hours were hounds
  Which chased the Day, like a bleeding deer
And it limped and stumbled with many wounds                        75
  Through the nightly dells of the desert year.

But now—oh weave the mystic measure
  Of music and dance and shapes of light,
Let the Hours, and the Spirits of might and pleasure
  Like the clouds and sunbeams unite.

A VOICE

                    Unite!                                          80

PANTHEA

See where the Spirits of the human mind
Wrapt in sweet sounds, as in bright veils, approach.

CHORUS OF SPIRITS

      We join the throng
      Of the dance and the song
By the whirlwind of gladness borne along;                          85
      As the flying-fish leap
      From the Indian deep,
And mix with the sea birds half asleep.

CHORUS OF HOURS

Whence come ye so wild and so fleet,
For sandals of lightning are on your feet                          90
And your wings are soft and swift as thought,
And your eyes are as Love which is veiled not?

CHORUS OF SPIRITS

      We come from the mind
      Of human kind
Which was late so dusk and obscene and blind;                      95
      Now 'tis an Ocean
      Of clear emotion,
A Heaven of serene and mighty motion.

      From that deep Abyss
      Of wonder and bliss                                          100
Whose caverns are chrystal palaces;
      From those skiey towers
      Where Thought's crowned Powers
Sit watching your dance, ye happy Hours!

From the dim recesses                                    105
Of woven caresses
Where lovers catch ye by your loose tresses,—
From the azure isles
Where sweet Wisdom smiles,
Delaying your ships with her syren wiles;                 110

From the temples high
Of Man's ear and eye,
Roofed over Sculpture and Poesy;
From the murmurings
Of the unsealed springs                                   115
Where Science bedews his Dædal wings.

Years after years
Through blood and tears,
And a thick hell of hatreds and hopes and fears,
We waded and flew                                        120
And the islets were few
Where the bud-blighted flowers of happiness grew.

Our feet now, every palm,[6]
Are sandalled with calm,
And the dew of our wings is a rain of balm;              125
And beyond our eyes
The human love lies
Which makes all it gazes on, Paradise.

CHORUS OF SPIRITS AND HOURS
Then weave the web of the mystic measure;
From the depths of the sky and the ends of the Earth     130
  Come, swift Spirits of might and of pleasure,
Fill the dance and the music of mirth,
  As the waves of a thousand streams rush by
  To an Ocean of splendour and harmony!

CHORUS OF SPIRITS
Our spoil is won,                                        135
Our task is done,
We are free to dive or soar or run . . .
Beyond and around
Or within the bound
Which clips the world with darkness round.               140

We'll pass the Eyes
Of the starry skies
Into the hoar Deep to colonize;
Death, Chaos and Night,

6. Sole of the foot.

From the sound of our flight                              145
Shall flee, like mist from a Tempest's might.

And Earth, Air and Light
And the Spirit of Might
Which drives round the Stars in their fiery flight;
And Love, Thought, and Breath,                           150
The powers that quell Death,
Wherever we soar shall assemble beneath!

And our singing shall build,
In the Void's loose field,
A world for the Spirit of Wisdom to wield;               155
We will take our plan
From the new world of man
And our work shall be called the Promethean.

CHORUS OF HOURS
Break the dance, and scatter the song;
Let some depart and some remain.                         160

SEMICHORUS I
We, beyond Heaven, are driven along—

SEMICHORUS II
Us, the inchantments of Earth retain—

SEMICHORUS I
Ceaseless and rapid and fierce and free
With the Spirits which build a new earth and sea
And a Heaven where yet Heaven could never be—           165

SEMICHORUS II
Solemn and slow and serene and bright
Leading the Day and outspeeding the Night
With the Powers of a world of perfect light—

SEMICHORUS I
We whirl, singing loud, round the gathering sphere
Till the trees and the beasts, and the clouds appear     170
From its chaos made calm by love, not fear—

SEMICHORUS II
We encircle the Oceans and Mountains of Earth
And the happy forms of its death and birth
Change to the music of our sweet mirth.

CHORUS OF HOURS AND SPIRITS
Break the dance and scatter the song—                    175
Let some depart and some remain;

Wherever we fly we lead along
In leashes, like starbeams, soft yet strong,
   The clouds that are heavy with Love's sweet rain.

PANTHEA

Ha, they are gone!

IONE

            Yet feel you no delight          180
From the past sweetness?

PANTHEA

               As the bare green hill
When some soft cloud vanishes into rain
Laughs with a thousand drops of sunny water
To the unpavilioned sky!

IONE

           Even whilst we speak
New notes arise . . . What is that awful sound?          185

PANTHEA

'Tis the deep music of the rolling world
Kindling within the strings of the waved air
Æolian modulations.

IONE

          Listen too,
How every pause is filled with under-notes,
Clear, silver, icy, keen, awakening tones          190
Which pierce the sense and live within the soul
As the sharp stars pierce Winter's chrystal air
And gaze upon themselves within the sea.

PANTHEA

But see, where through two openings in the forest
Which hanging branches overcanopy,          195
And where two runnels[7] of a rivulet
Between the close moss violet-inwoven
Have made their path of melody, like sisters
Who part with sighs that they may meet in smiles,
Turning their dear disunion to an isle          200
Of lovely grief, a wood of sweet sad thoughts;
Two visions of strange radiance float upon
The Ocean-like inchantment of strong sound
Which flows intenser, keener, deeper yet
Under the ground and through the windless air.          205

---

7. Small streams.

IONE

I see a chariot like that thinnest boat
In which the Mother of the Months[8] is borne
By ebbing light into her western cave
When she upsprings from interlunar dreams,
O'er which is curved an orblike canopy                        210
Of gentle darkness, and the hills and woods
Distinctly seen through that dusk aery veil
Regard[9] like shapes in an enchanter's glass;
Its wheels are solid clouds, azure and gold,
Such as the genii of the thunderstorm                        215
Pile on the floor of the illumined sea
When the Sun rushes under it; they roll
And move and grow as with an inward wind.
Within it sits a winged Infant, white
Its countenance, like the whiteness of bright snow,          220
Its plumes are as feathers of sunny frost,
Its limbs gleam white, through the wind-flowing folds
Of its white robe, woof of ætherial pearl.
Its hair is white,—the brightness of white light[1]
Scattered in strings, yet its two eyes are Heavens           225
Of liquid darkness, which the Deity
Within, seems pouring, as a storm is poured
From jagged clouds, out of their arrowy lashes,
Tempering the cold and radiant air around
With fire that is not brightness;[2] in its hand             230
It sways a quivering moonbeam, from whose point
A guiding power directs the chariot's prow
Over its wheeled clouds, which as they roll
Over the grass and flowers and waves, wake sounds
Sweet as a singing rain of silver dew.                       235

PANTHEA

And from the other opening in the wood
Rushes with loud and whirlwind harmony
A sphere, which is as many thousand spheres,
Solid as chrystal, yet through all its mass
Flow, as through empty space, music and light:               240
Ten thousand orbs involving and involved,[3]
Purple and azure, white and green and golden,
Sphere within sphere, and every space between
Peopled with unimaginable shapes

8. The moon, seen as the thin crescent of the new moon bearing the shadowy old moon.
9. Appear or look.
1. The multiple references to the *whiteness* of the moon emphasize both its cold sterility and
   the beauty of its light, undistorted by an atmosphere.
2. As Shelley knew from Sir Humphry Davy's account of the findings of Herschel (1800), there
   are "dark rays"—infrared emanations that produce heat without light—which, Davy suggested, might be given off by the moon.
3. This description of the earth and the spirit asleep within it draws heavily on Milton's descriptions of angels (*Paradise Lost*, V.620–24) and of the Chariot of Paternal Deitie (*Paradise
   Lost*, VI.749ff.), which in turn echo visions in Ezekiel (chaps. 1 and 10) and Dante (*Purgatorio*, Canto XXIX); *involving and involved*: entwining and enfolded or enwrapped.

Such as ghosts dream dwell in the lampless deep                245
Yet each intertranspicuous,[4] and they whirl
Over each other with a thousand motions
Upon a thousand sightless[5] axles spinning
And with the force of self-destroying swiftness,
Intensely, slowly, solemnly roll on—                          250
Kindling with mingled sounds, and many tones,
Intelligible words and music wild.—
With mighty whirl the multitudinous Orb
Grinds the bright brook into an azure mist
Of elemental subtlety, like light,                            255
And the wild odour of the forest flowers,
The music of the living grass and air,
The emerald light of leaf-entangled beams
Round its intense, yet self-conflicting[6] speed,
Seem kneaded into one aerial mass                             260
Which drowns the sense. . . . Within the Orb itself,
Pillowed upon its alabaster arms
Like to a child o'erwearied with sweet toil,
On its own folded wings and wavy hair
The Spirit of the Earth is laid asleep,                       265
And you can see its little lips are moving
Amid the changing light of their own smiles
Like one who talks of what he loves in dream.—


IONE

'Tis only mocking the Orb's harmony . . .


PANTHEA

And from a star upon its forehead, shoot,                     270
Like swords of azure fire, or golden spears
With tyrant-quelling myrtle[7] overtwined,
Embleming Heaven and Earth united now,
Vast beams like spokes of some invisible wheel
Which whirl as the Orb whirls, swifter than thought,          275
Filling the abyss with sunlike lightenings,
And perpendicular now, and now transverse,
Pierce the dark soil, and as they pierce and pass
Make bare the secrets of the Earth's deep heart—
Infinite mine of adamant[8] and gold,                         280
Valueless[9] stones and unimagined gems,
And caverns on chrystalline columns poised
With vegetable silver[1] overspread,

4. That can be seen through or between each other.
5. Invisible.
6. Because its various component spheres are spinning in different directions.
7. The myrtle was associated with Venus and love.
8. Extremely hard rock.
9. Valuable beyond calculation.
1. In Milton's Eden, the Tree of Life bore "Ambrosial Fruit / Of vegetable Gold" (*Paradise Lost*, IV.218–20).

Wells of unfathomed fire, and watersprings
Whence the great Sea, even as a child, is fed                              285
Whose vapours clothe Earth's monarch mountain-tops
With kingly, ermine snow; the beams flash on
And make appear the melancholy ruins
Of cancelled cycles;[2] anchors, beaks of ships,
Planks turned to marble, quivers, helms and spears                        290
And gorgon-headed targes,[3] and the wheels
Of scythed chariots,[4] and the emblazonry
Of trophies, standards and armorial beasts
Round which Death laughed, sepulchred emblems
Of dead Destruction, ruin within ruin!                                    295
The wrecks beside of many a city vast,
Whose population which the Earth grew over
Was mortal but not human; see, they lie,
Their monstrous works and uncouth skeletons,
Their statues, homes, and fanes;[5] prodigious shapes                     300
Huddled in grey annihilation, split,
Jammed in the hard black deep; and over these
The anatomies[6] of unknown winged things,
And fishes which were isles of living scale,
And serpents, bony chains, twisted around                                 305
The iron crags, or within heaps of dust
To which the tortuous strength of their last pangs
Had crushed the iron crags;—and over these
The jagged alligator and the might
Of earth-convulsing behemoth,[7] which once                               310
Were monarch beasts, and on the slimy shores
And weed-overgrown continents of Earth
Increased and multiplied like summer worms
On an abandoned corpse, till the blue globe
Wrapt Deluge round it like a cloak, and they                              315
Yelled, gaspt and were abolished; or some God
Whose throne was in a Comet, past, and cried—
"Be not!"—and like my words they were no more.


                    THE EARTH
The joy, the triumph, the delight, the madness,
The boundless, overflowing bursting gladness,                             320
The vapourous exultation, not to be confined!
    Ha! ha! the animation of delight
    Which wraps me, like an atmosphere of light,
And bears me as a cloud is borne by its own wind!

2. Many details in this passage come from a book Shelley read in 1812: James Parkinson's
*Organic Remains of a Former World* (3 vols., 1800–1811).
3. Light shields or bucklers carried by archers, embossed with gorgon's head; *helms:* helmets.
4. War chariots with scythes fastened to the axles.
5. Temples.
6. Skeletons.
7. A general expression for a huge and powerful animal.

THE MOON

Brother mine, calm wanderer,          325
Happy globe of land and air,
Some Spirit is darted like a beam from thee
     Which penetrates my frozen frame
     And passes with the warmth of flame—
With love and odour and deep melody       330
     Through me, through me!—


THE EARTH

Ha! ha! the caverns of my hollow mountains,
My cloven fire-crags,[8] sound-exulting fountains
Laugh with a vast and inextinguishable laughter.
     The Oceans and the Desarts and the Abysses     335
     Of the deep air's unmeasured wildernesses
Answer from all their clouds and billows, echoing after.

     They cry aloud as I do—"Sceptred Curse,[9]
     Who all our green and azure Universe
Threatenedst to muffle round with black destruction, sending    340
     A solid cloud to rain hot thunderstones,
     And splinter and knead down my children's bones,
All I bring forth, to one void mass battering and blending,

     "Until each craglike tower and storied column,
     Palace and Obelisk and Temple solemn,      345
My imperial mountains crowned with cloud and snow and fire,
     My sea-like forests, every blade and blossom
     Which finds a grave or cradle in my bosom,
Were stamped by thy strong hate into a lifeless mire,

     "How art thou sunk, withdrawn, cover'd—drunk up    350
     By thirsty nothing, as the brackish[1] cup
Drained by a Desert-troop—a little drop for all!
     And from beneath, around, within, above,
     Filling thy void annihilation, Love
Bursts in like light on caves cloven by the thunderball."     355


THE MOON

The Snow upon my lifeless mountains
Is loosened into living fountains,
My solid Oceans flow and sing and shine:
     A spirit from my heart bursts forth,
     It clothes with unexpected birth      360
My cold bare bosom—oh! it must be thine
     On mine, on mine!

---

8. Volcanoes.
9. Jupiter—or, rather, the more general principle of tyrannical rule.
1. Salty.

Gazing on thee I feel, I know,
Green stalks burst forth, and bright flowers grow
And living shapes upon my bosom move:                    365
    Music is in the sea and air,
    Winged clouds soar here and there,
Dark with the rain new buds are dreaming of:
        'Tis Love, all Love!


THE EARTH

It interpenetrates my granite mass,                      370
Through tangled roots and trodden clay doth pass
Into the utmost leaves and delicatest flowers;
    Upon the winds, among the clouds 'tis spread,
    It wakes a life in the forgotten dead,
They breathe a spirit up from their obscurest bowers     375


And like a storm, bursting its cloudy prison
With thunder and with whirlwind, has arisen
Out of the lampless caves of unimagined being,
    With earthquake shock and swiftness making shiver
    Thought's stagnant chaos, unremoved forever,         380
Till Hate and Fear and Pain, light-vanquished shadows, fleeing,


Leave Man, who was a many-sided mirror
Which could distort to many a shape of error
This true fair world of things—a Sea reflecting Love;
    Which over all his kind, as the Sun's Heaven          385
    Gliding o'er Ocean, smooth, serene and even,
Darting from starry depths radiance and life, doth move,


Leave Man, even as a leprous child is left
Who follows a sick beast to some warm cleft
Of rocks, through which the might of healing springs is poured;  390
    Then when it wanders home with rosy smile
    Unconscious, and its mother fears awhile
It is a Spirit—then weeps on her child restored.[2]


Man, oh, not men! a chain of linked thought,
Of love and might to be divided not,                     395
Compelling the elements with adamantine stress—
    As the Sun rules, even with a tyrant's gaze,
    The unquiet Republic of the maze
Of Planets, struggling fierce towards Heaven's free wilderness.


Man, one harmonious Soul of many a soul                  400
Whose nature is its own divine controul
Where all things flow to all, as rivers to the sea;
    Familiar acts are beautiful through love;


2. The stanza alludes to the legend of King Bladud, mythical king of Britain, a banished leper
who, while following a lost swine, stumbled upon the healing hot springs of the English
town of Bath and returned home cured (Richard Warner's *History of Bath* [Bath, 1801]).

Labour and Pain and Grief in life's green grove
Sport like tame beasts—none knew how gentle they could be!     405

His Will, with all mean passions, bad delights,
And selfish cares, its trembling satellites,
A spirit ill to guide, but mighty to obey,
  Is as a tempest-winged ship, whose helm
  Love rules, through waves which dare not overwhelm,     410
Forcing Life's wildest shores to own its sovereign sway.

All things confess his strength.—Through the cold mass
Of marble and of colour his dreams pass;
Bright threads, whence mothers weave the robes their children
    wear;[3]
  Language is a perpetual Orphic song,[4]     415
  Which rules with Dædal harmony a throng
Of thoughts and forms, which else senseless and shapeless were.

The Lightning is his slave; Heaven's utmost deep
Gives up her stars, and like a flock of sheep
They pass before his eye, are numbered, and roll on!     420
  The Tempest is his steed,—he strides the air;
  And the abyss shouts from her depth laid bare,
"Heaven, hast thou secrets? Man unveils me, I have none."

THE MOON

The shadow of white Death has past
From my path in Heaven at last,     425
A clinging shroud of solid frost and sleep—
  And through my newly-woven bowers
  Wander happy paramours
Less mighty, but as mild as those who keep
    Thy vales more deep.     430

THE EARTH

As the dissolving warmth of Dawn may fold
A half-unfrozen dewglobe, green and gold
And chrystalline, till it becomes a winged mist
  And wanders up the vault of the blue Day,
  Outlives the noon, and on the Sun's last ray     435
Hangs o'er the Sea—a fleece of fire and amethyst—

THE MOON

Thou art folded, thou art lying
In the light which is undying
Of thine own joy and Heaven's smile divine;

---

3. That is, the ideals and culture that parents give their children are shaped by their artistic
   heritage.
4. *Orphic song . . . Dædal harmony:* Orpheus, the mythical Greek bard, sang so beautifully that
   he tamed wild beasts and even stopped the tortures of Hades; Daedalus was the mythical
   Athenian artist; both represent the creative human spirit.

All suns and constellations shower                                    440
  On thee a light, a life, a power
Which doth array thy sphere—thou pourest thine
    On mine, on mine!

THE EARTH

I spin beneath my pyramid of night[5]
Which points into the Heavens, dreaming delight,                      445
Murmuring victorious joy in my enchanted sleep;
  As a youth lulled in love-dreams, faintly sighing,
  Under the shadow of his beauty lying
Which round his rest a watch of light and warmth doth keep.

THE MOON

  As in the soft and sweet eclipse                            450
  When soul meets soul on lovers' lips,
High hearts are calm and brightest eyes are dull;
  So when thy shadow falls on me
  Then am I mute and still,—by thee
Covered; of thy love, Orb most beautiful,                             455
  Full, oh, too full!—

  Thou art speeding round the Sun,
  Brightest World of many a one,
  Green and azure sphere, which shinest
  With a light which is divinest                                 460
  Among all the lamps of Heaven
  To whom life and light is given;
  I, thy chrystal paramour
  Borne beside thee by a power
  Like the polar Paradise,                                       465
  Magnet-like, of lovers' eyes;
  I, a most enamoured maiden
  Whose weak brain is overladen
  With the pleasure of her love—
  Maniac-like around thee move,                                  470
  Gazing, an insatiate bride,
  On thy form from every side[6]
  Like a Mænad round the cup
  Which Agave lifted up
  In the weird Cadmæan forest.[7]—                               475
  Brother, wheresoe'er thou soarest
  I must hurry, whirl and follow
  Through the Heavens wide and hollow,

5. The cone-shaped shadow a planet casts out into space on the side away from the sun, as
Earth's shadow sometimes darkens the Moon in lines 453–55.
6. The moon, in circling the earth, always keeps the same side toward the earth because the
period of its rotation exactly equals that of its revolution.
7. Agave, daughter of Cadmus, became a maenad (one of the female devotees of Dionysus); in
a fit of blind intoxication, she killed her own son Pentheus. See Euripides, *The Bacchae.*

Sheltered by the warm embrace
Of thy soul, from hungry space,                              480
Drinking, from thy sense and sight
Beauty, majesty, and might,
As a lover or chameleon
Grows like what it looks upon,
As a violet's gentle eye                                     485
Gazes on the azure sky
Until its hue grows like what it beholds,
    As a grey and watery mist
    Glows like solid amethyst
Athwart the western mountain it enfolds,                     490
    When the sunset sleeps
        Upon its snow—

                THE EARTH
    And the weak day weeps
        That it should be so.
O gentle Moon, the voice of thy delight                      495
Falls on me like thy clear and tender light
Soothing the seaman, borne the summer night
    Through isles forever calm;
O gentle Moon, thy chrystal accents pierce
The caverns of my Pride's deep Universe,                     500
Charming the tyger Joy, whose tramplings fierce
    Made wounds, which need thy balm.

                PANTHEA
I rise as from a bath of sparkling water,
A bath of azure light, among dark rocks,
Out of the stream of sound—

                IONE
                        Ah me, sweet sister,                 505
The stream of sound has ebbed away from us
And you pretend to rise out of its wave
Because your words fall like the clear soft dew
Shaken from a bathing wood-nymph's limbs and hair.

                PANTHEA
Peace! peace!—a mighty Power, which is as Darkness,          510
Is rising out of Earth, and from the sky
Is showered like Night, and from within the air
Bursts, like eclipse which had been gathered up
Into the pores[8] of sunlight—the bright Visions
Wherein the singing spirits rode and shone                  515
Gleam like pale meteors through a watery night.

---

8. Minute spaces between the particles of light.

IONE
There is a sense of words upon mine ear—


PANTHEA
A universal sound like words . . . O list!


DEMOGORGON
Thou Earth, calm Empire of a happy Soul,
    Sphere of divinest shapes and harmonies,                          520
Beautiful orb! gathering as thou dost roll
    The Love which paves thy path along the skies:


THE EARTH
I hear,—I am as a drop of dew that dies!


DEMOGORGON
Thou Moon, which gazest on the nightly Earth
    With wonder, as it gazes upon thee,                               525
Whilst each to men and beasts and the swift birth
    Of birds, is beauty, love, calm, harmony:


THE MOON
I hear—I am a leaf shaken by thee!


DEMOGORGON
Ye Kings of suns and stars, Dæmons and Gods,
    Ætherial Dominations, who possess                                 530
Elysian, windless, fortunate abodes
    Beyond Heaven's constellated wilderness:[9]


A VOICE: *from above*
Our great Republic hears . . . we are blest, and bless.


DEMOGORGON
Ye happy Dead, whom beams of brightest verse
    Are clouds to hide, not colours to portray,                      535
Whether your nature is that Universe
    Which once Ye saw and suffered—


A VOICE: *from beneath*
                                        Or as they
Whom we have left, we change and pass away.—


9. Shelley creates a hierarchy of Heaven like those described in Dante's *Paradiso* (XXVIII.121–
26, for example) and *Paradise Lost* (II.310–11, V.772), with *Dæmons* and *Gods* ruling heavenly bodies within human ken and *Dominations* existing at rest beyond the active universe.
As Carl Grabo notes, even Newton had allowed for the possibility of "some body absolutely
at rest," though this region would be beyond human power to identify.

DEMOGORGON

Ye elemental Genii,[1] who have homes
   From man's high mind even to the central stone     540
Of sullen lead, from Heaven's star-fretted domes
   To the dull weed some sea-worm battens[2] on—

A *confused* VOICE

We hear—thy words waken Oblivion.

DEMOGORGON

Spirits whose homes are flesh—ye beasts and birds—
   Ye worms and fish—ye living leaves and buds—     545
Lightning and Wind—and ye untameable herds,
   Meteors and mists, which throng Air's solitudes:

A VOICE

Thy voice to us is wind among still woods.

DEMOGORGON

Man, who wert once a despot and a slave,—
   A dupe and a deceiver,—a Decay,     550
A Traveller from the cradle to the grave
   Through the dim night of this immortal Day:

ALL

Speak—thy strong words may never pass away.

DEMOGORGON

This is the Day which down the void Abysm
At the Earth-born's spell yawns for Heaven's Despotism,     555
   And Conquest is dragged captive through the Deep;
Love from its awful throne of patient power
In the wise heart, from the last giddy hour
   Of dread endurance, from the slippery, steep,
And narrow verge of crag-like Agony, springs     560
And folds over the world its healing wings.

Gentleness, Virtue, Wisdom and Endurance,—
These are the seals of that most firm assurance
   Which bars the pit over Destruction's strength;
And if, with infirm hand, Eternity,     565
Mother of many acts and hours, should free
   The serpent that would clasp her with his length,—
These are the spells by which to reassume
An empire o'er the disentangled Doom.

To suffer woes which Hope thinks infinite;     570
To forgive wrongs darker than Death or Night;

---

1. The animating spirits of the elements.
2. Feeds gluttonously.

> To defy Power which seems Omnipotent;
> To love, and bear;[3] to hope, till Hope creates
> From its own wreck the thing it contemplates;
>     Neither to change nor falter nor repent:[4]                    575
> This, like thy glory, Titan! is to be
> Good, great and joyous, beautiful and free;
> This is alone Life, Joy, Empire and Victory.

# THE SENSITIVE-PLANT

"The Sensitive-Plant" was the first of the "other poems" included in the *Prometheus Unbound* volume, perhaps because it is both the longest of these poems and a mythopoeic fable that harmonizes with *Prometheus* itself. Shelley composed it during Spring 1820, quite possibly in March, the date Mary Shelley assigns it at the end of the fair copy she transcribed in the larger Silsbee notebook at Harvard, MS Eng.258.3, pp. 47–60 (*MYR: Shelley*, V). We have consulted her transcription in revising the orthography and punctuation to approximate Shelley's customary practice. The first edition remains authoritative for the words of the text. Drafts of the poem can be found at the Bodleian Library, Bod. MS Shelley adds. e.12, pp. 44–48, 134–40, 142–43, 145–46a, 147, 161–63, 167–70, 185–87, 220 (*BSM*, XVIII); and at the Huntington Library, HM 2176, fol. *33r. (*MYR: Shelley*, VI).

The sensitive-plant itself is a small variety of mimosa (*Mimosa pudica*), native to Brazil, that closes up and recoils when touched; it is hermaphroditic—needing only a single plant to reproduce (hence, *companionless*, line 12). Earl Wasserman has noted that late-eighteenth-century biologists were debating the sensitive-plant's place as a bridge between the animal and vegetable kingdoms.

Though interpretations of the poem's fable have varied, it seems likely that the sensitive-plant represents, not Shelley or any individual, but either mankind amid natural creation or else the type of the poet with creative sensibility amid general mankind. For some of the ecological implications of the poem, see the essay by Alan Bewell in this volume (pp. 627–36).

## The Sensitive-Plant

### PART FIRST

> A Sensitive-plant in a garden grew,
> And the young winds fed it with silver dew,
> And it opened its fan-like leaves to the light
> And closed them beneath the kisses of night.
>
> And the Spring arose on the garden fair                    5
> Like the Spirit of love felt every where;

---

3. Appropriately, Demogorgon expresses these timeless admonitions in timeless infinitives.
4. Here Shelley has adapted Satan's sentiment from Milton's *Paradise Lost* and reversed its moral implications: "yet not for those / Nor what the Potent Victor in his rage / Can else inflict, do I repent or change" (I.94–96).

And each flower and herb on Earth's dark breast
Rose from the dreams of its wintry rest.

But none ever trembled and panted with bliss
In the garden, the field or the wilderness,　　　　　　　　　10
Like a doe in the noontide with love's sweet want
As the companionless Sensitive-plant.[1]

The snow-drop and then the violet
Arose from the ground with warm rain wet
And their breath was mixed with fresh odour, sent　　　15
From the turf, like the voice and the instrument.

Then the pied[2] wind-flowers and the tulip tall,
And narcissi, the fairest among them all
Who gaze on their eyes in the stream's recess
Till they die of their own dear loveliness;[3]　　　　　　20

And the Naiad-like[4] lily of the vale
Whom youth makes so fair and passion so pale,
That the light of its tremulous bells is seen
Through their pavilions of tender green;

And the hyacinth[5] purple, and white, and blue,　　　　25
Which flung from its bells a sweet peal anew
Of music so delicate, soft and intense,
It was felt like an odour within the sense;

And the rose like a nymph to the bath addresst,
Which unveiled the depth of her glowing breast,　　　30
Till, fold after fold, to the fainting air
The soul of her beauty and love lay bare:

And the wand-like lily, which lifted up,
As a Mænad,[6] its moonlight-coloured cup
Till the fiery star, which is its eye,　　　　　　　　　　35
Gazed through clear dew on the tender sky;

---

1. Whereas the sensitive-plant is an annual, all of the other flowers mentioned in Part First, lines 13–57, are perennials.
2. Of varied colors.
3. *marcissi . . . loveliness:* An allusion to the myth of Narcissus, who fell in love with his own beautiful image in a pool and killed himself in despair because he could not communicate with the image he believed to be a nymph. He was transformed into a flower.
4. A *Naiad* was a nymph of a stream or fountain; naiads, according to Hesiod, initiated youths into sexual experience.
5. According to Greek legend, Hyacinthus was a youth beloved by both Apollo and Zephyrus, one of the winds; the latter, in a fit of jealousy, blew a quoit that Apollo had thrown out of its course, killing the young man. Apollo changed his blood into a flower.
6. A fanatical female devotee of Bacchus. Note that all the mythical creatures compared with the flowers are highly passionate and sexual, whereas the sensitive-plant, being unisexual, has no such relations with the other flowers.

And the jessamine faint, and the sweet tuberose,
The sweetest flower for scent that blows;[7]
And all rare blossoms from every clime
Grew in that garden in perfect prime.                              40

And on the stream whose inconstant bosom
Was prankt[8] under boughs of embowering blossom
With golden and green light, slanting through
Their Heaven of many a tangled hue,

Broad water-lilies lay tremulously,                                45
And starry river-buds glimmered by,
And around them the soft stream did glide and dance
With a motion of sweet sound and radiance.

And the sinuous paths of lawn and of moss,
Which led through the garden along and across—                     50
Some open at once to the sun and the breeze,
Some lost among bowers of blossoming trees—

Were all paved with daisies and delicate bells
As fair as the fabulous asphodels,[9]
And flowrets which drooping as day drooped too                     55
Fell into pavilions, white, purple and blue,
To roof the glow-worm from the evening dew.

And from this undefiled Paradise
The flowers, as an infant's awakening eyes
Smile on its mother, whose singing sweet                           60
Can first lull, and at last must awaken it,

When Heaven's blithe winds had unfolded them,
As mine-lamps enkindle a hidden gem,
Shone smiling to Heaven; and every one
Shared joy in the light of the gentle sun,                         65

For each one was interpenetrated
With the light and the odour its neighbour shed
Like young lovers, whom youth and love make dear,
Wrapt and filled by their mutual atmosphere.

But the Sensitive-plant, which could give small fruit              70
Of the love which it felt from the leaf to the root,
Received more than all—it loved more than ever,
Where none wanted but it, could belong to the giver.

7. Blooms.
8. Spangled or brightened with colors.
9. A common flower in Italy; in poetic usage from Homer through Milton and Pope it has been
the name given to the immortal flowers that bloom in the Elysian fields.

For the Sensitive-Plant has no bright flower;
Radiance and odour are not its dower—                                    75
It loves—even like Love—its deep heart is full—
It desires what it has not—the beautiful![1]

The light winds which from unsustaining wings
Shed the music of many murmurings;
The beams which dart from many a star                                     80
Of the flowers whose hues they bear afar;

The plumed[2] insects swift and free
Like golden boats on a sunny sea,
Laden with light and odour which pass
Over the gleam of the living grass;                                       85

The unseen clouds of the dew which lie
Like fire in the flowers till the Sun rides high,
Then wander like spirits among the spheres,
Each cloud faint with the fragrance it bears;

The quivering vapours of dim noontide,                                    90
Which like a sea o'er the warm earth glide
In which every sound, and odour, and beam
Move, as reeds in a single stream;

Each, and all, like ministering angels were
For the Sensitive-plant sweet joy to bear                                 95
Whilst the lagging hours of the day went by
Like windless clouds o'er a tender sky.

And when evening descended from Heaven above,
And the Earth was all rest, and the Air was all love;
And delight, though less bright, was far more deep,                      100
And the day's veil fell from the world of sleep,

And the beasts, and the birds, and the insects were drowned
In an ocean of dreams without a sound
Whose waves never mark, though they ever impress
The light sand which paves it—Consciousness.                             105

(Only over head the sweet nightingale
Ever sang more sweet as the day might fail
And snatches of its Elysian[3] chant
Were mixed with the dreams of the Sensitive-plant).

1. This stanza closely parallels a passage in Plato's *Symposium* that Shelley cited with approval
   in his review of Peacock's *Rhododaphne* (1817). Shelley translated *The Symposium* in July
   1818, rendering the relevant passage (in which Socrates records his earlier conversation with
   Diotima) thus: " 'It is conceded, then, that Love loves that which he wants but possesses
   not?'—'Yes, certainly.'—'But Love wants and does not possess beauty?'—'Indeed it must
   necessarily follow' " (Notopoulos, *Platonism of Shelley*, p. 440).
2. Delicately winged.
3. Glorious or perfect, like Elysium, Greek mythological abode of the blessed dead.

The Sensitive-plant was the earliest                          110
Upgathered into the bosom of rest;
A sweet child weary of its delight,
The feeblest and yet the favourite—
Cradled within the embrace of night.


PART SECOND

There was a Power in this sweet place,
An Eve in this Eden; a ruling grace
Which to the flowers did they waken or dream
Was as God[4] is to the starry scheme:


A Lady—the wonder of her kind,                                5
Whose form was upborne by a lovely mind
Which, dilating, had moulded her mien and motion,
Like a sea-flower unfolded beneath the Ocean—


Tended the garden from morn to even:
And the meteors[5] of that sublunar Heaven                     10
Like the lamps of the air when night walks forth,
Laughed round her footsteps up from the Earth.


She had no companion of mortal race,
But her tremulous breath and her flushing face
Told, whilst the morn kissed the sleep from her eyes          15
That her dreams were less slumber than Paradise:


As if some bright Spirit for her sweet sake
Had deserted heaven while the stars were awake
As if yet around her he lingering were,
Though the veil of daylight concealed him from her.           20


Her step seemed to pity the grass it prest;
You might hear by the heaving of her breast,
That the coming and going of the wind
Brought pleasure there and left passion behind,


And wherever her aery footstep trod,                          25
Her trailing hair from the grassy sod
Erased its light vestige, with shadowy sweep
Like a sunny storm o'er the dark green deep.


---

4. In Shelley's conception God did not create matter but merely organized it into a universe.
In letters and conversations Shelley compared two women with the *Lady* in this poem—
Margaret, Countess of Mount Cashell ("Mrs. Mason") and Jane Williams. His references
seem to imply that they gave emotional support and harmony to those about them.
5. Any atmospheric phenomenon; in this context, healthful winds (cf. Part Third, line 78);
*sublunar:* earthly; within the realm of mutability.

I doubt not the flowers of that garden sweet
Rejoiced in the sound of her gentle feet;                    30
I doubt not they felt the spirit that came
From her glowing fingers through all their frame.

She sprinkled bright water from the stream
On those that were faint with the sunny beam;
And out of the cups of the heavy flowers                    35
She emptied the rain of the thunder showers.

She lifted their heads with her tender hands
And sustained them with rods and ozier bands;[6]
If the flowers had been her own infants she
Could never have nursed them more tenderly.                    40

And all killing insects and gnawing worms
And things of obscene and unlovely forms
She bore, in a basket of Indian woof,[7]
Into the rough woods far aloof,

In a basket of grasses and wild flowers full,                    45
The freshest her gentle hands could pull
For the poor banished insects, whose intent,
Although they did ill, was innocent.

But the bee and the beam-like ephemeris[8]
Whose path is the lightning's, and soft moths that kiss                    50
The sweet lips of the flowers, and harm not, did she
Make her attendant angels be.

And many an antenatal tomb
Where butterflies dream of the life to come
She left clinging round the smooth and dark                    55
Edge of the odorous cedar bark.

This fairest creature from earliest spring
Thus moved through the garden ministering
All the sweet season of summertide,
And ere the first leaf looked brown—she died!                    60

### PART THIRD

Three days the flowers of the garden fair,
Like stars when the moon is awakened, were;

---

6. Slender willow branches.
7. A woven pattern.
8. The ephemerid, dayfly or mayfly, has a slender body and small, transparent wings. In its imago or winged stage, it lives for only a single day. Shelley also mentions the insect in his note to *Queen Mab*, VIII.203–07, and alludes to it in *Adonais*, line 254.

Or the waves of Baiæ,[9] ere luminous
She floats up through the smoke of Vesuvius.

And on the fourth, the Sensitive-plant                    5
Felt the sound of the funeral chant
And the steps of the bearers heavy and slow,
And the sobs of the mourners deep and low,

The weary sound and the heavy breath
And the silent motions of passing death                   10
And the smell, cold, oppressive and dank,
Sent through the pores of the coffin plank.

The dark grass and the flowers among the grass
Were bright with tears as the crowd did pass;
From their sighs the wind caught a mournful tone,         15
And sate in the pines and gave groan for groan.

The garden once fair became cold and foul
Like the corpse of her who had been its soul
Which at first was lovely as if in sleep,
Then slowly changed, till it grew a heap                  20
To make men tremble who never weep.

Swift summer into the autumn flowed,
And frost in the mist of the morning rode,
Though the noonday sun looked clear and bright,
Mocking the spoil of the secret night.                    25

The rose leaves like flakes of crimson snow
Paved the turf and the moss below:
The lilies were drooping, and white, and wan,
Like the head and the skin of a dying man.

And Indian plants, of scent and hue                       30
The sweetest that ever were fed on dew;
Leaf after leaf, day by day,
Were massed into the common clay.

And the leaves, brown, yellow, and grey, and red,
And white, with the whiteness of what is dead,            35
Like troops of ghosts on the dry wind past—
Their whistling noise made the birds aghast.

And the gusty winds waked the winged seeds
Out of their birthplace of ugly weeds,
Till they clung round many a sweet flower's stem          40
Which rotted into the earth with them.

9. Baiae is a small bay of the Gulf of Naples, west of the city itself; volcanic Mt. Vesuvius is
within sight of the bay, though on the other side of Naples.

The water-blooms under the rivulet
Fell from the stalks on which they were set;
And the eddies drove them here and there
As the winds did those of the upper air. 45

Then the rain came down, and the broken stalks
Were bent and tangled across the walks;
And the leafless network of parasite bowers
Massed into ruin; and all sweet flowers.

Between the time of the wind and the snow 50
All loathliest weeds began to grow,
Whose coarse leaves were splashed with many a speck
Like the water-snake's belly and the toad's back.

And thistles, and nettles, and darnels[1] rank,
And the dock, and henbane, and hemlock dank,[2] 55
Stretched out its long and hollow shank
And stifled the air, till the dead wind stank.

And plants, at whose names the verse feels loath,
Filled the place with a monstrous undergrowth,
Prickly, and pulpous,[3] and blistering, and blue, 60
Livid, and starred with a lurid[4] dew.

And agarics[5] and fungi with mildew and mould
Started like mist from the wet ground cold;
Pale, fleshy,—as if the decaying dead
With a spirit of growth had been animated! 65

Their moss rotted off them, flake by flake,
Till the thick stalk stuck like a murderer's stake,
Where rags of loose flesh yet tremble on high,
Infecting the winds that wander by.[6]

Spawn,[7] weeds and filth, a leprous scum, 70
Made the running rivulet thick and dumb

1. Harmful grasses.
2. *Dock* is the common name for several thick-rooted, coarse plants; both *henbane* and *hemlock* are poisonous.
3. Soft or fleshy; flabby.
4. *Livid:* bruised; *lurid:* pale and sickly in color.
5. Gill mushrooms. Lines 64–69 describe in detail (Hélène Dworzan informs us) the maturing of the *Amanita phalloides* ("Death Cap") and the *Amanita virosa* ("Destroying Angel"), two of the deadliest agarics.
6. Some editors have omitted this stanza (which describes a body rotting on a gibbet) on the grounds that it is canceled in Mary Shelley's transcript and that she omits it from her collected editions. But the first fact probably explains the second, and since all editors follow the other substantive features of the first edition rather than Mary Shelley's quite different safekeeping transcript, it seems logical to retain this stanza also. The gibbet was a sort of gallows on which the body of a criminal executed for a particularly heinous crime was, by order of the sentencing judge, chained to an iron frame near the scene of the crime as a warning to others. Its use was legal in England only from 1752 to 1834. See the use of an actual gibbet at the end of "Zeinab and Kathema."
7. The vegetative part (white filamentous tubes) of mushrooms or other fungi.

And at its outlet flags[8] huge as stakes
Dammed it up with roots knotted like water snakes.

And hour by hour when the air was still
The vapours arose which have strength to kill:          75
At morn they were seen, at noon they were felt,
At night they were darkness no star could melt.

And unctuous[9] meteors from spray to spray
Crept and flitted in broad noonday
Unseen; every branch on which they alit          80
By a venomous blight was burned and bit.

The Sensitive-plant like one forbid
Wept, and the tears, within each lid
Of its folded leaves which together grew,
Were changed to a blight of frozen glue.          85

For the leaves soon fell, and the branches soon
By the heavy axe of the blast were hewn;
The sap shrank to the root through every pore
As blood to a heart that will beat no more.

For Winter came—the wind was his whip—          90
One choppy finger was on his lip:
He had torn the cataracts[1] from the hills
And they clanked at his girdle like manacles;

His breath was a chain which without a sound
The earth and the air and the water bound;          95
He came, fiercely driven, in his Chariot-throne
By the tenfold blasts of the arctic zone.

Then the weeds which were forms of living death
Fled from the frost to the Earth beneath.
Their decay and sudden flight from frost          100
Was but like the vanishing of a ghost!

And under the roots of the Sensitive-plant
The moles and the dormice died for want.
The birds dropped stiff from the frozen air
And were caught in the branches naked and bare.          105

First there came down a thawing rain
And its dull drops froze on the boughs again;
Then there steamed up a freezing dew
Which to the drops of the thaw-rain grew;

8. Reeds or rushes.
9. Oily; *meteors*: bad air or winds; *spray*: a slender twig or shoot.
1. Large waterfalls.

And a northern whirlwind, wandering about                            110
Like a wolf that had smelt a dead child out,
Shook the boughs thus laden and heavy and stiff
And snapped them off with his rigid griff.[2]

When winter had gone and spring came back
The Sensitive-plant was a leafless wreck;                            115
But the mandrakes and toadstools and docks and darnels
Rose like the dead from their ruined charnels.

CONCLUSION

Whether the Sensitive-plant, or that
Which within its boughs like a spirit sat
Ere its outward form had known decay,
Now felt this change,—I cannot say.

Whether that Lady's gentle mind,                                     5
No longer with the form combined
Which scattered love—as stars do light,
Found sadness, where it left delight,

I dare not guess; but in this life
Of error, ignorance and strife—                                     10
Where nothing is—but all things seem,
And we, the shadows of the dream,

It is a modest creed, and yet
Pleasant if one considers it,
To own that death itself must be,                                   15
Like all the rest,—a mockery.

That Garden sweet, that lady fair
And all sweet shapes and odours there
In truth have never past away—
'Tis we, 'tis ours, are changed—not they.                          20

For love, and beauty, and delight
There is no death nor change: their might
Exceeds our organs—which endure
No light—being themselves obscure.[3]

2. A claw.
3. *their might . . . obscure:* The statement of the conclusion is simply that, since we know *our organs* (of sensation, reasoning, etc.) to be *obscure* (dark, dim), the sequence of events related in Parts First, Second, and Third may not be the true picture. Because he knows human perceptions to be fallible, the poet can still hold his *modest creed* (line 13), even after relating the apparent death of the Lady and the destruction of the beautiful garden.

# Ode to Heaven[1]

Palace-roof of cloudless nights,
Paradise of golden lights,
  Deep, Immeasurable, Vast,
    Which art now, and which wert then;
Of the present and the past,                  5
  Of the eternal Where and When,
    Presence chamber, Temple, Home,
    Ever-canopying Dome
  Of acts and ages yet to come!

Glorious shapes have life in thee—           10
Earth and all Earth's company,
  Living globes which ever throng
  Thy deep chasms and wildernesses,
And green worlds that glide along,
  And swift stars with flashing tresses,      15
    And icy moons most cold and bright,
    And mighty suns, beyond the Night,
  Atoms[2] of intensest light!

Even thy name is as a God,
Heaven! for thou art the abode            20
  Of that Power which is the glass
    Wherein man his nature sees;—
  Generations as they pass
    Worship thee with bended knees—
      Their unremaining Gods and they      25
    Like a river roll away—
    Thou remainest such—alway!—

---

1. In the larger Silsbee notebook at Harvard, MS Eng.258.3, Mary Shelley concluded her transcript of "Ode to Heaven," "Florence—December. 1819" (*MYR: Shelley*, V). This transcription appears to be based on an untitled holograph fair copy located in the same Bodleian notebook containing Shelley's intermediate fair copy of Act III of *Prometheus Unbound*, Bod. MS Shelley, e.3, fols. 17r, 18r, 19r, 20r (*BSM*, IX). Shelley drafted the poem in a notebook now at the Huntington Library, HM 2177, fols.*42r–*45r (*MYR: Shelley*, IV).
   "Ode to Heaven" shares the same mythopoeic impulse that inspired Act IV of *Prometheus Unbound*, and it was first published in 1820 in the *Prometheus* volume. Our text, which differs considerably in form from those in the collected editions, is based on a detailed comparison of the first edition with the holograph manuscripts at the Huntington and Bodleian libraries and with Mary Shelley's transcript. The three parts of the poem represent three perspectives on humanity's place in the universe. The first is the viewpoint of eighteenth-century deists, represented by Joseph Addison's famous hymn, "The Spacious Firmament on High." The second enunciates the Platonic doctrine that the present world is an imperfect and darkened delusion compared to the spiritual reality. The third deplores the presumption of thinking that human existence is so important in the scheme of things. Cf. the opening canto of *Queen Mab*.
2. The smallest conceivable portions or fragments of anything.

A REMOTER VOICE

Thou art but the Mind's first chamber,
Round which its young fancies[3] clamber
  Like weak insects in a cave                                    30
    Lighted up by stalactites;
  But the portal of the grave,
    Where a world of new delights
      Will make thy best glories seem
      But a dim and noonday gleam                            35
    From the shadow of a dream.

A LOUDER AND STILL REMOTER VOICE

Peace! the abyss is wreathed with scorn
At your presumption, Atom-born![4]
  What is Heaven? and what are ye
    Who its brief expanse inherit?                             40
  What are suns and spheres which flee
    With the instinct of that spirit
      Of which ye are but a part?
      Drops which Nature's mighty heart
    Drives through thinnest veins. Depart!                    45

What is Heaven? a globe of dew
Filling in the morning new
  Some eyed flower[5] whose young leaves waken
    On an unimagined world.
  Constellated suns unshaken,                                    50
    Orbits measureless, are furled
      In that frail and fading sphere
      With ten million gathered there
    To tremble, gleam, and disappear![6]—

# ODE TO THE WEST WIND

Though the basic imagery of this poem dates from at least 1817, when
Shelley developed it in Canto IX of *Laon and Cythna* (see pp. 105–07),
this best known of all Shelley's shorter poems was begun October 20–25,
1819, under circumstances described in the poet's own note: "This poem
was conceived and chiefly written in a wood that skirts the Arno, near
Florence, and on a day when that tempestuous wind, whose temperature
is at once mild and animating, was collecting the vapours which pour down
the autumnal rains. They began, as I foresaw, at sunset with a violent

3. Fantasies.
4. I.e., born of one of the dust particles rendered visible by light, a mote in a sunbeam.
5. Probably a flower such as the daisy or the cosmos.
6. In lines 45–54 the entire visible universe is seen as a microcosm existing as a tiny part of a
   dewdrop in an infinitely bigger universe.

tempest of hail and rain, attended by that magnificent thunder and lightning peculiar to the Cisalpine regions."

In drafting "Ode to the West Wind," Shelley used parts of three different
notebooks. A draft of stanzas I–III appears in a Huntington Library notebook, HM 2176, fols. *6r–*4r (*MYR: Shelley*, VI); these stanzas are revised in Bodleian MS Shelley adds. e.12, pp. 63–65 (*BSM*, XVIII), which
also contains a draft of stanza IV (p. 155). A revision of stanza IV and a
draft of stanza V appear in Bodleian MS Shelley adds. e.6, pp. 138 rev.–
137 rev. (*BSM*, V). The Pforzheimer Collection contains a notebook (SC
546) in which Shelley drafted his note to the poem (SC 547; see *SC*, VI,
1066–69). "Ode to the West Wind" was first published in the *Prometheus
Unbound* volume of 1820.

Structurally the poem consists of five terza-rima sonnets, the first three
of which describe the effect of autumn on the foliage of the land, the sea,
and (figuratively) the sky. The fourth stanza contrasts the poet's situation
with these natural elements, and the final stanza is a prayer or request to
the West Wind, as mover of the seasonal cycle, to assist the poet's aims
by spreading his message and, thereby, helping him to contribute to a
moral or political revolution paralleling the seasonal change. For a detailed
reading of the poem, see the excerpts from James Chandler's *England in
1819* in this volume (pp. 711–21).

# Ode to the West Wind

## I

O wild West Wind, thou breath of Autumn's being,
Thou, from whose unseen presence the leaves dead
Are driven, like ghosts from an enchanter fleeing,

Yellow, and black, and pale, and hectic[1] red,
Pestilence-stricken multitudes:[2] O Thou,                                    5
Who chariotest to their dark wintry bed

The winged seeds, where they lie cold and low,
Each like a corpse within its grave, until
Thine azure sister of the Spring[3] shall blow

Her clarion[4] o'er the dreaming earth, and fill                             10
(Driving sweet buds like flocks to feed in air)
With living hues and odours plain and hill:

---

1. Wasting or consuming (referring to the "hectic flush" of tuberculosis).
2. *the leaves dead . . . multitudes:* Shelley embodies in lines 2–5 the traditional epic simile
   found in Homer, Virgil, Dante, and Milton, in which souls of the dead are compared to
   fallen leaves driven by the wind (see also "The Triumph of Life," lines 49–51). G. M. Matthews notes that the four colors are not only actually found in dead leaves, but represent
   the traditional four races of humans—Mongoloid, Negroid, Caucasian, and American
   Indian.
3. The traditional name of the autumnal west wind was Ausonius. (Italy was poetically known
   as Ausonia.) Though the spring west wind was masculine in both Greek (Zephyrus) and
   Latin (Favonius) mythology, Shelley revises the tradition by making the restorative force of
   the spring mildly feminine.
4. A narrow shrill-sounding war trumpet.

Wild Spirit, which art moving everywhere;
Destroyer and Preserver;[5] hear, O hear!

## II

Thou on whose stream, 'mid the steep sky's commotion,          15
Loose clouds[6] like Earth's decaying leaves are shed,
Shook from the tangled boughs of Heaven and Ocean,[7]

Angels[8] of rain and lightning: there are spread
On the blue surface of thine aery surge,
Like the bright hair uplifted from the head                    20

Of some fierce Mænad,[9] even from the dim verge
Of the horizon to the zenith's height,
The locks of the approaching storm. Thou Dirge[1]

Of the dying year, to which this closing night
Will be the dome of a vast sepulchre,                          25
Vaulted with all thy congregated might

Of vapours,[2] from whose solid atmosphere
Black rain and fire and hail will burst: O hear!

## III

Thou who didst waken from his summer dreams
The blue Mediterranean, where he lay,                          30
Lulled by the coil of his chrystalline streams,

Beside a pumice isle in Baiæ's bay,[3]
And saw in sleep old palaces and towers
Quivering within the wave's intenser day,

5. These titles come directly from the titles of the Hindu gods Siva the Destroyer and Vishnu
the Preserver, known to Shelley from both the translations and writings of Sir William Jones
and Edward Moor's *Hindu Pantheon* (1810).
6. High, wispy cirrus clouds (the word means "curl" or "lock of hair" in Latin).
7. Along the coasts of the Mediterranean from Genoa to Leghorn the autumn brought storms
accompanied by waterspouts that rose like tree trunks on the horizon, as Shelley and other
travelers of his time described them.
8. Literally, "messengers."
9. *hair . . . Mænad:* The cirrus clouds seem scattered ahead of the storm like locks thrown
forward by the wild orgiastic dance of a maenad. Shelley had seen four depicted in a relief
sculpture at Florence, which he described thus: "The tremendous spirit of superstition aided
by drunkenness . . . seems to have caught them in its whirlwinds, and to bear them over
the earth as the rapid volutions of a tempest bear the ever-changing trunk of a water-spout.
. . . Their hair loose and floating seems caught in the tempest of their own tumultuous
motion, their heads are thrown back leaning with a strange inanity upon their necks, and
looking up to Heaven, while they totter and stumble even in the energy of their tempestuous
dance" (*Works*, VI, 323). See "The Triumph of Life," lines 137–47.
1. A song of mourning.
2. Clouds.
3. From a boat beside an island of *pumice* (porous lava) Shelley had the previous December
seen the overgrown ruins of villas from the days of imperial Rome reflected in the waters of
the Bay of Baiae (*Letters*, II, 61).

All overgrown with azure moss and flowers          35
So sweet, the sense faints picturing them! Thou
For whose path the Atlantic's level powers

Cleave themselves into chasms, while far below
The sea-blooms and the oozy woods which wear
The sapless foliage of the ocean,[4] know          40

Thy voice, and suddenly grow grey with fear,
And tremble and despoil themselves: O hear!

### IV

If I were a dead leaf thou mightest bear;
If I were a swift cloud to fly with thee;
A wave to pant beneath thy power, and share          45

The impulse of thy strength, only less free
Than thou, O Uncontroulable! If even
I were as in my boyhood, and could be

The comrade of thy wanderings over Heaven,
As then, when to outstrip thy skiey speed          50
Scarce seemed a vision; I would ne'er have striven

As thus with thee in prayer in my sore need.
Oh! lift me as a wave, a leaf, a cloud!
I fall upon the thorns of life![5] I bleed!

A heavy weight of hours has chained and bowed          55
One too like thee: tameless, and swift, and proud.

### V

Make me thy lyre, even as the forest is:
What if my leaves are falling like its own!
The tumult of thy mighty harmonies

Will take from both a deep, autumnal tone,          60
Sweet though in sadness. Be thou, Spirit fierce,
My spirit! Be thou me, impetuous one!

Drive my dead thoughts over the universe
Like withered leaves to quicken a new birth!
And, by the incantation of this verse,          65

4. "The phenomenon alluded to at the conclusion of the third stanza is well known to natu-
   ralists. The vegetation at the bottom of the sea, of rivers, and of lakes, sympathizes with that
   of the land in the change of seasons, and is consequently influenced by the winds which
   announce it" (Shelley's note).
5. Behind Shelley's image—besides other literary references—lie Jesus' crown of thorns and
   Dante's metaphor of life as "a dark wood . . . rough and stubborn" (*Inferno*, I.1–5).

Scatter, as from an unextinguished hearth
Ashes and sparks, my words among mankind!
Be through my lips to unawakened Earth

The trumpet of a prophecy![6] O Wind,
If Winter comes, can Spring be far behind?                    70

# THE CLOUD

"The Cloud" was composed sometime between Fall 1819 and June 1820,
as Carlene Adamson has argued (*BSM*, V, xxxviii), and was published with
*Prometheus Unbound*. A fair copy of lines 59–66 appears in Bodleian MS
Shelley adds. e.6, pp. 35–37 (*BSM*, V), a notebook that also contains a
rough draft of the final stanza (pp. 21, 31). We have reverted to the readings in the holograph fair copy in lines 42 (*depths*) and 75 (*oceans*), adding
in each case a final "s" that is missing in *1820*, but clearly present in the
MS; both of these could have been overlooked by the transcriber (probably
Mary Shelley) or the compositor.

The poem was inspired, not so much by an event or scene in Italy,
as by the first-person plural song of the Nepheliads (cloud nymphs) in
Part II of Leigh Hunt's poem "The Nymphs," which was admired by Shelley at least from its publication in *Foliage* (1818), and probably before.
That song begins:

> Ho! We are the Nepheliads, we,
> Who bring the clouds from the great sea,
> And have within our happy care
> All the love 'twixt earth and air.
> We it is with soft new showers
> Wash the eyes of the young flowers. . . .
> (*Foliage*, p. xxxi)

Throughout the song are lines like these that suggest ideas that Shelley
develops in "The Cloud." As Desmond King-Hele points out (*Shelley: His
Thought and Work,* [London: Macmillan, 1960], pp. 219–27), Luke Howard's *Essay on Clouds*, published in a journal in 1803, established the modern system of classification and generated interest in describing clouds.
Reiman has argued (*Percy Bysshe Shelley* [Updated edition, 1990], pp. 96–
97) that, besides creating the mythopoeic autobiography of a cloud, Shelley uses the cloud here, as in other poems, as "an analogue of the human
mind" and that the poem portrays "the life-cycle of the human soul."

# The Cloud

I bring fresh showers for the thirsting flowers,
    From the seas and the streams;

---

6. *Be . . . prophecy!*: "It is impossible to read the productions of our most celebrated writers . . . without being startled with the electric life which there is in their words. . . . They
are the priests of an unapprehended inspiration, the mirrors of gigantic forms which futurity
casts upon the present, the words which express what they conceive not, the trumpet which
sings to battle and feels not what it inspires, the influence which is moved not but moves"
(*A Philosophical View of Reform*; see also *A Defence of Poetry*, p. 535).

I bear light shade for the leaves when laid
    In their noon-day dreams.
From my wings are shaken the dews that waken          5
    The sweet buds every one,
When rocked to rest on their mother's[1] breast,
    As she dances about the Sun.
I wield the flail[2] of the lashing hail,
    And whiten the green plains under,                10
And then again I dissolve it in rain,
    And laugh as I pass in thunder.

I sift the snow on the mountains below,
    And their great pines groan aghast;
And all the night 'tis my pillow white,               15
    While I sleep in the arms of the blast.
Sublime on the towers of my skiey bowers,
    Lightning my pilot sits;[3]
In a cavern under is fettered the thunder,
    It struggles and howls at fits;[4]                20
Over Earth and Ocean, with gentle motion,
    This pilot is guiding me,
Lured by the love of the genii that move
    In the depths of the purple sea;
Over the rills, and the crags, and the hills,         25
    Over the lakes and the plains,
Wherever he dream, under mountain or stream,
    The Spirit he loves remains;
And I all the while bask in Heaven's blue smile,
    Whilst he is dissolving in rains.                 30

The sanguine Sunrise, with his meteor eyes,[5]
    And his burning plumes[6] outspread,
Leaps on the back of my sailing rack,[7]
    When the morning star shines dead;
As on the jag of a mountain crag,                     35
    Which an earthquake rocks and swings,
An eagle alit one moment may sit
    In the light of its golden wings.
And when Sunset may breathe, from the lit Sea beneath,
    Its ardours of rest and of love,                  40

---

1. I.e., the earth's.
2. A military weapon consisting of an iron handle, at the end of which a stouter striking part armed with spikes swings freely; also a similarly constructed implement for threshing grain.
3. In his published lectures entitled *A System of Familiar Philosophy* (2 vols., 1799), Adam Walker (who lectured at both Syon House Academy and Eton during Shelley's school days there) argued that "water rises through the air, flying on the wings of electricity" and that rains are caused when positively charged clouds react with the negatively charged earth, either in a violent electrical storm (lines 19–20) or in more gentle precipitation (line 30). Shelley personifies the attraction of the two kinds of electrical charge as love (lines 23–28).
4. Spasmodically, or at varying intervals.
5. I.e., like a fireball or shooting star; *sanguine*: blood-red.
6. A poetic description of the sun's corona.
7. A mass of clouds driven before the wind in the upper air.

And the crimson pall[8] of eve may fall
  From the depths of Heaven above,
With wings folded I rest, on mine aëry nest,
  As still as a brooding dove.[9]

That orbed maiden with white fire laden      45
  Whom mortals call the Moon,
Glides glimmering o'er my fleece-like floor,
  By the midnight breezes strewn;
And wherever the beat of her unseen feet,
  Which only the angels hear,      50
May have broken the woof,[1] of my tent's thin roof,
  The stars peep behind her, and peer;
And I laugh to see them whirl and flee,
  Like a swarm of golden bees,
When I widen the rent in my wind-built tent,      55
  Till the calm rivers, lakes, and seas,
Like strips of the sky fallen through me on high,
  Are each paved with the moon and these.[2]

I bind the Sun's throne with a burning zone
  And the Moon's with a girdle of pearl;[3]      60
The volcanos are dim, and the stars reel and swim
  When the whirlwinds my banner unfurl.
From cape to cape, with a bridge-like shape,
  Over a torrent sea,
Sunbeam-proof, I hang like a roof—      65
  The mountains its columns be!
The triumphal arch, through which I march
  With hurricane, fire, and snow,
When the Powers of the Air, are chained to my chair,
  Is the million-coloured Bow;      70
The sphere-fire above its soft colours wove
  While the moist Earth was laughing below.

I am the daughter of Earth and Water,
  And the nursling of the Sky;[4]

---

8. A canopy or coverlet of rich cloth.
9. *With wings . . . brooding dove:* A significant echo of the invocation that begins Book I of *Paradise Lost,* in which the "Heav'nly Muse," whom Milton identifies with the Holy Spirit, is described at the creation as sitting "Dove-like . . . brooding on the vast Abyss" (I.21).
1. Fabric.
2. That is, the earthly waters reflect the images of the moon and stars (*these*).
3. *I bind . . . girdle of pearl:* Cirrostratus nebulosus clouds—high, transparent, whitish cloud-veils covering the sky—produce the halo phenomenon when the sun or moon shines behind them. Shelley's universalized Cloud changes constantly throughout the poem, assuming roles played by different types of clouds; for example, the cloud described in lines 45–58 is probably the middle-altitude altocumulus radiatus, a sheet of cloud that seems to be torn in *strips*; that *Sunbeam-proof . . . roof* in line 65 is the low gray sheet stratocumulus opacus; and that which marches through the *triumphal arch* of the rainbow (lines 67–70) is probably a cumulonimbus capillatus, a low rain-cloud, often featuring an anvil-shaped "thunderhead." *zone* (line 59): *girdle,* belt.
4. As in the parentage of "The Witch of Atlas," the emphasis is on the Cloud's middle station on the metaphysical scale of being, between Earth and Heaven.

I pass through the pores, of the oceans and shores;                     75
   I change, but I cannot die—
For after the rain, when with never a stain
   The pavilion of Heaven is bare,
And the winds and sunbeams, with their convex gleams,[5]
   Build up the blue dome of Air—                                  80
I silently laugh, at my own cenotaph,[6]
   And out of the caverns of rain,
Like a child from the womb, like a ghost from the tomb,
   I arise, and unbuild it again.—

# To a Sky-Lark[1]

Hail to thee, blithe Spirit!
   Bird thou never wert—
That from Heaven, or near it,
   Pourest thy full heart
In profuse strains of unpremeditated art.                               5

Higher still and higher
   From the earth thou springest
Like a cloud of fire;
   The blue deep thou wingest,
And singing still dost soar, and soaring ever singest.                  10

In the golden lightning
   Of the sunken Sun—
O'er which clouds are brightning,
   Thou dost float and run;
Like an unbodied joy whose race is just begun.                          15

The pale purple even
   Melts around thy flight,
Like a star of Heaven[2]
   In the broad day-light
Thou art unseen,—but yet I hear thy shrill delight,                     20

5. The course of sunlight is refracted by the earth's atmosphere, bending around the earth in a convex arc, when viewed from above. Violet and blue, at the end of the visible color spectrum with the shortest wave length, dominate in the sky when the sunbeams are least distorted by clouds of dust or moisture.
6. A sepulchral monument erected to honor a deceased person whose body is elsewhere.
1. This poem was composed near Leghorn (Livorno) in late June 1820 and published with *Prometheus Unbound*. Lines 1–4, 31–35, and 76–77 were drafted in Bodleian MS Shelley adds. e.6, pp. 97 rev.–96ᴬ rev. (*BSM*, V). Shelley's holograph fair copy, with his own corrections, is in Harvard MS Eng.258.2, pp. 100–105 (*MYR: Shelley*, V).
   Thematically, "To a Sky-Lark" can be divided into three parts: lines 1–30; 31–60; and 61–105. The first describes the flight of an actual skylark (*Alauda arvensis*), a small European bird that sings only in flight, usually when it is too high to be clearly visible. The second part attempts but fails to find a fitting analogue for the bird and its song; the third asks the bird to teach humanity its secret joy.
2. Venus as the evening star.

Keen as are the arrows
   Of that silver sphere,[3]
Whose intense lamp narrows
   In the white dawn clear
Until we hardly see—we feel that it is there.        25

All the earth and air
   With thy voice is loud,
As when Night is bare
   From one lonely cloud
The moon rains out her beams—and Heaven is overflowed.        30

What thou art we know not;
   What is most like thee?
From rainbow clouds there flow not
   Drops so bright to see
As from thy presence showers a rain of melody.        35

Like a Poet[4] hidden
   In the light of thought,
Singing hymns unbidden,
   Till the world is wrought
To sympathy with hopes and fears it heeded not:        40

Like a high-born maiden
   In a palace-tower,
Soothing her love-laden
   Soul in secret hour,
With music sweet as love—which overflows her bower:        45

Like a glow-worm golden
   In a dell of dew,
Scattering unbeholden
   Its aerial hue
Among the flowers and grass which screen it from the view:        50

Like a rose embowered
   In its own green leaves—
By warm winds deflowered—
   Till the scent it gives
Makes faint with too much sweet these heavy-winged thieves:        55

Sound of vernal showers
   On the twinkling grass,
Rain-awakened flowers,
   All that ever was
Joyous, and clear and fresh, thy music doth surpass.        60

3. Venus as the morning star.
4. The similes in stanzas 8–12 both involve all five senses and descend from human poet and
lover through the animal, vegetable, and mineral realms.

Teach us, Sprite or Bird,
   What sweet thoughts are thine;
I have never heard
   Praise of love or wine[5]
That panted forth a flood of rapture so divine:          65

Chorus Hymeneal[6]
   Or triumphal chaunt
Matched with thine would be all
   But an empty vaunt,
A thing wherein we feel there is some hidden want.     70

What objects are the fountains
   Of thy happy strain?
What fields or waves or mountains?
   What shapes of sky or plain?
What love of thine own kind? what ignorance of pain?   75

With thy clear keen joyance
   Languor cannot be—
Shadow of annoyance
   Never came near thee;
Thou lovest—but ne'er knew love's sad satiety.      80

Waking or asleep,
   Thou of death must deem
Things more true and deep
   Than we mortals dream,
Or how could thy notes flow in such a chrystal stream?  85

We look before and after,
   And pine for what is not[7]—
Our sincerest laughter
   With some pain is fraught—
Our sweetest songs are those that tell of saddest thought.  90

Yet if we could scorn
   Hate and pride and fear;
If we were things born
   Not to shed a tear,
I know not how thy joy we ever should come near.    95

Better than all measures
   Of delightful sound—
Better than all treasures
   That in books are found—
Thy skill to poet were, thou Scorner of the ground!  100

---

5. Short poems in *praise of love or wine*, called Anacreontics, were an established tradition descending from the Greek poet Anacreon (ca. 563–478 B.C.).
6. Wedding song; Hymen was the Greek god of marriage.
7. Shelley echoes *Hamlet*, IV.iv.33–39, where Hamlet distinguishes between human beings' "god-like reason" and mere animal life.

Teach me half the gladness
　　That thy brain must know,
Such harmonious madness
　　From my lips would flow,
The world should listen then—as I am listening now.[8]　　105

# Ode to Liberty[1]

Yet, Freedom, yet thy banner torn but flying,
Streams like a thunder-storm against the wind.[2]

BYRON

## I.

A glorious people vibrated again
　　The lightning of the nations:[3] Liberty
From heart to heart, from tower to tower, o'er Spain,
　　Scattering contagious fire into the sky,
Gleamed. My soul spurned the chains of its dismay,　　5
　　And in the rapid plumes of song
　　Clothed itself, sublime and strong;
As a young eagle soars the morning clouds among,
　　Hovering in verse o'er its accustomed prey;
　　Till from its station in the heaven of fame　　10
The Spirit's whirlwind rapt it, and the ray
Of the remotest sphere of living flame
Which paves the void was from behind it flung,
　　As foam from a ship's swiftness, when there came
A voice out of the deep: I will record the same.　　15

## II.

The Sun and the serenest Moon sprang forth:
　　The burning stars of the abyss were hurled

---

8. Shelley's estimate of the effects of poetic joy in lines 101–05 contrasts with the isolation that Coleridge sees as its result in "Kubla Khan," lines 42–54. See also *Julian and Maddalo*, lines 544–46.

1. This ode was written between March and July 1820—perhaps in May, as Carlene Adamson suggests (*BSM*, V, xxxix)—in celebration of the Spanish liberal revolution of that spring. Published later that year with *Prometheus Unbound*, it traces the progress of liberty as Thomas Gray had earlier traced the "Progress of Poesy." Except for the first and last stanzas, which frame the poem, the poet addresses the personified goddess of Liberty directly as "thou" in the form of a prayer.
　　Shelley's draft is in Bodleian MS Shelley adds. e.6, pp. 147–42, 135–118, 108–106, 103–98—all with the notebook reversed (*BSM*, V). His translation into Italian of stanzas I–XIII and XIX is in Bodleian MS Shelley adds. e.4, fols. 84–91 (*BSM*, III). Mary Shelley transcribed lines 1–21 in the larger Harvard Shelley Notebook (MS 258.2), p. 87 (*MYR: Shelley*, V).
2. Byron's *Childe Harold's Pilgrimage*, IV.xcviii.1–2; the lines begin the last of twenty-one stanzas in which Byron traces the struggle between tyranny and liberty.
3. The Spanish people's spontaneous resistance to the French in 1807–08 had inspired the British to engage in the Peninsular Campaign in Portugal and Spain, the prelude to the downfall of Napoleon's empire.

Into the depths of heaven. The dædal[4] earth,
  That island in the ocean of the world,
Hung in its cloud of all-sustaining air:                    20
    But this divinest universe
    Was yet a chaos and a curse,
For thou wert not: but power from worst producing worse,
  The spirit of the beasts was kindled there,
    And of the birds, and of the watery forms,      25
  And there was war among them, and despair
    Within them, raging without truce or terms:
The bosom of their violated nurse
  Groan'd, for beasts warr'd on beasts, and worms on worms,
And men on men; each heart was as a hell of storms.      30

### III.

Man, the imperial shape, then multiplied
  His generations under the pavilion
Of the Sun's throne: palace and pyramid,
  Temple and prison, to many a swarming million
Were, as to mountain-wolves their ragged caves.      35
    This human living multitude
    Was savage, cunning, blind, and rude,
For thou wert not; but o'er the populous solitude,
  Like one fierce cloud over a waste of waves
    Hung tyranny; beneath, sate deified      40
The sister-pest,[5] congregator of slaves;
    Into the shadow of her pinions[6] wide
Anarchs[7] and priests, who feed on gold and blood
  Till with the stain their inmost souls are dyed,
Drove the astonished herds of men from every side.      45

### IV.

The nodding promontories, and blue isles,
  And cloud-like mountains, and dividuous[8] waves
Of Greece, basked glorious in the open smiles
  Of favouring heaven: from their enchanted caves
Prophetic echoes flung dim melody      50
    On the unapprehensive wild.
    The vine, the corn, the olive mild,
Grew savage yet, to human use unreconciled;
  And, like unfolded flowers beneath the sea,
    Like the man's thought dark in the infant's brain,      55
  Like aught that is which wraps what is to be,
    Art's deathless dreams lay veiled by many a vein

---

4. Intricately wrought (from Daedalus, the Greek craftsman).
5. Fideistic religion, exaggerating the importance of blind faith and subservience to priests.
6. Wings.
7. Tyrants.
8. Separate, individual.

Of Parian stone;[9] and, yet a speechless child,
  Verse murmured, and Philosophy did strain
  Her lidless eyes for thee; when o'er the Ægean main     60

### V.

Athens arose: a city such as vision
  Builds from the purple crags and silver towers
Of battlemented cloud, as in derision
  Of kingliest masonry: the ocean-floors
Pave it; the evening sky pavilions it;     65
     Its portals are inhabited
     By thunder-zoned winds, each head
Within its cloudy wings with sunfire garlanded,—
  A divine work! Athens diviner yet
    Gleamed with its crest of columns, on the will     70
  Of man, as on a mount of diamond, set;
     For thou[1] wert, and thine all-creative skill
Peopled with forms that mock the eternal dead
  In marble immortality that hill[2]
  Which was thine earliest throne and latest oracle.     75

### VI.

Within the surface of Time's fleeting river
  Its[3] wrinkled image lies, as then it lay
Immovably unquiet, and for ever
  It trembles, but it cannot pass away!
The voices of its bards and sages thunder     80
     With an earth-awakening blast
     Through the caverns of the past;
Religion veils her eyes; Oppression shrinks aghast:
  A winged sound of joy, and love, and wonder,
    Which soars where Expectation never flew,     85
  Rending the veil of space and time asunder!
     One ocean feeds the clouds, and streams, and dew;
  One sun illumines heaven; one spirit vast
    With life and love makes chaos ever new,
    As Athens doth the world with thy delight renew.     90

### VII.

Then Rome was, and from thy deep bosom fairest,
  Like a wolf-cub from a Cadmæan Mænad,[4]
She drew the milk of greatness, though thy dearest

9. Fine white marble from the island of Paros (one of the Cyclades), used by classical sculptors.
1. The poet addresses the spirit of Liberty as the creator of Athens, seen as a permanent ideal
  of human civilization.
2. The Acropolis.
3. Athens'.
4. In Euripides' play *The Bacchae*, the maenads, who are worshipers of Dionysus, are led by
  Cadmus' daughter Agave. (See *Prometheus Unbound*, IV.473–75.)

From that Elysian food was yet unweaned;[5]
And many a deed of terrible uprightness                              95
    By thy sweet love was sanctified;
    And in thy smile, and by thy side,
Saintly Camillus lived, and firm Atilius died.[6]
    But when tears stained thy robe of vestal whiteness,
      And gold prophaned thy Capitolian throne,[7]          100
    Thou didst desert, with spirit-winged lightness,
      The senate of the tyrants: they sunk prone
Slaves of one tyrant: Palatinus sighed
    Faint echoes of Ionian song; that tone
    Thou didst delay to hear, lamenting to disown.                105


## VIII.

From what Hyrcanian[8] glen or frozen hill,
    Or piny promontory of the Arctic main,
Or utmost islet inaccessible,
    Didst thou lament the ruin of thy reign,
Teaching the woods and waves, and desert[9] rocks,                  110
      And every Naiad's[1] ice-cold urn,
      To talk in echoes sad and stern
Of that sublimest lore which man had dared unlearn?
    For neither didst thou watch the wizard flocks
      Of the Scald's dreams, nor haunt the Druid's sleep.[2]    115
    What if the tears rained through thy scattered locks
      Were quickly dried? for thou didst groan, not weep,
When from its sea of death, to kill and burn,
    The Galilean serpent[3] forth did creep,
    And made thy world an undistinguishable heap.                120


## IX.

A thousand years the Earth cried, Where art thou?
    And then the shadow of thy coming fell
On Saxon Alfred's olive-cinctured brow:[4]

---

5. *thy dearest . . . yet unweaned:* Athens was still nourished by Liberty from which Rome now also drew inspiration. Shelley's metaphor draws upon the story of Romulus and Remus, the legendary founders of Rome, who were suckled by a wolf.
6. Camillus, the Roman general, rejected the proposal by a traitorous teacher that Camillus secure the surrender of Falerii by using the teacher's pupils—the sons of that city's leading men—as hostages (Livy, 5.27). According to Roman legend, Atilius Regulus (third century B.C.) urged Rome to continue the war with Carthage even though failure of the peace mission meant his own cruel death. Cf. *A Defence of Poetry*, paragraph 21 and note 5.
7. The Capitoline and Palatine line (line 103), two of Rome's seven hills, represent republican Rome and imperial Rome, respectively.
8. Hyrcania was a province of Persia near the Caspian (Hyrcanian) Sea.
9. I.e., deserted.
1. Nymphs of fountains and streams, who poured out waters from urns.
2. Scalds (skalds) were Norwegian and Icelandic poets from the Viking period to about A.D. 1250; *Druids:* Celtic priests.
3. The Christian religion.
4. Alfred the Great (870–901), the West Saxon king and scholar who made peace with the raiding Danes, united the English people and encouraged the intellectual growth of his nation. He is depicted as crowned with olive leaves, traditionally the highest tribute that could be paid to the honorable and brave.

And many a warrior-peopled citadel,
Like rocks which fire lifts out of the flat deep,                    125
    Arose in sacred Italy,
    Frowning o'er the tempestuous sea
Of kings, and priests, and slaves, in tower-crowned majesty;
    That multitudinous anarchy did sweep
        And burst around their walls, like idle foam,                    130
    Whilst from the human spirit's deepest deep
        Strange melody with love and awe struck dumb
Dissonant arms; and Art, which cannot die,
    With divine wand traced on our earthly home
    Fit imagery to pave heaven's everlasting dome.⁵                    135

### X.

Thou huntress swifter than the Moon!⁶ thou terror
    Of the world's wolves! thou bearer of the quiver,
Whose sunlike shafts pierce tempest-winged Error,
    As light may pierce the clouds when they dissever
In the calm regions of the orient day!                    140
        Luther⁷ caught thy wakening glance,
        Like lightning, from his leaden lance
Reflected, it dissolved the visions of the trance
    In which, as in a tomb, the nations lay;
        And England's prophets hailed thee as their queen,⁸                    145
    In songs whose music cannot pass away,
        Though it must flow for ever: not unseen
Before the spirit-sighted countenance
    Of Milton didst thou pass, from the sad scene
    Beyond whose night he saw, with a dejected mien.                    150

### XI.

The eager hours and unreluctant years
    As on a dawn-illumined mountain stood,
Trampling to silence their loud hopes and fears,
    Darkening each other with their multitude,
And cried aloud, Liberty! Indignation                    155
        Answered Pity from her cave;
        Death grew pale within the grave,
And Desolation howled to the destroyer,⁹ Save!
    When like heaven's sun girt by the exhalation
        Of its own glorious light, thou didst arise,                    160
    Chasing thy foes from nation unto nation
        Like shadows: as if day had cloven the skies

---

5. The rise of the communes, independent city-state republics in medieval Italy, led to a revival of the arts.
6. The moon as the goddess Diana, the virgin huntress.
7. Cf. *A Defence of Poetry*, pp. 527–28.
8. Cf. the end of Shelley's pamphlet "An Address to the People on the Death of Princess Charlotte," where he imagines the possibility of Liberty arising from the grave and deems that it should be worshiped "as our Queen."
9. Death (line 157).

At dreaming midnight o'er the western wave,
   Men started, staggering with a glad surprise,
   Under the lightnings of thine unfamiliar eyes.[1]    165


## XII.

Thou heaven of earth! what spells could pall thee then
   In ominous eclipse? a thousand years
Bred from the slime of deep oppression's den,
   Dyed all thy liquid light with blood and tears,
Till thy sweet stars could weep the stain away;    170
      How like Bacchanals of blood
      Round France, the ghastly vintage, stood
Destruction's sceptred slaves, and Folly's mitred brood![2]
   When one, like them, but mightier far than they,
     The Anarch[3] of thine own bewildered powers,    175
   Rose: armies mingled in obscure array,
     Like clouds with clouds, darkening the sacred bowers
Of serene heaven. He, by the past pursued,
   Rests with those dead, but unforgotten hours,
   Whose ghosts scare victor kings in their ancestral towers.   180


## XIII.

England yet sleeps: was she not called of old?
   Spain calls her now, as with its thrilling thunder
Vesuvius wakens Ætna,[4] and the cold
   Snow-crags by its reply are cloven in sunder:[5]
O'er the lit waves every Æolian isle    185
      From Pithecusa to Pelorus[6]
      Howls, and leaps, and glares in chorus:
They cry, Be dim; ye lamps of heaven suspended o'er us.
   Her[7] chains are threads of gold, she need but smile
     And they dissolve; but Spain's were links of steel,    190
   Till bit to dust by virtue's keenest file.
     Twins of a single destiny! appeal
To the eternal years enthroned before us
   In the dim West; impress as from a seal
   All ye have thought and done! Time cannot dare conceal.   195

---

1. Lines 159–65 depict the Enlightenment and subsequent reform and revolutionary movements of the eighteenth century.
2. The kings, aristocrats, and bishops during the French Revolution.
3. Napoleon.
4. Volcanoes near Naples and in eastern Sicily, respectively. See G. M. Matthews's essay on "A Volcano's Voice in Shelley" in this volume (pp. 550–68).
5. Split apart.
6. *Aeolian isles:* islands north of eastern Sicily, including Stromboli; *Pithecusa:* island of Ischia, west of Naples and Cumae; *Pelorus:* Cape Faro, the northeast point of Sicily. Lines 183–88 refer to the 1820 constitutional revolution in the Kingdom of the Two Sicilies, which included also Naples and the lower half of Italy.
7. England's.

## XIV.

Tomb of Arminius![8] render up thy dead
  Till, like a standard from a watch-tower's staff,
His soul may stream over the tyrant's head;
  Thy victory shall be his epitaph,
Wild Bacchanal[9] of truth's mysterious wine,        200
    King-deluded Germany,
      His dead spirit lives in thee.
Why do we fear or hope? thou art already free!
  And thou,[1] lost Paradise of this divine
    And glorious world! thou flowery wilderness!    205
Thou island of eternity! thou shrine
    Where desolation, clothed with loveliness,
Worships the thing thou wert! O Italy,
  Gather thy blood into thy heart; repress
  The beasts who make their dens thy sacred palaces.    210

## XV.

O, that the free would stamp the impious name
  Of KING into the dust! or write it there,
So that this blot upon the page of fame
  Were as a serpent's path, which the light air
Erases, and the flat sands close behind!    215
      Ye[2] the oracle have heard:
    Lift the victory-flashing sword,
And cut the snaky knots of this foul gordian word,[3]
  Which weak itself as stubble, yet can bind
    Into a mass, irrefragably[4] firm,    220
  The axes and the rods which awe mankind;[5]
    The sound has poison in it, 'tis the sperm
Of what makes life foul, cankerous, and abhorred;
  Disdain not thou,[6] at thine appointed term,
  To set thine armed heel on this reluctant worm.    225

## XVI.

O, that the wise from their bright minds would kindle
  Such lamps within the dome of this dim world,
That the pale name of PRIEST might shrink and dwindle
  Into the hell from which it first was hurled,

8. Germanic tribal leader (18 B.C.–A.D. 19), who annihilated a Roman army (A.D. 9) and freed the German tribes from foreign oppression.
9. An occasion of drunken revelry.
1. Italy.
2. The free (line 211).
3. "King" (line 212).
4. Indisputably.
5. The "facses"—axes bound in bundles of rods—were the symbols of authority in ancient Rome (and later in fascist Italy).
6. Liberty.

A scoff of impious pride from fiends impure;                     230
　　Till human thoughts might kneel alone,
　　Each before the judgment-throne
Of its own aweless soul, or of the power[7] unknown!
　　O, that the words which make the thoughts obscure
　　　From which they spring, as clouds of glimmering dew     235
　　From a white lake blot heaven's blue portraiture,
　　　Were stript of their thin masks and various hue
And frowns and smiles and splendours not their own,
　　Till in the nakedness of false and true
　　They stand before their Lord,[8] each to receive its due!     240

### XVII.

He[9] who taught man to vanquish whatsoever
　　Can be between the cradle and the grave
Crowned him the King of Life. Oh, vain endeavour!
　　If on his own high will, a willing slave,
He has enthroned the oppression and the oppressor.              245
　　　What if earth can clothe and feed
　　　Amplest millions at their need,[1]
And power in thought be as the tree within the seed?
　　　Or what if Art, an ardent intercessor,
　　　　Diving on fiery wings to Nature's throne,                 250
　　Checks the great mother stooping to caress her,
　　　And cries: Give me, thy child, dominion
Over all height and depth?[2] if Life can breed
　　New wants, and wealth from those who toil and groan
　　Rend of thy gifts and hers[3] a thousandfold for one!         255

### XVIII.

Come Thou, but lead out of the inmost cave
　　Of man's deep spirit, as the morning-star
Beckons the Sun from the Eoan[4] wave,
　　Wisdom. I hear the pennons of her car
Self-moving, like cloud charioted by flame;                      260
　　　Comes she not, and come ye not,
　　　Rulers of eternal thought,
To judge, with solemn truth, life's ill-apportioned lot?
　　Blind Love, and equal Justice, and the Fame
　　　Of what has been, the Hope of what will be?                 265
　　O, Liberty! if such could be thy name
　　　Wert thou disjoined from these, or they from thee:
If thine or theirs were treasures to be bought

---

7. As in "Mont Blanc," *power* refers to the ultimate Cause or the Deity.
8. Either *aweless soul* or *power unknown* (line 233); Shelley may be purposely (skeptically) ambiguous here.
9. Lord (line 240).
1. Shelley here attacks Malthusian pessimism.
2. In lines 249–53, Art intercedes between Nature (*the great mother*) and human beings.
3. *thy:* Liberty's; *hers:* Art's.
4. Eastern; Eos was the Greek name of Aurora, goddess of the dawn.

By blood or tears, have not the wise and free
Wept tears, and blood like tears?—The solemn harmony    270

### XIX.

Paused, and the spirit of that mighty singing
    To its abyss was suddenly withdrawn;
Then, as a wild swan, when sublimely winging
    Its path athwart the thunder-smoke of dawn,
Sinks headlong through the aerial golden light    275
        On the heavy-sounding plain,
        When the bolt has pierced its brain;
    As summer clouds dissolve, unburthened of their rain;
        As a far taper fades with fading night,[5]
        As a brief insect dies with dying day,—    280
    My song, its pinions disarrayed of might,
        Drooped; o'er it closed the echoes far away
Of the great voice which did its flight sustain,
    As waves which lately paved his watery way
Hiss round a drowner's head in their tempestuous play.    285

## THE MASK OF ANARCHY

On August 16, 1819, in St. Peter's Field, Manchester, a riot occurred when a group of drunken mounted militiamen and cavalrymen misinterpreted their orders and charged into a peaceful crowd of men, women, and children who were attending a rally in support of Parliamentary reform. At least six persons were killed and more than eighty wounded. (Some authorities give figures as high as eleven killed and five hundred injured.) Shelley, isolated in Italy, first learned of the so-called Peterloo Massacre (a name alluding to the Tories' great pride in the victory at Waterloo) in a letter from Thomas Love Peacock that reached him on September 5. Writing to Charles Ollier, his publisher, Shelley said that the "torrent of my indignation has not yet done boiling in my veins." He drafted *The Mask of Anarchy* and reworked it into an intermediate fair copy, and Mary Shelley recopied it for the press and mailed it to Leigh Hunt to publish in the *Examiner* on September 23, 1819. Hunt—fearful of prosecution because of the volatile temper of the country and the new repressive legislation passed late in 1819 and 1820—refrained from publishing the poem until 1832, after the Reform Bill had won the battle for which Shelley had intended his poem as a kind of rallying hymn.

The tetrameter couplets and triplets, set in stanzas of four and five lines, embody Shelley's characteristic symbols and imagery, but this poem is intended to produce more immediate effects upon a less educated audience than the one for which Shelley usually wrote. It apparently was one of a group of poems that Shelley later hoped to publish in what he described to Hunt as "a little volume of *popular songs* wholly political, & destined to awaken & direct the imagination of the reformers" (*Letters*, II, 191). For a good discussion of the poem's cultural contexts and significance, see

---

5. Compare this simile with "Hymn to Intellectual Beauty," lines 44–45: "Thou—that to human thought art nourishment, / Like darkness to a dying flame!"

Steven E. Jones, *Shelley's Satire* (1994), 95–123; within this volume, see
the essays by Donald H. Reiman (pp. 589–99) and Susan J. Wolfson
(pp. 722–35).

The two authoritative manuscripts, Shelley's intermediate holograph and
Mary Shelley's fair copy with Shelley's corrections, are in the Ashley Collection of the British Library (Ashley MS 4086) and in the Manuscript Division
of the Library of Congress (MMC 1399), respectively; both appear in photofacsimile in *MYR: Shelley*, II. Shelley's draft can be found in the
Huntington Library, HM 2177, fols. 6(c)v, 7r–16r, 17r–24r, *21r (*MYR:
Shelley*, IV); and the Bodleian Library, Bodleian MS Shelley adds. e. 12,
p. 205 (*BSM*, V). Our text is based on the press transcript (which Shelley reviewed), with some corrections from Shelley's intermediate holograph.

# The Mask of Anarchy

### *Written on the Occasion of the Massacre at Manchester*

As I lay asleep in Italy
There came a voice from over the Sea,
And with great power it forth led me
To walk in the visions of Poesy.

I met Murder on the way—                          5
He had a mask like Castlereagh[1]—
Very smooth he looked, yet grim;
Seven bloodhounds[2] followed him:

All were fat; and well they might
Be in admirable plight,                           10
For one by one, and two by two,
He tossed them human hearts to chew
Which from his wide cloak he drew.

Next came Fraud, and he had on,
Like Eldon,[3] an ermined gown;                   15
His big tears, for he wept well,
Turned to mill-stones as they fell.

And the little children, who
Round his feet played to and fro,
Thinking every tear a gem,                        20
Had their brains knocked out by them.

1. Robert Stewart, Viscount Castlereagh, at this time Foreign Secretary and leader of the Tories
   in the House of Commons, had earlier been infamous for his bloody suppression of unrest
   in Ireland; now Shelley (and Byron) blamed him for supporting Austria and the reactionary
   Holy Alliance in Europe.
2. In 1815, Britain joined seven other nations (Austria, France, Russia, Prussia, Portugal, Spain,
   and Sweden) in agreeing to postpone final abolition of the slave trade; the pro-war advocates
   in Pitt's administration had been popularly known as the "bloodhounds" (cf. "hawks").
3. John Scott, Baron Eldon, was the Lord Chancellor (hence the *ermined gown*); his decision
   in court had denied Shelley custody of his children by Harriet. He was notorious for weeping
   in public.

Clothed with the Bible, as with light,[4]
And the shadows of the night,
Like Sidmouth,[5] next, Hypocrisy
On a crocodile[6] rode by.                                          25

And many more Destructions played
In this ghastly masquerade,
All disguised, even to the eyes,
Like Bishops, lawyers, peers or spies.

Last came Anarchy:[7] he rode                                      30
On a white horse, splashed with blood;
He was pale even to the lips,
Like Death in the Apocalypse.

And he wore a kingly crown,
And in his grasp a sceptre shone;                                  35
On his brow this mark I saw—
"I AM GOD, AND KING, AND LAW!"

With a pace stately and fast,
Over English land he past,
Trampling to a mire of blood                                       40
The adoring multitude.[8]

And a mighty troop around,
With their trampling shook the ground,
Waving each a bloody sword,
For the service of their Lord.                                     45

And with glorious triumph, they
Rode through England proud and gay,
Drunk as with intoxication
Of the wine of desolation.

O'er fields and towns, from sea to sea,                            50
Passed the Pageant swift and free,

---

4. Shelley had marked an "x" in his manuscript, as if to indicate the reference to a footnote (which remained unwritten).
5. Henry Addington, Viscount Sidmouth, was as Home Secretary responsible for internal security. He hired spies and agents who first provoked discontented workingmen to illegal acts and then betrayed them to be hanged or deported. In 1818 he persuaded Parliament to vote a million pounds for new churches to help pacify the half-starved workers in the new industrial towns.
6. The crocodile, which according to legend wept in order to attract or while devouring its prey, was a symbol of hypocrisy.
7. Shelley's personification of Anarchy, besides drawing on Revelation 6:8, alludes to Benjamin West's celebrated painting of *Death on the Pale Horse*, in which Death is portrayed as wearing a crown and, with sword-bearing followers, is trampling a crowd. In using the name Anarchy for the supreme personification of evil, Shelley was following Milton and Pope, who termed Chaos "Anarch" (*Paradise Lost*, II.988; *Dunciad*, IV.655).
8. Another of Shelley's allusions to the Hindu procession of the Juggernaut. See note to *Queen Mab*, VII.36.

Tearing up, and trampling down;
Till they came to London town.

And each dweller, panic-stricken,
Felt his heart with terror sicken          55
Hearing the tempestuous cry
Of the triumph of Anarchy.

For with pomp to meet him came
Clothed in arms like blood and flame,[9]
The hired Murderers, who did sing          60
"Thou art God, and Law, and King.

"We have waited, weak and lone
For thy coming, Mighty One!
Our purses are empty, our swords are cold,
Give us glory, and blood, and gold."          65

Lawyers and priests, a motley crowd,
To the earth their pale brows bowed;
Like a bad prayer not over loud,
Whispering—"Thou art Law and God."—

Then all cried with one accord;          70
"Thou art King, and God, and Lord;
Anarchy, to Thee we bow,
Be thy name made holy now!"

And Anarchy, the Skeleton,
Bowed and grinned to every one,          75
As well as if his education
Had cost ten millions to the Nation.[1]

For he knew the Palaces
Of our Kings were rightly his;
His the sceptre, crown, and globe,[2]          80
And the gold-inwoven robe.

So he sent his slaves before
To seize upon the Bank and Tower,[3]
And was proceeding with intent
To meet his pensioned[4] Parliament          85

9. I.e., the red coats of the British soldiers.
1. Alluding to the millions of pounds voted for the Prince Regent's debts run up during his youthful dissipations.
2. The golden ball or orb borne along with the scepter as a sign of sovereignty.
3. *Bank:* The Bank of England, which manages the government's money; *Tower:* The Tower of London, where the crown jewels are kept.
4. Pensions were government annuities given for services rendered, not as retirement money; the word implies that Parliament was open to bribery.

When one fled past, a maniac maid,
And her name was Hope, she said:
But she looked more like Despair,
And she cried out in the air:

"My father Time is weak and grey                    90
With waiting for a better day;
See how idiot-like he stands,
Fumbling with his palsied hands!

"He has had child after child
And the dust of death is piled                    95
Over every one but me—
Misery, oh, Misery!"

Then she lay down in the street,
Right before the horses' feet,
Expecting, with a patient eye,                    100
Murder, Fraud and Anarchy.

When between her and her foes
A mist, a light, an image rose,
Small at first, and weak, and frail
Like the vapour of a vale:                    105

Till as clouds grow on the blast,
Like tower-crowned giants striding fast
And glare with lightnings as they fly,
And speak in thunder to the sky,

It grew—a Shape arrayed in mail                    110
Brighter than the Viper's scale,
And upborne on wings whose grain
Was as the light of sunny rain.

On its helm, seen far away,
A planet, like the Morning's,[5] lay;                    115
And those plumes its light rained through
Like a shower of crimson dew.

With step as soft as wind it past
O'er the heads of men—so fast
That they knew the presence there,                    120
And looked,—but all was empty air.

As flowers beneath May's footstep waken
As stars from Night's loose hair are shaken
As waves arise when loud winds call
Thoughts sprung where'er that step did fall.                    125

5. Venus as the morning star.

And the prostrate multitude
Looked—and ankle-deep in blood,
Hope that maiden most serene
Was walking with a quiet mien:

And Anarchy, the ghastly birth,          130
Lay dead earth upon the earth—
The Horse of Death tameless as wind
Fled, and with his hoofs did grind
To dust, the murderers thronged behind.

A rushing light of clouds and splendour,    135
A sense awakening and yet tender
Was heard and felt—and at its close
These words of joy and fear arose

As if their own indignant Earth
Which gave the sons of England birth     140
Had felt their blood upon her brow,
And shuddering with a mother's throe

Had turned every drop of blood
By which her face had been bedewed
To an accent unwithstood,—       145
As if her heart had cried aloud:

"Men of England, heirs of Glory,
Heroes of unwritten story,
Nurslings of one mighty Mother,
Hopes of her, and one another;      150

"Rise like Lions after slumber
In unvanquishable number
Shake your chains to Earth like dew
Which in sleep had fallen on you—
Ye are many—they are few.      155

"What is Freedom?—ye can tell
That which slavery is, too well—
For its very name has grown
To an echo of your own.

" 'Tis to work and have such pay      160
As just keeps life from day to day
In your limbs, as in a cell
For the tyrants' use to dwell

"So that ye for them are made
Loom, and plough, and sword, and spade,     165

With or without your own will bent
To their defence and nourishment.

" 'Tis to see your children weak
With their mothers pine and peak,[6]
When the winter winds are bleak,—                    170
They are dying whilst I speak.

" 'Tis to hunger for such diet
As the rich man in his riot
Casts to the fat dogs that lie
Surfeiting beneath his eye;                           175

" 'Tis to let the Ghost of Gold[7]
Take from Toil a thousand fold
More than e'er its substance could
In the tyrannies of old.

"Paper coin—that forgery                              180
Of the title deeds, which ye
Hold to something of the worth
Of the inheritance of Earth.

" 'Tis to be a slave in soul
And to hold no strong controul                        185
Over your own wills, but be
All that others make of ye.

"And at length when ye complain
With a murmur weak and vain
'Tis to see the Tyrant's crew                         190
Ride over your wives and you—
Blood is on the grass like dew.

"Then it is to feel revenge
Fiercely thirsting to exchange
Blood for blood—and wrong for wrong—                  195
Do not thus when ye are strong.

"Birds find rest, in narrow nest
When weary of their winged quest;
Beasts find fare, in woody lair
When storm and snow are in the air.                   200

"Asses, swine, have litter spread
And with fitting food are fed;

6. Waste away in health and spirits.
7. Paper money, which Shelley considered a trick to inflate currency, thereby depressing the
   relative cost of labor.

All things have a home but one—
Thou, Oh, Englishman, hast none![8]

"This is Slavery—savage men,                   205
Or wild beasts within a den
Would endure not as ye do—
But such ills they never knew.

"What art thou Freedom? O! could slaves
Answer from their living graves                 210
This demand—tyrants would flee
Like a dream's dim imagery:

"Thou art not, as impostors say,
A shadow soon to pass away,
A superstition, and a name                   215
Echoing from the cave of Fame.[9]

"For the labourer thou art bread,
And a comely table spread
From his daily labour come
In a neat and happy[1] home.                   220

"Thou art clothes, and fire, and food
For the trampled multitude—
No—in countries that are free
Such starvation cannot be
As in England now we see.                   225

"To the rich thou art a check,
When his foot is on the neck
Of his victim, thou dost make
That he treads upon a snake.[2]

"Thou art Justice—ne'er for gold          230
May thy righteous laws be sold
As laws are in England—thou
Shield'st alike the high and low.

"Thou art Wisdom—Freemen never
Dream that God will damn for ever       235
All who think those things untrue
Of which Priests make such ado.

---

8. Shelley alludes ironically to a saying of Jesus: "The foxes have holes, and the birds of the air have nests; but the Son of man hath not where to lay his head" (Matthew 8:20; Luke 9:58).
9. Common talk or rumor.
1. Free from want; fortunate (rather than joyful).
2. This image had been used by the American Revolutionists in their "Don't Tread on Me" flag picturing a coiled snake. Shelley—and/or the English radicals who used the image earlier— may have adopted it from the Americans.

"Thou art Peace—never by thee
Would blood and treasure wasted be
As tyrants wasted them, when all                    240
Leagued to quench thy flame in Gaul.[3]

"What if English toil and blood
Was poured forth, even as a flood?
It availed, Oh, Liberty!
To dim, but not extinguish thee.                    245

"Thou art Love—the rich[4] have kist
Thy feet, and like him following Christ,
Give their substance to the free
And through the rough world follow thee

"Or turn their wealth to arms, and make            250
War for thy beloved sake
On wealth, and war, and fraud—whence they
Drew the power which is their prey.

"Science, Poetry and Thought
Are thy lamps; they make the lot                    255
Of the dwellers in a cot[5]
So serene, they curse it not.

"Spirit, Patience, Gentleness,
All that can adorn and bless
Art thou—let deeds not words express              260
Thine exceeding loveliness.

"Let a great Assembly be
Of the fearless and the free
On some spot of English ground
Where the plains stretch wide around.              265

"Let the blue sky overhead,
The green earth on which ye tread,
All that must eternal be
Witness the solemnity.

"From the corners uttermost                         270
Of the bounds of English coast,
From every hut, village and town
Where those who live and suffer moan
For others' misery or their own,

"From the workhouse and the prison                 275
Where pale as corpses newly risen,

3. France, during the Revolution.
4. Shelley obviously includes himself in this group dedicated to Liberty through Love.
5. Cottage.

Women, children, young and old
Groan for pain, and weep for cold—

"From the haunts of daily life
Where is waged the daily strife          280
With common wants and common cares
Which sows the human heart with tares⁶—

"Lastly from the palaces
Where the murmur of distress
Echoes, like the distant sound          285
Of a wind alive around

"Those prison halls of wealth and fashion
Where some few feel such compassion
For those who groan, and toil, and wail
As must make their brethren pale—          290

"Ye who suffer woes untold,
Or to feel, or to behold
Your lost country bought and sold
With a price of blood and gold—

"Let a vast assembly be,          295
And with great solemnity
Declare with measured words that ye
Are, as God has made ye, free—

"Be your strong and simple words
Keen to wound as sharpened swords,          300
And wide as targes⁷ let them be
With their shade to cover ye.

"Let the tyrants pour around
With a quick and startling sound,
Like the loosening of a sea          305
Troops of armed emblazonry.

"Let the charged artillery drive
Till the dead air seems alive
With the clash of clanging wheels,
And the tramp of horses' heels.          310

"Let the fixed bayonet
Gleam with sharp desire to wet
Its bright point in English blood
Looking keen as one for food.

6. Deleterious weeds; see Matthew 13:24ff. for the parable of the wheat and the tares.
7. Large lightweight shields or bucklers.

"Let the horsemen's scimitars                                    315
Wheel and flash, like sphereless stars
Thirsting to eclipse their burning
In a sea of death and mourning.

"Stand ye calm and resolute,
Like a forest close and mute,                                    320
With folded arms and looks which are
Weapons of unvanquished war,

"And let Panic, who outspeeds
The career of armed steeds
Pass, a disregarded shade                                        325
Through your phalanx undismayed.

"Let the Laws of your own land,
Good or ill, between ye stand
Hand to hand, and foot to foot,
Arbiters of the dispute,                                         330

"The old laws of England—they
Whose reverend heads with age are grey,
Children of a wiser day;
And whose solemn voice must be
Thine own echo—Liberty!                                          335

"On those who first should violate
Such sacred heralds in their state
Rest the blood that must ensue,
And it will not rest on you.

"And if then the tyrants dare                                    340
Let them ride among you there,
Slash, and stab, and maim, and hew,—
What they like, that let them do.

"With folded arms and steady eyes,
And little fear, and less surprise                               345
Look upon them as they slay
Till their rage has died away.

"Then they will return with shame
To the place from which they came
And the blood thus shed will speak                               350
In hot blushes on their cheek.

"Every woman in the land
Will point at them as they stand—
They will hardly dare to greet
Their acquaintance in the street.                                355

"And the bold, true warriors
Who have hugged Danger in wars
Will turn to those who would be free,
Ashamed of such base company.


"And that slaughter to the Nation                    360
Shall steam up like inspiration,
Eloquent, oracular;
A volcano heard afar.[8]


"And these words shall then become
Like oppression's thundered doom               365
Ringing through each heart and brain,
Heard again—again—again—


"Rise like lions after slumber
In unvanquishable number—
Shake your chains to earth like dew             370
Which in sleep had fallen on you—
Ye are many—they are few."

THE END.


# England in 1819[1]

An old, mad, blind, despised and dying King;[2]
Princes, the dregs of their dull race, who flow
Through public scorn,—mud from a muddy spring;[3]
Rulers who neither see nor feel nor know,
But leechlike to their fainting country cling          5
Till they drop, blind in blood, without a blow.
A people starved and stabbed in th'untilled field;[4]
An army, whom liberticide[5] and prey
Makes as a two-edged sword to all who wield;

---

8. For Shelley's general use of volcanic imagery, see G. M. Matthews's "A Volcano's Voice in Shelley," in this volume (pp. 550–68).
1. Shelley sent this sonnet to Leigh Hunt from Florence on December 23, 1819 (*Letters*, II, 167). An early partial draft appears in Bodleian Shelley MS adds. e.12, p. 178, preceding a fair copy in Shelley's hand on p. 182 (*BSM*, XVIII). Our text is based on the fair copy. Shelley did not provide a title for the poem in either the drafts or the fair copy, although heavy blotting obscures what is probably the start of a title in the latter. Mary Shelley—who transcribed the poem in Bodleian Shelley MS adds. d.9, p. 153, under the title "England in 1820"—first published it under the present title in her edition of Shelley's *Poetical Works* (1839). See Susan J. Wolfson's discussion of the poem in this volume (pp. 733–35).
2. King George III, who had reigned since 1760, had been acknowledged violently insane in 1811, when his son was made Prince Regent; he died on January 29, 1820.
3. The sons of George III had among them sired numerous illegitimate children but only two legitimate ones. In addition, they had engaged in such diverse activities as gluttony, gambling, incest with a sister, and selling army commands to those who bribed a favorite mistress.
4. An allusion to the Peterloo Massacre (see "The Mask of Anarchy").
5. The killing of liberty.

Golden and sanguine[6] laws which tempt and slay;                    10
Religion Christless, Godless—a book sealed;
A senate, Time's worst statute, unrepealed[7]—
Are graves from which a glorious Phantom may
Burst, to illumine our tempestuous day.

## Sonnet: To the Republic of Benevento[1]

Nor[2] happiness nor majesty nor fame
Nor peace nor strength nor skill in arms or arts
Shepherd[3] those herds whom Tyranny makes tame;
Verse echoes not one beating of their hearts,
History is but the shadow of their shame—                           5
Art veils her glass, or from the pageant starts
As to Oblivion their blind millions fleet,[4]
Staining that Heaven with obscene imagery
Of their own likeness.[5]—What are numbers knit
By force or custom? Man who man would be,                           10
Must rule the empire of himself; in it
Must be supreme, establishing his throne
On vanquished will,—quelling the anarchy
Of hopes and fears,—being himself alone.—

## Sonnet[1]

Lift not the painted veil[2] which those who live
Call Life; though unreal shapes be pictured there

6. Gold and blood are recurring emblems of the twin roots and forms of tyranny. (See *Queen Mab*, IV.195; "Ode to Liberty," lines 43–44; *The Cenci*, I.i.127; "Written on . . . the Death of Napoleon," line 35; *Hellas*, line 1094; "The Mask of Anarchy," lines 65, 294; "The Triumph of Life," line 287.)
7. Shelley details his objections to Parliament for being unrepresentative of the British people in his *Philosophical View of Reform* (see SC, VI, 997ff.).
1. Better known as "Political Greatness," the title that Mary Shelley gave it when she first published it in *Posthumous Poems* (1824), this sonnet records Shelley's interest in the revival of one of the medieval Italian communes that Sismondi celebrates in his *History of the Italian Republics in the Middle Ages*. (See "Ode to Liberty" and Shelley's first note to *Hellas*, p. 462 below.) After a popular revolt in July 1820 drove Ferdinand, the reactionary Bourbon King of the Two Sicilies, from absolute rule in Naples, the town of Benevento northeast of Naples established a short-lived "republic," until the entire revolutionary movement was crushed by an Austrian army in the spring of 1821. A fair copy of the poem, upon which we base our text, was written on page 152 of the large Silsbee notebook, Harvard MS Eng.258.2 (*MYR: Shelley*, V), between July and September 1820.
2. The first *nor* in a series of this kind means "neither."
3. Though each subject of this verb is technically discrete and singular, grammarians of Shelley's day accepted the practice of using plural verbs in such situations.
4. Speed or hasten.
5. *Staining . . . likeness*: See *Queen Mab*, VI.88–107 and "The Triumph of Life," ll. 288–92.
1. The date Shelley composed this sonnet is uncertain, but probably sometime between fall of 1818 and spring of 1820, to judge from its position in Shelley's notebooks. A draft of the poem appears in Bodleian Shelley MS adds. e.12, 23–22 rev. (*BSM*, XVIII). An intermediate fair copy at the Pierpont Morgan Library, on which our text is based (MA 406, p. 2; *MYR: Shelley*, V), is written on the back of a leaf containing the concluding lines of "Stanzas Written in Dejection." Both poems were torn from the large Silsbee notebook at Harvard. This sonnet was first published in Shelley's *Posthumous Poems* of 1824.
2. Compare and contrast the veil figure in *Prometheus Unbound*, III.iv.190–92.

And it but mimic all we would believe
With colours idly spread,—behind, lurk Fear
And Hope, twin Destinies, who ever weave                5
Their shadows o'er the chasm, sightless[3] and drear.
I knew one who had lifted it . . . . he sought,
For his lost heart was tender, things to love
But found them not, alas; nor was there aught
The world contains, the which he could approve.          10
Through the unheeding many he did move,
A splendour among shadows—a bright blot
Upon this gloomy scene—a Spirit that strove
For truth, and like the Preacher,[4] found it not.—

## Sonnet[1]

Ye hasten to the grave! What seek ye there,
Ye restless thoughts, and busy purposes
Of the idle brain, which the world's livery wear?
O thou quick Heart, which pantest to possess
All that pale Expectation feigneth fair!                 5
Thou vainly curious mind which wouldest guess
Whence thou didst come, and whither thou must go,
And all that never yet was known, would[2] know,
O whither hasten ye, that thus ye press
With such swift feet life's green and pleasant path      10
Seeking alike from happiness and woe
A refuge in the cavern of grey death?
O Heart and Mind and Thoughts what thing do you
Hope to inherit in the grave below?

# LETTER TO MARIA GISBORNE

Shelley's verse letter, addressed to Maria James Reveley Gisborne—and obviously also meant to be read by her husband John and Henry Reveley, her son by her first marriage—was written soon after the Shelleys occupied the Leghorn home of their friends, who were in London attempting to find a suitable professional position for Henry, an aspiring engineer. Shelley mailed the letter to England on either July 1 or July 2, 1820. That copy of the verse letter, transcribed by either Shelley or Mary W. Shelley, may not survive, although Shelley's draft and one transcript by Mary Shelley do. The poem was first published in *Posthumous Poems* (1824), with some

---

3. Lacking anything to see.
4. I.e., the skeptical speaker in Ecclesiastes, who begins by saying "Vanity of vanities . . . all is vanity" (emptiness). In Shelley's rough draft, lines 13 and 14 read: "I should be happier had I ne'er known / This mornful man—he was himself alone."
1. Leigh Hunt first published this sonnet in *The Literary Pocket-Book for 1823* (1822). Mary Shelley reprinted it in *Posthumous Poems* (1824). In her collected edition of Shelley's *Poetical Works* (1839), she placed this sonnet among Shelley's poems of 1820. Our text follows the holograph press-copy manuscript in the Pierpont Morgan Library, MA 3223 (*MYR: Shelley*, VIII).
2. The verb is subjunctive (*thou . . . wouldst* being the correct indicative form).

of the personal references omitted and others disguised. It reached its present length in Harry Buxton Forman's edition of 1876. Our text is based on Forman's, with punctuation generally lightened on the basis of Shelley's draft (Bodleian MS Shelley adds. e.9, 97–111, 115; *BSM*, XIV), and with a few verbal emendations from the draft and from Mary's transcription of it in the Huntington Library (HM 12338; *MYR: Shelley*, III, 91–111), which—though it contains errors—may embody some revisions attributable to Shelley.

The poem has an air of easy, conversational informality, as Shelley describes the objects in Henry Reveley's study, imagines the Gisbornes and Henry in London and mutual friends whom they would be seeing there, and recalls their happy times together in Italy. Also running through it is a strong unifying theme contrasting mechanical and scientific knowledge with the magical powers of the imagination.

# Letter to Maria Gisborne

## *Leghorn, July 1, 1820*

The spider spreads her webs, whether she be
In poet's tower, cellar, or barn, or tree;
The silkworm in the dark green mulberry leaves
His[1] winding sheet and cradle ever weaves;
So I, a thing whom moralists call worm,[2]                           5
Sit spinning still round this decaying form,
From the fine threads of rare and subtle thought—
No net of words in garish colours wrought
To catch the idle buzzers of the day—
But a soft cell, where when that fades away,                         10
Memory may clothe in wings my living name
And feed it with the asphodels[3] of fame,
Which in those hearts which must remember me
Grow, making love an immortality.


Whoever should behold me now, I wist,[4]                             15
Would think I were a mighty mechanist,
Bent with sublime Archimedean[5] art
To breathe a soul into the iron heart
Of some machine portentous, or strange gin,[6]

---

1. Though Shelley's draft reads "Her winding sheet," in revising the simile that identified him with the silkworm (sexless larva of the moth *Bombyx mori*), Shelley changed the pronoun to *His*.
2. Shelley alludes to personal attacks on his morals in reviews of his and Leigh Hunt's poems in the *Quarterly Review* and to personal criticisms of himself with which, as Shelley suspected, William Godwin (bitter because Shelley refused to "lend" him more money) was then filling the Gisbornes' ears.
3. The immortal flowers of the Elysian fields.
4. "I know" or "certainly."
5. Here, mechanical or scientific, from Archimedes (ca. 287–12 B.C.), the Greek mathematician and inventor who lived at Syracuse in Sicily.
6. Engine, mechanical device; Shakespeare and other Renaissance writers used the word *gin* to refer to traps or snares.

Which by the force of figured spells might win                          20
Its way over the sea,[7] and sport therein;
For round the walls are hung dread engines, such
As Vulcan never wrought for Jove to clutch
Ixion or the Titan:[8]—or the quick
Wit of that man of God, St. Dominic,[9]                                 25
To convince Atheist, Turk or Heretic
Or those in philanthropic council[1] met,
Who thought to pay some interest for the debt
They owed to Jesus Christ for their salvation,
By giving a faint foretaste of damnation                                30
To Shakespeare, Sidney, Spenser and the rest
Who made our land an island of the blest,
When lamp-like Spain, who now relumes her fire
On Freedom's hearth, grew dim with Empire:—
With thumbscrews, wheels, with tooth and spike and jag,                 35
Which fishers found under the utmost crag
Of Cornwall and the storm-encompassed isles,[2]
Where to the sky the rude sea rarely smiles
Unless in treacherous wrath, as on the morn
When the exulting elements in scorn                                     40
Satiated with destroyed destruction, lay
Sleeping in beauty on their mangled prey,
As Panthers sleep;—and other strange and dread
Magical forms the brick floor overspread,—
Proteus[3] transformed to metal did not make                           45
More figures, or more strange; nor did he take
Such shapes of unintelligible brass,
Or heap himself in such a horrid mass
Of tin and iron not to be understood,
And forms of unimaginable wood,                                         50
To puzzle Tubal Cain[4] and all his brood:
Great screws, and cones, and wheels, and grooved blocks,
The elements of what will stand the shocks
Of wave and wind and time.—Upon the table
More knacks and quips there be than I am able                          55
To catalogize in this verse of mine:—
A pretty bowl of wood—not full of wine,

7. With Shelley's financial help, Henry Reveley had been building a steamboat to travel between
   Leghorn (Livorno) and Marseilles.
8. Vulcan (Greek Hephaestus) made both an ever-turning wheel on which Ixion was tied in
   Hades and the bands that chained Prometheus to his mountain of torture.
9. The Spanish founder of the Dominican order (lived 1170–1221) took a leading role in the
   bloody suppression of the Albigensian heresy in southern France, an activity that led to the
   Dominicans' control of the Inquisition for centuries thereafter.
1. Syntactically parallel to *Vulcan* and *St. Dominic*, this line alludes to the ecumenical councils
   of the Roman Catholic Church—especially the Council of Trent (1545–63), which initiated
   the Counter-Reformation.
2. The Hebrides, north of Scotland, where many ships from the Spanish Armada, which sailed
   against England in 1588, were wrecked. Some ships contained instruments of torture (line
   35) that the Spanish Inquisition intended to use against English Protestants.
3. A Greek mythological sea-god who could assume numerous different forms.
4. Tubal Cain, the first metalsmith of biblical myth (Genesis 4:22), was the third son of La-
   mech, who was the great-great-great-grandson of Cain, the son of Adam.

But quicksilver; that dew which the gnomes drink
When at their subterranean toil they swink,[5]
Pledging the demons of the earthquake, who                    60
Reply to them in lava—cry halloo!
And call out to the cities o'er their head,—
Roofs, towers, and shrines, the dying and the dead,
Crash through the chinks of earth—and then all quaff
Another rouse,[6] and hold their sides and laugh.             65
This quicksilver no gnome has drunk—within
The walnut bowl it lies, veined and thin,
In colour like the wake of light that stains
The Tuscan deep, when from the moist moon rains
The inmost shower of its white fire—the breeze               70
Is still—blue Heaven smiles over the pale seas.
And in this bowl of quicksilver—for I
Yield to the impulse of an infancy
Outlasting manhood—I have made to float
A rude idealism of a paper boat[7]—                          75
A hollow screw with cogs—Henry will know
The thing I mean and laugh at me,—if so
He fears not I should do more mischief.—Next
Lie bills and calculations much perplext,
With steam-boats, frigates and machinery quaint              80
Traced over them in blue and yellow paint.
Then comes a range of mathematical
Instruments, for plans nautical and statical;[8]
A heap of rosin, a queer broken glass
With ink in it;—a china cup that was                         85
What it will never be again, I think,
A thing from which sweet lips were wont to drink
The liquor doctors rail at—and which I
Will quaff in spite of them—and when we die
We'll toss up[9] who died first of drinking tea,             90
And cry out, heads or tails? where'er we be.
Near that a dusty paint box, some odd hooks,
A half-burnt match, an ivory block, three books,
Where conic sections, spherics, logarithms,
To great Laplace, from Sanderson and Sims,[1]               95

---

5. Gnomes are diminutive spirits fabled to inhabit the interior of the earth as the guardians of its treasures; *swink:* labor.
6. A full draught of liquor.
7. Shelley was famous among his friends for sailing paper boats on any small body of water that he happened to encounter.
8. Referring to the science of statics, or bringing weights into balance to achieve equilibrium (as opposed to "dynamics," the science of facilitating motion by means of the unequal distribution of weight).
9. I.e., toss a coin to settle the question.
1. Marquis Pierre Simon de Laplace (1749–1827), French mathematician and astronomer, was most famous in Shelley's day for his theory of the universe (1796) that introduced the nebular hypothesis; Nicholas Saunderson or Sanderson (1682–1739), an early teacher of Newtonian science at Cambridge and eventually professor of mathematics who wrote important books on algebra and elementary mathematical physics; *Sims* is either Thomas Simpson (1710–61), who wrote treatises on the laws of chance and the theory of fluctuations, as well as textbooks on algebra, geometry, and trigonometry, or Robert Simson (1687–1768), who wrote books on geometry and conic sections.

Lie heaped in their harmonious disarray
Of figures,—disentangle them who may.
Baron de Tott's Memoirs² beside them lie,
And some odd volumes of old chemistry.
Near those a most inexplicable thing,                    100
With lead in the middle—I'm conjecturing
How to make Henry understand; but no—
I'll leave, as Spenser says, with many mo,
This secret in the pregnant womb of time,³
Too vast a matter for so weak a rhyme.                   105

And here like some weird Archimage⁴ sit I,
Plotting dark spells, and devilish enginery,
The self-impelling steam-wheels of the mind
Which pump up oaths from clergymen, and grind
The gentle spirit of our meek reviews                    110
Into a powdery foam of salt abuse,
Ruffling the ocean of their self-content—
I sit—and smile or sigh as is my bent,
But not for them—Libeccio⁵ rushes round
With an inconstant and an idle sound,                    115
I heed him more than them—the thunder-smoke
Is gathering on the mountains, like a cloak
Folded athwart their shoulders broad and bare;
The ripe corn under the undulating air
Undulates like an ocean—and the vines                    120
Are trembling wide in all their trellised lines—
The murmur of the awakening sea doth fill
The empty pauses of the blast—the hill
Looks hoary through the white electric rain,
And from the glens beyond, in sullen strain,             125
The interrupted thunder howls—above
One chasm of Heaven smiles, like the eye of Love
On the unquiet world—while such things are,
How could one worth your friendship heed the war
Of worms?—the shriek of the world's carrion jays,        130
Their censure, or their wonder, or their praise?

You are not here . . . the quaint witch Memory sees,
In vacant chairs, your absent images,
And points where once you sat, and now should be
But are not.—I demand if ever we                         135
Shall meet as then we met—and she replies,
Veiling in awe her second-sighted eyes;

2. Baron François de Tott's *Mémoires sur les Turcs et les Tartares* (1785; English trans., 1786).
3. Shelley coalesces Spenser's phrase "many mo" (*Faerie Queene*, IV.i.8) with "many events in the womb of time," in Shakespeare's *Othello*, I.iii.377.
4. Archimago is the evil wizard or magician in *The Faerie Queene*; Shelley sardonically describes his own imagination as evil because it ruffles the feelings of such clergymen as his Eton and Oxford contemporary and rival poet, the Rev. Henry Hart Milman, who wrote for the *Quarterly Review*.
5. The southwest wind.

"I know the past alone—but summon home
My sister Hope,—she speaks of all to come."
But I, an old diviner, who know well                    140
Every false verse of that sweet oracle,[6]
Turned to the sad enchantress once again,
And sought a respite from my gentle pain,
In citing every passage o'er and o'er
Of our communion—how on the sea shore              145
We watched the ocean and the sky together,
Under the roof of blue Italian weather;
How I ran home through last year's thunder-storm,
And felt the transverse lightning linger warm
Upon my cheek—and how we often made               150
Feasts for each other, where good will outweighed
The frugal luxury of our country cheer,
As well it might, were it less firm and clear
Than ours must ever be—and how we spun
A shroud of talk to hide us from the Sun            155
Of this familiar life, which seems to be
But is not—or is but quaint mockery
Of all we would believe, and sadly blame
The jarring and inexplicable frame
Of this wrong world:—and then anatomize[7]          160
The purposes and thoughts of men whose eyes
Were closed in distant years—or widely guess
The issue of the earth's great business,
When we shall be as we no longer are—
Like babbling gossips safe, who hear the war        165
Of winds, and sigh, but tremble not—or how
You listened to some interrupted flow
Of visionary rhyme,[8] in joy and pain
Struck from the inmost fountains of my brain,
With little skill perhaps—or how we sought          170
Those deepest wells of passion or of thought
Wrought by wise poets[9] in the waste of years,
Staining their sacred waters with our tears;
Quenching a thirst ever to be renewed!
Or how I, wisest lady! then indued                  175
The language of a land which now is free,[1]
And winged with thoughts of truth and majesty
Flits round the tyrant's sceptre like a cloud,
And bursts the peopled prisons—cries aloud,
"My name is Legion!"[2]—that majestic tongue        180
Which Calderon over the desert flung

6. That is, Hope; the *sad enchantress* (line 142) is Memory.
7. Analyze minutely.
8. Shelley had read *Prometheus Unbound* to the Gisbornes the previous autumn.
9. Maria Gisborne had taught Shelley to read Spanish; together they had read several plays by
   Pedro Calderón de la Barca.
1. In January 1820 there had been an almost bloodless revolution is Spain that had resulted
   in the abolition of the Inquisition and the establishment of a constitutional monarchy.
2. I.e., "innumerable" (Mark 5:9; Matthew 26:53).

Of ages and of nations, and which found
An echo in our hearts, and with the sound
Startled Oblivion—thou wert then to me
As is a nurse—when inarticulately                                    185
A child would talk as its grown parents do.
If living winds the rapid clouds pursue,
If hawks chase doves through the ætherial way,
Huntsmen the innocent deer, and beasts their prey,
Why should not we rouse with the spirit's blast                      190
Out of the forest of the pathless past
These recollected pleasures?[3]

                                                    You are now
In London, that great sea whose ebb and flow
At once is deaf and loud, and on the shore
Vomits its wrecks, and still howls on for more.                      195
Yet in its depth what treasures! You will see
That which was Godwin,—greater none than he
Though fallen—and fallen on evil times[4]—to stand
Among the spirits of our age and land
Before the dread Tribunal of *to come*                               200
The foremost . . . while Rebuke cowers pale and dumb.
You will see Coleridge—he who sits obscure
In the exceeding lustre and the pure
Intense irradiation of a mind
Which, with its own internal lightning blind,                        205
Flags wearily through darkness and despair—
A cloud-encircled meteor of the air,
A hooded eagle among blinking owls.—
You will see Hunt[5]—one of those happy souls
Who are the salt of the Earth, and without whom                      210
This world would smell like what it is, a tomb—
Who is, what others seem—his room no doubt
Is still adorned with many a cast from Shout,[6]
With graceful flowers tastefully placed about,
And coronals[7] of bay from ribbons hung,                            215
And brighter wreaths in neat disorder flung,
The gifts of the most learn'd among some dozens
Of female friends, sisters-in-law and cousins.

---

3. Lines 132–92 treat the past and Memory, the traditional "mother of the Muses." The next
   section (lines 192–253) is an imaginative flight across space, rather than time, to London
   in the present.
4. Shelley describes Mary Shelley's father—once his mentor but now his bitter accuser—in a
   phrase that Milton used of himself (*Paradise Lost*, VII.25) and with a generous appreciation
   of Godwin's place in intellectual history. In the 1790s Maria Gisborne and her first husband,
   Willey Reveley, had been members of London intellectual circles that included Godwin and
   Samuel Taylor Coleridge (lines 202–08), both, in 1820, near the low ebb of their literary
   reputations.
5. (James Henry) Leigh Hunt (1784–1859), Shelley's closest friend, was a poet and journalist
   who, at this period, was best known as editor of the *Examiner*, a weekly political and literary
   newspaper.
6. Robert Shout was a London maker of plaster copies of great statues, such as the Venus de
   Medici and the Apollo Belvedere.
7. Garlands worn on the head.

And there is he with his eternal puns,
Which beat the dullest brain for smiles, like duns[8]                220
Thundering for money at a poet's door.
Alas, it is no use to say "I'm poor!"
Or oft in graver mood, when he will look
Things wiser than were ever read in book,
Except in Shakespeare's wisest tenderness.—                225
You will see Hogg[9]—and I cannot express
His virtues, though I know that they are great,
Because he locks, then barricades the gate
Within which they inhabit—of his wit
And wisdom, you'll cry out when you are bit.                230
He is a pearl within an oyster shell,
One of the richest of the deep. And there
Is English Peacock,[1] with his mountain fair,
Turned into a Flamingo, that shy bird
That gleams i' the Indian air—have you not heard                235
When a man marries, dies, or turns Hindoo,
His best friends hear no more of him?—but you
Will see him, and will like him too, I hope,
With the milk-white Snowdonian antelope
Matched with this cameleopard[2]—his fine wit                240
Makes such a wound, the knife is lost in it;
A strain too learned for a shallow age,
Too wise for selfish bigots—let his page
Which charms the chosen spirits of the time
Fold itself up for the serener clime                245
Of years to come, and find its recompense
In that just expectation.—Wit and sense,
Virtue and human knowledge, all that might
Make this dull world a business of delight,
Are all combined in Horace Smith.[3]—And these,                250
With some exceptions, which I need not tease
Your patience by descanting on,—are all
You and I know in London.[4]

                    I recall
My thoughts, and bid you look upon the night.
As water does a sponge, so the moonlight                255
Fills the void, hollow, universal air—
What see you?—unpavilioned heaven is fair
Whether the moon, into her chamber gone,

8. Collection agents.
9. Thomas Jefferson Hogg (1792–1862), Shelley's closest friend at Oxford, had now grown somewhat distant from him.
1. Thomas Love Peacock (1785–1866), Shelley's friend and a comic novelist, had recently taken a post at the East India Company and married Jane Gryffydh from the area of northwest Wales to which Mount Snowdon gave its regional name (line 239).
2. A giraffe.
3. Famous as one of the authors (with his brother James) of *Rejected Addresses* (1812), which included parodies of many famous writers of the day, Horace Smith (1779–1849) was a stockbroker, poet, wit, and later a novelist.
4. That is, all their mutual friends who lived in London.

Leaves midnight to the golden stars, or wan
Climbs with diminished beams the azure steep,                    260
Or whether clouds sail o'er the inverse deep
Piloted by the many-wandering blast,
And the rare stars rush through them dim and fast—
All this is beautiful in every land—
But what see you beside?—a shabby stand                    265
Of Hackney coaches,[5] a brick house or wall
Fencing some lonely court, white with the scrawl
Of our unhappy politics; or worse—
A wretched woman reeling by, whose curse
Mixed with the watchman's, partner of her trade,[6]                    270
You must accept in place of serenade—
Or yellow-haired Pollonia murmuring
To Henry, some unutterable thing.[7]—
I see a chaos of green leaves and fruit
Built round dark caverns, even to the root                    275
Of the living stems that feed them—in whose bowers
There sleep in their dark dew the folded flowers;
Beyond, the surface of the unsickled corn
Trembles not in the slumbering air, and borne
In circles quaint, and ever changing dance,                    280
Like winged stars the fire-flies flash and glance
Pale in the open moonshine, but each one
Under the dark trees seems a little sun,
A meteor tamed, a fixed star gone astray
From the silver regions of the Milky Way;—                    285
Afar the contadino's[8] song is heard,
Rude, but made sweet by distance—and a bird
Which cannot be the Nightingale, and yet
I know none else that sings so sweet as it
At this late hour—and then all is still—                    290
Now Italy or London—which you will!

    Next winter you must pass with me; I'll have
My house by that time turned into a grave
Of dead despondence and low-thoughted care
And all the dreams which our tormentors are.                    295
Oh, that Hunt, Hogg, Peacock and Smith were there,
With everything belonging to them fair!
We will have books, Spanish, Italian, Greek;
And ask one week to make another week
As like his father as I'm unlike mine,[9]                    300
Which is not his fault, as you may divine.
Though we eat little flesh and drink no wine,
Yet let's be merry! we'll have tea and toast;

---

5. Horse-drawn carriages for hire.
6. I.e., the watchmen (the only police of that time) pimped for the prostitutes.
7. Apollonia Ricci, daughter of the Gisbornes' landlord in Leghorn, had a crush on Henry
   Reveley, as Mary Shelley repeatedly reminded him in teasing letters.
8. Italian peasant or farmhand.
9. Shelley alludes to his estrangement from his own father, Sir Timothy Shelley.

Custards for supper, and an endless host
Of syllabubs[1] and jellies and mince-pies,                    305
And other such lady-like luxuries—
Feasting on which we will philosophize!
And we'll have fires out of the Grand Duke's wood,[2]
To thaw the six weeks' winter in our blood.
And then we'll talk—what shall we talk about?                  310
Oh, there are themes enough for many a bout
Of thought-entangled descant;—as to nerves,
With cones and parallelograms and curves
I've sworn to strangle them if once they dare
To bother me—when you are with me there,                       315
And they shall never more sip laudanum,
From Helicon or Himeros;[3]—well, come,
And in despite of God and of the devil
We'll make our friendly philosophic revel
Outlast the leafless time—till buds and flowers               320
Warn the obscure inevitable hours
Sweet meeting by sad parting to renew—
"To-morrow to fresh woods and pastures new."[4]

# PETER BELL THE THIRD

Wordsworth's *Peter Bell*, published at the end of April 1819, tells the story of an itinerant potter who leads a completely immoral life until a series of natural events, centering on an ass that is dumbly faithful to its dead master, so work upon the ignorant man's superstitious imagination that he "Forsook his crimes, renounced his folly, / And, after ten months' melancholy, / Became a good and honest man." In a scathing review in the *Examiner* for May 2, 1819, Leigh Hunt charged that the moral of the poem (a "didactic little horror") was "founded on the bewitching principles of fear, bigotry, and diseased impulse," and after quoting the stanza that Shelley uses as his epigraph, Hunt asks whether "Mr. Wordsworth is earnest . . . in thinking that his fellow-creatures are to be damned?" (*RR*, Part A, II, 538–39). Shelley's poem treats a Methodist Peter Bell, predestined to damnation, whose life resembles, in a wild way, Wordsworth's own career.

In June or July 1819, Shelley read Hunt's review, together with a review in the April 25 issue of the *Examiner* by John Keats of John Hamilton Reynolds's parody entitled *Peter Bell; A Lyrical Ballad* (which Reynolds had contrived without seeing Wordsworth's poem and published just before "the real Simon Pure" appeared). Mary Shelley wrote in 1839, "A critique on Wordsworth's *Peter Bell* reached us at Leghorn, which amused

---

1. A sweetened drink or dish made from milk (often freshly drawn from the cow) and cider or wine.
2. Ferdinand III was the Grand Duke of Tuscany.
3. Laudanum, opium dissolved in wine or other alcohol, is used figuratively here. Shelley says (lines 312–17) that he will *strangle* his *nerves* with mathematical studies rather than use the opiates of either writing poetry (the summit of *Helicon* contains the sanctuary of the Muses and the spring of poetic inspiration) or falling in love. *Himeros:* "A synonym of Love" (Shelley's note).
4. The final line of Milton's *Lycidas*.

Shelley exceedingly and suggested this poem." But the drafts of the poem were probably not complete until October–November 1819 (*BSM*, VII, 4–5). Some believe that Shelley read Wordsworth's poem itself by that date (e.g., Cameron, *Shelley: The Golden Years*, pp. 626–27), but because different portions of *Peter Bell* were quoted in other reviews available to Shelley, the case remains moot (*BSM*, I, 6–8).

By Sunday, October 24, 1819, Shelley had completed his poem and read it to Mary Shelley, who transcribed it for the press by October 28. Shelley mailed it to Leigh Hunt on November 2 with instructions to ask Charles Ollier "to print & publish immediately . . . NOT however with my name . . . as I have only expended a few days on this party squib . . . & I am about to publish more serious things this winter" (*Letters*, II, 135). On December 15, Shelley asked Ollier what he had done with the poem, adding, "I think *Peter* not bad in his way; but perhaps no one will believe in anything in the shape of a joke from me" (*Letters*, II, 164). Though Shelley tried as late as May 1820 to persuade Ollier to publish it, the poem remained unknown to the public until Mary Shelley added it to the one-volume second edition of Shelley's *Poetical Works* late in 1839. Though she had earlier omitted the poem because she found its humor at the expense of Wordsworth and Coleridge embarrassing by that time, she added to her apologetic remarks: "No poem contains more of Shelley's peculiar views, with regard to the errors into which many of the wisest have fallen, and of the pernicious effects of certain opinions on society. Much of it is beautifully written—and though . . . it must be looked on as a plaything, it has so much merit and poetry—so much of *himself* in it, that it cannot fail to interest greatly. . . ."

Our text is based directly on the Bodleian press-copy manuscript (MS Shelley adds. c.5, fols. 50–68; facsimile in *BSM*, I), which Mary Shelley transcribed for the press and to which P. B. Shelley added headings, some notes, and verbal corrections. Part of the Preface (suppressed by Mary in 1839 because it attacked the powerful publisher John Murray) initially appeared in the first edition of *Shelley's Poetry and Prose*, which also corrected numerous readings to conform to Shelley's manifest intention. We have now rechecked the text and notes in the light of additional research on the poem by the Reimans in Volumes I and VII of *BSM*. For a penetrating analysis of this poem and Shelley's other satirical writing, see Steven E. Jones, *Shelley's Satire* (1994).

# Peter Bell the Third

## By Miching Mallecho, Esq<sup>r</sup>.

Is it a party in a parlour—
Crammed just as they on earth were crammed,
    Some sipping punch—some sipping tea;
    But, as you by their faces see,
All silent and all——damned!

*Peter Bell*, by W. Wordsworth.[1]

*Ophelia*: What means this, my lord?
*Hamlet*: Marry, this is miching mallecho; it means mischief.[2]

## Dedication
### To Thomas Brown, Esq<sup>r</sup>., the Younger, H.F.[3]

Dear Tom—Allow me to request you to introduce Mr. Peter Bell to the respectable family of the Fudges; although he may fall short of those very considerable personages in the more active properties which characterize the Rat and the Apostate,[4] I suspect that even you their historian will be forced to confess that he surpasses them in the more peculiarly legitimate qualification of intolerable dulness.

You know Mr. Examiner Hunt. That murderous and smiling villain at the mere sound of whose voice our susceptible friend the *Quarterly* fell into a paroxysm of eleutherophobia[5] and foamed so much acrid gall that it burned the carpet in Mr. Murray's upper room,[6] and eating a hole in the floor fell like rain upon our poor friend's head,[7] who was scampering from room to room like a bear with a swarm of bees on his nose:—it caused an incurable ulcer and our poor friend has worn a wig ever since. Well, this monkey[8] suckled with tyger's milk, this odious thief, liar, scoundrel, coxcomb and monster presented me to two of the Mr. Bells. Seeing me in his presence they of course uttered very few words and those with much caution. I scarcely need observe that they only kept company with him—at least I can certainly answer

1. The stanza, later omitted by Wordsworth at the remonstrance of friends, appeared in the first edition on page 39, the fourth stanza from the end of Part I. Shelley punctuates the text as he found it in the *Examiner*, but (unlike Wordsworth and Hunt) he indents lines 3–4 to mark the rhyme-scheme, as he did in his own poetry.
2. Shakespeare, *Hamlet*, III.ii.148–49. Ophelia's question follows the opening scene of the dumb show that reenacts Claudius' murder of Hamlet's father. Scholars have glossed "miching mallecho" as "lying in wait for the evildoer." Presumably Shelley, like Hamlet, hoped to "catch the conscience" of his political foes by eliciting self-exposing reactions to his poem.
3. I.e., Thomas Moore, Byron's friend, who had written popular doggerel satires including *The Twopenny Post-Bag* (1813) and *The Fudge Family in Paris* (1818) under the pseudonym "Thomas Brown, the Younger." "H.F." (Historian of Fudges) plays off Wordsworth's Dedication to "Robert Southey, Esq., P.L." (Poet Laureate).
4. Presumably the *Rat* is Reynolds' *antenatal Peter* (Prologue, line 3) and the *Apostate* is Wordsworth's *legitimate* poem (i.e., one supporting king and church).
5. *eleutherophobia*: "fear of defenders of freedom" (Shelley's coinage from the Greek).
6. William Gifford, who edited the Tory *Quarterly Review* in an upper room at John Murray's Albemarle Street publishing house, was Hunt's greatest enemy.
7. I.e., John Murray's head.
8. I.e., Leigh Hunt.

for one of them—in order to observe whether they could not borrow colours from any particulars of his private life for the denunciation they mean to make of him, as the member of an "infamous and black conspiracy for diminishing the authority of that venerable canon, which forbids any man to mar his grandmother"; the effect of which in this on our moral and religious nation is likely to answer the purpose of the controversy. My intimacy with the younger Mr. Bell naturally sprung from this introduction to his brothers. And in presenting him to you, I have the satisfaction of being able to assure you that he is considerably the dullest of the three.

There is this particular advantage in an acquaintance with any one of the Peter Bells; that if you know one Peter Bell, you know three Peter Bells; they are not one but three, not three but one. An awful mystery after having caused torrents of blood, and having been hymned by groans enough to deafen the music of the spheres is at length illustrated to the satisfaction of all parties in the theological world, by the nature of Mr. Peter Bell.

Peter is a polyhedric Peter, or a Peter with many sides. He changes colours like a chameleon, and his coat like a snake. He is a Proteus[9] of a Peter. He was at first sublime, pathetic, impressive, profound; then dull; then prosy and dull; and now dull—o so dull! it is an ultra-legitimate dulness.

You will perceive that it is not necessary to consider Hell and the Devil as supernatural machinery. The whole scene of my epic is in "this world which is"—so Peter informed us before his conversion to White Obi[1]—

> the world of all of us, *and where*
> *We find our happiness, or not at all.*

Let me observe that I have spent six or seven days in composing this sublime piece;—the orb of my moonlike genius has made the fourth part of its revolution round the dull earth which you inhabit, driving you mad whilst it has retained its calmness and its splendour, and I have been fitting this its last phase "to occupy a permanent station in the literature of my country."[2]

Your works, indeed, dear Tom, Sell better; but mine are far superior. The public is no judge; posterity sets all to rights.

Allow me to observe that so much has been written of Peter Bell, that the present history can be considered only, like the *Iliad*, as a continuation of that series of cyclic poems which have already been candidates for bestowing immortality upon, at the same time that they

9. Greek demigod of the sea who could change shape at will (e.g., *Odyssey*, IV.360ff.).
1. Among black slaves in the West Indies, "Obi" was the name of a magical power that sorcerers used to afflict their enemies; the "White Obi" would be white magic, or (in this context) Christianity. The indented quotation is from Wordsworth's "The French Revolution as It Appeared to Enthusiasts at Its Commencement," which was first published in Coleridge's periodical *The Friend* (1809) and reprinted in his collected poems of 1815, before finally appearing in *The Prelude* in 1850 (XI.142–44).
2. Wordsworth wrote that he had taken pains with his *Peter Bell* since 1798 "to make the production less unworthy of a favourable reception; or, rather, to fit it for filling *permanently* a station however humble, in the Literature of my Country."

receive it from, his character and adventures. In this point of view, I have violated no rule of syntax in beginning my composition with a conjunction; the full stop which closes the poem continued by me being, like the full stops at the end of the *Iliad* and *Odyssey*, a full stop of a very qualified import.

Hoping that the immortality which you have given to the Fudges, you will receive from them; and in the firm expectation that when London shall be an habitation of bitterns,[3] when St. Paul's and Westminster Abbey shall stand, shapeless and nameless ruins in the midst of an unpeopled marsh; when the piers of Waterloo bridge shall become the nuclei of islets of reeds and osiers[4] and cast the jagged shadows of their broken arches on the solitary stream,—some transatlantic commentator will be weighing in the scales of some new and now unimagined system of criticism, the respective merits of the Bells and the Fudges, and of their historians; I remain, Dear Tom, Yours sincerely,

Miching Mallecho.

*December* 1, 1819.

P.S. Pray excuse the date of place; so soon as the profits of this publication come in, I mean to hire lodgings in a more respectable street.[5]

*Prologue*

Peter Bells, one, two and three,
O'er the wide world wandering be:—
First, the antenatal Peter,
Wrapt in weeds of the same metre,
The so long predestined raiment          5
Clothed in which to walk his way meant
The second Peter; whose ambition
Is to link the proposition
As the mean of two extremes—
(This was learnt from Aldric's themes)[6]   10
Shielding from the guilt of schism
The orthodoxal syllogism:
The first Peter—he who was
Like the shadow in the glass
Of the second, yet unripe,                15
His substantial antitype.—
Then came Peter Bell the Second,
Who henceforward must be reckoned
The body of a double soul—

3. Marsh-dwelling birds related to the heron; compare *Queen Mab*, II. 109–224, especially the end of that disquisition on the rise and fall of cities and empires.
4. Willow trees.
5. I.e., Miching Mallecho does not name his humble address, as Tom Brown did his fashionable one ("245, Piccadilly") in *The Fudge Family in Paris*.
6. *Artis Logicae Compendium*, written in 1691 by Henry Aldrich (1647–1710), remained the standard school logic text until the late nineteenth century.

> And that portion of the whole                                      20
> Without which the rest would seem
> Ends of a disjointed dream.—
> And the third is he who has
> O'er the grave been forced to pass
> To the other side, which is,—                                      25
> Go and try else,—just like this.
> Peter Bell the First was Peter
> Smugger, milder, softer, neater,
> Like the soul before it is
> Born from *that* world into *this*.[7]                             30
> The next Peter Bell was he
> Predevote[8] like you and me
> To good or evil as may come;
> His was the severer doom,—
> For he was an evil Cotter[9]                                        35
> And a polygamic Potter.[1]
> And the last is Peter Bell,
> Damned since our first Parents fell,
> Damned eternally to Hell—
> Surely he deserves it well!                                         40

## PART FIRST

### *Death*

> And Peter Bell, when he had been
>   With fresh-imported Hell-fire warmed,
> Grew serious—from his dress and mien
> 'Twas very plainly to be seen
>   Peter was quite reformed.                                          5

> His eyes turned up, his mouth turned down;
>   His accent caught a nasal twang;
> He oiled his hair;[2] there might be heard
> The grace of God in every word
>   Which Peter said or sang.                                          10

---

7. The idea underlying this *antenatal Peter* is the Platonic (or Pythagorean) doctrine of the transmigration of souls, which are reborn in various bodies.
8. Predestined, foredoomed.
9. A Scottish peasant renting a cottage and small plot of ground; a *potter* (line 36) makes and sells ceramic pots.
1. "The oldest scholiasts read—
   A *dodecagamic* Potter.
   This is at once descriptive and more megalophonous—but the alliteration of the text had captivated the vulgar ears of the heard of later commentators" (Shelley's note); *polygamic:* having many wives; *dodecagamic:* having twelve wives ("He had a dozen wedded wives."— Wordsworth, *Peter Bell* [1819], p. 21); *megalophonous:* big-sounding.
2. "To those who have not duly appreciated the distinction between *whale* and *Russia* oil this attribute might rather seem to belong to the Dandy than the Evangelic. The effect, when to the windward, is indeed so similar, that it requires a subtle Naturalist to discriminate the animals. They belong, however, to distinct genera" (Shelley's note). Oil of birch trees, imported from Russia, was used as hair oil by Shelley and the upper classes; whale oil, which had an equally strong odor, served as a cheap substitute.

But Peter now grew old, and had
  An ill no doctor could unravel;
His torments almost drove him mad;—
Some said it was a fever bad—
  Some swore it was the gravel.[3]           15

His holy friends then came about
  And with long preaching and persuasion,
Convinced the patient, that without
The smallest shadow of a doubt
  He was predestined to damnation.         20

They said—"Thy name is Peter Bell;
  Thy skin is of a brimstone hue;
Alive or dead—aye, sick or well—
The one God made to rhyme with hell;
  The other, I think, rhymes with you."[4]     25

Then Peter set up such a yell!—
  The nurse, who with some water gruel
Was climbing up the stairs as well
As her old legs could climb them—fell,
  And broke them both—the fall was cruel.     30

The Parson from the casement leapt
  Into the lake of Windermere[5]—
And many an eel—though no adept
In God's right reason for it—kept
  Gnawing his kidneys half a year.        35

And all the rest rushed through the door,
  And tumbled over one another,
And broke their skulls.—Upon the floor
Meanwhile sate Peter Bell, and swore,
  And cursed his father and his mother;    40

And raved of God, and sin, and death,
  Blaspheming like an infidel;
And said, that with his clenched teeth,
He'd seize the Earth from underneath,
  And drag it with him down to Hell.      45

As he was speaking came a spasm,
  And wrenched his gnashing teeth asunder,—
Like one who sees a strange phantasm
He lay,—there was a silent chasm
  Between his upper jaw and under.       50

3. Kidney stones: a disease involving aggregations of urinary crystals; popularly used to indicate
   pain or difficulty in passing urine. (Shelley himself suffered from the condition.)
4. *one . . . other:* i.e., *Peter Bell* and *brimstone hue.*
5. A large lake in Westmorland frequently mentioned in Wordsworth's poetry.

And yellow death lay on his face;
   And a fixed smile that was not human
Told, as I understand the case,
That he was gone to the wrong place:—
   I heard all this from the old woman.       55

Then there came down from Langdale Pike[6]
   A cloud with lightning, wind and hail;
It swept over the mountains like
An Ocean,—and I heard it strike
   The woods and crags of Grasmere vale.[7]     60

And I saw the black storm come
   Nearer, minute after minute,
Its thunder made the cataracts[8] dumb,
With hiss and clash, and hollow hum
   It neared as if the Devil was in it.     65

The Devil *was* in it:—he had bought
   Peter for half a crown;[9] and when
The storm which bore him vanished, nought
That in the house that storm had caught
   Was ever seen again.     70

The gaping neighbours came next day—
   They found all vanished from the shore:
The Bible, whence he used to pray,
Half scorched under a hen-coop lay;
   Smashed glass—and nothing more!     75

## PART SECOND

### The Devil

The Devil, I safely can aver,
   Has neither hoof, nor tail, nor sting;[1]
Nor is he, as some sages swear,
A spirit, neither here nor there,
   In nothing—yet in every thing.     80

He is—what we are; for sometimes
   The Devil is a gentleman;
At others a bard bartering rhymes

6. The Langdale Pikes (or Peaks) are a group of mountains east of Grasmere.
7. Wordsworth lived in the village of Grasmere, near the lake of the same name, from December 1799 until May 1813; when Shelley tried to visit him in 1811, he was not home.
8. Waterfalls of considerable size.
9. *half a crown:* a coin worth two and a half shillings—an eighth of one pound sterling.
1. Shelley discussed the Devil at length in his early poem entitled *The Devil's Walk* (see *CPPBS*, I, 121–29). For the satire by Southey and Coleridge that inspired Shelley then, as well as Byron's poem and others on the same theme, see our hypertext edition of *The Devil's Walk* on the *Romantic Circles* website.

For sack;[2] a statesman spinning crimes,
   A swindler, living as he can;         85

A thief, who cometh in the night,
   With whole boots and net pantaloons,
Like some one whom it were not right
To mention;—or the luckless wight
   From whom he steals nine silver spoons.     90

But in this case he did appear
   Like a slop-merchant[3] from Wapping
And with smug face, and eye severe
On every side did perk and peer
   Till he saw Peter dead or napping.     95

He had on an upper Benjamin
   (For he was of the driving schism[4])
In the which he wrapt his skin
From the storm he travelled in,
   For fear of rheumatism.     100

He called the ghost out of the corse;[5]—
   It was exceedingly like Peter,—
Only its voice was hollow and hoarse—
It had a queerish look of course—
   Its dress too was a little neater.     105

The Devil knew not,[6] his name and lot;
   Peter knew not that he was Bell:
Each had an upper stream of thought,
Which made all seem as it was not;
   Fitting itself to all things well.     110

Peter thought he had parents dear,
   Brothers, sisters, cousins, cronies,
In the fens o' Lincolnshire;
He perhaps had found them there
   Had he gone and boldly shewn his     115

Solemn phiz[7] in his own village;
   Where he thought, oft when a boy

2. The Poet Laureate (at this time, Robert Southey) was paid with a butt of *sack*, a class of white and amber wines, including sherries, imported from Spain and the Canary Islands. In *Nightmare Abbey* (1818), Peacock used this fact and the title of Southey's poem *Roderick, the Last of the Goths* to satirize Southey as "Roderick Sackbut."
3. A dealer in cheap sailor's clothes; *Wapping*: a poor seamen's quarter (and traditional place of executions) in London's East End, along the Thames; *perk* (line 94): to assume . . . a lively, self-assertive, or self-conceited attitude or air" (*OED* I.1).
4. I.e., one of his great pleasures was driving his own carriage, like Sir Telegraph Paxarett in Peacock's *Melincourt*; an *upper Benjamin* was a short overcoat.
5. Corpse.
6. Shelley usually uses medial commas to mark internal rhymes in poetic lines.
7. Face (short for "physiognomy").

He'd clombe[8] the orchard walls to pillage
The produce of his neighbour's tillage
    With marvellous pride and joy.                    120

And the Devil thought he had,
    'Mid the misery and confusion
Of an unjust war, just made
A fortune by the gainful trade
Of giving soldiers rations bad—                       125
    The world is full of strange delusion.

That he had a mansion planned
    In a square like Grosvenor square,[9]
That he was aping fashion, and
That he now came to Westmorland                       130
    To see what was romantic[1] there.

And all this, though quite ideal,—
    Ready at a breath to vanish,—
Was a state not more unreal
Than the peace he could not feel,                     135
    Or the care he could not banish.

After a little conversation
    The Devil told Peter, if he chose
He'd bring him to the world of fashion
By giving him a situation                             140
    In his own service—and new clothes.

And Peter bowed, quite pleased and proud,
    And after waiting some few days
For a new livery—dirty yellow
Turned up with black—the wretched fellow              145
    Was bowled[2] to Hell in the Devil's chaise.

### PART THIRD

#### Hell

Hell is a city much like London—
    A populous and a smoky city;
There are all sorts of people undone
And there is little or no fun done;                   150
    Small justice shewn, and still less pity.

8. Climbed.
9. Then a relatively new section of London, inhabited by both old nobility and gentry (such as Lord Grosvenor, William Gifford's patron) and such *nouveaux riches* as Shelley's first father-in-law, the wealthy coffeehouse owner John Westbrook.
1. The word *romantic* had several meanings in Shelley's time; for tourists it could mean "unusual" or "picturesque," though here the poet's reference contains a note of irony or satire.
2. *bowled*: carried or conveyed in a vehicle.

There is a Castles, and a Canning,
  A Cobbett, and a Castlereagh;[3]
All sorts of caitiff corpses planning
All sorts of cozening for trepanning[4]         155
  Corpses less corrupt than they.

There is a Southey,[5] who has lost
  His wits, or sold them, none knows which;
He walks about a double ghost,
And though as thin as Fraud almost—         160
  Ever grows more grim and rich.

There is a Chancery Court,[6] a King,
  A manufacturing mob; a set
Of thieves who by themselves are sent
Similar thieves to represent;[7]         165
  An Army;—and a public debt.

Which last is a scheme of Paper money,
  And means—being interpreted—
"Bees, keep your wax—give us the honey
And we will plant while skies are sunny         170
  Flowers, which in winter serve instead."[8]

There is great talk of Revolution—
  And a great chance of Despotism—
German soldiers[9]—camps—confusion—
Tumults—lotteries—rage—delusion—         175
  Gin—suicide and methodism;

Taxes too, on wine and bread,
  And meat, and beer, and tea, and cheese,[1]

3. John Castle(s), a government spy and agent provocateur, led workmen into illegal conspir-acies and then betrayed them, sending them to the gallows; George Canning, brilliant Tory wit of the *Anti-Jacobin*, government official, and later prime minister; William Cobbett, pop-ular journalist and demagogue whose *Political Register* urged radical reform; John Stewart, Viscount Castlereagh, an Anglo-Irish politician who at this time, as foreign secretary, was the strong man in the reactionary government. Shelley labels them as equally unsavory, whatever their politics.
4. *caitiff*: vile, base, mean; *cozening*: deception or defrauding by deceit; *trepanning*: cheating, entrapping.
5. The press-copy manuscript read *Southey*, though the name was later crossed out by one of the Shelleys (as were parts of each name in the previous stanza, probably to avoid libel actions).
6. The court of equity presided over by the Lord Chancellor ruled on matters of equity between individuals (see Dickens's *Bleak House*); after the death of Harriet Westbrook Shelley in 1816, Lord Chancellor Eldon had ruled against Shelley's right to raise his children by Har-riet, placing them instead under the guardianship of strangers at Shelley's expense.
7. The unreformed Parliament.
8. Shelley attacked the evils arising from a standing army, the national debt, and paper money in his *Philosophical View of Reform* (see SC, VI, 945ff.).
9. Rumors periodically circulated among the liberals that King George III or George IV (who ruled as electors of Hanover as well as kings of England) was bringing in German soldiers or even Russian Cossacks to suppress dissent among the English people.
1. In 1817 new regressive commodity taxes, passed to pay the interest on the national debt, added to the burdens on the poor.

From which those patriots pure are fed
Who gorge before they reel to bed                           180
   The tenfold essence of all these.

There are mincing women, mewing,
   (Like cats, who amant misere,[2])
Of their own virtue, and pursuing
Their gentler sisters to that ruin,                         185
   Without which—what were chastity?[3]

Lawyers—judges—old hobnobbers[4]
   Are there—Bailiffs—Chancellors—
Bishops—great and little robbers—
Rhymesters—pamphleteers—stock-jobbers[5]—                  190
   Men of glory in the wars,—

Things whose trade is, over ladies
   To lean, and flirt, and stare, and simper,
Till all that is divine in woman
Grows cruel, courteous,[6] smooth, inhuman,                 195
   Crucified 'twixt a smile and whimper.

Thrusting, toiling, wailing, moiling,[7]
   Frowning, preaching—such a riot!
Each with never ceasing labour
Whilst he thinks he cheats his neighbour                    200
   Cheating his own heart of quiet.

And all these meet at levees;[8]—
   Dinners convivial and political;—
Suppers of epic poets;—teas,
Where small talk dies in agonies;—                          205
   Breakfasts professional and critical;

Lunches and snacks so aldermanic
   That one would furnish forth ten dinners,
Where reigns a Cretan-tongued[9] panic

2. Love miserably. "One of the attributes in Linnaeus's description of the Cat. To a similar cause the caterwauling of more than one species of this genus is to be referred;—except indeed that the poor quadruped is compelled to quarrel with its own pleasures, whilst the biped is supposed only to quarrel with those of others" (Shelley's note).
3. "What would this husk and excuse for a Virtue be without its kernal prostitution, or the kernal prostitution without this husk of a Virtue? I wonder the Women of the Town do not form an association, like the Society for the Suppression of Vice, for the support of what may be considered the 'King, church, and Constitution' of their order. But this subject is almost too horrible for a joke.——" (Shelley's note).
4. Those who drink together and toast each other, or who are on familiar terms.
5. Brokers and speculators in stocks and bonds.
6. I.e., with manners characteristic of the court of a prince; hence, insincere.
7. Drudging, working in wet and mire.
8. In Great Britain, assemblies held in the early afternoon by the sovereign or his representative, at which only men are received.
9. Lying. The Cretans were proverbially thought to be liars at least as early as the time of the New Testament (see Titus 1:12).

Lest news Russ, Dutch, or Alemannic[1]    210
    Should make some losers, and some winners

At conversazioni[2]—balls—
    Conventicles[3] and drawing-rooms.
Courts of law—committees—calls
Of a morning—clubs—book stalls—    215
    Churches—masquerades and tombs.

And this is Hell—and in this smother
    All are damnable and damned;
Each one damning, damns the other;
They are damned by one another,    220
    By none other are they damned.

'Tis a lie to say, "God damns!"[4]
    Where was Heaven's Attorney General
When they first gave out such flams?[5]
Let there be an end of shams,    225
    They are mines of poisonous mineral.

Statesmen damn themselves to be
    Cursed; and lawyers damn their souls
To the auction of a fee.
Churchmen damn themselves to see    230
    God's sweet love in burning coals.

The rich are damned beyond all cure
    To taunt, and starve, and trample on
The weak and wretched: and the poor
Damn their broken hearts to endure    235
    Stripe on stripe,[6] with groan on groan.

Sometimes the poor are damned indeed
    To take,—not means for being blest,—
But Cobbett's snuff, revenge;[7] that weed
From which the worms that it doth feed    240
    Squeeze less than they before possessed.

And some few, like we know who,
    Damned—but God alone knows why—
To believe their minds are given

1. German.
2. Social assemblies, often with discussions of literature, art, or science.
3. Nonconformist or dissenting meeting-houses, or the meetings themselves.
4. "This libel on our national oath, and this accusation of all our countrymen of being in the daily practise of solemnly asseverating the most enormous falshood I fear deserves the notice of a more active Attorney General than that here alluded to" (Shelley's note).
5. Deceptions, humbugs.
6. A stroke or lash with a whip or scourge.
7. Alluding to journalistic calls for revenge on the ruling class in Cobbett's *Political Register*.

To make this ugly Hell a Heaven;                    245
    In which faith they[8] live and die.

Thus, as in a Town, plague-stricken,
    Each man be he sound or no
Must indifferently sicken;
As when day begins to thicken                       250
    None knows a pigeon from a crow,—

So good and bad, sane and mad,
    The oppressor and the oppressed;
Those who weep to see what others
Smile to inflict upon their brothers;               255
    Lovers, haters, worst and best;

All are damned—they breathe an air
    Thick, infected, joy-dispelling:
Each pursues what seems most fair,
Mining like moles, through mind, and there          260
Scoop palace-caverns vast, where Care
    In throned state is ever dwelling.

### Part Fourth

#### Sin

Lo! Peter in Hell's Grosvenor square,
    A footman in the Devil's service!
And the misjudging world would swear                265
That every man in service there
    To virtue would prefer vice.

But Peter, though now damned, was not
    What Peter was before damnation.
Men oftentimes prepare a lot                        270
Which ere it finds them, is not what
    Suits with their genuine station.

All things that Peter saw and felt
    Had a peculiar aspect to him;
And when they came within the belt                  275
Of his own nature, seemed to melt
    Like cloud to cloud, into him.

And so the outward world uniting
    To that within him, he became
Considerably uninviting                             280
To those, who meditation slighting,
    Were moulded in a different frame.

8. I.e., Hunt, Shelley himself, and other idealistic reformers.

And he scorned them, and they scorned him;
 And he scorned all they did; and they
Did all that men of their own trim⁹
Are wont to do to please their whim,            285
 Drinking, lying, swearing, play.


Such were his fellow servants; thus
 His virtue, like our own, was built
Too much on that indignant fuss             290
Hypocrite Pride stirs up in us
 To bully out another's guilt.


He had a mind which was somehow
 At once circumference and centre
Of all he might or feel or know;            295
Nothing went ever out, although
 Something did ever enter.


He had as much imagination
 As a pint pot:—he never could
Fancy another situation                 300
From which to dart his contemplation,
 Than that wherein he stood.


Yet his was individual mind,
 And new created all he saw
In a new manner, and refined            305
Those new creations, and combined
 Them, by a master-spirit's law,


Thus—though unimaginative,
 An apprehension clear, intense,
Of his mind's work, had made alive          310
The things it wrought on; I believe
 Wakening a sort of thought in sense.¹


But from the first 'twas Peter's drift
 To be a kind of moral eunuch
He touched the hem of Nature's shift,        315
Felt faint—and never dared uplift
 The closest, all-concealing tunic.


She laughed the while, with an arch smile,
 And kissed him with a sister's kiss,

9. Nature, character, or manner.
1. Lines 293–312 can probably be taken as Shelley's candid (if sardonically expressed) evaluation of Wordsworth's genius.

And said—"My best Diogenes,[2]                         320
I love you well—but, if you please,
   Tempt not again my deepest bliss.

"Tis you are cold—for I, not coy,
   Yield love for love, frank, warm and true:
And Burns, a Scottish Peasant boy,—                    325
His errors prove it—knew my joy
   More, learned friend, than you.

   *"Bocca baciata non perde ventura*
     *Anzi rinnuova come fa la luna:*[3]—
So thought Boccaccio, whose sweet words might cure a   330
Male prude like you from what you now endure, a
   Low-tide in soul, like a stagnant laguna."

Then Peter rubbed his eyes severe,
   And smoothed his spacious forehead down
With his broad palm;—'twixt love and fear,            335
He looked, as he no doubt felt, queer,
   And in his dream sate down.

The Devil was no uncommon creature;
   A leaden-witted thief—just huddled
Out of the dross and scum of nature;                   340
A toadlike lump[4] of limb and feature,
   With mind, and heart, and fancy muddled.

He was that heavy, dull, cold thing
   The Spirit of Evil well may be:
A drone[5] too base to have a sting;                   345
Who gluts, and grimes his lazy wing,
   And calls lust, luxury.

Now he was quite, the kind of wight[6]
   Round whom collect, at a fixed æra,[7]
Venison, turtle, hock[8] and claret,—                  350
Good cheer—and those who come to share it—
   And best East Indian Madeira!

---

2. The Cynic philosopher of Athens who scoffed at everything; the name suggests that Peter is unwilling to commit himself in support of his beliefs.
3. "A mouth that's been kissed does not lose its charm; / Rather, it renews itself as does the moon" (Boccaccio, *Decameron*, Second Day, end of the Seventh Novella).
4. In two stanzas Shelley has coalesced reminiscences of two classic passages—*Paradise Lost*, IV.799ff., where guardian angels discover Satan "Squat like a Toad, close at the eare of *Eve*," and Pope's character of Sporus in "Epistle to Dr. Arbuthnot" (lines 305–33), where Pope echoes that passage in Milton.
5. The non-working male honeybee whose function is to impregnate the queen; hence, a lazy or unproductive member of society.
6. A person; here used with contempt.
7. A memorable or important date.
8. White German wine; *claret:* red Bordeaux wines; *Madeira:* wines of a type imported from this Portuguese island west of Africa.

It was his fancy to invite
  Men of science, wit and learning
Who came to lend each other light:—                         355
He proudly thought that his gold's might
  Had set those spirits burning.

And men of learning, science, wit,
  Considered him as you and I
Think of some rotten tree, and sit                          360
Lounging and dining under it,
  Exposed to the wide sky.

And all the while, with loose fat smile
  The willing wretch sat winking there,
Believing 'twas his power that made                         365
That jovial scene—and that all paid
  Homage to his unnoticed chair.

Though to be sure this place was Hell;
  He was the Devil—and all they—
What though the claret circled well,                        370
And wit, like ocean, rose and fell?—
  Were damned eternally.

### PART FIFTH

#### *Grace*

Among the guests who often staid
  Till the Devil's petits soupers,[9]
A man[1] there came, fair as a maid,                        375
And Peter noted what he said,
  Standing behind his master's chair.

He was a mighty poet—and
  A subtle-souled Psychologist;
All things he seemed to understand                          380
Of old or new—of sea or land—
  But his own mind—which was a mist.

This was a man who might have turned
  Hell into Heaven—and so in gladness
A Heaven unto himself have earned;                          385
But he in shadows undiscerned
  Trusted,—and damned himself to madness.

9. Suppers to which only a few intimates are invited.
1. Samuel Taylor Coleridge. Shelley, who admired Coleridge's writings, may have heard him
   lecture but seems never to have met him socially; he certainly learned much about him from
   such mutual acquaintances as Southey, Godwin, Hunt, Byron, and Maria Gisborne.

He spoke of Poetry, and how
  "Divine it was—a light—a love—
A spirit which like wind doth blow           390
As it listeth, to and fro;
  A dew rained down from God above

"A power which comes and goes like dream,
  And which none can ever trace—
Heaven's light on Earth—Truth's brightest beam."    395
And when he ceased there lay the gleam
  Of those words upon his face.

Now Peter when he heard such talk
  Would, heedless of a broken pate,
Stand like a man asleep, or baulk           400
Some wishing guest of knife or fork,[2]
  Or drop and break his master's plate.

At night he oft would start and wake
  Like a lover, and began
In a wild measure songs to make          405
On moor, and glen, and rocky lake,
  And on the heart of man.

And on the universal sky;—
  And the wide earth's bosom green;—
And the sweet, strange mystery          410
Of what beyond these things may lie,
  And yet remain unseen.

For in his thought he visited
  The spots in which, ere dead and damned,
He his wayward life had led;           415
Yet knew not whence the thoughts were fed
  Which thus his fancy crammed.

And these obscure remembrances
  Stirred such harmony in Peter,
That whensoever he should please,        420
He could speak of rocks and trees
  In poetic metre.

For though it was without a sense
  Of memory, yet he remembered well
Many a ditch and quickset fence;        425
Of lakes he had intelligence
  He knew something of heath and fell.[3]

---

2. I.e., intentionally omit the silverware.
3. *heath:* flat, uncultivated land covered with low vegetation; *fell:* elevated waste or pasture land.

He had also dim recollections
  Of pedlars tramping on their rounds,
Milk pans and pails, and odd collections        430
Of saws,[4] and proverbs; and reflexions
  Old parsons make in burying grounds.

But Peter's verse was clear, and came
  Announcing from the frozen hearth
Of a cold age, that none might tame        435
The soul of that diviner flame
  It augured to the Earth:

Like gentle rains, on the dry plains,
  Making that green which late was grey,
Or like the sudden moon, that stains        440
Some gloomy chamber's window panes
  With a broad light like day.

For language was in Peter's hand
  Like clay while he was yet a potter,
And he made songs for all the land        445
Sweet both to feel and understand
  As pipkins[5] late to mountain Cotter.

And Mr.——, the Bookseller,[6]
  Gave twenty pounds for some:—then scorning
A footman's yellow coat to wear,        450
Peter, too proud of heart I fear,
  Instantly gave the Devil warning.

Whereat the Devil took offence,
  And swore in his soul a great oath then,—
That for his damned impertinence,        455
He'd bring him to a proper sense
  Of what was due to gentlemen!—

## PART SIXTH

### Damnation

"O, that mine enemy had written
  A book!"—cried Job:[7]—A fearful curse;
If to the Arab, as the Briton,        460
'Twas galling to be critic-bitten:—
  The Devil to Peter wished no worse.

4. Traditional maxims and sayings.
5. Small earthenware pots or pans.
6. Though Shelley clearly did not know all the details, he may be alluding to Joseph Cottle's purchase (for 30 guineas) of the copyright to *Lyrical Ballads*.
7. See Job 31:35, where Job's "adversary" is God.

When Peter's next new book found vent,
　　The Devil to all the first Reviews
A copy of it slyly sent                                      465
With five-pound note as compliment,
　　And this short notice—"Pray abuse."⁸

Then *seriatim*,⁹ month and quarter,
　　Appeared such mad tirades.—One said—
"Peter seduced Mrs. Foy's daughter,                          470
Then drowned the Mother in Ullswater,¹
　　The last thing as he went to bed."

Another—"Let him shave his head!
　　Where's Dr. Willis?²—Or is he joking?
What does the rascal mean or hope,                           475
No longer imitating Pope,
　　In that barbarian Shakespeare poking?"

One more,—"Is incest not enough,
　　And must there be adultery too?
Grace after meat? Miscreant³ and liar!                       480
Thief! Blackguard! Scoundrel! Fool! Hellfire
　　Is twenty times too good for you.

"By that last book of yours WE think
　　You've double damned yourself to scorn:
We warned you whilst yet on the brink                        485
You stood. From your black name will shrink
　　The babe that is unborn."

All these Reviews the Devil made
　　Up in a parcel, which he had
Safely to Peter's house conveyed.                            490
For carriage ten-pence Peter paid—
　　Untied them—read them—went half mad.

"What!"—Cried he, "this is my reward
　　For nights of thought, and days of toil?

8. The leading "Reviews" of Shelley's day (as opposed to "magazines" and weekly "newspapers")
were the quarterly *Edinburgh Review* (1802ff.), *Quarterly Review* (1809ff.), and *British Review* (1811–25); and the monthly *Monthly Review* (1749–1845), *Critical Review* (1756–1817), and *British Critic* (1793–1826). Though Francis Jeffrey's attacks on Wordsworth in
the *Edinburgh Review* are the most (in)famous, many reviewers—including Byron—handled
roughly his *Poems: In Two Volumes* (1807). For facsimiles of these and other contemporary
reviews of Wordsworth, Coleridge, and their friends, see the two-volume Part A of Reiman,
ed., *The Romantics Reviewed*. (1972)
9. One by one in succession.
1. Betty Foy, the mother of Wordsworth's "Idiot Boy," had no daughter, but Shelley needed
one for his rhyme; *Ullswater* is one of the larger lakes in the Lake Country of Westmorland
and Cumberland counties.
2. Francis Willis (1718–1807) and his sons John (1751–1835) and Robert Darling Willis
(1760–1821), physicians specializing in the treatment of mental illness, were famous for
treating King George III during his madness. Robert Willis (1799–1878) later wrote on
insanity, but he was too young for Shelley to have known of him.
3. Vile evil-doer, villain.

Do poets, but to be abhorred                                    495
By men of whom they never heard,
   Consume their spirits' oil?

"What have I done to them?—and Who
   *Is* Mrs. Foy? 'Tis very cruel
To speak of me and Betty so!                                    500
Adultery! God defend me! Oh!
   I've half a mind to fight a duel.

"Or," cried he, a grave look collecting,
   "Is it my genius, like the moon,
Sets those who stand her face inspecting,                       505
(That face within their brain reflecting,)
   Like a crazed bell chime, out of tune?"[4]

For Peter did not know the town,
   But thought, as country readers do,
For half a guinea or a crown,                                   510
He bought oblivion or renown
   From God's own voice[5] in a review.

All Peter did on this occasion
   Was, writing some sad stuff in prose.[6]
It is a dangerous invasion                                      515
When Poets criticise: their station
   Is to delight, not pose.

The Devil then sent to Leipsic fair,
   For Born's translation of Kant's book;[7]
A world of words, tail-foremost, where                          520
Right—wrong—false—true—and foul and fair
   As in a lottery wheel are shook.

Five thousand crammed octavo pages
   Of German psychologics,—he
Who his *furor verborum*[8] assuages                            525
Thereon, deserves just seven months' wages
   More than will e'er be due to me.

I looked on them nine several days,
   And then I saw that they were bad;

4. Cf. Shakespeare, *Hamlet*, III.i.165–66: "Now see that noble and most sovereign reason, / Like sweet bells jangled, out of tune and harsh."
5. "*Vox populi, vox dei.* As Mr. Godwin truly observes of a more famous saying, of *some merit as a popular maxim, but totally destitute of philosophical accuracy*" (Shelley's note). *Vox populi, vox dei:* The voice of the people [is] the voice of god.
6. Wordsworth's preface to *Lyrical Ballads* (1800), his preface to the collected *Poems* of 1815, and the "Essay, Supplementary to the Preface" in the same volume (I, 341ff.).
7. F. G. Born's Latin translation of the works of Immanuel Kant: *Opera ad philosophiam criticam pertinentia* (4 vols., Leipzig, 1796–98). Kant (1724–1804), of Koenigsburg, Prussia, was a leading philosopher of the late eighteenth century.
8. The inspired frenzy of poets and prophets.

A friend, too, spoke in their dispraise,—                    530
  He never read them;—with amaze
I found Sir William Drummond had.[9]

When the book came, the Devil sent
  It to "P. Verbovale[1] Esquire,"
With a brief note of compliment,                             535
By that night's Carlisle mail. It went
  And set his soul on fire.

Fire, which *ex luce præbens fumum*,[2]
  Made him beyond the bottom see
Of truth's clear well—when I and you, Ma'am,                 540
Go, as we shall do, *subter humum*,[3]
  We may know more than he.

Now Peter ran to seed in soul
  Into a walking paradox;—
For he was neither part nor whole,                           545
Nor good, nor bad—nor knave, nor fool,
  —Among the woods and rocks.

Furious he rode, where late he ran,
  Lashing and spurring his lame hobby;
Turned to a formal Puritan,                                  550
A solemn and unsexual man,—
  He half believed *White Obi*![4]

This steed in vision he would ride,
  High trotting over nine-inch bridges,
With Flibbertigibbet,[5] imp of pride,                       555
Mocking and mowing by his side—
  A mad brained goblin[6] for a guide—
  Over cornfields, gates and hedges.

After these ghastly rides, he came
  Home to his heart, and found from thence                   560
Much stolen of its accustomed flame:
His thoughts grew weak, drowsy, and lame
  Of their intelligence.

9. Sir William Drummond (1770–1828) criticized Kant's ideas in *Academical Questions* (London, 1805), a book that greatly influenced Shelley.
1. "Quasi, *Qui valet verba:*—*i.e.* all the words which have been, are, or may be expended by, for, against, with, or on him. A sufficient proof of the utility of this History. Peter's progenitor who selected this name seems to have possessed *a pure anticipated cognition* of the nature and modesty of this ornament of his posterity" (Shelley's note).
2. "From light he then gives smoke"; this inverts Horace's praise of Homer's low-key opening of the *Odyssey*: "His thought is not to give flame first and then smoke, but from smoke to let light appear" (*Ars poetica*, 143–44).
3. Under the ground, i.e., die.
4. Christianity; see the note on *White Obi* in the Dedication to *Peter Bell the Third*.
5. A devil or fiend named in Shakespeare's *King Lear* (III.iv.120); *mowing:* making faces, grimacing.
6. Will-o'-the-wisp, the elusive light-goblin who leads travelers astray.

To Peter's view, all seemed one hue;
   He was no Whig, he was no Tory: 565
No Deist[7] and no Christian he;—
He got so subtle, that to be
   Nothing, was all his glory.

One single point in his belief
   From his organization sprung, 570
The heart-enrooted faith, the chief
Ear in his doctrine's blighted sheaf,
   That "happiness is wrong,"

So thought Calvin and Dominic;[8]
   So think their fierce successors, who 575
Even now would neither stint nor stick
Our flesh from off our bones to pick,
   If they might "do their do."

His morals thus were undermined:—
   The old Peter—the hard, old Potter— 580
Was born anew within his mind:
He grew dull, harsh, sly, unrefined,
   As when he tramped beside the Otter.[9]

In the death hues of agony
   Lambently[1] flashing from a fish, 585
Now Peter felt amused to see
Shades, like a rainbow's, rise and flee,
   Mixed with a certain hungry wish.[2]

So in his Country's dying face
   He looked—and, lovely as she lay, 590
Seeking in vain his last embrace,

---

7. One who believes in a deity that created the universe and rules it through natural law, but who does not believe in divine intervention in earthly affairs or in the divinity of Jesus.
8. Both St. Dominic (1170–1221), Spanish founder of the Catholic Dominican order, and John Calvin (1509–64), Reformed theologian at Geneva, burned others as "heretics."
9. "A famous river in the new Atlantis of the Dynastophylic Pantisocratists" (Shelley's note). In one early sonnet, Coleridge addressed the River *Otter* near his boyhood home; in another, he praised Pantisocracy, the plan that he, Southey, their wives (the Fricker sisters), and friends had concocted in 1794 to establish a utopian community on the banks of the Susquehanna River. *Dynastophylic* refers to Southey's and Coleridge's later *love* of the established *dynasties* of Europe.
1. Gliding or flickering on a surface.
2. "See the description of the beautiful colours produced during the agonising death of a number of trout, in the fourth part of a long poem in blank verse, published within a few years. [*The Excursion*, VIII.568–71.] That poem contains curious evidence of the gradual hardening of a strong but circumscribed sensibility, of the perversion of a penetrating but panic stricken understanding. The Author might have derived a lesson which he had probably forgotten from these sweet and sublime verses:—

   This lesson, Shepherd, let us two divide,
   Taught both by what she [i.e., Nature] shews and what conceals,
   Never to blend our pleasure or our pride
   With sorrow of the meanest thing that feels."

(Shelley's note, quoting the last four lines of Wordsworth's "Hart-Leap Well" [1800].)

Wailing her own abandoned case,
　　With hardened sneer he turned away:

And coolly to his own soul said;—
　　"Do you not think that we might make　　　　　　595
A poem on her when she's dead?—
Or, no—a thought is in my head—
　　Her shroud for a new sheet I'll take:

"My wife wants one.—Let who will bury
　　This mangled corpse!—And I and you,　　　　　　600
My dearest Soul, will then make merry,
As the Prince Regent did with Sherry,³—"
　　"Aye—and at last desert me too."

And so his Soul would not be gay,
　　But moaned within him; like a fawn,　　　　　　605
Moaning within a cave, it lay
Wounded and wasting, day by day,
　　Till all its life of life was gone.

As troubled skies stain waters clear,
　　The storm in Peter's heart and mind,　　　　　　610
Now made his verses dark and queer;
They were the ghosts of what they were,
　　Shaking dim grave clothes in the wind.

For he now raved enormous folly
　　Of Baptisms, Sunday-schools and Graves,　　　　615
'Twould make George Colman⁴ melancholy
To have heard him, like a male Molly,⁵
　　Chaunting those stupid staves.

Yet the Reviews, who heaped abuse
　　On Peter, while he wrote for freedom,　　　　　620
So soon as in his song they spy
The folly which soothes Tyranny,
　　Praise him, for those who feed 'em.

"He was a man, too great to scan;—
　　A planet lost in truth's keen rays:—　　　　　625
His virtue, awful and prodigious;—

---

3. Richard Brinsley Sheridan (1751–1816), dramatist, wit, and liberal Whig member of Parliament, was a friend and drinking companion of George IV in his younger days as Prince of Wales. As Prince Regent, George turned reactionary and abandoned Sheridan along with the Whigs; (false) rumor had it that George allowed "Sherry" to be arrested for debt and die in poverty without attempting to assist him. Line 603 is spoken by Peter's soul in reply to his speech in lines 595–602.
4. George Colman, the Younger (1762–1836), a dramatist and writer of farces long noted for his wit and off-color humor, later became a hypocritical government censor of plays.
5. *male Molly:* an effeminate or homosexual man; *staves:* stanzas.

He was the most sublime, religious,
  Pure-minded Poet of these days."

As soon as he read that—cried Peter,
  "Eureka! I have found the way                                    630
To make a better thing of metre
Than e'er was made by living creature
  Up to this blessed day."

Then Peter wrote odes to the Devil;—
  In one of which he meekly said:—                                635
"May Carnage and Slaughter,
Thy niece and thy daughter,[6]
May Rapine and Famine,
Thy gorge ever cramming,[7]
  Glut thee with living and dead!                                 640

"May death and Damnation,
And Consternation,
Flit up from Hell with pure intent!
  Slash them at Manchester,[8]
  Glasgow, Leeds and Chester;                                     645
Drench all with blood from Avon to Trent!

"Let thy body-guard yeomen
Hew down babes and women,
And laugh with bold triumph till Heaven be rent!
  When Moloch[9] in Jewry                                         650
  Munched children with fury
It was thou, Devil, dining with pure intent."[1]


PART SEVENTH

*Double Damnation*

The Devil now knew, his proper cue.—
  Soon as he read the ode, he drove

---

6. Cf. lines 636–37 with Wordsworth's "Ode, 1815" (celebrating the defeat of Napoleon at Waterloo): ". . . Almighty God! / . . . Thy most dreaded instrument, / In working out a pure intent, / Is Man—arrayed for mutual slaughter, / —Yea, Carnage is thy daughter." After *Peter Bell the Third* appeared in 1840, Wordsworth drastically revised these lines before reprinting his poem in 1845.
7. Pronounced "crammin'."
8. An allusion to the Peterloo Massacre; see "The Mask of Anarchy."
9. The name of both a Canaanite god to whom children were sacrificed as burnt offerings (Leviticus 18:21) and one of Milton's devils in *Paradise Lost* (II.43). Moloch, as Milton knew—and Shelley may have known—means "king" in Hebrew.
1. "It is curious to observe how often extremes meet. Cobbett and Peter use the same language for a different purpose: Peter is indeed a sort of metrical Cobbett. Cobbett is however more mischievous than Peter, because he pollutes a holy and now unconquerable cause with the principles of legitimate murder; whilst the other only makes a bad one ridiculous and odious.
    "If either Peter or Cobbett should see this note, each will feel more indignation at being compared to the other than at any censure implied in the moral perversion laid to their charge" (Shelley's note).

To his friend Lord M<sup>c</sup>Murderchouse's,² 655
A man of interest in both houses,
   And said:—"For money or for love


"Pray find some cure or sinecure,
   To feed from the superfluous taxes
A friend of ours—a Poet—fewer 660
Have fluttered tamer to the lure
   Than he."—His Lordship stands and racks his


Stupid brains, while one might count
   As many beads as he had boroughs,—³
At length replies;—from his mean front, 665
Like one who rubs out an account,
   Smoothing away the unmeaning furrows:—


"It happens fortunately, dear Sir,
   I can. I hope I need require
No pledge from you, that he will stir 670
In our affairs;—like Oliver,⁴
   That he'll be worthy of his hire."


These words exchanged, the news sent off
   To Peter:—home the Devil hied;
Took to his bed; he had no cough, 675
No doctor,—meat and drink enough,—
   Yet that same night he died.


The Devil's corpse was leaded down.—
   His decent heirs enjoyed his pelf;⁵
Mourning coaches, many a one, 680
Followed his hearse along the town:—
   Where was the Devil himself?


When Peter heard of his promotion
   His eyes grew like two stars for bliss:
There was a bow of sleek devotion 685
Engendering in his back; each motion
   Seemed a Lord's shoe to kiss.

---

2. *M<sup>c</sup>Murderchouse: chouse* meant to cheat or swindle, or (as a noun) one who is a swindler.
The nobleman who actually obtained a government position for Wordsworth was (as Shelley
knew) William Lowther, Earl of Lonsdale, the son of ("M<sup>c</sup>") Lord Lowther, who had cheated
Wordsworth and his siblings out of money that Lowther owed to their father.
3. *boroughs:* political units that elected one or two members to Parliament; a nobleman was
said to "own" boroughs when he could influence enough of the few voters in it to elect his
hand-picked candidate(s).
4. W. J. Richards ("Oliver") was a government spy and agent like Castle (line 152).
5. A deprecatory term for money or wealth.

He hired a house,[6] bought plate, and made
  A genteel drive up to his door,
With sifted gravel neatly laid,—       690
As if defying all who said
  Peter was ever poor.

But a disease soon struck into
  The very life and soul of Peter—
He walked about—slept—had the hue      695
Of health upon his cheeks—and few
  Dug better—none a heartier eater.

And yet, a strange and horrid curse
  Clung upon Peter, night and day—
Month after month the thing grew worse,     700
And deadlier than in this my verse
  I can find strength to say.

Peter was dull—he was at first
  Dull—O, so dull—so very dull!
Whether he talked—wrote—or rehearsed—    705
Still with this dulness was he cursed—
  Dull—beyond all conception—dull.—

No one could read his books—no mortal,
  But a few natural friends, would hear him:—
The parson came not near his portal;—    710
His state was like that of the immortal
  Described by Swift[7]—no man could bear him.

His sister, wife, and children yawned,
  With a long, slow and drear ennui,
All human patience far beyond;      715
Their hopes of Heaven each would have pawned,
  Any where else to be.

But in his verse, and in his prose,
  The essence of his dullness was
Concentred and compressed so close,    720
'Twould have made Guatimozin doze
  On his red gridiron of brass.[8]

6. In 1813, Wordsworth received a government appointment as Distributor of [Tax] Stamps for Westmorland and Cumberland countries and moved into Rydal Mount, the larger house that he was to occupy until his death in 1850.
7. One of the Struldbruggs in *Gulliver's Travels*, Part III, chap. x, who are doomed to live forever.
8. *Guatimozin*, the nephew and successor of Montezuma, led the Aztec defense of Mexico City against Cortes; after his capture, he and a friend were tortured on a hot metal grid. In order to keep up his companion's courage, Guatimozin said, "Am I now reposing on a bed of flowers?"

A printer's boy, folding those pages,
    Fell slumbrously upon one side:
Like those famed seven who slept three ages.[9]          725
To wakeful frenzy's vigil rages
    As opiates were the same applied.

Even the Reviewers who were hired
    To do the work of his reviewing,
With adamantine nerves, grew tired;—                     730
Gaping and torpid they retired,
    To dream of what they should be doing.

And worse and worse, the drowsy curse
    Yawned in him—till it grew a pest—
A wide contagious atmosphere,                            735
Creeping like cold through all things near;
    A power to infect, and to infest.

His servant maids and dogs grew dull;
    His kitten, late a sportive elf;
The woods and lakes, so beautiful,                       740
Of dim stupidity were full,
    All grew dull as Peter's self.

The earth under his feet—the springs,
    Which lived within it a quick life—
The Air—the Winds of many wings—                         745
That fan it with new murmurings,
    Were dead to their harmonious strife.

The birds and beasts within the wood,
    The insects—and each creeping thing,
Were now a silent multitude;                             750
Love's work was left unwrought:—no brood
    Near Peter's house took wing.

And every neighbouring Cottager
    Stupidly yawned upon the other;
No jackass brayed;—no little cur                         755
Cocked up his ears;—no man would stir
    To save a dying mother.

Yet all from that charmed district went
    But some, half idiot and half knave,
Who, rather than pay any rent,                           760
Would live, with marvellous content,
    Over his father's grave.

9. Seven Christian youths of Ephesus, sealed up in a cave during the Decian persecution of
A.D. 250, awoke after a sleep of 187 years (Gibbon calculates in *Decline and Fall*, Chap.
xxxiii), or as Shelley here estimates, about three lifetimes.

No bailiff dared within that space,
  For fear of the dull charm, to enter:
A man would bear upon his face,                    765
For fifteen months, in any case,
  The yawn of such a venture.

Seven miles above—below—around—
  This pest of dulness holds its sway:
A ghastly life without a sound;                    770
To Peter's soul the spell is bound—
  How should it ever pass away?

———

Finis

# THE WITCH OF ATLAS

In August 1820, Shelley went on foot from Lucca to a shrine high in the Apennines atop Monte San Pellegrino, completing the entire journey in three days (August 11–13). Inspired during this walk, Shelley spent the next three days (August 14–16) writing "The Witch of Atlas."

The poem is written in the *ottava rima* stanzas of Italian seriocomic poetry. In June and July, Shelley and Mary Shelley had been reading aloud *Il Ricciardetto* (1738) by Niccolò Forteguerri, an imitator of Luigi Pulci, whose *Morgante Maggiore* had been the ultimate source of Byron's style in *Beppo, Don Juan*, and *A Vision of Judgment*. But Shelley's *ottava rima* in "The Witch of Atlas" (and in the Homeric "Hymn to Mercury," which he translated during this period) is as distinctively different from Byron's *ottava rima* as it is from Keats's use of the same form in *Isabella*.

Shelley treats the Witch seriously but with lightness and without a note of sentimentality. Yet she plays pranks with mortal creatures, and they—including the poet and his readers—are aware that the consequences of her actions are not as satisfactory to humankind as they might be. The tone holds the reader's feelings in suspension, as the poet describes the incomparable beauty and perfection of the Witch and, at the same time, her lack of understanding sympathy with the problems of mortal creatures. Jerrold Hogle, who notes Leigh Hunt's oft-cited argument that the Witch is an allegorical personification of the imagination at work, recalls Shelley's own warnings in the introductory stanzas to Mary Shelley against reading the poem allegorically. Hogle then offers a long list of figures with whom Shelley's Witch shares some characteristics, including Isis; Venus; Juno; Minerva; Hermes (at his most prankish); Milton's *L'Allegro* nymph; Byron's "Witch of the Alps" in *Manfred*; Spenser's Una, Belphoebe, and Phaedria; Dante's Beatrice and Petrach's Laura, when they appear to the poets in dream-visions; the Massylian priestess described by Dido as casting spells near Mount Atlas in Virgil's *Aeneid*; and—from Shelley's own poetry—the "Witch Poesy" in "Mont Blanc," Intellectual Beauty, Queen Mab, the dream-maiden from *Alastor*, Cythna, Asia, Panthea, the cloud, the west wind, and the sky-lark (*Shelley's Process* [1988], pp. 211–12).

Though most of such "plot" as the poem exhibits is self-explanatory, a few comments on particular matters may be helpful. According to some classical geographers, the Atlas Mountains, which were the Witch's home, were the source of one branch of the Nile River, which was imagined to loop from Morocco below the Sahara Desert and flow eastward into the Sudan. So the Witch's final journey down the populated Nile Valley has some connection with her childhood among the remote mountains. Roland A. Duerksen has suggested that the Witch's flight into the skies of the Southern Hemisphere (lines 423–48) was Shelley's response to the Prologue of Wordsworth's *Peter Bell the Third*, in which the prosaic narrator rejects the talking boat's offer to take him to a calm, cool oasis in sub-Saharan Africa ("Wordsworth and the Austral Retreat in Shelley's 'Witch of Atlas,' " *KSJ* XXXIV [1985]: 18–19). And Frederick Colwell argues that Shelley's portrait of an "Austral lake" that is a calm haven has its origin in reports Shelley would have heard of "a vast lake far to the south through which the Nile or one of its arms was reputed to pass," later to be named Lake Victoria ("Shelley's 'Witch of Atlas' and the Mythic Geography of the Nile," *ELH* XLV [1978]: 83). Indeed, as Debbie Lee has noted, contemporary interest in travel accounts of sub-Saharan Africa was keen, piqued by such books as Françoise Le Vaillant's *Travels into the Interior Parts of Africa* (1790), Mungo Park's *Travels in the Interior Districts of Africa* (1799), and C. F. Damberger's (faked) *Travels through the Interior of Africa* (1801). Lee's essay connects the exploration of Africa's interior and Romantic writers' exploration of the human interior—and both these subjects to gender codes (*European Romantic Review* VIII [Spring 1997]: 169–83).

Mary Shelley transcribed "The Witch of Atlas" in December 1820, and Shelley mailed the poem to Ollier on January 20, 1821. On February 22 he instructed Ollier to publish it with his name—but not to include it with *Julian and Maddalo*. Ollier neglected issuing "The Witch," and it was first published by Mary Shelley in Shelley's *Posthumous Poems* (1824), though without the introductory stanzas in which Shelley mocks her, the critics, and Wordsworth's *Peter Bell*. She added these stanzas when she reprinted the poem in the one-volume second edition of Shelley's *Poetical Works* (1839/40).

Besides the first edition and Mary Shelley's subsequent collected editions of 1839, the chief textual authorities are Shelley's intermediate fair copy, Bodleian MS Shelley d.1, fols. 15–32 (*BSM*, IV.i), and a transcript in Mary Shelley's hand that Forman collated in his edition of 1876. Drafts for the poem can be found in Bodleian MS Shelley adds. e.6, rev., pp. 94–70, 68–66, 30, 9–8 (*BSM*, V). Shelley's fair copy is missing some lines and phrases, as is Mary Shelley's transcript, which obviously derives from it. The fair copy by Mary Shelley sent to Ollier in January 1821 presumably served as press copy for *Posthumous Poems* (1824); it is now lost. Her other transcript, the one collated by Forman, may have been done in Italy after Shelley's death, before Mary Shelley had retrieved the completed version sent to Ollier. We have followed 1824 on most verbal differences but have followed the manuscripts on several matters of spelling, capitalization, and punctuation and on a few verbal points where the 1824 reading could have resulted from Mary Shelley's error in transcribing Shelley's manuscript or the typesetter's in setting her transcript.

# The Witch of Atlas

## To Mary

(ON HER OBJECTING TO THE FOLLOWING POEM, UPON THE SCORE
OF ITS CONTAINING NO HUMAN INTEREST)

### I

How, my dear Mary, are you critic-bitten
  (For vipers kill, though dead)[1] by some review,
That you condemn these verses I have written
  Because they tell no story, false or true?
What, though no mice are caught by a young kitten,      5
  May it not leap and play as grown cats do,
Till its claws come? Prithee, for this one time,
Content thee with a visionary rhyme.

### II

What hand would crush the silken-winged fly,[2]
  The youngest of inconstant April's minions,[3]      10
Because it cannot climb the purest sky
  Where the Swan sings, amid the Sun's dominions?[4]
Not thine. Thou knowest 'tis its doom to die
  When Day shall hide within her twilight pinions[5]
The lucent[6] eyes, and the eternal smile,      15
Serene as thine, which lent it life awhile.

### III

To thy fair feet a winged Vision[7] came
  Whose date should have been longer than a day,
And o'er thy head did beat its wings for fame
  And in thy sight its fading plumes display;      20
The watery bow burned in the evening flame,
  But the shower fell,—the swift Sun went his way.
And that is dead:[8] O, let me not believe
That anything of mine is fit to live!

1. "Experiments have shown that a snake head severed from its body will remain alive and able to inflict a deadly bite for 15 to 30 minutes after being cut off" (Joan Arehart-Treichel, *Poisons and Toxins* [New York, 1976], pp. 146–47). We have not identified the contemporary source for Shelley's information.
2. Ephemerid, or dayfly, which lives for only a few hours to a few days (see "The Sensitive-Plant," II.49).
3. Favorites or darlings.
4. In classical mythology the swan, believed to sing shortly before its death, was sacred to Apollo (the *sun*); the swan appears in astronomy as the northern constellation Cygnus.
5. Wings.
6. Shining or bright.
7. Shelley alludes to his longest poem, *Laon and Cythna* (*The Revolt of Islam*), also dedicated to Mary Shelley.
8. Both the sales and the reviews of *The Revolt* disappointed Shelley.

## IV

Wordsworth informs us he was nineteen years                             25
    Considering and retouching Peter Bell;[9]
Watering his laurels[1] with the killing tears
    Of slow, dull care, so that their roots to hell
Might pierce, and their wide branches blot the spheres
    Of Heaven, with dewy leaves and flowers; this well          30
May be, for Heaven and Earth conspire to foil
The over busy gardener's blundering toil.

## V

My Witch indeed is not so sweet a creature
    As Ruth or Lucy,[2] whom his graceful praise
Clothes for our grandsons—but she matches Peter                        35
    Though he took nineteen years, and she three days
In dressing. Light the vest of flowing metre
    She wears: he, proud as dandy with his stays,
Has hung upon his wiry limbs a dress
Like King Lear's "looped and windowed raggedness."[3]                  40

## VI

If you strip Peter, you will see a fellow
    Scorched by Hell's hyperequatorial climate
Into a kind of a sulphureous yellow,
    A lean mark hardly fit to fling a rhyme at;
In shape a Scaramouch, in hue Othello.[4]                              45
    If you unveil my Witch, no Priest or Primate
Can shrive[5] you of that sin, if sin there be
In love, when it becomes idolatry.

## The Witch of Atlas

## I

Before those cruel Twins, whom at one birth
    Incestuous Change bore to her father Time,                    50
        Error and Truth, had hunted from the earth
        All those bright natures which adorned its prime,
    And left us nothing to believe in, worth
        The pains of putting into learned rhyme,

9. For Wordsworth's Peter Bell, see the headnote to Peter Bell the Third, above.
1. The emblem of distinction in poetry.
2. Idealized young women in Wordsworth's Lyrical Ballads.
3. The reference is to Shakespeare, King Lear, III.iv.31.
4. Probably the puppet representing the stock character in Italian farce, Scaramouche, a coward and boaster constantly being cudgeled by Harlequin; Othello: i.e., black.
5. Impose penance on and administer absolution for.

A lady-witch there lived on Atlas' mountain[6]                    55
Within a cavern, by a secret fountain.

## II

Her mother was one of the Atlantides[7]—
    The all-beholding Sun[8] had ne'er beholden
In his wide voyage o'er continents and seas
    So fair a creature, as she lay enfolden                    60
In the warm shadow of her loveliness . . .
    He kissed her with his beams, and made all golden
The chamber of grey rock in which she lay—
She, in that dream of joy, dissolved away.[9]

## III

'Tis said, she first was changed into a vapour,                    65
    And then into a cloud, such clouds as flit,
Like splendour-winged moths about a taper,
    Round the red West when the sun dies in it:
And then into a meteor,[1] such as caper
    On hill-tops when the moon is in a fit:[2]                    70
Then, into one of those mysterious stars
Which hide themselves between the Earth and Mars.

## IV

Ten times the Mother of the Months[3] had bent
    Her bow beside the folding-star,[4] and bidden
With that bright sign the billows[5] to indent                    75
    The sea-deserted sand—like children chidden
At her command they ever came and went—
    Since in that cave a dewy Splendour hidden
Took shape and motion: with the living form
Of this embodied Power, the cave grew warm.                    80

## V

A lovely lady garmented in light
    From her own beauty—deep her eyes, as are
Two openings of unfathomable night

6. The Atlas Mountains run from southwestern Morocco to northeastern Algeria. According to the myth, Atlas, a brother of Prometheus, when shown Medusa's head by Perseus, was changed into the mountain; he was believed to support the heavens on his shoulders.
7. Daughters of Atlas and Hesperus or Pleione, the *Atlantides* (also called Hesperides or Pleiades) were nymphs or goddesses made into a constellation after their deaths.
8. I.e., Apollo; see line 293 and note.
9. *The all-beholding . . . dissolved away*: The circumstances of the Witch's birth are very similar to those of Spenser's Belphoebe and Amoret (*Faerie Queene*, III.vi.7ff.).
1. Aurora or halo.
2. An interval of inaction; perhaps a period when the moon is obscured by clouds.
3. I.e., the moon; nine full months *she bent / Her bow* by expanding from a thin crescent to the full moon.
4. Venus, the evening star, rising at folding time (when sheep are put into their folds for the night).
5. Waves (figuratively, the tides).

Seen through a Temple's cloven roof—her hair
Dark—the dim brain whirls dizzy with delight                    85
    Picturing her form—her soft smiles shone afar,
And her low voice was heard like love, and drew
All living things towards this wonder new.


### VI

And first the spotted cameleopard[6] came,
    And then the wise and fearless Elephant;                    90
Then the sly Serpent, in the golden flame
    Of his own volumes intervolved;[7]—all gaunt
And sanguine[8] beasts her gentle looks made tame—
    They drank before her at her sacred fount—
And every beast of beating heart grew bold,                     95
Such gentleness and power even to behold.


### VII

The brinded[9] lioness led forth her young
    That she might teach them how they should forego
Their inborn thirst of death—the pard[1] unstrung
    His sinews at her feet, and sought to know                  100
With looks whose motions spoke without a tongue
    How he might be as gentle as the doe.
The magic circle of her voice and eyes
All savage natures did imparadise.


### VIII

And old Silenus,[2] shaking a green stick                       105
    Of lilies, and the wood-gods in a crew
Came, blithe, as in the olive copses thick
    Cicadæ[3] are, drunk with the noonday dew:
And Dryope and Faunus[4] followed quick,
    Teasing the God to sing them something new                  110
Till in this cave they found the lady lone,
Sitting upon a seat of emerald stone.

---

6. Giraffe.
7. Wound up within his coils (*volumes*).
8. Bloody; i.e., carnivorous or predatory.
9. Tawny or brownish color, marked with streaks of a different hue.
1. Leopard or panther.
2. A demigod, attendant of Bacchus. See *Prometheus Unbound*, II.ii; *wood-gods*: probably the Sileni—fauns and satyrs in general.
3. Insects with large, transparent wings, sometimes called locusts and often erroneously identified as grasshoppers; the male makes a shrill chirping sound.
4. *Dryope*: a nymph; the name designates both the Arcadian mother of Pan by Mercury and an Italian nymph who was the mother of Tarquitus by *Faunus*, the brave and wise legendary ruler of Italy, who was revered as a satyr-deity.

## IX

And Universal Pan,[5] 'tis said, was there,
   And though none saw him,—through the adamant
Of the deep mountains, through the trackless air,          115
   And through those living spirits, like a want[6]
He past out of his everlasting lair
   Where the quick heart of the great world doth pant—
And felt that wondrous lady all alone—
And she felt him upon her emerald throne.                  120

## X

And, every Nymph of stream and spreading tree
   And every shepherdess of Ocean's flocks[7]
Who drives her white waves over the green Sea;
   And Ocean with the brine on his grey locks,
And quaint Priapus[8] with his company                     125
   All came, much wondering how the enwombed rocks
Could have brought forth so beautiful a birth;—
Her love subdued their wonder and their mirth.

## XI

The herdsmen and the mountain maidens came
   And the rude kings of Pastoral Garamant[9]—             130
Their spirits shook within them, as a flame
   Stirred by the air under a cavern gaunt:
Pigmies, and Polyphemes,[1] by many a name,
   Centaurs and Satyrs,[2] and such shapes as haunt
Wet clefts,—and lumps neither alive nor dead,             135
Dog-headed, bosom-eyed[3] and bird-footed.

## XII

For she was beautiful—her beauty made
   The bright world dim, and every thing beside
Seemed like the fleeting image of a shade:
   No thought of living spirit could abide—               140
Which to her looks had ever been betrayed,

5. As god of shepherds, huntsmen, and inhabitants of Arcadia (an area in Greece in the center of the Peloponnesus), *Pan* (sometimes identified with *Faunus*) appears as a ruddy, flat-nosed, horned man with the feet and legs of a goat—a satyr.
6. Mole (*OED*, sb.1); identified by Curt R. Zimansky.
7. Daughters of Oceanus, the Oceanides, who also protected seamen.
8. The deity of gardens and genitalia, *Priapus* was the deformed son of Aphrodite and Dionysus; he is represented with a human face, goat's ears, a stick to drive away birds, and a pruning hook.
9. The Garamantes were an African (north central Libyan) people who lived in common and "scarce clothed themselves" because of the warm climate.
1. One-eyed giants; after Polyphemus, the Cyclops (*Odyssey*, IX).
2. *Centaurs*: a race of imaginary creatures, half man and half horse, of Thessaly; *Satyrs*: see note 5, above. These creatures are both lascivious and generally playful.
3. The syntax of the entire line indicates that the creatures have eyes like bosoms—i.e., bulging eyes, not (as has been suggested) breasts filled with eyes.

On any object in the world so wide,
On any hope within the circling skies,
But on her form, and in her inmost eyes.

### XIII

Which when the lady knew she took her spindle          145
    And twined three threads of fleecy mist, and three
Long lines of light such as the Dawn may kindle
    The clouds and waves and mountains with, and she
As many star-beams, ere their lamps could dwindle
    In the belated moon, wound skilfully;              150
And with these threads a subtle veil she wove—
A shadow for the splendour of her love.

### XIV

The deep recesses of her odorous dwelling
    Were stored with magic treasures—Sounds of air,
Which had the power all spirits of compelling,         155
    Folded in cells[4] of chrystal silence there;
Such as we hear in youth, and think the feeling
    Will never die—yet ere we are aware,
The feeling and the sound are fled and gone,
And the regret they leave remains alone.               160

### XV

And there lay Visions swift and sweet and quaint,
    Each in its thin sheath like a chrysalis,[5]
Some eager to burst forth, some weak and faint
    With the soft burthen of intensest bliss;
It was its work to bear to many a saint                165
    Whose heart adores the shrine which holiest is,
Even Love's—and others white, green, grey and black,
And of all shapes—and each was at her beck.

### XVI

And Odours in a kind of aviary
    Of ever blooming Eden-trees she kept,              170
Clipt[6] in a floating net a love-sick Fairy
    Had woven from dew beams while the moon yet slept—
As bats at the wired window of a dairy
    They beat their vans;[7] and each was an adept,
When loosed and missioned, making wings of winds,      175
To stir sweet thoughts or sad, in destined minds.

4. Small rooms in monasteries.
5. Cocoon.
6. Embraced or held tightly.
7. Wings.

## XVII

And liquors clear and sweet, whose healthful might
   Could medicine the sick soul to happy sleep
And change eternal death into a night
   Of glorious dreams—or if eyes needs must weep,     180
Could make their tears all wonder and delight,
   She in her chrystal vials did closely keep—
If men could drink of those clear vials, 'tis said
The living were not envied of[8] the dead.

## XVIII

Her cave was stored with scrolls of strange device,     185
   The works of some Saturnian Archimage,
Which taught the expiations at whose price
   Men from the Gods might win that happy age
Too lightly lost, redeeming native vice[9]—
   And which might quench the earth-consuming rage     190
Of gold and blood—till men should live and move
Harmonious as the sacred stars above.

## XIX

And how all things that seem untameable,
   Not to be checked and not to be confined,
Obey the spells of wisdom's wizard skill;     195
   Time, Earth and Fire—the Ocean and the Wind
And all their shapes—and man's imperial Will—
   And other scrolls whose writings did unbind
The inmost lore of Love—let the prophane[1]
Tremble to ask what secrets they contain.     200

## XX

And wondrous works of substances unknown,
   To which the enchantment of her father's power
Had changed those ragged blocks of savage stone,
   Were heaped in the recesses of her bower;
Carved lamps and chalices and phials which shone     205
   In their own golden beams—each like a flower
Out of whose depth a fire-fly shakes his light
Under a cypress in the starless night.

8. By.
9. Unlike Archimago's books, which contain recipes for evil charms (Spenser's *Faerie Queene*, I.i.36), the Witch's *scrolls* show how men can return to *that happy age*: the Golden Age of Saturn or the time before the Fall, when men acquired *native vice*, or original sin. (Cf. "Letter to Maria Gisborne," lines 106ff.)
1. The uninitiated.

## XXI

At first she lived alone in this wild home,
    And her own thoughts were each a minister,        210
Clothing themselves or[2] with the Ocean foam,
    Or with the wind, or with the speed of fire,
To work whatever purposes might come
    Into her mind; such power her mighty Sire
Had girt them with, whether to fly or run,       215
Through all the regions which he shines upon.

## XXII

The Ocean-Nymphs and Hamadryades,
    Oreads and Naiads with long weedy locks,
Offered to do her bidding through the seas,
    Under the earth, and in the hollow rocks,      220
And far beneath the matted roots of trees
    And in the knarled heart of stubborn oaks,
So they might live forever in the light
Of her sweet presence—each a satellite.[3]

## XXIII

"This may not be—" the wizard Maid replied;      225
    "The fountains where the Naiades bedew
Their shining hair at length are drained and dried;
    The solid oaks forget their strength, and strew
Their latest leaf upon the mountains wide;
    The boundless Ocean like a drop of dew      230
Will be consumed—the stubborn centre must
Be scattered like a cloud of summer dust—

## XXIV

"And ye with them will perish one by one—
    If I must sigh to think that this shall be—
If I must weep when the surviving Sun      235
    Shall smile on your decay—Oh, ask not me
To love you till your little race is run;
    I cannot die as ye must . . . over me
Your leaves shall glance—the streams in which ye dwell
Shall be my paths henceforth, and so, farewell!"      240

## XXV

She spoke and wept—the dark and azure well
    Sparkled beneath the shower of her bright tears,
And every little circlet where they fell

2. Either.
3. I.e., an attendant to an important person. The nymphs are beautiful young girls and inferior
deities, each of whom lasts only as long as her special habitat: forests and trees (*Hamadryades*), mountains (*Oreads*), and fountains and streams (*Naiads*).

Flung to the cavern-roof inconstant spheres
And intertangled lines of light—a knell[4]                    245
    Of sobbing voices came upon her ears
From those departing Forms, o'er the serene
Of the white streams and of the forest green.

### XXVI

All day the wizard lady sate aloof
    Spelling out scrolls of dread antiquity,                    250
Under the Cavern's fountain-lighted roof;
    Or broidering the pictured poesy
Of some high tale upon her growing woof,[5]
    Which the sweet splendour of her smiles could dye
In hues outshining Heaven—and ever she                    255
Added some grace to the wrought poesy.

### XXVII

While on her hearth lay blazing many a piece
    Of sandal wood, rare gums and cinnamon;
Men scarcely know how beautiful fire is—
    Each flame of it is as a precious stone                    260
Dissolved in ever moving light, and this
    Belongs to each and all who gaze upon.
The Witch beheld it not, for in her hand
She held a woof that dimmed the burning brand.[6]

### XXVIII

This lady never slept, but lay in trance                    265
    All night within the fountain—as in sleep. .
Its emerald crags glowed in her beauty's glance:
    Through the green splendour of the water deep
She saw the constellations reel and dance
    Like fire-flies—and withal[7] did ever keep                    270
The tenour[8] of her contemplations calm,
With open eyes, closed feet and folded palm.

### XXIX

And when the whirlwinds and the clouds descended
    From the white pinnacles of that cold hill
She past at dewfall to a space extended                    275
    Where in a lawn of flowering asphodel
Amid a wood of pines and cedars blended
    There yawned an inextinguishable well

4. A doleful cry or dirge, reminiscent of a funeral bell.
5. The weft, or threads that intertwine at right angles with the warp (the lengthwise threads on the loom). In "Mont Blanc" (line 44) Shelley calls Poesy a witch.
6. Wood burning on the hearth; *woof*: here, a piece of woven fabric.
7. Nevertheless.
8. The procedure or course of progress.

Of crimson fire, full even to the brim
And overflowing all the margin trim.                                   280

### XXX

Within the which she lay when the fierce war
 Of wintry winds shook that innocuous liquor[9]
In many a mimic[1] moon and bearded star[2]
 O'er woods and lawns—the serpent heard it flicker
In sleep, and dreaming still, he crept afar—                           285
 And when the windless snow descended thicker
Than autumn leaves she watched it as it came
Melt on the surface of the level flame.

### XXXI

She had a Boat which some say Vulcan wrought
 For Venus, as the chariot of her star;[3]                        290
But it was found too feeble to be fraught
 With all the ardours in that Sphere which are,
And so she sold it, and Apollo[4] bought
 And gave it to this daughter: from a car
Changed to the fairest and the lightest boat                           295
Which ever upon mortal[5] stream did float.

### XXXII

And others say, that when but three hours old
 The first-born Love out of his cradle leapt[6]
And clove dun Chaos with his wings of gold,
 And like an horticultural adept,                                  300
Stole a strange seed, and wrapt it up in mould
 And sowed it in his mother's star,[7] and kept
Watering it all the summer with sweet dew,
And with his wings fanning it as it grew.

### XXXIII

The plant grew strong and green—the snowy flower                       305
 Fell, and the long and gourd-like fruit began
To turn the light and dew by inward power

---

9. The fire.
1. An artistic or playful imitation of.
2. A comet with its tail (which always points away from the sun) preceding it.
3. *Venus* is goddess of beauty, laughter, grace, and pleasure, and mother of Love; *Vulcan*, craftsman among the gods, is her deformed husband.
4. The sun and inventor and god of the fine arts, including medicine, poetry, music, and eloquence.
5. I.e., accessible to human beings, as opposed to the sphere of Venus.
6. Cf. Shelley's translation of Plato's *Symposium*: "Hesiod says . . . that after Chaos these two were produced, the Earth and Love": *clove dun Chaos*: i.e., split (*clove*) the dark or murky (*dun*) void (*Chaos*).
7. The *star*, called Lucifer or the morning star, is actually the planet Venus. Here Shelley combines the myth from Hesiod with that of Cupid, the son of Venus.

To its own substance; woven tracery ran
Of light firm texture, ribbed and branching, o'er
   The solid rind, like a leaf's veined fan—         310
Of which Love scooped this boat—and with soft motion
Piloted it round the circumfluous[8] Ocean.


### XXXIV

This boat she moored upon her fount, and lit
   A living spirit within all its frame,
Breathing the soul of swiftness into it—         315
   Couched on the fountain, like a panther tame,
One of the twain at Evan's[9] feet that sit—
   Or as on Vesta's[1] sceptre a swift flame—
Or on blind Homer's heart a winged thought—
In joyous expectation lay the Boat.         320


### XXXV

Then by strange art she kneaded fire and snow
   Together, tempering the repugnant mass
With liquid love—all things together grow
   Through which the harmony of love can pass;
And a fair Shape out of her hands did flow—         325
   A living Image, which did far surpass
In beauty that bright shape of vital stone
Which drew the heart out of Pygmalion.[2]


### XXXVI

A sexless thing it was, and in its growth
   It seemed to have developed no defect         330
Of either sex, yet all the grace of both—
   In gentleness and strength its limbs were decked;
The bosom swelled lightly with its full youth—
   The countenance was such as might select
Some artist that his skill should never die,         335
Imaging forth such perfect purity.

---

8. Flowing around; in ancient geography Ocean was thought to be a river flowing around the land.
9. *Evan:* Bacchus (Dionysus).
1. Roman goddess of the sacred hearth, which was tended by the vestal virgins.
2. *Pygmalion:* a legendary king of Cyprus who, after he had vowed never to love a woman or to marry, sculptured and fell in love with a beautiful statue, which Venus changed into a living (*vital*) woman in response to his prayers (Ovid, *Metamorphoses*, X). In the classical legend, Hermaphroditus was the son of Hermes (Mercury) and Aphrodite (Venus); a nymph united her body with his, giving Hermaphroditus the perfect beauty of both sexes. Though the Witch's hermaphrodite is made of snow like the wicked witch's False Florimell in *The Faerie Queene*, III.viii.6, Shelley's Witch adds fire instead of the wax, mercury, and vermilion that inhabit the creature made by Spenser's witch.

## XXXVII

From its smooth shoulders hung two rapid wings,
　　Fit to have borne it to the seventh sphere,[3]
Tipt with the speed of liquid lightenings—
　　Dyed in the ardours of the atmosphere—                    340
She led her creature to the boiling springs
　　Where the light boat was moored, and said: "Sit here!"
And pointed to the prow, and took her seat
Beside the rudder, with opposing feet.[4]

## XXXVIII

And down the streams which clove those mountains vast      345
　　Around their inland islets, and amid
The panther-peopled forests, whose shade cast
　　Darkness and odours and a pleasure hid
In melancholy gloom, the pinnace[5] past
　　By many a star-surrounded pyramid                        350
Of icy crag cleaving the purple sky
And caverns yawning round unfathomably.

## XXXIX

The silver noon into that winding dell
　　With slanted gleam athwart the forest tops
Tempered like golden evening, feebly fell;                 355
　　A green and glowing light like that which drops
From folded lilies in which glow worms dwell
　　When Earth over her face night's mantle wraps;
Between the severed mountains lay on high
Over the stream, a narrow rift[6] of sky.                  360

## XL

And ever as she went, the Image lay
　　With folded wings and unawakened eyes;
And o'er its gentle countenance did play
　　The busy dreams, as thick as summer flies,
Chasing the rapid smiles that would not stay,             365
　　And drinking the warm tears, and the sweet sighs
Inhaling, which, with busy murmur vain,
They had aroused from that full heart and brain.

## XLI

And ever down the prone[7] vale, like a cloud
　　Upon a stream of wind, the pinnace went:                370

3. The transparent hollow globe carrying Saturn; this sphere was next to that of the fixed stars,
   according to classical and medieval astronomy.
4. I.e., the Witch and the Hermaphrodite sat facing each other.
5. Small boat.
6. An interval.
7. Having a descending slope.

Now lingering on the pools, in which abode
  The calm and darkness of the deep content
In which they paused, now o'er the shallow road
  Of white and dancing waters all besprent[8]
With sand and polished pebbles . . mortal Boat        375
In such a shallow rapid could not float.

### XLII

And down the earthquaking cataracts[9] which shiver
  Their snowlike waters into golden air,
Or under chasms unfathomable ever
  Sepulchre[1] them, till in their rage they tear       380
A subterranean portal for the river,
  It fled . . the circling sunbows[2] did upbear
Its fall down the hoar[3] precipice of spray,
Lighting it far upon its lampless way.

### XLIII

And when the wizard lady would ascend               385
  The labyrinths of some many winding vale
Which to the inmost mountain upward tend—
  She called "Hermaphroditus!"—and the pale
And heavy hue which slumber could extend
  Over its lips and eyes, as on the gale             390
A rapid shadow from a slope of grass,
Into the darkness of the stream did pass.

### XLIV

And it unfurled its heaven-coloured pinions[4]
  With stars of fire spotting the stream below;
And from above into the Sun's dominions             395
  Flinging a glory, like the golden glow
In which Spring clothes her emerald-winged minions,[5]
  All interwoven with fine feathery snow
And moonlight splendour of intensest rime[6]
With which Frost paints the pines in winter time.    400

### XLV

And then it winnowed the Elysian[7] air
  Which ever hung about that lady bright,

8. Sprinkled or scattered.
9. Large waterfalls.
1. Entomb; the subject is *which* (line 377).
2. An arch of prismatic colors like a rainbow, formed by refraction of light in mist or vapor.
3. Grayish white.
4. *it*: the Hermaphrodite; *pinions*: wings.
5. Favorites or darlings.
6. Frozen mist.
7. Gloriously fragrant, as in Elysium, the Greek abode of the honorable dead; *winnowed*: beat or flapped.

With its ætherial vans—and speeding there
  Like a star up the torrent of the night
Or a swift eagle in the morning glare                               405
  Breasting the whirlwind with impetuous flight,
The pinnace, oared by those enchanted wings,
Clove the fierce streams towards their upper springs.

### XLVI

The water flashed, like sunlight by the prow
  Of a noon-wandering meteor[8] flung to Heaven;               410
The still air seemed as if its waves did flow
  In tempest down the mountains—loosely driven
The lady's radiant hair streamed to and fro:
  Beneath, the billows[9] having vainly striven
Indignant and impetuous, roared to feel                             415
The swift and steady motion of the keel.

### XLVII

Or, when the weary moon was in the wane
  Or in the noon of interlunar[1] night
The lady-witch in visions could not chain
  Her spirit; but sailed forth under the light                     420
Of shooting stars, and bade extend amain[2]
  Its storm-outspeeding wings, th' Hermaphrodite;
She to the Austral[3] waters took her way
Beyond the fabulous Thamondocana,[4]—

### XLVIII

Where like a meadow which no scythe has shaven,               425
  Which rain could never bend, or whirl-blast shake,
With the Antarctic constellations paven,
  Canopus[5] and his crew, lay th' Austral lake—
There she would build herself a windless haven
  Out of the clouds whose moving turrets make               430
The bastions of the storm, when through the sky
The spirits of the tempest thundered by.

### XLIX

A haven beneath whose translucent floor
  The tremulous stars sparkled unfathomably,
And around which, the solid vapours hoar,                          435
  Based on the level waters, to the sky

8. A flash or reflection of light.
9. Great waves.
1. The period between the old and the new moon.
2. With full force and speed.
3. Of the Southern Hemisphere.
4. The ancient name for Tombouctou (Timbuktu), located in Mali, south of the Sahara Desert.
5. One of the brightest stars in the southern sky, in the constellation Argo.

Lifted their dreadful crags; and like a shore
   Of wintry mountains, inaccessibly
Hemmed in with rifts and precipices grey
And hanging crags, many a cove and bay.        440

## L

And whilst the outer lake beneath the lash
   Of the wind's scourge,[6] foamed like a wounded thing,
And the incessant hail with stony clash
   Ploughed up the waters, and the flagging wing
Of the roused cormorant[7] in the lightning flash        445
   Looked like the wreck of some wind-wandering
Fragment of inky thundersmoke,—this haven
Was as a gem to copy Heaven engraven.[8]—

## LI

On which that lady played her many pranks,
   Circling the image of a shooting star,        450
Even as a tyger on Hydaspes'[9] banks
   Outspeeds the antelopes which speediest are,
In her light boat; and many quips[1] and cranks
   She played upon the water, till the car
Of the late moon, like a sick matron wan,        455
To journey from the misty East began.

## LII

And then she called out of the hollow turrets
   Of those high clouds, white, golden and vermilion,
The armies of her ministering Spirits—
   In mighty legions million after million        460
They came, each troop emblazoning its merits
   On meteor flags,[2] and many a proud pavilion
Of the intertexture of the atmosphere
They pitched upon the plain of the calm mere.[3]

## LIII

They framed the imperial tent of their great Queen        465
   Of woven exhalations,[4] underlaid

6. A flail or whip.
7. Black sea bird about three feet long, noted for its voracious appetite.
8. I.e., was like a gem engraved with a copy of Heaven.
9. A river of northeast Pakistan, now called the Jhelum; it marked the eastern limit of Alexander's conquests.
1. Fanciful turns of speech; *cranks*: odd or fantastic actions. The expression is from Milton's *L'Allegro*, line 27.
2. I.e., inscribing conspicuously (*emblazoning*) on flashes of lightning (*meteor flags*). Shelley evokes Milton's description of an "Empyreal Host of Angels" in *Paradise Lost*, V.583–94.
3. Lake.
4. Cf. Milton's Pandemonium: "a Fabric huge / Rose like an Exhalation" (*Paradise Lost*, I.710–11).

With lambent[5] lightning-fire, as may be seen
    A dome of thin and open ivory inlaid
With crimson silk . . cressets from the Serene[6]
    Hung there, and on the water for her tread          470
A tapestry of fleecelike mist was strewn,
Dyed in the beams of the ascending moon.

### LIV

And on a throne o'erlaid with starlight, caught
    Upon those wandering isles of aëry dew
Which highest shoals of mountain shipwreck not          475
    She sate, and heard all that had happened new
Between the earth and moon since they had brought
    The last intelligence—and now she grew
Pale as that moon lost in the watery night—
And now she wept and now she laughed outright.          480

### LV

These were tame pleasures—She would often climb
    The steepest ladder of the crudded rack[7]
Up to some beaked cape of cloud sublime,
    And like Arion on the dolphin's back[8]
Ride singing through the shoreless air. Oft time          485
    Following the serpent lightning's winding track
She ran upon the platforms of the wind
And laughed to hear the fireballs[9] roar behind.

### LVI

And sometimes to those streams of upper air
    Which whirl the earth in its diurnal round          490
She would ascend, and win the spirits there
    To let her join their chorus. Mortals found
That on those days the sky was calm and fair,
    And mystic snatches of harmonious sound[1]
Wandered upon the earth where'er she past,          495
And happy thoughts of hope too sweet to last.

### LVII

But her choice sport was, in the hours of sleep
    To glide adown old Nilus,[2] where he threads

5. Shining with a soft, clear light without fierce heat.
6. Iron lamps (Milton's Pandemonium also contains *cressets*); *Serene:* clear blue sky.
7. A bank of clouds (*rack*) resembling coagulated curds (*crudded*).
8. *Arion*, seventh-century B.C. lyric poet and musician, was threatened with death while aboard a ship but was saved when dolphins, attracted by his music, carried him away.
9. Lightning in a globular form.
1. Lines 489–94 allude to the music of the spheres. (Cf. *Prometheus Unbound*, IV.186–88, and "With a Guitar. To Jane," lines 75–78.)
2. The Nile River.

Egypt and Æthiopia, from the steep
   Of utmost Axumè,[3] until he spreads,         500
Like a calm flock of silver-fleeced sheep,
   His waters on the plain: and crested heads
Of cities and proud temples gleam amid
And many a vapour-belted pyramid.[4]

### LVIII

By Mœris and the Mareotid lakes,[5]        505
   Strewn with faint blooms like bridal chamber floors,
Where naked boys bridling tame Water snakes
   Or charioteering ghastly alligators
Had left on the sweet waters mighty wakes
   Of those huge forms—within the brazen doors     510
Of the great Labyrinth[6] slept both boy and beast,
Tired with the pomp of their Osirian feast.[7]

### LIX

And where within the surface of the River
   The shadows of the massy[8] temples lie
And never are erased—but tremble ever       515
   Like things which every cloud can doom to die,
Through lotus-pav'n canals, and wheresoever
   The works of man pierced that serenest sky
With tombs, and towers, and fanes,[9] 'twas her delight
To wander in the shadow of the night.     520

### LX

With motion like the spirit of that wind
   Whose soft step deepens slumber, her light feet
Past through the peopled haunts of humankind;
   Scattering sweet visions from her presence sweet
Through fane and palace-court and labyrinth mined     525
   With many a dark and subterranean street
Under the Nile, through chambers high and deep
She past, observing mortals in their sleep.—

3. Probably the present site of Aksum in mountainous northeast Ethiopia.
4. Enveloped in mist or fog.
5. Lake Mareotis is located in the Nile Delta; Lake Moeris (now called Birket-Qarun) is south-west of Cairo and about 120 miles southeast of Lake Mareotis.
6. A magnificent tomb and commemorative structure of Egyptian royalty, containing 3,000 chambers.
7. Osiris, one of the chief Egyptian gods, was variously considered by the Greeks to be a son of Jupiter or Saturn. In legends he is depicted as a wise and good king of Egypt who taught his people agriculture, good morals, and civilized ways, and as a bloodless conqueror (like Dionysus) of other peoples, bringing them civilization. The most important religious myths depict him as a vegetation god, killed and cut to pieces by Set or Typhon and then brought together and revived by his wife Isis and their son Horus. Thus comparative mythologists identified him with Adonis and with aspects of Christ.
8. Massive.
9. Temples.

## LXI

A pleasure sweet doubtless it was to see
   Mortals subdued in all the shapes of sleep.     530
Here lay two sister-twins in infancy;
   There, a lone youth who in his dreams did weep;
Within, two lovers linked innocently
   In their loose locks which over both did creep
Like ivy from one stem—and there lay calm     535
Old age with snow bright hair and folded palm.

## LXII

But other troubled forms of sleep she saw,
   Not to be mirrored in a holy song—
Distortions foul of supernatural awe,
   And pale imaginings of visioned wrong     540
And all the code of custom's lawless law
   Written upon the brows of old and young:
"This," said the wizard maiden, "is the strife
Which stirs the liquid[1] surface of man's life."

## LXIII

And little did the sight disturb her soul—     545
   We, the weak mariners of that wide lake
Where'er its shores extend or billows roll,
   Our course unpiloted and starless make
O'er its wild surface to an unknown goal—
   But she in the calm depths her way could take     550
Where in bright bowers immortal forms abide
Beneath the weltering[2] of the restless tide.

## LXIV

And she saw princes couched under the glow
   Of sunlike gems, and round each temple-court
In dormitories ranged, row after row,     555
   She saw the priests asleep—all of one sort
For all were educated to be so—
   The peasants in their huts, and in the port
The sailors she saw cradled on the waves,
And the dead lulled within their dreamless graves.     560

## LXV

And all the forms in which those spirits lay
   Were to her sight like the diaphanous
Veils, in which those sweet ladies oft array
   Their delicate limbs, who would conceal from us

---

1. I.e., changeable in shape.
2. Surging.

Only their scorn of all concealment: they                565
  Move in the light of their own beauty thus.
But these and all now lay with sleep upon them
And little thought a Witch was looking on them.

### LXVI

She, all those human figures breathing there
  Beheld as living spirits—to her eyes                570
The naked beauty of the soul lay bare,
  And often through a rude and worn disguise
She saw the inner form most bright and fair—
  And then, she had a charm of strange device,
Which murmured on mute lips with tender tone                575
Could make that Spirit mingle with her own.

### LXVII

Alas, Aurora! what wouldst thou have given
  For such a charm when Tithon became grey?[3]
Or how much, Venus, of thy silver Heaven
  Wouldst thou have yielded, ere Proserpina                580
Had half (oh! why not all?) the debt forgiven
  Which dear Adonis had been doomed to pay,[4]
To any Witch who would have taught you it?
The Heliad[5] doth not know its value yet.

### LXVIII

'Tis said in after times her spirit free                585
  Knew what love was, and felt itself alone—
But holy Dian could not chaster be
  Before she stooped to kiss Endymion[6]
Than now this lady—like a sexless bee[7]
  Tasting all blossoms and confined to none—                590
Among those mortal forms the wizard-maiden
Passed with an eye serene and heart unladen.

### LXIX

To those she saw most beautiful, she gave
  Strange panacea[8] in a chrystal bowl . . .

---

3. Aurora (Eos in Greek), goddess of the dawn, loved Tithonus and at her request Zeus gave him immortality, but she forgot to ask also for the gift of eternal youth. When old age made him decrepit, she changed him into a cicada (see note to line 108).
4. Adonis, beloved of Venus, was killed while hunting a wild boar; Proserpina (Greek Persephone), queen of the underworld and wife of Pluto (Hades), restored Adonis to life on the condition that he spend six months with Venus and the rest of the year with her.
5. The Witch of Atlas; literally, child of Helius, or the sun.
6. Diana, virgin goddess of the moon, became so enamored of the beauty of Endymion, a shepherd of Caria (in modern Turkey), that she descended nightly from heaven to make love to him as he slept his eternal sleep on Mt. Latmos.
7. The undeveloped female (neuter) bee is the worker that collects honey and produces wax, to store the honey for food in the winter.
8. A medicine reputed to heal all diseases.

They drank in their deep sleep of that sweet wave—          595
    And lived thenceforward as if some control
Mightier than life, were in them; and the grave
    Of such, when death oppressed the weary soul,
Was as a green and overarching bower
Lit by the gems of many a starry flower.          600

## LXX

For on the night that they were buried, she
    Restored the embalmer's ruining, and shook
The light out of the funeral lamps, to be
    A mimic⁹ day within that deathly nook;
And she unwound the woven imagery          605
    Of second childhood's swaddling bands and took
The coffin, its last cradle, from its niche
And threw it with contempt into a ditch.

## LXXI

And there the body lay, age after age,
    Mute, breathing, beating, warm and undecaying          610
Like one asleep in a green hermitage
    With gentle smiles about its eyelids playing
And living in its dreams beyond the rage
    Of death or life, while they were still arraying
In liveries ever new, the rapid, blind          615
And fleeting generations of mankind.

## LXXII

And she would write strange dreams upon the brain
    Of those who were less beautiful, and make
All harsh and crooked purposes more vain
    Than in the desert is the serpent's wake          620
Which the sand covers—all his evil gain
    The miser in such dreams would rise and shake
Into a beggar's lap—the lying scribe¹
Would his own lies betray without a bribe.

## LXXIII

The Priests would write an explanation full,          625
    Translating hieroglyphics into Greek,
How the god Apis, really was a bull²
    And nothing more; and bid the herald stick
The same against the temple doors, and pull

---

9. Artistic imitation.
1. A public official in charge of writing and keeping accounts.
2. A bull with special markings was much venerated as the Egyptian god Apis, with a festival, consultation for omens, and offerings of money.

The old cant down; they licensed all to speak                630
Whate'er they thought of hawks and cats and geese[3]
By pastoral letters to each diocese.

### LXXIV

The King would dress an Ape up in his crown
    And robes, and seat him on his glorious seat,[4]
And on the right hand of the sunlike throne                635
    Would place a gaudy mock-bird to repeat
The chatterings of the monkey.—Every one
    Of the prone courtiers crawled to kiss the feet
Of their great Emperor when the morning came,
And kissed—alas, how many kiss the same!                640

### LXXV

The soldiers dreamed that they were blacksmiths, and
    Walked out of quarters in somnambulism,
Round the red anvils you might see them stand
    Like Cyclopses in Vulcan's sooty Abysm,[5]
Beating their swords to ploughshares[6]—in a band                645
    The jailors sent those of the liberal schism
Free through the streets of Memphis, much, I wis,[7]
To the annoyance of King Amasis.[8]

### LXXVI

And timid lovers who had been so coy
    They hardly knew whether they loved or not,                650
Would rise out of their rest, and take sweet joy
    To the fulfilment of their inmost thought;
And when next day the maiden and the boy
    Met one another, both, like sinners caught,
Blushed at the thing which each believed was done                655
Only in fancy[9]—till the tenth moon shone;

### LXXVII

And then the Witch would let them take no ill:
    Of many thousand schemes which lovers find

3. The hawk was sacred to Horus. Diana Bubastis transformed herself into a cat when the gods
    fled into Egypt. Though the sacred geese of Juno's temple were famous for warning the
    besieged Romans of the Gauls' attack on the Capitoline Hill, the reference to geese as
    Egyptian gods may be intended as the reductio ad absurdum of animal worship, because
    "goose" was a name commonly applied in Shelley's time to a foolish person ("silly goose").
4. Cf. Spenser's *Prosopopoia*, in which the Ape "upon his head / The Crowne, and on his backe
    the skin he did, / And the false Foxe him helped to array" (lines 1061–63).
5. Vulcan, god of fire and patron of artists who worked metals, forged Jupiter's thunderbolts
    and arms for heroes and gods with the aid of the Cyclopes under Mt. Aetna in Sicily.
6. Micah 4:3.
7. I.e., "I know"; a corruption of "iwis," an adverb meaning "certainly."
8. Amasis (570–526 B.C.), according to Herodotus (II.161ff.), rose from a common soldier to
    king of Egypt.
9. Fantasy or dream.

The Witch found one,—and so they took their fill
   Of happiness in marriage warm and kind;      660
Friends who by practice of some envious skill,
   Were torn apart, a wide wound, mind from mind!
She did unite again with visions clear
Of deep affection and of truth sincere.

## LXXVIII

These were the pranks she played among the cities    665
   Of mortal men, and what she did to sprites
And gods, entangling them in her sweet ditties
   To do her will, and shew their subtle slights,
I will declare another time; for it is
   A tale more fit for the weird winter nights     670
Than for these garish summer days, when we
Scarcely believe much more than we can see.

# Song of Apollo[1]

The sleepless Hours who watch me as I lie
   Curtained with star-enwoven tapestries
From the broad moonlight of the open sky;
   Fanning the busy dreams from my dim eyes,
Waken me when their mother, the grey Dawn,     5
Tells them that Dreams and that the moon is gone.

Then I arise; and climbing Heaven's blue dome,
   I walk over the mountains and the waves,
Leaving my robe upon the Ocean foam.
   My footsteps pave the clouds with fire; the caves    10
Are filled with my bright presence, and the air
Leaves the green Earth to my embraces bare.

The sunbeams are my shafts with which I kill
   Deceit, that loves the night and fears the day.
All men who do, or even imagine ill     15
   Fly me;[2] and from the glory of my ray

1. The following two "Songs" were written in 1820 by Shelley for inclusion in Mary Shelley's mythological drama *Midas*. In this blank-verse play, as in the well-known account in Ovid's *Metamorphoses* (Book XI, fables 4 and 5), Midas arrives on the scene just as Tmolus, spirit of the mountain of the same name, is about to judge a singing contest between Apollo and Pan. In Ovid's version Pan sings first and Apollo overpowers him; Mary Shelley reverses the order of the contest, having Apollo perform first and leaving the last word to Pan. Shelley's poems, each thirty-six lines long, tend to give static power and dignity (along with considerable self-satisfaction) to Apollo and a historical progression toward a tragedy (and, hence, considerable human sympathy) to Pan.
    Mary Shelley could not find a publisher for her verse drama and published Shelley's poems under the titles "Hymn of Apollo" and "Hymn of Pan" in Shelley's *Posthumous Poems* (1824). The present texts are based on Shelley's draft in Bodleian MS Shelley adds. e.6, pp. 23–29 (*BSM*, V). Mary Shelley's transcription of this draft (with some alterations) appears in Bodleian MS Shelley d.2, fols. 22r–23v (*BSM*, X). For an important reading of these two poems, see Earl R. Wasserman's discussion in this volume (pp. 570–79).
2. Flee from me.

Good minds, and open actions take new might
Until diminished, by the reign of night.


I feed the clouds, the rainbows and the flowers
　　With their ætherial colours; the moon's globe                    20
And the pure stars in their eternal bowers
　　Are cinctured³ with my power as with a robe;
Whatever lamps on Earth or Heaven may shine
Are portions of one spirit; which is mine.


I stand at noon upon the peak of Heaven;                             25
　　Then with unwilling steps, I linger down
Into the clouds of the Atlantic even.⁴
　　For grief that I depart they weep and frown—
What look is more delightful, than the smile
With which I soothe them from the Western isle?                      30


I am the eye with which the Universe
　　Beholds itself, and knows it is divine.
All harmony of instrument and verse,
　　All prophecy and medicine are mine;
All light of art⁵ or nature—to my song                               35
Victory and praise, in its own right, belong.


# Song of Pan¹

From the forests and highlands
　　We come, we come,
From the river-girt islands
　　Where loud waves were dumb
Listening my sweet pipings.²                                          5
　　　　The wind in the reeds and the rushes,
　　　　The bees on the bells of thyme,
　　　　The birds in the myrtle bushes,
　　　　The cicadæ above in the lime,
　　　　　　And the lizards below in the grass,                        10
Were silent as even old Tmolus was,
　　　　Listening my sweet pipings.


Liquid Peneus was flowing—
　　And all dark Tempe lay

3. Encircled, girdled.
4. I.e., "evening."
5. Apollo, god of the fine arts, music, poetry, eloquence, and medicine, received from Jupiter
　the power of knowing the future and was the only god whose oracles were in general repute
　throughout the ancient world.
1. For the textual history of this poem, see note 1 to "Song of Apollo."
2. The use of the transitive form *listening* here and in line 12 was a poeticism used by such
　favorites of Shelley as Milton and Southey; it was probably obsolescent in Shelley's day.

In Olympus' shadow,[3] outgrowing                    15
    The light of the dying day,
    Speeded with my sweet pipings.
        The sileni and sylvans and fauns[4]
        And the nymphs of the woods and the waves,
    To the edge of the moist river-lawns            20
    And the brink of the dewy caves,
        And all that did then attend and follow
Were as silent for love, as you now, Apollo,
    For envy of my sweet pipings.

I sang of the dancing stars,                         25
    I sang of the dædal[5] Earth,
And of Heaven, and the giant wars,[6]
    And Love and Death and Birth;
        And then I changed my pipings,
        Singing how, down the vales of Mænalus       30
    I pursued a maiden and clasped a reed.[7]
    Gods and men, we are all deluded thus!—
        It breaks in our bosom and then we bleed;
        They wept as, I think, both ye[8] now would,
If envy or age had not frozen your blood,            35
    At the sorrow of my sweet pipings.

# EPIPSYCHIDION

In late November 1820, Mary Shelley and Claire Clairmont were introduced to Teresa Viviani, the nineteen-year-old daughter of the governor of Pisa, who was confined in the Convent of St. Anna there. Shelley—always struck by the plight of teen-age girls confined by strict (or tyrannical) fathers—took an interest in Teresa; he, Mary, and Claire all visited and corresponded with her until her arranged marriage (September 8, 1821). Teresa's biographer has argued that the Shelleys called her "Emilia" because her position in a triangle involving two suitors was analogous to that of Emilia, the heroine of Boccaccio's *Teseida* (the story that was the model for Chaucer's *Knight's Tale*).

Shelley composed the lines that were to become *Epipsychidion* amid a welter of other verses that were later sorted out to form two fragmentary narrative poems on Italian themes—"Ginevra" and "Fiordispina." The poem proper was written sometime between December 1820 and early

---

3. *Peneus*: a river in Thessaly that flows northeastward through the beautiful Valley of *Tempe*, which lies between Mt. *Olympus* to the northwest and Mt. Ossa to the southeast.
4. *sileni*, *sylvans*, and *fauns* are various male woodland and rural demigods, like satyrs. The nymphs are their (beautiful) female equivalents.
5. Intricately, artistically wrought (after Daedalus).
6. The giants, who first aided Zeus (Jupiter) and the Olympians in their overthrow of the Titans, later rose up and attacked the Olympian gods, who—after a severe fright—defeated them with help of Hercules.
7. The nymph Syrinx, when Pan tried to make love to her, was turned into a reed (from which Pan made his musical pipes). *Mænalus*: a mountain in Arcadia sacred to Pan.
8. Apollo and Tmolus; the first is accused of being silent through *envy*, the second because of *age*.

February 1821, though Shelley seems to have incorporated lines he had drafted earlier (primarily between late October 1819 and early March 1820) for other purposes. On February 16, 1821, Shelley sent the (now lost) fair copy of *Epipsychidion* to his publisher Charles Ollier, asking him to publish it anonymously: "indeed, in a certain sense, it is a production of a portion of me already dead; and in this sense the advertisement is no fiction" (*Letters*, II, 262–63). After Shelley's death Ollier told Mary Shelley that "it was the wish of Mr. Shelley that the whole of the 'Epipsychidion' should be suppressed"; he turned over to John Hunt (on Mary's instructions) a remainder of 160 copies (showing that at least 200 or 250 copies were printed). One reason for the poem's suppression is cited in a letter published in *Blackwood's Edinburgh Magazine* over the pseudonym "John Johnes," who was apparently Ollier himself: "The poem was published anonymously, but as people began to apply it to a certain individual, and make their own inferences, it was, I believe, suddenly withdrawn from circulation." Shelley later wrote to John Gisborne: "The 'Epipsychidion' I cannot look at; . . . If you are anxious, however, to hear what I am and have been, it will tell you something thereof. It is an idealized history of my life and feelings" (*Letters*, II, 434).

In addition to Shelley's indications of deep personal involvement in the sentiments of *Epipsychidion* (and Mary Shelley's failure to write a note on this alone among Shelley's major poems), we have the evidence of the text itself that it involves the core of Shelley's personal aspirations. Kenneth Neill Cameron's essay "The Planet-Tempest Passage in *Epipsychidion*" (*PMLA* 63 [1948]: 950–72) first judiciously sorted out the probable significance of some of the allegorized autobiography, a subject more recently pursued well in Stuart Sperry's *Shelley's Major Verse* (1988), pp. 158–82. At the same time, it has been cogently argued that the poem is essentially about the role of poetry as the most appropriate object of human desires. Those who accept this view base their analysis on the comparison of this work with Dante's *Vita Nuova*, to which Shelley calls attention in his Advertisement, and with the biblical Song of Solomon or Song of Songs, to the language and imagery of which there are frequent parallels in *Epipsychidion*.

In the absence of a fair-copy manuscript, our sole textual authority of any consequence is the first edition of 1821. Drafts for various parts of the poem can be found in Bodleian MSS Shelley d.1.i (*BSM*, IV), adds. e.12 (*BSM*, XVIII), adds. e.8 (*BSM*, VI), adds. e.9 (*BSM*, XIV), adds. c.4 (*BSM*, XXI), and adds. e.6 (*BSM*, V). We have normalized a few spellings according to Shelley's consistent practice (e.g., *Ay* to *Aye* in line 33) and have adopted a few minor or conventional changes included in other editions (such as italicizing the words "*Vita Nuova*" in the Advertisement), but we have otherwise followed the printed text that is based on Shelley's final holograph.

*Epipsychidion* can be divided into the following major sections: (1) lines 1–189 tell of the poet's relationship to "Emily"—first in an invocation (1–71), then in an allegorical history of his encounter with her (72–129), and finally in an address to her about the nature of love (130–89); (2) lines 190–383 form the main part of the "idealized history of [Shelley's] life and feelings," concluding with an address to Emily, Mary Shelley, and (probably) Claire Clairmont under the symbols Sun, Moon, and Comet, respectively; (3) after a short transitional prayerful address to Emily, Shelley concludes the poem proper with a proposal that Emily elope with him to an island paradise; and (4) the concluding envoy addressed to the poem.

Shelley's title is coined from the Greek preposition *epi-* (upon) and the
diminutive noun *psychidion* ("little soul") and means "On the Subject of
the Soul" (as in the Emperor Hadrian's poem *De animula*). For a discussion of the poem that considers its meaning in terms of its process of
composition, see Nancy Moore Goslee's "Dispersoning Emily: Drafting as
Plot in *Epipsychidion*" in this volume (pp. 735–52).

# Epipsychidion:

VERSES ADDRESSED TO THE NOBLE AND
UNFORTUNATE LADY, EMILIA V——, NOW IMPRISONED
IN THE CONVENT OF ——

L'anima amante si slancia fuori del creato, e si crea nel infinito un Mondo
tutto per essa, diverso assai da questo oscuro e pauroso baratro.
                                                    HER OWN WORDS.[1]

## ADVERTISEMENT

The Writer of the following Lines died at Florence, as he was preparing
for a voyage to one of the wildest of the Sporades,[2] which he had
bought, and where he had fitted up the ruins of an old building, and
where it was his hope to have realised a scheme of life, suited perhaps
to that happier and better world of which he is now an inhabitant, but
hardly practicable in this. His life was singular; less on account of the
romantic vicissitudes which diversified it, than the ideal tinge which
it received from his own character and feelings. The present Poem,
like the *Vita Nuova* of Dante, is sufficiently intelligible to a certain
class of readers without a matter-of-fact history of the circumstances
to which it relates; and to a certain other class it must ever remain
incomprehensible, from a defect of a common organ of perception for
the ideas of which it treats. Not but that, *gran vergogna sarebbe a colui,
che rimasse cosa sotto veste, di figura, o di colore rettorico: e domandato
non sapesse denudare le sue parole da cotal veste, in guisa che avessero
verace intendimento.*[3]
    The present poem appears to have been intended by the Writer as
the dedication to some longer one. The stanza on the opposite page[4]
is almost a literal translation from Dante's famous Canzone

*Voi, ch' intendendo, il terzo ciel movete, etc.*

1. The quotation from Teresa Viviani may be translated: "The loving soul launches beyond
   creation, and creates for itself in the infinite a world all its own, far different from this dark
   and terrifying gulf."
2. Greek islands in the Aegean Sea.
3. "Great would be his shame who should rhyme anything under the garb of metaphor or
   rhetorical figure; and, being requested, could not strip his words of this dress so that they
   might have a true meaning."
4. I.e., the nine lines that follow, which are translated from the final lines of the first canzone
   of Dante's *Convito*, Trattato II, the opening line of which may be translated, "Ye who intelligent, the third sphere move . . ." (see note to line 117).

The presumptuous application of the concluding lines to his own composition will raise a smile at the expense of my unfortunate friend: be
it a smile not of contempt, but pity.                                        S.

> My Song, I fear that thou wilt find but few
> Who fitly shall conceive thy reasoning,
> Of such hard matter dost thou entertain;
> Whence, if by misadventure, chance should bring
> Thee to base company (as chance may do),
> Quite unaware of what thou dost contain,
> I prithee, comfort thy sweet self again,
> My last delight! tell them that they are dull,
> And bid them own that thou art beautiful.

## Epipsychidion

Sweet Spirit! Sister of that orphan one,
Whose empire is the name thou weepest on,[5]
In my heart's temple I suspend to thee
These votive[6] wreaths of withered memory.

Poor captive bird! who, from thy narrow cage,                    5
Pourest such music, that it might assuage
The rugged hearts of those who prisoned thee,
Were they not deaf to all sweet melody;
This song shall be thy rose: its petals pale
Are dead, indeed, my adored Nightingale!                        10
But soft and fragrant is the faded blossom,
And it has no thorn left to wound thy bosom.

High, spirit-winged Heart! who dost for ever
Beat thine unfeeling bars with vain endeavour,
'Till those bright plumes of thought, in which arrayed          15
It over-soared this low and worldly shade,
Lie shattered; and thy panting, wounded breast
Stains with dear blood its unmaternal nest!
I weep vain tears: blood would less bitter be,
Yet poured forth gladlier, could it profit thee.                20

Seraph of Heaven![7] too gentle to be human,
Veiling beneath that radiant form of Woman
All that is insupportable in thee
Of light, and love, and immortality!

---

5. From Shelley's own Italian version of these lines, it appears that the *orphan one* is Shelley's soul, to which Teresa's *Sweet Spirit* is a sister. The word "Percy" means "lost" (*persi*) in Italian. A contrary explanation sees *that orphan one* as Mary Shelley's soul, in which case the empire would be the name of "wife" or "Mrs. Shelley." In Teresa's correspondence with Shelley and Mary Shelley she called and referred to them as her "Brother" and "Sister."
6. Consecrated or dedicated, in fulfillment of a vow.
7. In medieval and Renaissance theology the Seraphim, excelling in love, were the highest of the nine orders of angels, just above the Cherubim (who excelled in wisdom). Milton first used the singular form "seraph" in English (*Paradise Lost*, III.667).

Sweet Benediction in the eternal Curse!                              25
Veiled Glory of this lampless Universe!
Thou Moon beyond the clouds! Thou living Form
Among the Dead! Thou Star above the Storm!
Thou Wonder, and thou Beauty, and thou Terror!
Thou Harmony of Nature's art! Thou Mirror                           30
In whom, as in the splendour of the Sun,
All shapes look glorious which thou gazest on!
Aye, even the dim words which obscure thee now
Flash, lightning-like, with unaccustomed glow;
I pray thee that thou blot from this sad song                        35
All of its much mortality and wrong,
With those clear drops, which start like sacred dew
From the twin lights thy sweet soul darkens through,
Weeping, till sorrow becomes ecstasy:
Then smile on it, so that it may not die.                            40

    I never thought before my death to see
Youth's vision thus made perfect. Emily,
I love thee; though the world by no thin name
Will hide that love from its unvalued[8] shame.
Would we two had been twins of the same mother![9]                  45
Or, that the name my heart lent to another
Could be a sister's bond for her and thee,
Blending two beams of one eternity!
Yet were one lawful and the other true,
These names, though dear, could paint not, as is due,               50
How beyond refuge I am thine. Ah me!
I am not thine: I am a part of *thee*.

    Sweet Lamp! my moth-like Muse has burnt its wings;
Or, like a dying swan who soars and sings,[1]
Young Love should teach Time, in his own grey style,                55
All that thou art. Art thou not void of guile,
A lovely soul formed to be blest and bless?
A well of sealed and secret happiness,
Whose waters like blithe light and music are,
Vanquishing dissonance and gloom? A Star                            60
Which moves not in the moving Heavens, alone?[2]
A smile amid dark frowns? a gentle tone
Amid rude voices? a beloved light?
A Solitude, a Refuge, a Delight?
A lute, which those whom love has taught to play                     65
Make music on, to soothe the roughest day

8. Extremely great, beyond measure.
9. Cf. the Song of Songs: "O that thou wert as my brother, that sucked the breasts of my
   mother! . . . I would kiss thee, yea, I should not be despised" (8:1).
1. According to classical and medieval fables, the swan, mute in its lifetime, was supposed to
   fly and sing a beautiful, plaintive song just before its death ("swan song").
2. I.e., the polestar, around which all the other "fixed" stars seem to move as the earth rotates
   and revolves around the sun.

And lull fond[3] grief asleep? a buried treasure?
A cradle of young thoughts of wingless pleasure?
A violet-shrouded grave of Woe?[4]—I measure
The world of fancies, seeking one like thee,                    70
And find—alas! mine own infirmity.

She met me, Stranger,[5] upon life's rough way,
And lured me towards sweet Death; as Night by Day,
Winter by Spring, or Sorrow by swift Hope,
Led into light, life, peace. An antelope,                      75
In the suspended impulse of its lightness,
Were less ethereally light: the brightness
Of her divinest presence trembles through
Her limbs, as underneath a cloud of dew
Embodied in the windless Heaven of June                        80
Amid the splendour-winged stars, the Moon
Burns, inextinguishably beautiful:
And from her lips, as from a hyacinth full
Of honey-dew,[6] a liquid murmur drops,
Killing the sense with passion; sweet as stops                 85
Of planetary music[7] heard in trance.
In her mild lights the starry spirits dance,
The sun-beams of those wells which ever leap
Under the lightnings of the soul—too deep
For the brief fathom-line[8] of thought or sense.              90
The glory of her being, issuing thence,
Stains the dead, blank, cold air with a warm shade
Of unentangled intermixture, made
By Love, of light and motion: one intense
Diffusion, one serene Omnipresence,                            95
Whose flowing outlines mingle in their flowing,
Around her cheeks and utmost fingers glowing
With the unintermitted[9] blood, which there
Quivers, (as in a fleece of snow-like air
The crimson pulse of living morning quiver,)                   100
Continuously prolonged, and ending never,
Till they are lost, and in that Beauty furled
Which penetrates and clasps and fills the world;
Scarce visible from extreme loveliness.
Warm fragrance seems to fall from her light dress,             105
And her loose hair; and where some heavy tress

3. Profound, but also possibly misguided—suggesting the way that one can become attached to one's own sorrows. Cf. Shelley's earlier poem "Mutability," line 12.
4. The violet, a persistent perennial that blooms early in the spring, recurs as one of Shelley's symbols of rebirth and hope.
5. From Shelley's draft it is clear that "Stranger" is the unknown reader of the poem, addressed directly.
6. A sweet, sticky substance found on plants in very hot weather (Shelley repeats the phrase at line 262; it also appears in Coleridge's "Kubla Khan," line 53).
7. The harmonious music of the spheres was supposed to have been audible by human beings in the state of innocence, or, since then, in ecstasy.
8. A weighted line thrown over the side of a boat to measure the depth of water.
9. Uninterrupted.

The air of her own speed has disentwined,
The sweetness seems to satiate the faint wind;
And in the soul a wild odour is felt,
Beyond the sense, like fiery dews that melt          110
Into the bosom of a frozen bud.—
See where she stands! a mortal shape indued
With love and life and light and deity,
And motion which may change but cannot die;
An image of some bright Eternity;          115
A shadow of some golden dream; a Splendour
Leaving the third sphere pilotless;[1] a tender
Reflection of the eternal Moon of Love
Under whose motions life's dull billows move;
A Metaphor of Spring and Youth and Morning;          120
A Vision like incarnate April, warning,
With smiles and tears, Frost the Anatomy[2]
Into his summer grave.

              Ah, woe is me!
What have I dared? where am I lifted? how
Shall I descend, and perish not? I know          125
That Love makes all things equal: I have heard
By mine own heart this joyous truth averred:
The spirit of the worm beneath the sod
In love and worship, blends itself with God.

      Spouse! Sister! Angel! Pilot of the Fate          130
Whose course has been so starless! O too late
Beloved! O too soon adored, by me!
For in the fields of immortality[3]
My spirit should at first have worshipped thine,
A divine presence in a place divine;          135
Or should have moved beside it on this earth,
A shadow of that substance, from its birth;
But not as now:—I love thee; yes, I feel
That on the fountain of my heart a seal[4]
Is set, to keep its waters pure and bright          140
For thee, since in those *tears* thou hast delight.
We—are we not formed, as notes of music are,
For one another, though dissimilar;
Such difference without discord, as can make
Those sweetest sounds, in which all spirits shake          145
As trembling leaves in a continuous air?

     Thy wisdom speaks in me, and bids me dare
Beacon the rocks on which high hearts are wreckt.

---

1. *Splendour . . . pilotless: Splendor* is one of Dante's words for angels; the third sphere in Dante's cosmology was that of Venus, the realm of lovers (cf. Advertisement).
2. Skeleton.
3. The Elysian fields, the classical abode of the blessed after death.
4. Such as the wax seal of a letter to keep it private.

I never was attached to that great sect,
Whose doctrine is, that each one should select                    150
Out of the crowd a mistress or a friend,
And all the rest, though fair and wise, commend
To cold oblivion, though it is in the code
Of modern morals, and the beaten road
Which those poor slaves with weary footsteps tread,              155
Who travel to their home among the dead
By the broad highway of the world, and so
With one chained friend, perhaps a jealous foe,
The dreariest and the longest journey go.

   True Love in this differs from gold and clay,        160
That to divide is not to take away.
Love is like understanding, that grows bright,
Gazing on many truths; 'tis like thy light,
Imagination! which from earth and sky,
And from the depths of human phantasy,                           165
As from a thousand prisms and mirrors, fills
The Universe with glorious beams, and kills
Error, the worm, with many a sun-like arrow
Of its reverberated lightning.[5] Narrow
The heart that loves, the brain that contemplates,              170
The life that wears, the spirit that creates
One object, and one form, and builds thereby
A sepulchre for its eternity.

   Mind from its object differs most in this:
Evil from good; misery from happiness;                           175
The baser from the nobler; the impure
And frail, from what is clear and must endure.
If you divide suffering and dross,[6] you may
Diminish till it is consumed away;
If you divide pleasure and love and thought,                    180
Each part exceeds the whole; and we know not
How much, while any yet remains unshared,
Of pleasure may be gained, of sorrow spared:
This truth is that deep well, whence sages draw
The unenvied light of hope; the eternal law                     185
By which those live, to whom this world of life
Is as a garden ravaged,[7] and whose strife
Tills for the promise of a later birth
The wilderness of this Elysian earth.

   There was a Being whom my spirit oft               190
Met on its visioned wanderings, far aloft,
In the clear golden prime of my youth's dawn,
Upon the fairy isles of sunny lawn,

5. An allusion to Apollo's slaying of Python, a monstrous serpent.
6. Worthless, impure matter.
7. See "The Sensitive-Plant," pp. 291–95.

Amid the enchanted mountains, and the caves
Of divine sleep, and on the air-like waves                                        195
Of wonder-level dream, whose tremulous floor
Paved her light steps;—on an imagined shore,
Under the grey beak of some promontory
She met me, robed in such exceeding glory,
That I beheld her not. In solitudes                                               200
Her voice came to me through the whispering woods,
And from the fountains, and the odours deep
Of flowers, which, like lips murmuring in their sleep
Of the sweet kisses which had lulled them there,
Breathed but of *her* to the enamoured air;                                       205
And from the breezes whether low or loud,
And from the rain of every passing cloud,
And from the singing of the summer-birds,
And from all sounds, all silence. In the words
Of antique verse and high romance,—in form,                                       210
Sound, colour—in whatever checks that Storm
Which with the shattered present chokes the past;[8]
And in that best philosophy,[9] whose taste
Makes this cold common hell, our life, a doom[1]
As glorious as a fiery martyrdom;                                                 215
Her Spirit was the harmony of truth.—


    Then, from the caverns of my dreamy youth
I sprang, as one sandalled with plumes of fire,
And towards the loadstar[2] of my one desire,
I flitted, like a dizzy moth, whose flight                                        220
Is as a dead leaf's in the owlet light,[3]
When it would seek in Hesper's setting sphere[4]
A radiant death, a fiery sepulchre,
As if it were a lamp of earthly flame.—
But She, whom prayers or tears then could not tame,                               225
Past, like a God throned on a winged planet,
Whose burning plumes to tenfold swiftness fan it,
Into the dreary cone of our life's shade;[5]
And as a man with mighty loss dismayed,
I would have followed, though the grave between                                   230
Yawned like a gulph whose spectres are unseen:
When a voice said:—"O Thou of hearts the weakest,
The phantom is beside thee whom thou seekest."
Then I—"where?"—the world's echo answered "where!"

8. *that Storm . . . past:* The random experience of everyday current activity (*shattered present*) ordinarily obscures the great achievements scattered through cultural history, or the moments of value within an individual's life.
9. Shelley probably refers not to any particular philosophical school but to a general attitude, described in lines 213–15, that sees suffering as meaningful.
1. Fate or destiny.
2. More commonly "lodestar"—a "guiding star."
3. The dim light in which owls fly about.
4. The planet Venus as the evening star.
5. The "cone of night," or shadow cast by the earth away from the sun.

And in that silence, and in my despair,                                   235
I questioned every tongueless wind that flew
Over my tower of mourning, if it knew
Whither 'twas fled, this soul out of my soul;[6]
And murmured names and spells which have controul
Over the sightless tyrants of our fate;                                   240
But neither prayer nor verse could dissipate
The night which closed on her; nor uncreate
That world within this Chaos, mine and me,
Of which she was the veiled Divinity,
The world I say of thoughts that worshipped her:                          245
And therefore I went forth, with hope and fear
And every gentle passion sick to death,
Feeding my course with expectation's breath,
Into the wintry forest of our life;[7]
And struggling through its error with vain strife,                        250
And stumbling in my weakness and my haste,
And half bewildered by new forms, I past,
Seeking among those untaught foresters[8]
If I could find one form resembling hers,
In which she might have masked herself from me.                           255
There,—One,[9] whose voice was venomed melody
Sate by a well, under blue night-shade bowers;[1]
The breath of her false mouth was like faint flowers,
Her touch was as electric poison,—flame
Out of her looks into my vitals came,                                     260
And from her living cheeks and bosom flew
A killing air, which pierced like honey-dew
Into the core of my green heart, and lay
Upon its leaves; until, as hair grown grey
O'er a young brow, they hid its unblown[2] prime                          265
With ruins of unseasonable time.

    In many mortal forms I rashly sought
The shadow of that idol of my thought.[3]
And some were fair—but beauty dies away:
Others were wise—but honeyed words betray:                                270
And One was true—oh! why not true to me?

6. See Shelley's essay "On Love," pp. 503–04.
7. The image of the hero's journey of life passing through a dark, hostile forest appears at the opening of Dante's *Divine Comedy*, among other works.
8. I.e., other human beings who had not experienced such a revelation.
9. The relationship with a woman depicted symbolically in lines 256ff. has been variously interpreted as a youthful encounter with a prostitute or simply the first serious arousal of the youth's sexual desires.
1. A poisonous plant, probably deadly nightshade (belladonna).
2. Not yet flowered.
3. K. N. Cameron's discussion in "Planet-Tempest Passage" of the biographical elements in lines 267–383 identifies the "One" untrue (271) as Harriet Westbrook Shelley, the poet's first wife, whose suicide in 1816 is represented by the quenching of the "Planet" (313); the comforting but cold Moon (281) as Mary Shelley; the "Tempest" (312) as Shelley's persecution after Harriet's suicide by her sister Eliza Westbrook, including the Chancery suit she and her father undertook to deprive him of custody of his two children, "the twin babes, a sister and a brother" (303); the "Sun" (335) as Teresa Viviani; and the "Comet" (368) as Claire Clairmont.

Then, as a hunted deer that could not flee,
I turned upon my thoughts, and stood at bay,
Wounded and weak and panting;[4] the cold day
Trembled, for pity of my strife and pain.                    275
When, like a noon-day dawn, there shone again
Deliverance. One stood on my path who seemed
As like the glorious shape which I had dreamed,
As is the Moon, whose changes ever run
Into themselves, to the eternal Sun;                         280
The cold chaste Moon, the Queen of Heaven's bright isles,
Who makes all beautiful on which she smiles,
That wandering shrine of soft yet icy flame
Which ever is transformed, yet still the same,
And warms not but illumines. Young and fair                  285
As the descended Spirit of that sphere,
She hid me, as the Moon may hide the night
From its own darkness, until all was bright
Between the Heaven and Earth of my calm mind,[5]
And, as a cloud charioted by the wind,                       290
She led me to a cave in that wild place,
And sate beside me, with her downward face
Illumining my slumbers, like the Moon
Waxing and waning o'er Endymion.[6]
And I was laid asleep, spirit and limb,                      295
And all my being became bright or dim
As the Moon's image in a summer sea,
According as she smiled or frowned on me;
And there I lay, within a chaste cold bed:
Alas, I then was nor alive nor dead:—                        300
For at her silver voice came Death and Life,
Unmindful each of their accustomed strife,
Masked like twin babes, a sister and a brother,
The wandering hopes of one abandoned mother,
And through the cavern without wings they flew,              305
And cried "Away, he is not of our crew."
I wept, and though it be a dream, I weep.

    What storms then shook the ocean of my sleep,
Blotting that Moon, whose pale and waning lips
Then shrank as in the sickness of eclipse;—                  310
And how my soul was as a lampless sea,
And who was then its Tempest; and when She,
The Planet of that hour, was quenched, what frost
Crept o'er those waters, 'till from coast to coast

4. For Shelley's other uses of this image of the Actaeon-like poet pursued by his own thoughts
(hounds), see *Prometheus Unbound*, I.454–57, and *Adonais*, lines 274–79.
5. I.e., the poet's mind is between heaven and earth, like the cloud used in the following simile.
6. In the traditional myth Jupiter granted the shepherd Endymion immortality and eternal youth
on the condition that he should sleep forever. Diana, the moon goddess, fell in love with his
sleeping form and made love to him every night. (See "The Witch of Atlas," line 588 and
note.)

The moving billows of my being fell      315
Into a death of ice, immoveable;—
And then—what earthquakes made it gape and split,
The white Moon smiling all the while on it,
These words conceal:—If not, each word would be
The key of staunchless tears. Weep not for me!      320

     At length, into the obscure Forest[7] came
The Vision I had sought through grief and shame.
Athwart that wintry wilderness of thorns[8]
Flashed from her motion splendour like the Morn's,
And from her presence life was radiated      325

Through the grey earth and branches bare and dead;
So that her way was paved, and roofed above
With flowers as soft as thoughts of budding love;
And music from her respiration spread
Like light,—all other sounds were penetrated      330
By the small, still, sweet spirit of that sound,
So that the savage winds hung mute around;
And odours warm and fresh fell from her hair
Dissolving the dull cold in the frore air:
Soft as an Incarnation of the Sun,      335
When light is changed to love, this glorious One
Floated into the cavern where I lay,
And called my Spirit, and the dreaming clay
Was lifted by the thing that dreamed below
As smoke by fire, and in her beauty's glow      340
I stood, and felt the dawn of my long night
Was penetrating me with living light:
I knew it was the Vision veiled from me
So many years—that it was Emily.

     Twin Spheres of light who rule this passive Earth,      345
This world of love, this *me*; and into birth
Awaken all its fruits and flowers, and dart
Magnetic might into its central heart;
And lift its billows and its mists, and guide
By everlasting laws, each wind and tide      350
To its fit cloud, and its appointed cave;
And lull its storms, each in the craggy grave
Which was its cradle, luring to faint bowers
The armies of the rainbow-winged showers;
And, as those married lights, which from the towers      355
Of Heaven look forth and fold the wandering globe
In liquid sleep and splendour, as a robe;

---

7. I.e., dark forest (the *selva oscura* in Dante's *Inferno*, I.2).
8. As in the mechanics' performance of "Pyramus and Thisbe" in Shakespeare's *A Midsummer Night's Dream*, a "bush of thorn" was a traditional property of the moon, as well as of the dark forest of life.

And all their many-mingled influence blend,
If equal, yet unlike, to one sweet end;—
So ye, bright regents, with alternate sway                          360
Govern my sphere of being, night and day!
Thou, not disdaining even a borrowed might;
Thou, not eclipsing a remoter light;
And, through the shadow of the seasons three,
From Spring to Autumn's sere maturity,                             365
Light it into the Winter of the tomb,
Where it may ripen to a brighter bloom.
Thou too, O Comet beautiful and fierce,
Who drew the heart of this frail Universe
Towards thine own; till, wreckt in that convulsion,                370
Alternating attraction and repulsion,
Thine went astray and that was rent in twain;
Oh, float into our azure heaven again!
Be there love's folding-star[9] at thy return;
The living Sun will feed thee from its urn                         375
Of golden fire; the Moon will veil her horn
In thy last smiles; adoring Even and Morn
Will worship thee with incense of calm breath
And lights and shadows; as the star of Death
And Birth[1] is worshipped by those sisters wild                   380
Called Hope and Fear—upon the heart are piled
Their offerings,—of this sacrifice divine
A World shall be the altar.

                         Lady mine,
Scorn not these flowers of thought, the fading birth
Which from its heart of hearts that plant puts forth              385
Whose fruit, made perfect by thy sunny eyes,
Will be as of the trees of Paradise.


    The day is come, and thou wilt fly with me.
To whatsoe'er of dull mortality
Is mine, remain a vestal sister still;                             390
To the intense, the deep, the imperishable,
Not mine but me, henceforth be thou united
Even as a bride, delighting and delighted.[2]
The hour is come:—the destined Star has risen
Which shall descend upon a vacant prison.                          395
The walls are high, the gates are strong, thick set
The sentinels—but true love never yet
Was thus constrained: it overleaps all fence:
Like lightning, with invisible violence

9. Venus as the evening star—"The Star that bids the Shepherd fold [his sheep]" (Milton,
   *Comus*, line 93). See also "The Witch of Atlas," line 74, and *Hellas*, line 1029.
1. Venus, as both the morning and the evening star. (Cf. "The Triumph of Life," lines 412–
   19.)
2. Lines 389–93, with their reference to the vestal virgins (see "The Witch of Atlas," line 318),
   have been cited to prove that the overt sexual imagery in the last part of the poem is not to
   be taken literally.

Piercing its continents; like Heaven's free breath,                    400
Which he who grasps can hold not; liker Death,
Who rides upon a thought, and makes his way
Through temple, tower, and palace, and the array
Of arms: more strength has Love than he or they;
For it can burst his charnel, and make free                    405
The limbs in chains, the heart in agony,
The soul in dust and chaos.

                         Emily,
A ship is floating in the harbour now,
A wind is hovering o'er the mountain's brow;
There is a path on the sea's azure floor,                    410
No keel has ever ploughed that path before;
The halcyons[3] brood around the foamless isles;
The treacherous Ocean has forsworn its wiles;
The merry mariners are bold and free:
Say, my heart's sister, wilt thou sail with me?                    415
Our bark[4] is as an albatross, whose nest
Is a far Eden of the purple East;
And we between her wings will sit, while Night
And Day, and Storm, and Calm, pursue their flight,
Our ministers, along the boundless Sea,                    420
Treading each other's heels, unheededly.
It is an isle under Ionian skies,[5]
Beautiful as a wreck of Paradise,
And, for[6] the harbours are not safe and good,
This land would have remained a solitude                    425
But for some pastoral people native there,
Who from the Elysian,[7] clear, and golden air
Draw the last spirit of the age of gold,
Simple and spirited; innocent and bold.
The blue Ægean girds this chosen home,                    430
With ever-changing sound and light and foam,
Kissing the sifted sands, and caverns hoar;
And all the winds wandering along the shore
Undulate with the undulating tide:
There are thick woods where sylvan forms abide;                    435
And many a fountain, rivulet, and pond,
As clear as elemental diamond,
Or serene morning air; and far beyond,

---

3. According to the myth, when Ceyx and Alcyone were turned into kingfishers (*halcyons*),
Alcyone's father, Aeolus, god of the winds, granted his daughter "seven days of calm in winter
[in which] Alcyone broods on the sea, wings outstretched over her nest" (Ovid, *Metamorphoses*, XI.10).
4. A small ship.
5. Though the Ionian Sea lies between southern Italy and western Greece, the area called Ionia
in classical times was the western coast of Asia Minor, together with the adjacent islands in
the Aegean Sea, which had been colonized by Greeks who spoke the Ionian dialect. Among
these islands were the Sporades (see Shelley's Advertisement).
6. Because.
7. Having the quality of the Elysian fields, the classical version of paradise (see note to line
133).

The mossy tracks made by the goats and deer
(Which the rough shepherd treads but once a year,)          440
Pierce into glades, caverns, and bowers, and halls
Built round with ivy, which the waterfalls
Illumining, with sound that never fails
Accompany the noon-day nightingales;[8]
And all the place is peopled with sweet airs;          445
The light clear element which the isle wears
Is heavy with the scent of lemon-flowers,
Which floats like mist laden with unseen showers,
And falls upon the eye-lids like faint sleep;
And from the moss violets and jonquils peep,          450
And dart their arrowy odour through the brain
'Till you might faint with that delicious pain.
And every motion, odour, beam, and tone,
With that deep music is in unison:
Which is a soul within the soul—they seem          455
Like echoes of an antenatal dream.—
It is an isle 'twixt Heaven, Air, Earth, and Sea,
Cradled, and hung in clear tranquillity;
Bright as that wandering Eden Lucifer,[9]
Washed by the soft blue Oceans of young air.          460
It is a favoured place. Famine or Blight,
Pestilence, War and Earthquake, never light
Upon its mountain-peaks; blind vultures, they
Sail onward far upon their fatal way:
The winged storms, chaunting their thunder-psalm          465
To other lands, leave azure chasms of calm
Over this isle, or weep themselves in dew,
From which its fields and woods ever renew
Their green and golden immortality.[1]
And from the sea there rise, and from the sky          470
There fall, clear exhalations, soft and bright,
Veil after veil, each hiding some delight,
Which Sun or Moon or zephyr draw aside,
Till the isle's beauty, like a naked bride
Glowing at once with love and loveliness,          475
Blushes and trembles at its own excess:
Yet, like a buried lamp, a Soul no less
Burns in the heart of this delicious isle,
An atom[2] of th' Eternal, whose own smile
Unfolds itself, and may be felt not seen          480
O'er the grey rocks, blue waves, and forests green,
Filling their bare and void interstices.—
But the chief marvel of the wilderness
Is a lone dwelling, built by whom or how

8. Ordinarily the nightingale sings only at night.
9. Venus as the morning star ("Light-Bearer") is imagined as the home of unfallen Eden.
1. The ever-renewing of the seasonal cycle of green foliage and golden harvests is cited as a kind of immortality.
2. The smallest possible particle.

None of the rustic island-people know:                    485
'Tis not a tower of strength, though with its height
It overtops the woods; but, for delight,
Some wise and tender Ocean-King,³ ere crime
Had been invented, in the world's young prime,
Reared it, a wonder of that simple time,                    490
An envy of the isles, a pleasure-house
Made sacred to his sister and his spouse.
It scarce seems now a wreck of human art,
But, as it were Titanic;⁴ in the heart
Of Earth having assumed its form, then grown                    495
Out of the mountains, from the living stone,
Lifting itself in caverns light and high:
For all the antique and learned imagery
Has been erased, and in the place of it
The ivy and the wild-vine interknit                    500
The volumes⁵ of their many twining stems;
Parasite flowers illume with dewy gems
The lampless halls, and when they fade, the sky
Peeps through their winter-woof of tracery
With Moon-light patches, or star atoms keen,                    505
Or fragments of the day's intense serene;—
Working mosaic on their Parian floors.⁶
And, day and night, aloof, from the high towers
And terraces, the Earth and Ocean seem
To sleep in one another's arms, and dream                    510
Of waves, flowers, clouds, woods, rocks, and all that we
Read in their smiles, and call reality.

    This isle and house are mine, and I have vowed
Thee to be lady of the solitude.—
And I have fitted up some chambers there                    515
Looking towards the golden Eastern air,
And level with the living winds, which flow
Like waves above the living waves below.—
I have sent books and music there, and all
Those instruments with which high spirits call                    520
The future from its cradle, and the past
Out of its grave, and make the present last
In thoughts and joys which sleep, but cannot die,
Folded within their own eternity.
Our simple life wants little, and true taste                    525
Hires not the pale drudge Luxury, to waste
The scene it would adorn, and therefore still,

3. One underlying myth may be that of Nereus, the eldest son of Oceanus; Hesiod in the
   *Theogony* says that Nereus "is always right and always gentle; he never forgets the laws, and
   is full of just and gentle wisdom." His wife, Doris, was also a child of Oceanus.
4. The origins are set back into the era of the Titans—Kronus (Saturn) and his siblings—
   before the advent of Zeus (Jupiter) and the Olympian gods, who introduced *crime* as a
   category of thought.
5. Coils.
6. Of fine white marble from the island of Paros in the Cyclades.

Nature, with all her children, haunts the hill.
The ring-dove, in the embowering ivy, yet
Keeps up her love-lament, and the owls flit                      530
Round the evening tower, and the young stars glance
Between the quick bats in their twilight dance;
The spotted deer bask in the fresh moon-light
Before our gate, and the slow, silent night
Is measured by the pants of their calm sleep.                   535
Be this our home in life, and when years heap
Their withered hours, like leaves, on our decay,
Let us become the over-hanging day,
The living soul of this Elysian isle,
Conscious, inseparable, one. Meanwhile                          540
We two will rise, and sit, and walk together,
Under the roof of blue Ionian weather,
And wander in the meadows, or ascend
The mossy mountains, where the blue heavens bend
With lightest winds, to touch their paramour;[7]                545
Or linger, where the pebble-paven shore,
Under the quick, faint kisses of the sea
Trembles and sparkles as with ecstacy,—
Possessing and possest by all that is
Within that calm circumference of bliss,                        550
And by each other, till to love and live
Be one:—or, at the noontide hour, arrive
Where some old cavern hoar seems yet to keep
The moonlight of the expired night asleep,
Through which the awakened day can never peep;                   555
A veil for our seclusion, close as Night's,
Where secure sleep may kill thine innocent lights;
Sleep, the fresh dew of languid love, the rain
Whose drops quench kisses till they burn again.
And we will talk, until thought's melody                        560
Become too sweet for utterance, and it die
In words, to live again in looks, which dart
With thrilling tone into the voiceless heart,
Harmonizing silence without a sound.
Our breath shall intermix, our bosoms bound,                    565
And our veins beat together; and our lips
With other eloquence than words, eclipse
The soul that burns between them, and the wells
Which boil under our being's inmost cells,
The fountains of our deepest life, shall be                     570
Confused in passion's golden purity,
As mountain-springs under the morning Sun.[8]
We shall become the same, we shall be one

7. Lover, i.e., the island.
8. wells (line 568) . . . *morning Sun:* Accompanying the fairly explicit sexual imagery is an
allusion to the myth of Alpheus, the river-god, who pursued Arethusa, a virgin nymph who
served Diana. Both became streams, and Alpheus followed Arethusa from Greece under the
ocean to Sicily, where their waters finally mingled. (Shelley wrote two versions of a poem
on Arethusa.)

Spirit within two frames, oh! wherefore two?
One passion in twin-hearts, which grows and grew,                    575
'Till like two meteors of expanding flame,
Those spheres instinct with[9] it become the same,
Touch, mingle, are transfigured; ever still
Burning, yet ever inconsumable:
In one another's substance finding food,                            580
Like flames too pure and light and unimbued[1]
To nourish their bright lives with baser prey,
Which point to Heaven and cannot pass away:
One hope within two wills, one will beneath
Two overshadowing minds, one life, one death,                       585
One Heaven, one Hell, one immortality,
And one annihilation. Woe is me!
The winged words on which my soul would pierce
Into the height of love's rare Universe,
Are chains of lead around its flight of fire.—                      590
I pant, I sink, I tremble, I expire!

———————

    Weak Verses, go, kneel at your Sovereign's[2] feet,
And say:—"We are the masters of thy slave;[3]
What wouldest thou with us and ours and thine?"
Then call your sisters from Oblivion's cave,                         595
All singing loud: "Love's very pain is sweet,
But its reward is in the world divine
Which, if not here, it builds beyond the grave."
So shall ye live when I am there. Then haste
Over the hearts of men, until ye meet                               600
Marina, Vanna, Primus,[4] and the rest,
And bid them love each other and be blest:
And leave the troop which errs, and which reproves,
And come and be my guest,—for I am Love's.[5]

# ADONAIS

Shelley learned of John Keats's serious consumptive illness from Leigh
Hunt and from John and Maria Gisborne during their visit to England.
Late in July 1820, Shelley wrote, inviting Keats to visit him in Italy. Keats
conditionally accepted, and he and Joseph Severn sailed for Naples in mid-
September 1820, reached there on October 21, started for Rome on No-

9. Animated by.
1. Unstained.
2. I.e., Emily's.
3. The poet.
4. *Marina, Vanna, Primus: Mary* Shelley, Jane (*Giovanna*) Williams, Edward Williams (Shelley's
   first [i.e., *primary*] friend).
5. This envoy, addressed to the poem in Dante's manner, restates the central theme of the
   entire composition.

vember 7 or 8, where they arrived on November 15, and took lodgings on
the Piazza di Spagna. There Keats died on February 23, 1821. Shelley did
not learn of this event until April 11, 1821, in a letter from Horace Smith,
and almost immediately began his elegy on Keats's death. By June 8, 1821,
Shelley wrote to Charles Ollier that he had completed his poem "of about
forty Spenser stanzas"; he finished the entire fifty-five stanzas, had the
poem printed in Pisa, and sent a copy to the Gisbornes on July 13. Though
Shelley instructed Ollier to have another edition printed in England, *Adonais* sold so poorly that Ollier did no more than sell the copies he had
received (perhaps less than one hundred).

Shelley called *Adonais* "a highly wrought piece of art" and "the least
imperfect of my compositions." Later poets and critics have generally
agreed, and its artistry, its place in the long, distinguished tradition of the
pastoral elegy, and its subject have made it the most widely known of
Shelley's book-length poems. That is not to say that *Adonais* has been
easily understood; although earlier commentators—particularly W. M.
Rossetti in his Clarendon Press Series edition of the poem (1891)—had
pointed out the poem's numerous parallels to Bion's Greek "Lament for
Adonis" and the "Elegy for Bion" attributed to Moschus, the coherence of
its imagery and structure were not well understood until Earl R. Wasserman's seminal analysis (*The Subtler Language*, 1959). Taking up the suggestion that the name Adonais embodies both the Greek Adonis and the
Hebrew word "Adonai" (Lord), Wasserman shows how this conflation reflects the ideas of contemporary syncretic mythologizers and raises the
story above the level of mere fertility myth. Wasserman divides the poem
into three movements of seventeen, twenty-one, and seventeen stanzas, a
structure Donald H. Reiman has elaborated by separating out the three
central stanzas (27–29) to leave sections of seventeen, nine, three, nine,
and seventeen stanzas (*Percy Bysshe Shelley*, 1969). Edwin R. Silverman,
in *Poetic Synthesis in Shelley's "Adonais"* (1972), finds the key to the
poem's structure in that of *Astrophel*, Spenser's pastoral elegy on the death
of Sir Philip Sidney.

As the epigraph from the elegy for Bion suggests, there are two chief
biographical focuses in the poem—Keats and the anonymous *Quarterly*
reviewer, whom Shelley believed to be Robert Southey. The relevance to
*Adonais* of Shelley's relations with Southey was first demonstrated in Kenneth Neill Cameron's "Shelley vs. Southey: New Light on an Old Quarrel"
(*PMLA*, 1942), and Reiman gives the fullest treatment of the other question in "Keats and Shelley: Personal and Literary Relations" (*SC*, V, 399–
427). For a detailed reading of the poem, see Michael Scrivener, "Defending the Imagination," in this volume (pp. 753–60).

There being no surviving fair-copy manuscript, the chief authorities for
the text are the first edition, which, Shelley wrote to Ollier, "is beautifully
printed, & what is of more consequence, correctly . . ." (*Letters*, II, 311),
and Mary Shelley's first edition of 1839, which contains (along with several
errors) at least three verbal changes that must have had Shelley's authority
behind them (lines 72, 143, 252). Drafts of *Adonais* appear in Bodleian
MS Shelley adds. e.20 (*BSM*, VII), adds. e.9 (*BSM*, XIV), adds. e.8 (*BSM*,
VI), and adds. e.6 (*BSM*, V). See especially the facsimile reconstruction
of the extensive drafts in adds. e.20 by Reiman, as well as his detailed
account of the poem's composition (*BSM*, VII, 97–104). Anthony Knerr's
edition of *Adonais* (New York: Columbia University Press, 1984) includes
a transcription of the drafts and a useful chapter on the poem's reception
history (pp. 137–248 and 119–35, respectively).

Beyond adopting the three emendations by Mary Shelley mentioned above, we have printed book titles in the Preface in italics, altered a few minor points of punctuation and orthography to conform to the consistent practice in Shelley's manuscripts (e.g., *ancient* to *antient*, *gray* to *grey*), and changed the possessive *it's* to *its*, to conform to the correct usage of Shelley's day as found in his poems printed in England.

# Adonais

## An Elegy on the Death of John Keats, Author of Endymion, Hyperion, Etc.

Ἀστὴρ πρὶν μὲν ἔλαμπες ἐνὶ ζωοῖσιν Ἑῷος·
νῦν δὲ θανὼν λάμπεις Ἕσπερος ἐν φθιμένοις.—PLATO[1]

### PREFACE

Φάρμακον ἦλθε, Βίων, ποτὶ σὸν στόμα, φάρμακον εἶδες.
πῶς τευ τοῖς χείλεσσι ποτέδραμε, κοὐκ ἐγλυκάνθη;
τίς δὲ βροτὸς τοσσοῦτον ἀνάμερος, ἢ κεράσαι τοι,
ἢ δοῦναι λαλέοντι τὸ φάρμακον; ἔκφυγεν ᾠδάν.
                    —MOSCHUS, EPITAPH. BION.[2]

It is my intention to subjoin to the London edition of this poem, a criticism upon the claims of its lamented object to be classed among the writers of the highest genius who have adorned our age. My known repugnance to the narrow principles of taste on which several of his earlier compositions were modelled, proves, at least that I am an impartial judge. I consider the fragment of *Hyperion*, as second to nothing that was ever produced by a writer of the same years.[3]

John Keats, died at Rome of a consumption, in his twenty-fourth year, on the —— of —— 1821; and was buried in the romantic and lonely cemetery of the protestants in that city, under the pyramid which is the tomb of Cestius, and the massy walls and towers, now mouldering and desolate, which formed the circuit of antient Rome. The cemetery is an open space among the ruins covered in winter with

---

1. An epigram attributed to Plato, which Shelley translated:

    Thou wert the morning star among the living,
        Ere thy fair light had fled—
    Now, having died, thou art as Hesperus, giving
        New splendour to the dead.

2. From the "Elegy for Bion" (attributed to Moschus): "Poison came, Bion, to thy mouth—poison didst thou eat. How could it come to such lips as thine and not be sweetened? What mortal was so cruel as to mix the drug for thee, or to give it to thee, who heard thy voice? He escapes [shall be nameless in] my song." The poem's next clause, not given by Shelley, states, "Yet justice overtakes all."

3. Shelley, thinking that Keats died *in his twenty-fourth year* (before his twenty-fourth birthday), and reading in the Advertisement to the *Lamia* volume (dated June 26, 1820) that *Hyperion* had been left unfinished because of the unfavorable reception of *Endymion* (1818), must have thought that the fragmentary *Hyperion* had been written by Keats by late 1818 or early 1819, when (according to Shelley's information) he would have been only twenty-one years old.

violets and daisies. It might make one in love with death, to think that one should be buried in so sweet a place.[4]

The genius of the lamented person to whose memory I have dedicated these unworthy verses, was not less delicate and fragile than it was beautiful; and where cankerworms abound, what wonder if its young flower was blighted in the bud? The savage criticism on his *Endymion*, which appeared in the *Quarterly Review*, produced the most violent effect on his susceptible mind; the agitation thus originated ended in the rupture of a blood-vessel in the lungs;[5] a rapid consumption ensued, and the succeeding acknowledgements from more candid critics,[6] of the true greatness of his powers, were ineffectual to heal the wound thus wantonly inflicted.

It may be well said, that these wretched men know not what they do. They scatter their insults and their slanders without heed as to whether the poisoned shaft lights on a heart made callous by many blows, or one, like Keats's composed of more penetrable stuff. One of their associates, is, to my knowledge, a most base and unprincipled calumniator. As to *Endymion*, was it a poem, whatever might be its defects, to be treated contemptuously by those who had celebrated, with various degrees of complacency and panegyric, *Paris*, and *Woman*, and a *Syrian Tale*, and Mrs. Lefanu, and Mr. Barrett, and Mr. Howard Payne, and a long list of the illustrious obscure?[7] Are these the men, who in their venal good nature, presumed to draw a parallel between the Rev. Mr. Milman and Lord Byron? What gnat did they strain at here, after having swallowed all those camels? Against what woman taken in adultery, dares the foremost of these literary prostitutes to cast his opprobrious stone?[8] Miserable man! you, one of the meanest, have wantonly defaced one of the noblest specimens of the workmanship of God. Nor shall it be your excuse, that, murderer as you are, you have spoken daggers, but used none.[9]

The circumstances of the closing scene of poor Keats's life were not

4. Shelley's son William had been buried there in 1819, as he himself was to be in 1822.
5. Shelley wrote to Byron on May 4, 1821: "Hunt tells me that in the first paroxysms of his disappointment he burst a blood-vessel; and thus laid the foundation of a rapid consumption" (*Letters*, II, 289). The review in question appeared in the April 1818 number of the *Quarterly*, which was published in September 1818. See Reiman, *The Romantics Reviewed*, Part C, II, 767–70.
6. Shelley may allude to Francis Jeffrey's favorable review of *Endymion* and the *Lamia* volume that appeared in the *Edinburgh Review* for August 1820 (see *The Romantics Reviewed*, Part C, I, 385–90).
7. *Paris in 1815* (1817) by the Rev. George Croly was published anonymously and favorably reviewed in the *Quarterly* for April 1817. (Croly wrote a vicious review of *Adonais* for the *Literary Gazette*.) A later edition of *Woman* (1810) by Eaton Stannard Barrett, a Tory wit, was reviewed by the *Quarterly* in the April 1818 number. John Howard Payne, an American dramatist who later courted the widowed Mary Shelley, was reviewed harshly, not favorably, in the *Quarterly* for January 1820. Works by the Rev. Henry Hart Milman (Shelley's contemporary at both Eton and Oxford) were favorably reviewed in the *Quarterly* issues dated April 1816, July 1818, and May 1820. (Milman himself was a reviewer for the *Quarterly*, and Shelley later came to suspect him of having written the scurrilous attack on *Laon and Cythna* in the number for April 1819.)
8. The language of this sentence, like that of the one that precedes it and the first sentence in the paragraph, comes straight from the New Testament; see Luke 23:34, Matthew 23:24, and John 8:3–11.
9. Shakespeare, *Hamlet*, III.ii.414.

made known to me until the Elegy was ready for the press.[1] I am given
to understand that the wound which his sensitive spirit had received
from the criticism of *Endymion*, was exasperated by the bitter sense
of unrequited benefits; the poor fellow seems to have been hooted
from the stage of life, no less by those on whom he had wasted the
promise of his genius, than those on whom he had lavished his fortune
and his care. He was accompanied to Rome, and attended in his last
illness by Mr. Severn, a young artist of the highest promise, who, I
have been informed "almost risked his own life, and sacrificed every
prospect to unwearied attendance upon his dying friend." Had I known
these circumstances before the completion of my poem, I should have
been tempted to add my feeble tribute of applause to the more solid
recompense which the virtuous man finds in the recollection of his
own motives. Mr. Severn can dispense with a reward from "such stuff
as dreams are made of."[2] His conduct is a golden augury of the success
of his future career—may the unextinguished Spirit of his illustrious
friend animate the creations of his pencil, and plead against Oblivion
for his name!

# Adonais

### 1

I weep for Adonais—he is dead!
O, weep for Adonais! though our tears
Thaw not the frost which binds so dear a head!
And thou, sad Hour,[3] selected from all years
To mourn our loss, rouse thy obscure compeers,          5
And teach them thine own sorrow, say: with me
Died Adonais; till the Future dares
Forget the Past, his fate and fame shall be
An echo and a light[4] unto eternity!

### 2

Where wert thou mighty Mother,[5] when he lay,          10
When thy Son lay, pierced by the shaft which flies
In darkness?[6] where was lorn Urania

1. Shelley alludes to a letter to John Gisborne from the Rev. Robert Finch, who gave a senti-
mentalized account of Keats's last days.
2. Shakespeare, *The Tempest*, IV.i.156–57.
3. As in *Prometheus Unbound*, Shelley follows the classical poetic convention of personifying
the Horae (Hours), goddesses of the seasons.
4. The distinction between the senses of sound and sight plays a significant part in the poem's
symbolism.
5. Urania (line 12), a name used for the Muse of astronomy, the "Heavenly Muse" invoked by
Milton in *Paradise Lost* (Books I, VII), and Uranian Venus, the goddess seen as patroness
of ideal love. In the draft, Urania appears as an abstract and decidedly non-Miltonic "great
Poesy."
6. Cf. "Thou shalt not be afraid for the terror by night, nor for the arrow that flieth by day"
(Psalms 91:5). Shelley alludes to the anonymous attack on Keats's *Endymion* in the *Quarterly
Review* XIX (April 1818): 204–08. *lorn*: forsaken.

When Adonais died? With veiled eyes,
'Mid listening Echoes, in her Paradise
She sate, while one,[7] with soft enamoured breath,                    15
Rekindled all the fading melodies,
With which, like flowers that mock the corse[8] beneath,
He had adorned and hid the coming bulk of death.


                                      3

O, weep for Adonais—he is dead!
Wake, melancholy Mother, wake and weep!                                 20
Yet wherefore? Quench within their burning bed
Thy fiery tears, and let thy loud heart keep
Like his, a mute and uncomplaining sleep;
For he is gone, where all things wise and fair
Descend;—oh, dream not that the amorous Deep[9]                         25
Will yet restore him to the vital air;
Death feeds on his mute voice, and laughs at our despair.


                                      4

Most musical of mourners, weep again!
Lament anew, Urania!—He died,[1]
Who was the Sire of an immortal strain,                                 30
Blind, old, and lonely, when his country's pride,
The priest, the slave, and the liberticide,
Trampled and mocked with many a loathed rite
Of lust and blood;[2] he went, unterrified,
Into the gulph of death; but his clear Sprite                           35
Yet reigns o'er earth; the third among the sons of light.[3]


                                      5

Most musical of mourners, weep anew!
Not all to that bright station dared to climb;
And happier they their happiness who knew,
Whose tapers yet burn through that night of time                        40
In which suns perished;[4] others more sublime,
Struck by the envious wrath of man or God,
Have sunk, extinct in their refulgent prime;
And some yet live, treading the thorny road,
Which leads, through toil and hate, to Fame's serene abode.[5]          45

---

7. One of the personified Echoes.
8. Corpse.
9. An unfathomable abyss.
1. I.e., Milton.
2. Lines 31–34 refer to the Restoration of the Stuart monarchy, when the "regicides"—those
responsible for executing King Charles I—were killed.
3. In *A Defence of Poetry*, Shelley says that Milton was the third great epic poet, along with
Homer and Dante; *Sprite*: spirit.
4. Lines 38–41 characterize minor poets who were content to have minor fame during their
lifetime.
5. *some . . . serene abode*: Byron and Shelley, among others.

### 6

But now, thy youngest, dearest one, has perished
The nursling of thy widowhood,[6] who grew,
Like a pale flower by some sad maiden cherished,
And fed with true love tears, instead of dew;[7]
Most musical of mourners, weep anew!                          50
Thy extreme hope, the loveliest and the last,
The bloom, whose petals nipt before they blew[8]
Died on the promise of the fruit, is waste;
The broken lily lies—the storm is overpast.

### 7

To that high Capital,[9] where kingly Death                    55
Keeps his pale court in beauty and decay,
He came; and bought, with price of purest breath,
A grave among the eternal.—Come away!
Haste, while the vault of blue Italian day
Is yet his fitting charnel-roof! while still                  60
He lies, as if in dewy sleep he lay;
Awake him not! surely he takes his fill
Of deep and liquid rest, forgetful of all ill.

### 8

He will awake no more, oh, never more!—
Within the twilight chamber spreads apace,                    65
The shadow of white Death, and at the door
Invisible Corruption waits to trace
His extreme way to her dim dwelling-place;
The eternal Hunger sits, but pity and awe
Soothe her pale rage, nor dares she to deface                 70
So fair a prey, till darkness, and the law
Of change, shall o'er his sleep the mortal curtain draw.[1]

### 9

O, weep for Adonais!—The quick Dreams,[2]
The passion-winged Ministers of thought,
Who were his flocks, whom near the living streams             75
Of his young spirit he fed, and whom he taught
The love which was its music, wander not,—
Wander no more, from kindling brain to brain,
But droop there, whence they sprung; and mourn their lot

6. Keats as a poet is depicted as the posthumous child of Milton (Sire of line 30). Shelley admired Keats's *Hyperion*, his most Miltonic poem.
7. Lines 48–49 allude to the story of Keats's poem "Isabella; or, The Pot of Basil."
8. Bloomed or achieved perfection.
9. Rome, the Eternal City, where Keats died.
1. In the first edition this line read: "Of mortal change, shall fill the grave which is her maw."
2. I.e., "living Dreams"; Shelley personifies various aspects of Keats's mental life as his *flocks*, according to the tradition of the pastoral elegy.

Round the cold heart, where, after their sweet pain,[3]        80
They ne'er will gather strength, or find a home again.

### 10

And one[4] with trembling hands clasps his cold head,
And fans him with her moonlight wings, and cries;
"Our love, our hope, our sorrow, is not dead;
See, on the silken fringe of his faint eyes,                   85
Like dew upon a sleeping flower, there lies
A tear some Dream has loosened from his brain."
Lost Angel of a ruined Paradise!
She knew not 'twas her own; as with no stain
She faded, like a cloud which had outwept its rain.            90

### 11

One from a lucid[5] urn of starry dew
Washed his light limbs as if embalming them;
Another clipt her profuse locks, and threw
The wreath upon him, like an anadem,[6]
Which frozen tears instead of pearls begem;                    95
Another in her wilful grief would break
Her bow and winged reeds,[7] as if to stem
A greater loss with one which was more weak;
And dull the barbed fire against his frozen cheek.

### 12

Another Splendour[8] on his mouth alit,                        100
That mouth, whence it was wont to draw the breath
Which gave it strength to pierce the guarded wit,
And pass into the panting heart beneath
With lightning and with music: the damp death
Quenched its caress upon his icy lips;                         105
And, as a dying meteor stains a wreath
Of moonlight vapour, which the cold night clips,[9]
It flushed through his pale limbs, and past to its eclipse.

### 13

And others came . . . Desires and Adorations,
Winged Persuasions and veiled Destinies,                       110
Splendours, and Glooms, and glimmering Incarnations
Of hopes and fears, and twilight Phantasies;
And Sorrow, with her family of Sighs,

3. Such use of oxymoron is common in Keats's poetry, but relatively unusual in Shelley's.
4. One of the Dreams, etc., of stanza 9.
5. Luminous.
6. Garland for the head, usually of flowers.
7. I.e., arrows; Shelley is here paraphrasing Bion's "Lament for Adonis," where the mourning
   creatures are Loves (Cupids) rather than *Dreams, Ministers of thought*, etc.
8. Cf. Dante's word *"splendori"* (*Paradiso*, XXIII.82).
9. Embraces.

And Pleasure, blind with tears, led by the gleam
Of her own dying smile instead of eyes,                    115
Came in slow pomp;—the moving pomp might seem
Like pageantry of mist on an autumnal stream.[1]

### 14

All he had loved, and moulded into thought,
From shape, and hue, and odour, and sweet sound,
Lamented Adonais. Morning sought                    120
Her eastern watchtower, and her hair unbound,
Wet with the tears which should adorn the ground,
Dimmed the aerial eyes that kindle day;
Afar the melancholy thunder moaned,
Pale Ocean in unquiet slumber lay,                    125
And the wild winds flew round, sobbing in their dismay.

### 15

Lost Echo sits amid the voiceless mountains,
And feeds her grief with his remembered lay,
And will no more reply to winds or fountains,
Or amorous birds perched on the young green spray,                    130
Or herdsman's horn, or bell at closing day;
Since she can mimic not his lips, more dear
Than those for whose disdain she pined away
Into a shadow of all sounds:[2]—a drear
Murmur, between their songs, is all the woodmen hear.                    135

### 16

Grief made the young Spring wild, and she threw down
Her kindling buds, as if she Autumn were,
Or they dead leaves; since her delight is flown
For whom should she have waked the sullen year?
To Phœbus was not Hyacinth so dear[3]                    140
Nor to himself Narcissus, as to both
Thou Adonais: wan they stand and sere[4]
Amid the faint companions of their youth,
With dew all turned to tears; odour, to sighing ruth.[5]

### 17

Thy spirit's sister, the lorn nightingale[6]                    145
Mourns not her mate with such melodious pain;

---

1. Lines 116–17 allude to Keats's "To Autumn."
2. When the nymph Echo was rebuffed by Narcissus, whom she loved, she faded into an echo of sounds; Narcissus scorned Echo, fell in love with his own reflection, and was transformed into a flower.
3. Hyacinthus was a youth beloved by Phoebus Apollo, who mourned him when jealous Zephyrus caused his death. Apollo turned Hyacinthus into a flower.
4. Dry or withered.
5. Pity.
6. Besides echoing the elegy on Bion, this image alludes to Keats's "Ode to a Nightingale."

Not so the eagle, who like thee could scale
Heaven, and could nourish in the sun's domain
Her mighty youth with morning,[7] doth complain,
Soaring and screaming round her empty nest,       150
As Albion[8] wails for thee: the curse of Cain[9]
Light on his head who pierced thy innocent breast,
And scared the angel soul that was its earthly guest!

### 18

Ah woe is me! Winter is come and gone,
But grief returns with the revolving year;       155
The airs and streams renew their joyous tone;
The ants, the bees, the swallows reappear;
Fresh leaves and flowers deck the dead Seasons' bier;
The amorous birds now pair in every brake,
And build their mossy homes in field and brere;[1]       160
And the green lizard, and the golden snake,
Like unimprisoned flames, out of their trance awake.

### 19

Through wood and stream and field and hill and Ocean
A quickening life from the Earth's heart has burst
As it has ever done,[2] with change and motion,       165
From the great morning of the world when first
God dawned on Chaos; in its steam immersed
The lamps of Heaven flash with a softer light;
All baser things pant with life's sacred thirst;
Diffuse themselves; and spend in love's delight,       170
The beauty and the joy of their renewed might.

### 20

The leprous corpse touched by this spirit tender
Exhales itself in flowers of gentle breath;[3]
Like incarnations of the stars, when splendour
Is changed to fragrance, they illumine death       175
And mock the merry worm that wakes beneath;
Nought we know, dies. Shall that alone which knows[4]
Be as a sword consumed before the sheath

---

7. *eagle . . . morning:* According to tradition, the eagle could renew its youthful vision by first flying toward the sun (which burned the scales from its eyes) and then diving into a fountain.
8. England.
9. The first murderer was cursed to be "a fugitive and a vagabond in the earth" (Genesis 4:14).
1. The original form of "brier": thorny bushes in general, or wild rosebushes; *brake:* thicket or clump of bushes.
2. The renewal of the animal and vegetable species in the spring, contrasted with the linear termination of the individual human life, leads to a lament (in the manner of the late Latin poem *Pervigilium Veneris*) that destroys the comfort earlier provided by the myth in which Adonais was reborn annually.
3. Anemones, or windflowers.
4. The human mind.

By sightless[5] lightning?—th'intense atom glows
A moment, then is quenched in a most cold repose.                      180

### 21

Alas! that all we loved of him should be,
But for our grief, as if it had not been,
And grief itself be mortal! Woe is me!
Whence are we, and why are we? of what scene
The actors or spectators? Great and mean                               185
Meet massed in death, who lends what life must borrow.
As long as skies are blue, and fields are green,
Evening must usher night, night urge the morrow,
Month follow month with woe, and year wake year to sorrow.

### 22

*He* will awake no more, oh, never more!                               190
"Wake thou," cried Misery, "childless Mother, rise
Out of thy sleep, and slake,[6] in thy heart's core,
A wound more fierce than his with tears and sighs."
And all the Dreams that watched Urania's eyes,
And all the Echoes whom their sister's song[7]                         195
Had held in holy silence, cried: "Arise!"
Swift as a Thought by the snake Memory stung,
From her ambrosial rest the fading Splendour sprung.

### 23

She rose like an autumnal Night, that springs
Out of the East, and follows wild and drear                            200
The golden Day, which, on eternal wings,
Even as a ghost abandoning a bier,
Had left the Earth a corpse. Sorrow and fear
So struck, so roused, so rapt Urania;
So saddened round her like an atmosphere                               205
Of stormy mist; so swept her on her way
Even to the mournful place where Adonais lay.

### 24

Out of her secret Paradise she sped,
Through camps and cities rough with stone, and steel,
And human hearts, which to her aery tread                              210
Yielding not, wounded the invisible
Palms[8] of her tender feet where'er they fell:
And barbed tongues, and thoughts more sharp than they

---

5. Both invisible and blind, amoral.
6. Render less acute or painful.
7. The sister is Echo (line 127), who repeated Adonais' poem.
8. Shelley's use of *palm* for "sole" of the foot here and in *Prometheus Unbound* (IV.123) and
   "The Triumph of Life" (line 361) is, so far as we can discover, entirely without precedent.

Rent the soft Form they never could repel,
Whose sacred blood, like the young tears of May,          215
Paved with eternal flowers that undeserving way.

### 25

In the death chamber for a moment Death
Shamed by the presence of that living Might
Blushed to annihilation, and the breath
Revisited those lips, and life's pale light          220
Flashed through those limbs, so late her dear delight.
"Leave me not wild and drear and comfortless,
As silent lightning leaves the starless night!
Leave me not!" cried Urania: her distress
Roused Death: Death rose and smiled, and met her vain caress. 225

### 26

"Stay yet awhile! speak to me once again;
Kiss me, so long but as a kiss may live;
And in my heartless breast and burning brain
That word, that kiss shall all thoughts else survive,
With food of saddest memory kept alive,          230
Now thou art dead, as if it were a part
Of thee, my Adonais! I would give
All that I am to be as thou now art!
But I am chained to Time, and cannot thence depart!

### 27

"Oh gentle child, beautiful as thou wert,          235
Why didst thou leave the trodden paths of men
Too soon, and with weak hands though mighty heart
Dare the unpastured dragon[9] in his den?
Defenceless as thou wert, oh where was then
Wisdom the mirrored shield,[1] or scorn the spear?          240
Or hadst thou waited the full cycle, when
Thy spirit should have filled its crescent[2] sphere,
The monsters of life's waste had fled from thee like deer.

### 28

"The herded wolves, bold only to pursue;
The obscene ravens, clamorous o'er the dead;          245
The vultures to the conqueror's banner true
Who feed where Desolation first has fed,
And whose wings rain contagion;—how they fled,

9. The hostile critic(s) who, Shelley believed, had crushed Keats's spirit.
1. A mirrored shield appears in the legend of Perseus, who succeeds in slaying Medusa by
viewing her only indirectly in the shield.
2. Growing.

When like Apollo, from his golden bow,
The Pythian of the age[3] one arrow sped                    250
And smiled!—The spoilers tempt no second blow,
They fawn on the proud feet that spurn them lying low.[4]

### 29

"The sun comes forth, and many reptiles spawn;
He sets, and each ephemeral insect[5] then
Is gathered into death without a dawn,                      255
And the immortal stars awake again;
So is it in the world of living men:
A godlike mind soars forth, in its delight
Making earth bare and veiling heaven, and when
It sinks, the swarms that dimmed or shared its light        260
Leave to its kindred lamps[6] the spirit's awful night."

### 30

Thus ceased she: and the mountain shepherds[7] came
Their garlands sere, their magic mantles rent;
The Pilgrim of Eternity,[8] whose fame
Over his living head like Heaven is bent,                   265
An early but enduring monument,
Came, veiling all the lightnings of his song
In sorrow; from her wilds Ierne sent
The sweetest lyrist of her saddest wrong,[9]
And love taught grief to fall like music from his tongue.   270

### 31

Midst others of less note, came one frail Form,[1]
A phantom among men; companionless
As the last cloud of an expiring storm
Whose thunder is its knell; he, as I guess,
Had gazed on Nature's naked loveliness,                     275
Actæon-like, and now he fled astray

3. Byron, his *one arrow* being his poem *English Bards and Scotch Reviewers*, which silenced
   the critics as Apollo killed the Python.
4. The first edition read "as they go" instead of *lying low*; Mary Shelley's emendation of this
   line and line 72 certainly reflects Shelley's wishes.
5. For Shelley's other uses of the ephemerid, see "The Sensitive-Plant" (II.49) and "The Witch
   of Atlas" (line 9).
6. The stars (other creative minds) that the glare of sunlight, diffused through the atmosphere,
   had "veiled" (line 259).
7. In pastoral elegies the fellow poets of the poet being mourned are also characterized as
   shepherds; here they are mountain shepherds because of the traditional associations of
   mountains with independence and liberty (see especially Milton's *L'Allegro*, line 36, and
   Wordsworth's poetry *passim*). The garlands these poet-mourners wear in their hair have become withered, and they have torn their cloaks as a sign of their grief.
8. Byron, alluding particularly to *Childe Harold's Pilgrimage*.
9. Thomas Moore from Ireland (*Ierne*), famous for his *Irish Melodies*, his translations of the
   love songs of Anacreon, and his anti-government satirical poetry (see notes to the Dedication
   of *Peter Bell the Third*).
1. I.e., Shelley.

With feeble steps o'er the world's wilderness,
And his own thoughts, along that rugged way,
Pursued, like raging hounds, their father and their prey.[2]

## 32

A pardlike[3] Spirit beautiful and swift—            280
A Love in desolation masked;—a Power
Girt round with weakness;—it can scarce uplift
The weight of the superincumbent hour;[4]
It is a dying lamp, a falling shower,
A breaking billow;—even whilst we speak           285
Is it not broken? On the withering flower
The killing sun smiles brightly: on a cheek
The life can burn in blood, even while the heart may break.

## 33

His head was bound with pansies overblown,
And faded violets, white, and pied, and blue;     290
And a light spear topped with a cypress cone,
Round whose rude shaft dark ivy tresses grew[5]
Yet dripping with the forest's noonday dew,
Vibrated, as the ever-beating heart
Shook the weak hand that grasped it; of that crew  295
He came the last, neglected and apart;
A herd-abandoned deer struck by the hunter's dart.

## 34

All stood aloof, and at his partial[6] moan
Smiled through their tears; well knew that gentle band
Who in another's fate now wept his own;           300
As in the accents of an unknown land,
He sung new sorrow; sad Urania scanned
The Stranger's mien, and murmured: "who art thou?"
He answered not, but with a sudden hand
Made bare his branded and ensanguined brow,       305
Which was like Cain's or Christ's[7]—Oh! that it should be so!

2. For the association of the Actaeon myth (in which the hunter Actaeon was destroyed by his own dogs because he saw Diana naked) with the Shakespearean image of thoughts pursuing their *father*-mind, see note to *Prometheus Unbound*, 1.454–57.
3. A *pard* is a panther or leopard, sacred to Dionysus (Bacchus).
4. Lines 281–83: The "overlying" or "overhanging" *hour* is that which marks the death of Adonais (see lines 4–9); this hour masks Cupid (*Love*) with *desolation*, godlike *Power* with *weakness*.
5. The thyrsus, a staff tipped with an evergreen cone and wrapped with ivy or grape leaves. In the Dionysia, the festival honoring Dionysus, the Greeks carried the thyrsus (which had clear phallic symbolism) and garlanded their heads with ivy, violets, and other flowers.
6. Having a bias.
7. The forehead of Cain was *branded* by God with a mark to distinguish him; the crown of thorns bloodied (*ensanguined*) Christ's brow.

### 35

What softer voice is hushed over the dead?
Athwart what brow is that dark mantle thrown?
What form leans sadly o'er the white death-bed,
In mockery of monumental stone,[8]                        310
The heavy heart heaving without a moan?
If it be He,[9] who, gentlest of the wise,
Taught, soothed, loved, honoured the departed one;
Let me not vex, with inharmonious sighs
The silence of that heart's accepted sacrifice.            315

### 36

Our Adonais has drunk poison—oh!
What deaf and viperous murderer could crown
Life's early cup with such a draught of woe?[1]
The nameless worm[2] would now itself disown:
It felt, yet could escape the magic tone                   320
Whose prelude held all envy, hate, and wrong,
But what was howling in one breast alone,
Silent with expectation of the song,
Whose master's hand is cold, whose silver lyre unstrung.

### 37

Live thou, whose infamy is not thy fame!                   325
Live! fear no heavier chastisement from me,
Thou noteless blot on a remembered name!
But be thyself, and know thyself to be!
And ever at thy season be thou free
To spill the venom when thy fangs o'erflow:                330
Remorse and Self-contempt shall cling to thee;
Hot Shame shall burn upon thy secret brow,
And like a beaten hound tremble thou shalt—as now.

### 38

Nor let us weep that our delight is fled
Far from these carrion kites[3] that scream below;         335
He wakes or sleeps with the enduring dead;

8. The figure leans silent and still, posing like a memorial statue, yet *mocking* such a statue because his *heart* continues to beat.
9. Leigh Hunt, Keats's first literary patron and champion; he took Keats into his house and cared for him at the beginning of his final illness.
1. Throughout this and the following stanza Shelley attacks the anonymous author of the *Quarterly Review*'s attack on Keats. Shelley believed him to be Robert Southey, who (Shelley thought) was also the hostile reviewer of works by Hunt and himself. The actual reviewer of Keats was John Wilson Croker, while the attacks on Hunt and Shelley had been written by John Taylor Coleridge, nephew of S. T. Coleridge.
2. Snake.
3. Birds of the hawk family.

Thou canst not soar where he is sitting now.[4]—
Dust to the dust! but the pure spirit shall flow
Back to the burning fountain whence it came,[5]
A portion of the Eternal, which must glow                    340
Through time and change, unquenchably the same,
Whilst thy cold embers choke the sordid hearth of shame.

### 39

Peace, peace! he is not dead, he doth not sleep—
He hath awakened from the dream of life—
'Tis we, who lost in stormy visions, keep                    345
With phantoms an unprofitable strife,
And in mad trance, strike with our spirit's knife
Invulnerable nothings.—*We* decay
Like corpses in a charnel; fear and grief
Convulse us and consume us day by day,                       350
And cold hopes swarm like worms within our living clay.

### 40

He has outsoared the shadow of our night;[6]
Envy and calumny and hate and pain,
And that unrest which men miscall delight,
Can touch him not and torture not again;                     355
From the contagion of the world's slow stain
He is secure, and now can never mourn
A heart grown cold, a head grown grey in vain;[7]
Nor, when the spirit's self has ceased to burn,
With sparkless ashes load an unlamented urn.                 360

### 41

He lives, he wakes—'tis Death is dead, not he;
Mourn not for Adonais.—Thou young Dawn
Turn all thy dew to splendour, for from thee
The spirit thou lamentest is not gone;
Ye caverns and ye forests, cease to moan!                    365
Cease ye faint flowers and fountains, and thou Air
Which like a mourning veil thy scarf hadst thrown
O'er the abandoned Earth, now leave it bare
Even to the joyous stars which smile on its despair![8]

4. Again addressing the *Quarterly* reviewer, Shelley adapts (and inverts the implications of) an
   image from *Paradise Lost*, IV.828–29, in which fallen Satan rebukes the angels Ithuriel and
   Zephon for failing to recognize him, who had once been "sitting where ye durst not soare."
5. The concept of spirit as a fiery emanation flowing from the divine fire appears in the writings
   of the neoplatonic philosopher Plotinus (*Enneads*, IV.iii.9–10) and had been widely disseminated in the Platonic tradition.
6. The shadow cast by the earth away from the sun. That shadow can eclipse the moon but
   none of the planets.
7. Shelley undoubtedly thought of Southey, whose youthful liberalism had hardened into conservatism by the time Shelley met him at Keswick late in 1811.
8. If there were no moisture-laden air to diffuse sunlight into a general glow, the stars would
   be visible in daytime, as well as at night.

## 42

He is made one with Nature: there is heard 370
His voice in all her music, from the moan
Of thunder, to the song of night's sweet bird;[9]
He is a presence to be felt and known
In darkness and in light, from herb and stone,
Spreading itself where'er that Power[1] may move 375
Which has withdrawn his being to its own;
Which wields the world with never wearied love,
Sustains it from beneath, and kindles it above.

## 43

He is a portion of the loveliness
Which once he made more lovely: he doth bear 380
His part, while the one Spirit's plastic[2] stress
Sweeps through the dull dense world, compelling there,
All new successions to the forms they wear;
Torturing th'unwilling dross that checks its flight
To its own likeness, as each mass may bear; 385
And bursting in its beauty and its might
From trees and beasts and men into the Heaven's light.

## 44

The splendours of the firmament of time[3]
May be eclipsed, but are extinguished not;
Like stars to their appointed height they climb 390
And death is a low mist which cannot blot
The brightness it may veil. When lofty thought
Lifts a young heart above its mortal lair,
And love and life contend in it, for what
Shall be its earthly doom, the dead live there[4] 395
And move like winds of light on dark and stormy air.

## 45

The inheritors of unfulfilled renown[5]
Rose from their thrones, built beyond mortal thought,

9. The nightingale.
1. *Power* was the eighteenth-century philosophical term for an impersonal God (note the pronoun *its* in line 376).
2. Capable of shaping or molding formless matter.
3. Adonais and other creative spirits are now called *splendours*, which at line 100 was the term used to designate one of Adonais' imaginative creations.
4. The examples of the illustrious dead influence the lives of young imaginative persons torn between the ideals pursued by their desires (*love*) and the sordid realities of everyday *life*; *doom:* destiny.
5. Those who died young before receiving their just recognition. Thomas *Chatterton*, to whose memory Keats had dedicated *Endymion*, committed suicide in 1770 at the age of seventeen while facing starvation, after writing brilliant poetry (purporting to be the work of a medieval monk named Thomas Rowley). Sir Philip *Sidney* (1554–1586), courtier and poet, while dying from wounds, directed that a cup of water intended for himself be given to a wounded

Far in the Unapparent. Chatterton
Rose pale, his solemn agony had not 400
Yet faded from him; Sidney, as he fought
And as he fell and as he lived and loved
Sublimely mild, a Spirit without spot,
Arose; and Lucan, by his death approved:
Oblivion as they rose shrank like a thing reproved. 405

### 46

And many more, whose names on Earth are dark
But whose transmitted effluence[6] cannot die
So long as fire outlives the parent spark,
Rose, robed in dazzling immortality.
"Thou art become as one of us," they cry, 410
"It was for thee yon kingless sphere has long
Swung blind in unascended majesty,
Silent alone amid an Heaven of song.[7]
Assume thy winged throne, thou Vesper of our throng!"

### 47

Who mourns for Adonais? oh come forth 415
Fond[8] wretch! and know thyself and him aright.
Clasp with thy panting soul the pendulous Earth;[9]
As from a centre, dart thy spirit's light
Beyond all worlds, until its spacious might
Satiate the void circumference:[1] then shrink 420
Even to a point within our day and night;
And keep thy heart light lest it make thee sink
When hope has kindled hope, and lured thee to the brink.[2]

### 48

Or go to Rome,[3] which is the sepulchre
O, not of him, but of our joy: 'tis nought 425
That ages, empires, and religions there

---

common soldier, saying, "Thy necessity is yet greater than mine." He is the subject of Spenser's pastoral elegy *Astrophel*. *Lucan*: Marcus Annaeus Lucanus (A.D. 39–65) was the author of the *Pharsalia* (*Bellum Civile*), which praised the republican ideals of Pompey and Cato in their war against Caesar; forced to commit suicide when his role in a plot against Nero was discovered, Lucan recited a passage from his own poetry to his friends while bleeding to death.
6. Emanation.
7. Traditionally each *sphere* that encircled the earth was thought to be piloted by a particular god or genius—a spirit that gave vitality to it. Adonais is to be the genius of the third sphere of Venus, also known as Lucifer (morning star) and Hesperus or *Vesper* (evening star).
8. Unreasonable or foolish.
9. Floating in air or space; yet another echo from *Paradise Lost*: "Wherein all things created first he weighd, / The pendulous round Earth with balanc't Aire / In counterpoise (IV.999–1001).
1. "Poetry is indeed something divine. It is at once the centre and circumference of knowledge . . ." (*Defence of Poetry*, paragraph 39).
2. The edge of a precipice or a grave.
3. When the imagination *shrinks* to a single *point* (a *centre*) after having reached out to scan the universe in stanza 47, the poet suggests Rome as the proper point within time (*our day and night*) to explore.

Lie buried in the ravage they have wrought;
For such as he can lend,—they[4] borrow not
Glory from those who made the world their prey;
And he is gathered to the kings of thought                    430
Who waged contention with their time's decay,
And of the past are all that cannot pass away.

### 49

Go thou to Rome,—at once the Paradise,
The grave, the city, and the wilderness;
And where its wrecks like shattered mountains rise,[5]          435
And flowering weeds, and fragrant copses dress
The bones of Desolation's nakedness
Pass, till the Spirit of the spot shall lead
Thy footsteps to a slope of green access
Where, like an infant's smile,[6] over the dead,              440
A light of laughing flowers along the grass is spread.[7]

### 50

And grey walls[8] moulder round, on which dull Time
Feeds, like slow fire upon a hoary brand;[9]
And one keen pyramid with wedge sublime,[1]
Pavilioning the dust of him who planned                       445
This refuge for his memory, doth stand
Like flame transformed to marble; and beneath,
A field is spread, on which a newer band
Have pitched in Heaven's smile their camp of death[2]
Welcoming him we lose with scarce extinguished breath.        450

### 51

Here pause: these graves are all too young as yet
To have outgrown the sorrow which consigned
Its charge to each; and if the seal is set,
Here, on one fountain of a mourning mind,[3]

---

4. I.e., those *such as he*, creative spirits as opposed to political and ecclesiastical rulers, who merely *ravage* the world.
5. The remains of Nero's palace and other imperial buildings, the city walls, and the Baths of Caracalla, where Shelley wrote *Prometheus Unbound*, were overgrown with vegetation and almost seemed to have returned to natural hills.
6. Shelley and Mary's son, William Shelley, had died in Rome on June 7, 1819; his grave was in the Protestant Cemetery (Cimitero Acattolico) near the spot where Keats was later buried.
7. Before he died, Keats had asked Severn to look at the cemetery, and he had expressed pleasure at the "description of the locality . . . , particularly the innumerable violets" and the daisies among the grass.
8. The twelve-mile walls of Rome begun under Aurelian (emperor, A.D. 270–275) form one boundary of the cemetery; the Porta San Paolo is the nearby gate in the Aurelian wall.
9. A log that has been covered with white ash while burning on the hearth.
1. The pyramidal tomb of Caius Cestius, praetor and tribune of Rome during the latter half of the first century B.C., had been incorporated into the Aurelian wall.
2. One common name for a cemetery in Italy is *camposanto*, "holy camp." Shelley is punning seriously on the Italian word.
3. Shelley alludes to his sorrow at the death of his son.

Break it not thou! too surely shalt thou find                                    455
Thine own well full, if thou returnest home,
Of tears and gall. From the world's bitter wind[4]
Seek shelter in the shadow of the tomb.
What Adonais is, why fear we to become?

### 52

The One remains, the many change and pass;                                        460
Heaven's light forever shines, Earth's shadows fly;
Life, like a dome of many-coloured glass,
Stains the white radiance of Eternity,
Until Death tramples it to fragments.[5]—Die,
If thou wouldst be with that which thou dost seek!                                 465
Follow where all is fled!—Rome's azure sky,
Flowers, ruins, statues, music, words, are weak
The glory they transfuse with fitting truth to speak.

### 53

Why linger, why turn back, why shrink, my Heart?
Thy hopes are gone before;[6] from all things here                                470
They have departed; thou shouldst now depart!
A light is past from the revolving year,
And man, and woman; and what still is dear
Attracts to crush, repels to make thee wither.
The soft sky smiles,—the low wind whispers near:                                  475
'Tis Adonais calls! oh, hasten thither,
No more let Life divide what Death can join together.

### 54

That Light whose smile kindles the Universe,[7]
That Beauty in which all things work and move,
That Benediction which the eclipsing Curse                                         480
Of birth can quench not, that sustaining Love
Which through the web of being blindly wove
By man and beast and earth and air and sea,
Burns bright or dim, as each are mirrors of
The fire for which all thirst; now beams on me,                                    485
Consuming the last clouds of cold mortality.

---

4. William Shelley died in an epidemic of *malaria* (Italian for "bad [or evil] air"), possibly another Italian-English serious pun.
5. As the atmosphere refracts the sun's white light into the colors of the rainbow, Life distorts the universal *One* into *many* imperfect particulars, *until Death* permits the individual to reunite with the One.
6. Shelley at this period regretted the deaths of his children William and Clara (as well as the legal loss of his children by Harriet), alienation from Mary Shelley, animosity from the reviewers, neglect by his publisher and the reading public, and exile from his country and his few closest friends. Most of his early hopes, personal and poetical, had apparently failed.
7. This line and several others in stanza 54 echo the opening lines of Dante's *Paradiso*: "The glory of him who moves all things penetrates throughout the universe and rekindles [glows again] in one part more, and in another less. I have been in that sphere which most receives his light."

55

The breath whose might I have invoked in song
Descends on me; my spirit's bark is driven,
Far from the shore, far from the trembling throng
Whose sails were never to the tempest given;[8]                490
The massy earth and sphered skies are riven!
I am borne darkly, fearfully, afar:
Whilst burning through the inmost veil of Heaven,
The soul of Adonais, like a star,
Beacons from the abode where the Eternal are.[9]                495

# HELLAS

In December 1820, Professor Francesco Pacchiani, who introduced the
Shelleys to Teresa Viviani, also introduced them to a group of exiled Greek
aristocrats living in Pisa, the leading figure of which was Prince Alexandros
Mavrokordatos (1791–1865). Mavrocordato (as his name is usually West-
ernized) remained friendly with them—especially with Mary W. Shelley,
to whom he taught Greek in return for English lessons, and kept them
informed of plans to liberate his people, who had been subject to Turkey
for several centuries. As early as mid-March 1821, Mary Shelley's journal
records the taking of a Turkish citadel by Greeks in Crete, and on April 1
news reached Pisa that the Greeks had openly revolted and declared their
independence. In June, Mavrocordato left Italy to take part in the fight,
which lasted in various forms until 1832, after which he served as prime
minister of independent Greece on four different occasions between 1833
and 1855.

Though it was once thought that Shelley wrote most of *Hellas* during
the first three weeks of October 1821, new evidence from his draft notebook (Bodleian MS Shelley adds. e.7; *BSM*, XVI) indicates that he drafted
three or four false starts for a poem on the Greek uprising before news of
Keats's death inspired him to write *Adonais* between April and June 1821.
He first returned to the subject of the Greek struggle for independence in
an abortive *Faust*-like "Prologue in Heaven," but he rejected that genre
and selected instead as his model Aeschylus' *The Persians* (the only surviving Greek tragedy with a contemporary setting), by means of which he
could use the convention of messengers bringing timely news from the
sites of distant battles so as to incorporate into his drama the latest accounts of his self-styled "newspaper erudition" on the progress of the war.

By October 11, 1821, Shelley wrote to Ollier that his "dramatic poem
called 'Hellas' will soon be ready." (Edward Williams's note in his journal

8. Lines 488–90 echo but recast the idea of the opening lines of Canto II of Dante's *Paradiso*:
"O ye who in your little skiff [*barca*], longing to hear, have followed behind my keel that
goes singing, turn back to your own shores; do not give yourself to the open sea, lest, losing
me, you would remain lost."
9. In a letter to Claire Clairmont, written June 8, 1821, Shelley declares about his troubled
health: "I have a great desire & interest to live, & I would submit to any inconveniences to
attain that object. . . . the only relief I find springs from the composition of poetry, which
necessitates contemplations that lift me above the stormy mist of sensations which are my
habitual place of abode. I have lately been composing a poem on Keats: it is better than any
thing that I have yet written, & worthy both of him & of me" (*Letters*, II, 296).

for October 25 that he suggested the name to Shelley was, therefore, after the fact.) Williams transcribed *Hellas* for the press, November 6–10; Shelley corrected and mailed the manuscript to London on November 11, with a cover letter instructing Ollier to "send the Ms. instantly to a Printer, & the moment you get a proof, dispatch it to me by the Post," adding that the publisher was at "liberty to suppress" anything in the *notes* he considered dangerous under the laws of the time. Ollier canceled some lines in the poem, as well as a paragraph in Shelley's Preface and some passages in the notes, but he did not send proofs for Shelley's approval.

*Hellas* had not been printed by February 19, 1822, according to Maria Gisborne; but when a copy first reached Pisa early in April, Shelley wrote to Ollier that it was "prettily printed, & with fewer mistakes than any poem I ever published." In a letter written the following day, Shelley sent Ollier a few important errata (some being errors in the manuscript rather than the printing), but because both the press-copy manuscript and the errata list survive (at the Huntington Library; HM 329 and HM 20152; facsimiles in *MYR: Shelley*, III), our text of *Hellas* can be more nearly authoritative than those for several of Shelley's other works, especially now that we include the full texts of all eight of Shelley's notes, placed at the end of the poetic text, where they appear both in the press-copy manuscript and in the first edition of 1821. Shelley presumably placed them there not only because they are longer than the notes to any of his poems except *Queen Mab*, but also because he did not wish the unorthodox views he expressed there to prejudice readers against his poem before they progressed into it.

In *The Persians* of Aeschylus, the defeat by the Greeks of the Persian grand army led by Xerxes is reported to the Persian capital by means of a series of messengers. There Atossa, the queen mother, a chorus of Persian elders, and the ghost of Darius the Great, Xerxes father, whom Atossa has summoned from the dead, all lament the misdirected pride of Xerxes that has resulted in the destruction of their empire's greatness. Shelley likewise sets his drama at the capital of the Greeks' antagonist, the Sultan Mahmud II, where a chorus of Greek slaves and concubines reflect upon the struggle of their people for liberty. Shelley's drama is purely Greek in its external form, observing the unities of time (twenty-four hours), place (the Sultan's palace in Constantinople), and action (news of the fortunes of the war between the Greeks and the Turks). Structurally, it consists of seven parts: four sections of intricate choral lyrics that flank three long sections of dialogue in blank verse.

Shelley's characterization of Mahmud II, known to history as "the Reformer," becomes clearer once we know that the Sultan's mother was a French woman—Aimée Dubucq de Rivery from Martinique, the cousin of Joséphine Bonaparte (also from that island). After Algerian corsairs captured Aimée while she was sailing home from France and gave her as a present to Sultan Abdul Hamid I (then fifty-nine), she became his favorite consort and gave birth to Mahmud in 1783. Until the death of Abdul Hamid and later as confidante and adviser to his successor Selim (about Aimée's age) and to her son, she influenced the Ottoman Empire toward a pro-French foreign policy, aided by her correspondence with Joséphine Bonaparte. When Mahmud came to the throne in 1808, he narrowly escaped death at the hands of the janizaries after Selim's half-brother Mustafa (in whose favor Selim had abdicated during an uprising) was killed by Selim's supporters. Mahmud then and there determined to replace the feudal army with a modern professional one, eventually doing so in 1826 after ordering the janizaries slaughtered during another of their revolts.

Much of Shelley's poem is aimed at British public opinion, urging his country to come to the aid of the people whose early history set the course of Western civilization. In *Hellas* Shelley's understanding of international politics is so astute that the poem, though not always precise about the details of current events, presciently forecasts the course of the war that would unfold only after his death. In 1824, when Sultan Mahmud finally agreed to the terms of Egypt's ruler Mohammed Ali (see lines 583–85 and note), the arrival of the Egyptian fleet under Mohammed Ali's son Ibrahim Pasha so changed the momentum of the war and made such great advances against the Greeks that a combined British, French, and Russian fleet, activated by the pressure of public opinion largely aroused by such philhellenes as Shelley and Byron, had to destroy the Egyptian fleet off Navarino in October 1827 to assure the Greeks their independence.

Noel Barber narrates the politics of the seraglio in *The Sultans* (Simon and Schuster, 1973). For an analysis of the dating, composition, and changing forms of *Hellas*, with an outline of Shelley's goals and his philosophical perspective, see the Introduction to *BSM*, XVI, by Reiman and Michael J. Neth. Carl Woodring succinctly characterizes the British political implications of the drama in *Politics in English Romantic Poetry* (Harvard University Press, 1970), and William St. Clair evokes the grim realities of the War of Greek Independence, of which Shelley—like other Western liberals—was partially ignorant, in *That Greece Might Still Be Free* (Oxford University Press, 1972). For Shelley's knowledge about Greek actions during the war and his turn to Greek tragedy, particularly Aeschylus' *Persians* as a model, see Michael Erkelenz, "Inspecting the Tragedy of Empire: Shelley's *Hellas* and Aeschylus' *Persians* (*PQ* 76 [1997], pp. 313–37). There is a bilingual edition of *Hellas* published in Athens, with a Greek translation by M. Byron Raizis, Professor of English at the University of Athens, containing an excellent introduction and useful notes in both languages (ISBN 960-7133-11-0).

# Hellas

## A Lyrical Drama

---

ΜΑΝΤΙΣ ΕΙΜ' ΕΣΘΛΩΝ 'ΑΓΩΝΩΝ.—oedip. colon.[1]

---

To His Excellency

Prince Alexander Mavrocordato

late Secretary for foreign affairs to the Hospodar of Wallachia

The drama of Hellas is inscribed as an imperfect token of the admiration, sympathy, and friendship of the Author.

Pisa, November 1st, 1821.

## Preface

THE Poem of *Hellas*, written at the suggestion of the events of the moment, is a mere improvise, and derives its interest (should it be found to possess any) solely from the intense sympathy which the Author feels with the cause he would celebrate.

The subject in its present state, is insusceptible of being treated otherwise than lyrically, and if I have called this poem a drama from the circumstance of its being composed in dialogue, the licence is not greater than that which has been assumed by other poets who have called their productions epics, only because they have been divided into twelve or twenty-four books.

*The Persæ* of Æschylus afforded me the first model of my conception, although the decision of the glorious contest now waging in Greece being yet suspended forbids a catastrophe parallel to the return of Xerxes and the desolation of the Persians. I have, therefore, contented myself with exhibiting a series of lyric pictures, and with having wrought upon the curtain of futurity which falls upon the unfinished scene such figures of indistinct and visionary delineation as suggest the final triumph of the Greek cause as a portion of the cause of civilization and social improvement.

The drama (if drama it must be called) is, however, so inartificial that I doubt whether, if recited on the Thespian waggon to an Athenian village at the Dionysiaca, it would have obtained the prize of the goat.[2] I shall bear with equanimity any punishment greater than the loss of such a reward which the Aristarchi[3] of the hour may think fit to inflict.

---

1. "I am a prophet of glorious struggles." Sophocles, *Oedipus at Colonus*, line 1080.
2. The word "tragedy" is generally supposed to derive from the Greek for "goat-song," the common explanation being that the winner of a dramatic competition at the festival of Dionysus received a goat as prize.
3. Aristarchus of Samothrace (ca. 220-143 B.C.) was an Alexandrian grammarian, editor, and critic who was noted for his rigorous analyses of the texts of the Greek classics.

The only *goat-song* which I have yet attempted[4] has, I confess, in spite of the unfavourable nature of the subject, received a greater and a more valuable portion of applause than I expected or than it deserved.

Common fame is the only authority which I can alledge for the details which form the basis of the poem, and I must trespass upon the forgiveness of my readers for the display of newspaper erudition to which I have been reduced. Undoubtedly, until the conclusion of the war, it will be impossible to obtain an account of it sufficiently authentic for historical materials; but poets have their privilege, and it is unquestionable that actions of the most exalted courage have been performed by the Greeks, that they have gained more than one naval victory, and that their defeat in Wallachia[5] was signalized by circumstances of heroism, more glorious even than victory.

The apathy of the rulers of the civilized world to the astonishing circumstance of the descendants of that nation to which they owe their civilization rising as it were from the ashes of their ruin is something perfectly inexplicable to a mere spectator of the shews of this mortal scene. We are all Greeks—our laws, our literature, our religion, our arts have their root in Greece. But for Greece, Rome, the instructor, the conqueror, or the metropolis of our ancestors would have spread no illumination with her arms, and we might still have been savages, and idolaters; or, what is worse, might have arrived at such a stagnant and miserable state of social institution as China and Japan possess.

The human form and the human mind attained to a perfection in Greece which has impressed its image on those faultless productions whose very fragments are the despair of modern art, and has propagated impulses which cannot cease, through a thousand channels of manifest or imperceptible operation to ennoble and delight mankind until the extinction of the race.

The modern Greek is the descendant of those glorious beings whom the imagination almost refuses to figure to itself as belonging to our Kind, and he inherits much of their sensibility, their rapidity of conception, their enthusiasm and their courage. If in many instances he is degraded, by moral and political slavery to the practise of the basest vices it engenders, and that below the level of ordinary degradation; let us reflect that the corruption of the best produces the worst, and that habits which subsist only in relation to a peculiar state of social institution may be expected to cease so soon as that relation is dissolved. In fact, the Greeks, since the admirable novel of *Anastasius*[6] could have been a faithful picture of their manners, have undergone most important changes; the flower of their Youth, returning to their Country from the universities of Italy, Germany and France have communicated to their fellow citizens the latest results of that social perfection of which their ancestors were the original source. The uni-

4. I.e., *The Cenci*.
5. Then a Turkish province north of the Danube; now part of Romania.
6. *Anastasius; or, Memoirs of a Greek*, a three-volume novel by Thomas Hope published anonymously in 1819.

versity of Chios contained before the breaking out of the Revolution eight hundred students, and among them several Germans and Americans. The munificence and energy of many of the Greek princes and merchants, directed to the renovation of their country with a spirit and a wisdom which has few examples, is above all praise.

The English permit their own oppressors to act according to their natural sympathy with the Turkish tyrant, and to brand upon their name the indelible blot of an alliance with the enemies of domestic happiness, of Christianity and civilization.

Russia desires to possess not to liberate Greece, and is contented to see the Turks, its natural enemies, and the Greeks, its intended slaves, enfeeble each other until one or both fall into its net. The wise and generous policy of England would have consisted in establishing the independence of Greece, and in maintaining it both against Russia and the Turk;—but when was the oppressor generous or just?

Should the English people ever become free they will reflect upon the part which those who presume to represent their will, have played in the great drama of the revival of liberty, with feelings which it would become them to anticipate. This is the age of the war of the oppressed against the oppressors, and every one of those ringleaders of the privileged gangs of murderers and swindlers, called Sovereigns, look to each other for aid against the common enemy and suspend their mutual jealousies in the presence of a mightier fear. Of this holy alliance all the despots of the earth are virtual members. But a new race has arisen throughout Europe, nursed in the abhorrence of the opinions which are its chains, and she will continue to produce fresh generations to accomplish that destiny which tyrants foresee and dread.[7]

The Spanish peninsula is already free. France is tranquil in the enjoyment of a partial exemption from the abuses which its unnatural and feeble government are vainly attempting to revive. The seed of blood and misery has been sown in Italy and a more vigorous race is arising to go forth to the harvest. The world waits only the news of a revolution of Germany to see the Tyrants who have pinnacled themselves on its supineness precipitated into the ruin from which they shall never arise. Well do these destroyers of mankind know their enemy when they impute the insurrection in Greece to the same spirit before which they tremble throughout the rest of Europe, and that enemy well knows the power and the cunning of its opponents, and watches the moment of their approaching weakness and inevitable division to wrest the bloody sceptres from their grasp.—

---

7. This paragraph, deleted by Ollier from the first edition, was first published by H. Buxton Forman in his Aldine Edition of Shelley's *Poetical Works* (1892), IV, 41–42.

## Dramatis Personae

| | |
|---|---|
| Mahmud. | Daood. |
| Hassan. | Ahasuerus, a Jew. |

Chorus of Greek Captive Women.
Messengers, Slaves, and Attendants.
Scene, Constantinople. Time, Sunset.

SCENE. A terrace on the Seraglio.[8] Mahmud sleeping, an Indian slave
sitting beside his couch.

CHORUS OF GREEK CAPTIVE WOMEN.
We strew these opiate flowers
    On thy restless pillow,—
They were stript from Orient bowers,
    By the Indian billow.
        Be thy sleep                                    5
        Calm and deep,
Like theirs who fell, not ours who weep!

INDIAN.
Away, unlovely dreams!
    Away, false shapes of sleep!
Be his, as Heaven seems                                 10
    Clear and bright and deep!
Soft as love, and calm as death,
Sweet as a summer night without a breath.

CHORUS.
Sleep, sleep! our song is laden
    With the soul of slumber;                           15
It was sung by a Samian[9] maiden
    Whose lover was of the number
        Who now keep
        That calm sleep
Whence none may wake, where none shall weep.            20

INDIAN.
I touch thy temples pale!
    I breathe my soul on thee!
And could my prayers avail,
    All my joy should be
Dead, and I would live to weep,                         25
So thou might'st win one hour of quiet sleep.

CHORUS.
Breathe low, low!
The spell of the mighty mistress now

8. Turkish palace (or, sometimes, the palace in which the harem was located).
9. From the Aegean island of Samos, off the coast of Asia Minor.

When Conscience lulls her sated snake
And Tyrants sleep, let Freedom wake.                    30
   Breathe! low—low
The words which like secret fire shall flow
Through the veins of the frozen earth—low, low!

#### SEMICHORUS I.

Life may change, but it may fly not;
Hope may vanish, but can die not;                       35
Truth be veiled but still it burneth;
Love repulsed,—but it returneth!

#### SEMICHORUS II.

Yet were Life a charnel where
Hope lay coffined with despair;
Yet were Truth a sacred lie,                            40
Love were Lust—

#### SEMICHORUS I.

   If Liberty
Lent not Life its soul of light,
Hope its iris of delight,
Truth its prophet's robe to wear,
Love its power to give and bear.                        45

#### CHORUS.

In the great Morning of the world
The spirit of God with might unfurled
The flag of Freedom over chaos,
   And all its banded Anarchs[1] fled
Like Vultures frighted from Imaus[2]                    50
   Before an Earthquake's tread.—
So from Time's tempestuous dawn
Freedom's splendour burst and shone.—
Thermopylæ and Marathon[3]
Caught, like mountains beacon-lighted,                  55
   The springing Fire.—The winged Glory
On Philippi[4] half-alighted,
   Like an Eagle on a promontory.
Its unwearied wings could fan

---

1. Tyrants who band together in a group or pack (cf. *Adonais*, line 244).
2. A mountain in central Asia; in *Paradise Lost*, Milton describes Satan as "a Vultur on *Imaus* bred" (III.431).
3. In 490 B.C. eleven thousand Athenians and Plataeans destroyed the much larger invading Persian army of Darius I on the plain of Marathon; ten years later (480 B.C.) the Spartans and their allies under Leonidas held the host of Xerxes at bay in the narrow defile of Thermopylae, between the mountains and the sea, for three bloody days until Leonidas and all the Spartans had been killed.
4. A city in Macedonia where, in 42 B.C., Mark Antony and Octavius Caesar put an end to the power of the senatorial (republican) party by defeating the army of Brutus and Cassius.

The quenchless ashes of Milan.[5]                                    60
From age to age, from man to man,
    It lived; and lit from land to land
    Florence, Albion,[6] Switzerland.
Then Night fell—and as from night
Re-assuming fiery flight                                             65
From the West swift Freedom came
    Against the course of Heaven and doom,
A second sun arrayed in flame
    To burn, to kindle, to illume.
From far Atlantis[7] its young beams                                 70
Chased the shadows and the dreams
France, with all her sanguine steams[8]
    Hid but quench'd it not; again
    Through clouds its shafts of glory rain
    From utmost Germany to Spain.                                    75
As an eagle fed with morning
Scorns the embattled tempest's warning
When she seeks her aiëry hanging
    In the mountain-cedar's hair
And her brood expect the clanging                                    80
    Of her wings through the wild air
Sick with famine—Freedom so
To what of Greece remaineth now
Returns; her hoary ruins glow
Like orient mountains lost in day.                                   85
    Beneath the safety of her wings
Her renovated nurslings prey,
    And in the naked lightnings
Of truth they purge their dazzled eyes.
Let Freedom leave, where'er she flies,                               90
A Desart, or a Paradise:
    Let the beautiful and the brave
    Share her glory, or a grave.


SEMICHORUS I.

With the gifts of gladness
    Greece did thy cradle strew—                                    95


SEMICHORUS II.

With the tears of sadness
    Greece did thy shroud bedew!

5. In the twelfth and thirteenth centuries Milan was the leading city of the Lombard League
of Italian communes, or city-states, that defied and eventually defeated the Holy Roman
Emperor Frederick I (Barbarossa). See Shelley's note 1, p. 462.
6. England.
7. The United States of America.
8. The French Revolution.

SEMICHORUS I.
With an orphan's affection
    She followed thy bier through Time

SEMICHORUS II.
And at thy resurrection                                    100
    Reappeareth, like thou, sublime!

SEMICHORUS I.
If Heaven should resume thee,
    To Heaven shall her spirit ascend;

SEMICHORUS II.
If Hell should entomb thee,
    To Hell shall her high hearts bend.                    105

SEMICHORUS I.
If annihilation——

SEMICHORUS II.
    Dust let her glories be!
And a name and a nation
    Be forgotten, Freedom, with thee!

INDIAN.
His brow grows darker—breathe not—move not!               110
He starts—he shudders—ye that love not,
    With your panting loud and fast,
    Have awakened him at last.

*Mahmud* (*starting from his sleep*).
Man the Seraglio-guard!—make fast the gate.
What! from a cannonade of three short hours?              115
'Tis false! that breach towards the Bosphorus⁹
Cannot be practicable yet—who stirs?
Stand to the match! that when the foe prevails
One spark may mix in reconciling ruin
The conqueror and the conquered! Heave the tower          120
Into the gap—wrench off the roof!
    (*Enter* HASSAN.)                    Ha! what!
The truth of day lightens upon my dream
And I am Mahmud, still,—
    *Hassan.*                Your sublime highness
Is strangely moved.
    *Mahmud.*        The times do cast strange shadows
On those who watch and who must rule their course,        125
Lest they being first in peril as in glory

---

9. Constantinople (Greek), or Istanbul (Turkish), is on the west side of the Bosporus (Bosphorus in Shelley's day), the strait that connects the Black Sea with the Sea of Marmara (then "Marmora"), which also connects with the Aegean Sea through the Dardanelles.

Be whelmed in the fierce ebb:—and these are of them.
Thrice has a gloomy vision hunted me
As thus from sleep into the troubled day;
It shakes me as the tempest shakes the sea,                            130
Leaving no figure upon memory's glass.
Would that—no matter—thou didst say thou knewest
A Jew, whose spirit is a chronicle
Of strange and secret and forgotten things.[1]
I bade thee summon him—'tis said his tribe                            135
Dream, and are wise interpreters of dreams.
    *Hassan.* The Jew of whom I spake is old—so old
He seems to have outlived a world's decay;
The hoary mountains and the wrinkled ocean
Seem younger still than he—his hair and beard                         140
Are whiter than the tempest-sifted snow.
His cold pale limbs and pulseless arteries
Are like the fibres of a cloud instinct[2]
With light, and to the soul that quickens them
Are as the atoms of the mountain-drift                                145
To the winter wind—but from his eye looks forth
A life of unconsumed thought which pierces
The present, and the past, and the to-come.
Some say that this is he whom the great prophet
Jesus, the Son of Joseph, for his mockery                             150
Mocked with the curse of immortality.—
Some feign that he is Enoch[3]—others dream
He was preadamite and has survived
Cycles of generation and of ruin.
The sage, in truth, by dreadful abstinence                            155
And conquering penance of the mutinous flesh,
Deep contemplation and unwearied study
In years outstretched beyond the date of man,
May have attained to sovereignty and science[4]
Over those strong and secret things and thoughts                      160
Which others fear and know not.
    *Mahmud.*                              I would talk
With this old Jew.
    *Hassan.*            Thy will is even now
Made known to him, where he dwells in a sea cavern
Mid the Demonesi,[5] less accessible
Than thou or God! He who would question him                           165
Must sail alone at sunset where the stream
Of ocean sleeps around those foamless isles,

---

1. From the period of Shelley's earliest poetry, he was fascinated by the legend of the Wandering Jew. For a sketch of his early poetic interest, see our general commentary on his first completed book-length poem, *The Wandering Jew; or, The Victim of the Eternal Avenger* (written 1810), in *CPPBS*, I, 189–204.
2. *instinct:* imbued or permeated.
3. "And Enoch [Methuselah's father] walked with God: and he was not, for God took him" (Genesis 5:24); this ambiguous poetic phrasing led some commentators to say that Enoch never died but was taken alive by God and would return.
4. Mastery.
5. Islands in the Sea of Marmara.

When the young moon is westering as now
And evening airs wander upon the wave;
And when the pines of that bee-pasturing isle,                    170
Green Erebinthus, quench the fiery shadow
Of his gilt prow within the sapphire water.
Then must the lonely helmsman cry aloud,
Ahasuerus! and the caverns round
Will answer Ahasuerus! If his prayer                             175
Be granted, a faint meteor will arise
Lighting him over Marmora, and a wind
Will rush out of the sighing pine forest
And with the wind a storm of harmony
Unutterably sweet, and pilot him                                 180
Through the soft twilight to the Bosphorus:
Thence at the hour and place and circumstance
Fit for the matter of their conference
The Jew appears. Few dare and few who dare
Win the desired communion—but that shout      [a shout within.
Bodes——
  *Mahmud.* Evil doubtless like all human sounds,              186
Let me converse with spirits.
  *Hassan.*      That shout again.
  *Mahmud.* This Jew whom thou hast summoned—
  *Hassan.*        Will be here—
  *Mahmud.* When the omnipotent hour to which are yoked
He, I, and all things shall compel.—Enough,                      190
Silence those mutineers—that drunken crew,
That crowd about the pilot in the storm.
Aye! strike the foremost shorter by a head.—
They weary me and I have need of rest.
Kings are like stars—they rise and set, they have                195
The worship of the world but no repose.[6]      [*exeunt severally.*

CHORUS.[7]

  Worlds on worlds are rolling ever
   From creation to decay,
  Like the bubbles on a river
   Sparkling, bursting, borne away.                         200
   But they are still immortal
   Who through Birth's orient portal
  And Death's dark chasm hurrying to and fro,
   Clothe their unceasing flight
   In the brief dust and light                             205
  Gathered around their chariots as they go;
   New shapes they still may weave,
   New Gods, new Laws receive,
  Bright or dim are they as the robes they last
   On Death's bare ribs had cast.                          210

6. Lines 195–96 echo Francis Bacon's essay "Of Empire": "Princes are like to Heavenly Bodies,
 which . . . have much Veneration, but no Rest."
7. See Shelley's note 2, p. 462.

A Power from the unknown God,
    A Promethean Conqueror,[8] came;
Like a triumphal path he trod
    The thorns of death and shame.
A mortal shape to him                                    215
    Was like the vapour dim
Which the orient planet[9] animates with light;
    Hell, Sin, and Slavery came
    Like bloodhounds mild and tame,
Nor preyed, until their Lord had taken flight;          220
    The moon of Mahomet[1]
    Arose, and it shall set,
While blazoned as on Heaven's immortal noon
    The cross leads generations on.[2]

    Swift as the radiant shapes of sleep              225
        From one whose dreams are Paradise
    Fly, when the fond wretch wakes to weep,
        And Day peers forth with her blank eyes;
    So fleet, so faint, so fair,
        The Powers of earth and air                   230
    Fled from the folding star[3] of Bethlehem;
        Apollo, Pan, and Love—
        And even Olympian Jove—
    Grew weak, for killing Truth had glared on them;[4]
        Our hills and seas and streams—,             235
        Dispeopled of their dreams—
    Their waters turned to blood, their dew to tears—
        Wailed for the golden years.


    Enter MAHMUD, HASSAN, DAOOD, and others.
Mahmud. More gold? our ancestors bought gold with victory,
And shall I sell it for defeat?
    Daood.                    The Janizars[5]             240
Clamour for pay—
    Mahmud.        Go! bid them pay themselves
With Christian blood! Are there no Grecian virgins
Whose shrieks and spasms and tears they may enjoy?

8. Jesus Christ.
9. Venus as the morning star.
1. The crescent moon is the chief symbol of Islam.
2. The Roman emperor Constantine I ("the Great"), who changed the name of the capital of the eastern Roman Empire from Byzantium to Constantinople, converted to Christianity (according to his own account) because before the decisive battle that secured his empire, he saw a cross of light superimposed on the sun.
3. The evening star, which appears about the time that shepherds bring their sheep back to the fold.
4. This stanza alludes to the downfall of the pagan gods that Milton describes in "On the Morning of Christ's Nativity" (lines 165–236). See also Shelley's note 8, p. 464.
5. From the end of the fourteenth century on, the janizaries (various English spellings) were the chief standing army of the Turkish Empire. Though originally recruited from captive Christian children who were converted to Islam and trained as soldiers, by 1700 they were an elite corps recruited from the Turkish upper classes and they rebelled every time their privileges were threatened. See the headnote for Mahmud's attitude toward them.

No infidel children to impale on spears?
No hoary priests after that Patriarch[6]                        245
Who bent the curse against his country's heart,
Which clove his own at last? Go! bid them kill—
Blood is the seed of gold.
   *Daood.*                    It has been sown,
And yet the harvest to the sicklemen
Is as a grain to each.
   *Mahmud.*               Then, take this signet.          250
Unlock the seventh chamber in which lie
The treasures of victorious Solyman,[7]—
An Empire's spoil stored for a day of ruin.
O spirit of my sires, is it not come?
The prey-birds and the wolves are gorged and sleep,          255
But these, who spread their feast on the red earth,
Hunger for gold, which fills not—see them fed;
Then, lead them to the rivers of fresh death.     [*Exit* DAOOD.
O, miserable dawn after a night
More glorious than the day which it usurped!                 260
O, faith in God! O power on earth! O word
Of the great prophet, whose o'ershadowing wings
Darkened the thrones and idols of the West:
Now bright!—for thy sake cursed be the hour,
Even as a father by an evil child                            265
When th'orient moon of Islam roll'd in triumph
From Caucasus to white Ceraunia![8]
Ruin above, and anarchy below;
Terror without, and treachery within;
The chalice of destruction full, and all                     270
Thirsting to drink, and who among us dares
To dash it from his lips? and where is hope?
   *Hassan.* The lamp of our dominion still rides high,
One God is God—Mahomet is his prophet.
Four hundred thousand Moslems, from the limits              275
Of utmost Asia, irresistibly
Throng, like full clouds at the Sirocco's[9] cry;
But not like them to weep their strength in tears:
They bear destroying lightning and their step
Wakes earthquake to consume and overwhelm                   280
And reign in ruin. Phrygian Olympus,
Tmolus and Latmos and Mycale[1] roughen

6. After the Greeks rebelled and slaughtered the Turks living among them, the Turks retaliated by massacring the Greeks in Asia Minor, including Gregorios, the Orthodox Patriarch of Constantinople, who was hanged on April 22, 1821. See Shelley's note 3, pp. 462–63.
7. Suleiman I, the Magnificent (sultan 1520–66), defeated Persia; conquered Rhodes, the Venetian strongholds in southern Greece, and Hungary (threatening Austria); and defeated the combined fleets of Spain and Venice off Preveza (1538). His reign also saw the highest achievements of the Ottoman Empire in law, literature, art, and architecture.
8. The Caucasus Mountains are between the Black Sea and the Caspian Sea; the Ceraunian (or Acroceraunian) Mountains of Epirus are in northwestern Greece.
9. The sultry southeast wind from Africa.
1. Mountains in northwestern Asia Minor, near the Ottoman homeland.

With horrent arms; and lofty ships even now
Like vapours anchored to a mountain's edge,
Freighted with fire and whirlwind, wait at Scala[2]     285
The convoy of the ever-veering wind.
Samos is drunk with blood;—the Greek has paid
Brief victory with swift loss and long despair.
The false Moldavian serfs[3] fled fast and far
When the fierce shout of Allah-illa-allah![4]     290
Rose like the war-cry of the northern wind
Which kills the sluggish clouds, and leaves a flock
Of wild swans struggling with the naked storm.
So were the lost Greeks on the Danube's day![5]
If night is mute, yet the returning sun     295
Kindles the voices of the morning birds;
Nor at thy bidding less exultingly
Than birds rejoicing in the golden day,
The Anarchies of Africa[6] unleash
Their tempest-winged cities of the sea     300
To speak in thunder to the rebel world.
Like sulphurous clouds half shattered by the storm
They sweep the pale Ægean, while the Queen
Of Ocean,[7] bound upon her island-throne
Far in the West sits mourning that her sons     305
Who frown on Freedom spare a smile for thee.
Russia still hovers as an Eagle might
Within a cloud, near which a kite and crane
Hang tangled in inextricable fight,
To stoop upon the victor—for she fears     310
The name of Freedom even as she hates thine.
But recreant[8] Austria loves thee as the Grave
Loves Pestilence, and her slow dogs of war
Fleshed with the chase come up from Italy
And howl upon their limits; for they see     315
The panther Freedom fled to her old cover
'Mid seas and mountains and a mightier brood
Crouch round. What Anarch wears a crown or mitre,
Or bears the sword, or grasps the key of gold,
Whose friends are not thy friends, whose foes thy foes?     320
Our arsenals and our armouries are full;
Our forts defy assault—ten thousand cannon
Lie ranged upon the beach, and hour by hour

2. The port of Scala Tyriorum in Phoenicia.
3. Moldavia, north of the River Prut, was in 1821 controlled by Russia, though it had been under Turkish rule for the previous 300 years.
4. The Islamic war cry: "There is no god but God."
5. Alexandros Ypsilantis, who was Mavrocordato's cousin, began the War of Greek Independence in March 1821 by crossing the River Prut from Russian-controlled Bessarabia into Moldavia, but he was soon defeated and fled to Austria, where he was imprisoned until 1827.
6. The corsair (pirate) states of Algiers, Tunis, and Tripoli—all Ottoman dependencies.
7. Great Britain.
8. Cowardly.

Their earth-convulsing wheels affright the city;
The galloping of fiery steeds makes pale                          325
The Christian merchant; and the yellow Jew
Hides his hoard deeper in the faithless earth.
Like clouds and like the shadows of the clouds
Over the hills of Anatolia[9]
Swift in wide troops the Tartar chivalry                          330
Sweep—the far flashing of their starry lances
Reverberates the dying light of day.
We have one God, one King, one hope, one law;
But many-headed Insurrection stands
Divided in itself, and soon must fall.                          335
    *Mahmud.* Proud words when deeds come short are seasonable.
Look, Hassan, on yon crescent moon emblazoned
Upon that shattered flag of fiery cloud
Which leads the rear of the departing day,
Wan emblem of an empire fading now.                          340
See! how it trembles in the blood-red air
And like a mighty lamp whose oil is spent
Shrinks on the horizon's edge while from above
One star[1] with insolent and victorious light
Hovers above its fall, and with keen beams                          345
Like arrows through a fainting antelope
Strikes its weak form to death.
    *Hassan.*                          Even as that moon
Renews itself——
    *Mahmud.*          Shall we be not renewed!
Far other bark[2] than ours were needed now
To stem the torrent of descending time;                          350
The spirit that lifts the slave before his lord
Stalks through the capitals of armed kings
And spreads his ensign in the wilderness,
Exults in chains, and when the rebel falls
Cries like the blood of Abel[3] from the dust;                          355
And the inheritors of the earth, like beasts
When earthquake is unleashed, with idiot fear
Cower in their kingly dens—as I do now.
What were Defeat when Victory must appal?
Or Danger when Security looks pale?                          360
How said the messenger who from the fort
Islanded in the Danube, saw the battle
Of Bucharest?[4]—that—
    *Hassan.*                          Ibrahim's scymitar

9. The central plateau of Asia Minor.
1. Venus as the evening star.
2. Small ship.
3. The second son of Adam, who was killed by his brother, Cain.
4. Though Alexandros Ypsilantis briefly held Bucharest, the capital of Wallachia, he soon re-
   treated in the face of the advancing Turks led by Ibrahim (line 363), the *Pacha* (now "Pasha":
   a title given to a high governmental official, governor of a province, or leader of an army),
   who is represented (lines 385–88) as demanding the Greeks' surrender. The decisive defeat
   of Ypsilantis and his army, which Shelley describes as a heroic stand, took place at Drăgasăni,
   about one hundred miles to the west-northwest of Bucharest.

Drew with its gleam swift victory from heaven,
To burn before him in the night of battle,                        365
A light and a destruction——
   *Mahmud.*                    Aye! the day
Was ours—but how?——
   *Hassan.*                The light Wallachians,
The Arnaut, Servian, and Albanian allies
Fled from the glance of our artillery
Almost before the thunderstone alit.                              370
One half the Grecian army made a bridge
Of safe and slow retreat with Moslem dead;
The other—
   *Mahmud.* Speak—tremble not.—
   *Hassan.*                        Islanded
By victor myriads formed in hollow square
With rough and steadfast front, and thrice flung back            375
The deluge of our foaming cavalry;
Thrice their keen wedge of battle pierced our lines.
Our baffled army trembled like one man
Before a host, and gave them space, but soon
From the surrounding hills the batteries blazed,                 380
Kneading them down with fire and iron rain:
Yet none approached till like a field of corn
Under the hook of the swart sickleman
The band, intrenched in mounds of Turkish dead,
Grew weak and few—then said the Pacha, "Slaves,                  385
Render[5] yourselves—they have abandoned you,
What hope of refuge, or retreat or aid?
We grant your lives." "Grant that which is thine own!"
Cried one, and fell upon his sword and died!
Another—"God, and man, and hope abandon me                       390
But I to them and to myself remain
Constant"—he bowed his head and his heart burst.
A third exclaimed, "There is a refuge, tyrant,
Where thou darest not pursue and canst not harm
Should'st thou pursue; there we shall meet again."               395
Then held his breath and, after a brief spasm
The indignant spirit cast its mortal garment
Among the slain;—dead earth upon the earth!
So these survivors, each by different ways,
Some strange, all sudden, none dishonorable,                     400
Met in triumphant death; and when our army
Closed in, while yet wonder and awe and shame
Held back the base hyenas of the battle
That feed upon the dead and fly the living,
One rose out of the chaos of the slain:                          405
And if it were a corpse which some dread spirit
Of the old saviours of the land we rule
Had lifted in its anger, wandering by;—

5. *Render:* surrender.

Or if there burned within the dying man
Unquenchable disdain of death, and faith                    410
Creating what it feigned;—I cannot tell—
But he cried, "Phantoms of the free, we come!
Armies of the Eternal, ye who strike
To dust the citadels of sanguine[6] kings,
And shake the souls throned on their stony hearts          415
And thaw their frostwork diadems like dew;—
O ye who float around this clime, and weave
The garment of the glory which it wears,
Whose fame though earth betray the dust it clasped,
Lies sepulchred in monumental thought;—                    420
Progenitors of all that yet is great,
Ascribe to your bright senate, O accept
In your high ministrations, us, your Sons.
Us first, and the more glorious yet to come!
And ye, weak conquerors! giants who look pale              425
When the crushed worm rebels beneath your tread,
The vultures and the dogs, your pensioners tame,
Are overgorged, but like oppressors, still
They crave the relic of destruction's feast;
The exhalations and the thirsty winds                      430
Are sick with blood; the dew is foul with death;
Heaven's light is quenched in slaughter; thus, where'er
Upon your camps, cities, or towers, or fleets
The obscene birds the reeking remnants cast
Of these dead limbs,—upon your streams and mountains,     435
Upon your fields, your gardens, and your housetops,
Where'er the winds shall creep or the clouds fly
Or the dews fall or the angry sun look down
With poisoned light—Famine and Pestilence
And Panic shall wage war upon our side;                    440
Nature from all her boundaries is moved
Against ye;—Time has found ye light as foam;
Earth rebels; and Good and Evil stake
Their empire o'er the unborn world of men
On this one cast;—but ere the die be thrown                445
The renovated Genius[7] of our race,
Proud umpire of the impious game, descends,
A seraph-winged Victory, bestriding
The tempest of the Omnipotence of God
Which sweeps all things to their appointed doom            450
And you to oblivion!"—More he would have said
But—
    *Mahmud.* Died—as thou shouldst ere thy lips had painted
Their ruin in the hues of our success—
A rebel's crime gilt with a rebel's tongue!
Your heart is Greek, Hassan.

6. Bloody.
7. Protective guiding spirit.

*Hassan.*                    It may be so:                          455
A spirit not my own wrenched me within
And I have spoken words I fear and hate;
Yet would I die for—
*Mahmud.*            Live! O live! outlive
Me and this sinking Empire. But the fleet—
*Hassan.* Alas!——
*Mahmud.*            The fleet which like a flock of clouds        460
Chased by the wind flies the insurgent banner.
Our winged castles from their merchant ships!
Our myriads before their weak pirate bands![8]
Our arms before their chains! our years of Empire
Before their centuries of servile fear!                            465
Death is awake! Repulse is on the waters!
They own no more the thunder-bearing banner
Of Mahmud, but like hounds of a base breed,
Gorge from a stranger's hand and rend their master.
*Hassan.* Latmos, and Ampelos and Phanæ[9] saw                    470
The wreck——
*Mahmud.* The caves of the Icarian isles
Told each to the other in loud mockery,
And with the tongue as of a thousand echoes
First of the sea convulsing fight—and, then,—
Thou darest to speak—senseless are the mountains;                  475
Interpret thou their voice!
*Hassan.*                    My presence bore
A part in that day's shame. The Grecian fleet
Bore down at day-break from the North, and hung,
As multitudinous on the ocean line
As cranes upon the cloudless Thracian wind.                        480
Our squadron convoying ten thousand men
Was stretching towards Nauplia[1] when the battle
Was kindled.—
First through the hail of our artillery
The agile Hydriote[2] barks with press of sail                     485
Dashed—ship to ship, cannon to cannon, man
To man were grappled in the embrace of war,
Inextricable but by death or victory—
The tempest of the raging fight convulsed
To its chrystalline depths that stainless sea                      490
And shook Heaven's roof of golden morning clouds
Poised on a hundred azure mountain-isles.
In the brief trances of the artillery

8. For many years the Turkish navy had depended upon the seamanship of subject Greek sailors
   and navigators, who during the war either deserted or could not be trusted. The irregular
   Greek ships outsailed and frequently defeated the Turks early in the war.
9. Latmos and Ampelos are mountains and Phanae is a mountainous promontory on the mainland of Asia Minor to the east; the Icarian isles are to the north and south of the island of
   Icaria and the Icarian Sea (near Samos).
1. Nauplia, at the head of the Gulf of Argolis, on the east coast of the Peloponnesus, the large
   peninsula south of the Gulf of Corinth, was the center of Greek rebels led by Dimitrios
   Ypsilantis (younger brother of Alexandros).
2. From the island of Hydra (Idhra), off the eastern coast of the Peloponnesus.

One cry from the destroyed and the destroyer
Rose, and a cloud of desolation wrapt                                495
The unforeseen event till the north wind
Sprung from the sea lifting the heavy veil
Of battle-smoke—then Victory—Victory!
For as we thought three frigates from Algiers
Bore down from Naxos[3] to our aid, but soon                         500
The abhorred cross glimmered behind, before,
Among, around us; and that fatal sign
Dried with its beams the strength in Moslem hearts,
As the sun drinks the dew—what more? We fled!—
Our noonday path over the sanguine foam                              505
Was beaconed,—and the glare struck the sun pale
By our consuming transports; the fierce light
Made all the shadows of our sails blood red
And every countenance blank. Some ships lay feeding
The ravening fire even to the water's level;                         510
Some were blown up—some settling heavily
Sunk; and the shrieks of our companions died
Upon the wind that bore us fast and far
Even after they were dead.—Nine thousand perished!
We met the vultures legioned in the air                              515
Stemming the torrent of the tainted wind;
They, screaming from their cloudy mountain peaks,
Stooped through the sulphurous battle-smoke and perched
Each on the weltering carcase that we loved
Like its ill angel or its damned soul,                               520
Riding upon the bosom of the sea.
We saw the dog-fish hastening to their feast,
Joy waked the voiceless people of the sea,
And ravening Famine left his ocean cave
To dwell with war, with us and with despair.                         525
We met Night three hours to the west of Patmos[4]
And with Night, tempest——
    *Mahmud.*              Cease!—


    *Enter a Messenger.*
  *Messenger.*                Your sublime Highness,
That Christian hound, the Muscovite Ambassador,
Has left the city—if the rebel fleet
Had anchored in the port, had Victory                                530
Crowned the Greek legions in the hippodrome,[5]
Panic were tamer—Obedience and Mutiny
Like giants in contention, planet-struck,[6]
Stand gazing on each other—there is peace
In Stamboul—

3. A large island of the Cyclades, halfway between Rhodes and Nauplia.
4. An island east-northeast of Naxos; there John wrote the Book of Revelation (1:9).
5. A *hippodrome* was the site of chariot races in classical times.
6. Paralyzed with fear.

*Mahmud.*   Is the grave not calmer still?      535
Its ruins shall be mine.
   *Hassan.*              Fear not the Russian:
The tiger leagues not with the stag at bay
Against the hunter—cunning, base, and cruel,
He crouches watching till the spoil be won
And must be paid for his reserve in blood.      540
After the war is fought yield the sleek Russian
That which thou can'st not keep, his deserved portion
Of blood, which shall not flow through streets and fields,
Rivers and seas, like that which we may win,
But stagnate in the veins of Christian slaves!      545

     *Enter second Messenger.*
   *Second Messenger.* Nauplia, Tripolizza, Mothon, Athens,
Navarin, Artas, Monembasia,[7]
Corinth and Thebes are carried by assault
And every Islamite who made his dogs
Fat with the flesh of Galilean slaves      550
Passed at the edge of the sword; the lust of blood
Which made our warriors drunk, is quenched in death;
But like a fiery plague breaks out anew
In deeds which make the Christian cause look pale
In its own light. The garrison of Patras[8]      555
Has store but for ten days, nor is there hope
But from the Briton; at once slave and tyrant
His wishes still are weaker than his fears
Or he would sell what faith may yet remain
From the oaths broke in Genoa and in Norway;[9]      560
And if you buy him not, your treasury
Is empty even of promises—his own coin.—
The freedman of a western poet chief[1]
Holds Attica with seven thousand rebels
And has beat back the Pacha of Negropont[2]—      565
The aged Ali sits in Yanina[3]
A crownless metaphor of empire:

7. *Tripolizza* (Tripolis) was in the interior of the Peloponnesus, not far from Nauplia (see note to line 482); *Mothon* (Methoni) and *Navarin* (Pilos) were near the southwest corner of the peninsula (off which the decisive Battle of Navarino was to be fought in 1827 in which the Turkish and Egyptian fleets were destroyed by French and British fleets). *Artas* (Arta) was far to the northwest in southern Epirus, and *Monembasia* (Monemvasia) is in the far southeast corner of the Peloponnesus. Things, the messenger says, are going badly for the Turks all over Greece.
8. *Patras* (Pátrai) is on the northwest coast of the Peloponnesus, just outside the narrows of the Gulf of Corinth. The British controlled the nearby Ionian Islands.
9. During the Napoleonic Wars, Sir William Bentinck had incited the people of Genoa to rebel against the French, promising that Britain would help restore the Genovese Republic, only to deliver the city to the kingdom of Sardinia. In 1814 Sweden took Norway; when the Norwegians rebelled and set up a constitutional monarchy, their independence was again curtailed in 1818 by a Swedish invasion to which Britain and the Holy Alliance acquiesced.
1. See Shelley's note 4, p. 463.
2. Euboea, a large island in the Aegean off the coast of Attica.
3. *Ali* (1741–1822), the pasha (governor) in Albania whom Byron had visited in 1813, was a famous warrior, intriguer, and murderer who by 1810 had established a virtually independent state with *Yanina* (Ioannina) as its capital. He was finally defeated and killed by the army of Sultan Mahmud II in May 1822.

His name, that shadow of his withered might,
Holds our besieging army like a spell
In prey to Famine, Pest, and Mutiny;                                     570
He, bastioned in his citadel, looks forth
Joyless upon the sapphire lake that mirrors
The ruins of the city where he reigned
Childless and sceptreless. The Greek has reaped
The costly harvest his own blood matured,                                575
Not the sower, Ali—who has bought a truce
From Ypsilanti[4] with ten camel loads
Of Indian gold—

      *Enter a third Messenger.*
  *Mahmud.*     What more?
   *Third Messenger.*       The Christian tribes
Of Lebanon and the Syrian wilderness
Are in revolt—Damascus, Hems, Aleppo                                     580
Tremble—the Arab menaces Medina,
The Ethiop has intrenched himself in Senaar,
And keeps the Egyptian rebel well employed
Who denies homage, claims investiture[5]
As price of tardy aid—Persia demands                                     585
The cities on the Tigris, and the Georgians
Refuse their living tribute.[6] Crete and Cyprus
Like mountain-twins that from each other's veins
Catch the volcano-fire and earthquake spasm,
Shake in the general fever. Through the city                             590
Like birds before a storm the Santons[7] shriek
And prophesyings horrible and new
Are heard among the crowd—that sea of men
Sleeps on the wrecks it made, breathless and still.
A Dervise learned in the Koran preaches                                  595
That it is written how the sins of Islam
Must raise up a destroyer even now.
The Greeks expect a Saviour from the West[8]
Who shall not come, men say, in clouds and glory:
But in the omnipresence of that spirit                                   600
In which all live and are. Ominous signs

---

4. Alexandros Ypsilantis (see notes to lines 289 and 294) had timed his invasion of Moldavia to take advantage of the conflict between the Sultan and Ali Pacha. Quite possibly (as Shelley may have heard) Ali and Ypsilantis had agreed to cooperate against their common enemy.
5. Mohammed Ali (ruled Egypt 1805–48), an Albanian officer in the Turkish service, had been raised to control of Egypt in 1805 by his troops and the war-weary populace during a period of chaos following the departure of Napoleon and the British forces that had dislodged him; in July 1805 he received from the Turks a "firman," or document of *investiture*—ceremonial appointment to the governorship he already held by force. Later, he, like his fellow Albanian Ali Pasha, ruled as an independent monarch and refused to aid the Turks in their war against the Greeks until they recognized his—and Egypt's—independence from Turkish rule.
6. Georgia, in the Caucasus Mountains, was famous for the beautiful girls who were sent to the Sultan's harem.
7. Islamic holy men, or dervishes (line 595)—an order whose members took vows of poverty and expressed religious fervor through their emotional dances; Shelley may have used both words with less specific meanings (like "priests and monks").
8. See Shelley's note 5, p. 463.

Are blazoned broadly on the noonday sky.
One saw a red cross stamped upon the sun;
It has rained blood, and monstrous births declare
The secret wrath of Nature and her Lord.                                605
The army encamped upon the Cydaris,[9]
Was roused last night by the alarm of battle
And saw two hosts conflicting in the air,
The shadows doubtless of the unborn time
Cast on the mirror of the night;—while yet                              610
The fight hung balanced, there arose a storm
Which swept the phantoms from among the stars.
At the third watch the spirit of the plague
Was heard abroad flapping among the tents;
Those who relieved watch found the sentinels dead.                      615
The last news from the camp is that a thousand
Have sickened, and——

      *Enter a fourth Messenger.*
  *Mahmud.*          And, thou, pale ghost, dim shadow
Of some untimely rumour—speak!
  *Fourth Messenger.*        One comes
Fainting with toil, covered with foam and blood:
He stood, he says, on Chelonites'                                       620
Promontory,[1] which o'erlooks the isles that groan
Under the Briton's frown, and all their waters
Then trembling in the splendour of the moon—
When as the wandering clouds unveiled or hid
Her boundless light, he saw two adverse fleets                          625
Stalk through the night in the horizon's glimmer,
Mingling fierce thunders and sulphurious gleams,
And smoke which strangled every infant wind
That soothed the silver clouds through the deep air.
At length the battle slept, but the Sirocco                             630
Awoke and drove his flock of thunder clouds
Over the sea-horizon, blotting out
All objects—save that in the faint moon-glimpse
He saw, or dreamed he saw, the Turkish admiral
And two—the loftiest—of our ships of war                               635
With the bright image of that Queen of Heaven
Who hid, perhaps, her face for grief, reversed;
And the abhorred cross—

      *Enter an Attendant.*
  *Attendant.*        Your sublime highness,
The Jew, who—
  *Mahmud.*    Could not come more seasonably:

---

9. A small river in Thrace, at the northern end of the Aegean Sea (identified by M. Byron Raizis in his bilingual edition; see headnote).
1. The westernmost point on the mainland of the Peloponnesus in Elis, in the northwest part of the peninsula, near the British-occupied Ionian islands, which included Ithaca, Odysseus' island-kingdom.

Bid him attend—I'll hear no more! too long                    640
We gaze on danger through the mist of fear,
And multiply upon our shattered hopes
The images of ruin—come what will!
Tomorrow and tomorrow are as lamps
Set in our path to light us to the edge                       645
Through rough and smooth, nor can we suffer aught
Which he inflicts not in whose hand we are.          [*exeunt.*

SEMICHORUS I.
Would I were the winged cloud
Of a tempest swift and loud.
                I would scorn                              650
                The smile of morn
And the wave where the moon rise is born!
                I would leave
                The spirits of eve
A shroud for the corpse of the day to weave               655
From other threads than mine!
Bask in the deep blue noon divine
                Who would,—not I.

SEMICHORUS II.
                Whither to fly?

SEMICHORUS I.
Where the rocks that gird th' Ægean                         660
Echo to the battle pæan[2]
                Of the free—
                I would flee,
A tempestuous herald of Victory,
                My golden rain                              665
                For the Grecian slain
Should mingle in tears with the bloody main
                And my solemn thunder knell
                Should ring to the world the passing bell
                Of Tyranny!                                670

SEMICHORUS II.
                Ha king! wilt thou chain
                The rack[3] and the rain,
Wilt thou fetter the lightning and hurricane?
                The storms are free
                But we?                                     675

CHORUS.
O Slavery! thou frost of the world's prime,
    Killing its flowers and leaving its thorns bare!

2. A Greek war song addressed to Ares (Roman Mars) while advancing to battle.
3. Cloud mass in the upper air driven by the wind.

Thy touch has stamped these limbs with crime,
   These brows thy branding garland bear,
      But the free heart, the impassive soul              680
         Scorn thy controul!

SEMICHORUS I.

Let there be light! said Liberty,[4]
And like sunrise from the sea,
Athens arose!—around her born,
Shone like mountains in the morn                          685
Glorious states,—and are they now
Ashes, wrecks, oblivion?

SEMICHORUS II.
Go,

Where Thermæ and Asopus swallowed
Persia,[5] as the sand does foam.
Deluge upon deluge followed,—                             690
   Discord, Macedon and Rome:
And lastly Thou!

SEMICHORUS I.
Temples and towers,

   Citadels and marts and they
Who live and die there, have been ours
   And may be thine, and must decay,                      695
But Greece and her foundations are
Built below the tide of war,
Based on the chrystalline sea
Of thought and its eternity;
Her citizens, imperial spirits,                           700
Rule the present from the past,
On all this world of men inherits
   Their seal is set—

SEMICHORUS II.
Hear ye the blast

Whose Orphic[6] thunder thrilling calls
   From ruin her Titanian walls?                          705
Whose spirit shakes the sapless bones
   Of Slavery? Argos, Corinth, Crete
Hear, and from their mountain thrones
   The dæmons and the nymphs[7] repeat
The harmony.

---

4. Lines 682–703 echo and partially recapitulate the "Ode to Liberty" that Shelley published
   with *Prometheus Unbound*.
5. The rivers near which were fought Thermopylae (480 B.C.) and Plataea (479 B.C.)—the first
   and last land battles during Xerxes' unsuccessful invasion of Greece.
6. Associated with Orpheus, the mythical Thracian whose music charmed all nature.
7. In Greek mythology supernatural beings intermediate between gods and men.

SEMICHORUS I.
I hear! I hear!                                          710


SEMICHORUS II.
The world's eyeless charioteer
    Destiny is hurrying by!
What faith is crushed, what empire bleeds
Beneath her earthquake-footed steeds?
What eagle-winged victory sits                          715
At her right hand? what shadow flits
    Before? what splendour rolls behind?
    Ruin and Renovation cry
"Who but we?"


SEMICHORUS I.
I hear! I hear.
The hiss as of a rushing wind,                          720
The roar as of an ocean foaming,
The thunder as of earthquake coming.
        I hear! I hear!
The crash as of an empire falling,
The shrieks as of a people calling                      725
"Mercy? Mercy!" how they thrill!
Then a shout of "Kill! Kill! Kill!"
And then a small still voice,[8] thus—


SEMICHORUS II.
                            For
Revenge and wrong bring forth their kind,
    The foul cubs like their parents are,                730
Their den is in the guilty mind
    And Conscience feeds them with despair.[9]—


SEMICHORUS I.
In sacred Athens, near the fane
    Of Wisdom, Pity's altar stood.
Serve not the unknown God in vain,                      735
But pay that broken shrine again,
    Love for hate and tears for blood!


*Enter* MAHMUD *and* AHASUERUS.
*Mahmud.* Thou art a man, thou sayest, even as we.
*Ahasuerus.* No more!

---

8. Lines 720–28 draw their emotional force from the story of how the Lord came to speak to the prophet Elijah—not in the earthquake, wind, or fire, but in "a still small voice" (1 Kings 19:11–13).
9. Lines 729–32, as Richard Garnett first pointed out in 1884, are based on lines 758–60 of Aeschylus' *Agamemnon*, which F. L. Lucas's free-verse translation renders: "Pride . . . bringeth forth / . . . / A ruinous younger Pride, a child of Wrath, / . . . / Foul as its parentage." Shelley quotes part of the Greek text at the end of his letter to Mary Shelley written at Ravenna on August [8–10], 1821 (*Letters*, II, 325).

*Mahmud.*              But raised above thy fellow men
By thought, as I by power.
  *Ahasuerus.*              Thou sayest so.                          740
  *Mahmud.* Thou art an adept in the difficult lore
Of Greek and Frank[1] philosophy; thou numberest
The flowers, and thou measurest the stars;
Thou severest element from element;
Thy spirit is present in the past, and sees            745
The birth of this old world through all its cycles
Of desolation and of loveliness,
And when man was not, and how man became
The monarch and the slave of this low sphere,
And all its narrow circles—it is much—                 750
I honour thee, and would be what thou art
Were I not what I am—but the unborn hour,
Cradled in fear and hope, conflicting storms,
Who shall unveil? Nor thou, nor I, nor any
Mighty or wise. I apprehended not                      755
What thou has taught me, but I now perceive
That thou art no interpreter of dreams;
Thou dost not own that art, device, or God,
Can make the future present—let it come!
Moreover thou disdainest us and ours;                  760
Thou art as God whom thou contemplatest.
  *Ahasuerus.* Disdain thee? not the worm beneath thy feet!
The Fathomless has care for meaner things
Than thou canst dream, and has made Pride for those
Who would be what they may not, or would seem          765
That which they are not—Sultan! talk no more
Of thee and me, the future and the past;
But look on that which cannot change—the One,
The unborn and the undying. Earth and ocean,
Space and the isles of life or light that gem          770
The sapphire floods of interstellar air,
This firmament pavilioned upon chaos,
With all its cressets[2] of immortal fire
Whose outwall bastioned impregnably
Against the escape of boldest thoughts, repels them    775
As Calpe[3] the Atlantic clouds—this Whole
Of suns, and worlds, and men, and beasts, and flowers
With all the silent or tempestuous workings
By which they have been, are, or cease to be,
Is but a vision—all that it inherits                   780
Are motes[4] of a sick eye, bubbles and dreams;
Thought is its cradle and its grave, nor less

1. The Greeks, Turks, and other peoples of the eastern Mediterranean referred to those from
   western Europe as "Franks" (the Germanic tribe from which France takes its name).
2. Lamps containing burning oil, usually atop a pole or suspended from a roof; here, stars.
3. The ancient name for the Rock of Gibraltar.
4. The small dust particles visible in a sunbeam.

The future and the past are idle shadows
Of thought's eternal flight—they have no being.
Nought is but that which feels itself to be.                                      785
    *Mahmud.* What meanest thou? thy words stream like a tempest
Of dazzling mist within my brain—they shake
The earth on which I stand, and hang like night
On Heaven above me. What can they avail?
They cast on all things surest, brightest, best,                            790
Doubt, insecurity, astonishment.
    *Ahasuerus.* Mistake me not! All is contained in each.
Dodona's forest[5] to an acorn's cup
Is that which has been, or will be, to that
Which is—the absent to the present. Thought                          795
Alone, and its quick elements, Will, Passion,
Reason, Imagination, cannot die;
They are, what that which they regard, appears,
The stuff whence mutability can weave
All that it hath dominion o'er, worlds, worms,                             800
Empires and superstitions—what has thought
To do with time or place or circumstance?
Would'st thou behold the future?—ask and have!
Knock and it shall be opened—look and, lo!
The coming age is shadowed on the past                                    805
As on a glass.
    *Mahmud.*  Wild—wilder thoughts convulse
My spirit—did not Mahomet the Second[6]
Win Stamboul?
    *Ahasuerus.*  Thou would'st ask that giant spirit
The written fortunes of thy house and faith—
Thou would'st cite one out of the grave to tell                              810
How what was born in blood must die—
    *Mahmud.*                              Thy words
Have power on me!—I see——
    *Ahasuerus.*                    What hearest, thou?
    *Mahmud.* A far whisper——
Terrible silence—
    *Ahasuerus.*      What succeeds?
    *Mahmud.*                          The sound
As of the assault of an imperial city[7]——                                    815
The hiss of inextinguishable fire,—
The roar of giant cannon;—the earthquaking
Fall of vast bastions and precipitous towers,
The shock of crags shot from strange engin'ry,
The clash of wheels, and clang of armed hoofs                          820

---

5. Dodona, in Epirus (northwest Greece), was in ancient times the site of a famous oak grove
surrounding an oracle of Zeus (Jupiter). The rustling of the leaves of these trees was interpreted by the oracle as messages from the god.
6. Sultan Mohammed II (1432–81), "the Conqueror," captured Constantinople (Istanbul) in
1453.
7. See Shelley's note 6, p. 463.

And crash of brazen mail as of the wreck
Of adamantine mountains—the mad blast
Of trumpets, and the neigh of raging steeds,
And shrieks of women whose thrill[8] jars the blood
And one sweet laugh most horrible to hear                         825
As of a joyous infant waked and playing
With its dead mother's breast, and now more loud
The mingled battle cry,—ha! hear I not
"Εν τούτῳ νίκη—" "Allah-Illa, Allah!"[9]
    *Ahasuerus.* The sulphurous mist is raised thou see'st—
    *Mahmud.*                              A chasm  830
As of two mountains in the wall of Stamboul
And in that ghastly breach the Islamites
Like giants on the ruins of a world
Stand in the light of sunrise. In the dust
Glimmers a kingless diadem, and one                               835
Of regal port has cast himself beneath
The stream of war: another proudly clad
In golden arms spurs a Tartarian barb[1]
Into the gap and with his iron mace
Directs the torrent of that tide of men                           840
And seems—he is, Mahomet!
    *Ahasuerus.*                    What thou see'st
Is but the ghost of thy forgotten dream.
A dream itself, yet, less, perhaps, than that
Thou callest reality. Thou mayest behold
How cities, on which empire sleeps enthroned,                     845
Bow their tower'd crests to Mutability.
Poised by the flood, e'en on the height thou holdest,
Thou may'st now learn how the full tide of power
Ebbs to its depths.—Inheritor of glory,
Conceived in darkness, born in blood, and nourished               850
With tears and toil, thou see'st the mortal throes
Of that whose birth was but the same. The Past
Now stands before thee like an Incarnation
Of the To-come; yet would'st thou commune with
That portion of thyself which was ere thou                        855
Didst start for this brief race whose crown is death,
Dissolve with that strong faith and fervent passion
Which called it from the uncreated deep
Yon cloud of war with its tempestuous phantoms
Of raging death; and draw with mighty will                        860
The imperial shade hither—                    [*Exit* AHASUERUS.
    *The Phantom of* MAHOMET THE SECOND *appears.*
    *Mahmud.*                    Approach!

---

8. Vibration.
9. The war cries of the Byzantine Greeks ("In this [sign; i.e., the cross], Victory") and the Turks
    ("There is no god but God!").
1. A breed of horse from Tartary, noted for speed and endurance.

*Phantom.*                              I come
Thence whither thou must go! the grave is fitter
To take the living than give up the dead;
Yet has thy faith prevailed and I am here.
The heavy fragments of the power which fell                    865
When I arose like shapeless crags and clouds
Hang round my throne on the abyss, and voices
Of strange lament soothe my supreme repose,
Wailing for glory never to return.——
    A later Empire nods in its decay:                          870
The autumn of a greener faith is come,
And wolfish Change, like winter howls to strip
The foliage in which Fame, the eagle, built
Her aiëry, while Dominion whelped below.
The storm is in its branches, and the frost                    875
Is on its leaves, and the blank deep expects
Oblivion on oblivion, spoil on spoil,
Ruin on ruin—thou art slow my son;
The Anarchs of the world of darkness keep
A throne for thee round which thine empire lies                880
Boundless and mute, and for thy subjects thou,
Like us, shalt rule the ghosts of murdered life,
The phantoms of the powers who rule thee now—
Mutinous passions, and conflicting fears
And hopes that sate themselves on dust and die,                885
Stript of their mortal strength, as thou of thine.
Islam must fall, but we will reign together
Over its ruins in the world of death—
And if the trunk be dry, yet shall the seed
Unfold itself even in the shape of that                        890
Which gathers birth in its decay—Woe! woe!
To the weak people tangled in the grasp
Of its last spasms.
    *Mahmud.*        Spirit, woe to all!—
Woe to the wronged and the avenger! woe
To the destroyer, woe to the destroyed!                        895
Woe to the dupe; and woe to the deceiver!
Woe to the oppressed; and woe to the oppressor!
Woe both to those that suffer and inflict,
Those who are born and those who die! but say,
Imperial shadow of the thing I am,                             900
When, how, by whom, Destruction must accomplish
Her consummation?
    *Phantom.*          Ask the cold pale Hour
Rich in reversion of impending death
When he shall fall upon whose ripe grey hairs
Sit Care and Sorrow and Infirmity,                             905
The weight which Crime whose wings are plumed with years
Leaves in his flight from ravaged heart to heart
Over the heads of men, under which burthen
They bow themselves unto the grave: fond wretch!

He leans upon his crutch and talks of years                          910
To come, and how in hours of youth renewed
He will renew lost joys, and——
   *Voice without.*       Victory! Victory!
                *[The Phantom vanishes.*
   *Mahmud.* What sound of the importunate earth has broken
My mighty trance?
   *Voice without.*   Victory! Victory!
   *Mahmud.* Weak lightning before darkness! poor faint smile     915
Of dying Islam! Voice which art the response
Of hollow weakness! Do I wake and live?
Were there such things or may the unquiet brain,
Vexed by the wise mad talk of the old Jew,
Have shaped itself these shadows of its fear?                        920
It matters not!—for nought we see or dream,
Possess or lose or grasp at can be worth
More than it gives or teaches. Come what may,
The Future must become the Past, and I
As they were to whom once this present hour,                         925
This gloomy crag of Time to which I cling,
Seemed an Elysian isle of peace and joy
Never to be attained.——I must rebuke
This drunkenness of triumph ere it die
And dying, bring despair. Victory? poor slaves!     *[Exit* MAHMUD.
   *Voice without.* Shout in the jubilee of death! the Greeks    931
Are as a brood of lions in the net
Round which the kingly hunters of the earth
Stand smiling. Anarchs, ye whose daily food
Are curses, groans and gold, the fruit of death,                     935
From Thule[2] to the Girdle of the World,
Come, feast! the board groans with the flesh of men;
The cup is foaming with a nation's blood,
Famine and Thirst await! eat, drink and die!

SEMICHORUS I.

   Victorious Wrong with vulture scream                     940
   Salutes the risen sun, pursues the flying day!
    I saw her, ghastly as a tyrant's dream,
   Perch on the trembling pyramid of night
   Beneath which earth and all her realms pavilioned lay
   In Visions of the dawning undelight.—                     945
      Who shall impede her flight?
      Who rob her of her prey?

*Voice without.* Victory! Victory! Russia's famished Eagles
Dare not to prey beneath the crescent's light.[3]
Impale the remnant of the Greeks? despoil?                           950
Violate! make their flesh cheaper than dust!

2. In classical poetry, the northernmost inhabited land.
3. The flag of Russia under the Romanov czars featured a double-headed eagle; the Turkish
   flag, a crescent moon.

### SEMICHORUS II.

Thou Voice which art
The herald of the ill in splendour hid!
Thou echo of the hollow heart
Of monarchy, bear me to thine abode                                955
    When Desolation flashes o'er a world destroyed.
O bear me to those isles of jagged cloud
    Which float like mountains on the earthquake, mid
The momentary oceans of the lightening,
    Or to some toppling promontory proud                          960
    Of solid tempest whose black pyramid,
Riven, overhangs the founts intensely brightening
    Of those dawn-tinted deluges of fire
    Before their waves expire
When Heaven and Earth are light, and only light                    965
    In the thunder night!

*Voice without.* Victory! Victory! Austria, Russia, England
And that tame Serpent, that poor shadow, France,
Cry Peace, and that means Death when monarchs speak.[4]
Ho, there! bring torches,—sharpen those red stakes,               970
These chains are light, fitter for slaves and poisoners
Than Greeks. Kill, plunder, burn! let none remain.

### SEMICHORUS I.

Alas! for Liberty!
If numbers, wealth or unfulfilling years
    Or fate can quell the free!                                   975
Alas! for Virtue when
Torments or contumely or the sneers
    Of erring judging men
Can break the heart where it abides.
Alas! if Love whose smile makes this obscure world splendid        980
    Can change with its false times and tides,
    Like hope and terror,—
    Alas for Love!
And Truth, who wanderest lone and unbefriended,
If thou can'st veil thy lie consuming mirror                        985
Before the dazzled eyes of Error,[5]
Alas for thee! Image of the Above.

### SEMICHORUS II.

Repulse, with plumes from Conquest torn,
Led the Ten Thousand from the limits of the morn

---

4. In this line and 1008, Shelley echoes the famous sentence that Tacitus puts into the mouth of Galgacus, a leader of the Britons, when rousing them to fight for their freedom against the invading Romans: "They make a desert [or solitude] and call it peace" (Life of Agricola, 30).
5. As Arthur's shield dazzles Duessa (Spenser, *Faerie Queene*, I.viii.20).

Through many an hostile Anarchy!                               990
At length they wept aloud and cried, "The sea! the sea!"⁶
Through exile, persecution and despair,
  Rome was, and young Atlantis⁷ shall become
  The wonder, or the terror or the tomb
Of all whose step wakes Power lulled in her savage lair:      995
  But Greece was as a hermit child,
    Whose fairest thoughts and limbs were built
  To woman's growth, by dreams so mild,
    She knew not pain or guilt;
And now—O Victory, blush! and Empire, tremble                 1000
  When ye desert the free—
  If Greece must be
A wreck, yet shall its fragments reassemble
And build themselves again impregnably
  In a diviner clime                                     1005
To Amphionic music⁸ on some cape sublime
Which frowns above the idle foam of Time.


SEMICHORUS I.
  Let the tyrants rule the desart they have made⁹—
  Let the free possess the paradise they claim,
  Be the fortune of our fierce oppressors weighed           1010
  With our ruin, our resistance and our name!


SEMICHORUS II.
  Our dead shall be the seed of their decay,
    Our survivors be the shadow of their pride,
    Our adversity a dream to pass away—
    Their dishonour a remembrance to abide!                 1015


  *Voice without.* Victory! Victory! The bought Briton sends
The Keys of Ocean to the Islamite—
Now shall the blazon of the cross be veiled
And British skill directing Othman might,
Thunderstrike rebel Victory. O keep holy                      1020
This jubilee of unrevenged blood—
Kill, crush, despoil! Let not a Greek escape!


SEMICHORUS I.
  Darkness has dawned in the East
    On the noon of Time:
  The death-birds descend to their feast,                   1025
    From the hungry clime.—
  Let Freedom and Peace flee far

---

6. The reference is to the ten thousand Greek mercenaries who fought their way back out of
Persia to the Black Sea, as recounted by Xenophon (one of them) in his *Anabasis*.
7. The United States of America.
8. Amphion, son of Zeus by Antiope, built the walls of Thebes by playing his lyre.
9. See note to line 969.

To a sunnier strand,
And follow Love's folding star[1]
To the Evening-land![2]                                    1030

SEMICHORUS II.

The young moon has fed
    Her exhausted horn
        With the sunset's fire.
The weak day is dead,
    But the night is not born,                             1035
And like Loveliness panting with wild desire
    While it trembles with fear and delight,
    Hesperus flies from awakening night
And pants in its beauty and speed with light
    Fast flashing, soft and bright.                        1040
Thou beacon of love, thou lamp of the free!
    Guide us far, far away,
To climes where now veiled by the ardour of day
    Thou art hidden
From waves on which weary noon                             1045
Faints in her summer swoon
Between Kingless continents sinless as Eden,
Around mountains and islands inviolably
    Prankt[3] on the sapphire sea.

SEMICHORUS I.

Through the sunset of Hope                                 1050
    Like the shapes of a dream
What Paradise islands of glory gleam!
    Beneath Heaven's cope,[4]
Their shadows more clear float by—
The sound of their oceans, the light of their sky,        1055
The music and fragrance their solitudes breathe
Burst, like morning on dream or like Heaven on death,
    Through the walls of our prison;
And Greece which was dead is arisen!

CHORUS.[5]

The world's great age begins anew,                        1060
    The golden years return,[6]
The earth doth like a snake renew
    Her winter weeds[7] outworn;
Heaven smiles, and faiths and empires gleam
Like wrecks of a dissolving dream.                        1065

---

1. Venus as Vesper or Hesperus (line 1038), the evening star, which is seen at the time sheep are returned to the fold.
2. The West (German: *Abendland*); more specifically, America.
3. Set, as jewels.
4. Vault or canopy.
5. See Shelley's note 7, pp. 463–64.
6. The mythical reign of Saturn, which the Greeks believed had been a Golden Age.
7. Clothing (i.e., skin).

A brighter Hellas rears its mountains
   From waves serener far,
A new Peneus[8] rolls his fountains
   Against the morning-star,
Where fairer Tempes bloom, there sleep                        1070
Young Cyclads[9] on a sunnier deep.

A loftier Argo[1] cleaves the main,
   Fraught with a later prize;
Another Orpheus sings again,
   And loves, and weeps, and dies;[2]                         1075
A new Ulysses leaves once more
Calypso for his native shore.[3]

O, write no more the tale of Troy,
   If earth Death's scroll must be!
Nor mix with Laian rage[4] the joy                            1080
   Which dawns upon the free;
Although a subtler Sphinx renew
Riddles of death Thebes never knew.

Another Athens shall arise,
   And to remoter time                                        1085
Bequeath, like sunset to the skies,
   The splendour of its prime,
And leave, if nought so bright may live,
All earth can take or Heaven can give.

Saturn and Love their long repose                             1090
   Shall burst,[5] more bright and good
Than all who fell, than One who rose,
   Than many unsubdued;
Not gold, not blood their altar dowers
But votive tears and symbol flowers.                          1095

O cease! must hate and death return?
   Cease! must men kill and die?
Cease! drain not to its dregs the urn
   Of bitter prophecy.

---

8. A river in Thessaly (northeastern Greece) that flowed through the valley of *Tempe* (line 1070), famed for its beauty.
9. The Cyclades, a chain of about fifty islands in the Aegean southeast of Attica.
1. The ship in which Jason and the Argonauts sailed in the quest for the Golden Fleece.
2. Reputed by some to be the son of Apollo by the muse Calliope, Orpheus charmed all natural things with the music of his lyre. He felt the loss of his wife Eurydice twice—first when she died and afterward when he failed to rescue her from the realm of Hades because he looked back too soon. He was torn apart by maenads—maddened female devotees of Dionysus (Bacchus).
3. In the *Odyssey*, Odysseus leaves the island of Calypso, a nymph whose love has detained him for seven years, to return to Ithaca and his wife, Penelope.
4. King Laius of Thebes ordered the death of Oedipus, his son; instead, the infant was raised by others and, after killing his father in an argument, solved the riddle of the monstrous *Sphinx* (line 1082), became king of Thebes, and unknowingly married his mother, Jocasta.
5. See Shelley's note 8, p. 464.

The world is weary of the past,                    1100
O might it die or rest at last!

## Notes. [By Shelley]

NOTE 1. *The quenchless ashes of Milan* [line 60]: Milan was the centre of the resistance of the Lombard league against the Austrian tyrant. Frederic Barbarossa burnt the city to the ground, but Liberty lived in its ashes and it rose like an exhalation from its ruin. See Sismondi's *Histoire des Républiques Italiennes*, a book which has done much towards awakening the Italians to an imitation of their great ancestors.

NOTE 2. The Chorus [line 197 et seq.]: The popular notions of Christianity are represented in this chorus as true in their relation to the worship they superseded, and that which in all probability they will supersede, without considering their merits in a relation more universal. The first stanza contrasts the immortality of the living and thinking beings which inhabit the planets, and to use a common and inadequate phrase, *clothe themselves in matter*, with the transience of the noblest manifestations of the external world.

The concluding verses indicate a progressive state of more or less exalted existence according to the degree of perfection which every distinct intelligence may have attained. Let it not be supposed that I mean to dogmatize upon a subject concerning which all men are equally ignorant, or that I think the Gordian knot of the origin of Evil can be disentangled by that or any similar assertions. The received hypothesis of a Being resembling men in the moral attributes of his nature having called us out of non-existence, and after inflicting on us the misery of the commission of error, should superadd that of the punishment and the privations consequent upon it, still would remain inexplicable and incredible. That there is a true solution of the riddle and that in our present state that solution is unattainable by us, are propositions which may be regarded as equally certain; meanwhile as it is the province of the poet to attach himself to those ideas which exalt and ennoble humanity let him be permitted to have conjectured the condition of that futurity towards which we are all impelled by an inextinguishable thirst for immortality. Until better arguments can be produced than sophisms which disgrace the cause, this desire itself must remain the strongest and the only presumption that eternity is the inheritance of every thinking being.

NOTE 3. *No hoary priests after that Patriarch* [line 245]: The Greek Patriarch after having been compelled to fulminate an anathema against the insurgents was put to death by the Turks.

Fortunately the Greeks have been taught that they cannot buy security by degradation, and the Turks though equally cruel are less cunning than the smooth-faced Tyrants of Europe. As to the anathema, his Holiness might as well have thrown his mitre at Mount Athos for any effect that it produced. The Chiefs of the Greeks are almost all men of comprehension and enlightened views on religion and politics.

NOTE 4. *The freedman of a Western Poet Chief* [line 563]: A Greek who had been Lord Byron's servant commands the insurgents in Attica.[1] This Greek, Lord Byron informs me, though a poet and an enthusiastic patriot, gave him rather the idea of a timid and unenterprising person. It appears that circumstances make men what they are and that we all contain the germ of a degree of degradation or of greatness whose connexion with our character is determined by events.

NOTE 5. *The Greeks expect a Saviour from the West* [line 598]: It is reported that this Messiah had arrived at a sea-port near Lacedæmon in an American brig. The association of names and ideas is irresistibly ludicrous, but the prevalence of such a rumour strongly marks the state of popular enthusiasm in Greece.

NOTE 6. *The sound as of the assault of an imperial city* [line 815]: For the vision of Mahmud of the taking of Constantinople in 1445, See Gibbon's *Decline and Fall of the Roman Empire*, vol. 12, p. 223.[2]

The manner of the invocation of the spirit of Mahomet the Second will be censured as over subtle. I could easily have made the Jew a regular conjuror and the phantom an ordinary ghost. I have preferred to represent the Jew as disclaiming all pretension or even belief in supernatural agency and as tempting Mahmud to that state of mind in which ideas may be supposed to assume the force of sensations through the confusion of thought with the objects of thought, and the excess of passion animating the creations of imagination.

It is a sort of natural magic, susceptible of being exercised in a degree by any one who should have made himself master of the secret associations of another's thoughts.

NOTE 7. The Chorus [line 1060 et seq.]: The final chorus is indistinct and obscure as the event of the living drama whose arrival it foretells. Prophecies of wars, and rumours of wars &c. may safely be made by poet or prophet in any age, but to anticipate, however darkly, a period of regeneration and happiness is a more hazardous exercise of the faculty which bards possess or feign. It will remind the reader "magno

1. Demetrios Zographos (Demetrius Zograffo, as Byron Westernizes the name) was Byron's servant during parts of 1809 through 1812, traveling to England with him in 1811, but returning to Greece the next year (*Byron's Letters and Journals*, ed. Leslie A. Marchand, IX, 23), presumably to be with his wife and two young sons—who (Byron says) he had named Miltiades and Alcibiades, after two generals of Athens' Golden Age. M. Byron Raizis further identifies Zographos as a member of a patriotic family in Attica and says that he died from wounds received at the battle of Haidari in 1826.
2. Although the date given for the fall of Constantinople in Gibbon's *Decline and Fall*, as elsewhere, is 1453, both the manuscript and first edition of *Hellas* give the date as 1445. Apparently Shelley here wrote either from memory or after glancing hastily at an edition of Gibbon with misleading date- or subject-glosses in its headers or margins.

*nec* proximus intervallo" of Isaiah and Virgil,[3] whose ardent spirits overleaping the actual reign of evil which we endure and bewail, already saw the possible and perhaps approaching state of society in which the "lion shall lie down with the lamb" and "omnis feret omnia tellus." Let these great names be my authority and my excuse.

NOTE 8. *Saturn and Love their long repose shall burst* [line 1090]: Saturn and Love were among the deities of a real or imaginary state of innocence and happiness. *All* those *who fell*, or the Gods of Greece, Asia, and Egypt; the *One who rose* or Jesus Christ, at whose appearance the idols of the Pagan world were amerced of their worship;[4] and *the many unsubdued* or the monstrous objects of the idolatry of China, India, the Antarctic islands, and the native tribes of America, certainly have reigned over the understandings of men in conjuction or in succession, during periods in which all we know of evil has been in a state of portentous, and until the revival of learning and the arts, perpetually increasing activity. The Grecian gods seem indeed to have been personally more innocent, although it cannot be said that as far as temperance and chastity are concerned they gave so edifying an example as their successor. The sublime human character of Jesus Christ was deformed by an imputed identification of it with a Demon, who tempted, betrayed and punished the innocent beings who were called into existence by his sole will; and for the period of a thousand years the spirit of this the most just, wise, and benevolent of men, has been propitiated with myriads of hecatombs of those who approached the nearest to his innocence and his wisdom, sacrificed under every aggravation of atrocity and variety of torture.[5] The horrors of the Mexican, the Peruvian, and the Indian superstitions are well known.

3. Shelley's note cites and quotes from chapter 11 of Isaiah and Virgil's fourth Eclogue— "Pollio." Many lines of Virgil's Eclogue were said to be based on the Sybilline prophecies, and both it and the passage in Isaiah were believed to "prophesy of our Saviour's birth" (Dryden). The concluding Chorus to *Hellas* is filled with close paraphrases of ideas and lines from Virgil's poem.
4. *the One who rose . . . their worship* omitted from first edition of *Hellas* (1822); *amerced of* means "deprived of" with a suggestion of being penalized or punished.
5. *The sublime human character . . . variety of torture:* omitted from *Hellas* (1822).

# Written on Hearing the News
## of the Death of Napoleon[1]

### 1

What! alive and so bold, oh Earth?
  Art thou not overbold?
What! leapest thou forth as of old
  In the light of thy morning mirth,
The last of the flock of the starry fold?        5
Ha! leapest thou forth as of old?
Are not the limbs still when the ghost is fled,
And canst thou move, Napoleon being dead?

### 2

How! is not thy quick heart cold?
  What spark is alive on thy hearth?[2]       10
How! is not *his* death-knell knolled?
  And livest *thou* still, Mother Earth?
Thou wert warming thy fingers old
  O'er the embers covered and cold
Of that most fiery spirit, when it fled—       15
What, Mother, do you laugh now he is dead?

### 3

"Who has known me of old," replied Earth,
  "Or who has my story told?
It is thou who art overbold."
And the lightning of scorn laughed forth       20
As she sung, "To my bosom I fold
All my sons when their knell is knolled
And so with living motion all are fed
And the quick spring like weeds out of the dead.

---

1. Napoleon Buonaparte died in exiled captivity on the island of St. Helena in the South Atlantic on May 5, 1821, but news of his death was not confirmed in Europe for several weeks. Claire Clairmont at Florence first heard the official report on July 16 (*Journals*, p. 242); Byron first alludes to the death in a letter to Moore on August 2, suggesting that his friend write a poem on the subject. The Shelleys' journals and letters do not mention the event before Shelley sent his poetic reaction to Ollier with the manuscript of *Hellas* on November 11, 1821, instructing him to print it "at the end"; Ollier did so, making this Shelley's last short poem to be published during his lifetime.

    For the title (once given as "*Lines* Written on Hearing . . .") we follow Mary Shelley's transcript in the Huntington Library (HM 330; *MYR: Shelley*, III, 85–89) that Shelley sent to Ollier as press copy, as well as the first edition of the *Hellas* volume (1821). The draft (Bodleian MS Shelley adds. e.17, pp. 206–02 *reverso*; *BSM*, XII, 367–58) is relatively clean, but it lacks a title. Shelley's letter to Ollier refers to the poem as "the ode to Napoleon." Indeed, as R. D. Havens pointed out (*PMLA*, 1950), the eight-line stanzas intricately interweave three basic rhyme-sounds, even repeating the same exact rhyme words in different sequences, in the manner of the sestina.
2. Vesta (identified with Tellus) was one of the names under which the ancients worshiped the Earth-goddess. This dialogue with Earth builds upon that in Act I of *Prometheus Unbound*.

### 4

"Still alive and still bold," shouted Earth,          25
  "I grow bolder and still more bold.
The dead fill me ten thousand fold
Fuller of speed and splendour and mirth.
I was cloudy, and sullen, and cold,
Like a frozen chaos uprolled          30
Till by the spirit of the mighty dead
My heart grew warm. I feed on whom I fed.

### 5

"Aye, alive and still bold," muttered Earth,
  "Napoleon's fierce spirit rolled
    In terror, and blood, and gold,          35
A torrent of ruin to death from his birth.
Leave the millions who follow to mould
The metal before it be cold,
And weave into his shame, which like the dead
Shrouds me, the hopes that from his glory fled."     40

## The Indian Girl's Song[1]

I arise from dreams of thee
In the first sleep of night—
The winds are breathing low
And the stars are burning bright.
I arise from dreams of thee—          5
And a spirit in my feet
Has borne me—Who knows how?
To thy chamber window, sweet!—

The wandering airs they faint
On the dark silent stream—          10
The champak[2] odours fail
Like sweet thoughts in a dream;
The nightingale's complaint—
It dies upon her heart—

---

1. The correct title of this poem proved to be the key to its meaning. New Critics hostile to Shelley used this minor lyric as an example of his "sentimental" verse—the personal lament of an effeminate poet—even though students of Shelley's major works pointed out that the titles under which the poem had been known, "Song, Written for an Indian Air" (as first published in the *Liberal*, no. II, 1823), "Lines to an Indian Air" (*Posthumous Poems*, 1824), and "The Indian Serenade" (transcripts by Mary Shelley in the larger Harvard Shelley notebook and in the Pierpont Morgan Library; *MYR: Shelley*, V and VIII), showed that it was a dramatic lyric. In 1962 this point was proved when Shelley's own fair copy reemerged bearing his title "The Indian Girl's Song" (Bodmer Library, near Geneva, Switzerland; *MYR: Shelley*, VIII, 329–35). Drafts in Bodleian MSS Shelley adds. e.7, pp. 144–45 and 153, and adds. e.17 (*BSM*, XVI, 146–47, 154–55; and *BSM*, XII, 355–52 *reverso*) suggest that the poem may have been written in 1821 or early 1822; some complicating questions about the poem are discussed in *BSM*, XVI, l–liii, and *MYR: Shelley*, V, 329–49.
2. A tree of India (a species of magnolia) bearing fragrant orange flowers.

As I must die on thine                    15
O beloved as thou art!

O lift me from the grass!
I die, I faint, I fail!
Let thy love in kisses rain
On my lips and eyelids pale.              20
My cheek is cold and white, alas!
My heart beats loud and fast.
Oh press it close to thine again
Where it will break at last.

# Song[1]

Rarely, rarely comest thou,
    Spirit of Delight!
Wherefore hast thou left me now
    Many a day and night?
Many a weary night and day              5
'Tis since thou art fled away.

How shall ever one like me
    Win thee back again?
With the joyous and the free
    Thou wilt scoff at pain.             10
Spirit false! thou hast forgot
All but those who need thee not.

As a lizard with the shade
    Of a trembling leaf,
Thou with sorrow art dismayed;           15
    Even the sighs of grief
Reproach thee, that thou art not near,
And reproach thou wilt not hear.

Let me set my mournful ditty
    To a merry measure;                  20
Thou wilt never come for pity—
    Thou wilt come for pleasure;
Pity then will cut away
Those cruel wings, and thou wilt stay.—

1. Like "The Indian Girl's Song," this cheerful lament—though on a favorite Shelleyan theme—
is probably a highly successful conventional exercise. In the larger Harvard Shelley notebook
Shelley's holograph fair copy of this poem was dated in Mary Shelley's hand, "Pisa—May—
1820" (MYR: Shelley, V, 82–83). If written by then, the poem was not included among those
that he asked her to transcribe for inclusion in Prometheus Unbound in mid-May 1820. Mary
Shelley first published it in Posthumous Poems (1824) without a date, but she later placed
it with "Poems written in 1821" in both her editions of 1839. Since no rough draft for this
"Song" has been identified to aid us in settling her contradictory dates of May 1820 and
1821, uncertainty about the circumstances of its composition and Mary Shelley's knowledge
of its origins has led us to base our text primarily on Shelley's Harvard holograph, rather
than on her printed versions.

I love all that thou lovest,                                    25
   Spirit of Delight!
The fresh Earth in new leaves drest,
   And the starry night,
Autumn evening, and the morn
When the golden mists are born.                          30

I love snow, and all the forms
   Of the radiant frost;
I love waves and winds and storms—
   Every thing almost
Which is Nature's and may be                              35
Untainted by man's misery.

I love tranquil Solitude,
   And such society
As is quiet, wise and good;
   Between thee and me                              40
What difference? but thou dost possess
The things I seek—not love them less.

I love Love—though he has wings,
   And like light can flee—
But above all other things,                                    45
   Spirit, I love thee—
Thou art Love and Life! O come,
Make once more my heart thy home.


# The Flower That Smiles Today[1]

The flower that smiles today
   Tomorrow dies;
All that we wish to stay
   Tempts and then flies;
What is this world's delight?                                5
Lightning, that mocks the night,
   Brief even as bright.—

Virtue, how frail it is!—
   Friendship, how rare!—
Love, how it sells poor bliss                               10
   For proud despair!
But these though soon they fall,

---

1. First published in *Posthumous Poems* under the title "Mutability," this lyric was reedited from Shelley's fair copy in Bodleian MS Shelley adds. e.7, p. 154, by Judith Chernaik (*The Lyrics of Shelley*, pp. 252–53). We also base our text on the holograph fair copy—now available in *BSM*, XVI (*The Hellas Notebook*), 156–57—with the evidence of the close relationship of its drafts to those of *Hellas*, first suggested by G. M. Matthews in his essay "Shelley's Lyrics" (see the Selected Bibliography, p. 781).

Survive their joy, and all
Which ours we call.—

Whilst skies are blue and bright,                    15
   Whilst flowers are gay,
Whilst eyes that change ere night
   Make glad the day;
Whilst yet the calm hours creep,
Dream thou—and from thy sleep          20
   Then wake to weep.

# Memory

Rose leaves, when the rose is dead,
Are heaped for the beloved's bed,
And so thy thoughts, when thou art gone,
Love itself shall slumber on. . . .

Music, when soft voices die,                    5
Vibrates in the memory.—
Odours, when sweet violets sicken,
Live within the sense they quicken.—

# To ———[1]

Music, when soft voices die,
Vibrates in the memory.—
Odours, when sweet violets sicken,
Live within the sense they quicken.—

Rose leaves, when the rose is dead,          5
Are heaped for the beloved's bed—
And so thy thoughts, when thou art gone,
Love itself shall slumber on. . . .

1. "To ———" and "Memory" are different versions of a poem Shelley drafted (or began to draft) in Bodleian MS Shelley adds. e.8, p. 154 *reverso*. The first version was initially published by Mary Shelley in *Posthumous Poems* (1824); the second version (below) and its alternative title were proposed by Irving Massey in *JEGP* 59 (1960): 430–38, as a revisionist view that was first supported by E. D. Hirsch (*JEGP* 60 [1961]: 296–98), then challenged by Chernaik in *The Lyrics of Shelley*, but recently upheld by Carlene A. Adamson in her edition of adds. e.8 (*BSM*, VI, 41–43). We consider the manuscript evidence on the order and significance of the two stanzas (both canceled in pencil by one of the Shelleys) to be inconclusive and the issues still open for discussion.

470

# When Passion's Trance Is Overpast[1]

When passion's trance is overpast,
If tenderness and truth could last
Or live—whilst all wild feelings keep
Some mortal slumber, dark and deep—
I should not weep, I should not weep!       5

It were enough to feel, to see
Thy soft eyes gazing tenderly . . .
And dream the rest—and burn and be
The secret food of fires unseen,
Could[2] thou but be what thou hast been!       10

After the slumber of the year
The woodland violets reappear;
All things revive in field or grove
And sky and sea, but two, which move
And form all others—life and love.—       15

# To Jane. The Invitation[1]

Best and brightest, come away—
Fairer far than this fair day

---

1. In her collected edition of 1839, Mary Shelley placed this lyric—first published in *Posthumous Poems* (1824)—among Shelley's poems written in 1821. Our text follows the only known contemporary manuscript, Shelley's very rough draft in Bodleian MS Shelley adds. e.12, pp. 7 and 6. As Nancy Moore Goslee suggests in *BSM*, XVIII, this poem, like some others scattered through that notebook, strongly reflects Mary Shelley's estrangement from Shelley during their last years together. The phrase "dream the rest" (line 8) echoes line 124 of Pope's "Eloisa to Abelard," in which Eloisa urges her former priest, teacher, and lover—now castrated by her relatives—to "Give all thou canst—and let me dream the rest." Cf. "Julian and Maddalo," lines 420ff.
2. The verb is subjunctive: "if thou could only be."
1. The two poems known as "To Jane. The Invitation" and "To Jane. The Recollection" were originally published by Mary Shelley in *Posthumous Poems* (1824) from Shelley's rough draft (which no longer survives) as a single poem entitled "The Pine Forest of the Cascine, near Pisa." Though there was a hitherto unnoted printing of "To Jane. The Invitation" in No. 2 of the short-lived *New Anti-Jacobin* (May 1833), pp. 196–97, the fair-copy manuscripts of the two poems, which had been given to Jane Williams, came to Mary's attention late, and she first included the finished versions of both in the second (one-volume) edition of her collected *Poetical Works of Percy Bysshe Shelley* (1839–40). Mary Shelley's friends probably did not bring these poems to her attention earlier because, though the walk on January 2, 1822, that inspired these poems was taken by Mary, Jane, and Shelley together, Jane alone evoked Shelley's happiness and the bittersweet memories of the departed joys here commemorated. For Shelley's artistry in these and the other poems addressed to Jane Williams, see Michael O'Neill's essay in this volume (pp. 616–26).
   Our texts are based on Shelley's fair copies—that of "The Invitation" in Cambridge University Library (add. MS 4444) and of "The Recollection" in the British Library (add. MS 37538, fols. 40–41)—which are edited, with facsimiles, in *MYR: Shelley*, VIII, 370–91. Although Mary Shelley published "The Recollection" with four numbered sections of couplets after the unnumbered introductory lines, Rossetti and subsequent editors show a stanza break after line 68 and group lines 69–88 as section 5. But Shelley's fair-copy manuscript (Bodleian adds. MS 37538, fols. 40–41) not only shows no break between lines 68 and 69, but Shelley's numeral 5 *follows* line 88, the end of the text he sent to Williams, and is followed by a row of five x's (such as he used to mark breaks within the Maniac's speeches in *Julian and Maddalo*). This suggests that either Shelley considered this poem to be unfin-

Which like thee to those in sorrow
Comes to bid a sweet good-morrow
To the rough year just awake                5
In its cradle on the brake.[2]—
The brightest hour of unborn spring
Through the winter wandering
Found, it seems, this halcyon morn
To hoar February born;                     10
Bending from Heaven in azure mirth
It kissed the forehead of the earth
And smiled upon the silent sea,
And bade the frozen streams be free
And waked to music all their fountains,    15
And breathed upon the frozen mountains,
And like a prophetess of May
Strewed flowers upon the barren way,
Making the wintry world appear
Like one on whom thou smilest, dear.       20

Away, away from men and towns
To the wild wood and the downs,
To the silent wilderness
Where the soul need not repress
Its music lest it should not find          25
An echo in another's mind,
While the touch of Nature's art
Harmonizes heart to heart.—
I leave this notice on my door
For each accustomed visitor—               30
"I am gone into the fields
To take what this sweet hour yields.
Reflexion, you may come tomorrow,
Sit by the fireside with Sorrow—
You, with the unpaid bill, Despair,        35
You, tiresome verse-reciter Care,
I will pay you in the grave,
Death will listen to your stave—
Expectation too, be off!
To-day is for itself enough—               40
Hope, in pity mock not woe
With smiles, nor follow where I go;
Long having lived on thy sweet food,
At length I find one moment's good
After long pain—with all your love         45
This you never told me of."

---

ished, or—more likely—he was indicating that he had purposely omitted a fifth stanza, written or imagined, in which he opened his heart more than he considered appropriate to send to the wife of a friend.
2. Thicket.

Radiant Sister of the day,
Awake, arise and come away
To the wild woods and the plains
And the pools where winter-rains          50
Image all their roof of leaves,
Where the pine its garland weaves
Of sapless green and ivy dun
Round stems that never kiss the Sun—
Where the lawns and pastures be          55
And the sand hills of the sea—
Where the melting hoar-frost wets
The daisy-star that never sets,
And wind-flowers, and violets
Which yet join not scent to hue          60
Crown the pale year weak and new
When the night is left behind
In the deep east dun and blind
And the blue noon is over us,
And the multitudinous          65
Billows murmur at our feet
Where the earth and ocean meet,
And all things seem only one
In the universal Sun.—


# To Jane. The Recollection[3]

### Feb. 2, 1822

Now the last day of many days,
All beautiful and bright as thou,
The loveliest and the last, is dead.
Rise, Memory, and write its praise!
Up to thy wonted work! come, trace          5
The epitaph of glory fled;
For now the Earth has changed its face,
A frown is on the Heaven's brow.


### 1.

We wandered to the pine forest
    That skirts the ocean foam;          10
The lightest wind was in its nest,
    The Tempest in its home;
The whispering waves were half asleep,
    The clouds were gone to play,
And on the bosom of the deep          15
    The smile of Heaven lay;
It seemed as if the hour were one

---

3. See the introductory note for "To Jane. The invitation," above.

Sent from beyond the skies,
Which scattered from above the sun
   A light of Paradise.                    20

### 2.

We paused amid the pines that stood
   The giants of the waste,
Tortured by storms to shapes as rude
   As serpents interlaced,
And soothed by every azure breath      25
   That under Heaven is blown
To harmonies and hues beneath,
   As tender as its own;
Now all the tree-tops lay asleep
   Like green waves on the sea,       30
As still as in the silent deep
   The Ocean woods may be.

### 3.

How calm it was! the silence there
   By such a chain was bound
That even the busy woodpecker          35
   Made stiller with her sound
The inviolable quietness;
   The breath of peace we drew
With its soft motion made not less
   The calm that round us grew.—      40
There seemed from the remotest seat
   Of the white mountain-waste,
To the soft flower beneath our feet
   A magic circle traced,
A spirit interfused around             45
   A thrilling silent life:
To momentary peace it bound
   Our mortal nature's strife;—
And still I felt the centre of
   The magic circle there              50
Was *one* fair form that filled with love
   The lifeless atmosphere.

### 4.

We paused beside the pools that lie
   Under the forest bough—
Each seemed as 'twere, a little sky     55
   Gulfed in a world below;
A firmament of purple light
   Which in the dark earth lay
More boundless than the depth of night
   And purer than the day,             60

In which the lovely forests grew
    As in the upper air,
More perfect, both in shape and hue,
    Than any spreading there;
There lay the glade, the neighbouring lawn,          65
    And through the dark green wood
The white sun twinkling like the dawn
    Out of a speckled cloud.
Sweet views, which in our world above
    Can never well be seen,          70
Were imaged in the water's love
    Of that fair forest green;
And all was interfused beneath
    With an Elysian glow,
An atmosphere without a breath,          75
    A softer day below—
Like one beloved, the scene had lent
    To the dark water's breast,
Its every leaf and lineament
    With more than truth exprest;          80
Until an envious wind crept by,
    Like an unwelcome thought
Which from the mind's too faithful eye
    Blots one dear image out.—
Though thou art ever fair and kind          85
    And forests ever green,
Less oft is peace in S[helley]'s mind
    Than calm in water seen.


# One Word Is Too Often Profaned[1]

One word is too often profaned
    For me to profane it,
One feeling too falsely disdained
    For thee to disdain it;
One hope is too like despair          5
    For prudence to smother,
And Pity from thee more dear
    Than that from another.

I can give not what men call love,—
    But wilt thou accept not          10
The worship the heart lifts above

1. Mary Shelley first published this poem in *Posthumous Poems* (1824) from a fair copy she
had made in one of her notebooks (Bodleian MS Shelley adds. d.7, p. 15; *BSM*, II, 32–33).
Her transcript is our copy-text, because the poem is one of the few short lyrics of Shelley's
later years for which no manuscript in the poet's own hand (holograph) is known to exist.
The central theme of the poem (which many critics have associated with Jane Williams) is
that also found in "On Love" and "The Sensitive-Plant"—the Platonic concept that love is
produced by a vacancy, or lack, felt by the lover, who desires and seeks the good or beautiful
seen in other beings.

And the Heavens reject not?
The desire of the moth for the star,
Of the night for the morrow,
The devotion to something afar          15
From the sphere of our sorrow.

## The Serpent Is Shut Out from Paradise[1]

### 1

The serpent is shut out from Paradise[2]—
The wounded deer must seek the herb no more
In which its heart's cure lies—
The widowed dove must cease to haunt a bower
Like that from which its mate with feigned sighs          5
Fled in the April hour.—
I, too, must seldom seek again
Near happy friends a mitigated pain.

### 2

Of hatred I am proud,—with scorn content;
Indifference, which once hurt me, now is grown          10
Itself indifferent.
But not to speak of love, Pity alone
Can break a spirit already more than bent.
The miserable one
Turns the mind's poison into food:          15
Its medicine is tears, its evil, good.

### 3

Therefore, if now I see you seldomer,
Dear friends, dear *friend*,[3] know that I only fly
Your looks, because they stir

1. Shelley gave these stanzas, enclosed in a note, to Edward Williams on January 26, 1822, with the injunction that he show them to no one else except Jane Williams, and preferably not even to her. Williams noted in his journal, "S sent us some beautiful but too melancholy lines"—the *us* suggesting that both he and Jane read them. First published in *Fraser's Magazine* in 1832, the poem was included in John Ascham's two-volume pirated edition of 1834, as simply "Stanzas to * * * *." William Michael Rossetti supplied its popular title, "To Edward Williams," in his edition of 1870, but lines 17–20 suggest that it was written primarily with Jane in mind.
   Before the first edition of *Shelley's Poetry and Prose*, the poem was usually reprinted in a corrupt state deriving from the Ascham version, though Shelley's fair-copy manuscript, which has been available for years in the University of Edinburgh Library (Dc. 1.100⁴), shows no less than five significant verbal variants from the Oxford Standard Authors text. (A more or less correct transcription appears in Shelley, *Letters*, II, 385–86.) Our text is based on Shelley's holograph, which has been edited, with a facsimile of the original, in *MYR: Shelley*, VIII, 409–16.
2. See Genesis 3:14, 24. Byron and others in the Pisan circle called Shelley "the snake"— probably punning on the name "Bysshe Shelley" and the Italian *bischelli*, a small snake.
3. The plural certainly refers to Jane and Edward Williams; the reference in the emphatic singular is less clear, but why would Edward's *looks* "stir / Griefs that should sleep, and hopes that cannot die"?

Griefs that should sleep, and hopes that cannot die.     20
The very comfort which they minister
    I scarce can bear; yet I,
(So deeply is the arrow gone)
Should quickly perish if it were withdrawn.

### 4

When I return to my cold home, you ask     25
   Why I am not as I have lately been?
    *You* spoil me for the task
   Of acting a forced part in life's dull scene.
Of wearing on my brow the idle mask
    Of author, great or mean,     30
In the world's carnival. I sought
Peace thus, and but in you I found it not.

### 5

Full half an hour, to-day I tried my lot
   With various flowers, and every one still said,
    "She loves me, loves me, not."     35
   And if this meant a Vision long since fled—
If it meant Fortune, Fame, or Peace of thought,
    If it meant—(but I dread
To speak what you may know too well)
Still there was truth in the sad oracle.     40

### 6

The crane o'er seas and forests seeks her home.
   No bird so wild, but has its quiet nest
    When it no more would roam.
   The sleepless billows on the Ocean's breast
Break like a bursting heart, and die in foam     45
    And thus, at length, find rest.
Doubtless there is a place of peace
Where *my* weak heart and all its throbs will cease.[4]

### 7

I asked her[5] yesterday if she believed
   That I had resolution. One who *had*     50
    Would ne'er have thus relieved
   His heart with words, but what his judgment bade
Would do, and leave the scorner unrelieved.—
    These verses were too sad
To send to you, but[6] that I know,     55
Happy yourself, you feel another's woe.

---

4. The imagery here suggests that only death could give peace to the poet's heart.
5. Mary Shelley.
6. Except; *were* (line 54): subjunctive verb to express a condition contrary to fact.

# With a Guitar.
# To Jane.[1]

*Ariel* to *Miranda*;—Take
This slave of music for the sake
Of him who is the slave of thee;
And teach it all the harmony,
In which thou can'st, and only thou,                    5
Make the delighted spirit glow,
'Till joy denies itself again
And too intense is turned to pain;
For by permission and command
Of thine own *prince Ferdinand*                          10
Poor Ariel sends this silent token
Of more than ever can be spoken;
Your guardian spirit Ariel, who
From life to life must still pursue
Your happiness, for thus alone                           15
Can Ariel ever find his own;
From Prospero's enchanted cell,
As the mighty verses tell,
To the throne of Naples he
Lit you o'er the trackless sea,                          20
Flitting on, your prow before,
Like a living meteor.
When you die, the silent Moon
In her interlunar[2] swoon
Is not sadder in her cell                                25
Than deserted Ariel;
When you live again on Earth
Like an unseen Star of birth[3]
Ariel guides you o'er the sea
Of life from your nativity;                              30
Many changes have been run
Since Ferdinand and you begun
Your course of love, and Ariel still
Has tracked your steps and served your will.

---

1. Shelley purchased an Italian guitar for Jane Williams, accompanying the gift with this urbane poem that depicts her, Edward Williams, and Shelley himself in the roles of Miranda, her beloved Ferdinand, and the spirit Ariel from Shakespeare's *The Tempest.*
   Edward John Trelawny, who tells of coming upon Shelley while he was drafting the poem in a secluded retreat in the marshy pine forest near Pisa, described the initial draft as a "frightful scrawl" that he found virtually illegible, though the only known surviving draft—of the poem's first twelve lines (in Bodleian MS Shelley adds. e.18, p. 105; *BSM*, XIX, 204–05)—does not fit that description. The copy that Shelley gave to Jane, beautifully written and punctuated in his best copying hand, is also in the Bodleian Library (MS Shelley adds. e.3), as is the guitar itself. Our text follows that manuscript, which is reproduced, transcribed, and edited in *BSM*, XXI, 432–37. The earliest published texts (the first appearing in the *Athenæum*, October 20, 1832) derived from copies made by Thomas Medwin.
2. The dark period between the old and the new moon.
3. According to various astrological traditions, all individuals live under the influence of natal stars that shape their temperament and destiny.

Now, in humbler, happier lot                                    35
This is all remembered not;
And now, alas! the poor sprite[4] is
Imprisoned for some fault of his
In a body like a grave.—
From you, he only dares to crave                                40
For his service and his sorrow
A smile today, a song tomorrow.

The artist who this idol[5] wrought
To echo all harmonious thought
Felled a tree, while on the steep                               45
The woods were in their winter sleep
Rocked in that repose divine
On the wind-swept Apennine;
And dreaming, some of autumn past
And some of spring approaching fast,                            50
And some of April buds and showers
And some of songs in July bowers
And all of love,—and so this tree—
O that such our death may be—
Died in sleep, and felt no pain                                 55
To live in happier form again,
From which, beneath Heaven's fairest star,[6]
The artist wrought this loved guitar,
And taught it justly to reply
To all who question skilfully                                   60
In language gentle as thine own;
Whispering in enamoured tone
Sweet oracles of woods and dells
And summer winds in sylvan cells
For it had learnt all harmonies                                 65
Of the plains and of the skies,
Of the forests and the mountains,
And the many-voiced fountains,
The clearest echoes of the hills,
The softest notes of falling rills,                            70
The melodies of birds and bees,
The murmuring of summer seas,
And pattering rain and breathing dew
And airs of evening;—and it knew
That seldom heard mysterious sound,                            75
Which, driven on its diurnal[7] round
As it floats through boundless day
Our world enkindles on its way—
All this it knows, but will not tell

---

4. In *The Tempest*, Ariel is a disembodied spirit of the elements of fire and air.
5. I.e., the guitar.
6. Venus, the evening/morning star of love.
7. Daily; lines 74–78 describe the music of the spheres, as described by Plato and invoked, at least metaphorically, down to Shelley's day.

To those who cannot question well                    80
The spirit that inhabits it:
It talks according to the wit
Of its companions, and no more
Is heard than has been felt before
By those who tempt it to betray                      85
These secrets of an elder day.—
But, sweetly as its answers will
Flatter hands of perfect skill,
It keeps its highest holiest tone
For our beloved Jane alone.—                         90

# To Jane[1]

The keen stars were twinkling
And the fair moon was rising among them,
     Dear Jane.
The guitar was tinkling
But the notes were not sweet 'till you sung them      5
     Again.—
As the moon's soft splendour
O'er the faint cold starlight of Heaven
     Is thrown—
So your voice most tender                            10
To the strings without soul had then given
     Its own.

The stars will awaken,
Though the moon sleep a full hour later,
     Tonight;                                        15
No leaf will be shaken
While the dews of your melody scatter
     Delight.
Though the sound overpowers
Sing again, with your dear voice revealing            20
     A tone
Of some world far from ours,
Where music and moonlight and feeling
     Are one.

1. The draft of this poem—written near the seaside village of Lerici during the last month of Shelley's life—is scattered in three separate folios of the Bodleian manuscript of "The Triumph of Life" (Bodleian MS Shelley adds. c.4, 56r, 33v, and 38v *reverso*; facsimile in *BSM*, I, 290–91, 194–95, and 214–15); a holograph fair copy is in the John Rylands University Library of Manchester (Box A; edited facsimile in *MYR: Shelley*, VIII, 433–37).
   The first printed version, entitled "An Ariette for Music," published by Thomas Medwin in the *Athenæum* (November 17, 1832) and again in *The Shelley Papers* (1833), was incomplete. Mary Shelley followed this text in her first edition of Shelley's *Poetical Works* (1839); her second one-volume edition of *Poetical Works* (1839/40) finally included the complete poem. Our text follows the fair-copy holograph, which also contains this note from Shelley to Jane: "I sate down to write some words for an ariette which might be profane— but it was in vain to struggle with the ruling spirit, who compelled me to speak of things sacred to yours & Wilhelmeister's [i.e., Edward Williams's] indulgence— I commit them to your secrecy & your mercy & will try & do better another time."

# Lines written in the Bay of Lerici[1]

Bright wanderer,[2] fair coquette of Heaven,
To whom alone it has been given
To change and be adored for ever. . . .
Envy not this dim world, for never
But once within its shadow grew     5
One fair as [thou], but far more true.
She left me at the silent time
When the moon had ceased to climb
The azure dome of Heaven's steep,
And like an albatross asleep,     10
Balanced on her wings of light,
Hovered in the purple night,
Ere she sought her Ocean nest
In the chambers of the west.—
She left me, and I staid alone     15
Thinking over every tone,
Which though now silent to the ear
The enchanted heart could hear
Like notes which die when born, but still
Haunt the echoes of the hill:     20
And feeling ever—O too much—
The soft vibrations of her touch
As if her gentle hand even now
Lightly trembled on my brow;
And thus although she absent were     25
Memory gave me all of her
That even fancy dares to claim.—
Her presence had made weak and tame
All passions, and I lived alone,
In the time which is our own;     30
The past and future were forgot
As they had been, and would be, not.—
But soon, the guardian angel gone,
The demon reassumed his throne

1. Shelley probably wrote this lyric, which has Jane Williams as its main subject, within three weeks of his death. Drafted on two conjugate leaves of the paper on which Shelley wrote "The Triumph of Life" and still kept with that MS (Bodleian MS Shelley adds. c.4, fols. 35–36; *BSM*, I, 200–207), it was probably composed before line 373 of "The Triumph" and presumably dates from between June 16 and June 30, 1822 (see Reiman, *Shelley's "The Triumph of Life": A Critical Study*, pp. 244–50). The poem was first published and its title devised by Richard Garnett in a truncated version in *Macmillan's Magazine* VI (June 1862): 122–23, and—with the opening lines of it given as a separate fragment—in Garnett's *Relics of Shelley* (1862). The first complete text was published by G. M. Matthews in "Shelley and Jane Williams," *RES*, n.s., XII (February 1961): 40–48. Later emendations were proposed by Reiman in *Shelley's "The Triumph of Life"* and by Chernaik in *The Lyrics of Shelley*. Since the last couplet in the draft is manifestly incomplete, the poem in its present state is probably unfinished. Though we were tempted to devise an aphoristic couplet to end the poem, this task can instead be assigned to readers of *Shelley's Poetry and Prose*.
2. The moon.

In my faint heart . . . I dare not speak                35
My thoughts; but thus disturbed and weak
I sate and watched the vessels glide
Along the ocean bright and wide,
Like spirit-winged chariots sent
O'er some serenest element                              40
To ministrations strange and far;
As if to some Elysian star
They sailed for drink to medicine
Such sweet and bitter pain as mine.
And the wind that winged their flight                   45
From the land came fresh and light,
And the scent of sleeping flowers
And the coolness of the hours
Of dew, and the sweet warmth of day
Was scattered o'er the twinkling bay;                   50
And the fisher with his lamp
And spear, about the low rocks damp
Crept, and struck the fish who came
To worship the delusive flame:
Too happy, they whose pleasure sought                   55
Extinguishes all sense and thought
Of the regret that pleasure [          ]³
Destroying life alone not peace.

# THE TRIUMPH OF LIFE

Written, probably in May and June 1822, at Villa Magni, near San Terenzo on the Bay of Lerici, "The Triumph of Life" was Shelley's final major effort. Though most of it was left in a very unfinished rough-draft manuscript, the poem exhibits such vitality and incisiveness that even Mary W. Shelley, who disliked the dark tone and "lack of human interest" (i.e., the philosophical nature) of the fragment, gave it a prominent place among Shelley's *Posthumous Poems* (1824). In the twentieth century it was hailed by T. S. Eliot as Shelley's finest work (see our essay on "Shelley's Reputation before 1960," p. 544). Recently, after years of discussion of the poem's meaning and its relation to his life and earlier writings, leading critics have concluded with Earl R. Wasserman that, because it remains a fragment, it cannot and should not be read as if it were a finished *poem*, even though it contains great *poetry*.

"The Triumph of Life" is written in terza-rima, the difficult interlocking

---

3. Editors have added a concluding word to line 57 and/or read a slightly different version of line 58 to complete the poem as follows:

> Of the regret that pleasure leaves
> Destroying life alone not peace.     (Garnett)
>
> Of the regret that pleasure [      ]
> Seeking Life alone *not peace*.     (Matthews)
>
> Of the regret that pleasure [      ]
> Seeking life not peace.   (Chernaik)

rhyme scheme that Dante employs in the *Divine Comedy* and Petrarch uses in his *Trionfi*, a sequence of seven poems recounting the successive "Triumphs" of Love over Man, Chastity over Love, Death over Chastity, Fame over Death, Time over Fame, and God over Time. Besides Dante and Petrarch, Milton, Wordsworth, Lucretius, and Plato figure prominently as recognizable influences on the thought and language of particular passages. Also important, both as a literary influence on the poem and as an epitomizing character who appears in it, is Jean Jacques Rousseau, whose novel *Julie; ou, La Nouvelle Héloïse* provides the organizing metaphor for large sections of "The Triumph of Life." In Book IX of his *Confessions*, Rousseau wrote of the year 1756: "I believed that I was approaching the end of my days almost without having tasted to the full any of the pleasures for which my heart thirsted, . . . without having ever tasted that passion which, through lack of an object, was always suppressed. . . . The impossibility of attaining the real persons precipitated me into the land of chimeras; and seeing nothing that existed worthy of my exalted feelings, I fostered them in an ideal world which my creative imagination soon peopled with beings after my own heart." (*The Confessions of Jean-Jacques Rousseau*, trans. J. M. Cohen [Penguin Books, 1954], pp. 396, 398). Out of these reveries grew *Julie*, in which a young tutor named Saint-Preux falls in love with his pupil Julie (as the medieval French theologian Peter Abelard fell in love with his pupil Héloïse). After their love has been consummated just once, Julie sends Saint-Preux away and—out of her sense of duty—marries her father's friend Wolmar. Saint-Preux later returns to Vevey, where Julie and Wolmar are living quietly, and he eventually learns to control his passions sufficiently to achieve happiness, if not ecstasy, as a friend and confidant of his beloved. This temporary happiness ends for all the idealized circle (including Julie's friend Claire and Saint-Preux's English friend Lord Bomston) when Julie drowns in Lake Geneva. As Rousseau tells in his *Confessions*, he wrote *Julie* while caught up in his last great passion—that for the Countess d'Houdetot, a love that remained chaste because of Mme. d'Houdetot's love for Rousseau's friend Saint-Lambert. As Shelley's lyrics to Jane Williams indicate, there was a parallel between Rousseau's situation in 1756 and that of Shelley in 1822, in which his emotional estrangement from Mary Shelley was compounded by his attachment to both Jane and Edward Williams; while Shelley was writing this poem, the two couples were living in isolation at Villa Magni.

In "The Triumph of Life," Rousseau, representing writers of the generation that prepared Europe for the French Revolution and for the Romantic age that followed, acts as the interpreter of the pageant seen by Shelley's persona, just as Virgil guides Dante through the Inferno and as Love's Triumph is explained to Petrarch by a Florentine acquaintance in the pageant. Shelley uses Rousseau to comment on historical events and processes and also, through Rousseau's symbolic autobiography (which Shelley abstracted from *Julie*), to provide an analogue of Shelley's own quest for ideal love (cf. *Epipsychidion*), together with a warning against the pursuit of shadows.

Although "The Triumph of Life" was left incomplete by Shelley's accidental drowning, the fragment shows a firm structural development: after an introduction (lines 1–40) that alludes to an unstated personal crisis, which disturbs the Poet in spite of the harmony of Nature, he encounters a visionary triumphal pageant (lines 41–175). His desire to know more explicitly the meaning of what he sees evokes the shade of Rousseau (as

Mahmud's concern with the fate of the Ottoman Empire evokes the imagined spirit of Mahomet II in *Hellas*); this phantasm identifies many of the
great persons in the train of Life and warns the Poet against giving way
to despair, pointing out the various degrees of resistance to Life's evil
influence (lines 176–295). In the last completed section of the fragment
(lines 296–543), Rousseau tells his own story through a series of allegories. Another question by the Poet—"Then, what is Life?"—has just introduced a new section of the poem when the fragment breaks off amid
the first words of Rousseau's reply. Critics vigorously disagree about how
—or even whether—Shelley would have continued the poem.

Mary Shelley published "The Triumph of Life" in Shelley's *Posthumous
Poems* (1824), and this text—slightly modified by Mary herself in 1839
and by other editors over the years—remained standard until the 1960s,
when new redactions were published by G. M. Matthews (in *Studia Neophilologica* 32 [1960]: 271–309) and Donald H. Reiman (*Shelley's "The
Triumph of Life"* [1965]), based on their studies of the Bodleian manuscript from which Mary Shelley first published the text (Bodleian MS Shelley adds. c.4, fols. 19–58; edited facsimile and transcription in *BSM*, I,
115ff.). The present text is based on Reiman's 1965 edition, revised in the
light of suggestions by Matthews in his review of Reiman (*JEGP*, 1967),
joint analysis by Matthews and Donald and Mary W. Reiman at the Bodleian Library in August 1971 with the manuscript before them, and later
work by Donald and Hélène Dworzan (Reiman) while preparing *BSM*, I
(1986). On the crisis in Shelley's life at the time he began writing "The
Triumph," see Reiman's essay "Shelley's 'The Triumph of Life': The Biographical Problem" (*PMLA* 78 [December 1963]: 536–50; reprinted in
Reiman, *Romantic Texts and Contexts*, pp. 289–320). Hugh Roberts usefully examines the central issues raised by "The Triumph" in excerpts from
his book *Shelley and the Chaos of History*, reprinted in this volume
(pp. 760–68). For an analysis of the important role that this poem has
played in the history of Deconstruction since Paul de Man's controversial
essay "Shelley Disfigured" (in *Deconstruction and Criticism*, ed. Harold
Bloom [Seabury (Continuum), 1979], pp. 39–73) and for a critique of de
Man's reading of history in the poem, see Orrin Wang's *Fantastic Modernity:
Dialectical Readings in Romanticism and Theory* (1996), pp. 37–68.

# The Triumph of Life

Swift as a spirit hastening to his task
  Of glory and of good, the Sun sprang forth
Rejoicing in his splendour, and the mask

Of darkness fell from the awakened Earth.
  The smokeless altars of the mountain snows       5
  Flamed above crimson clouds, and at the birth

Of light, the Ocean's orison arose
  To which the birds tempered their matin lay.[1]
All flowers in field or forest which unclose

---

1. A morning song; *orison:* a prayer.

Their trembling eyelids to the kiss of day,                    10
Swinging their censers[2] in the element,
    With orient incense lit by the new ray

Burned slow and inconsumably, and sent
    Their odorous sighs up to the smiling air,
And in succession due, did Continent,                          15

        Isle, Ocean, and all things that in them wear
The form and character of mortal mould
    Rise as the Sun their father rose, to bear

Their portion of the toil which he of old
    Took as his own and then imposed on them;                  20
But I, whom thoughts which must remain untold

    Had kept as wakeful as the stars that gem
The cone of night,[3] now they were laid asleep,
    Stretched my faint limbs beneath the hoary stem

Which an old chestnut flung athwart the steep                  25
    Of a green Apennine:[4] before me fled
The night; behind me rose the day; the Deep

    Was at my feet, and Heaven above my head
When a strange trance over my fancy grew
    Which was not slumber, for the shade it spread             30

Was so transparent that the scene came through
    As clear as when a veil of light is drawn
O'er evening hills they[5] glimmer; and I knew

    That I had felt the freshness of that dawn,
Bathed in the same cold dew my brow and hair                   35
    And sate as thus upon that slope of lawn

Under the self same bough, and heard as there
    The birds, the fountains and the Ocean hold
Sweet talk in music through the enamoured air.
    And then a Vision on my brain was rolled. . . .            40

———————

As in that trance of wondrous thought I lay
    This was the tenour of my waking dream.
Methought I sate beside a public way

---

2. Vessels in which incense is burned.
3. The cone-shaped shadow (umbra) cast by the earth away from the sun.
4. A peak of the Apennines, a mountain range constituting most of the Italian peninsula south of the Po Valley.
5. I.e., the hills.

Thick strewn with summer dust, and a great stream
Of people there was hurrying to and fro 45
   Numerous as gnats upon the evening gleam,

All hastening onward, yet none seemed to know
   Whither he went, or whence he came, or why
He made one of the multitude, yet so

   Was borne amid the crowd as through the sky 50
One of the million leaves of summer's bier.[6]—
   Old age and youth, manhood and infancy,

Mixed in one mighty torrent did appear,
   Some flying from the thing they feared and some
Seeking the object of another's fear, 55

   And others as with steps towards the tomb
Pored on the trodden worms that crawled beneath,
   And others mournfully within the gloom

Of their own shadow walked, and called it death . . .
   And some fled from it[7] as it were a ghost, 60
Half fainting in the affliction of vain breath.

   But more with motions which each other crost
Pursued or shunned the shadows the clouds threw
   Or birds within the noonday ether lost,

Upon that path where flowers never grew; 65
   And weary with vain toil and faint for thirst
Heard not the fountains whose melodious dew

   Out of their mossy cells forever burst
Nor felt the breeze which from the forest told
   Of grassy paths, and wood lawns interspersed 70

With overarching elms and caverns cold
   And violet banks where sweet dreams brood, but they
Pursued their serious folly as of old. . . .

   And as I gazed methought that in the way
The throng grew wilder, as the woods of June 75
   When the South wind[8] shakes the extinguished day.—

6. The phrase *public way* (line 43) and the comparison of the souls of men with crowds of *gnats* (line 46) are found in Petrarch's "Triumph of Death" and Dante's *Inferno*, respectively; the simile comparing the dead with fallen leaves had earlier been used by Homer, Virgil, Dante, and Milton.
7. I.e., shadow.
8. The *libeccio*, the southwest wind in Italy, is the wind of hot storms and of the evening onshore breeze on the western coast.

And a cold glare, intenser than the noon
    But icy cold, obscured with [      ] light[9]
The Sun as he the stars. Like the young Moon

    When on the sunlit limits of the night                    80
Her white shell trembles amid crimson air
    And whilst the sleeping tempest gathers might

Doth, as a herald of its coming, bear
    The ghost of her dead Mother, whose dim form
Bends in dark ether from her infant's chair,[1]              85

    So came a chariot on the silent storm
Of its own rushing splendour, and a Shape
    So sate within as one whom years deform

Beneath a dusky hood and double cape
    Crouching within the shadow of a tomb,                    90
And o'er what seemed the head a cloud like crape[2]

    Was bent, a dun and faint œtherial gloom
Tempering the light; upon the chariot's beam
    A Janus-visaged[3] Shadow did assume

The guidance of that wonder-winged team.                     95
    The Shapes which drew it in thick lightnings
Were lost: I heard alone on the air's soft stream

    The music of their ever moving wings.
All the four faces of that charioteer
    Had their eyes banded . . . little profit brings          100

Speed in the van and blindness in the rear,
    Nor then avail the beams that quench the Sun[4]
Or that these banded eyes could pierce the sphere

    Of all that is, has been, or will be done.—
So ill was the car guided, but it past                       105
    With solemn speed majestically on . . .

The crowd gave way, and I arose aghast,
    Or seemed to rise, so mighty was the trance,
And saw like clouds upon the thunder blast

9. Mary Shelley filled this blank with the adjective "blinding."
1. The image in lines 79–85 is that of the crescent new moon (shaped like a chariot body) with
   the shadow of the rest of the moon over it; Coleridge, in "Dejection: An Ode," quotes the
   "Ballad of Sir Patrick Spence" on "the new Moon, / With the old Moon in her arms" as the
   sign of an approaching storm.
2. *cloud* is the subject of *Was bent* (line 92); *crape*: black material worn on the clothes of those
   in mourning.
3. Janus, the Roman god of beginnings and endings, was represented in art as having either
   two faces (*Janus Bifrons*) or four faces, one on each side of his head (*Janus Quadrifrons*).
4. I.e., the *cold glare* of line 77.

The million with fierce song and maniac dance                110
Raging around; such seemed the jubilee
    As when to greet some conqueror's advance

Imperial Rome poured forth her living sea
    From senatehouse and prison and theatre
When Freedom left those who upon the free                    115

Had bound a yoke which soon they stooped to bear.[5]
Nor wanted here the true similitude
    Of a triumphal pageant, for where'er

The chariot rolled a captive multitude
    Was driven; all those who had grown old in power          120
Or misery,—all who have their age[6] subdued,

    By action or by suffering, and whose hour
Was drained to its last sand in weal or woe,
    So that the trunk survived both fruit and flower;

All those whose fame or infamy must grow                     125
    Till the great winter lay the form and name
Of their green earth with them forever low—

All but the sacred few who could not tame
Their spirits to the Conqueror, but as soon
    As they had touched the world with living flame           130

Fled back like eagles to their native noon,
    Or those who put aside the diadem
Of earthly thrones or gems, till the last one

Were there; for they of Athens and Jerusalem[7]
Were neither mid the mighty captives seen                    135
    Nor mid the ribald crowd that followed them

Or fled before. . . . Swift, fierce and obscene
    The wild dance maddens in the van, and those
Who lead it, fleet as shadows on the green,

5. *jubilee . . . stooped to bear:* in the Old Testament the Year of Jubilee was the "year of release" in which slaves were freed (Deuteronomy 15), but Shelley ironically uses the word to describe a Roman triumph, in which a victorious army displayed the people that they had conquered, marching them under a yoke to symbolize their subservience. Such public triumphs began about the end of the Republic, when the Romans themselves were enslaved by emperors, and variants of these pageants continued in Western civilization, both in literature—as in triumphal processions of Lucifera (*Faerie Queene*, I.iv.2) and Dulness (Pope, *Dunciad*, IV), where the pageants are associated with evil—and in life, such as displays in London in 1815 celebrating the fall of Napoleon. See Patrick Story, *KSJ* XXI–XXII (1972–73): 145–59.
6. *age:* i.e., era, historical period.
7. The *sacred few* (line 128) include the leading representatives of the Hellenic and Hebraic civilizations, among them Socrates and Jesus.

Outspeed the chariot and without repose                    140
    Mix with each other in tempestuous measure
        To savage music. . . . Wilder as it grows,

They, tortured by the agonizing pleasure,
    Convulsed and on the rapid whirlwinds[8] spun
Of that fierce spirit, whose unholy leisure              145

    Was soothed by mischief since the world begun,
Throw back their heads and loose their streaming hair,
    And in their dance round her who dims the Sun

Maidens and youths fling their wild arms in air
    As their feet twinkle; now recede and now           150
Bending within each other's atmosphere

    Kindle invisibly; and as they glow
Like moths by light attracted and repelled,
    Oft to new bright destruction come and go:

Till like two clouds into one vale impelled            155
    That shake the mountains when their lightnings mingle
And die in rain—the fiery band which held

    Their natures, snaps . . . the shock still may tingle—
One falls and then another in the path
    Senseless, nor is the desolation single,            160

Yet ere I can say *where* the chariot hath
    Past over them; nor other trace I find
But as of foam after the Ocean's wrath

    Is spent upon the desert shore.—Behind,
Old men, and women foully disarrayed                   165
    Shake their grey hair in the insulting wind,

Limp in the dance and strain with limbs decayed
    To reach the car of light which leaves them still
Farther behind and deeper in the shade.

    But not the less with impotence of will            170
They wheel, though ghastly shadows interpose
    Round them and round each other, and fulfill

Their work and to the dust whence they arose
    Sink and corruption veils them as they lie
And frost in these performs what fire in those.[9]     175

8. The carnal sinners of the Second Circle in Dante's *Inferno* (Canto V) are blown about by whirling winds.
9. The coldness (*frost*) of the *old men and women* (line 165) destroys them just as uncontrolled passions (*fire*) destroy the maidens and youths (line 149). J. C. Maxwell has pointed out that the line echoes *Paradise Lost*, II.594–95: "the parching Air / Burns frore, and cold performs th' effect of Fire."

Struck to the heart by this sad pageantry,
Half to myself I said, "And what is this?
  Whose shape is that within the car? & why"—

I would have added—"is all here amiss?"
  But a voice answered . . "Life" . . . I turned and knew          180
(O Heaven have mercy on such wretchedness!)

  That what I thought was an old root which grew
To strange distortion out of the hill side
  Was indeed one of that deluded crew,

And that the grass which methought hung so wide          185
  And white, was but his thin discoloured hair,
And that the holes it vainly sought to hide

  Were or had been eyes.—"If thou canst forbear
To join the dance, which I had well forborne,"
  Said the grim Feature,[1] of my thought aware,          190

"I will now tell that which to this deep scorn
  Led me and my companions, and relate
The progress of the pageant since the morn.

  "If thirst of knowledge doth not thus abate,
Follow it even to the night, but I          195
  Am weary" . . . Then like one who with the weight

Of his own words is staggered, wearily
  He paused, and ere he could resume, I cried,
"First who art thou?" . . . "Before thy memory

  "I feared, loved, hated, suffered, did, and died,[2]          200
And if the spark with which Heaven lit my spirit
  Earth had with purer nutriment supplied

"Corruption would not now thus much inherit
  Of what was once Rousseau—nor this disguise
Stain that within which still disdains to wear it.—          205

  "If I have been extinguished, yet there rise
A thousand beacons from the spark I bore."—
  "And who are those chained to the car?" "The Wise,

---

1. The shade of Rousseau (see line 204); Milton describes Death in *Paradise Lost* (X.279) as a
   "grim Feature," using "feature" in the sense of its Latin root-word, *factura*, as a "shaped,"
   or "created," thing.
2. Jean Jacques Rousseau lived from 1712 to 1778.

"The great, the unforgotten: they who wore
   Mitres and helms and crowns, or wreathes of light,[3]     210
Signs of thought's empire over thought; their lore

"Taught them not this—to know themselves; their might
   Could not repress the mutiny within,
   And for the morn of truth they feigned, deep night

"Caught them ere evening." "Who is he with chin     215
   Upon his breast and hands crost on his chain?"
"The Child of a fierce hour;[4] He sought to win

"The world, and lost all it did contain
   Of greatness, in its hope destroyed; and more
   Of fame and peace than Virtue's self can gain     220

"Without the opportunity which bore
   Him on its eagle's pinion to the peak
From which a thousand climbers have before

"Fall'n as Napoleon fell."—I felt my cheek
   Alter to see the great form pass away     225
   Whose grasp had left the giant world so weak

That every pigmy kicked it as it lay—
   And much I grieved to think how power and will
   In opposition rule our mortal day—

And why God made irreconcilable     230
Good and the means of good;[5] and for despair
   I half disdained mine eye's desire to fill

With the spent vision of the times that were
   And scarce have ceased to be . . . "Dost thou behold,"
Said then my guide, "those spoilers spoiled, Voltaire,     235

"Frederic, and Kant, Catherine, and Leopold,
Chained hoary anarchs, demagogue and sage
   Whose name the fresh world thinks already old[6]—

---

3. The headgear respectively of bishops, warriors, kings, and (as line 211 explains) sages.
4. Napoleon.
5. The Poet's despair is contradicted by the phantasm of Rousseau (lines 234–43). Compare Prometheus' rejection of the Furies, who try to drive him to despair (*Prometheus Unbound*, I.625–31).
6. King Frederick II, "the Great," of Prussia (1712–86); Czarina Catherine II, "the Great," of Russia (1729–96); and Leopold II (1747–92), Grand Duke of Tuscany and later Holy Roman Emperor—three of the so-called enlightened despots. Shelley called such self-willed absolute rulers *anarchs*—i.e., those who obey no law but their own whims and desires—following similar usages of the word by Milton in *Paradise Lost* (II.988) and Pope in *The Dunciad* (IV.655), in both instances used as a name for Chaos. The *demagogue* and the *sage* are Voltaire (1694–1778), who both influenced these despots intellectually and inspired the French people to revolt against their successors, and Immanuel Kant (1724–1804), who lived and wrote quietly, away from the centers of power.

"For in the battle Life and they did wage
    She remained conqueror—I was overcome                    240
By my own heart alone; which neither age

"Nor tears nor infamy nor now the tomb
Could temper to its object."—"Let them pass"—
    I cried—"the world and its mysterious doom

"Is not so much more glorious than it was                    245
    That I desire to worship those who drew
New figures on its false and fragile glass

"As the old faded."—"Figures ever new
Rise on the bubble, paint them how you may;
    We have but thrown, as those before us threw,            250

"Our shadows on it as it past away.
    But mark, how chained to the triumphal chair
The mighty phantoms of an elder day—

"All that is mortal of great Plato there
Expiates the joy and woe his master knew not;               255
    That star that ruled his doom was far too fair⁷—

"And Life, where long that flower of Heaven grew not,
    Conquered the heart by love which gold or pain
Or age or sloth or slavery could subdue not.—

"And near [       ] walk the [       ] twain.⁸              260
The tutor and his pupil, whom Dominion
    Followed as tame as vulture in a chain.—

"The world was darkened beneath either pinion
    Of him whom from the flock of conquerors
Fame singled as her thunderbearing minion;                  265

"The other long outlived both woes and wars,
Throned in new thoughts of men,⁹ and still had kept
    The jealous keys of truth's eternal doors

---

7. Socrates (Plato's *master*) refrained from passionate love affairs with boys, but Plato loved a
youth named Aster (which means "star" in Greek and is the name of a flower—hence, *flower
of Heaven*). See the epigram attributed to Plato that Shelley uses as an epigraph to *Adonais*.
8. Mary Shelley filled in the first blank with "him"; a later editor suggested "Macedonian" as a
proper adjective for *twain*, inasmuch as the *tutor* and his *pupil* are Aristotle and Alexander
the Great.
9. Sir Francis Bacon wrote of Aristotle: "I will think of him that he learned the humour of his
scholar, with whom it seemeth he did emulate, the one to conquer all opinions, as the other
to conquer all nations."

"If Bacon's spirit[1] [          ] had not leapt
   Like lightning out of darkness; he compelled          270
The Proteus shape[2] of Nature's as it slept

"To wake and to unbar the caves that held
   The treasure of the secrets of its reign[3]—
     See the great bards of old[4] who inly quelled

"The passions which they sung, as by their strain          275
   May well be known: their living melody
     Tempers[5] its own contagion to the vein

"Of those who are infected with it—I
   Have suffered what I wrote, or viler pain!—

"And so my words were seeds of misery—          280
   Even as the deeds of others."[6]—"Not as theirs,"[7]
     I said—he pointed to a company

In which I recognized amid the heirs
   Of Cæsar's crime from him to Constantine[8]
     The Anarchs old whose force and murderous snares          285

Had founded many a sceptre bearing line
And spread the plague of blood and gold abroad,
   And Gregory and John[9] and men divine

Who rose like shadows between Man and god
   Till that eclipse, still hanging under Heaven,          290
     Was worshipped by the world o'er which they strode

For the true Sun it quenched.—"Their power was given
But to destroy," replied the leader—"I
     Am one of those who have created, even

1. Bacon's introduction of the foundations of the scientific method broke the hold of scholastic dogmatism by encouraging experimental testing of rational hypotheses.
2. In *The Wisdom of the Ancients*, Bacon discusses the myth of Proteus as an allegory of physical matter and its transformations.
3. These are allusions to the Cave of Mammon in Spenser's *Faerie Queene* (II.vii) and to Bacon's quotation from Democritus that "the truth of nature lieth hid in certain deep mines and caves."
4. A canceled reading in the manuscript: "Homer & his brethren."
5. Restrains or checks.
6. Whereas the classical writers sublimated their passions into their harmonious poetry (see *Defence of Poetry*, paragraph 20), Rousseau acted out his passions before writing them, so that his writings lack tranquillity, and therefore they enflame others just as do ill-considered actions.
7. The Poet replies that Rousseau's writings are not as bad as the deeds of the political and ecclesiastical rulers of the Roman Empire and medieval Europe.
8. Julius Caesar established the power of the Roman emperors; Constantine first made Christianity the state religion of the empire, combining political and ecclesiastical tyranny.
9. Gregory VII (Hildebrand) established the temporal power of the papacy; John was the name most frequently used by popes in the Middle Ages.

"If it be but a world of agony."—                                      295
    "Whence camest thou and whither goest thou?
How did thy course begin," I said, "and why?


"Mine eyes are sick of this perpetual flow
Of people, and my heart of one sad thought.—
    Speak."—"Whence I came, partly I seem to know,      300


"And how and by what paths I have been brought
    To this dread pass, methinks even thou mayst guess;
Why this should be my mind can compass not—


"Whither the conqueror hurries me still less.
But follow thou, and from spectator turn                      305
    Actor or victim in this wretchedness


"And what thou wouldst be taught I then may learn
    From thee.—Now listen . . . In the April prime
When all the forest tops began to burn


"With kindling green, touched by the azure clime      310
Of the young year, I found myself asleep
    Under a mountain, which from unknown time


"Had yawned into a cavern high and deep,
    And from it came a gentle rivulet
Whose water like clear air in its calm sweep            315


    "Bent the soft grass and kept for ever wet
The stems of the sweet flowers, and filled the grove
    With sound which all who hear must needs forget


"All pleasure and all pain, all hate and love,
    Which they had known before that hour of rest:      320
A sleeping mother there would dream not of


    "The only child who died upon her breast
At eventide, a king would mourn no more
    The crown of which his brow was dispossest


"When the sun lingered o'er the Ocean floor              325
    To gild his rival's new prosperity.—
Thou wouldst forget thus vainly to deplore


    "Ills, which if ills, can find no cure from thee,
The thought of which no other sleep will quell
    Nor other music blot from memory—                        330

"So sweet and deep is the oblivious[1] spell.—
　Whether my life had been before that sleep
The Heaven which I imagine, or a Hell

"Like this harsh world in which I wake to weep,
I know not. I arose and for a space　　　　　335
　The scene of woods and waters seemed to keep,

"Though it was now broad day, a gentle trace
　Of light diviner than the common Sun
Sheds on the common Earth, but all the place

"Was filled with many sounds woven into one　　340
Oblivious melody, confusing sense
　Amid the gliding waves and shadows dun;

"And as I looked the bright omnipresence
　Of morning through the orient cavern flowed,
And the Sun's image radiantly intense　　　　　345

"Burned on the waters[2] of the well that glowed
Like gold, and threaded all the forest maze
　With winding paths of emerald fire—there stood

"Amid the sun, as he amid the blaze
　Of his own glory, on the vibrating　　　　　350
Floor of the fountain, paved with flashing rays,

"A shape all light,[3] which with one hand did fling
Dew on the earth, as if she were the Dawn
　Whose invisible rain forever seemed to sing

"A silver music on the mossy lawn,　　　　　355
　And still before her on the dusky grass
Iris[4] her many coloured scarf had drawn.—

"In her right hand she bore a chrystal glass
Mantling with bright Nepenthe;[5]—the fierce splendour
　Fell from her as she moved under the mass　　360

"Of the deep cavern, and with palms[6] so tender
　Their tread broke not the mirror of its billow,
Glided along the river, and did bend her

1. Attended by forgetfulness.
2. The sun, symbol of the deity, is reflected from water, symbol of mortality.
3. Literally the glare of the light from the *Sun* (line 345) reflected from the *waters of the well* (line 346).
4. The rainbow.
5. In *Comus*, lines 63–66, 672–77, Milton describes Comus, the evil magician who is the son of Circe, the daughter of the Sun, as seducing virtuous travelers by offering them "orient liquor in a Crystal Glasse" greater than "that *Nepenthes*," a drug to erase all pain, anger, and sorrow, which Helen of Troy gives to Telemachus (*Odyssey*, IV).
6. See *Adonais*, line 212 and note.

"Head under the dark boughs, till like a willow
Her fair hair swept the bosom of the stream 365
That whispered with delight to be their pillow.⁷—

"As one enamoured is upborne in dream
O'er lily-paven lakes mid silver mist
To wondrous music, so this shape might seem

"Partly to tread the waves with feet which kist 370
The dancing foam, partly to glide along
The airs that roughened the moist amethyst,

"Or the slant morning beams that fell among
The trees, or the soft shadows of the trees;
And her feet ever to the ceaseless song 375

"Of leaves and winds and waves and birds and bees
And falling drops moved in a measure new
Yet sweet, as on the summer evening breeze

"Up from the lake a shape of golden dew
Between two rocks, athwart the rising moon, 380
Dances i' the wind where eagle never flew.—

"And still her feet, no less than the sweet tune
To which they moved, seemed as they moved, to blot
The thoughts of him who gazed on them, and soon

"All that was seemed as if it had been not— 385
As if the gazer's mind was strewn beneath
Her feet like embers, and she, thought by thought,

"Trampled its fires into the dust of death,
As Day upon the threshold of the east
Treads out the lamps of night, until the breath 390

"Of darkness reillumines even the least
Of heaven's living eyes—like day she came,
Making the night a dream; and ere she ceased

"To move, as one between desire and shame
Suspended, I said—'If, as it doth seem, 395
Thou comest from the realm without a name,

"'Into this valley of perpetual dream,
Shew whence I came, and where I am, and why—
Pass not away upon the passing stream.'

7. The *shape all light* (line 352) assumes the shape of a rainbow.

" 'Arise and quench thy thirst,' was her reply.    400
And as a shut lily, stricken by the wand
   Of dewy morning's vital alchemy,

"I rose; and, bending at her sweet command,
   Touched with faint lips the cup she raised,
And suddenly my brain became as sand    405

"Where the first wave had more than half erased
The track of deer on desert Labrador,
   Whilst the fierce wolf from which they fled amazed

"Leaves his stamp visibly upon the shore
   Until the second bursts—so on my sight    410
Burst a new Vision never seen before.—

"And the fair shape waned in the coming light
As veil by veil the silent splendour drops
   From Lucifer,[8] amid the chrysolite

"Of sunrise ere it strike the mountain tops—    415
   And as the presence of that fairest planet
Although unseen is felt by one who hopes

"That his day's path may end as he began it
In that star's smile,[9] whose light is like the scent
   Of a jonquil when evening breezes fan it,    420

"Or the soft note in which his dear lament
   The Brescian shepherd breathes,[1] or the caress
That turned his weary slumber to content.—

"So knew I in that light's severe excess
The presence of that shape which on the stream    425
   Moved, as I moved along the wilderness,

"More dimly than a day appearing dream,
   The ghost of a forgotten form of sleep,
A light from Heaven whose half extinguished beam

"Through the sick day in which we wake to weep    430
Glimmers, forever sought, forever lost.—
   So did that shape its obscure tenour keep

8. Lucifer, the Light-Bearer, is the morning star (always the planet Venus in Shelley's poetry); *Chrysolite* is a gem, olivine, of pale yellowish-green color.
9. Venus, as morning and evening star.
1. "The favorite song, 'Stanco di pascolar le peccorelle' is a Brescian national air," (Mary Shelley's note). Burton R. Pollin located the Italian song with this title (English: "I am weary of pasturing my sheep"), published in Paris in "année 6" (i.e., September 22, 1798–September 21, 1799), as sung by Angelica Catalani, an Italian soprano (1780–1845) who starred in London from 1806 to 1813 and was admired by Shelley's friend Edward Fergus Graham. See line 14 of Shelley's second verse-letter to him, beginning, "Dear dear dear dear dear dear Græme" (Shelley, *CPPBS*, I, 143; *SC*, IX, 146–68).

"Beside my path, as silent as a ghost;
　But the new Vision, and its cold bright car,
With savage music, stunning music, crost                          435

"The forest, and as if from some dread war
Triumphantly returning, the loud million
　Fiercely extolled the fortune of her star.—

"A moving arch of victory, the vermilion
　And green and azure plumes of Iris had              440
Built high over her wind-winged pavilion,[2]

"And underneath ætherial glory clad
The wilderness, and far before her flew
　The tempest of the splendour which forbade

"Shadow to fall from leaf or stone;—the crew          445
　Seemed in that light like atomies[3] that dance
Within a sunbeam;—some upon the new

"Embroidery of flowers that did enhance
The grassy vesture of the desart, played,
　Forgetful of the chariot's swift advance;            450

"Others stood gazing till within the shade
　Of the great mountain its light left them dim.—
Others outspeeded it, and others made

"Circles around it like the clouds that swim
Round the high moon in a bright sea of air,            455
　And more did follow, with exulting hymn,

"The chariot and the captives fettered there,
　But all like bubbles on an eddying flood
Fell into the same track at last and were

"Borne onward.—I among the multitude                  460
Was swept; me sweetest flowers delayed not long,
　Me not the shadow nor the solitude,

"Me not the falling stream's Lethean[4] song,
　Me, not the phantom of that early form
Which moved upon its motion,—but among                 465

"The thickest billows of the living storm
I plunged, and bared my bosom to the clime
　Of that cold light, whose airs too soon deform.—

2. The rainbow forms an arch of triumph for the conquering chariot of Life.
3. Tiny particles (motes) of dust.
4. In Greek mythology, drinking the waters of the River Lethe induced forgetfulness of the
   past.

"Before the chariot had begun to climb
   The opposing steep of that mysterious dell,          470
Behold a wonder worthy of the rhyme

"Of him[5] who from the lowest depths of Hell
Through every Paradise and through all glory
   Love led serene, and who returned to tell

"In words of hate and awe the wondrous story          475
   How all things are transfigured, except Love;
For deaf as is a sea which wrath makes hoary

"The world can hear not the sweet notes that move
The sphere whose light is melody to lovers—
   A wonder worthy of his rhyme—the grove          480

"Grew dense with shadows to its inmost covers,
   The earth was grey with phantoms,[6] and the air
Was peopled with dim forms, as when there hovers

"A flock of vampire-bats before the glare
Of the tropic sun, bringing ere evening          485
   Strange night upon some Indian isle,—thus were

"Phantoms diffused around, and some did fling
   Shadows of shadows, yet unlike themselves,
Behind them, some like eaglets on the wing

"Were lost in the white blaze, others like elves          490
Danced in a thousand unimagined shapes
   Upon the sunny streams and grassy shelves;

"And others sate chattering like restless apes
   On vulgar hands and voluble like fire.
Some made a cradle of the ermined capes          495

"Of kingly mantles, some upon the tiar[7]
Of pontiffs sate like vultures, others played
   Within the crown which girt with empire

"A baby's or an idiot's brow, and made
   Their nests in it; the old anatomies[8]          500
Sate hatching their base broods under the shade

5. Dante; *who* is the object of *Love led* (line 474), and some editors alter the word to "whom," but the awkward sound of "him whom from" might well have led Shelley to find another solution, even to retaining the ungrammatical *who*.
6. In *De rerum natura*, IV, Lucretius describes how people exude ideas, superstitions, and passions in the form of *simulacra* or masks that peel off and float around in the air. Contrast the reversal of this process in *Prometheus Unbound*, III.iv.
7. Tiara or triple crown, symbolic of the sovereignty and dignity of the papacy.
8. Skeletons.

"Of demon wings, and laughed from their dead eyes
To reassume the delegated power
   Arrayed in which these worms did monarchize

"Who make this earth their charnel.⁹—Others more          505
   Humble, like falcons sate upon the fist
Of common men, and round their heads did soar,

   "Or like small gnats and flies as thick as mist
On evening marshes thronged about the brow
   Of lawyer, statesman, priest and theorist,          510

"And others like discoloured flakes of snow
   On fairest bosoms and the sunniest hair
Fell, and were melted by the youthful glow

   "Which they extinguished; for like tears, they were
A veil to those from whose faint lids they rained          515
   In drops of sorrow.—I became aware

"Of whence those forms proceeded which thus stained
   The track in which we moved; after brief space
From every form the beauty slowly waned,

   "From every firmest limb and fairest face          520
The strength and freshness fell like dust, and left
   The action and the shape without the grace

"Of life; the marble brow of youth was cleft
   With care, and in the eyes where once hope shone
Desire like a lioness bereft          525

   "Of its last cub, glared ere it died; each one
Of that great crowd sent forth incessantly
   These shadows, numerous as the dead leaves blown

"In Autumn evening from a poplar tree—
   Each, like himself and like each other were,¹          530
At first, but soon distorted seemed to be

   "Obscure clouds moulded by the casual air,
And of this stuff the car's creative ray
   Wrought all the busy phantoms that were there

"As the sun shapes the clouds—thus, on the way          535
   Mask after mask fell from the countenance
And form of all, and long before the day

---

9. A charnel house, where bones of the dead are collected.
1. Each shadow was like *himself* who gave it off and, therefore, resembled all the other *simulacra* emanating from the same person.

"Was old, the joy which waked like Heaven's glance
The sleepers in the oblivious valley, died,
   And some grew weary of the ghastly dance          540

"And fell, as I have fallen by the way side,
   Those soonest, from whose forms most shadows past
And least of strength and beauty did abide."—

"Then, what is Life?" I said . . . the cripple cast
His eye upon the car which now had rolled          545
   Onward, as if that look must be the last,

And answered. . . . "Happy those for whom the fold
   Of

# THE PROSE

The prose writings that Shelley composed in Italy, like many of his later poems and poetic fragments, are not yet available in modern critical texts in a standard collective edition. Although limits of space have not permitted us to include additional prose works, we have taken particular pains to update the texts of the three pieces that are included according to the best available scholarly evidence based on the surviving manuscripts. For the essays "On Love" and "On Life," there is a single holograph draft manuscript of each. *A Defence of Poetry* survives not only in Shelley's (incomplete) first draft and his holograph fair copy, but also in Mary W. Shelley's fair copy of 1821 that Shelley read over and corrected before sending it to Charles Ollier to publish, and in a (less authoritative) transcript that she made when she finally published *A Defence* in 1840.

# On Love[1]

What is Love?—Ask him who lives what is life; ask him who adores what is God.

I know not the internal constitution of other men, or even of thine whom I now address. I see that in some external attributes they resemble me, but when misled by that appearance I have thought to appeal to something in common and unburthen my inmost soul to them I have found my language misunderstood like one in a distant and savage land. The more opportunities they have afforded me for experience the wider has appeared the interval between us, and to a greater distance have the points of sympathy been withdrawn. With a spirit ill fitted to sustain such proof,[2] trembling and feeble through its tenderness, I have every where sought and have found only repulse and disappointment.

*Thou* demandest what is Love. It is that powerful attraction towards all that we conceive or fear or hope beyond ourselves when we find within our own thoughts the chasm of an insufficient void and seek to awaken in all things that are a community with what we experience within ourselves. If we reason we would be understood; if we imagine we would that the airy children of our brain were born anew within another's, if we feel, we would that another's nerves should vibrate to our own, that the beams of their eyes should kindle at once and mix and melt into our own, that lips of motionless ice should not reply to

---

1. The original draft of "On Love" appears on pp. 1–9 of Bodleian MS Shelley adds. e.11 (*BSM*, XV, 2–11), having been written (the contents of the notebook suggest) in Bagni di Lucca in the summer of 1818—very likely July 20–25, after Shelley finished his translation of Plato's *Symposium* and before he began his "Discourse on the Manners of the Antient Greeks Relative to the Subject of Love." Mary Shelley first published "On Love" in the annual *Keepsake For 1829* (1828), from which it was immediately reprinted in England and New York and translated in a French periodical. Thomas Medwin published a somewhat different version in *The Shelley Papers* (1833). For a full discussion of the essay's date, text, and ideas, see *SC*, VI (1973), 633–47. Our text is based on Shelley's Bodleian holograph.

2. *proof*: testing.

lips quivering and burning with the heart's best blood. This is Love. This is the bond and the sanction which connects not only man with man, but with every thing which exists. We are born into the world and there is something within us which from the instant that we live and move thirsts after its likeness. It is probably in correspondence with this law that the infant drains milk from the bosom of its mother. This propensity developes itself with the development of our nature. We dimly see within our intellectual nature a miniature as it were of our entire self, yet deprived of all that we condemn or despise, the ideal prototype of every thing excellent or lovely that we are capable of conceiving as belonging to the nature of man. Not only the portrait of our external being, but an assemblage of the minutest particulars of which our nature is composed:[3] a mirror whose surface reflects only the forms of purity and brightness: a soul within our soul that describes a circle around its proper Paradise which pain and sorrow or evil dare not overleap.[4] To this we eagerly refer all sensations, thirsting that they should resemble or correspond with it. The discovery of its antitype: the meeting with an understanding capable of clearly estimating the deductions of our own, an imagination which should enter into and seize upon the subtle and delicate peculiarities, which we have delighted to cherish and unfold in secret, with a frame whose nerves, like the chords of two exquisite lyres strung to the accompaniment of one delightful voice, vibrate with the vibrations of our own; and of a combination of all these in such proportion as the type within demands: this is the invisible and unattainable point to which Love tends; and to attain which it urges forth the powers of man to arrest the faintest shadow of that without the possession of which there is no rest or respite to the heart over which it rules. Hence in solitude, or in that deserted state when we are surrounded by human beings and yet they sympathise not with us, we love the flowers, the grass and the waters and the sky. In the motion of the very leaves of spring in the blue air there is then found a secret correspondence with our heart. There is eloquence in the tongueless wind and a melody in the flowing of brooks and the rustling of the reeds beside them which by their inconceivable relation to something within the soul awaken the spirits to a dance of breathless rapture, and bring tears of mysterious tenderness to the eyes like the enthusiasm of patriotic success or the voice of one beloved singing to you alone. Sterne says that if he were in a desart he would love some cypress . . .[5] So soon as this want or power is dead, man becomes the living sepulchre of himself, and what yet survives is the mere husk of what once he was.—

3. "These words are inefficient and metaphorical—Most words so—No help—" (Shelley's note).
4. Shelley alludes to *Paradise Lost*, IV.179–83, where Satan "disdain'd" to enter Eden through its single gate on the East side, but instead "At one slight bound overleap'd all bound / Of Hill or highest Wall, and sheer within / Lights on his feet."
5. In the third of the unnumbered sections called "In the Street: *Calais*" in *A Sentimental Journey through France and Italy*, Laurence Sterne wrote: "I declare . . . that was I in a desart, I would find out wherewith in it to call forth my affections—If I could not do better, I would fasten them upon some sweet myrtle, or seek some melancholy *cypress* to connect myself to" (2nd ed., 1768; Chadwyck-Healy, *Literature Online*).

# On Life[1]

Life, and the world, or whatever we call that which we are and feel, is an astonishing thing. The mist of familiarity obscures from us the wonder of our being. We are struck with admiration at some of its transient modifications; but it is itself the great miracle. What are changes of empires, the wreck of dynasties with the opinions which supported them; what is the birth and the extinction of religions and of political systems to life? What are the revolutions of the globe which we inhabit, and the operations of the elements of which it is composed, compared with life? What is the universe of stars and suns [of][2] which this inhabited earth is one and their motions and their destiny compared with life. Life, the great miracle, we admire not, because it is so miraculous. It is well that we are thus shielded by the familiarity of what is at once so certain and so unfathomable from an astonishment which would otherwise absorb and overawe the functions of that which is [its][3] object.

If any artist (I do not say had executed) but had merely conceived in his mind the system of the sun and stars and planets, they not existing, and had painted to us in words or upon canvas, the spectacle now afforded by the nightly cope of Heaven and illustrated it by the wisdom of astronomy, great would be our admiration. Or had he imagined the scenery of this earth, the mountains, the seas and the rivers, and the grass and the flowers and the variety of the forms and masses of the leaves of the woods and the colours which attend the setting and the rising sun, and the hues of the[4] atmosphere, turbid or serene, these things not before existing, truly we should have been astonished

1. Shelley's fragmentary essay "On Life" grew directly from an early passage in his *Philosophical View of Reform*, his longest (though unfinished) work in prose, and was written (late in 1819), in the back of the notebook in which he drafted that treatise, the manuscript of which is in the Pforzheimer Collection, New York Public Library (see *SC*, VI, 945ff.). The leaves containing "On Life," as well as Shelley's fragment on contraception, had earlier been removed from the notebook by a previous owner and are now a few blocks away in the Pierpont Morgan Library (MA 408). Thomas Medwin first published a version of "On Life" in the *Athenæum* for September 29, 1832, and again the next year in *The Shelley Papers*. Mary W. Shelley provided a more correct version in her edition of Shelley's *Essays, Letters from Abroad, Translations and Fragments* (1840).
   Our text, based on Shelley's manuscript in the Pierpont Morgan Library, contains important changes not only from those early texts and others deriving from them, but also from the text in the first edition of *Shelley's Poetry and Prose* (*SPP*). Through anomalies in the division of materials reproduced in the *MYR: Shelley* series, this Pierpont Morgan manuscript has not yet been reproduced in facsimile and was used as the basis of a modern critical text only in the first edition of *SPP*. Like many of Shelley's draft manuscripts, this one contains cruxes where its unfinished state of thought, or changes in the syntax during the heat of composing and revising, necessitate personal interpretations of the evidence. We, therefore, annotate the text where the manuscript differs from—or has caused differences between—Mary Shelley's version of "On Life" and ours. In quoting from the manuscript, we expand the ampersands, as Shelley regularly did when publishing his works.
   For discussions of the ideas and implications of "On Life" and what Shelley calls "the intellectual system," see C. E. Pulos's *The Deep Truth: A Study of Shelley's Scepticism*, Reiman's *Shelley's "The Triumph of Life,"* pp. 3–18, and the excerpt from Cameron's *Shelley: The Golden Years* in this volume (pp. 580–89).
2. [*of*]: the manuscript appears to give "by"; we follow Mary Shelley's emendation.
3. [*its*]: this word, lacking in the draft, was supplied by Mary Shelley.
4. *the atmosphere: the* is canceled in the manuscript, but we follow Mary Shelley in including it as parallel to the other phrases in the sequence.

and it would have been more than a vain boast to have said of such a man, "Non merita nome di creatore, sennon Iddio ed il Poeta."[5] But now these things are looked on with little wonder and to be conscious of them with intense delight is esteemed to be the distinguishing mark of character[6] of a refined and extraordinary person. The multitude of those men care not for them. It is thus with Life—that which includes all.

What is life? Thoughts and feelings arise, with or without our[7] will, and we employ words to express them. We are born, and our birth is unremembered and our infancy remembered but in fragments. We live on, and in living we lose the apprehension of life. How vain is it to think that words can penetrate the mystery of our being. Rightly used they may make evident our ignorance to ourselves, and this is much. For what are we? Whence do we come, and whither do we go? Is birth the commencement, is death the conclusion of our being? What is birth and death?

The most refined abstractions of logic conduct to a view of life which, though startling to the apprehension, is in fact that which the habitual sense of its repeated combinations has extinguished in us. It strips, as it were, the painted curtain from this scene of things. I confess that I am one of those who am unable to refuse my assent to the conclusions of those philosophers, who assert that nothing exists but as it is perceived.

It is a decision against which all our persuasions struggle, and we must be long convicted, before we can be convinced that the solid universe of external things is "such stuff as dreams are made of."[8]— The shocking absurdities of the popular philosophy of mind and matter, and its fatal consequences in morals, their violent dogmatism concerning the source of all things, had early conducted me to materialism. This materialism is a seducing system to young and superficial minds. It allows its disciples to talk and dispenses them from thinking. But I was discontented with such a view of things as it afforded; man is a being of high aspirations "looking both before and after,"[9] whose "thoughts that wander through eternity,"[1] disclaim alliance with transience and decay, incapable of imagining to himself annihilation, existing but in the future and the past, being, not what he is, but what he has been, and shall be. Whatever may be his true and final destination, there is a spirit within him at enmity with change and extinction [nothingness and dissolution].[2] This is the character of

5. "None deserves the name of Creator except God and the Poet." Shelley quotes from a saying attributed to the Italian epic poet Tasso in Pierantonio Serassi's *Life of Torquato Tasso*.
6. *of character:* Mary Shelley omits these words, apparently thinking them to have been superseded by the prepositional phrase that follows.
7. *our:* miswritten "or" in the manuscript.
8. Shakespeare, *The Tempest*, IV.i.156–57.
9. Shakespeare, *Hamlet*, IV.iv.37. See also, "To a Sky-Lark," lines 86–87.
1. Milton, *Paradise Lost*, II.148. Because Shelley changed his syntax while drafting this sentence, the word "disclaiming" in the manuscript must be changed to *disclaim* (as Mary Shelley did) to provide a finite verb for this clause.
2. Shelley wrote *change and extinction* above *nothingness and dissolution* but all remain uncanceled.

all life and being.—Each is at once the centre and the circumference; the point to which all things are referred, and the line in which all things are contained.—Such contemplations as these materialism and the popular philosophy of mind and matter, alike forbid; they are consistent only with the intellectual system.

It is absurd to enter into a long recapitulation of arguments sufficiently familiar to those enquiring minds whom alone a writer on abstruse subjects can be conceived to address. Perhaps the most clear and vigorous statement of the intellectual system is to be found in Sir W. Drummond's Academical Questions.[3] After such an exposition it would be idle to translate into other words what could only lose its energy and fitness by the change. Examined point by point and word by word, the most discriminating intellects have been able to discover no train of thoughts in the process of its reasoning, which does not conduct inevitably to the conclusion which has been stated.

What follows from the admission? It establishes no new truth, it gives us no additional insight into our hidden nature, neither its action, nor itself. Philosophy, impatient as it may be to build, has much work yet remaining as pioneer[4] for the overgrowth of ages. It makes one step towards this object however; it destroys error, and the roots of error. It leaves, what is too often the duty of the reformer in political and ethical questions to leave, a vacancy. It reduces the mind to that freedom in which it would have acted, but for the misuse of words and signs, the instruments of its own creation.—By signs, I would be understood in a wide sense, including what is properly meant by that term, and what I peculiarly mean. In this latter sense almost all familiar objects are signs, standing not for themselves but for others, in their capacity of suggesting one thought which shall lead to a train of thoughts.—Our whole life is thus an education of error.

Let us recollect our sensations as children. What a distinct and intense apprehension had we of the world and of ourselves. Many of the circumstances of social life were then important to us, which are now no longer so. But that is not the point of comparison on which I mean to insist. We less habitually distinguished all that we saw and felt from ourselves. They seemed as it were to constitute one mass. There are some persons who in this respect are always children. Those who are subject to the state called reverie feel[5] as if their nature were dissolved into the surrounding universe, or as if the surrounding universe were absorbed into their being. They are conscious of no distinction. And these are states which precede or accompany or follow an unusually intense and vivid apprehension of life. As men grow up, this power commonly decays, and they become mechanical and habit-

3. In *The Deep Truth*, Pulos emphasizes the influence on Shelley of Sir William Drummond's *Academical Questions* (1805); for later and broader perspectives on the subject, see Earl R. Wasserman's *Shelley: A Critical Reading*, pp. 3–56, Reiman's *Intervals of Inspiration*, especially the first and fifth chapters, and Terence Allan Hoagwood's *Skepticism and Ideology*, pp. 1–66.
4. A foot soldier who went ahead to clear a path for the main body of troops.
5. *feel*: "fell" in manuscript; we agree with Mary Shelley that Shelley must simply have miswritten the word.

ual agents. Their feelings and their reasonings are the combined result of a multitude of entangled thoughts, of a series of what are called impressions, blunted[6] by reiteration.

The view of life presented by the most refined deductions of the intellectual philosophy, is that of unity. Nothing exists but as it is perceived. The difference is merely nominal between those two classes of thought which are vulgarly distinguished by the names of ideas and of external objects. Pursuing the same thread of reasoning, the existence of distinct individual minds similar to that which is employed in now questioning its own nature, is likewise found to be a delusion. The words, I, you, they are not signs of any actual difference subsisting between the assemblages[7] of thoughts thus indicated, but are merely marks employed to denote the different modifications of the one mind.[8] Let it not be supposed that this doctrine conducts to the monstrous presumption, that I, the person who now write and think, am that one mind. I am but a portion of it. The words I, and you and they are grammatical devices invented simply for arrangement and totally devoid of the intense and exclusive sense usually attached to them. It is difficult to find terms adequately to express so subtle a conception as that to which the intellectual philosophy has conducted us. We are on that verge where words abandon[9] us, and what wonder if we grow dizzy to look down the dark abyss of—how little we know.

The relations of things remain unchanged by whatever system. By the word things is to be understood any object of thought, that is, any thought upon which any other thought is employed, with an apprehension of distinction. The relations of these remain unchanged; and such is the material of our knowledge.

What is the cause of life?—that is, how was it preceded,[1] or what agencies distinct from life, have acted or act upon life? All recorded generations of mankind have wearily busied themselves in inventing answers to this question. And the result has been . . Religion. Yet, that the basis of [cause of][2] all things cannot be, as the popular philosophy alledges, mind is sufficiently evident. Mind, as far as we have any experience of its properties, and beyond that experience how vain is argument, cannot create, it can only perceive. It is said also to be the Cause? But cause is only a word expressing a certain state of the human mind with regard to the manner in which two thoughts [things][3] are apprehended to be related to each other.—If any one desires to know how unsatisfactorily the popular philosophy employs itself upon this great question, they need only impartially reflect upon the manner

6. *blunted*: Mary Shelley read this word as "planted" but in *A Defence of Poetry*, compare the penultimate sentence of paragraph 42.
7. *assemblages*: "assemblage" in Mary Shelley's edition.
8. At this point in her edition, Mary Shelley begins a new paragraph that, we believe, neither the manuscript evidence nor the logic of Shelley's argument supports.
9. The manuscript seems to read "abandoned" but we accept Mary Shelley's emendation of the word to *abandon* as Shelley's likely final choice.
1. *preceded*: "produced" in Mary Shelley's text, though the manuscript seems clear on the point.
2. *basis of* is interlined above *cause of* (uncanceled in the draft manuscript); in such cases, Shelley often went back to the earlier reading when he prepared a fair copy.
3. *things* is written minutely above *thoughts* (uncanceled).

in which thoughts develope themselves in their minds.—It is infinitely improbable that the cause of mind, that is, of existence, is similar to mind. It is said that mind produces motion and it might as well have been said that motion produces mind.

# A DEFENCE OF POETRY

Thomas Love Peacock published a half-serious essay entitled "The Four Ages of Poetry" in the first—and only—issue of *Ollier's Literary Miscellany* (1820), a periodical issued by Shelley's publisher Charles Ollier. There Shelley's friend argued that poetry passed through repeated four-stage cycles: first, an Iron Age, in which literature was crude and simple (the period of court bards, folk ballads, and romances, both primitive and medieval); second, an Age of Gold, in which genius develops the great epic and tragic forms (from Homer to Euripides and from Dante to Milton); third, a Silver Age of polished and civilized, but derivative, poetry governed by fixed rules (the Augustan age in Rome and the English Augustan age of Dryden, Pope, and their successors); and, finally, the Age of Bronze, in which the narrow vein of polished social poetry and satire having been exhausted, poets sought novelty in pseudo-simplicity. This is the stage that Peacock saw in the England of his own time: "Mr. Scott digs up the poachers and cattle-stealers of the ancient border. Lord Byron cruizes for thieves and pirates on the shores of the Morea and among the Greek islands. . . . Mr. Wordsworth picks up village legends from old women and sextons; and Mr. Coleridge, to the valuable information acquired from similar sources, superadds the dreams of crazy theologians and the mysticisms of German metaphysics. . . ."

Peacock, who after failing as a poet had recently begun work at the East India Company, urged intelligent men to stop wasting their time writing poetry and apply themselves to the new sciences, including economics and political theory, that could improve the world. Shelley, angrier than he pretended to be about this judgment on the work to which he had dedicated his life, in February and March 1821 wrote an answer that he hoped would appear in a subsequent issue of the *Literary Miscellany*. When Ollier informed him that the periodical would not be continued, Shelley suggested that his *Defence* be issued as a pamphlet, but he died before he could complete the arrangements. Late in 1822, Mary W. Shelley tried to include the paper in the *Liberal*, but that publication also failed before the *Defence* could appear. Ultimately Mary Shelley, after removing the references to Peacock's by then long-forgotten essay, included it in *Essays, Letters from Abroad, Translations and Fragments* (1840).

The *Defence of Poetry* exists in four major manuscripts: in Shelley's hand there are both a rough draft (Bodleian MS Shelley d.1; *BSM*, IV, part ii, 93–305) and a fair copy, begun in Bod. MS Shelley adds. e.20 and continued on the loose sheets now catalogued as Bod. MS Shelley adds. c.4, fols. 212–46 (*BSM*, VII, 132–235; 397–525, with notes and commentaries elsewhere in the volume), as well as two transcripts by Mary Shelley— one, containing Shelley's corrections, which was sent as press copy to Ollier in 1821 (Bod. MS Shelley e.6; *BSM*, XX, 3–117), and the other from Mary's transcript book of 1822–1824, which was removed in 1840 to serve as press copy for the first edition (Bod. MS Shelley adds. d.8; *BSM*, XX, 121–259). Although many editions derive from Mary Shelley's published version and some recent texts are based on Shelley's fair copy, the transcript by Mary Shelley with Shelley's corrections that he sent to Ollier for publication in 1821 is clearly the most authoritative single document. We have, therefore, followed Bodleian MS Shelley e.6, while restoring some words, spellings, and marks of punctuation from Shelley's holographs, which include a few words that may have been accidentally miswritten or omitted by Mary Shelley while transcribing. Our text differs more radically from the early printed texts of *Defence*. Most such corrections were first suggested by transcriptions and notes either in *BSM*, VII, ed. Reiman and Hélène Dworzan Reiman, or in *BSM*, XX, ed. Michael O'Neill, who provides a detailed collation of all the manuscripts and primary printed texts. For ease of reference, we have here numbered the paragraphs of this final text.

There have been many studies of *A Defence of Poetry* and its place in the tradition of literary theory from Plato, Aristotle, Longinus, the Italian Renaissance, Sidney, Dryden, Wordsworth, and Coleridge, down to the post-structuralists and New Historicists. For the relation between *A Defence* and Shelley's own life and poetry, however, the reader might well begin with the general books on Shelley, especially Earl R. Wasserman's discussion of the philosophical context of *A Defence of Poetry* in *Shelley: A Critical Reading* (1971), pp. 204–20, or Michael Scrivener's approach through the political and social issues in *Radical Shelley* (1982), pp. 250–67. John Wright's *Shelley's Myth of Metaphor* (1970) and Jerrold Hogle's "Shelley's Poetics: The Power as Metaphor" (*KSJ* 31[1982]: 159–97) remain seminal discussions of metaphor as the foundation of Shelley's poetics in *A Defence*.

# A Defence of Poetry;
## or, Remarks Suggested by an Essay Entitled "The Four Ages of Poetry"

{1}   According to one mode of regarding those two classes of mental action, which are called reason and imagination, the former may be considered as mind contemplating the relations borne by one thought to another, however produced; and the latter as mind acting upon those thoughts so as to colour them with its own light, and composing from them as from elements, other thoughts, each containing within itself the principle of its own integrity. The one is the τὸ ποιεῖν or the principle of synthesis, and has for its objects those forms which are common to universal nature and existence itself; the other is the τὸ λογιζειν,[1] or principle of analysis, and its action regards the relations of things, simply as relations; considering thoughts, not in their integral unity, but as the algebraical representations which conduct to certain general results. Reason is the enumeration of quantities already known; Imagination the perception of the value of those quantities, both separately and as a whole. Reason respects the differences, and Imagination the similitudes of things. Reason is to Imagination as the

---

1. The two Greek terms can be transliterated (and translated) *poiein* (making) and *logizein* (reasoning).

instrument to the agent, as the body to the spirit, as the shadow to the substance.

{**2**}   Poetry, in a general sense, may be defined to be "the expression of the Imagination": and poetry is connate with the origin of man. Man is an instrument over which a series of external and internal impressions are driven, like the alternations of an ever-changing wind over an Æolian lyre, which move it by their motion to ever-changing melody. But there is a principle within the human being, and perhaps within all sentient beings, which acts otherwise than in the lyre, and produces not melody alone, but harmony, by an internal adjustment of the sounds or motions thus excited to the impressions which excite them. It is as if the lyre could accommodate its chords to the motions of that which strikes them, in a determined proportion of sound; even as the musician can accommodate his voice to the sound of the lyre. A child at play by itself will express its delight by its voice and motions; and every inflexion of tone and every gesture will bear exact relation to a corresponding antitype in the pleasurable impressions which awakened it; it will be the reflected image of that impression; and as the lyre trembles and sounds after the wind has died away, so the child seeks, by prolonging in its voice and motions the duration of the effect, to prolong also a consciousness of the cause. In relation to the objects which delight a child, these expressions are, what Poetry is to higher objects. The savage (for the savage is to ages what the child is to years) expresses the emotions produced in him by surrounding objects in a similar manner; and language and gesture, together with plastic or pictorial imitation, become the image of the combined effect of those objects and of his apprehension of them. Man in society, with all his passions and his pleasures, next becomes the object of the passions and pleasures of man; and additional class of emotions produces an augmented treasure of expressions; and language, gesture and the imitative arts, become at once the representation and the medium, the pencil and the picture, the chisel and the statue, the chord and the harmony. The social sympathies, or those laws from which as from its elements society results, begin to develope themselves from the moment that two human beings coexist; the future is contained within the present as the plant within the seed; and equality, diversity, unity, contrast, mutual dependence become the principles alone capable of affording the motives according to which the will of a social being is determined to action, inasmuch as he is social; and constitute pleasure in sensation, virtue in sentiment, beauty in art, truth in reasoning, and love in the intercourse of kind. Hence men, even in the infancy of society, observe a certain order in their words and actions, distinct from that of the objects and the impressions represented by them, all expression being subject to the laws of that from which it proceeds. But let us dismiss those more general considerations which might involve an enquiry into the principles of society itself, and restrict our view to the manner in which the imagination is expressed upon its forms.

{**3**}   In the youth of the world, men dance and sing and imitate natural objects, observing in these actions, as in all others, a certain rhythm or order. And, although all men observe a similar, they observe not the same order, in the motions of the dance, in the melody of the song, in the combinations of language, in the series of their imitations of natural objects. For there is a certain order or rhythm belonging to each of these classes of mimetic representation, from which the hearer and the spectator receive an intenser and purer pleasure than from any other: the sense of an approximation to this order has been called taste, by modern writers. Every man, in the infancy of art, observes an order which approximates more or less closely to that from which this highest delight results: but the diversity is not sufficiently marked, as that its gradations should be sensible, except in those instances where the predominance of this faculty of approximation to the beautiful (for so we may be permitted to name the relation between this highest pleasure and its cause) is very great. Those in whom it exists in excess are poets, in the most universal sense of the word; and the pleasure resulting from the manner in which they express the influence of society or nature upon their own minds, communicates itself to others, and gathers a sort of reduplication from that community. Their language is vitally metaphorical; that is, it marks the before unapprehended relations of things, and perpetuates their apprehension, until the words which represent them, become through time signs for portions or classes of thoughts[2] instead of pictures of integral thoughts; and then if no new poets should arise to create afresh the associations which have been thus disorganized, language will be dead to all the nobler purposes of human intercourse. These similitudes or relations are finely said by Lord Bacon to be "the same footsteps of nature impressed upon the various subjects of the world"[3]—and he considers the faculty which perceives them as the storehouse of axioms common to all knowledge. In the infancy of society every author is necessarily a poet, because language itself is poetry; and to be a poet is to apprehend the true and the beautiful, in a word the good which exists in the relation, subsisting, first between existence and perception, and secondly between perception and expression. Every original language near to its source is in itself the chaos of a cyclic poem: the copiousness of lexicography and the distinctions of grammar are the works of a later age, and are merely the catalogue and the form of the creations of Poetry.

{4}   But Poets, or those who imagine and express this indestructible order, are not only the authors of language and of music, of the dance and architecture and statuary and painting: they are the institutors of laws and the founders of civil society and the inventors of the arts of life and the teachers, who draw into a certain propinquity with the beautiful and the true that partial apprehension of the agencies of the invisible world which is called religion. Hence all original religions are

2. I.e., abstract concepts.
3. Bacon, *The Advancement of Learning*, Book III, chap. 1.

allegorical or susceptible of allegory, and like Janus[4] have a double
face of false and true. Poets, according to the circumstances of the
age and nation in which they appeared, were called in the earlier epochs of the world legislators or prophets:[5] a poet essentially comprises
and unites both these characters. For he not only beholds intensely
the present as it is, and discovers those laws according to which present things ought to be ordered, but he beholds the future in the present, and his thoughts are the germs of the flower and the fruit of latest
time. Not that I assert poets to be prophets in the gross sense of the
word, or that they can foretell the form as surely as they foreknow the
spirit of events: such is the pretence of superstition which would make
poetry an attribute of prophecy, rather than prophecy an attribute of
poetry. A Poet participates in the eternal, the infinite and the one; as
far as relates to his conceptions, time and place and number are not.
The grammatical forms which express the moods of time, and the
difference of persons and the distinction of place are convertible with
respect to the highest poetry without injuring it as poetry, and the
choruses of Æschylus, and the book of Job, and Dante's Paradise
would afford, more than any other writings, examples of this fact, if
the limits of this essay did not forbid citation. The creations of sculpture, painting and music, are illustrations still more decisive.

{5}   Language, colour, form, and religious and civil habits of action
are all the instruments and materials of poetry; they may be called
poetry by that figure of speech which considers the effect as a syn-
onime of the cause. But poetry in a more restricted sense expresses
those arrangements of language, and especially metrical language
which are created by that imperial faculty, whose throne is curtained
within the invisible nature of man. And this springs from the nature
itself of language, which is a more direct representation of the actions
and passions of our internal being, and is susceptible of more various
and delicate combinations, than colour, form or motion, and is more
plastic and obedient to the controul of that faculty of which it is the
creation. For language is arbitrarily produced by the Imagination and
has relation to thoughts alone; but all other materials, instruments
and conditions of art have relations among each other, which limit and
interpose between conception and expression. The former is as a mirror which reflects, the latter as a cloud which enfeebles, the light of
which both are mediums of communication. Hence the fame of sculptors, painters and musicians, although the intrinsic powers of the great
masters of these arts, may yield in no degree to that of those who have
employed language as the hieroglyphic of their thoughts, has never
equalled that of poets in the restricted sense of the term; as two per-
formers of equal skill will produce unequal effects from a guitar and
a harp. The fame of legislators and founders of religions, so long as

4. Janus, the Roman god of endings and beginnings ( January), is represented with two (sometimes four) faces on a single head.
5. As Sir Philip Sidney pointed out in his *Defence of Poesie* (1595), *vates*, the Romans' term
   for poet, means "a diviner, fore-seer, or Prophet."

their institutions last, alone seems to exceed that of poets in the restricted sense; but it can scarcely be a question whether, if we deduct the celebrity which their flattery of the gross opinions of the vulgar usually conciliates, together with that which belonged to them in their higher character of poets, any excess will remain.

{6} We have thus circumscribed the meaning of the word Poetry within the limits of that art which is the most familiar and the most perfect expression of the faculty itself. It is necessary however to make the circle still narrower, and to determine the distinction between measured and unmeasured language; for the popular division into prose and verse is inadmissible in accurate philosophy.

{7} Sounds as well as thoughts have relations, both between each other and towards that which they represent, and a perception of the order of those relations has always been found connected with a perception of the order of the relations of thoughts. Hence the language of poets has ever affected a certain uniform and harmonious recurrence of sound, without which it were not poetry, and which is scarcely less indispensable to the communication of its influence, than the words themselves without reference to that peculiar order. Hence the vanity of translation; it were as wise to cast a violet into a crucible that you might discover the formal principle of its colour and odour, as seek to transfuse from one language into another the creations of a poet. The plant must spring again from its seed or it will bear no flower—and this is the burthen of the curse of Babel.

{8} An observation of the regular mode of the recurrence of this harmony in the language of poetical minds, together with its relation to music, produced metre, or a certain system of traditional forms of harmony and language. Yet it is by no means essential that a poet should accommodate his language to this traditional form, so that the harmony which is its spirit, be observed. The practise is indeed convenient and popular, and to be preferred, especially in such composition as includes much form and action: but every great poet must inevitably innovate upon the example of his predecessors in the exact structure of his peculiar versification. The distinction between poets and prose writers is a vulgar error. The distinction between philosophers and poets has been anticipated. Plato was essentially a poet—the truth and splendour of his imagery and the melody of his language is the most intense that it is possible to conceive. He rejected the measure of the epic, dramatic, and lyrical forms, because he sought to kindle a harmony in thoughts divested of shape and action, and he forbore to invent any regular plan of rhythm which would include, under determinate forms, the varied pauses of his style. Cicero[6] sought to imitate the cadence of his periods but with little success. Lord Bacon was a poet.[7] His language has a sweet and majestic rhythm, which

6. Marcus Tullius Cicero (106–43 B.C.), Roman statesman, man of letters, and philosopher. Shelley alludes to the style of his speeches in law courts and before the Senate.
7. "See the *Fillium Labyrinthi* and the *Essay on Death* particularly" (Shelley's note). Francis Bacon—Baron Verulam and Viscount St. Albans (1561–1626), Lord Chancellor of England, leading philosopher, and man of letters—also developed the English essay.

satisfies the sense, no less than the almost superhuman wisdom of his philosophy satisfies the intellect; it is a strain which distends, and then bursts the circumference of the hearer's[8] mind, and pours itself forth together with it into the universal element with which it has perpetual sympathy. All the authors of revolutions in opinion are not only necessarily poets as they are inventors, nor even as their words unveil the permanent analogy of things by images which participate in the life of truth; but as their periods are harmonious and rhythmical and contain in themselves the elements of verse; being the echo of the eternal music. Nor are those supreme poets, who have employed traditional forms of rhythm on account of the form and action of their subjects, less capable of perceiving and teaching the truth of things, than those who have omitted that form. Shakespeare, Dante and Milton (to confine ourselves to modern writers) are philosophers of the very loftiest power.

{**9**}   A Poem is the very image of life expressed in its eternal truth. There is this difference between a story and a poem, that a story is a catalogue of detached facts, which have no other bond of connexion than time, place, circumstance, cause and effect; the other is the creation of actions according to the unchangeable forms of human nature, as existing in the mind of the creator, which is itself the image of all other minds. The one is partial, and applies only to a definite period of time, and a certain combination of events which can never again recur; the other is universal, and contains within itself the germ of a relation to whatever motives or actions have place in the possible varieties of human nature. Time, which destroys the beauty and the use of the story of particular facts, stript of the poetry which should invest them, augments that of Poetry, and for ever developes new and wonderful applications of the eternal truth which it contains. Hence epitomes have been called the moths of just history;[9] they eat out the poetry of it. The story of particular facts is as a mirror which obscures and distorts that which should be beautiful: Poetry is a mirror which makes beautiful that which is distorted.

{**10**}   The parts of a composition may be poetical, without the composition as a whole being a poem. A single sentence may be considered as a whole though it be found in the midst of a series of unassimilated portions; a single word even may be a spark of inextinguishable thought. And thus all the great historians, Herodotus, Plutarch, Livy, were poets;[1] and although the plan of these writers, especially that of Livy, restrained them from developing this faculty in its highest degree,

---

8. Shelley wrote "hearers" in his fair copy (adds. e.20); Mary Shelley changed the word to "reader's" in her press copy (e.6), and though Shelley did not reverse her change, the context supports "hearer's."
9. Bacon, *The Advancement of Learning*, II.ii.4: "As for the corruptions and moths of history, which are epitomes, the use of them deserveth to be banished"; *epitomes:* abridgments or summaries of facts.
1. Herodotus (fifth century B.C.) wrote the first Greek history in nine books, which outline events in the kingdoms of the eastern Mediterranean that lead up to the wars between the Greek states and the Persian Empire; Plutarch (ca. A.D. 46–120) wrote the *Parallel Lives* of eminent Greeks and Romans in Greek; Titus Livius (ca. 59 B.C.–A.D. 17) wrote a history of Rome in 142 books, 35 of which survive.

they make copious and ample amends for their subjection, by filling all the interstices of their subjects with living images.

{11}   Having determined what is poetry, and who are poets, let us proceed to estimate its effects upon society.

{12}   Poetry is ever accompanied with pleasure: all spirits on which it falls, open themselves to receive the wisdom which is mingled with its delight. In the infancy of the world, neither poets themselves nor their auditors are fully aware of the excellency of poetry: for it acts in a divine and unapprehended manner, beyond and above consciousness; and it is reserved for future generations to contemplate and measure the mighty cause and effect in all the strength and splendour of their union. Even in modern times, no living poet ever arrived at the fulness of his fame; the jury which sits in judgement upon a poet, belonging as he does to all time, must be composed of his peers: it must be impanelled by Time from the selectest of the wise of many generations. A Poet is a nightingale who sits in darkness, and sings to cheer its own solitude with sweet sounds; his auditors are as men entranced by the melody of an unseen musician, who feel that they are moved and softened, yet know not whence or why.[2] The poems of Homer and his contemporaries were the delight of infant Greece; they were the elements of that social system which is the column upon which all succeeding civilization has reposed. Homer embodied the ideal perfection of his age in human character; nor can we doubt that those who read his verses were awakened to an ambition of becoming like to Achilles, Hector and Ulysses: the truth and beauty of friendship, patriotism and persevering devotion to an object, were unveiled to the depths in these immortal creations: the sentiments of the auditors must have been refined and enlarged by a sympathy with such great and lovely impersonations, until from admiring they imitated, and from imitation they identified themselves with the objects of their admiration. Nor let it be objected, that these characters are remote from moral perfection, and that they can by no means be considered as edifying patterns for general imitation. Every epoch under names more or less specious has deified its peculiar errors; Revenge is the naked Idol of the worship of a semi-barbarous age; and Self-deceit is the veiled Image of unknown evil before which luxury and satiety lie prostrate. But a poet considers the vices of his contemporaries as the temporary dress in which his creations must be arrayed, and which cover without concealing the eternal proportions of their beauty. An epic or dramatic personage is understood to wear them around his soul, as he may the antient armour or the modern uniform around his body; whilst it is easy to conceive a dress more graceful than either. The beauty of the internal nature cannot be so far concealed by its accidental vesture, but that the spirit of its form shall communicate itself to the very disguise, and indicate the shape it hides from the manner in which it is worn. A majestic form and graceful motions will express themselves through the most barbarous and tasteless costume. Few poets of the

---

2. Cf. "To a Sky-Lark," lines 36–40.

highest class have chosen to exhibit the beauty of their conceptions in its naked truth and splendour; and it is doubtful whether the alloy of costume, habit, etc., be not necessary to temper this planetary music[3] for mortal ears.

{13}   The whole objection however of the immorality of poetry rests upon a misconception of the manner in which poetry acts to produce the moral improvement of man. Ethical science arranges the elements which poetry has created, and propounds schemes and proposes examples of civil and domestic life: nor is it for want of admirable doctrines that men hate, and despise, and censure, and deceive, and subjugate one another. But Poetry acts in another and a diviner manner. It awakens and enlarges the mind itself by rendering it the receptacle of a thousand unapprehended combinations of thought. Poetry lifts the veil from the hidden beauty of the world, and makes familiar objects be as if they were not familiar; it reproduces all that it represents, and the impersonations clothed in its Elysian light stand thenceforward in the minds of those who have once contemplated them, as memorials of that gentle and exalted content which extends itself over all thoughts and actions with which it coexists. The great secret of morals is Love; or a going out of our own nature, and an identification of ourselves with the beautiful which exists in thought, action, or person, not our own.[4] A man, to be greatly good, must imagine intensely and comprehensively; he must put himself in the place of another and of many others; the pains and pleasures of his species must become his own. The great instrument of moral good is the imagination; and poetry administers to the effect by acting upon the cause. Poetry enlarges the circumference of the imagination by replenishing it with thoughts of ever new delight, which have the power of attracting and assimilating to their own nature all other thoughts, and which form new intervals and interstices whose void for ever craves fresh food. Poetry strengthens that faculty which is the organ of the moral nature of man, in the same manner as exercise strengthens a limb. A Poet therefore would do ill to embody his own conceptions of right and wrong which are usually those of his place and time in his poetical creations, which participate in neither. By this assumption of the inferior office of interpreting the effect, in which perhaps after all he might acquit himself but imperfectly, he would resign the glory of a participation in the cause. There was little danger that Homer, or any of the eternal poets, should have so far misunderstood themselves as to have abdicated this throne of their widest dominion. Those in whom the poetical faculty, though great, is less intense, as Euripides, Lucan,[5]

---

3. The "music of the spheres" that was thought to accompany the movements of the planets but could not be heard by sinful humans after the fall of Adam and Eve.
4. In Plato's *Symposium*, Socrates explains to Agathon that love arises not from richness and fulfillment, but from lack and need. One of Socrates' key sentences in Shelley's translation of the dialogue reads: "Love, therefore, and every thing else that desires anything, desires that which is absent and beyond his reach, that which it has not, that which is not itself, that which it wants . . ." ( James A. Notopoulos, *The Platonism of Shelley* [1949], p. 440).
5. For Lucan, author of the *Pharsalia* (or *Civil War*), see paragraph 28 below and *Adonais*, line 404 and note.

Tasso, Spenser, have frequently affected a moral aim, and the effect of their poetry is diminished in exact proportion to the degree in which they compel us to advert to this purpose.

{14}   Homer and the cyclic poets were followed at a certain interval by the dramatic and lyrical Poets of Athens; who flourished contemporaneously with all that is most perfect in the kindred expressions of the poetical faculty; architecture, painting, music, the dance, sculpture, philosophy, and we may add the forms of civil life. For although the scheme of Athenian society was deformed by many imperfections which the poetry existing in Chivalry and Christianity have erased from the habits and institutions of modern Europe;[6] yet never at any other period has so much energy, beauty, and virtue, been developed; never was blind strength and stubborn form so disciplined and rendered subject to the will of man, or that will less repugnant to the dictates of the beautiful and the true, as during the century which preceded the death of Socrates. Of no other epoch in the history of our species have we records and fragments stamped so visibly with the image of the divinity in man. But it is Poetry alone, in form, in action or in language, which has rendered this epoch memorable above all others, and the storehouse of examples to everlasting time. For written poetry existed at that epoch simultaneously with the other arts, and it is an idle enquiry to demand which gave and which received the light, which all as from a common focus have scattered over the darkest periods of succeeding time. We know no more of cause and effect than a constant conjunction of events: Poetry is ever found to coexist with whatever other arts contribute to the happiness and perfection of man. I appeal to what has already been established to distinguish between the cause and the effect.

{15}   It was at the period here adverted to, that the Drama had its birth; and however a succeeding writer may have equalled or surpassed those few great specimens of the Athenian drama which have been preserved to us, it is indisputable that the art itself never was understood or practised according to the true philosophy of it, as at Athens. For the Athenians employed language, action, music, painting, the dance, and religious institution to produce a common effect in the representation of the highest idealisms of passion and of power; each division in the art was made perfect in its kind by artists of the most consummate skill, and was disciplined into a beautiful proportion and unity one towards the other. On the modern stage a few only of the elements capable of expressing the image of the poet's conception are employed at once. We have tragedy without music and dancing; and music and dancing without the highest impersonations of which they are the fit accompaniment, and both without religion and solemnity. Religious institution has indeed been usually banished from the stage. Our system of divesting the actor's face of a mask, on which the many expressions appropriated to his dramatic character might be moulded

6. Shelley elsewhere identifies slavery and the subjugation of women as the two chief blots on Athenian society (see paragraph 25 below).

into one permanent and unchanging expression, is favourable only to
a partial and inharmonious effect; it is fit for nothing but a monologue,
where all the attention may be directed to some great master of ideal
mimicry. The modern practise of blending comedy with tragedy,
though liable to great abuse in point of practise, is undoubtedly an
extension of the dramatic circle; but the comedy should be as in King
Lear, universal, ideal and sublime. It is perhaps the intervention of
this principle which determines the balance in favour of King Lear
against the Œdipus Tyrannus or the Agamemnon, or, if you will the
trilogies with which they are connected; unless the intense power of
the choral poetry, especially that of the latter, should be considered
as restoring the equilibrium.[7] King Lear, if it can sustain this comparison, may be judged to be the most perfect specimen of the dramatic
art existing in the world; in spite of the narrow conditions to which
the poet was subjected by the ignorance of the philosophy of the
Drama which has prevailed in modern Europe. Calderon in his religious Autos has attempted to fulfil some of the high conditions of
dramatic representation neglected by Shakespeare; such as the establishing a relation between the drama and religion, and the accommo-
dating them to music and dancing; but he omits the observation of
conditions still more important, and more is lost than gained by a
substitution of the rigidly-defined and ever-repeated idealisms of a distorted superstition for the living impersonations of the truth of human
passion.[8]

{16}   But we digress.—The Author of the Four Ages of Poetry has
prudently omitted to dispute on the effect of the Drama upon life and
manners. For, if I know the knight by the device of his shield, I have
only to inscribe Philoctetes or Agamemnon[9] or Othello upon mine to
put to flight the giant sophisms which have enchanted him, as the
mirror of intolerable light, though on the arm of one of the weakest
of the Paladins, could blind and scatter whole armies of necromancers
and pagans. The connexion of scenic exhibitions with the improvement
or corruption of the manners of men, has been universally recognized:
in other words, the presence or absence of poetry in its most perfect
and universal form has been found to be connected with good and evil
in conduct and habit. The corruption which has been imputed to the
drama as an effect begins, when the poetry employed in its constitution, ends: I appeal to the history of manners whether the gradations
of the growth of the one and the decline of the other have not corresponded with an exactness equal to any other example of moral
cause and effect.

{17}   The drama at Athens or wheresoever else it may have approached to its perfection, coexisted with the moral and intellectual

7. Shakespeare's King Lear is compared with plays by Sophocles and Aeschylus, each the first
   play of a trilogy—Sophocles' Theban cycle of Oedipus the King, Antigone, and Oedipus at
   Colonus and Aeschylus' trilogy of Argos, known as the Oresteia—Agamemnon, The Libation-
   Bearers, and The Eumenides.
8. Shelley learned Spanish primarily to read the dramas and autos sacramentales (allegorical or
   religious plays) of Pedro Calderón de la Barca (1600–81), parts of which he translated.
9. Two tragedies by Sophocles.

greatness of the age. The tragedies of the Athenian poets are as mirrors in which the spectator beholds himself, under a thin disguise of circumstance, stript of all but that ideal perfection and energy which every one feels to be the internal type of all that he loves, admires, and would become. The imagination is enlarged by a sympathy with pains and passions so mighty that they distend in their conception the capacity of that by which they are conceived; the good affections are strengthened by pity, indignation, terror and sorrow; and an exalted calm is prolonged from the satiety of this high exercise of them into the tumult of familiar life; even crime is disarmed of half its horror and all its contagion by being represented as the fatal consequence of the unfathomable agencies of nature; error is thus divested of its wilfulness; men can no longer cherish it as the creature[1] of their choice. In a drama of the highest order there is little food for censure or hatred; it teaches rather self-knowledge and self-respect. Neither the eye nor the mind can see itself, unless reflected upon that which it resembles. The drama, so long as it continues to express poetry, is as a prismatic and many-sided mirror, which collects the brightest rays of human nature and divides and reproduces them from the simplicity of these elementary forms, and touches them with majesty and beauty, and multiplies all that it reflects, and endows it with the power of propagating its like wherever it may fall.

{18}   But in periods of the decay of social life, the drama sympathizes with that decay. Tragedy becomes a cold imitation of the form of the great masterpieces of antiquity, divested of all harmonious accompaniment of the kindred arts; and often the very form misunderstood: or a weak attempt to teach certain doctrines, which the writer considers as moral truths; and which are usually no more than specious flatteries of some gross vice or weakness with which the author in common with his auditors are infected. Hence what has been called the classical and domestic drama. Addison's "Cato" is a specimen of the one; and would it were not superfluous to cite examples of the other! To such purposes Poetry cannot be made subservient. Poetry is a sword of lightning, ever unsheathed, which consumes the scabbard that would contain it. And thus we observe that all dramatic writings of this nature are unimaginative in a singular degree; they affect sentiment and passion: which, divested of imagination, are other names for caprice and appetite. The period in our own history of the grossest degradation of the drama is the reign of Charles II when all forms in which poetry had been accustomed to be expressed became hymns to the triumph of kingly power over liberty and virtue. Milton stood alone illuminating an age unworthy of him. At such periods the calculating principle pervades all the forms of dramatic exhibition, and poetry ceases to be expressed upon them. Comedy loses its ideal universality: wit succeeds to humour; we laugh from self-complacency and triumph instead of pleasure; malignity, sarcasm and contempt, succeed to sympathetic

---

1. *creature*, the probable reading in adds. e.20, was copied by Mary Shelley as "creation."

merriment; we hardly laugh, but we smile. Obscenity, which is ever blasphemy against the divine beauty in life, becomes, from the very veil which it assumes, more active if less disgusting: it is a monster for which the corruption of society for ever brings forth new food, which it devours in secret.

{19}   The drama being that form under which a greater number of modes of expression of poetry are susceptible of being combined than any other, the connexion of poetry and social good is more observable in the drama than in whatever other form: and it is indisputable that the highest perfection of human society has ever corresponded with the highest dramatic excellence; and that the corruption or the extinction of the drama in a nation where it has once flourished, is a mark of a corruption of manners, and an extinction of the energies which sustain the soul of social life. But, as Machiavelli says of political institutions, that life may be preserved and renewed, if men should arise capable of bringing back the drama to its principles. And this is true with respect to poetry in its most extended sense: all language, institution and form, require not only to be produced but to be sustained: the office and character of a poet participates in the divine nature as regards providence, no less than as regards creation.

{20}   Civil war, the spoils of Asia, and the fatal predominance first of the Macedonian, and then of the Roman arms were so many symbols of the extinction or suspension of the creative faculty in Greece. The bucolic writers, who found patronage under the lettered tyrants of Sicily and Egypt, were the latest representatives of its most glorious reign.[2] Their poetry is intensely melodious; like the odour of the tuberose, it overcomes and sickens the spirit with excess of sweetness; whilst the poetry of the preceding age was as a meadow-gale of June which mingles the fragrance of all the flowers of the field, and adds a quickening and harmonizing spirit of its own which endows the sense with a power of sustaining its extreme delight. The bucolic and erotic delicacy in written poetry is correlative with that softness in statuary, music, and the kindred arts, and even in manners and institutions which distinguished the epoch to which we now refer. Nor is it the poetical faculty itself, or any misapplication of it, to which this want of harmony is to be imputed. An equal sensibility to the influence of the senses and the affections is to be found in the writings of Homer and Sophocles: the former especially has clothed sensual and pathetic images with irresistible attractions. Their superiority over these succeeding writers consists in the presence of those thoughts which belong to the inner faculties of our nature, not in the absence of those which are connected with the external; their incomparable perfection consists in an harmony of the union of all. It is not what the erotic writers have, but what they have not, in which their imperfection con-

---

2. Theocritus (ca. 310–250 B.C.), Callimachus (fl. 260 B.C.), Moschus (fl. 150 B.C.), and Bion (fl. 100 B.C.) were poets writing in Greek who lived in Alexandria, Egypt, under the Ptolemy kings, or at Syracuse in Sicily. They developed such slighter forms of Greek poetry as the pastoral idyll.

sists. It is not inasmuch as they were Poets, but inasmuch as they were
not Poets, that they can be considered with any plausibility as connected with the corruption of their age. Had that corruption availed
so as to extinguish in them the sensibility to pleasure, passion and
natural scenery, which is imputed to them as an imperfection, the last
triumph of evil would have been atchieved. For the end of social corruption is to destroy all sensibility to pleasure; and therefore it is corruption. It begins at the imagination and the intellect as at the core,
and distributes itself thence as a paralyzing venom, through the affections into the very appetites, until all become a torpid mass in which
sense hardly survives. At the approach of such a period, Poetry ever
addresses itself to those faculties which are the last to be destroyed,
and its voice is heard, like the footsteps of Astræa, departing from the
world.[3] Poetry ever communicates all the pleasure which men are capable of receiving: it is ever still the light of life; the source of whatever
of beautiful, or generous, or true can have place in an evil time. It will
readily be confessed that those among the luxurious citizens of Syracuse and Alexandria who were delighted with the poems of Theocritus,
were less cold, cruel and sensual than the remnant of their tribe. But
corruption must have utterly destroyed the fabric of human society
before Poetry can ever cease. The sacred links of that chain have never
been entirely disjoined, which descending through the minds of many
men is attached to those great minds, whence as from a magnet the
invisible effluence is sent forth, which at once connects, animates and
sustains the life of all. It is the faculty which contains within itself the
seeds at once of its own and of social renovation. And let us not cir-
cumscribe the effects of the bucolic and erotic poetry within the limits
of the sensibility of those to whom it was addressed. They may have
perceived the beauty of those immortal compositions, simply as fragments and isolated portions: those who are more finely organized, or
born in a happier age, may recognize them as episodes to that great
poem, which all poets, like the co-operating thoughts of one great
mind, have built up since the beginning of the world.

{21}   The same revolutions within a narrower sphere had place in
antient Rome; but the actions and forms of its social life never seem
to have been perfectly saturated with the poetical element. The Romans appear to have considered the Greeks as the selectest treasuries
of the selectest forms of manners and of nature, and to have abstained
from creating in measured language, sculpture, music or architecture,
anything which might bear a particular relation to their own condition,
whilst it should bear a general one to the universal constitution of the
world. But we judge from partial evidence; and we judge perhaps partially. Ennius, Varro, Pacuvius, and Accius, all great poets, have been

3. Astraea—variously said to be the daughter of Astraeus, the Titan king of Arcadia, of Titan
(Saturn's brother) and Aurora, or of Zeus (Jupiter) and Themis ("law")—was the goddess
of justice, sometimes identified with Rhea, wife of Saturn. During the Golden Age she lived
on earth, but the evil of men drove her into heaven as the zodiacal constellation Virgo. She
is represented as a stern virgin holding balance scales in one hand and a sword in the other.

lost.[4] Lucretius is in the highest, and Virgil in a very high sense, a creator. The chosen delicacy of the expressions of the latter is as a mist of light which conceals from us the intense and exceeding truth of his conceptions of nature. Livy is instinct with poetry. Yet Horace, Catullus, Ovid, and generally the other great writers of the Virgilian age, saw man and nature in the mirror of Greece. The institutions also and the religion of Rome were less poetical than those of Greece, as the shadow is less vivid than the substance. Hence poetry in Rome, seemed to follow rather than accompany the perfection of political and domestic society. The true Poetry of Rome lived in its institutions; for whatever of beautiful, true and majestic they contained could have sprung only from the faculty which creates the order in which they consist. The life of Camillus, the death of Regulus; the expectation of the Senators, in their godlike state, of the victorious Gauls; the refusal of the Republic to make peace with Hannibal after the battle of Cannae, were not the consequences of a refined calculation of the probable personal advantage to result from such a rhythm and order in the shews of life, to those who were at once the poets and the actors of these immortal dramas.[5] The imagination beholding the beauty of this order, created it out of itself according to its own idea: the consequence was empire, and the reward ever-living fame. These things are not the less poetry, *quia carent vate sacro.*[6] They are the episodes of the cyclic poem written by Time upon the memories of men. The Past, like an inspired rhapsodist, fills the theatre of everlasting generations with their harmony.

{22}   At length the antient system of religion and manners had fulfilled the circle of its revolution. And the world would have fallen into utter anarchy and darkness, but that there were found poets among the authors of the Christian and Chivalric systems of manners and religion, who created forms of opinion and action never before conceived; which, copied into the imaginations of men, became as generals to the bewildered armies of their thoughts. It is foreign to the present purpose to touch upon the evil produced by these systems: except that we protest, on the ground of the principles already established, that no portion of it can be imputed to the poetry they contain.

4. Quintus Ennius (239–169 B.C.), the fathering genius of Latin literature, wrote his epic entitled *Annales* in Latin hexameter verse adapted from the Greek; about 600 lines survive. Of his 19 tragedies, 420 lines remain. Marcus Pacuvius (220–ca. 130 B.C.), his nephew, was the first important Latin tragic dramatist; of his 13 known plays, only 400 lines survive. Marcus Terentius Varro (116–27 B.C.), the leading scholar of his day, wrote 74 works, of which only his *Res rusticae*, a dialogue about managing a farm, survives intact. Lucius Accius or Attius (170–ca. 85 B.C.) was the greatest Roman tragic poet. Of his 40 or more plays, only 700 lines survive.
5. Marcus Furius Camillus (fl. 396, d. 365 B.C.), though rejected by the Roman common people, continued to return to aid the young republic whenever it was threatened, while his humanity to conquered enemy cities gained Rome many allies. Marcus Atilius Regulus, captured in 255 B.C., was paroled by the Carthaginians in order to have him persuade his Roman countrymen to make peace; instead, he urged them to continue the war. Then, to honor the terms of his parole, he returned to Carthage, where he was tortured to death. When the Gauls entered Rome in 390 B.C., the Senators sat so still, in such dignified poses, that the Gauls at first mistook them for statues. After Hannibal invaded Italy and destroyed two Roman armies (217 and 216 B.C.), many of Rome's Italian allies went over to the Carthaginians, but the Romans persisted until the defeat of Carthage.
6. "Because they lack a sacred poet" (Horace, *Odes*, IX.28).

{**23**}  It is probable that the astonishing poetry of Moses, Job, David, Solomon and Isaiah had produced a great effect upon the mind of Jesus and his disciples. The scattered fragments preserved to us by the biographers of this extraordinary person, are all instinct with the most vivid poetry. But his doctrines seem to have been quickly distorted. At a certain period after the prevalence of a system of opinions founded upon those promulgated by him, the three forms into which Plato had distributed the faculties of mind underwent a sort of apotheosis, and became the object of the worship of the civilized world. Here it is to be confessed that "Light seems to thicken," and

> The crow makes wing to the rooky wood,
> Good things of day begin to droop and drowze,
> And night's black agents to their preys do rouze.[7]

But mark how beautiful an order has sprung from the dust and blood of this fierce chaos! how the World, as from a resurrection, balancing itself on the golden wings of knowledge and of hope, has reassumed its yet unwearied flight into the Heaven of time. Listen to the music, unheard by outward ears, which is as a ceaseless and invisible wind, nourishing its everlasting course with strength and swiftness.

{**24**}  The poetry in the doctrines of Jesus Christ, and the mythology and institutions of the Celtic[8] conquerors of the Roman empire, outlived the darkness and the convulsions connected with their growth and victory, and blended themselves into a new fabric of manners and opinion. It is an error to impute the ignorance of the dark ages to the Christian doctrines or the predominance of the Celtic nations. Whatever of evil their agencies may have contained sprung from the extinction of the poetical principle, connected with the progress of despotism and superstition. Men, from causes too intricate to be here discussed, had become insensible and selfish: their own will had become feeble, and yet they were its slaves, and thence the slaves of the will of others: lust, fear, avarice, cruelty and fraud, characterised a race amongst whom no one was to be found capable of *creating* in form, language, or institution. The moral anomalies of such a state of society are not justly to be charged upon any class of events immediately connected with them, and those events are most entitled to approbation which could dissolve it most expeditiously. It is unfortunate for those who cannot distinguish words from thoughts, that many of these anomalies have been incorporated into our popular religion.

{**25**}  It was not until the eleventh century that the effects of the poetry of the Christian and Chivalric systems began to manifest themselves. The principle of equality had been discovered and applied by Plato in his Republic, as the theoretical rule of the mode in which the materials of pleasure and of power produced by the common skill and labour of human beings ought to be distributed among them. The

7. Shakespeare, *Macbeth*, III.ii.50–53.
8. Shelley uses "Celt" and "Celtic" in their original Greek meaning: barbarian tribes to the north of the classical Mediterranean civilizations.

limitations of this rule were asserted by him to be determined only by the sensibility of each, or the utility to result to all. Plato, following the doctrines of Timæus and Pythagoras, taught also a moral and intellectual system of doctrine comprehending at once the past, the present, and the future condition of man.[9] Jesus Christ divulged the sacred and eternal truths contained in these views to mankind, and Christianity, in its abstract purity, became the exoteric expression of the esoteric doctrines of the poetry and wisdom of antiquity. The incorporation of the Celtic nations with the exhausted population of the South, impressed upon it the figure of the poetry existing in their mythology and institutions. The result was a sum of the action and reaction of all the causes included in it; for it may be assumed as a maxim that no nation or religion can supersede any other without incorporating into itself a portion of that which it supersedes. The abolition of personal and domestic slavery, and the emancipation of women from a great part of the degrading restraints of antiquity were among the consequences of these events.

{26}   The abolition of personal slavery is the basis of the highest political hope that it can enter into the mind of man to conceive. The freedom of women produced the poetry of sexual love. Love became a religion, the idols of whose worship were ever present. It was as if the statues of Apollo and the Muses had been endowed with life and motion and had walked forth among their worshippers; so that earth became peopled by the inhabitants of a diviner world. The familiar appearance and proceedings of life became wonderful and heavenly; and a paradise was created as out of the wrecks of Eden. And as this creation itself is poetry, so its creators were poets; and language was the instrument of their art: "Galeotto fù il libro, e chi lo scrisse."[1] The Provençal Trouveurs, or inventors, preceded Petrarch, whose verses are as spells, which unseal the inmost enchanted fountains of the delight which is in the grief of Love. It is impossible to feel them without becoming a portion of that beauty which we contemplate: it were superfluous to explain how the gentleness and the elevation of mind connected with these sacred emotions can render men more amiable, more generous, and wise, and lift them out of the dull vapours of the little world of self. Dante understood the secret things of love even more than Petrarch. His *Vita Nuova* is an inexhaustible fountain of purity of sentiment and language: it is the idealized history of that period, and those intervals of his life which were dedicated to love. His apotheosis of Beatrice in Paradise and the gradations of his own

9. Pythagoras (fl. ca. 530 B.C.), a Greek from Samos, founded a religio-philosophical sect at Crotona in southern Italy, which was influential in ancient thought in mathematics, music, science, morals, and religion. The Timaeus mentioned here was probably Pythagoras' pupil, who wrote a (still extant) treatise on the nature and soul of the world.
1. "Gallehaut [Galahad] was the book and he who wrote it" (Dante, *Inferno*, V.137). In medieval romances Lancelot and Guinevere began their adultery after being introduced by Galahad; Dante and other Italians therefore used Galahad's name (as English-speaking readers use Pandarus) to signify any go-between—in this case, the book that Paolo and Francesca read together—that facilitates an illicit romance.

love and her loveliness, by which as by steps he feigns himself to have
ascended to the throne of the Supreme Cause, is the most glorious
imagination of modern poetry. The acutest critics have justly reversed
the judgement of the vulgar, and the order of the great acts of the
"Divine Drama," in the measure of the admiration which they accord
to the Hell, Purgatory and Paradise. The latter is a perpetual hymn of
ever-lasting love. Love, which found a worthy poet in Plato alone of
all the antients, has been celebrated by a chorus of the greatest writers
of the renovated world; and the music has penetrated the caverns of
society, and its echoes still drown the dissonance of arms and superstition. At successive intervals, Ariosto, Tasso, Shakespeare, Spenser,
Calderon, Rousseau, and the great writers of our own age, have celebrated the dominion of love, planting as it were trophies in the human
mind of that sublimest victory over sensuality and force. The true relation borne to each other by the sexes into which human kind is
distributed has become less misunderstood; and if the error which
confounded diversity with inequality of the powers of the two sexes
has become partially recognized in the opinions and institutions of
modern Europe, we owe this great benefit to the worship of which
Chivalry was the law, and poets the prophets.

{27}    The poetry of Dante may be considered as the bridge thrown
over the stream of time, which unites the modern and antient world.
The distorted notions of invisible things which Dante and his rival
Milton have idealized, are merely the mask and the mantle in which
these great poets walk through eternity enveloped and disguised. It is
a difficult question to determine how far they were conscious of the
distinction which must have subsisted in their minds between their
own creeds and that of the people. Dante at least appears to wish to
mark the full extent of it by placing Riphæus, whom Virgil calls *jus-
tissimus unus*, in Paradise,[2] and observing a most heretical caprice in
his distribution of rewards and punishments. And Milton's poem contains within itself a philosophical refutation of that system of which,
by a strange and natural antithesis, it has been a chief popular support.
Nothing can exceed the energy and magnificence of the character of
Satan as expressed in Paradise Lost. It is a mistake to suppose that he
could ever have been intended for the popular personification of evil.
Implacable hate, patient cunning, and a sleepless refinement of device
to inflict the extremest anguish on an enemy, these things are evil;
and although venial in a slave are not to be forgiven in a tyrant; although redeemed by much that ennobles his defeat in one subdued,
are marked by all that dishonours his conquest in the victor. Milton's
Devil as a moral being is as far superior to his God as one who per-
severes in some purpose which he has conceived to be excellent in
spite of adversity and torture, is to one who in the cold security of

2. Riphaeus, whom Virgil's Aeneas in his tale to Dido called the "one man who was most just"
among the Trojans and whose senseless death led the Trojan hero to reflect that "the gods'
ways are not as ours" (*Aeneid*, II.424–27), appears in Dante's *Paradiso* in the Circle of the
Just: "Who would believe, in the erring world below, that Ripheus the Trojan would be in
this circle the fifth of the holy lights?" (XX.67–69).

undoubted triumph inflicts the most horrible revenge upon his enemy, not from any mistaken notion of inducing him to repent of a perseverance in enmity, but with the alleged design of exasperating him to deserve new torments. Milton has so far violated the popular creed (if this shall be judged to be a violation) as to have alleged no superiority of moral virtue to his God over his Devil. And this bold neglect of a direct moral purpose is the most decisive proof of the supremacy of Milton's genius. He mingled as it were the elements of human nature, as colours upon a single pallet, and arranged them into the composition of his great picture according to the laws of epic truth; that is, according to the laws of that principle by which a series of actions of the external universe and of intelligent and ethical beings is calculated to excite the sympathy of succeeding generations of mankind. The Divina Commedia and Paradise Lost have conferred upon modern mythology a systematic form; and when change and time shall have added one more superstition to the mass of those which have arisen and decayed upon the earth, commentators will be learnedly employed in elucidating the religion of ancestral Europe, only not utterly forgotten because it will have been stamped with the eternity of genius.

{**28**}   Homer was the first, and Dante the second epic poet: that is, the second poet the series of whose creations bore a defined and intelligible relation to the knowledge, and sentiment, and religion, and political conditions of the age in which he lived, and of the ages which followed it, developing itself in correspondence with their development. For Lucretius had limed the wings of his swift spirit in the dregs of the sensible world; and Virgil, with a modesty which ill became his genius, had affected the fame of an imitator even whilst he created anew all that he copied; and none among the flock of mock-birds, though their notes were sweet, Apollonius Rhodius, Quintus Calaber Smyrnaeus, Nonnus, Lucan, Statius, or Claudian,[3] have sought even to fulfil a single condition of epic truth. Milton was the third Epic Poet. For if the title of epic in its highest sense be refused to the Æneid, still less can it be conceded to the Orlando Furioso, the Gerusalemme Liberata, the Lusiad, or the Fairy Queen.[4]

{**29**}   Dante and Milton were both deeply penetrated with the antient religion of the civilized world; and its spirit exists in their poetry probably in the same proportion as its forms survived in the unreformed worship of modern Europe. The one preceded and the other followed the Reformation at almost equal intervals. Dante was the first religious

3. Apollonius of Rhodes (born ca. 295 B.C.) wrote his Greek romance-epic, the *Argonautica*, in Alexandria. Quintus Smyrnaeus (fl. ca. A.D. 375) was called "Calaber" because the manuscript of his *Posthomerica*, a fourteen-book Greek sequel to Homer's *Iliad*, was discovered in Calabria. Nonnus (fl. ca. A.D. 425–450) wrote *Dionysiaca*, a Greek epic in forty-eight books about Dionysus' conquest of India. (He was a favorite poet of Peacock, who in "The Four Ages of Poetry" labeled the classical "Bronze Age" of poetry the "Nonnic" age.) Publius Papinius Statius (ca. A.D. 45–96), a Roman court poet, wrote two Latin epics, the finished twelve-book one entitled *Thebais*, on the struggle between Polynices and Eteocles for Thebes. Claudius Claudianus (ca. A.D. 370–404) wrote a mythological Latin epic on the rape of Proserpine.
4. Romance epics of the Renaissance period by Ariosto and Tasso (in Italian), Luis de Camoens (in Portuguese), and Spenser.

reformer, and Luther surpassed him rather in the rudeness and acrimony, than in the boldness of his censures of papal usurpation. Dante was the first awakener of entranced Europe; he created a language in itself music and persuasion out of a chaos of inharmonious barbarisms. He was the congregator of those great spirits who presided over the resurrection of learning; the Lucifer[5] of that starry flock which in the thirteenth century shone forth from republican Italy, as from a heaven, into the darkness of the benighted world. His very words are instinct with spirit; each is as a spark, a burning atom of inextinguishable thought; and many yet lie covered in the ashes of their birth, and pregnant with a lightning which has yet found no conductor. All high poetry is infinite; it is as the first acorn, which contained all oaks potentially. Veil after veil may be undrawn, and the inmost naked beauty of the meaning never exposed. A great Poem is a fountain for ever overflowing with the waters of wisdom and delight; and after one person and one age has exhausted all its divine effluence which their peculiar relations enable them to share, another and yet another succeeds, and new relations are ever developed, the source of an unforeseen and an unconceived delight.

{30} The age immediately succeeding to that of Dante, Petrarch, and Boccaccio, was characterized by a revival of painting, sculpture, music, and architecture. Chaucer caught the sacred inspiration, and the superstructure of English literature is based upon the materials of Italian invention.

{31} But let us not be betrayed from a defence into a critical history of Poetry and its influence on Society. Be it enough to have pointed out the effects of poets, in the large and true sense of the word, upon their own and all succeeding times and to revert to the partial instances cited as illustrations of an opinion the reverse of that attempted to be established in the Four Ages of Poetry.

{32} But poets have been challenged to resign the civic crown to reasoners and mechanists on another plea. It is admitted that the exercise of the imagination is most delightful, but it is alleged that that of reason is more useful. Let us examine as the grounds of this distinction, what is here meant by Utility. Pleasure or good in a general sense, is that which the consciousness of a sensitive and intelligent being seeks, and in which when found it acquiesces.[6] There are two kinds of pleasure, one durable, universal, and permanent; the other transitory and particular. Utility may either express the means of producing the former or the latter. In the former sense, whatever strengthens and purifies the affections, enlarges the imagination, and adds spirit to sense, is useful. But the meaning in which the Author of the Four Ages of Poetry seems to have employed the word utility is the

5. "Light-Bearer," or morning star.
6. Shelley here challenges the growing school of radical reformers now known as "utilitarians," many of them followers of Jeremy Bentham (1748–1832), who argued that the goal of life was to provide the greatest quantity of "good"—always defined simply as "pleasure"—to the greatest number of people. Shelley here anticipates John Stuart Mill's interest in *qualitative* as well as quantitative elements in the calculation of pleasure.

narrower one of banishing the importunity of the wants of our animal nature, the surrounding men with security of life, the dispersing the grosser delusions of superstition, and the conciliating such a degree of mutual forbearance among men as may consist with the motives of personal advantage.

{33}  Undoudtedly the promoters of utility in this limited sense, have their appointed office in society. They follow the footsteps of poets, and copy the sketches of their creations into the book of common life. They make space, and give time. Their exertions are of the highest value so long as they confine their administration of the concerns of the inferior powers of our nature within the limits due to the superior ones. But whilst the sceptic destroys gross superstitions, let him spare to deface, as some of the French writers have defaced, the eternal truths charactered upon the imaginations of men. Whilst the mechanist abridges, and the political œconomist combines, labour, let them beware that their speculations, for want of correspondence with those first principles which belong to the imagination, do not tend, as they have in modern England, to exasperate[7] at once the extremes of luxury and want. They have exemplified the saying, "To him that hath, more shall be given; and from him that hath not, the little that he hath shall be taken away."[8] The rich have become richer, and the poor have become poorer; and the vessel of the state is driven between the Scylla and Charybdis[9] of anarchy and despotism. Such are the effects which must ever flow from an unmitigated exercise of the calculating faculty.

{34}  It is difficult to define pleasure in its highest sense; the definition involving a number of apparent paradoxes. For, from an inexplicable defect of harmony in the constitution of human nature, the pain of the inferior is frequently connected with the pleasures of the superior portions of our being. Sorrow, terror, anguish, despair itself are often the chosen expressions of an approximation to the highest good. Our sympathy in tragic fiction depends on this principle; tragedy delights by affording a shadow of the pleasure which exists in pain. This is the source also of the melancholy which is inseparable from the sweetest melody. The pleasure that is in sorrow is sweeter than the pleasure of pleasure itself. And hence the saying, "It is better to go to the house of mourning, than to the house of mirth."[1] Not that this highest species of pleasure is necessarily linked with pain. The delight of love and friendship, the extacy of the admiration of nature, the joy of the perception and still more of the creation of poetry is often wholly unalloyed.

{35}  The production and assurance of pleasure in this highest sense is true utility. Those who produce and preserve this pleasure are Poets or poetical philosophers.

---

7. *exasperate:* to make more painful, to aggravate (*OED* 2.b.).
8. One of the sayings of Jesus (Matthew 25:29; Mark 4:25; Luke 8:18, 19:26).
9. A legendary group of rocks and a whirlpool that flanked the Straits of Messina, between Sicily and the toe of Italy, and endangered ships (Homer's *Odyssey*, XII); the names came to represent dangers from any two opposite extremes.
1. Cf. Ecclesiastes 7:2.

{**36**}   The exertions of Locke, Hume, Gibbon, Voltaire, Rousseau,[2] and their disciples, in favour of oppressed and deluded humanity, are entitled to the gratitude of mankind. Yet it is easy to calculate the degree of moral and intellectual improvement which the world would have exhibited, had they never lived. A little more nonsense would have been talked for a century or two; and perhaps a few more men, women, and children, burnt as heretics. We might not at this moment have been congratulating each other on the abolition of the Inquisition in Spain.[3] But it exceeds all imagination to conceive what would have been the moral condition of the world if neither Dante, Petrarch, Boccaccio, Chaucer, Shakespeare, Calderon, Lord Bacon, nor Milton, had ever existed; if Raphael and Michael Angelo had never been born; if the Hebrew poetry had never been translated; if a revival of the study of Greek literature had never taken place; if no monuments of antient sculpture had been handed down to us; and if the poetry of the religion of the antient world had been extinguished together with its belief. The human mind could never, except by the intervention of these excitements, have been awakened to the invention of the grosser sciences, and that application of analytical reasoning to the aberrations of society, which it is now attempted to exalt over the direct expression of the inventive and creative faculty itself.

{**37**}   We have more moral, political and historical wisdom, than we know how to reduce into practise; we have more scientific and œconomical knowledge than can be accommodated to the just distribution of the produce which it multiplies. The poetry in these systems of thought, is concealed by the accumulation of facts and calculating processes. There is no want of knowledge respecting what is wisest and best in morals, government, and political œconomy, or at least, what is wiser and better than what men now practise and endure. But we let "*I dare not* wait upon *I would,* like the poor cat i' the adage."[4] We want the creative faculty to imagine that which we know; we want the generous impulse to act that which we imagine; we want the poetry of life: our calculations have outrun conception; we have eaten more than we can digest. The cultivation of those sciences which have enlarged the limits of the empire of man over the external world, has, for want of the poetical faculty, proportionally circumscribed those of the internal world; and man, having enslaved the elements, remains himself a slave. To what but a cultivation of the mechanical arts in a degree disproportioned to the presence of the creative faculty, which is the basis of all knowledge, is to be attributed the abuse of all invention for abridging and combining labour, to the exasperation of the inequality of mankind? From what other cause has it arisen that the discoveries which should have lightened, have added a weight to

---

2. "I follow the classification adopted by the author of the Four Ages of Poetry. But Rousseau was essentially a poet. The others, even Voltaire, were mere reasoners" (Shelley's note).
3. The Spanish Inquisition had been suppressed after the Spanish Revolution of 1820; it was restored in 1823 and finally abolished in 1834.
4. Shakespeare, *Macbeth,* I.vii.44–45.

the curse imposed on Adam?[5] Poetry, and the principle of Self, of which money is the visible incarnation, are the God and the Mammon of the world.[6]

{38} The functions of the poetical faculty are two-fold; by one it creates new materials of knowledge, and power and pleasure; by the other it engenders in the mind a desire to reproduce and arrange them according to a certain rhythm and order which may be called the beautiful and the good. The cultivation of poetry is never more to be desired than at periods when, from an excess of the selfish and calculating principle, the accumulation of the materials of external life exceed the quantity of the power of assimilating them to the internal laws of human nature. The body has then become too unwieldy for that which animates it.

{39} Poetry is indeed something divine. It is at once the centre and circumference of knowledge; it is that which comprehends all science, and that to which all science must be referred. It is at the same time the root and blossom of all other systems of thought: it is that from which all spring, and that which adorns all; and that which, if blighted, denies the fruit and the seed, and withholds from the barren world the nourishment and the succession of the scions of the tree of life. It is the perfect and consummate surface and bloom of things; it is as the odour and the colour of the rose to the texture of the elements which compose it, as the form and the splendour of unfaded beauty to the secrets of anatomy and corruption. What were Virtue, Love, Patriotism, Friendship &c.—what were the scenery of this beautiful Universe which we inhabit—what were our consolations on this side of the grave—and what were our aspirations beyond it—if Poetry did not ascend to bring light and fire from those eternal regions where the owl-winged faculty of calculation dare not ever soar? Poetry is not like reasoning, a power to be exerted according to the determination of the will. A man cannot say, "I will compose poetry." The greatest poet even cannot say it: for the mind in creation is as a fading coal which some invisible influence, like an inconstant wind, awakens to transitory brightness: this power arises from within, like the colour of a flower which fades and changes as it is developed, and the conscious portions of our natures are unprophetic either of its approach or its departure. Could this influence be durable in its original purity and force, it is impossible to predict the greatness of the results: but when composition begins, inspiration is already on the decline, and the most glorious poetry that has ever been communicated to the world is probably a feeble shadow of the original conception of the poet. I appeal to the greatest Poets of the present day, whether it be not an error to assert that the finest passages of poetry are produced by labour and study.

5. "In the sweat of thy face shalt thou eat bread, till thou return unto the ground; for out of it wast thou taken: for dust thou art, and to dust shalt thou return" (Genesis 3:19).
6. "No man can serve two masters: for either he will hate the one, and love the other; or else he will hold to the one, and despise the other. Ye cannot serve God and mammon" (Matthew 6:24; see also Luke 16:13).

The toil and the delay recommended by critics can be justly interpreted to mean no more than a careful observation of the inspired moments, and an artificial connexion of the spaces between their suggestions by the intertexture of conventional expressions; a necessity only imposed by a limitedness of the poetical faculty itself. For Milton conceived the Paradise Lost as a whole before he executed it in portions. We have his own authority also for the Muse having "dictated" to him the "unpremeditated song,"[7] and let this be an answer to those who would alledge the fifty-six various readings of the first line of the Orlando Furioso. Compositions so produced are to poetry what mosaic is to painting. This instinct and intuition of the poetical faculty is still more observable in the plastic and pictorial arts: a great statue or picture grows under the power of the artist as a child in the mother's womb, and the very mind which directs the hands in formation is incapable of accounting to itself for the origin, the gradations, or the media of the process.

{**40**}   Poetry is the record of the best and happiest moments of the happiest and best minds. We are aware of evanescent visitations of thought and feeling sometimes associated with place or person, sometimes regarding our own mind alone, and always arising unforeseen and departing unbidden, but elevating and delightful beyond all expression: so that even in the desire and the regret they leave, there cannot but be pleasure, participating as it does in the nature of its object. It is as it were the interpenetration of a diviner nature through our own; but its footsteps are like those of a wind over a sea, which the coming calm erases, and whose traces remain only as on the wrinkled sand which paves it. These and corresponding conditions of being are experienced principally by those of the most delicate sensibility and the most enlarged imagination; and the state of mind produced by them is at war with every base desire. The enthusiasm of virtue, love, patriotism, and friendship is essentially linked with these emotions; and whilst they last, self appears as what it is, an atom to a Universe. Poets are not only subject to these experiences as spirits of the most refined organization, but they can colour all that they combine with the evanescent hues of this etherial world; a word, a trait in the representation of a scene or a passion, will touch the enchanted chord, and reanimate, in those who have ever experienced these emotions, the sleeping, the cold, the buried image of the past. Poetry thus makes immortal all that is best and most beautiful in the world; it arrests the vanishing apparitions which haunt the interlunations of life, and veiling them or in language or in form sends them forth among mankind, bearing sweet news of kindred joy to those with whom their sisters abide—abide, because there is no portal of expression from the caverns of the spirit which they inhabit into the universe of things.[8] Poetry redeems from decay the visitations of the divinity in man.

---

7. ". . . my Celestial Patroness, who deignes / Her nightly visitation unimplor'd, / And dictates to me slumb'ring, or inspires / Easie my unpremeditated Verse" (*Paradise Lost*, IX.21–24).
8. I.e., all people have kindred visions, and even those unable to communicate them to others can respond to poets' articulation of their sister dreams.

{41}  Poetry turns all things to loveliness; it exalts the beauty of that which is most beautiful, and it adds beauty to that which is most deformed: it marries exultation and horror, grief and pleasure, eternity and change; it subdues to union under its light yoke all irreconcilable things. It transmutes all that it touches, and every form moving within the radiance of its presence is changed by wondrous sympathy to an incarnation of the spirit which it breathes; its secret alchemy turns to potable gold the poisonous waters which flow from death through life; it strips the veil of familiarity from the world, and lays bare the naked and sleeping beauty which is the spirit of its forms.

{42}  All things exist as they are perceived: at least in relation to the percipient. "The mind is its own place, and of itself can make a heaven of hell, a hell of heaven."[9] But poetry defeats the curse which binds us to be subjected to the accident of surrounding impressions. And whether it spreads its own figured curtain or withdraws life's dark veil from before the scene of things, it equally creates for us a being within our being. It makes us the inhabitants of a world to which the familiar world is a chaos. It reproduces the common universe of which we are portions and percipients, and it purges from our inward sight the film of familiarity which obscures from us the wonder of our being. It compels us to feel that which we perceive, and to imagine that which we know. It creates anew the universe after it has been annihilated in our minds by the recurrence of impressions blunted by reiteration. It justifies that bold and true word of Tasso—*Non merita nome di creatore, se non Iddio ed il Poeta.*[1]

{43}  A Poet, as he is the author to others of the highest wisdom, pleasure, virtue and glory, so he ought personally to be the happiest, the best, the wisest, and the most illustrious of men. As to his glory, let Time be challenged to declare whether the fame of any other institutor of human life be comparable to that of a poet. That he is the wisest, the happiest, and the best, inasmuch as he is a poet, is equally incontrovertible: the greatest poets have been men of the most spotless virtue, of the most consummate prudence, and, if we could look into the interior of their lives, the most fortunate of men: and the exceptions, as they regard those who possessed the poetic faculty in a high yet inferior degree, will be found on consideration to confirm rather than destroy the rule. Let us for a moment stoop to the arbitration of popular breath, and usurping and uniting in our own persons decide without trial, testimony, or form, that certain motives of those who are "there sitting where we dare not soar"[2] are reprehensible. Let us assume that Homer was a drunkard, that Virgil was a flatterer, that Horace was a coward, that Tasso was a madman, that Lord Bacon was a peculator, that Raphael was a libertine, that Spenser was a poet lau-

9. Milton, *Paradise Lost*, I.254–55.
1. "None deserves the name of Creator except God and the Poet." Quoted in Pierantonio Serassi's Italian *Life of Torquato Tasso* (1785).
2. Milton, *Paradise Lost*, IV.829. See also *Adonais*, line 337.

reate.[3] It is inconsistent with this division of our subject to cite living poets, but Posterity has done ample justice to the great names now referred to. Their errors have been weighed and found to have been dust in the balance; if their sins "were as scarlet, they are now white as snow";[4] they have been washed in the blood of the mediator and the redeemer Time. Observe in what a ludicrous chaos the imputations of real or fictitious crime have been confused in the contemporary calumnies against poetry and poets; consider how little is, as it appears—or appears, as it is; look to your own motives, and judge not, lest ye be judged.

{**44**} Poetry, as has been said, in this respect differs from logic, that it is not subject to the controul of the active powers of the mind, and that its birth and recurrence has no necessary connexion with consciousness or will. It is presumptuous to determine that these are the necessary conditions of all mental causation, when mental effects are experienced insusceptible of being referred to them. The frequent recurrence of the poetical power, it is obvious to suppose, may produce in the mind an habit of order and harmony correlative with its own nature and with its effects upon other minds. But in the intervals of inspiration, and they may be frequent without being durable, a poet becomes a man, and is abandoned to the sudden reflux of the influences under which others habitually live. But as he is more delicately organized than other men, and sensible to pain and pleasure, both his own and that of others, in a degree unknown to them, he will avoid the one and pursue the other with an ardour proportioned to this difference. And he renders himself obnoxious to calumny, when he neglects to observe the circumstances under which these objects of universal pursuit and flight have disguised themselves in one another's garments.

{**45**} But there is nothing necessarily evil in this error, and thus cruelty, envy, revenge, avarice, and the passions purely evil, have never formed any portion of the popular imputations on the lives of poets.

{**46**} I have thought it most favourable to the cause of truth to set down these remarks according to the order in which they were suggested to my mind by a consideration of the subject itself, instead of following that of the treatise that excited me to make them public. Thus although devoid of the formality of a polemical reply, if the views which they contain be just, they will be found to involve a refutation of the "Four Ages of Poetry," so far at least as regards the first division of the subject. I can readily conjecture what should have moved the gall of the learned and intelligent author of that paper; I confess myself like him unwilling to be stunned by the Theseids of the hoarse Codri of the day. Bavius and Mævius undoubtedly are, as they ever were,

3. Shelley, believing that Robert Southey, then the Poet Laureate, had slandered him in articles and reviews (see Kenneth Neill Cameron, *Shelley: The Golden Years*, pp. 428–31), here alludes to the laureateship as a post for hirelings and flatterers.
4. Isaiah 1:18.

insufferable persons.[5] But it belongs to a philosophical critic to distinguish rather than confound.

{**47**}  The first part of these remarks has related to Poetry in its elements and principles; and it has been shewn, as well as the narrow limits assigned them would permit, that what is called Poetry, in a restricted sense, has a common source with all other forms of order and of beauty according to which the materials of human life are susceptible of being arranged, and which is Poetry in an universal sense.

{**48**}  The second part will have for its object an application of these principles to the present state of the cultivation of Poetry, and a defence of the attempt to idealize the modern forms of manners and opinion, and compel them into a subordination to the imaginative and creative faculty.[6] For the literature of England, an energetic developement of which has ever preceded or accompanied a great and free developement of the national will, has arisen as it were from a new birth. In spite of the low-thoughted envy which would undervalue contemporary merit, our own will be a memorable age in intellectual achievements, and we live among such philosophers and poets as surpass beyond comparison any who have appeared since the last national struggle for civil and religious liberty. The most unfailing herald, companion, and follower of the awakening of a great people to work a beneficial change in opinion or institution, is Poetry. At such periods there is an accumulation of the power of communicating and receiving intense and impassioned conceptions respecting man and nature. The persons in whom this power resides, may often, as far as regards many portions of their nature, have little apparent correspondence with that spirit of good of which they are the ministers. But even whilst they deny and abjure, they are yet compelled to serve, the Power which is seated upon the throne of their own soul. It is impossible to read the compositions of the most celebrated writers of the present day without being startled with the electric life which burns within their words. They measure the circumference and sound the depths of human nature with a comprehensive and all-penetrating spirit, and they are themselves perhaps the most sincerely astonished at its manifestations, for it is less their spirit than the spirit of the age. Poets are the hierophants of an unapprehended inspiration, the mirrors of the gigantic shadows which futurity casts upon the present, the words which express what they understand not, the trumpets which sing to battle and feel not what they inspire: the influence which is moved not, but moves. Poets are the unacknowledged legislators of the World.

---

5. Codrus (author of the *Thesiad*), Bavius, and Maevius were inferior Latin poets castigated by Juvenal, Virgil, and Horace.
6. Though no draft for this projected second part survives, Shelley probably had clear ideas that he was prepared to set down if encouraged by Ollier or a public response.

# CRITICISM

# Shelley's Reputation Before 1960: A Sketch

Readers will better understand the tone and focus of some of the selections from recent criticism reprinted below if they have in mind the issues raised during the rise and fall of Shelley's reputation between about 1860 and 1960. The struggle to establish Shelley's poetic reputation after his death in 1822[1] was led initially by Mary W. Shelley and Shelley's close friends Leigh Hunt and Thomas Medwin. Beginning in the late 1820s and carrying through the 1840s, this cause was taken up by such younger writers as Alfred Tennyson and his friends in the Cambridge Apostles group and, independently, by Robert Browning and members of his circle. By the 1860s, poets and artists associated with Dante Gabriel Rossetti and the Pre-Raphaelite Brotherhood—particularly William Michael Rossetti and Algernon Swinburne—added their voices, and during the 1870s W. M. Rossetti and Harry Buxton Forman critically reedited the texts of Shelley's poetry and prose. As a result of these efforts, by the 1880s Shelley was not only accepted as a canonical poet, but he was much revered by a plethora of minor literary figures.[2]

Any passionate orthodoxy will breed dissent, and Matthew Arnold was one of the first of the major Victorian writers to suggest that Shelley was not quite up to High Victorian standards. During Arnold's honeymoon in France and Italy in 1851—in a poem that, seen in retrospect, marked his withdrawal from poetry—he characterized the careers of Byron and Shelley as essentially useless to society:

> What helps it now, that Byron bore,
> With haughty scorn which mocked the smart,
> Through Europe to the Ætolian shore
> The pageant of his bleeding heart?
> That thousands counted every groan,
> And Europe made his woe their own?

1. The reviews of Shelley's works published during his lifetime are available in *RR*, Part C, and Newman Ivey White's *The Unextinguished Hearth* (Durham, NC: Duke University Press, 1938).
2. For a readable full-length account of the vissitudes of Shelley's reputation, see Sylva Norman, *The Flight of the Skylark: The Development of Shelley's Reputation* (Norman: University of Oklahoma Press, 1954), as well as "Dip of the Skylark" (*KSJ* IX [1960]: 10–13), an amusing coda in which Carl Woodring discusses the (mostly) negative views of Shelley found in fiction and plays after the First World War, such as that articulated by a character in Aldous Huxley's *Point Counter Point* (1928) to whom Shelley was "only a kind of fairy slug with the sexual appetites of a schoolboy."

What boots it, Shelley! that the breeze
Carried thy lovely wail away,
Musical through Italian trees
Which fringe thy soft blue Spezzian bay?
Inheritors of thy distress
Have restless hearts one throb the less?[3]

Shortly before Arnold's death, there appeared his review-article of Edward Dowden's *The Life of Percy Bysshe Shelley*,[4] the official biography based on the archives collected at Boscombe Manor by Mary Shelley and her son, Sir Percy Florence Shelley—i.e., the bulk of the Shelleyan books and papers now at the Bodleian Library, Oxford. Arnold first recalled how he had loved the poetry of Shelley and the sense of his life and personality found in Mary Shelley's notes to her editions of 1839–40. He went on to regret that Dowden's more detailed biography made him realize that, though Shelley meant well, he was a very flawed individual. Yet, Arnold writes, "I propose to mark firmly what is ridiculous and odious in the Shelley brought to light by the new materials, and then to show that our former beautiful and lovable Shelley nevertheless survives." Like Mark Twain, whose later essay on Dowden's biography compared it to a "literary cake-walk,"[5] Arnold felt particularly pained by its account of how Shelley abandoned Harriet Westbrook Shelley and his young daughter Ianthe, as well as by Dowden's strained rationalization of Shelley's behavior leading up to the suicides of Harriet and Mary Shelley's half-sister Fanny [Imlay] Godwin. Arnold attributes some of Shelley's errors to the poet's "inflammability" around women and other flaws to the bad influence of the poet's companions: of the Godwins, Leigh Hunt, Shelley's father, "and Lord Byron with his deep grain of coarseness, his affectation, his brutal selfishness" Arnold famously exclaims, "What a set! what a world!" The concluding paragraph of the review, ostensibly intended to rehabilitate Shelley's image, as Arnold had promised in his opening, instead ends with an aphorism that was to haunt Shelley's reputation for decades:

> To all this we have to add the charm of the man's writings—of Shelley's poetry. It is his poetry, above everything else, which for many people establishes that he is an angel. Of his poetry I have not space now to speak. But let no one suppose that a want of humour and a self-delusion such as Shelley's have no effect upon a man's poetry. The man Shelley, in very truth, is not entirely sane, and Shelley's poetry is not entirely sane either. The Shelley of actual life is a vision of beauty and radiance, indeed,

---

3. "Stanzas from the Grande Chartreuse," lines 133–44.
4. "Shelley," *The Nineteenth Century* XXIII (Jan. 1888): 23–29. This essay was reprinted in two other periodicals in 1888 and republished posthumously in Arnold's *Essays in Criticism, Second Series* (London: Macmillan, 1888), pp. 205–52.
5. Samuel Clemens's essay "In Defense of Harriet Shelley" appeared in three parts in *The North American Review* in July, August, and September 1894 and was reprinted in *How to Tell a Story and Other Essays* (New York: Harper & Brothers, 1897).

but availing nothing, effecting nothing. And in poetry, no less than in life, he is "a beautiful *and ineffectual* angel, beating in the void his luminous wings in vain."[6]

Arnold's characterization (as well as later remarks by the Roman Catholic writer G. K. Chesterton) was belatedly challenged in the memoirs of Henry Salt, a pioneer socialist, vegetarian, animal rights advocate, and member of the Shelley Society in the 1880s, though with evidence unlikely to win Shelley many friends among the more conservative members of British society:

> In mentioning . . . poets . . . I come last to Shelley, the poet who in my estimation has always been the first. As I have said, it was in my school-days that I heard of him; then through Mr. Kegan Paul, who was a friend of Sir Percy and Lady Shelley, I learnt more and more of his life, and found myself writing articles and books to show that, far from being the "ineffectual angel" of Matthew Arnold's foolish epigram, he had a very precious and important message for his fellow-men. This brought me into conflict with many prominent writers, among others with Mr. G. K. Chesterton, who had said that Shelley's work amounted "to a great epic about an inspiring example of nothing in particular that was done nowhere in particular at no particular time."
>
> Our difference, according to Mr. Chesterton, lay in my regarding Shelley as a pioneer rather than a poet; as a fact I regarded him as *both*. The poet is much the greater; but it is no slur on the poet to credit him with a clear mind as well as a skiey imagination. The early contemporary abuse of Shelley as a "fiend-writer" was hardly more foolish than the later apologetic view, in which he was depicted as an amiable visionary who knew not what he did.
>
> This is what Eleanor Marx, daughter of Karl Marx, wrote to me (in a letter of 1892) of the great part which Shelley's poetry played in the Chartist movement: "I have heard my father and Engels again and again speak of this; and I have heard the same from the many Chartists it has been my good fortune to know as a child and young girl—Ernest Jones, Richard Moore, the Watsons, George Julian Harney, and others. Only a very few months ago, I heard Harney and Engels talking of the Chartist times, and of the Byron and especially Shelley-worship of the Chartists; and on Sunday last Engels said: 'Oh, we all knew Shelley by heart then.' Surely to have been one of the inspirers of such a movement isn't bad for an 'ineffectual angel' and 'dreamer'."[7]

---

6. Arnold places quotation marks around this aphorism because he had earlier used it in his essay "Byron," published in *MacMillan's Magazine* XLIII (Mar. 1881): 367–77, seven years before his review of Dowden's Shelley biography: "But these two, Wordsworth and Byron, stand, it seems to me, first and pre-eminent in actual performance, a glorious pair, among the English poets of this century. . . . I for my part can never even think of equalling with them any other of their contemporaries;—either Coleridge, poet and philosopher wrecked in a mist of opium; or Shelley, beautiful and ineffectual angel, beating in the void his luminous wings in vain" (p. 377).

7. Henry S. Salt, *Company I Have Kept* (London: George Allen & Unwin, 1930), pp. 49–51.

Such major writers and thinkers as George Bernard Shaw, William Butler Yeats, and George Santayana also defended Shelley, but in contradictory ways, while each conceded the truth of some of the charges leveled at his character by his detractors. For Yeats, Shelley exhibited a great mythopoetic imagination and metrical genius and, withdrawn from contemporary society, drew his poetic imagery from the deepest wells of the racial memory to reveal mystical truths. For Shaw, a Fabian socialist like his friend Salt, Shelley's greatness lay, on the contrary, in his clear-sighted understanding of the social and political workings of British society, as well as in his enthusiasm for vegetarianism, atheism, women's rights, and other causes dear to Shaw, who believed *Queen Mab* to be Shelley's greatest poem. In his "Epistle Dedicatory" to *Man and Superman* (1903), Shaw distinguished between "normal" writers (epitomized by Shakespeare and Dickens) and his own "peculiar" culture-heroes, who included Bunyan, Blake, the artists Hogarth and Turner, Goethe, Shelley, Schopenhauer, Wagner, Ibsen, William Morris, Tolstoy, and Nietzsche—all of whom, he implies, carried to the level of quasi-religious fanaticism their efforts to change society radically. Shaw had articulated his views on Shelley even more emphatically in 1892, during the celebration of the centennial of Shelley's birth. When invited to speak at ceremonies to be held at Horsham, Sussex, to support the building of a free library in the poet's honor, he refused, with this explanation:

> If I spoke at Horsham I should say that the Shelley library was the damnedest nonsense from the Shelleyan point of view . . . [unless] it contained, as it ought, the most complete collection outside the British Museum of works on Atheism, Free Love, Republicanism, Socialism and the like. The whole affair will simply be a conspiracy to persuade the silly Sussexers that Shelley was a model Churchman & country gentleman who attained great distinction in literature. If there is one man in the district who has the gumption to get up and ask the audience whether they know that Shelley was expelled from Oxford as an atheist, and that he ran away from his wife with the daughter of an atheist anarchist, and that he taught that it was just as natural for a man to sleep with his own sister as with any other woman, your library will come tumbling down around your ears before the foundation stone is laid.[8]

Yeats, on the other hand, rejected Shelley as a revolutionary thinker. He speaks of having been told by "a learned scholar" (probably Edward Dowden, who as Professor of English at Trinity College, Dublin, befriended Yeats early in his career) that *Prometheus Unbound* "was Godwin's *Political Justice* put into rhyme, and that Shelley was a crude revolutionist, and believed that the overturning of kings and priests

---

8. *Bernard Shaw: Collected Letters, 1874–1897*, ed. Dan H. Laurence (New York: Dodd, Mead & Co., 1965), p. 352. See also Shaw's essay "Shaming the Devil about Shelley," *The Albemarle* II (Sept. 1892): 91–98; reprinted in *Pen Portraits and Reviews* (London: Constable, 1932), pp. 236–46.

would regenerate mankind." Yeats himself, however, "had hoped that my fellow-students would have studied [*Prometheus Unbound*] as a sacred book," and he wrote his long two-part essay entitled "The Philosophy of Shelley's Poetry" to explain the occult images and "ruling symbols" in Shelley's poetry that, he believed, "elude the ordinary reader by their abstraction and delicacy of distinction."[9]

George Santayana (1863–1952), the Spanish-born Harvard philosopher and critic, attempted in his essay "Shelley: or the Poetic Value of Revolutionary Principles" to answer the condescending tone of Dowden, Arnold, and other Victorian critics of Shelley. Santayana based his defense on the premise that Shelley's genius was entirely inner-directed, but he underestimated (like most of his contemporaries) the intelligence, learning, and worldly wisdom of the Romantics who had died young.

> Matthew Arnold said that Shelley was not quite sane; and certainly he was not quite sane, if we place sanity in justness of external perception, adaptation to matter, and docility to the facts; but his lack of sanity was not due to any internal corruption; it was not even an internal eccentricity. He was like a child, like a Platonic soul just fallen from the Empyrean; and the child may be dazed, credulous, and fanciful; but he is not mad. On the contrary, his earnest playfulness, the constant distraction of his attention from observation to day-dreams, is the sign of an inward order and fecundity appropriate to his age. If children did not see visions, good men would have nothing to work for.[1]

After the horrors of the First World War, ineffectual angels, Platonic souls just fallen from the Empyrean, and even playful and childlike innocents were no longer deemed admirable guides for human action, whether personal or social. The younger generation who had witnessed, or had lost friends in, that global carnage reacted against the easy optimism for eternal progress that (in spite of long-time protests by the avant garde) had become both the dominant social attitude and the official reading of Shelley's message. Shelley, who had been adopted as a mascot and model by the bland newspaper versifiers of the pre-war age, thus became an easy target for those intent upon introducing a new aesthetic sensibility into society. Traditionalists who were shocked by the free verse and stark imagery of T. S. Eliot's *The Waste Land* and the overt complexities of James Joyce's *Ulysses* contrasted Modernist writings with the beautiful images and rhymes of Shelley, Tennyson, and Swinburne, thereby further alienating the younger generation from the earlier poets. Thereafter, the condescend-

---

9. *Ideas of Good and Evil* (1903), pp. 90–141; reprinted in W. B. Yeats, *Essays and Introductions* (New York: Macmillan, 1961), pp. 65–95.

1. From *Winds of Doctrine* (London: J. M. Dent; New York: Charles Scribners' Sons, 1913), pp. 155–81; quotation, p. 175. Santayana regretted that Shelley did not have "time to read Spinoza—an author with whom he would have found himself largely in sympathy" (p. 173). In fact, Shelley not only read Spinoza early and quoted him in the notes to *Queen Mab* (1813), but late in life he completed a translation of one of Spinoza's major works, which he planned to publish with a biography to make Spinoza and his writings better known (see SC, VIII, 737–43).

ing attitude that had characterized detractors *and* defenders of the
Romantics by the turn of the century was taken up with greater hostility, as in these dismissive lines by John Crowe Ransom—academic
poet, Southern Agrarian mentor, editor of literary quarterlies, and de-
finer of *The New Criticism* (1941)—in his "Survey of Literature":

> Sing a song for Percy Shelley,
> Drowned in pale lemon jelly,
>
> And for precious John Keats,
> Dripping blood of pickled beets.
>
> Then there was poor Willie Blake,
> He foundered on sweet cake.[2]

The New Critics who targeted Shelley included both social and political conservatives such as Ransom, his Southern Agrarian disciples,
and Eliot—all of whom who disliked Shelley's libertarian ideals—and
a number of would-be practical reformers who (like Hazlitt in the
poet's lifetime) viewed Shelley as being so far ahead of the social norms
that he gave reform a bad name. In 1931, about the time that Eliot
described himself as a "classicist in literature, royalist in politics, and
anglo-catholic in religion,"[3] he declared in his Charles Eliot Norton
Lectures at Harvard that although during his youth he had been influenced by Shelley, he could no longer read him with pleasure:

> The ideas of Shelley seem to me always to be ideas of ado-
> lescence—as there is every reason why they should be. And an
> enthusiasm for Shelley seems to me also to be an affair of ado-
> lescence: for most of us, Shelley has marked an intense period
> before maturity, but for how many does Shelley remain the com-
> panion of age? I confess that I never open the volume of his
> poems simply because I want to read poetry, but only with some
> special reason for reference. I find his ideas repellent; and the
> difficulty of separating Shelley from his ideas and beliefs is still
> greater than with Wordsworth.[4]

After conceding that Shelley may have been gaining maturity ("in his
last, and to my mind greatest though unfinished poem, *The Triumph
of Life*, there is evidence not only of better writing than in any previous
long poem, but of greater wisdom"), Eliot added more negative opinions and, in support of them, quoted brief passages from Shelley's
poetry that he judged either intellectually "puerile" or else fluent verse
that is "just bad jingling."
Though these judgments were later surgically imploded by C. S.
Lewis's brilliant essay "Dryden, Shelley, and Mr. Eliot,"[5] the influence

2. From "Survey of Literature," in *Poems and Essays*, by John Crowe Ransom, as "selected, edited, and arranged by the author" (New York: Vintage Books [Alfred A. Knopf], 1955), p. 63.
3. *For Lancelot Andrewes: Essays on Style and Order* (London: Faber and Gwyer, 1928; New York: Doubleday Doran, 1929), p. vii.
4. These lectures were published as *The Use of Poetry and the Use of Criticism* (London: Faber and Faber, 1933); that entitled "Shelley and Keats" occupies pp. 87–102.
5. Lewis, *Rehabilitations and Other Essays* (London: Oxford University Press, 1939), pp. 3–34.

of Eliot's comments on Shelley was magnified both by his own reputation as a poet, then nearing its apogee as he converted to Anglo-
Catholicism, and by the qualified "Amen!" to his view of Shelley that
was soon voiced by F(rank) R. Leavis (1895–1978), then in his heyday
at Cambridge University as founder of *Scrutiny* and leader of a school
of young British anti-establishment literary critics. Leavis took up Eliot's superficial remarks and, like a patient teacher after a student has
answered a question badly, proceeded to explain to the world just why
Eliot could no longer read Shelley's poetry. After quoting a passage
late in Eliot's lecture that ends, "I can only regret that Shelley did not
live to put his poetic gifts, which were certainly of the first order, at
the service of more tenable beliefs—which need not have been, for
my purposes, beliefs more acceptable to me," Leavis continues:

> This is, of course, a personal statement; but perhaps if one
> insists on the more obvious terms of literary criticism—more
> strictly critical terms—in which such a change might be ex-
> plained, and suggests that the terms actually used might be found
> unfortunate in their effect, the impertinence will not be unpar-
> donable. It does, in short, seem worth endeavouring to make
> finally plain that, when one dissents from persons who, sympa-
> thizing with Shelley's revolutionary doctrines and with his ideal-
> istic ardours and fervours—with his 'beliefs,' exalt him as a poet,
> it is strictly the 'poetry' one is criticizing. There would also appear
> to be some reason for insisting that in finding Shelley almost un-
> readable one need not be committing oneself to a fashionably
> limited taste—an inability to appreciate unfashionable kinds of
> excellence or to understand a use of words that is unlike Hop-
> kins's or Donne's.[6]

After quoting lines 15–23 of "Ode to the West Wind," Leavis attempted to show that they had little precise meaning and that the
powerful effects of the poem resulted from what he characterized as
"[t]he sweeping movement of the verse, with the accompanying plan-
gency" (or, as Shelley's poem puts it—in words that Leavis did *not*
quote—"by the incantation of this verse").

> It is only the vague general sense of windy tumult that associates
> the clouds and the leaves; and, accordingly, the appropriateness
> of the metaphor 'stream' in the first line is not that it suggests a
> surface on which, like leaves, the clouds might be 'shed,' but that
> it contributes to the general 'streaming' effect in which the in-
> appropriateness of 'shed' passes unnoticed. What again, are those
> 'tangled boughs of Heaven and Ocean'? They stand for nothing
> that Shelley could have pointed to in the scene before him; the
> 'boughs,' it is plain, have grown out of the 'leaves' in the previous
> line, and we are not to ask what the tree is.   (pp. 204–05)

After a few more such assertions, Leavis climaxes this argument thus:

---

6. F. R. Leavis, "Shelley," in *Revaluation: Tradition and Development in English Poetry* (London:
Chatto & Windus, 1949), pp. 203–04; the essay occupies pp. 203–31.

Here, clearly, in these peculiarities of imagery and sense, peculiarities analysable locally in the mode of expression, we have the
manifestation of essential characteristics—the Shelleyan characteristics as envisaged by the criticism that works on a philosophical plane and makes judgments of a moral order. In the growth
of those 'tangled boughs' out of the leaves, exemplifying as it does
a general tendency of the images to forget the status of the metaphor or simile that introduced them and to assume an autonomy
and a right to propagate, so that we lose in confused generations
and perspectives the perception or thought that was the ostensible
*raison d'être* of imagery, we have a recognized essential trait of
Shelley's: his weak grasp upon the actual. This weakness, of
course, commonly has more or less creditable accounts given
of it—idealism, Platonism and so on; and even as unsentimental
a judge as Mr. Santayana correlates Shelley's inability to learn
from experience with his having been born a 'nature preformed,'
a 'spokesman of the *a priori*,' 'a dogmatic, inspired, perfect and
incorrigible creature.'   (p. 206)

Subsequently, in the "Letters to the Editor" of the *Times Literary Supplement*, several younger students and teachers of Shelley (including
G. M. Matthews) argued that Shelley's language in his "Ode" and
elsewhere is firmly grounded in realities of science and sense, as well
as moral philosophy, and suggested that Leavis was not always a careful reader of Shelley's poetic tropes. Nevertheless, Leavis's phrase
"weak grasp upon the actual" became a scourge that those who disliked
Shelley for literary, biographical, or ideological reasons used to flog
him.

As the Fugitive, Agrarian, New Critics in America (including
Cleanth Brooks, Robert Penn Warren, and Allen Tate) gained influence throughout the American academy, Shelley's reputation sank so
low that for over two decades only a handful of teachers and scholars
on this side of the Atlantic openly defended his competence as a poet,
and most of the students who wrote dissertations on Shelley (including
Floyd H. Stovall, Carlos Baker, Roy R. Male, C. E. Pulos, Milton Wilson, and Ross Grieg Woodman) went on to study American or Cana-
dian literature, rather than be typed as "Shelleyans." Henri Peyre
(1901–1988), who had written his French thesis on *Shelley et la
France*, was told not to mention Shelley when he interviewed for a
teaching position at Yale, lest he be thought to have bad taste in
literature.

The chief Shelleyans in America during the 1930s, 1940s, and early
1950s were Newman Ivey White of Duke, whose masterly two-volume
biography, *Shelley*, appeared in 1940; Carl H. Grabo at the University
of Chicago, who demonstrated that a number of Shelley's images were
drawn directly from the scientific literature of his time, his major study
being an intellectual biography entitled *The Magic Plant* (1936); Frederick L. Jones, who wrote essays on P. B. Shelley and edited the letters
(1944) and journals (1947) of Mary W. Shelley and of Shelley's friends
the Gisbornes and Edward Williams (1951), before capping his career

at Penn by editing *The Letters of Percy Bysshe Shelley* (1964); and
Kenneth Neill Cameron, a Marxist born in England, raised in Mon-
treal, and educated at McGill, Pembroke College, Oxford, and the
University of Wisconsin, who pursued the study of Shelley's political
thought in a series of major historical and explicatory essays in academic quarterlies before reaching a larger audience with *The Young
Shelley: Genesis of a Radical* (1950). Among the other Shelleyan studies published in America during this period, those of lasting value
included Ellsworth Barnard's *Shelley's Religion* (1937), still the best
analysis of this major topic; Carlos Baker's *Shelley's Major Poetry*
(1948), a series of critical readings of individual poems that surpassed
those in most earlier books; *Shelley's Platonism*, an expansive exploration of that topic by James A. Notopoulos, a professor of classics at
Trinity College in Hartford, Conn. (1949); and C. E. Pulos's *The Deep
Truth: A Study of Shelley's Scepticism* (1954).

These authors all helped to counter the fashion of making Shelley
a whipping-boy, a quiet rehabilitation that finally came to light through
a long process that Asia describes in *Prometheus Unbound*:

> the rushing snow
> The sun-awakened avalanche! whose mass,
> Thrice sifted by the storm, had gathered there
> Flake after flake, in Heaven-defying minds
> As thought by thought is piled, till some great truth
> Is loosened, and the nations echo round,
> Shaken to their roots: . . .                    (II.iii.36–42)

The years 1958–59 saw the publication of four major books that
heralded a new attitude toward Shelley. Most important was Earl R.
Wasserman's *The Subtler Language*,[7] which contrasted poems by Dryden, Denham, and Pope with "Mont Blanc," "The Sensitive Plant,"
and *Adonais*. Through detailed analysis of poetic structure, diction,
and tropes, Wasserman showed how the private symbolic imagination
of a Romantic poet necessarily differed from the more public discourse
of the earlier poets, who enjoyed a common cultural inheritance. Wasserman went on to write an important, if controversial, reading of
*Prometheus Unbound* (1965) before completing his comprehensive
masterwork, *Shelley: A Critical Reading* (1971). In *The Subtler Language,* Wasserman, who had previously studied the traditions of English poetry from the Renaissance through the eighteenth century and
had gained stature as a Romanticist with *The Finer Tone: Keats' Major
Poems* (1956), made the study of Shelley intellectually respectable by
applying to his poetry not only the close verbal analysis that the New
Critics demanded, but also a rigorous scrutiny of its relationship to
Western intellectual history, thereby elucidating both Shelley's sources
and the cultural value of his poetic mode. Wasserman demonstrated
what C. S. Lewis had earlier asserted when he wrote that those un-
prepared to give Shelley's poems "a fair hearing . . . may doubtless be

---

7. Wasserman, *The Subtler Language* (Baltimore, MD: Johns Hopkins University Press, 1959).

very worthy people, but they have no place in the European tradition."[8]

The second major book of 1959 was Lawrence John Zillman's *Shelley's Prometheus Unbound: A Variorum Edition*. Its 800 tightly packed pages collected the bulk of the textual evidence found in the intermediate fair-copy manuscripts in the Bodleian Library and in previous printed editions, as well as a generous sampling of commentary on every aspect of *Prometheus* from Shelley's lifetime till the early 1950s. Though not a far-sighted edition, Zillman's volume demonstrated how much valuable information could be assembled through patient and careful research; moreover, it proclaimed that Shelley, like Shakespeare, was worthy of such efforts.

Finally, two students of Frederick A. Pottle at Yale (who himself had written his Yale dissertation on Shelley and Browning and who in 1952 contributed a classic essay defending Shelley[9]) produced important books. The first, published in 1958, was a slim but significant bibliographical study by Charles H. Taylor, Jr., entitled *The Early Collected Editions of Shelley's Poems*. The second, in 1959, was *Shelley's Mythmaking* by Harold Bloom. Though Bloom's theoretical framework was questionable, his fine taste in poetry, his infectious enthusiasm for Shelley's writings, and his acute sense of how important life-issues are embodied in poetic forms made *Shelley's Mythmaking* a book to argue with that is more valuable than are most books to which one gives unqualified assent.[1]

Within the next decade there appeared numerous books and essays that took up the methods, issues, and attitudes unlocked by these studies—many of them in dialogue with Wasserman or Bloom. The new textual, biographical, and critical materials that began to be unearthed during this period provided additional evidence on issues—once ignored but now hotly debated—that proved to be crucial to later scholarship and criticism of Shelley. Thus the mere willingness to give Shelley's poetry "a fair hearing" was enough to produce the knowledge that raised the status of his writings to the high level that they now enjoy. The following selections from recent essays and books are a small but typical sample of the many excellent studies of Shelley's thought and art that have appeared during the past forty years. They have been carefully chosen and edited (with the cooperation of their authors) to save space so that we could include a broad representation of perspectives to help students and teachers approach Shelley's major writings. First are selections by some scholar-critics whose work

8. From "Dryden, Shelley, and Mr. Eliot," in *Rehabilitations and Other Essays*; as quoted in Reiman, *The Study of Modern Manuscripts* (Baltimore, MD: Johns Hopkins University Press, 1993), p. 144.
9. Pottle, *Shelley and Browning: A Myth and Some Facts* (1923) and "The Case of Shelley," *PMLA* LXVII (1952): 589–608.
1. One other book—Neville Rogers's *Shelley at Work* (Oxford: Clarendon Press, 1956)—deserves mention here. Though prone to errors in its transcriptions from Shelley's poetic manuscripts, it provoked a period of intensive study of the manuscripts in the Bodleian Library, leading to *The Bodleian Shelley Manuscripts* (*BSM*) and the *Manuscripts of the Younger Romantics* (*MYR*) series, which joined *Shelley and his Circle* (*SC*, begun in the mid-1950s) in providing photofacsimiles and/or detailed analyses of the bulk of Shelley's manuscripts, together with most of Keats's poetic manuscripts and a generous selection of Byron's.

helped lay the foundation for recent Shelley studies; these are followed by a section of general essays on Shelley and then by papers focused on his individual works. Other titles, including studies by other authors whose work was represented in the selections found in the first edition of *Shelley's Poetry and Prose,* will be found in the Selected Bibliography.

# Foundations

## G. M. MATTHEWS

## A Volcano's Voice in Shelley[†]

There is still a perilous tendency towards dualism in Shelley studies. Those preoccupied by the poet's "symbols" maintain, or assume, that what is worth attention on the profoundest level in his work is to be sought in domes of poetic consciousness, veils of unreality, and caves of gnostic power; Professor Grabo has made it clear that he regards even Shelley's use of science as ultimately mystical. Those concerned with his social interests, on the other hand, concentrate on biography and Radical theory, and will not touch the symbols at any price.

If this division is justifiable, it would mean that Shelley's Left hand did not want to know what his Right hand was doing; that while his prose mind declaimed about Reform, his poetic soul was quietly navigating up the Stream of Life towards the Bases of Being (whatever they are). A fair case has of course been made out for Shelley as a poor mixed-up boy. Yet his life and letters hardly give the impression that his over-riding interest lay in the lifehistory of the individual soul. It was poetry he chose, not metaphysics; and poetry intended (so he said) to cast what weight was possible "into the scale of that balance, which the Giant of Arthegall holds."[1] One of two things must be true: either the writer's political dedication, so often repeated, was essentially superficial and the "symbolism" proves it, or else the "symbolism" involves more than its interpreters suspect. I suggest, and shall try to demonstrate from one special field, that the latter alternative is the right one. * * *

* * *

During the mutual exchange of dreams in Act II sc. 1, Asia and Panthea discover the command to "follow" explicit in nature and in each other's eyes. Invisible echoes then invite them

> Through the caverns hollow,
> Where the forest spreadeth. . . .
> (II. i. 175–6)

† From *ELH* 24 (1957): 191, 204–28. Copyright © The Johns Hopkins University Press. Reprinted by permission of the Johns Hopkins University Press. The author's notes have been edited.
1. Letter of 26 Jan. 1819.

We need not hesitate to recognize these caverns as volcanic, since the
Echoes definitely tell us they are: the nymphs are urged to follow

> Through the many-folded mountains;
> To the rents, and gulfs, and chasms,
> Where the Earth reposed from spasms,
> On the day when He and thou
> Parted, to commingle now. . . .
>                                    (II. i. 201–5)

Without doubt Shelley had the 1794 eruption of Vesuvius—the last
before his own visit—in mind when depicting the path of the ocean
nymphs. The mountains above Torre del Greco (a village obliterated
in this eruption) he described in language closely similar to that of the
poem as

> covered with the rare and divine vegetation of this climate, with
> many-folding vales, and deep dark recesses, which the fancy
> scarcely could penetrate. . . .[2]

The forcible separation of Asia and Prometheus, therefore, either
caused, or resulted from, volcanic upheavals—presumably caused,
since Earth recalls the outbreak of "new fire From earthquake-rifted
mountains of bright snow" when Prometheus was first enchained
(I. 166–7).

As the pair approach these mountains, they enter "A Forest, intermingled with Rocks and Caverns"; here the lush exuberance of the
flora and fauna, the interwoven bowers and voluptuous nightingales,
have been criticized as excessive, but the lushness is neither fanciful
nor gratuitous. Asia and her companion have reached an area of volcanic fall-out, long famous for extreme fertility. Since classical times
observers had recognized that "the Campania Felice . . . owes its exuberant fertility to frequent showers of volcanic ashes,"[3] and those of
Shelley's letters which describe this area show that the passage was by
no means exaggerated. Shelley's scene is, of course, over-determined:
the mention of Silenus (II. ii. 90) suggests that Etna and Sicily were
also in his mind; but the clearest influence—and, indeed, the clearest
scenic influence on the whole of *Prometheus* apart from Act I—is not
Rome, but the area round Naples which Shelley explored with such
delight in late 1818 and early 1819, especially the Phlegraean Fields,
where, by some accounts, the Titans and Giants had fought their vain
risings against Jupiter. Lake Agnano and the Astroni crater had particularly impressed him: they were the first places he mentioned after
telling Peacock that the scenery surrounding Naples was "more delightful than any within the immediate reach of civilized man."[4] The
prose and the verse must be compared at some length to establish this

2. Letter of 25 Feb 1819.
3. *Edinburgh Review,* April 1804, 27.
4. Letter of 25 Feb 1819.

more precise connection. "They are both the craters of extinguished volcanos," Shelley wrote,

> and Nature has thrown forth forests of oak and ilex, and spread mossy lawns and clear lakes over the dead or sleeping fire. . . . [The Astroni crater] is a royal chace, and is surrounded by steep and lofty hills, and only accessible through a wide gate of mossy oak. . . . The hills are covered with thick woods of ilex, myrtle, and laurustirus. . . . The plain so surrounded is at most three miles in circumference. It is occupied partly by a lake, with bold shores wooded by evergreens, and interrupted by a sylvan promontory of the wild forest, whose mossy boughs overhang its expanse, of a silent and purple darkness, like an Italian midnight; and partly by the forest itself, of all gigantic trees, but the oak especially, whose jagged boughs, now leafless, are hoary with thick lichens, and loaded with the massy and deep foliage of the ivy.[5]

The effect, he added, was "of an enchanting solemnity." Here is part of the verse:

> The path through which that lovely twain
> Have passed, by cedar, pine, and yew,
> And each dark tree that ever grew,
> Is curtained out from Heaven's wide blue;
> Nor sun, nor moon, nor wind, nor rain
> Can pierce its interwoven bowers,
> Nor aught, save where some cloud of dew,
> Drifted along the earth-creeping breeze,
> Between the trunks of the hoar trees,
> Hangs each a pearl in the pale flowers
> Of the green laurel, blown anew . . .
> And the gloom divine is all around,
> And underneath is the mossy ground.
>                                    (II. ii. 1–23)

Shelley's cedars and pines may be Roman (or Spenserian) imports; but the ivy, evergreens, and hoar trees of the poem, the mossy ground, the gloom divine, the green laurel, all have counterparts in the letter.

The "clear lakes" of the Second Faun also derive from the scene of the letter. For this rich forest harbours the echoes (or exhalations) which draw (or drive) those destined to be agents of historical change towards the "fatal" mountain of Demogorgon. In it dwell nightingales, the "poets" or imaginative thinkers: among others, Spenser (in echoes of the opening canto of the *Faerie Queene*); Shakespeare (the opening of *Twelfth Night*); Milton (the opening of the *Nightingale* sonnet); probably Gray, whose *Progress of Poesy* had adopted the same idea of successive schools of poetry; perhaps the "frail form" of Shelley himself (the anemone). It is difficult to share the enthusiasm of Professor Grabo and more recent commentators for the scientific knowledge displayed in the dialogue of the Fauns, where it is suggested that the

5. *Ibid.*

spirits causing these echoes live in bubbles sucked up from lakes by the sun and return to the earth on shooting-stars. For one thing, what the sun raised from *live* conferva in *clear* water, according to Priestley and Darwin, was not hydrogen, but oxygen.[6] And for another thing, it was a mere poetic fancy by 1819 to suppose that hydrogen raised from the earth and ignited was the cause of meteors; Humphry Davy had indeed proved this to be impossible before the Shelleys left England.[7] Like much of Shelley's science, therefore, it did not intend to be scientific; and the passage was in any case interpolated so as to give time for Asia and Panthea to reach their destination.[8] But it is true that in popular folklore all kinds of similar exhalations continued to ignite into meteors, and were particularly common in volcanic country. Hamilton was told by the 1794 survivors of Torre del Greco that

> they often see a vapour issue from the body of the lava, and taking fire in air, fall like those meteors vulgarly called falling stars.[9]

Shelley would have seen gases liberated under water or mud in the Burning Fields, and possibly at Matlock Bath (which he must have visited on about 7 Oct 1813), and the passage is over-determined.

The volcanic tract through which the ocean-nymphs pass, then, corresponds broadly to the country near Naples, where, as a contemporary journal put it,

> we find . . . the whole territory . . . rough with craters, and fuming with exhalations; and near these half-extinct remains, we find the formidable Vesuvius resting from the work of desolation, and concentrating his energies for another overwhelming explosion.[1]

This association points a way through the complexities of the third Semichorus:

> . . . And first there comes a gentle sound
> To those in talk or slumber bound,
> And wakes the destined: soft emotion
> Attracts, impels them: those who saw
> Say from the breathing earth behind
> There steams a plume-uplifting wind
> Which drives them on their path, while they
> Believe their own swift wings and feet
> The sweet desires within obey. . . .
> (II. ii. 48–63. Locock's punctuation)

*Sleep*, in Shelley, is another over-determined concept which awaits investigation. It may imply what is now known as hibernization, an artificial state of cold insensibility, or a "detested trance" like that of

6. ". . . pure dephlogisticated air" (Erasmus Darwin, *The Botanic Garden*, IV. 195 note).
7. *Phil. Trans.* CVII Pt. I (1817), 75–6.
8. See C. D. Locock's note to line 64 in his edition of *The Poems of Percy Bysshe Shelley* (London 1911), I, 610.
   The episode seems to have been suggested by the dialogue of the Shepherds in Leigh Hunt's *The Descent of Liberty* (1815), Sc. I.
9. *Phil. Trans.* XVII abr. ed., 502.
1. *Edinburgh Review*, April 1804, 28.

winter; but *winter* is also "the winter of the world," an era of bondage or of apathy in the face of social injustice. This is why the West Wind wakened the Mediterranean from dreams of Roman grandeur and oppression; why the news of Peterloo (that "tremendous storm") roused Shelley as he "lay asleep in Italy" to write *The Mask of Anarchy,* and why in the same poem the working-men were summoned to "Rise like lions after slumber." "Those in talk or slumber bound" therefore means something like "those who are too shallow or insensible to heed the summons of history." I have tried earlier[2] to indicate the heavy overdetermination of the "plume-uplifting wind" that blows the destined along their path. Volcanoes had always been thought to contain caves, and to generate underground winds; where else could the lava come from, and how else was combustion to be maintained? "Omnibus est porro in speluncis ventus et aër," Lucretius remarked of Etna,[3] and the moderns supported him: "The immense quantities of such matter [as] we see above ground must necessarily suppose very great hollows underneath."[4] Hamilton had investigated the *ventaroli* near the base of Etna; possibly Shelley, too, had felt an underground wind in what is now called the Great Rutland Cavern at Matlock Bath. He certainly introduces volcanic winds and caves into his address to Athens in the *Ode to Liberty* (1820):

> The voices of thy bards and sages thunder
> With an earth-awakening blast
> Through the caverns of the past (80–2)

Of course, the "plume-uplifting wind" not only lifts the wings of the chosen and wafts them onward, but involves other volcanic associations: the *mofette,* like that of the Solfatara (illustrated with "plumes" in Plate XXVII of Hamilton's *Campi Phlegraei*); the geyser (illustrated in Mackenzie's book); the steam from hot springs (Bladud's springs at Bath), and so on. Fumaroles were commonly described as emitting "plumes," for instance in Captain Tillard's striking account of the birth of Sabrina Island in 1811, when the sea erupted jets of vapour like "innumerable plumes of black and white ostrich feathers."[5] Other determining factors such as the tricolored plumes worn by the French revolutionaries are important but irrelevant to this inquiry. The point is that the "destined" think they are doing as they choose, while they are really doing as Demogorgon chooses. This is a hard nut to crack for those who think Shelley abandoned his belief in "Necessity" as applied to the individual will; but he stated repeatedly, throughout his life, that "poets" are subject to coercive forces which they are powerless to evade, although they themselves form part of those forces. In the Preface to *The Revolt of Islam* (1818), he put it like this:

2. *Essays in Criticism,* July 1954.
3. *De Rerum Natura,* VI. 684.
4. Sir William Hamilton, *Observations on Mount Vesuvius, Mount Etna, and other Volcanoes,* 2 ed., 1773, p. 67.
5. *Phil. Trans.* CII Pt. I, 164.

. . . there must be a resemblance, which does not depend upon their own will, between all the writers of any particular age. They cannot escape from subjection to a common influence which arises out of an infinite combination of circumstances belonging to the times in which they live; though each is in a degree the author of the very influence by which his being is thus pervaded.

All artists, he said again two years later in the preface to *Prometheus* itself, being companions and prophets of social change, "are, in one sense, the creators, and, in another, the creations of their age. From this subjection the loftiest do not escape." And in *A Defence of Poetry* (1821), almost the last piece of prose he wrote, he reiterated that "Poets are the hierophants of an unapprehended inspiration" (i.e. the servants of an unconscious influence), that "even while they deny and abjure, they are yet compelled to serve the power which is seated upon the throne of their own soul . . . it is less their spirit than the spirit of the age."

It is an influence of the same sort that surrounds Asia and Panthea as they approach the realm of Demogorgon. Swept along by the movement of chance, they are borne like clouds to the fatal mountain. For it was observed of volcanoes that they not only generated their own "clouds of fire," but attracted more orthodox clouds from elsewhere. Breislak watched the 1794 eruption of Vesuvius from June to July, "and during that period," he declared, "every cloud that appeared on the horizon was attracted to Vesuvius."[6] In the same way the sound bears the sea-nymphs

> to the realm
> Of Demogorgon, and the mighty portal
> Like a volcano's meteor-breathing chasm,
> Whence the oracular vapour is hurled up
> Which lonely men drink wandering in their youth,
> And call truth, virtue, love, genius, or joy. . . .
>                                        (II. iii. 1–6)

It is hard to see why, in order to undertake what C. S. Lewis has eloquently called "this descent into hell, this return to the womb, this death,"[7] the two sisters should have done so much climbing. *Facilis descensus Averno.* And why seek a return to the womb on a dizzy "Pinnacle of Rock among Mountains"? To make the real position clear it is helpful to recall Shelley's letter to Peacock describing Vesuvius:

On the summit is a kind of irregular plain . . . riven into ghastly chasms. . . . In the midst stands the conical hill from which volumes of smoke, and the fountains of liquid fire, are rolled forth forever. The mountain is at present in a slight state of eruption; and a thick heavy white smoke is perpetually rolled out, interrupted by enormous columns of an impenetrable black bi-

6. *Edinburgh Review,* April 1804, 31.
7. *Rehabilitations,* 1939, 32.

tuminous vapour, which is hurled up, fold after fold, into the
sky. . . .[8]

We may note in passing that what alarms Jupiter, at the opening of
Act III, is that the soul of man ("like unextinguished fire") is busy
"Hurling up insurrection," just as the vapour is "hurled up" from Demogorgon's spiraculum and from Vesuvius itself. But the objective setting seems unchallengeable: the nymphs have been attracted
(impelled) to the terminal cone of a colossal volcano.[9] The pinnacle
of rock corresponds to the "conical hill" of Vesuvius, and the "oracular
vapour," like the earlier "plume-uplifting wind," patently flies the same
flag as the militant volcanic exhalation which, Shelley said, forced him
to write the *Ode to Naples*:

> From the Typhaean mount, Inarime,[1]
> There streamed a sunbright vapour, like the standard
> Of some aetherial host;
> Whilst from all the coast,
> Louder and louder, gathering round, there wandered
> Over the oracular woods and divine sea
> Prophesyings which grew articulate—
> They seize me—I must speak them!—be they fate! (44–51)

Later, in Demogorgon's presence, Asia's tongue will be loosened by
these *venti loquaces*. "When this divine inspiration has been conceived
in the virgin's breast," according to Lucan, ". . . it re-echoes, and opens
the mouth of the prophetess, just as the Sicilian peaks undulate when
the flames press upon Aetna; or as Typhoeus, buried beneath the everlasting mass of Inarime, roaring aloud, heats the Campanian rocks."[2]
Before becoming drugged by inspiration, however, Asia bids her companion admire the view ("ere the vapour dim thy brain"); and the description which follows has been recognized as deriving from the Alps,
where the poem was first conceived. Nevertheless, Alpine as it is, Asia's
description confirms the poet's intentions. "Beneath is a wide plain of
billowy mist," she says, "islanding the peak whereon we stand"—a peak
that is naked at the top (if we take the makeshift adverbs "midway,
around" as qualifying "encinctured"), but belted lower down by the
forest through which they had come. All round them and "far on high"
stand mountains, in such a way that "The vale is girdled with their
walls"—the idea of a *circle* being insistently enforced by the vocabulary: *islanding* the peak, *around*, *encinctured*, *girdled*. A familiar picture
emerges: a cone of rock in the centre of a luxuriant elevated valley,
encircled by a mountainous wall. One remembers the "circular vale"

8. Letter of 22 Dec 1818.
9. It is no objection to this reading that Panthea describes the realm of Demogorgon as "*Like
a volcano's meteor-breathing chasm.*" Panthea has not been there before, and does not know
whether it is a volcano or not; in the same way, Ione compares the moon to itself before
identifying it in IV. 206–13.
1. Inarime was an old name for the island of Ischia in the Bay of Naples, under whose volcano,
Epomeo, the Earth-born Typhon, or Typhoeus, was said to have been imprisoned after re-
belling against Jupiter.
2. *Pharsalia*, V. 97–101 (Bohn translation).

"surrounded by steep and lofty hills" of the Astroni crater. There is little doubt that Asia and Panthea are conceived as standing in a gigantic *caldera*, the bowl-shaped crater of a quiescent volcano with a tall cindercone in the middle. Both Astroni (splendidly illustrated in Plate XX of Hamilton, *op. cit.*) and Vesuvius are calderas, and although the latter was "the most horrible chaos that can be imagined" in 1818, Shelley had probably seen Bracini's description of it as it had been prior to the eruption of 1631, when boars were hunted and cattle grazed in the wooded crater. He is known to have read a guide-book which states—following Bracini—that at this time the summit "and even the hollow of the crater, was covered with verdure and forest trees, as *Astroni*, a long extinguished volcano, is at present."[3] Other regions may well have contributed to the scene: Las Faldas on Teneriffe,[4] for example, or Morne Garou in the Canaries, which is said to have had a moss-lined circular crater, with a conical hill in the centre and a terminal cone of granite-like rock on top, the apex emitting smoke.[5] The Alpine associations reinforce as well as modify the volcanic. The "sun-awakened avalanche," compared by Asia to the accumulation of thoughts in a great mind,

> till some great truth
> Is loosened, and the nations echo round,
> Shaken to their roots, as do the mountains now,"
> (II. iii. 40–2)

no doubt owes its existence to the avalanche Shelley witnessed in Switzerland, but the shaking of the nations round must refer to the collapse of Mont d'Anterne, which in 1751 had sent people "from Turin to investigate whether a volcano had not burst from among the Alps."[6] Shelley himself saw the fallen mountain the day after writing the letter.

Meanwhile Asia and Panthea are urged downward by a "Song of Spirits," one of which has burning "An azure fire within its golden locks." Grabo thinks, not unexpectedly, that this Spirit must be some kind of electricity, but it is more likely to be gaseous oxide of carbon, described by Davy as burning blue at the base of yellow flames, which—together with what the old mineralogists called "the inflammable breath of the pyrites"—was sometimes suggested among the causes of volcanic activity. Asia is now told that she must

> Resist not the weakness—
> Such strength is in meekness
> That the Eternal, the Immortal,
> Must unloose through life's portal
> The snake-like Doom coiled underneath his throne,
> By that alone,          (II. iii. 93–8)

---

3. J. C. Eustace, *A Classical Tour through Italy* (1812), 1818 ed., III, 40 note. Mary's *Journal* notes that Shelley read this work 3–5 Aug 1818.
4. *Geological Transactions*, II (1814), 293.
5. *Phil. Trans.* XIII abr. ed., 636–7.
6. Letter of 25 July 1816.

Earlier analysis has shown that Locock's interpretation of these lines must be correct: it is only by submitting to the wind of doctrine that the ocean-nymphs can assist the desired change. A reasonably close modern equivalent would be the Hegelian "freedom is the consciousness of necessity." The nymphs are guided, "As steel obeys the spirit of the stone," as the needle follows the magnet, but their submission to the influence is conscious and co-operative. A note to *Mab* had observed that "In the only true sense of the word power, it applies with equal force to the lodestone as to the human will."[7]

The "Cave of Demogorgon" is attained at last. In his metaphysical study "The Motivation of Shelley's *Prometheus Unbound*," B. Rajan observes at this point, with sudden disconcerting facetiousness, that "Demogorgon lives in a cave, because a cave is dramatically more appropriate than Bayswater."[8] But if Demogorgon inhabits a quiescent volcano, a cave is not only appropriate but unavoidable. Shelley had visited the Solfatara, Strabo's *forum Vulcani*, and had doubtless heard the guide thump with his stick on the hollow ground "thrown like a vault over an abyss of fire," and listened where "the workings of the furnace beneath are heard distinctly through it."[9] In this cave, Panthea senses Demogorgon as he sits enthroned:

> I see a mighty darkness
> Filling the seat of power, and rays of gloom
> Dart round, as light from the meridian sun.
> (II. iv. 2–4)

The reference to the infra-red rays discovered in 1800 was first detected by Grabo; but as unluckily often happens with Shelley's scientific allusions, no one has troubled to explain its relevance to the scene it occurs in. *Why* should Demogorgon emit infra-red rays? There is naturally only one answer—because he is extremely hot; too hot to be visible. It was known, in Herschel's own words on the solar spectrum, that "the full red falls still short of the maximum of heat; which perhaps lies even beyond visible refraction."[1] Demogorgon is, in fact, realized in terms of molten magma, the obscure and terrible volcanic agent hidden in the depths of the earth. His further connections with Milton's Satan, and with the Snake in Canto I of *Islam*, lie outside the scope of this article.

It is now time to inquire what caused the magmatic reservoirs to explode and discharge their contents, in the opinions of Shelley's contemporaries. Here the explanation of the ancients seems to have survived modern scepticism. Strabo and Pliny declared that volcanoes erupted when their caves were invaded by sea-water; and this theory was applied to Etna by Lucretius, whose influence on *Prometheus* is appreciable:

7. Note to VI. 198.
8. *RES*, July 1943, 299.
9. Eustace, *op. cit.*, II, 495.
1. *Phil. Trans.* XVIII abr. ed., 683.

Ex hoc usque mari speluncae montis ad altas perveniunt subter
fauces. Hac ire fatendumst et penetrare maris penitus percocta
in apertum atque efflare foras, ideoque extollere flammam sax-
aque suiectare et arenae tollere nimbos.[2]

Shelley had read an article in which Breislak (a Plutonist) was quoted
as stating that "the access of the waters of the sea" contributed to
volcanic activity.[3] There were doubters, admittedly, Humboldt among
them; and it was hard to conceive how sea-water could provoke an
effusion of lava; but the theory was generally accepted, and indeed,
according to *Chambers' Encyclopedia*, Breislak's cautious statement
would still have been acceptable in 1950. After the great eruption of
Vesuvius in 1794, Hamilton found

> that the majority of the people here were convinced that the tor-
> rents of mud and water, that had done them so much mischief,
> came out of the crater of Vesuvius, and that it was sea-water.[4]

Shelley himself believed that Pompeii had been overwhelmed by "torrents of boiling water" from Vesuvius.

It is clear what was to be expected, scientifically speaking, if children
of Ocean were drawn into contact with the magma of a volcanic
cavern—a violent eruption, accompanied by the classic symptoms:
earthquakes; mephitic vapours; the familiar pine-tree cloud; the bursting of a storm, with *ferilli* or volcanic lightning; and of course destruction—in this case final destruction of the heavenly dictatorship
which Demgorgon tells Jupiter,

none may retain,
Or reassume, or hold, succeeding thee.
(III. i. 57–8)

All these symptoms occur. First Asia breathes the divine vapour and
is inspired to be her own oracle,[5] until her ultimate question: "When
shall the destined hour arrive?" And at this point she is answered by
a volcanic explosion. The rocks are cloven; blackening the night, that
terrible shadow, Demogorgon, floats

Up from its throne, as may the lurid smoke
Of earthquake-ruined cities o'er the sea.
(II. iv. 150–2)

2. *De Rerum Natura* VI. 696–700. "From this sea subterranean caverns penetrate all the way
   to the depth of its throat. It cannot be doubted that by this channel a blend of wind and
   water from the open sea is forced into the heart of the mountain. From here it spouts out,
   shooting up flame, volleying stones and disgorging clouds of sand." (R. E. Latham's Penguin
   Books translation, London 1951).
3. *Edinburgh Review,* Sept 1816, 161.
4. *Phil. Trans.* XVII abr. ed., 502.
5. Asia's exasperating "dialogue" with Demogorgon only makes sense, and becomes dramatically
   satisfying, if it is realized that she is talking to herself. She is made to interrogate her own
   soul; and Demogorgon can supply no answer that she cannot supply herself at this moment
   of supreme prophetic consciousness, or for which she has insufficient knowledge even to
   frame the question meaningfully.

Any of a dozen accounts of major eruptions would serve to gloss this scene. I select one from Hamilton (Vesuvius, 1767) which Shelley may have read:

> . . . the mountain split; and, with much noise, from this new mouth, a fountain of liquid fire shot up many feet high, and then, like a torrent, rolled on directly towards us. The earth shook, at the same time that a volley of pumice stones fell thick upon us; in an instant, clouds of black smoak and ashes caused almost a total darkness; the explosions from the top of the mountain were much louder than any thunder I ever heard. . . . the pumice-stones, falling upon us like hail, were of such a size as to cause a disagreeable sensation upon the part where they fell.[6]

Shelley himself had seen identical "fountains of liquid fire" rolled forth from Vesuvius; and the Earth, who might be presumed to know a good deal of geology, was right to warn the Spirit of the Hour that the flight of its horses "must be swifter than fire." It would not do to be caught in the "bursting cloud" that overwhelmed Jupiter, like an eagle blinded by lightning and struck down by hail.

Apollo is held in heaven by wonder: the "sun will rise not until noon." The reason for the apparent anachronism initiated by this statement is that hinted at (but dismissed) by "B. V." in his amusing summary of the time-problems in *Prometheus*,[7] as anyone interested in volcanoes would assume at once. The sun is eclipsed by the eruption, and day "dawns" only at noon, when Jupiter has been overthrown. Pliny, Cicero, Seneca, and other classical authors read by Shelley had described a similar volcanic darkness. Breislak, a witness of the 1794 outburst of Vesuvius, wrote that

> At Caserta, more than ten miles from Vesuvius, torches were obliged to be used at mid-day, and the gloom was only broken by the frequent flashes of lightning which partially displayed the mountain. . . .[8]

Hamilton had shared this experience at Somma, where "the darkness was such, though it was mid-day, that even with the help of torches it was scarcely possible to keep in the high road."[9] Artificial night was an expected result of eruptions. In 1768 "the quantity of ashes ejected by the mouth of Cotopaxi was so great, that, in the towns of Hambato and Tacunga, day broke only at three in the afternoon. . . ."[1] Shelley had no first-hand knowledge of this phenomenon; but his night view of Vesuvius on 16 December 1818 perhaps contributed to his picture of the defeated Jupiter illumining heaven with "sanguine light" through the "thick ragged skirts" of the victorious darkness.

6. *Observations, op. cit.*, 26–8.
7. *Shelley, a Poem: with other writings relating to Shelley, by the late James Thomson* ('B. V.'), London pvtly ptd, 1884, 56.
8. Quoted by the *Edinburgh Review*, April 1804, 31.
9. *Phil. Trans.* XVII abr. ed., Pt. I, 502.
1. Humboldt's *Researches, op. cit.*, quoted by the *Quarterly Review*, July 1816, 461.

With astounding unanimity, critics have contrived to find that Jupiter's overthrow is an essentially peaceful process. "Tyranny always falls without a struggle";[2] "no real conflict is possible";[3] "Jupiter simply falls."[4] No doubt in these days of nuclear intimidation, respect for merely volcanic power may seem a little naive. Nevertheless, it must be allowed that a dispute which eclipses the sun and shakes the planets (possibly even the Milky Way) has its claim to seriousness. A hotter war could hardly have been imagined with the resources of 1819, though for the normal Aristotelian reasons its climax is not staged but reported. Perhaps the root of the error still lies in the old fallacy that determinism exempts its adherents from the need to act. In fact, Shelley's bloodless revolutionism existed more in his hopes than in his expectations, which were less optimistic; both his major pictures of social revolution involve catastrophic violence. "So dear is power," he believed at the time of writing *Prometheus*, "that the tyrants themselves neither then, nor now, nor ever, left or leave a path to freedom but through their own blood."[5] Nothing could be more explicit than that. A conflict was inescapable because the "tyrants" were habitually the first to resort to force.

The fall of Jupiter under a "bursting cloud" brings the concept of *volcanic activity* into close relation with that of the *storm*. Violent rains mixed with black ash, hail, and lightning, commonly accompanied volcanic eruptions. In that of 1794 Hamilton said:

> . . . the discharge of the electrical matter from the volcanic clouds during this eruption . . . caused explosions like those of the loudest thunder; and indeed the storms raised evidently by the sole power of the volcano resembled in every respect all other thunder storms; the lightning falling and destroying every thing in its course.[6]

Jupiter's thunderbolts thus provided a metaphorical connection between the concepts. "Sceptred curse," Earth cries later in the poem,

> Who all our green and azure universe
> Threatenedst to muffle round with black destruction, sending
> A solid cloud to rain hot thunder-stones,
> And splinter and knead down my children's bones. . . .
> (IV. 337–341)

Again the origin of these lines is likely to have been Hamilton and the 1794 eruption; his report for the 18th June includes this sentence:

> One cloud heaped on another, and succeeding each other incessantly, formed in a few hours such a gigantic and elevated column of the darkest hue over the mountain, as seemed to threaten Na-

2. Crane Brinton, *Political Ideas of the English Romanticists*, 1926, 169.
3. C. M. Bowra, *The Romantic Imagination*, 1950, 122.
4. Graham Hough, *The Romantic Poets*, 1953, 137.
5. *A Philosophical View of Reform*, 1819.
6. *Phil. Trans.* XVII abr. ed., 495–6.

ples with immediate destruction, having at one time been bent
over the city, and appearing to be much too massive and ponderous to remain long suspended in the air.[7]

The following day, "thunder-stones" fell near Sienna during a storm,
the biggest weighing over five pounds.[8] The affinities of these phenomena with the congregated might of vapours, solid atmosphere, black
rain and fire and hail of the *Ode to the West Wind* make it patent that
the sepulchral "dome" in that poem—a favourite word of Humboldt's
for the cones of the Cordillera—has its strong volcanic overtones as
well as its share of starlight.

## VI

Who or what, then, is Demogorgon, and what underlies this volcanic
symbolism, these "characters and mechanism of a kind yet unat-
tempted"[9] of *Prometheus*? He can scarcely be literally what he pre-
tends, "Eternity," though some have accepted the paragram at its face
value. This is rather as if an arrested rioter gave his name as "Swing,"
and saw it solemnly inscribed on the indictment. We must expect him,
naturally, to be an over-determined, not an allegorical figure, and his
interpretation is therefore limited to the aspects isolated in this study.
Several critics have felt Demogorgon to be uncomfortably alien among
the classical *personae* of the poem; D. G. James even says—almost
incredibly—that "at least, through him Shelley was able to fill up his
second Act."[1] But Demogorgon in his volcanic capacity is, in typical
Shelley fashion, at once a denizen of the Jupiter-Prometheus cosmos
and an intruder into it. His close affinity with Earth's "prostrate sons,"
who had revolted against Jupiter over the Burning Fields, is sufficiently
evident. Like these, Demogorgon is located at the bottom of a volcano;
according to one of Shelley's most admired authorities, his name cannot be mentioned without causing an earthquake;[2] and Jupiter himself,
in Act III, hoped to use the "earthquake" of his arrival for destructive
purposes, unless indeed this metaphor represents the irony of ignorance (contrary to traditional teaching, *Prometheus* contains brilliant
and savage irony). Demogorgon is accurately described in terms of
shapeless molten magma or lava; he erupts in order to overthrow Jupiter; and Jupiter's impulse, when he sees the danger, is to deal with
him exactly as he had dealt with the Titans and the Giants—that is,
to attack him with lightning and incarcerate him underground:

> Detested prodigy!
> Even thus beneath the deep Titanian prisons
> I trample thee!
>
> (III. i. 61–3)

7. *Phil. Trans.* XVII abr. ed., 498–9.
8. *Ibid.*, 503.
9. Letter of 6 April 1819.
1. *The Romantic Comedy*, 1948, 130.
2. "quo nunquam terra vocato Non concussa tremit"—(Lucan, *Pharsalia*, VI. 745–6).

Demogorgon's novelty consists in the fact that, unlike earlier rebels, he genuinely possesses the power to overthrow Jupiter, so that no figure named by Hesiod could have served Shelley's purpose. Shelley thought that his own contemporary society contained a force which was familiar and alien in the same way. He believed that since 1688 a new social class and ideology had been acquiring separate existence, destined ultimately to give the death-blow to political oppression, and he expressed this belief on many occasions, notably in the suppressed paragraph of the preface to *Hellas* (1821), and in *A Philosophical View of Reform*, from which, as it was written with the same impulse as *Prometheus*, my quotations are taken. After William III's accession, Shelley said, the number of "hands" increased greatly in proportion to that of the upper classes.

> A fourth class therefore appeared in the nation, the unrepresented multitude . . . the nation universally became multiplied into a denomination which had no constitutional presence in the state. This denomination had not existed before—

or, at least, had not been conscious of having independent interests. But as the growth of a middle class came to impose a "double aristocracy," intensified exploitation impoverished it and drove it to seek redress in an after-life, yet to its members

> The gleams of hope which speak of Paradise seem like the flames in Milton's hell only to make darkness visible. . . .

Shelley knew that in 1818–9 this class had few enlightened leaders, little organization, and no common plan of action, that it was, in fact, shapeless, with neither limb, nor form, nor outline; but he felt passionately that it was a living Spirit. "He believed that a clash between the two classes of society was inevitable, and he eagerly ranged himself on the people's side," Mary wrote in her note to his 1819 poems. It is likely, therefore, that scholars were wasting their time in pursuing the name "Demogorgon" to its unilluminating origins in Lactantius and Hyginus. Shelley was of the school of Peacock in his etymologies, as *Swellfoot* demonstrates, and it is impossible that the combination δεμος-γοργώ did not commend itself as one reason for the choice of name. To take the physical significance of Demogorgon any further within the limits set is hardly practicable.

The basis of much of the volcanic imagery in Shelley's mature poetry must now be clear. This is the perception of revolutionary activity in the external world and in the human mind—of irrepressible collective energy contained by repressive power. (Such a usage, it will be remembered, by no means prohibits others, including its opposite, that which implies despotic energy exerted against the oppressed). The Naples area presented a perfect mythological background. The classical tales of the risings of Earth's sons against Jupiter clearly record the volcanic upheavals that shaped the landscape in this part of Italy. Hamilton quotes an earlier witness as writing, during the 1538 eruption of Monte Nuovo,

G. M. MATTHEWS

"It appeared to me as if Typheus and Enceladus from Ischia and Etna with innumerable giants, of those from the Campi Phlegrei (which, according to the opinions of some, were situated in this neighbourhood), were come to wage war again with Jupiter."[3]

Hamilton used the comparison himself when his powers of description failed;[4] and the same tradition is to be found in many authors read by Shelley.[5] With his volcanoes, Shelley was really making use of a myth or "symbol" at least as old as *Exodus*, which has survived with formidable vitality into quite recent times.[6] There are, in fact, grounds for regarding the volcano as an archetypal image; which poses an interesting question for followers of Jung: how Collective is the Collective Unconscious?

It is understandable that the literature of the French Revolution should exploit this inviting analogy between social upheaval and the highly topical science of geology. Shelley must have met it early, in the Abbé Barruel's *Memoirs Illustrating the History of Jacobinism*, "a favourite book at college," according to Hogg, of which "he went through the four volumes again and again."[7] To Barruel, subversion appeared "to arise from the bowels of the earth";[8] the disaffected hid their purposes under "the black cloud . . . round the summit of the volcano,"[9] but "at length the erruption denotes the abyss where so great a convulsion was generated."[1] After the suppression of the Jacobins, warned Barruel,

The sect, weakened, may slumber for a while, but such a sleep is the calm preceding the irruption of the volcano. It no longer sends forth its curling flames; but the subterraneous fire winds its course, penetrates, and preparing many vents, suddenly bursts forth and carries misery and devastation wherever its fiery torrent rolls.   (I. xix)

Shelley's prose establishes beyond doubt that these associations were deliberate. When in 1821 the Holy Alliance mandated Austria to intervene against the rebels of southern Italy, Shelley declared that notwithstanding the soldierly advantages of the invaders,

3. *Observations, op. cit.*, 131.
4. *Phil. Trans.* XIV abr. ed., 618:—"It may have been from a scene of this kind, that the ancient poets took their ideas of the giants waging war with Jupiter" (11 Aug 1779).
5. E.g. in Pindar, *1st Pythian Ode*; and Bacon, *De Sapientia Veterum*, under "Typhon, sive rebellis." Shelley speaks of "many-headed Insurrection" in *Hellas*, 334.
6. The first line of the English version of the *Internationale*, "Arise, ye starvelings, from your slumbers!" was directly influenced by Shelley; the French original continues:

"La raison tonne en sa cratère,
C'est l'éruption de la fin!"
(Pottier, 1871).

7. Hogg, *op. cit.*, I, 376. The English translation in four volumes was published in 1797. Shelley was reading it again in 1814 (see Mary's *Journal* for 23, 25 Aug and 9, 11 Oct 1814).
8. Abbé Barruel, *Memoirs, illustrating the History of Jacobinism. A translation from the French of the Abbé Barruel* . . . 4 vols. (London: T. Burton and Co., 1797), I, x.
9. *Ibid.*, IV, 3.
1. *Ibid.*, IV, 356–7.

all these things, if the Spirit of Regeneration is abroad, are chaff before the storm, the very elements and events will fight against them, indignation and shameful repulse will burn after them to the valleys of the Alps.[2]

The image of the pursuing lava would perhaps go unnoticed but for the letter to Peacock a month later, employing less indefinite terms:

We are surrounded here at Pisa by revolutionary volcanoes which as yet give more light than heat: the lava has not yet reached Tuscany.[3]

It is useful to find the importance of Demogorgon's heat confirmed by this remark. Nor are these the only confirmatory passages in the prose. In weighing the chances of an Irish rising in 1821, for example, Shelley lamented that "there are no regular bodies of men in opposition to the government, nor have the people any leaders. In England," he continued, "all bears for the moment the aspect of a sleeping volcano."[4] Shelley's description of the vegetation spread "over the dead or sleeping fire" in the Astroni crater will be remembered. Some of the associations he attached to the concept *sleep* have already been pointed out; and a sleeping volcano carried a double significance. Demogorgon remained quiescent until visited by the sea-sisters. "In the world unknown," the Echoes had told Asia,

> Sleeps a voice unspoken;
> By thy step alone
> Can its rest be broken;
> Child of Ocean!
> (II. i. 190–4)

In other contexts the "sleep" of a nation or people might be broken by the summons or the inspiring example of a neighbor; and this idea, much cherished by Shelley, commonly involves imagery drawn from a related geological discovery:

> England yet sleeps: was she not called of old?
> Spain calls her now, as with its thrilling thunder
> Vesuvius wakens Aetna, and the cold
> Snow-crags by its reply are cloven in sunder:
> O'er the lit waves every Aeolian isle
> From Pithecusa to Pelorus
> Howls, and leaps, and glares in chorus. . . .[5]

These lines, with their pounding rhetoric and comically inappropriate visual evocation ("Volcanoes of the World, Unite!"), are scarcely among Shelley's best, but for contemporary readers the comedy would

2. Letter of 15 Feb 1821.
3. Letter of 20 Mar 1821.
4. Letter of 31 Dec 1821.
5. *Ode to Liberty* (1820), xiii. The Aeolian or Lipari Islands contain Vulcano and Stromboli; Pithecusa was another early name for volcanic Ischia.

not be quite so apparent. Only since Michell's impressive essay of 1760 had it been fully realized that the volcanic regions of the globe were interconnected, and could and did communicate at enormous distances.[6] The Lisbon earthquake had been felt in the mines of Derbyshire. Humboldt remarked in his *Personal Narrative* that in Chile and Guatamala "the active volcanoes are grouped in rows,"[7] and noted that those of Mexico, too, "are ranged in a line from east to west."[8] These and other facts led to a disturbing conviction

> that the subterraneous fire has pierced through an enormous crevice, which exists in the bowels of the Earth . . . and stretches from the Pacific to the Atlantic Ocean.[9]

Some thought with Humboldt that the world's volcanoes were ganged together along isolated crevices; others that they penetrated direct to the central fires;[1] but in either case the recognition permitted an alarming analogy to be drawn between international political subversion and volcanic activity.[2] It was this consciousness of interconnection that enabled Barruel to say of Jacobinism that "the subterraneous fire winds its course," and Shelley to write of the "contagious" fires of revolutionary sentiment; it explains why the curses of Laone's fellow-captives could be compared to "the voice of flames far underneath";[3] and why the Greek Captive Women in *Hellas* long to hear

> The words which, like secret fire, shall flow
> Through the veins of the frozen earth,
>                         (32–3)

until, as a messenger announces later in the same poem,

> Crete and Cyprus,
> Like mountain-twins that from each other's veins
> Catch the volcano-fire and earthquake-spasm,
> Shake in the general fever.
>                         (587–590)

Readers should be wary of referring every outbreak of "fire" in Shelley's poetry to the electrical fire of Beccaria or the occult fire of Ficinus: even his purest flame is apt to have some relish of damnation in it. Again it will be noted that his "tingling joy" extends equally to the earthquake and the eruption. For both, in his symbolic usage, repre-

---

6. John Michell, *Conjectures concerning the cause . . . of earthquakes . . .* (London: n.p., 1760), 454–6; 461–2.
7. *Op. cit.,* I, 200.
8. *Researches, op. cit.,* II, 103.
9. *Ibid.*
1. Erasmus Darwin held the latter view. See *The Botanic Garden* (1791), I. 141–2, and *The Temple of Nature, or The Origin of Society* (1803), I. 321.
2. "If we consider a burning crater only as an isolated phenomenon . . . the volcanic action at the surface of the Globe will appear neither very powerful, nor very extensive. But the image of this action swells in the mind, when we study the relations that link together volcanoes of the same group; for instance those of Naples and Sicily, of the Canary islands, of the Azores . . . or the distance to which, by subterranean communications, they at the same moment shake the Earth" (Humboldt, *Personal Narrative, op. cit.,* IV, 31–2).
3. *The Revolt of Islam,* VII. vii.

sent an essentially preservative and creative force as well as a destructive one. On a social and political level they connote reform, liberation,[4] the indomitable and united energies of oppressed mankind, besides the destructiveness and destruction of Jupiter. On a physical level they involve, as we have seen, the fertility of nature. More, they involve the creation or renewal of the earth. It is unquestionable that the "bright garden-isles" of *Queen Mab* and the "fortunate isles" of *Prometheus Unbound*, like the pumice-isles and *faraglioni* which Shelley had seen off the coast of Naples, are to be imagined as rising from the wastes of the sea by volcanic action.[5] Contemporary records of the birth of new islands, from Iceland to the Aleutians, are too common to enumerate, but the *Quarterly Review* justly observed that they constituted "the most recent act of creation in the western world."[6] Of the Naples region, Sir William Hamilton roundly declared:

> The more opportunities I have of examining this volcanic country, the more I am convinced of the truth of what I have already ventured to advance, which is, that volcanoes should be considered in a creative rather than a destructive light. . . .[7]

This attitude, it should be added, was thoroughly in accord with the most advanced geogenic theory of Shelley's day, that of Hutton, who thought that the continents and islands of the globe, worn continually down into the sea by attrition, were continually replaced by subaqueous material thrust up by volcanic fire. One might say that according to the Huttonian Hypothesis, the renaissance of the earth depended on volcanic change, and it would not be surprising if Shelley accepted this hypothesis in a literal as he incontestably did in a metaphorical sense.

VII

"It is a mistake," Shelley wrote in his preface to *Prometheus*, "to suppose that I dedicate my poetical compositions solely to the direct enforcement of reform." Present-day critics are perhaps less liable to this particular mistake than the writer anticipated; yet it *must* be inferred from Shelley's words that the poem is at least partly so dedicated. The pursuit of "symbols" can become an evasion of reality. Some of the poet's most energetic concepts have never been allowed their full significance in his work, and others have been examined too exclusively from a mystical point of view. The eruption, the earthquake, the volcanic dome, cloud, cavern, and fire, the burning fountain or *girandole*, the storm, the spark blown from the metallurgical "hearth" (a technical word probably picked up from Henry Reveley)—

4. Cf. *A Philosophical View of Reform*: "The great monarchies of Asia cannot, let us confidently hope, remain unshaken by the earthquake which shatters to dust the "mountainous strongholds" of the tyrants of the western world."
5. "Like rocks which fire lifts out of the flat deep" (*Ode to Liberty*, ix. 125). The name "fortunate isles" itself derives from Plutarch's name for the volcanic Canaries.
6. April 1814, 194.
7. *Phil. Trans.* XVI abr. ed., 134.

all these, and others, contribute to a meaning which has been more and more attenuated by specialized metaphysical assumptions. It would be falling into an equal error to claim that the volcano is the "key-symbol" of *Prometheus Unbound*, or that its recognition in the imagery and structure of the work exhausts the significance of the scenes discussed. Obviously many problems set by the poem are outside the present terms of reference, while others have been raised as a result of them. What is the relation of Demogorgon to Prometheus? Of volcanic to electrical energy? What is the purport on a social level of Asia's part in the drama? What modifications are necessary in the orthodox "moral myth" view, which presupposes a forgiveness of Jupiter which is demonstrably absent? These questions remain to be answered. What is obviously wrong, however, is to acknowledge on the one hand Shelley's passionate and lifelong interest in the progress of social relations, and on the other hand to study his major poetry as if its symbolism had no bearing except on the progress of the individual soul. Shelley's boyhood recognition of Intellectual Beauty was a simultaneous recognition of the social and political principles which, in his opinion, illustrated and indeed constituted that Beauty. Whatever full reading may be given to the great poems of 1818–19, it must, I am sure, remain constantly attentive to the principles Shelley regarded as central: the beauty and grandeur (to redistribute his own words) of the doctrines of equality and liberty and disinterestedness, which first determined him to devote his life to the inculcation of them.

# HAROLD BLOOM

## Urbanity and Apocalypse†

and where death, if shed,
Presumes no carnage, but this single change,—
Upon the steep floor flung from dawn to dawn
The silken skilled transmemberment of song.

HART CRANE

Shelley is a prophetic and religious poet whose passionate convictions are agnostic, and a lyrical poet whose style is a deliberate gamble with the limits of poetry. He is in consequence likely to remain controversial, but no single generation of critics will dispose of him. Of all the Romantics, he needs the closest reading, and a reading whose context ought to be found in traditions of poetry, and not in philosophy or politics. But the critical fate of his poetry has been obscured by allegorizers who have read it as Plato versified, or as an apotheosis of Godwin, his father-in-law and mentor in revolutionary theory.

† From "Percy Bysshe Shelley," in *The Visionary Company: A Reading of English Romantic Poetry*, rev. ed., by Harold Bloom (Ithaca, NY: Cornell University Press, 1971), pp. 282–84. Copyright © 1971 by Cornell University. Used by permission of the publisher, Cornell University Press.

Shelley drowned at twenty-nine, and made no single poem that shows all his powers working together. His major completed poem, *Prometheus Unbound*, was written a little too early; like Keats, he found his myth before he had matured his style. His unfinished last poem, *The Triumph of Life*, is probably as complete as it could be; like the two *Hyperions* of Keats, it resolves itself by breaking off. The *Triumph* has a more severe and finished style than *Prometheus*, but it is a work that attempts less, for *Prometheus* shares with Blake and Wordsworth an ambition to replace *Paradise Lost*. What distinguishes Shelley from Blake, whom he otherwise resembles, is the urbanity of his apocalypse. Usually intense, Shelley is yet always at ease, though few of his critics want to note this. Shelley's irony is neither the "romantic irony" of pathos, brilliantly manipulated by Byron, nor the "metaphysical" irony so valued in the generation just past. It has more in common with the prophetic and cyclic irony of Blake; like Blake, Shelley is always alert to the combative possibilities of interweaving an antinomian rhetoric with a dialectic that exposes the inadequacies of both the orthodox in morality and religion and any position that seeks merely to negate orthodoxy by an inversion of categories. But Blake's irony is always at the expense of some position, and is usually bitter. Shelley's irony is gentler and relies on incongruities that can suddenly startle us in the midst of the sublime without dropping us into the bathetic. Indeed, Shelley's urbanity is unique in literature in that it can manifest itself on the level of the, sublime. We can even say that in *Prometheus*, Acts III and IV, Shelley *civilizes the sublime*, and makes a renovated universe a subject for gentlemanly conversation.

The notions of urbanity and civility rely upon the image of a city, and Blake more than Shelley understands that a redeemed universe must be a city of art and not a garden of happier nature. But it is Shelley who has an instinctive sense of the manners of Blake's City.

When Blake gives us the complete trumpet rhapsody of his Last Judgment ("Night the Ninth," *The Four Zoas*), the aim of his astonishing invention is to compel in us a total response as exuberant as our creative energies can supply. Nothing can exceed the sense of a more human world that Blake gives us, but the solitary reaction within that world is one of exultant wonder:

> The roots shoot thick thro' the solid rocks bursting their way
> They cry out in joys of existence; the broad stems
> Rear on the mountains stem after stem the scaly newt creeps
> From the stone and the armed fly springs from the rocky
>    crevice
> The spider, the bat burst from the harden'd slime crying
> To one another: "What are we, and whence is our joy and
>    delight?"

In Act III, scene iv, of *Prometheus Unbound* the Spirit of Earth observes the renovation of mankind, as all ugly shapes and images depart upon the winds:

> and those
> From whom they passed seemed mild and lovely forms
> After some foul disguise had fallen.

In Blake this would be followed by something strenuous; in Shelley it flows on with an urbane rhythm, as the marvelous is civilized into the ordinary:

> and all
> Were somewhat changed, and after brief surprise
> And greetings of delighted wonder, all
> Went to their sleep again.

The "somewhat" is masterly; the "brief" not less so, and the concluding turn a triumph of gracious underemphasis.

This spirit of urbanity is so prevalent in Shelley that one learns to distrust the accuracy of any critic who finds Shelley's poetry shrill, without humor, self-centered, or exhibiting only "primary impulses." Ideologically Shelley is of the permanent Left, in politics and religion, and his morality insists on the right of private judgment in every possible human matter. He is nothing short of an extremist, and knew it; he says of himself, "I go on until I am stopped, and I never am stopped." Perhaps it is inevitable that so passionately individual a poet will always make ideological enemies. Nevertheless, it is to be hoped that such enemies will in time cease to misrepresent Shelley's poetry, and not continue to pretend to an aesthetic condemnation that is usually a mask for their own sense of moral and religious outrage.

# EARL R. WASSERMAN

## The Poetry of Skepticism[†]

It may well be that Shelley encouraged Mary to write her drama of 1820 on Midas in order to be provided with a pretext—and context—for composing the so-called "hymns" of Apollo and Pan that he contributed to it.[1] Ovid's tale of Midas and the singing contest between the two gods invites interpretation as the archetypal myth of the claims of two opposing orders, and a singing match lends itself as a variant form of the skeptical dialogue. The myth therefore offered Shelley a

---

[†] From "The Poetry of Skepticism," in *Shelley: A Critical Reading*, by Earl R. Wasserman (Baltimore, MD: Johns Hopkins University Press, 1971), pp. 46–56. Copyright © 1971. Reprinted by permission of The Johns Hopkins University Press.

1. Mary was apparently responsible for supplying the titles "Hymn of Apollo" and "Hymn of Pan" when she published the poems independently of her play in the 1824 volume of her husband's poems. The songs are without title in Shelley's working manuscript (Bodleian Shelley MS e. 6, pp. 22–29) and, of course, in Mary's manuscript of the entire play, where they are incorporated into the dramatic action. Her play, entitled *Midas*, remained in manuscript until 1922, when it was published by A. Koszul.

   A hymn *of* a god is, of course, an anomaly, and the songs by the two gods are not hymns in the customary sense of prayers. The title is appropriate only inasmuch as, in accordance with some of the conventional features of the classical hymn, each song is in (self-) praise of a deity and describes his domain, attributes, powers, and history.

renewed challenge to explore and dramatize the irreconcilable affilia-
tions of man's dual nature, and this time he did so with a technical
virtuosity and a total artistic functionalism unparalleled in his poetry.

According to the Ovidian myth, Tmolus, a hill god, heard the contest
between the two deities and adjudged Apollo's song the superior, but
King Midas, a worshipper of Pan, disputed the decision and was given
ass's ears by Apollo as punishment. Ovid of course represented Apollo
and Pan as gods of a higher and a lower order of values, and his myth
leads almost necessarily to such typical interpretations as George Sandys's: "Pan presents illiterate rusticity; Apollo is a mind imbued with
the divine endowments of art and nature. . . . For there is a two fold
harmony of musick; the one of divine providence, and the other of
humane reason." Midas, by preferring Pan's music and electing the
"vile" instead of the "excellent," denotes "the brutish and ignorant life."
The myth must have appeared to Shelley the archetypal form of the
dilemma that persisted in confronting him: a contest between "universal Pan" and Apollo, god of the heavens, dramatizes man's divisive
desires for mortal life and for the absolute values that he can conceive
of but that exceed the world's resources. As established myth it is a
traditional and therefore universal statement of the oppositions of
which *Alastor*, "The Two Spirits," and "Lift Not the Painted Veil" are
enactments in a variety of more special modes—human history, allegory, dream vision, and popular beliefs. That Ovid's two gods, presiding
over opposing realms—earth and heaven, human and divine, mutability and immutability, experience and desire—embraced all possible
domains for Shelley is suggested by his representing the sum of the
classical pantheon elsewhere as Jove (the overriding spirit), Love (the
operative principle of the universe), Apollo, and Pan.[2]

Shelley's Apollo boasts not only of his role as source of all natural
light but also of the mental realms over which he presides. As the
destroyer of Python, or Error, the god of Truth[3] slays with his sun-
beam-arrows "Deceit, that loves the night and fears the day"; and, as
Ovid illustrated in his story of Apollo's disclosure of Venus' adultery
with Mars,

> All men who do, or even imagine ill
> Fly me; and from the glory of my ray
> Good minds, and open actions, take new might.[4]

In his various roles, he is god of poetry, music, medicine, and
prophecy—"All light of art or nature."[5] He is not symbolic of an oth-
erworld, as has been suggested, but is god of all that the human mind
is capable of conceiving, "all of wonderful, or wise, or beautiful, which
the poet, the philosopher, or the lover could depicture," however much
actual experience may be at odds with those mental ideals. It is for

---

2. *Hellas*, 232–33.
3. For this traditional interpretation of the myth of Apollo and Python, see Sandys's Ovid.
4. Shelley is probably also alluding indirectly to the tradition that the eagle renews its youth
   and regains clarity of sight by flying into the sun. * * *
5. The MS (e. 6, p. 25) shows that Shelley also tried "All light of mind or nature."

this reason that, transforming the sun's speech in Ovid—"I am he . . .
who beholds all things, by whom the earth beholds all things, the
world's eye [*mundi oculus*]"[6]—Shelley has Apollo sing,

> I am the eye with which the Universe
> Beholds itself, and knows it is divine,

just as in his "Ode to Heaven" Shelley described the sun as the "Power
which is the glass / Wherein man his nature sees." Apollo's words may
well reflect, as has been proposed, Plato's association of the sun with
the spiritual eye and with the Good, which supplies the "light" that
allows the soul's eye to see Truth.[7] But if so—and the analogy is
enriching—Apollo's words do not carry with them anything else of
Plato's supposed philosophy, such as the postulation of the real existence of a transcendent ideal world distinct from the world of appear-
ances. Their import is that there is a mode of self-knowledge whereby
the universe can see truly its own divinity, a mental view from "above"
in which its inherent perfection, or true potential nature, can be dis-
cerned. In one of its aspects, then, the universe is divine and has
access to a special mode of vision in which its own divinity is evident
to it. For the distinction between Shelley's Apollo and Pan is not really
one between two realms of being, one here and now, the other "there"
and hereafter; it is between the contradictory aspects shared by both
the self and the world—the one aspect perfect, eternal, conceptual,
and transcendent (in the sense that it is outside lived experience), and
the other inadequate, mutable, and experiential. Like the Visionary of
*Alastor*, like the one who lifted the veil of life, and like the aspiring
Spirit, Apollo, presiding over absolutes alone, is "superior" to life and
not engaged in it, while nevertheless transfiguring it with his light—a
splendor among shadows who makes night day.

Yet there are disturbing counterstatements in Apollo's song that seriously qualify his tone of easy perfection and degrade it at length to
the too-insistent boastfulness with which the lyric ends: "to my song
/ Victory and praise, in its own right, belong." Deceit flees Apollo's
light, but it "loves the night"—and to that night Apollo must give way.
Good minds and open actions gain their renewed power from the light
of day—"Until diminished by the reign of night." And however "unwilling" Apollo's descent from his absoluteness at noon "upon the peak
of Heaven," he must yield to night and leave the clouds weeping with
rain and frowning with darkness where he had brought them the light
of smiles:

> Then with unwilling steps, I linger down
> Into the clouds of the Atlantic even;
> For grief that I depart they weep and frown—

6. *Metamorphoses* iv. 226–28.
7. *Republic* 507 seq.

What look is more delightful, than the smile
With which I soothe them from the Western isle.[8]

In his inevitable sinking he can at best "soothe" the clouds with his twilight from a distant Hesperides, a far-off paradise of hope. Although he is the power with which the universe sees its own divinity, he does not have omnipotent sway over the universe, but must share his reign equally with night and deceit, just as he shares with Pan exactly the same number of lines of poetry in their singing contest. For man, paradoxically, the absolute exists in the context of mutability; the eternal is occasional.

On the other hand, universal Pan appropriately sings, not of the mind's ideal and abstract powers, but of lived experience and its objects—of the natural elements, creatures, and nature deities who come to hear him pipe of stars, earth, and heaven, and of the range of human events, conflict, love, death, and birth. He sings not of the earth as an abstraction or an undifferentiated entity but of the "daedal Earth." He sings of the "dancing stars," that mystic movement supposed to be the model for the human dance that traditionally attends upon Pan's pipe, not, as Apollo does, of the "pure" stars—stars as deathless and immutable spirits—and of their "eternal" bowers.[9] But his central theme is love, love as a contingent earthly experience and not as a mental concept; and this is what essentially distinguishes him from Apollo. Apollo's subjects are absolutes—Love, Truth, Beauty, Virtue, and Divinity—not the relational act of love, whereas Pan's themes are his love of Syrinx and the enraptured silence of love with which all of nature and her creatures have listened to his songs of life and the world. Apollo therefore is entirely self-contained subjectivity, the absolute ego, concentrating exclusively on defining himself and attributing everything to himself: "I arise," "I kill Deceit," "I feed the clouds," all lights are "portions of one spirit, which is mine," "I am the eye with which the Universe / Beholds itself," all harmony, prophecy, medicine "are mine." All forms of the first person singular of the pronoun flood each of his stanzas. Like the Solitary who lifted life's veil, he is "himself alone," the same term with which Shelley elsewhere addressed the Absolute. Pan, on the other hand, concerned centrally with the love-response of Syrinx and of his past audiences, and even preoccupied with how Apollo and Tmolus are at this moment responding to his song, is entirely oriented to a subject-object relationship that is signalled by his beginning his song not with Apollo's egotism but with a sense of community and shared experience: "From the forests and highlands / *We* come, *we* come." And he ends not with his private sorrow but with the fact that all of us share it with him: "Gods and men, we are all deluded thus." By embracing his audience he has also,

8. All quotations from the two songs are derived from Shelley's manuscript, which differs at a number of places from the text Mary published. For "Atlantic" Shelley first wrote "Hesperian" (MS e. 6, p. 25).
9. It may be that the distinction between Apollo's pure stars in eternal bowers and Pan's dancing stars is meant to be the distinction between the fixed stars and the wandering planets.

unlike Apollo, implicated us, the readers. Correspondingly, the song of Apollo is cast in the present tense of universal statement, for the abstract perfections he represents are atemporal; Pan's lyric, except for his references to the immediate moment of the contest, is a narrative entirely in the past tense,[1] the dimension of that constantly vanishing time in which mutable human beings live and experience.

As a description of vital experience, Pan's song opens with rhythmic verve; yet, for all its sprightly energy, an ominous and contravening note intrudes into the center of it, just as Apollo's song makes counterstatements that undermine that god's sovereignty. For not only are Apollo and Pan irreconcilable opposites, neither the mind's ideals nor the actualities of human experience that they respectively preside over are self-sustaining. Like the Christian and Deist of *A Refutation of Deism* and the Narrator and Visionary of *Alastor,* each god repudiates the other and at the same time opens up the flaws in his own domain. Pan tells that when he sang, idyllic Tempe lay dark

> In Pelion's shadow, outgrowing
> The light of the dying day,
> Speeded with my sweet pipings.

For Pan's reign begins only as Apollo's reign of sunlight declines, and although his songs of the world's beauty and of mortal life enamor worldly creatures, they also contribute to dispelling and displacing Apollo's ideal light of mind. Lived experience hastens the inevitable fading of conceptual perfection and lengthens the shadows over existence. But, as Apollo has told, at night, when the light of Apollo's day no longer nourishes good minds and open actions and no longer shows the world its divinity, Deceit returns and flourishes. Lovely and captivating though the world of human experience is, it is a world of deceit and inconstancy. Correspondingly, after Pan has sung joyously of the dancing stars, the daedal earth, and the heavens, and of conflict, love, death, and birth, he abruptly "changed" the tenor of his pipings to bitter sorrow and so incorporated into the structure of his narrative the very inconstancy of which he is singing, the very Deceit that is native to his reign. What he changed to in his inconstant piping is itself a tale of the world's deceit, the product of Shelley's ingenious mythopoeia, richly reinterpreting the myth of Pan's pursuit of Syrinx and of her change into a reed in a world where all mutability is an Ovidian metamorphosis from a higher to a baser form:

> And then I changed my pipings
> Singing how down the vales of Maenalus
> I pursued a maiden and clasped a reed.
> Gods and men,[2] we are all deluded thus!
> It breaks in our bosom and then we bleed.

---

1. The received text, "Where loud waves are dumb" (line 4), should read, according to Shelley's manuscript, "were dumb" (MS e. 6, p. 27); "are" is cancelled and replaced by "were."
2. Pan's distinction is not between two orders of beings, but between the two natures of man, one divine and ideal, the other earthly and experiential. Both are deluded in their search in the world for fulfillment.

> They wept as I think both ye now would,
> If envy or age had not frozen your blood,
> At the sorrow of my sweet pipings.

Pan's experience is that of the Maniac in *Julian and Maddalo* and of Shelley's Prince Athanase, who seeks the Uranian Venus but, until death, can meet only the Pandemic: what the mind pursues in the world through love proves inconstant, untrue, inferior to the mind's perfect pattern that sought to be fulfilled by an outward correspondence, and the deluded pursuing heart is pierced by what it pursues. Both Julian and Maddalo also lament the ill wrought on the Maniac by his lady's "falsehood":

> . . . it were a grief indeed
> If he had changed one unsustaining reed
> For all that such a man might else adorn.

Pan's whole story is told in the evolution of his song's internal refrains:

> Listening my sweet pipings. . . .
> Pelion's shadow . . . Speeded with my sweet pipings. . . .
> And then I changed my pipings. . . .

And at another level it is told by the course of the final refrains:

> Listening my sweet pipings. . . .
> For envy of my sweet pipings. . . .
> At the sorrow of my sweet pipings. . . .

As Shelley wrote elsewhere, mortal man's "sweetest songs," unlike those of the skylark or of Apollo, "are those that tell of saddest thought." The unsustaining reed into which Syrinx was metamorphosed not only pierced Pan's heart, according to Shelley's myth, but also, according to the original myth, is the instrument on which he pipes his songs. To Shelley it is because the reed pierces the heart that it is the instrument for songs of sweet sorrow: to use Shelley's language, poets who "transcribe" human reality instead of creating poetry that is "wholly ideal," like Apollo's, are those who "learn in suffering what they teach in song."[3] Apollo brings grief only because of his necessary departure; the equal mixture of sweetness and sorrow is the very substance of Pan's mortal song.

Shelley gave his gods equal opportunity, granting each exactly thirty-six lines in which to assert his superiority by singing of his own domain, powers, and attributes; but each elects to shape his allotted space into a different rhythmic form, the emotional character of which corresponds to the god's special ethos. Since a choice is to be made between the two songs, there is no distinction between each song's lyric power and its thematic content: what each god declares of his own powers and domain is identical with the esthetic character of his singing, and any judge's esthetic preference is also his determination of the realm to which he has bound himself and the way in which he defines him-

---

3. *Julian and Maddalo*, 546.

self. Both lyrics are therefore brilliant tours de force directed toward fusing form and content; singing, song, and singer; the god's art and the character of the domain over which he presides.

The lines of Pan's song vary in number of syllables, but the preponderant tendency toward anapests imparts a vivacity and forward thrust, especially in the opening two-stress lines:

> From the forests and highlands
>      We come, we come;
> From the river-girt islands
>      Where the loud waves were dumb.

The poem, in its "inconstancy," never returns to this two-stress unit, and the basic pattern thereafter is the rapid three-stress line that lengthens out to one four-stress line toward the end of the first stanza ("Were silent as ever old Tmolus was") and two toward the end of the second, the deceleration and growing deliberateness being furthered by the increasing number of syllables and the irregularity of the meter:

> And all that did then attend and follow
> Were as silent for love, as you now, Apollo.

Progressively this new tempo foreshadows the third stanza, for with Pan's announcement of the change of his piping from joy to the sadness of the story of Syrinx, all six lines (quoted above) preceding the final refrain have four stresses or hesitate between four and five, slowing the reader with iambs and spondees where he anticipates more anapests, and moving with wistful solemnity. Moreover, in each of the first two stanzas the internal refrain (the fifth line) terminates the first unit of thought: for example,

> Liquid Peneus was flowing,
>      And all dark Tempe lay
> In Pelion's shadow, outgrowing
>      The light of the dying day,
>           Speeded with my sweet pipings.

But, as Milton Wilson has observed in his sensitive analysis,[4] in the third stanza the thought breaks at the end of the fourth line, and the refrain initiates the next unit instead of closing the previous one:

> I sang of the dancing stars,
>      I sang of the daedal Earth,
> And of Heaven, and the giant wars
>      And Love and Death and Birth;
>           And then I changed my pipings
> Singing how down the vales of Maenalus
>      I pursued a maiden and clasped a reed.

The consequence is not only to throw the momentum and emphasis forward upon the story of Syrinx rather than back upon Pan's vivacious songs of the universe and life; the reorganization of the rhetorical pat-

---

4. *Shelley's Later Poetry* (New York, 1959), pp. 30–37.

tern, together with the shift to successive four-foot lines in the rest of the stanza, is the structural enactment of the very "change" Pan here speaks of from joyous to sorrowful song, of the "change" which is Syrinx' metamorphosis into a reed, and, at the profoundest level, of the "change" which is the inevitable inconstancy and deceit of all earthly things in the realm over which Pan presides.

Yet, the rhythm of Pan's song, modulating from sprightly joy to the disillusioned languor in which all earthly pleasure and vitality must end, is the authentic rhythm of life. Apollo's song, on the other hand, so squarely of six stanzas of six ten-syllable lines, is consistently stately and majestic, invariable in form and quality. But it is more than that: the recurrent clashes between the metrical and rhetorical emphases, the repeated and unexpected substitution of one kind of foot for another, the occasional spondees, all tend to frustrate forward movement and require that the reader advance deliberately enough to readjust his psychological momentum to new and unanticipated rhythms. Without being unrhythmical, it is a rhythm to which the living voice has difficulty adapting itself:

> The sleepless Hours who watch me as I lie,
>   Curtained with star-enwoven tapestries
> From the broad moonlight of the open sky,
>   Fanning the busy dreams from my dim eyes
> Waken me when their mother, the grey Dawn,
> Tells them that Dreams and that the moon is gone.
>
> Then I arise; and climbing Heaven's blue dome
>   I walk over the mountains and the waves,
> Leaving my robe upon the Ocean foam.
>   My footsteps pave the clouds with fire; the caves
> Are filled with my bright presence, and the air
> Leaves the green Earth to my embraces bare.

Apollo's song is that of the lyre; each line measured exactly to ten syllables, it is appropriate to lyric recitative. Pan's is that of the pipe, the lines of constantly changing length being suggestive of the dancing chorus, with which his pipe was traditionally associated. Yet both rhythms are defective, each in a different way. One can at least understand why, in Mary's play, Midas prefers Pan's "sprightly" song of sweet sorrow, which "in melody outweighs" Apollo's "drowsy tune"; Apollo, she has Midas say, "put me fast asleep," but Pan's "gay notes awoke me." Pan's varying rhythm is that of experience felt in the blood and felt along the heart; Apollo's, that of the purer mind's abstract aspirations, a constant but cold ideal harmony that is lifeless and dull to Midas' "blunted sense," as Apollo calls it. For Mary was careful to point out that whereas Tmolus, the hill god who finds in Apollo's song the "wisdom, beauty, and the power divine / Of highest poetry," is an immortal, Midas is only a man. Like all mortals, Midas is foolish, incapable of appreciating highest poetry, or what Shelley elsewhere calls "poetic idealisms"; and for his devotion to the earth god, Midas, like all mortals and like everything else in Pan's song, suffers a debasing metamorphosis that symbolizes the world's inconstancy—according to Mary's play, his "soul's oppressed with the sad change" when Apollo gives him ass's ears. But his choice is really an impossible one for mortals: the lovely and vital night of life in which the heart is inevitably crossed by deceit and saddened by the incompatibility of its desires with what the false, disappointing world has to offer, or, on the other hand, the grand but unvital day of the mind's ideal conceptions of immutable truth, in the light of which the world reveals its divinity but not its humanity. In a sense, the contest between Pan and Apollo reflects the dispute between Mary and Shelley on the subject of Shelley's poetic talents and duty. She urged him to write "in a style that commanded popular favour" and to devote himself to "the delineations of human passion"; but "the bent of his mind went the other way," and he believed "he was too metaphysical and abstract—too fond of the theoretical and the ideal," too Apollonian for that kind of poetry.[5] Of Shelley's *Witch of Atlas* Mary wrote: "This poem is peculiarly characteristic of his tastes—wildly fanciful, full of brilliant imagery, and discarding human interest and passion, to revel in the fantastic ideas that his imagination suggested."[6]

In his "hymn," Apollo himself has subtly explained Midas' preference for Pan: "to my song," he sings, "Victory and praise, *in its own right*, belong." In its own right—but not as an object of vital encounter. It is of the highest worth intrinsically, independent of its effect upon any auditors, of whom, indeed, Apollo as absolute subjectivity is oblivious. Or Apollo is what Maddalo describes as "a system refutation-tight / As far as words go"; in *Julian and Maddalo* the Maniac's "wild talk will show / How vain are such aspiring theories." But the only touchstone that Pan can conceive is his effect upon an experiencing audience, since his song has no worth in its own right. Not only is his song itself a proud recounting of the audiences he has sung to and the spells he has cast upon them, each of his stanzas ends with a comment on the response of his present auditors, first Tmolus, then Apollo, and then both. Even as he sings he is troubled that he is failing to move them, and he ends each of his last two stanzas by incorporating into his song a direct address to them, explaining why they are unmoved. At the end of his first stanza he draws in Tmolus: all creatures who have heard Pan's songs

> Were silent as ever old Tmolus was
> Listening my sweet pipings.

Then he tells that his past audiences, in their responses,

> Were as silent for love, as you now, Apollo,
> For envy of my sweet pipings.

And at last, when he used to sing of the deceitfulness of love, his auditors would weep,

---

5. Mary's note to *The Cenci* (*Works*, II, 156, 158).
6. *Julian*, IV, 78.

> as I think both ye now would
> If envy or age had not frozen your blood
> At the sorrow of my sweet pipings.

Tmolus was once enthralled into silence by engagement in life and the love of it. But although Tmolus is immortal, he is not, like Apollo, an eternal youth outside time; bridging the immortal and the human, he endlessly ages, and therefore he, too, is subject to and illustrative of the change, the disappointing metamorphosis, the deceit, which is everywhere the subject and form of Pan's lament. Now old, Tmolus has voted for Apollo because age has frozen his blood until he is silent through indifference to life or incapacity for it; and Pan's song is of blood, not of Apollonian mind, or soul.

Apollo, on the other hand, is silent with envy, the opposite of love. As the absolute subject he has laid claim to everything—all is "mine"— and would also assume the domain of Pan, if he could. His blood is frozen because he would assume everything into his own absoluteness and so has nothing to do with life, which is the relationship of love, however disappointing. At least, tragic Pan is aware of a possession unavailable to Apollo. Life mourns that its experiences of the world have not the eternity and truth of conceptual ideals; the ideal envies what it is incapable of, human life. Keats, too, had recognized that essence cannot engage in existence unimpaired, that the ideal cannot be superimposed on reality, that divinity is no longer divine when incarnated in the world. The Titans of *Hyperion*, divine from birth, lose their "strong identity," their "real self," when they descend into the world and take on human experience. But unlike Keats, Shelley cannot conceive of an Apollo born on earth who becomes a god through enormous knowledge of life. For him the human and divine, although co-present in man, refuse to compromise their conflict and become one.

Shelley, however, is not merely unfolding the continuous conflict between the mutually exclusive ideal and human. In this singing contest he is also raising the question of the role and possibilities of poetry, for Apollo is the god of poetry, and the reed which pierced Pan's heart is the instrument on which that god pipes his songs of sweet sorrow. It was for the same reason that he made both the Visionary and the Narrator of *Alastor* poets. There are, then, two fundamental kinds of poetry: the inhuman, unvital, and possibly futile ideal and the tragic, disappointing human. Each is flawed, and option for either would be blind negligence of the other. Here and in *Alastor* Shelley has made no choice, but one purpose of his waging the unresolved contest is to learn, clear-eyed, all the pitfalls as he searches for a poetic mode and matter that will allow him, in good conscience, to take a stand without compromising his skepticism.

# KENNETH NEILL CAMERON

## Philosophy, Religion, and Ethics[†]

Shelley was—like Lucretius or Goethe—primarily a poet of ideas, ranging widely into social thought, philosophy, science, and ethics. His greatest poetry combines ideas from all four. * * *

The general ideas of philosophy as Shelley knew them fall mainly into four groups: materialist, idealist, dualist, and skeptic. Materialists, such as Lucretius or Holbach, argue that the universe is a material entity, consisting of matter in various forms—solid, liquid, gaseous— and having qualities such as motion and energy inherent within it. It was not "created" but has existed from all time. The human mind is only another manifestation of matter. It follows that there is no God, either as creator or as a force within the universe. The idealist view falls into two main streams, the Platonic and the Berkeleian, although both, in fact, had early origins in Asia. According to the Platonists, there is both matter and God, but the world of matter is an imperfect shadow of the mind of God, the One, which has as its attributes the Good, the True, and the Beautiful. Berkeley simplified this concept by asserting that the world *is* the mind of God, that what looks like matter is, in fact, a spiritual substance. The dualists, such as Locke, argue that both mind and matter exist and are different entities, each subject to its own laws of action. The external world is simply a world of shapes and solidity; the mind supplies it with colors, sounds, and so on. The skeptics, such as Hume, argue that all one can know are sensations. There may be an external world, there may be a God, there may be mind, or there may be none of them.

The earliest influences on Shelley's philosophy came from Locke, Hume, Godwin, and Holbach. At Oxford he had accepted the proposition from Locke that the mind is a blank tablet at birth and all ideas come from the senses. He also accepted Locke's dualistic concept of an external world of matter clothed by the mind with color and sound. From the first of these propositions he derived the argument, put forward in *The Necessity of Atheism*, that the idea of God cannot be a divine implantation but must come from the senses. Hence the existence of God is a matter for reasoned argument, not merely acceptance as an article of "faith" (with the corollary that a lack of acceptance implies "sin").

*The Necessity of Atheism* also presents two propositions from Hume: it is more likely that those reporting miracles lied than that the miracles took place; and if God created the world, who created God (and

† Reprinted by permission of the publisher from "Philosophy, Religion, and Ethics," in *Shelley: The Golden Years*, by Kenneth Neill Cameron (Cambridge, MA: Harvard University Press, 1974), pp. 150–58. Copyright © 1974 by the President and Fellows of Harvard College. The author's notes have been edited.

so on in an infinite regress of creating and created Gods)? In the *Queen Mab* Note on necessity Hume's arguments on causality are used against the existence of a deity: if we know only sequence and not cause, then we do not know that there was a First Cause. Shelley did not at this time, however, accept Hume's skeptical epistemological views, as he told his friend Hogg: "I have examined Hume's reasonings with respect to the non-existence of external things, & I confess, they appear to me to follow from the doctrines of Locke. What am I to think of a philosophy which conducts to such a conclusion?"[1] From Godwin, first read in 1809 at Eton, came the idea of necessity: both mind and matter operate by inexorable laws, inherent in their nature, to produce an inevitable chain of events in the universe and in society. But Shelley disagreed with Godwin's idealistic concepts that mind was a unique entity, quite different from matter, was always active, even in sleep, and was the source of motion.[2] On the contrary, he agreed with Holbach that mind was similar to certain manifestations of matter, such as electricity, and that motion was inherent in the nature of matter. Holbach also strengthened his concept of necessity.

At Keswick in 1812 Robert Southey introduced Shelley to Berkeley's subjective idealism—the universe *is* the mind of God; there is no mind-matter dilemma, for all is mind—and Shelley rejected it: "I have read Berkeley, and the perusal of his arguments tended more than anything to convince me that immaterialism & other words of general usage deriving all their force from mere *predictates* in *non* were invented by the pride of philosophers to conceal their ignorance even from themselves."[3]

Later, however, according to Mary Shelley, he became a "disciple of the Immaterial Philosophy of Berkeley. This theory gave unity and grandeur to his ideas, while it opened a wide field for his imagination."[4] Shelley had perhaps discussed these matters with Mary, but it seems more likely that she was basing her views on an interpretation of his essay *On Life*. She may have been echoing the phrasing of that essay, and by the time of its composition (1819–1820), Shelley seems to have been discussing his works very little with her. Few critics have gone so far as to consider Shelley a Berkeleian, but some have argued that he was an immaterialist. More have contended that he became a Platonist, others a Neoplatonist. In recent years the "Platonist" tide has begun to turn, and the emphasis has been placed on the British empiricists, especially Hume.

Shelley's later views on mind, matter, and perception—his epistemology—were expressed primarily in two works, the short essay *On Life* and the first fragment of *Speculations on Metaphysics. On Life* also contains his repudiation of "materialism." In 1814, following the

1. To Hogg, November 22–23, 1813, SC, III, 260.
2. For Godwin's influence on Shelley's philosophy, see Cameron, *The Young Shelley: Genesis of a Radical* (New York: Macmillan, 1950), pp. 194–95; Ross Woodman, *The Apocalyptic Vision in the Poetry of Shelley* (Toronto: University of Toronto Press, 1964), pp. 6–9. * * *
3. July 29, 1812, *Letters*, II, 316.
4. Preface to *Essays, Letters from Abroad, Works*, V, ix.

publication of *Queen Mab*, Shelley had advanced a materialist position in *A Refutation of Deism*:

> The greatest, equally with the smallest motions of the Universe, are subjected to the rigid necessity of inevitable laws. These laws are the unknown causes of the known effects perceivable in the Universe. Their effects are the boundaries of our knowledge, their names the expressions of our ignorance.
>
> To assert that God is intelligent, is to assert that he has ideas; and Locke has proved that ideas result from sensation. Sensation can exist only in an organized body, an organized body is necessarily limited both in extent and operation. The God of the rational Theosophist is a vast and wise animal.
>
> Mind cannot create, it can only perceive. Mind is the recipient of impressions made on the organs of sense, and without the action of external objects we should not only be deprived of all knowledge of the existence of mind, but totally incapable of the knowledge of any thing. It is evident therefore that mind deserves to be considered as the effect, rather than the cause of motion.[5]

Shelley here presumes four entities: a material universe, a biological body, sensation, and mind. The material universe is controlled by natural laws that can be investigated by science but whose fundamental nature is unknown. Sensation arises from the interaction of biological body and universal matter and provides the material for thought. Mind is not basically creative but works with what is provided for it by the senses. It can, of course, create new combinations from this sense data—as in poetry or art—but it does not create the sense data. In the mind-matter relationship, matter is primary. Mind is perhaps a form of material motion. Without matter, mind would not be aware of its own existence. If there is any divine mind or God, it too must have a similar nature and be dependent on sensation, body, and the material universe; hence, by implication, there is no divine mind.

The repudiation passage in *On Life* (1819–1820), runs as follows:

> I confess that I am one of those who am unable to refuse my assent to the conclusions of those philosophers who assert that nothing exists but as it is perceived.
>
> It is a decision against which all our persuasions struggle, and we must be long convicted before we can be convinced that the solid universe of external things is "such stuff as dreams are made of." The shocking absurdities of the popular philosophy of mind and matter, its fatal consequences in morals, and their violent dogmatism concerning the source of all things, had early conducted me to materialism. This materialism is a seducing system to young and superficial minds. It allows its disciples to talk, and dispenses them from thinking. But I was discontented with such a view of things as it afforded; man is a being of high aspirations,

5. *Works* VI, 48, 55, 56. In a letter to Leigh Hunt on Sept. 27, 1819 Shelley states that he first came across the phrase, "Mind cannot create, it can only perceive," as a pencil note in a copy of Berkeley owned by Southey's friend Charles Lloyd, the poet, at Keswick, where Shelley lived November 1811–February 1812. (*Letters*, II, 122–123.)

"looking both before and after," whose "thoughts wander through eternity," disclaiming alliance with transience and decay; incapable of imagining to himself annihilation; existing but in the future and the past; being, not what he is, but what he has been and shall be. Whatever may be his true and final destination, there is a spirit within him at enmity with nothingness and dissolution. This is the character of all life and being. Each is at once the centre and the circumference; the point to which all things are referred, and the line in which all things are contained. Such contemplations as these, materialism and the popular philosophy of mind and matter alike forbid; they are only consistent with the intellectual system.

Although the statement that "the solid universe of things is 'such stuff as dreams are made of' " gives the impression that Shelley is advocating immaterialism, a comparison with other passages shows that he is really advancing a skeptical position. He is not denying the existence of an external universe, but is arguing only that whatever is known is known only through the senses, and the senses disclose nothing more than sensation. Knowledge is knowledge of thought substance only. Some sensations or thoughts are stronger than others. Although the stronger ones are presumed to have an origin in "external objects," all we actually know is that they are stronger:

> Thoughts, or ideas, or notions, call them what you will, differ from each other, not in kind, but in force. It has commonly been supposed that those distinct thoughts which affect a number of persons, at regular intervals, during the passage of a multitude of other thoughts, which are called *real*, or *external objects*, are totally different in kind from those which affect only a few persons, and which recur at irregular intervals, and are usually more obscure and indistinct, such as hallucinations, dreams, and the ideas of madness . . . A specific difference between every thought of the mind, is, indeed, a necessary consequence of that law by which it perceives diversity and number; but a generic or essential difference is wholly arbitrary.[6]

Those who have argued that Shelley became an immaterialist have usually argued also that he abandoned his beliefs in an ordered universe, in science, and in rational logic, substituting for them God, intuition, and mysticism. But that this cannot be so is apparent even in *On Life*:

> The relations of things remain unchanged, by whatever system. By the word things is to be understood any object of thought, that is, any thought upon which any other thought is employed, with an apprehension of distinction. The relations of these remain unchanged; and such is the material of our knowledge.
> What is the cause of life? that is, how was it produced, or what agencies distinct from life have acted or act upon life? All re-

6. *Speculations on Metaphysics, Works,* VII, 59–60. For Shelley's skepticism in these essays, see Pulos, pp. 49–53 *passim.*

corded generations of mankind have wearily busied themselves in inventing answers to this question; and the result has been,— Religion. Yet, that the basis of all things cannot be, as the popular philosophy alleges, mind, is sufficiently evident. Mind, as far as we have any experience of its properties, and beyond that experience how vain is argument! cannot create, it can only perceive. It is said also to be the cause. But cause is only a word expressing a certain state of the human mind with regard to the manner in which two thoughts are apprehended to be related to each other. If any one desires to know how unsatisfactorily the popular philosophy employs itself upon this great question, they need only impartially reflect upon the manner in which thoughts develop themselves in their minds. It is infinitely improbable that the cause of mind, that is, of existence, is similar to mind.[7]

Shelley here seems almost to be harking back to A *Refutation of Deism,* with his attack on Christian theology ("the popular philosophy" of such theologians as Paley), his argument on the noncreativity of mind and his implication that this rules out a creative God (the divine cosmic mind). Shelley also includes his former *Necessity of Atheism* argument from Hume that causation may be simply unmotivated succession; hence, there is no First Cause (or God). Regardless of one's epistemological view, the "relations of things" remain "unchanged," a position also implied in Hume and other skeptics. Only in their specific philosophical arguments do they assert their epistemological skepticism. Usually they write and act as though they were, like the rest of us, inhabiting a universe of "things." So also in Shelley's poetry. Unless he is directly expressing his epistemological view, he writes in terms of things and thoughts. Presumably in his poems written before his repudiation of "this materialism" he actually meant things, and afterward meant only the more powerful sensations, but there is usually no way of telling. A star is a star in both cases, or a bird a bird.

Not only do the "relations of things" remain the same, but the laws of nature also remain: "By considering all knowledge as bounded by perception, whose operations may be indefinitely combined, we arrive at a conception of Nature inexpressibly more magnificent, simple and true, than accord [s with] the ordinary systems of complicated and partial consideration. Nor does a contemplation of the Universe, in this comprehensive and synthetical view, exclude the subtlest analysis of its modifications and parts."[8] If the universe is still to be analyzed in all its "modifications and parts," such analysis—as Shelley's interest in science and use of it in his poetry indicate—must be carried on by scientific investigation.

Shelley's empirical and scientific attitude holds true also for the analysis of mind itself: "Mind, so far as we have any experience of its properties, and beyond that experience how vain is argument!" Mind is not only noncreative in essence and neither a unique nor an ultimate

7. *Works,* VII, 196.
8. *Ibid.,* p. 60.

substance, but it has to be examined and its properties determined by analysis and "experience."

The epistemological picture is further developed in another passage in *On Life*:

> What follows from the admission [that "nothing exists but as it is perceived"]? It establishes no new truth, it gives us no additional insight into our hidden nature, neither its action nor itself. Philosophy, impatient as it may be to build, has much work yet remaining, as pioneer for the overgrowth of ages. It makes one step towards this object; it destroys error, and the roots of error. It leaves, what is too often the duty of the reformer in political and ethical questions to leave, a vacancy. It reduces the mind to that freedom in which it would have acted, but for the misuse of words and signs, the instruments of its own creation.[9]

Skepticism does not, of itself, contribute to knowledge, but it does clear away "error" and its "roots." Shelley is apparently referring primarily to theological concepts. If skepticism shows that all we know are our own sensations, then we cannot know whether God exists (which was one of Hume's points in his attack on Berkeley). Philosophy, if it is to move ahead, must begin with a "vacancy"—"we grow dizzy to look down the dark abyss of how little we know"—but it is better to begin with a vacancy that one can build from than to be lost in theological fantasies. Light can be thrown into the "abyss" only by philosophical investigation and the "subtlest analysis" of science. Eventually, Shelley indicates, in a future higher social order, the fundamental nature of the universe and of mankind will be known: "That there is a true solution of the riddle, and that in our present state the solution is unattainable by us are propositions which may be regarded as equally certain."[1]

Shelley implies that he was convinced of the falsity of "materialism" by the argument that "nothing exists but as it is perceived," a proposition that was basic to Berkeley and Hume alike. Berkeley used it to support his contention that "there is not any other substance than *Spirit*, or that which perceives."[2] Hume used it to support his skeptical view that all cognition can be reduced to "a bundle of perceptions." Shelley differed from Berkeley in that he did not believe in the Berkeleian all-inclusive "Spirit", and from Hume in that he posited the existence of mind. The materialist view was both "complicated" and "partial"—complicated because, assuming both mind and matter, it had to account for their interaction; partial because it placed an exclusive emphasis on matter. Once, however, we realize that our knowledge is limited by our perceptions, everything becomes much simpler. The so-called world of matter and the world of mind blend into one. This latter thought Shelley derived from neither Berkeley nor Hume but from a contemporary philosopher, Sir William Drummond: "Per-

9. *Ibid.*, VI, 195.
1. *Ibid.*, p. 196; Note to *Hellas*, ll. 197–238, *ibid.*, III, 56.
2. *Principles of Human Knowledge*, para. 7.

haps the most clear and vigorous statement of the intellectual system is to be found in Sir William Drummond's Academical Questions. After such an exposition, it would be idle to translate into other words what could only lose its energy and fitness by the change."[3]

Sir William Drummond became known mainly for his anticlerical argument in *Oedipus Judaicus* (1811) that the biblical stories were myths. Shelley had early read this work and by the time of writing *A Refutation of Deism* had also read Drummond's philosophical study *Academical Questions*, and was impressed by Drummond's argument for the nonexistence of God, which Shelley summarized: "If Power be an attribute of existing substance, substance could not have derived its origin from power."[4] This is simply an extension of the argument that if motion is inherent in matter, a "prime mover" is not needed, but Drummond placed it in a skeptical framework and added to it, rather incongruously, the contention of Parmenides that all existence was a unity (the one "ens"): "There is One that is all, which is the principle of all, by which extension and mind exist, and in which all things are contained contractedly and unitedly, in one unity . . . the nominal difference between physical forces, and mental faculties, concealed from the inattentive observer their common origin and their real similitude."[5] It was perhaps this concept that inspired Shelley's comment: "It is difficult to find terms adequate to express so subtle a conception as that to which the Intellectual Philosophy had conducted us."[6] In Drummond, Shelley found a philosopher who was anticlerical and yet avoided the sterility of an absolute skepticism, imaginatively viewing all reality as essentially one.

By "materialism" Shelley must mean mainly the doctrines of Holbach, for Holbach was the only materialist who had deeply influenced him, and in regard to Holbach he appears to be thinking mainly of his scoffing at all hope of immortality and his mechanistic picture of man: "The moral man is nothing more than this physical being considered under a certain point of view."[7] On the contrary, man is "a being of high aspirations . . . disclaiming alliance with transience and decay." Shelley felt that the concept of man as a primarily "physical being" responding to self-serving instincts (as Hobbes had earlier argued and Malthus implied) was a degrading one. Such a "being" could never build a new world based on humanitarian principles. Whatever Shelley's reasoning, he is certainly cavalier in his sweeping dismissal of materialism, implying that its arguments are over simplified and its

---

3. *On Life, Works*, VI, 195.
4. *Works*, VI, 55.
5. William Drummond, *Academical Questions* (London, 1805), p. 244. Shelley was influenced in other ideas by Drummond. For instance, the passage quoted above giving Shelley's reasons for renouncing materialism is partly derived from Drummond. Shelley's contention that materialism seems logical at first, but that on further examination skepticism, despite its seeming absurdity, is more tenable is typical of Drummond: "Nothing, I know, appears at first view more singular or visionary, than the philosophic doctrine of ideas. The human mind does not easily abandon its early habits of association." * * *
6. *Works*, VI, 196.
7. Baron d'Holbach, *The System of Nature*, trans. H. D. Robinson (Boston, 1889), I, 11–12.

"disciples" superficial. A more modest appraisal might have been in order, especially as his new philosophy was not without pitfalls:

> The view of life presented by the most refined deductions of the intellectual philosophy, is that of unity. Nothing exists but as it is perceived. The difference is merely nominal between those two classes of thought, which are vulgarly distinguished by the names of ideas and of external objects. Pursuing the same thread of reasoning, the existence of distinct individual minds, similar to that which is employed is now questioning its own nature, is likewise found to be a delusion. The words *I, you, they,* are not signs of any actual difference subsisting between the assemblage of thoughts thus indicated, but are merely marks employed to denote the different modifications of the one mind.
>
> Let it not be supposed that this doctrine conducts to the monstrous presumption that I, the person who now write and think, am that one mind. I am but a portion of it.[8]

Shelley, then, was uneasily aware of the solipsism inherent in his new epistemology: if "I" know nothing except "my" sensations, how do I know that the world is not just my dream? This awkward question—the bugbear of idealism and skepticism alike—he chose not to pursue but contented himself with labeling it a "monstrous presumption."

As corollaries of this solipsist theme came other problems. If "the" mind is not "my" mind but a universal mind, then there are really no individual minds. But in *Speculations on Metaphysics* as in his works in general Shelley assumes the existence of individual minds: "We are intuitively conscious of our own existence, and of that connection in the train of our successive ideas, which we term our identity. We are conscious also of the existence of other minds; but not intuitively." It was perhaps partly in response to this problem—which gave Berkeley and Hume trouble also—that Shelley suggested the rather desperate expedient of a graduated "scale" by which one could measure the "intensity, duration, connexion" and so on of one's sensations.[9] But he failed to provide a reference base for such a scale.

Such, then, were the main epistemological changes in Shelley's philosophy. The indications are that these changes took place in 1816–1817. In a passage in *The Queen of the Universe*, probably written in the fall of 1815, Shelley presumes the existence of a "universal mind" or "Spirit," the individual human mind, and the "vast world" of matter.[1]

8. *On Life, Works*, VI, 196.
9. *Ibid.,* VII, 60, 61.
1. SC, IV, 496–502, 564–565 (ll. 1064–1072). Wasserman argued that Shelley intended the passage to reflect Drummond's exposition of a Platonic concept of the "universal mind" achieving "intelligence," but this does not seem to be his object. The "main" difference between the *Queen Mab* text and *The Queen of the Universe* revisions, according to Wasserman, lies in the use of "universal mind" instead of "spirit," but the *Queen of the Universe* text shows that Shelley there first used "Spirit," then crossed it out and inserted "universal mind," so that he apparently intended both to signify the same thing. (Earl Wasserman, *Shelley's Prometheus Unbound* [Baltimore: Johns Hopkins University Press, 1965], p. 25n.) Shelley appears to be arguing that the "universal mind" or "spirit" inherent in the universe achieves human significance only when human mind perceives it.

In the summer of 1816, a similar dualistic assumption apparently underlies *Mont Blanc*. In fragment IV of *Speculations on Metaphysics* and in the essay *On the Punishment of Death*, both written circa 1816–1817, the change is apparent. In the essay, Shelley refers to the "accurate philosophy" of the "modern Academy" (of Drummond), which shows "the prodigious depth and extent of our ignorance respecting the causes and nature of sensation."[2] The fragment contains the following observation: "It imports little to inquire whether thought be distinct from the objects of thought. The use of the words *external* and *internal*, as applied to the establishment of this distinction, has been the symbol and the source of much dispute. This is merely an affair of words and as the dispute deserves, to say, that when speaking of the objects of thought, we indeed only describe one of the forms of thought—or that, speaking of thought, we only apprehend one of the operations of the universal system of beings."[3] The position in this fragment is the same as that in *On Life* (1819–1820).

Just as it was formerly assumed that Shelley was a Platonist, now there seems to be a tendency to assume that he was a thoroughgoing skeptic, both in philosophy and in social thought. But an all-embracing philosophical skepticism should not be confused with a selective reserving of judgment where evidence is lacking or with a specifically epistemological skepticism. Shelley's own efforts to solve "the riddle" had been in vain. There might perhaps be an ultimate creative force behind phenomena, but then again there might be nothing beyond what can be perceived, and the whole answer might lie in scientific analysis. Whatever the answer, Shelley believed, as the true skeptic does not, that mankind would in time discover it. But for the present, evidence on which to base a conclusion was lacking, and rather than propose one, he withheld judgment. However, he was always hopefully seeking for answers, and often he felt he had found them. When he did, he expressed them vigorously and positively. He was not skeptical about the existence of God; he was sure there was none. He was certain that mind was not creative but perceptive, its deductions and fantasies alike ultimately dependent on "sensation." In *A Defence of Poetry* he included Hume among the "mere reasoners" and not among the great creative intellects. Shelley, that is, resorted to noncommittal and agnostic responses on certain questions because intellectual honesty demanded that he do so, but he felt that skepticism as a system of philosophy, while essential for the abolition of theological "error," was negative rather than creative. It made for the beginning of wisdom, but the beginning only.

This was true also of Shelley's concept of political thought. As he stated, it is often the "duty" of the philosopher as well as of the "reformer in political questions to leave a vacancy."[4] He did this himself

2. *Works*, VI, 186.
3. *Ibid.*, VII, 65, 343 ("beings" or "being"?).
4. *On Life, Ibid.*, VI, 195.

from time to time in *A Philosophical View of Reform*; for instance, when he did not know whether intellectual or social forces were primary in causing social change, he argued only that change arose from their interaction. Yet his political and social views were essentially positive. Although he withheld judgment on some social questions, he had a clear position on others. Human nature was conditioned by social forces. The source of political oppression lay in the ruling classes, with their "standing army," their "legion of spies," and their control of the press and pulpit. He was confident that this "tyranny" would be eliminated by "reform" or "revolution." He was convinced that humanity was advancing to an egalitarian society. He dedicated his life and writing to the battle against social evils. Indeed, it is difficult to think of works that are more the antithesis of social skepticism—with its cynical concept of the uselessness of human endeavor—than *A Philosophical View of Reform* or *Prometheus Unbound*.

# DONALD H. REIMAN

## Shelley as Agrarian Reactionary[†]

Leigh Hunt noted that "the family connexions of Mr. Shelley belonged to a small party in the House of Commons, itself belonging to another party. They were Whig Aristocrats. . . ."[1] Though (as Hunt goes on to point out) Shelley was offended by the moral and political hypocrisy and the anti-intellectualism of the country gentry as he knew them in his youth, he never lost some perspectives that developed with his character from the very fact that he was brought up as the heir to large landed estates in Sussex in an area of prosperous grain and foodstuff farming. As Hunt (with benign humor) and Peacock (with general sympathy) also noted, Shelley never quite outgrew his predisposition to think of social, economic, and moral questions from the viewpoint of a landed aristocrat.

In transcribing and commenting on Shelley's ideas and even his imagery in *A Philosophical View of Reform*,[2] I became aware of some of the implications of Shelley's background for his political and social ideas; since then, I have had a greater opportunity to study the lives and politics of landed Whig aristocrats and the transformation of Whig and Tory politics from the mid-eighteenth century to the agitation for repeal of the Corn Acts in the 1830s and 1840s that tore both parties asunder and gave entirely new meanings in British politics to the terms

† From *Keats-Shelley Memorial Bulletin* 30 (1979): 5–15, as reprinted in *Romantic Texts and Contexts*, by Donald H. Reiman (Columbia: University of Missouri Press, 1987), pp. 262–74. Reprinted by permission of the University of Missouri Press. Copyright © 1987 by the Curators of the University of Missouri.
1. *Lord Byron and Some of His Contemporaries* (London: Henry Colburn 1828), p. 178.
2. SC, vol. 6 (Cambridge: Harvard University Press, 1973), pp. 945–1066.

*liberal* and *conservative* (with or without capital letters).[3] The conclusion I have reached is that it may be a historical error to call Shelley simply a "radical" in terms of the larger sweep of British social and political development during this period. Rather, when Shelley's political and social program is measured by the massive changes in British economic, social, and political activity and institutions, many of his ideas must be judged "reactionary" by virtue of their emphasis on forms characteristic of and beneficial to the agricultural estate system of the eighteenth century and earlier. Like Wordsworth, Coleridge, and William Cobbett (to name only three contemporaries whose thinking to some degree parallels his), Shelley generally opposed laws and programs that favored monetary, commercial, and industrial expansion. He ignored the Corn Laws, which maintained artificially high prices for grain and thereby increased the profits of farmers while squeezing the growing urban population (whose prosperity depended upon foreign trade) between high food prices and low wages or—when foreign competition increased in the 1830s and 1840s—chronic unemployment. Shelley did not oppose—and in his dealings with tradesmen and moneylenders personally took advantage of—laws that prohibited the confiscation and sale of hereditary landed estates to pay the owner's debts.[4] In 1807 Sir Samuel Romilly (the leading barrister who later acted in important legal battles involving Shelley and Byron) was serving as solicitor general and introduced in the House of Commons legislation designed to correct this legal vestige of the feudal system. William Lamb (later Lord Melbourne) wrote in his journal on the occasion:

> The third reading of the Solicitor-General's (Sir S. Romilly's) Bill for making the freehold estates of persons dying insolvent assets for the payment of their simple contract debts. The landed interest were much alarmed, and all the old topics of the danger of innovation, the value of country gentlemen, the sanctity of family settlements, the antiquity of the present law, were very strongly insisted upon. . . . The Bill was rejected—sixty-nine to forty-seven—the majority having in it many landed proprietors, either in possession or expectancy; a most disgraceful division, and one

3. Among secondary sources (besides the *DNB, Annual Registers*, peerages, and encyclopedias), I have found the following useful in studying the political background: F. O'Gorman, *The Whig Party and the French Revolution* (London: Macmillan, 1967); Michael Roberts, *The Whig Party, 1807–1812* (London: Frank Cass, 1965); A. S. Turberville, *The House of Lords in the Age of Reform, 1784–1837* (London: Faber and Faber, 1958); G. E. Mingay, *English Landed Society in the Eighteenth Century* (London: Routledge and Kegan Paul, 1963); F. M. L. Thompson, *English Landed Society in the Nineteenth Century* (London: Routledge and Kegan Paul, 1963); E. P. Thompson, *The Making of the English Working Class* (London: Victor Gollancz, 1963); Douglas Hay et al., *Albion's Fatal Tree: Crime and Society in Eighteenth-Century England* (New York: Pantheon, 1975); J. P. D. Dunbabin, *Rural Discontent in Nineteenth-Century Britain* (New York: Holmes & Meier, 1974); Norman McCord, *The Anti-Corn Law League, 1838–1846* (London: George Allen & Unwin, 1958); Travis L. Crosby, *English Farmers and the Politics of Protection, 1815–1852* (Hassocks, Sussex: Harvester Press, 1977).
4. Some instances of this penchant have been discussed by Kenneth Neill Cameron and Donald H. Reiman in SC; see, for example, "Shelley's Chariot" (vol. 3 [1970], pp. 153–78), SC 262, Commentary (vol. 3, pp. 333–39), SC 454, Commentary (vol. 5 [1973], pp. 478–84), and "Shelley and the Upholsterers of Bath" (vol. 8 [1986], pp. 827–38).

which really hurt and mortified me deeply, as I could see no plausible argument *ab inconvenienti* . . . that . . . ought to prevail
against the glaring injustice of the law as it at present stands.[5]

As social and political historians have noted, the members of the
House of Lords effectively controlled the House of Commons at least
until the passage of the first reform bill of 1832. But as F. M. L.
Thompson also observes, the nobility had such great power during
most of the period between 1660 and 1832 that they were divided by
private interests and personal rivalries. Though I have not all the facts
at hand to sketch the interactions of the various factions that called
themselves "Whigs" and "Tories" during the late eighteenth century, I
will observe (and this is far from a truism among the social and political historians of England that I have read) that the heart of the "Whig
Connexion"—the great magnates such as the Howard dukes of Norfolk and the Russell dukes of Bedford—had their chief estates in the
east or south of England and derived the bulk of their income from
the rents of tenant farmers with long-term leases who raised cereal
grains ("corn") and other foodstuffs.[6] The Tory lords, on the other
hand, included a much larger number who derived their chief
income—or, at least, whose family fortunes had been recently
established—from activities other than rents from corn farming: for
example, the Lowther earls of Lonsdale derived a large part of their
income from coal mines at Whitehaven and from the development of
the port there. Many of the peers whose estates were in Ireland, Wales,
the Border and Highlands of Scotland, and the west of England drew
their chief income from raising sheep to supply the textile industry or
from land development of the new industrial cities and towns that were
springing up in the Midlands, Lancashire, the West Riding of York-
shire, and the Scottish Lowlands. The family of Lord Grosvenor (patron of William Gifford) had built its chief fortune from subdividing
and developing one rather small manor (acquired through marriage in
1677) into what is now the part of London surrounding Grosvenor
Square (in Shelley's time the most fashionable address in London).[7]
The wealth of Robert Banks Jenkinson, Earl of Liverpool and long-

5. *Lord Melbourne's Papers*, ed. L. C. Sanders (London: Longmans, Green, 1889), pp. 32–33.
6. F. M. L. Thompson's *English Landed Society in the Nineteenth Century* includes a map
(p. xiii) reproducing a line of demarcation between "the predominantly corn counties of the
east from the grazing counties of the west . . . from J. Caird, *English Agriculture in 1850–
51*." In addition to major seats at Arundel Castle in Sussex and Worksop Manor, Notting-
hamshire, the Duke of Norfolk had a northern seat at Greystoke (or Graystock) Castle, near
Penrith, Cumberland, where Shelley, Harriet Shelley, and Eliza Westbrook were his guests
from 1 December to 8 or 9 December 1811. Though this estate falls on the "grazing" side
of Caird's line, I recall from a brief visit to Greystoke in 1971 that the area surrounding it
is relatively level rather than hilly and was at the time of my visit devoted to raising grain
rather than sheep. Kenneth Neill Cameron's assertion in *The Young Shelley: Genesis of a
Radical* (New York: Macmillan, 1950) that Sir Bysshe Shelley and the Duke of Norfolk,
because they were Whigs, supported the mercantile interests and drew a great part of their
wealth from sheep farming and timber (pp. 37–38) was based on insufficient information
about the Shelley estates and the agricultural situation in the southern and eastern parts of
England, as well as on generalizations made about the dominant Whigs of the seventeenth
and eighteenth centuries that were not valid for the Foxite Whigs of the 1790s. Walpole was
a mercantilist; Bedford and Norfolk certainly were not.
7. See A. I. Dasant, *A History of Grosvenor Square* (London: Macmillan, 1935).

time Tory prime minister, came in the first instance from his father's and his own lucrative government positions and sinecures and from involvement in foreign (particularly East Indian) trade. Other leading Tories drew their wealth from West Indian plantations or from supplying goods and services to the British army and navy. (The same owners of forested lands in the west of England, Wales, Scotland, or the colonies profited, for example, from the sale of timber for shipbuilding and repairs.) These Tories, with deep personal interests in foreign trade, the colonial empire, and open markets throughout the world, and in expanding the amount of money that passed through their hands as government officials and contractors, naturally tended to identify British national interest with defeating French expansion, controlling the seas, and seizing new colonies and overseas markets. The agrarian Whig magnates, on the other hand, saw the French Wars only as an excuse to increase their taxes, draw off their labor force for the military, and add to the wealth of the capitalists, industrialists, and overseas slaveowners who were their rivals for political control of the country. (Some of the Whigs would have favored the increase in the bureaucracy, government spending, and peculations of officialdom if they had been the "ins" instead of the "outs.") In short, the "radicalism" of such Whig magnates as Francis, Duke of Bedford (whose attacks on the Pitt administration's aggressive policies of containing the French Revolution elicited Burke's *Letter to a Noble Lord*), and Charles, Duke of Norfolk (who was the political ally and sponsor of Sir Bysshe Shelley and Timothy Shelley, M.P.), was essentially an attack by the older landed aristocracy on government policies designed to enrich the capitalist-commercial interests. These so-called "radical" Whigs of the 1790s hoped to rally a coalition of the food-farming interests in the populous agricultural areas of the south and east of England, small merchants, craftsmen, and professional men, and ideological humanitarians who opposed slavery and the bloodshed of war (some of whom also favored broadening the franchise, particularly in the growing towns and cities). France when ruled by the old aristocracy had competed with the British agricultural interests, whereas France ruled by the bourgeoisie would compete with British capital, manufacturing, and commercial interests. Why shouldn't Bedford and Norfolk favor the French Revolution? But should a modern historian call Bedford and Norfolk radicals or reactionaries?

According to G. E. Mingay, in 1790 "there were some 400 families [in all Great Britain] who could be described as great landlords" with incomes of at least £5,000 to £10,000 per year.[8] Certainly Sir Bysshe Shelley fell into that category, for after his death—when his estates were divided between his two principal heirs (Sir Timothy Shelley, his eldest son by his first wife, and Sir John Shelley Sidney of Penshurst, his eldest son by his second wife) and after all the younger siblings of each had been provided for (as well as Sir Bysshe's mistress Eleanor

---

8. *English Landed Society in the Eighteenth Century*, pp. 19–20.

Nicholls of Canterbury and his four children by her)—the rent-rolls of the lands in trust for Sir Timothy Shelley's estates totaled about £4,500 per year and the trustees held at least £15,000 in unencumbered mortgages and accounts receivable for Sir Timothy and his heirs.[9] (Sir Bysshe had also directed that the residue of his personal property be used to purchase additional land in England.) Thus Bysshe Shelley's heirs in Sussex and Kent grew up in the knowledge that Bysshe was one of the small number of very wealthy landowners in Britain, and yet—when the estates were divided—found themselves on the lower edge of this elite class. As time passed and great fortunes were made in trade, manufacturing, and government appointments (with their vast opportunities for speculation and peculation added to the acknowledged emoluments), all the landed families sank in relation to these *nouveaux riches*.[1] On the growth of this new class of wealthy men, Shelley (like Peacock, for example, in his genealogical account of "Ebenezer Mac Crotchet, Esquire" in *Crotchet Castle* [1831]) expressed himself very negatively in *A Philosophical View of Reform* (1819–1820):

> Instead of one aristocracy, the condition which in the present state of human affairs, the friends of justice and liberty are willing to subscribe as to an inevitable evil, they have supplied us with two aristocracies: The one, consisting [of] the great land proprietors and wealthy merchants, receive and interchange the produce of this country with the produce of other countries; in this because all other great communities have as yet acquiesced in it we acquiesce. . . . [But there] is an aristocracy of attornies and excisemen and directors and government pensioners, usurers, stock jobbers, country bankers with their dependents and descendants. These are a set of pelting wretches in whose employment there is nothing to exercise, even to their distortion, the more majestic faculties of the soul. Though at the bottom it is all trick, there is something magnificent in the chivalrous disdain of infamy connected with a gentleman. . . . But in the habits and lives of this new aristocracy created out of an increase [in] the public calamities, and whose existence must be determined by their termination, there is nothing to qualify our disapprobation. They eat and drink and sleep, and in the interval of those [actions] being performed with the most ridiculous ceremony and accompaniments, they cringe and lie.[2]

9. These facts are drawn from two legal documents in The Carl H. Pforzheimer Library: (1) "Analysis of the Will and Codicils of Sir Bysshe Shelley Bart. deceased" (Shelleyana 170B) and (2) a list of "Property & Estates under the Settlement of 1782[,] Settlement of 1791 & Will of John Shelley Esq." (Shelleyana 173). This second document, dated 20 January 1815 for delivery to Shelley's solicitor P. W. Longdill, contains a full list of landed properties under the settlements, together with the names of tenants and the lengths and terms of leases. These documents are cited by permission of The Carl and Lily Pforzheimer Foundation, Inc.
1. Mingay, *English Landed Society in the Eighteenth Century*, p. 4; details on the decline are given in F. M. L. Thompson's companion volume, *English Landed Society in the Nineteenth Century*.
2. Edited from the literal transcription published in SC, 6:1016–17.

Shelley goes on to pillory the *nouveaux riches* in several equally sting-ing sentences, and he writes that, because "the merchant and the country gentleman," the "instruments of the fraud," are "as usual" the people first deceived, they "may be excused for believing" that the existence of this second aristocracy "is connected with the permanence of the best practicable forms of the social order."[3] In short, Shelley believes that custom, tradition, and the higher nature of their char-acter and utility sanction the landed and older merchant aristocracy, but denies the value of those whose wealth was newly created by the need to fund the national debt, the issuing of paper money and credit, and the expansion of governmental bureaucracy during the American and French wars, 1775–1815. Shelley does not, at this point, mention wealth created by industrialists. In another part of *A Philosophical View of Reform*, he presents "two descriptions of property"—a legiti-mate one deriving from "labour, industry, economy, skill, genius, or any similar power honourably and innocently exerted" and another that was procured "by fraudulent and violent means" or "has its foundation in usurpation or violence, without which, by the nature of things, im-mense aggregations of possessions of gold or land could never have been accumulated." Here, we see, he lumps all substantial gains from capital investments, rather than from "skill" or "genius," as illegitimate property of the second kind.

Shelley then proceeds to state that the second kind of property "be-ing transmitted from father to son, acquires, as property of the more legitimate kind loses, force and sanction, but in a more limited man-ner." And he suggests that all such property, in excess of the needs of common life, might be liable to expropriation by the nation to pay off the "national debt"—but at a discount, since that debt is not truly national, but "is a debt contracted by the whole of a particular class in the nation towards a portion of that class."[4]

As radical as this solution seems to be, it would merely, as he said earlier, "determine" (i.e., "to put an end to," *OED* I.1) the entire race of "pelting wretches" in the second aristocracy. Once the national debt, paper money, and other "fraudulent . . . means" had been abol-ished, thought Shelley, these drones would be forced to earn their livings by their "labour, industry, . . . skill, genius." That would, we note, leave only the older landed and commercial aristocracy, though reduced in wealth by the nation's expropriation of the gross excess acquired by their ancestors by "grants from feudal sovereigns, . . . lands of the antient Catholic clergy, . . . or the products of patents and monopolies" (*Shelley and his Circle*, 6:1035).

It would be interesting to know the full history of Sir Bysshe Shel-ley's acquisition of land and money. The supposition is that his original lands came chiefly from directly inheriting small holdings that had been in the family for generations and from marrying two heiresses of estates—in the case of Shelley's own grandmother, Mary Catherine

3. Edited from ibid., 6:1017.
4. Edited from ibid., 6:1033–37.

Michell, the sixteen-year-old orphan daughter of Rev. Theobald Michell of Horsham, perhaps herself the heiress of a series of small holdings inherited by her father from various relatives. The Michells and Shelleys had earlier intermarried, and Field Place itself had belonged to the Michells through the sixteenth and seventeenth centuries.[5] If these inferences are true, then it just happens that the bulk of landed wealth held in trust by the terms of Sir Bysshe Shelley's will for his son Sir Timothy, grandson Percy Bysshe, and *his* eldest surviving son, might be of that class of property—according to Shelley's arguments in *A Philosophical View of Reform* (an unfinished draft, to be sure)—that would be exempt from national confiscation.

Shelley, I suggest—benevolent and generous though he was and possessing a highly sensitive social conscience though he did—was not himself exempt from being unconsciously swayed in his social, economic, and political theories by inbred class prejudices.[6] He might agree (with Burke) that the Russell dukes of Bedford, whose lands were gifts of Henry VIII for service in the suppression of the Roman Catholic church, or the Howard dukes of Norfolk, whose lands descended from the feudal titles of the Norman barons who followed William the Conqueror, should have their patrimony reduced or entirely confiscated, but his arguments led toward the conclusion that, in the name of justice, *his* ox should not be gored. These observations are not meant to discredit Shelley's social thought, which is, in many respects, altruistic and far ahead of both his time and ours. They merely point to a few limitations of perspective that even the best persons exhibit because of their interests or experience.[7]

Shelley's political ideas sound, at the theoretical level, extremely radical. From his *Proposals for an Association* and *Declaration of Rights* (both 1812) to *A Proposal for Putting Reform to the Vote* (1817) and *A Philosophical View of Reform* (1818–1820), Shelley continually holds up as his ideal a free, classless society in which there would be unlimited freedom of speech and interposition of government only to stop one person from infringing the rights of another. Like Jefferson, he believed that the less government, the better, and thus his social thought parallels Godwin's brand of philosophical anarchism. But at the practical level, Shelley believed compromise and an orderly, step-by-step progression to be necessary. In his note to *Queen Mab* on "and statesmen boast / Of wealth" (V.94), Shelley observes: "I will not insult

5. See Roger Ingpen, *Shelley in England* (London: Kegan Paul, Trench, Trubner, 1917), pp. 7–8.
6. Kenneth Neill Cameron has noted in *Humanity and Society: A World History* (Bloomington: Indiana University Press, 1973) how Plato's ideas were influenced by his connection with "the landowning aristocracy of Athens" and how Aristotle's ideal of the "middle path" reflects "the views of his own class, the professional class, which occupied a middle position in society," as well as the fact that, because he "came from Stageira . . . a Greek colony," he could "view Athenian society and thought with critical objectivity" (pp. 216–18).
7. David V. Erdman has noted an ambivalence similar to Shelley's in Byron's attitude toward "the economic and social and especially the political conditions of his heritage" (see SC, 3:283ff.). Recently I observed in an account of Tadeuz Kosciuszko that, though he fought bravely, honorably, and well for the freedom of the American colonies and of Poland and though, when he was released from a Russian prison in 1796 and returned to America, he used the money awarded him by Congress to buy the freedom of Negro slaves, he (like Thomas Jefferson) did not free the serfs on his own Polish estates until near the time of his death.

common sense by insisting on the doctrine of the natural equality of man. The question is not concerning its desirableness, but its practicability: so far as it is practicable, it is desirable." At the end of *A Proposal for Putting Reform to the Vote*, Shelley also enunciates his ideals as "Universal Suffrage" and "a pure republic," and yet temporizes by arguing that, because of the "imprepared state of public knowledge and feeling," "I think that none but those who register their names as paying a certain small sum in *direct taxes* ought, at present, to send Members to Parliament" (direct taxes in 1817 being chiefly real estate taxes) and that "nothing can less consist with reason . . . than the plan which should abolish the regal and the aristocratical branches of our constitution, before the public mind, through many gradations of improvement, shall have arrived at the maturity which can disregard these symbols of its childhood."[8]

Even in *The Mask of Anarchy*, Shelley's most radical major poem, his agrarian and aristocratic biases are apparent. The identifiable social institutions that he attacks as evil are the slave trade (line 8; see footnote glosses to "bloodhounds"); the Court of Chancery (lines 14–21); the church heirarchy, lawyers, the House of Lords, and the use of spies and *agents provocateurs* (line 29); the standing army (lines 42–49); royal prerogatives (lines 78–81); the Bank of England, Tower of London (another symbol of royal power), and the corrupt, unreformed Parliament (lines 82–85); the practice of hiring (industrial) workers by the day at subsistence wages (lines 160ff.); paper currency (lines 176–83); and the thirst for revenge. All these had been from time immemorial enemies to the untitled landed gentry.

And what positive goals does Shelley put before the wretched populace in *The Mask of Anarchy*? Fundamentally, enough "clothes, and fire, and food" in "a neat and happy home" (lines 217–25; "happy" here means free from want). Beyond those basics, the people must possess enough boldness to redress excessive wrongs by the rich (lines 226–29); they must enjoy equal protection under the law, freedom from religious superstition (lines 230–33), and peace—especially from such liberticide wars as those against France (lines 239–41). Finally, Shelley praises "Love" that leads some of the rich (such as Shelley) to "give their substance" or even "turn their wealth to arms" in a war against "wealth, and war, and fraud" and "power" (lines 246–53). He goes on to set his ideal for the common people:

> "Science, Poetry, and Thought
> Are thy [Freedom's] lamps; they make the lot
> Of the dwellers in a cot
> So serene, they curse it not." (lines 254–57)

Did Shelley actually believe that a knowledge of science and poetry would make the poor content in their relative poverty, even if they possessed an adequate supply of food, fuel, and clothing "in a neat and happy home," or was this assurance mere rhetoric to calm the

8. Shelley, *Works* (Julian Edition), 6:68.

fears of the upper classes? In neither interpretation are his words exactly the sentiments of an egalitarian leveler, arousing farm laborers and the urban proletariat to claim full legal and economic equality.

Shelley in his lifetime certainly gave ample evidence of his benevolent disposition to help those less fortunate than himself, from giving sheets, blankets, and medicines to the poor weavers of the Marlow area to funding the follies of Godwin, Hunt, and Henry Reveley. But he also found it difficult to avoid sounding patronizing, as he and Mary Shelley learned to their sorrow in their dealings with William Thomas Baxter and his family (see *Shelley and his Circle*, 5:333–92, 505–8). Thomas Love Peacock, apparently, also resented the situation in which, for a few years, Shelley maintained his services as a factotum for an annual stipend of £100 to £125. Not only did Peacock suppress all evidence of this arrangement after Shelley's death by destroying letters of his own and letters from Shelley to him in which this annuity was mentioned, but at the time he even made out the quarterly checks (at least four of which survive) to his friends Thomas Hookham and Robert Madocks or Maddocks, as though in payment of Shelley's debts to them.[9] Yet Peacock seems to have understood and appreciated Shelley's need to patronize others, for he depicts it very sympathetically in his characterizations of Shelley both as Sylvan Forester in *Melincourt* (1817), where (as David Garnett has observed) Peacock's tone and ideas most nearly coincide with Shelley's, and as Algernon Falconer in *Gryll Grange* (1860), where Peacock idealizes the young Shelley as he never did during Shelley's lifetime. Both Forester and Falconer are aristocrats in the best sense of that term—wealthy, cultured, well-educated, and strongly motivated by *noblesse oblige*. Falconer protects (as his servants) seven orphaned sisters, whom he determines never to abandon, even at the cost of his own happiness. When it is explained that they, like him, wish to marry, he gives each a generous dowry. Sylvan Forester in *Melincourt* is more identifiably a country squire—what Shelley might have become had he inherited his patrimony in 1816–1817, when he was disposed toward a life of retirement as the "hermit" of Bishopsgate or Marlow. Besides sponsoring his friend Oran Haut-ton (an orangutan who becomes both a baronet and a member of Parliament), Forester is benevolent to individuals and encourages such direct social action as refusing to use sugar or other products of slave plantations (see especially Chapter 5). But in a number of speeches (as well as in his general behavior), Forester refuses to renounce fully the class distinctions of the day. In answer to a criticism of his radicalism by Mr. Fax, Forester replies:

> I am no revolutionist. I am no advocate for violent and arbitrary changes in the state of society. I care not in what proportions property is divided (though I think there are certain limits which

---

9. For some of the checks, see Walter E. Peck, *Shelley: His Life and Work* (Boston: Houghton Mifflin, 1927), 2:392–93. We know from Peacock's surviving correspondence that Shelley's debts to Hookham and Maddocks were never paid. From the evidence of others, summarized in SC, 4:590–92, we know that Peacock for an undetermined period received financial help from Shelley.

it ought never to pass, and approve the wisdom of the American laws in restricting the fortune of a private citizen to twenty thousand a year), provided the rich can be made to know that they are but the stewards of the poor, that they are not to be the monopolizers of solitary spoil, but the distributors of general possession; that they are responsible for that distribution to every principle of general justice, to every tie of moral obligation, to every feeling of human sympathy: that they are bound to cultivate simple habits in themselves, and encourage most such arts of industry and peace, as are most compatible with the health and liberty of others.[1]

This chapter of *Melincourt* and Chapter 26, "The Cottagers," show more clearly than any of Shelley's own theoretical pronouncements how he might have carried out his social philosophy, had he inherited the life-interest in the estates entailed to him. And if the picture of the life of Forester's estate—"the neatness and comfort of the dwellings, the exquisite order of the gardens, the ingenuous air of happiness and liberty that characterized the simple inhabitants, and the health and beauty of the little rosy children that were sporting in the fields"—owes something to Peacock's own ideals, as well as to eighteenth-century nostalgic or utopian scenes from Squire Allworthy's estate to "sweet Auburn" to Rasselas's Happy Valley, we can be sure from Shelley's own publications and letters that it accords with his ideals as well. Peacock, as a semi-objective observer of his friend and patron, knew what Shelley often refused to admit, even to himself—the importance to Shelley of an appropriate response to his generosity:

> Mr. Forester had been recognised from a distance. The cottagers ran out in all directions to welcome him: the valley and the hills seemed starting into life, as men, women, and children poured down, as with one impulse, on the path of his approach, while some hastened to the residence of Miss Evergreen, ambitious of being the first to announce to her the arrival of her nephew. Miss Evergreen came forward to meet the party, surrounded by a rustic crowd of both sexes and of every age, from the old man leaning on his stick, to the little child that could just run alone, but had already learnt to attach something magical to the sound of the name of Forester. (Peacock, *Complete Novels*, 1:251)

If this idyll and others like it, expressed or implied, in Shelley's own works and those of his close friends writing about him strike us as being excessively paternalistic—even dangerously close to "Massa's in de cold, cold ground"—we must remember that such more recent ideals as that which sees the poor but rugged individualist who maintains his independence by always triumphing over adversity and that which imagines the abolition of poverty and dependence through an equitable state system of social welfare are also conditioned by particular times, backgrounds, and experiences and that each of these also

1. Peacock, *The Complete Novels*, ed. David Garnett (London: Rupert Hart-Davis, 1963), 1:243–44.

may strike other people with different ideals as either naive or immoral. Shelley's social ideals were, like ours, limited by his perspective within the human condition. To recognize that fact helps us understand certain patterns of behavior that might otherwise seem inexplicable.[2] But it does not invalidate his claim to our attention. As Morse Peckham has pointed out more cogently than any other theorist that I know, "complete historical interpretation" not only takes into account the historical context being analyzed, with a view to seeing the circumstances and limitations of those persons and works being studied, but also recognizes that the historian is himself a limited human being caught within the partial blindness of his own historical perspective.[3] Recognizing this truth, we can come to terms with Shelley's inevitable limitations without condescending to him. We can acknowledge of him—as he acknowledged of Keats (whose limitations Shelley keenly recognized)—that though he like us was once caught within the unwilling dross that checks the Spirit's flight, his poetry and the general tendency of his life and thought rank him, along with a few others of his age (a minority even more select than the rich landed gentry of England), as one of the splendors of the firmament of time.

2. For example, Peacock relates that as "we were walking . . . through a village where there was a good vicarage house, with a nice garden," Shelley, impressed by the quiet beauty of the scene, "suddenly said to me,—'I feel stronly inclined to enter the church' " ("Memoirs of Percy Bysshe Shelley" in Peacock, *Works*, ed. H. F. B. Brett-Smith and C. E. Jones [London: Constable, 1934], 8:76). Peacock calls this "the most singular" of Shelley's many schemes of life, but, viewed from his delight in magnanimously patronizing and teaching others, it is no stranger than his later desire for a position in the East India Company.

3. Peckham outlines his important theory in "On the Historical Interpretation of Literature," reprinted in Peckham's *The Triumph of Romanticism: Collected Essays* (Columbia: University of South Carolina Press, 1970), especially pp. 449–50. Another useful theoretical position relevant to this paper is outlined by Terry Eagleton in *Marxism and Literary Criticism* (Berkeley: University of California Press, 1976). Eagleton, unlike less perceptive Marxist critics, recognizes that great works such as Conrad's *Nostromo* or Eliot's *The Waste Land* can be written by political conservatives or even reactionaries: "in the absence of genuinely revolutionary art, only a radical conservatism, hostile like Marxism to the withered values of liberal bourgeois society, could produce the most significant literature" (p. 8).

# General Studies

## STUART CURRAN

## Shelley and the End(s) of Ideology[†]

Liberation was the driving passion of Shelley's life. His 'far goal of time' is the symphonic anarchy of the fourth act of *Prometheus Unbound*:

> . . . one harmonious Soul of many a soul
> Whose nature is its own divine controul
> Where all things flow to all, like rivers to the sea.
> (IV. 400–2)

If that paradise to us seems unattainable, its terms at least can be reasonably comprehended. A more difficult question than the utopian goal of liberation is from what exactly we are to liberate ourselves. Just how shall we define, how do we even recognize in their protean multiplicity,

> . . . those foul shapes, abhorred by God and man—
> Which under many a name and many a form
> Strange, savage, ghastly, dark and execrable
> Were Jupiter, the tyrant of the world
> (III. iv. 180–3)?

My contention is that Jupiter is constituted by interlocking systems of ideology and that Shelley spent his entire life in an endeavor to locate the root from which this vast and ever-spreading upas—a 'poison-tree, / Beneath whose shade all life is withered up,' he called it in *Queen Mab* (VI 207–8)—derived its sustenance.

It all seemed easy enough to him at first. Following Godwin, Shelley determined that all external sources of power were inimical to human well-being. In the central cantos of *Queen Mab*, and particularly in the remarkable notes appended to them, he traced with brilliant clarity an interdependence of civil, commercial, and religious power, each component protecting itself through its association with the others, functioning together collectively to deprive individuals of their natural rights: 'Kings, priests, and statesmen, blast the human flower / Even

† From *The Most Unfailing Herald: Percy Bysshe Shelley 1792–1992*, ed. Alan M. Weinberg and Romaine Hill (Pretoria: Unisa Press, 1996), pp. 21–30. Reprinted by permission of Unisa Press. Page references have been changed to correspond to this Norton Critical Edition.

in its tender bud' (IV 104–5). The organic metaphor is central here: 'How withered all the buds of natural good! / No shade, no shelter from the sweeping storms / Of pitiless power!' (IV 125–7). Such systems of power are of their essence inhuman, inimical to natural growth: state power through its physical constraints, religion through shackling the mind, commerce through treating human beings as 'Scarce living pulleys of a dead machine, / Mere wheels of work and articles of trade' (V 76–7). Shelley's identification of an interlocking power structure remains even today a compelling feature of the social analysis of *Queen Mab*, but the poem fails exactly at the point of explaining why so monstrous a structure exists in the first place; for without that understanding of the foundation there can be no hope of toppling the edifice reared upon it.

The same problem dogged Shelley's forays into political activism of the previous year, forays whose lack of real consequence had to have been a major spur to his attempt to integrate a social vision in his philosophical poem. In *An Address to the Irish People* (Dublin, 1812), Shelley twice admonishes the Irish, as a means to their liberation, to '[t]hink, read, and talk' (49), surely aware that empty rhetoric is the articulation of mere good intentions. The inadequacy of his prescription for Ireland's alleviation notwithstanding, Shelley seems to have determined that good intentions, if sufficiently magnified or perhaps mystified, might provide the platform on which like Archimedes he could hope to stand and move the universe, as his epigraph to *Queen Mab* indicates. The Necessity on which his poem so depends for motive power is intentionality constituted as a universal force, an ideology to overthrow ideologies. Yet, even as Shelley had himself cautioned the Irish 'to take great care . . . that while one tyranny is destroyed, another more fierce and terrible does not spring up' (43), his Necessity looks suspiciously like the interlocked system of repression it would drive from existence. It is even figured repeatedly, if incongruously, as a chain (VI 186, VII 17) that will free us from 'the darkness of our prison, / Whose chains and massy walls / We feel, but cannot see' (VI 194–6). Godwin's Necessity had been construed as an accumulated weight of historical consequence, rather in the manner of Derridean traces, driving toward an ever-receding future. Shelley, desperate, as Godwin's admonishing letters recognized,[1] for a more certain means of social amelioration, transforms Necessity into omnipotence, 'Apportioning with irresistible law / The place each spring of its machine shall fill' (VI 163–4). Doubtless, Shelley intended no new tyranny to succeed the old; rather, he was emphasizing, through the natural composition of society as a collection of individual wills contending for self-fulfillment, the inevitable failure of any individual or oligarchy to exercise hegemonic control. But that he cannot find a metaphor that does not reconstitute (chain, spring, machine) what it would overthrow is indicative of a serious intellectual fault beneath

---

1. In particular, see Godwin's letter of 14 March 1812, reprinted in *Letters* II, 269–70 n.

the avowed stability of his platform.[2] A totalizing force must by its conceptual nature enforce, compelling submission to its dictates.

At what point Shelley abandoned this faith in a crude necessitarianism is debatable. I am myself unsure that he ever held it, except for the rhetorical purposes of his poem.[3] Certainly, by 1819, when he traced his philosophical development in 'On Life,' he looked back on these conceptions from a bemused distance we do not usually associate with him: 'The shocking absurdities of the popular philosophy of mind and matter, and its fatal consequences in morals, their violent dogmatism concerning the source of all things, had early conducted me to materialism. This materialism is a seducing system to young and superficial minds' [506]. By his second major attempt to create a myth of liberation from tyranny, *The Revolt of Islam*, Shelley has abandoned the notion of a totalizing counter-force to tyranny. Under the generalized impress of Napoleon's example, he may even have abandoned the notion of ideology; for what sustains the Tyrant of Islam on his throne is raw fear, and its specular inversion is responsible for the psychosis driving the Iberian Priest's persecution: 'fear of God did in his bosom breed / A jealous hate of man, an unreposing need' (X 4097–8). The Priest is self-victimized before he sets out to persecute others, and his victims reinforce the vicious circle in which that self-victimization plays itself out. What can dispel the fear and undermine the despotic system it sustains are mere words, the power of oratory. This may seem at first to involve an even greater mystification than the intentionality of *Queen Mab*, yet in recognizing that the sources of tyranny are not external but psychological, Shelley has taken a major step toward his mature political understanding. Cythna's rhetoric disintegrates the protective covering of social roles, forcing those who have identified their selves with their consigned roles to acknowledge their common and inherent humanity. But not enough of them, it would seem, are able to—or care to. What defeats Laon and Cythna is not the residual force of ideology, social structures whose integrated power defies challenge, but merely the force of arms that a league of petty tyrants can together muster to support one of their own. In identifying the underlying problem as psychological, Shelley might seem in *The Revolt of Islam* to have discounted much too easily the strength of those external institutions whose interconnections he had so skillfully anatomized in *Queen Mab*.

Yet, whether from mere wish-fulfillment, or from the desire to have his poem as a whole actually reflect the oratorical powers of its fictive heroine, or (the alternative I prefer) from a shrewd self-questioning of

2. In Shelley's *Annus Mirabilis: The Maturing of an Epic Vision*, San Marino, California, Huntington Library, 1975, 18–19, I saw these contradictions in the light of Shelley's epic ambitions. They appear to me now to be even more serious in their ramifications than they seemed in that earlier account.

3. I do not mean cavalierly to dismiss the distinguished critics who have argued for the significance of a concept of Necessity in Shelley's work. Kenneth Neill Cameron, *The Young Shelley: Genesis of a Radical*, New York, Macmillan, 1950—see esp. 270–3—assumes the notion as a given. The subtlest rendering of how necessitarian values continue in Shelley's works is that of Stuart Sperry, 'Necessity and the Role of the Hero in Shelley's *Prometheus Unbound*', PMLA XCVI, 1981, 242–54.

his only means of securing a liberating influence in the real world, writing, Shelley has located the source of the power of ideologies and the problem of dispelling them: words. Once in Italy Shelley is displaced from his earlier political fantasies and, perhaps shocked by a prolonged experience of his own linguistic instability, begins to question the extent to which words, as the names of objects, can themselves assume the function of roles. Demogorgon, reclaiming the part of the earlier Necessity, shifts its axis, refusing in his sublime confrontation with Asia to answer her repeated request for names, for an external and objective embodiment of the source of evil. Similarly, in the first act Prometheus cannot hear his own words except as they are voiced by the Other whose power those words have helped sustain. In both cases Shelley underscores the extent to which ideological formulations are psychic arrangements and, in the mirrored face-off between Prometheus and the Phantasm of Jupiter, he even suggests that they can continue to determine mental reality after a repression so severe that their very terms are forgotten.

Although I believe that *The Cenci*, as a representation of 'sad reality' against the 'idealisms of moral excellence' of *Prometheus Unbound*, systematically inverts the issues and tropes of that work, an argument I attempted to demonstrate in *Shelley's Annus Mirabilis*,[4] in respect to the issue I am pursuing here, the tragedy represents the logical outgrowth of the ideological repression revealed in Act I of the lyrical drama. Christianity is the hegemonic ideological force of the tragedy as well as the categorical imperative for each of its characters, and in his unfolding plot Shelley brilliantly dramatizes what must eventuate from the panoply of hidden contradictions within Italian Catholicism he so cogently remarks in his 'Preface': 'interwoven with the whole fabric of life. . . . Religion pervades intensely the whole frame of society, and is according to the temper of the mind which it inhabits, a passion, a persuasion, an excuse, a refuge; never a check' [143]. Cenci appeals to God to support his sadism; the Pope his temporal power; Cardinal Camillo his ineffectual sentimentality; and Beatrice her demand for justice. Each has a psychological investment in a system incompatible with the claims of all: thus, it is ideology that rapes Beatrice, as it is ideology that murders her father. And yet, Beatrice, alone of the characters, recognizes how the word betrays. To the puzzlement of her family and Orsino she will not name the act perpetrated against her as rape, nor in the trial scene and after will she name her own action as parricide. To name is to replace the unique act with an idea of it, with an abstract representation that distorts and necessarily destroys. Once the church and state have reduced Beatrice herself to that abstract representation, she may be safely, even routinely, executed.

At the end of the tragedy Beatrice glimpses what it might be like to

---

4. See Chapter 4, 119–36. For useful insight on the Italian bases of *The Cenci*, see Chapter 3 ('Shelley and Renaissance Italy: *The Cenci*') in Alan M. Weinberg, *Shelley's Italian Experience*, New York, St Martin's Press, 1991, 71–100.

live outside ideological bounds, but she cannot realistically attain that
realm, and not just because she is in prison. In her culture no woman
can live outside the boundaries of ideological control. Indeed, it is
questionable, as Orsino's final monologue allows us to see, how much
even an 'unaccommodated man' can continue to manipulate a world
on whose systems of power he has no grasp. Inevitably, ideology destroys the individual, and yet it appears the be-all and end-all of human
culture. In that massive contradiction lies a tragic conception reminiscent of the Greeks.

Yet, why should human beings willingly cede their autonomy to such
stifling bondage? Shelley is clear about his sense of the reason—clear,
and penetrating, as well, in the care with which he traces its implications. We give ourselves over to system, he suggests, rather than
tempt chaos. We crave a totalizing order, for it excludes the menace
of the unknown, excludes it even to the point of literally sacrificing it
when it threatens to obtrude. No wonder Jupiter sits on his throne
serenely unconscious of his impending doom. As the avatar of all ideological systems whatsoever, his only threat can come from their total
rejection, and that he cannot foresee. Yet, it is precisely this Prometheus accomplishes when he steps outside the system of antagonism
he has created in collusion with Jupiter; and his achievement is simultaneously doubled by Asia as she finds herself unable, perhaps
unwilling, to scapegoat Jupiter by naming him the source of evil. Jupiter's reality therefore simply disintegrates: 'No pity, no release, no
respite! . . . No refuge! no appeal! (III. i. 64, 70). He is negated as a
form of thought. Here is what I would surmise is the relevant commentary on the fall of Jupiter from 'On Life,' written in the same year:

> Philosophy, impatient as it may be to build, has much work yet
> remaining as pioneer for the overgrowth of ages. It makes one
> step towards this object; it destroys error, and the roots of error.
> It leaves, what is too often the duty of the reformer in political
> and ethical questions to leave, a vacancy. It reduces the mind to
> that freedom in which it would have acted, but for the misuse of
> words and signs, the instruments of its own creation. [507]

Jupiter falls into vacancy and we too become lodged in that mental
kingdom which is its counterpart, he leaves behind his instruments, a
wreckage of signs the Spirit of the Hour will, at the end of Act III,
observe 'are now / But an astonishment' (III. iv. 175–6). These 'foul
shapes' remain behind, 'not o'erthrown, but unregarded now' (III. iv.
179–80). In other words, Jupiter disappears, but his words do not.
That is why Demogorgon ends the drama with a timely warning about
historical repetitions. We are dependent upon words, and, since they
are arbitrary representations of unique things in unique combinations
caught in a unique moment of time, they are susceptible—more than
susceptible, they are prone—to ideological abstraction.

The distrust of language carefully laid out by William Keach in the
opening chapter of *Shelley's Style*, which has kindled one of the truly
significant debates in modern Shelley studies, to me seems rooted in

the poet's obsession with signs as the instruments of ideology.[5] Listened to from that vantage, these words from Shelley's fragmentary metaphysical speculations assume a dire connotation:

> We combine words, combined a thousand times before. In our minds we assume entire opinions; and in the expression of those opinions, entire phrases, when we would philosophize. Our whole style of expression and sentiment is infected with the tritest plagiarisms. Our words are dead, our thoughts are cold and borrowed.[6]

This is Jupiter's language: ready-made, systematized, dead and deadening. This is the language, Shelley proclaims, that poets combat. They are legislators because, without acknowledging their purpose, they ceaselessly reformulate the building blocks of culture, the conceptual structures that are words:

> Their language is vitally metaphorical; that is, it marks the before unapprehended relations of things, and perpetuates their apprehension, until the words which represent them, become through time signs for portions or classes of thoughts instead of pictures of integral thoughts; and then if no new poets should arise to create afresh the associations which have been thus disorganized, language will be dead to all the nobler purposes of human intercourse. [512]

Yet again, even in the *Defence of Poetry*, a tolling knell: 'Our words are dead', 'language will be dead'. An ideology is exactly not 'vitally metaphorical': it is constituted, in fact, wholly from dead metaphors.

But if that is the case, how immense the task, how demanding the responsibility, the poet faces! And it is small wonder that Shelley's utopia in Act IV of *Prometheus Unbound* is described in such resolutely linguistic terms: there 'Language is a perpetual Orphic song' (IV 415); that is, endlessly, insistently creative. It can be seen in this guise only because Prometheus and Asia have stepped outside Jupiter's system of signification; yet all poetry in the end relies on some system of signification, and what poet in the history of the earth has been able to transcend the very instruments essential to the craft? Can Shelley, however acute his awareness of the problem, not, if only because of his own psychological needs, succumb to the trap of his own creation?

If we had only *Prometheus Unbound*, perhaps we would not need to express the bind Shelley confronts in such extreme terms. But the poetry of his last years, with what I think we should recognize is a certain bravery, increasingly focuses on the inadequacies of metaphor. Part of this questioning of means and ends stems from the practical reality that Shelley could not export the demands he might make on

5. *Shelley's Style*, New York and London, Methuen, 1984: 'The Mirror and the Veil: Language in Shelley's *Defense*', 1–41. On the relation of language and ideology, consult also Jerrold E. Hogle, *Shelley's Process: Radical Transference and the Development of His Major Works*, New York and Oxford, Oxford University Press, 1988.
6. *Shelley's Prose; or, The Trumpet of a Prophecy*, ed. David Lee Clark (Albequerque: University of New Mexico Press, 1954), 184.

himself to a dependable readership, and without a public his refined sense of the problematics of language would be still-born in irony, simply unread. Part of it, too, reflects a near despair over the cost he and those who depended on him had sustained from his rigorous adherence to principle. Yet, even without such professional and family concerns to remind him of the shaky foundation on which he had pitched his existence, the self-questioning, given the purity of its definition, would have persisted. One sees its operations in the litany of apostrophes to Emily in *Epipsychidion*, as Shelley ransacks his mind and experience to find a metaphor adequate to her definition, yet at the same time attempts the precarious balance of maintaining his conception of her within the bounds of metaphor.[7] I believe myself that this is all artfully intended so as to exemplify the way in which the mind constitutes its ideals, but that does not alter the aura of poetic crisis in which the process is staged. The sense in *Adonais* that nothing remains of Keats but his poetic conceptions and that the transformation of the self through the creative act risks dissolution of all stabilities testifies to similar plaguing doubts. But the major questions are reserved for Shelley's last poem, *The Triumph of Life*, where they rest, and with them this entire discourse, because quite simply they remain unanswered there.

The triumph of life, in so far as its success can be gauged, is a triumph of metaphor and of the ideologies created through its means. The long train of captives includes the principal philosophers, poets, politicians, churchmen, who are fittingly introduced not by name but by sign: they who wore 'Mitres and helms and crowns, or wreathes of light, / Signs of thought's empire over thought' (209–11). Signs of signs: the process seems inescapable, as experience turns into a concept of experience and these in turn aggregate into categories of experience which rigidify into the conceptual systems that are ideologies.[8] The creative act, at least as Rousseau reflects on his career, is simply and essentially part of the process, helping to bring into being what he acknowledges is 'a world of agony' (295). In his narrative he refuses to name the 'Shape all light,' leaving that task to the by-now hundreds of commentators on this poem. Perhaps his refusal, like Beatrice Cenci's, stems from Shelley's recognition that the imaginative process is infinitely complex and ambiguous, not simply a sign to be demarcated and presumed as known. Perhaps it could even be construed as a cynical trap of this self-reflexive poem, to see if we as its readers will convert the living metaphor into the static ideological counter and enact the very triumph of life whose enactment we are vicariously witnessing. There is no way to know for certain and thus no way to convert the poem into a firm conceptual order.

In a remarkable paradox, then, this poem that sees all of history and certainly all writers in the shadow of ideological fixity refuses to par-

---

7. Finally, Shelley must admit that he cannot penetrate the resistance of his linguistic veil: Emily, he acknowledges, is simply 'A Metaphor of Spring and Youth and Morning' (120).
8. The most extensive commentary on the way signs function in objectification in *The Triumph of Life* is offered by Hogle: *Shelley's Process*, 325 ff.

ticipate in the process it enacts. It stands as the actual embodiment of the condition of its author, staring at the stars after the sun comes up, falling into dream as the world awakes. The poet who transcribes this vision is profoundly uncertain about its terms and its extent, but he is decidedly not a participant in the procession he witnesses for us. Of its temptations he is well aware; of its costs he is stoically assured; of its grim irony, that the triumph of life is one of death, he demands our acquiescence. And yet the very depth of the pessimism driving this poem may be an aspect of the paradox I am remarking at its center, that it veils a fiercely determined optimism not to give in to the seeming logic of metaphors to harden into systems. If in his last major poem Shelley wholly recasts the notion of ideology that had impelled his first one, now seeing the interlocking external forms as deeply embedded in mental formulation and psychic need, the insistent aim has not changed at all. The end is still liberation of the self from the strictures surrounding it. Even if those strictures may here be acknowledged not as the snares of tyrants and priests, but as the potentiality in all of us to become tyrants and priests, first imposing on ourselves the temptations by which we would betray others, still the poem resolutely refuses the despair that haunts its margins. We continue to have the right to our liberty, Shelley would assert, all the more so since we can see so fully, so painfully, so intimately, the ideological forces that are its enemy.

## ANNETTE WHEELER CAFARELLI

## The Transgressive Double Standard: Shelleyan Utopianism and Feminist Social History[†]

* * *

In his early letters, Shelley felt obliged to justify repeatedly to Godwin, Byron, and others his decision to succumb to the convention of marriage in order to ameliorate the burden of public opprobrium transgressive women unequally bear—an argument he seems to have gotten from his friend Thomas Jefferson Hogg. Beyond Godwin's own work, there were other influences on Shelley's antimatrimonialism, notably the preface to James Lawrence's novel *The Empire of the Nairs* (1811), whence he appropriated the term "superstition" to refer to chastity and the marriage ceremony.[1] The preface (condensed from an essay

---

[†] From *Shelley: Poet and Legislator of the World*, ed. Betty T. Bennett and Stuart Curran (Baltimore: Johns Hopkins University Press, 1996), pp. 96–104. Copyright © 1996. Reprinted by permission of the author and The Johns Hopkins University Press.

1. Shelley's "Even love is sold" note to *Queen Mab* (1813) called "chastity" a "monkish and evangelical superstition"; his September 26, 1814, letter to Harriet Shelley said, "The pure & liberal principles of which you used to boast you were a disciple, served only for display. In your heart it seems you were always enslaved to the vilest superstitions"; his October 4, 1814, letter to T. J. Hogg called marriage one of the "vulgar superstitions." *Letters*, 1:377, 403.

Lawrence wrote in 1793) may have been a response to Godwin, but its purported investigation of polyandry essentially depicts a male utopian paradise of sexual opportunities bereft of any concrete ideas for instituting social reform. The book depicts a society without marriage in which women are honored for their prolific motherhood, oblivious to the fact that contemporary women were burdened by the lack of adequate reproductive control.[2]

Despite Shelley's enthusiasm for the book, it is not surprising that female response to the *Nairs* was cool (he had Mary Shelley, Claire Clairmont, and Harriet Shelley read it)—about as cool as Shelley's to Amelia Opie's *Adeline Mowbray* (1805), which Harriet sent him in 1811.[3] Opie's inverse view of antimatrimonialism shows how the burden of unlegitimated marriage falls upon women and children; reappropriating the Godwinian phrase "things as they are," her novel shows its antimatrimonialists recanting under the force of public custom just before they expire. Indeed, the disjuncture between male and female marital agendas is rather interestingly illuminated in Thomas Love Peacock's parodic novel *Nightmare Abbey* (1818): The Wollstonecraftian Stella dismays the Shelleyan free-love hero by announcing that her antimatrimonialism is monogamous.

## Queen Mab: The Politics of Prostitution

Shelley wrote Lawrence in 1812 to say that Lawrence's book "succeeded in making me a perfect convert . . . I then retained no doubts of the evils of marriage,—Mrs. Wollstonecraft reasons too well for that; but I had been dull enough not to perceive the greatest argument against it, until developed in the 'Nairs,' viz., prostitution both *legal* and *illegal*."[4] As incorrect as the letter is on Wollstonecraft's ideological goals, it reveals the thoughts that lay behind the "Even love is sold" footnote to *Queen Mab*, on which I shall focus here.

As with Godwin, practical experience altered Shelley's outlook on the nature of matrimonial politics and other issues. Both Mary Shelley and Thomas Medwin wondered whether he would have included the poem in his collected works; at the time of its piracy in 1821, Shelley

---

2. James Lawrence, *Das Faradies der Liebe* (1801); *L'Empire des Nairs* (1803); *The Empire of the Nairs; or, the Rights of Women, an Utopian Romance* (London: Hookham, 1811); the original 1793 essay, "Nair System of Gallantry and Inheritance," was published four months after *Political Justice*; see Walter Graham, "Shelley and the *Empire of the Nairs*," *Publications of the Modern Language Association of America* 50 (1925): 881.

3. Shelley, to Hogg, July 15, 1811, *Letters*, 1:122; on Harriet's reading of the *Nairs*, see Boas, *Harriet Shelley: Five Long Years* (London: Oxford Univ. Press, 1962), 227; from the September 26, 1814, *Journals of Mary Shelley*, ed. Paula R. Feldman and Diana Scott-Kilvert (Oxford: Clarendon, 1987), 1:29, and *Journals of Claire Clairmont*, ed. Marion Kingston Stocking (Cambridge, Mass.: Harvard Univ. Press, 1968), 46, it appears neither expended much time on this four-volume tome.

4. If male successors were likely to get Godwin wrong, they were even more likely to misappropriate Wollstonecraft's use of the expression "legal prostitution" to describe marriage; *A Vindication of the Rights of Woman* (London: Johnson, 1792); rpt. *Works of Mary Wollstonecraft*, ed. Janet Todd and Marilyn Butler (New York: New York Univ. Press, 1989), 5:129, 218.

claimed that he hardly remembered the poem.[5] But examination of *Queen Mab* sheds light on the collision of the naive idealism of 1813 and the realities he encountered later in life. In any case, I think we should regard Shelley's views, like Godwin's, as well intentioned, but as nevertheless sharing the blindness to gender-based issues that bedeviled the sexual ideology of the men of the era.

The understanding behind the "Even love is sold" note is fundamentally Godwin's equation of marriage with property,[6] infused with the inspired libertarian discourse of the early Romantic poets. The language of social revolution is carried to the rhetoric of love: "its very essence is liberty," its enforcement in marriage "intolerable tyranny," "servitude," a "system of constraint," and the "usurpation of the right of private judgment."

Shelley follows Godwin's reasoning. Constancy is nothing virtuous in itself (indeed he bolsters the Godwinian argument against monopolization by vindicating it as the right to free "enquiry").[7] Like Godwin, he evades the question of the duration of the union, asking, "How long then ought the sexual connection to last?" and answering, "This is a subject which it is perhaps premature to discuss." And like other post-Godwinian male radicals, Shelley's emphasis is on facilitating dissolution of marriage, rather than on the female radical agenda of property rights within marriage and educational and labor opportunities. As with Godwin, matters will simply sort themselves out: "from the abolition of marriage, the fit and natural arrangement of sexual connection would result."

More problematic, however, is the poem's treatment of prostitution, the undernote we have heard all along in an era that reductively used the term *gallantry* as a euphemism for male libertinism and the term *prostitution* as the accusatory equivalent for unchaste women.[8] The poem's analysis of prostitution hinges on the declaration "Prostitution is the legitimate offspring of marriage and its accompanying errors. Women, for no other crime than having followed the dictates of a natural appetite, are driven with fury from the comforts and sympathies of society." As with the parliamentary debates, adultery and prostitution are conflated. But what is the precise connection between prostitution and indissoluble marriage? Will cultural acceptance of

---

5. *Queen Mab* (London: for the author, 1813), 144–52; *Letters*, 2:298–302, 350, 355; Mary's 1839 note on *Queen Mab* says that "it is doubtful whether he would himself have admitted it into a collection of his works"; but Thomas Medwin, *Life of Percy Bysshe Shelley*, ed. H. Buxton Forman (1824; rpt. Oxford: Oxford Univ. Press, 1913), 186, said of the poem, "however he might have modified, and did modify his opinions, he was the last man to have recanted them."

6. Shelley's fragment "On Marriage" (circa 1817) developed Godwin's concept of "the female the possession . . . the property of men. . . . Those laws or opinions which defend the security of property suggested also the institution of marriage."

7. "Love is free: to promise for ever to love the same woman, is not less absurd than to promise to believe the same creed: such a vow, in both cases, excludes us from all inquiry."

8. Even Shelley, angry that the birth of William (named after Mary Shelley's father) did not bring reconciliation with Godwin, invoked the popular dichotomy: "a young family, innocent and benevolent and united, should not be confounded with prostitutes and seducers"; March 6, 1816, letter to Godwin, *Letters*, 1:459.

multiple relationships and branding women with less infamy prevent prostitution? Herein lies the troubling error of the age: assuming that prostitution is simply the consequence of female sexual desires, rather than regarding the economic imperatives behind it.

Although Shelley elicits sympathy for the life of misery, disease, and social ostracism ("Theirs is the right of persecution, hers the duty of endurance"), he actually masks the more direct causes of prostitution: assault, desertion, seduction, illegitimacy, and poverty. Indeed, in personifying both the persecutor and the victim as female—"Society avenges herself on the criminals of her own creation"—the text implicitly assists in removing the blame from men.

Curiously, Shelley's strategy is to deflect pity onto men as the chief cultural victims: "Young men, excluded by the fanatical idea of chastity from the society of modest and accomplished women, associate with these vicious and miserable beings, destroying . . . exquisite and delicate sensibilities . . . annihilating all genuine passion . . . debasing that to a selfish feeling." Shelley's sensitive young men are compelled by society to consort with prostitutes; though in real terms, gallants were not excluded from modest and uncorrupted society, merely deterred from prenuptial sexual liaisons. Shelley's young men are not indicted for perpetuating prostitution, and there is no articulation of the fact that the miserable and diseased women to whom they resort were made so by other young men.

As Wollstonecraft pointed out in her *Vindication of the Rights of Woman* (1792), "Necessity never makes prostitution the business of men's lives; though numberless are the women who are thus rendered systematically vicious."[9] With his character of the "Magdalene" Ann in his *Confessions of an English Opium Eater* (1821), De Quincey was to be one of the first male Romantics to elicit sympathy for the prostitute as a cultural victim of men rather than as a purveyor of vice. Yet Shelley's earlier strategy is certainly less judgmental than the Victorian redemptive evangelicism of such artworks as William Holman Hunt's "Awakening," the Henry Mayhew and William Acton anatomizations of prostitution, or the scapegoating Contagious Diseases Acts of the 1860s, attitudes that dominated the spiritual and scientific response of the later nineteenth century.

## Male and Female Radical Agendas

\* \* \* Whatever we may think of Shelley's marriages, it becomes clear that, in contrast to Byron, for example, Shelley, like Godwin, upheld his ethical responsibility to children of free love or antimatrimonial unions. Leigh Hunt was one of many who testified to Shelley's integrity, explaining how Shelley refuted "that extraordinary privilege to indulge one sex at the expense of the other," vowed to live by Godwin's *Political Justice* and Milton's doctrine of divorce, and shocked a village ballroom by dancing with a woman who had been shamed by the rep-

9. Wollstonecraft, *Vindication*, 5:140.

utation of having once been seduced ("probably," Hunt says, "by some well-dressed gentleman in the room, who thought himself entitled nevertheless to the conversation of the most flourishing ladies present").[1]

It is clear that Shelley above all loved the language of rebellion (Harriet Shelley was held in "prison"; "her father has persecuted her in a most horrible way, & endeavours to compel her to go to school. She asked my advice: resistance was the answer").[2] His ecstatic writings catalyzed others who had never met him. The Owenite socialist Anna Wheeler closed a letter to Robert Owen by quoting Shelley's declaration, "Can man be free if woman be a slave?"[3] and although Owen never met Shelley, when he visited a spiritualist medium in later years, he seems to have greeted the spirit of the poet with the words "my old friend Shelley." Medwin attended an Owenite meeting with Lawrence and found *Queen Mab* and the *Empire of the Nairs* on sale; when he introduced himself as a friend of Shelley's, Owen "made a long panegyric on him, and taking up one of the *Queen Mabs* from the table, read . . . the following passage: 'How long ought the sexual connection to last?' "[4]

Thomas Poole observed that the planners of the Pantisocracy scheme of 1794, Coleridge and Southey, were not sure what to do with Godwin's matrimonial policy and noted that their chief problems had to do with the position of women: "the regulations relating to the females strike them as the most difficult."[5] Although Owen linked the rise of private property with marriage and sought to alleviate women's domestic "drudgery" and childrearing through collectivism, women historians have come to distinguish the female Owenite agenda from the male: Whereas men popularized free love and divorce reform to solve the risks of perpetual marriage, women were more concerned with rights within marriage, educational equality, and destigmatizing female transgressors. Lack of control over reproduction was a crucial factor shaping the female radical view. It is interesting that, in the female utopian schemes of bluestocking novels written by women, such as Sarah Scott's *Millenium Hall* (1762) and Mary Walker Hamilton's *Munster Village* (1778), and in Shakerism itself, led by Anna Lee, utopian communities were connected with celibacy.[6]

Incongruities exist within the Romantic era and indeed within any era, and we can only measure any gesture of radicalism or social re-

---

1. Leigh Hunt, *Lord Byron and Some of his Contemporaries* (London: Colburn, 1828), 1:308–12.
2. Shelley to Hogg, August 3, 1811, *Letters*, 1:131.
3. *Laon and Cythna* (2:xliii); on the popularity of this phrase among the Owenites, see Paul Foot, *Red Shelley* (London: Sidgwick and Jackson, 1980), 153, and M. Siddiq Kalim, *The Social Orpheus: Shelley and the Owenites* (Lahore: Research Council, 1973), 108–12.
4. Frank Podmore, *Robert Owen* (1907; rpt. New York: Haskell, 1971), 2:647; Medwin, *Life of Shelley*, 97–98, refers to the John Brooks edition of *Queen Mab*, which, if reliable, would date the episode as 1829 or later.
5. "Whether the marriage contract shall be dissolved if agreeable to one or both parties, and many other circumstances, are not yet determined," Poole to Mr. Haskins, March 24, 1820; Margaret E. Sandford, *Thomas Poole and His Friends* (London: Macmillan, 1888), 1:95–98.
6. On female Owenites, see Barbara Taylor, *Eve and the New Jerusalem* (London: Virago, 1983), xv, 40–43, 69, 213–16; Carol A. Kolmerten, *Women in Utopia* (Bloomington: Indiana Univ. Press, 1990), 10, 25–27, 79–85, 133–35.

form within its historically relative context. But it is also clear—and not only from the Romantic male-centered discourse on illegitimacy, divorce, and prostitution—that female and male radical priorities have not always coincided—although male radicals have tended to assume the correspondence of women's interests. Simple assessments, however, are not easy to make.

The dissonance of male and female political agendas is evident in the history of suffrage reform. Despite the interest of Wollstonecraft and Benthamite radicals in female suffrage, Shelley's opposition to the female vote as "somewhat immature" in the *Philosophical View of Reform* (1819),[7] voiced the unreadiness argument that beleaguered suffrage activists until the twentieth century. The London Working Men's Association similarly allowed the discourse of universal suffrage to lapse into the more expedient male suffrage; indeed, within early-nineteenth-century industrial reform there was considerable male unionist hostility to women, and their attempt to remove the cheaper female labor pool from the skilled trades often masqueraded as concern for affirming the home.[8]

Let us take another example. While Shelley's "Discourse on the Manners of the Ancients Relative to the Subject of Love" (circa 1818) places him in the vanguard of male feminist thought (denouncing the "degraded" state of women in Greek and Roman culture, "educated as slaves" and relegated to "inferiority"), his 1813 letter to Godwin on the subject of Classical education illustrates the conflict between male theories and female praxis. It was rebellious for Shelley as a man to denounce the emphasis on ancient learning as "a literary despotism . . . intended to shut out from real knowledge . . . all who . . . will not support the established systems of politics, religion & morals";[9] but the fact that Mary Shelley, Claire Clairmont, and Harriet Shelley took advantage of the opportunity to learn Latin from him reflected the widespread intellectual feminist goal of acquiring Classical learning to overcome the traditional exclusion of women from high literary discourse.

The ideological contradictions of antimatrimonialism surround the radical publisher William Clark[e], who was prosecuted by the Society for the Suppression of Vice and subsequently jailed for reissuing *Queen Mab* in 1821 (preempting Shelley's own attempt to suppress the edition). That summer he seems to have also published a *Reply to the Anti-Matrimonial Hypothesis . . . as laid down in "Queen Mab,"* which pointed out that Shelley's system failed to protect women from

7. "Mr Bentham and other writers have urged the admission of females to the right of suffrage; this attempt seems somewhat immature"; Wollstonecraft, *Vindication*, 5:217. On early suffrage initiatives, see Miriam Williford, "Bentham on the Rights of Women," *Journal of the History of Ideas* 36 (1975): 134, 167–76; Claire Tomalin, *The Life and Death of Mary Wollstonecraft* (London: Penguin, 1992), 341–43.

8. Edward Royce and James Walvin, *English Radicals and Reformers* (Brighton, U.K.: Harvester Press, 1987), 134, 186; Neil J. Smelser, *Social Change in the Industrial Revolution* (Chicago: Univ. of Chicago Press, 1959), 236, 306; Taylor, *Eve*, 98; K. D. M. Snell, *Annals of the Labouring Poor* (Cambridge: Cambridge Univ. Press, 1985), 313–18; Anna Clark, "The Politics of Seduction in English Popular Culture," in *The Progress of Romance*, ed. Jean Radford (London: Routledge, 1986), 59–62.

9. Shelley to Godwin, July 29, 1813, *Letters*, 1:318.

desertion in old age and distress, that affections are unlikely to subside simultaneously, and that Shelley considered women only as "the mere instrument of male gratification—the passive and unconsulted medium of his transports." The gender of the author is unclear, but viewed from a feminist perspective it echoes the radical critique of the sexual double standard put forth by female radicals in the late eighteenth century. Observing that "the evils of prostitution . . . spring, in a great measure, from the want of laws, which *man* has neglected to frame, lest his gratifications should be limited," the pamphlet calls for "punishment of seduction" and requiring men to support the women who, after being discarded, have no way of finding employment once branded with illegitimate offspring: "it is considered *disgraceful* for a *gentleman* to degrade himself by a marriage with a poor, fond, deluded woman. . . . A small sum paid to the parish compensates for the crime, and annihilates the necessity of feeling. It is ONLY an illegitimate child. . . . What becomes of the mother, is a matter of still less consideration with the seducer. She is old enough to work. The parish does not insist upon a maintenance for her."[1]

## Middle-Class Fallen Women

Although most male radical commentators failed to perceive that prostitution and nuptiality trends were connected with economic disenfranchisement, radical women writers directly addressed the politics of seduction. It is not surprising to find fallen women suggesting the most concrete plans for remedying the transgressive double standard. Long before male radicals argued against desecration of female character, Laetitia Pilkington proclaimed in her 1748 *Memoirs*, "Is it not monstrous, that our seducers should be our accusers?" The unpublished *Female Protector* (1800) suggested making seduction a criminal offence. Wollstonecraft's *Vindication* (1792) repeatedly declared that laws should compel men to maintain women they seduced.[2]

\* \* \*

Women who tried to espouse a sexual ideology resembling that of Romantic men, however, found themselves economically and socially marginalized; they paid a high price for demanding equality, and there were far greater punishments for female freethinkers than for male. Indeed, the middle-class fallen woman was an immensely radicalizing force. The women surrounding Shelley provide an interesting chronicle of the economic and social realities for women of the era who challenged conventional assumptions about female transgression.

1. *Queen Mab* (London: W. Clarke, 1821); *Reply to the Anti-Matrimonial Hypothesis and Supposed Atheism of Percy Byssche* [sic] *Shelley, as laid down in* Queen Mab (London: W. Clark, 1821), 11, 19, 33–37. Newman Ivey White slightly conjectures William Johnson Fox as its author; see *Shelley* (New York: Knopf, 1940), 2:304–5, 405–6, and *The Unextinguished Hearth* (1938; rpt. New York: Octagon, 1966), 63, 95–97, 370–73.
2. Laetitia Pilkington, *Memoirs*, ed. Iris Barry (New York: Dodd, Mead, 1928), 103, 221; Alice Browne, *The Eighteenth-Century Feminist Mind* (Detroit: Wayne State Univ. Press, 1987), 134, 204; Wollstonecraft, *Vindication*, 5:139–40, 209.

Like other legally separated wives, Harriet Shelley was condemned to a life of loneliness or to the furtive amours that branded her as having "descended the steps of prostitution." Elizabeth Hitchener, who joined the "glorious cause" Shelley described, found her retreat to schoolteaching blocked until she laundered her past on the continent with a brief marriage. Claire Clairmont, whose intense commitment to independence made her a true daughter of Wollstonecraft, supported herself for over twenty years as a companion, governess, and day teacher. Like Wollstonecraft, she adhered to feminist theories of education ("my pupil should be left at liberty as much as possible . . . her own reason should be the prompter of her actions"), but she too found governessing a "life which lies stagnant from inactivity." Her situation was worse than Wollstonecraft's: Hounded by her unwed motherhood and her Godwinian past ("issued from the very den of freethinkers"), she was forced to change employers each time her reputation became known—an experience Medwin recounted using the words of *Queen Mab*: "theirs is the right of persecution—hers the duty of endurance." Experiencing a life of slander herself, Claire Clairmont came to sympathize with the traduced Harriet Shelley, defending her from tales about being the prostitute of a stableman.[3]

Unlike that of her stepsister, Mary Shelley's experience of hardship was long postponed, as she moved from the girlhood shelter of her father's household to the protection of a freethinking noble scion. She was eager to have Claire Clairmont's natural child removed from her house as soon as possible lest it injure her own precarious reputation—without realizing that, had Shelley died in his illness of 1815 or had Harriet Shelley induced him to return, she would have been in the same position as Claire Clairmont. Mary Shelley's stepmother worried, "everybody tells [Harriet Shelley] that love affairs last but a little time and her husband will be sure to return to her. . . . That is indeed but too true and what a gloomy prospect it opens to us."[4] Mary Shelley's radicalization, however, only occurred after she was left a widow, when she realized the isolation and circumscribed life of a woman without a male protector. Frustrated in her attempts to secure a settlement from Shelley's family and faced with the difficulty of supporting herself, she came to understand the position of Claire Clairmont and joined the unsuccessful attempt of Lady Mount Cashell, who had been Wollstonecraft's favorite student, to persuade Byron to provide Claire

---

3. On rumors about Harriet Shelley, see *Letters*, 1:521, 525, 527–28; Alan Lang Strout, "Knights of the Burning Epistle: The *Blackwood* Papers in the National Library of Scotland," *Studia Neophilologica* 26 (1954): 89. Mary Shelley also came to sympathize with Harriet Shelley on some level, according to the February 12, 1839, journal entry excised by Lady Jane Gibson Shelley from most copies of *Shelley and Mary* (London: privately printed, 1882), 1222: "[T. J.] Hogg has written me an insulting letter because I left out the dedication to Harriet [prefacing *Queen Mab*]. Poor Harriet, to whose sad fate I attribute so many of my own heavy sorrows as the atonement claimed by fate for her death." Claire Clairmont, to Mary Shelley, April 29, 1825, *Journals of Claire Clairmont*, ed. Marion Kingston Stocking (Cambridge, MA: Harvard University Press, 1968), 298, 401–5; R. Glynn Grylls, *Claire Clairmont* (London: Murray, 1939), 199, 201; Medwin, *Life of Shelley*, 176.

4. Grylls, *Claire Clairmont*, 38.

Clairmont with an annuity.[5] Her own shock at Byron's recommendation that she give her boy away to his male relations compelled her to reconfront the recommendations she had given Claire Clairmont about Allegra, and the rumors she had to combat upon returning home to England made her solicitous to protect Claire Clairmont's reputation from the scandal sheets at Byron's death.

Shelley, too, came to hard realizations in the course of his life. It must have been infuriating to have had to defend his morality to Byron in order to secure Claire Clairmont's visitation rights with Allegra ("I smiled at your protest about what you consider my creed. On the contrary, I think a regard to chastity is quite necessary, as things are, to a young female—that is, to her happiness—and at any time a good habit").[6] Likewise, he had to instruct his solicitor P. W. Longdill to propose a highly conventionalized (and gendered) plan of instruction in the attempt to gain educational custody of his children after Harriet's demise.[7]

It is disturbing to realize that as hard as their lives were, Claire Clairmont and Mary Shelley were in fact insulated from the full brunt of the transgressive double standard solely by Shelley's intercession. As tragic as her pleading letters to Byron are to read, Claire Clairmont's interests in Allegra were protected to the extent they were only by Byron's nominal concern with how he appeared to Shelley. She was in this sense protected, unlike the chambermaids on whom Byron "fell like a thunderbolt,"[8] or Margherita Cogni, who was trivialized to posterity as "the fornarina." The other side of the class-based implications of seduction, however, shielded the transgressive behavior of aristocrats such as Lady Mount Cashell, Lady Melbourne (aunt of Byron's wife), and Countess Guiccioli, whose second husband would introduce her as "Ma femme, ancienne maîtresse de Byron."[9] Only when Lady Caroline Lamb exceeded the farthest bounds of public propriety was she censured (characteristic of the era, she was ostracized while her husband conducted his liaison and went on to be Queen Victoria's prime minister).

It is also worth noting that not every middle-class woman was as heroic in her endeavors as Claire Clairmont or Mary Shelley. Jane Williams and Byron's supposed natural daughter Medora accepted support from a series of male "protectors" rather than forging their independence. But for both Claire Clairmont and Mary Shelley, it was

5. Clairmont, *Journals*, 294–96; Edward C. McAleer, *The Sensitive Plant: A Life of Lady Mount Cashell* (Chapel Hill: Univ. of North Carolina Press, 1958), 119, 174–76; *The Letters of Mary Wollstonecraft Shelley*, ed. Betty T. Bennett (Baltimore, MD: The Johns Hopkins University Press, 1980–93), I:306–7, 312, 437.
6. Shelley to Byron, May 26, 1820, *Letters*, 1:199.
7. Longdill's document emphasized "being very circumspect (particularly as far as respects Girls) in the Books which are permitted to be brought before them"; Leslie Hotson, *Shelley's Lost Letters to Harriet* (London: Faber and Faber, 1980), 66–67, 70–71.
8. Entry for April 26, 1816, *The Diary of Dr. John William Polidori*, ed. William Michael Rossetti (London: Elkin Mathews, 1911), 32–33.
9. Marchand, *Byron's Letters and Journals*, ed. Leslie A. Marchand (Cambridge, MA: Harvard University Press, 1972–94), 6:278.

the memory of Shelley's undaunted optimism that they credited in this
uphill struggle—not his systems, but his inspiriting exhortation to
action.

This is to say that mooring Shelley's utopian ideals in the context of
practical schemes of reform * * * does not mean that we want *no*
better bread than is made of wheat. Perhaps the concept most helpful
in understanding Shelley's idealizations and his gift of inspiring others
is the statement of his early biographer Edward Dowden, who in 1886
wrote that Shelley believed it was "a poet's duty to sustain the hopes
and aspirations of men in their movement of advance, and at the same
time to endeavour to hold their passions in check by presenting high
ideals, and showing that the better life of society is not to be won out
of the air."[1] This may in fact be the key importance of Shelley within
contemporary reform movements: He was no demagogue—but he had,
and has, the gift of inspiring others.

# MICHAEL O'NEILL

## Shelley's Lyric Art[†]

Critics of Shelley have tended, in recent years, either to highlight the
significance and complexity of his political and philosophical vision, or
to deconstruct this vision. There has been rather less emphasis on
Shelley's lyric gift and achievement. Whereas book after book on the
narrative and dramatic poems has appeared, discussion of the poet's
shorter pieces has concentrated on only a handful of poems. This is
understandable as a reaction against the Victorian praise of Shelley as
a spinner of magical, apolitical lyrics and the New Critical condemnation of Shelley as the purveyor of incantatory gush. But contemporary criticism has, with notable exceptions (principally work by
Judith Chernaik and William Keach),[1] underplayed a central part of
Shelley's artistic achievement: his ability to write crafted, affecting,
and richly suggestive short poems.

These are poems that require and reward close attention. And yet

1. Edward Dowden, *Life of Percy Bysshe Shelley* (London: Kegan Paul, 1886), p. 286.
† The bulk of this essay was originally published as the introduction to *Fair-Copy Manuscripts of Shelley's Poems in European and American Libraries*, ed. Donald H. Reiman and Michael O'Neill (New York: Garland, 1997), volume VIII of the Shelley volumes in the *Manuscripts of the Younger Romantics* series, gen. ed. Donald H. Reiman, and referred to as *MYR: Shelley*, VIII. It is reprinted by permission. Ideally, readers of the essay should consult the volume. Quotations from manuscripts are based on the transcriptions in *MYR: Shelley*, VIII (and occasionally elsewhere), tidied up where appropriate (that is, cancellations, false starts, and idiosyncratic details of layout are not recorded or reproduced, and the occasional apostrophe is silently introduced or omitted). Line numbers for poems quoted from these manuscripts are not given. Elsewhere, Shelley's poetry is quoted, if possible, from this edition of *SPP*; if that is not possible, it is quoted from *Shelley: Poetical Works* (*PW*), ed. Thomas Hutchinson, rev. G. M. Matthews (London: Oxford University Press, 1970). Shortened references are given to the Bodleian Shelley Manuscripts series and to the standard edition of Shelley's letters.
1. See Judith Chernaik, *The Lyrics of Shelley* (Cleveland and London: The Press of Case West-ern Reserve University, 1972), and William Keach, *Shelley's Style* (New York and London: Methuen, 1984).

what such attention will discover is not fixities or definites. Characteristically, the Shelleyan lyric will not be pigeon-holed; its kind of verbal precision is at one with a fascinating openness to interpretation. If these lyrics employ syntactical, metrical and stanzaic patterns of great ingenuity, they occupy the space of their own suggestiveness.

*   *   *

As "Hymn to Intellectual Beauty" and "Mont Blanc" reveal, concern with poetic voice, or with the operations of consciousness, is nearly always in Shelley twined round concern with the ends to which poetic voice and operations of consciousness might be put. In the "Hymn" Shelley concludes (in the Scrope Davies fair copy; hereafter SD: Hymn) by invoking the "fleeting power" in terms that are at once heterodox and spiritual:

> Thus let thy shade—which like the truth
> Of Nature on my passive youth
> Descended, to my onward life supply
> Its hues, to one that worships thee
> And every form containing thee
> Whom fleeting power! thy spells did bind
> To fear himself & love all human Kind.

Subversively the last line replaces orthodox fear (in the sense of awe) of God with reverence for self: a reverence that underpins the poet's seemingly grandiose claim to "love all human Kind." But the claim earns our sympathy when we review the tensions and struggles which it resolves, and in relation to which it is as much a brave rejoinder as a necessary consequence. That opening "Thus," so apparently confident, refers to the interplay of presence and absence which has just been evoked (Autumn's "lustre" is not "heard or seen" in summer, as if, Shelley writes with fine excitement, "it could not be—as if it had not been"). The argumentative drive of the poem co-exists with an alert sense, conveyed through minute details of diction, rhythm, and syntax, that the "power" worshipped is also a power which Shelley is creating as he writes. Here, for instance, "spells" recalls even as it overturns the earlier dismissal of orthodox "Frail spells." Again, as in the version which Shelley published in *The Examiner*, 19 January 1817 (when it would appear that he was forced to return to his draft), the repetition of "thee" in the rhyme position suggests an almost yearning drive to reach out to the presence which Shelley is invoking. The sense of Intellectual Beauty's flickering and transience is more marked at the end of SD: *Hymn* than at the end of the published version (hereafter Ex: *Hymn*). In Ex: *Hymn* "shade" becomes "power" (78), "hues" becomes "calm" (81), and "fleeting power" becomes "SPIRIT fair" (83). Ex: *Hymn*, in contrast to SD: *Hymn*, comes close to stabilizing what it hopes is the object of apprehension.

Comparison between the two versions suggests fascinating variations on a theme. If at the end of SD: *Hymn* Intellectual Beauty's presence is more shadowy and "fleeting" than at the end of Ex: *Hymn*, the two openings are also intriguingly different. *SD: Hymn* starts, "The lovely shadow of some awful Power / Walks though unseen amongst us, visiting / This peopled world." *Ex: Hymn* begins, "The awful shadow of some unseen Power / Floats though unseen amongst us,—visiting / This various world" (1–3). *SD: Hymn* stresses the Power's mingled loveliness and awfulness, and attributes the loveliness to the Power's "shadow," as though there were ample gains for the fact that the "shadow" is "unseen." In *SD: Hymn*, too, the "shadow" "Walks" rather than "Floats," visiting a "peopled" rather than "various" world. *Ex: Hymn* emphasizes the awe-inspiring, "unseen" nature of the Power's shadow, and is marginally less interested in loveliness; again marginally, but perceptibly, it is more abstractly concerned with the relations between source and "various" manifestations than is the opening of *SD: Hymn*. Differences of diction between the two versions show Shelley wrestling with nuances of significance, as he tries to articulate his apprehension of the presence and status possessed by the Power. The published version makes this presence at the outset more august, its status more apparently transcendent. One variation between the two texts shows Shelley widening the scope of, yet possibly lessening the personal anxiety apparent in, *SD: Hymn*. In stanza 4 *SD: Hymn* reads, "Thou that to the poet's thought art nourishment / As darkness to a dying flame," but *Ex: Hymn* prefers, "Thou—that to human thought art nourishment, / Like darkness to a dying flame!" (44–5). There is about "the poet's thought" an energy of self-concern; the phrase reminds us that this poet's thought—the poem we are reading—is nourished in the paradoxical and frail way described by the simile. Arguably, however, "human thought" encompasses this recognition while assuming wider applicability. Again, whereas *SD: Hymn* has "wisest poets" (the reading in the draft, Bodleian MS. Shelley adds. e. 16), *Ex: Hymn* alters and extends the reference to "sage or poet" (26)—one instance which shows that, though Shelley almost certainly did return to his draft (in Bodleian MS Shelley adds. e. 16) after mislaying the Scrope Davies fair copy, he did not always abide by his draft formulations.

Readings of this poem and "Mont Blanc" need to take full account of the implications of the Scrope Davies fair copies as well as the rough draft of "Mont Blanc" and the draft of the "Hymn" available in Bodleian MS Shelley adds. e. 16 (ed. Erkelenz, *BSM* (1992), XI). It is clear that in both cases textual complications have bequeathed two versions of each poem; in each case the two versions point up one another's distinctly individual outlook. For example, *SD: Hymn* proves to be more overt than *Ex: Hymn* about the fear-tinged feelings of need and fugitiveness of perception in the important passage from lines 32 to 36. Where *Ex: Hymn* addresses "Thy light alone" (32), *SD: Hymn* invokes "Thy shade alone"; where *Ex: Hymn* imagines "some still instrument" (34), *SD: Hymn* is more haunted by a potential loss of voice, speaking of "some mute instrument"; and where *Ex: Hymn* refers with fine reticence to "life's unquiet dream" (36), *SD: Hymn* paints a turbulent picture of "life's tumultuous dream." In the two versions of

"Mont Blanc" the most famous difference is that between "But for such faith" in *History of a Six Weeks' Tour* (hereafter *1817*) (79) and "In such a faith" in the Scrope Davies fair copy (hereafter *SD: MB*). "In such a faith" makes the more evident sense, though it possibly sacrifices some of the tension of a poem which elsewhere is not easily reconciled with nature (or "Nature," as *SD: MB*, perhaps revealingly, has it); "But for such faith" is cryptic and tortuous, and yet the fact remains that Shelley chose to print the poem with this reading in his lifetime. Again, consultation of the draft does not simplify matters; in it Shelley has canceled the phrase "But for such" and left "In such a faith" uncanceled. Presumably, therefore, when he came to publish the poem in *1817* and looked again at his draft, he decided against the uncanceled reading. The immediately preceding line speaks of this "faith" as "So simple, so serene" in *SD: MB*, but as "So solemn, so serene" (78) in *1817*; the switch from "simple" to "solemn" indicates that Shelley backed away from representing any "faith" as uncomplicated.

The two versions of "Mont Blanc" are full of fascinating differences of inflection and emphasis. The openings diverge. *SD: MB* has "In day the eternal universe of things", subliminally preparing the reader for the "gleams of a remoter world" that "Visit the soul in sleep" when the rules that govern by "day" are relaxed; *1817* reads, "The everlasting universe of things" (1), as if Shelley had decided to let go of a possible distinction between day and night. In the vital second section of the poem, *1817* is, for all its excitement, more expressive of control than *SD: MB*. *1817* describes "an unremitting interchange" (39), whereas *SD: MB* speaks of "an unforeseeing interchange". In *1817* Shelley seems "as in a trance sublime and strange" (35), whereas in *SD: MB* he seems "as in a vision deep & strange": "vision" may seem profounder than "trance," but "sublime" claims to have access to a quality of apprehension not aimed at by "deep." And in *1817* the "legion of wild thoughts" (41) rests "In the still cave of the Witch Poesy" (44), not "Near" it, as *SD: MB*, more circumspectly, phrases the possibility of poetic intuition. One is conscious, too, that the lines describing "The sudden pause" in *SD: MB*, which disappear from *1817*, strike a louder note of forlornness than one finds in *1817*.

The point to stress is that we are given a rare opportunity of watching one of our greatest poets writing one of his greatest poems twice. For instance, in the magnificent final section of the poem, Shelley stages his haunting double-take of absence and presence differently in the two versions. As "the snows descend", in *SD: MB*, "none beholds them there— / Nor when the sunset wraps their flakes in fire"; in *1817*, "none beholds them there, / Nor when the flakes burn in the sinking sun" (132–3). In *SD: MB* the flakes are passively wrapped; in *1817* they actively "burn", offsetting (even as they are lit up by) the "sinking" sun. The effect of the change is to give the flakes in *1817* a more dynamic affinity with earlier "gleams" in the poem: gleams that have suggested the power of "imaginings". In accord with this stronger suggestion in *1817* of some hidden excitement about the mind's coun-

terbalancing power, the "Winds" (134) "heap the snow with breath /
Rapid and strong" (135–6), where "Rapid and strong" seem more
transferrable to the imagining mind than the adjectives used of the
winds in SD: MB, "Blasting & swift". Later, SD: MB remarks, "The
secret strength of things / Which governs thought, and to the infinite
dome / Of Heaven is a column, rests on thee." By contrast, 1817 reads,
for that last line, "Of Heaven is as a law, inhabits thee" (141). The
changes make for greater abstraction (the column becomes a law) and
stronger presence (the secret strength no longer rests on, it inhabits).
Even capital letters slip and slide, will not stay still. Reading SD: MB
in manuscript one is struck by the way the author attached importance, perhaps only while making that particular copy, to certain
nouns: the concluding "Vacancy," with its capital "V," absorbs the attention rather more than "the human mind's imaginings" pitted against
it (yet partly responsible for it since only "imaginings" can produce the
idea of "vacancy").

                            *    *    *

    "Stanzas Written in Dejection—December 1818, near Naples," a
fair copy of which (entitled "Naples—December 1818") is in the Pierpont Morgan Library, is among Shelley's most famous lyrics, [and]
reveals how he was able to articulate "morbid but too natural bursts
of discontent and sadness" (Mary Shelley's "Note on Poems of 1818,"
PW, 570) without loss of artistic authority. Indeed, the poem's power
to affect is inseparable from its measured control, just as the poet's
sense of having "nor hope nor health / Nor peace within, nor calm
around" sharpens his responsiveness to the beauty of the Neapolitan
scene:

               The sun is warm, the sky is clear
               The waves are dancing fast & bright
               Blue isles & snowy mountains wear
               The purple noon's transparent might . . .[2]

Shelley's indirect presentation of "dejection" owes something to the
great crisis poems of Wordsworth ("Ode: Intimations of Immortality")
and Coleridge ("Dejection: An Ode"), poems in which clarity of description speaks volumes about loss of visionary power. Certainly, the
opening lines pay tribute, as Shelley always does, even in the depths
of personal sorrow, to the dancing energies that animate the natural
world. As his wife observes, "enjoying as he appeared to do every sight
or influence of earth or sky, it was difficult to imagine that any melancholy he showed was aught but the effect of the constant pain to
which he was a martyr" (PW, 570–71). The near-oxymoron, "transparent might," sets the tone of Shelley's response to the material world,
discovering here a blend of the substantial and the transpicuous, a
spiritualized materiality. In this condition opposites melt into one an-

2. There is a photofacsimile of the manuscript in Donald H. Reiman (ed.), MYR: Shelley, V
(1991), pp. 73–75.

other, so that in the alexandrine which concludes Shelley's modified form of a Spenserian stanza (same rhyme scheme but tetrameters rather than pentameters for lines 1–8) he is able to assert, "The City's voice itself is soft, like Solitude's." This view of solitude emerges as a pleasing deception in the next stanza when the crucial fifth line takes one to an emotional dead-centre: "I sit upon the sands alone."

But, far from wallowing in self-pity, the poem passes through its different emotional phases with a curious dignity: the result of Shelley's attention to each developing stage of the poetic experience, attention shown in the calm, unhurried movement of the lines, emphasized by the sure, elegant hand in which he wrote the Pierpont Morgan fair copy. Stanza 3 evokes the positive values whose absence is lamented by the poet, such as "that content, surpassing wealth, / The sage in meditation found / And walked with inward glory crowned." The stanza concludes on a note of almost shoulder-shrugging resignation—"To me that cup has been dealt in another measure." But stanza 4 redefines "despair" as "mild" "Even as the winds & waters are," and the stanza's death-wish is a longing to simplify consciousness into a state where it no longer impinges with its "untimely moan" on "this sweet day." That last phrase occurs in the final stanza; it shows the poet withdrawing from his wish for cessation of consciousness, and reasserting a sense of otherness, as he does in the final lines which are marked by a reticent refusal to mourn:

> They might lament—for I am one
> Whom men love not, & yet regret
> Unlike this day, which when the Sun
> Shall on its cloudless glory set
> Will linger, though enjoyed, like joy in memory yet.

As Judith Chernaik has observed, "the poem ends, indeed, with the sweet day, rather than the poet's dejection".[3] Shelley's ending recalls the close of Wordsworth's "The Solitary Reaper" with its emphasis on the continuing nourishment made possible by memory: "The music in my heart I bore, / Long after it was heard no more."[4] But Wordsworth's "joy" does not have to contend with the impulse to "lament" evident in Shelley's lines, and it is the ability to express deep grief yet realize that the prospect of "joy in memory" remains for others (and possibly himself) which helps to make "Stanzas Written in Dejection" a lyric masterpiece.

\*    \*    \*

Several of Shelley's shorter poems are accompanied by notes which flirt with an addressee (woman and muse) yet withdraw into a psychological and creative privacy. Running up the right margin of the manuscript of "To Jane [The keen stars were twinkling]" are the words, "I sate down to write some words for an ariette which might be

3. Chernaik, *The Lyrics of Shelley*, p. 77.
4. Quoted from Stephen Gill (ed.), *William Wordsworth*, The Oxford Authors (1984; Oxford: Oxford University Press, 1990).

622 Michael O'Neill

profane.——but it was in vain to struggle with the ruling spirit, who compelled me to speak of things sacred to yours & Wilhelmeister's indulgence.—I commit them to your secrecy & your mercy & will try & do better another time." The reference to the "ruling spirit" implies the imperious sway over the poet of inspiration; and the notion that the "profane" may be indistinguishable from "things sacred" prepares one for the emotional cliff-edge along which the poems to Jane make their way. The inadequacy topos with which the note finishes also permits the poet to keep writing, in order to "do better another time." Even more tantalizingly oblique is the note accompanying the gift of "Remembrance" to Jane Williams (in Eton College Library): ". . . if this melancholy old song suits any of your tunes or any that humour of the moment may dictate you are welcome to it.—Do not say it is mine to any one even if you think so;—indeed it is from the torn leaf of a book out of date." As he does elsewhere, Shelley presents the poem as wrested from another context and adapted to a new one. This re-presentation prevents the poem from being read as a straightforward declaration of present feelings. Such jotted, enigmatic notes attached to poems seem like leaves torn out of a latter-day, unsystematized *Vita Nuova*, where poems and commentary interact. In the case of the poems to Jane Williams, this interaction is richly oblique, and makes a telling contrast with the more straightforward relationship between text and comment established in the poems that Shelley sent in letters to Elizabeth Hitchener. After transcribing poems in a letter of 14 February 1812 Shelley wrote, "These are merely sent as lineaments in the picture of my mind on these topics. I find that I can sometimes write poetry when I feel." (*Letters*, I, 254). That earlier remark reveals Shelley as working far more explicitly within a poetics of sincerity than he does in the poems to Jane Williams. The earlier poems downgrade aesthetic indirection and recreation; they locate value in the degree to which poetry communicates accurately "the picture of [the] mind." The "mind" in the later poems gives artistic representation an altogether less straightforward challenge.

\* \* \*

To read Shelley's poems in manuscript is to be brought into intimate proximity with the idiosyncratic way he shapes on paper the emerging or chosen syllables of a piece. It is also to be made aware that poetic greatness is inseparable from, but never reducible to, technical skill. Shelley's concern with detail, so evident in his manuscripts, should scotch once and for all the notion that he was indifferent to nuance. \* \* \* The use of rhyme by Shelley makes one admiringly aware, once again, of the poet's awareness that every detail in a poem counts, that technical considerations are always significant. In "To Jane. The Recollection", for example, Shelley's rhymes are far more conversationally natural than in earlier poems (such as the poems contained in letters to Elizabeth Hitchener).[5] Here Shelley is prepared to rhyme "forest"

5. I am indebted to Donald H. Reiman for this observation.

with "nest," "breath" with "beneath," "there" with "woodpecker," and "lent" with "lineament." Such rhymes hover on the verge of being quasi- or near-rhymes, and anticipate the practice of twentieth-century poets; they employ a soft-pedal rather than striving for anything too climactic and grand. In so doing they are consonant with a poetic mood of great subtlety, and help to catch on the wing those "evanescent visitations of thought and feeling" [532] which Shelley describes in *A Defence of Poetry*. Indeed, the poems to Jane Williams are among the most impressive examples of his poetic artistry. Each of the so-called Trelawny manuscripts—including "To Jane. The Invitation," "To Jane—The Recollection," "To Jane [The keen stars were twinkling]," "Remembrance," "The Serpent Is Shut Out from Paradise," and "When the Lamp Is Shattered"—was given by his daughter Laetitia, Mrs Charles F. Call, to a different library. In the Trelawny manuscripts Shelley writes at the height of his lyrical powers, though out of the depths of entangled and difficult feelings. In the case of possibly the most confessional of the poems, "The Serpent Is Shut Out from Paradise," which is accompanied by a note to Jane Williams's common-law husband, Edward, there is a striking difference between the way the poem is written (beautifully) and the way the letter to Williams is written (very "distrait," possibly deliberately so). The handwriting enforces awareness of the gap between experiential pain and lyric art. The poem plays on this recognition, even exploits it. The reader is made to sense a painful rawness of feeling, even as he or she is persuaded that the poem has pain under artistic control. So private a poem makes the reader of the manuscript feel like a priveleged voyeur. Edward (and Jane) Williams may well have been both flattered and disturbed by the role which the poem assigns them:

> When I return to my cold home, you ask
> Why I am not as I have lately been?
> You spoil me for the task
> Of acting a forced part in life's dull scene.
> Of wearing on my brow the idle mask
> Of author, great or mean,
> In the world's carnival.

Like the other Trelawny manuscripts the fair copy is punctuated with care, and one notes here the artful effect of the rhetorical stop at the end of the fourth line. It is as if the effort of "acting a forced part in life's dull scene" brings the syntax to a brief, exhausted halt, before the next line takes up the struggle. "The Serpent Is Shut Out from Paradise" has in common with other late poems a deep concern with the psychology and poetics of survival; like them it invents a form (modified *ottava rima*) that communicates intricate present-tense experience but looks before and after. "When the Lamp Is Shattered" subtly misleads the reader into thinking that it describes a once-and-for-all emotional catastrophe; its central concern emerges (in the "second part" of the Trelawny fair copy in Glasgow University Library) as endurance, living on: "The weak one is singled / To endure what it once possest." By the time of the fair copy of the poem in the British Library Shelley has got rid of an explicitly contrapuntal form, but a dialogue between inner voices—one saying "everything is over," the other saying "life must drag out its course"—is even more apparent.

Frequently the poems given to Jane Williams communicate moods which suggest self-division. In the act of communicating this self-division, however, Shelley displays control and perceptiveness. For instance, the assertion, at the end of "To Jane. The Invitation," that "all things seem only one / In the universal Sun" balances utopian longing against the element of doubt unostentatiously implied by "seem." Throughout the poems, Shelley brings into play the workings of a sensitive, emotionally complex consciousness. These lyrics are aware of themselves as crafted linguistic structures, but they recognize that their artistic symmetries and successes must be set against the experiential silences, isolation and imperfection which they set themselves less to redeem than to take on board. A central concern is the gap between a privileged moment made available through art and temporal pressures arising from memory and anticipation which bring into the writing a continual, niggling sense of anxiety.

"To Jane—the Recollection" yields up new insights when read in manuscript. For one thing, the process makes one more attentive to the self-reflexive suggestions of the stoic opening when "Memory" is told to get on with its "wonted work" and "trace / The epitaph of glory dead." "Dead" is almost certainly a transcription slip for "fled." Yet the "deadness" of writing, however remarkable, that is trying to recapture past experience is momentarily borne in upon one as one reads the manuscript, and retraces Shelley's own epitaphic traces. I say "momentarily" because the poem (rather like *Epipsychidion*) soon abandons the wry, defeated note with which it begins. In fact, it builds towards a beautiful suspension of anxiety as Shelley recalls his intuition of "A spirit interfused around / A thrilling silent life." But if "interfused" brings "Tintern Abbey" (97) to mind, the "peace" it betokens is only "momentary," as the ending shows: "Though thou art ever fair and kind / And forests ever green / Less oft is peace in ———'s mind / Than calm in water seen." No prizes, of course, for supplying Shelley's omitted name, yet the omission, disrupting the possibility of saying the line, has an uncanny effect. Shelley seems both to introduce and erase himself in the same breath; the lines hold together the prospect of unchanging kindness and beauty, and the scarcity of "peace" in the poet's troubled mind. But the cumulative impact of the final section is a question of the deftest insinuations of disquiet, the most understated of emotional diminuendos. The steady iambic control of the poem curbs and shapes feeling. "To Jane. The Invitation" also thrives on bringing together different moods; it modulates from a vigorous, but care-attended, rejection of care to the eloquent tour-de-force of the final section: a single sentence made up of twenty-three lines (ten couplets and one triplet). In this case the trochaic measure is expressive of the poem's desire to "Awake, arise and come away," the echo of Satan rousing his fallen troops (*Paradise Lost*, I, 330) merely confirming the poet's turning away from political rebellion to a search for some sense of oneness under "the universal Sun."[6]

It would, however, be wrong to over-emphasize any retreat from politics in the late poems to Jane Williams. They are better seen as giving a yearning, oblique, and individualist slant to the utopian politics typical of Shelley's poetic imaginings. "To Jane [The keen stars were twinkling]" shows Shelley's ability to use form mimetically; the movement of the lines, the deployment of rhyme, the choice of diction—all these elements combine to create a tour-de-force. But the poem is more than an exquisite trifle, or "ariette," the title given to it by Medwin and the word used by Shelley in his accompanying note. Rather, it gathers into its crystalline structure Shelley's intuition of "some world far from ours / Where music & moonlight & feeling / Are one." The farness of this world is hinted at by the breakdown of the analogy between "voice" and "strings" and "moon" and "stars" which governs the first stanza. The second stanza appeals more directly to the power of song; Jane becomes in her singing and playing the poet's muse and surrogate. At the end of his career Shelley is still possessed and buoyed up by a sense of the "human mind's imaginings," a sense which finds expression in the word "overpowers." Here the poem cunningly takes itself by surprise and assumes far greater force. The verb implies that beauty is too overwhelming to be endured; the paradisal glimpse which, embodied in a work of art, it affords haunts and taunts our post-lapsarian condition.

In "The Magnetic Lady to her Patient" Shelley refers to "the world's dull scorn," not simply alluding to the reception of his poetry. However, personal strains lead to double-binds that cannot be solved by the incantation of politicized formulae. Wryly and sadly, the poem ends with the poet's words: "What would cure that would kill me, Jane / And as I must on earth abide / Awhile yet, tempt me not to break / My chain." The "chain" of endurance, whether of physical or emotional suffering, is captured by the terse rhyme with which the poem concludes. What makes the poem confessionally modern, as with all the poems to Jane, is the implication that Shelley has transferred his utopian hopes onto a particular, named person. It is doubtful that Shelley would have published the poem in unaltered form had he lived; and one assumes that his shade acquiesced in the omission of Jane's name in the version published by Thomas Medwin in *The Athenæum*, 11 August 1832, reprinted in *The Shelley Papers* (1833); this version is the probable source of a fair copy in Trinity College Dublin. This fair copy possesses no intrinsic textual authority, but it is of interest as showing the early dissemination of Shelley's work. It draws attention, too, to the superior quality of Shelley's own text. For the changes derived from Medwin simplify its impact. For example, the Trelawny manuscript reads "Sleep, sleep on, forget thy pain"; the Trinity College

---

6. Shelley used the line from *Paradise Lost* referred to in this sentence at the end of his *Declaration of Rights*. See E. B. Murray (ed.), *The Prose Works of Percy Bysshe Shelley*, Volume I (Oxford: Clarendon Press, 1993), p. 60.

Dublin copy offers the robustly comforting "Sleep on! sleep on!" "Sleep, sleep on" reveals a poet writing with a sure ear for the intimacies of affectionate speech. A similar loss of nuance is apparent in the omission of the dash before "forever" in stanza 3, line 4, which, in the Trelawny manuscript, lends a gathering urgency to the catalogue of desired forgetfulness. Medwin's coarsening piracies meant that some of Shelley's most carefully phrased poems were for many years known only through inferior versions.

*  *  *

Very often Shelley's lyric poetry uses its copious resources to adumbrate a tale of consciousness, a tale with implications for the lives of "another and of many others" (*A Defence of Poetry* [517]); whether it be a "Tale of Society as it is" (the title given to "She was an aged woman, and the years" in the *Esdaile Notebook*), or a tale of existence as it ought to be or might be, the Shelleyan lyric tale frequently lures us on by leaving another tale partly "untold." In "With a Guitar to Jane", central to the suite of poems written for Jane Williams, Shelley casts himself with a certain humor as Ariel, yet he attributes the capacity for magical transformation to the skilled player of "this loved guitar" (58). The poem draws an enchanted circle round performer, fit audience, and art itself. But this circle is never closed, remaining open to the hurts and yearnings of experience, an openness which finds formal expression in a variety of ways in the poetry (the question at the end of "The Question" is an example of one such way). This openness sometimes involves a valuable interrogation of the limits of art, a sense both that art creates structures of its own and that these structures need to remain alert to their own assumptions and presumptions. "The Sunset", a text of which is now in the Pforzheimer Collection and is soon to be published in volume IX of *Shelley and his Circle*, vividly illustrates the poet's truncated yet spun-out handling of a "tale." Here, too, powerful lyric emotion seeks accommodation within a narrative that ends without being ended. The "subtle being" elegized by the poem dies and rises again throughout Shelley's oeuvre, until his physical death confirmed the unfinished fragment, "The Triumph of Life," as the most questing, mysterious work of English Romantic poetry.

ALAN BEWELL

## Percy Bysshe Shelley and Revolutionary Climatology[†]

\* \* \*

In this chapter I explore the important ways Shelley's geographies are shaped by his medicalizing of social life. He shares with medical meteorologists and topographers the view that it is not people but places that are sick, yet whereas most saw disease as primarily a symptom of the physical environment, as climatological factors combine with specific aspects of a rural or urban landscape (marshes, forests, narrow streets, dockyards, etc.) to produce harmful poisons or miasmas, Shelley sees the physical environment itself as a social product. It is "kings, and priests, and statesmen" who produce the "venomed exhalations" that "spread / Ruin, and death, and woe" (*Queen Mab* 4.80–85). Geography is thoroughly a social construction. To "socialize the natural," to take up such seemingly "natural" aspects of the environment as "soil" and "climate" and rewrite them as expressions of social relations, is thus a central aspect of Shelley's medical thought that has not received the attention it deserves. In confronting disease, the poet believed he was confronting not a physical organism but social spaces fundamentally shaped by power and ideas. Shelley's social theory is profoundly influenced by medical geography, but rather than seeing the physical environment as a given, he understands it as a product of social relations. This is why he refuses to separate ideopathology from the analysis of power. "Power" is a "desolating pestilence" that "Pollutes whate'er it touches" (3.176–77). Literature has often employed epidemics as metaphors for social ills, but the environmental and demographic aspects of "desolating" go beyond metaphor to suggest that power *is* disease; it is the force that creates pathogenic spaces in the world. Pathology *is* the study of power. Ignorance, vice, misery, and disease are not just useful metaphors for describing its effects but are part of its being. Alluding to the upas tree of tropical Asia, Shelley argues that "commerce" is a "poison-breathing shade" beneath which "no solitary virtue dares to spring" (5.44–45). This link between power, disease, and the environment can be seen again in his description of the world that meets the eyes of the human soul:

> Ah! to the stranger-soul, when first it peeps
> From its new tenement, and looks abroad
> For happiness and sympathy, how stern
> And desolate a tract is this wide world!
> How withered all the buds of natural good!

† From *Romanticism and Colonial Disease*, by Alan Bewell (Baltimore, MD: Johns Hopkins University Press, 1999), pp. 209–19. Copyright © 2000. Reprinted by permission of the author and The Johns Hopkins University Press. The author's notes have been edited.

No shade, no shelter from the sweeping storms
Of pitiless power.                    (4.121–27)

Anticipating the "living storm" (466) of the *Triumph of Life*, Shelley describes power in meteorological terms as the "sweeping storms" that "desolate" the earth, withering "the buds of natural good." In confronting disease, Shelley was therefore confronting social spaces that he believed derived their pathogenic character from the desolating power of "evil, the immedicable plague" (*Prometheus Unbound* 2.4.101). Medicine provided him with a vocabulary for reading social geographies as disease environments. As he suggests in the conclusion to "The Sensitive Plant," one of the primary tasks of the poet is to provide a visionary alternative to such landscapes, the vision of a healthy world:

> That garden sweet, that lady fair
> And all sweet shapes and odours there
> In truth have never past away—
> 'Tis we, 'tis ours, are changed—not they.
>                         (4.17–20)

Shelley's social therapeutics are constituted as a recovery of a nature that preceded the fall into sickness, but this recovery proceeds through a radical critique of contemporary disease geographies as preeminently social formations.

Shelley's writings constitute an extended reflection on the intertwining of social power and disease. The understanding of this relation, however, was not fixed but underwent significant changes of emphasis. After the utopian optimism of the early writings, in which he celebrated people's power to control and transform their environments through social reason, an increasing pessimism dominates his work. In *Mont Blanc* this pessimism derives from his recognition of the limits of our control of nature. In the *Triumph of Life* a far deeper pessimism emerges as he recognizes the depths of social power and disease. In this poem social evils have become pandemic. Shelley's comprehension of the ideopathology of space was not removed from the colonial world but frequently advanced through a reflection on colonial spaces, for it was there that the dynamic interaction of social and natural forces was writ large. As the embodiment of a pathogenic space that had come into being through the misuse of power, colonial space thus provided Shelley with a means and vocabulary for understanding European society. His increasing pessimism about the world's human environments can be said, then, to express anxiety about the direction British society was heading and fear that its imperial contact with other nations was becoming as great a plague to them as the East had originally seemed to be for England.

## The Social Environment

With the exception of *Prometheus Unbound*, *Queen Mab* represents Shelley's greatest articulation of a biosocial utopia. In book 8 he envisions a total conquest and transformation of the world's diseased environments, a global ecological revolution made possible by science and love:

> All things are recreated, and the flame
> Of consentaneous love inspires all life:
> The fertile bosom of the earth gives suck
> To myriads, who still grow beneath her care,
> Rewarding her with their pure perfectness:
> The balmy breathings of the wind inhale
> Her virtues, and diffuse them all abroad:
> Health floats amid the gentle atmosphere,
> Glows in the fruits, and mantles on the stream.
> (8.107–15)

As in much of Shelley's writing, social revolution is here registered by a change in the physical environment. Countering the miasmas, those "terrestrial emanations . . . [or] causes of disease which float in the atmosphere,"[1] Shelley presents a world in which love, health, and reason are diffused everywhere. Man, with "taintless body" (8.199), rules and guides the changes taking place on earth: "his being notes / The gradual renovation, and defines / Each movement of its progress on his mind" (8.142–44). Shelley's biosocial utopia remains centered in human beings as he describes how reason and passion, no longer at war with each other, extend over the entire earth "Their all-subduing energies, and wield / The sceptre of a vast dominion there" (8.233–34).

*    *    *

Shelley's geographical ideas are similar to those of Comte Georges-Louis Leclerc de Buffon, whom he first read in 1811. Like the French naturalist, he believes that large areas of the earth need improvement if they are to be adequate human habitats. Thomas Hogg notes the scientific culture shaping Shelley's geography. "What is the cause of the remarkable fertility of some lands, and of the hopeless sterility of others?" Shelley asked. "A spadeful of the most productive soil, does not to the eye differ much from the same quantity taken from the most barren. The real difference is probably very slight; by chemical agency the philosopher may work a total change, and may transmute an unfruitful region into a land of exuberant plenty."[2] Shelley's belief that chemical fertilizers can make an "unfruitful region" produce "exuberant plenty" was not, as Hogg believed, fanciful but instead shows the influence of Sir Humphry Davy's lectures on behalf of the Board of Agriculture early in 1802. There Davy argued that agriculture is "an

1. James Annesley, *Researches into the Causes, Nature, and Treatment of the More Prevalent Diseases of India, and of Warmer Climates Generally*, 2d ed. (London: Longman, Brown, Green, and Longmans, 1841), 45.
2. Thomas Jefferson Hogg, *The Life of Percy Bysshe Shelley*, introd. Edward Dowden (London: Routledge, 1906), 48–49.

art intimately connected with chemical science."[3] Having already suffered ridicule for his enthusiasm over the medical benefits of nitrous
oxide, Davy was careful to avoid looking "to distant ages . . . [to] amuse
ourselves with brilliant, though delusive dreams concerning the infinite improveability of man, the annihilation of labour, disease, and
even death. . . . We consider only a state of human progression arising
out of its present condition" (323). The infertility of the soil, however,
was not the only factor standing in the way of agricultural improvement. Finding adequate water supplies was just as important. Shelley
believed that chemistry would ultimately discover "a simple and sure
method of manufacturing the useful fluid, in every situation and in
any quantity," a knowledge that would produce a total ecological transformation of North Africa. "The arid deserts of Africa may then be
refreshed by a copious supply," he declared, "and may be transformed
at once into rich meadows, and vast fields of maize and rice." Nor
would the coldness of some climates constitute an insurmountable
obstacle to human ingenuity; it might be possible "perhaps at no very
distant period . . . to produce heat at will, and to warm the most
ungenial climates as readily as we now raise the temperature of our
apartments to whatever degree we may deem agreeable or salutary."
Shelley's science provides the means for making the entire earth serve
human needs. We make a serious mistake if we treat his notions about
ecological revolution as simply visionary. They also express many of
the ideas that led to the radical transformation of the landscapes of
England and that informed the engineering megaprojects of later
nineteenth-century colonialism.[4] An anti-imperialist on one level,
Shelley nevertheless shares with the promoters of empire the "tech-
notopian" belief that European science should contribute to the transformation of global environments.[5]

In *Queen Mab*, Shelley follows Hippocrates in drawing a parallel
between different climates and the health of the people who inhabit
them. He divides the world into three primary environmental zones—
the polar, the tropical, and the temperate. The first two are extreme
pathogenic spaces. Whatever might be said about the extreme environment of those who dwell in "the gloom of the long polar night," a
much harsher world awaits them in the poem. Shelley speaks of people
who are biologically degenerate. Man "shrank with the plants, and
darkened with the night," he writes:

> His chilled and narrow energies, his heart,
> Insensible to courage, truth, or love,
> His stunted stature and imbecile frame,
> Marked him for some abortion of the earth,

3. For Shelley's interest in agriculture, see Timothy Morton, *Shelley and the Revolution in Taste: The Body and the Natural World* (Cambridge: Cambridge UP, 1994), 232–34. *The Collected Works of Sir Humphry Davy*, ed. John Davy (London: Smith, Elder, and Cornhill, 1839), 2:315.
4. For more on colonialism and ecology, see Richard Grove's work.
5. Morton uses the word "technotopianism" in "Shelley's Green Desert" 417. For an argument that Shelley is a "confirmed orientalist and liberal imperialist," see Nigel Leask, *British Romantic Writers and the East: Anxieties of Empire* (Cambridge: Cambridge UP, 1992), 70.

> Fit compeer of the bears that roamed around,
> Whose habits and enjoyments were his own:
> His life a feverish dream of stagnant woe.
>
> (8.149–56)

Drawing on Buffon's description of the disastrous impact of the cold American climate on its indigenous people, Shelley produces an even more negative picture of environmental and reproductive degeneration as he repeatedly speaks of the narrowing of moral and biological energies, of shrinking, stunting, imbecility, and abortiveness, and the absence of the Shelleyan virtues of "courage, truth, and love." Disease has often been understood as a punishment for moral offenses. Shelley applies this idea to entire regions, as if the world's pathogenic spaces were a punishment upon their inhabitants: "All was inflicted here that Earth's revenge / Could wreak on the infringers of her law" (8.163–64).

Since Shelley associates sickness and fever with social stasis—the word "stagnant" deriving from *stagnum* ("swamp")—the people who inhabit the tropics are little different:

> Nor where the tropics bound the realms of day
> With a broad belt of mingling cloud and flame,
> Where blue mists through the unmoving atmosphere
> Scattered the seeds of pestilence, and fed
> Unnatural vegetation, where the land
> Teemed with all earthquake, tempest and disease,
> Was man a nobler being . . .          (8.166–72)

Again disease is understood as a deviation from nature, as the "blue mists" of miasma, their color suggesting death, are born from "*unnatural* vegetation" and an "unmoving" atmosphere. One popular explanation for the unhealthy character of tropical environments during the dry season was "the want of the free ventilation afforded by the tradewinds during the rest of the year."[6] Shelley draws on this idea, but for him the "unmoving" state of the atmosphere or of the swamp—both productive of miasmas—is a *symptom* of social stagnancy, not its *cause*. Shelley goes on to argue that disease combines with slavery and constant warfare to make the tropics a bane to human existence.

Given the analogy drawn in medical geography between the moral and intellectual qualities of a people and the qualities of the environments they inhabit, Shelley's contemporaries would not have been surprised by his turn from these extreme environments to the "milder zone" (8.187), the "favoured clime" (8.193) of England, where "truth" has finally arisen to combat disease. Yet Shelley describes it as also being diseased:

> Even where the milder zone afforded man
> A seeming shelter, yet contagion there,
> Blighting his being with unnumbered ills,

6. Alexander M. Tulloch and Henry Marshall, "Statistical Report of the Sickness, Mortality, and Invaliding among the Troops of the West Indies," *Accounts and Papers* (*Parliamentary Papers*, 1837–38, 40 [417]), 102.

Spread like a quenchless fire; nor truth till late
Availed to arrest its progress.          (8.187–91)

Shelley does not celebrate the enviromedical superiority of Europe as
a physical space, although he does place it higher in the scale of world
regions. Instead, he values its role in bringing truth to light. For Shelley, disease environments are not "essentialized" but are symptoms of
the absence of truth, which is the only force needed to "arrest" their
development.

Michael Scrivener argues that Shelley's " 'nature' not only presents
no insuperable obstacles to reason, but is itself rational."[7] From such
a viewpoint, disease-bearing environments are unnatural because they
deviate from reason. Their cure is seen as a "recovery" both of reason
and of their "nature." Shelley supports this idea through an interesting
revision of the extensive "ruins of empire" literature. Where the contemplation of the ruins of ancient cities frequently gave rise to a melancholy sense of historical change and to the moral that all empires
must eventually fall victim to time, Shelley focuses on the destruction
of habitable environments indicated by such ruins. Take Palmyra, for
instance, where "the aspect of a great city deserted, the memory of
times past, compared with its present state" ushers in the political
reverie of Volney.[8] Shelley follows the French ideologue in using these
ruins to reflect on the course of empires and on social and political
decay. "Monarchs and conquerors there / Proud o'er prostrate millions
trod— / The earthquakes of the human race" (2.121–23). Yet his association of the rulers with destructive geological forces suggests that
the poet is more fascinated by the clear evidence these ruins provide
of a physical environment that no longer exists. To the obvious question raised by such ruins—Why would a people build a great city in
the middle of a desert?—Shelley drew the obvious conclusion that
Palmyra had not always been in the desert, that some massive change
had radically altered its character. His explanation is political: a change
in moral and political institutions, notably the advent of an increasingly despotic government, caused depopulation and with it a progressive decline in the people's capacity to maintain the fertility and
moderate climate of the region. The emergence of the desert, as both
a demographic and a physical process, is thus a political development,
concomitant with the emergence of despotism.[9]

The contemporary condition of Jerusalem evokes a similar sense of
the link between politics and environmental degradation:

7. Michael Henry Scrivener, *Radical Shelley: The Philosophical Anarchism and Utopian Thought
of Percy Bysshe Shelley* (Princeton: Princeton UP, 1982), 68.
8. Constantin-F. Volney, *The Ruins, or Meditation on the Revolution of Empires; and The Law
of Nature* (Baltimore: Black Classic, 1991), 3–4.
9. Current climatological studies suggest that the Romantics were correct in recognizing that
a major climatic change had occurred in the region. Between A.D. 300 and 800, two major
drought periods saw the collapse of several of the cities along the Great Silk Road to the
East. "In Arabia," H. H. Lamb notes, "places where agriculture had been carried on with
the aid of elaborate irrigation works, which had survived earlier periods of desiccation, were
abandoned around AD 600" *Climate, History and the Modern World*, 2nd ed. (London: Methuen, 1995), 168.

Behold yon sterile spot;
Where now the wandering Arab's tent
Flaps in the desart-blast.
There once old Salem's haughty fane
Reared high to heaven its thousand golden domes,
And in the blushing face of day
Exposed its shameful glory.            (2.134–40)

After noting that "where Athens, Rome, and Sparta stood / There is
a moral desert now" (2.162–63), Shelley turns to the ancient Mayan
civilization. Where once "arose a stately city / Metropolis of the western continent," there is now only a wilderness (2.187–88). States that
deviate from the virtues of independence, labor, and equality produce
wildernesses. Shelley takes his republican environmentalism further to
reach the extraordinary visionary conclusion that there is no spot on
earth, no matter how wild, that was not once a populous city. "There's
not one atom of yon earth," he writes:

But once was living man;
Nor the minutest drop of rain,
That hangeth in its thinnest cloud,
But flowed in human veins:
And from the burning plains
Where Libyan monsters yell,
From the most gloomy glens
Of Greenland's sunless clime,
To where the golden fields
Of fertile England spread
Their harvest to the day,
Thou canst not find one spot
Whereon no city stood.
                    (2.211–24)

Here Shelley articulates a social ecology more radical than anything
currently claimed by contemporary social constructionists, arguing
that all nature "once was living man." He thus inverts the traditional
understanding of the relation between the city and the wilderness by
claiming that *cities come first*. In *Queen Mab* the wilderness and the
depopulated desert—emblems of environments that have proved uninhabitable to humankind—are not viewed as an "essential" nature
that precedes social life but instead are seen as the vestiges of cities
in ruin. Diseased environments are not the cause of social and political
disorder but are their result, the effects of a power that is truly a
"desolating pestilence" (3.176). Shelley denies that nature is conceivable apart from human life. The wilderness is always the signature of
a population decline produced by social inequity, resulting in the collapse of the habitable environments produced by rational, social labor:
it is always the city gone wild. Whereas Wordsworth argues for the
need to humanize nature, Shelley understands revolution as the recovery of the human face of nature, the cities that once existed
everywhere on earth.

Shelley's belief that the wilderness is a "depopulated nature" contributes to a century-old demographic debate, begun by the *Persian Letters* (1721), in which Montesquieu argued that the modern world was suffering from depopulation. "After a calculation as exact as is possible in such matters," Rhedi writes to Uzbek, "I have found that hardly one-tenth as many people are now on the earth as there were in ancient times." Even "more astonishing," he goes on to argue, "is that this depopulation goes on daily, and if it continues, the earth will be a desert in a thousand years."[1] He concludes that there must be "a secret and hidden poison, a corrupting disease afflicting human nature itself" (188). Uzbek responds that the problem lies not in nature, but in the sphere of morals and government, as the small, densely populated Greek city-states were replaced by large, ineffective empires shaped by anti-republican values. Shelley is a population pessimist who employs the idea of depopulation to argue against vice and bad government. Cities become deserts through changes in the moral and civil nature of human beings.[2] In *Hellas*, both the desert and paradise are politically determined: "Let the tyrants rule the desert they have made; / Let the free possess the paradise they claim" (1008–9).

As Shelley and his contemporaries looked at various parts of the globe, they saw ample evidence that some regions had undergone substantial climatic changes. They were quite aware that North Africa and the Middle East had once been immensely fertile, with sufficient rainfall to allow them to serve as the granary of the Roman Empire. Seeing deserts where there once were major croplands, they reached the not unwarranted conclusion that these environmental changes were linked to changes in social and political institutions. Colonial regions, associated with poverty, disease, and depopulation, far from being "naturally" this way, were seen as having undergone ecological degradation. Early on, as Richard Grove notes, Europeans had seen in the Canary Islands and Madeira how quickly deforestation can produce a radical decline in rainfall and consequent desiccation.[3] Shelley shares the anxieties that shaped early conservationist thinking as he sees in tropical colonial regions the forces that produce social ruin. "Ozymandias" is probably Shelley's most powerful depiction of the relation between poor government and a degraded physical environment. A traveler recounts his encounter with the "colossal Wreck" of a monument to Ramses II in the desert of an "antique land." The poem has long been read as a classic example of dramatic irony. The words on the pedestal of the broken statue read, "My name is Ozymandias, King of Kings, / Look on my Works, ye Mighty, and despair!" Kelvin Everest sees them

---

1. Montesquieu, *The Persian Letters*, ed. George R. Healey (Indianapolis: Bobbs-Merrill, 1964), 188.
2. Since population increase is a sign of good government, Shelley cannot conceive of a social revolution that does not lead to an increase in pleasure and erotic fulfillment—in Scrivener's words, "a renovated erotic nature" (69). In the ideal world that concludes *Queen Mab*, "impotence" is in the catalog of evils (the others being crime, languor, disease, and ignorance) that are exiled from earth (see 9.9–10).
3. Richard H. Grove, *Ecology, Climate, and Empire: Colonialism and Global Environmental History, 1440–1940* (Cambridge: White Horse, 1997), 6.

as conveying "a simple moral. The tyrant's affirmation of his omnipotence, sneeringly arrogant and contemptuous of its human cost, has been ironised by time. . . . It is simply true that tyranny does not last."[4] Such a view, though correct on one level, does not recognize how far-reaching is the desolating power of Ozymandias, so that his true works are still everywhere present in the "lone and level sands" that "stretch far away." The tyrant's words should be taken literally, though in a manner the speaker did not intend. Shelley looked at depopulated nature—the *desert*—as a far more ominous monument than the broken sculpture, showing not tyranny's susceptibility to time, but its continuing presence not only *in*, but *as* physical space. Tyranny *is* ruin, and Shelley intended his readers to recognize that "those passions . . . *yet survive* stamped on these lifeless things." "Ozymandias" is thus very much a poem about colonial space, which sees the ecologically degraded and depopulated character of such regions as a sign of the continuing survival of desolating power. Ecology and politics are inseparably allied.

Because Shelley denies that climate is "natural" because he sees all climates as "climates of power," addressing climate in his poetry is always a political gesture. * * * [C]olonial regions were seen not only as sites of social ruin, but also as places whose environments were undergoing radical renewal. Rather than seeing it as an "immovable barrier to the political improvement of the species,"[5] many writers thought that climate itself could be radically transformed, as appeared to be the case in America. Climate change was indeed seen as one of the chief benefits of the introduction of European technologies, knowledge, and political institutions. In the concluding utopian vision of *Queen Mab*, the fairy describes a world in which a total ecological transformation has taken place: "The habitable earth is full of bliss" (8.58). Social revolution engenders a world in which the polar wastes and tropical deserts no longer exist and the climatic differences that once characterized the globe have been eliminated:

> Those wastes of frozen billows that were hurled
> By everlasting snow-storms round the poles,
> Where matter dared not vegetate or live,
> But ceaseless frost round the vast solitude
> Bound its broad zone of stillness, are unloosed;
> And fragrant zephyrs there from spicy isles
> Ruffle the placid ocean-deep
>
> . . . . . . . . . .
>
> Those desarts of immeasurable sand,
> Whose age-collected fervors scarce allowed
> A bird to live, a blade of grass to spring,
> Where the shrill chirp of the green lizard's love
> Broke on the sultry silentness alone

4. Kelvin Everest, " 'Ozymandias': The Text in Time" in *Percy Bysshe Shelley: Bicentenary Essays*, ed. Kelvin Everest (Cambridge: Brewer, 1992), 26–27.
5. William Godwin, *Enquiry concerning Political Justice and Its Influence on Modern Morals and Happiness* (1793; Hammondsworth, Eng.: Penguin, 1985), 146.

Now teem with countless rills and shady woods,
Corn-fields and pastures and white cottages.
(8.59–76)

The centrality of "Corn-fields, pastures, white cottages" in this renovated earth shows how difficult it is, even for the most radical of English anti-imperial poets, to avoid using English landscapes as the
measure of utopia. Yet Shelley criticized English society not for its
utopian self-representation as an "island garden" but because it did
not live up to this ideal.[6] Having provided Ianthe with a vision of what
the earth can become, the fairy brings her back to reality. "The present
now recurs. / Ah me! a pathless wilderness remains / Yet unsubdued
by man's reclaiming hand" (9.143–45). Revolution is ecological reclamation, the recovery of a nature produced by human labor and love
that has been destroyed by social degradation.

# STEPHEN C. BEHRENDT

## Audiences and the Later Works[†]

> There is thus another man gone, about whom the world was ill-naturedly, and
> ignorantly, and brutally mistaken. It will, perhaps, do him justice now, when
> he can be no better for it.
>
> BYRON TO THOMAS MOORE, ON SHELLEY'S DEATH

In her "note" to the poems of 1819, Mary Shelley wrote:

> Shelley loved the People; and respected them as often more vir-
> tuous, as always more suffering, and therefore more deserving of
> sympathy, than the great. He believed that a clash between the
> two classes of society was inevitable, and he eagerly ranged him-
> self on the people's side. He had an idea of publishing a series of
> poems adapted expressly to commemorate their circumstances
> and wrongs. He wrote a few; but, in those days of prosecution for
> libel, they could not be printed. They are not among the best of
> his productions, a writer being always shackled when he endeav-
> ours to write down to the comprehension of those who could not
> understand or feel a highly imaginative style; but they show his

---

6. The idea that a total global climatic change might make health universally available to all
   human beings continued to fascinate Shelley throughout his career. In *Prometheus Unbound*,
   the union of Promethean science with the love of Asia makes possible the recovery of a
   temperate world:

   > a soft influence mild;
   > Shall clothe the forests and the fields—aye, even
   > The crag-built desarts of the barren deep—
   > With ever-living leaves and fruits and flowers.
   > (3.3.120–24)

† From *Shelley and His Audiences*, by Stephen C. Behrendt (Lincoln: University of Nebraska
   Press, 1989), pp. 227–35. Copyright © 1989 by the University of Nebraska Press. Reprinted
   by permission of the University of Nebraska Press. The author's notes have been edited.

earnestness, and with what heartfelt compassion he went home to the direct point of injury—that oppression is detestable as being the parent of starvation, nakedness, and ignorance. Besides these outpourings of compassion and indignation, he had meant to adorn the cause he loved with loftier poetry of glory and triumph: such is the scope of the *Ode to the Assertors of Liberty.*

(*Works,* 588)

She is propagandizing here, to be sure, to some extent inventing and mythologizing both Shelley and his relation to "the People." For the poet to have ranged himself "on the people's side" would have been to profess an alliance rather than to affirm any inhering egalitarian relationship, for Shelley never was "one of the people." Born into an aristocratic family and afforded a privileged—though truncated—education, Shelley ended by publishing poems not for "the People" but for a deliberately narrowed audience of cognoscenti, an audience neither broad nor populist.

But even in 1839, nearly two decades after her husband's death, Mary Shelley had to be careful. Sir Timothy Shelley, upon whom her income largely depended, had forced the suppression of the *Posthumous Poems* (1824), which she had edited, and had only grudgingly consented to the editions of 1839 and 1840 when she had promised not to include a biographical memoir of the poet.[1] Like her husband, Mary Shelley had to consider her audiences, and Sir Timothy was a hostile audience of one who had to be mollified by painful concessions if she was to publish Shelley's works. Seen in their proper context, her occasionally disparaging remarks in many ways resemble devices Shelley employed in his works and his statements about those works: they are devices of exigency, tactical concessions. If we put together her annual "Notes" in the 1839 and 1840 volumes, we find in them—as any perceptive reader must have—the general outline of the biographical memoir against which Sir Timothy had specifically warned her. It is singularly appropriate that such strategic manipulations should have been a part of the first "official" edition of Shelley's writings.

Mary Shelley's comments, here and elsewhere, about Shelley's ability (or inability) to capitalize on a popular style accord with the opinions of Hunt and Peacock. They also echo the sentiments of the reviewer for Gold's *London Magazine,* who spoke for those of his colleagues inclined to view Shelley at all favorably: in a generally positive and laudatory essay "On the Philosophy and Poetry of Shelley" published in 1821 the reviewer nevertheless observes that "with all the combined attractions of mind and verse, we feel that Mr. Shelley can never become a popular poet. He does not sufficiently link himself with man; he is too visionary for the intellect of the generality of his readers, and is ever immersed in the clouds of religious and metaphysical speculations. His opinions are but skeletons, and he does not sufficiently embody them to render them intelligible. They are mag-

---

1. Newman Ivey White, *Shelley,* 2 vols. (New York: Alfred A, Knopf, 1940), II, 401.

nificent abstractions of mind,—the outpourings of a spirit 'steeped to the very full' in humanity and religious enthusiasm."[2] The comments seem at first self-contradictory: the reviewer's assertion that Shelley's works are steeped in humanity scarcely accords with his subsequent claim that the poet "does not sufficiently link himself with man." But the reviewer had not seen the suppressed exoteric writings and does not mention *The Cenci*, although the same journal had reviewed Shelley's tragedy (negatively) in April 1820. In distinguishing between the broadly humanistic intent or sentiment of Shelley's work and the forbidding aesthetic and semantic vehicles by which the poet chose to convey that intent or sentiment, though, these remarks are not far from the judgments rendered by Shelley's own circle.

The *London Magazine*'s reviewer insightfully assesses the "religious enthusiasm" of Shelley's writing, although Shelley would probably have regretted his choice of that particular adjective. This reviewer recognized the missionary zeal that energizes all of Shelley's works. That this aspect of his work should be acknowledged would doubtless have pleased Shelley, had he ever seen the review, as would the reviewer's observations on his relation to Byron: "In intensity of description, depth of feeling, and richness of language, Mr. Shelley is infinitely superior to Lord Byron. He has less versatility of talent, but a purer and loftier imagination."[3]

The accusation that he insufficiently linked himself with humanity would have disheartened Shelley, although the reviewer's observations are not unjust. Although Shelley's writings reveal that he had moved from the general liberal Whig position of his early works toward the more distinctively radical stance of the later ones, he came increasingly to feel that his energy was largely wasted on a contemporary audience. When he was disappointed by Covent Garden's rejection of *The Cenci* and the suppression of the exoteric poems and the Carlile letter, he not surprisingly reassessed his position and opted realistically to reaffirm the opinion he had angrily voiced to Godwin in 1812: he would devote himself to becoming the cause of effects that would not become apparent until long after his own death. What changed increasingly with the passage of time was not the nature of his ideas but the manner and direction of their expression in his poetry and prose as he began to see that the directness he had termed "virtue and truth" in 1812 (*Letters*, I, 259) had apparently cut him off from his intended audiences. His comment to the Gisbornes upon learning of the death of Elena Adelaide Shelley in Naples (on 9 June 1820) epitomizes his state of mind in the summer of 1820: "It seems as if the destruction that is consuming me were as an atmosphere which wrapt & infected everything connected with me" (*Letters*, II, 211; ?7 July 1820).

2. Theodore Redpath, *The Young Romantics and Critical Opinion, 1807–1824* (London: Harrap, 1973), p. 361. For the sensitive, favorable review of *Prometheus Unbound and Other Poems* (published in September and October 1820), see Donald H. Reiman, ed., *The Romantics Reviewed*, 2 vols. (New York: Garland, 1972), pt. C, II, 627–38.
3. Ibid., p. 361.

Trelawny reports that when a reviewer characterized *Epipsychidion* as "the rhapsody of a madman," Shelley responded that "all the mass of mankind consider everyone eccentric or insane who utters sentiments they do not comprehend."[4] But his reviewers' repeated accusations both of insanity and of moral and aesthetic infamy, coupled with their complaints about unintelligibility, took a toll on Shelley, and his work after 1819 reflects a change of heart. The self-preserving declaration Trelawny reports is telling: "I have the vanity to write only for poetical minds, and must be satisfied with few readers. Byron is ambitious; he writes for all, and all read his works."[5] Inevitably, Shelley sees himself in relation to Byron, and if Trelawny's recollection of Shelley's words is at all accurate, Shelley's candid comparison suggests that he regards Byron's universal appeal as in some respects almost a point against that poet, an indication of questionable sincerity and commitment. Shelley is engaging in self-justification, of course, but not without reason.

Even if Shelley was writing "only for poetical minds" now, though, the major works he undertook in his final years exhibit great range and diversity. *Epipsychidion* may well be addressed to the SUNETOI, or cognoscenti, as Shelley claimed to John Gisborne (*Letters*, II, 363; 22 October 1821) and to Ollier, whom he instructed to print the poem in a limited run of only one hundred copies, "for the esoteric few" who "are capable of judging and feeling rightly with respect to a composition of so abstruse a nature" and who "certainly do not arrive at that number" (*Letters*, II, 263; 16 February 1821). Such an invented audience of ideal readers, which at least partially overlaps the envisioned audience for *A Philosophical View of Reform*, would also appreciate that *Adonais* was a complex manipulation of the Adonis myth and the scriptural concept of the Adonai; that *The Triumph of Life* directly invoked not only its Italian Renaissance predecessors (Dante's *Divine Comedy* and Petrarch's *Triumphs*) but also Plato, Milton, and Rousseau (particularly *Julie*) as keys to its meaning; that *A Defence of Poetry* demanded of its reader a sophisticated understanding of literary and cultural history; and that *Hellas* was a serious "imitation of the Persae of Aeschylus, full of lyrical poetry" and not the "lyrical, dramatic, nondescript piece of business" he later offhandedly termed it to Horace Smith (*Letters*, II, 364; 22 October 1821, to John Gisborne; II, 411; 11 April 1822). Given Hunt's inability or unwillingness to assist him in publishing his more overtly political poetry and prose and Ollier's real or assumed unreliability, Shelley cannot be faulted for deciding to write for a distinctly elite audience, particularly as it became clear to him that he would not return to England, where he might have taken matters into his own hands and secured new publishers. Nor can he be faulted for building into his prefaces the rhetorical and

4. Edward John Trelawny, *Records of Shelley, Byron, and the Author* (London: Basil Montague Pickering, 1878), I, 116.
5. Ibid., p. 118.

semantic gestures that explicitly limit this range of readers and exclude both hostile and inept readers, as Elise Gold has claimed.[6] In these considerations the particular case of *Hellas* dramatizes Shelley's dilemma.

Some six months after he had completed *Hellas*, Shelley asked John Gisborne's reaction to the poem, adding that "it was written without much care, in one of those few moments of enthusiasm which now seldom visit me, & which make me pay dear for their visits" (*Letters*, II, 406; 10 April 1822). If his work on *Hellas* (or any creative project) now made him "pay dear," it may have been because of the mixed emotions that attended composition: his enthusiasm for his work, and for the creative process itself, was necessarily tempered by the sober realization that his efforts were likely to meet once again with public rebuffs. So he struck the familiar pose of nonchalance as a defensive and self-preserving measure. Shelley was always enthusiastic about seeing his works into print quickly: indeed, his occasional rashness in this respect cost him more than once. With *Hellas* he likewise sought immediate publication, giving Ollier very particular instructions: "I send you the Drama of Hellas, relying on your assurance that you will be good enough to pay immediate attention to my *literary* requests.— What little interest this Poem may ever excite, depends upon it's [sic] *immediate* publication; I entreat you therefore to have the goodness to send the Ms. instantly to a Printer, & the moment you get a proof, dispatch it to me by the Post. . . . If any passages should alarm you in the notes, you are at liberty to suppress them; . . . the *Poem* contains nothing of a tendency to danger" (*Letters*, II, 365; 11 November 1821). Shelley's offer to let Ollier suppress any of the manuscript is both a compliment and a concession. Given Shelley's increasing dissatisfaction with Ollier, the offer is clearly a calculated attempt to press him into action.

Like Shelley's letter on Carlile's trial or *The Mask of Anarchy*, *Hellas* seemed to him to require immediate circulation because the events it commemorated were, for Shelley, of immediate concern to English readers, to whom the poem's particular relevance would have been underscored by its preface. Significantly, while he gives Ollier the option of suppressing passages from the notes to the poem, he attempts to preserve poem and preface alike by declaring the poem (and, by extension, presumably its preface as well) free of dangerous (that is, seditious or blasphemous) material. Not only did Ollier proceed slowly, however—the poem was not yet printed late in February of 1822, and a copy reached Shelley only in early April—but he also suppressed passages not only from the notes but from poem and preface alike, including the entire penultimate paragraph of the latter. This deletion, coupled with the long delay in publishing the poem, seriously undermined Shelley's attempt to define the poem's specific relevance to English affairs.

6. Elise M. Gold, "Touring the Inventions: Shelley's Prefatory Writing," *Keats-Shelley Journal* 36 (1987): 72ff. and passim.

Shelley intended his poem as "a political action" that would promote the cause of both Greek independence and English liberty by rallying public opinion in England around the Greek cause.[7] This intention is borne out by the Shelleys' earlier involvement with Prince Alexander Mavrocordato, the exiled Greek patriot they had met at Pisa in December 1820 and who joined their circle until June 1821, when he returned to Greece to play a leading role in the revolution. As Charles Robinson has revealed, the Shelleys—apparently working together as they had done when they translated Spinoza in June 1820—prepared a translation of Alexander Ypsilanti's rousing proclamation of Greek liberation, a copy of which (in Mary's hand with corrections by Shelley) exists among the Bodleian Shelley manuscripts.[8] Shelley (or perhaps his wife) subsequently sent a copy to Hunt, together with a cover letter, for insertion in the *Examiner* (though Hunt printed only the letter, having already on 15 April printed another translation). Shelley meantime sent another copy of the translation—and another cover letter—to the Whiggish *Morning Chronicle* (which had also already published the translated proclamation and so printed only Shelley's letter). Both letters call attention to the rise of the Greek national liberation movement and explicitly link the Greek cause with the interests of all lovers of national independence and personal liberty.

In *Hellas*, as in these letters, Shelley's increasingly ardent Hellenism (he had originally taken a much more negative view of the Greek contribution to Western culture) converges with his own resilient patriotism. In dramatically commemorating the momentous struggle of present-day Greece to liberate itself from "alien" occupation and oppression and thus, by reanimating it, to recapture the glory of its historical contributions to Western society, Shelley offers his perceptive readers yet another analogy. England had long congratulated itself on what it considered its position as the bastion of all that was accounted great and good in the modern world, as illustrated, for instance, in the self-congratulatory manner in which England, particularly in 1788–89, regarded its "glorious" bloodless revolution of 1688, or in Wordsworth's 1802 sonnets, or in the countless expressions of nationalistic pride published after Waterloo. In rallying his English audience around the Greek cause, Shelley meant to rally them also around their own analogous English cause. The restoration of independence to Greece might commemorate past glory but it could not reinstate it: in the modern world that glory could only belong to the most fitting inheritors of the Greek legacy, the English nation. Furthermore, Shelley's stress in *Hellas* and in his letters upon the Christian orientation of the revolutionary Greeks of 1821 (as opposed to their barbarous Turkish oppressors), and upon their position as the descendants of the

7. See Michael Scrivener, *Radical Shelley* (Princeton, NJ: Princeton University Press, 1982), p. 287; and Kenneth Neill Cameron, *Shelley: The Golden Years* (Cambridge, MA: Harvard University Press, 1974), p. 381.
8. See Charles E. Robinson, "The Shelleys to Leigh Hunt: A New Letter of 5 April 1821," and "Shelley to the Editor of the *Morning Chronicle*: A Second New Letter of 5 April 1821," *Keats-Shelley Memorial Bulletin* 31 (1980): 52–56, and 32 (1981): 55–58. The translation is the "Cry of War to the Greeks" (Bodleian MS Shelley adds. c. 5).

founders of Western civilization, further underscores the parallel with
the would-be reformers of late Regency England (and perhaps specifically with victims of political violence, like the victims of Peterloo,
whose historic rights and freedom as English citizens have been violated by a repressive Tory "occupation"). But as in *The Cenci* and the
never-completed *Charles the First*, Shelley elevates history to mythic
status, as may be seen in part in his choice for title of *Hellas* rather
than the modern *Greece*.[9] In each case Shelley's intention is to reveal
the importance to the overall welfare of his English audiences of studying the parallels between their present situation—and the options
available to them—and particular events of past and contemporary
history.

*Hellas* shares with many of Shelley's later works the multistability
inherent in productions that simultaneously address different messages to their audiences. On one hand, it counsels moderation: a sort of
wait-and-see attitude for which the poem offers one precedent and the
preface several others. On the other, it may be seen to advocate active
intervention by the people, as in the case of the revolutionary Greeks,
to speed up the process by which oppression is cast off. Both messages
are viable instructions to members of the same sophisticated audience,
which differs only in its preference for one alternative or the other as
the best means of achieving reform. Properly speaking, if both these
factions were to set things in motion, even simultaneously, the two
groups might recognize their natural affinity and join together in service to the cause of reform that presumably motivated both: this is the
point Shelley makes at the end of his letter on Carlile's trial.

One cannot be much surprised that Ollier deleted a paragraph beginning with the phrase "should the English people ever become free"
and referring to "the privileged gangs of murderers and swindlers,
called Sovereigns." Given their already troubled relations, it is in many
ways surprising that Ollier published Shelley's poem at all. Did Ollier,
whose connection with *Blackwood's Edinburgh Magazine* had already
begun, and whose profession may have lent him a better perspective
on the book trade than Hunt had as a periodical journalist, perceive
that Shelley's reputation was rising and that the association that had
to date been unprofitable might yet prove quite the reverse? Shelley's
relative ignorance of his own reputation in England appears to have
been as profound as his ignorance of English political and social affairs. Cautious friends like Hunt kept him in silence or, perhaps worse,
misinformed, while others like Peacock sought to persuade him to
redirect his efforts into channels more in keeping with their own opinions. It is tempting to consider what might have happened had Shelley's ties been with publishers like Carlile or, earlier, Eaton—or even
John Murray—and had he earlier on acquired Horace Smith and John
Gisborne as agents to represent his interests in England.

I have stressed this point because *Hellas* marks the end of Shelley's

9. See Earl R. Wasserman, *Shelley: A Critical Reading* (Baltimore, MD: Johns Hopkins University Press, 1971), p. 374.

overt public attempts on behalf of immediate and practical reform. Rather than merely lapsing into bitter (or suicidal) silence because of the apparent unpopularity of his public writings, however, in his final years Shelley devoted himself more consciously to writing primarily for an audience of posterity, for virtual readers of the future who might yet prove to be ideal readers. Embarking upon so ambitious a poem as *The Triumph of Life*, once he was away from Byron, suggests anything but the terminal despondency some have attributed to him.

In looking at Shelley's final years, we should also consider, briefly, his unfinished drama, *Charles the First*. He had originally encouraged his wife to take up the subject in a tragedy, according to Mary Shelley's note to the poems of 1822 (*Works*, 676). In September 1818 he twice prodded her to "remember *Charles the 1st*" (*Letters*, II, 39), but she never took up the assignment. Shelley wrote Medwin in 1820 that he had taken up the gauntlet and would write the play himself, "in the spirit of human nature, without prejudice or passion" (*Letters*, II, 219–20; 20 July 1820). He seems to have worked at it sporadically, expressing his doubts about the project to Ollier twice in 1820 and in greater detail in 1821: "*Charles the First* is conceived, but not born. Unless I am sure of making something good, the play will not be written. Pride, that ruined Satan, will kill *Charles the First*, for his midwife would be only *less than him whom thunder has made greater*" (*Letters*, II, 354; 25 September 1821).[1] Even though he told Ollier that "the Historical Tragedy of 'Charles the First' will be ready by the Spring" (*Letters*, II, 372; 11 January 1822) and offered to sell him the work's copyright, he told Peacock at about the same time that "a devil of a nut it is to crack" (*Letters*, II, 573; ?11 January 1822).

The nut never did get cracked, though Shelley had good reason to persist in his efforts. Horace Smith had informed him in April 1821 of Brooks and Co.'s failure to pay the spring quarter of his annuity and freezing of his account pending a suit brought by Dr. Thomas Hume, guardian of Shelley's children by his first wife. Though Smith proved invaluable to Shelley in resolving the crisis, Shelley was painfully reminded of the pressing need for additional income. The play was, he thought, a potential moneymaker worth pursuing, but on 19 February 1822 Gisborne wrote that the Olliers "decline paying any price whatever for 'Charles Ist'." Even though Gisborne sensibly tried to persuade Shelley to allow him to seek out other potential publishers for this and his future works, Shelley seems to have lost interest in the drama.

Shelley wrote Hunt in the spring of 1822 that work on *Charles the First* had come to a virtual standstill. His explanation is interesting: "What motives have I to write.—I *had* motives—and I thank the god of my own heart they were totally different from those of the other apes of humanity who make mouths in the glass of time—but what are *those* motives now? The only inspiration of an ordinary kind I could

---

1. The italics are Shelley's, an allusion to Satan's reference to God the Father, *Paradise Lost*, I, 257–58.

descend to acknowledge would be the earning of £100 for *you*—& that it seems I cannot" (*Letters*, II, 394; 2 March 1822). Shelley's remarks make greater sense when we recall his comment less than four months previously to Claire Clairmont about the *"unprofitable"* nature of writing in solitude and without sympathy (*Letters*, II, 368), that is, without a buyer in sight. But Shelley's original motives seem to have been other than merely economic. Trelawny reports that Shelley's intentions for *Charles the First* were like those for *The Cenci*: "I am now writing a play *for the stage. It is affectation to say we write a play for any other purpose.* The subject is from English history; in style and manner I shall approach as near our great dramatist as my feeble powers will permit. 'King Lear' is my model, for that is nearly perfect."[2] Perhaps Shelley recalled that in refusing *The Cenci* Covent Garden had invited him to submit another play and felt that the opportunity to influence affairs at home through the vehicle of the theater might not yet have slipped away.

But the fragments of Shelley's play suggest that it would have met with little enthusiasm at Covent Garden or Drury Lane, for even in its uncharacteristically austere form it contained a rather too overt attack on the English power structure. Like *The Cenci*, it aimed to educate by reminding the audience of the nearness with which the present appeared mistakenly to be repeating the errors of the past. Presumably the play would have developed the antirevenge line his other works consistently take, perhaps treating the insulted and degraded aristocrats, and the people generally, much as *The Cenci* had treated Beatrice Cenci. But Shelley found himself in an impossible position. Beatrice had been beautiful and virtuous: a theatre audience would warm to her immediately. But how could he make *Charles's* aristocrats—Leighton, Bastwick, Bishop Williams of Lincoln, even branded and tortured as they are—attractive, when for most of his adult life he had portrayed aristocracy's unattractive nature? Although the several scenes in which Charles I figures are relatively well developed, those with the oppressed aristocrats and the rebels-to-be are fragmentary and undeveloped. Mary Shelley's speculation that Shelley abandoned the project because "he could not bend his mind away from the broodings and wanderings of thought, divested from human interest, which he best loved" (*Works*, 676) surely underestimates the practical side of Shelley's character that hoped yet to discover not only an avenue to real public influence but also one that would produce some measurable financial security. The seventeen years following Shelley's death, taken together with her stated preference for Shelley's less esoteric works, influenced Mary Shelley's misremembering (or her misrepresentation) of the practical exigencies of the Italian years, as did her understandable desire to create for a new generation a more distinctly ethereal Shelley than history reveals.

---

2. Trelawny, *Records*, I, 117; my italics.

## NEIL FRAISTAT

## Shelley Left and Right: The Rhetorics of the Early Textual Editions[†]

Unquestionably, of the 170 years that have passed since Shelley's death, the two most crucial years for establishing his texts, textualizing his life, and securing his reputation were 1824 and 1839, the years of Mary Shelley's truly monumental editions. But any account of these authoritative editions becomes complicated by the fact that they had their dark cultural doubles, their evil twins, so to speak, in the unauthorized, "illegitimate," pirated editions of Shelley that proliferated between 1821 and 1840. Here I pursue specific ways in which the authorized and illegitimate Shelleys so reproduced might be said to be in cultural dialogue with each other.

As a start, let us think of the textual edition as a type of prosopopoeia, a giving of face and figure that is always—whatever else it may be—inevitably a defacement and disfiguration, a culturally specific form of what Paul de Man has helped us to see as "monumentalized" discourse.[1] The materiality of that discourse might then be conceived in terms of Jerome McGann's distinction between a book's bibliographical codes—which include such material details as the page format, paper, typefaces, price, advertising mechanisms, and distribution venues—and its linguistic codes, which include not only all of the linguistic text of the poems as such but also what Gérard Genette has termed the set of surrounding "paratexts": "prefaces, dedications, . . . advertisements, footnotes, and the like."[2] Shelley's textual body, so to speak, could then be located within the "laced network" (13) of linguistic and bibliographical codes that ultimately comprise each edition's own monumentalized discourse. That discourse might itself be thought of as a rhetoric of Shelley, a cultural performance locating the textual space of the edition within the particularized social space of its production and reception. For the purposes of this chapter, I examine both Mary Shelley's 1824 edition of *Posthumous Poems* and William Benbow's piracy of that volume in 1826 as such cultural performances, considering the rhetoric of Shelley each produces as both a product of and a participant in a larger set of social discourses.

Mary Shelley's editorial efforts must be understood as cultural performances in the broadest sense of the term. The etherialized, dis-

† From *Shelley: Poet and Legislator of the World*, ed. Betty T. Bennett and Stuart Curran (Baltimore, MD: Johns Hopkins University Press, 1996), pp. 105–13. This chapter is an earlier version of the author's "Illegitimate Shelley: Radical Piracy and the Textual Edition as Cultural Performance," *Publications of the Modern Language Association of America* 110 (May 1994): 409–23. Reprinted by permission of the copyright owner, The Modern Language Association of America.

1. See especially "Shelley Disfigured," in Paul de Man, *The Rhetoric of Romanticism* (New York: Columbia Univ. Press, 1984), 93–123.
2. See McGann, *The Textual Condition* (Princeton, N.J.: Princeton Univ. Press, 1991), 12–13, which includes a discussion of Genette.

embodied, and virtually depoliticized poet to emerge from her textual editions was the corporate product of an entire cultural apparatus: sponsored by a nascent set of middle-class Victorian ideological positions, propagated by the publishing and reviewing institutions, undergirded as well as undercut by copyright law, mediated by the workings of the marketplace, and challenged by competing appropriations of Shelley.

Taking its impetus from a tendency in Shelley's own self-representations, both in his poetry and in his life, to slight the body for the mind or the spirit, the etherializing and disembodying of Shelley was, in fact, a project fostered by most of the Shelley circle, and also, importantly, by John Stuart Mill, F. D. Maurice, and the Cambridge Apostles—in particular Hallam and Tennyson. It took the form of various sorts of reductive readings of Shelley and his poetry: the reduction to sensation, the reduction to the lyric moment, the reduction to spirituality, the reduction to beauty. The master trope of these reductions was "purity" and its product was "pure poetry." Shelley thus became at once a signifier of "pure poetry" and a means by which pure poetry could be argued for as a cultural standard of England's national literature.

Mary Shelley's first entrance into the marketplace as an editor came in 1824, with the publication of *Posthumous Poems of Percy Bysshe Shelley*, a volume designed, as she explained to Leigh Hunt, as "a specimen of how . . . [Shelley] could write without shocking any one" (*MWSL* I:397).[3] Her desire for a shockproof Shelley was especially conditioned by two moments in the early 1820s that played major roles in further polarizing the already polarized rhetoric through which Shelley was received: the reviews prompted by the pirating of *Queen Mab* in 1821, not to mention the trial of William Clark for pirating it; and the controversy in the obituary notices in 1822 over the significance of Shelley's life and work. In both instances, the vehement attacks from the political right worked, sometimes literally, to demonize Shelley, as the following quotation from the *Literary Gazette*'s review of *Queen Mab* (May 19, 1821) illustrates well: "We declare against receiving our social impulses from a destroyer of every social virtue; our moral creed, from an incestuous wretch; or our religion, from an atheist, who denied God, and reviled the purest institutes of human philosophy and divine ordination, did such a demon exist."[4] Out to show that the "demon" existed only as an ideological illusion of right-wing

---

3. *The Letters if Mary Wollstonecraft Shelley*, ed. Betty T. Bennett (Baltimore, MD: The Johns Hopkins University Press, 1980–88), cited as *MWSL*. I have commented in much greater detail on Mary Shelley's construction of Shelley through her editions in " 'I Hate to Mutilate': Mary Shelley and the Transmission of Shelley's Textual Corpus," a lecture delivered at the CUNY Graduate Center in November 1990. This subject is also well developed, as I have recently discovered, in an essay by Susan Wolfson, "Editorial Privilege: Mary Shelley and Percy Shelley's Audiences," in *The Other Mary Shelley*, ed. Audrey Fisch, Anne K. Mellor, and Esther Schor (New York: Oxford Univ. Press, 1993): 39–72. Wolfson's essay also considers how Mary Shelley's editions of Shelley's works function to construct Mary Shelley herself.

4. *Literary Gazette and Journal of Belles Lettres* 226 (May 19, 1821): 305.

critics, Mary Shelley followed the rhetorical tracks of Shelley's defenders on the left who were quick to fix a halo in place. Paratext and
text work hand in hand in *Posthumous Poems* to produce a powerful
rhetoric of Shelley, the master tropes of which are "unearthliness" and
"elevation"—that is to say, purity inscribed by upper-class status, the
rhetoric of high culture.

These tropes are most explicitly developed in the paratext of the
volume, with its opening epigraph from Petrarch, which crossdresses
a description of Laura to become one of Shelley that, as translated by
Robert Durling, reads "In noble blood a humble and quiet life, / with
a high intellect a / pure heart, the fruit of age in the flower of youth,
and with / thoughtful aspect a happy soul."[5] The preface reenacts the
rhetoric of the epigraph in its brief biographical sketch of Shelley's
"unearthly and elevated" nature.[6] Rather than scanting the fact that
Shelley was a devoted political reformer, the preface uses this fact to
explain Shelley's notoriety: "like other illustrious reformers, [he] was
pursued by hatred and calumny" (iv). This same strategy had already
been employed in Horace Smith's obituary for Shelley in the *Paris
Monthly Review* for August 1822, which, after anointing Shelley as the
new Lycidas, comments, "yet never was there a name associated with
more black, poisonous, and bitter calumny than his," a fact it explains
by stating that Shelley "had the misfortune to entertain, from his very
earliest youth, opinions, both in religion and politics, diametrically opposed to established systems."[7] But whereas Smith concedes that he
does not intend to "exculpate Mr. Shelley from the charge of sometimes adopting crude and rash opinions" (32), there is little rash and
nothing crude about the Shelley of *Posthumous Poems*. After dealing
with Shelley's politics in only the most general frame of reference, the
preface uses a class-coded language of sensibility to stress his refinement, describing in the process his ill health, his elegant scholarship,
and his extraordinary emotional responsiveness both to nature and to
others.

Perhaps the most crucial decision Mary Shelley made about the
volume was to defer trying to publish Shelley's complete works, which
would have prompted all of the by-now-familiar complaints and resistances, in favor of an edition of primarily posthumous works selected
to show how Shelley could "write without shocking any one." As finally
published, *Posthumous Poems* contained thirteen poems that had already gone out of print, five translations, and sixty-five formerly

5. Robert Durling, *Petrarch's Lyric Poems: The "Rime Sparse" and Other Lyrics* (Cambridge,
  Mass.: Harvard Univ. Press, 1976), 370. For a second epigraph from Petrarch that Mary
  Shelley ultimately decided not to print in *Posthumous Poems*, see Emily W. Sunstein, *Mary
  Shelley: Romance and Reality* (Boston: Little, Brown, 1989), 235. For Mary Shelley's continued use of untranslated epigraphs from Petrarch in her 1839 edition, see Wolfson, "Editorial Privilege."
6. *Posthumous Poems of Percy Bysshe Shelley*, ed. Mary Wollstonecraft Shelley (London: John
  and Henry L. Hunt, 1824), vii. All quotations of *Posthumous Poems* are from this edition.
7. The obituary appears in the *Paris Monthly Review* 2, no. 7 (August 1822): 392–96. I quote
  from Stuart Curran, "Horace Smith's Obituary Panegyric on Shelley," *Keats-Shelley Journal*
  37 (1988): 31.

unpublished poems. Approximately one-quarter of the unpublished poems consisted of fragments, most of which were no longer than one or two stanzas, and several no more than two lines. Unlike Shelley's most ideologically contestatory poems—all of which were suppressed from the volume—these brief, nonnarrative fragments were politically safe, irreducibly poetic, and calculated to foreground Shelley as a writer of lyrics in whose work, as the preface explains, "more than [in] any other poet of the present day, every line and word . . . is instinct with peculiar beauty" (viii). Mary Shelley's judgment in printing these fragments and such poems as "Stanzas, Written in Dejection, near Naples," "Song, on a Faded Violet," "When passion's trance," and "To Night" was rewarded by the enthusiasm of readers and reviewers, the latter quoting these lyrics at length.[8]

C. H. Reynell printed *Posthumous Poems* handsomely in octavo format on fine paper with wide margins for John Hunt and Henry L. Hunt, who published the book at the not inexpensive price of fifteen shillings. In its material production, its price, and its selection of poems, the book's bibliographical codes made clear what was already implicit in its linguistic codes: that it was designed for consumption by the middling and upper classes—certainly not the working class and artisan readers who were eagerly consuming inexpensive pirated editions of *Queen Mab*. Indeed, the volume succeeded in making Shelley accessible and acceptable to more of its targeted readers than he had ever reached in his lifetime. Within two months of its publication, over three hundred copies had been sold. Once put into social circulation by *Posthumous Poems*, the lyrics of the volume took on a cultural life of their own, so to speak, and were reproduced in articles, anthologies, musical settings, and critical discussions; quotations from the lyrics appeared as epigraphs to chapters in novels and to short fiction.[9] In this way, Mary Shelley successfully monumentalized Shelley as, in the words of her preface, "a bright vision, whose radiant track, left behind in the memory, is worth all the realities that society can afford" (iv). The pure poet of the lyric moment took textual form.

This text-based rhetoric of Shelley might have quickly become more complicated if Mary Shelley had been able to pursue her original plan, which was to follow the publication of *Posthumous Poems* immediately, first with an edition of Shelley's prose and then with a complete edition of the poetry, in which "any thing too shocking" for *Posthumous Poems* could finally be included. There were, however, to be no further authorized editions of Shelley's poetry for fifteen years, and Mary Shelley was even forced to recall all of the unsold volumes of *Posthumous Poems* itself some two months after publication, because—as is well known—Sir Timothy Shelley, upon whom she depended for financial

---

8. For the reception and reproduction of Shelley's lyrics, see, for instance, Karsten Klejs Engelberg, *The Making of the Shelley Myth: An Annotated Bibliography of Criticism of Percy Bysshe Shelley 1822–1860* (London: Mansell, 1988), 78–82. Two other essential sources are Sylva Norman, *Flight of the Skylark: The Development of Shelley's Reputation* (Norman: Univ. of Oklahoma Press, 1954), and "Shelley's Posthumous Reputation," the penultimate chapter of Newman Ivey White, *Shelley* (1940; rpt. New York: Octagon, 1972), 2:389–418.
9. Engelberg, *Making of the Shelley Myth*, 78.

support, forced her to promise not to bring Shelley's name before the public again during Sir Timothy's lifetime.[1]

Consequently, the rhetoric of Shelley fostered by the production and reception of *Posthumous Poems* took firm root in the developing middle-class culture. But this impression was not uncontested, both because of the culture's prior reception of Shelley and because, given the workings of copyright law and the marketplace, a number of literary pirates rushed in where authorized textual reproductions of Shelley could tread no more. Between 1822 and 1841 there were at least twenty-six pirated editions of Shelley's poetry, nine among which were of *Queen Mab* alone.[2] These piracies were primarily the work of radical pressmen, some of whom—including Richard Carlile—defiantly produced inexpensive pamphlets on birth control for sale to the lower classes, while others—including William Benbow and John Ascham—published obscene and pornographic literature.[3] "Pure poetry" found strange bedfellows here.

One might even say that, somewhat like Prometheus meeting the phantasm of Jupiter, Mary Shelley's 1824 *Posthumous Poems of Percy Bysshe Shelley* met its textualized other, also called up from the underworld, when in 1826 William Benbow pirated virtually the entire volume for his own edition, *Miscellaneous and Posthumous Poems of Percy Bysshe Shelley*. With the exception of the translations, Benbow printed all of the texts in *Posthumous Poems* as they had been arranged by Mary Shelley, simply adding at the opening and close of his edition eight more texts: the four poems of the *Rosalind and Helen* volume; "A Vision of the Sea," "The Sensitive Plant," and "To a Sky-Lark" from the *Prometheus Unbound* volume; and "Lines, Written on Hearing the Death of Napoleon," the lyric accompanying *Hellas*.

Benbow's paratext retains Mary Shelley's footnotes and the untranslated epigraphs to poems such as *Alastor* but, significantly, omits her epigraph from Petrarch and her biographical sketch of Shelley. There is, in fact, no prefatory material at all to contextualize Shelley's texts for the reader; that part of the volume's performance is consigned to its bibliographical codes. In place of the large octavo format of *Posthumous Poems*, with its fine print and wide margins, Benbow's edition is a much smaller duodecimo, with inexpensive wove paper and narrow margins, whose print is in the generic fonts characteristic of inexpensive books and pamphlets published in London at the time. Priced at five shillings, sixpence, Benbow's volume cost nearly two-thirds less than *Posthumous Poems*. Moreover, in place of the authorizing name of Mary Shelley, the title page of *Miscellaneous and Posthumous Poems* carried only the name of William Benbow, printer and bookseller, who,

---

1. For a recent discussion of Mary Shelley's plans for publishing Shelley's works, see Neil Fraistat, ed., *The "Prometheus Unbound Notebooks," The Bodleian Shelley Manuscripts*, vol. 9 (New York: Garland, 1991), xxxiv–xxxv.
2. These numbers are given in White, *Shelley*, 2:398, 397.
3. William St Clair contends that one reason *Queen Mab* "caused such deep hatred was that it was published by the author of this book [i.e., *Every Woman's Book; or What is Love*, Richard Carlile's pamphlet on contraception] and sold in his shop." See *The Godwins and the Shelleys: A Biography of a Family* (New York: W. W. Norton, 1989), 479.

along with William Hone and Carlile, was one of the three most notorious radical pirates of the day. Thus the material form of the edition
itself, as well as its venue of distribution, announce the book's appropriation of Shelley into a network of production and distribution that
provided its own distinct cultural context from which to read the poet.[4]

The cultural space for radical literary piracy was, in effect, created
by Lord Eldon's landmark decision in *Southey v. Sherwood* that Robert
Southey could not stop the embarrassing piracy of *Wat Tyler* because
"a person cannot recover in damages for a work which is, in its nature,
calculated to do injury to the public."[5] In other words, the status as
property of a literary work depended upon its propriety as determined
by the courts, not on what might seem to be a natural relation between
the author as producer and the fruits of his or her work.[6] Politically
or religiously subversive work thus could not be claimed as legal property, a principle intended to punish authors and publishers who over-
stepped the line, as when it was first deployed by Lord Chief Justice
Eyre in 1791 against Joseph Priestley, who wanted to sue for damages
done to his manuscripts by a Church and King mob. But as Eldon
himself recognized in *Murray v. Benbow*, this principle "opens a door
for . . . wide dissemination" of works "calculated to produce mischievous effects."[7]

And mischief there was. A brief return to the reviewer for the *Literary Gazette*, whom we last left foaming at the mouth over *Queen
Mab*, will illustrate the point. For this reviewer, Shelley's demonic tendencies were all the more threatening because they were embodied in
"a book of so blasphemous a nature, as to have no claim to the protection of copy-right; it may be published by Scoundrels at all prices,
to destroy the moral feeling of every class of the community" (305).
Shelley's work, in short, was both morally and legally out of control.
Too subversive to qualify as property over which Shelley could claim
ownership, it could be reproduced by "Scoundrels" inexpensively
enough to circulate freely throughout the social system, becoming, in

4. The most extensive studies of the literary pirates' modes of production as well as their cultural
   contexts are Iain McCalman's *Radical Underworld: Prophets, Revolutionaries and Pornogra-
   phers in London, 1795–1840* (Cambridge: Cambridge Univ. Press, 1988), and Hugh J. Luke's
   dissertation, "Drams for the Vulgar': A Study of Some Radical Publishers and Publications
   in Early Nineteenth-Century London" (Univ. of Texas, 1963). More specifically for the pirating of Shelley, see Charles H. Taylor, Jr., *The Early Collected Editions of Shelley's Poems*
   (New Haven, Conn.: Yale Univ. Press, 1958); and appendix 3, "Shelley and the Pirates" in
   St Clair, *The Godwins and the Shelleys*, 512–18.
5. I cite the account of the case in J. H. Merivale, *Reports of Cases Argued and Determined in
   the High Court of Chancery from the Commencement of Michaelmas Term, 1815 to the End
   of the Sittings after Michaelmas Term, 1817* (London: Joseph Butterworth and Son, 1818),
   2:439.
6. This point is well made by Peter Manning, "The Hone-ing of Byron's *Corsair*," in *Textual
   Criticism and Literary Interpretation*, ed. Jerome McGann (Chicago: Univ. of Chicago Press,
   1985), 124.
7. In *Walcot* [sic for Wolcot, i.e., "Peter Pindar"] v. *Walker* (1802), Eldon first cites the precedent set by Eyre, which he repeats in *Southey v. Sherwood*. For Eldon's opinion in *Walcot
   v. Walker*, see Francis Vesey, *Reports of Cases Argued and Determined in the High Court of
   Chancery during the Time of Lord Chancellor Eldon. Containing from Easter Term to the
   Sittings after Trinity Term Inclusive*, 42, Geo. III (London: Brooke and Clarke, 1804), 7:1–
   2. For Eldon's opinion in *Murray v. Benbow*, see *Quarterly Review* 27, no. 54 (April 1822):
   130.

the words of our reviewer, "dangerous to the ignorant and weak, hateful to the lovers of social felicity, and an enemy to all that is valuable in life, or hopeful in eternity" (306).

Benbow, an ultraradical who styled himself a publisher for the "ignorant and weak," seized on pirating as a form of proto-class warfare: "The enormous high price of books has long prevented the humble in place and purse from acquiring information, and we are not sorry to see the 'gates of knowledge' opened so that all ranks may enter therein for a mere trifle," he wrote in the *Rambler's Magazine* for March 1822.[8] Originally a shoemaker from the Manchester area, Benbow began his career as a literary pirate in 1821, with the financial backing of the by-now-notorious ultraradical George Cannon (a.k.a. "Erasmus Perkins")—a career beginning with a surreptitious piracy of *Queen Mab* in 1821, the so-called "New York edition," and ending in 1827 with a piracy of *The Cenci*.[9]

During this time, most, though not all, of Benbow's publications implicitly attacked the ideological underpinnings of church and state. Many were overtly political, like the several pro-Caroline pamphlets he authored and his compilation *Crimes of the Clergy* (1823); some were pornographic, like *The Confessions of Julia Johnstone* (1826), or the soft-core *Rambler's Magazine* he edited and published, which featured, along with literary and dramatic gossip and criticism, erotic verse and pictures. In response to attacks in *Blackwood's* and the *Quarterly* that his literary piracies were doing injury "to the lower orders of society," he proudly claimed in the *Rambler's Magazine* for September 1822 that his piracies "all tend to unmask those systems of corruption and hypocrisy which the *Quarterly* and *Blackwood* so devoutly adore."[1] Benbow, in short, was attacking "Old Corruption" with a vengeance.

In 1826, the year Benbow pirated *Posthumous Poems* and planned on being the first publisher ever to produce a complete poetical works of Shelley, Robert Southey described Benbow's second shop, "The Byron's Head," as "one of those preparatory schools for the brothel and gallows; where obscenity, sedition, and blasphemy are retailed in drams for the vulgar."[2] Thus connected to the radical underground and retailed among obscenity, sedition, and blasphemy in inexpensive editions for working-class and artisan readers, Shelley's poetry in general—but especially *Queen Mab*—gained or regained its most transgressive implications. As reproduced by low publishers primarily for "vulgar" readers, then, the unauthorized or illegitimate Shelley took textual form as an earthbound body with a vengeance, circulating through the culture as a signifier of certain kinds of culturally pro-

8. *Rambler's Magazine; or, Fashionable Emporium of Polite Literature . . . and All the Gay Variety of Supreme Bon Ton* 1, no. 3 (March 1822): 119.
9. For general background on Benbow's career, see *The Biographical Dictionary of Modern British Radicals*, ed. Joseph O. Baylen and Norbert Grossman (Sussex, U. K.: Harvester Press, 1979), 1:35–36, and especially Luke, "Drams for the Vulgar," 25–77.
1. *Rambler's Magazine* 1, no. 9 (September 1822): 396.
2. Quoted from *The Works of Lord Byron*, ed. Rowland E. Prothero (London: John Murray, 1901), 6:399.

hibited knowledge and behavior. The "purity" of Shelley's poetry, if not of poetry itself, was thereby reinterrogated by the radical counter-rhetoric of the early pirated textual editions.

Although the repressed in Shelley and his works might thereby be seen as staging a return, the extent to which Shelley's works—and, in particular, the shockproof Shelley of *Posthumous Poems*—could also resist the rhetoric of radicalism itself should not be underestimated, as the fate in the marketplace of Benbow's attempt to appropriate that collection in *Miscellaneous and Posthumous Poems* suggests. Writing in the *Metropolitan Quarterly Magazine* for September 1826, in an essay on Shelley upon which I have not seen previous critical comment, Derwent Coleridge states, "A surreptitious edition of Shelley's works has lately been attempted in cheap numbers, but the sale has not been sufficient to induce the publisher, (Mr. Benbow) to proceed with it."[3] Coleridge attributes the failure of Benbow's edition to the fact that Shelley's works "have no charm for the ignorant or half-informed [as] is proved by their narrow sale, notwithstanding all the arts of low and venal publishers. They are indeed addressed to the highest order of readers, to whom the nature both of the thoughts and the diction confines them, much more effectually than a learned or even a technical language" (195).

Whether or not Coleridge accurately accounts for the financial failure of Benbow's edition, his claim that the linguistic codes of *Posthumous Poems* successfully resisted appropriation by the bibliographical codes of the piracy invites us to reimagine the differences in the rhetoric of Shelley produced by the early textual editions as functions of a cultural semiotic in which "high" and "low" are terms as crucial as "left" or "right." Considered from the bottom up, in light of Gareth Stedman Jones's argument that for radicalism "the dividing line between classes was not that between employer and employed, but that between the represented and the unrepresented," the piracy of Shelley, an aristocrat writing against aristocracy, can be seen as one means for radicals to gain a purchase on the system of representation itself, a way in which low culture could attempt to appropriate high culture so as to come to know itself better as a public—and, ultimately, as a class.[4]

Jon Klancher has observed that "Radical discourse was not as much 'expressed' by a nascent working class as it formed the latter's ideological and interpretive map. Yet, like an atlas in which one map overlaps another . . . the boundaries between middle-class and working-class discourses were not immobile lines but strategic, shifting latitudes of

3. Derwent Coleridge, "An Essay on the Poetic Character of Percy Bysshe Shelley, And on the Probable Tendency of his Writings," *Metropolitan Quarterly Magazine* 2, no. 3 (September 1826): 197.
4. Gareth Stedman Jones, *Languages of Class: Studies in English Working Class History, 1832–1982* (Cambridge: Cambridge Univ. Press, 1983), 106–07. Jones is specifically referring here to *political* representation. I am following Jon Klancher in extending the implications of Jones's comment to encompass a broader notion of representation within the semiotics of the culture itself. See Klancher, *The Making of English Reading Audiences, 1790–1832* (Madison: Univ. of Wisconsin Press, 1987), 102.

force" (103). Few others of his day would have been more aware of these shifting boundaries or the need for radical discourse to provide the working-class with such an interpretive map than William Benbow, himself a shoemaker become an artisan intellectual, a man socially dislocated from his own class who nonetheless still attempted to identify himself with it. Dislocated in many ways from *his* own class during his lifetime, Shelley became as monumentalized text a figure of tremendous mobility, simultaneously underwriting and undercutting both the rhetoric of "purity" and the rhetoric of "radicalism." As reproduced in both high and low cultural registers in the mid-1820s, he becomes a telling sign for what Klancher calls "the very separation of publics and the deeper division of class it designates" (102). This separation in reading publics and classes, this "wound of a fracture"[5] in the social semiotics of late Georgian England, is almost uncannily reflected in the self-contending rhetorics of, and the cultural performance enacted by, William Benbow's piracy of *Posthumous Poems*.

5. De Man, *Rhetoric of Romanticism*, 120.

# Studies of Individual Works

## MICHAEL FERBER

### Alastor[†]

We may disagree with Mary Shelley's judgement that *Queen Mab* belongs with her husband's juvenile poems, but most of his readers sense that Shelley becomes Shelley—he arrives at the modes, themes, and style distinctive of his 'mature' poetry—with the poems he wrote in 1815 and early 1816 and published as *Alastor . . . and Other Poems*. This impression may owe something to the surprising contrast between the mood of the sermonizing poem of social reform of 1813 and the mood of the self-absorbed and sometimes despairing poems of two and three years later. In her note on the title poem, Mary Shelley explains that 'A very few years, with their attendant events, had checked the ardour of Shelley's hopes, though he still thought them well grounded', events not political, such as the final defeat of Napoleon and the restoration of the Bourbons in France, but personal, such as poverty, loss of friends, and the expectation that he would soon die of consumption. She considers the poem 'an outpouring of his own emotions', and if that commonplace Romantic phrase can apply to a long narrative poem then it certainly seems to fit *Alastor; or, The Spirit of Solitude.*

Recent criticism, however, has tried to demonstrate that *Alastor* is not an outpouring at all but a carefully staged dialogue of sorts between the main character and the narrator, neither of which stands for Shelley, who could not decide the issue between them. We shall look more closely at this reading, but we should note first that, whatever personal grief Shelley may have felt at the time of writing *Alastor*, within a year he was writing *Laon and Cythna*, an ambitious epic of social revolution, and within another year he was starting his optimistic masterpiece, *Prometheus Unbound*. He was to alternate between anguished personal quests and hopeful public prophecies throughout his life. We have already seen, too, that *Queen Mab* is enclosed in a meditation on death, while *Laon and Cythna*, though full of revolutionary action, is obsessed with martyrdom, so it is not always easy to separate the social poetry from the personal, nor to attribute some poems to emotional outpourings and others to calculated craft.

The first difficulty with *Alastor* is the title. A careful reader of Homer

---

[†] From *Critical Studies: The Poetry of Shelley*, by Michael Ferber (New York: Penguin Books, 1993), pp. 23–33. Reprinted by permission of the author.

might recognize it as the name of at least three characters in the *Iliad*, but only a reader who knew Greek tragedy in the original Greek could guess at its sense as (1) a wanderer, outcast, one who is pursued by an avenging spirit, a suppliant, or (2) the avenging spirit itself. Shelley's friend Thomas Love Peacock claimed that he suggested the title to Shelley, and that an *alastor* is an evil genius, not the name of the hero. Peacock was to use the word in this sense himself in his poem *Rhododaphne* in 1818. But if we take Peacock as authoritative we not only needlessly eliminate the first sense of *alastor* (found in Aeschylus and Sophocles) but we import the tragic Greek sense of nemesis into the spirit whom the wandering poet-protagonist encounters, a spirit who is not vengeful in any moral sense and whom the poet conjures up in his own dream in the first place. The poet, moreover, pursues the spirit, not the other way round, and she is better described as a spirit of love than of solitude. On the other hand, the Preface states that 'The Poet's self-centred seclusion was avenged by the furies of an irresistible passion pursuing him to speedy ruin.' That seems to warrant Peacock's view, but many readers feel that the Preface is not consistent with the poem and should have no more weight than Peacock's comment. In any case, it is perfectly justifiable to take the title as referring to the wandering poet, either as his name or as a Greek near-synonym for 'spirit of solitude'. 'Spirit of solitude', in turn, is a good epithet for the poet, for he seems to be a spirit to those he meets, 'the Spirit of wind / With lightning eyes' (259–60), and at the end he is called a 'surpassing Spirit' (714) by the narrator himself.

Except for the opening (1–49) and closing (672–720), and one or two brief interventions, the narrator devotes the poem to the story of the life of a Poet (whom I shall capitalize henceforth, as Shelley does). "There was a Poet,' he begins, and we never learn his name, nationality, date, or any other worldly circumstances except the route of his extraordinary journey. They are left so obviously vague that the Poet seems to be a spirit or a symbol from the first. Indeed the most important fact about him seems to be that he died young and unknown. 'There was a Poet whose untimely tomb / No human hands with pious reverence reared, / . . . —no mourning maiden decked / With weeping flowers, or votive cypress wreath, / The lone couch of his everlasting sleep' (49–57). We are immediately in the elegiac mode, in the spirit of Gray's 'Elegy Written in a Country Churchyard' and Wordsworth's 'Lines (Left upon a Seat in a Yew-tree)', both of which Shelley knew well.

The Poet's life is sketched very briefly until he sets out on his wandering quest 'To seek strange truths in undiscovered lands' (77). First he pursues 'Nature's most secret steps' (81) in volcanic caves and lonesome vales; then he visits the ruins of ancient civilizations and gazes on the mysterious hieroglyphs 'till meaning on his vacant mind / Flashed like strong inspiration, and he saw / The thrilling secrets of the birth of time' (126–8). That seems to define his quest more precisely, for he makes his way across Arabia and Persia to the vale of Kashmir which, his hieroglyphs may have told him, was the birthplace of the human race. While he had been studying these signs, however, an Arab maiden had been tending him. She was 'Enamoured, yet not daring for deep awe / To speak her love' (132–3), while for his part he seems not to have noticed her at all. When he arrives in Kashmir, in 'Its loneliest dell, where odorous plants entwine / Beneath the hollow rocks a natural bower' (146–7), he has 'a dream of hopes' (150) in which a 'veiled maid / Sate near him' (151–2) and spoke, or sang, in a voice 'like the voice of his own soul' (153). Like him she is a poet, and sings of knowledge, truth, virtue, and 'lofty hopes of divine liberty' (159), the themes of *Queen Mab* and many of Shelley's later poems. These themes lead her to sing in 'wild numbers' (163) (verses); overcome by emotion, she stops, rises, and spreads her bare arms to embrace the Poet. He rises to meet her, and she 'With frantic gesture and short breathless cry / Folded his frame in her dissolving arms' (186–7). It ends as suddenly as it began: 'Now blackness veiled his dizzy eyes, and night / Involved and swallowed up the vision; sleep, / Like a dark flood suspended in its course, / Rolled back its impulse on his vacant brain' (188–91), and he drowns, as it were, in sleep. He suddenly awakens to the cold light of morning and the 'vacant woods' (195) and 'His wan eyes / Gaze on the empty scene as vacantly / As ocean's moon looks on the moon in heaven' (200–2).

We notice that twice the Poet's mind or brain has been 'vacant' as he has gone into a visionary trance: first he learns the secrets of the hieroglyphs and then he discovers love, or an ideal beloved. They are both revelations or unveilings—indeed the maid is veiled at first, he then sees 'Her glowing limbs beneath the sinuous veil' (176), and finally she embraces him with bare arms, only to leave him veiled in blackness himself—and we seem invited to see more similarities between them. Hieroglyphs, not yet fully understood in Shelley's day, were sometimes taken to be poetry, the primordial poetry of the human race; the maiden is a poet, and one scholar has recently called her a visionary hieroglyph herself. She is, after all, only the representation of a maiden, not a real one, as hieroglyphs are representations of things, not the things themselves. Shelley was probably aware, too, of the tradition (found in Philo and others) that interpreting a sacred text is analogous to unveiling and marrying a maiden. We may wonder if the two revelations are not linked causally, for the hieroglyphs, as we noted, seem to have sent him to Kashmir, where another tradition placed the birth of the human race, if not of time itself. Perhaps there is a curse contained in the ancient writings. If his mind was vacant before the revelations, the world now seems vacant after them, and the Poet reflects that emptiness as if he has become for the moment no more than a mirror of his surroundings, a moon on the ocean reflecting the moon in the sky, itself shining with only a reflected light.

Most readers, however, have been struck with the connection between the veiled dream-maiden and the Arab maid whom the Poet neglected while pondering the hieroglyphs, and the next passage makes it explicit: 'The spirit of sweet human love has sent / A vision to the sleep of him who spurned / Her choicest gifts' (203–5). Is this spirit of love a fury or an *alastor* in Peacock's sense? Is the Poet punished for spurning love, the way Hippolytus in Euripides' play is punished for neglecting Aphrodite? The narrator may not be fair to the Poet here, for if we reread lines 129–39 we see the Poet has not so much 'spurned' the Arab maid as simply failed to notice her. We shall discuss the narrator's own biases later. It is hard to resist, meanwhile, the sense that the dream-maiden is a 'return of the repressed', as Freudians say, a version of the Arab maid herself.

In his desolation, the Poet wonders if the vision is forever lost in the 'pathless desart of dim sleep' (210) or if it may be found in sleep's paradise, through the gates of death, sleep's twin. It does not occur to him to seek her anywhere but in sleep, as if he knows that it is already too late for him to find an earthly counterpart of his ideal. The only question is whether he should seek death as a way to find her. Like the flood that rolled over his brain at the end of his dream, 'This doubt with sudden tide flowed on his heart, / The insatiate hope which it awakened, stung / His brain even like despair' (220–22). This hopeless hope, so different from the social or political hopes the maiden sang, sends him fleeing to yet remoter parts of central Asia, while death seems to have his way with him: his whitened hair sings dirges in the wind, his hand hangs like a dead bone in its withered skin—only his eyes show the fire of life. Not surprisingly, in a poem about visions, eyes are an insistent motif throughout it. As if to remind him of the Arab maiden he ignored, youthful maidens press his hand and weep as he departs from their homes.

On the 'lone Chorasmian shore' (272), probably the Caspian Sea but perhaps the Aral Sea, the Poet is struck by the contrast between a swan, now flying to its home, and his own homelessness. The words he addresses to the swan are the closest thing to a poem we actually get from this Poet, and it is a very 'poetic' utterance, for swans are ancient symbols of poets, they are said to sing when they die, and—according to Horace—they are birds of exile. All the more poignant, then, is the Poet's assumption that this swan is on his way home. At this, another 'desperate hope' leads him to contemplate suicide, though he is still doubtful if death will bring him to the realm of sleep which holds his vision. He decides to meet lone death on the sea, as if to make literal the metaphors of flooding and overwhelming we have seen, and he sets out in a little boat. In Shelley's poetry from this point on voyages in boats become as frequent as flights in chariots, and typically the voyages, like this one, are passive, the boats simply given to the winds or currents to take them where they will. This boat is blown by a whirlwind and tossed by fierce waves, but it is 'Safely fled— / As if that frail and wasted human form, / Had been an elemental god' (349–51).

At midnight on the other side of the sea the cliffs of the Caucasus appear in the moonlight, the European Caucasus if this is the Caspian, the Indian Caucasus or Hindu Kush (at a great distance) if this is the Aral. Shelley was to set *Prometheus Unbound* in the Indian Caucasus, perhaps to allude to the putative birthplace of the 'caucasian' race while shifting it eastward so as to include the oriental races, and perhaps he has the same purpose here. If so, the setting has the same significance as Kashmir earlier.

The boat is drawn into a cavern, which the Poet hails as the gate of death and the approach to his 'Vision and Love' (366), and in a mysterious movement it is taken along a river, apparently upstream (or perhaps on a tidal bore) into a whirlpool that rises in a rocky funnel until the highest ridge of water, bearing the boat, overflows the bank and deposits it safely on to a smooth spot, where a gentle breeze carries it on to a placid stream and then, presumably downstream, into a quiet cove. If, as the Poet later says to the rivulet, it is an image of his life (and rivers have been commonplace figures for human life since ancient times), then this strange voyage through the cave and upward to a stream is a journey backward through time to one's birth. We are for the third time in a setting of birth or origin.

The cove has banks 'whose yellow flowers / For ever gaze on their own drooping eyes, / Reflected in the crystal calm' (406–8). The Poet feels akin to these narcissi, and suppresses an impulse to deck his hair with them. This moment gives us a hint, if we needed one, that *Alastor* is in large part a reworking of the story of Narcissus and Echo as Ovid told it. Narcissus is a beautiful youth whom girls and boys both love, but he feels no interest in any of them. Echo, a maid who only spoke when spoken to, and whom Juno punished by limiting her speech to the last few words of another's, falls in love with Narcissus, but when she tries to embrace him he flees her touch; she wastes away and dies. Nemesis sends him to a hidden pool in the forest, and when he bends to drink he is smitten with his own image, whose eyes meet his. After many frustrating attempts to kiss his beloved, he plunges into the pool and drowns. The differences between the plots are obvious enough, but Ovid's story pervades Shelley's thoroughly enough to serve as a continuous allusion—from the 'flood' imagery and the Poet's impulse to drown himself to the Arab maid who cannot speak her love—and perhaps a framework for judging the Poet's tragic flaw.

The cove is a kind of Bower of Bliss (Spenser) or Garden of Eden, described in maternal and infantile terms. It is in a vale that the forest 'embosoms' (423). Overhead are 'meeting boughs and implicated leaves' (426). The oak 'Embraces' (433) the beech, and flowery vines or ivy

> flow around
> The grey trunks, and, as gamesome infants' eyes,
> With gentle meanings, and most innocent wiles,
> Fold their beams round the hearts of those that love,
> These twine their tendrils with the wedded boughs
> Uniting their close union [.]              (440–45)

With this last simile Shelley teeters on the brink of the unbearably namby-pamby (and we may wonder how one folds a beam), but he gives us an extraordinarily vivid embodiment of nature's 'cradle'. It reminds us too of the 'cold fireside and alienated home' he left as a youth, or the 'cold home' (138) of the Arab maid: here is the regressive fantasy of what he was denied in his childhood. But nature's cradle is the Poet's 'sepulchre' (430), for he knows this is no more his home than the swan's nest had been.

Just beyond the dell is a deep well that reflects the foliage overhead and an occasional 'inconstant star' (463). The Poet looks down into it, like Narcissus, gazing into his own eyes as if it were a dream of a gloomy grave. This is the third trance the Poet falls into, and we are not surprised that 'A Spirit seemed / To stand beside him' (479–80), perhaps the one he has been pursuing all along. This time, however, she is not robed in bright light but seems identical with the woods, well, and rivulent, as if she is the *genius loci*, the spirit of that place. As he looks up, 'two eyes, / Two starry eyes, hung in the gloom of thought' (489–90)—as if he is still looking at his own two eyes in his own thought—And seemed with their serene and azure smiles / To beckon him' (491–2). And off he goes again.

This time he follows the rivulet downstream. As he himself proclaims, the rivulet is an image of the mystery of his life, with its darkness and brightness, unknown source and unknown course. As we can see, too, the rivulet rehearses the course of any human life, 'like childhood laughing' (499) as it begins, then flowing through 'changed' scenery, where rocks 'stemmed / The struggling brook' (527–8) and dry windlestraw grows and ancient pines 'clenched with grasping roots / The unwilling soil' (531–2). If we missed the symbolism the narrator makes it explicit in a simile:

> For, as fast years flow away,
> The smooth brow gathers, and the hair grows thin
> And white, and where irradiate dewy eyes
> Had shone, gleam stony orbs:—so from his steps
> Bright flowers departed, and the beautiful shade
> Of the green groves, with all their odorous winds
> And musical motions.                    (533–9)

We know that he was already old and withered by the time he came to the lone Chorasmian shore, and that he was not rejuvenated when he came to nature's cradle, so it is a little odd that his ageing and dying, however vicariously, should be repeated here. This and the other repetitions we have noted suggest that *Alastor* is only outwardly a narrative; it is really a set of variations on a theme. It is as if Shelley found the situation of the self-secluded and death-drawn poet so interesting in itself that he constructed a thin and artificial plot by stringing together analogous scenes.

In any case, the Poet and his river arrive at the precipice of a vast ravine. The river 'Fell into that immeasurable void / Scattering its waters to the passing winds' (569–70) but the Poet pauses, in keeping with the symbolic single rock-rooted pine that 'stretched athwart the vacancy / Its swinging boughs, to each inconstant blast / Yielding one only response' (562–4), like a wind harp, and like the Poet stretched across the vacancies of his world. And here another bower appears, the third in the poem and the fourth 'birthplace': 'a tranquil spot, that seemed to smile / Even in the lap of horror' (577–8). Ivy wraps 'entwining arms' (579) around the stones, embowering the space with leaves. There are 'children' at play here, too, this time not the ivy but bright coloured leaves, 'children of the autumnal whirlwind' (583). Flowers grow out of the blue cavern mould. Though this 'green recess' (625) is surrounded by the realm of death, it seems to signify what the Poet has always hoped, that on the far side of death's gateway there may be a paradise. The Poet does not, in any case, plunge over the cliff, but placing his hand on the old pine trunk he lays his head on an ivy-covered stone and yields to the 'final impulses' (638) of life, or death. His last sight is of the setting crescent moon. As the two tips of the horn linger at the western horizon they must look to him, as they remind us, of the eyes of the lost dream-maiden. As they sink into the dark he dies.

This long narration is enclosed, and occasionally interrupted, by more meditative and personal passages that help us characterize the Narrator. To some of his poems it may do no harm to call the narrator or *persona*, 'Shelley', but the distinction between narrator and author, possible to draw in any literary work, is often crucial in Shelley's poetry. Recent criticism of *Alastor*, as we noted at the outset, has made much of the differences between Narrator and Poet. On the model of an inconclusive prose dialogue, Shelley's *Refutation of Deism* (1814), *Alastor* can be seen as a confrontation of world views as one poet tries to understand another. The Narrator begins by invoking the 'brotherhood' (1) of the elements and cites his own 'natural piety' (3) towards 'our great Mother' (2), his love of the sequence of hours and seasons, and his kinship with bird and beast, as evidence of his fitness to tell the story of the Poet. He then invokes the 'Mother of this unfathomable world' (18) and tells how he has 'loved / Thee ever, and thee only' (19–20), pursuing her mysteries day and night, and though failing to penetrate her 'inmost sanctuary' (38) he is ready for her inspiring breath 'as a long-forgotten lyre' (42) receives the wind. These and other details of the opening section seem to define the Narrator as a nature-poet, bound by the natural world and more or less content to be so bound, much like the author of *Queen Mab*. The Poet, on the other hand, has rightly or wrongly gone beyond nature, seeking union with a transcendent spirit or ideal self, denying natural human ties, and hovering on the brink of the supernatural world. The mutual love between the Narrator and nature is embodied in the bowers the Poet visits, but these, as we saw, do not satisfy the Poet or restore him to health.

But lest we think the Narrator's natural limits must serve as the frame of reference for judging the Poet, we find, besides the sympathy and admiration shown for the Poet during his wanderings, the Narrator's expression of irretrievable loss in the final section. There the Narrator wishes he had the power of a witch or alchemist, agents of the supernatural, to prolong the life of the lost Poet. He becomes his sole mourner: 'ah! thou hast fled! / The brave, the gentle, and the

beautiful, / The child of grace and genius' (688–90). But art and eloquence and even sobs and groans are vain 'when some surpassing
Spirit, / Whose light adorned the world around it, leaves / Those who
remain behind' (714–16). All that is left to us is 'pale despair and cold
tranquillity, / Nature's vast frame, the web of human things' (718–
19)—inadequate to our needs as they were inadequate to the Poet's
—and 'Birth and the grave, that are not as they were' (720). Any judgement that we might have passed on the Poet, to the effect that he
'went too far' or failed to outgrow his adolescent narcissism, is brought
up short by all this praise and grief. The naturally pious Narrator ends
by railing against nature's limits.

So a good case can be made (there are many more details one could
bring in) that *Alastor* presents two contrary standpoints, a natural and
a supernatural, or an immanent and a transcendent, or a worldly and
an otherworldly, and shows the limitations and uncertainties of each.
If, as the Preface says, 'The picture is not barren of instruction to
actual men', what the poem instructs us in is scepticism, an enlightened doubt as to which standpoint, if either, is true or right. The
Preface, in fact, complicates this case, for it seems to side with the
Narrator, and even goes beyond his view in using the language of
vengeance, as we saw, implicit in Peacock's notion of an *alastor*: 'The
Poet's self-centred seclusion was avenged by the furies of an irresistible
passion pursuing him to speedy ruin.' A chief advocate of the sceptical-
dialogue case even attributes the Preface to the Narrator, not to Shelley; that is, Shelley wrote it while adopting the mask of the Narrator,
consciously or unconsciously, and we are not to take its opinions as
gospel.

Against this case one may point out that it is a tricky business to
separate the interpretations and judgements the Narrator may offer,
implicitly in the poem or explicitly in the Preface, from the description
of the Poet's life and death. To do so we must take the Narrator's word
for the facts but bracket out his personal comments on the facts as
inadequate. Are we to doubt the Narrator's assertion, for instance, that
'The spirit of sweet human love has sent / A vision to the sleep of him
who spurned / Her choicest gifts' (203–5), because we saw nothing
we could quite call spurning and because we dislike the idea that any
'spirit' other than the Poet's own imagining can exist? What really
makes this passage less reliable than others, or in special need of correction? It is a little like the bottomless problem of the quest for the
historical Jesus by means of the four Gospel texts alone; it is worse,
because there is only one testimony concerning the Poet. Moreover
we tend to ignore the contradiction at the heart of the poem: that
much of the Poet's life, everything the Poet is quoted as saying, and
above all his death had no witnesses! We might imagine the Narrator
following the Poet's path and interviewing maidens, cottagers, and
mountaineers, but the bulk of his story is either a supernatural revelation, unlikely for this naturalistic poet, or a fabrication.

The Narrator and the Poet have more in common, too, than the
dialogue theory allows. The Narrator is also a poet, and we might note

that he alone seems actually to have written anything. (Those critics who claim the Narrator's imagination is limited also neglect the evidence of his highly imaginative narration.) Like the Poet, the Narrator was fascinated with death. 'I have made my bed / In charnels and on coffins,' he tells us in the opening, 'where black death / Keeps record of the trophies won from thee' (23–5), hoping to force 'some lone ghost, / Thy messenger, to render up the tale / Of what we are' (27–9). He imagines himself trafficking in the supernatural in the closing passage as well, searching for an elixir of life, and he seems to believe in the story of the Wandering Jew (677–81). The Poet pursues the same interests as the Narrator, and seems to have gone one step farther; though the Mother has not yet unveiled her mysteries to the Narrator, the Poet does have a revelation into the 'secrets of the birth of time' (128) and, very equivocally, a vision of ideal love. Yet the Narrator also claims that 'Enough [of the mysteries] from incommunicable dream, / And twilight phantasms, and deep noonday thought, / Has shone within me' (39–41) that he feels ready to tell the story. This inner light is not a product of nature, it is not the usual inspiration of a nature poet.

It is also interesting that both Narrator and Poet, like their creator, are vegetarians. As a sign of his devotion to 'our great Mother' the Narrator claims 'no bright bird, insect, or gentle beast / I consciously have injured, but still loved / And cherished these my kindred' (13–15), while the Poet would linger in lonesome vales 'Until the doves and squirrels would partake / From his innocuous hand his bloodless food' (100–1).

There is an analogy that might be enlisted by both those who see the poets as fundamentally different and those who see them as much alike. The relationship between the Narrator and the Poet is similar to that between the Poet and his dream-maiden. The Poet is an ideal projection of the Narrator, and, while not explicitly erotic, the Narrator's feelings for the Poet are intense. As the loss of the maiden leads the desperate Poet to a passive suicide, the loss of the Poet leaves the Narrator in 'pale despair' (718), perhaps only a step from suicide himself. The difference, of course, is that the Poet dies, and the Narrator lives to write a poem about him. As the Poet dies, the Narrator likens him (among other things) to 'A fragile lute, on whose harmonious strings / The breath of heaven did wander' (667–8); that image echoes the one that begins the narrative: 'the charmed eddies of autumnal winds / Built o'er his mouldering bones a pyramid / Of mouldering leaves in the waste wilderness' (53–4). They both hearken to the conclusion of the opening, where the Narrator likens himself to "a long-forgotten lyre' (42) awaiting the breath of the 'Great Parent' (45). That breath evidently comes, for the remarkable story gets told.

It has also been argued that Shelley did not, in the end, make it clear if we are to take *Alastor* as a sceptical dialogue or an anguished monologue, so we must be meant to take it as a second-order dialogue between these alternatives. In other words we are to be sceptical about scepticism! Occam's razor and common sense dictate that this idea is

a non-starter, as well as a non-stopper, for it breeds an infinite re-
gression. It seems wiser to allow that Shelley might not have sorted
everything out properly than to elevate the seeming inconsistencies
into a deliberate programme. Critics are always in search of a formula
that would sublate, or simultaneously cancel and preserve at a higher
level (as in Hegel's dialectic) all the contradictions of a text. *Alastor* in
particular has attracted more commentary per line than any other
poem of Shelley's, more than it deserves, no doubt, for few of the many
commentators would rate it a great poem. But because it is the first
long poem of Shelley's maturity it is important to try to understand it.

## FOREST PYLE

## "Frail Spells": Shelley and the Ironies of Exile[†]

### 1. Spirit in Exile

The "frail spells" of my title appear in the third stanza of Shelley's
"Hymn to Intellectual Beauty" (1816) where they follow the series of
questions addressed to the "Spirit of BEAUTY." The celebrated questions that constitute the hymn's second stanza are elaborations of the
first question posed to the spirit: "where art thou gone?" (l. 15). "Why,"
asks the speaker, "dost thou pass away and leave our state, / This dim
vast vale of tears, vacant and desolate?" (ll. 16–17). "Intellectual
Beauty," that which unlike church or state most deserves our "vows"
of worship and celebration, has "pass[ed] away" without explanation;
and the poem announces the withdrawal of the spirit of beauty in the
form of hymn to its absence or, more precisely, to the "path of its
departure." The spirit of this beauty is nothing if not divine, for it
is a spirit that "consecrates" with its own "hues" all "it dost shine
upon / Of human thought or form" (ll. 13–15). Why, asks the poem's
speaker, has this divine spirit of beauty been exiled from us, an exile
which, whether self-imposed or enforced by wordly powers, leaves our
state, our worldly actuality, a place of desolation.

Far from proposing an answer to this question—which would, after
all, require the poem to speak in the name of the spirit—the subsequent stanza serves instead to nullify the entire history of proposed
answers, to demystify the claims of all those "sage[s] or poet[s]" who
may fancy that they have heard a response:

> No voice from some sublimer world hath ever
> To sage or poet these reponses given—
> Therefore the name of God and ghosts and Heaven,
> Remain the records of their vain endeavour,
> Frail spells—whose uttered charm might not avail to sever,

† From *Irony and Clerisy*, ed. Deborah Elise White, in the online *Romantic Circles Praxis
Series*, Aug. 1999. Reprinted by permission of the author. Page references have been changed
to correspond to this Norton Critical Edition.

From all we hear and all we see,
Doubt, chance, and mutability. (ll. 25–31)

Placing God and Heaven in the company of ghosts, the lines appear to be a straightforward declaration of Shelley's radical philosophical skepticism. The passage spells out his critique of the "uttered charms" of the various religious and philosophical ideologies that, try as they might to seduce us into belief, cannot "avail to sever" the irreducible condition of "doubt, chance, and mutability" from the sensual world. But the critique is not so straightforward as it first appears, for Shelley qualifies his refusal of the power of these "frail spells": their "uttered charm *might not* avail to sever" "doubt, chance, and mutability" from our worldly perception. If this qualification does not diminish the force of the poem's repudiations, it does nonetheless demonstrate the *necessity* of countering the "uttered charm" of onto-theology with the act of a demystification: a spell can be rendered "frail" only when the "charm" of its utterance is revealed.

Shelley's demystification of the "frail spells" of poetry, theology, and philosophy can be extended to his political critique of the nation-state and the nationalisms that institute and preserve it. From Shelley's effort to vacate all false groundings comes a poetics of the idea that conducts a politics of love and liberty beyond the "frail spells" of national character or identity. In the idiom of Shelley's critical neoplatonism, there can be no idea of the nation: the idea is always in exile and the nation always the scene of the actuality of power. Thus, the idea is in a perpetually ironic relation to the nation and to the clerisies that would institute it. Which is why, according to Shelley, the poet must in an entirely positive sense remain an "unacknowledged legislator of the World." If "all authors of revolutions are poets," as Shelley declares in the *Defence*, it is because as "hierophants of an unapprehended inspiration," they liberate us from what in *The Triumph of Life* he calls "thought's empire over thought." The moment poetic legislation is *acknowledged* is the moment that poets begin laying down the law, the moment they cease their service to the idea and enlist themselves in the actualities of institution. It is, in other words, the moment they claim to pass from the "awful shadow of some unseen Power" to the light of the aesthetic state.

Shelley's critique of the desire for the state places the poet's famous lament in the hymn—"why dost thou pass away and leave our state, / This dim vast vale of tears, vacant and desolate?" (ll. 16–17)—in a curiously ironic light: statelessness, it seems, is an originary condition; and beauty only "lends" "for some uncertain moments" (l. 37) its "glorious train" (l. 41). Beauty's perpetual disappearance leaves a "vacancy" in "our state"; but it is also by virtue of that very vacancy that the "voices" which sage and poet alike call truth—the "voices" of God and ghost and Heaven—can be recognized as echoes of their own "uttered charms." Shelley would voice his commitment to the power of "vacancy" in his 1819 prose fragment "On Life" where it is quite explicitly the "duty" of critical philosophy not to "establish" or institute truth but "it destroys error, and the roots of error" [507]. The destruction of error, an interminable critique, necessarily results in the "leaving" of a vacancy: "It leaves, what is too often the duty of the reformer in political and ethical questions to leave, a vacancy" [507]. This is, moreover, not merely the "duty of the reformer in political and ethical questions," but the role of the poetic imagination as Shelley conceives it in a poem as late as *Epipsychidion*: it is an illuminating negation, a "reverberated lightning" that "As from a thousand prisms and mirrors, fills / The Universe with glorious beams and kills / Error" (ll. 166–69).

To sing a hymn to intellectual beauty is to invoke the incantatory "charm" of the hymn form and defiantly sing in praise of vacancy, the vacancy left by this aesthetic spirit's exile from our state. To sing a hymn to intellectual beauty is thus to be both perverse and reverent and to join one's voice to a non-nationalist chorus which, like the silent voice of the mountain in "Mont Blanc," has the capacity to "repeal large codes of fraud and woe" such as those "sealed" in English statutes. To sing this godless but still sacred hymn is to give worship to the absent spirit of beauty and every form and thought it consecrates. If the proper worship of the spirit of beauty demands an initial demystification of the "frail spells" of god and ghosts and heaven, this worship nonetheless makes good on its vows only through the conjuring, the "calling" of phantoms: in the sixth stanza, the poet, asking the silent spirit to confirm that he has indeed "kept his vows," declares that "even now / I call the phantoms of a thousand hours / Each from his voiceless grave . . ." (ll. 63–65).

Ghosts, gods, spirits, phantoms: if each of these figures by turns haunts or inspires Shelley's poem, its success as a "*hymn* to intellectual beauty" depends upon a rigorous distinction between them. It is not, in other words, a matter of opposing anything like actual reality or the living present to the spectral properties of the ghost; it is, rather, a question of distinguishing the differences between God and Spirit, between ghosts and phantoms. While the phantom, for instance, may suggest the spectral qualities of the ghost, the phantom for Shelley is not mere ideological delusion but the shadowing forth of something ideal, such as the appearance of the Spirit of "Intellectual Beauty" addressed by the poem. But since one cannot see this Spirit, the distinctions the poem insists upon between spirit and ghost or phantom and god depend on measuring and evaluating their various effects, which might be characterized as the difference between the theological and the aesthetic. It amounts to measuring the differences between the "frail spells" of "God and ghosts and Heaven" on the one hand and the "hues and harmonies of evening" or the "memory of music fled" (ll. 8,10) on the other. But such distinctions are not so easily maintained, as the poem's early praise to the "grace" and "mystery" of the spirit beauty demonstrates. It may well appear that the poem has challenged the "frail spells" of theology only to succumb to the theologizing charms of the aesthetic. Thus, the speaker declares to the spirit of beauty that its "light alone" "gives grace and truth to life's unquiet dream" (ll. 32,35).

And yet, as many readers have stressed, intellectual beauty is not to be confused with sensuous beauty; and thus the hymn is addressed not to the aesthetic as such—not to the sensory manifestation of the spirit—but to the spirit of beauty itself. This means that the aesthetic exists only in the realm of likeness and that its figural model is that of the simile. But if the "visitations" of the "awful shadow of some unseen Power" leave us with a string of similes, they are similes that, as Carol Jacobs has rightly noted, do not operate in the service of similarity: "The first stanza of the 'Hymn to Intellectual Beauty' . . . is an attempt to define that elusive poetic force through a long series of similes whose terms of comparison seem peculiarly at odds with one another."[1] Our "state" is thus one of failed likenesses, a potentially interminable series of figures which, in Jacobs's words, "mark the refusal of language to define by affirming an identity" (171). No linguistic system based upon a principle of identity could "define" a spirit which not only remains unseen but whose own "seeing" is nothing more than an "inconstant glance" (l. 6).

If such a "spirit fair" does not preside over the idea or form of any national community, it does nonetheless exert deep binding powers of its own. In the poem's last lines, where this hymn becomes supplication, the poet-suppliant beseeches the spirit of beauty to lend him its power as "one who worships thee, / And every form containing thee, / Whom, SPIRIT fair, thy spells did bind / To fear himself, and love all human kind" (ll. 81–84). No one is likely to confuse this with the International, but it is a hymn which, after sounding the emptiness of the "frail spells" of "God and ghosts and heaven," turns its praise to an exiled spirit whose genuinely binding spells are those solely of universal love. If a hymn is not merely a song of praise or adoration but also a form of spell, then one of the intended effects of this hymn to intellectual beauty is to extend its sacred powers to its singers and readers: it is intended to place those who utter it under the spell of love. This is its effect on the poem's own speaker who feels the "shadow" of Beauty's spirit fall upon him as a kind of counter-charm, an antidote to the "poisonous names with which our youth is fed" (l. 53). The result is something like a conversion experience in which the eruption of an ecstatic "shriek"—"I shrieked, and clasped my hands in extasy" (l. 60)—prompts the declaration of poetic vows. Thus, the comings and goings of the spirit of beauty, a power both unseen and unheard as such, are according to Shelley figured through its phantoms and known only through its effects, like the blind falling of a shadow. And yet it is by its very inconstancy that the spirit of beauty generates the binding force of love, that which the poem's last line identifies as the "love of all human kind." The hymn declares the "hope" that it is within the scope of Beauty's "unseen Power" to "free / This world from its dark slavery" (ll. 69–70). If this sounds more than a little like the "spectropoetics" that Derrida unearths in his reading of Marx, perhaps this likeness accounts more than a little for Marx's

---

1. Carol Jacobs, "On Looking at Shelley's Medusa," *Yale French Studies* 69 (1985): 171.

famously sympathetic assessment of the poet. And perhaps it is because Marx and Shelley, both illegitimate heirs of the Platonic tradition, recognize in this cluster of specters—ghosts, gods, spirits, phantoms—the elements of a theory of ideology.

To evaluate the nature of this idealist but genuinely political critique of the actuality of the nation-state, one needs only to situate it alongside *On the Constitution of Church and State* (1829). For Coleridge, of course, there is an idea of the nation; and what he calls the "ever-originating idea" of nation is understood to precede and inform the "Idea of a Constitution"[2] and the institutions of the nation-state. The origins of this "ever-originating idea" are not, moreover, empirical in nature: Coleridge regards the origin of the nation as a "pure fiction" (14), but one which is the very condition of its effectivity. For the idea of the nation to secure the state and overcome the class divisions that threaten to undo the sense of a national community, the national fiction must be entrusted to what he calls a "permanent class of order," a "national clerisy." It is thus this national clerisy—a secular poetic intelligentsia—that would effect and adminster what Coleridge would openly acknowledge as the "spell" of that "ideal object" called the nation.

When Shelley's poems address the state of the nation, as in those works provoked by the Peterloo massacre, the nation finds its truest expression as the vehicle of oppression: England is itself the "veil" or "mask of anarchy." "England in 1819," a sonnet which Shelley sent to Leigh Hunt with no illusions that it would be published, identifies the institutions of the English state as a set of graves:

> An old, mad, blind, despised, and dying King;
> Princes, the dregs of their dull race, who flow
> Through public scorn,—mud from a muddy spring;
> Rulers who neither see nor feel nor know,
> But leechlike to their fainting country cling
> Till they drop, blind in blood, without a blow.
> A people starved and stabbed in th'untilled field;
> An army, whom liberticide and prey
> Makes as a two-edged sword to all who wield;
> Golden and sanguine laws which tempt and slay;
> Religion Christless, Godless—a book sealed;
> A senate, Time's worst statute, unrepealed—
> Are graves from which a glorious Phantom may
> Burst, to illumine our tempestuous day.

The dating in the title (which, it seems, was Mary's addition) is significant not because things might be better in 1820 or, say, 1832 but because the phrase "England in 1819" demonstrates that the nation is bound to this date: the nation itself is now "Time's worst statute," imprisoned to actuality. Indeed, the very form of the sonnet seems to be oppressed by the actualities of the nation it describes: this

2. Samuel Taylor Coleridge, *On the Constitution of Church and State*, ed. John Colmer (Princeton: Princeton UP, 1976), 12.

strange sonnet is a static catalogue of phrases and clauses, an enumeration of the ills that characterize the English state in 1819: "An
old, mad, blind, despised, and dying King"; "Princes, the dregs of their
dull race"; "Rulers who neither see nor feel nor know"; "A people
starved and stabbed"; "Religion Christless, Godless"; "A senate, Time's
worst statute, unrepealed." The litany extends for twelve lines without
hint of turn or, in Shelley's words, "repeal." It is not until the closing
couplet that this poem finds its verb, its agreement secured in the
static form of the copula: the institutions of the state "are graves."
Significantly, the poem turns after this agreement has been reached
or, as Adorno might have said, after this identity between subject and
copula has been "extorted." The poem's final prepositional phrases herald, through the explosive enjambment of the last lines, the disruptive
force of the "glorious Phantom": these institutions "Are graves from
which a glorious Phantom may / Burst, to illumine our tempestuous
day."

*   *   *

The England in 1819 that is represented to us in Shelley's "England
in 1819" thus qualifies as what Walter Benjamin, in an essay written
during his own exile, would call a "state of emergency"[3] from which
the messianic phantoms of the poem "may / Burst, to illumine our
tempestuous day." That the sonnet—its method and its effects—
should be so precisely illuminated by Benjamin's "Theses on History"
demonstrates Shelley's incompatibility with historicism: for Shelley as
for Benjamin history is not composed of events unfolding through "ho-
mogenous, empty time" (261). And like Benjamin's "historical materialist," Shelley "cannot do without the notion of a present which is
not a transition, but in which time stands still and has come to a stop
(262). *This* is "England in 1819": the poetic "sign of a Messianic cessation of happening, . . . a revolutionary chance in the fight for the
oppressed past" (263). As with Benjamin's sense of a "*weak* messianic
power (*eine* schwache *messianische Kraft*), a power to which the past
has a claim" (254), a messianism without the messiah, Shelley's phantoms would "blast" the state "out of the continuum of history," a revolutionary break with its historical conditions (262).

One might assert that Shelley's manipulation of the sonnet form,
the sudden force of the enjambment in the closing couplet, expresses
his sense of the disruptive power of revolutionary illumination; but it
would be more to the point of Shelley's own "Benjaminian" poetics
and politics to say that the poem is less an *expression* of his historico-
political understanding than that the poem itself—the poetic resources
that are conjured in and by the sonnet—*produces* this sense of historical and political possibility. Much of the power of the "Hymn to
Intellectual Beauty" derives from a similar poetic act, its performance
of the call to "the phantoms of a thousand hours / Each from his

---

3. Walter Benjamin, "Theses on the Philosophy of History," in *Illuminations*, trans. Harry Zohn
(New York: Schocken Books, 1969), 257.

voiceless grave," a call intended to invoke the spell of redeeming love
in the phantom conjuring of futurity. In the later sonnet the subjunctive agency of the phantom is conjured to "repeal" not the spell of
"God and ghosts and Heaven" but the spell of actuality. Thus, what
we might call the critical redemption value of Shelley's poetry, including the sonnet "written at the suggestion of the events of the moment,"
resides not in its reference to the present or the empirical but in its
blank opening onto futurity.

\* \* \*

# WILLIAM KEACH

## [*Mont Blanc*]†

### II

'Before the chariot had begun to climb
  The opposing steep of that mysterious dell,
Behold a wonder worthy of the rhyme

  'Of him who from the lowest depths of Hell
Through every Paradise and through all glory
    Love led serene . . .'

           (469–74)

It is no accident that Shelley should rhyme on the word 'rhyme' in an
allusion to Dante, nor was the decision to compose *The Triumph of
Life* in terza rima an arbitrary one. But his decision some six years
earlier that Mont Blanc was a wonder worthy of rhyme presents a
much more challenging formal situation. Shelley's own note says that
*Mont Blanc* 'rests its claim to approbation on an attempt to imitate
the untameable wildness and inaccessible solemnity from which [his]
feelings sprang.'[1] 'Untameable wildness' and 'inaccessible solemnity',
without and within, both suggest that blank verse might have been the
appropriate form for this subject. Wordsworth (in *The Prelude*), Coleridge (in the 'Hymn Before Sunrise, in the Vale of Chamouni')—and
John Hollander too (in a wonderful parody of Shelley's poem called
'Mount Blank')[2]—all write about *Mont Blanc* in blank verse. But Shelley's poem, while creating the impression of blank verse with its massive periods and very frequent enjambment, uses rhyme in its 'attempt
to imitate' an experience of the untameable and the inaccessible. Why?
    The facts about rhyme in *Mont Blanc* are in themselves striking,
particularly when measured against what must have been one of Shel-

---

† From "Rhyme and the Arbitrariness of Language," in *Shelley's Style*, by William Keach (New
   York: Methuen, 1984), pp. 194–200. Reprinted by permission of the publisher. Page references to this Norton Critical Edition appear in brackets after the original citations.
1. Shelley's note appears at the end of the Preface to *History of a Six Weeks' Tour through a Part
   of France, Switzerland, Germany, and Holland*, London, T. Hookham Jr, C. and J. Ollier, 1817.
2. The poem is in *Tales Told of the Fathers*, New York, Atheneum, 1975.

ley's formal models, Milton's *Lycidas*.[3] Of the 144 lines in *Mont Blanc*, only three end in words which have no rhyme elsewhere in the poem.[4] Three of the 193 lines in *Lycidas* are also unrhymed. There are only fifteen couplets in Shelley's poem, contrasted with thirty-four in Milton's (ten of these contain lines of different length), and six of the fifteen are relatively faint or imperfect. Curiously, however, two of these six imperfect couplets are repeated: 'for ever' / 'river' in lines 910 are reversed as 'River' / 'for ever' in lines 123–4; 'down' / 'throne' in lines 16–17 are repeated phonetically though not semantically in 'down' / 'over-thrown' in lines 111–12. Even more curiously, there are eleven instances in *Mont Blanc* of words rhyming with themselves (usually over long stretches of verse), and in three of these eleven instances the same word appears in rhyming position not twice but three times.

One of the remarkable features of this extensive rhyming is the degree to which it is disguised or muted by enjambment. In the text Shelley published in 1817, seventy-three of the poem's 144 lines (one more than half) have no punctuation at the end. In *Lycidas*, by contrast, thirty-three of Milton's 193 lines are without terminal punctuation. In the *Defence* Shelley says of the language of Bacon's prose that 'it is a strain which distends, and then bursts the circumference of the hearer's mind, and pours itself forth . . . into the universal element with which it has perpetual sympathy' (*SPP*, 485) [515]. The images Shelley uses about Bacon in this passage all have their parallels in the imagery of *Mont Blanc* (*burst* actually appears twice in the poem, at lines 11 and 18). There is much in the syntax and versification of *Mont Blanc* that invites us to apply these images—the recurrent Shelleyan pun on 'strain'; the activities of distending, bursting and pouring—to Shelley's own style. But noticing the rhymes in *Mont Blanc* makes us think differently about the straining swell and flow of Shelley's lines. To treat the poem as if it were written in blank verse is to close our eyes, ears and minds to one of its greatest sources of poetic power.

3. See Judith Chernaik, *The Lyrics of Shelley*, Cleveland, Case Western Reserve University Press, 1972, 288 n.4. She points out that the rhymes in the Bodleian MS. of *Mont Blanc* are more regularly interwoven than those of the 1817 printed text and suggests that 'Shelley may have been consciously striving in 1817 for the more irregular rhyme effects of *Lycidas*.' I refer here to the text of *Lycidas* in the *Complete Poems and Major Prose*, ed. Merritt Y. Hughes, New York, Odyssey, 1957. For excellent accounts of Milton's rhyming in *Lycidas*, see Ants Oras, 'Milton's early rhyme schemes and the structure of *Lycidas*', *Modern Philology*, 52, 1954–55, 12–22, and Joseph A. Wittreich Jr, 'Milton's "Destin'd urn": the art of *Lycidas*', *PMLA*, 84, 1968, 60–70. Wittreich's analysis is particularly relevant to Shelley's rhyming in *Mont Blanc*, since he argues that Milton's 'encompassing scheme' is not confined to patterns within individual verse paragraphs but 'envelops the poem and its various parts in a massive unity' (61). *Lycidas* is listed among the poems read by Shelley and Mary Shelley in 1815, the year before *Mont Blanc* was written (*Mary Shelley's Journal*, ed. Frederick L. Jones [Norman: University of Oklahoma Press, 1947], 48).
4. The unrhymed words in *Mont Blanc* are 'forms' (62), 'spread' (65) and 'sun' (133). Neville Rogers, *The Complete Poetical Works of Percy Bysshe Shelley*, Oxford, Clarendon Press, 1975, II, 355, says that Locock also counted 'sky' (108) and 'world' (113) as rhymeless. But if we look at the poem as a whole, 'sky' (108) repeats 'sky' at the end of line 60 and rhymes with 'lie' (19, 54), 'by' (45) and 'high' (52, 70); 'world' (113) repeats 'world' at the end of line 49 and rhymes with 'unfurled' (53). *Lycidas* had traditionally been analyzed paragraph by paragraph, in which case there appear to be ten unrhymed lines. But looking at the total rhyme pattern of the poem as Wittreich does yields only three; see 'Art of *Lycidas*', 63, 69–70.

There is no precedent for Shelley's crossing of extended blank-verse enjambment with irregular rhyme in a poem which raises such fundamental questions about the mind's powers and limitations. That he should rhyme with pervasive and provocative irregularity while going so far to create the feeling of blank verse is in keeping with a poem in which questions simultaneously propose and interrogate, in which the experience of blankness itself is both acknowledged and challenged. Considered from this inclusive perspective, rhyme in *Mont Blanc* is one important way in which Shelley's verbal imagination structures and shapes, without giving a closed or determinate pattern to, an experience which defies structuring and shaping. In a more specific sense, the cognitive play between or among rhyme words shows Shelley taking advantage of the way in which the very arbitrariness of linguistic signs he speaks of in the *Defence* can produce an expressive coincidence and thus a resource for a mind contending, ultimately, with its own and nature's blankness. There is no prior reason, for example, why 'waves' (2) and 'raves' (11) should rhyme. But they do, and the fact affords Shelley a distant yet powerful phonetic link that spans and condenses the relation in this opening verse paragraph between the mad rush of the 'vast river' and the 'everlasting universe of things' to which it metaphorically corresponds. As a dimension of poetic form wrought from the mysterious arbitrariness of language, Shelley's rhyme becomes both a stay against and a means of marking the chaos and blankness which are *Mont Blanc*'s special concerns.

In thinking about the purposes rhyme serves in *Mont Blanc*, we need to look at the way it functions both in terms of its own inherent possibilities and in relation to the syntax and rhythm of Shelley's periods. We must be careful not to isolate rhyme as the vehicle of the structuring, organizing intellect in easy contrast to the sweeping, impetuous emotional energy of the long, overflowing sentences: both are aspects of Shelley's 'attempt to imitate' an experience in which philosophical skepticism and impassioned intuition are held in suspension. Take the second couplet in the opening verse paragraph:

> Where waterfalls around it leap for ever,
> Where woods and winds contend, and a vast river
> Over its rocks ceaselessly bursts and raves.
>
> (9–11)

'For ever' and 'river' here seem at once to confirm the proposition with which the poem opens—'The everlasting universe of things / Flows through the mind' (1–2)—and yet to convey a certain probing openness, both because the rhyme is partial, imperfect (the imperfection stands out against the initial repetition of 'Where' / 'Where'), and because the absence of any pause after 'river' leaves that line open to flow into the next. This couplet is again left open in part iv, where its reversal shifts the emphasis from 'river' to 'for ever' ('all seems eternal now' the speaker has said in line 75, after first taking in the summit of Mont Blanc). The couplet is followed by 'raves' in line 11, by 'waves' in line 125:

> and one majestic River,
> The breath and blood of distant lands, for ever
> Rolls its loud waters to the ocean waves,
> Breathes its swift vapours to the circling air.
>                                                    (123–6)

The last word in this passage, 'air', is part of what is perhaps the most striking group of postponed or suspended rhyme-words in *Mont Blanc*. Part II ends with the word 'there', with no immediate companion or echo: 'till the breast / From which they fled recalls them, thou art there!' (47–8). That this line appears to be unrhymed is appropriate in a passage about the momentary, precarious apprehension of 'some faint image' (47) of the awesome, personified Ravine of Arve. But 'there' does eventually get its complement in the insubstantial 'air' at the end of part IV. Once this very distant rhyme has been completed, it is immediately confirmed at the end of the first line of part V: 'Mont Blanc yet gleams on high:—the power is there' (127). This is the only point in the poem where a couplet spans two verse paragraphs (although 'raves' and 'Ravine' between parts I and II, both of which contain anagrams of the name 'Arve', and 'feel' and 'streams' between parts III and IV, may seem to foreshadow such a spanning). Yet to link two separate sections together by rhyme in this way is also to pull the couplet apart: every resolution in *Mont Blanc* has at least an undertow of dissolution. The 'there' / 'air' / 'there' sequence is extended a few lines later in part V, but this time the sense of the passage cuts across even the tentativeness of those previous assertions that some presence is 'there': 'in the lone glare of day, the snows descend / Upon that Mountain; none beholds them there' (131–2). The internal rhyme in these lines ('glare' / 'there') illuminates the discrepancy between the mind's power of perception and its limitations in gaining access to reality's ultimate source. The same daylight which renders things visible in the speaker's immediate realm of experience 'glares' upon the snows of Mont Blanc—but 'there', remote and apart from any beholder, daylight itself seems to lose all connection with human intellection.

The 'there' (48) / 'there' (127) / 'there' (132) pattern is Shelley's finest exploitation in *Mont Blanc* of identical rhyme, of a word rhyming (and re-rhyming) with itself. Homonymic rhyme (punning rhyme, *rime très riche*) in which entire rhyme-words are phonetically identical but semantically different, is a related but distinct phenomenon. John Hollander assents to the prejudice against such rhyme when he argues that because of 'the crucial relation between the effect of word stress and the quality of rhyme in English . . . *rime très riche* is always in a sense, *rime pauvre*.'[5] But the two instances of it in *Mont Blanc* indicate how alert Shelley could be to the ways in which even flamboyantly fortuitous rhyme could help him mark the mind's response to the wild

---

5. *Vision and Resonance: Two Senses of Poetic Form* (New York: Oxford University Press, 1975), 118. See Derek Attridge on the different functions of rhyme in English and French verse in 'Dryden's dilemma, or, Racine refashioned: the problem of the English dramatic couplet', *Yearbook of English Studies*, 9, 1979, 62–65.

and the inaccessible. 'Throne' (17) / 'overthrown' (112) is not a pure example (it is analogous phonetically, though not semantically, to 'form' / 'deform' in *The Triumph of Life*), but given Shelley's politics it might appear to be a suggestive one. The suggestiveness is not, however, exactly predictable. Although earthly thrones, so often the embodiments for Shelley of 'Large codes of fraud and woe' (81), are implicitly included in what will be 'over-thrown' by the 'Power' in part IV as it flows down from its remote abode, that 'Power' has itself been imaged as occupying a 'secret throne'. So 'throne' stands distantly and indirectly in relation to 'overthrown' as subject, not object, a relation in keeping with Shelley's skeptical ambivalence towards the 'Power'. The fact that both 'throne' and 'overthrown' form imperfect couplets with 'down' (16, 111) further complicates the suggestiveness of this rhyme group.

The other homonymic rhyme in *Mont Blanc* affords a purer example of this phenomenon and more telling evidence of Shelley's resourcefulness in handling what would appear to be deliberately restricted verbal possibilities. At the beginning of part II, when he first names the Ravine of Arve as the immediate location of his experience, he addresses the ravine as 'Thou many-coloured, many-voiced vale' (13). Twelve lines later, when the first of these compound adjectives is expanded and particularized, the 'vale' becomes, or is seen to contain, a 'veil':[6]

> Thine earthly rainbows stretched across the sweep
> Of the ethereal waterfall, whose veil
> Robes some unsculptured image . . .
>
> (25–7)

'Poetry', Shelley says in the *Defence*, '. . . arrests the vanishing apparitions which haunt the interlunations of life, and veiling them, or in language or in form, sends them forth among mankind'. One is again tempted to follow this line of thought and figuration and apply the images in *Mont Blanc* to the poem itself, to see the 'ethereal waterfall' as a metaphor for the poem's own verbal veiling of what may be accessible only to momentary, vanishing intuition. The 'veil' in these lines, as so often in Shelley, has a double valence—it simultaneously conceals and reveals—and the movement from 'vale' to 'veil' is by no means entirely negative (compare the function of Iris and 'her many coloured scarf' in *The Triumph of Life*, 357). There is a sense in which this aspect of the 'vale' hides the 'unsculptured image' behind it; there is also a sense, partly enforced by the verb 'Robes', that the 'veil' is what makes this unspecified ('some'), uncreated image exist for the mind at all. Shelley's homonymic rhyme signals the precarious balance and interaction between skepticism and visionary imagination so important in this section and throughout the poem.

Rhyme in *Mont Blanc* is not, then, as 'wildly irregular' as it has been

---

6. Cf. David Simpson, *Irony and Authority in Romantic Poetry*, Totowa, N.J., Rowan & Littlefield, 1979, 233, n. 15.

thought to be. It is sufficiently irregular to help evoke the 'untameable wildness' Shelley spoke of: some of the most interesting rhymes in the poem are so distant and so muted by distended syntax that the reader may find them as 'remote' and 'inaccessible' as Mont Blanc itself. With the three unrhymed lines Shelley's rhyme remains open, partly unresolved. Yet rhyme is there as one of the resources with which the poet verbally counters as well as encounters an experience of threatening power and sublimity. A glance at Shelley's final question, together with the sentence that precedes it, may help to confirm our sense of why he did not ask about Mont Blanc in blank verse:

> The secret strength of things
> Which governs thought, and to the infinite dome
> Of heaven is as a law, inhabits thee!
> And what were thou, and earth, and stars, and sea,
> If to the human mind's imaginings
> Silence and solitude were vacancy?
>
> (139–44)

At the beginning of the poem, 'things' (1) became Shelley's first rhyme-word by finding its phonetic complement in 'secret springs' (4), a phrase which appears prominently and characteristically in the opening section of Hume's *Enquiry Concerning Human Understanding* as a metaphor for the unknowable first principle 'by which the human mind is actuated in its operations'.[7] Here at the end of *Mont Blanc*, 'things' finds a rhyme with a different, apparently less skeptical resonance in 'imaginings', although the difference diminishes when one takes in the immediate context of those words: the 'secret strength of things' in line 139; the if-clause and interrogative syntax surrounding 'the human mind's imaginings'. 'Thee' in line 140 forms a couplet with 'sea' and thus supports the initial 'And' through which the final question is joined logically to what precedes it. And does 'vacancy' belong in this rhyming sequence with 'thee' and 'sea'? It both does and does not: the '-cy' suffix rhymes with 'thee' and 'sea', but imperfectly, because it is rhythmically unstressed and because it is attached to the root *vacan(s)*. Shelley simultaneously draws that critical last word into and separates it from the central rhyme of the entire passage—'vacancy' seems both to yield to and to resist the rhyming power of the compositional will—and in the process he makes us conscious of the ambiguous categorizations on which rhyme depends in the first place.

The rhymes of *Mont Blanc* are part of Shelley's response to a landscape and to a philosophical tradition—'to the Arve's commotion, / A loud, lone sound no other sound can tame' (31–2), and to Hume's

---

7. Ed. L.A. Selby-Bigge, rev. P.H. Nidditch, Oxford, Clarendon Press, 1975, 14. See also 30, 33, 42, 66. 'Secret springs' receives additional emphasis by forming the poem's first couplet with 'brings' in line 5. If this phrase is a Humean allusion, it developed late in Shelley's revisions; he wrote 'secret caves' both in the Bodleian draft and in the recently discovered fair copy. See Chernaik, *The Lyrics of Shelley*, 288, and Judith Chernaik and Timothy Burnett, 'The Byron and Shelley notebooks in the Scrope Davies find', *Review of English Studies*, n.s. 29, 1978, 45–49.

argument that the 'ultimate springs and principles' of phenomenal reality 'are totally shut up from human curiosity and enquiry', that the mind's attempts to make sense of them as necessity are nothing more than arbitrary impositions:

> every effect is a distinct event from its cause. It could not, therefore, be discovered in the cause, and the first invention or conception of it, *a priori*, must be entirely arbitrary. And even after it is suggested, the conjunction of it with the cause must appear equally arbitrary.[8]
>
> (*An Enquiry Concerning Human Understanding*, IV.1)

Shelley's irregular rhymes do not tame the wildness of a 'sound no other sound can tame', nor can they break the inaccessible silence at the summit of Mont Blanc. But they impose on his and our experience of both an order of language that accepts the arbitrary and submits it to the deliberations of art. They are part of the evidence the poem offers that the arbitrary connections of thought and language need not leave the 'human mind's imaginings' in vacancy.

# KELVIN EVEREST

## Shelley's Doubles:
## An Approach to *Julian and Maddalo*[†]

My purpose is to offer some thoughts on two problems often encountered in reading and teaching Shelley's poetry. These problems share enough features to suggest some significant relation between them, and it is the possibility of such a relationship, and its implications, that I wish to explore.

One problem arises out of a simple and striking paradox of Shelley's poetry that is easy for the 'specialist' reader to gloss over. How do we reconcile the very sophisticated, and often very difficult manner of Shelley's most characteristic visionary poetry with the essentially radical character of the ideas—their 'levelling' cast, in the contemporary idiom—that inform all the major poems? Is there not the persistent and sometimes worrying impression that the social reference of Shelley's poetic style, in its use of conventions and traditions (with their concomitant assumptions about the kind of audience in mind), is curiously at odds with the social analyses and aspirations—unmistakably revolutionary, in a direct way—that are articulated? This paradox is scarcely a *weakness* in the poetry, for it is precisely in their transformation of received conventions that the great poems generate their distinctive strength. Shelley's handling of traditional forms, the Greek

---

8. Ed. Selby-Bigge, 30.
† From *Shelley Revalued: Essays from the Gregynog Conference*, ed. Kelvin Everest (Leicester: Leicester University Press, 1983), pp. 63–64, 79–88. Reprinted by permission.

mythic drama, the persona of the poet, the pastoral elegy, exerts a pressure which can shift the base of assumptions that had seemed to support such forms. Shelley's literary idiom is fundamentally subversive in this sense, and this is a quality in his poetry with which the reader must come to terms. But a properly positive alertness to the subversive function of Shelley's rhetoric need not blind us to that persistent paradoxical ambivalence to which I have drawn attention. Shelley's poetry appears to operate from within a literary culture that is the possession and medium of the ruling class that his revolutionary critique is directed towards, and while this is not a damaging criticism of the poetry, I think that it produces a considerable part of its difficulty.

That difficulty bears an immediately recognizable affinity to the other Shelleyan problem that I have in mind, and again it is a problem simple in outline, and involving a paradox. Shelley's passionate and thoroughgoing radicalism was yet the conviction of a temperament in some ways decidedly aristocratic. It was the natural product of a family background, upbringing, and education that placed Shelley, in accomplishments and social manner, as a member of the dominant class into which he was born. I do not mean to imply anything specious in Shelley's radicalism (although I will suggest that some of his contemporaries may have seen it that way); but there is evidence that points to his consciousness of this paradox, and which does imply that he felt his own class position to be a problem that he resolved in his poetry, but which remained rather more discomfiting in the actual experience of his life in English society, and as an exile in Italy. An informed and highly intelligent subversion of received literary modes is shadowed in the life by a nagging contradiction between manner and commitment, at least in the view of contemporaries who we might have expected to be sympathetic. And this misunderstanding has been reproduced by readers of the *poetry* who, taking their cue from various associations of the literary manner, continue to minimize the political and social orientation of the poetry in favour particularly of what is seen as a significantly determining 'Platonic' cast of thought.

The following discussion explores various related aspects of the two problems proposed, and suggests one way in which our awareness of these paradoxical elements may help us to read the major poetry, by a detailed examination of *Julian and Maddalo*.

\* \* \*

Shelley explained to Hunt how he had attempted, in *Julian and Maddalo*, to imitate the manner of conversation between people whom 'education and a certain refinement of sentiment have placed above the use of vulgar idioms'. Shelley's 'sermo pedestris' style, as he himself called it, was a manner adapted to the familiar idiom of the poetic audience, and as such it was preferred and encouraged by Mary Shelley. In *Julian and Maddalo*, and in *The Cenci*, it is a style appropriate to a specific poetic intention; to present 'sad reality', as opposed to 'visions which impersonate apprehensions of the beautiful and just', 'dreams of what ought to be, or may be'.[1] The style is interestingly problematic for a radical poet, for it involves the danger of acceding to the ideological implications of that familiar idiom. And there is a strong possibility that Shelley was fully alert to this problem in *Julian and Maddalo*, where the single most striking rhetorical effect of the poem is the violently contrasting idiom of the maniac's soliloquy, which is set against the gentlemanly discourse of Maddalo and Julian.

There is a passage in Donald Davie's discussion of Shelley, in his *Purity of Diction in English Verse*, that points up the problem:

> The conversation that we have attended to in the poem is just as civilized as the intercourse of Maddalo and Julian here described. It is in keeping that Julian should know little of Maddalo and not approve of all that he knows, but should be prepared to take him, with personal reservations, on his own terms. It is the habit of gentlemen; and the poet inculcates it in the reader, simply by taking it for granted in his manner of address. The poem civilizes the reader; that is its virtue and its value.[2]

This does indeed catch a certain quality of tone in the poem; but Professor Davie's own tone here is more arresting, not simply in its oblivion to Shelley's whole manner of proceeding in the poem, where we are constantly offered qualifying and contrasting contexts for each passage, but in its bewildering identification of civilizing virtues and values with 'the habit of gentlemen'. It may be suggested that this identification is something that the whole movement of *Julian and Maddalo* is directed against, in its presentation of Julian's creative, 'poetic' potential as frozen within his quiescent commitment to the manner of a repressive and repressed dominant social group. The fig-ure of the maniac may then emerge in the poem as the externalized representation of this buried poetic potential in Julian, a potential trag-ically unmediated for any audience and thus possessing the aspect of a tragic incoherence.

*Julian and Maddalo* opens in a tone of cultivated and relatively cool self-possession, which introduces into the voice of Julian, who speaks the poem, a note of wry self-distance, worldly, and not in fact very far from Maddalo's frank disillusionment. This tone is picked up from the preface, which we assume to be in some other voice, but a voice close in its estimate of Julian to Julian's own self-awareness. The preface tells us of Julian's 'passionate attachment' to certain 'philosophical no-tions', of how he is 'for ever speculating' how good may be made su-perior to evil. This is all good-humoured, of course, well-mannered; more *amusedly* tolerant than the sympathetic tolerance extended in the preface to Maddalo's lofty gloom, but still quite definitely not dis-affected. The tone is echoed at various points by Julian's own per-spective on his radical views:

1. Preface to *The Cenci*, *Works*, 274–75. Shelley's own position here is probably influenced by Hunt's views on poetic diction in his Preface to *The Story of Rimini* (1816), xv–xix (this important document has never been reprinted).
2. D. Davie, *Purity of Diction in English Verse* (1952), 144.

> I love all waste
> And solitary places; where we taste
> The pleasure of believing what we see
> Is boundless, as we wish ourselves to be.   (ll. 14–17)

The phrasing and diction here—'taste . . . pleasure . . . believing'—
suggest something agreeably luxurious in the indulgence of such a
whim. And again, in

> as we rode, we talked; and the swift thought,
> Winging itself with laughter, lingered not,
> But flew from brain to brain,—such glee was ours,
> Charged with light memories of remembered hours,
> None slow enough for sadness: till we came
> Homeward, which always makes the spirit tame.   (ll. 28–33)

Talk is fine, but the possibilities it seems to open out must always be
chastened as we recall the familiar substance of our actual lives. The
tone of the poem's opening section is really the best medium for Maddalo, who, convinced in spite of his powers of the nothingness of human life, supports social life, as the preface tells us, by being in his
manners surpassingly 'gentle, patient, and unassuming'. For all the
balanced objectivity of Shelley's presentation of the argument between
the two men, that argument is conducted in a manner in which Maddalo's position is more at home than Julian's. It is no more than we
would expect from a style adapted to 'sad realities', rather then 'dreams
of what ought to be, or may be'. Julian's radicalism is bound to appear
diminished in strength, to have too much the aspect of a theory,
'refutation-tight/As far as words go', when the words are organized on
Maddalo's gentlemanly terms. And it does seem that this effect in the
poem is intended by Shelley; for in the context of the whole poem,
the argument between Maddalo and Julian will itself be diminished in
strength, because we are exposed, in the maniac's soliloquy, to just
precisely what it lacks. What unsettles us in Julian's manner is the
absence of any critically disruptive emotional engagement with the
conflict between social aspiration and social reality. His cultivated
composure is tantamount to consent; so that the potential for change
embodied in his ideas—a poetic potential, in Shelley's large sense of
the 'poet'—is rendered inoperable. The maniac combines a passionate
restatement of Julian's radical creed, with a grim enactment of its fate
in the response of a society—an audience—that does not understand
the language of that radicalism. This is in the order of a *poetic* failure,
a failure of communication; Julian's ideals are not mediated for his
society, and this consigns those ideals to an inarticulate limbo, like
the madhouse.

*Julian and Maddalo* has grown steadily in critical esteem over the
last 15 years, and recent studies have rated it very highly indeed.[3] It

---

3. See for example Earl R. Wasserman, *Shelley: A Critical Reading* (Baltimore, MD: Johns
   Hopkins University Press, 1971), ch. 2, and G. M. Matthews, " 'Julian and Maddalo': The
   Draft and the Meaning," *Studia Neophilologica*, xxxv (1963), 57–84.

is now assumed that the poem is a coherent whole, an executed design, and not the hotch-potch of autobiographical and other fragments that it once seemed. The difficulty of the poem's structure has always lain in what we are to make of the maniac, but it is now generally agreed that whatever his function in the poem he clearly provides us with a further perspective on the contrasting views of Julian and Maddalo. Julian believes, we can agree, that man has the capacity to imagine and create for himself a better world; Maddalo thinks that experience proves life to be unconquerably inimical to human aspirations and desires. The maniac, it is argued, shows us that the questions involved are too large for resolution, and that his presence in the poem throws the debate open for the reader's participation, to be decided in his own response to the maniac. As the preface says, 'the unconnected exclamations of his agony will perhaps be found a sufficient comment for the text of every heart'.

The progress of this argument is underpinned by the changing implications of the natural setting, however; and this makes a difference. The poem opens on:

> a bare strand
> Of hillocks, heaped from ever-shifting sand,
> Matted with thistles and amphibious weeds,
> Such as from earth's embrace the salt ooze breeds . . .   (ll. 3–6)

An ambiguously neutral territory, potentially fertile but barren in the immediate prospect, like the opposed grounds of the argument. Julian's optimism is confirmed in the beautiful Italian light, and in the lingering sunset over the distant mountains, and over Venice: 'in evening's gleam,/Its temples and its palaces did seem/Like fabrics of enchantment piled to Heaven'. But Maddalo manoeuvres Julian into what he calls 'a better station', from which the madhouse is seen outlined against the fading sunset, the emblem of mortality in Maddalo's view. As the discussion takes its sombre turn, nature assumes an increasing hostility: 'The following morn was rainy, cold and dim', and, as they approach the madhouse on their visit, they sail 'Through the fast-falling rain and high-wrought sea'. This development implies the poem's tacit assent to Maddalo's pessimism, and for the maniac himself, at the nadir of hope, nature takes on an almost Hardyesque malicious indifference; human achievement perishes in its imperious and irrelevant necessities. Through the bars of the madhouse Julian sees 'like weeds on a wrecked palace growing,/Long tangled locks flung wildly forth'. The maniac himself is discovered 'sitting mournfully/Near a piano, his pale fingers twined/One with the other, and the ooze and wind/Rushed through an open casement, and did sway/His hair, and starred it with the brackish spray'. This specification of the natural context appears to imply man's subjection to the natural forces that govern him, independently and oblivious of the uniquely human consciousness that is the only part of nature not made immortal in its cycles. It is a position that Shelley arrives at, and transcends, in the first, darker half of *Adonais*. The ooze and brackish spray are tugging

at the maniac's independent consciousness, threatening to resolve it
back into meaningless elemental constituents; and this contrasts with
Julian's earlier cheerful contemplation of the embrace of earth with
the salt ooze, and his exultation at the way that 'the winds drove/The
living spray along the sunny air/Into our faces'. The negative implication of nature in the poem, up to the maniac's soliloquy, is countered
to a certain extent by the more hopeful implication of the stress on
perspective in the early part of the poem. From where Julian stands,
and in his concentration on the sunset, nature can be made a beautiful
and sympathetic setting for mind. Maddalo's differently chosen perspectives and emphases can confirm his different views; so that the
status of nature is a matter determined by consciousness, which fits
with Julian's argument. But this possibility is very definitely subdued
in the first section of the poem, and the maniac's soliloquy opens to
the accompaniment of a hostile natural world:

> all the while the loud and gusty storm
> Hissed through the window, and we stood behind
> Stealing his accents from the envious wind
> Unseen.   (ll. 295–8)

The maniac's soliloquy begins at a point in the poem where Maddalo's
perspective has as it were infected the rhetorical strategies of the
poem.

  The figure of the maniac is apparently based on parts of the real
experience of Shelley and Byron, as of course are the figures of Julian
and Maddalo, and this in itself suggests Shelley's concern to explore
a disjunction of social and poetic identity that has some context in his
own life. The maniac incorporates too details derived from Shelley's
contemporary interest in Torquato Tasso, a striking example of the
poet isolated and driven to madness, or the appearance of madness in
the eyes of his audience, and thus frustrated by his social context. But
we do not need to know these things to think of the maniac as a poet
frustrated by the failure to achieve an audience. He is 'as a nerve o'er
which do creep/The else unfelt oppressions of this earth'; he strikes
Julian as 'one who wrought from his own fervid heart/The eloquence
of passion', and he speaks 'as one who wrote, and thought/His words
might move some heart that heeded not,/If sent to distant lands'. He
speaks of his 'sad writing', and says at one point

>                            How vain
> Are words! I thought never to speak again,
> Not even in secret,—not to my own heart—
> But from my lips the unwilling accents start,
> And from my pen the words flow as I write,
> Dazzling my eyes with scalding tears . . . my sight
> Is dim to see that charactered in vain
> On this unfeeling leaf which burns the brain
> And eats into it . . .   (ll. 472–80)

The maniac has two audiences in the poem; the absent ex-lover that his speech is addressed to, and the unseen Julian and Maddalo who overhear him, and whose urbane discussion pales into a passionless inadequacy in comparison with his words: 'our argument was quite forgot'. It is understandable that the maniac's suffering is the result of a broken love affair; the poet's need for an audience merges, in Shelley's thought, into his need for love (as in the lyric 'An Exhortation', published in the *Prometheus Unbound* volume), and the withholding of love by his audience, the failure of sympathetic and responsive consciousness, makes the poet seem inarticulate because he will not be understood. The maniac's state of mind is comparable with that expressed by the sixth Spirit in act I of *Prometheus Unbound*, in the lines beginning 'Ah, sister, Desolation is a delicate thing'. The passage seems to have developed out of Shelley's recent work on a translation of Plato's *Symposium*, at Bagni di Lucca; he had been particularly impressed by the broad terms of Diotima's discussion of love, which expand the reference of the word to embrace the spirit of all creative human endeavour, in whatever sphere. The sixth Spirit's speech, closely following a passage in Diotima's discussion, articulates the especially devastating emotional effects of disappointment in our highest ideals; those who are most sensitive, and most delicately responsive to the human condition, are most severely vulnerable to its buffetings. But it is interesting to note that in the maniac's case, his desperate inarticulacy is itself partly the product of a hostility in the audience whose loss his manner of speech confirms.

This reading of the maniac's soliloquy, as a dramatization of the poet's position in a society whose attitudes severely hamper his creative potential, has been suggested by Donald Davie, although in a curiously inverted form:

> It is in [his dealings with the abstractions of moral philosophy] that Shelley's diction is woefully impure. He expressed, in *The Defence of Poetry*, his concern for these large abstractions, and his Platonic intention to make them apprehensible and 'living' in themselves. In *The Witch of Atlas* he came near to effecting this; but more often, this programme only means that an abstraction such as Reason, or Justice must always be tugged about in figurative language. The moment they appear in Shelley's verse (and they always come in droves) the tone becomes hectic, the syntax and punctuation disintegrate. In *Julian and Maddalo*, by inventing the figure and the predicament of the maniac, Shelley excuses this incoherency and presents it (plausibly enough) as a verbatim report of the lunatic's ravings.[4]

Even given the extreme and grossly misrepresenting hostility of this passage, Professor Davie has settled on a telling quality in Shelley's creation of the maniac; introduced into the discourse of Julian and

---

4. Davie, *op. cit.*, 143.

Maddalo, the maniac's speech has an effect that reproduces the effect of Shelley's poetry on its contemporary audience (and indeed the effect that it frequently still has on readers unsympathetic or new to Shelley). It is worth emphasizing once more that the single most dramatic effect of reading the poem is its violent contrast of styles, between the urbane and wholly familiar manner of the two gentlemen, and the uncomprehended and thus despairingly isolated words of the maniac. His inarticulacy is simply the reflex, in Julian and Maddalo and in the ex-lover, of a consciousness that will not change until it can understand, and cannot understand except by being changed. The dramatic situation of the poem here externalizes a conflict that is implicit in the contradiction of Julian's radical creed and his passive acquiescence in the manners of a gentleman. Maddalo's attitude to the maniac is that he can but treat him with the decency owing to any man, 'evidently a very cultivated and amiable person when in his right senses', who has been defeated by life into a touching but wholly inarticulate intensity of despair. Maddalo attempts to alleviate the maniac's suffering by creating the illusion of a gentlemanly normality like the personal style with which Maddalo in fact supports his own sense of 'the nothingness of human life':

> I fitted up for him
> Those rooms beside the sea, to please his whim,
> And sent him busts and books and urns for flowers,
> Which had adorned his life in happier hours,
> And instruments of music—you may guess
> A stranger could do little more or less
> For one so gentle and unfortunate   (ll. 252–8)

Julian's response similarly reveals an inadequacy that is the measure of the limitations imposed by his social identity. He rightly detects something retrievable in the maniac's raving—it is very difficult for the reader too to decide whether the maniac is in fact mad, or really inarticulate—but his intention to work at the task of healing the maniac, of making him articulate again, is smothered by the commitment to a social existence that has no room for the maniac's experience. It is a perfectly appropriate irony that we can recognize in the maniac the outlines of Julian's own radicalism, and that this intellectual commitment is no less potently realized in the maniac's speech than in Julian's. The maniac is 'ever still the same/In creed as in resolve', and, like Julian, he is especially sensitive to 'the else unfelt oppressions of the earth'. The maniac is recognizably Shelleyan too in his rejection of revenge, his sense of the fruitlessness of the desire to reciprocate wrongs. Shelley's ironic juxtapositioning of Julian and the maniac seems most overt in his representation of Julian's awareness of the poetic potential of the maniac, a potential that Maddalo is the more alert to:

> The colours of his mind seemed yet unworn;
> For the wild language of his grief was high,

Such as in measure were called poetry;
And I remember one remark which then
Maddalo made. He said: 'Most wretched men
Are cradled into poetry by wrong,
They learn in suffering what they teach in song.'    (ll. 540–6)

The maniac's 'high' language *is* 'in measure'; his speech is controlled and heightened by the same metrical convention that animates the speech of Maddalo and Julian. Here Shelley quite manifestly stands beyond his gentlemanly creations, and places them for us within the limitations that prevent them from recognizing themselves in the maniac.

The poem ends with Julian's failure or refusal to explain to 'the cold world' the story of the maniac, given to him by Maddalo's daughter. The daughter is a positive and hopeful but silent figure in the poem; she appears for the reader only through the idealizing medium of Julian's somewhat watery perception of her. We receive the impression, perhaps, from Julian's account of her—'a wonder of this earth,/Where there is little of transcendent worth,—/Like one of Shakespeare's women'—that he is not prepared in practice to countenance the existence in his real world of simple human goodness, without the distancing perspective that experiences a realized ideal as somehow transcendent and remote in character. This note sounds more strongly in the passage towards the end of the poem in which Julian rationalizes his failure to attempt the rehabilitation of the maniac (ll. 547–83). We witness here the process by which Julian accommodates his ideas to a social life which consigns them, inevitably, to the realm of the unrealizably ideal. He leaves the maniac, and Venice—the 'bright Venice' of his optimistic perception—and returns to the familiar tenor of his accustomed existence. Julian chooses not to articulate the maniac in himself, and aspires rather, appropriately, more to the life of Maddalo than of the maniac. It is Maddalo, and not the maniac, in whom Julian seeks to know himself.

*Julian and Maddalo* dramatizes the dangers that operate to nullify the creative radical potential of a man whose way of life identifies him with the class against which his radical critique is directed. These dangers were real enough, certainly in the view of contemporaries, in Shelley's own life, and they beset him still in the different form of the misleading expectations that his sophisticated literary medium produces in his readers. *Julian and Maddalo* overcomes the problem by building its rhetorical strategies upon it; so that the damaging limitations of Julian's situation emerge as the condition of his failure, in forming the materials of Shelley's poetic success.

# JERROLD E. HOGLE

## Transference Perverted:
## *The Cenci* as Shelley's Great Exposé[†]

\* \* \*

*The Cenci* aims at being so comprehensive in what it exposes that it is almost a meta-tragedy in relation to the tradition it furthers and alters. To begin with, it tries to highlight and then explicitly answer *the* question posed in tragedy since Aeschylus and even before: to what extent is personal choice responsible for the evil that finally destroys some individuals, and how much is a tragic figure the nearly helpless victim of fate or cultural pressure? Shelley's preface grants some importance to both "causes," so much so that he has spawned a running debate among critics over which factor is dominant or if they counterbalance each other in the course of his play. Shelley flatly states that Beatrice Cenci's conspiracy to murder her tyrannical father the Count in 1599 is the act of an "amiable" and brilliant young woman "violently thwarted from her nature by the necessity of circumstance and opinion" (Preface, *SPP*, p. 239) [141]. Yet he just as firmly condemns her "revenge" and "retaliation" as "pernicious mistakes." They are prompted for Shelley by her blind determination to see the Count's rape of her as true dishonor (which it need not be) and her refusal "to convert the injurer from his dark passions by [postures] of peace and love" in a going out of herself overcoming the "dogmas" that she has chosen to accept (p. 240) [142]. The foundation of all "tragic character," as Shelley sees it (p. 240) [142], lies in what places Beatrice at the Sophoclean crossroads where "external" pressure and "internal" choice become coterminous and supportive of each other, then rigidly dictatorial in making the later choices of the psyche subject to this set of "commands." The play, in other words, sets out to explain the apparent contradictions in the preface and in Shelley's principal source, the "Relation of the Death of the Family of the Cenci" (*Works*, II, 160–63), by pointing to the basis of tragedy that both dictates to and is dictated by individual characters.

\* \* \*

\* \* \* In order for his play to reveal what instigates human tragedy most often and makes people the functions of master scripts at the same time, Shelley must see all the methods by which people abase themselves as interacting to produce both the errors of personal choice and the cultural, even patriarchal, oppression of individuals. *The Cenci*

---

† From "The Key to All Tyrannies: From *Laon and Cythna* to *The Cenci*," in *Shelley's Process: Radical Transference and the Development of His Major Works*, by Jerrold E. Hogle (New York: Oxford University Press, 1988), pp. 148–55, 159–61. Copyright © 1988 by Oxford University Press, Inc. Used by permission of Oxford University Press, Inc. The author's notes have been edited, and page references to this Norton Critical Edition appear in brackets after the original citations.

therefore stages all the ways that he has discovered over several years by which the preconscious process of transference undergoes perversion into tyrannies. While some other works prior to *The Cenci* isolate one type of perversion, or occasionally two that are closely related, this ambitious tragedy sees them as inextricably mixed and inclined to generate all the others to reinforce any one of them, almost as soon as one or more are accepted by the will—and their actual base is deceptively obscured. Certainly it is such an interplay of tyrannical modes of thought in people that accounts for tragedy as Shelley redefines it, and it is the tendency of people, even some brilliant and generous people, to stage themselves according to such patterns in such a combination that underlies Shelley's use and critique of Shakespeare in this play, not to mention the stances of nearly all the characters in *The Cenci*. Indeed, the "human heart" gains a "knowledge of itself" by confronting the mirrors in this play (Preface, p. 240) [142] because the characters reflect the destructive methods by which we are still tempted to mirror ourselves or let ourselves be used as reflectors by tyrants who need us (as audience) to achieve their stagings of domination.

Theatrical mirroring, it turns out, is the key to Count Cenci's will to power, even in that opening scene when he decides to debase his sons and especially his daughter. What he wants most in choosing that course is neither mere sensual license nor a vague supremacy but the "sight of agony" on the faces of those he asserts himself against. He craves "the dry fixed eyeball, the pale quivering lip, / Which tell [him] that the spirit weeps within" and that he may exult in "joy" because he is not that being (I. i. 82–83 and 111–12). He is so much a theatrical character that his very significance—and certainly his continued power over others—depends on the reaction of an auditor to his aggression,[1] on a reflection that appears to recognize his self-assertion and so allows him to seem a figure who causes fear instead of one who might feel it himself. * * * "Any design [his] captious fancy makes" projects a "picture of his wish" similar to their dreams of an ideal ego, and yet that wish "forms none," leads to no visible result or recognition of its existence, "But such as men [reacting to it] would start to know" (I. i. 87–89). There is no mastery in a performance without the "reading" of the other that acknowledges enslavement and so seems to give mastery back, or at least to offer signs in a visage that can be read by the performer as suggesting an inner weeping, a "soul within [his] power" (I. i. 115).

This exchange of readings, though, while necessary for an actor so that he may feel himself to be what he seems, is a two-sided source of identity for anyone producing his "selfhood" with such a device on

---

1. All this, of course, is partly because Shelley is extending—and critiquing—the stock figure of the raging or vengeful aristocrat on the tragic stage of his own day, designed as that Gothic type was for an Edmund Kean and for the "thrill of terror" it supposedly aroused, usually in the women of a Covent Garden audience. See Curran, *Shelley's Cenci: Scorpions Ringed with Fire* (Princeton: Princeton UP, 1970), pp. 160–71. * * *

the stage of the world. True, the constitution of power by the Other's look and "knowledge" can place the responsibility and sanction for power outside the would-be tyrant, as though someone else has given him title to power and the title can never be taken from him on the grounds that he has stolen it. The Count seeks and, for the present, secures that license from the Pope's emissary in the opening scene. Cardinal Camillo is the most immediate person whose "start[ing] to know" will grant real force, and thus a kind of permission, to the "picture of [the Count's] wish," even though only some of Cenci's intentions have been declared to this appalled, but obligingly fearful, auditor. At the same time, any dependence on an "appropriate" response means that the auditor is in a position of control. The Count's aggression must be counterbalanced frequently by a nagging paranoia, as several have noted, mainly because he senses his own "quivering lip" submitting to a Sartrean "gaze of the Other." He realizes that the "reader" on whom he so depends may have the freedom to deny him the response he wants, and he especially fears that apparent self-sufficiency in Beatrice, who has long refused the trembling reaction he so desperately needs for the effect he pursues.

As he reveals to open the second act, the Count has been placed in an abject position, like a Lear facing a Cordelia, by his daughter's "fearless eye, / And brow superior, and unaltered cheek" on the most recent occasions when he has asserted himself in her presence (II. i. 116–17). In the not-too-distant past, moreover, her "mirror" has reacted to his power-plays with inappropriate, dissociated responses ranging from the look of a Madonna's pitying "tenderness" to a glance of "scorn" from a lofty position of moralistic judgment (II. i. 118). None of these gazes will offer his declarations the facial signifiers or "weeping" inner signifieds that can be read as submitting to his power and thereby granting its existence. This possibility is terrifying to him because it exposes the merely staged, rhetorical, and dependent basis of his power. It shows that the needed response is not automatically the Count's to command and that he has given all decisive force to the Other's gaze in looking to it for definition. Unable to deny that so much significance resides in the Other, since he needs it to be there if the "mirror" is to reflect any power back to him, the Count therefore sets out to reappropriate that capacity for determining meaning from his most resistant auditor so as to seem the gaze of the Other himself. One reason he decides to rape Beatrice is how much this invasion of her body will belie her Madonna-like removal from the imposition of masculine and patriarchal authority. Once ravished, he hopes, she will reflect the "quivering lip" of the "meek and tame" at last (I. i. 167). If he has his way, she will even come to seem to herself the location of the very dishonor that she has ascribed to him in her looks of scorn. With what makes him seem inferior thus transferred from him to her, he will seem as superior to her, he fancies, as she once seemed to him. In other words, he will become Sartre's Other as "seducer . . . producing in the other [he faces] a consciousness of a state of nothingness [in juxtaposition to] a fullness of being" that the seducer will seem to contain absolutely in his phallic aggression.[2]

Still, the Count finds, it takes more than an assertion of bodily force—indeed, even the rape will have to include more dimensions than that—if the would-be tyrant is to seem to introject a self-determining ability to turn desire into effective performance, "to act the thing [he] thought" (I. i. 97). * * * The degradation of Beatrice proposed in act I may seem to promise her father the sense of conquering "Manhood" he needs (I. i. 97). But the power to act can seem unlicensed by an Other and usurped from one—a stigma we have seen the Count determined to avoid so that no authority can hold him fully accountable—when "frail" woman appeals, as Beatrice does before the guests at a banquet, to higher male authorities thought of as separate from him and greater in power: "the Pope's chamberlain" and "offended God" (I. iii. 127 and 157). Cenci must attach himself to these underpinnings if the illusion of his self-contained right to violence is to stay in force.

His technique is multifaceted but very effective rhetorically. First he makes the papacy so dependent on the "revenue" with which he bribes the church to escape prosecution (I. i. 27–33) that he becomes linked to the drive for male dominance already pervading the Catholic Fathers. Cardinal Camillo, as a result, rebuffs Beatrice with the "law" that "paternal power" is the "shadow" of the Pope's, setting up Cenci as underwritten by papal prerogatives (II. ii. 28 and 55–56). Then, aided by this supposed connection to God's earthly representative, the Count styles himself as a temporal extension of "the great father of us all" (I. iii. 23), an Italian Renaissance version of the Jupiter who has given himself the right to rape Thetis in *Prometheus Unbound*. The power desired by a patriarch to create reflectors of his dominance is projected up to a father-figure (a "soul upthrown"), one both exalted beyond all other beings and reflected within the projector most of all, who then does not seem as dependent on earth-bound mirrors as he really is.[3] Beatrice has gained the superiority of her gaze, after all, by

2. I quote Sartre from *Being and Nothingness*, trans. Hazel Barnes (New York: Philosophical Library, 1956), p. 372. * * *

3. Shelley's Cenci thus departs in very significant ways from the Count as he is rendered in the "Relation of the Death of the Family of the Cenci" (the already mentioned chief source for the play). The Francesco Cenci of the "Relation" remains a thoroughgoing "atheist," though he does build a "small chapel . . . in the court of his palace" for burying—and thus concealing his crimes against—his children (*Works*, II, 159). He therefore does not answer Beatrice's appeals to Catholicism and God (noted in the "Relation," *Works*, II, 160) with similar forms of justification for his insistence on patriarchal power. Indeed, he approaches Beatrice sexually in the "Relation" (without ever quite completing the act) not to match her assertions of supremacy with a reverse-reflection of them but because she really appeals to his senses, as do concubines in his palace whom Shelley does not mention, and because he wants to prevent a costly marriage like the one that her elder sister (not in Shelley's play) has made against his will. Shelley's version makes a point of mirroring-reactions and imitative performances that the "Relation" does not emphasize nearly as much. There could hardly be clearer evidence that Shelley is deliberately skewing the basic story he receives to depict mirrored power plays as the basis of action in *The Cenci*. A similar point can be made about what Shelley does with the few elements he borrowed from Vincenzio Pieracci's *Beatrice Cenci*, a tragedy published in 1816 and circulated in Italy while Shelley was there. See a translation of that play and some comparisons between it and *The Cenci* in George Yost, *Pieracci and Shelley: An Italian* Ur-Cenci (Potomac, MD: Scripta Humanistica, 1986).

suggesting an "awe-inspiring" depth in her visage (I. ii. 84). The mystery in that face has seemed a "protecting presence" looking inward to a "firm mind" that itself looks back, as a Madonna should, to "God to Heaven" (II. i. 30, 48, and I. iii. 52). Again adopting a pattern from her to stage himself, the Count conquers this powerful stance by aping its layers in his public posture. His pronouncements, often vicious prayers that Heaven does appear to answer at first (I. iii. 22–44), now claim to rest on a "sober truth" behind which lies "the word of God" (I. iii. 55–56). The "knowing" apparently at the heart of his daughter's glance that abashes the Count with its reflection of his insufficiency appears to be *his* "sober" possession henceforth, just as much as it seems to be the Pope's, backed as both men say they are by the absolute Word. With this dimension added, the rape becomes an assertion of the right and the will to "knowledge," the status and drive we saw Prometheus seek by recasting himself as a rapacious King of Heaven. Such an act so underwritten constitutes "knowing" as the total penetration and domination of any targeted person. From this point on, that person's subjection will be "deployed" as the patriarch wishes—to quote Michel Foucault—in a rhetoric that he (as God's spokesman) seems authorized to control. The barriers between the lust for power and tyrannical action have now been removed by a grounding of the self in a supremacy where motivation, utterance, and action are allowed to be simultaneous. The Count therefore begins his assault by bringing that presumption home to Beatrice. He simply utters "one word" (II. i. 63), somewhat in the manner of God at the Beginning, and that in itself makes her try (like fallen Eve) to conceal her oncepowerful face from his gaze of the Other. Her initial reaction is to run for a hiding place away from the assault of a phallic discourse betokening the force of the phallus itself (the sign of the Father on earth).

Seen from this angle, Beatrice is far more sinned against than sinning. She can hardly be said to consent willfully to this onslaught, since it is directed quite specifically against her. In the initial two acts, at least, she is a real threat to a male-dominated discourse and worthy of the audience's admiration because of that stance. She is first, by her own admission, the champion and strong representative of all the women who have contended with the patriarchy in the Cenci family. Being quite capable of attaching her emotions to numerous other beings analogous to herself, she is haunted, quite gladly, by "the ghost / Of [her] dead Mother," and, as if at her mother's request, she protects and guides Lucretia, the stepmother "who filled the [mother's] place," and thereby stands as a "refuge and defense" between the Father's "moody wrath" and the wives (now composited) whom he has victimized over the years (II. i. 94–96 and 49). In this role as Woman defending her entire sex, Beatrice can challenge male supremacy in a number of ways. She can situate herself partly inside and partly outside the hegemonic ideology striving to secure the dominance of men. She can consequently read and articulate the ironies in the system, having been both intimately involved with and sometimes distant from them. She can expose at the banquet how unfairly "honour and obedience" are granted to a man who is really a "torturer" and how much the men given supremacy by their observers, while denying the fact of the gift, must rhetorically "cover [their actual] faces from every living eye" if they do not want their duplicity revealed (I. iii. 148–49 and 54). Meanwhile, too, Beatrice challenges the unity as well as the dominance of the "Manhood" achieved by such deceptions. When the Count finds himself the subject of her gaze of the Other, he feels his "masculinity" compromised because he has been placed in what he thinks ought to be (and in male discourse *is*) the feminine position. He is for a time in a very mixed state, male but figuratively "gendered" as female, and must (like Hamlet) theatrically throw this "frailty" off if he is to have a strictly masculine dominance. Even Beatrice, being positioned as the "knowing gaze," is a mixture of genders herself in acting out the authority that patriarchal discourse wants to restrict to men alone.

Herein lies the problem. To challenge such a discourse by being an authorized speaker of it is to discover oneself forced into its deployments, whatever one's intentions may have seemed. Beatrice finds that even a public utterance declaring "a father's hoary hair" a "shelter" for lawless "tyranny" (as in II. iii. 99–129) can express itself only as an appeal to "the father of all" (I. iii. 118) or to the princes, cardinals, and chamberlains who gain much of their authority from the widely held assumption that the primal speaker and ultimate auditor of language is male. Just to speak and so to create personal thoughts by confronting the psyche with verbal forms of them, Beatrice comes to see, is to be read *and* to read oneself as the master language and the father set up behind it want to construe a speaker's words. Count Cenci's utterance of a single phallic "word" horrifies her in part because it shows how the dictates of male supremacist discourse have become virtually inescapable, even in attempts to resist them.

Beatrice appears to have only two choices under this "necessity of circumstance and opinion." One option is not to let "the tongue . . . fashion [desire] into words" at all, as her brother suggests (II. ii. 85), since any concrete utterance will turn around to oppress the "I" and skew its aims with a configuration of the words according to the confining standards attributed to the father.[4] The other choice, it seems, is to combat the patriarchy by deliberately adopting some of the most effective devices in patriarchal discourse: its claim of being grounded in God's Word, its suppression of possible word-patterns and meanings that might undercut assertions of power sanctioned by the Lord, its supposed right to penetrate and debase its targets according to its will, and its attempt to cover over the merely human power-play underlying its restrictions with the assertion that its dictates are or can be "chronicled in heaven" (IV. i. 159) and so imposed on humankind as if they were among the givens of Creation. The first alternative plays too obviously into Count Cenci's hands and would serve to lock Beatrice

---

4. This problem throughout the play is thoroughly assessed by Michael Worton, "Speech and Silence in *The Cenci*," in *Essays on Shelley*, ed. Miriam Allott (Liverpool: U of Liverpool P, 1982), pp. 105–24. I write here to further what Worton suggests by revealing the larger causes in cultural discourse for the fear of language he notes.

JERROLD E. HOGLE

away in a silence that would leave patriarchal assumptions completely unchallenged. For that reason, especially after the rape, she chooses the second option more often than the first. Asserting God's law as her own sanction even more than she did before, she finally denies all verbal renderings of the Count but those that place a "Hell within him" justifying his eradication (IV. ii. 33); she makes herself the "accusing" priestess of the ultimate knower demanding her father's full confession and the right to pierce to his "dying heart" (IV. i. 34–37); and she refers to the justness of a God beyond this "judging world" for license to obscure her involvement in the murder (IV. iv. 113–28). She even urges her stepmother on these grounds to use signs for concealment and not to "write on unsteady eyes . . . / All that thou wouldst hide" (IV. iv. 39–40). This choice, of course, although not obviously, contorts her into the patterns of patriarchal language, thus making her hiring of assassins easily detected by the male Catholic authorities who finally put her to death. There seems no place for her to go that does not suit the aims of the father's master text, so she becomes a version of its own violence against its subjects,[5] and that makes her one of its victims even more than she already was.

Nevertheless, "seems" is an accurate verb in this statement. Such an eventuality, though sometimes the victim's own view of the situation, is not simply inevitable in the world of the play—and Beatrice is not completely free of responsibility. She does not submit willingly to such deployment, at least not during the first three acts, but she has already set herself up for conscription before her first entrance in act 1. She has, quite simply, refused at the outset, even in supposing that her choices are only two, some of the options really available to her all along. Given her definite capacity for carrying through positive forms of transference, she could have used the imagination she genuinely possesses in more telling ways than she has. She could have "gone out of herself" in her thinking sufficiently to comprehend the uncertain and multi-leveled otherness-from-himself in her father-adversary. Then she could have responded in kind to that sense of him rather than imitating the Count's apparent posture of self-determination underwritten by God's Will. She could have continued playing out in her own behavior something like Asia's otherness-from-herself in *Prometheus Unbound*, just as we have heard that Beatrice used to do in her shifts from maidenly "tenderness" to moralistic "scorn" during visits by her father. Such a pluralistic manner, as we have noted, responds to visitations in terms of one set of metaphors and then suddenly in terms of a different set. The result undercuts the Promethean projection of a Jupiter by transforming both speaker and visitor from role to role without any single role coming to dominate the scene completely and claiming to rival one illusion of self-sufficiency with another. As Shelley claims in his preface, then, Beatrice

---

5. It is mainly this dimension of Shelley's play that Antonin Artaud intensifies in his 1935 version of *The Cenci*, first staged with himself as both the director and Count Cenci (as well as the rewriter—or should one say *dewriter*?—of the script). * * *

could have reacted to the "injuries" her father has inflicted by returning both an outpouring, sympathetic "kindness" and a held-in or un-
revealing, albeit nonviolent, "forebearance" (*SPP*, p. 240) [142]. If she
had kept up this imaginative movement that would have refused to be
contained by her father's sense of human relations, the Count would
have been kept off balance and held in a more impotent anxiety, considering how anomalous the entire response would be according the
context in which he wants to place his aggression. Certainly Cenci
would have had no visible basis, under these circumstances, to construe her as a violator of patriarchal laws on the grounds that she had
revealed herself publically as stealing the postures of male dominance
to deny the absolute authority of fathers. In addition, through all this,
Beatrice could have consistently attached her "vitally metaphorical"
role-playing to the attitude (and subtle verbal skill) of the noncom-
bative yet unsettling poet, who surely, again in words from the preface,
is one of those who strives "to convert [an] injurer from his dark passions by [devices of] peace and love." Even so, once she has decided,
as transference permits, to abash, and thus to try neutralizing, her
father with a disdain and religious language resembling his own, she
has rendered potentially deconstructive roles impossible for herself.[6]
Despite the pull of liberating transference that she feels on occasion,
she willfully goes on to act out all the perversions of transference that
we have seen her father use against her.

   Her seemingly sanctified gaze at him, we must admit, narcissistically
imitates the Count's staging of an apparent self-sufficiency, though
admittedly in an inverted, goddesslike form. It depends, as his look
does, for much of its "reality" on the effect, and thus acceptance, it
achieves in its observer. When the desired reaction no longer appears
in Cenci's occasional acknowledgments that he has been "rebuked"
(II. i. 45), Beatrice's seeming confidence and distance from his control
disappear at once to show how much of an act they have been all
along (II. i. 12–21, 53–57, and 63–66). In addition, she has deliberately pursued an underwriter for her posture that is exactly the same
as the one grounding her father's claim to power. Accepting the "submission" most pervasive in her culture for the sake of her own counter-
staging of his rhetoric, she becomes as "blind[ed]" and "excuse[d]" by
Catholicism in her own mind as the Count has sought to be himself
(*SPP*, Preface, p. 241) [143]. That decision, which could have been
avoided despite this religion's domination of the era in question (as
poets have repeatedly shown, according to the *Defence*, p. 498) [526–
27], sets up Beatrice's appeal to God as a sanction, then her desire to
"knowingly" penetrate the facades of sinners, and it is those stances
that suck her completely into patriarchal patterns when she sets out
to murder her patriarch with these motivators among her justifications.
The tragedy of Beatrice Cenci includes, though it is not limited to, the

---

6. Jean Hall quite rightly points out this failure in Beatrice to "achieve poetic distancing" from
hegemonic modes of thought in "The Socialized Imagination: Shelley's *The Cenci* and *Prometheus Unbound*," *Studies in Romanticism*, 23 (1984), 339–50.

692 JERROLD E. HOGLE

combined social *and* personal acceptance of the narcissism, the deferral to an Other, and the will to "penetrating" knowledge (the suppressor of feminine diffusion) with which she is assaulted by her male enemy and according to which, notwithstanding her less rigid tendencies, she decides to stage herself for the sake of some mastery over her immediate audience.

\* \* \*

Meanwhile, however, Beatrice matches the force of this admitted imposition upon her by willfully, almost ruthlessly, adopting one mimed posture after another for the sake of the supremacy and distance from responsibility that each one seems to provide. Her deliberate inventiveness with such postures is especially apparent in the final act of the play, where Shelley is faced with the difficulty of establishing "tragic heroism" for a woman who, in the main source document on "the Family of the Cenci," is famous for letting her father's murder be pinned initially on the hired assassins alone, thereby sending others to their deaths so as to conceal her own and her family's involvement.[7] Shelley stages an explanation for this apparent cowardice by having Beatrice react mimetically when her priest-judges come close to discovering the imitated stance she has taken as God's avenging angel (what Giacomo calls her at V. i. 43). As soon as she learns that their evidence is the testimony of the assassin Marzio, she orally prints on his "countenance," as Count Cenci had attempted to write on hers (I. i. 42), the "shame and misery" of "dar[ing] not to look the thing he speaks" (V. ii. 85), of having an obedient (feminine) facade hiding deeper sentiments of envious (male) aggression. By ascribing to him what has been imputed to her and thus making him the scapegoat that she is being made, she regains, as the Count did, the penetrating gaze of the Other that her Catholic judges want to cast on her. She makes Marzio react as she once did to her father's worst glance ("Let her not look on me!"), so much so that he recants his testimony and reverses the duplicity she has attributed to him by trying to look like an independently "guilty criminal wretch" and claiming that she is completely innocent of the crime she really instigated (V. ii. 90–91 and 158–59). Later, after other confessions and Orsino's absence have convicted Beatrice anyway, she leaps back to the posture of removed and Godlike uninvolvement, this time giving that figuration the features of "white innocence" compelled to "wear the mask of guilt to hide [a most] awful and serenest countenance" (V. iii. 24–26). This pose expressed in those terms imitates the position and appearance of the always off-stage pontiff, the authority behind her judges. The Pope, after all, is now reported to be "as calm and keen as [an] engine . . . exempt itself / From aught that it inflicts [through the pronouncers of guilt]: a marble form [of Heavenly and patriarchal] law . . . not a man" (V. iv. 2–5). Beatrice answers the claims of her accusers, then, astonishing others aside from Marzio into assertions of her innocence

7. *Works*, II, 162.

(V. ii. 185–88), by acting out the two-faced attitudes and mimetic underpinnings that have given her judges the power to try her. She has in effect put them on trial, and so they are naturally reluctant to find her guilty of their culpabilities. She is "heroic" in the sense that she fights illegitimate authority by performatively recommitting its crimes and thus exposing them (and their pressure on her), at least to Shelley's audience. There is undeniable nobility in the resolve and intelligence of her resistance, and the audience in a good production must feel the force of some moral grandeur in her attitude. Yet she is also "tragic" in showing how much the logic she assaults has become so thoroughly her own, how much it has led her by her own consent to be as prone to scapegoating and self-concealment as the mimetic power-plays directed so brutally against her.

This doubleness, in fact, does not exhaust the extent of the resolute cleverness in Beatrice's final posture. In the hope of leaving a character-pattern in memory that will belie what "ill tongues" may henceforth attribute to her "name" (V. ii. 150), she works through all the maneuvers of perverted transference, albeit mimetically, in the two concluding scenes of the last act. She reinforces her imitated noninvolvement by drawing quite clearly on the pose of the objectivist. Answering one judge's assertion of her guilt, she reminds him of the position taken by "high judging God" when "he beheld" her father's crimes against her and let the Count's "death" be the natural "consequence" (V. iii. 78–82). She places her thinking at this locus of seemingly disinterested subjectivity * * * so as to render quite logical, yet keep her deepest psyche disconnected from, the demand in one objective fact (the rape) for a matching external enactment (the murder). Indeed, if she does not try to be this gaze of the Other, she feels doomed to behold a form of it as the sole object of her consciousness at the moment of and even after her death. For a time, once her sentence is made unalterable, she trembles at being possibly condemned to face eternally what she has imitated most of all: her father's "eye [and] voice [and] shape" standing between her and the ultimate Father just as he once claimed to do and her priestly judges have done (V. iv. 60–67). She briefly gives in to the Catholic, Dantean fear that the roles she has played on earth and the objects of hate she has set up in playing them will come back in the afterlife to haunt her with their effects, turning her again into the sort of object that Italian culture has made her and she had made others. To counteract this possibility she has to reconfigure herself as part of a greater level of "knowing" above and prior to the patriarchal gaze that has so long confined her in this world.[8]

She therefore falls back on narcissism in a way that apparently returns her to a lost purity and thus, it would seem, to an unfallen, Godlike level still existing at the foundations of her nature. She asks

---

8. This vision of creation as therefore divided into hierarchical levels of true and false gods is what James Rieger discusses as "Paterin" about Beatrice in *The Mutiny Within: The Heresies of Percy Bysshe Shelley* (New York: Braziller, 1967), pp. 111–28. I am here suggesting what impels Beatrice to construct the universe in the fashion Rieger describes.

to be judged in the end with the eyes of her surviving and youngest brother, Bernardo, who still regards her as the "mirror" in which he learned "pure innocence," even though *he* is now the youthful mirror reflecting that innocence back on her (V. iv. 130). Beatrice also finds and becomes a mirror by asking Lucretia to knot her hair for her and urging this affectionate "Mother" to put her own tresses up in the same way so that they seem very like each other as they proceed to their execution (V. iv. 159–62). That restyling of her features connects Beatrice, even if Lucretia is only her stepmother, with what Bernardo has called the "Mother, / Whose love was a bond to all our loves" quite outside the father's power (V. iv. 135–36). Beatrice, aided by all these reflectors, has thereby * * * made oncoming "Death" seem like "a fond mother" retaking possession of her innocent child (V. iv. 115–17) and restoring this child to that ideal-ego existence of loving inter-relationship that occurs much earlier than the state of subjection to the culturally established patriarch. In the restored state, Beatrice imagines, she can be permanently thought of, Madonna-like again, as "holy and unstained . . . Though wrapped [throughout her life] in a strange cloud of crime and shame" (V. iv. 148–49). She can mentally attain what she has always claimed to be grounded in, a divine knowl-edge, gaze, and objectivity previous to patriarchal claims to all those powers. Hence she dies hoping for a situation beyond this need to imitate that is clearly bound up with several other transfers aimed at establishing hierarchical levels. All of these maneuvers together as Be-atrice uses them appear to aim at a location, even an origin, beyond earthbound dominations only to reveal how much the aspirant, in cre-ating another hierarchy (mother before father) to have this "beyond," has constructed that hope out of, and so is still conscripted by, the very sources of tyranny she has been trying so brilliantly to overcome.

* * *

# TIMOTHY WEBB

## The Unascended Heaven: Negatives in *Prometheus Unbound*†

For a poet who was committed to an essentially optimistic philoso-phy Shelley had an extraordinary predilection for the negative. Con-sider the eloquent celebration of the poetic faculty which brings the *Defence of Poetry* to its climax: 'Poets are the hierophants of an *un-apprehended* inspiration; the words which express what they *under-*

---

† From *Shelley Revalued: Essays from the Gregynog Conference*, ed. Kelvin Everest (Leicester: Leicester University Press, 1983), pp. 37, 40–45, 47–54, 56–62. Reprinted by permission.
  The italics in the quotations from Shelley are mine. They are intended to give some indi-cation of the extent of Shelley's negatives; however, for reasons of legibility I have had to confine these indications to grammatical negatives. These markings should not be taken as a complete guide to the negative element in Shelley's ideas (Author's note).

*stand not*; the trumpets which sing to battle and *feel not* what they inspire; the influence which is *moved not*, but moves. Poets are the *unacknowledged* legislators of the world'. The way in which this passage adumbrates its positives through a series of negatives suggests both the limitations of human understanding and the possibility of a realm in which the seemingly negative is caught up, transformed, redeemed, or even regenerated, by some higher reality. Such an approach, tentative in its definition yet adulatory in its tone, bears some resemblance to the language of theology and religious contemplation.

In spite of its poetic intensity and the richness of its imagery, the *Defence of Poetry* is, of course, prose; yet a similar preference for the negative can be detected in much of the poetry. Sometimes Shelley's negative embodies the joy of liberty after the cramping restraints of confinement: 'And the green lizard, and the golden snake,/Like *unimprisoned* flames, out of their trance awake.' (*Adonais*, 161–2). Sometimes it is an acknowledgement of forces which challenge our recognition: 'Thou art *unseen*', Shelley addresses the skylark, 'but yet I hear thy shrill delight'. The West Wind, too, is an *unseen presence*, while Intellectual Beauty is 'The awful shadow of some *unseen* Power'. Sometimes the negative may be suggested by a problem of definition: 'Hail to thee, blithe spirit! / Bird thou *never* wert' in 'To a Skylark', or the sequence of negatives used to approximate the nature of Emilia and of Shelley's reaction to her in *Epipsychidion*. Sometimes it is a drastic reversal of our expectations as, for example, in *Adonais*: 'Peace, peace! he is not dead, he doth not sleep'.

\* \* \*

\* \* \* It would seem . . . that Shelley's fascination with the negative arose out of a necessity of his own imagination or temperament; its use is sufficiently widespread, consistent, and peculiar to Shelley to suggest that it is more than a stylistic device or a flourish of the vocabulary or an irritating *tic* inherited from the eighteenth century. If we examine it carefully, it may lead us to the very centre of his thinking and illuminate areas of his work which have been neglected or inadequately understood.

Since the negative is most richly represented in *Prometheus Unbound* and since this is arguably his most complex and ambitious work, it should provide a suitable case for scrutiny. How, then, does the negative function in *Prometheus Unbound*? How does the high proportion of negative adjectives relate to the revolutionary structure of that play? And what does it reveal about Shelley's political views and what about his metaphysics? Any approach to answering these questions must be based on the recognition that the play acknowledges more than one variety of negative and that the validity of its moral and political content depends on our ability to discriminate between them and to disentangle their connections. To begin with: Jupiter is close to Blake's Nobodaddy or Urizen; he is the lord of repressive rule, of restrictive commandments. The decalogue, with which Jupiter as Je-

hovah is associated, is a supremely negative expression of religious
values ('Thou shalt Not . . .'). Jupiter denies the natural instincts of
humanity; he betrays man into nihilistic cynicism—

> . . . that common, false, cold, hollow talk
> Which makes the heart deny the *yes* it breathes,
> Yet question that *unmeant* hypocrisy
> With such a self-mistrust as has *no* name.   (III, iv, 149–52)

If Joyce's Molly Bloom represents the life-force and her characteristic
word is *yes*, Shelley's Jupiter seduces men into saying *no*, to their own
confusion and despair.

The bleak scene into which we are introduced in the opening speech
is the world as dominated by this life-denying Jupiter—a world of negatives. To his slaves and worshippers the rule of Jupiter is manifested
as fear and self-contempt and barren hope; for the defiant Prometheus
it takes the form of

> Three thousand years of *sleep-unsheltered* hours,
> And moments aye divided by keen pangs
> Till they seemed years, torture and solitude,
> Scorn and despair . . .                    (I, 12–15)

This physical and mental suffering is graphically bodied forth and objectified by the geography of despair, in which Prometheus is 'Nailed
to this wall of eagle-baffling mountain,/Black, wintry, dead, *unmeasured; without* herb,/Insect, or beast, or shape or sound of life' (I, 20–
2). The relentless sequence of adjectives ('Black, wintry, dead, *unmeasured*') corresponds, one might think, to the painful hammer-blows by
which Prometheus is nailed to his precipice, while suggesting the
blank hopelessness of this world of deprivation. Jupiter's world defines
itself partly through absences—it is *without* the normal signs of life in
plant, insect or animal, 'to one void mass battering and blending' all
the productions of the earth (IV, 343). It is a world of disease and
death, based on a cycle of 'unseasonable seasons' (II, iv, 52), without
form or colour or the variety of sounds which are associated with animation and activity. It is not unlike Milton's

> Universe of death, which God by curse
> Created evil, for evil onely good,
> Where all life dies, death lives, and Nature breeds,
> Perverse, all monstrous, all prodigious things . . .
>                         (*Paradise Lost*, II, 622–25)

Like the world in which Milton's Satan finds himself, Jupiter's realm
is also the product of a curse; like Satan, Prometheus is faced by a
world whose most terrifying property is its vertiginous sense of endlessness both in space and in time.

So potent is the threat of endlessness that Prometheus even employs
it against his own persecutor when he consigns Jupiter to a 'lagging
fall through *boundless* space and time' (though Prometheus is out of
order in cursing the tyrant, Jupiter does eventually meet an appropriate

fate in a 'shoreless sea', a 'bottomless void').[1] Before his regeneration
has taught him to see things differently, Prometheus is himself vulnerable to this powerful threat. Time is cruelly slow (the hours are
'wingless', 'sleep-unsheltered' and 'slumberless') so that Prometheus laments that there is 'no Hope' and that his only prospect is 'pain, pain
ever, forever'; while the horror of seemingly endless space is manifested in the eagle-baffling mountain, which Prometheus sees as 'unmeasured'.[2] Unmeasured is particularly powerful because it implies the
insignificance of life and hope against the towering negation which is
Jupiter, here represented by the stern rock-face of the Caucasus. Mercury who acts as agent for Jupiter plays on this fear when he reminds
Prometheus that continued defiance will have the most terrifying consequences:

> Yet pause, and plunge
> Into eternity, where recorded time,
> Even all that we imagine, age on age,
> Seems but a point, and the reluctant mind
> Flags wearily in its *unending* flight,
> Till it sink, dizzy, blind, lost, *shelterless*;
> Perchance it has *not numbered* the slow years
> Which thou must spend in torture, *unreprieved*.    (I, 416–23)

These lines demonstrate Shelley's ability to concretize the abstract
processes of time but they also show Mercury pressurizing Prometheus
to acquiesce in the world of negation by an insistence on its very
negativity. *Unending, shelterless, unreprieved*, are forcefully deployed
but Prometheus rejects the temptation through his own negative, the
negative of heroic resistance: 'I *would not quit*/This bleak ravine, these
*unrepentant* pains' (matching Mercury's Miltonic *unreprieved* with the
equally Miltonic *unrepentant*).

Throughout the first act, we inhabit a world of negation, a world
which, as the imagery suggests, is endlessly empty. Emptiness and
hollowness are everywhere: Jupiter's ministers, the Furies, are 'hollow
underneath, like death' while even Heaven itself is 'hollow'.[3] Recognizing this, Prometheus anticipates the fall of Jupiter in terms which
appropriately suggest his emptiness and the means he employs to ter-
rify others:

> What Ruin
> Will hunt thee *undefended* through wide Heaven!
> How will thy soul, cloven to its depth with terror
> Gape like a hell within!    (I, 53–6)

1. III, i, 74, 76.
2. The adjective can be traced back to Aeschylus, where its implications are rather different.
   In his appeal to the elements, Prometheus invokes ποντιων τε κυματων / ἀνεϱιθμον
   γελασμα [pontion te kumaton / anerithmon gelasma] (89–90) (the unnumbered laughter of
   the waves of the sea); here, the emphasis is on the power and beauty of the natural world,
   with which Prometheus allies himself. Milton's geography may also have some relevance,
   particularly *the vast immeasurable Abyss* (Paradise Lost, VII, 211).
3. I, 442, 108, 478. Cf. Paradise Lost, I, 314, II, 518, 953.

When Jupiter does fall, the Universe rejoices in lines which powerfully
evoke the force of nothingness:

> How art thou sunk, withdrawn, covered—drunk up
> By thirsty *nothing*, as the brackish cup
> Drained by a desert troop, a little drop for all!
> And from beneath, around, within, above,
> Filling thy *void annihilation*, Love
> Bursts in like light on caves cloven by the thunder-ball:
> (IV, 350–5)

The power of Jupiter is based on emptiness, he is himself a negation;
therefore, it is entirely appropriate that he should be consumed by
nothing. But Shelley discriminates here between the active force of
*thirsty nothing* (associated with Demogorgon) which consumes Jupiter,
and the *void annihilation*, the vacuum he leaves behind.

Yet, if Jupiter is a negation, he is none the less potent for that. Like
a minus quantity in mathematics, he is a force to be reckoned with, a
tangible influence on human behaviour. If Jupiter is dependent for his
existence on the collaboration of Prometheus, on *our* collaboration, he
represents all the same a real temptation and a dangerous tendency
of the mind. Shelley suggests at least two ways in which we can allow
Jupiter to impose himself on us. First, there is the curse. This is no
mere Gothic device but is invested with some of the solemnity of the
operatic curse and the profound moral consequence of the curse in
Greek tragedy (as, for example, in the Oresteian trilogy). To curse is
to give verbal expression to hate; it is to employ the negative powers
of language to achieve a tangible and injurious effect. It is to deny the
creative powers of language (that 'perpetual Orphic song') and to pervert them to destructive ends. The curse not only belongs to Jupiter's
world; it is an expression of that all-miscreative divinity, whose 'strong
hate' transforms every blade and blossom produced by the earth into
a 'lifeless mire' (IV, 349). Near the end of the play we discover that
Jupiter is not only cursed and cursing but that he is the incarnation
of the curse ('Sceptred Curse,/Who all our green and azure universe/
Threatendst to muffle round with black destruction').[4] The instinctive
and unthinking reaction of Prometheus had been to curse Jupiter; by
doing so, he immediately identified himself with the tyrant and temporarily lost his own independence. Shelley suggests this unhealthy
identification both through the syntax of the opening speech and
through the ironic device of calling up the Phantasm of Jupiter to
repeat the curse which was directed at himself. This is a strange conjunction between the tyrant and the revolutionary but a psychologically
compelling one, which Blake also recognized. By cursing Jupiter, Prometheus has in some sense collaborated in his world of negation. The
extent of the consequences is made clear in a long and vivid report by
the Earth, in which she describes the change in her condition after

4. IV, 338–40.

Prometheus has uttered his curse. She makes it clear, too, that following the contagious example of her son Prometheus she has been guilty of hatred; thus, she has submitted herself to the rule and influence of Jupiter and has collaborated in cursing herself.

Second, through the agency of the Furies, Jupiter offers the temptation to despair. By presenting Prometheus with carefully edited extracts designed to illustrate the futility of history and the vanity of human wishes, the Furies attempt to reconcile him with his torturer. The temptation is at its most compelling in this sombre catalogue presented by the final Fury:

> They *dare not* devise good for man's estate,
> And yet they *know not* that they *do not dare*.
> The good want power, but to weep barren tears;
> The powerful goodness want—worse need for them;
> The wise want love; and those who love want wisdom;
> And all best things are thus confused to ill.
> Many are strong and rich, and would be just,
> But live among their suffering fellow-men
> As if *none felt*; they *know not* what they do.   (I, 623–31)

Here the failure of reform is presented as a *fait accompli*: the moral and political negative, it is suggested, is eternal and unchanging. The insidiousness of this temptation is based on the fact that what the Fury tells Prometheus is, in a sense, true; Prometheus acknowledges this but he does not accept the implied conclusion, that there is nothing which can be done to remedy the situation. The temptation here is nothing less than despair—the refusal to believe that we can ever escape from the negative conditions imposed by Jupiter (or, if you prefer, that man and society can ever become any better). The shrewdest and most telling touch is the final phrase ('they *know not* what they do'). These are the words of Christ who, in the supreme act of forgiveness, asked for pardon for his executioners; but where Christ had spoken in the spirit of charitable forgiveness, the Fury suggests that human incapacity is such that even the well-intentioned are inevitably frustrated and diverted from their goals. So the message of charity becomes the insinuating whisper of despair; far from being a pretext for forgiveness, 'they know not what they do' becomes an imprisoning negative. Were Prometheus to accept it, he would be guilty of a cynical disbelief in human capacity.

This failure of nerve is possible even for the tender-hearted and those to whom the miseries of the world are misery and will not let them rest. This was one of the lessons of the French Revolution, as Shelley noted in the preface to *The Revolt of Islam*:

> many of the most ardent and tender-hearted of the worshippers of public good have been morally ruined by what a partial glimpse of the events they deplored appeared to show as the melancholy desolation of all their cherished hopes. Hence gloom and misanthropy have become the characteristics of the age in which we

live, the solace of a disappointment that unconsciously finds relief
only in the wilful exaggeration of its own despair.

(Hutchinson, *Poetical Works*, 33)

Indeed, the Fury seems to imply, those of sympathetic disposition may
be particularly vulnerable because of their very sensitivity: 'The good
want power, but to weep barren tears'.

This idea is developed in a striking passage where, having described
the architectural remains of the old way of life, the Spirit of the Hour
goes on to explore its implications—the fall of the old nexus of power
which bound together Church and State:

> And those foul shapes, abhorred by God and man—
> Which, under many a name and many a form,
> Strange, savage, ghastly, dark and execrable,
> Were Jupiter, the tyrant of the world;
> And which the nations, panic-stricken, served
> With blood, and hearts broken by long hope, and love
> Dragged to his altars soiled and *garlandless*,
> And slain amid men's *unreclaiming* tears,
> Flattering the thing they feared, which fear was hate—
> Frown, mouldering fast, o'er their abandoned shrines.
>
> (III, iv, 180–9)

\* \* \*

Unreclaiming tears are not only tears of cowardice and moral weakness but unpractical tears, tears which reject the possibilities of redemption which are open to humankind (or, to be more specific, to
England in the year 1819). Since Jupiter has only reigned by the consent of man, love can still be rescued from the altar of sacrifice and
human society can still be redeemed. Of course, in the passage in
question *unreclaiming tears* are *not* a part of the new society; they are
recalled as one of the features of the old *régime* presided over by Jupiter. Nonetheless, it is part of Shelley's moral purpose that so vividly
realized a negative should appear in a passage which joyfully celebrates
the Promethean revolution. Shelley (or the Spirit of the Hour) does
not want his readers to forget all those dark forces which threaten the
establishment of a better society, a reformed government, a fertility
based on reclamation. As Shelley was only too well aware, England in
1819 was still a country in which the people were 'starved and stabbed
on the *untilled* field'.[5] The present danger from *unreclaiming tears* is
subtly underlined by the use of the present participle: such tears are
unproductive now, as they always have been.

Jupiter, then, is associated with negation; he represents a variety of
temptations all of which may be summed up under another of Shelley's
favourite words, *self-contempt*, the failure to acknowledge or pursue
our own best possibilities. Prometheus feels the force of these temptations; in the past, he has even been guilty of hatred in cursing Ju-

5. 'England in 1819', line 7. The MS has *on* in place of the received *in*.

piter. Now he resists by practising the positive virtues of patience, hope and love. His resistance and the eventual overthrow of Jupiter involve another set of negatives whose implications are directly opposed to the negatives associated with Jupiter. These negatives cancel or reverse the negative conditions of Jupiter's kingdom.

First, and most obviously, there is the negative of defiance embodied in the title *Prometheus Unbound*: this refusal to endorse the reigning tyranny in religious matters stems from Shelley's own revolutionary *a-theism* which, if we are to believe Trelawny, he took up 'as a knight took up a gauntlet, in defiance of injustice'.[6] In the play, the defiance is directed not only at Jupiter but also perhaps at Aeschylus who failed to rescue Prometheus to Shelley's moral satisfaction: 'The moral interest of the fable, which is powerfully sustained by the sufferings and endurance of Prometheus, would be annihilated if we could conceive of him as *unsaying* his high language and quailing before his successful and perfidious adversary.' Here, Milton's influence can be detected behind the heroic recoil from *unsaying* his high language,[7] while in *Prometheus Unbound* itself the negative of defiance has a strong Miltonic ring in phrases like *these unrepentant pains*. This negative is associated not only with defiance but with a refusal to give in to threats or torture: in spite of all that Jupiter can do to him, Prometheus will not break down—his eyes remain *tearless*, his head is *undeclining*, he is *the Invincible*.[8]

Second, there are the negatives which proclaim the success of the revolution:

> The painted veil, by those who were called life,
> Which mimicked, as with colours idly spread,
> All men believed or hoped, is torn aside;
> The loathsome mask has fallen, the man remains
> *Sceptreless*, free, *uncircumscribed*—but man:
> Equal, *unclassed*, *tribeless* and *nationless*;
> Exempt from awe, worship, degree; the king
> Over himself; just, gentle, wise—but man . . .    (III, iv, 190–7)

*Sceptreless*, *uncircumscribed*, *unclassed*, *tribeless*, *nationless* and (to extend the category beyond adjectives with negative prefixes or suffixes) *Exempt from awe, worship, degree*; here as in most evocations of the ideal society, much of the emphasis is placed upon what it is not.[9] The *unJupitered* world is a free and equal society because it is able to dispense with those limiting conditions which have marked the reign of the tyrant: the negatives in this category are the negatives of liberation. Here Shelley is concerned with morals (or politics, if one

---

6. *Records of Shelley, Byron, and the Author* (1878), ed. David Wright (1973), 107.
7. 'How soon/Would highth recall high thoughts, how soon unsay' (*Paradise Lost*, IV, 94–5).
8. I, 636, 281, 536.
9. See, for example, this description of America in *A Philosophical View of Reform*:

    It has no King, that is it has no officer to whom wealth & from whom corruption flows. It has no hereditary oligarchy, that is it acknowledges no order of men priveledged to cheat & insult the rest of the members of the state . . . It has no established Church . . . (SC, VI, p. 975 (with spelling of *priviledged* adjusted).

prefers, since for Shelley politics were the morals of the nations); elsewhere in the third and fourth acts he indicates that the
moral regeneration of man has been mirrored in the natural world.
For instance, Ocean prophesies that 'Henceforth the fields of heaven-
reflecting sea/Which are my realm, will heave, *unstained* with blood,/
Beneath the uplifting winds, like plains of corn/Swayed by the summer
air . . .' (II, ii, 18–21). Here the reference is to naval battles, to the
wretched conditions in the Navy which had led to recent mutinies,
and to slavery (as in Turner's dramatic painting 'Slavers throwing over-
board the dead and dying—Typhon coming on'); this is replaced by a
harmonious natural world, with hints of the reappearance of Atlantis
and the reclamation of land from the sea. Not only is nature '*untainted*
by man's misery' as in 'Rarely, rarely comest thou' but, it is implied,
nature itself is regenerated. The sea is no longer a threat to man, and
the ice and snow of the opening setting are gradually melted by the
growing warmth of the revolutionary day. Paradise, in fact, is regained
and the usual paradisal weather conditions prevail. Shelley had already
rehearsed this scene at some length in *Queen Mab* and *The Daemon
of the World*.[1] Here the sky is *unpavilioned* (that is, cloudless), the
pool by the temple of Prometheus is *windless*, the waves are *unerasing*.[2]

So far this is easily understood; but is Shelley offering anything more
than a simple series of reversals? Is H. N. Brailsford right when he
complains: 'There is something amiss with an ideal which is constrained to express itself in negatives. What should be the climax of a
triumphant argument becomes its refutation'?[3] One answer to this criticism is that Shelley's negatives are more various than Brailsford would
allow. In addition to the negatives of reversal and liberation, the final
speech of the third act finds space for cautionary and restraining negatives (*but man; Passionless? no; Nor yet exempt*) and for the ironical
negatives which record the irrelevance of the monuments of ancient
religion, the *ghosts of a no-more-remembered fame*, with their *unworn*
obelisks, . . . /*not o'erthrown*, but *unregarded* now.

A second and irresistibly potent answer is provided by the last act,
which had not been part of Shelley's original design. Had he brought
his play to a finish at the end of the third act, it might have suffered
from its concentration on the overthrow of Jupiter and its negative
formulation of the new society; but the final act embodies through the
animation of delight not only a new society but a regenerated universe,
a universe from which the curse of tyranny has been lifted. This new
heaven and earth manifests itself, for the most part, not through the
mediation of negatives but through joyful self-expression:

> The joy, the triumph, the delight, the madness!
> The boundless, overflowing, bursting gladness!
> The vaporous exultation not to be confined!
>                                   (IV, 319–21)

---

1. VIII, 58ff.; II, 339ff.
2. IV, 184; II, iii, 159–60; cf. *unwithering hues* (III, iii, 102).
3. H. N. Brailsford, *Shelley, Godwin, and their Circle* (1919 edn), 241–2.

The energy of this celebration marks a new freedom from the cramps and restraints of tyranny; the emphatically affirmative note which dominates the play after the fall of Jupiter must be seen as a direct response to the negativity which Jupiter had once tried to impose. In the third act the new world is defined by the use of negatives to show what it is not, as well as by positive expressions to show what it is; in the final act Shelley almost shakes himself clear from negatives, though the very fervour of the affirmation acknowledges the difficulty of the struggle which has just resolved itself so triumphantly.

And the new liberation offers a new perspective. From this vantage point we can begin to see that the world of negation is not perhaps so substantial as we had supposed. As we have seen already, the restrictions imposed by Jupiter can be abolished by the application of negatives (*sceptreless, throneless, uncircumscribed*). But there is a sense in which many of the negatives associated with Jupiter can and should be recognized as potentially positive: they do not need to be removed or abolished but rather to be reinterpreted. For example, the mountain associated with Jupiter is 'Black, wintry, dead, *unmeasured*' but in the joyful final act *unmeasured* is introduced again in one of the ironic reversals in which Shelley delights. In this case the regenerated universe is celebrating its liberty; while at the beginning of the play it can do no more than cry 'Misery', now freed from the curse of Jupiter it can 'Laugh with a vast and *inextinguishable* laughter' (like the Greek gods as Homer unforgettably described them).[4] Among the celebrators are 'the abysses/Of the deep air's *unmeasured* wildernesses';[5] thus, when *unmeasured* ceases to be a threat and becomes a potentiality, one of Jupiter's most formidable properties is taken from him and regenerated. *Wildernesses*, too, are suggestive here of infinite potentiality, that free range of possibility which is available to the human mind when it has liberated itself from the shadow of the darker forces; the Fourth Spirit had hinted at such creative possibilities in its picture of the Poet feeding on the kisses of 'shapes that haunt thought's wilderness' but, so long as man fell under the distorting influence of Jupiter's permitted tyranny, wildernesses would more obviously have represented one of the threatening aspects of endless, bottomless, unwelcoming space. If space is redeemed from fear, so too is the element of time: if Jupiter depends for his power on the threat of eternity 'where the reluctant mind/Flags wearily in its *unending* flight', Demogorgon the redeemer announces himself to Jupiter in the character of Eternity.

Jupiter's world is chaotic. Under his jurisdiction, '*shapeless* sights come wandering by,/The ghastly people of the realm of dream/Mocking me';[6] presumably these shapeless mockers can be identified with his ministers, the Furies, who are '*shapeless* as our mother Night'.[7]

4. I, 107–11; IV, 334. For Shelley and the laughter of the Greek gods see my "Shelley and the Religion of Joy," *Studies in Romanticism*, xv (1976), 357–82.
5. IV, 335–6.
6. I, 36–38.
7. I, 472.

Jupiter's world is also a world of emptiness and absences (the Furies are 'Hollow underneath, like death'). Ultimately and ironically, he and his ministers are defeated through the agency of Demogorgon, who bears an interesting resemblance to them. He is '*Ungazed upon and shapeless*', he is 'A mighty Darkness/Filling the seat of power', he is *unbodied*, he can be found in 'the grey, void abysm/ . . . Where the air is *no prism*' (that is, a world devoid of light and colour).[8] Jupiter himself is mistaken in Demogorgon, only realizing at the last moment that this *tremendous Gloom* is not his ally but his executioner.

This is perhaps the moral pivot of the whole play and it is based very largely on the use of negatives. On first examination, it might appear that Jupiter and Demogorgon both share in a world of negations and absences; it is part of the play's ironical purpose that this resemblance should be so close. Jupiter, who is the emanation of nothing, is finally devoured by a power which has '*neither limb,/Nor form, nor outline*'.[9] Nothing returns to nothing. Yet Shelley insists that we distinguish between Jupiter and Demogorgon, that we learn to peer through the darkness until we recognize that Demogorgon is 'A living spirit'. Everything depends on the observer: it is, if you like, a question of epistemology. The darkness may be the darkness of negation, of winter, of death; on the other hand, it may be the matrix of potentiality, the cradle of possibility, the rich seedbed of the future. If Jupiter the all-miscreative is associated with the shapelessness of chaos, Demogorgon is associated with the shapelessness that can be ordered and organized by the human mind: 'Language is a perpetual Orphic song,/ Which rules with daedal harmony a throng/Of thoughts and forms, which else *senseless* and *shapeless* were' (IV, 415–17). If Jupiter represents the darkness of the grave, Demogorgon inhabits the '*lampless* caves of *unimagined* being' (IV, 378), an address whose powerful pair of negatives suggests its unmeasured potentiality. Eternity is not a threat but an open promise.

The close resemblance between Jupiter and Demogorgon is crucial since it helps to show that potentiality can be potentiality either for good or for evil. Mercury threatens Prometheus with the prospect of 'the strange might of *unimagined* pains' (I, 366); *unimagined*, which elsewhere marks the almost unlimited potentialities for self-improvement, here represents another facet of the punitive endlessness of Jupiter's world. So, when the Furies call their confederates to assist in the temptation of Prometheus with their macabre visions of history, they encourage them to 'Leave the self-contempt implanted/In young spirits, sense-enchanted,/Misery's yet *unkindled* fuel' (I, 510–12): the image of the burning spark beneath the ashes, so characteristic of Shelley's optimism, here is used to suggest the untapped potentialities of evil. These powerful auxiliaries are also enjoined to 'Leave Hell's secrets *half-unchanted*/To the maniac dreamer' (I, 513–14): *unchanted* is Shelley's invention and indicates not only that the Furies must re-

8. II, iv, 5; II, iv, 2–3; III, i, 44; II, iii, 72–4.
9. II, iv, 5–6.

linquish their torturing practices (*half-chanted* would convey that meaning) but that Hell's secrets offer a great reservoir of possibility which has not been exhausted. Thus, when Prometheus has endured the spectacle of the crucifixion and the wars of religion which have perverted the positive teaching of Christ so that he has become a Jupiter ('Thy name I will not speak;/It hath become a curse.' (I, 603–4)), the Fury sums up with ominous calm: 'Blood thou canst see, and fire; and canst hear groans:/Worse things *unheard, unseen*, remain behind.' (I, 616–17). Evil, it would seem, is a potentiality which can be infinitely developed. In *The Cenci* Shelley does indicate how 'Evil minds/Change good to their own nature' but in *Prometheus Unbound* he is more concerned to assert the power of the human will, together with the shaping influence of love, to defy evil and to escape the dark corridors of despair. The emphasis is on the positive but the first act demonstrates in detail and the last act pointedly reminds us that the void's loose field, the free range of Promethean man, is the other side of a universe which is built over the void abysm and the deep gulf of man's capacity for evil.

Man's potential for evil is embodied in Jupiter; his potential for goodness is associated with Demogorgon, who so closely resembles the tyrant. Originally, the name of Demogorgon was derived from a scribal error in copying the word *Demiourgos*;[1] Shelley's Demogorgon is not a creator but he is associated with the creative possibilities of human existence. 'In the world *unknown*/Sleeps a voice *unspoken*' (II, i, 190–1): Demogorgon is not only an oracle to be consulted but an unrealized potential to be recognized, respected and made actual. Together Prometheus and Asia initiate the sequence of events by which Demogorgon eventually removes Jupiter from his throne and consigns him to void annihilation. Demogorgon is closely connected with the '*voiceless and invisible* Consequence' of the Aeschylus fragment which Shelley translated. He is a result not a precondition of human action. Potentiality must be activated, set in motion: without the intervention of Asia and Prometheus, Demogorgon would be '*unremoved*' from the lampless caves of unimagined being.[2]

Man can liberate himself from the tyranny of history through the exercise of love, hope, patience and the other Shelleyan virtues: as Shelley was to suggest in the 'Ode to Liberty' a few months after he finished *Prometheus Unbound*, the positive achievements of the past remain endlessly potential ('and for ever/It trembles, but it cannot pass away!'). Thus, the Spirits of the human mind announce their arrival with a negative which embodies the enduring potential of the past:

> From *unremembered ages* we
> Gentle guides and guardians be
> Of Heaven-oppressed mortality . . .   (I, 672–4).

1. Introduced in the scholia on Statius, Demogorgon is 'a ghost-word which owes its existence to a slip of the pen' (R. Pfeiffer, *History of Classical Scholarship from 1300 to 1850* (1976), 21–2).
2. IV, 380; cf. *Paradise Lost*, IV, 987 ('Like *Teneriff* or *Atlas* unremov'd').

Shelley's *unremembered* may owe a debt to Wordsworth, who uses it twice within four lines in *Tintern Abbey*:

> . . . feelings too
> Of *unremembered* pleasure: such, perhaps,
> As have no slight or trivial influence
> On that best portion of a good man's life,
> His little, nameless, *unremembered* acts
> Of kindness and of love.          (30–5)

Like Wordsworth, Shelley acknowledges that the unrecognized pressure of the past may shape our actions in the present, even though we are unconscious of its influence; but whereas Wordsworth is primarily concerned with the individual, Shelley is concerned with humankind as a whole. Shelley's concept seems to have something in common with Jung's collective unconscious but it seems to involve also a creative connection with all that is best in human experience.

In their rôle as guardians, the Spirits perform a function which aligns them with the angels of Christianity or with Neo-Platonic daemons; but, though they do not succumb to the infections of human thought, their potency is limited by such weaknesses and it is not till the final act that they fully collaborate in the achievement of man's Promethean potentiality. Here man's capacity makes him lord not only of himself but also of the natural world, which in a sense provides an external reflection of his own inner condition. After the change has taken place, Panthea has a vision of nature which reveals the evolutionary graph of historical development and suggests the infinite potentiality of the earth itself. In place of *Hell's secrets* which the Furies had chanted to the maniac dreamer, Panthea now celebrates

> . . . the secrets of the earth's deep heart—
> Infinite mines of adamant and gold,
> *Valueless* stones, and *unimagined* gems . . .   (IV, 279–81)

(*valueless* meaning without value, a usage attributed to Shelley by the *Oxford English Dictionary*). Among the catalogue of nature's wonders Panthea also mentions 'Wells of *unfathomed* fire':[3] both the vindictive flames of the underworld and their boundless extent are here transformed into a positive image of Promethean import.

So, if man follows the example of Prometheus, he can become master of the universe and assume control over his own history. The key to mastery lies in the recognition of the potential. This emphasis on potentiality is characteristic of Shelley and links *Prometheus Unbound* to many of his other works, where it is often discovered, with a negative prefix. In 'Stanzas Written in Dejection', for example, 'The breath of the moist earth is light/Around its *unexpanded* buds': before Shelley

---

3. *Unfathomed* makes a notable appearance in Gray's *Elegy*, which offers an extensive exploration of potentiality: 'full many a gem of purest ray serene,/The dark unfathom'd caves of ocean bear:/Full many a flower is born to blush unseen,/And waste its sweetness on the desert air' (53–6). Gray also offers a counterpoint to Shelley in his use of *unseen*.

*unexpanded* was essentially a technical word,[4] but here it carries an almost magical sense of the possibilities of growth hidden in the fecund darkness under the earth. In 'Ode to the West Wind' the *unawakened earth* and the *unextinguished hearth* both suggest the possibilities of resurrection behind the image of apparent decay and death. Indeed, 'Ode to the West Wind' is an interesting analogy to *Prometheus Unbound* since in both poems we are asked to confront the seeming darkness and to descry in it the sparks of life and hope. Again, in the *Defence of Poetry* we read of *an unforeseen and an unconceived delight*,[5] just as in *Prometheus Unbound* we are told of 'arts, though *unimagined*, yet to be' (III, iii, 56).

\* \* \*

Like the poet's creations [I, 740–6], like the glorious manifestations of Prometheus and Asia [II, i, 79–82; II, v, 48ff.], the journey to Demogorgon involves the transcendence of materiality. Although the approach is made through negatives the experience is permeated by implications which are elusive and intangible but strongly positive. So Panthea attempts to describe Demogorgon in a vivid sequence of negatives and achieves as a result the adumbration of something beyond definition:

> I see a mighty Darkness
> Filling the seat of power; and rays of gloom
> Dart round, as light from the meridian sun,
> *Ungazed upon and shapeless—neither limb*,
> *Nor form, nor outline*; yet we feel it is
> A living Spirit.                    (II, iv, 2–7)

As some previous readers have noticed, this draws on Milton's accounts both of the shapelessness of Death (*Paradise Lost*, II, 666–7) and of the paradoxical radiance of his God, 'Dark with excessive bright' (III, 380). It is obviously also a development of Milton's evocation of Hell—'No light, but rather darkness visible'—but, unlike Milton, Shelley wants us to see the darkness as richly potential.

What links together all these passages concerning Demogorgon, Asia and Prometheus is a sense of the limitations of phenomenal experience and an implicit awareness of the inadequacy of language. Both theologians and mystics have always acknowledged these obstacles to comprehension and to communication. Consider, for example, this passage from Plato's *Symposium* in Shelley's own translation:

> It is eternal, unproduced, indestructible: neither subject to encrease or decay: not, like other things, partly beautiful and partly deformed; not at one time beautiful and at another time not; not

---

4. 'So every foetus bears a secret hoard,/With sleeping unexpanded issue stor'd (Blackmore, *Creation* (1712), VI, 290). The *Oxford English Dictionary* cites another example from Withering's *British Plants* (1796) as well as a seventeeth-century passage which refers to unexpanded air.
5. *The Prose Works of Percy Bysshe Shelley*, Volume I, ed. E. B. Murray (1993), p. 291.

beautiful in relation to one thing and deformed in relation to another; not here beautiful and there deformed; not beautiful in the estimation of one person and deformed in that of another; nor can this supreme beauty be figured to the imagination like a beautiful face or beautiful hands or any portion of the body, nor like any discourse or any science. Nor does it subsist in any other thing that lives or is, either in earth or in heaven, or in any other place: but it is eternally uniform and consistent and monoeidic with itself.[6]

Or consider this statement from Thomas Aquinas: 'Because we cannot know what God is, but rather what God is not, our method has to be merely negative . . . What kind of being God is not can be known by eliminating characteristics which we cannot apply to him, like composition, change, and so forth.'[7] That Shelley recognized this means of defining the undefinable is shown by a passage in 'On Christianity' where he says, 'The universal being can only be described or defined by negatives, which deny his subjection to the laws of all inferior existences. Where indefiniteness ends idolatry and anthropomorphism begin.'[8] *Prometheus Unbound* comes close to the practice of Plato and to the theory of Aquinas. As a whole the play creates an ambience which is undeniably positive yet Shelley also insists on the difficulty of definition, the problems of communication, the cramping boundaries of language. *Prometheus Unbound* emphasizes the intricacies of communication and it is not surprising to find Shelley using negatives such as *unimaginable, tongueless, inarticulate, uncommunicating* and *wordless*.[9] Most important of all, Demogorgon informs us that 'the deep truth is *imageless*' (II, iv, 116). This is not a sceptical cry of despair which absolves the poet from responsibility. There are transcendent realities which cannot be expressed directly but which we must try to approach, not least through the assistance of negatives. The *via negativa* is the road not of despair but of hope.

The negative, then, often indicates not only a negative negated but an energy unquenched or a potential not realized, perhaps not even recognized. It is easy to mistake this kind of negative for the negative of deprivation, of limitation, of denial, associated with Jupiter. The task which Shelley sets before us is that of discovering that so many apparent negatives are really positives, that if we peel away the veil of seeming negativity we will find the potentiality slumbering within.[1] Here Shelley imposes a moral burden on his readers and his interpreters. He recognizes how easy it is to mistake one kind of darkness

---

6. James A. Notopoulos, *The Platonism of Shelley: A Study of Platonism and the Poetic Mind* (1949), p. 449 (corrected).
7. *Summa Theologica*, 1a, 3, prologue; cited from F. C. Copleston, *Aquinas* (Harmondworth, repr. ed., 1961), p. 126.
8. *Prose*, 252.
9. IV, 244; I, 107; I, 183; III, iii, 112; II, i, 52. In his other works Shelley extended the range of *expressionless, speechless* and *voiceless.*
1. For Shelley's use of this image, see T. Webb, *Shelley: A Voice Not Understood* (1977), 25–58. For a pioneering study of potentiality, see D. J. Hughes, "Potentiality in *Prometheus Unbound*," reprinted in *Shelley: Modern Judgements*, ed. R. B. Woodings (1969), 142–61.

for the other—as he puts it in *The Mask of Anarchy*, 'And her name was Hope, she said:/But she looked more like Despair'. He knew that one of the temptations facing reformers after the apparent failure of the French Revolution was to surrender their ideals; like Prometheus, they had to learn to 'hope, till hope creates/From its own wreck the thing it contemplates'. This difficulty in assessing the true meaning of negatives, in recognizing that the conditions imposed by Jupiter need only be temporary and not the permanent setting for human existence, may help to explain Shelley's use of the oracular imagery in *Prometheus Unbound*. Oracles, he suggests, can be deceptive; or rather, we can project our own wishes on to what they tell us. Oracles, like negatives, are ambiguous and must be handled with care. Ultimately the responsibility rests with us:

> So much I asked before, and my heart gave
> The response thou hast given; and of such truths
> Each to itself must be the oracle.   (II, iv, 121–3)

Perhaps that is why, even after the revolution, the chariot belonging to the Spirit of the Hour bears a yoke in the form of an amphisbaenic snake. According to legend, the amphisbaena was a snake with a head at each end, which was capable of moving in either direction. Although Shelley had in mind here a specific statue which he had seen in the Vatican,[2] the choice of statue was not an idle one and the amphisbaena is not a decorative excrescence. This mysterious snake had already made its appearance in *The Revolt of Islam* in a scene of Gothic horror (VIII, xxi) where it might be exchanged for any other snake of challenging proportions; but in *Prometheus Unbound* its appearance is entirely appropriate to Shelley's moral purpose. Whether we enact and perpetuate a Promethean revolution depends on us; we have the opportunity to move in either direction. This can be related to the fact that Asia sees two chariots before the fall of Jupiter; one is the chariot of violent revolution while the other is associated with a more peaceful exchange of power. Or again it can be related to the ambivalence of Demogorgon himself—Demogorgon may be a monster symbolizing the repressed and threatening energies of the people,[3] or he may be a force for good who is identified with Asia. The ambiguity reflects a real dilemma. Shelley saw his contemporaries as poised between the insinuating whispers of the Furies and the inspiring intimations of the Spirits, balanced on a knife-edge not only between despair and hope but also between despotism and revolution:

> These . . . are awful times. The tremendous question is now agitating, whether a military or judicial despotism is to be established by our present rulers, or some form of government less

---

2. D. H. Reiman, "Roman Scenes in *Prometheus Unbound* III, iv" in *Philological Q.*, XLVI (1967), 69–78.
3. ". . . it is impossible that the combination δεμος-γοργώ [*dēmos-gorgo*] did not commend itself as one reason for the choice of name" (G. Matthews, "A Volcano's Voice in Shelley," reprinted in Woodings, *op. cit.*, 187).

unfavourable to the real and permanent interests of all men is to arise from the conflict of passions now gathering to overturn them.  (*Letters*, II, 148; 3 November 1819)

Shelley insists on the moral responsibility and on the importance of avoiding complacency or apathy. That perhaps is why he presents the scene of Iphigenia's sacrifice so brutally and with such strong negative accompaniments even in the moment of triumph. That, too, may be what he had in mind in these lines addressed to Prometheus by the Earth, in which she describes his temple which stood in the Academy at Athens:

> It is deserted now, but once it bore
> Thy name, Prometheus; there the emulous youths
> Bore to thy honour through the divine gloom
> The lamp which was thine emblem—even as those
> Who bear the *untransmitted* torch of hope
> Into the grave, across the night of life . . .   (III, iii, 167–72)

The imagery here deserves careful scrutiny. During their great festivals it was the custom of the Greeks to run relay races through the city streets in which, instead of a baton, the runners handed on a lighted torch; in order to win, a team had to keep its torch alight to the end of the race.[4] One of the most popular of these Greek festivals was the one held at Athens in honour of the fire gods, when a race was run from the altar of Prometheus to the city.  * * *

Where Shelley differs from this classical tradition is in his insistence that the race of life is not a team effort. Though the prowess and example of others may be inspiring and though we may encourage each other to greater efforts (the youths are *emulous* in the best Homeric tradition), this is a race which each must run on his own. The crucial word is *untransmitted*, which limits the scope of optimism; this is not a relay race and each man has to carry the torch for himself. Yet, because this is so, each man has a responsibility which must not be shirked. *Untransmitted* balances precisely the nature of the predicament: it is possible for man to go either way, to remain shrouded inside his negative condition or to turn grave into cradle and transform his negatives into positives. A similar point is made in the Preface, where Shelley states that although writers may be influenced by the spirit of the age, the success and significance of their work depends ultimately on their own contribution, on the quality of their imagination: that 'must be the *uncommunicated* lightning of their own mind'.

As this second example indicates, the choice applies not only to morality and politics but also to literature. Perhaps the best illustration of this is *Prometheus Unbound* itself. In one of Shelley's Bodleian notebooks (adds. e. 12) there is a neglected fragment in which he seems to be exploring this question. The lines appear to be addressed to Prometheus:

4. See H. A. Harris, *Sport in Greece and Rome* (1972), plates 24–28 and p. 33.

One sung of thee, who left the tale *untold*,
Like the false dawns which perish on the bursting . . .[5]

'One sung of thee'—surely this is Aeschylus, who provided the starting point for Shelley's play? Aeschylus left the tale *untold* not because he failed to finish his trilogy but because in Shelley's view he did not satisfactorily realize the best possibilities of his own subject. False dawns are associated in Shelley with hopes of reform and revolution that are dashed because of premature expectations and which can easily turn into hopelessness or apathy. Thus, it would be true to say that in *Prometheus Unbound* Shelley attempts to realize the potential of a tale *untold*. Perhaps one might even say that in the Prometheus trilogy Shelley discovered a myth which was, in his view, still *unreclaimed* and that *Prometheus Unbound* is itself an example of how a poet can address himself to the process of reclamation, never ignoring the force of the negative but seeking where possible to replace it with the positive which lies behind.

## JAMES CHANDLER

### History's Lyre:
### The "West Wind" and the Poet's Work[†]

#### 2. A Revolution in the Turns of Season

The problems posed by the *Ode*, as commentators have long recognized, begin with the opening lines. Before we have any reason to associate the "West Wind" with, let us say, the "Spirit of the Age," with which we are now familiar from Shelley's other writings of the period, we run into a grammatical problem traceable to the alignment of the initial metaphors in which the West Wind is represented:

> O wild West Wind, thou breath of Autumn's being,
> Thou, from whose unseen presence the leaves dead
> Are driven, like ghosts from an enchanter fleeing,
>
> Yellow, and black, and pale, and hectic red,
> Pestilence-stricken multitudes. (ll. 1–5)

After "breath of Autumn's being," one is disposed to see in the ensuing figure a picture of Autumn sitting like Aeolus in his cave and driving

---

5. See *Percy Bysshe Shelley: The Homeric Hymns and Prometheus Draft Notebook: Bodleian MS Shelley adds. e. 12*, ed. Nancy Moore Goslee (1996), pp. 6–7. Goslee notes: "we might take this poem as an answer first to Byron's 'Prometheus' and then, more indirectly, to Aeschylus' *Prometheus Bound*. Thus it might not be a fragment written for *Prometheus Unbound*, but a lyric that leads into it" (p. 278).
† From *England in 1819: The Politics of Literary Culture and the Case of Romantic Historicism*, by James Chandler (Chicago: University of Chicago Press, 1998), pp. 532–45, 549–54. Reprinted by permission of The University of Chicago Press. The author's notes have been edited, and page references to this Norton Critical Edition appear in brackets following the original citations.

the leaves away with his mighty exhalations. It is the unseen presence of the wind itself, however, from which the leaves are said to be driven, and precisely by *what* the leaves are driven is left, as it were, up in the air. The ensuing simile of the ghosts and the enchanter ought to settle this question, but in fact it only complicates matters further. The ghosts that are likened to the leaves are not depicted as being driven from the enchanter (the counterpart of the unseen presence) by anything in particular. Moreover, they are not depicted as being *driven* from him at all; they are depicted as *fleeing* him. Further still, insofar as some force is involved in the metaphor, it seems to work in the other direction, for the enchanter's power would presumably tend to hold the ghosts against their will.[1]

Metaphorical mismatching is by no means rare in Shelley. It is surely not unusual for him to compose a catalogue of figures that do not neatly add up, and commentators have developed various ways of generalizing about the significance of the practice, whether as a sign of Shelley's incompetence, as in the Leavisite tradition, or of his protodeconstructive half-insight, in poststructuralist criticism. But even the contradictions of the opening lines might not demand special attention if it were not for what Shelley does with the metaphors in the ensuing lines, which comprise the stanza's second movement:

> O Thou,
> Who chariotest to their dark wintry bed
>
> The winged seeds, where they lie cold and low,
> Each like a corpse within its grave, until
> Thine azure sister of the Spring shall blow
>
> Her clarion o'er the dreaming earth, and fill
> (Driving sweet buds like flocks to feed in air)
> With living hues and odours plain and hill. . . . (ll. 5–12)

Having left behind the apparently destructive effects of the Autumn wind, its scattering of the pestilence-stricken multitudes, this passage focuses on the wind's function in delivering the seeds to their place of implantation. The presence of similar words and tropes in this movement signals that it reunites the first movement, but the differences show strongly conventionalizing tendencies. Indeed, the passage amounts to a miniature nature poem rendered in the familiar Christianized pastoral framework of the redemption of the soul after the death of the body. Eschatologically, it is the apocalypse of the beautiful rather than the sublime.

If we focus on the operation of the figures, the tropes or tunes of these lines, we see that the metaphors cooperate, corroborate, and cohere. By contrast with what we noted in the opening movement, for example, we find nothing especially complicated about "driving" in this

---

1. Paul Fry calls this last contradiction "the crux of the simile, and of the ode," in *The Poet's Calling in the English Ode* (New Haven: Yale University Press, 1980), p. 210. The figure is also jarring in respect to its predecessor, as Fry points out, because it implies that the ghosts are visible and the enchanter unseen.

context, and metaphorical elaboration of the term now runs not against the grain but very much with it: "like flocks to feed in air." This is the wind of Autumn comprehended in its azure sister-wind of the Spring. (Their "sisterhood" itself will prove to be a function of the passage's vernal perspective.)

The clarity that results from the alignment of the metaphors in this movement is perhaps explicitly marked in the reference to the clarion (l. 10), a horn noted for, and indeed named for, its clear tone: *Clarion*, from *clario*, from *clarus* (clear), as the polyglot Shelley would certainly have known. The poem's second movement is as clear as the first is obscure, and the juxtaposition of the two movements suggests that both the obscurity and the clarity are tellingly motivated.[2] The two movements comprise an introduction to the *Ode* only, therefore, when they are read together.[3]

To gain a better idea of what is at stake in the *Ode*'s opening juxtaposition of two diverse manners or modes, we must consult the lines that have long been recognized as a prototype for the theme's topoi of the *Ode*, one of the climactic passages in Shelley's *The Revolt of Islam*.[4] The passage in question is the speech that Cythna makes to Laon in canto 9 at a time when the two of them, having been the intellectual leaders of the revolution in the Golden City, are weathering a counter revolution much like the one that Shelley and other reformers saw themselves confronting in the years after Waterloo. Here, as in Lukács's account of this same period, the experience of counter revolution lends motive and perspective to an attempt to make sense of the entire Revolutionary epoch. Cythna represents the epoch through a sustained conceit. It is a seasonal topos that develops in two distinct cycles, although its cycles are themselves rhetorical rather than meteorological. The first is completed in a single stanza:

> The blasts of autumn drive the winged seeds
>   Over the Earth,—next come the snows, and rain,
> And frosts, and storms, which dreary winter leads
>   Out of his Scythian cave, a savage train;
>   Behold! Spring sweeps over the world again,
> Shedding soft dews from her aetherial wings;
>   Flowers on the mountains, fruits over the plain,

2. Paul de Man's analysis of figuration in "The Triumph of Life" is a precedent for what follows in that it too discriminates second-order considerations of coherence/incoherence in the play of Shelley's tropes. I refer especially to de Man's analysis of how, unlike most images in the poem, "light" tends to be figured coherently: "Shelley Disfigured," in *Deconstruction & Criticism*, ed. Harold Bloom (New York: Seabury Press, 1979), p. 57.
3. Two of the most suggestive recent interpretations of the *Ode* focus only on one or the other of the these related movements, in effect not seeing them as movements, or related, in the relevant respects. Fry's deconstructionist account sees the poem as a coming to terms with what I have been calling the initial, destructive movement: "There is enough mystery in the first tercet to supply a whole poem," he begins (*Poet's Calling*, pp. 208–210). Edward Duffy's Christianizing and Eliotic reading finds the poem's seminal beginning the second, preservative movement, in which the "verbal seeds" of the poem's traditionalizing renaming of Golgotha as part of a broader "resurrection *logos*" are "already embedded." See "Where Shelley Wrote and What He Wrote For: The Example of "The Ode to the West Wind," *Studies in Romanticism* 23 (fall 1984): 365–67.
4. Stuart Curran, for example, calls it the "long first draft" of the *Ode*. See Stuart Curran, *Shelley's Annus Mirabilis* (San Marino, Calif.: Huntington Library, 1975).

> And music on the waves and woods she flings,
> And love on all that lives, and calm on lifeless things. (st. 21)

This account of the seasonal cycle obviously employs certain figures, chiefly prosopopeia (personification), but, like the opening stanza of the "West Wind" *Ode*, it offers no explicit allegorization of its terms. That sort of gloss must await the second movement of Cythna's speech beginning two stanzas later. But it is already clear from this stanza why the speech should prompt Stuart Curran to call it the long first draft of the *Ode*. In recognizing the features that allow us to see the passage that way, however, we must not fail to notice the crucial ways in which the *Ode* revises in rewriting. One crucial revision in this first stanza, for example, is that the wind of autumn is represented only in its capacity as charioteer of the seeds. The destructive powers are all given to the winter. This fact suggests that Cythna's speech may be called a "first draft" for the *second movement* of the "West Wind" *Ode*, but not for the *Ode* itself. * * *

In the second movement of the *Ode*, the Wind's preserving function, to chariot the seeds to their wintry bed, stands side by side with the clearing of the leaves of the previous year's growth, as represented in the first movement: this is all summarized pointedly in the exclamation that closes the first part, "Destroyer and Preserver; hear, oh hear!" Because of the movement structure of the first stanza—in which the wind is treated first as the driver of the leaves and then as the charioteer of the seeds—one may be inclined at this point to see the destructive and preservative functions of the wind as quite separable. It scatters the leaves, and it also happens to implant the seeds. But by ascribing to the autumnal power two functions conventionally (as in *The Revolt of Islam*) relegated to different seasons—autumn and winter—the *Ode* forces one to see destruction and preservation as unified at some level of abstraction, despite their apparent autonomy. By the end of the *Ode*'s last stanza, we are also invited to recognize a similar unity in the functions that were, even in the first stanza of this ode, relegated to autumn and *spring*. In the first stanza, the autumn's sister spirit of the spring fulfills the process of regeneration. She blows her clarion over the dreaming earth. In the final stanza, however, it is the autumn wind itself that is to be, through the poet's lips, the trumpet of an awakening prophecy to the earth. Since in the *Ode* "Autumn" subsumes the opposed functions of destruction and preservation, as well as the functions of the two rival sisterwinds, we are forced as readers to a second-order thematic synthesis in an attempt to comprehend the topos of the wind. The play of themes or topoi, in other words, confronts us with a question: How are we to conceive of the power in which the thematic distinctions conventionally made between both autumn and winter, on the one hand, and autumn and spring, on the other, are overcome?

The play of tropes leads us by different means to roughly the same place. The corroborative or analogous organization of the figures in the destruction movement and the disanalogous organization of the figures in the preservation movement can themselves be regarded as second-order tropes, tropes of tropes. The wind then becomes that trope which constitutes the conjunction of these two, apparently incompatible, second-order tropes. This move likewise forces a question: If the wind is neither the power of analogy nor the power of disanalogy, how are we to represent the relationship of these tropes-of-tropes with each other? I will be suggesting below that the answers to both of these questions, and others like them, are not "understood" but only *imagined* by the *Ode*, in Shelley's late and somewhat technical sense of that term. For now it is perhaps enough to suggest that the dialectic of the tropes in the *Ode* elevates it to meet the criterion of true poetry set forth in the *Defence*. The language of the poem is "vitally metaphorical" in that it marks the before unapprehended relations of things.

## 3. The Elementary Case

The most controversial issue in the criticism of Shelley's *Ode* is probably the question of its structure, particularly in respect to the five-stanza organization of the poem. Some of the conclusions we have reached in the analysis of topoi and tropes can be corroborated in the analysis of structure. The progression of the first three stanzas through the zones of the land, the atmosphere, and the sea would have been obvious to most readers even if Shelley had not recapitulated it at the start of stanza 4: "If I were a leaf, . . . a cloud, . . . a wave." But like so many of the individual simplicities of this poem—the line about falling on the thorns of life, for example—this one resists ready analysis. One key question is whether this triadic formation is "structural" in the sense of constituting a principle of the poem's making, one that can be understood as generating it? Many commentators have linked this triangulation of terms to the poem's reliance on tercets and to the sonnetlike stanzaic form in which rhymes occur in threes. But what then is the structural relation of stanzas 4 and 5 to the first three?

No progress can be made with the poem, I think, without first challenging the exclusively tripartite model of the poem's structure as Eben Bass did many years ago, when he noticed the poem's implicit invocation of the ancient quartet of the natural elements.[5] To see in the initial trio of stanzas a passage from earth to air to water is inevitably to expect a stanza on fire. Fire in fact dominates the closing movement of the poem, in stanza 5, and it is present *in potentia* as the threat of lightning in the middle of the initial three-part movement. But where one would *expect* to see fire, at the opening of four, one is confronted instead with the figure of the poet, in the appearance of the first-person pronoun that had hitherto been withheld. Harold Bloom once urged that the poem be read as "a poem about Shelley's relationship

---

5. Eben Bass, "The Fourth Element in 'Ode to the West Wind,' " *Papers on Language and Literature* 3 (1967): 327–38.

to 'Prometheus Unbound.' "⁶ We could certainly read the poem in worse ways, and the suggestion is useful to keep in mind in stanza 4 especially. Like the mythic character who gives his name to Shelley's most important poetic work to this date, and indeed to the volume in which the *West Wind* initially appeared, the poet is evidently introduced to bring fire into the poem and thus to complete its four-part elemental structure.⁷ But why does it require two parts for the poem to complete this act of fire bringing? This is the question that Bass could not answer. Drawing on Pythagorean and Oriental cosmologies, respectively, James Rieger and Stuart Curran have suggested that Shelley builds his poem on five elements, including a master element that subsumes the other four: ether, for Rieger, and the wind itself, for Curran.⁸ But this does not answer the question of why fire comes last. Nor does it do full justice to the evidence on the basis of which so many readers before Bass read the *Ode* as a poem of triads.⁹

Since fire is what is looked for to complete the quartet, the question of why there are two stanzas beyond the first triad is perhaps better approached through the recognition that the Promethean poet of the *Ode* is identified with fire in the poem under two antithetical aspects. He (his fire) is both the subject and object of the wind's operation. As object, the poet would be understood to participate in the world of the elements on which the wind acts; as subject, he would act on it—with, or as, or like the wind. In rhetorical terms, this duality of aspect appears as a problem about whether the poet's relation to the wind will be metonymic or metaphoric; the play of metonymy against metaphor is, indeed, one of the poem's most conspicuous rhetorical features from the start. In grammatical terms, the duality of aspect appears in the play of objective and subjective cases in the last two parts of the poem, as for example in the famous lines—"O lift me as a wave, a leaf, a cloud! / I fall upon the thorns of life! I bleed!"—a fortunate fall into the subjective case. It also appears in the grammar of the poet's climactic imperative—"Be thou me, impetuous one!"—a solecism with respect to case that at once enacts the speaker's windlike impetuosity and casts a shade of doubt on the hoped-for resolution.

The structure of the *Ode*'s five sections, then, must be understood as complex in the precise sense of involving two substructures that interlock, and this interlocking must be understood to occur in the figure of the firebringing Promethean poet.¹ The ambiguous status of fire perfectly suits it to help play the role of the zeugma that holds the

6. Bloom, *Shelley's Mythmaking* (New Haven, CT: Yale University Press, 1959), p. 67.
7. Neil Fraistat argues for a complex interrelation of the poems in this volume in *The Poem and the Book: Interpreting Collections of Romantic Poetry* (Chapel Hill: University of North Carolina Press, 1985), pp. 141–87.
8. Curran, *Shelley's Annus Mirabilis*, p. 162; James Rieger, *The Mutiny Within* (New York: G. Brazillier, 1967), pp. 169–71.
9. Rieger's Pythagorean reading of the poem does, however, acknowledge the importance of competing three-to-five, four-to-five, and four-to-one ratios in the poem: ibid., pp. 170–71.
1. For an analysis of the rhyme scheme of the poem that I think tends to support this view, see J. J. Oversteegen, "Shelley's 'Ode to the West Wind,' A Case of Whig History" in *Comparative Poetics*, ed. D. W. Fokkema, Elrud Kune-Ibsch, and A. J. A. van Zoest (Amsterdam: Editions Rodolpi, 1975), p. 115.

two substructures in relation to each other *and* to function as the dialectical wild card among the quartet of elements. * * * More simply put, the point is that, in the *Ode*, as in *Prometheus Unbound*, "fire" involves two ranges of connotation—not only light, heat, and electricity but also the ability to control these things: intelligence. It stands both *as* an element and *for* the power to control the elements.

The double binding or bonding of this poetic element, in the context of the *Ode*'s interlocking substructures, thus leads us back to the sort of conclusion we reached in looking closely at the first stanza: that the poem is the site of conceptual contest, a negotiation of competing claims about fire as a case and a cause. Is the operation of fire to be understood *among* the play of the objective elements of nature or as over *against* the other three elements? Is it an instrument of divine change in an ultimately fixed order of things or of human change in a world where destinies are forged as time moves on? In the terms of the myth, was Prometheus, in man's behalf, the thief of fire or the agent by which it was restored to its rightful place? The central question for the *Ode* might therefore be posed: is the poet's fire like the other elements in the lawlike way it is subject to that force for change that is represented by the wind? If so, then how is any real change possible, how do we escape the persistent regularity which governs the interaction of the elements? Or is the poet like the wind in giving the law to change? Is he legislator or legislated?

We know that just (perhaps even days) after composing the *Ode*, Shelley set to work on *A Philosophical View of Reform*. The first chapter of the *View* culminates in the famous paragraph, reused in the *Defence*, in which Shelley pronounced that poets were "the unacknowledged legislators of the world." As I noted earlier, this celebrated pronouncement is consistently read out of its problematizing context. Insofar as the previous claims in this paragraph are about a failure of acknowledgment, they suggest that this failure is on the poets' side. The celebrated writers of England in 1819, Shelley argues, and by extension the inspired writers of any age, fail to acknowledge the power that operates in and through them to enable them to imagine what they imagine. It is precisely at the moment in the text when writers seem to be reduced to the status of objective instrumentality in the service of higher laws and powers that they are suddenly given the status of subjects, agents, and lawmakers.

A similarly problematic instance of chiasmas occurs when some of the same language appears in the concluding section of the *Ode to the West Wind*. In that stanza, the metaphor of instrumentality (in the fullest sense) first occurs in the poet's opening imperative "Make me thy lyre, even as the forest is." Everyone recognizes that this invokes the sense of instrumentality implicit in the Romantic topos of the Aeolian harp. Less widely acknowledged is the fate met by this sense of instrumentality before the section is completed, for the final imperative in this section is the one that involves the trumpet: "Be through my lips to unawakened Earth / The trumpet of a prophecy!" In one of the best commentaries on the poem we have, Earl Wasserman takes the common view that the sense of instrumentality in this metaphor points in the same direction as was implicit in the lyre metaphor.[2] Insofar as "trumpet" might be understood as the sound of the prophecy, its trumpet*ing*, this reading can be defended. The breath that winds the trumpet is that of the West Wind, just as in *A Philosophical View of Reform* (earlier in that paragraph used to conclude the *Defence*), the spirit of the age is understood to animate the poet's work. Read in another way, however, the lines from the *Ode* reverse the directionality implicit in the earlier command. In the context of the initial imperative about the lyre, it is difficult not to read the "trumpet" of the penultimate line as an instrument, and, read this way, the metaphor turns itself inside out. This is so because, not only does the wind become in two senses the poet's instrument, it is the work of the poet that is "making" the wind that instrument. The wind will be the trumpet of a prophecy through the poet's lips: "through," in the sense now not of passive access but of active agency. The phrase is here roughly analogous with "By the incantation of this verse." Both prepositions convey the sense of "by virtue of" or "by the power of."

This representation of mutual making may be said to elaborate the paradox of Shelley's suggestion in the preface to *The Revolt of Islam* that writers are in some sense the authors of the influence (authors, that is, of the spirit of the age) by which their being is unwillingly pervaded. Perhaps some such idea of the mutuality of causation also lurks in Shelley's endorsement of Tasso's comment that there are only two creators in the world, God and the poet (*Letters*, 2:530), the unstated conclusion being that God and the poet are the creators, or authors, of one another. God makes the poet to make God, and vice versa. The Wind makes Shelley make the Wind make Shelley make the Wind and so on.

\*    \*    \*

## 5. *Fallen Leaves*

The *Ode*'s special self-consciousness about its words and figures has been implicit in much that we have already noted about it. It remains only to consider, in the light of "imagination," one doubly pertinent word/figure: the "leaves" of the *Ode*. The fullest anticipation of the *West Wind*'s seasonal topoi, Cythna's speech in the *Revolt*, gives the leaves very little play. They do not appear in either of the elaborations of the cyclical pattern, and what mention they receive in the intervening stanza about Spring's filial relation to Autumn is casual: spring is said to bear fresh flowers for her mother, "with gentle feet, / Disturbing not the leaves which are her winding-sheet." We know that, in *Queen Mab*, the leaves play a far more prominent role, as they would again

2. In Wasserman, *Shelley: A Critical Reading* (Baltimore: Johns Hopkins University Press, 1971), p. 250.

in the *Ode*, and they are seen as problematic in the cycle of things.[3] The leaves in this passage, scattered by the Autumn wind, as in the *Ode*, are seen first as choking the seeds and deforming the earth on which they lie and only on second thought as fertilizing the soil to make regeneration possible.[4] None of this is accommodated in Cythna's account. The *Ode* addresses the issue of decay in its very first lines, but the leaves on which pestilence makes its mark take on a very different coloration. They become the poet's leaves—"what if my leaves are falling like its [the forest's] own?" These may be considered the leaves of laurel, the sibylline leaves recently recalled by Coleridge's volume, and, perhaps, too, the leaves of the Biblical topos of the tree of man. But we must not fail to see them as the fallen pages of Shelley's text, lapses from the initial inspiration that is the encounter with the *West Wind*'s power. "[W]hen composition begins," Shelley said in the *Defence*, "inspiration is already on the decline" (*SPP*, p. 504) [531]. Taking the "declension" seriously, we may say that composition establishes the *case* of inspiration.[5]

The topos of the leaf as the page of text is, of course, not a novel one with Shelley. Rousseau and Dante, to take only two authors Shelley knew well, both pun in this way. * * *

It would be like Shelley, and perhaps also an enactment of the point at issue, to have developed his new sense of textuality out of a pun, rather than the other way around. In any case, this new dimension of the autumn leaves as pages of text is responsive to the development in Shelley's self-consciousness about textuality that culminates in the *Defence*, and Shelley's sense of the relationship between textuality and Prometheanism is best approached through the *Defence*'s central discussion of Dante, the poet with whom Shelley increasingly identifies as he moves toward *The Triumph of Life*. The *Defence* represents Dante in persistently Promethean terms; he becomes indeed, for Shelley, nothing less than the great prototype of the promethean poet. He is "the first religious reformer," "the first awakener of entranced Europe," and, most explicitly, the "Lucifer [or 'Light-bearer'] of that starry flock which in the thirteenth century shone forth from republican Italy, as from a heaven, into the darkness of the benighted world" (*SPP*, 499–500) [528]. Most relevant to the *Ode*, though, is the account of how this light was generated out of the poetry: "His very words are instinct with spirit; each is as a spark, a burning atom of inextinguishable thought; and many yet lie covered in the ashes of their birth, and pregnant with a lightning which has yet found no conductor."[6] "Spirit,"

---

3. See I. J. Kapstein, "The Symbolism of the Wind and the Leaves in Shelley's 'Ode to the West Wind,'" *PMLA* 51 (1936): 1069–79.

4. *Queen Mab* sect 5, ll. 1–15.

5. For an account of "the case" in terms of declension and the "fall" into circumstances, see Chandler, *England in 1819*, pp. 234–52.

6. Cf. the use of this last term in connection with the spirit of the age in the letter of November 6, 1819, less than two weeks after the composition of the *Ode*: "[T]he people are nearly in a state of insurrection, & the least unpopular noblemen perceive the necessity of conducting a spirit which it is no longer possible to oppose" (*Letters*, 2:149). * * *

"spark," "inextinguishable," "ashes," "lightning," "conductor"—these are the sorts of terms that figure prominently in the *Ode*'s development of an alternative to the organic or "cultural" model of social regeneration.

In the *Ode*, the paronomasia of the leaves works subterraneously from the start but emerges at the end in the third and final use of the key verb "drive," which is associated with "conductor," just as other terms are associated with the terms from the discussion of Dante's Prometheanism:

> Be thou, Spirit fierce,
> My spirit! Be thou me, impetuous one!
> Drive my dead thoughts over the universe
> Like withered leaves to quicken a new birth! (ll. 61–64)

If we take the account in the *Defence* as understood in this passage, then the simile "like withered leaves" is problematic in the extreme. For if thought decays as composition begins, then the pages of text, "withered leaves," are not so much a metaphor for the dead thoughts as the form that thought takes when it dies. The dead thoughts are driven not *like* withered leaves, but *as* withered leaves; they ride the boundary between metaphor and metonymy. Such paronomasia is a function of the textuality to which it playfully alludes. It marks yet another revision of the trope in Cythna's speech in which the blasts of autumn drive the winged seeds over the earth, and in which this work is explicitly identified with the driving of truth's deathless germs to thought's remotest caves by the whirlwind of the intellectuals' spirit. Although this may at first seem to augur a return to the mode of *Queen Mab*, where the leaves are understood to fertilize the seeds, seeds have in fact disappeared from the scene of the *Ode*'s final stanza.

In *Poet's Grammar*, Francis Berry sees the problem, but not the point, when he says of this passage: "Leaves, dead or living, do not bear seeds." "Shelley's mistake," he says, "is not deeply relevant."[7] But Shelley's mistake could scarcely be more deeply relevant in that it challenges the very metaphor of cultural seminality in social regeneration. The presence of fire creates the possibility of writing the leaves into a very differently conceived model of change:

> And, by the incantation of this verse,
> Scatter, as from an unextinguished hearth
> Ashes and sparks, my words among mankind! (ll. 65–67)

The withered leaves of text have not disappeared. Instead, they constitute the substance slowly being consumed on the unextinguished hearth. Their figurative status in the poem is being transformed by the figure of fire. The seeds of thought that had independent status and a very different relationship to the wind in the earlier treatments of

---

7. In Francis Berry, *Poet's Grammar: Person, Time, and Mood in Poetry* (London: Routledge and Paul, 1958), p. 152.

the question, now give way to the sparks that lie next to the ashes. Under this new dispensation, the scattering of the leaves and the production of the new thoughts would both be accomplished by the inspiring wind. Fire is the element that is itself preserved only at the expense of destroying something else, and wind is the power that sustains this twofold process at the same time, in the same breath. Many more ideas can be constructed from words and figures than from the principles and notions on which the whole fabric of reasoned knowledge is reared, as Spinoza argued, but every construction (including mine here) will involve some destruction.

After discussing the production and reception of Dante's poetry, Shelley generalized his remarks to suggest that all genuine poetry is Promethean in mission and at the same time entered an important qualification about the role of will in carrying out that mission:

> What were Virtue, Love, Patriotism, Friendship &c.—what were the scenery of this beautiful Universe which we inhabit—what were our consolations on this side of the grave—and what were our aspirations beyond it—if Poetry did not ascend to bring light and fire from those eternal regions where the owl-winged faculty of calculation dare not ever soar? Poetry is not like reason, a power to be exerted according to the determination of the will. A man cannot say, "I will compose poetry." The greatest poet even cannot say it: for the mind in creation is as a fading coal which some invisible influence, like an inconstant wind, awakens to transitory brightness. . . . (*SPP* pp. 503–04) [531]

Early on, a skeptical Shelley may have been unwillingly drawn into a reckoning with the movement of history in his calculations, poetic and prosaic, for improving the social order. Later, in the period he saw as critical for English society, his hopes for improvement seemed to rest on an act of political faith that he hoped would be self-fulfilling. It had to do with defining poetry against the rational will, and aligning it with the spirit of the age, precisely because this alignment lifted it clear of the calculating faculty, and indeed of the entire utilitarian calculus in which he had once invested his energy. God makes the poet to make God, and vice versa. The Wind makes Shelley make the Wind make Shelley make the Wind. But perhaps better: Shelley is led by the events of post-Revolution history to construct an account whereby he and post-Revolution history make each other. It is as if Shelley had glimpsed that profound lesson later articulated by Marx at mid-century, still in force with Sartre and Lévi-Strauss a century later, and then reworked into the "historicism" that Jameson fashioned from Althusser's Spinozist principle of structural causality: that human beings make their own history, but not just as they please.[8]

\* \* \*

8. For specific linkages of Shelley's Spinozist sense of "imagination" to Jameson's post-structuralist use of Althusser, see Chandler, *England in 1819*, pp. 51–93 and 545–49.

# SUSAN J. WOLFSON

## Poetic Form and Political Reform:
## *The Mask of Anarchy* and "England in 1819"†

> The system of society as it exists at present must be overthrown from the
> foundations with all its superstructure of maxims & of forms before we shall
> find anything but disappointment in our intercourse with any but a few select
> spirits. [. . .] I wish to ask you if you know of any bookseller who would like
> to publish a little volume of *popular songs* wholly political, & destined to
> awaken & direct the imagination of the reformers. I see you smile but answer
> my question.
>
> —Shelley to Leigh Hunt, May 1, 1820

> . . . let us dismiss those more general considerations which might involve an
> enquiry into the principles of society itself, and restrict our view to the manner
> in which the imagination is expressed upon its forms.
>
> —Shelley, *A Defence of Poetry*

Shelley is nothing if not ambivalent about poetic form as a medium
of transmission. In the affirmative motions of *A Defence* he argues
that poetic form, by revealing "the spirit of [earthly] forms," "redeems
from decay the visitations of the divinity in man" (*SPP* 505) [532].
But other motions plea-bargain, reducing its claim to mere "instruments and materials," of a piece with "grammatical forms" which are
"convertible with respect to the highest poetry without injuring it as
poetry" (483) [513]. Even the metrical line is no necessity (484) [513].
This ambivalence extends to Shelley's sense of a specifically "poetic"
audience. His disdain of "didactic poetry" seems to dismiss the agency
of poetic form in the "reform" of other minds: "nothing can be equally
well expressed in prose that is not tedious and supererogatory in verse"
(Preface to *Prometheus Unbound*, *SPP* 135) [209]. Yet the double negative implies a positive: when poetry *is* the expression, it communicates
something that mere prose cannot. This is the point on which the
*Defence* rests, designating for poetry a form at once embodying visionary information and signifying visionary authority. The laws of poetry,
by creating "actions according to the unchangeable forms of human
nature, as existing in the mind of the creator, which is itself the image
of all other minds" (485) [515], are those of a "social system" (486)
[516]. It is in this spirit, and with a hope of political agency, that
Shelley wrote to Leigh Hunt from Italy in May 1820, asking him to
find an English publisher for "a little volume of *popular songs* wholly

† Adapted from *Formal Charges: The Shaping of Poetry in British Romanticism* by Susan J.
Wolfson (Stanford University Press, 1997), pp. 193–206. Used with the permission of Stan-
ford University Press. Copyright © 1997 by the Board of Trustees of the Leland Stanford
Junior University. The author's notes have been edited, and page references to this Norton
Critical Edition appear in brackets following the original citations.

political, & destined to awaken & direct the imagination of the reformers." (*Letters* 2:191)[1]

*   *   *

Making this request, Shelley also imagined Hunt's reaction—"I see
you smile"—and knew its point: self-censorship for fear of prosecution
for libel, sedition, or treason. Still unpublished was a reform polemic
Shelley had sent to Hunt eight months earlier for the *Examiner*, with
either a guileless or a stubborn disregard of legal risk. This was *The
Mask of Anarchy*, written in a fury over the "Peterloo Massacre."[2]
    The prestige of *The Mask* as the epitome of political poetry is pe-
culiarly idealizing (and idolizing).[3] But it does dramatize the *problem*
of Shelley's "political poetry," especially in the conflicting investments
of its poetic forms, which for all their calibration to move and inspire
a vast audience, also expose a poetic self-absorption. If, as David
Punter argues, Shelley was "painfully aware" that the translation of

1. The probable contents would have included *The Mask of Anarchy*, "Lines Written During
   the Castlereagh Administration," "Song to the Men of England," "Similes for Two Poetical
   Characters," "What Men Gain Fairly," "A New National Anthem," "Sonnet: England in
   1819," "Ballad of the Starving Mother," "Ode to Liberty," and "Ode to the West Wind." The
   last two were published in 1820 with *Prometheus Unbound* and all but the "Ballad" appeared
   in the 1830s. *Athenæum* published "Lines" late in 1832 ("Original Papers: Lines Written
   during the Castlereagh Administration. By the Late Percy Bysshe Shelley," *The Athenæum:
   Journal of English and Foreign Literature, Science, and the Fine Arts* 267 [December 8, 1832]
   794), with a caution: although "there is something fearful in the solemn grandeur of these
   lines," they may "be now published without the chance of exciting either personal or party
   feeling." Yet not until 1990 was a unified publication effected, when Paul Foot, noting "the
   enthusiasm of members of the S[ocialist] W[orkers] P[arty] for Shelley's revolutionary writings," packaged the poems with *A Philosophical View of Reform*, in a "marvellous, cheap
   volume" (£3.95 in 1990), which he exhorts socialists to use in "duty to their children to
   bribe or bully them to learn the poetry which carries revolutionary ideas through the centuries" (*Shelley's Revolutionary Year: The Peterloo Writings of the Poet Shelley* [London: Red-
   words, 1990] 9, 26).
2. The "Peterloo Massacre"—a name codified by the left press in parody of the celebrated
   English victory at Waterloo, and now the standard reference—was a savage, sabre-wielding
   attack by drunken local yeomanry (a militia of property-owners) on an orderly, non-violent
   demonstration of 80,000–100,000 men, women, and children in St. Peter's Fields, near
   Manchester, on August 16, 1819, gathered to hear Henry "Orator" Hunt urge parliamentary
   reform, specifically, greater representation for the Manchester working-class population. The
   militia killed about a dozen people and brutally wounded hundreds more (for detailed accounts, in addition to the several reports in the *Examiner* of August 22, 1819, see E.P.
   Thompson, *The Making of the English Working Class* [London: Victor Gollancz, 1964] 681–
   89, and Richard Holmes, *Shelley: The Pursuit* [New York: E. P. Dutton, 1975 (1974)] 529–
   31). It is unclear whether the London Home Office collaborated in advance, in order to
   suppress the reform movement, or, with the Prince Regent, found it irresistible to "make
   themselves accomplices after the fact" with lavish congratulations (Thompson 684). Shelley
   was reading the *Examiner* and other radical newspapers sent by his friend Peacock; the
   *Examiner* featured its report on the front page of its August 22 issue and reprinted notices
   from the *Times* and a set of seven "Letters from Manchester," and continued for weeks after
   with a barrage of front-page reports, follow-ups, letters, and protest poetry. In a torrent of
   indignation (*Letters* 2:117–20, 136), Shelley posted *The Mask of Anarchy* to Hunt on September 23, hoping for publication in the *Examiner*.
3. Holmes calls *The Mask* not only "the greatest poem of political protest ever written in English," but perhaps "the most powerfully conceived, the most economically executed and the
   most perfectly sustained" of Shelley's poems (532), and to Foot, it is "one of the great
   political protest poems of all time" (*Revolutionary Year* 15; in *Red Shelley* [London: Sidgwick
   and Jackson, 1980] 175). Even F. R. Leavis admires *The Mask* for "its unusual purity and
   strength," its departure from "the usual Shelleyan emotionalism" ("Shelley," in *Revaluation:
   Tradition and Development in English Poetry* [Harmondsworth, Eng.: Penguin, 1972 (1936)]
   215).

political vision into potent revelation rarely "actually worked,"[4] what does seem clearly represented is an aesthetic processing of politics. This question—can poetry have political agency, or is it "supereroga-tory" to political action?—energizes the contradictions of *The Mask*. What evokes admiration (however delayed the broadcast) is its daring equation of Anarchy and King, of mask and legitimacy;[5] its proto-Marx-ist analysis of labor and consumption; and the rhetorical dazzle of its call to the "Men of England" to recognize their claims (147–372; fully three-fifths of the poem).[6] Yet the material fact is that the bolder as-pects of this performance are exactly what rendered the poem unpub-lishable, unable to affect the struggle it addresses. Between its writing in 1819 and its popular reading in 1832 is a gap of over a decade in which its poet languishes as unacknowledged legislator.

In this aspect, *The Mask*, one of Shelley's most passionately charged "exoteric species" of poetry (*Letters* 2:152), is weirdly kin to the elitist visionary poem of the same period with which it is sometimes con-trasted, *Prometheus Unbound*, a poem he projected "only for the elect" (2:200).[7] The "unacknowledged legislator" is a product of a poetics that had a share in the adjective as well as the noun, and the outcome could not have been unanticipated.[8] Nonpublication is not just an

---

4. "Shelley: Poetry and Politics," in David Aers, Jonathan Cook, and David Punter, *Romanticism and Ideology: Studies in English Writing 1765–1830* (London and Boston: Routledge and Kegan Paul, 1981) 165.

5. Shelley detaches "Anarchy" from the standard sense of social chaos that Lord Chancellor Eldon meant in judging the Manchester meeting "an overt act of treason" posing a "shocking choice between military government and anarchy" (Thompson 684) and turns the term back on the Government itself to name its perversion by tyranny (Foot, *Revolutionary Year* 15); "anarchy will only be the last flash before despotism," Shelley wrote before he knew of the events at Manchester [August 24, 1819; *Letters* 2:115]). Yet by spring of 1822, frustrated over the prospects for reform, he was resorting to the standard sense: "anarchy is better than despotism—for this reason, that the former is for a season & that the latter is eternal" (April 11; *Letters* 2:412). For a succinct genealogy of anarchy from Milton to Shelley, see William Keach, "Radical Shelley?" *Raritan* 5:2 (Fall 1985) 120–29.

6. Ronald Tetreault comments on the variety of oratorical devices (*The Poetry of Life: Shelley and Literary Form* [Toronto: University of Toronto Press, 1987] 205–6), and argues that this rich "aesthetic experience" is "a function of form and not just of content" (199). Stephen C. Behrendt (*Shelley and His Audiences* [Lincoln: University of Nebraska Press, 1989] 199–202) remarks on the several audiences variously addressed: the aristocracy (with warning and instruction), the oppressed workers (with encouragement, instruction, and inspiration), and the liberal readers of the *Examiner* (with urgency). Stuart Curran considers the more precisely formalist poetics, a "considerable achievement in the low style, shrewdly coupling its radical politics to a balladlike meter and framing its exhortations within the iconography of chapbooks, penny pamphlets, and folk pageants" (*Shelley's Annus Mirabilis: The Maturing of an Epic Vision* [San Marino, Calif.: Huntington Library, 1975] 186).

7. For the contrasting senses of audiences, see Roger Sales (*English Literature in History 1780–1830: Pastoral and Politics* [New York: St. Martin's Press, 1983] 196–99), Tetreault (199), and Stephen Goldsmith (*Unbinding Jerusalem: Apocalypse and Romantic Imagination* [Ith-aca: Cornell University Press, 1993] 243, 252–54).

8. Apologists such as Behrendt contend that Shelley's "physical and emotional distance from events in England, together with a certain characteristic naive rashness in all such matters, prevented him from understanding that Hunt would not publish the piece at the time" (202). But Shelley was closely following the developing indictment of Richard Carlile for having published Paine's *Age of Reason*. It was clear, moreover, that the Hunts would reap a pros-ecution for publishing a poem denouncing the king in an address to the laboring poor (as opposed to aristocrats) and, as Michael Henry Scrivener notes (*Radical Shelley: The Philo-sophical Anarchism and Utopian Thought of Percy Bysshe Shelley* [Princeton: Princeton Uni-versity Press, 1982] 210), rooting liberty in an argument for their rights; while Shelley remained in Italy, the Hunts would be left to bear the legal and material penalties. See also Donald Reiman's remarks in his introduction (*"The Mask of Anarchy": A Facsimile Edition, with Scholarly Introductions, Bibliographical Descriptions, and Annotations*, vol. 2 of *Percy*

unlucky effect of state repression or the poet's exile in Italy; it is troped by the poem itself: the news "from over the Sea" (2) reaches its poet in a dream state from which he is never seen to awaken. While this modality—what *The Mask* calls "the visions of Poesy" (4)—is one that apologists elide or grant a licence of prophetic vision, it is an awkward finesse.[9] This is "a public poem with revolutionary intentions having to face and cope with the fact that its generating consciousness, the poet's mind, is in no position to do more than write a poem," remarks Thomas Edwards.[1] The effect is to make *The Mask* seem ultimately self-addressed, a masque in the mind of a poet dreaming about being a political orator and projecting this figure as a fantastic epipsyche.[2] This inwardness is spelled by Shelley's full title:

*The Mask of Anarchy*
*Written on the Occasion of the Massacre at Manchester*

The "occasion" is not his witnessing, but his reading, after the fact and a continent away. If the "infernal business" at Manchester had Shelley fuming in the voice of his incestuously raped and desperately parricidal Beatrice Cenci, "something must be done" (*Letters* 2:117, 120), all he wanted to do was to write, and in behalf of restraint: "Let a vast assembly be . . . // Stand ye calm and resolute" (295 ff).[3] Envisioning this formation of public performance art, Shelley puns his

---

Bysshe Shelley in *The Manuscripts of the Younger Romantics* [New York and London: Garland Press, 1985] xiv).

Hunt did publish *The Mask* in 1832, when the reformers gained control of Parliament and a mollifying Reform Bill was secured. By this time, the poem's hotter rhetoric could be read with historical distance and its cooler rhetoric admired as a sensibly prophetic recommendation of passive resistance, the means by which (shallow) parliamentary reform had been brought about—and by which time, too, as Thompson notes, the notoriety of the event "as a massacre and as 'Peter-Loo' " was established, along with a national "moral consensus" about the right of peaceful assembly and the unlawful "riding down and sabreing of an unarmed crowd" (710). That *The Mask* was not publishable in 1819 (or in the repressive dispensation soon thereafter) is frankly conceded by Mary Shelley in her edition of 1839: Shelley "had an idea of publishing a series of poems adapted expressly to commemorate [the] circumstances and wrongs" of "the People," and "he wrote a few, but in those days of prosecution for libel they could not be printed" (*The Poetical Works of Percy Bysshe Shelley*, 4 vols. [London: Edward Moxon, 1839] 3:205–7). For details on repression and prosecution "in those days," see Holmes 539–41 and Foot, *Red Shelley* 34–36; Foot, however, is hard on Hunt: although he realizes that "Shelley could not reasonably blame" him for his caution (221), he himself indicts Hunt as "the censor of some of the most powerful political writing in the English language" (219).

9. Even so sardonic a critic of the politics of Romantic poets as Sales endorses Holmes's praise of the poem (193) and generously grants Shelley the argument that "the poet's dream was more important than the politician's programme," although he concedes that the first stanza awkwardly raises a "contradiction between the dormant activist and the prophesying poet" (196). To Scrivener, Shelley's exile bears only on the poem's idiom of "symbolic reference," which he still wants to see as politically potent, a "proposal for massive nonviolent resistance" that would "push the reform movement leftwards" even at the risk of revolution (208, 198).

1. Thomas R. Edwards, *Imagination and Power: A Study of Poetry on Public Themes* (New York: Oxford University Press, 1971) 160.

2. Raymond Williams comments on the eruption of this doubleness at the close of the *Defence*, another declaration unpublished in Shelley's lifetime: "The last pages [. . .] are painful to read. The bearers of a high imaginative skill become suddenly the 'legislators,' at the very moment when they were being forced into practical exile; their description as 'unacknowledged,' which, on the theory, ought only to be a fact to be accepted, carries with it also the felt helplessness of a generation" (*Culture and Society, 1780–1950* [New York: Harper and Row, 1966 (1958)] 47).

3. See *The Cenci* 3.1.86–91. Although the play was written a few months before Peterloo, its publication in 1820 made its reception virtually inseparable from this contemporary reference.

*Mask* in the aristocratic genre of "masque" and uses this pun to create a new force-field of forms: allegorical modes worked into ballad and broadsheet stanzas, political oratory investing highly literary conceptions, social critique in visionary figures, etc. Yet, if this literary assembly bodes a symbolic revolution in its genre-collapsing and satirical tropings on traditional forms, the extravaganza also seems a symptom of the strain of trying to charge poetry as a comprehensive public discourse, "the centre and circumference of knowledge" (*Defence* 503) [531]. Can poetry inspire reform and insert its own forms into the process of social reform? Or is its work only a symbolic politics? Or even, a merely aesthetic self-satisfaction?

These questions come into sharpest focus, aptly, in the two moments where *The Mask* refers to concurrent social events. One is the internal orator's report that mothers and children "are dying whilst I speak" (171). The other seems quite opposite: the poet's pose of dormancy:

> As I lay asleep in Italy
> There came a voice from over the Sea. (1–2)

Is the poem's immediacy in its oratory or its dormancy, its speaking or sleeping? The disparity is seemingly reconciled by the keynote of the political argument, which tropes a poet's pre-visionary sleep as a pre-revolutionary stage of consciousness:

> Rise like Lions after slumber
> In unvanquishable number—
> Shake your chains to Earth like dew
> Which in sleep had fallen on you—
> Ye are many—they are few.   (151–55)

Shelley liked this reveille enough to repeat it as the close of the poem's internal oration, simultaneously the close of *The Mask* (368–72). But what of the simile that casts material oppression as ephemeral, insubstantial "chains . . . like dew"? This may be analogy only; what is more significant is the way this stirring, epipsychic oratory about awakening displaces the poem's formal frame—the slumber from which the poet never rises. The close of the poem, in which the internal oratory becomes the stirring drama, all but effaces the opening tableau, of a poet's quiescence and self-imposed isolation from the distant political scene:

> As I lay asleep in Italy
> There came a voice from over the Sea,
> And with great power it forth led me
> To walk in the visions of Poesy.   (1–4)

Poetic form produces nothing so much as nodding languor. The origin of its hypnotic, nearly claustrophobic single rhyme is "as*leep*" (itself oozing suggestively out of the initial *As I*). The quadruple end-rhyme is a dreamy extension of *sleep* into its site in *Italy*; the *Sea* across which lies England; the poet's sign of self, *me*; and the field of action, *Poesy*.

Poesy, moreover, is not securely located in the syntax: *of* situates it both as the producer of visions and as object of envisioning. That this specular object is not fully distinguishable from the masquerade figures soon to follow spells the perplexed logic of Shelley's political poetics.

*The Mask* never really unmasks this dreamy origin. Its first verbal form, "*As* I lay asleep," imprints a syntax that binds its dream of political oratory, whose "words of joy and fear arose" (138)

> As *if* their Own indignant Earth
>
> . . . . .
>
> Had turned every drop of blood
> By which her face had been bedewed
> To an accent unwithstood,—
> As *if* her heart had cried aloud:
>
> "Men of England, heirs of Glory . . .
> (139, 143–47, my italics)

Echoing the initial *As* that opens to visions of Poesy, the syntax of *As if* has a reflexive effect of restraining the imagination of potent political oratory to a dream. The words arise by inexplicable agency and are borne by fantastic illusion.

Even as this dreamy shimmer sustains the poem's idealism, it exposes the ideological bind of proffering poetry as the thing to be "done" in political crisis. Part of this bind is the symbolic work of its keyword *Mask*.[4] The political value of representing anarchy in and as a "Mask" is to provoke unmasking; the pun on *masque* assists by denoting an elaborate artifice with which a poet's art may or may not comply. Thus, in the reign of Charles II (Shelley remarks in his *Defence*), "all forms in which poetry had been accustomed to be expressed became hymns to the triumph of kingly power over liberty and virtue," demonstrating how in such epochs "the calculating principle pervades all the forms of dramatic exhibition, and poetry ceases to be expressed upon them" (491) [520]. In the "ghastly masquerade" of *The Mask* (5–81), Shelley

---

4. Shelley's manuscript reads *Mask*, perhaps inspired by the report in the *Examiner* referring to the government and its henchmen as "Men in the Brazen Masks of power" (608 [August 22, 1819] 530), or more distantly by Keats's cry at the top of *Endymion* III, "Are then regalities all gilded masks?" (22), the last line of verses that *Blackwood's* "Z" cited as evidence of Keats's "sedition" (3:524; August 1818). Shelley's pun on the literary-theatrical masque is obvious enough, however; he refers to the poem as the "Masque of Anarchy" in his letter of November 1819 to Hunt (*Letters* 2:152), and Hunt's edition uses this word. While Hunt defanged the poem by dropping its historically specifying subtitle and its namings of Eldon and Sidmouth, Shelley's generic designation of a "masque" is not an aesthetic evasion of the more politically demystifying metaphor, *Mask*. It is another version of it: the pun on *Masque* is amplified by the "ghastly masquerade" of government figures (27), a theatrical register that lets Shelley satirize the historical consolidation of the masque in the early seventeenth century as "the artistic property of the rich and powerful, performed as a ritual enactment of the received order of society and as a recommitment to its structures of authority" (Curran, *Annus Mirabilis* 188). Tetreault sees Shelley deploying masque conventions ironically "in order to condemn the values of the corrupt and anarchic court party"; "the dramatic ritual that would ordinarily confirm the monarch's power is turned against him" (201). Even Shelley's mixing of ballad and visionary poetry is a critique, for the dissonance contrasts how the mixture of forms in the Stuart masque (drama, song, dance, spectacle) is meant to reflect "a variety of social forms, each preserving its decorum within the ordered structure of the whole" (Curran ibid.).

unveils this pervasiveness in the historical moment of 1819 by staging kingly power itself as a dramatic exhibition. This parade is a linguistic masquerade as well, an array of the discursive forms through which official power commands and permeates social organization. In the trappings of kingship, anarchy is logos: "I AM GOD, AND KING, AND LAW!" (37). His "hired Murderers" echo, "Thou art God, and Law, and King" (60–61); the agents, "Lawyers and priests," whisper, "Thou art Law and God" (66–69); "Then all cried with one accord; / 'Thou art King, and God, and Lord'" (70–71)—an establishment vision of Poesy proliferated and masked in different syntaxes and grammars. The "stifling repetition," remarks Stephen Goldsmith, "encourages belief that words are limited in supply, belong to few, and can be combined only in prescribed, mechanical ways that endlessly reproduce the structure of power."[5]

Shelley uses poetic form to satirize this calculating principle. The couplet, "The hired Murderers, who did sing / 'Thou art God, and Law, and King' " (60–61), aligns the embodied authority, *King*, to *sing*, its official hymn. As another quatrain-rhyme mimes the claustrophobic effect—

> Lawyers and priests, a motley crowd,
> To the earth their pale brows bowed;
> Like a bad prayer not over loud,
> Whispering—"Thou art Law and God."—    (66–69)

Shelley lets the dissonance of *God* suggest the specious conscription of deity to party ideology. Against this ritual of language, Shelley envisions the Men of England as "Heroes of unwritten story" (148), whose consciousness he would shape with poetic oratory:

> "What is Freedom?—ye can tell
> That which slavery is, too well—
> For its very name has grown
> To an echo of your own.    (156–59)

In this didactic poetics, Shelley's punning of *groan* in *grown* and the absorption of *own* into *grown* spell the total claim on identity by economic oppression. He then produces a figure of outrageous equivalence for the oppressors' regard of their laborers:

> ye for them are made
> Loom, and plough, and sword, and spade,
> With or without your own will bent
> To their defence and nourishment.    (164–67)

The proto-Marxist sting of "ye for them" is its very syntax: tools are not made "for" the laborers; the laborers themselves "are made" into tools "for the tyrants' use" (163).

Yet, just as remarkably, these political stings fade with the emergence of allegorical figures:

---

5. *Unbinding Jerusalem* 243.

"What art thou Freedom? O! could slaves
Answer from their living graves
This demand—tyrants would flee
Like a dream's dim imagery.   (209–12)

This call does propose a linguistic politics—that the naming of an idea
of freedom gives it conceptual force and helps generate new ideas of
social existence: "For the labourer thou art bread" (217); "To the rich
thou art a check" (226); "Thou art Justice" (230); "Thou art Wisdom"
(234); "Thou art Peace" (238); "Thou art Love" (246); "Spirit, Patience, Gentleness, / All that can adorn and bless / Art thou" (258–
60). Yet the simile of "a dream's dim imagery" opens a difficulty related
both to the master-trope of "mask" and the genre of dream vision.
Fighting tyranny with allegorical signs, "the sing-song of instructive
nursery-rhymes or routine political oration" is a rarefied political poetics: "If the poem does not express a total loss of faith in politics,"
remarks Thomas Edwards, "it at best shows such faith sustained only
by the mythologizing of political issues, making them rhetorical and
symbolic 'properties' in a moral drama whose relation to the actual
public case grows increasingly tenuous."[6]
    This tenuousness even attends aesthetically complex poetic lan-
guage. Shelley intends his words and poetic forms to pattern political
action against "God and Law and King":

"Let a vast assembly be,
And with great solemnity
Declare with measured words that ye
Are, as God has made ye, free—

"Be your strong and simple words
Keen to wound as sharpened swords,
And wide as targes let them be
With their shade to cover ye.   (295–302)

A declaration "with measured words" is not only a speech act, but also
a poetic act: "measured" involves rational self-possession with poetic
form as its prestigious expression ("poetry" is "measured" language,
says A Defence, 484) [514]. With simple but insistent poetic
measures—the chime of e-rhymes and tones (assembly, be, solemnity,
Declare, ye, ye, free, be ye); the drumbeat of meter, the artful repetition
of syntax—Shelley asserts the authority of poetry in this fantasy of
political performance. As is often the case with his most invested imaginings, however, they seed their own subversion. The seed here is
the critical poetic figure in these verses, the analogy of words to weapons, with a troping of poetic form to sharpen the point: words are not
just likened to and rhymed with swords, but are literally infused into
them: swords. This semantic wit, however, is also the event that ex-

---

6. *Imagination and Power* 165, 168. See also Goldsmith: "the transformation from silence to
speech, from death to life [. . .] ends oppression automatically, as if the dismantling of power
on the terrain of political discourse were somehow a *generic* dismantling of domination
itself"; "power appears to be insubstantial, a mere language effect that evaporates the moment one brings to an end its monopoly over representation" (256).

poses the poetic self-service of Shelley's fantasy. The rhyme-force and
the graphemic pun of *words/swords* are forms that register in writing
and reading rather than in speech and listening. The poetic forms that
make Shelley's political point do not translate into oration.[7]

Moving from the definition of "Freedom" to the agenda of "Let a
great Assembly be / Of the fearless and the free" (262 ff.)—these are
rhymes that really chime—Shelley's orator first argues that the transition from the idea ("Freedom") to the political fact ("free") has to be
expressed in "deeds, not words" (260–61). Yet Shelley's medium of
words soon makes them (a substitution for) deeds, and soon even
deeds are being cast into the silent signifying of a readable text:

> "Stand ye calm and resolute,
> Like a forest close and mute,
> With folded arms and looks which are
> Weapons of unvanquished war.   (319–22)

The allegorical version and justification for this translation of deeds
into mute spectacle is the sudden death of Anarchy. This is a phan-
tasmic event initiated by a "maniac maid" who lies down before the
onrushing army of tyrants—an outward action, or mask, that covers
the identity that her voice claims: "her name was Hope, she said: / But
she looked more like Despair" (86–88). Shelley's point is that what
looks like surrender is a potentially revolutionary performance, a political art. Prefiguring the later call for vast passive resistance, the
maid's risk of martyrdom is redeemed by a miraculous epiphanic female intervention, an advent that simultaneously leaves Anarchy dead
and releases the oratory to the "Men of England":

> between her and her foes
> A mist, a light, an image rose,
> Small at first, and weak, and frail
> Like the vapour of a vale:
>
> Till as clouds grow on the blast,
> Like tower-crowned giants striding fast
> And glare with lightnings as they fly,
> And speak in thunder to the sky,
>
> It grew—a Shape arrayed in mail
> Brighter than the Viper's scale,
> And upborne on wings whose grain
> Was as the light of sunny rain.
>
> On its helm, seen far away,
> A planet, like the Morning's, lay,
> And those plumes its light rained through
> Like a shower of crimson dew.

---

7. In "Ode to Liberty," by contrast, Shelley does not rhyme *sword* and *word* or claim their
congruity, but exerts the former against the latter: "Ye the oracle have heard: / Lift the
victory-flashing sword, / And cut the snaky knots of this foul gordian word" (i.e., "the impious
name / Of KING"); "The sound has poison in it, 'tis the sperm / Of what makes life foul,
cankerous, and abhorred" (216–23). The strong rhymes are *heard/word* and *sword/abhorred*.

With step as soft as wind it past
O'er the heads of men—so fast
That they knew the presence there,
And looked,—but all was empty air.

As flowers beneath May's footstep waken
As stars from Night's loose hair are shaken
As waves arise when loud winds call
Thoughts sprung where'er that step did fall.    (102–25)

This is a "vision of Poesy" as politics that bears a recognizable Shelleyan cast, of ideals sustained and simultaneously attenuated by their mode of representation. Notwithstanding its ground in "Hope" and the array in quasi-military mail, the political work of this "Shape" in Shelley's rhetoric is both tentative and ambivalent. Some read a political allegory in the way the verse accumulates comparisons and analogies, a Shelleyan signature of visionary access.[8] Yet the central agency, the "Shape" (its visionary status marked with a capital) is elevated and limited to an intangible, phenomenal "presence" that finally produces "empty air"—in other words, visionary poetry, rather than material change, or even a practical program for the crises of 1819. When the *Athenæum* noted the publication of 1832, it felt compelled to explain that while *The Masque of Anarchy* (the title Hunt applied) is "political" in subject, "Shelley was too much of a poet to be a good politician, and, with every wish to be simple and plain, he is much too lofty in his conceptions to be either," and it went on to alert readers that Shelley's "account of the Peterloo affair [. . .] is not in the customary style of reports."[9]

Admirers of the poem's political vision shift uncomfortably at Shelley's summary appeal to "the old laws of England" (331), as if this social form were discontinuous with the modern sale of "laws . . . in England" (231–32). Paul Foot tries to rescue the contradiction and Shelley in general ("at the end of the poem, he seems to be openly advocating revolution"), but he has to concede that for "much of the poem Shelley seems to be counselling the people to behave constitutionally, and to protest within the system."[1] The contradiction that finally stumps Foot (who sees it in other of Shelley's political poems) has to do with the way passivity, even (or especially) in a heroic masquerade, can serve the interests of tyranny. While Shelley never consciously put his art to such service, his anxiety about the historical processes of change is related to this effect. Behind the contradiction

8. See Scrivener for Shelley's evasion of the question of revolutionary action (209). David Simpson (thinking of the "libertarian theory of history" in *A Defence*) discerns a political allegory: "The principle of creativity and liberation from habit is embodied in the unstable qualities of [Shelley's] metaphoric mode as it continues to create new metaphors in an ongoing displacement of figures already formed," and this is a dynamic "Shelley means to relate very directly to the nature of, and prospects for, historical change in society at large" (*Wordsworth and the Figurings of the Real* [Atlantic Highlands, N.J.: Humanities Press, 1982] 117). I think this extension problematic, but what interests me is Shelley's capacity to charge his forms with such appeal.
9. *Athenæum* 262 (November 3, 1832) 705.
1. *Shelley's Revolutionary Year* 16.

is a lively specter of anarchy, not in the Crown but in the Men of England. Before he heard of Peterloo, Shelley worried to Peacock about a radical monetary reform from which working classes would benefit (replacing the "fraud" of paper currency and the sinking fund with "paying in gold"): "England seems to be in a very disturbed state. [. . .] But the change should commence among the higher orders, or anarchy will only be the last flash before despotism. I wonder & tremble" (August 24, 1819; *Letters* 2:115).

Some of this trembling appears in the contradictory elements that Shelley writes into the aftermath of the revolutionary Shape's advent:

> And the prostrate multitude
> Looked—and ankle-deep in blood,
> Hope that maiden most serene
> Was walking with a quiet mien.   (126–29)

The prostrate multitude—the political class that extends the maniac maid's political theater—sees two things: the quiet serenity with which this courageous maid survives, and the sea of blood on which she survives. The ringing refrain, "Rise like Lions . . . / In unvanquishable number," remarks Michael Scrivener, is no appeal to "moral argument, but a political exhortation, an appeal to *physical* superiority."[2] The Tories, for their part, were alarmed by the working-class formation at St. Peter's Fields: a disciplined, carefully rehearsed, display of grievance —a kind of embodied public poetry boding revolution.[3] Shelley's caution is to be sensed in his exhortation of this class to value the work of poetry. The epiphanic female orator instructs the assembly that

> "Science, Poetry, and Thought
> Are thy lamps; they make the lot
> Of the dwellers in a cot
> So serene, they curse it not.   (254–57)

This "delicious stanza," Hunt says in his Preface of 1832, produces "a most happy and comforting picture in the midst of visions of blood and tumult"[4] and he was happy to review its imagery as a striking "*political anticipation*" (his italics) of what could be judged, in retrospect, as the right policy: "the Poet recommends that there should be no active resistance, come what might; which is a piece of fortitude, however effective, which we believe was not contemplated by the Political Unions: yet, in point of the spirit of the thing, the success he anticipates has actually occurred, and after his very fashion. [. . .] The battle was won without a blow" (x–xi).

---

2. *Radical Shelley* 209.
3. It was "the *discipline* of the sixty or a hundred thousand who assembled on St. Peter's Fields which aroused such alarm"; beyond the frightening size of the demonstration was the "profounder fear evoked by the evidence of the translation of the rabble into a disciplined *class*" (Thompson 682).
4. Leigh Hunt, Preface, *The Masque of Anarchy. A Poem. by Percy Bysshe Shelley* (London: Edward Moxon, 1832) x.

The Reformists' view of success, however, is not equivalent to the sum of Shelley's ambivalent vision of Poesy, which wavers between a call to revolutionary resistance and an aesthetic fantasy of melioration. Or to put this issue in the language of Shelley's contradictory imaginings: will anarchy be reformed by a visionary light that looks like "crimson dew" (117), or by a violence "ankle-deep in blood" (127)? Foot privileges what the framing rhetoric of the oratory also privileges by its repetition and its summary position: "Rise like lions after slumber." This is the activist language that the political unions *did* take up. The frame shaped by its two stanzas (151–55, 368–72) is the most critical form in *The Mask*, for it not only occludes but usurps the initial dream frame. It frames a substitute reality. That the poem remains in the rhetoric of its fantasized oratory (a draft does not even apply closing quotation marks, merely a prospective dash)[5] suggests Shelley's imaginative investment in this voice. At the same time, the suppression of the poem's initiating frame marks an aesthetic ideology that is as delimited as it is motivated by its challenge to political ideology. Shedding the dream frame, Shelley positions the fantasy oration for a potentially wider circulation, implying that a political action has emerged from visionary Poesy, that the dream song has scripted a voice for the "Men of England." If the frame were to return, it would cast the oration as an unreal event—a wish and a dream, a fantasy wrought by visions of Poesy—at the very moment that Shelley wants to insist on its political potency.[6]

A sonnet written later the same year, whose scope extends beyond Peterloo, also tropes poetic fantasy as political—but with a sense of craft now cannily managing the strains as figures of the dilemma. Shelley did not delude himself about the prospect of publishing "England in 1819."[7] Yet the absence of an historically immediate audience gave him the license to write a political poem for the ends of self-arousal. The effect is nowhere more in evidence than in the dramatic drive of syntax toward a predicate that seems a symbolic poetics for the action it describes.

> An old, mad, blind, despised, and dying King;
> Princes, the dregs of their dull race, who flow
> Through public scorn,—mud from a muddy spring;
> Rulers who neither see nor feel nor know,
> But leechlike to their fainting country cling
> Till they drop, blind in blood, without a blow.
> A people starved and stabbed in th'untilled field;

5. See Reiman's edition (32); even if this "intermediary" holograph fair copy was "not intended as press copy" (1), Mary Shelley's later press-copy manuscript, which Shelley reviewed and corrected, also lacks a closing quotation mark.
6. My thinking about the ideological function of *The Mask*'s unclosed frame has been helped by Richard A. Burt's shrewd analysis of a similar structure in *The Taming of the Shrew* ("Charisma, Coercion, and Comic Form in *The Taming of the Shrew*," *Criticism* 26 [1984] 295–31).
7. See the letter to Hunt in which he enclosed the sonnet (December 23, 1819; *Letters* 2:167); "England in 1819" was first published much later than *The Mask of Anarchy*, in Mary Shelley's edition of 1839.

> An army, whom liberticide and prey
> Makes as a two-edged sword to all who wield;
> Golden and sanguine laws which tempt and slay;
> Religion Christless, Godless—a book sealed;
> A senate, Time's worst statute, unrepealed—
> Are graves from which a glorious Phantom may
> Burst, to illumine our tempestuous day.

With impressive skill, Shelley defies Italian and Shakespearean forms, increasing the syntactic pressure of his list of ills and grievances toward the predicate, the blunt statement of line 13, "Are graves." Even here the syntax does not close, but extends into a couplet that defies rhyme pattern with a push toward *Burst*.

Yet as forceful as this play against formal prescription is, it registers with uncertain effect, as three sample readings show. For Stuart Curran, the drama of form is set against the idea of form:

> The sudden enjambment of the final couplet, with its ambiguous modal auxiliary—"may"—throw[s] the accumulated weight of the single-sentence catalog onto the active, explosive verb so long awaited. The melding of form and content appears seamless. Yet ultimately the appearance is a paradox, for the informing idea of this marriage is an impossibility: the subject, as Shelley conceives it, is pitted against the form itself. [. . .] Shelley pivots his poem on a syntactic potentiality—"may"—that yields to the bursting of its formal bonds in a movement parallel to the revolutionary explosion that will invert the anti-forms repressing contemporary society. The form symbolically consumes itself, as surely as does the society it catalogs.[8]

For Curran, *may* caps a rhetorical feat that takes precedence over its ambiguous mode. For F. R. Leavis, it is a sign of hesitation coinciding with a "pathetic weakness" of both form and statement: the "oddly ironical stress" that "results from the rime position" sustains no more than a Phantom of miraculous agency.[9] Timothy Webb finds the stress on *may* tough-minded: "Shelley's intellectual honesty prevents him from even believing wholeheartedly in such an incarnation: the rhyme scheme insists that we underline the improbability of this redemption by stressing the word *may*. [. . .] A mere escapist would not have allowed that ironical and limiting stress on *may*. Surely the point is that Shelley's sense of evil is too strong rather than too weak?"[1]

What these divergent readings show is that the question Webb poses rhetorically is one Shelley's formalist poetics produce as genuine and genuinely unresolvable. It is no overstatement to say that Shelley's sonnet stakes the force of its predicate—a force both conceptual and, more specifically, political—on a simultaneous apprehension of form

---

8. *Poetic Form and British Romanticism* (New York: Oxford University Press, 1986) 55.
9. "Shelley" 213.
1. *Shelley: A Voice Not Understood* (Atlantic Highlands, N.J.: Humanities Press International, 1977) 107–8.

and grammar. In the register of form, *may* has significance as a rhyme form weakened in the rush to *Burst*; in the register of grammar, it designates a merely tentative hope. Curran argues for the former, in effect a signifying form, and Webb and Leavis for the reverse, seeing weak rhyme conveying, for better or for worse, limited confidence. There is, moreover, a semantic indeterminacy in the two incompatible senses of *may*. If it means "perhaps," it is tentative, whether optimistically or skeptically, in the way that Leavis and Webb recognize. But if it means "is enabled," or even "is empowered to," then it is energized in the way that Curran suggests.[2]

The array of signals in this climactic couplet—fantasy, hesitation, faint hope, affirmative prophesy—make the question ultimately undecidable. Shelley's poetic form keeps the possibilities in tension. Even his letter to Hunt pivots interestingly on the point: "I do not expect you to publish it, but you may show it to whom you please," he said of the sonnet (*Letters* 2:167). Publication would provoke two audiences, the oppressed for whom the sonnet articulates political grievance and the oppressors for whom it articulates a political threat. The compromise of giving it to Hunt with no demands, but with yet another calculated overload on *may*, places the agency on him: either with Shelley's permission, or as a possibility from his own judgment, he "may" show the poem to readers in England in 1819.

\* \* \*

## NANCY MOORE GOSLEE

### Dispersoning Emily:
### Drafting as Plot in *Epipsychidion*†

Just over thirty years ago Daniel Hughes argued that the apparent formlessness of Shelley's poetry was a deliberate artistic choice, the representation of the mind's process in the act of creation. "I would suggest," Hughes writes, "a method of reading Shelley, and particularly *Epipsychidion*, which sees calculated coherence and calculated collapse, the whole to mirror in its progress the process of mind as it creates the poem." Hughes argues that these collapses are deliberate and artistically controlled for thematic purposes. The theme, he says, is to show the mind—Shelley's own mind, yet also all minds, consid-

2. Paul de Man reads such syntaxes as a deconstructive contest between semiology and rhetoric: "the same grammatical pattern engenders two meanings that are mutually exclusive" ("Semiology and Rhetoric," in *Allegories of Reading* [New Haven: Yale University Press, 1979] 9). Jerome McGann reads a sad ambivalence in the grammatical mood: if Shelley's subjunctive *may* "hopes for a future promise, a glimpse of some far goal in time," it is also "deeply [. . .] allied to his sense of hopelessness"—"the consciousness out of which Shelley's greatest works were created" (*The Romantic Ideology: A Critical Investigation* [Chicago: University of Chicago Press, 1983] 112–13).
† An earlier version of this article appeared in *Keats-Shelley Journal* 42 (1993): 104–19. Reprinted by permission of the publisher, The Keats-Shelley Association of America, Inc.

ered more universally—in the process of creation.[1] Using *Epipsychidion* as Hughes did, in this paper I want to pursue the relationship, the gap or abyss, between rhetoric and history. Using the draft notebooks as well as the final printed text, I will argue that Shelley's conversion of Teresa Viviani from person to rhetorical personification leads in the draft notebooks not only to the insufficiency of the speaker's language to represent, but also to the power of the writer's metaphor to create. I will also argue that the drafts redefine what we might call compositional impasses, collapses in the actual writing process, as several different kinds of rhetorical collapses. Through these two different sorts of collapses—one that tries to evoke and praise an objective other yet recognizes the mind's creation of the object, and another that tries to move the subject-in-creation from an actual, snarled process to the representing of that process—we can see how the interplay between the intentions of the poet and the intentionality of figure and genre creates the autobiography of a life-giving experience of love—Shelley's *Vita Nuova*.[2]

The most central "figure" in the poem, both in the sense of a person or character and in the sense of a rhetorical figure or the lodestone for most of the poem's rhetorical figures, is of course Emilia: Teresa Viviani, daughter of the governor of Pisa, but also Dantean courtly mistress, synechdoche of all good and beauty (Hogle), woman transformed into an allegorical personification like Intellectual Beauty (Essick, but also Shelley himself in his preface drafts).[3] Because this figure occupies the boundary or liminal space between history and rhetoric, an unusually well-defined and narrow boundary between person and personification, she conveys not only the ecstatic joy of a life-redeeming vision but the uneasiness Stephen Knapp describes as a characteristic effect of allegorical personification—of words taking on daemonic or demonic force, of deities convertible to words.[4] In the *Ode to Liberty*, as I have argued elsewhere, Shelley begins with an abstract word or figure, evokes an increasingly powerful mythic and sculptural figure of "Liberty" as mother and as maenad, and then con-

---

1. D. J. Hughes, "Coherence and Collapse in Shelley, with Particular Reference to *Epipsychidion*," *ELH* 28, no. 3 (Sept. 1961), pp. 261, 263. For more recent developments of Hughes's approach, see William Keach, *Shelley's Style* (New York: Methuen, 1984), pp. 152–53, and Jerrold E. Hogle, *Shelley's Process* (Oxford: Oxford University Press, 1988), pp. 279–86. Though William A. Ulmer includes political and feminist interpretations of the poem, following Michael Scrivener's *Radical Shelley* (Princeton: Princeton University Press, 1982), pp. 267–73, his interpretation, like Hogle's, is primarily based on a theory of language and rhetorical figure that undermines "historical" interpretations: in *Shelleyan Eros: The Rhetoric of Romantic Love* (Princeton: Princeton University Press, 1990), ch. 6. See Angela Leighton, "Love, Writing, and Scepticism in *Epipsychidion*," in *The New Shelley: Later Twentieth Century Views*, ed. G. Kim Blank (London: Macmillan, 1991), pp. 220–41, for a helpful alignment of historical vs. rhetorical criticism on this poem and for the implications of this conflict for a feminist reading.
2. Richard E. Brown, "The Role of Dante in *Epipsychidion*," *Comparative Literature* 30, no. 3 (Summer 1978), pp. 224–25, notes that Carlos Baker was the first to make this analogy but did so without pursuing its implications.
3. See Hogle, p. 279, and Robert N. Essick, " 'A shadow of some golden dream': Shelley's Language in *Epipsychidion*," *PPL* 22, no. 2 (Spring 1986), p. 167.
4. See Knapp, *Personification and the Sublime*, p. 2. See also Jerome Mazzaro, *The Figure of Dante: an Essay on the Vita Nuova* (Princeton: Princeton University Press, 1981), pp. 127–31 for suggestions that the *Vita Nuova* enacts such a presentation and withdrawal of "deity."

trols this powerful force both by recognizing her place in an established genre—the progress ode—and by recognizing her as a word, as a figure of speech for which we are responsible.[5]

In *Epipsychidion* genre is far more elusive, but it seems to grow out of the reflexive difficulties in developing and sustaining the praise of this almost but not quite abstract figure of Emily. The most apt illustration of this reflexiveness in the poem is, surely, the speaker's moment of despair as like Actaeon he turns on his own thoughts—thoughts he had been pursuing but which have now taken on their own momentum and have like hounds pursued and torn at him. Unlike Schulze and Hogle, I do not see this moment as a single turning-point of the poem but as an extremely powerful example of the way in which Shelley turns and re-reads the impasses or blocked moments in his pursuit, his drafting, of the poem.[6]

Thus, I will argue, the series of "collapses" of the subject-as-speaker in the 1821 printed text seems to originate in the drafts as what we might, however naively, call "genuine"—that is, historical or biographical—falterings of inspiration, particularly in the nominating lyric sections of the poem. Shelley then re-reads these marks of faltering or fading and makes them thematic. Their full thematic significance as plot for the whole poem, however, does not emerge until he has re-evaluated the language that describes the figure of the object, of "this phantom of the idol of my thought"—that is, the series of addresses and visions culminating in the presence of Emilia. By looking at one cluster of revisions for a sequence of "phantom" and "idol" images that define the object of his visionary quest, and at a series of faltering and collapses in the drafting process that come to define the composing subject, we may move toward a clearer understanding of the differing kinds of potentiality and process Shelley enacts as well as those he represents. If we can distinguish degrees and differences within the collapses, we may be able to avoid the reductionism that often plagues linguistically-based rhetorical readings, a reduction of all collapses to the recognition of allegorical difference in the signifying process of language.[7] Thus we can also begin to negotiate this gap—or abyss—between historical, contextual research and the rhetorical criticism of figurative language, a gap that Shelley's own linguistic scepticism has helped, with great brilliance, to create.

To read multiple drafts of any of Shelley's poems and to speculate about their sequence is to be drawn into a circular process, a hermeneutics we would do well to be somewhat suspicious about. When we have a relatively clear end-point, as we do in the 1821 printed text of

5. In a paper presented at the Society for Textual Scholarship conference, New York, April 1991; since published as "Pursuing Revision in Shelley's 'Ode to Liberty'," *Texas Studies in Literature and Language* 36, no. 2 (Summer 1994), pp. 166–83.
6. See Earl Schulze, "The Dantean Quest of *Epipsychidion*," *SiR* 21, no. 2 (Summer 1982), pp. 206–07, and Hogle, p. 281.
7. Here I am protesting the sort of reading that follows Paul de Man's "The Rhetoric of Temporarily" (1969; rpt. in *Blindness and Insight: Essays in the Rhetoric of Contemporary Criticism*, 2nd ed., rev., intro. by Wlad Godzich [Minneapolis: University of Minnesota Press, 1983], pp. 187–228). Both Hogle and Ulmer, as well as de Man himself, occasionally fall into this predictable "deconstructive turn."

*Epipsychidion*, we must keep it in mind as a manifest final intention of the poet.[8] Simultaneously, we must examine evidence from letters, journals, and other historical or contextual sources. Within that framework of hypothetical origins and assumed telos, we then turn to look at the various drafts, not only from these two vantage points but from within. We imagine that we are the author, proposing alternate drafts, re-reading and choosing one metaphor, one word, one lyric or narrative trajectory over another. One way to avoid some of this circularity is to affirm a radical intertextuality in which the reader declares that each draft or fragment is in effect an independent work which we are free to interpret and then relate, as one among many versions, to the final version. Although I do agree with such a radical position as an intermediate one, to clear our heads of that teleology of the final text so that we may see intermediate choices more clearly and thus recognize the final choices more fully, such a position ignores the sequences, the history of the revising process as clues to the meanings of figures and formal patterns in the final text. As we watch an image transform itself through several pages and even through several notebooks, we understand better a range of possible meanings though not necessarily limits for interpreting it in the final text. * * * Both Donald Reiman and E. B. Murray have warned that Shelley often writes pieces of drafts almost at random in three or four notebooks and then, in a kind of architectonic miracle, pulls them together in an intermediate draft.[9] Thus premature teleology based on notebook order is a constant danger.

* * *

The sense that we can read and imagine ourselves sharing Shelley's choices in revising—that as readers of the drafts we somehow can move from text to consciousness and enter the historical Shelley's mind—is one of the most seductive and exhilarating yet also one of the most tricky aspects of interpreting these drafts. With its intensely emotional lyric voice and its complex biographical background, *Epipsychidion* is particularly open to the reader's hubris that she shares the subjectivity of authorial intent. Yet it also prompts particularly strong resistance to such identification. For me that very background sets salutary limits on such a process of identifying with the author who writes these drafts for the speaker: what is the relationship be-

---

8. I am following the text (pp. 373–88) and textual information (371–72) from Donald H. Reiman and Sharon B. Powers, *Shelley's Poetry and Prose* (New York: Norton, 1977). Later editing decisions by Mary Shelley and others have influenced our perception of the poem, as Neil Fraistat reminds me, but for *Epipsychidion* the 1821 printed text is a relatively stable resting-point for the purposes of discussing authorial intention.

9. I owe my formulation of this Nietzschean or Riffaterrean view of intertextuality to conversation with my colleague B. J. Leggett; a version of this position is proposed by Tilottama Rajan, in her reading of *The Triumph of Life* (*Supplement*, ch. 12), though she has not extended this approach to drafts of more stable printed works or, for that matter, to works earlier than *The Triumph of Life*. For warnings about interpreting Shelley's uses of several draft notebooks for long works, see Donald H. Reiman, ed., *Percy Bysshe Shelley, Volume VII: "Shelley's Last Notebook": Bodleian MS. Shelley adds. e. 20* (New York: Garland, 1990), pp. 97–103, in a discussion of *Adonais*, and E. B. Murray, ed., *Percy Bysshe Shelley, Volume IV: A Facsimile of Bodleian MS. Shelley d. 1* (New York: Garland, 1988), p. 367.

tween the historical Teresa Viviani and the muse-like Emilia of the poem? What voice does she have, as Ulmer asks, in her own representation? If she is its intended audience, how does she read it? Even more disturbing, how does Mary Shelley, normally the first reader of the notebook drafts, respond as resisting reader to these drafts? Why do we have no drafts for the section describing the crisis in the speaker's relationship to the Moon—that is, to Mary?[1] These questions are not intended at all to dismiss the poem but instead to emphasize the complexity of readers' responses to the drafts and to possible judgments about them. Once these tensions are acknowledged, however, it becomes easier to see how important the role and masks of rhetorical figure and literary convention become in the writing of the poem, to codify attitudes and to evade, defer, or transform personal pain as well as joy.

Searching for such literary models and conventions in the poem also involves a certain element of circularity: if we hold in mind the conventions of courtly love and particularly the model of an autobiographical narrative of its difficulties and its idealizations, we can conjecture that Shelley has Dante's *Vita Nuova* in mind and and is shaping his own poem either toward it or in response to it. Because Shelley both names this work and quotes from it in his preface to the printed poem, surely we are meant to pursue it as ideal. Further, in the finished poem we do find something like its peculiar mixture of lyric, narrative, and discursive modes; of the writer's frequent collapses as he recognizes his own inadequacy, both social and poetic; and the complex near-allegorizing of the woman as object of the speaker's love.[2]

Most important for my exploring of personification, the lines Shelley quotes in his preface come from the twenty-fifth chapter of the *Vita Nuova*, a reflexive chapter in which Dante argues that personification—in this case not of Beatrice but of Love—should be transferred from classical to vernacular literature. Here Dante's own uncertainty about the rhetorical status of Love in the chapter Shelley quotes from destabilizes and makes more clearly teasing the lines he does quote—that is, that we should not doubt the presence of a stable, existent signified beyond the "garment of figuration," the "colors of rhetoric."[3] Yet if we look closely at the draft notebooks, the *Vita Nuova* seems to become almost like Emily herself in the poem—a late-comer, a figure fulfilling and completing the form but not the source for the structuring vision or visions. For the first explicit reference to the *Vita* comes not only in Bodleian MS. Shelley d. l, but in its third draft of the advertisement—and aside from the preface drafts, all drafts of

1. For Ulmer's question, see *Shelleyan Eros*, p. 147. The lines of the 1821 printed text for which we have no known notebook drafts run from lines 310–67 and then 384–512. We have neither an intermediate fair copy nor a printer's fair copy of this poem.
2. See Timothy Webb, *The Violet in the Crucible: Shelley and Translation* (Oxford: Clarendon Press, 1976), p. 297. Alan Weinberg's reading of *Epipsychidion* in *Shelley's Italian Experience*, while extremely sensitive to the subtlety of Shelley's revisions of Dante, discounts, I think, too fully what we might call the domestic function of his idealizing rhetoric (London: Macmillan, 1991), pp. 142–43.
3. See *Dante's "Vita Nuova", a Translation and an Essay*, by Mark Musa, rev. ed. (Bloomington: Indiana University Press, 1973), pp. 54–56. See also Mazzaro, *The Figure of Dante*, p. 127.

*Epipsychidion* in this notebook come from the final section of the poem.

Let me turn, now, to look more closely at the development of the two forms of collapse I began with: the "depersoning" of Teresa and the despair of the writer or the speaker at his inadequacy. Most of my examples are drawn from Bod. MS. Shelley adds. e. 8, and particularly from drafts of the two autobiographical narratives.[4]

We hardly need turn to Dante, of course, for models of an intensely physical woman as intellectual and spiritual muse veiled behind a screen of music and light, since this figure occurs repeatedly in Shelley's own poems. He was translating passages from *Prometheus Unbound* for Teresa, including the lyric celebrating Asia's transfiguration at the end of Act II; and in Bod. MS. Shelley adds. e. 12, the drafts of the opening lines of *Epipsychidion*, beginning "To Teresa Emilia Viviani," are written over drafts of Asia's quest in that act.[5]

In Bod. MS. Shelley adds. e. 8, pages 47–51, Shelley revises these transcendent addresses begun, I speculate, in adds. e. 12, and then begins a narrative of the speaker's encounter with the woman who is their focus: "She met me ~~stranger~~ reader in a ~~dell of cave by~~ ⟨upon⟩ life's dark way" (p. 61, lines 1a–2). In the shift from categorizing metaphors in his direct address to a more discursive description, he approaches and then backs away from "the color of your eyes—& hair" —a phrase I borrow from adds. e. 12, p. 69—leaving us guessing. At the point where he most strongly evokes her physical presence, his draft first enacts a deliberate rhetorical collapse, then cancels this literary collapse in an actual compositional collapse—and then constructs Emily deliberately as "Metaphor." Yet this "depersoning" leads to the emergence and autonomy of another personification and, through their opposition and interchange, to the emergence of a more sustained narrative.

Astonishingly, however, the first sub-narrative, the one that develops from pages 61–69, emerges from another faltering narrative that Shelley had apparently drafted a month or two before meeting Teresa Viviani. Tatsuo Tokoo's 1992 paper and Carlene Adamson's edition both identify those drafts on pages 60–68 in adds. e. 8 as first written for the fictional narrative *Fiordispina*, a poem probably thought of, Adamson suggests, as a response to Keats's *Eve of St. Agnes*.[6] Whatever Keatsian concreteness Shelley at first attributes to his imaginary heroine, however, begins to dissolve into a Shelleyan envisioning resembling Asia's transfiguration in *Prometheus Unbound*, Act III. This

4. I wish to thank the Bodleian Library Oxford, for permission to quote from Bodleian MSS. Shelley adds. e. 8 and e. 12. My citations from Bod. MS. Shelley d. 1 are from Murray's facsimile edition.

5. For the translations, see Neville Rogers, *Shelley at Work*, 2nd ed. (Oxford: Clarendon Press, 1967), p. 242.

6. Carlene Adamson, *Percy Bysshe Shelley, Volume VI: Shelley's Pisan Winter Notebook (1820–21), A Facsimile of Bodleian MS. Shelley adds. e. 8* (New York: Garland, 1992), and *Percy Bysshe Shelley, Volume XVIII: The Homeric Hymns and 'Prometheus' Drafts Notebook: Bodleian MS. Shelley adds. e. 12* (New York: Garland, 1996). Tatsuo Tokoo's conference paper, "The Composition of *Epipsychidion*: Some Manuscript Evidence," appears in *KSJ* 42 (1993), pp. 97–103; the present essay originally appeared in the same issue, pp. 104–19.

description of the heroine, Adamson argues, dominates or even usurps the already under-developed plot of *Fiordispina*. After Shelley meets Teresa Viviani in December 1820, he incorporates this highly-figurative sequence of descriptive phrases into the new poem addressed to her. Rededicating his description of a fictional woman—Fiordispina— to an actual one—Teresa or Emilia Viviani—he then intensifies the process of making her less and less actual. At the same time the narrative speaker also moves from his position outside the fiction of *Fiordispina* to the far more central position of lover within the reportedly "autobiographical" narrative of *Epipsychidion*. The second sub-narrative, drafted later in the notebook, seems to have emerged more directly from Shelley's relationship with Viviani—or at least from this new, recast narrative for Emilia.

In the middle of page 62, transcendent and physical responses begin to merge: "beyond the fathom-line of ~~passions thought~~ / ~~love's own search~~ / ~~Upon From her ⟨dusky⟩~~ / ~~sense or~~ thought / ~~Out of her loose hair~~, & sense ~~felt not~~" (lines 8–9). Then two more half lines describing her hair are cancelled and deferred, replaced with "flowing outlines" (p. 63) of "inutterable power" (both phrases cancelled), now "invisible power which wraps the world" (p. 63, line 3). Fairly smooth composition flows from the bottom of page 63 through the middle of p. 64. At that point, either his first draft of the deictic phrase "There she stands" on line 11 of that page or the sexually evocative similes that refuse to move "Beyond the sense . . . Like fiery Dews that melt / Into the bosom of a frozen ~~flower~~ bud," evoke all too much presence. By addressing the inadequacy of his own speaking or writing to describe her presence and by establishing images of distance and light instead of heat, the next lines cool off the representation of the writer's feelings:

> Alas, ~~poor Verse, well may it overpower~~
> Th~~y feeble sight to gaze upon thee~~
> ~~Their/Thine eyes to gaze~~        upon ~~this~~
> Thine . . . ~~dazzled~~ eyes to gaze        maiden
>            ~~feeble~~

The "poor verse" personified with its "feeble eyes" may describe Shelley's own problems with eyesight in mid-December to mid-January.[7] Yet the passage also has trouble with whose eyes are gazing upon whom, with locating the subject. Perhaps for this reason, he goes on to cancel this whole passage—which itself deliberately dramatizes a collapse of poetic power. He then turns to a passage in which deictic gesture and the recognized play of metaphoric signifiers deliberately confront one another:

> Their ⟨eyes⟩
>        ⟨~~wings~~⟩        mortal shape

---

7. Such an autobiographical allusion would work only after Shelley rededicates these lines to Viviani; though there is a change of ink and pen cut after the second line in this passage, both sections were probably drafted earlier in the fall.

> See where she stands! . . . a ~~Human form~~ endued
> . . .
> With ~~life & light & immortality~~
>              of          deity
> A ~~form of it must change which cannot die~~
> . . . . . . . . . . . . . . . . .
> A metaphor ~~of morning & of spring~~   (p. 65)

To show the power of this "metaphor" of spring, Shelley creates an antagonist—but the antagonist, a personified Frost, keeps developing intentions of his own, taking over 2 1/2 pages of the draft. In the course of this usurpation, however, the figure metamorphoses into the "golden" Being of the next narrative segment—that is, into the vision Emily will manifest in the next section of the adds. e. 8 drafts of *Epipsychidion*.

On page 65 this antagonist is first "~~the tempests~~," then "~~The Spirit~~" (though that phrase may refer to the vision herself), then the "⟨~~sullen clouds~~⟩," then the "~~cold snake Frost~~," then in the next line "The ~~Phantom~~ Frost" with a cancelled "spectre" below the line. Next appears twice the phrase "Frost ⟨the⟩ Anatomy," first fully and then partially cancelled. Thus this figure changes from natural phenomenon to metaphor to Gothic spirit to skeleton. Like Milton's representation of the personified Death as Knapp describes it, this figure threatens readers with an unstable oscillation between deity and mere word.[8]

Here, however, this deity is reborn as another deity. Sent to his "~~chrystalline cave~~," Frost is again "~~a Phantom flown / From the embraces of the a ⟨dreaming⟩~~ . . ." but the next line reads "A ~~spirit~~ A ~~Dream of some ⟨?to⟩~~ dream of / A ~~Phantom from ⟨ineffable⟩ the~~," and at the top of p. 66,

>              ~~beautiful as a Ghost~~
>       ~~A Phantom~~
>              ~~—a Phantom from the dream~~
>       . . . . . . . . . . . . . .
>       Leaving the imperial   (lines 1–3)

As if by the witch-like play of the figure itself, this phantom of opposition now becomes the spring vision. For, in a new hand—either stopping to fix his pen or starting again later—Shelley backs up to revise the earlier lines directly describing Emily but now carrying into them a transformed and cross-gendered phantom:

>       With love, & light & life & d[ie]eity
>              A
>       ~~The~~ Shadow of some bright eternity
>              A              ~~unremembered~~
>       ~~The Phantom of some Poets        dream~~
>       ~~Wandring into awakened life, the Beam~~
>       . . . . . . . . . . . . . .
>              Leaving the morning planet pil~~o~~tless
>                        (lines 10–13, 15)

---

8. See Knapp, *Personification and the Sublime*, p. 59.

At the bottom of p. 67, she is again the "Phantom [from]of some golden dream . . . And her planet ⟨?wanderd⟩ planet is / Leaving some wandering." Although this draft segment stops here and the next section of *Epipsychidion* does not begin again until page 93, the "wandering" off of his wording may represent here, rough as the draft looks, not the failure of inspiration but instead a reshaping of it. For this passage about the planet Venus seems to be the first allusion to Dante in the drafts. As Webb and Schulze have pointed out, it comes from the first canzone in the *Convito*, which Shelley translated probably sometime in 1820 in adds. e. 9 and commented on in the back of this notebook, adds. e. 8; and that lyric describes a debate over two women, one earthly and one transcendent.[9] Shelley's flight from the deictic "There she stands" into metaphor and then into a psychomachia with the Phantom Frost who is reborn as the Vision leads not only into a more idealizing form for Emily but also into the more extended narrative of pilgrimage and quest drawn, in broad form, from Dante's reflexive, allegorical quest for his ideal woman in the *Convito* and the *Divine Comedy*.

When Shelley begins the next unit of the *Epipyschidion* draft on page 93, below a drawing of someone in a tube or a coffin or a peculiar boat, he begins, revising in ink over pencil, "I loved a lady from / My Spirit, in the golden dreams dawn of youth / Met one . . . "—and in pencil below, "My spirit in the golden dreams." As he begins a new part of the draft in ink, he changes emphasis and objectifies: "There was a Being who . . . Ther was a Being . . . whom my Spirit oft / Met in on the its winged visioned wandering far aloft / In the bright golden dawn prime of my youth youths prime / dawn." His elaboration of this "bright dawn," however, stalls him in an idyllic landscape that he escapes only by what seems to be a compositional collapse in a passage on page 96.

With this compositional collapse, I'll shift my emphasis from the figures of the object—"idol" or phantom—to the figure of the composing and discomposed subject. In the final printed text this collapse—the passage reading "Ah woe is me! What have I dared? where am I lifted? how / Shall I descend and perish not?" follows the passage in which Shelley turns from pointing to Emily's physical presence to praising her as Metaphor incarnate. In the draft notebook, it follows the beginning of the second narrative sequence, the historicizing autobiography, as this narrative too stalls in its idyllic originating scene. After repeated attempts to describe that early paradise, he writes, in a small rough hand, "Ah woe is me" and then, below it, begins again in a firmer hand, "What have I dared. . . ." These lines seem to record a felt breakdown of inspiration, of power either to describe that early paradise or of despair at retrieving it in later experience; but they are quickly recognized and incorporated into the definition of that place's ineffability. At this point, we might say that he has only begun to realize the structural possibilities in the reading

9. See Webb, *Violet*, p. 302 and Schulze, "Dantean Quest," pp. 200–01.

and reshaping of breakdowns, in their conversion into rhetoric. Further, he has only begun to recognize the narrative form which will eventually become lines 190–344 of the completed poem.

Though he continues over nine pages with increasing confidence, through a draft of the poisonous figure by the well (lines 255–66 in the printed version), on page 106 he begins to revise the opening of that passage, writes two half-lines, and then—with white space all around—prints the word "chaos" and goes over it and darkens it with the pen-point. After that reflective pause, page 107 continues in the same fairly sure script as that of the preceding pages but is in content a collapse into or "~~Across~~ an open g grave: . . . —I leapt in . . . ~~what hope~~ / What ~~hope what~~ / Angels lifted me,; & kept at bay / ~~Oblivion~~ sexton who / The swarming [?hours] ~~that heap the heavy clay~~ / . . . ~~Upon the scull~~ . . . coffin lid" (lines 2, 7, 16–19). Not used in the final poem, these lines are a dead-end in several senses.

On page 108 he begins again, "In many ~~forms in many hopes I sought~~ / The shadow of the/is idol of my thought" and moves easily into the Actaeon-image that Schulze and Hogle see as a turning-point of the poem, the turning on his own thoughts as he recognizes that they have been his chimerical goal: "~~when~~ as hunted deer that cd. not flee / ~~And I turned on the thoughts~~ / ~~Those winged sextons of the soul~~ / I turned upon ~~the~~ my thoughts & stood at bay / ~~Bleeding~~ Wounded & torn & ~~famished~~ panting . . . ." Because the discarded "gothic" or graveyard passage also used the metaphor "kept at bay," rhyming with the "heavy clay" that threatens to bury him, we might see this passage on the following page as a more vivid and more fully allusive development of the dead-end draft, leading again from his own turn to read his drafts and recognize their potentiality. In this sweep of inspiration, however, such a reading would have been the work of a moment, for he goes on with relatively great fluidity to describe his "deliverance" from this assault of his own thoughts. In terms of the Actaeon myth echoed so powerfully here, he has been pursued by his own hound-like thoughts for seeking and not for finding his goddess—or for believing, too many times, that he has found her. Yet no physical figure of a bathing Diana appears here—not even a figure like Beatrice in Dante's dream in the *Vita Nuova*, naked but wrapped in a red cloth.[1] Instead, just as the quester turns into the pursued, then turns to confront his own thoughts, he becomes the observed, passive body. Though he recognizes the moon as a simulacrum of the earlier vision, the "deliverance" is "As like the glorious Shape which I had dreamd / As is the ~~cold cold~~ ~~Moon~~ / Eye of night . . . whose changes ever run / Into ~~themselves~~, to the Eternal Sun." A creative subject converting him to observed object, she "makes all beautiful on which she smiles." As he tries alternative phrases for "transformed," he writes—off to the right, in a smaller hand and finer point—"Endymion," a marginal note acknowledging his changed myth and changed situating of subjectivity.

1. See ch. 3 of the *Vita Nuova*; see also Robert Payne Harrison, *The Body of Beatrice* (Baltimore: Johns Hopkins University Press, 1988), pp. 24–29.

About 12 lines later in the printed text, and in the middle of the next page in the notebook draft, he works his resemblance to Endymion into the text. On pages 110–11 his Endymion-like dream turns not to a Keatsian Adam's dream but to nightmare. Yet the composing hand seems fluid until the bottom of p. 111. Here the draft of this section breaks off, just at the beginning of the most damning descriptions of crisis in the printed poem.

He does not return to *Endymion* until p. 142, and those pages are very rough drafts of the last movement, the invitation to the voyage. Although he begins on pages 142–3 with a version of lines 573-89— "we shall become the same, we shall be one—," he then breaks off and turns to the more urbane and colloquial promise of walking around the island. When he breaks off, however, there is no collapse, no failure of vision or language in the narrative. It is at the opening of the Bod. MS. Shelley d. 1 drafts that the collapse develops—as if he had re-read adds. e. 8, recognized its patterns, and then begun this new stage of composition.

Although adds. e. 8, then, develops a two-stage autobiographical narrative—"She met me" and "There was a Being"—and begins to suggest a narrative for escape in the third part, it does not yet integrate the preaching, the doctrinal passages begun several years earlier in adds. e. 12 (pp. 67, 153–4), nor does it develop very explicitly the voyage to the semi-actual Greek island. D. 1 begins with the latter, mixing poetry with preface drafts, and finally in the third preface draft adds the explicit reference to the *Vita Nuova*. At some point before he sent the final fair copy (now missing) to Ollier, Shelley decided—in generic imitation and in thematic opposition to Dante's new life—to include the sermons on "free" or "true" love. In a complicated series of revisions through and beyond d. 1, he also decides to affirm physical love as a model for transcendental knowledge of the good and the beautiful, and yet to make the collapses of composition a model for the inadequacy of sustaining such ecstatic vision.

In d. 1, he begins the *Epipsychidion* drafts with the passage "Woe is me / the ~~plumed~~ / the ~~plumed~~ wings of words in which my ~~heart~~ soul would ~~soar~~ pierce / Beyond the ~~height~~ depth of Loves rare universe / Are ~~lead~~ chains of lead ~~upon its flight~~ which upon its fiery flight / I sink" (f102v rev; facsim 29). They are immediately followed by a draft of the preface, in which the fictional "young Englishman . . . leaped from the Ponte della Trinita" into the flooded Arno (and Shelley apparently and wisely decides that such a jump risked bathos). They do not yet, however, include the printed version's "I tremble, I expire!" Thus the text of the poem so far ends by lamenting the failure of words but not the failure of the sexual union: in "depth" that union exceeds words. By 99v rev, he has added to the physical description just preceding these lines, the phrase "and one annihilation"—and has thus brought death into the poem's text, as a description of sexual climax and yet also as a loss of consciousness of that experience. On the next page, the poem's speaker addresses Emilia by saying, "we shall meet in death"—here a literal death—if the events of life keep them

746    NANCY MOORE GOSLEE

separate; and on 97r rev, he proposes an *Adonais*-like merger of their
spirits, after physical death, with all of nature. On 96v rev comes the
draft of the preface in which Shelley explicitly proposes the *Vita Nuova*
as a model for readers,[2] and on 94r rev, still showing great uncertainty
about the conclusion, he has the speaker say that Emily will survive
him and pour libations on his grave, that she will either become
"Heaven's Spouse" or be supported by "her"—as if Beatrice is to be
her mentor in divinity. The final lines in d. 1, on 92v rev, which find
their way earlier in the completed poem, describe the two as "A living
soul of this Elysian isle / Conscious & ~~autonomous~~ united one." There
is still a clear range of possibilities here for the union or separateness
of this "living soul"—from "united" to "one," with "autonomous" ambiguously referring to the individual selves, to their merged self, or to
the personified island.

   Thus, although he explores more explicit and literal ideas of death
in these drafts, the primary meaning of the final "woe is me" collapse
seems to be the inadequacy of words to represent an achieved and
meaningful sexual union. When we turn to the printed poem, the inclusion of "annihilation" just before it and the use of "expire" within
the "woe passage" intensify this interpretation by the metaphoric use
of death for climax, but also make it more ambiguous and return us
to the hesitations about the possibility of becoming one that Shelley
expresses earlier in the final section of the poem. Rejecting the denial
of fulfilled physical love in Dante's *Vita Nuova*, Shelley affirms a merg-
ing of self and the actual other gestured to earlier in the poem—
"There she stands." At first words fail because other communication
is complete. Yet consciousness gives way to "one annihilation"; words
fail to preserve their ideal, and this elysium cannot sustain itself even
in a prophetic narrative. We might well say that this is a Keatsian
failure, in which the admission of temporality and mortality frees us
from the "cold pastoral" of a transformative, idealizing rhetoric into a
"burning forehead, and a parching tongue." Thus words fail in order
to succeed, and the allegorization of Teresa as Emily sets up the possibilities of this failure and this success—through the artifice of conventions, of courtly love and the colors of rhetoric which veil the body;
through the linguistic artifices of metaphor and of personification
which make that veil so nearly opaque that we must see it as well as
her; and through the setting of this final encounter in a prophesied
future.

   I would like to argue that this conclusion is Keatsian and experiential instead of rhetorical or linguistic, and thus to remain outside
the veil of an allegory which would necessarily predict such an outcome. If the completed poem enacts the history of its drafting crises

2. Mary Shelley's journal records that she and Percy began reading the *Vita Nuova* on Tuesday January 30 (p. 351) and that they completed it on Monday February 12, just four days before Shelley writes Ollier that he is mailing a completed copy of the poem to him (p. 353, *Journal; Letters* 2: 262–63). Feldman and Scott-Kilvert, the editors of the journal, agree with White's suggestion (2:606, n. 16) that PBS's decision to spend the evening of February 16 at Casa Silva, Lady Mountcashell's house, allowed him "to prepare and dispatch the poem without awkward questions from Mary" (353n.).

or collapses as a form of its figuration, then with the interpretive context of the drafts we may be able to combine history and rhetoric. If this claim for including the otherness of circumstances and person in the poem brings me closer to accepting the drafts as a part of the completed poem and thus to a more radical intertextuality, this is surely one of the effects that Shelley represents as his intention, through his faltering speaker and through his ambiguous, often autonomous figures.

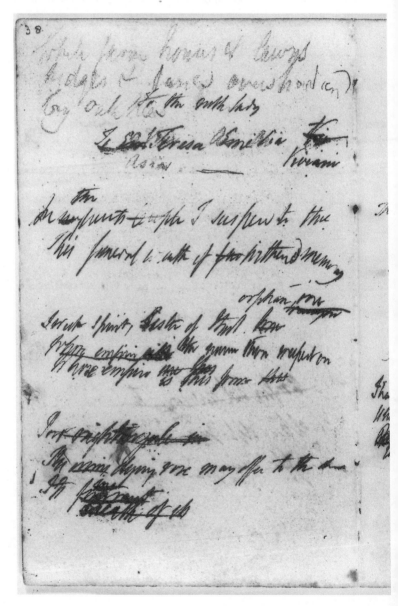

Courtesy of the Bodleian Library, Oxford University.

Courtesy of the Bodleian Library, Oxford University.

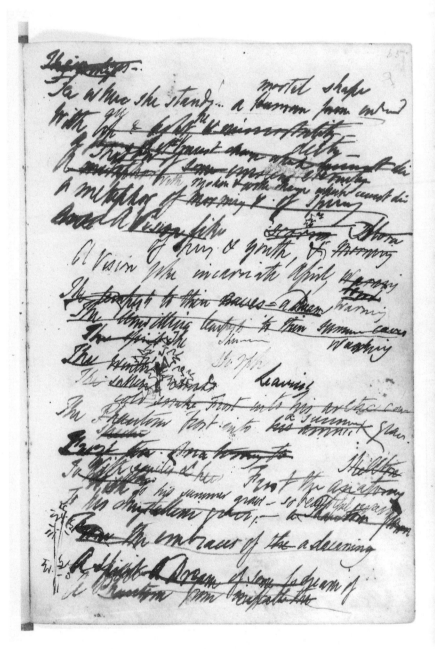

Courtesy of the Bodleian Library, Oxford University.

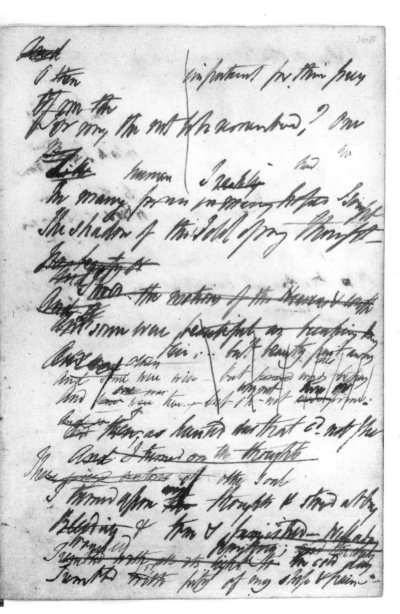

Courtesy of the Bodleian Library, Oxford University.

# MICHAEL SCRIVENER

## [*Adonais*: Defending the Imagination]†

\* \* \*

Some critics have suggested that the trajectory of Shelley's development can be charted as veering away from politics, society, even life
itself, and toward a Platonic mysticism, an asocial spirituality, a *con-
temptus mundi* akin to that of the medieval ascetics. Earl Wasserman,
for example, points to *Adonais* as the poem where Shelley finally gives
up his earthly hopes and locates the Ideal in the afterlife.[1] Milton
Wilson, drawing a distinction between a political millennium and a
Platonic apocalypse, sees *Adonais* declaring an "uncompromising Platonism which Shelley could not accept wholeheartedly elsewhere."
Shelley the radical is eclipsed by the Platonist who sees human life
itself as an evil from which death delivers us.[2] Ross Woodman, who
calls *Adonais* Shelley's most "Shelleyan" poem, reads it in terms of an
absolute conflict between life and death, matter and spirit, so that the
triumph of spirit is identical with spirit's release from the body after
death.[3] Although each of these critics offers many valuable insights, I
nevertheless think that the dualism operating in the poem is not new,
is consistent with Shelley's previous poetry, and in no way contradicts
his utopianism. First, however, one must distinguish between poems
and prose, because Shelley always permits himself more hope in poetry
than in prose, where he is much more skeptical. One can scan the
entire corpus of Shelley's prose for his statements concerning death
and immortality without finding a single dogmatic sentence affirming
immortality. Without question, Shelley wanted death to provide what
life had not, but he unwaveringly maintained his skepticism on the
issue. Desire for immortality is clearly present in *Adonais*, particularly
in the third part, but the Neoplatonic One to which the postmortal
spirit returns is a metaphor, a symbol, and must be understood as a
poetically useful fiction, like the flight with Emily to the island in
*Epipsychidion*.

*Adonais* is yet another defense of imagination, an angry protest
against the mistreatment of Keats at the hands of hostile critics, especially one in particular, the author of a review in the *Quarterly* which
attacked Keats's *Endymion* volume. Shelley assumes the murdering
critic is Southey, whom he suspected of writing the negative review of

† From "Defending the Imagination" in *Radical Shelley: The Philosophical Anarchism and
Utopian Thought of Percy Bysshe Shelley*, by Michael Scrivener (Princeton, NJ: Princeton
University Press, 1982), pp. 272–81. Copyright © 1982 by Princeton University Press. Reprinted by permission of Princeton University Press.
1. Earl R. Wasserman, *Shelley: A Critical Reading* (Baltimore, MD: Johns Hopkins Univ. Press,
1971), pp. 462; 472.
2. Milton Wilson, *Shelley's Later Poetry* (New York: Columbia Univ. Press, 1959), pp. 235; 252.
3. Ross Woodman, *The Apocalyptic Vision in the Poetry of Shelley* (Toronto: Univ. of Toronto
Press, 1964), pp. 3; 158–79.

*The Revolt of Islam* which also appeared in the *Quarterly*.[4] At one level
*Adonais* accuses the forces of cultural reaction of murderous insensi-
tivity, of actually killing John Keats who, unlike Shelley, could not
sustain the abuse with which his creations were met. Keats's death
and the myth of his murder (a myth without any foundation in fact
because Keats died, of course, from tuberculosis) provided Shelley
with an opportunity for publicly attacking his own detractors. Ever
since the publication of the *Quarterly Review*'s essay on *The Revolt of
Islam*, he had wanted to fight back, but had been restrained by a sense
of decorum and a Promethean conviction that it was inappropriate to
combat one's enemies using their tactics. *Peter Bell the Third* assaults
a member of the apostate Lake poets, Wordsworth, who is briefly criticized in *The Witch of Atlas*, too, but Southey is never mentioned by
name, not even in *Adonais*. Indeed, Wordsworth would not have been
so openly criticized if he had not intervened so vigorously on the side
of the Tories, especially in publishing the infamous lines on "carnage."
Shelley did not, however, put his name to *Peter Bell the Third*, which
is comic and, moreover, tempered by praise for Wordsworth, and the
three stanzas of anti-Wordsworthian jest in *The Witch of Atlas* are
lightly satirical. *Adonais*, however, launches a thoroughly serious and
uncompromising attack on the cultural Toryism that Shelley identified
with Southey.

Like so many of Shelley's poems, this one falls into three parts: part
one (stanzas 1–17) is a lamentation; part two (18–38) offers several
consolations to the mourners; part three (39–55) is the triumphant
celebration of Adonais's spirit immortally reborn in the living imagination as his spirit returns to the "One." The murderous Critic, who
is first attacked in the Preface, is implicitly criticized throughout the
lamentations, since Adonais is portrayed as such an invaluable member
of the human community. Moreover, the first part concludes with a
curse: "the curse of Cain / Light on his head who pierced thy innocent
breast, / And scared the angel soul that was its earthly guest!" (st. 17).
The second part also concludes with a curse on the Critic (st. 36–38),
which identifies his worst fate as to continue living, being himself and
knowing himself because "Remorse and Self-contempt shall cling to
thee" (st. 37). While the pure spirit of Adonais "shall flow / Back to
the burning fountain whence it came" (st. 38), the Critic's "cold embers choke the sordid hearth of shame" (st. 38). Like Jupiter, the Critic
will self-destruct from his own evil which can destroy, but not create.
In the triumphant third part, the Critic is left far behind as an insig-
nificant cipher while Adonais becomes one with the universe of beauty
and spirit.

One theme I want to develop is the existential situation of the utopian poet. The pain and stress so evident in *Adonais*'s portrait of the
utopian poet can be traced back to the shamanistic or prophetic role

4. Kenneth Neill Cameron, *Shelley: The Golden Years* (Cambridge, MA: Harvard Univ. Press,
1974), pp. 422–31; also, SC, V, 399–418.

Shelley assigned to the true poet. Existing wholly in neither actuality nor potentiality, his inspiration destroys his mortality, and he is in the unique position of being able to cultivate libertarian images that are not "tainted" by self-interest. The Godwinian ideal of disinterested benevolence finds its most reliable exponent in the utopian poet, who appeals to an Ideal that claims universality, while most political ideals are partial and vitiated by class interests (of course, in reality, Shelley's own Ideal is far from pure). *Adonais*, then, records the living situation experienced by the disinterested mediator between utopian ideals and an interest-ridden actuality. As in "Lines written among the Euganean Hills" and Act I of *Prometheus Unbound*, whatever pain the utopian endures is necessary and justified by the moments of beauty.

In one movement of the poem, Adonais starts as a "broken lily" (st. 6), and becomes flowers "exhaling" from the corpse (st. 20). The speaker consoles himself by realizing that "death feeds life" and, as Wasserman says, "the impersonal sum total of animation persists even though individualized matter disintegrates."[5] The theme of nature's cyclicity is apparent, but after the speaker consoles himself with "Nought we know, dies," he asks himself the question which sabotages the consolation: "Shall that alone which knows / Be as a sword consumed before the sheath / By sightless lightning?" The movement from broken lily to corpse-flowers is a remarkable consolation which, however, depends on the angle of perception. Viewed within a massive scheme of cyclical time and immense space, the death of Adonais is a passage from one mode of life to another. Nothing, in fact, *dies*. Viewed from the ordinary perspective of a living person, the passage still represents loss because the unique presence—the mind, the soul—is no longer alive.

The transition that begins midway in stanza 38 depends upon a new perspective on the immortality of the soul. In the preceding stanza, the soulless Critic, living as he lives, has no life, but "lives" a death-in-life, a self-destructive prolongation of sterility, an invulnerable nothing. In fact, only in death will the Critic be creative, because his corpse will renew nature and make possible a new beginning. The loss of mere existence, the poem now sees, is not as lamentable as the death of a creative poet, because what matters most is beauty, not mere existence. The dead Adonais has a fate more enviable than the live Critic, whose life, without beauty, is not worth living.

If an eternity is possible through the activities of memory, then Adonais lives on through his poetry as it is reborn in the living imagination. In this case, memory is unequivocally a blessing, but if one changes focus slightly, memory becomes a curse. What it is that feeds the memory, and the identity of the rememberer, are crucial variables. "Loss" and "regain" define the ambiguity of paradise. As long as one forgets the harsh reality that is the actual context in which memory

---

5. Earl R. Wasserman, *The Subtler Language*, (Baltimore, MD: Johns Hopkins Univ. Press, 1959), p. 321.

occurs, then one can dwell in beauty. Beauty, however, is vulnerable. The soft tenderness of beauty requires protection and necessitates struggle. The struggle itself to create beauty in an ugly world is so wearying that to forget is also to escape from pain, and so there is a kinship between death and paradise. One sleeps and dreams of pleasure, but awakens to a world of pain. And if paradise is only a memory, why continue to endure the torturing discrepancy between predatory reality and the paradise of dream? This question draws one to Keats's "Ode to a Nightingale," where the speaker is half in love with easeful death because living is so painful. Pleasure is escape, but death is the ultimate escape. Just as "the snake Memory" (st. 22) can be a blessing or a curse, so can "Paradise" shift its allegiance to life or death. Paradise exists in *Adonais*, unlike utopia in *Prometheus Unbound*, as a limited potentiality, coexisting with a dominant actuality which is the very negation of paradise.

Urania's "Paradise" is a familiar Shelleyan place. "With veiled eyes, / 'Mid listening Echoes, in her Paradise / She sate, while one with soft enamoured breath, / Rekindled all the fading melodies" (st. 2). Shelley locates an intense aesthetic moment in the process of reviving songs of beauty, reliving the creative process. *Fading* beauty is echoed and rekindled: thus, memory is eternity.[6] The erotic playfulness that characterized utopia in *Prometheus Unbound* reappears here too. The breath is soft and enamoured, and like Panthea and Ione, Urania and her attendants are able to maintain the cyclicity of beauty and pleasure by remembering, and thus reenacting, the past. However, because Urania's paradise does not exist absolutely, but only as a green isle in a sea of misery, it is ambiguous. First, Urania was unable to protect her son, Adonais, because she was in *her* paradise. Also, Urania is told to *awaken*, "wake and weep!" (st. 3).

In stanza 22, the ambiguities of sleep and death, dream and paradise, come into fullest expression.

> *He* will awake no more, oh, never more!
> "Wake thou," cried Misery, "childless Mother, rise
> Out of thy sleep, and slake, in thy heart's core,
> A wound more fierce than his with tears and sighs."
> And all the Dreams that watched Urania's eyes,
> And all the Echoes whom their sister's song
> Had held in holy silence, cried: "Arise!"
> Swift as a Thought by the snake Memory stung,
> From her ambrosial rest the fading Splendour sprung.

This stanza pictures paradise as a sleep from which one awakens only to grieve. In Keats's words, it is "Where but to think is to be full of sorrow / And leaden-eyed despairs, / Where Beauty cannot keep her lustrous eyes, / Or new Love pine at them beyond tomorrow." It is, aptly enough, *Misery* who tells Urania to awaken. The Dreams and Echoes of paradise behave uncharacteristically, and urge Urania to go

6. See Irving Massey, on Shelleyan memory, in "Shelley's 'Music, When Soft Voices Die': Text and Meaning," *Journal of English and Germanic Philology*, 59 (1960), 430–38.

out into the world. Here, Memory is a stinging snake, because to re-member Adonais is to awaken into a nightmare-world. The implication here and elsewhere is that being unable to awaken is not nearly as bad a fate as one had thought at first; indeed, it is similar to paradise itself.

Stanza 24 makes explicit a number of themes only partially devel-oped before.

> Out of her secret Paradise she sped,
> Through camps and cities rough with stone, and steel,
> And human hearts, which to her aery tread
> Yielding not, wounded the invisible
> Palms of her tender feet where'er they fell:
> And barbed tongues, and thoughts more sharp then they,
> Rent the soft Form they never could repel,
> Whose sacred blood, like the young tears of May,
> Paved with eternal flowers that undeserving way.

One recalls *Prometheus Unbound*, Act I, where the Sixth Spirit sings, "Desolation is a delicate thing" (772–79). This song has its source in Agathon's speech in the *Symposium*, where Agathon pictures Love, instead of Homer's Ate, delicately inhabiting the soft places of men and gods. Shelley's innovation is to equate desolation with "the mon-ster, Love." The first line of the song speaks appropriately to the stanza at hand: "[The best and gentlest dream visions of joy] And wake, and find the shadow Pain. . . ." The hardness of actuality pierces and cuts the soft places where tenderness lives in Urania. In this stanza, her paradise is "secret," thus implying a need for secrecy. The verb "wounded" sets in motion important reverberations. Beauty, love, pleasure, tenderness—that is, the qualities of paradise—are soft and vulnerable, whereas ugliness and hate are piercing, cutting, like stone and steel, sharp but invulnerable. Adonais was killed by a piercing shaft of poisonous hate to which he was vulnerable because he was a creator of beauty and dreamer of paradise.

A struggle between softness and hardness takes place throughout the poem. Adonais is "pierced" (st. 3 and 17), "broken" (st. 6), and defenseless, lacking a shield or spear (st. 27). The road to Fame is "thorny" (st. 5). In a reversal, the beauty of Adonais's song is said to "pierce the guarded wit, / And pass into the panting heart beneath / With lightning and with music" (st. 12). In stanza 20, the image of sword and sheath suggests that creative beauty has to wage war with its opponents, even though the essence of beauty is the antithesis of battle. In stanza 39, in a mad trance we "strike with our spirit's knife / Invulnerable nothings." Whether struggle is thought to be futile or necessary, the softness of paradise must penetrate a resisting hardness, or defend itself, or suffer inevitable wounds at the hands of harsh reality. For these reasons, the poem's speaker says: "From the world's bitter wind / Seek shelter in the shadow of the tomb" (st. 51).

The first two lines in the twenty-fourth stanza have rich associations. From Urania's wounds fertilizing blood flows and paves her way with eternal flowers. As in "Ode to the West Wind," the poet must fall upon the thorns of life in order to create beauty: blood is creative fire.[7] As in "Orpheus," the wounded poet indulges his grief and creates exquisite beauty, for which he must pay the price of destruction. In a historical, rather than millennial world, the effort to expand the circumference of beauty, pleasure, sympathy, love, and the other utopian attributes, necessitates wounding. Urania survives the ordeal of bleeding, but Adonais does not.

Shelley's alleged self-portrait in stanzas 31 through 34 makes sense in this context. The frail Form is somewhere between Adonais's weakness and the strength of Urania, who cannot die. The Form is an oxymoron of strength and weakness: frail, but like a leopard; like a storm, but feeble; expiring, but beautiful and swift. Unlike Adonais, the Form survives, but only *just* survives. The Actaeon image unites the predatory theme with the memory theme. The ugly brutality of the world is predatory and orally destructive. Wolves, ravens, vultures and cannibalism characterize the sadistic power of the Jupiter-world. When the Form gazes on nature's pure beauty, he glimpses paradise, which, instead of becoming his residence, becomes his haunting demon. He experiences Paradise as something lost and inaccessible. Not the promise, but the impossibility of happiness, has been the consequence of the Form's communion with beauty. The other poets keep their distance because he indeed represents a dangerous possibility. Whereas Adonais was killed by the direct attack of reality, the Form tortures himself with the memory of a beauty that is inconstant and powerless to overthrow the Jupiter-world. In stanza 33, the Form, as Carlos Baker has said, wears the apparel of a devotee of Bacchus.[8] If a poet is dressed like a Maenad, then the implication seems clear enough: the poet calls into existence his own destruction; the Form creates beauty for others, but for himself creates only pain; inspiration and creativity lead to death because remembering Paradise while still in the historical world is to create hell.

The eternity Adonais achieves is the work of memory, and so forgetting is another kind of death. The Critic is a "nameless worm" (st. 36) contrasted with Adonais, who is a "remembered name" (st. 37); the "nameless" is also a reference to the poem's inscription from Moschus, who will not "name" the poisoner of Bion, just as Shelley will not grant immortality to Keats's murderer. In stanza 44, the "dead live" as living poems. The poet lives on through the survival of poetry, and as the world remembers the poetry, so it breathes life into the dead, and keeps alive the hope of utopian transformation. But the poem's speaker does not rest content with his consolation after he discovers that Adonais, in death, is closer to Paradise than the living who must suffer.

7. Stuart Curran, *Shelley's Annus Mirabilis*, (San Marino, CA: Huntington Library, 1975) p. 165. Cf. Daniel Hughes' statement on the poet's self-destruction: Prometheus "is *sacrificed* like the Bard of the West Wind in order that the great age of millennium and apocalypse can come to consciousness." "Prometheus Made Capable Poet in Act One of *Prometheus Unbound*," *Studies in Romanticism*, 17 (1978), 4.
8. Carlos Baker, *Shelley's Major Poetry*, (Princeton, NJ: Princeton Univ. Press, 1948), pp. 245–46.

"Fear and grief / Convulse us and consume us day by day, / And cold hopes swarm like worms within our living clay" (st. 39). If life is a bad dream, then it is a nightmare made even more unbearable by hope. As in the case of Actaeon, the image of something better makes endurance that much more wearying. The struggle to create beauty is, in some ways, antithetical to the essence of Paradise, which is erotic play and unity. In death at least there is an end to alienation: Adonais "is made one with Nature" (st. 42). Within Nature's cycle, where all things "pant with life's sacred thirst; / Diffuse themselves; and spend in love's delight / The beauty and the joy of their renewed might" (st. 19), Adonais can participate in the cyclicity of love. During the climax of the speaker's triumphant rhapsody on death, he says, "Die, / If thou wouldst be with that which thou dost seek! / Follow where all is fled!" (st. 52). The last words remind one of the injunction in Act II, *Prometheus Unbound*: in order to liberate the world's potentiality, one must descend and retrace one's steps back to the source; as in Asia's song, one must go as far back as death and birth. Existence and nature, at their origin, are fundamentally pure, and in death, one returns to the source.

Here is Shelley's grimmest portrait of hope. But one must also put this in its poetic context because Adonais's death came after and as a result of a life of poetic creativity. The yearning for purity expressed in the poem is also the desire for peacefulness by someone who has struggled and endured. Could anyone deny that there are situations in which to continue living is by no means the only reasonable way to affirm life in all its utopian possibilities? The crucial question is whether, in Shelley's praise of death, he is transforming what used to be political and psychological categories into metaphysical ones.

Shelley is not, I believe, making a metaphysical defense of suicide. For example, when he says, "what still is dear / Attracts to crush, repels to make thee wither" (st. 53), he is not arguing against desire itself, only its frustration; there is still the feeling that desire *ought* to be satisfied. I interpret the last stanzas to mean that Shelley is carried toward suicide, which he nevertheless refuses to accept. I emphasize the fact that he is driven there by forces outside his control. The "low wind" that "whispers" in stanza 53 becomes the "breath whose might I have invoked in song" in the last stanza. The West Wind, destroyer and preserver, *descends* upon the speaker. He has not willed himself to the brink, but has found himself there anyway. If the possibility of utopia is to be maintained from the position of the inspired poet-prophet, then the poet must accept his social isolation and esteem poetry as a spiritual activity which has been ostracized. Poetry and society also divide into their separate spheres in *A Defence of Poetry*; but in the essay poetry returns to society in the form of unacknowledged legislation, while in *Adonais* the split seems permanent. Despite these consequences, Shelley remains committed to poetry, whether it leads to self-destruction or new possibility.

The difference between the divinity of *Adonais* and that of earlier poems is not its location in a dualism but its inability to make existence more bearable for the utopian poet. Although in stanza 43, a panthe-istic presence is "bursting in its beauty and its might / From trees and beasts and men into Heaven's light," the living utopian poet is "far from the trembling throng," and is "borne darkly, fearfully, afar" (st. 55). When Shelley feels actuality might be transformed by the Ideal, he is capable of responding with a wide range of literary projects, but when he perceives actuality as a resistant surface, impermeable to Spirit, he returns then to potentiality as it exists in its purer states. The divinity celebrated in *Adonais*'s third part is alternately human and natural, the product of past and present Poets, but it is not anything even close to the "heaven" of Christian mythology. If the poem's speaker does decide to die, he has no hope in a *personal* immortality; rather, he hopes to return to the One from which his spirit came initially. The primary meaning of immortality in the poem is the en-tirely naturalistic process by which dead poets live by being read cre-atively by successive generations. As to whether the Neoplatonic One is simply a metaphorical symbol for this process, or is to be understood more literally, the poem is characteristically unclear. Adonais, as in stanza 38, "wakes or sleeps with the enduring dead," and the poem refuses to erase the ambiguous "or."

The poem is skeptical concerning the nature of a postmortal exis-tence, but there is no skepticism over the imagination, whose values Shelley asserts unequivocally. Although individual poets might be lured toward death by the anguish of utopian creativity, poetry itself, represented by Urania, is "chained to Time" (st. 26), and cannot es-cape into a postmortal One. To win a place in Fame among the dis-tinguished poets, one has to walk the thorny road of struggle, desire, will, endurance, hope—the Promethean virtues. In Act I of *Prome-theus Unbound* the Titan knows that "Peace is in the grave," but death "hides all things beautiful and good," and it would be "defeat . . . not victory" (638–42).

# HUGH ROBERTS

## [Spectators Turned Actors: "The Triumph of Life"]†

\* \* \*

The question of death is particularly relevant to how we approach the "Triumph," because it lies at the center of one of the recurrent cruxes in criticism of this poem. Shelley's own death, which left the poem "unfinished," has revealed the profound uncertainties in our cultural and critical attitudes toward death and authorship. On the one hand, there has been a tendency to look in the "Triumph" for "last words,"

† From "Skepticism Versus Idealism: An Old Problem Reconsidered" and "Spectators Become Actors: The Politics of Temporality," in *Shelley and the Chaos of History: A New Politics of Poetry*, by Hugh Roberts (University Park: Pennsylvania State University Press, 1997), pp. 198–200; 398–407. Reprinted by permission of The Pennsylvania State University Press.

not just those words that, as chance would have it, were the last Shelley could write, but words that give us a clue to the nature of Shelley's poetic enterprise, that at some level mark a closure or fulfillment (or recantation) of Shelley's life and oeuvre considered as a "whole." This is to read Shelley's death therapeutically as, in Dilthey's terms, that "last moment of a life" when "the balance of its meaning [can] be struck."[1]

If we read Shelley's life as a narrative totality, the "Triumph" gains special significance as the moment when he looks back on his life and work and seeks to capture its essence. Hence the vehemence of the critical debates over whether the "Triumph" is a pessimistic palinode to Shelley's previously optimistic idealism, or a fulfillment of that vision in a bleaker register, or the pure extreme of his "decentering" poetics. Each critic is claiming not just that this one poem is or is not consistent with many of Shelley's earlier poems but that either by exemplification or by contrast this poem determines our reception of "Shelley" and all that means.

Ironically, the "fact" of the poem's unfinishedness is precisely what opens it up to so many competing interpretations. The attempt to force Shelley's life and death into a unity resolved at the moment of death is a clear case of what Foucault calls the author function: "a certain functional principle by which, in our culture, one limits, excludes, and chooses; in short, by which one impedes the free circulation, the free manipulation, the free composition, decomposition, and recomposition of fiction. . . . The author . . . marks the manner in which we fear the proliferation of meaning."[2] Poetic fragmentation may prompt us to attempt a reconstitution of the "whole" of which the text is a "part," but our inability to decide upon which "whole" we are to reconcile the text with neither eliminates the possibility of finding meaning in the text nor makes the text seem any more intractable to interpretation. As Foucault suggests, meaning proliferates in the absence of imposed "wholes"; it does not dissipate. The "Triumph" 's fragmentary nature is irreducible, and irresolvable. Shelley's death makes it infinitely debatable how he might have finished the poem. It is even possible to assert the poem's openness and read this as a kind of "closure" at the same time. When Marjorie Levinson, for example, writes of the poem's "(in)conclusion . . . imaginatively confirm[ing] the work's skeptical idealism,"[3] she confirms how impossible it is for us not to recuperate the accidental within essentializing narratives.

* * * Shelley's accidental disappearance from the scene brings home sadly to us the infinite, incommensurable potential of his life, a potential that defeats the possibility of hermeneutical closure. Hence the persistence of attempts to read the death either as an outright suicide

1. *Meaning in History: W. Dilthey's Thoughts on History and Society*, ed. and trans., H. P. Rickman (London: George Allen & Unwin, 1961), pp. 74–75.
2. Michel Foucault, "What is an Author," in *Textual Strategies: Perspectives in Post-Structural Criticism*, ed. Jose Hararie (Ithaca, NY: Cornell University Press, 1979), p. 159.
3. Marjorie Levinson, *The Romantic Fragment Poem: A Critique of Form* (Chapel Hill: University of North Carolina Press, 1986), p. 129; see also p. 205.

or as a welcome end for a man who had drained life's cup to the dregs; we "fear the proliferation of meaning."

On the other hand, any reading of the poem, no matter how "faithful" to its metaphoric disruptions of "fidelity," reveals a certain hostility (the desire to kill off Shelley "neatly") to the openness and undecidability of the text, a point de Man notes at the end of his essay on the "Triumph" when he writes of the unavoidability of the "use" of texts "for the assertion of methodological claims made all the more pious by their denial of piety."[4]

\*    \*    \*

The "Triumph" has always been a crux in Shelley criticism: critics have divided sharply on the issue of whether the poem is a despairing vision of the pointlessness of life's ridiculous pageant or a grim warning that nonetheless leaves open the possibility of avoiding the "dance" if we take the right approach to life. One of the chief delights of the "Triumph" is that each time we read it, we seem to discover it anew. Any reading that argues that the poem's portrait of a life in perpetual flux, where we "to new bright destruction come and go" (154), is purely pessimistic conflicts with the joy and pleasure we derive from the poem itself, which "destroys" itself as frequently as any of the "atomies" in the dance of life. While no reading of the poem can, or should, hope to be definitive, a reading should be able to acknowledge the poem's beauty.

The key to a proper understanding of the "Triumph" is to throw into question the status of the voices in the poem in a way that does not seem to have been done before. So many of Shelley's major poems are written in the borrowed voice of more or less elaborately constructed personae (*Alastor*, "Julian and Maddalo," *Epipsychidion*, "Peter Bell the Third") that it is odd that this possibility has not, to my knowledge, been considered in criticism of the "Triumph."[5]

It is, perhaps, the desire for "last words" that makes us read this poem as Shelley's direct and unmediated vision of life. Many critics, however, have argued that we are to find Rousseau at fault in the poem, and any of the more optimistic readings of the poem have to assume that an engagement with life's career more successful than Rousseau's is possible. The poem's narrator, however—about whom no information is given that allows us to identify him with Shelley, or anyone else—shares Rousseau's viewpoint and, for the duration of the extant fragment of the poem, is subject to his tutelage. Should we trust what the narrator sees?

The "Triumph of Life" is a criticism, not of life, but of a certain way of looking at life. It is a criticism of the attempt to achieve the "view

---

4. Paul de Man, "Shelley Disfigured," in Bloom, et al., *Deconstruction and Criticism* (New York: Continuum, 1979), p. 68.

5. Jones notes the curiously "detached" nature of the narrator and Rousseau in the "Triumph" (*Shelley's Satire: Violence, Exhortation, and Authority* [DeKalb: Northern Illinois Press, 1994], 161–63), but from his perspective they are insufficiently "detached" to achieve true satiric distance. He does not seem to consider the possibility that they are to be criticized for their detachment.

from the citadel." At the time of writing the "Triumph," Shelley's early enthusiasm for Rousseau had been tempered by a more critical appraisal of his achievement; in the *Defence* he lists Rousseau, with some reservations, with Locke, Hume, Gibbon, and Voltaire, as one of those votaries of abstract reason the loss of whose works would not represent an incalculable blow to humanity (*SPP*, 502, 502 n. 8)[530]. Rousseau, in his aspiration to representative self-consciousness, is a form of Shelley's Apollo; in the "Triumph," he is an Apollo who is no longer capable of believing in his own myth of an eternal, absolute order, but who still cannot reconcile himself to the mutable world he inhabits.

Apollo does figure in the "Triumph," in the form of the sun. The sun's rising at the poem's opening, which obliterates "the stars that gem / The cone of night" (22–23), is related to the vision that visits the narrator. Shelley's sun is the sun of "reason," but reason seen in the coercive, ideologically restrictive form of the "Song of Apollo" or the "calculating faculty" of the *Defence*. This is a reason that insists that all data must be related to a single point of view; as such, Yeats was right to identify the sun in the "Triumph" as "the being and source of all tyrannies."[6] The narrator leaves the visionary realm of night, in which the multivocal stars shine forth, for the "single vision" of the sun:

> before me fled
> The night; behind me rose the day, the Deep
>
> Was at my feet, and Heaven above my head.
> (26–28)

The narrator's viewpoint merges with Apollo's;[7] his point of view becomes the all-embracing "view from the citadel" of Enlightenment reason, commonly symbolized by the sun. But the result is not Absolute Knowing. A "strange trance" (29) comes over him, the trance of reason itself. The trance represents the inability of this monological reason to perceive the complexity of a reality that it insists upon reducing to a unified story.

Under the tyrannical spell of this reason, the narrator has a vision of life. Who better to guide him than the man popularly identified as the foremost of the Enlightenment philosophes? Rousseau is an inspired choice because he was also so tempted by the irrational. He becomes, for Shelley, a gateway figure who allows us to imagine the possibility, within the poem, of a point of view different from that which is proposed to us.

Almost everywhere else in Shelley's writing the Lucretian vision of a world in a constant state of becoming is celebrated, as it is in the "Witch of Atlas," but in the "Triumph" it takes on a nightmare quality:

---

6. Harold Bloom, *Shelley's Mythmaking* (New Haven, CT: Yale University Press, 1959), 270.
7. It is unclear whether the narrator's viewpoint has *become* Apollo's or merely approximates to it. In a poem that is quite cautious about the sun's whereabouts, the very uncertainty of this passage suggests the former. The night apparently "flees" him as it would the sun, and to say that "day" rises "behind" him (not the "sun") may be an iconic representation of causal sequence: first there is night, then comes the sun, and "subsequently" there is "day."

why? The answer can be found, as David Quint suggests, in Rousseau's and the narrator's response to this world. They both search obsessively for guarantees of identity in the face of flux (177–79, 199, 208, 300–304, 543). The most dramatic example of this is Rousseau's response to the shape all light, to which he turns for a certainty that proves to be delusive:

> " 'Shew whence I came, and where I am, and why—
> Pass not away upon the passing stream.' "
>
> (398–99)

Shelley models this moment on another work he was reading (and translating) at the time of writing the "Triumph," a work he admired greatly: Goethe's *Faust*. According to Faust's pact with Mephistopheles, Faust's soul will be forfeit if he should ever tell the passing moment, "Oh stay! You are so beautiful!"[8] (1700). We know the passage struck Shelley, and was in his mind at the time of writing the "Triumph" (*Letters*, 2:436).

Rousseau's error is to fight against the inevitable forces of change and deformation in the world; he refuses to open himself to the future, and attempts to single out a particular moment of ideal beauty and fix it as a reference point forever: "Pass not away upon the passing stream." Like Faust, his "damnation" follows swiftly upon this attempt to transcend the flux of time in a moment of epiphany. As the shape offers to let him "quench his thirst" in the cup of nepenthe, a flood of atomistic change rushes through his brain, which becomes "as sand" and leaves him mourning the passing of the shape (which fades "veil by veil" [413] in perfectly Lucretian manner) in an unrecognizably transformed world.

Saint-Preux's career in *Julie: Ou, la nouvelle Héloïse* forms an ironic parallel to Rousseau's in the "Triumph." Saint-Preux inhabits a world of Lucretian flux when he is in the "torrent" of Paris, and much of the imagery of the "Triumph" comes from this part of Rousseau's novel. Paris is a place where one undergoes a constant "forgetting of initial conditions"; the "disfiguration" de Man notes in Shelley's poem is a key word, as well as a constant process, in Saint-Preux's Paris, a world where the faces of men are "masques"[9] that they discard at will, and where "tout change à chaque instant" in the "flux et reflux" of this "chaos."

Saint-Preux learns to loathe Paris, and looks back on it from the security of Julie's Elysée—which stands for the Epicurean Garden, a tranquil citadel removed from the flux of the world—as a place of horror. When he is in Paris, however, he is seduced by the "ivresse où cette vie agitée et tumultueuse plonge ceux qui la mènent" (*Julie*, 232).[1] This "ivresse" haunts the "Triumph" as an alternative to Rousseau's cynical despair in response to its giddying flux. Central to re-

8. "Verweile doch, du bist so schön!"
9. *Julie: ou, la nouvelle Héloïse* (Paris: Garnier Frères, 1960), p. 212.
1. "giddiness into which that agitated and tumultuous life plunges those who lead it" (my translation).

alizing this alternative is a piece of advice Shelley puts into Rousseau's mouth:

> "But follow thou, and from spectator turn
> Actor or victim in this wretchedness,
>
> "And what thou wouldst be taught I then may learn
> From thee."
>
> (305–8)

This advice stands rather oddly in the poem. Rousseau offers it, but immediately launches into his account of the encounter with the shape all light. The narrator does not act upon it, and Rousseau does not seem to expect him to. It stands as a contingent point of bifurcation, a road not taken that invites us to inquire what it might mean if the narrator did "turn actor or victim" in the dance of which they remain decidedly abstracted "spectators." We are particularly struck by the ambiguity of Rousseau's "what thou wouldst be taught I then may learn / From thee." Does this mean that the narrator would only then be able to state clearly what he wants to learn from Rousseau; or, more intriguingly, does Rousseau mean that he would then learn from the narrator what the narrator would have learned by entering the dance? If the latter reading is correct, this would be an implicit acknowledgment on Rousseau's part that he does not know the meaning of the spectacle before them.

The move from "spectator" to "actor" is central to the implications of chaos theory. * * * The implications of the "révolution quantique" are that all "spectators" inevitably become "actors"; the old pretense of a science abstracted above the flux of phenomena is shattered, and all knowledge exists at a finite human scale, not a divine or eternal one. Rousseau's advice—"from spectator turn / Actor"—is borrowed by Shelley from Saint-Preux, who also discovered the radical implications of being "portions and percipients" of an infinitely complex world in the irreversible, chaotic flux of Paris. This was the discovery that led to the "ivresse" he would later read as a fall: "Je trouve . . . que c'est une folie de vouloir étudier le monde en simple spectateur. Celui qui ne prétend qu'observer n'observe rien. . . . On ne voit agir les autres qu'autant qu'on agit soi-même; dans l'école du monde comme dans celle de l'amour, il faut commencer par pratiquer ce qu'on veut apprendre" (*Julie*, 222).[2] The parallel between "amour" and "le monde" is particularly striking, because in the pageant of life it is love, above all, that the narrator and Rousseau as abstract spectators seem least able to comprehend (149–69). This is the equivalent of Plato's view of the desiring life as an ill to be avoided by recourse to a suitable *technē*. There is nothing "incorrect" in this portrait of human desire and aging; it simply leaves out everything that gives them meaning. The problem is one of scale; from the detached, eternal viewpoint

2. "I find . . . that it is foolish to wish to study the world as a simple spectator. He who claims merely to observe, observes nothing. . . . One can only see how others act to the extent that one acts oneself; in the school of life as in that of love one must begin by practicing what one wishes to learn" (my translation).

of the narrator's and Rousseau's citadel, human *erōs* becomes a bad joke, of which the inexorable advance of age and death is the punchline.

But what if we follow Rousseau's advice * * * and from spectators turn actors in this dance? What if we adapt our knowledge to the finite and irreversible reality of human lives? What if we accept the inevitability of *tuchē* in our lives, and open ourselves to the chance and change of an unforeseeable and inconceivable future? From such a scale—the scale of Pan's inclusive, multivocal "we," not Apollo's uni-perspectival "I"—it is the knowledge that death is the inevitable outcome of their erotic minglings that makes real the intense fragile beauty of these "new bright destructions." This is that "quick tense splendour of human excellence" that, as Nussbaum points out, even the immortal Gods envy us.[3] Rousseau and the narrator are looking at life through the wrong end of the telescope, and are therefore unable to see the beauty that rises out of its constant disfigurations. Rousseau's constant efforts to find a still point of unchangeable identity from which to stand and view the world blind him to its possibilities. Like Apollo, he can only condemn and execrate the "errors" that constantly deform the world around him.

If we return to the "Triumph of Life" and, turning actor not spectator, avoid Rousseau's mistake of demanding a value that is not at risk in the flux of process, then we find the apparent nightmare of life's dance is a product of incorrect seeing, or choosing an inappropriate scale. The beauty within the "living storm" does not register at the scale of Rousseau's and the narrator's hunt for eternal verities. The image of the "dance of life" is a clue that the perspective of the "spectators"—Rousseau and the narrator—is to be distinguished from that of the poet. The "maniac dance" (110) is modeled on the maenadic fury of the followers of Dionysus. The maenad is for Shelley a positive image of the poetically inspired. The self-portrait of Shelley carrying the thyrsus in *Adonais* (291) indicates his perspective as that of an actor in, and not a spectator of, the maenad's maniac dance.

Similarly, the *simulacra*, which Rousseau can see only as fitting inhabitants of Dante's *Inferno*, produce, among many who lead the tragic lives of the victims of *tuchē*, "others" who

> "like elves
> Danced in a thousand unimagined shapes
> Upon the sunny stream and grassy shelves."
> (490–92)

This, with its echoes of the Witch of Atlas's free creativity, or the dancing hours of *Prometheus Unbound*'s fourth act, or the "unforeseen and unconceived delight" of poetic creativity (compare "unimagined shapes"), which in *Prometheus* figures as "arts, though unimagined, yet to be" (III, iii, 56), is too evidently a positive image in Shelley's

3. Martha Nussbaum, *The Fragility of Goodness: Luck and Ethics in Greek Tragedy and Philosophy* (Cambridge: Cambridge University Press, 1986), p. 342.

imaginative world to allow us to share Rousseau's horrified repugnance.

Abandoning Rousseau's demand for stable, self-identical values, we can even appreciate the beauty of the moment that is, for him, a nadir, his encounter with the shape all light. Most readers would agree that this passage is the most compelling in a poem of remarkable power. I read this moment, earlier, as Rousseau's "fall" into the ironic world of figuration. But if we take a "Shelleyan" attitude toward this passage, and not Rousseau's, we are freed to appreciate the ephemeral beauty of the shape's appearance. Even the rapid transitions of Rousseau's brain-become-as-sand take on an exhilarating energy that is only frightening if we demand, as Rousseau does, a rigid continuity of identity.

Hogle, who suggests that the shape represents the principle of radical transference, argues that Rousseau's error is that he merely "touched with faint lips" (404) her cup of transferential nepenthe, failing to drink unreservedly and enter into pure and joyful amnesiac transference.[4] I agree with Hogle that Rousseau's vision is distorted because he demands absolute certainty in a world that does not offer this, and that Rousseau's error is in too great an attachment to the "past" (321–39). It is important to emphasize the differences, however.

Carlos Baker was the first to suggest that the phrase "touched with faint lips" meant that Rousseau did not actually drink the nepenthe, but merely touched his lips to the cup.[5] One must agree with Bloom, however, that this is a perverse reading: "If Shelley meant to indicate that Rousseau did not drink, he would surely have made so important a point a bit clearer. As it is, he employs an idiom, to touch a cup with one's lips, which means that one drinks" (*Mythmaking*, 269); in the *Revolt*, Laon tells us how he was nursed by the Hermit, saying that "a potion to my lips / At intervals he raised" (III, xxxii, 1–2); Baker's reading would suggest either that the Hermit was teasing his patient or that the "potion" was a treatment for chapped lips.

Rousseau does drink of the shape's nepenthe, and the partial amnesia that follows is Shelley's view of ordinary, entropic process, the principle of evolutionary change that the shape represents. The absolute transferential amnesia that Hogle believes the cup to contain would, in Shelley's view, be an annihilation of meaning, which would eliminate any possibility of joy and hope along with regrets for the past. The shape is not a purely comforting figure, as Hogle wishes her to be. Some of what she "tramples into the dust of death" we are right to regret; Shelley does not attempt to replace the oversimplifications of the therapeutic Absolute with an equally oversimplified transferential Absolute. The world of *tuchē* is a world in which tragedy is possible, and to allow the possibility of genuinely negative political action as a normal part of political process is also to admit that we are exposed to considerable dangers.

4. Jerrold Hogle, *Shelley's Process: Radical Transference and the Development of His Major Works* (Oxford: Oxford University Press, 1988), pp. 329–30.
5. Carlos Baker, *Shelley's Major Poetry* (Princeton, NJ: Princeton University Press, 1948), pp. 264–65.

When Shelley writes that the shape tramples our thoughts "As Day upon the threshold of the east / Treads out the lamps of night, until the breath / Of darkness reillumines even the least / Of heaven's living eyes" (389–92), we cannot but agree with the majority of commentators that this must be read as a lamentable obliteration of "differences," and this may appear to be fatal for the reading I am constructing here. Although this image is, as we have seen, a common one in Shelley's poetry, which usually indicates the obliteration of poetic inspiration by the "light of common day," Reiman is right to point out that here Shelley is in part echoing Saint-Preux's description of Julie: "Ne te vis-je pas briller entre ces jeunes beautés comme le soleil entre les astres qu'il éclipse?" (81).[6] It is unlikely that Shelley regards Julie as a purely destructive force to be shunned at all costs. Rather, this seems persuasive evidence that Rousseau's error is in how he approaches the shape. The world of ironic division that the shape represents is not inherently "evil"—no more than is Julie—but it obliterates us and all possibility of joy and love in us if we refuse to accept its limitations, and demand that it reveal an underlying therapeutic Absolute. Similarly, Julie is fatal to Saint-Preux only because he makes his love for her an absolute principle of his identity, so that he is incapable of responding usefully to the unfortunate *tuchē* that makes their happiness impossible. The ironic world contains the potential for tragedy; we recognize that the shape represents both the entropic and negentropic aspects of evolutionary process and that we should fear her, at the same time as we recognize that without her there is neither hope nor beauty.

Everywhere, in fact, in this exceptionally lovely poem, there is beauty to be found. Rousseau and the narrator cannot get beyond their horror at the fact that the beauty is so ephemeral that it is always poised on the brink of destruction (445–60). But cannot we, knowing that we too will be carried away by this turbulent "eddying flood" whether or not we fight against its current, choose to live as fully as possible the moments when we "dance / Within a sunbeam" or play upon the "Embroidery of flowers," whose "quick, tense splendour" owes everything to the "chariot's swift advance"?

6. "Do I not see you shining among those young beauties like the sun among those stars that he eclipses?" (my translation). See Donald H. Reiman, *Shelley's "Triumph of Life": A Critical Study* (Urbana: University of Illinois Press, 1965), p. 66.

# Percy Bysshe Shelley: A Chronology

| | |
|---|---|
| 1792 | Percy Bysshe Shelley (PBS) born August 4 at Field Place, Warnham, near Horsham, West Sussex, the eldest child of Timothy Shelley, M.P., and Elizabeth Pilfold Shelley, and eldest grandchild of (Percy) Bysshe Shelley, a wealthy landowner. |
| 1797 | On March 29, William Godwin marries Mary Wollstonecraft, who gives birth to their daughter Mary Wollstonecraft Godwin (later Shelley—MWS) on August 30 and dies September 10. |
| 1798 | PBS studies with Warnham clergyman, the Reverend Evan ("Taffy") Edwards. |
| 1802–04 | PBS at boarding school in Syon House Academy, Isleworth, on the Great Western Road in Thames Valley. |
| 1804 | PBS begins studies at Eton in September, which continue through spring of 1810. |
| 1806 | Grandfather Bysshe Shelley becomes Sir Bysshe Shelley, baronet. Earliest possible year for any of PBS's poems in what is now *The Esdaile Notebook* (latest poems in it written 1813). |
| 1808 | PBS begins corresponding with his Wiltshire cousin Harriet Grove; their informal engagement ended by her late in 1810. |
| 1809 | PBS writes five or six poems now found in *The Esdaile Notebook*. |
| 1810 | PBS's earliest book-length poem, *The Wandering Jew*, begun in the winter of 1809/10, is submitted for publication late in the summer (but remains unpublished during his lifetime). His Gothic novel *Zastrozzi* published (spring); *Original Poetry* by "Victor" and "Cazire" (i.e., PBS and his sister Elizabeth) published and withdrawn (early autumn). In October, PBS begins residence at University College, Oxford, and meets Thomas Jefferson Hogg. PBS's *Posthumous Fragments of Margaret Nicholson* published in November and *St. Irvyne*, his second Gothic novel (this one containing poems), in December, though dated 1811. |
| 1811 | PBS meets Harriet Westbrook (January). After George III is declared insane, the Prince of Wales becomes prince |

regent in February. PBS, with Hogg, writes and circulates *The Necessity of Atheism*; both are expelled from University College on March 25. In August, PBS and Harriet Westbrook elope and marry in Edinburgh on August 29. After their return to York, Hogg tries to seduce Harriet; the Shelleys decamp to Keswick, where they are befriended by Robert Southey.

1812    Shelleys travel to Dublin, where PBS publishes two pamphlets in February—*Address to the Irish People* and *Proposals for an Association of . . . Philanthropists. Declaration of Rights* printed. Shelleys return to Wales (April 6) and move to Lynmouth, Devon, where PBS writes *Letter to Lord Ellenborough*, completes and prints *The Devil's Walk*; the Shelleys, Eliza Westbrook, Elizabeth Hitchener, and their Irish servant circulate these and *Declaration of Rights*; the Shelleys, under suspicion, flee to Wales, arriving at Tremadoc, North Wales, in September. In October, while in London to raise money, they meet Godwin.

1813    Shelleys, having made enemies and deeply in debt, leave their house hastily on February 27 and go to Dublin, where they recover manuscript of *The Esdaile Notebook* from printer there, returning to London on April 5. *Queen Mab* printed and circulated privately sometime between May and December. On June 23, Ianthe Shelley born; Shelleys live at Bracknell, west of London, with Newton-Boinville circle, while dodging creditors and trying to raise money for Godwin.

1814    In January or February, PBS publishes *A Refutation of Deism*. Allies invade France and capture Paris on March 31; Napoleon is first deposed and then abdicates; Louis XVIII proclaimed king on April 6. On July 28 PBS and Mary Wollstonecraft Godwin (MWS) elope to war-ravaged France, accompanied by MWS's step-sister, Mary Jane (later "Claire") Clairmont (b.? April 27, 1798); from Switzerland they return to England on September 13, after boating down the Rhine. Charles Shelley, PBS's first son (and heir), born to Harriet on November 30.

1815    Sir Bysshe Shelley dies on January 5. PBS involved with George Cannon and *Theological Inquirer* (January); PBS, MWS, Claire Clairmont, and Hogg engage in free-love experiment; MWS's first child (a daughter) born prematurely, probably on February 22, but dies on March 6. Napoleon returns to rule France for the Hundred Days, March through June (Waterloo, June 18). In settling legal claims to Sir Bysshe's estate, PBS receives from his father money to pay his debts (some cash he diverts to Godwin), as well as an annual income of £1,000 (£200 earmarked for Harriet; later for her children); PBS and MWS settle near Bishopgate in August and travel by boat up the

Thames with Thomas Love Peacock and Charles Clairmont in September; PBS writes *Alastor*.

1816     William Shelley born January 24; *Alastor . . . and Other
Poems* published in February, the first work to be pub-
lished under PBS's name. Byron leaves England April 25.
Princess Charlotte, the only legitimate child of the Prince
Regent (later George IV), marries Leopold of Saxe-Coburg
in May. PBS, MWS, and Claire Clairmont leave England
for Geneva (arrive mid-May) and remain near Byron till
August 29; in June, Byron and PBS tour Lake Geneva
(Leman); PBS writes "Hymn to Intellectual Beauty"; in
July, the Shelleys visit Mont Blanc and PBS writes "Mont
Blanc." After returning to England via Portsmouth in Sep-
tember, they settle at Bath; Fanny [Imlay] Godwin (MWS's
half-sister), feeling unwanted by both the Godwins and the
Shelleys, commits suicide in Wales on October 9; Harriet
Shelley, left pregnant by another lover, drowns herself in
London (her body found December 10); PBS and MWS
marry on December 30. Meanwhile, a year of social unrest
caused by post-war unemployment and food shortages culminates December 2 in the Spa Fields Riot in London,
suppressed by the army.

1817     Allegra Byron, Claire's daughter, born at Bath. The Lord
Chancellor denies PBS custody of his children Ianthe and
Charles. Habeas Corpus is suspended March 4 (till February 1818), causing many opposition journalists to flee or
be imprisoned. Shelleys settle at Marlow in March, when
PBS's pamphlet, *A Proposal for Putting Reform to the Vote*
is published. PBS writes *Laon and Cythna* from ?March to
September; it is printed in October–November, then revised (censored) and finally published as *The Revolt of Islam*, December 1817 (dated 1818). Clara Shelley born
September 2. PBS drafts "Essay on Christianity" (?Sep-
tember–December); *History of a Six Weeks' Tour* by MWS
and PBS (including "Mont Blanc") published in November. After Princess Charlotte dies in childbirth in November, PBS writes (and perhaps publishes) *An Address to the
People on the Death of the Princess Charlotte*. MWS's
*Frankenstein; or, The Modern Prometheus* published in December (dated 1818).

1818     Probably in January, PBS begins *Rosalind and Helen*; he
and MWS visit London before they leave for the Continent
on March 11, accompanied by Claire Clairmont, three
children, and two female servants—Amelia (Milly) Shields
and Louise (Elise) Duvillard; they reach Milan April 4,
visit the Italian lakes, send Allegra, with her nurse Elise,
to Byron April 28, visit Pisa and Livorno (Leghorn), and
meet the Gisbornes in May. In June they move to Bagni
di (Baths of) Lucca, where PBS translates Plato's *Sym-*

*posium*, writes "On Love," and completes *Rosalind and Helen*. PBS and Claire go to Venice to see Allegra, beginning August 17; PBS summons MWS and the children (with Milly and new servant, Paolo Foggi); he visits Byron, settles at Este, and begins *Prometheus Unbound* before the death of little Clara Shelley on September 24. PBS's depression reflected in "Euganean Hills" and beginning of "Julian and Maddalo," ?September 29–October 11. After visiting Venice, October 12–31, the Shelleys travel to Rome and Naples (November–December 1), remaining in Naples till February 28, 1819, with excursions to Vesuvius, Paestum, and other classical sites.

1819     Shelleys reach Rome on March 5; by early April PBS completes intermediate fair draft for the first three acts of *Prometheus*. After William Shelley dies of malaria on June 7, the Shelleys flee to Livorno, where MWS remains in depression, while PBS completes *The Cenci* in summer (printed in Italy, with 1819 date, then sent to England for publication in 1820). News of "Peterloo Massacre" (August 16) provokes PBS to write *The Mask of Anarchy* in September. On October 2, Shelleys move to Firenze (Florence), where son Percy Florence Shelley is born November 12 and PBS finishes *Prometheus Unbound* (published August 1820), writes "Ode to the West Wind" and *Peter Bell the Third* (October–November), and drafts "A Philosophical View of Reform," with "On Life" (?December–January 1820). In December 1819 and January 1820, Parliament, fearing revolution, passes the "Six Acts" to repress dissent.

1820     George III dies and George IV succeeds him in January; Cato Street Conspiracy to kill the English ministry is foiled in February and its leaders are executed. The Spanish army revolts in January and establishes constitutional monarchy in March. Shelleys move to Pisa January 26, where PBS writes "Sensitive-Plant" in March, "Ode to Liberty," and "Sky-Lark." Shelleys live in Gisbornes' house at Livorno while the Gisbornes are in England from June to August; PBS writes "Letter to Maria Gisborne," June 16ff. Constitutional revolution in Naples in July. Caroline of Brunswick, estranged wife of George IV, returns to England from Italy (July) to claim her rights as queen; she is "tried" by House of Lords (August–November), becoming a rallying symbol for the opposition. At Bagni di San Giuliano (Bagni di Pisa) from August to October, PBS writes *The Witch of Atlas*, "Ode to Naples," and *Swellfoot the Tyrant* (the last published and suppressed in November or December). Claire Clairmont moves to Firenze; flood forces the Shelleys (with Thomas Medwin) to return to Pisa at end of

October. There they meet Teresa ("Emilia") Viviani in November and Prince Alexander Mavrocordato in December.

1821   In January–February, PBS visits Teresa Viviani and writes *Epipsychidion* (published anonymously in May). Edward and Jane Williams arrive and meet Shelleys on January 13. PBS writes *A Defence of Poetry*, February–March, in response to Peacock's "The Four Ages of Poetry." The first two pirated editions of *Queen Mab* appear in England. The Austrians crush Neapolitan liberals and restore their hegemony throughout Italy (March). Greeks in Morea rise against Turkish rule in March; expatriate Greeks invade Turkish provinces from Russia in April. On April 11 a letter from London informs PBS of John Keats's death (Rome, February 23); PBS writes *Adonais* in May and June (printed at Pisa in July). Early in May, Edward and Jane Williams move to Pugnano, the Shelleys to Bagni di San Giuliano—both on the River Serchio. In August PBS visits Byron at Ravenna and urges him, his lover Countess Guiccioli, and her father and brother, the Counts Gamba, to move to Pisa (the Gambas arrive in August; Byron, on Nov. 1). During October and November, PBS completes *Hellas* (published February 1822).

1822   PBS writes scenes for "Charles the First" (?January). Edward John Trelawny arrives at Pisa January 14. The "Pisan Circle," centered on Byron and PBS, plan theatricals. Allegra Byron dies April 20 in a convent near Ravenna. The Shelleys and the Williamses move for the summer to San Terenzo, on the Bay of Lerici, April 30; PBS's boat, the "Don Juan," arrives there May 12. PBS begins writing "The Triumph of Life" after May 20. MWS miscarries on June 16. When Leigh Hunt arrives with his large family in Italy to join PBS and Byron in founding a new journal, to be called *The Liberal*, PBS and Williams sail to Leghorn July 1, meet the Hunts there, and settle them at Pisa, but both PBS and Williams drown on July 8 during the return voyage; their bodies wash up on shore several miles apart, and after temporary burial (mid-July) they are cremated on August 13 and 14. MWS and Hunts follow Byron to Genoa and live together at nearby Albaro from September 1822 till July 1823; there MWS begins to transcribe PBS's unpublished manuscripts.

1823   MWS returns to England in July.

1824   MWS's edition of PBS's *Posthumous Poems* published in June but is suppressed in September at the insistence of Sir Timothy Shelley.

# Selected Bibliography

## I. MANUSCRIPT FACSIMILES AND TRANSCRIPTIONS

*The Manuscripts of the Younger Romantics: Shelley (MYR: Shelley)*. 9 volumes. General Editor, Donald H. Reiman. New York & London: Garland Publishing, 1985–1996.

Volume I. *The Esdaile Notebook: A Facsimile of the Intermediate Fair-Copy Manuscript in The Carl H. Pforzheimer Library*. Ed. Donald H. Reiman (1985).

II. *The Mask of Anarchy: Facsimiles of the Intermediate Fair-Copy Holograph . . . , The Press-Copy Transcription by Mary W. Shelley . . . , Proofs of the First Edition, 1832. . . .* Ed. Donald H. Reiman (1985).

III. *Hellas: A Lyrical Drama: A Facsimile of the Press-Copy Transcript and Fair-Copy Transcripts of "Written on Hearing the News of the Death of Napoleon" and "Letter to Maria Gisborne," as well as a Fragment of the Press-Copy Transcript of "Lines written among the Euganean Hills": All in the Henry E. Huntington Library*. Ed. Donald H. Reiman (1985).

IV. *The Mask of Anarchy Draft Notebook: A Facsimile of Huntington MS. HM 2177: Including Drafts of The Mask of Anarchy, A Vision of the Sea, Preface to Prometheus Unbound, Preface to The Cenci, "Ode to Heaven," Together with Minor Poems, Fragments, and Prose Writings*. Ed. Mary A. Quinn (1990).

V. *The Harvard Shelley Poetic Manuscripts. . . .* Ed. Donald H. Reiman (1991).

VI. *Shelley's 1819–1821 Huntington Notebook: A Facsimile of Huntington MS. HM 2176: Including Drafts of Prometheus Unbound, "Ode to the West Wind," "The Sensitive Plant," "Fragment of a Satire on Satire," "Una Favola" Together with Minor Poems and Fragments*. Ed. Mary A. Quinn (1994).

VII. *Shelley's 1821–1822 Huntington Notebook . . . MS. HM 2111*. Ed. Mary A. Quinn (1996).

VIII. *Fair-Copy Manuscripts of Shelley's Poems in European and American Libraries. . . .* Eds. Donald H. Reiman and Michael O'Neill (1997).

IX. *The Frankenstein Notebooks . . . in Draft and Fair Copy . . . .* (in 2 parts). Ed. Charles E. Robinson (1996).

*The Bodleian Shelley Manuscripts (BSM)*. 23 volumes. General Editor, Donald H. Reiman. New York & London: Garland Publishing, 1986–2001.

Volume I. *Peter Bell the Third: A Facsimile of the Press-Copy Transcript . . . (Bodleian MS. Shelley adds. c. 5, folios 50–69); and The Triumph of Life: A Facsimile of Shelley's Holograph Draft (Bodleian MS. Shelley adds. c. 4, folios 18–58). . . .* Ed. Donald H. Reiman (1986).

II. *Bodleian MS. Shelley adds. d. 7: A Facsimile Edition with Full Transcriptions and Textual Notes*. Ed. Irving Massey (1987).

III. *Bodleian MS. Shelley adds. e. 4: A Facsimile Edition with Full Transcriptions and Textual Notes*. Ed. P. M. S. Dawson (1987).

IV. *A Facsimile of Bodleian MS. Shelley adds. d. 1: Including Drafts of Speculations on Morals and Metaphysics, A Defence of Poetry, Ode to Naples, The Witch of Atlas, Epipsychidion and Mary Wollstonecraft Shelley's The Fields of Fancy/Mathilda. . . .* (in 2 parts). Ed. E. B. Murray (1988).

V. *The Witch of Atlas Notebook . . . Bodleian MS. Shelley adds. e. 6*. Ed. Carlene A. Adamson (1997).

VI. *Shelley's Pisan Winter Notebook (1820–1821): A Facsimile of Bodleian MS. Shelley adds. e. 8*. Ed. Carlene A. Adamson (1992).

VII. *"Shelley's Last Notebook": Bodleian MS. Shelley adds. e. 20 (including . . . A Defence of Poetry and . . . Adonais . . . ) . . . with . . . Shelley adds. e. 15 (drafts for Peter Bell the Third) and adds. c. 4, folios 212–246 (conclusion of . . . A Defence of Poetry): A Facsimile Edition with Full Transcriptions and Notes*. Eds. Donald H. Reiman and Hélène Dworzan Reiman (1990).

VIII. *Bodleian MS. Shelley d. 3: A Facsimile Edition with Full Transcription and Textual Notes* [contains fair copy of parts of *Laon and Cythna*—later *The Revolt of Islam*]. Ed. Tatsuo Tokoo (1988).

IX. *Bodleian MS. Shelley e. 1, e. 2, and e. 3: Intermediate Fair Copies of Prometheus Unbound . . . : A Facsimile Edition with Full Transcriptions and Notes.* Ed. Neil Fraistat (1991).

X. *Mary Wollstonecraft Shelley's Mythological Dramas: Proserpine and Midas, Bodleian MS. Shelley d. 2.* Ed. Charles E. Robinson; and *"Relation of the Death of the Family of the Cenci," Bodleian MS. Shelley adds. e. 13.* Trans. Mary Wollstonecraft Shelley, ed. Betty T. Bennett. *Facsimile Editions with Full Transcriptions and Notes* (1992).

XI. *The Geneva Notebook of Percy Bysshe Shelley: Bodleian MS. Shelley adds. e. 16 and Bodleian MS. Shelley adds. c. 4, folios 63, 65, 71, and 72: A Facsimile Edition with Transcriptions and Textual Notes.* Ed. Michael Erkelenz (1992).

XII. *The "Charles the First" Draft Notebook, A Facsimile of Bodleian MS. Shelley adds. e. 17: Including Drafts of "Charles the First," "Buona Notte," "The Boat on the Serchio," "Written on Hearing the News of The Death of Napoleon," "The Zucca," Song "A Widowed Bird", "To the Moon ('Art Thou Pale')", "Sonnet to Byron," together with Mary Shelley's Fair-Copy Transcript of "Orpheus," Her Research Notes for Valperga, and Miscellaneous Fragments of Verse and Prose.* Ed. Nora Crook (1991).

XIII. *Drafts for Laon and Cythna: Facsimiles of Bodleian MSS. Shelley adds. e. 14 and adds. e. 19.* Ed. Tatsuo Tokoo (1992).

XIV. *Shelley's "Devils" Notebook: Bodleian MS. Shelley adds. e. 9: A Facsimile Edition with Full Transcription and Textual Notes.* Ed. P. M. S. Dawson and Timothy Webb (1993).

XV. *The Julian and Maddalo Draft Notebook: Bodleian MS. Shelley adds. e. 11: Including Drafts For Julian and Maddalo, Prometheus Unbound, "Stanzas Written in Dejection . . . Near Naples," "A Future State," "On Love," "A Discourse on the Manners of the Antient Greeks Relative to the Subject of Love," as well as other Fragments of Poems and Prose.* Ed. Steven E. Jones (1990).

XVI. *The Hellas Notebook: Bodleian MS. Shelley adds. e. 7: Including False Starts and Cancelled Passages for Hellas, Shelley's Research Notes for "Charles the First," and Drafts for Several Lyrics: A Facsimile Edition with Full Transcriptions, Textual Notes, and a Critical Introduction.* Eds. Donald H. Reiman and Michael J. Neth (1994).

XVII. *Drafts for Laon and Cythna, Cantos V–XII: Bodleian MS. Shelley adds. e. 10: A Facsimile Edition With Full Transcriptions, Textual Notes, and an Introduction.* Ed. Steven E. Jones (1994).

XVIII. *The Homeric Hymns and Prometheus Drafts Notebook: Bodleian MS. Shelley adds. e. 12.* Ed. Nancy Moore Goslee (1996).

XIX. *The Faust Draft Notebook: A Facsimile of Bodleian MS. Shelley adds. e. 18: Including Drafts of "Scenes from the Faust of Goethe," "Ginevra," "Scenes from the Magico Prodigioso of Calderon," "Fragments of an Unfinished Drama," "Lines: 'When the Lamp is Shattered,' " "From the Arabic," "A Lament" ("O World! O Life! O Time"), "With a Guitar, to Jane," and Miscellaneous Fragments of Verse and Prose.* Eds. Nora Crook and Timothy Webb (1997).

XX. *The Defence of Poetry Fair Copies: A Facsimile of Bodleian MSS. Shelley e. 6 and adds. d. 8: Including A Defence of Poetry: A Facsimile of the Fair-Copy Transcript by Mary W. Shelley, with Corrections by Percy Bysshe Shelley (Bodleian MS. Shelley e. 6); and A Defence of Poetry, The Banquet Translated from Plato, Essay on Love: A Facsimile of the Fair-copy Transcripts by Mary W. Shelley (Bodleian MS. Shelley adds. d. 8).* Ed. Michael O'Neill (1994).

XXI. *Miscellaneous Poetry, Prose, and Translations from Bodleian MS. Shelley adds. c. 4, etc.: Including Fair Copies of "Misery.—A Fragment," "Ode to Naples," "To a Faded Violet," "Letter on Richard Carlisle," "Una Favola," Drafts of "Speculations on Morals and Metaphysics," "The Coliseum," "On Vegetarianism," and Translations of Goethe's Faust, Along with Fifty Beta-radiograph Reproductions of Relevant Watermarks.* Ed. E. B. Murray (1995).

XXII. *Part One: A Facsimile and Full Transcript of Bodleian MS. Shelley adds. d. 6: Including Fair-Copies for A Philosophical View of Reform and Other Writings of Percy Bysshe Shelley in the Hand of Mary Wollstonecraft Shelley. Part Two: A Facsimile and Full Transcript of Bodleian MS. Shelley adds. c. 5: Including Drafts/Fair-Copies for The Fields of Fancy/Mathilda, The Coliseum (1st Part), The Assassins, Translations of Aeschylus's Prometheus Chained, Dante's First Canzone from The Convivio, and Ypsilanti's Cry of War to the Greeks, Mary Shelley's brief "Life of Shelley" and Other Writings Mainly in the Hand of Mary Wollstonecraft Shelley.* Ed. Alan Weinberg (1997).

XXIII. *A Catalogue and Index of the Shelley Manuscripts in the Bodleian Library and a General Index to the Facsimile Edition of the Bodleian Shelley Manuscripts, Vols. I–XXII,* by Tatsuo Tokoo; with *Shelleyan Writing Materials in the Bodleian Library: A Catalogue of Formats, Papers, and Watermarks,* by B. C. Barker-Benfield. Garland Publishing: New York & London, 2001.

## II. FIRST PUBLICATIONS IN BOOKS OF SHELLEY'S MAJOR POETRY AND PROSE

*Queen Mab; A Philosophical Poem: with Notes.* Anon. London, n.p., 1813.

*Alastor; or, The Spirit of Solitude: and Other Poems.* London: Baldwin, Cradock, and Joy; and Carpenter and Son, 1816.

*History of a Six Weeks' Tour through a Part of France, Switzerland, Germany, and Holland.* . . .

Anon. [Shelley and Mary Shelley]. London: T. Hookham, Jr., and C. and J. Ollier, 1817. Contains the first printing of "Mont Blanc."

*Laon and Cythna; or, The Revolution of the Golden City; A Vision of the Nineteenth Century.* London: Sherwood, Neely, & Jones; and C. and J. Ollier, 1818. Suppressed, emended, and reissued as *The Revolt of Islam; A Poem, in Twelve Cantos.* London: C. and J. Ollier, 1818.

*Rosalind and Helen, A Modern Eclogue; with Other Poems.* London: C. and J. Ollier, 1819.

*The Cenci: A Tragedy, in Five Acts.* Italy: for C. and J. Ollier, London, 1819.

*Prometheus Unbound: A Lyrical Drama in Four Acts, with Other Poems.* London: C. and J. Ollier, 1820.

*Œdipus Tyrannus: or, Swellfoot the Tyrant. A Tragedy in Two Acts.* Anon. London: The Author, 1820.

*Epipsychidion: Verses Addressed to the Noble and Unfortunate Lady Emilia V—— Now Imprisoned in the Convent of ———.* Anon. London: C. and J. Ollier, 1821.

*Adonais: An Elegy on the Death of John Keats, Author of Endymion, Hyperion etc.* Pisa: With the types of Didot, 1821; Cambridge: Printed by W. Metcalfe and sold by Gee & Bridges, 1829.

*Hellas: A Lyrical Drama.* London: Charles and James Ollier, 1822.

*Posthumous Poems of Percy Bysshe Shelley* [ed. Mary Shelley]. London: John and Henry L. Hunt, 1824.

*The Masque of Anarchy. A Poem.* Ed. Leigh Hunt. London: Edward Moxon, 1832.

*The Shelley Papers.* Ed. Thomas Medwin. London: Whittaker, Treacher, & Co., 1833.

*The Poetical Works of Percy Bysshe Shelley.* Ed. Mrs. Shelley. 4 vols. London: Edward Moxon, 1839.

*Essays, Letters from Abroad, Translations and Fragments.* Ed. Mrs. Shelley. 2 vols. London: Edward Moxon, 1840.

*Relics of Shelley.* Ed. Richard Garnett. London: Edward Moxon & Co., 1862.

*A Philosophical View of Reform, Now Printed for the First Time.* Ed. T. W. Rolleston. London: Oxford University Press, 1920.

*The Esdaile Notebook: A Volume of Early Poems.* Ed. Kenneth Neill Cameron. New York: Alfred A. Knopf, 1964.

## III. CRITICAL EDITIONS AND TEXTUAL CRITICISM

Cameron, Kenneth Neill, and Donald H. Reiman, eds. *Shelley and his Circle, 1773–1822.* (SC) To be completed in 12 vols. Cambridge, MA: Harvard University Press; Cameron's vols. I–II (1961) and III–IV (1971); Reiman's vols. V–VI (1973) and VII–VIII (1986); IX–X (2001). A catalogue-edition, with extensive commentaries, of the MSS of the Shelleys, Byron, Godwin, Wollstonecraft, Hunt, Peacock, et al. in the Pforzheimer Collection of Shelley and His Circle, New York Public Library.

Clark, David Lee, ed. *Shelley's Prose; or, The Trumpet of a Prophecy.* Albuquerque: University of New Mexico Press, 1954. The only accessible edition of PBS's later prose, but misleadingly inaccurate in both text and notes; for a more reliable text of the earlier prose see the Oxford Edition by E. B. Murray, below.

Forman, Harry Buxton, ed. *The Poetical Works of Percy Bysshe Shelley.* 4 vols. London: Reeves and Turner, 1876; with *Prose Works,* 4 vols., 1880, an eight-volume collected edition. Forman revised *Poetical Works* in condensed edition for Reeves and Turner, 1882 (2 vols.), and the "Aldine Edition" for George Bell, 1892 (5 vols.). All are accurate, outdated only where new evidence has since appeared.

Hutchinson, Thomas, ed. *The Complete Poetical Works of Shelley.* Oxford: Clarendon Press, 1904. Reset as *The Poetical Works of Percy Bysshe Shelley.* The Oxford Edition. London: Henry Frowde, 1905, et seq.; reset in 1943 for Oxford Standard Authors; corrected by G. M. Matthews, 1970. A conservative text, based chiefly on Forman; still the best one-volume, nearly complete edition.

Ingpen, Roger, and Walter E. Peck, eds. *The Complete Works of Percy Bysshe Shelley* (*Works*). 10 vols. (Julian Edition). London: Ernest Benn; New York: Charles Scribner's Sons, 1926–1930. The latest attempt at a complete edition, still useful for its texts of PBS's later prose and collations of poetic authorities.

Knerr, Anthony D. *Shelley's "Adonais": A Critical Edition.* New York: Columbia University Press, 1984. A critical edition of the poem, with a contextual study that incorporates much earlier commentary on the poem.

Locock, C. D., ed. *The Poems of Percy Bysshe Shelley.* 2 vols. London: Methuen, 1911. Useful for its notes, but introduces unauthorized readings from PBS's drafts into the final texts.

Matthews, G. M. and Kelvin Everest, eds. *The Poems of Shelley.* London: Longman, 1989. The first of a three-volume complete edition of PBS's poetry; done with scholarly care and editorial skill for the Longman Annotated English Poets series.

Murray, E. B., ed. *The Prose Works of Percy Bysshe Shelley.* Oxford: Clarendon Press, 1993. This volume presents authoritative texts of PBS's prose up until he leaves England in March 1818. Murray's untimely death prevented him from editing the later prose.

Notopoulos, James A. *The Platonism of Shelley: A Study of Platonism and the Poetic Mind.*

Durham, NC: Duke University Press, 1949. Most valuable for its texts of PBS's translations from Plato, supplemented by Notopoulos in "New Texts from Plato," *Keats-Shelley Journal* XV [Winter 1966]: 99–115; see also Webb, *The Violet in the Crucible*, below.

Reiman, Donald H. *Shelley's "The Triumph of Life": A Critical Study, Based on a Text Newly Edited from the Bodleian Manuscript*. Urbana: University of Illinois Press, 1965. A full textual and critical study of PBS's last major poetic fragment.

Reiman, Donald H. and Neil Fraistat, eds. *The Complete Poetry of Percy Bysshe Shelley* (*CPPBS*), Volume I. Baltimore, MD: Johns Hopkins University Press, 2000. A comprehensive edition, providing critically edited clear texts of all poems and translations that Shelley published or circulated among friends, as well as diplomatic texts of his significant incomplete poetic drafts and fragments.

Rossetti, William Michael, ed. *The Poetical Works of Percy Bysshe Shelley*. 2 vols. London: Moxon, 1870; revised in 3 vols., 1878. Rossetti's strength was his poetic sensitivity, but he sometimes emended PBS's text to correspond with his own taste and he rushed his editing to earn his living.

Taylor, Charles H., Jr., *The Early Collected Editions of Shelley's Poems: A Study in the History and Transmission of the Printed Text*. New Haven, CT: Yale University Press, 1958. Important bibliographical analysis of early pirated reprintings and Mary Shelley's editions of PBS's poems.

Webb, Timothy, ed. *Percy Bysshe Shelley: Poems and Prose*. London: J. M. Dent, 1995. Selection for students, critically edited from primary sources and annotated.

Woodberry, George E. *The Complete Poetical Works of Percy Bysshe Shelley*. 4 vols. in 8 parts (Centenary Edition). Cambridge, MA: Riverside Press, 1892. An ambitious critical text (the only one completed in America) that was widely disseminated in the one-volume Cambridge Edition (1901).

Zillman, Lawrence John, ed. *Shelley's "Prometheus Unbound": A Variorum Edition*. Seattle: University of Washington Press, 1959. Useful for summarizing earlier commentary and collating the early printed texts with the intermediate fair-copy MSS and with other editions.

## IV. BIBLIOGRAPHIES AND REFERENCE WORKS

Curran, Stuart. "Percy Bysshe Shelley," in *The English Romantic Poets: A Review of Research and Criticism*. 4th edition, ed. Frank Jordan. New York: Modern Language Association of America, 1985. Still the best critical survey of scholarship and opinion on PBS.

Dunbar, Clement. *A Bibliography of Shelley Studies: 1823–1950*. New York: Garland, 1976; 2nd edition, 1988. Detailed entries on publications in English discussing PBS from 1825 till the *Keats-Shelley Journal* (*KSJ*) began its bibliography.

Ellis, F. S. *A Lexical Concordance to the Poetical Works of Percy Bysshe Shelley*. London: Quaritch, 1892. Based on Forman's two-volume edition of 1882, this concordance—the first done for any of the Romantics—remains as indispensible as it is outdated.

Forman, Harry Buxton. *The Shelley Library: An Essay in Bibliography*. London: Reeves and Turner, 1886.

Green, David Bonnell, and Edwin Graves Wilson, eds. *Keats, Shelley, Byron, Hunt, and Their Circles, A Bibliography: July 1, 1950–June 30, 1962*. Lincoln: University of Nebraska Press, 1964. Collects and indexes the first twelve annual bibliographies from *KSJ*.

Hartley, Robert A. *Keats, Shelley, Byron, Hunt, and Their Circles. A Bibliography: July 1, 1962– December 31, 1974*. Lincoln: University of Nebraska Press, 1978. Collects and indexes more bibliographies from *KSJ*.

Hogle, Jerrold E. "Percy Bysshe Shelley," in *Literature of the Romantic Period: A Bibliographical Guide*, ed. Michael O'Neill. Oxford: Clarendon Press; New York: Oxford University Press, 1998. Most recent and updated bibliographical resource for Shelley studies.

*Keats-Shelley Journal* (*KSJ*). "Current Bibliography" (1951 to date). Besides its annual bibliography, *KSJ*—like *Keats-Shelley Memorial Bulletin* (*KSMB*), since 1986 *Keats-Shelley Review* (*KSR*)—publishes articles, notes, and reviews on Keats, Byron, PBS, and their circles.

Reiman, Donald H., *English Romantic Poetry, 1800–1835: A Guide to Information Sources*. Detroit, MI: Gale Research, 1979. Selective, annotated bibliography on each major poet (except Blake) and on the background poets and history of the period.

———, ed. *The Romantics Reviewed: Contemporary Reviews of British Romantic Writers* (*RR*) Part C: *Shelley, Keats, and London Radical Writers*. 2 vols. New York: Garland, 1972. Contains facsimiles of the original periodical texts of most of the known reviews of PBS, as well as relevant ancillary materials.

White, Newman Ivey. *The Unextinguished Hearth: Shelley and His Contemporary Critics*. Durham, NC: Duke University Press, 1938. Reprints reviews and other contemporary references to PBS through 1824.

Wise, Thomas James. *A Shelley Library*. London: Privately printed, 1924; reprinted as part of Wise's catalogue *The Ashley Library* (11 vols., 1922–1936). With Forman's earlier catalogue, the fullest description of first editions and other rare items relating to the Shelleys; Wise's Ashley Collection is now in the British Library.

## V. PRIMARY BIOGRAPHICAL SOURCES

Clairmont, Mary Jane Clara. *The Clairmont Correspondence: Letters of Claire Clairmont, Charles Clairmont, and Fanny Imlay Godwin,* ed. Marion Kingston Stocking. Baltimore: Johns Hopkins University Press, 1995. Stocking's editions of the Clairmont journals and letters provide unique information on the lives and writings of the Shelleys, Byron, Godwin, etc., in both readable and quotable form.

———. *The Journals of Claire Clairmont,* ed. Marion Kingston Stocking. Cambridge, MA: Harvard University Press, 1968.

Gisborne, Maria, and Edward E. Williams. *Maria Gisborne & Edward E. Williams, Shelley's Friends: Their Journals and Letters,* ed. Frederick L. Jones. Norman: University of Oklahoma Press, 1951. For corrections to the Gisborne journal, see George H. Ford's review, *Modern Philology* L (1952): 69–72; for corrections to Williams's journal, see *Journals of Mary Shelley,* I, 417–418n.

Hunt, Leigh. *Lord Byron and Some of His Contemporaries; with Recollections of the Author's Life, and of His Visit to Italy.* London: Henry Colburn, 1828. Hunt's comments on PBS also appear (with revisions) in his *Autobiography* (1850).

Medwin, Thomas. *The Life of Percy Bysshe Shelley: A New Edition . . . Amended and Extended by the Author . . .,* ed. H. Buxton Forman. London: Humphrey Milford / Oxford University Press, 1913. Contains useful notes and addenda by Forman.

Shelley, Mary W. *The Journals of Mary Shelley, 1814–1844,* ed. Paula R. Feldman and Diana Scott-Kilvert. 2 vols. Oxford: Clarendon Press, 1987.

———. *The Letters of Mary Wollstonecraft Shelley,* ed. Betty T. Bennett. 3 vols. Baltimore, MD: Johns Hopkins University Press, 1980–1988. For addenda, see Bennett's "Newly Uncovered Letters and Poems by Mary Wollstonecraft Shelley," *KSJ* 46 (1997): 51–74.

Shelley, Percy Bysshe. *The Letters of Percy Bysshe Shelley* (*Letters*), ed. Frederick L. Jones. 2 vols. Oxford: Clarendon Press, 1964. Additional letters appear in *SC, KSMB,* and *KSJ.*

*Shelley and Mary.* 3 vols., occasionally bound as 4 vols. "For private circulation only" [1882]. Sponsored by Sir Percy Florence Shelley and Jane, Lady Shelley, these volumes contain (sometimes censored) versions of letters, journals, and other documents relating to PBS and MWS.

Wolfe, Humbert, ed. *The Life of Percy Bysshe Shelley, as Comprised in "The Life of Percy Bysshe Shelley" by Thomas Jefferson Hogg, "The Recollections of Shelley & Byron" by Edward John Trelawny, "Memoirs of Shelley" by Thomas Love Peacock.* 2 vols. London: Dent, 1933. A convenient collection of three basic primary biographical records; for correction of the tampered texts of PBS's early letters to Hogg, see *SC,* II–IV.

## VI. BIOGRAPHIES AND BIOGRAPHICAL STUDIES

Cameron, Kenneth Neill. *Shelley: The Golden Years.* Cambridge, MA: Harvard University Press, 1974. Takes up chronology from *The Young Shelley,* with less emphasis on life, more on PBS's major writings.

———. *The Young Shelley: Genesis of a Radical.* New York: Macmillan, 1950. Supplements White's *Shelley* with scholarly Marxist account of PBS's early life and works.

Crook, Nora, and Derek Guiton. *Shelley's Venomed Melody.* Cambridge: Cambridge University Press, 1986. Explores PBS's possible health problems (including his possible encounters with venereal disease) and evidence from his writings of his reactions.

Dowden, Edward. *The Life of Percy Bysshe Shelley.* 2 vols. London: Kegan Paul, Trench, 1886. The "official" life, authorized by PBS's son; though reticent on some matters, a notably accurate work of scholarship.

Holmes, Richard. *Shelley: The Pursuit.* London: Weidenfeld & Nicholson, 1974; New York: E. P. Dutton, 1975. Imaginative and lively life, marred by factual errors, by a journalist-scholar with limited sympathy for PBS's poetry.

Ingpen, Roger. *Shelley in England: New Facts and Letters from the Shelley-Whitton Papers.* Sometimes bound as 2 vols. London: Kegan Paul, Trench, Trubner, 1917. Important information on PBS's finances, legal problems, and relations with his father.

Peck, Walter Edwin. *Shelley: His Life and Work.* 2 vols. Boston and New York: Houghton Mifflin, 1927. Flawed by Peck's idiosyncratic views, but filled with detailed information drawn from primary sources. The appendixes in vol. II are especially valuable.

Reiman, Donald H. *Percy Bysshe Shelley* (Twayne's English Authors). Updated edition. Boston: Twayne Publishers, a division of G. K. Hall, 1990.

St. Clair, William. *The Godwins and the Shelleys: The Biography of a Family.* Baltimore, MD: Johns Hopkins University Press, 1991. The best literary and historical biography of William Godwin, containing new information on his wives and their children, with ancillary comments on PBS and other contemporaries.

White, Newman Ivey. *Shelley.* 2 vols. New York: Alfred A. Knopf, 1940 (one-volume condensed revision, *Portrait of Shelley,* 1945). Still the best biography, a monument to a lifetime of devoted study, though it has been corrected and supplemented in Cameron and Reiman, eds., *Shelley and his Circle* and other subsequent studies.

## VII. STUDIES OF SHELLEY'S THOUGHT AND ART

Studies of the writings of Percy Bysshe Shelley now number in the hundreds, but the list of individual topics discussed is more manageable. The books and essays listed below retain their value in relation to other studies by virtue of: (1) comprehensive treatment of their chosen topics; (2) accurate and thorough scholarship; and/or (3) a unique perspective or persuasive exposition of a viable viewpoint.

• indicates works included or excerpted in this Norton Critical Edition.

Baker, Carlos. *Shelley's Major Poetry: The Fabric of a Vision.* Princeton, NJ: Princeton University Press, 1948. Excellent interpretive essays emphasizing PBS's use of earlier literature.
Barnard, Ellsworth. *Shelley's Religion.* Minneapolis: University of Minnesota Press, 1937. Still the best account of its important topic.
• Behrendt, Stephen C. *Shelley and His Audiences.* Lincoln: University of Nebraska Press, 1989. A perceptive analysis of the rhetoric in PBS's poetry and prose—his various attempts to portray himself and to influence the response of readers.
Bennett, Betty T., and Stuart Curran, eds. *Shelley: Poet and Legislator of the World.* Baltimore, MD: Johns Hopkins University Press, 1996. Twenty-three essays by top Shelleyans from several nations, celebrating the bicentenary of his birth.
• Bewell, Alan. "Percy Bysshe Shelley and Revolutionary Climatology." From *Romanticism and Colonial Disease.* Baltimore, MD: Johns Hopkins University Press, 1999. 209–19.
Blank, Kim, ed. *The New Shelley.* London: Macmillan; New York: St. Martin's, 1991. Twelve essays by leading Shelley critics.
Bloom, Harold, ed. *Deconstruction and Criticism.* New York: Continuum, 1979. Includes Paul de Man's influential essay, "Shelley Disfigured."
——. *Shelley's Mythmaking.* New Haven, CT: Yale University Press, 1959. Speculative and stimulating, though factually unreliable.
• ——. *The Visionary Company: A Reading of English Romantic Poetry.* Ithaca, NY: Cornell University Press, 1971.
Brown, Nathaniel. *Sexuality and Feminism in Shelley.* Cambridge, MA: Harvard University Press, 1979. A full study of PBS's thinking on sexuality and gender, illuminated from the thought of his own age, what he read from earlier times, and modern studies of human sexuality and gender difference.
Butter, P(eter) H. *Shelley's Idols of the Cave.* Edinburgh: Edinburgh University Press, 1954. Following Yeats, Butter explores characteristic symbols and modes of thought in PBS's writings.
• Cafarelli, Annette Wheeler. "The Transgressive Double Standard: Shelleyan Utopianism and Feminist Social History." From *Shelley: Poet and Legislator of the World,* ed. Betty T. Bennett and Stuart Curran. Baltimore, MD: Johns Hopkins University Press, 1996. 96–104.
• Cameron, Kenneth Neill. *The Golden Years.* Cambridge, MA: Harvard University Press, 1974.
• Chandler, James. "History's Lyre: The 'West Wind' and the Poet's Work." From *England in 1819: The Politics of Literary Culture and the Case of Romantic Historicism.* Chicago: University of Chicago Press, 1998. 532–54.
Chernaik, Judith. *The Lyrics of Shelley.* Cleveland, OH: Case Western Reserve University Press, 1972. Detailed readings of PBS's major lyrics from new texts (some now superseded by this Norton Critical Edition).
Clark, Timothy. *Embodying Revolution: The Figure of the Poet in Shelley.* Oxford: University Press, 1989. Traces the conflicts embedded in the figure of the poet in PBS's works.
Clark, Timothy, and Jerrold E. Hogle, eds. *Evaluating Shelley.* Edinburgh: Edinburgh University Press, 1996. Fourteen essays by leading Shelleyans from North America and the U.K. to celebrate PBS's bicentenary.
Cronin, Richard. *Shelley's Poetic Thoughts.* New York: St. Martin's, 1981. A cogent study of the interrelations among PBS's thought, language, and use of poetic form, with insightful readings of the major poems.
Curran, Stuart. *Shelley's Annus Mirabilis: The Maturing of an Epic Vision.* San Marino, CA: Huntington Library, 1975. A richly informed study of PBS's poems of 1819–1820.
——. *Shelley's "Cenci": Scorpions Ringed with Fire.* Princeton, NJ: Princeton University Press, 1970. The standard study of *The Cenci* both as a drama and as a poem.
• ——. "Shelley and the End(s) of Ideology." From *The Most Unfailing Herald: Percy Bysshe Shelley 1792–1992,* ed. Alan M. Weinberg and Romaine Hill. Pretoria: Unisa Press, 1996. 21–30.
Dawson, P(aul) M. S. *The Unacknowledged Legislator: Shelley and Politics.* Oxford: Clarendon Press, 1980. An important study of PBS's political perspective, set against the ideas current in his family and those of his own mentors.
Duffy, Edward. *Rousseau in England: The Context for Shelley's Critique of the Enlightment.* Berkeley: University of California Press, 1979. Explores British knowledge of and interest in Rousseau, focusing on PBS's portrait of him in *The Triumph of Life.*
• Everest, Kelvin, ed. *Shelley Revalued: Essays from the Gregynog Conference.* Leicester:

Leicester University Press, 1983. Ten significant essays by British and American Shelleyans.
• Ferber, Michael. *Critical Studies: The Poetry of Shelley*. New York: Penguin Books, 1993.
Fraistat, Neil. *The Poem and the Book: Interpreting Collections of Romantic Poetry*. Chapel Hill and London: University of North Carolina Press, 1985. Illustrates the "contexture" of the arrangement of poems within volumes by reading Wordsworth's and Coleridge's *Lyrical Ballads* (1798), Keats's *Lamia* volume, and PBS's *Prometheus Unbound; with Other Poems*.
• ———. "Shelley Left and Right: The Rhetorics of the Early Textual Editions." From *Shelley: Poet and Legislator of the World*, ed. Betty T. Bennett and Stuart Curran. Baltimore, MD: Johns Hopkins University Press, 1996. 105–13.
Gelpi, Barbara. *Shelley's Goddess: Maternity, Language, Subjectivity*. New York: Oxford University Press, 1992. An important feminist study of the mother-infant relationship in PBS's poetry and life, especially *Prometheus Unbound*, grounded in historical work on motherhood in England after 1790.
• Goslee, Nancy Moore. "Dispersoning Emily: Drafting as Plot in *Epipsychidion*." *KSJ* 42 (1993): 104–19.
Grabo, Carl. *The Magic Plant: The Growth of Shelley's Thought*. Chapel Hill: University of North Carolina Press, 1935. The culminating 1930s study of PBS's thought, with special attention to scientific and Neoplatonic influences on his ideas.
Hall, Jean. *The Transforming Image: A Study of Shelley's Major Poetry*. Urbana: University of Illinois Press, 1980. A lucid, useful study of the transformational—as opposed to the transcendental—character of PBS's imagery in the major poems.
Hoagwood, Terence Allan. *Skepticism and Ideology: Shelley's Political Prose and Its Philosophical Context from Bacon to Marx*. Iowa City: University of Iowa Press, 1988. A valuable study of PBS's philosophical prose as mediating between Marxism and older forms of skeptical argumentation.
• Hogle, Jerrold E. *Shelley's Process: Radical Transference and the Development of his Major Works*. New York and Oxford: Oxford University Press, 1988.
Jones, Steven E. *Shelley's Satire: Violence, Exhortation, and Authority*. DeKalb: Northern Illinois University Press, 1994. An important study that relates PBS's use of satire in his writings (and his ambivalence toward using this weapon) to both his life and times and later psychological and sociological insights.
• Keach, William. *Shelley's Style*. New York and London: Methuen, 1984. The best book on PBS's interest in language, on the relations between his linguistic ideas and those of his contemporaries, and on several specific stylistic topics.
• Matthews, G(eoffrey) M. Though Matthews, like Hughes, wrote mainly essays and reviews on PBS, he was recognized as England's major Shelleyan for nearly two decades (see the bibliographies listed above). See, for example, "Shelley's Lyrics" in *The Morality of Art*, ed. D. W. Jefferson (London: Routledge, 1969), pp. 195–209; and "A Volcano's Voice in Shelley," *ELH* 24 (1957):191–228.
Morton, Timothy. *Shelley and the Revolution in Taste: The Body and the Natural World*. Cambridge: Cambridge University Press, 1995. The best study of PBS's vegetarianism and its cultural context.
O'Neill, Michael. *The Human Mind's Imaginings: Conflict and Achievement in Shelley's Poetry*. Oxford: Oxford University Press, 1989.
• ———. Introduction to *Fair-Copy Manuscripts of Shelley's Poems in European and American Libraries*, ed. Donald H. Reiman and Michael O'Neill. New York: Garland, 1997. *MYR: Shelley*, VIII.
Pulos, C. E. *The Deep Truth: A Study of Shelley's Scepticism*. Lincoln: University of Nebraska Press, 1954. Seminal for later studies relating PBS's thought to Academic Skepticism.
• Pyle, Forest. " 'Frail Spells': Shelley and the Ironies of Exile." From *Irony and Clerisy*, ed. Deborah Elise White. *Romantic Circles Praxis Series* (online). Aug. 1999.
Rajan, Tilottama. *The Supplement of Reading: Figures of Understanding in Romantic Theory and Practice*. Ithaca, NY: Cornell University Press, 1990. Includes three chapters on PBS containing important deconstructive readings of *A Defence of Poetry*, *Prometheus Unbound*, and *The Triumph of Life*.
Reiman, Donald H. *Intervals of Inspiration: The Skeptical Tradition and the Psychology of Romanticism*. Greenwood, FL: Penkevill, 1988. Surveys the Skeptical tradition from the Hellenistic schools and Cicero through Ockham, Montaigne, and Hume and the use of this tradition by the English Romantics; Chapter 5: "Shelley: The Mythology of Aspiration."
• ———. *Romantic Texts and Contexts*. Columbia: University of Missouri Press, 1987. Six of its nineteen essays center on PBS or the editing of his writings.
• Roberts, Hugh. *Shelley and the Chaos of History: A New Politics of Poetry*. University Park: Pennsylvania State University Press, 1997.
Robinson, Charles E. *Shelley and Byron: The Snake and Eagle Wreathed in Fight*. Baltimore, MD: Johns Hopkins University Press, 1976. Carefully researched analysis of interactions between PBS and Byron in life and poetry.
• Scrivener, Michael. *Radical Shelley: The Philosophical Anarchism and Utopian Thought of Percy Bysshe Shelley*. Princeton, NJ: Princeton University Press, 1982. The fullest chronological account of PBS's political radicalism and his search for an audience.

Sperry, Stuart M. *Shelley's Major Verse: The Narrative and Dramatic Poetry*. Cambridge, MA: Harvard University Press, 1988. A major study and defense of PBS as a moral idealist.

Ulmer, William A. *Shelleyan Eros: The Rhetoric of Romantic Love*. Princeton, NJ: Princeton University Press, 1990. Investigates the interrelation of language, politics, and sexuality in PBS's poetry.

Wang, Orrin. *Fantastic Modernity: Dialectical Readings in Romanticism and Theory*. Baltimore, MD: Johns Hopkins University Press, 1996. Contains a chapter with a major reading of both *The Triumph of Life* and Paul de Man's influential interpretation of it.

• Wasserman, Earl R. *Shelley: A Critical Reading*. Baltimore, MD: Johns Hopkins University Press, 1971. A comprehensive reading incorporating Wasserman's earlier influential studies of particular works by PBS. Still the most influential critical analysis of PBS's poetry.

Weaver, Bennett. *Toward the Understanding of Shelley*. Ann Arbor: University of Michigan Press, 1932. Explores the impact of the Bible and the Hebraic prophetic tradition on PBS.

Webb, Timothy. *Shelley: A Voice Not Understood*. Atlantic Highlands, NJ: Humanities Press, 1977. A mature introduction to PBS, arranged topically to refute old myths about his life and poetry.

• ———. "The Unascended Heaven: Negatives in *Prometheus Unbound*." From *Shelley Revalued: Essays from the Gregynog Conference*, ed. Kelvin Everest. Leicester: Leicester University Press, 1983. 37–62.

———. *The Violet in the Crucible: Shelley and Translation*. Oxford: Clarendon Press, 1976. The standard study of Shelley as a translator, with much information on his reading in other languages.

Weisman, Karen A. *Imageless Truths: Shelley's Poetic Fictions*. Philadelphia: University of Pennsylvania Press, 1994. The most extensive study of PBS and language since William Keach's *Shelley's Style*, emphasizing the engagement of PBS's work with the quotidian.

Wheatley, Kim. *Shelley and His Readers: Beyond Paranoid Politics*. Columbia: University of Missouri Press, 1999. Critical analysis of the dialogue between Shelley's poetry and its contemporary reviewers.

Wilson, Milton. *Shelley's Later Poetry: A Study of His Prophetic Imagination*. New York: Columbia University Press, 1959. A wise appreciation of PBS's art, held somewhat in check by the anti-Shelleyan temper of the academy during the 1950s.

• Wolfson, Susan. *Formal Charges: The Shaping of Poetry in British Romanticism*. Stanford, CA: Stanford University Press, 1997. While arguing for the unity of ideas with the formal aspects of poetry, Wolfson's fine chapter on PBS treats the shaping of "The Mask of Anarchy" and PBS's shorter political poems, as well as his late personal lyrics to Jane Williams.

Woodring, Carl. *Politics in English Romantic Poetry*. Cambridge, MA: Harvard University Press, 1970. PBS receives an important chapter in this fine study of the interrelations of the Romantics' poetry with the political events and ideas of their time.

Young, Art. *Shelley and Nonviolence*. The Hague: Mouton, 1975. Expores PBS's philosophy of nonviolent action in relation to the ideas and practices of Gandhi, Martin Luther King, Jr., and others.

## VIII. CRITICAL SELECTIONS FROM THE FIRST EDITION OF *SHELLEY'S POETRY AND PROSE* (1977)

Abrams, M. H. "[Shelley's *Prometheus Unbound*]." From *Natural Supernaturalism: Tradition and Revolution in Romantic Literature*. New York: Norton, 1971. 299–307.

Baker, Carlos. "[*The Cenci*]." From Chapter 5, "The Human Heart: The Conversation Poems of 1818–1819," in *Shelley's Major Poetry: The Fabric of a Vision*. Princeton, NJ: Princeton University Press, 1948. 138–53.

Cameron, Kenneth N. "The Planet-Tempest Passage in *Epipsychidion*." *PMLA* 63 (1948): 950–72.

———. "The Social Philosophy of Shelley." *The Sewanee Review* (Autumn 1942): 457–66.

Chayes, Irene H. "['Ode to the West Wind']." From "Rhetoric as Drama: An Approach to the Romantic Ode." *PMLA* 79 (1964): 71–74.

Gibson, Evan K. "*Alastor*: A Reinterpretation." *PMLA* 62 (1947): 1022–42.

Hughes, D. J. "Potentiality in *Prometheus Unbound*." *SiR* 2 (1963): 107–26.

Matthews, G. M. "Shelley's Lyrics." From *The Morality of Art: Essays Presented to G. Wilson Knight*, ed. D. W. Jefferson. London: Routledge and Kegan Paul, 1969. 195–209.

Pulos, C. E. "[Shelley's Skepticism]." From Chapter VII, "Conclusion," in *The Deep Truth: A Study of Shelley's Scepticism*. Lincoln: University of Nebraska Press, 1954. 105–12.

Reiman, Donald H. "The Purpose and Method of Shelley's Poetry." From *Shelley's "The Triumph of Life": A Critical Study*. Urbana: University of Illinois Press, 1965. 3–18.

———. "Structure, Symbol, and Theme in 'Lines written among the Euganean Hills.' " *PMLA* 77 (1962): 404–13.

Vivian, Charles H. "The One 'Mont Blanc.' " *KSJ* 4 (1955): 55–65.

Wasserman, Earl R. "[Shelley's Use of Myth]." From *Shelley: A Critical Reading*. Baltimore, MD: Johns Hopkins University Press, 1971. 269–75.

Woodman, Ross. "*Adonais*." From *The Apocalyptic Vision in the Poetry of Shelley*. Toronto: University of Toronto Press, 1964. 159–78.

Woodring, Carl. "[*Hellas*]." From *Politics in English Romantic Poetry*. Cambridge, MA: Harvard University Press, 1970. 313–19.

# Index of Titles and First Lines